Reader's Guide to

WOMEN'S STUDIES

EDITORIAL ADVISORY COMMITTEE

Reader's Guide to

WOMEN'S STUDIES

Editor

ELEANOR B. AMICO

FITZROY DEARBORN PUBLISHERS
CHICAGO AND LONDON

For information write to:

FITZROY DEARBORN PUBLISHERS
70 East Walton Street
Chicago, Illinois 60611
USA

or

11 Rathbone Place
London W1P 1DE
England

British Library Cataloguing in Publication Data
Reader's guide to women's studies
1. Women's studies - Bibliography
I. Amico, Eleanor
016.3'054'07

ISBN 188496477X

Library of Congress Cataloging in Publication Data is available.

First published in the USA and UK 1998

Typeset by Print Means Inc., New York, New York
Printed by Braun-Brumfield, Inc., Ann Arbor, Michigan
Cover design by Chicago Advertising and Design, Chicago, Illinois

CONTENTS

EDITOR'S NOTE

Aims, Scope, and Selection of Entries

Women's Studies is a new field of inquiry, beginning only in the late 1960s, but since that time the literature on women and gender-related topics has burgeoned and multiplied to the point where scholars who once were able to remain aware of new publications are now unable to do so, often even within their own subfields. Part of the reason for this is the interdisciplinary nature of women's studies. Women's studies research and writing has taken place in virtually every field of academic endeavor, including each branch of the humanities, the sciences, the social sciences, and the fine arts. This volume is an attempt to guide the reader through the mass of published work on women and gender to date, and it, like the field of women's studies itself, is an interdisciplinary work, including contributions from scholars in every field of knowledge.

In addition to being interdisciplinary, women's studies is a global field, both in the sense that it is being researched and taught in countries throughout the world and also in the sense that the topics the field addresses include women's issues across the world, involving concerns as diverse as dowry in India, Australian Aboriginal women, and the American and British Industrial Revolutions. Therefore, an attempt was made, as far as possible within the English-language limitations of this volume, to include both contributors and topics from around the globe.

The purpose of the *Reader's Guide to Women's Studies* is to provide the reader with brief discussions of some of the best books on over 500 topics and individuals in women's studies. Some of the topics are specialized and very specific; others are much more general. Some overlap often occurs as more general topics encompass issues that are the subject of specific entries. The thematic list that follows this introductory note should guide readers in finding both specific and more general entries on topics of their interest.

This approach is designed to help readers of various interests and at various levels: students (both undergraduate and graduate) looking for assistance with research papers; teachers in schools, colleges, and universities, especially those faced with preparing courses or classes on topics in which they are not specialists; and other readers who are interested in a particular topic and seek guidance on what to read.

Within certain editorial guidelines, each contributor was free to select the books listed and discussed. In some cases, choices had to be made from a large body of possible works, and the bibliographies can be as long as 12 to 14 books, which only scratch the surface of the available literature. In others, on which there are yet few books available, the contributor attempted to find and review virtually all the available book-length literature, sometimes ending up with a bibliographic list containing as few as three volumes.

Only books available in English are listed, and in most cases only books that are completely or mostly about the subject; that is, books that mention the topic under consideration only briefly or that include only a chapter on the topic are generally not included. Similarly, journal articles are not included, and in general, juvenile books are not included, with the exception of a few that are aimed at a sufficiently high level that they provide valuable information to the adult reader. Finally, the *Reader's Guide* is a guide to secondary literature, particularly in the entries on individuals, and does not give primary source literature.

Unfortunately, even though books in women's studies are multiplying at a very fast rate, many important topics in the field have had to be omitted from this volume. Because the field is still so new, there are many topics on which few or no books have yet been published, most of the research still being in the form of articles in journals. Whenever possible, those issues are addressed as part of entries on broader topics. For example, not enough books exist for an entry on the crucial and emerging topic of the "comfort women" during World War II; however, that topic is addressed under the broader topic of "Sexual Slavery." In addition, a large number of important women have not been included in this *Reader's Guide* because very few if any books have been written on them. This surely reflects the relatively low interest (until recently) in women's lives and in highlighting women's contributions to society and culture. It also indicates a direction in which women's studies needs to go. Interestingly, several women have been written about only in juvenile literature, indicating a willingness, at least, to present these women's lives to young people.

A partial list of women who could not be discussed in this volume owing to a lack of adequate book-length material about them includes Jane Addams, Catherine Beecher, Amelia Bloomer, Barbara Bodichon, Rosario Castellanos, Prudence Crandall, Marian Wright Edelman, Ruth Bader Ginsburg, Fanny Lou Hamer, Grace Murray Hopper, Phillis Kaberry, Billy Jean King, Alexandra Kollantai, Charlotte Lennox, Clarice Lispector, Wilma Mankiller, Barbara McClintock, Gabriela Mistral, Maria Mitchell, Lucretia Mott, Martina Navratilova, Sandra Day O'Connor, Rosa Parks, Alice Paul, Ntozake Shange, Nancy Ward, Ida B. Wells Barnett, and Sarah Winnemucca. A number of these persons, however, are discussed briefly in entries that deal with issues with which they are or were involved. We can hope that by the time this *Reader's Guide* is ready for a revised edition, more of these important women can be included because increased interest in their valuable contributions will have resulted in more books written about them.

Arrangement of the Entries

Entries are listed in alphabetical order. In addition, there are a number of aids to help the reader find entries on topics of interest.

1. **Thematic List** (p. xxi). This list provides the reader with a guide to finding all entries on particular themes or in particular disciplines. There will be some overlap in these lists, as some entries easily fall into more than one category.
2. **Booklist Index** (p. 655). This list gives the alphabetical order by author of all books discussed in the entries. Some books are included in more than one entry, and the reader can then turn to the entry or entries to find discussions of a particular book, at times from more than one perspective.
3. **General Index** (p. 701). The general index includes events, individuals, and topics mentioned in any of the entries. It is especially useful in locating references to individuals or topics that have no entry of their own.
4. **Cross References**. At the end of many entries there are "*See also*" notes that refer the reader to entries on related topics.

Format within Entries

Each entry begins with a list of the books to be discussed, including publication details. In each case, first date and place of publication in the United States and/or the United Kingdom are included, as well as, when relevant, the dates of the most recent revision. Following this, the text of each essay provides brief discussions of the books listed. To help the reader identify the material on a particular book, the first significant mention of each author is in capital letters. When more than one work by the same author is included, the name is capitalized at the beginning of the discussion of each book, followed by the publication date in parentheses.

Acknowledgments

This project has been a pleasure to pursue, not the least because of the many fine scholars and writers with whom I have worked and corresponded. I am grateful to the advisers and contributors for their hard work in developing this complex interdisciplinary work.

ADVISERS

Marjorie Agosin
Virginia Crane
Claire Duchen
Marilyn French
Jerry Gems
Gabriele Griffin
Jill Johnston
Annis Pratt
Sue V. Rosser
Marilyn Safir
Ailbhe Smyth
Linda Wagner-Martin
Phyllis Holman Weisbard

CONTRIBUTORS

Pamela Abbott
Susan Kiernan Ahern
Tria Airheart-Martin
Julie S. Amberg
Elisabeth Armstrong
Chris Atmore
Alison Bailey
Billie Salisbury Baladouni
Ann Stewart Balakier
Paul Barton-Kriese
Ingrid Bartsch
Judith R. Baskin
Paulina Bazin
Frances R. Belmonte
Linda Benson
Cynthia A. Bily
Carol A. Blessing
Janet K. Boles
Mary Jo Bona
Beverly Greene Bond
Marilyn Bordwell
Eileen Bresnahan
Linda Czuba Brigance
Harry Brod
Barbara Brook
Elizabeth E. Brusco
Susan R. Burgess
Deirdre C. Byrne
Jenny Cameron
Donna M. Campbell
Victoria Carchidi
Francis Carleton
Jo Eldridge Carney
Allison Carter
Donald Baird Chae
Joanne A. Charbonneau

Wendy E. Chmielewski
Linda K. Christian-Smith
Dawn M. Cicero
Albrecht Classen
Andrew Clutterbuck
Helena Antolin Cochrane
Katherine Cockin
Lisa Gail Collins
Susan Conley
Susan P. Conner
Jane Connor
Elizabeth Cooley
Carlo Coppola
Gary D. Crane
Ralph J. Crane
Denise Cuthbert
Carol Klimick Cyganowski
Fabienne Darling-Wolf
Indra M. David
Doreen D'Cruz
Maryanne Dever
Mary Leah DeZwart
Carol E. Dickson
Heather Elise Dillaway
Sandi L. Dinger
Robert Dingley
Carolyn DiPalma
John C. Dixon
Colleen T. Donaldson
Nan H. Dreher
Ruth Evans
Barbara C. Ewell
Amy S. Farrell
Susan B. Feldman
Rachel Fensham
Bonnie L. Ford
Vivian Foss
Brigittine M. French
Elizabeth Lane Furdell
Theresa Strouth Gaul
Davida Gavioli
Mary M. Gergen
Amelia Gibson
Sharón Gordon
Val Gough
Melanie G. Green
Gabriele Griffin
Rita M. Gross
Michèle Grossman
Martin Gruberg
Deborah Bush Haffey
Joan Wylie Hall
Gina L. Hames
Alexandra M. Hart
Leslie Heaphy
Melissa Hellstern
Diane Andrews Henningfeld
Melanie A. Herzog
Nels P. Highberg
Bridget D. Holland
Sara R. Horowitz
Sharon Shih-jiuan Hou
Kate Pritchard Hughes
Kirsten Jamsen
Helen Johnson
Julie K. Johnston
Jyl J. Josephson
Cheryl Toronto Kalny
Meg Wilkes Karraker
Carolyn Keith
Ellin M. Kelly
Erna Kelly
Lori J. Kenschaft
Patricia Clark Kenschaft
Michelle Maria Keown
Catherine Pélissier Kingfisher
Laura F. Klein
Melvin A. Kulbicki
Rachel Simon Kumar
Priya A. Kurian
Janet M. LaBrie
Alice L. Laffey
Ralph L. Langenheim, Jr.
Robert W. Langran
Katharina von Ledersteger
Robin S. Lent
Carole Levin
Holli G. Levitsky
Jian Li
Sharon A. Locy
Jean Marie Lutes
Karen V. Lyons
Patricia MacCormack
Gina Macdonald
Suzanne H. MacRae
Edward A. Malone
Bill Manikas
Cecilia G. Manrique
Catherine L. Marston
Frances E. Mascia-Lees
Karol Maybury
Anne E. McCall
Mary A. McCay
Jennifer McDonell
Patricia McNeal
Carolyn Michelle
Angela R. Miles
Barbara B. Miller
Karen A.J. Miller
Radhika Mohanram
Jennifer R. Moore
Jennifer More
Susan L. Morrow
Jay Mullin
Lorri G. Nandrea
Nancy R. Nangeroni

Shyamala A. Narayan
Caryn E. Neumann
Pamela J. Nickless
Toula Nicolacopoulos
Norma C. Noonan
Soňa Nováková
Mary O'Connor
Christine O'Grady
Kathleen O'Grady
Laura Katz Olson
Brigitta Olubas
Andrea O'Reilly
Catherine M. Orr
Jo Ortel
Stephanie Oxendale
Robert J. Paradowski
Bob Pease
Kate L. Peirce
Cynthia Fabrizio Pelak
Barbara Penner
Linda Peterat
Barbara Bennett Peterson
Valerie Victoria Peterson
AnnMarie Phillips
Jan Pilditch
Melinda Plastas
Stacey B. Plichta
Judith L. Poxon
James J. Preston
Victoria Price
Vivian Price
Gwen Raaberg
Bette Adams Reagan
Michaela Crawford Reaves
H. Elizabeth Renfro
Katherine Roberts
Carol L. Robinson
Rinaldina Russell
Vicki A. Sanders
Rebecca Saunders
Monica C. Schraefel
Rose Secrest
Mark Sergi
Lynda Sexson
Margrit Shildrick
Stacey C. Short
Donald C. Simmons, Jr.
Pamela M. Smiley
Angela K. Smith
Gail K. Smith
Hilda D. Spear
Sharon L. Spray
Kathleen Staudt
Beverly A. Stitt
Carla A. Stoner
Annette Stott
Erin Striff
Banu Subramaniam
Timothy E. Sullivan
Susan M. Taylor
Anne N. Thalheimer
Alison Thomas-Cottingham
Helen Thompson
Jan Todd
Mary Todd
Sandy Toussaint
Paul B. Trescott
Anna Tripp
Susan Tucker
Tiffany Urwin
Kimberly A. VanHoosier-Carey
Denise Varney
Lynn Walter
Cecil Walters
Paula Wansbrough
Pat Washington
C. Kay Weaver
Batya Weinbaum
Merry E. Wiesner-Hanks
Tanya E. Williamson
Kerstin Wilsch
Amy L. Wink
Nancy Woloch
Effie Yiannopoulou

ALPHABETICAL LIST OF ENTRIES

THEMATIC LIST: ENTRIES BY CATEGORY

Activism

(*See also* Social Movements)

Anthony, Susan B.
Bethune, Mary McLeod
Catt, Carrie Chapman
Child, Lydia Maria
Davis, Angela Y.
Day, Dorothy
Dix, Dorothea
Feminist Activism
Fuller, Margaret
Goldman, Emma
Grimké, Angelina and Sarah
Keller, Helen
Kelley, Florence
Leadership
Luxemburg, Rosa
Mandela, Winnie
Mother Jones
Pankhurst, Christabel, Emmeline, and Sylvia
Roosevelt, Eleanor
Sanger, Margaret
Stanton, Elizabeth Cady
Stone, Lucy
Stopes, Marie
Tristan, Flora
Truth, Sojourner
Tubman, Harriet
Wald, Lillian D.
Willard, Frances
Woodhull, Victoria
Wright, Frances

Adventurers

Bly, Nellie
Earhart, Amelia
Kempe, Margery
Sacagawea

Ancient History

Amazons
Ancient Classical World
Ancient Egalitarian Cultures
Ancient Near East
Hatshepsut
History: Prehistory
Hunting/Gathering Cultures
Hypatia and Early Philosophers
Matriarchal Theory
Sappho

Anthropology

Anthropology: Feminist
Anthropology: Traditional
Benedict, Ruth
Hunting/Gathering Cultures
Matrifocal Cultures
Matriliny
Mead, Margaret
Migration

ARTS

Architecture
Art, Images of Women in
Art and Gender Issues

Dance
Dance
Duncan, Isadora
Fonteyn, Margot
Graham, Martha
Pavlova, Anna

Film
Film, Images of Women in
Filmmaking

Painting
Artists: General Surveys
Artists: Nineteenth Century
Artists: Twentieth Century
Carr, Emily
Cassatt, Mary
Grandma Moses
Kahlo, Frida
Kauffmann, Angelica
Kollwitz, Käthe Schmidt
Morisot, Berthe
O'Keeffe, Georgia

Photography
Bourke-White, Margaret
Cameron, Julia Margaret
Photography

Arts and Crafts, Traditional
Nevelson, Louise
Sculpture

Theater
Acting
Bernhardt, Sarah
Performance Art
Theater: Images of Women in
Theater: Women's Activity in

CHILDREN

Adolescence
Child Custody
Child Sexual Abuse
Child Support
Female Infanticide
Girlhood
Girls' Organizations
Literature: Modern Children's

COMMUNICATION

Communication Styles and Gender
Language, Gender Inclusive/Exclusive

ECONOMICS

Affirmative Action
Business and Entrepreneurship
Capitalism
Child Support
Class and Gender
Day, Dorothy
Division of Labor by Sex
Dowry
Dual Career Families
Dual Labor Markets
Earnings Gap
Economic Development: Africa
Economic Development: Asia
Economic Development: Latin America
Feminization of Poverty
Glass Ceiling
Great Depression
Industrial Revolution
Labor Unions
Mentoring
Multinational Corporations
Poverty
Property Rights
Welfare

EDUCATION

Coeducation
Consciousness-Raising
Curricular Transformation
Gender Bias in Education
Higher Education
Mathematics: Teaching to Women
Mentoring
Pedagogy, Feminist

Scholarship/Research, Feminist
Science: Teaching to Women
Sex-Segregated Education
Sexual Harassment in Education
Teaching: Primary and Secondary
Teaching: University
Willard, Emma
Women's Studies, General Works
Women's Studies: Introductory Works

FAMILY

Adultery
Child Custody
Child Support
Concubinage
Divorce: History
Divorce: Present-Day
Domestic Violence
Dowry
Dual Career Families
Family
Incest
Marriage
Matriliny
Mother-Daughter Relationships
Motherhood
Polygamy
Polygamy, Mormon
Purdah
Sexual Assault/Rape: Marital
Single-Parent Families
Sisterhood
Surrogate Motherhood
Widowhood

FEMINIST THEORY AND WOMEN'S STUDIES

Ecofeminism
Feminine Archetypal Theory
Feminism: Cultural
Feminism: Liberal
Feminism: Marxist/Socialist
Feminism: Postmodern
Feminism: Radical
Feminist Theory, Formative Works
Lesbian Studies
Literary Criticism, Feminist
Matriarchal Theory
Men and Feminism
Patriarchy
Queer Theory
Womanism
Women's Studies: General Works
Women's Studies: Introductory Works

FEMINIST APPROACHES TO VARIOUS DISCIPLINES

Anthropology: Feminist
Health: Women's Health Movement
Jurisprudence, Feminist
Language, Gender Inclusive/Exclusive
Pedagogy, Feminist
Psychological Theories about Women: Feminist
Psychotherapy, Feminist
Science Studies, Feminist
Spirituality, Feminist
Theology, Feminist
Women's History Movement

GENDER ISSUES

Art and Gender Issues
Communication Styles and Gender
Consciousness-Raising
Division of Labor by Sex
Femininity
Gender as a Social Construct
Gender Bias in Education
Gender Stereotyping
Health: Gender Politics of
Language, Gender Inclusive/Exclusive
Race/Ethnicity and Gender
Science: Gender Bias in Research
Separate Spheres
Sex Discrimination in the Workplace
Sexual Double Standard
Transgenderism

HEALTH

Addictions
AIDS and HIV

Barton, Clara
Blackwell, Elizabeth
Body Image
Breastfeeding
Caregiving
Codependency
Depression
Disability Issues
Doctors
Eating Disorders
Elder Abuse
Female Genital Mutilation
Gynecology, History and Development of
Healers and Herbalism
Health: Gender Politics of
Health: General Works
Health: Women's Health Movement
Infertility
Medical History
Menopause
Menstruation
Mental Health
Midwifery
Nightingale, Florence
Physical Fitness
Pregnancy and Childbirth
Self-Defense
Sterilization

HISTORY

(*See also* Ancient History, Politics and Government, Religion, Social Movements, Suffrage Struggle, War)

Ancient Classical World
Ancient Near East
History: American
History: British
History: Medieval
History: Prehistory
History: Renaissance
Oral History
Victorian Era
Women's History Movement

Historical Events
- American Revolutionary Era
- Great Depression
- Holocaust
- Industrial Revolution
- Women's Rights Convention, Seneca Falls, New York

LAW

Adultery
Criminal Punishment
Female Offenders
Lawyers
Jurisprudence, Feminist
Property Rights
Protective Legislation
Roe v. Wade (United States 1973)
Workplace Equality Legislation

LESBIANISM

Homophobia and Heterosexism
Lesbian Community
Lesbian History
Lesbian Identity
Lesbian Separatism
Lesbian Studies
Literature: Lesbian
Queer Theory

LIFE CYCLE

Adolescence
Aging
Girlhood
Menopause
Menstruation

LITERATURE

(*See also* Writers)

Literary Criticism, Feminist
Literature: Biography and Autobiography
Literature: Diaries and Journals
Literature: Drama

MEN

MUSIC

ORGANIZATIONS

POLITICS AND GOVERNMENT

POPULAR CULTURE

Film, Images of Women in
Filmmaking
Magazines and Periodicals
Romance
Soap Opera
Television, Images of Women in

PSYCHOLOGY

Body Image
Eating Disorders
Ethic of Care
Femininity
Freud, Anna
Freud, Sigmund
Horney, Karen
Klein, Melanie
Mental Health
Psychological Theories about Women: Pre-Feminist
Psychological Theories about Women: Feminist
Psychotherapy, Feminist
Self-Esteem

RACE/ETHNICITY

Apartheid
Holocaust
Race/Ethnicity and Gender
Slavery, Black

Groups
Arab Women
Asian Women
Black Women
Jewish Women
Latin American Women
Native American Women
White Women

RELATIONSHIPS

Friendship
Marriage
Motherhood
Sisterhood

RELIGION

Bible: General
Bible: New Testament
Bible: Old Testament/Hebrew Bible
Church Fathers
Clergywomen
Convents and Nuns
Fundamentalism: Christian
Fundamentalism: Islamic
Goddesses
Jewish Women
Polygamy, Mormon
Saints
Spirituality, Feminist
Theology, Feminist
Virgin Mary
Witch Hunts

Persons
Blavatsky, Helena Petrovna
Cabrini, Mother Frances
Day, Dorothy
Dyer, Mary
Eddy, Mary Baker
Hildegard of Bingen
Hutchinson, Anne
Joan of Arc
Julian of Norwich
Lee, Ann, Mother
Seton, Elizabeth Ann Bayley
Tekakwitha, Kateri
Teresa of Avila

Religions
Buddhism
Christianity: Pre-Reformation
Christianity: Post-Reformation
Hinduism
Judaism
Mormonism
Witchcraft: Ancient
Witchcraft/Wicca: Modern and Neo-Paganism

REPRODUCTIVE ISSUES

Abortion: Pre-Twentieth Century
Abortion: Twentieth Century
Birth Control Movement
Infertility
Menstruation
Midwifery
Pregnancy and Childbirth
Reproductive Freedom
Reproductive Technologies
Roe v. Wade (United States 1973)
Sanger, Margaret
Sterilization
Surrogate Motherhood

SCIENCES

Aviation
Biological Determinism
Computers and Cyberspace
Ecofeminism
Geography
Inventors
Mathematics: General
Mathematics: Teaching to Women
Nature
Reproductive Technologies
Science: Gender Bias in Research
Science: History
Science: Teaching to Women
Science: Women as Subject of
Sciences: Biological
Sciences: Physical
Science Studies, Feminist
Scientists
Technology

Persons

Byron, Ada, Countess of Lovelace
Carson, Rachel
Curie, Marie
Franklin, Rosalind, and the DNA Controversy
Hodgkin, Dorothy Mary Crowfoot

SEXUALITY

Bisexuality
Heterosexuality
Lesbian Identity
Pornography
Prostitution
Sex Customs in China, Japan, and India
Sexual Double Standard
Sexual Politics
Transsexualism

SOCIAL ISSUES

Antifeminism
Apartheid
Divorce: History
Divorce: Present-Day
Female Genital Mutilation
Gender-Role Socialization
Homophobia and Heterosexism
Misogyny
Prostitution
Sati
Sexism
Sex Tourism
Sexual Slavery
Slavery, Black

SOCIAL MOVEMENTS

Birth Control Movement
Black Woman's Club Movement
Consciousness-Raising
Cult of True Womanhood
Feminist Activism
Feminist Movement, Abolitionist Origins of
Feminist Movements: Global
Feminist Movements: Nineteenth Century
Feminist Movements: Twentieth Century
Greenham Common Women's Peace Camp
Intentional Communities
Labor Unions

Peace Movement
Settlement House Movement
Suffrage: Britain and Ireland
Suffrage: United States
Suffrage: Worldwide
United Nations
Volunteerism
Woman's Christian Temperance Union
Woman's Club Movement
Women's International League for Peace and Freedom
Women's Liberation Movement
Women's Rights Convention, Seneca Falls, New York

SPORTS

Athletes
Physical Fitness
Sport and Gender
Sport, History of
Zaharias, Mildred "Babe" Didrikson

SUFFRAGE STRUGGLE

Anthony, Susan B.
Catt, Carrie Chapman
Pankhurst, Christabel, Emmeline, and Sylvia
Stanton, Elizabeth Cady
Stone, Lucy
Suffrage: Britain and Ireland
Suffrage: United States
Suffrage: Worldwide
Truth, Sojourner

THIRD WORLD ISSUES

Concubinage
Economic Development: Africa
Economic Development: Asia
Economic Development: Latin America
Dowry
Dowry Murder/Bride Burning
Female Genital Mutilation
Multinational Corporations
Polygamy
Purdah
Sati
Sex Customs in China, Japan, and India
Sex Tourism
Sexual Slavery

VIOLENCE AND ABUSE

Child Sexual Abuse
Domestic Violence
Dowry Murder/Bride Burning
Elder Abuse
Female Genital Mutilation
Female Infanticide
Hill, Anita
Incest
Misogyny
Pornography
Sati
Self-Defense
Sex Tourism
Sexual Assault/Rape: Acquaintance
Sexual Assault/Rape: Marital
Sexual Assault/Rape: Other
Sexual Assault/Rape: War
Sexual Harassment in Education
Sexual Harassment in the Workplace
Sexual Slavery
Witch Hunts

WAR

Battlefield Nursing
Boadecia
British Women during World War II
Holocaust
Israeli-Palestinian Conflict
Joan of Arc
Military
Women at Work during World War II, United States

WORK AND PROFESSIONS

Business and Entrepreneurship
Clergywomen

Clerical Work
Day, Dorothy
Division of Labor by Sex
Doctors
Domestic Service
Dual Career Families
Dual Labor Markets
Earnings Gap
Glass Ceiling
Home-Based Work
Home Economics
Homemaking and Housework
Industrial Revolution
Lawyers
Management
Migrant Labor
Military
Mother Jones
Nontraditional Jobs
Protective Legislation
Scientists
Separate Spheres
Sex Discrimination in the Workplace
Sexual Harassment in the Workplace
Teaching: Primary and Secondary
Teaching: University
Women at Work during World War II, United States
Work
Workplace Equality Legislation

WRITERS: PRE-NINETEENTH CENTURY

Astell, Mary
Behn, Aphra
Bradstreet, Anne
Chaucer, Geoffrey
Christine de Pizan
Hildegard of Bingen
Kempe, Margery
Marie de France
Martineau, Harriet
Milton, John
Sappho
Sévigné, Marie, Marquise de
Shakespeare, William
Wheatley, Phillis
Wollstonecraft, Mary

WRITERS: NINETEENTH CENTURY

Alcott, Louisa May
Austen, Jane
Brontë, Charlotte and Emily
Browning, Elizabeth
Burney, Frances
Chopin, Kate
Dickinson, Emily
Eliot, George
Flaubert, Gustave
Gaskell, Elizabeth
Howe, Julia Ward
Radcliffe, Ann Ward
Rossetti, Christina
Sand, George
Shelley, Mary
Staël, Madame de, Anne-Louise-Germaine
Stowe, Harriet Beecher

WRITERS: TWENTIETH CENTURY

Akhmatova, Anna Andreeva
Angelou, Maya
Arendt, Hannah
Atwood, Margaret
Beauvoir, Simone de
Bishop, Elizabeth
Brooks, Gwendolyn
Carson, Rachel
Cather, Willa
Cixous, Hélène
Colette
Dinesen, Isak
Doolittle, Hilda (H.D.)
Duras, Marguerite
Frame, Janet
Gilman, Charlotte Perkins
Glasgow, Ellen
Gordimer, Nadine
Hall, Radclyffe
Head, Bessie
Hellman, Lillian
Hurston, Zora Neale
Irigaray, Luce
Jhabvala, Ruth Prawer
Laurence, Margaret
Le Guin, Ursula K.
Lessing, Doris
Lowell, Amy
Mansfield, Katherine
Millay, Edna St. Vincent
Moore, Marianne
Morrison, Toni

Munro, Alice
Murdoch, Iris
Nin, Anaïs
Oates, Joyce Carol
O'Connor, Flannery
Piercy, Marge
Plath, Sylvia
Porter, Katherine Anne
Rich, Adrienne
Sarton, May
Sayers, Dorothy Leigh
Sexton, Anne
Stead, Christina
Stein, Gertrude
Tsvetaeva, Marina
Walker, Alice
Weil, Simone
Welty, Eudora
Wharton, Edith
Woolf, Virginia
Yourcenar, Marguerite

A

Abolition Movement *see* Feminist Movement, Abolitionist Origins of; Slavery, Black

Aboriginal Women

Bell, Diane, *Daughters of the Dreaming*, Melbourne: McPhee Gribble, 1983; London: Allen and Unwin, 1984; revised edition, Sydney: Allen and Unwin, and Minneapolis: University of Minnesota Press, 1993

Brewster, Anne, *Reading Aboriginal Women's Autobiography*, Sydney: Sydney University Press, 1996

Brock, Peggy (ed.), *Women, Rites and Sites: Aboriginal Women's Cultural Knowledge*, Sydney and Boston: Allen and Unwin, 1989

Daylight, Phyllis, and Mary Johnstone, *Women's Business: Report of the Aboriginal Women's Task Force*, Canberra: Commonwealth of Australia, 1986

Gale, Fay (ed.), *We Are Bosses Ourselves: The Status and Role of Aboriginal Women Today*, Canberra: Australian Institute of Aboriginal Studies, and Atlantic Highlands, New Jersey: Humanities Press, 1983

Pring, Adele (ed.), *Women of the Centre*, Apollo Bay, Australia: Pascoe Press, 1990

Sykes, Roberta, *Murawina: Australian Women of High Achievement*, Sydney and New York: Doubleday, 1993

Vaarzon-Morel, Petronella (ed.), *Walpiri Karnta Karnta-Kurlangu Yimi/Warlpiri Women's Voices: Our Lives, Our History*, Alice Springs, Australia: IAD Press, 1995

The books reviewed here—a necessarily selective and hardly comprehensive list—are intended to provide multiple points of entry for readers wishing to pursue work concerned with Australian Aboriginal women, and readers should note that much excellent material in the area appears in essays, journal articles, book chapters, and primary sources beyond the scope of this survey. Until relatively recently, Aboriginal women neither appeared in print representing their own experiences and perspectives, nor did women's lives and business preoccupy the standard works of anthropology and ethnography that dominated twentieth-century European knowledge of Aboriginal peoples and cultures. Aboriginal women have thus historically been subject to a double silence, or absence, from the written record for much of the time from European invasion in the eighteenth century to the present. Since the late 1970s, however, there has been a steadily developing body of work that redresses this imbalance; most important are the contributions made by Aboriginal women themselves in the increasingly flourishing genres of biography, autobiography, life-writing, and oral history.

SYKES, in her collection of the narratives of thirty-four Aboriginal and Torres Strait Island "women of achievement," selected for their prominence in their own communities, draws on national contexts of Aboriginality and women's experiences in order to make more visible the contributions of Aboriginal women to mainstream readers. Including writers, politicians, artists, lawyers, community leaders, and others, the book introduces and celebrates both the diversity and the commonality characterising the experiences of contemporary Aboriginal and Torres Strait Islander women across the nation, although the selective number of entries makes it neither wholly representative nor fully inclusive of Aboriginal women in contemporary Australia, a limitation emphasized by Sykes herself.

By contrast, PRING focuses on the regional and the traditional in her grouping of the life stories of ten Aboriginal women whose traditional lands in Central Australia span various state borders, and whose lives attest to the extraordinary impact of successive government policies of forced resettlement, assimilation, and institutional dependence on Aboriginal women in personal, family, and community contexts. The Aboriginal historian Jackie Huggins has said that to understand Aboriginal history it is necessary to "read between the lines" of official documents of the day; it is also necessary, contributors to this book suggest, to bring the previously untold and unacknowledged history of many Aboriginal women into print for later generations to learn from and draw on.

VAARZON-MOREL's book brings together an impressive and moving range of narratives told by Walpiri women of Wirliyajarrayi (Willowra) in Australia's Northern Territory, collected, transcribed, and translated by a team of Aboriginal female academics and community members. The text is enriched both by its genuinely collaborative production and also by its bilingual format (accompanied by a Walpiri/Aboriginal English glossary), an editorial strategy all too rare in the presentation of Aboriginal narratives where traditional languages have survived into the present. The narratives are organised in relation to land and spirituality, the surviving and resisting of the often fatal brutality exercised by whites during the advent of European contact, and perspectives on the changes wrought by interaction with white Australian policies, technologies, and cultures.

GALE's book remains a highly valuable compendium of perspectives on a broad range of issues concerning Aboriginal women, from an equally broad range of Aboriginal and non-Aboriginal contributors. Ambitious in scope, cross-disciplinary in orientation, and productively linking academic and community voices, the chapters cover Aboriginal women and land rights, health, family, sexuality, culture, and the changing nature of Aboriginal women's social and cultural roles. The volume achieves a commendable balance by encouraging dialogue on the diversity of Aboriginal women's experiences in distinctive urban, traditional, and regional contexts, while maintaining respect for the complexities of the public sharing of Aboriginal "women's business."

Women's business is also the focus of the report of the Labor Government policy initiative conducted by Aboriginal authors DAYLIGHT and JOHNSTONE into the needs and issues confronted by Aboriginal women in health, welfare, housing, landrights, language and literacy, domestic and family issues, and interaction with government institutions and agencies. Much of the information is now outdated or superceded by new developments; the work remains relevant, however, for its commitment to an indigenous women-centred methodology, and its charting of issues facing Aboriginal women in both public and private spheres, many of which, such as the devastating impact of the "stolen children" generations, continue unabated in the present.

BELL's germinal work of feminist anthropology, revised for its second edition, documents the ceremonial and cultural life of Walpiri women and re-assesses models of gender relations in the process. The book remains pioneering in its dismantling of male-centred blindnesses in the anthropological and ethnographic literature to the importance of women in "traditional" Aboriginal cosmologies, belief systems, community maintenance, and cultural preservation and development. While the book has engendered controversy among both Aboriginal and non-Aboriginal feminist critics concerned with cross-cultural representation, knowledge formation, and the politics of academic inquiry, it remains an empathetically informed work of scholarship that argues passionately for the significance and status of "women's ways of knowing" in traditional cultural contexts.

Another re-valuation of the importance of Aboriginal women's roles as custodians for and authorities on cultural heritage and maintenance comes from BROCK's collection of essays on Aboriginal women's cultural knowledge. Nine contributors from a variety of disciplines explore the dynamics of Aboriginal women's relationship to land, community, and heritage, with a particular focus on cross-cultural interactions in specific locales and contexts, and the active role played by Aboriginal women in managing these complex processes.

BREWSTER offers a useful introductory text to contemporary Aboriginal women's autobiography and life-writing, which engages with contemporary issues of Aboriginality and gender. Drawing on indigenous-centred, postcolonial, and feminist interpretive practices, and focusing on writers including Alice Nannup, Sally Morgan, and Ruby Langford Ginibi, Brewster provides a stimulating and well-theorised examination of how such texts are linked—notwithstanding the author's attentiveness to issues of specificity and difference between individual works—by their focus on the family as a "site of resistance" for Aboriginal women. Her discussion centres on the specialised role that families play in the continued survival and flourishing of Aboriginal communities in the face of two centuries of colonial dispossession and interference, during which the long arm of European law frequently reached into the deepest recesses of Aboriginal family life and structures. This is a valuable addition to the analysis and appraisal of Aboriginal women's life-writing, as is the bibliography of primary and secondary sources for further reading.

—MICHÈLE GROSSMAN

See also Hunting/Gathering Cultures

Abortion: Pre-Twentieth Century

Brodie, Janet Farrell, *Contraception and Abortion in Nineteenth-Century America,* Ithaca, New York, and London: Cornell University Press, 1994

Browder, Clifford, *The Wickedest Woman in New York: Madame Restell, the Abortionist,* Hamden, Connecticut: Archon, 1988

Glendon, Mary Ann, *Abortion and Divorce in Western Law,* Cambridge, Massachusetts: Harvard University Press, 1987

Gordon, Linda, *Woman's Body, Woman's Right: A Social History of Birth Control in America,* New York: Grossman, and Harmondsworth: Penguin, 1976

Hurst, Jane, *The History of Abortion in the Catholic Church: The Untold Story,* Washington, D.C.: Catholics for a Free Choice, 1981
Mohr, James C., *Abortion in America: The Origins and Evolution of National Policy, 1800–1900,* New York: Oxford University Press, 1978; Oxford: Oxford University Press, 1979
Olasky, Marvin, *Abortion Rites: A Social History of Abortion in America,* Wheaton, Illinois: Crossway, 1992
Reagan, Leslie J., *When Abortion Was a Crime: Women, Medicine, and Law in the United States, 1867–1973,* Berkeley and London: University of California Press, 1997
Riddle, John M., *Contraception and Abortion from the Ancient World to the Renaissance,* Cambridge, Massachusetts: Harvard University Press, 1992

Any history of abortion written in the late twentieth century necessarily reflects contemporary debates about the nature, politics, and ethics of abortion. Historians who seek to guarantee women's access to abortion in the modern world tend to emphasize that abortion has always been a part of human societies. Historians who think that abortion should be subject to moral and/or legal sanctions tend to emphasize that it is only resorted to when something else has gone wrong—and that two wrongs do not make a right. Histories of abortion thus make it unusually clear that vastly differing conclusions can be drawn from historical evidence.

GORDON's classic volume makes clear its premise in its title: that reproductive control is a woman's inalienable right. Gordon's discussion of abortion, though not extensive, presents it as a normal if not always approved method of controlling births, which has been used in all times and cultures and social groups.

RIDDLE uses written documents and demographic data to demonstrate the use of contraceptives and abortifacients among a wide range of premodern peoples. He argues that the tendency of modern Westerners to dismiss such methods as superstition or magic blinds them to the existence of herbal and other traditional contraceptives and abortifacients. Women of all periods, he suggests, have acted to some degree as if fertility control were within their rights, but a historical trend toward restricting birth control information has deprived modern women of knowledge available to their ancestors.

HURST's goal is to encourage Catholics to reconsider abortion's theological status. She examines historical writings on abortion, starting in A.D. 100, and concludes that these sources present substantively different views on such basic questions as when an embryo becomes a human being, the relative values of actual and potential human life, and the purposes of human sexuality. Catholic writings on abortion, she argues, have never fallen within the realm of papal infallibility, so modern Catholics have an opportunity to develop a moral theology of abortion that is better grounded in historical church teachings than the recent and overly simplistic formula "abortion is homicide."

MOHR's study of abortion and abortion policy in nineteenth-century America concurs with the image of abortion as historically uncontroversial and not uncommon. English common law, Mohr points out, condoned abortion until "quickening," or the first time a woman felt fetal movement. The earliest American statutes regulating early abortion, passed around 1830, sought to preserve women's health and were part of general poison control measures. The incidence and visibility of abortion, as well as its acceptability to middle-class married women, increased during the first half of the nineteenth century. Starting around 1860, the nascent American Medical Association, as part of its drive to create a public professional role for "regular" physicians, led a crusade to make abortion illegal and socially unacceptable. Their success, and that of the anti-obscenity crusaders, was bequeathed to the twentieth century as "traditional" law and mores.

The basic structure of Mohr's study has been followed by many later writers. BRODIE's discussion of abortion generally follows Mohr's, although she gives more explicit attention to reproduction as a field of power struggles between men and women. She, like Gordon, sees abortion as one end of a spectrum of methods of birth control.

Avowedly Christian and pro-life, OLASKY presents a contrary interpretation of abortion's history, and specifically takes issue with Mohr's portrayal of nineteenth-century society as generally tolerant of abortion. Abortion, he argues, was generally seen as the last refuge of the desperate: the seduced, the abandoned, the prostitute. He correctly points out that nineteenth-century advocates of women's rights did not see abortion as part of the solution to women's oppression, but rather as a tool that men could use to justify their continued exploitation of women. While he acknowledges that by mid-century, middle-class married people were increasingly turning to abortion as a method of limiting their numbers of children, Olasky portrays this development as an aberration from a general moral consensus against abortion. Physicians, he suggests, were stirred to take action by the sight of middle-class women pursuing such misguided goals. The late nineteenth-century antiabortion movement, Olasky argues, was part of a broader attempt to extend "compassion" and practical aid to those who suffered from poverty, sexual exploitation, and social ostracism. Only in the twentieth century would compassion be redefined as allowing pregnant women to make their own mistakes and suffer the consequences alone.

BROWDER's portrayal of the nineteenth-century abortionist Ann Lohman, alias Madame Restell, concurs with Olasky's image of abortion as belonging to a marginal underworld. Restell was the most prominent of many practicing abortionists in antebellum New York: indeed, in her time abortion was often called "Restellism." The less sensational of two published biographies,

Browder's book portrays Restell as an unscrupulous woman, motivated solely by an insatiable greed for wealth and social stature. Generally uninterested in issues of gender, class, and power, Browder nevertheless provides vivid depictions of the idiosyncratic personalities and events that determined the changing availability of abortion in nineteenth-century New York.

REAGAN argues that the primary purpose of legal prohibition was not to eradicate abortion but to police boundaries of gender and sexuality. The publicity of abortion raids and prosecutions punished women who dared step outside acceptable bounds and sent a clear message to other women who might want to challenge gender norms. Nevertheless, abortion was commonly if erratically available until the 1950s, when organized medicine and law finally succeeded in destroying the networks on which women had relied. *Roe v. Wade,* Reagan argues, was not an instance of anomalous "judicial activism" but a response to general questioning of established ideologies of sexuality and gender and women's longstanding determination to control reproduction.

GLENDON's purpose is once again explicit: to suggest ways that the United States might end its turmoil over abortion while decreasing, though not eliminating, abortion's incidence. Arguing that law is an embodiment of social norms and appropriately has an instructive or "pedagogical" function, Glendon provides a comparative history of recent laws regarding abortion in 20 European and North American countries. France, she suggests, provides a useful model: since the 1970s, France has legally discouraged abortion and named it undesirable, while simultaneously making it available in early pregnancy to women who are "in distress." Discourse about abortion in the United States, Glendon concludes, has been polarized by the excessive individualism of U.S. culture and law, but legal compromise is possible if both sides recognize that their real target is not the law, but the climate of opinion surrounding abortion.

—LORI KENSCHAFT

See also Reproductive Freedom

Abortion: Twentieth Century

Blanchard, Dallas A., *The Anti-Abortion Movement and the Rise of the Religious Right: From Polite to Fiery Protest,* New York: Twayne, 1994

Bonavoglia, Angela, *The Choices We Made: Twenty-Five Women and Men Speak Out about Abortion,* New York: Random House, 1991

Costa, Marie, *Abortion: A Reference Handbook,* Santa Barbara, California: ABC-CLIO, 1991

Kaplan, Laura, *The Story of Jane: The Legendary Underground Feminist Abortion Service,* New York: Pantheon, 1995

Lader, Lawrence, *Abortion II: Making the Revolution,* Boston: Beacon Press, 1973

Luker, Kristin, *Abortion and the Politics of Motherhood,* Berkeley and London: University of California Press, 1984

Reagan, Leslie J., *When Abortion Was a Crime: Women, Medicine, and Law in the United States, 1867–1973,* Berkeley and London: University of California Press, 1997

Rosenblatt, Roger, *Life Itself: Abortion in the American Mind,* New York: Random House, 1992

Sachdev, Paul, *International Handbook on Abortion,* Westport, Connecticut: Greenwood, 1988

Tribe, Laurence, *Abortion: The Clash of Absolutes,* New York and London: Norton, 1990

Weddington, Sarah, *A Question of Choice,* New York: Putnam, 1992

Abortion is considered to be one of the most divisive social issues of our time. It polarizes Americans just as the issue of slavery did in the nineteenth century. This point is eloquently made by LADER, a pioneer in the 1960s who used the tactics of the abolitionists to bring abortion to the national consciousness prior to its becoming legal. He provides a moving, first-hand account of the social forces that came together finally to legalize abortion nationally in 1973.

KAPLAN provides an equally compelling historical summary of the rise of a grassroots movement as one of the original organizers of "Jane," an underground abortion service that operated from 1969 to 1973 in Chicago and provided more than eleven thousand women with safe, affordable abortions. The focus throughout the book is on the empowerment this grassroots effort gave to both the organizers and the women seeking abortions, at a time when there was no consumer health movement. She also includes a good description of the Clergy Abortion Referral Network and how they acted like an Underground Railroad for women prior to the national legalization of abortion. WEDDINGTON was a very young attorney from a small, rural Texas town who argued the landmark Supreme Court case, Roe v. Wade, that legalized abortion in 1973. The evolution of the case is detailed and followed by a discussion of the backlash against women's rights today. She concludes with a whole chapter on activism, with a plan of action to protect legal abortion.

Several authors in the field take a broad perspective and cover two or more aspects of abortion from a legal, historical, sociological, political, or philosophical perspective. Each expresses concern with the way in which the issue has divided, and continues to divide the United States and attempts to help find a common ground. REAGAN has written the first study of the entire era of illegal abortion in the United States and focuses on how private activities and conversations transform public policy. She divides the history of abortion from 1867 to 1973 into four sections and devotes considerable attention to how women's class, race, and marital status affected their availability to safe abortions in hospitals. Her rich case studies, based on primary sources in the city of Chicago, help the reader to understand the choices that women made and how they shaped public policy. The book also contains a focus on the often neglected aspect of African-American women's stories.

TRIBE has a unique perspective as a professor and Supreme Court litigator. He feels that America is at a crossroads as rights are being eroded and the country is becoming more divided on the issue of abortion. As others have noted, the two strongly-held competing sides on this issue are peculiar to the late twentieth century. His book covers several dimensions of the issue, including a good history of abortion in the twentieth century, abortion world-wide and how it has been used in many countries as a tool of control by governments, and abortion rights in the U.S. Constitution. In addition, a chapter is devoted to ways the two sides can come to a common ground. He develops a theme repeated by several authors, that opposition to abortion is often based upon a belief in traditional sex roles and a punitive attitude toward women's sexual freedoms.

LUKER is often cited as a reference in the field. Using a sociological perspective, she makes the point that abortion polarizes people just as slavery did. In a thoroughly researched book she interviewed a wide range of people on both sides of the debate in California. Unlike others, she found that people have few common premises on the issue, and she seeks to uncover how such differing viewpoints came about. To do this she examines how views of life, death, parenthood, sexuality, gender roles, and morality are formed. She puts forth four arguments for her theory and notes that the abortion issue is a debate about worldviews and personhood. She also takes a historical perspective and contrasts the nineteenth and twentieth centuries. Luker believes that this issue will separate us for years to come, because it involves our most strongly held beliefs about life, gender roles, and being human, concepts on which it is difficult to compromise.

BLANCHARD analyzes the organizations and the cultural, ideological, and political forces in the anti-abortion movement, also using a sociological perspective. He finds that religious networks are a primary source for people joining the anti-abortion movement. This is a factual and well-documented book that addresses important issues related to class and race. He summarizes that the anti-abortion movement is one of cultural fundamentalism that seeks to reestablish traditional sex roles.

ROSENBLATT, as a social commentator, traces the history of abortion and makes the point that all civilizations have had to deal with conflicts on abortion and have developed different ways of doing so.Through interviews and his own insights, he concludes that what makes abortion unique is the "sense of grief" it evokes, discouraging open discussion. Silence on this issue, he says, is the problem. He concludes that the United States is basically a religious country, and abortion is offensive to many because it does not coincide with middle-class values of sexual conduct. A chapter is devoted to suggestions as to how both sides can reach a compromise—he refers to it as "permit, but discourage" and uses the state of Iowa as an example. COSTA has developed a resource book with historical and factual information on abortion. Separate chapters are devoted to the history of abortion; key players in the debate; statistical and factual information about abortion laws and policies, medical techniques, harassment of providers, and public opinion; bibliography of print and non-print resources; and a directory of relevant organizations in the United States only.

For information on the international aspects of abortion one may refer to the thorough book edited by SACHDEV. This single volume contains data from all continents and thirty-three countries, each written by a different leading authority in the field. Each chapter addresses a different country and contains factual information on the historical development of abortion policy; the role of the medical profession, media, women's and religious organizations, and other groups affecting legislation; shifting attitudes over time towards abortion; demographic data including special populations; impact on family planning and fertility; illegal abortions; and abortion research. In contrast to strict resource books, BONAVOGLIA has edited a collection of highly personal stories of a wide variety of famous women who have had abortions. Many of the authors cited above note that we should never forget the women and their families whose lives have been affected by an unwanted pregnancy and an abortion, whether safe and legal or illegal and dangerous.

—COLLEEN DONALDSON

See also Reproductive Freedom; Roe v. Wade (United States 1973)

Acting

Berenstein, Rhona J., *Attack of the Leading Ladies: Gender, Sexuality, and Spectatorship in Classic Horror Cinema*, New York: Columbia University Press, 1996

Fischer, Lucy, *Shot/Countershot: Film Tradition and Women's Cinema*, Princeton, New Jersey: Princeton University Press, and London: Macmillan, 1989

Gilder, Rosamund, *Enter the Actress: The First Women in the Theatre*, London: Harrap, and Boston: Houghton Mifflin, 1931

Unterbrink, Mary, *Funny Women: American Comediennes*,

1860–1985, London and Jefferson, North Carolina: McFarland, 1987

Wexman, Virginia Wright, *Creating the Couple: Love, Marriage, and Hollywood Performance*, Princeton, New Jersey: Princeton University Press, 1993

Although acting is the most essential element of any theatrical or film presentation, to date it has been the least studied. There are varying opinions as to why this is so, but the reason probably has to do mainly with the difficulty of quantifying an event as ephemeral as a performance and the lack of specialized knowledge among most scholars that would enable them to successfully dissect the elements of acting. Therefore, there are very few texts that deal with live performances and almost none dealing particularly with those by women. There are many more texts written about women in film, but most of these focus on the director's role, and only a few attempt to analyze the performative act itself.

Though it predates the inception of women's studies as a discipline by several decades, GILDER's text remains a standard in the realm of theater history. She does not write from a specifically feminist perspective, but she was the first to offer a systematic study of women's participation in the theater. Beginning with the stage in ancient Greece, Gilder traces the progression of women there from priestesses who controlled the early rites that eventually became theatrical to passive non-participants who were perhaps not even in attendance at the great tragedies of the "Golden Age" of Greek drama. She also clearly points out the irony in the fact that many of the greatest tragic roles ever written for female characters—Electra, Medea, Antigone—were performed solely by men. She tracks the attitude of disdain for actresses through Roman society—where they were given the legal status of prostitutes—into the modern era of the nineteenth century, when a major change of attitudes allowed actress/managers such as Carolina Neuber and Madame Vestris to become highly admired performers as well as wealthy stockholders in their theater companies. Gilder also offers a view of Hrotsvitha of Gandersheim that differs sharply from previous scholars. Hrotsvitha, a tenth-century nun who is the only person known to have composed drama in the west between the fall of Rome and the late Middle Ages, had been viewed as a minor writer of closet drama, but Gilder offers a persuasive argument that she was in fact writing for performance, a fact that would further distinguish her as a singular dramatic pioneer.

UNTERBRINK's account of comediennes is valuable chiefly due to its exhaustive listing of almost every woman who ever performed in American comedy over 130-year span. Unterbrink begins with Lotta Crabtree, a burlesque vaudevillian of the mid-nineteenth century American west, and ends with Sandra Bernhard and Marsha Warfield, two well-known comic actresses of the 1980s. She provides fairly lengthy entries on Lucille Ball, the most important female pioneer in television, as well as lesser-known performers of the early era of television, such as Imogene Coca. This listing is valuable particularly since women have traditionally been heavily concentrated in the field of comedy and remain so today, especially in television. Although she provides little in the way of analysis of why women are more acceptable as comediennes than tragediennes, the book is valuable for its very broad scope, its inclusion of otherwise obscure performers, and its extensive bibliography.

Among the numerous feminist film theorists publishing since the 1970s, only a few have attempted to analyze the details of performance. One of the most cogent analyses is provided by FISCHER, particularly in her third chapter, "The Lives of Performers: The Actress as Signifier." She discusses the role of actresses, within films and without, as "stars"—as part of the entire signification process of movies. Although the creation of false star personas and their value to films has been discussed extensively by others, Fischer is one of the few scholars to focus on actresses in particular. She also provides an interesting discussion of films about actresses, including Ingmar Bergman's *Persona* and Mai Zetterling's *The Girls.*

BERENSTEIN's book is unusual, in that it focuses throughout on the centrality of actresses and acting styles to the classical horror genre in American film. Particularly in chapters four and five, she minutely investigates the elements of female performance—the upturned look of terror, the protracted high-pitched scream, the hypnotic stare—that form the indispensable vocabulary of horror on film. She also investigates why women have traditionally been the victims in horror films, and how the horror genre deals with the dread of gender confusion, homosexuality, and male loss of control.

Finally, WEXMAN's book also concerns itself primarily with the elements of acting, but within the genre of romantic drama and comedy. She supplies an especially detailed treatment of how certain actresses, actor/actress combinations, and actress/director combinations merged to create the culturally sanctioned and acceptable appearances and roles of romantic couples. She also deals extensively with how the "love goddess" character affects cultural notions of males and maleness, reinforcing the myths of the powerful, emasculating, sexual woman, and the need for men to control her by dominating her and restoring her to acceptability within traditional patterns of male-female relations, especially marriage. Although the book has a rather narrow focus, it provides an especially intriguing discussion of acting and actresses in American film, and how they contribute to our past and current attitudes toward sex, love, monogamy, and marriage.

—VICKI A. SANDERS

See also Theater, Women's Activity in

Adams, Abigail 1744–1818

American

Akers, Charles W., *Abigail Adams: An American Woman,* Boston: Little Brown, 1980

Gelles, Edith B., *Portia: The World of Abigail Adams,* Bloomington: Indiana University Press, 1992

Keller, Rosemary, *Patriotism and the Female Sex: Abigail Adams and the American Revolution,* Brooklyn, New York: Carlson, 1994

Levin, Phyllis Lee, *Abigail Adams: A Biography,* New York, St. Martin's Press, 1987

Nagel, Paul C., *The Adams Women: Abigail and Louisa Adams, Their Sisters and Daughters,* New York and Oxford: Oxford University Press, 1987

Whitney, Janet, *Abigail Adams,* Boston: Little Brown, 1947; London: Harrap, 1949

Withey, Lynne, *Dearest Friend: A Life of Abigail Adams,* New York: Free Press, and London: Macmillan, 1981

Although always recognized as a notable woman of the early republic, First Lady Abigail Adams received little attention from biographers until the publication of several critical works in the 1980s and 1990s. The relatively recent interest in Adams probably arose with the publication of several volumes of the Adams Family correspondence in the 1960s and 1970s, as well as with the rise of women's studies programs in the United States, which sought both to recover early women's texts and to rewrite American history to include women's contributions.

WHITNEY's book is the only modern biography of Abigail Adams published before 1980 and thus is still cited today. Actually a fictionalized account of Adams's life, Whitney writes scenes around quotations from Adams's letters, frequently inventing dialogue and the thoughts of her characters. Because Abigail's life is told essentially through those events in which her husband, John, took a prominent part, the book offers an incomplete picture of its heroine. Little mention is made, for instance, of more domestic and personal issues about which Adams wrote extensively in her letters, such as the stillborn birth of her sixth child and her despondency over her daughter Nabby's breast cancer and subsequent death. Impressive for its extensive citing of the Adams letters, Whitney's book serves as an adequate introduction to the Adams family and American politics in general in Revolutionary times.

AKERS's book is the first full biography of Abigail Adams written after the publication of the Adams correspondence in the 1960s and 1970s. Drawing upon over two thousand of Abigail Adams's letters, Akers constructs not only a compelling portrait of this important American woman, but also a comprehensive cultural study of the period. Akers suggests that although Adams recognized and accepted the different roles men and women played, she insisted upon equality with her husband in her marriage. Akers's biography is a useful source for information on late eighteenth-century American politics.

WITHEY's biography of Abigail Adams is part of the first wave of women's studies scholarship that, in an effort to recover and validate the lives of women previously neglected or ignored, often used twentieth-century standards to judge earlier women's lives. Thus, Withey writes of the "feminism" of Adams and her important role in the political life of the new nation, focusing almost exclusively upon her public life and neglecting other important aspects, such as her religion and her domesticity. The book quotes extensively from the Adams Papers and contains a useful bibliography of primary and secondary sources.

LEVIN's biography utilizes extensive quotation from the Adams Papers and casts Abigail in a supportive role to her husband, John. Like Withey, Levin suggests that Adams was something of a feminist, who disliked her domestic work and reveled in the politics of her day. Levin's argument would be stronger if she introduced some analysis of women's place and work into her discussions, but instead, the book is a pure narrative, composed of invented dialogue and thoughts of the characters. Levin's work serves as an entertaining introduction to Abigail's life.

Following the publication of his earlier work, *Descent from Glory: Four Generations of the John Adams Family* (1983), NAGEL writes a book that solely concerns the Adams women. Approximately one half of the volume is devoted to Abigail Adams. Nagel tells a very detailed, straightforward account of the Adams women's lives, yet he manages seemingly to disconnect them from almost all contemporary political events. He does this by focusing almost exclusively on their family and domestic affairs. Unfortunately, Nagel's text has no footnotes, so the specific sources of his many quotations can not be known.

Adding to what she has termed the "Abigail Industry," GELLES offers a valuable biography of Abigail Adams that differs from previous biographies in two ways. First, she has attempted to write from a specifically female point of view that acknowledges and accentuates the domesticity of Adams to see how it informs her character. Secondly, Gelles has examined Adams's letters within, as much as possible, an eighteenth-century context. Different from previous biographers, Gelles argues that Adams's intelligence and character, but not her values or attitudes, distinguish her from other eighteenth-century women. The book contains a valuable overview of contemporary writing on Adams, as well as an extensive bibliography on both Adams and her age.

KELLER is one among many scholars in the 1990s exploring the notion of men's and women's roles within the so-called public and private spheres, respectively. Keller investigates those junctions where American politics intersects Adams's domestic life and states that the American Revolution is a "focal point for understanding" Adams. Keller's book provides a rich cultural description of late eighteenth-century America and of the significant changes occurring in the position of and function of women's roles.

—JULIE S. AMBERG

See also American Revolutionary Era

Addams, Jane *see* Settlement House Movement

Addictions

Bepko, Claudia, *Feminism and Addiction,* New York: Haworth, 1991

Broom, Dorothy, *Double Bind: Women Affected by Alcohol and Other Drugs,* St. Leonards, Australia: Allen and Unwin, 1994

Cuskey, Walter, and Richard Wathey, *Female Addiction: A Longitudinal Study,* Lexington, Massachusetts: Lexington, 1982

Ettorre, E.M., *Women and Substance Use,* New Brunswick, New Jersey: Rutgers University Press, and London: Macmillan, 1992

Greaves, Lorraine, *Smoke Screen: Women's Smoking and Social Control,* Halifax: Fernwood, and London: Scarlet Press, 1996

Nellis, Muriel, *The Female Fix,* Boston: Houghton Mifflin, 1980; Harmondsworth: Penguin, 1981

Peluso, Emanuel, and Lucy Silvay Peluso, *Women and Drugs: Getting Hooked, Getting Clean,* Minneapolis: Minnesota CompCare, 1988

Roth, Paula, *Alcohol and Drugs Are Women's Issues,* London: Women's Action Alliance, and Metuchen, New Jersey: Scarecrow Press, 1991

Sargent, Margaret, *Women, Drugs, and Policy in Sydney, London, and Amsterdam: A Feminist Interpretation,* Aldershot and Brookfield, Vermont: Avebury, 1992

The feminist movement drastically changed the interpretation of addiction and its treatment modalities for women. During this movement, there was a growing realization that the understanding of addiction neglected to encompass the differing needs of the female population. Several resources emerged to fill this gap. These resources often focus on three general areas of women and addiction: treatment, research, and social policy.

While some authors seek to understand the origin of women's addiction, others attempt to determine the meaning of addiction in women's lives in order to develop adequate treatment modalities. ROTH and contributing authors explore a wide range of factors relating to women's substance abuse. These articles highlight the relationship between domestic violence, abuse, poverty, racism, sexism, and women's addiction. This text provides a structural and multi-cultural approach to the study of women and addiction. It is one of few resources that comprehensively demonstrate the importance for understanding the underlying antecedents of women's addiction when determining adequate treatment provision. Roth also promotes a feminist framework for addiction treatment that recognizes the need to address the imbalance of power and access to resources that often feed women's addiction.

PELUSO and PELUSO stray from a theoretical construction of women's addiction toward a more humanistic understanding of the effect of substance abuse on women. They compile a collection of stories written by women who have struggled with chemical dependency and addiction recovery. This book provides an intimate understanding of the emotional elements of addiction and is meant to be an inspiration and support for its readers. It is an excellent reference for anyone wanting insight into the psycho-social elements of women's experience with addiction and recovery. The final chapter of this book examines patterns of substance abuse developed out of the collection of a cross-section of women's stories. These patterns illustrate pertinent issues to consider for future addiction treatment.

BEPKO focuses on the field of women's addiction treatment within the context of family therapy, which is an area rarely examined by academics. Several authors collaborate to develop an exploration of the theoretical and clinical issues of female addiction. This book examines the gender issues underlying women and addiction treatment. The authors scrutinize several treatment modalities that lack a feminist perspective. They provide an illustration of the connection between addiction and women's lack of power and freedom. They also present feminist methods and clinical treatment alternatives for counselors and clinicians working with addicted women.

ETTORRE's philosophical perspective on women and addiction contains several theories spun out of a feminist ideology. She is one of few authors to examine several previously unexplored avenues of feminism and addiction, such as addictive eating and women's addiction to tobacco use. Ettorre reformulates traditional definitions of addiction in order to provide a women-centred approach to substance abuse. She conveys the need to transform and extend the perimeters of the addiction field to encompass the gender-specific needs of the female population.

CUSKEY and WATHEY also provide an examination of the barriers to treatment experienced by female addicts. They attempt to illustrate the gaps in women-centred services. They facilitate this study through a large-scale longitudinal research project to test several addiction treatment methodologies. This research takes place within a residential treatment centre for women who are addicted to several substances. The three-year study attempts to document the effectiveness of differing techniques utilized in women's addiction programming. This research is based on a disease model of addiction and is one of few studies to challenge some of its own medical model barriers in the provision of addiction treatment for women.

BROOM compiles a research collection from several authors who examine Australian women's substance use and abuse patterns. This comprehensive research makes the important distinction that the experience of men and women in relation to addiction is very different. It indicates that there are significant barriers for women's access to substance abuse intervention. In addition, this research examines the connection between past physical, sexual, and emotional abuse and women's addiction. It also illustrates the difficulty women experience when attempting to seek treatment without access to child care provision.

SARGENT provides a feminist interpretation of drug policies and heroine-addicted women in London, Sydney, and Amsterdam. She demonstrates how current government policy for treatment of female addiction services is punitive and contains elements of social control. Sargent's study evaluates current policy implementation through research using field observation. As there are few field observation studies on female drug addicts in relation to the intricacies of social policy, this research provides a fresh angle to women's addiction studies.

GREAVES diverges from standard addiction policy research. She examines the impact of women's smoking as a means of social adaptation and as a method of social control. Greaves examines women's addiction to tobacco from historical, social, and cultural contexts. She is one of few authors to present a picture of women's tobacco use with a primary focus on their experience of consumption. The final segment of her study attempts to define methods of cessation and prevention through the use of social policy restructuring.

NELLIS provides insight into the growing area of legal addictions and women. She examines the medical model and its contribution to legal female substance abuse. Nellis discusses the drastic increase in prescription medication to women who have difficulty coping with insurmountable life stresses. Although she presents this stress as primarily individualistic, she develops an extensive picture of the prescription drug industry and the medical profession as primary contributors to the problem of women's legal addiction. This information is presented through the use of stories about women's lives and their paths to prescription use. Nellis indicates the need for systemic and structural change to address this legal addiction issue.

—CHRISTINE O'GRADY

See also Codependency

Adolescence

Brown, Lyn Mikel, and Carol Gilligan, *Meeting at the Crossroads*, Cambridge, Massachusetts: Harvard University Press, 1992

Gilligan, Carol, Nona Lyons, and Trudy Hanmer, *Making Connections: The Relational Worlds of Adolescent Girls at Emma Willard School*, New York: Emma Willard School, 1989; London: Harvard University Press, 1990

Hancock, Emily, *The Girl Within*, New York: Dutton, 1989; London: Pandora, 1990

Konopka, Gisela, *Young Girls: A Portrait of Adolescence*, Englewood Cliffs, New Jersey: Prentice Hall, 1983

Mann, Judy, *The Difference: Growing Up Female in America*, New York: Warner, 1994

Orenstein, Peggy, *Schoolgirls: Young Women, Self-Esteem, and the Confidence Gap*, New York: Doubleday, 1994

Pipher, Mary, *Reviving Ophelia: Saving the Selves of Adolescent Girls*, New York: Putnam, 1994

Although studying the lives of females is not a new phenomenon, the approaches taken and topics studied in recent years are unique. The authors of the above books did as others had not and talked to adolescent girls about what they think, how they feel about the world, both global and personal, and what their lives are really like. Gilligan's work is perhaps the best known, and others have followed her lead in studying adolescent girls in depth by going into the schools and observing as well as interviewing. For BROWN and GILLIGAN's book, the authors went to the Laurel School to find out what happens to girls on the road to becoming women. What they found is that girls lose their "voices," because saying what they think or feel means risking losing their relationships and finding themselves powerless and alone. To empower women, the authors say, one must begin by giving girls their voices back—and by listening to those voices.

GILLIGAN, LYONS and HANMER went to the Emma Willard School, a private boarding school, to listen to girls talk about the meaning of self, relationship, and morality. The authors looked at moral conflicts among the high school girls, their conceptions of separation and connection (that is, their need for both closeness with others and autonomy), and their attachment to parents and relationships with mothers. They also examined eating disorders, leadership styles, racial issues, sexuality, and the girls' views of the future. In addition to adding to the scholarship on adolescent lives, the book teaches parents and educators alternate ways of interacting with adolescents.

HANCOCK also studied female development and the way in which girls put their identities aside during adolescence. By interviewing women about their adolescence rather than girls in the middle of it, she found that lost identities are rediscovered later. It is the childhood sense of self—the child within—that resurfaces after an adolescence spent in hiding. Other questions asked and examined include: How is it that this girl is lost or buried in the first place? What is her importance to a woman's identity? Who is this "girl within?" What deep truth does she possess?

KONOPKA also listened to voices—one thousand of them—to find out how they experience the world and to learn their hopes, concerns, and aspirations. Calling their struggle for personhood a touchstone of the times, she says it is more important than ever to listen to their thoughts and feelings and perhaps set wheels in motion for social change. As with the books discussed previously, this one is embedded in psychological and historical theory and research and includes frank discussions of most of the issues important to adolescents: sexuality and sex education, organizations and political concerns, friends, fear of isolation, suicide, and drugs. Konopka also injects personal history into the chapters and includes the poetry of teenage girls, making the book more intimate than others of its type.

MANN's work came into being because of her daughter, who was about to be an adolescent. Her daughter and her daughter's friends were important resources, but Mann also spent two years interviewing experts, visiting schools, listening to rock music, and talking with anyone who had knowledge of adolescent girls. Her goal was to go beyond the politics of gender and learn what really happens to girls that makes their experience so different from that of boys, and to explain her findings in lay terms for the general population. She does so without talking down to those who know something about the subject, thus making the book a good resource for all. Among her conclusions are that society will never effectively change the way girls are raised until it changes the way boys are raised, and boys must be raised to be more respectful of girls. We need, she says, to raise children with a new framework and a new set of values about what we want to see in boys and girls.

The American Association of University Women (AAUW) conducted a study in 1990 of adolescent girls and their decline of self esteem and concluded that there is a crisis in America regarding the way girls are educated. ORENSTEIN takes the poll to a higher level by introducing the human element to its findings. She spent a year at two middle schools observing and interviewing girls, administrators, teachers, and family members. Although her primary purpose was to find out gender differences in the academic experience, she put the academic experience in context with family life and relationships with girlfriends and boys. She documented gender bias in the classroom, such as teachers giving more attention to boys than to girls, as well as behavior differences between boys and girls, both in and out of the classroom, and the consequences of that behavior. And she found parents and teachers who not only did not know the detrimental effects to girls of these differences, but also did not know of their existence.

PIPHER, as a therapist and mother of an adolescent girl, wanted to know why so many adolescent girls were in therapy in the 1990s, why so many had sexually transmitted diseases, and why drugs and alcohol were so much a part of their lives—among other things. As she observed the world adolescents now live in by listening to their music, watching the television shows they watch, and talking with them, she too became convinced that something is very wrong with American culture and the way in which adolescent girls are taught to live in the world. She compares the problems of adolescent life in the 1990s with the problems of housewives, "the problem that has no name," which Betty Friedan had much earlier named in *The Feminine Mystique* (1963). The book is primarily case studies, stories of her clients, and her responses to them, but in and around the stories are facts and figures about American culture and suggestions for parents and educators about how to improve the quality of life for adolescent girls.

—KATE PEIRCE

See also Girlhood

Adultery

Atwater, Lynn, *The Extramarital Connection: Sex, Intimacy, and Identity*, New York: Irvington, 1982

Fisher, Helen, *Anatomy of Love: The Natural History of Monogamy, Adultery, and Divorce*, London: Simon and Schuster, and New York: Norton, 1992

Frayser, Suzanne G., *Varieties of Sexual Experience: An Anthropological Perspective on Human Sexuality*, New Haven, Connecticut: HRAF Press, 1985

Lawson, Annette, *Adultery: An Analysis of Love and Betrayal*, New York: Basic Books, 1988; Oxford: Basil Blackwell, 1989

Richardson, Laurel, *The New Other Woman: Contemporary Single Women in Affairs with Married Men*, New York: Free Press, 1985; London: Collier Macmillan, 1987

Wolfe, Linda, *Playing Around: Women and Extramarital Sex*, New York: Morrow, 1975

Although anthropologists have recorded adultery in many cultures, LAWSON found that there was almost no academic work by historians, sociologists, or anthropologists that focuses on adultery, and no book with the word *Adultery* as its title, when she wrote her book. The book starts with an interpretation of adultery as presented in western mythology, history, and literature, before dealing with the main topic—a quantitative and qualitative sociological study of a volunteer sample drawn from readers of three British newspapers. All subjects completed a 34-page questionnaire and about 100 also were interviewed. The sample, 59 percent female, is overwhelmingly middle class. The author also included seven percent of those who had "remained faithful" during their marriages, and some of those data were used to compare with those who had extramarital liaisons. Although Lawson finds much overlap in the extramarital attitudes and behaviors of men and women, she also notes some gender distinctions. Women tend to get involved more for "feeling" reasons; men more for calculated ("wouldn't hurt my marriage") reasons. When emotional involvement in the affairs deepens, women are more concerned about the effect on their children than are men. Lawson presents a multifaceted view of extramarital relations. This is a well-researched book with two appendices of the questionnaires and methods as well as a full bibliography. The book should be valuable to professionals and for supplementary reading in courses on gender, marriage, and divorce.

ATWATER's book is based on interviews with 50 women who answered a 1974 *Ms.* magazine's ad on participating in a study of extramarital relationships. Atwater points out in her introduction that those women who were interviewed were "feminist oriented" and were either "presently or recently engaged in extramarital relationships." The book describes initiations, the sexual and expressive intimacies, open marriage, self identities, and attitudes toward extramarital relations, with one chapter devoted to extramarital relationships with other women. This book is intended for two audiences: college students studying in the area of sexuality, gender roles, marriage and the family, and alternative lifestyles; and a general audience. The main thesis that the extramarital involvement provides emotional satisfaction and acts as a liberating force for women may be provocative to some readers.

Based on 66 lengthy interviews with middle- to upper middle-class women, WOLFE describes extramarital relationships of two groups of women: one group who attempt to be secretive about extramarital sexual experiences by virtue of traditional marriage vows; and another group who are committed to acknowledging such experiences to their husbands based on agreed-upon principles of open marriages. Each case study opens with a brief description of the person interviewed and ends with the author's reflection on the case. Wolfe demonstrates from the case studies that there are a variety of patterns in women's adultery: some seek to retaliate against their husband's emotional remoteness or sexual inadequacy or their infidelity; some act out of personal longings for adventure and variety; and still others believe such activities would help them hold onto and preserve their marriages. Wolfe is a sympathetic interviewer and writer who does not hesitate to inject her own feelings into her research. This book with its conversational style will interest general readers as well as researchers who study family, marriage, and divorce in the United States.

RICHARDSON examines both the social forces responsible for the increasing trend of liaisons between single women and married men, and the effect of such relationships on marriage and family. The book begins with an introduction of social conditions under which increasing numbers of single women are engaging in relationships with married men: the severe shortage of single males for women over the age of 25, women's socialization which impels them to seek heterosexual couplehood, the feminist movement's creation of needs in women for autonomy, and the increased likelihood of work-related interaction between men and women. Relying heavily on narratives from 55 interviews, Richardson continues in subsequent chapters to document how such relationships get started, how women become emotionally involved with their partners without intending to, and how, eventually, such relationships end, as almost all do. In the final chapter, Richardson speculates on the future of such liaisons and suggests some alternatives for single women who do not care to follow this route. Building on an extensive record of scholarship on the sociology of sex and gender, Richardson has produced a well-researched book that should be equally interesting to sociologists and the general public.

As an anthropologist, FISHER discusses monogamy, adultery, and divorce from evolutionary and comparative perspectives. By presenting evidence from nature and different societies, Fisher argues that the origin of monogamy and desertion, as well as worldwide patterns of adultery and divorce, can be traced to innate legacies of our ancestors' primitive mating games dating back to some two and a half million years ago. In chapter four about adultery, Fisher discusses the ambiguity of the definition of adultery, which is always affected by particular cultural mores. Fisher also explores what she argues are evolutionary forces behind adultery behavior: while men seek sexual variety for increasing chances of passing their genes, women look for more than one partner for extra goods and services, life insurance, better genes, and more varied DNA for their biological future. In the last chapter, Fisher examines the origins of the sexual double standard in farming communities and in the west. Fisher's work is well researched, witty, and fun to read, but it is also polemic, since much of her explanation of human sexual behavior is grounded in an bio-evolutionary framework.

FRAYSER adopts a highly comprehensive and interdisciplinary approach to the study of human sexual experience, including adultery. The author develops a theoretical model that integrates biological, social, and cultural aspects of sexuality by looking at sexuality from cross-species and cross-cultural perspectives. Although only a fraction of the book is devoted to the study of adultery, Frayser's coverage of adultery is the most extensive of all ethnographic studies on this subject. After surveying more than 30 societies regarding their sexually restrictive rules for women and men, Frayser concludes that societies that separate women's reproductive and sexual relationships allow women flexibility to engage in premarital and/or extramarital relationships; at the other extreme, societies that observe a female-restrictive regime—that is, confine the woman's intercourse to a single marital union—are likely to impose elaborate marriage celebrations, practice bride-price customs for finalizing the marriage, and use the wife's extramarital relationships as grounds for divorce. Between these two extremes lie societies that have some overlap between sexual and reproductive relationships. Societies that conform to the intermediate position display the greatest variation in the rules and social actions that govern the sexual and reproductive relationships of their members. Drawing on the principles of anthropological tradition, Frayser's book is an excellent reference for studying human sexuality, including adultery, for both scholars and general readers.

—JIAN LI

Advertising, Images of Women in

Barthel, Diane, *Putting On Appearances: Gender and Advertising,* Philadelphia, Pennsylvania: Temple University Press, 1988

Courtney, Alice E., and Thomas W. Whipple, *Sex Stereotyping in Advertising,* Lexington, Massachusetts: Lexington Books, 1983

Dispenza, Joseph E., *Advertising the American Woman,* Dayton, Ohio: Pflaum, 1975

Friedan, Betty, *The Feminine Mystique,* New York: Norton, and London: V. Gollancz, 1963

Goffman, Erving, *Gender Advertisements,* London: Macmillan, and Cambridge, Massachusetts: Harvard University Press, 1979

Macdonald, Myra, *Representing Women: Myths of Femininity in the Popular Media,* London: Arnold, 1995

Manca, Luigi, and Alessandra Manca, *Gender and Utopia in Advertising: A Critical Reader,* Lisle, Illinois: Procopian, 1994

Millum, Trevor, *Images of Woman: Advertising in Women's Magazines,* London: Chatto and Windus, and Totowa, New Jersey: Rowman and Littlefield, 1975

Feminists have long expressed concern about the cumulative effect of stereotypical images of women in print, magazine, and television advertising, particularly in relation to the way in which these images may lead women to perceive themselves in a negative light, and to limit their aspirations as a consequence. One of the earliest groundbreaking works of this nature is FRIEDAN's exposé of real attempts by American manufacturers to manipulate female consumption during the 1950s. Friedan reveals that within the context of a rapidly expanding economy, capitalists sought to expand the lucrative feminine consumer market for domestic products, by actively affirming the notion that the primary source of women's fulfilment, happiness, and creativity derived from their roles as mothers and housewives. Toward this end, advertisements promoted an ideal image of women as childlike, sexy, and preoccupied with their homes and families. Advertisements also portrayed women in a limited range of roles, which Friedan feared would curtail their future aspirations at work and in the public realm.

While Friedan's "manipulation model" and simplistic conception of audience "effects" have been subsequently challenged, this early work sparked considerable academic interest and research into women's portrayal in advertising. Numerous studies have since documented the content and connotation of advertising images of women, including DISPENZA's illustrated anthology and content analysis of visual images of women in North American magazine advertisements from 1900–1975. This study identifies a number of recurrent themes in the advertisements, including beauty and domesticity, heterosexual romance, marriage and motherhood, fashion, and the objectification of women's bodies.

Another early study is MILLUM's detailed survey and semiotic analysis of visual images of women in advertisements from six British women's magazines. Millum identifies the connotative meaning of the props, settings, and actors used in these advertisements, and concludes that women are typically portrayed as either mannequins, hostesses, wives/mothers, or narcissists. This study may be of some interest to readers wishing to conduct similar research in this area, due to its systematic presentation of the classification system employed, and its detailed discussion of the process of research and analysis.

GOFFMAN's semiotic analysis of visual imagery in American print and magazine advertisements is widely regarded as the most comprehensive research on this topic to date. A sociologist, Goffman argues that analysts need to do more than simply identify stereotypical images of women and men. His broad focus is on abstract and ritualized displays of gender in advertisements, which he suggests are so prominent because they provide an instantly recognizable, shorthand means of communicating information. Through a close examination of details such as the use of hands, and the size and positioning of men compared to women, Goffman finds that women are frequently depicted as deferent and child-like, and are portrayed in subordinate occupational roles. He concludes that in its need to convey information very quickly, advertising conventionalizes existing social relations and exaggerates them, creating new meanings in the process.

COURTNEY and WHIPPLE offer a very useful review of the extensive body of international research and literature on stereotypical advertising images of men and women in their book. The first section provides a comprehensive overview of content analyses of the portrayal of women and men in advertising until the late 1970s, the major finding of which is that advertisements inaccurately reflect sex roles within wider society, and continue to depict women's place as in the home. Research on public attitudes toward sex stereotyping in advertising, and its social impact on children and adults, is also surveyed in this section. The authors then consider the effectiveness of advertising, and strategies for changing sex stereotyping, in sections two and three. Here, they develop their central thesis that while advertising regulation and self-regulation are important factors in the eradication of stereotypical images of women and men, real change can only come through advertiser reeducation.

Influenced by semiology and poststructuralist theory, BARTHEL's book is a sociological discussion of the cultural content of images of women in magazine advertisements. Her primary focus is on representations constructed through the written text of these advertisements, as opposed to their visual imagery. Barthel discusses topics such as images of women as either "fair maidens" or "dark ladies," and examines the way in which certain advertisements co-opt a feminist vision of women as "liberated" for capitalist purposes. Throughout this book, Barthel suggests that there is a connection between representations of women in magazine advertisements and women's self-esteem. She argues that these images and their often adverse effects are symptomatic of a society in which women are encouraged to see themselves as the object of gaze, and to manage their appearance to best effect.

The essays in MANCA and MANCA's edited anthology all explore the idea that advertising images of women and men offer a vision of a better self and life—a utopia attainable through the consumption of material goods. The first contribution provides a very useful critical overview of existing research, and draws together findings from content analyses, audience and reaction studies, and critical studies of advertising images of women. Other essays address topics such as the relationship between contemporary images of women in magazine advertisements and their depiction in medieval literature, facets of femininity depicted in perfume advertisements, and the appropriation of feminist ideals in fashion magazine advertisements.

The most recent contribution to this field is MACDONALD's textual analysis of the production and reproduction of myths of "femininity" and "the feminine" in advertising, film, magazines, and television. Informed by Foucauldian discourse theory, Macdonald argues that the media constructs ideas and ways of talking about women, and from this perspective she explores the role of consumer discourses in affirming and reproducing various myths about femininity. She discusses the myths of femininity as "enigmatic and threatening," and "nurturing and caring," and also examines a number of myths about female sexuality and women's bodies. The role of advertising in reproducing these myths is most directly addressed in Chapters Three and Seven—the former contains particularly useful discussions of advertising's construction of multiple subjectivities for women during the inter-war period, the response of advertisers to the second wave of feminism, and the playful appropriation of quasi-feminist concepts in the "postfeminist" 1980s and 1990s. Throughout this book, Macdonald argues that despite significant changes in the social, cultural, and material conditions of many women's lives, advertising's meanings of femininity have remained relatively stagnant, and are continually reinvented in ways that merely toy with traditional notions of femininity, rather than transforming them.

—CAROLYN MICHELLE

See also Television, Images of Women in

Affirmative Action

Bergmann, Barbara, *In Defense of Affirmative Action,* New York: Basic Books, 1996

Clayton, Susan, and Faye Crosby, *Justice, Gender, and Affirmative Action,* Ann Arbor: University of Michigan Press, 1992

Eastland, Terry, *Ending Affirmative Action,* New York: Basic Books, 1996

Faundez, Julio, *Affirmative Action: International Perspectives,* Geneva, Switzerland: International Labour Organization, 1994

Urofsky, Melvin, *A Conflict of Rights: The Supreme Court and Affirmative Action,* New York: Scribner, 1991

Witt, Stephanie, *The Pursuit of Race and Gender Equity in American Academe,* New York: Praeger, 1990

Scholarly works that analyze affirmative action programs aimed specifically at women are few in number. The literature in this area, in fact, is weighted heavily toward a (typically damning) focus on the role of race in policies designed to diversify the government, workplace, and educational institutions. For example, the work of Glenn Loury, Thomas Sowell, Shelby Steele, and Stephen Carter deal almost exclusively not just with race, but with the black male (conservative) perspective on affirmative action. There are, nevertheless, at least some book-length treatments of affirmative action based on gender.

CLAYTON and CROSBY employ a psychological approach that is rooted in social context to make the case for affirmative action based on gender. They demonstrate the dynamics of what they call "the denial of personal disadvantage," whereby women overwhelmingly indicate an awareness of pervasive sex discrimination in the workplace, but rarely believe that they themselves are the victims of such behavior. As a result of this common dynamic, as well as other, related factors, antidiscrimination laws (such as Title VII of the Civil Rights Act of 1964) are rarely invoked by women in the workplace. Hence, Clayton and Crosby declare, proactive affirmative action policies are necessary if the United States is to remedy the workplace gap between men and women.

UROFSKY provides an in-depth account of a 1987 Supreme Court case (*Johnson v. Transportation Agency, Santa Clara*) that endorsed gender-based affirmative action programs in the workplace, albeit with significant reservations. He tells the competing stories of the two people at the heart of the case: Diane Joyce and Paul Johnson. Urofsky points out in his conclusion, however, that this case represented the high water mark for affirmative action policies, given more recent decisions handed down by a more conservative U.S. Supreme Court. Urofsky does a decent job of representing fairly the conflicting arguments over the merits of these controversial policies.

FAUNDEZ examines both the theory and practice of affirmative action in several countries. Faundez first lays out the various philosophical, legal, and economic debates over this controversial set of policies. He then compares the practice of affirmative action in Australia, Canada, India, Malaysia, and the United States. It is notable that outside the United States, the vast majority of affirmative action programs are aimed at such categories as race, ethnicity, and political status, rather than gender. He identifies the significance of several variables for the success of affirmative action policies. He notes, for example, that if such policies are built into a nation's constitution (as in India), then their legitimacy is likely to be enhanced considerably. Faundez also explores the impact of such factors as how affirmative action policies are implemented (central versus local), their enshrinement in legislation or bureaucratic regulations, and voluntary versus mandated programs.

WITT employs a focus on university faculty attitudes toward affirmative action, based on the faculty person's race and gender. She is especially interested in exploring the inherent tension within liberal societies between individual rights and justice for various groups that occupy the political and economic margins of American society. Witt also characterizes this conflict as one involving an emphasis on individualism versus egalitarianism. She presents a statistical analysis of how attitudes toward affirmative action policies are greatly affected by the categories of race and gender. She finds that white males are most likely to oppose affirmative action and believe that minorities and women have an advantage over them in academe, while blacks and women are more likely to favor affirmative action and believe that they are at a disadvantage in the university. Witt is concerned that this reflects the centrality of self-interest as conditioned by the categories of race and gender. She also believes that her findings reveal a disturbing gap between white males on the one hand, and women and minorities on the other, a situation that does not bode well for the integration of women and minority faculty into academic institutions in the United States.

BERGMANN provides a qualified endorsement of affirmative action based on race and gender. She recognizes the potential harm of reverse discrimination against white males, but argues that this cost is ultimately outweighed by the countervailing benefits of remedying both historical and, more importantly, contemporary discrimination in American society. Bergmann also questions the narrow definition of merit that is often used by opponents of affirmative action. She argues that merit is an inherently subjective and ambiguous gauge of human potential, which cannot be reduced to scores on standardized tests or other allegedly objective measures of a person's ability to do well in school or succeed in the workplace. Bergmann emphasizes in this volume the widespread practice of race and sex discrimination in the present, and supports the use of affirmative action programs based at least in part on class. She also advocates the stricter enforcement of antidiscrimination laws, better education and training for women and minorities, and aid for the poor, as necessary and important adjuncts in the war against racial and sexual inequality.

EASTLAND pens a polemical and divisive tract that seeks to demonize proponents of affirmative action, and portray opponents as noble defenders of an American tradition of justice for all. What is perhaps most notable about Eastland's book is its almost sole focus on affirmative action based on race and ethnicity, although it is clear that he also opposes the use of gender in such programs. Eastland quietly steers the reader away from gender, and emphasizes instead the demands being made by recent immigrants to the United States and the resident population of blacks. While he effectively tells the story of white litigants, both male and female, who have been affected negatively by affirmative action, he seems most interested in inflaming white anger toward nonwhites. It is also worth noting that Eastland supports the immediate abolition of all affirmative action programs (which he describes at one point as "a Bargain with the Devil"), but does not believe that any alternative action is necessary to remedy the economic and political gap between white males and nonwhites and women in America. Race and sex discrimination in the United States, Eastland believes, is only episodic rather than systemic, and so does not require any government action beyond that which is already being taken under existing antidiscrimination statutes.

—FRANCIS CARLETON

Africa *see* Apartheid; Black Women; Economic Development: Africa

Aging

Arber, Sara, and Jay Ginn, *Gender and Later Life: A Sociological Analysis of Resources and Constraints*, London and Newbury Park, California: Sage, 1991

——— (eds.), *Connecting Gender and Aging: A Sociological Approach*, Buckingham and Philadelphia: Open University, 1995

Bernard, Miriam, and Kathy Meade (eds.), *Women Come of Age: Perspectives on the Lives of Older Women*, London: Arnold, 1993

Garner, J. Dianne, and Susan O. Mercer (eds.), *Women as They Age: Challenge, Opportunity, and Triumph*, London: Harrington Park, 1988; New York: Haworth, 1989

Gibson, Mary Jo Storey, *Older Women around the World*, Washington, D. C.: International Federation on Aging, in cooperation with the American Association of Retired Persons, 1985

Sennott-Miller, Lee, *Midlife and Older Women in Latin America and the Caribbean*, Washington, D. C.: American Association of Retired Persons, 1989

Around the world, in both developed and developing nations, a growing proportion of the population is reaching old age. This statement, while true, hides another, even more startling demographic reality: among those aging survivors, it is women who predominate. Thus, it has rightly been said, aging is a women's issue. Yet society in general has tended to overlook older women's situations and needs. Even among feminists, the focus has been on younger women's issues. The available literature about older women is much limited in comparison to that about younger women. Still, a handful of volumes offer information about the lives of older women in North America, Great Britain, and the developing world (there is also, particularly in English-speaking countries, a growing literature of older women's personal essays and oral histories, which do not fall within the parameters of this review).

Though GARNER and MERCER introduce their book with an international overview about aged women, the volume in reality is largely limited to discussion of women in the United States. The edited volume reviews a variety of topics at a level appropriate to readers who do not yet have an extensive familiarity with women and aging: sociological and psychological perspectives on women's aging, developmental theories, and physical and mental health. A section on "Special Issues" examines sexuality and intimacy, minority feminist issues, and the intersection of family and work in older women's lives. Chapters on policy, programs, and services are of particular use to social providers and persons interested in affecting policy.

Three books from Great Britain may be useful to readers with varying levels of familiarity with the topic. BERNARD and MEADE, like Garner and Mercer, address such issues as work and poverty, health, intimacy and sexuality, and caring (referred to in the United States as caregiving or caretaking). While Garner and Mercer suggest that "The unique and frequently troublesome situation of older women is not just the result of growing older, [but rather] the result of invasive and historical patterns of socioeconomic and gender stratification in societies," Bernard and Meade explicitly place their discussion within the framework of two theories, political economy and feminism. The latter volume also includes thoughtful discussions of two topics absent from Garner and Meade, the lives of older lesbians, and the impact of built environments on older women. Data and discussion of U.S. and British women, as well as various minority women in Great Britain, are integrated throughout the book.

The two books by ARBER and GINN also are explicit in their political theoretical perspective, premised on the concept that age and gender are inextricably intertwined in shaping women's lives. The first book (1991) examines the effect differential access to resources, both material and human, has on the lives of older women, across both gender and class lines. Independence and dependence, health status, cultural stereotypes, and the politics of aging are among the issues addressed. Data from both the United States and Great Britain are drawn on for analysis.

Their second book (1995) casts a more theoretically sophisticated eye on some of the basic issues of aging discussed in the other volumes reviewed here. Theories are not merely presented as possible explanations for older women's situations in particular domains (retirement, elder abuse, etc.), but are critically analyzed for their strengths and weaknesses, and needs for further research are identified. This book requires of its reader some familiarity with relevant sociological theory. Drawing on both U.S. and British sources and data, this book is useful to understanding similarities and differences in women's aging in the two societies.

The books by Gibson and Sennott-Miller introduce the reader to the lives of older women "around the world," specifically in developing countries. GIBSON's volume is just 58 pages long, and was published more than a decade ago, so demographic data are somewhat out-of-date. Ten chapters comprise the monograph, covering the "basics" (demographics, living arrangements, family life, employment, health, etc.); each chapter has two sections, "Developing Nations" and "Developed Nations." The contents are brief, suggestive rather than comprehensive, and obviously reflect the sparsity of available data and research about older women. Nevertheless, the book has value, giving the nonspecialist reader a sense of some of the commonalities and differences in the aging experiences of women within and among the developing/developed sectors.

The book by Sennott-Miller is a collection of background papers and presentations at a meeting on midlife and older women in 1988. Together, the papers reveal something of the social and cultural diversity of women in Latin America and the Caribbean, and the political and cultural effects on their lives as they grow older in male-dominated and ageist societies. The background papers review such topics as economic situation, family context, education and literacy, and health. Papers presented at the group meeting focus on health, psychosocial, and economic aspects of women's lives, frequently using individual country case histories as demonstrations. The conference was convened to illuminate women's lives and forward the effort to make women full partners in society; the publication is an exemplar of the partnership of scholarly research and activist intent.

—CAROLYN KEITH

See also Caregiving; Elder Abuse

AIDS and HIV

Cohen, Felissa L., and Jerry D. Durham (eds.), *Women, Children, and HIV/AIDS,* New York: Springer, 1993

Corea, Gena, *The Invisible Epidemic: The Story of Women and AIDS,* New York: HarperCollins, 1992

Farmer, Paul, Janie Simmons, and Margaret Connors (eds.), *Women, Poverty, and AIDS: Sex, Drugs, and Structural Violence,* Monroe, Maine: Common Courage Press, 1996

Kaplan, Helen Singer, *The Real Truth about Women and AIDS: How to Eliminate the Risk without Giving Up Love and Sex,* New York: Simon and Schuster, 1987

Kurth, Ann (ed.), *Until the Cure: Caring for Women with HIV,* New Haven, Connecticut: Yale University Press, 1993

Pearlberg, Gerry, *Women, AIDS and Communities: A Guide for Action,* Metuchen, New Jersey: Scarecrow Press, 1991

Richardson, Diane, *Women and AIDS,* New York: Methuen, 1988

Rieder, Ines, and Patricia Ruppelt (eds.), *AIDS: The Women,* San Francisco: Cleis Press, 1988

Squire, Corinne (ed.), *Women and AIDS: Psychological Perspectives,* New York: Sage, 1993

Since the first reported case of Acquired Immune Deficiency Syndrome (AIDS) in 1981, Human Immunodeficiency Virus (HIV) and AIDS have become the focus of much research. There are many publications regarding HIV, but few of them focus on the impact of HIV on women. According to recent statistics, AIDS is the leading cause of death for women between the ages of 25 and 44. This dearth in the literature, in spite of the statistical data regarding HIV and women, is a cause for concern. The existing literature concerning women and AIDS is quite diverse, as it comes from a variety of disciplines. The literature on women and AIDS covers psychological, political, legal, medical, and sociological perspectives. Although some of the issues concerning medical treatment must be read cautiously, as advances in research yield new information about the illness on a frequent basis, the material regarding psychological, legal, and political perspectives remains current.

PEARLBERG's book is intended to serve as a guide for community-based programs that provide AIDS-related services for women. The target audience for this publication consists of those who have little or no previous experience with HIV/AIDS. Therefore, the content is at an introductory level. Information about HIV is provided, along with suggestions for community center staff training, and activities the centers may offer the women served. The guidebook also details the various issues staff may face with different clientele: adolescents, lesbians, incarcerated women, older women, women who are physically challenged, and prostitutes.

COHEN and DURHAM's publication presents HIV as it relates to women and children. Although the editors and the majority of the contributors are nurses, the target audience is not limited to those in the nursing profession. Any health care worker will find this text enlightening. The book is divided into four sections: an introduction, HIV infection and AIDS in women, HIV and AIDS in children and adolescents, and perspectives on selected issues. The first two sections include discussion of the controversy surrounding the reproductive choices of women who are HIV-positive, and prevention of HIV in women and children. The final half of the book examines concerns about HIV in women from developing countries, and the impact of working with HIV-positive clients on the mental well-being of health care providers.

SQUIRE examines psychological perspectives with regard to women and AIDS. The text is divided into four sections. The first addresses the reproductive rights of HIV-positive women, the second the transmission risk, the third females who work with HIV-positive women, and finally representations of women and AIDS in the media. A strength of this text is that the authors seem to draw from their own experience with affected women and are able to bring this material alive for the reader. The chapter on the drug culture and the great dangers faced by women who are a part of this culture is especially gripping.

FARMER, CONNORS, and SIMMONS take a global approach in examining women and AIDS. They explore the impact of the disease on women from different cultures and conclude that many of these infected women have one commonality: poverty. They then explore the influence of poverty on prevention, diagnosis, and treatment of HIV. Statistical information is intermingled with the stories of numerous women who are HIV-positive or have been diagnosed with AIDS. These women's stories supplement the statistical information and make the facts of this disease even more disturbing.

COREA's book also relays information regarding women and AIDS through the stories of women infected with the disease. More specifically, Corea chronicles the AIDS epidemic from 1981 to 1990 as seen through the eyes of Eileen Hogan, a nun living in the Bronx. Hogan's perspective on the disease is shared, along with the perspectives of health care professionals and women who are HIV-positive. These infected women come from a variety of racial/ethnic groups, backgrounds, and experiences. The book illustrates the extent to which the disease has affected a diverse group of women.

Similarly, RIEDER and RUPPELT explore the impact of HIV on the lives of a variety of women: health care providers, prostitutes, wives, mothers, and lesbians all share their stories. These stories are in the form of individually written essays. Each essay conveys one woman's point of view, and together they illustrate the diverse group of women affected by HIV. Interestingly, these essays vary in tone; whereas some resonate with regret and sadness, others reflect hope and even humor.

RICHARDSON's book contains general information about AIDS and serves as a good introductory text for someone who is unfamiliar with the disease. The work begins with a summary of basic information regarding transmission, symptoms, and treatment. The text also examines issues relevant to women and AIDS such as rape, pregnancy, and prostitution. Richardson discusses risk reduction, the psychological issues facing those who are infected, health care for people with HIV, and public policy issues regarding HIV.

KAPLAN has also written a book for the general population about women and AIDS. In her book, she attempts to dispel many of the myths about AIDS and replace this misinformation with accurate up-to-date information. Unlike most of the other texts, this publication is written for a diverse audience, and therefore the language is less technical and easier to read. Kaplan provides statistics on heterosexual transmission and briefly discusses the politics of AIDS and the history of AIDS in the United States. She provides suggestions regarding how to have pleasurable sex in spite of the fear and anxiety many have in the age of AIDS.

KURTH's edited book is very thorough in its coverage of the epidemic. Medical, legal, and ethical issues regarding HIV are covered. The book serves as a reference guide not only for the professionals who work with women with HIV/AIDS, but also for the women who are infected with and affected by the disease. Each chapter of the book begins with the story of a woman struggling with issues of HIV. Like many of the preceding books that use the same format, the personal tales of these women complement and bring life to the facts regarding HIV.

—ALISON THOMAS-COTTINGHAM and JANE CONNOR

Akhmatova, Anna Andreeva 1889–1966

Russian Writer

Chukovskaia, Lydia, *The Akhmatova Journals (1938–41)*, London: Collins-Harville, 1991; New York: Farrar, Straus and Giroux, 1994

Davies, Jessie, *Anna of All the Russias: The Life of Anna Akhmatova, 1889–1966*, Liverpool: Lincoln Davies, 1988

Haight, Amanda, *Anna Akhmatova: A Poetic Pilgrimage*, Oxford and New York: Oxford University Press, 1976

Leiter, Sharon, *Akhmatova's Petersburg*, Cambridge: Cambridge University Press, and Philadelphia: University of Pennsylvania Press, 1983

Nayman, Anatoly, *Remembering Anna Akhmatova*, London: Halban, and New York: Henry Holt, 1991

Polivanov, Konstantin, *Anna Akhmatova and Her Circle*, Fayetteville: University of Arkansas Press, 1994

Reeder, Roberta, *Anna Akhmatova: Poet and Prophet*, New York: St. Martin's Press, 1994; London: Allison and Busby, 1995

Wells, David, *Anna Akhmatova: Her Poetry*, Oxford and Dulles, Virginia: Berg, 1996

Anna Akhmatova, one of the great Russian poets of all time and one of the first Russian female poets, was a persecuted founder of the Acmeist literary movement, which promoted realism over symbolism. She has proven a difficult subject for indepth psychological portraiture because she was a very private person, and constant censorship made documentation scarce. However, recent criticism reads the poet through memoirs and poetry set against the turbulent historical and cultural changes out of which they grew, to portray courage amid bleak suffering and oppression, creativity out of wasteland, and a phoenix-like intellectual flame rising from the ashes of the poet's life.

HAIGHT wrote the first informal critical biography and analysis in English of Akhmatova and her work. British historian of ideas Sir Isaiah Berlin called it "the most accurate, lucid, truthful, . . . best organized, and most authoritative book on Akhmatova's life," while Peter Levi termed it "a subtle and exact account of a subtle and precise poet." Haight met Akhmatova in 1964, developed an immediate rapport, and followed her directions to friends and acquaintances who helped elucidate Akhmatova's life and work. The result is a poignant, sympathetic portrait of a brave woman finding in "splendid" poetry her source of strength and "giving voice to the woman's point of view in a culture where women's voices . . . were few and far between." Its value lies in its sensitive understanding of the tragic limitations and restraints under which Akhmatova wrote, and in her skill in overcoming these.

DAVIES's short, lucid biography addresses readers unfamiliar with Russia, and it offers the poetry and poet as truly representative of the best and worst of that enigmatic land—the terrible daily life, the turbulent, repressive politics, the personal losses, and yet the individual's ability to endure, create, and overcome. She calls Akhmatova's theme of wounded, idealized love unique—the first treatment of this theme in Russia from a woman's point of view—and juxtaposes biography and poetry to elucidate lines and to provide a moving tribute to Akhmatova's greatness.

Although NAYMAN knew Akhmatova only the last five years of her life, as a poet himself and Akhmatova's literary secretary from 1962 on, his authentic portrait of the poet's life and personality looks into her heart through the hidden compartments and interlocking drawers of her poetry. First published in Russia in 1969, this book won Russian praise for its affection for the poet felt in every page, and for the depiction of her personal perspective through her authentic, intelligent, free-spirited voice: "into what dirt they've trampled me—poverty, prison lines, fear, poems remembered only by heart." Nayman denounces the official Soviet view of Akhmatova as a pessimistic sexual deviant representative of empty reactionary values alien to Soviet literature. Instead, he captures her ability to joke even during those terrible years of horror and demonstrates the power of her erotic poetry, her ability to capture the essence of an event, idea, or character, and the values her poetry offers to help others resist oppression as she did.

POLIVANOV's collection of fifteen memoirs about Akhmatova by prominent friends and by Akhmatova herself provides multiple perspectives on the daily struggles, heartbreaks, hungers, and hardships of the poet, the paranoid restraints of state-controlled publications, and the threats of imprisonment or death from World War I through the Revolution, Civil War, and the horrifying 1920s and 1930s to Hitler's invasion and post-war Stalinist repressions. Together these memoirs are a story of courage and friendship in the face of terror, and of intellectual, literary, and personal struggles against tyranny and stupidity. A precise appendix of explanatory notes familiarizes non-Russian readers with key names, places, and historical events.

American-trained Russianist REEDER, editor of *The Complete Works of Anna Akhmatova*, writes an ambitious, exhaustively researched biography to illuminate both Akhmatova and her world. This major study is richly detailed, with an overwhelming breadth of material stitched together from numerous sources. Each section begins with a political and social-historical overview of the period to be covered, then provides a mosaic of quotations about and from the period studied, and ends with a sampler of poems from the works of Akhmatova and of writers with whom Akhmatova was linked, including a discussion of what they reveal and imply. The result is a vivid picture of the Russian intelligentsia and of the turmoil and complexities of Akhmatova's era—from the turn of the century to the 1960s. However, its very thoroughness is at the expense of a coherent and compelling interpretation of Akhmatova's life and work, and Reeder's translations of Akhmatova's poetry are at times infelicitous.

CHUKOVSKAIA's first of several projected volumes draws on her personal diaries and conversations with Akhmatova to provide fascinating glimpses of Akhmatova's life and thought during the critical, stressful period of Stalinist repressions. A novelist in her own right, Chukovskaia brings to the work the intimate view of a long-time friend (since 1938) whose husband was also sent to the work camps; a deep knowledge of Russian history, literature, social conditions, and conventions; and the skills of a memoirist who personally memorized risky, even compromising poems Akhmatova wrote and burned, who, without sentimentality, meticulously records lively, authentic details, and who helps readers understand how Akhmatova managed to remain alive and sane with her son imprisoned and her own life threatened. An appendix of fifty-four Akhmatova poems wonderfully translated by Peter Norman, copious explanatory footnotes, and Akhmatova's caustic comments on well-known Russian writers are added bonuses to an invaluable text. Overall, Chukovskaia projects an image of an intellectually honest artist, at times theatrical—a survivor with a penetrating wit and, by the standards of her day, scurrilous views—famous yet neglected, helpless yet strong, lonely yet courageous.

An earlier work by LEITER takes a much more limited focus: Akhmatova's Petersburg poems and their transformation of the nineteenth century's dark, tormented vision of Petersburg into "a triumphant metaphor of survival." Leiter calls Akhmatova "the last great poet in the Petersburg tradition" and argues that, despite having spent much of her life in that city, Akhmatova had only partially realized a planned historical prose chronicle of the city's incarnations, but in poetry written over a lifetime she captures the protean layers of her vision—the city as a shifting lyrical and mythical model of the world, where the personal and public intersect, and where a questing feminine sensibility miraculously regenerates and resurrects what aggressive male forces (both the Nazis and the Soviets) have laid waste.

WELLS warns of the biographical fallacy that has led to multiple and contradictory myths and constructed theories about Akhmatova based on scanty evidence, faulty memories, and biased public records, and he calls instead for a study of what is knowable: her poetry as literature. He lucidly analyzes Akhmatova's poetry in periods—early poetry, the poems of the 1930s and 1940s, and the poetry of the Kruschev thaw (1950s and 1960s)—and demonstrates her accessibility, which involves simple vocabulary and syntax to express complex themes. He juxtaposes transliterated Russian versions with English translations to demonstrate the sounds and melodies of her native tongue. He praises her courageous documentation of the Terror of the 1930s and her outspoken poetry of female love, but his main interest is in the principle of extratextuality—the intentional reliance on literary, historical, religious, musical, and visual associations to engage the reader emotionally and intellectually—which he argues unites her canon and is her legacy to the poets who succeeded her. He concludes that Akhmatova's poetic ideas have found an "ineradicable place in the Russian literary consciousness."

Isaiah Berlin summarized the tribute of these critics when he said that Akhmatova's "genius and monstrous persecution by the state" would be remembered as long as the history and literature of Russia continued to be known. The critical consensus is that the Stalinist police state tried to break this seemingly defenseless woman, but she was victorious over them; instead, her poetry trampled them under foot.

—GINA MACDONALD and PAULINA BAZIN

Alcoholism *see* Addictions

see Addictions

Alcott, Louisa May 1832–1888

American Writer

Anthony, Katharine Susan, *Louisa May Alcott,* New York and London: Knopf, 1938

Delamar, Gloria T., *Louisa May Alcott and "Little Women": Biography, Critique, Publications, Poems, Songs, and Contemporary Relevance,* Jefferson, North Carolina, and London: McFarland, 1990

Elbert, Sarah, *A Hunger for Home: Louisa May Alcott and Little Women,* Philadelphia: Temple University Press, 1984

Meigs, Cornelia, *Invincible Louisa,* Boston: Little Brown, 1933

Saxton, Martha, *Louisa May: A Modern Biography of Louisa May Alcott,* Boston: Houghton Mifflin, 1977; London: Deutsch, 1978

Stern, Madeleine B., *Louisa May Alcott,* Norman: University of Oklahoma Press, 1950; London: P. Neville, 1952

Among the earlier biographies of Louisa May Alcott, MEIGS's treatment is especially appropriate for the adolescent and young adult reader. Alcott is characterized as being devoted to the welfare of the family from her early years; in fact, she felt duty-bound to provide whatever they needed. She acknowledged the uneveness of her writing: stories dashed off for ready economic gain were not comparable to her best, which were based on family or close friends. Meigs captures the tomboyish heart of Alcott, who unabashedly wished that she could have been a man. Unable to enter the war effort as a soldier, she served as a nurse until serious illness squelched that effort. A major focus of the work is Alcott's devotion to family, and all in all, Meigs pens a family portrait rather than a literary biography. In following her literary career, however, Meigs provides the context out of which the works were born.

Organized largely around some key locations that were home to the Alcott family or to Louisa between 1835 and the year of the author's death in 1888, STERN fills in for a more mature reader many details surrounding incidents introduced by Meigs. As in most of the Alcott biographies, "Louy" is portrayed as a lively, adventurous, often tomboyish child who, as she matured, came to target herself as the one who could make the dreams of the rest of the family come true. Her role as breadwinner would at times provide the fuel needed to produce stories and novels. Stern also expands on the author's attachment to her family and her feelings of devastation when her sister Elizabeth (Lizzie) died, when her older sister Anna became engaged, and when her younger sister May died later in Europe. One chapter is devoted in part to Alcott's contributions to the women's suffrage movement, to *The Woman's Magazine,* and to other activities that place her in the ranks of determined, brave women who helped to bring equity for women closer to being reality.

A common thread that runs throughout the accounts of Meigs's and Stern's biographies continues in ANTHONY's early biography of Louisa May Alcott: a resistance to the restrictive aspects of being female. She is described as a child who enjoyed an out-of-doors life of climbing trees and leaping fences, and who hated gloves, bonnets, and done-up hair. In a number of chapters, the accounts of Alcott's enduring literary accomplishments are integrated into a portrayal of various relationships in her life, for example, that with her mother, who first noticed Louisa's powers of expression. She was prepared by her idealistic upbringing to uphold feminist ideals, even if shyness kept her out of more active fights for women's rights. Alcott's role as a working woman acknowledges the legacy of her Puritan ancestry and her willingness to do honest work in a simple and natural way. Another chapter reveals Alcott's charming and "proper" romance with her Polish comrade Ladislas Wisniewski, a relationship that did not alter her perceived role as "old maid." Anthony's treatment of Alcott's literary development focuses especially on the ultimate success of *Little Women.*

A distinctive feature of DELAMAR's biography is the addition of sections that provide reviews and critical analyses of Alcott's work, ratings that *Little Women* received on various polls and lists, her showing in a popular magazine poll as one of the twenty-five most important women in American history, and her appearance on a short list of persons honored in 1940 with commemorative postage stamps (Alcott appeared in the company of Washington Irving, James Fenimore Cooper, Ralph Waldo Emerson, and Samuel Clemens). One chapter identifies various kinds of uses to which the "little women" image has been put: a children's novel, a cookbook, a diary, playscripts, movies, television movies, and video cartoons, while another focuses on Alcott's reception abroad. By 1968, 31 countries had published the novel. Delamar's appraisal of Alcott concludes that her work still belongs on contemporary bookshelves, and that her support of women's suffrage grew naturally out of her earlier wish that she could have been male.

Much more so than the other biographers of Alcott, SAXTON takes a more psychological slant. Presumably, Bronson Alcott "never liked" Louisa, so she had kept a "critical distance" from him. After her mother's death, however, the two were closer and her father even penned a loving poem in which he labels Louisa "duty's faithful child." Regarding her writing, Saxton sees Alcott's novel *Little Women* as a step backward as a writer and as a woman. She portrays a much darker side of the family than do the other biographers. For example, Alcott is described as an embittered person who harbored many resentments. Her mother is credited with burdening Louisa with "hopeless guilt" and with the notion that, when anything needed to be fixed, it was Louisa's duty to do so. Saxton is complimentary of Alcott's *Hospital Sketches,* and she evaluates *Moods* as a complaint against the various restrictions placed upon women of the day. Like several of the other biographers, Saxton acknowledges Alcott's involvement in the women's suffrage movement, as well as her interest in an expanding role for women in the medical profession.

Like Saxton, ELBERT analyzes the dynamics between Louisa and the other family members. She depicts Louisa as a passionate baby, as a dominant and aggressive playmate, and as a stubborn girl who competed fiercely with her older sister Anna. Elbert points out that the self-sacrifice and repression instilled in Louisa was typical of society at large and not just of Bronson Alcott; in fact, more than the others, this biographer places the family's lifestyle and frequent upheaval in context. In an age of reform, Louisa felt that the new order offered genuine possibility for freeing women from a life of "household drudgery." The Civil War provided Louisa an opportunity for direct action. Following sections on the writing and reading of her best-known novel, *Little Women,* Elbert focuses on the author's "hunger for home" and makes the point that Alcott never had a permanent domestic environment. The final chapter identifies events in Alcott's life that spawned ideas for a number of her less well-known novels.

—VICTORIA PRICE

Amazons

Bennett, Florence Mary, *Religious Cults Associated with the Amazons,* New York: Columbia University Press, 1912

Blok, Josine, *The Early Amazons: Modern and Ancient Perspectives on a Persistent Myth,* New York: E.J. Brill, 1995

Kleinbaum, Abby Wettan, *The War against the Amazons,* New York: New Press, 1983

Sobol, Donald, J., *The Amazons of Greek Mythology,* New York: A.S. Barnes, 1972

Tiffany, Sharon W., and Kathleen J. Adams, *The Wild Woman: An Inquiry into the Anthropology of an Idea,* Cambridge, Massachusetts: Shenkman, 1985

Tyrrell, William Blake, *Amazons: A Study in Athenian Mythmaking,* Baltimore, Maryland, and London: Johns Hopkins University Press, 1984

The Amazons occupied a singular place in ancient Greek culture. Practically every genre of tradition and literature testifies to the fact that many stories were in circulation on these warriorlike women. BLOK centers her writing on a fundamental problem: how are we to determine the relation between two inconsistent mythical data? How are we to distinguish between fact and fiction? The interpretation of the Amazon myth led the writer to the study of myth as a scientific discipline, which indicates which questions arise and how they are to be formulated, as well as how they are to be answered. Blok's work focuses on the question of interpretation of the Amazon myth from the nineteenth and twentieth centuries. Blok shows how the view of the Amazons as extraordinary figures was created and reveals the perceptions of myth and history on which they are based.

KLEINBAUM's book is an attempt to investigate the long war against the Amazons. Its data are not mythical women, but the artistic and literary artifacts of western culture that document the long struggle against them. This book also is not a survey of the Amazons themselves but of the high endeavors for which the imaginary women were sacrificed. According to Kleinbaum, the Amazon is a dream that men created, an image of a superlative female that men constructed to flatter themselves. However,

Kleinbaum eloquently reveals her opinion that in the characteristically human, and even commendable, pursuit of excellence, men have often been marvelously silly.

SOBOL's work contains bits and pieces from funeral mounds to records of tremendous campaigns, all put together in order to form a narrative history that has a dramatic, rational, valid sequence. This book is intended neither to expose the warrior-women as figments of the imagination, nor to defend them against their detractors. It is, however, an unbiased handbook in which the curious reader may find collected all the essential data currently known on the subject of the Amazon women in mythology. The book is divided into two parts. The first part actually tells the story of the Amazons. The second part discusses the commentary, and tries to answer the long debated question: are Amazons myth or fact?

TYRRELL discusses the manner of myth-making. This book remains a powerful conception of the sexes and their roles in marriage and in every sphere of life. This study of the Amazon myth is not confined to classicists and other specialists. Chapter One traces the history of the Amazon myth at Athens. The central question in Chapter Two is the historicity of Amazons in view of the evidence or lack thereof for ancient matriarchies. Chapter Three establishes that the customs of the Amazons are imagined in the myth to be the reverse of those of patriarchy. In Chapter Four, the Amazons are studied in the light of the rites of transition every youth had to undergo to become a full member of society. Chapter Five deals with what it meant to kill an Amazon. Finally, Chapter Six deals with the examination of the myth, which leads to an understanding of the part played by the Amazon myth in Athenian myth-making.

BENNETT's book discusses the Amazons in Greek legend, including the theories concerning the Amazons. The earliest writings of the Greeks concerning the Amazons show them in part of Asia Minor where evidence for rites of the mother goddess appear throughout ancient times. The author speaks of conflicting theories concerning the provenience of the cult of Ares. The general tendency of the evidence is in the direction of the theory that Ares was an ancient god of the Thracians, of the pre-Hellenic peoples of Greece, and of the races who worshipped the mother goddess in Asia Minor and Crete. As a god whom the Amazons supposedly worshipped, he does not appear to have been as important as the mother goddess. The records of his association with them are few and somewhat confused. The best evidence is that furnished by the accounts of the saga of Theseus and the Amazons, to which Ares belongs, although the author is careful to note that it is impossible to define his position. However, the author states that the saga is of special importance in being analogous to the Ephesian tales of Heracles and Dionysus. The author looks at interpretations of Greek travelers in the age of Herodotus, who inferred that they had discovered the Amazons in the regions of Scythia and Libya.

Throughout the centuries, men have found women to be a mystery. Idealized as morally and spiritually superior to men, women are, alternately, denigrated as biologically and socially inferior. These ideas about women parallel the western imagination about primitive peoples. TIFFANY and ADAMS write about images of women. Women are the archetype of what men are not. Appearing in various roles as Amazons, virgins, and matriarchs, women represent a projection of civilized men's imaginations. Written in the spirit of feminist commitment and inquiry, this book demystifies the notion of the "wild women." The authors discard ideas about female nature as essentially wild and urge women to claim their own identities. This book addresses an audience concerned about the lives and experiences of women everywhere. It stimulates criticism and debate.

—SUSAN M. TAYLOR

See also Ancient Classical World

American Revolutionary Era

Akers, Charles W., *Abigail Adams: An American Woman,* Boston: Little Brown, 1980

Cott, Nancy F., *The Bonds of Womanhood: "Women's Sphere" in New England, 1780–1835,* New Haven, Connecticut: Yale University Press, 1977

Freeman, Lucy, and Alma Halbert Bond, *America's First Woman Warrior: The Courage of Deborah Sampson,* New York: Paragon, 1992

Gelles, Edith B., *Portia: The World of Abigail Adams,* Bloomington: Indiana University Press, 1992

Hoffman, Ronald, and Peter J. Albert, *Women in the Age of the American Revolution,* Charlottesville: University Press of Virginia, 1989

Kerber, Linda K., *Women of the Republic: Intellect and Ideology in Revolutionary America,* Chapel Hill: University of North Carolina Press, 1980

Nicolay, Theresa Freda, *Gender Roles, Literary Authority, and Three American Women Writers: Anne Dudley Bradstreet, Mercy Otis Warren, Margaret Fuller Ossoli,* New York: Lang, 1995

Norton, Mary Beth, *Liberty's Daughters: The Revolutionary Experience of American Women, 1750–1800,* Boston: Little Brown, 1980

Richards, Jeffrey H., *Mercy Otis Warren,* New York: Twayne, and London: Prentice Hall, 1995

Before 1975, studies of the American Revolutionary era (1770–1800) emphasized the lives of men, and either neglected women's lives altogether, or discussed women's experiences solely in terms of men's. In the last twenty years, scholars have attempted to rewrite the history of late eighteenth-century women to reflect the singularities of their experiences, and to describe their roles through a female interpretive model. Four of the books described here have been successful at this attempt, and are now standards in the field. The other works discussed are the best in-depth studies available on three notable women of the period.

To explain how the so-called cult of domesticity arose in 1830s New England, COTT examines private documents of over one hundred middle-class white women living between 1780 and 1835. Under chapter headings such as "Work," "Domesticity," "Education," and "Religion," Cott describes in detail women's lives, and concludes that women of this period were neither victims of social change, as historians had traditionally thought, nor truly mistresses of their own destinies. Cott's is the only study on women to bridge both centuries, and therefore remains a valuable source for scholars interested in late eighteenth- and early nineteenth-century American female culture.

NORTON's study draws upon the private papers of more than 450 families of various racial, economic, and geographic groups to explain the impact of the Revolutionary War on women's lives. In Part One of the book Norton traces patterns in women's lives that remained constant before, during, and after the war. In Part Two she discusses changes to women's status quo brought on by the war, which include women's increased "reverence of self," and the broadening of their educational opportunities. Norton's well-researched and documented book is scholarly, and yet highly readable. The work has become a standard for the study of women's lives in the revolutionary period.

KERBER's book, like Norton's, examines the effects of the Revolutionary War upon women. Different from Norton's conclusions, however, Kerber suggests that the war brought significant change to women's lives, despite the "conservatism" of the Revolution itself. Using women's diaries, journals, letters, and other private papers, in the first four chapters Kerber relates the feelings of women during wartime as they took on new duties at home and in the field camps. The last five chapters focus upon broader, post-war social changes that affected women's lives, including increased educational opportunities and the freedom to divorce. Kerber introduces here her well-known theory of "Republican Motherhood," which she uses to describe the role offered women in the new republic. She suggests that Republican Motherhood is a "revolutionary" invention, since it forces an intersection of the domestic and political spheres. Although critics have disagreed with the implications of Kerber's theory of Republican Motherhood, her analysis of women's lives in the Revolutionary era has become a standard.

HOFFMAN and ALBERT bring together essays by preeminent scholars of early American women's history. Essays by Kerber and Norton frame the collection, by reviewing what we already know of women's history, and where our knowledge is still lacking. The book's essays range from examination of the age, to more specific topics pertaining in particular to women. Topics include analyses of long-term trends in wills, the effects of the Revolutionary War on poet Phillis Wheatley, and the fusing of religious and secular values in the minds of women in late eighteenth-century America. Written expressly for this collection, these essays synthesize much of the information already known about the age, and add new knowledge as well.

FREEMAN and BOND's biography of Deborah Sampson, a woman who dressed as a male soldier and served in the Revolutionary War, is the first modern-day account of this extraordinary woman's life. Drawing upon original research, the authors contend that she was "America's first feminist," and that she entered the war partly because she sought equality with men. Perhaps a more sustainable argument is presented by Bond, a psychoanalyst who interprets Sampson's recurrent nightmare and childhood memories to offer another explanation for her desire to serve in the military. This book corrects and improves upon Herman Mann's original 1797 biography, written from interviews with Sampson after the war.

AKERS's book is the first full biography of Abigail Adams published after the opening of the Adams Papers. Drawing upon over two thousand of Abigail Adam's letters, Akers constructs not only a compelling portrait of this important American woman, but also a comprehensive cultural study of the period. Akers suggests that although Adams recognized and accepted the different roles men and women played, she insisted upon equality with her husband in her marriage. Akers's biography is an important addition to the growing corpus of works on this famous first lady.

Adding to what she has termed the "Abigail industry," GELLES offers a valuable biography of Abigail Adams, which differs from previous biographies in two ways. First, she has attempted to write from a specifically female point of view, which acknowledges and accentuates the domesticity of Adams to see how it informs her character. Secondly, Gelles has examined Adams's letters within, as much as possible, an eighteenth-century context. Different from previous biographers, Gelles argues that Adams's intelligence and character distinguish her from other eighteenth-century women, but that her values and attitudes were shared by others. The book contains a valuable overview of contemporary writing on Adams, as well as an extensive bibliography on both Adams and her age.

In her study of literary authority and female writers, NICOLAY devotes an extensive chapter to Mercy Otis Warren, Revolutionary playwright and historian. Nicolay argues that Warren's incorporation of political rhetoric into all of her work moved female authorship further into the public "male" world, and raised public consciousness about the range of possibility for women's writing. Nicolay suggests that the publishing industry became "democratic" more quickly than other public institutions because of the presence of women writers such as Warren. This work is valuable for scholars of Warren, since it is the only one that analyzes the reception of her work by the publishing industry and the public.

In the tradition of the Twayne series, RICHARDS offers a comprehensive introduction to Warren. Drawing upon numerous sources about the Revolutionary era in general, and Mercy Otis Warren in particular, Richards provides a comprehensive account of Warren's life and literary output. While discussion of the individual works is brief, the inclusiveness of the survey of her writings, including publishing history and public reception, makes the book a valuable tool for scholars. Extended notes and a bibliography of primary and secondary sources are included.

—JULIE S. AMBERG

Ancient Classical World

DuBois, Page, *Centaurs and Amazons: Women and the Pre-History of the Great Chain of Being*, Ann Arbor: University of Michigan Press, 1982

———, *Sowing the Body: Psychoanalysis and Ancient Representations of Women*, Chicago: University of Chicago Press, 1988

Halperin, David, John Winkler, and Froma Zeitlin (eds.), *Before Sexuality: The Construction of Erotic Experience in the Ancient Greek World*, Princeton, New Jersey: Princeton University Press, 1990

Laqueur, Thomas, *Making Sex: Body and Gender from the Greeks to Freud*, Cambridge, Massachusetts: Harvard University Press, 1990

Loraux, Nicole, *Tragic Ways of Killing a Woman*, translated by Anthony Forster, Cambridge, Massachusetts: Harvard University Press, 1987

Pomeroy, Sarah, *Goddesses, Whores, Wives and Slaves: Women in Classical Antiquity*, New York: Shocken, 1975; London: Hale, 1976

Winkler, John, and Froma Zeitlin (eds.), *Nothing to Do with Dionysos?: Athenian Drama in Its Social Context*, Princeton: New Jersey: Princeton University Press, 1989

Theories of femininity relating to the ancient classical age have traversed many fields, from the politics of Athens and the position of women within its rigid structure, to the "construction" of the ancient female body, in medical discourse, in theatre, in religion, and in poetry and epic texts. One of the earlier explorations of the woman in ancient classical history, text, and politics is POMEROY's book. It conforms well with the first wave of feminism in the 1970s, by dividing the figure of woman into stock binary types and recognising the limits of positing women at either end of a positive/negative dichotomy. This book reads women as constructed by, and as secondary in relation to, the male Greek, dividing Greek culture into a neat array of extremes of femininity, to emphasise the limits of the classical woman's options. As the title suggests, Pomeroy believes women were encouraged to fit into an established role, and any diversion was seen as a flaw in femininity. The book is extremely useful in explicating a more ancient version of the Madonna/whore dilemma, which remains relevant today. It also includes information on the position of Roman women.

Two books that follow this lead into the 1980s are those by DuBois. Taking a view of the binaries offered to women in a highly specific classical Greek context, DuBOIS (1982) mingles them with similar stock gender types offered to males of the classical world of myth. She uses apocryphal tales, ancient texts, and political culture successfully to explore the more intricate manifestations of masculinity and femininity, and she even insinuates the metamorphic potential of the gender roles assigned to classical men and women. This aim becomes more sophisticated in DuBOIS (1988), in which gender role focus shifts from text and culture to body theory, specifically the gendered body as metaphor in classical culture. From architecture to agriculture, the deification, worship, and fear of the gendered body is revealed as "creating" conceptions about women. This is a beautifully visual book in its language and the art and architecture objects DuBOIS chooses in order to elucidate the body as metaphor. Both of DuBois's books are very useful in gaining a more specific knowledge about classical culture and its social practice, often surprisingly dispelling, rather than perpetuating ideas about woman being trapped in a series of limiting social positions.

LORAUX has created a fascinating insight into the popular classical image of the dying body, but specifically in this book it is the body of the woman. Although this may sound unusual, by focusing upon the tragic stage, as well as myth, Loraux excavates patterns within classical culture of the meaning of tragic deaths, which pervade ancient literature. Certain forms of death (suicide, sacrifice) hold radically different meanings than others, and the manner of death (rope, sword) recreates how the body is remembered in life. Death and burial was a crucial ceremony in Athens, and the mode of depicting the body of a mythic hero or heroine encouraged society to re-read their being in life, and the being of other women like them. This book is a unique and essential source for reading tragic drama.

LAQUEUR's book is useful mainly for the first few chapters, which deal with medical discourse and its role in formulating the notion of gendered citizens in classical Greece. Some of the anatomical theories that were held as true and affected daily life in Athens seem outrageous, but their influence on marriage, illness, and birth were supreme. The foreign nature of the treatise on medicine is good evidence that the formulation of gender comes frequently from sources other than those that are accessible to the academy, such as drama and poetry. This section of the book is vital for those wishing to have a broad sociological knowledge of how the creation of women's roles in the classical world were formulated. It also makes interesting reading for anyone interested in medical discourse in general.

HALPERIN, WINKLER, and ZEITLIN bring together a collection of essays that traverse everything from philosophy, myth, and drama to medicine, the normativity of homo-eroticism, and pot painting. It is a rich tome, which includes essays by the editors as well as academicians from around the world, all focusing on sexuality. The great use of this book is its revelation that the pristine world modern culture imagines classical Greece to have been was actually a highly sexual, frequently androgynous, and defiantly liberal realm. It gives the reader a broad overview of a polyphony of sexualities prevalent in classical culture, but it is also useful because of the great range of cultural areas these sexualities are read into: Herakles as a super-woman, female bodies as leaking vessels akin to pots, homosexuality, and the semiotics of age. It emphasises eros as constructed rather than natural. This book therefore provides readers with new knowledge but also with the utensils to reinterpret their own interests in Greek culture through an alternate angle.

WINKLER and ZEITLIN's anthology is concerned with the classical dramatic stage and its influences on the polis. It is a book that uses historical and dramatic theory but pulls these to a more postmodern arena in order to contemporise the study of classical drama. Many of the essays grapple with the historical conventions about drama: that women were absent both from stage and audience, and that young boys "became" women when on stage. Theories of performativity and a mistrust of historical convention are the main drives of this book. It is a welcome intrusion on the prevalent idea that women did not figure in drama at all, and for this reason it is valuable for any feminist reinterpretation of the ancient stage.

—PATRICIA MacCORMACK

See also Amazons

Ancient Egalitarian Cultures

Ehrenberg, Margaret, *Women in Prehistory*, London: British Museum Publications, and Norman: University of Oklahoma Press, 1989

Eisler, Riane, *The Chalice and the Blade: Our History, Our Future*, San Francisco: Harper and Row, 1987; London: Unwin, 1990

Gimbutas, Marija, *The Civilization of the Goddess*, San Francisco: Harper SanFrancisco, 1991

Hughes, Sarah Shaver, and Brady Hughes, *Women in World History: Vol. I—Readings from Prehistory to 1500*, Armonk, New York: M.E. Sharp, 1995

Lerner, Gerda, *The Creation of Patriarchy*, New York: Oxford University Press, 1986; Oxford: Oxford University Press, 1987

Stone, Merlin, *When God Was a Woman*, London: Virago, and San Diego, California: Harcourt Brace, 1976

The possibility of the existence of ancient cultures in which women held equal socio-political status to that of men has been tantalizing scholars of women's studies since the second wave of feminism thrust the women's movement into the academic arena. There are many reasons that feminist historians and anthropologists would want to prove that such societies existed, not the least of which is to combat the popular notion that patriarchy is the "natural" political structure in civilized societies. The present almost universal existence of male dominance over women is too often considered proof of male superiority and female dependency. The existence of ancient cultures that celebrated and respected both women and men help discredit such beliefs.

The task of reconstructing the history of preliterate societies demands that traditional research methods and academic assumptions about ancient cultures be critiqued in light of the cultural and gender biases of those who conducted the original research. The speculative nature of research based solely on archaeological evidence cannot be denied. EHRENBERG provides a framework for understanding the nature of archaeological and anthropological evidence in hypothesizing about the roles of women in ancient cultures. Her work discusses how and why the study of present-day societies with simple economic and technological advancements may help us understand how ancient societies with similar technology may have lived. One particularly interesting example discussed by Ehrenberg is that of the study of the Iroquois by Lewis Henry Morgan in the late 1800s. Morgan noticed that women in the Iroquois society held much greater status than European-American women of that time. The Iroquois were a matrilineal society (where lineage is determined and inheritance passed through the female line), which has sometimes accompanied higher status for women in a given culture. The Iroquois shared their political ideologies with early European settlers in North America and were influential in the development of U.S. democracy, if not in the treatment of women within that political system.

Ehrenberg also discusses how archaeologists arrive at theories based on material evidence left at the sites of ancient societies. Often archaeological evidence (artifacts, bones, remnants of structures) provide the only clues of how a preliterate culture may have developed. An important theme of this work is that the biases and cultural backgrounds of those hypothesizing about preliterate societies, be they nineteenth-century anthropologists or present-day feminist scholars, must always be considered, regardless of the method of inquiry.

The work of GIMBUTAS has been both controversial and ground-breaking in the area of feminist anthropology. Gimbutas uses her vast knowledge of archaeology to explain the development of civilization in western Europe. Her work posits that in order to understand ancient societies, we must assume the possibility that such cultures bore no resemblance to our own, and that allegedly matriarchal societies were not merely a mirror image of our patriarchal societies. Her suggestion is that so-called matriarchal societies were much more likely to have been egalitarian than simply systems where women forcefully dominated men. Such societies would have had a greater focus on collaborative endeavors and would have shared respect and responsibilities. Archaeological evidence suggests that where such societies may have existed, the veneration of goddesses was in evidence. Gimbutas's research has been extremely influential and was the impetus for much of the research that followed in this area.

STONE's work focuses on the socio-political implications of the worship of goddesses as the primary deities of a culture. She hypothesizes that many "patriarchal images, stereotypes, customs and laws . . . were developed as direct reactions to Goddess worship by leaders of the later male-worshipping religions." It was necessary to enforce loyalty to a male god who demanded the obedience of woman to man. Stone gives a historical analysis of the development of goddess religions and the egalitarian societies in which they flourished. While Stone's research has also been heavily criticized for not adhering to methodological standards, it is a very popular introduction to the imagining of goddess-centered cultures where women held political and private power with men.

It is virtually impossible to discuss egalitarianism without examining the origins of patriarchy. LERNER has written one of the most influential and scholarly works on the evolution of patriarchy and the historical roles of women. Her work refutes the idea that matrilineality and matrilocality necessarily indicate matriarchy (that is, a female-dominated society reflecting patriarchy). Her work also focuses on the division of labor and economic production and distribution as indicators of status in a given society. Lerner notes that "most egalitarian societies are to be found among hunting/gathering tribes, which are characterized by economic interdependency."

EISLER's research also asserts that it "does not make sense to conclude that societies in which men did not dominate women were societies in which women dominated men." Her historical analysis seeks to promote the idea that at certain times in history, egalitarianism was, and therefore could again be, the preferred mode of survival. Her Cultural Transformation theory hypothesizes that there are two general models of society. One is the dominator model under which both patriarchy and matriarchy would fall. The other is called the partnership model, in which "diversity is not equated with inferiority or superiority." While Eisler's research and methodology have been heavily criticized, she does offer an interesting vision of what ancient egalitarian cultures may have been. However speculative, this work has inspired scholars and sparked more thorough research.

HUGHES and HUGHES's survey of the history of women is an invaluable source book for the study of women in culture and the exploration of ancient egalitarianism. It provides interesting essays that guide the reader though the ages and that are supplemented with articles by scholars in specific areas of study, including some interesting primary sources. This work is an important resource for women's studies scholars and provides a framework for understanding ancient egalitarian cultures, although they are not the specific focus of this work. Topics of discussion include gender as a category of analysis, women's roles in the social and economic development of prehistorical cultures, goddess worship, and a cross-cultural historical perspective.

—DAWN M. CICERO

See also Hunting/Gathering Cultures; Matrifocal Cultures; Matriliny

Ancient Near East

Boulding, Elise, *The Underside of History: A View of Women through Time*, Boulder, Colorado: Westview Press, 1976

Cameron, Averil, and Amelie Kuhrt (eds.), *Images of Women in Antiquity*, London: Croom Helm, and Detroit, Michigan: Wayne State University Press, 1983

Leon, Vicki, *Uppity Women of Ancient Times*, Berkeley, California: Conari Press, 1995

Lerner, Gerda, *The Creation of Patriarchy*, New York: Oxford University Press, 1986; Oxford: Oxford University Press, 1987

Lesko, Barbara, *The Remarkable Women of Ancient Egypt*, Berkeley, California: B.C. Scribe, 1978

Seibert, Ilse, *Women in the Ancient Near East*, New York: Abner Schram, 1974

Watterson, Barbara, *Women in Ancient Egypt*, Stroud: Alan Sutton, and New York: St. Martin's Press, 1991

The ancient Near East spans the period from 100,000 years ago with settlements at Shanidar, to the Uruk period of civic communities around 5,000 years ago, to the occupation of Mesopotamia and Egypt by Alexander the Great in 331 B.C. Historically this broad expanse of time includes ancient Egypt, settlements at Ur, Hammurabi in the second millenium B.C., the Assyrians, Babylonians, Hyksos, Hittites, Kassites, and Persians, just to name a few. With such an expanse of time and cultures there are obvious problems with the comparison of women from one culture and time period to another. Moreover, studies of women in antiquity have generally focused on the women of Greece and Rome who have been studied for years, rather than the Near East.

BOULDING presents a very comprehensive view of the Near East as she explores the development of humankind from sex role differentiation in the Paleolithic age to the transition from hunter to gatherer and then urbanite. Her book not only addresses the history of this development, but the anthropological, sociological, and archaeological changes that took place. Boulding explores dominance theory, matrilineal societies, the growth of horticulture versus agriculture, and the metamorphosis in sex roles that transmutes the powerful to the powerless. Boulding's book is well researched, dense, and extremely comprehensive. Her wealth of information, however, includes aspects of all early civilizations, not just those in the Near East, although the development of civic habitation there does make it the primary focus.

Another study of patriarchy as a theme for women's studies in the Near East is that of LERNER. Her investigation, which is the first volume of a set that elucidates a feminist theory of world history, is intensely centered on the Near East, from Catal Huyuk to the genesis of Jewish monotheism. This is an exceptional work, with the constructs and conceptual framework of patriarchy carefully outlined in terms of historiography from Marx and Darwin. From there she explores her hypothesis that patriarchy antedated western civilization, a hypothesis she finds difficult to support. Patriarchy, she argues, was based not on economic control of women in the Near East, but on control of their sexuality and productivity. This evolution toward "slavery" was reinforced by the monotheistic god of Israel, who controlled all fertility and left women only the role of mother by which to achieve power. Lerner's work is impressive, tightly argued, and well researched. Her attention to feminist theory is superior. Two things especially stand out about this work. The first is her ability to write cogently on historical theory and make it interesting and clear to the reader. The second is her assertion that a male god based monotheistic belief system "codified" western patriarchy. Near Eastern women for Lerner then become a linchpin for the development of the patriarchy in world history.

Editors CAMERON and KUHRT's work includes many images of women from antiquity. Their intention was to present articles on comparing women from ancient societies, using the varying approaches of the contributors to unite sections around major themes and questions for current feminism. For instance, perceptions of women as "other" or evil include a discussion of witchcraft in Assyria as delineated in cuneiform texts. The discussion of women and power includes the women of the Eighteenth Dynasty in Egypt while the question of "biological sorting" addresses birth rituals among Hittite women. Discussion of economic roles of women delves into bride wealth in the Akkadian and Hurrian periods of Mesopotamia, while that of the cultic roles of women in Babylonia form the focus of another essay. This work is solidly grounded in feminist studies, and the contributors represent the best in their respective fields. Each article stands on its own merits, but the attempt to address the female experience across time and culture makes this especially tantalizing. The essays are superbly researched, but very complicated and probably not understandable to a novice reader.

Much more readable and entertaining is LEON's work in a more popular style. In it she has compiled short biographies of historical women grouped by geographical area. The majority of the work includes Babylon and Mesopotamia, Egypt and North Africa, and Asia Minor and the Holy Land. Her avowed purpose in this work is to discover the evolution of women into individuals whose "consent mattered." Although much of the book is tongue in cheek and a bit irreverent, the facts are solid and the presentation is witty and entertaining. Although Leon is staunchly feminist in approach, her levity can sometimes trivialize these women and their experiences. Overall, the book is a valuable resource, although not the definitive one.

Such an attempt to define women in the ancient Near East was made by SEIBERT. Her work is roughly divided into two parts, one half prose and one half a photo essay of women from the ancient Near East. Although the work deals with women in power, it is an attempt to uncover the daily roles of women through texts, codes, and imagery from the harem to the throne room. Written early in the development of women's studies, the work addresses the issues of power, the male-female relationship, professional roles, and motherhood, in an interesting and readable format. The notes are extensive, but many are not in English. It is also important to note that this work omits any mention of Egyptian women.

Egyptian women are directly explored in LESKO's short work, which is beautifully illustrated. Lesko argues persuasively that women in ancient Egypt were expected to, and did, take an active part in public and private life. This premise is recounted by example and short narratives. Very little theory or philosophic examination is included in the text or thesis.

Egyptian women receive more complete treatment in WATTERSON's history. Little effort is made to apply feminist theory, but the work is dedicated to evaluating the status of women in ancient Egypt as a civic, non-oppressed group. Divided according to topical themes, which vary from love and marriage to adornment and dress, this book carefully recreates the lives of women five millenia ago, based on primary and secondary sources from ancient history. Both the lives of commoners and royalty receive careful treatment. These readings about the ancient Near East from Egypt to Assyria highlight the fact that women sharing roughly the same geographic portion of the globe and the same time period received very different social and civic status.

—MICHAELA CRAWFORD REAVES

Angelou, Maya 1928–

American Writer

McPherson, Dolly, *Order out of Chaos: The Autobiographical Works of Maya Angelou,* London: Virago, and New York: Lang, 1990

Shapiro, Miles, *Maya Angelou,* New York: Chelsea, 1994

Shuker, Nancy, *Maya Angelou,* Englewood Cliffs, New Jersey: Silver Burdett, 1990

Perhaps because Maya Angelou's primary works are autobiographies, relatively little has been written about her by others for adult readers. Beginning with *I Know Why the Caged Bird Sings,* published in 1970 to both critical acclaim and controversy, she has documented her life with an honesty and detail not often found in autobiographical narratives. Rising from cook and streetcar conductor to author, performer, playwright, producer, and activist, Angelou stands as one of the foremost contemporary role models for young African-Americans. While a number of informative, photo-documented books for young readers have appeared in the last decade, adult readers should turn to contemporary reviews and articles, and to Angelou's own writing to learn about her life and works. Her autobiographies are more than the story of her personal life; as she has said, her works "speak to the black experience," but are always "talking about the human condition."

First published as the premier volume in the Studies in African-American Culture Series (1990), McPHERSON's book is the most scholarly, placing Angelou's autobiographies within a literary and cultural tradition. African-American autobiography began with slave narratives, and is still a primary form of literary expression among African-American writers. As one of a long line of such autobiographers, Angelou defines and redefines herself; presents a corrective social, political, and moral image; celebrates Southern black life; and inspires future generations through her serial autobiography. McPherson sees Angelou's work as offering instruction into the "range of survival strategies available to women in America," as well as providing insights into twentieth-century African-American culture and traditions. The book ends with a conversation with Angelou, and provides notes and bibliographical material.

Memory and the expression of the personal and cultural past are again important for SHAPIRO, in his more general study of Angelou's life and works. While classified as juvenile literature, this book is appropriate for adult audiences as well. Quoting extensively from Angelou's poetry and prose, as well as from interviews and other sources, Shapiro gives us a portrait of a woman struggling against societal and personal forces. In this struggle, memory is a necessary component leading to self-awareness and progress, from a child who wanted to be someone other than herself, to a woman who "brought herself...to a place that no African-American, and no woman" before her had ever been: at the side of the president on Inauguration Day. A volume in the Black Americans of Achievement series, this book includes an introduction by Coretta Scott King, as well as a chronology, an index, and informative photographs of Angelou, her family, and her historical and cultural context.

Writing primarily for a young audience, SHUKER gives a clear overview of Angelou's life in this volume of the Genius: The Artist and the Process series. The book includes a glossary, chronology, bibliography, and index, which together make a good, quick reference guide to Angelou's career. In addition, photographs of Angelou, and of historical figures and events of the Civil Rights Movement, give a visual context for this brief biography.

—ELIZABETH COOLEY

Anorexia *see* Eating Disorders

Anthony, Susan B. 1820–1906

American Suffragist

Anthony, Katharine, *Susan B. Anthony: Her Personal History and Her Era,* Garden City, New York: Doubleday, 1954

Barry, Kathleen, *Susan B. Anthony: A Biography of a Singular Feminist,* New York: Free Press, and London: Collier Macmillan, 1987

Dorr, Rheta Childe, *Susan B. Anthony: The Woman Who Changed the Mind of a Nation,* New York: Stokes, 1928

Edwards, G. Thomas, *Sowing Good Seeds: The Northwest Suffrage Campaigns of Susan B. Anthony,* Portland: Oregon Historical Society Press, 1990

Harper, Ida Husted, *The Life and Work of Susan B. Anthony,* 3 vols., Indianapolis, Indiana: Hollenbeck, 1898–1908

Lutz, Alma, *Susan B. Anthony: Rebel, Crusader, Humanitarian*, Boston: Beacon, 1959

Pellauer, Mary D., *Toward a Tradition of Feminist Theology: The Religious Social Thought of Elizabeth Cady Stanton, Susan B. Anthony, and Anna Howard Shaw*, Brooklyn, New York: Carlson, 1991

The life of Susan Brownell Anthony is synonymous with the nineteenth-century American women's suffrage movement, as evidenced by the designation of the Nineteenth Amendment to the U.S. Constitution, granting voting rights to women, as the "Susan B. Anthony Amendment." Despite characterization by various of her contemporaries and historians as "the Napoleon," "the Bismarck," and "the George Washington" of women's rights, relatively few academic works have been written about her. The majority of these are biographical rather than critical. Fortunately for women's history scholars, exhaustive records of Anthony's women's rights efforts have been preserved and well utilized by her biographers.

HARPER's three-volume biography could rightly be called an autobiography, as the first two books were written under the close supervision of Anthony herself (Harper wrote the volumes in Anthony's attic study) as a companion to *History of Woman Suffrage* (1881–1922, 6 vols.), the official record of the National Woman Suffrage Association (edited by Anthony, Elizabeth Cady Stanton, Matilda Gage, and Harper). This biography was intended as a defense against inaccurate representations of the radical arm of the woman's rights movement by the press and other individuals. The only biographical work to be written during Anthony's lifetime, it is based on letters, diaries, financial records, scrapbooks, and pictures from Anthony's personal library. The 1610-page work is a painstakingly detailed account of the "evolution of a life and a condition"—Susan B. Anthony and the status of women. A unique feature of this book is the reproduction of the autographs of 114 of Anthony's contemporaries. The final volume, written after Anthony's death, includes a comprehensive account of America's remembrance of one of its first female heroes, including eulogies from over eighty newspapers from throughout the United States.

DORR's biography is a worshipful tribute from another contemporary of Anthony. The author's interest in Anthony began at the age of twelve, when Dorr attended a woman's suffrage rally led by Anthony and Elizabeth Cady Stanton, and continued as she covered the activities of the National American Woman Suffrage Association as a newspaper reporter. Dorr was motivated to write this book because she believed Harper's account suffered, owing to Anthony's refusal to let herself be characterized as "the towering figure she actually was." Anthony's life is recounted against the backdrop of nineteenth-century America's political and social development, and the tumultuous battles concerning equality and citizenship, and she is characterized as a "history maker of this Republic." This heroic portrayal of Anthony is inspired by Dorr's idealistic belief that the Nineteenth Amendment (ratified only six years earlier) signified a "complete victory" for women's rights in America.

ANTHONY's book was written to balance Dorr's almost mythical portrayal of Susan B. Anthony by focusing on the private life behind the public persona. Anthony achieves her goal to "depict [Susan B. Anthony] as a human being—not as the figurehead of the feminist cause"—by emphasizing her personal relationships and their influence on her life work. This well-documented biography draws on Susan B. Anthony's personal letters and diaries, as well as interviews with friends and relatives.

LUTZ's biography, written at the request of two of Anthony's nieces, is full of anecdotal accounts of Anthony's relationship with friends and family. Like Katharine Anthony's work, this book emphasizes the human side of the suffragist, and the personal influences that motivated her to devote her entire life to women's civil and political rights. Written in a highly accessible literary style, Lutz bases this work on extensive archival research, including letters and journals of Anthony, as well as a heavy reliance on Harper's *Life and Work of Susan B. Anthony* and the *History of Woman Suffrage.*

BARRY's work, the most recent biography of Anthony, charts her private and public life within the moral, social, cultural, and political context of nineteenth-century America. While Anthony may be presented as the "leading lady" of this story, it is really the story of a country. Although this book is more theoretical than the other biographies, it is exceedingly accessible. Barry addresses the intellectual and ideological influences on Anthony's political consciousness, including Jacksonian democracy, the liberalism of John Stuart Mill, Victorian attitudes about sexuality, and Marx's critique of capitalism. In addition, Barry chronicles the various argumentative and rhetorical strategies considered and utilized by women's rights advocates. She also weaves in the stories of a number of Anthony's contemporaries, including Elizabeth Cady Stanton, Anna Howard Shaw, Lucretia Mott, Ernestine Rose, Lucy Stone, and Frederick Douglass.

EDWARDS's book focuses on Anthony's involvement in campaigns for women's suffrage in Oregon, Washington, and Idaho in 1871, 1896, and 1905, which she undertook on her own—"out of [Elizabeth Cady] Stanton's shadow." Despite the failure of these efforts, Edwards attributes Anthony with laying the political groundwork that ultimately saw success, but not until after her death in 1906. This groundwork included formal training sessions for local women in the basics of grassroots mobilization. These sessions generated suffrage leaders such as Oregon's Abigail Scott Duniway, who eventually engaged Anthony in an internal battle for leadership of the campaign. Anthony's work is set within the context of other reform movements important in the nineteenth-century Pacific Northwest—better schools, safer medicine, and establishment of cooperatives and temperance, as well as women's rights. Edwards analyzes Anthony's strategies for balancing the much needed financial and personnel support of temperance organizations, particularly the Woman's Christian Temperance Union and the Prohibition Party, with the political liability such endorsements represented in one of the most liberal parts of the United States. This chapter of Anthony's efforts is offered as a lesson for modern social reformers (especially advocates of an Equal Rights Amendment), who lack historical perspective because they have not "kept an eye on the past."

PELLAUER's analysis of three pioneering feminists as religious thinkers is the most non-traditional treatment of Anthony's life and work. Asserting that religion was an especially serious concern for nineteenth-century women, whose very womanhood was judged, in part, by piety, Pellauer says we must understand their religiousness in order to understand their secularity. The section devoted to Anthony includes a brief biography, and an explication of Anthony's focus on women's economic powerlessness and social-sexual dependency. Pellauer also examines Anthony's uncompromising principles, which motivated her to reject those solutions to women's inequality that were merely politically expedient. The author compares Anthony's religious views to modern liberation theology and its focus on social action. Pellauer draws heavily on Anthony's public and private writings as evidence for her interpretation of the integration of religion and politics.

—LINDA C. BRIGANCE

See also Suffrage: United States

Anthropology: Feminist

Behar, Ruth, *Translated Woman: Crossing the Border with Esperanza's Story,* Boston: Beacon, 1993

Behar, Ruth, and Deborah A. Gordon (eds.), *Women Writing Culture*, Berkeley: University of California Press, 1995

Brettell, Carolyn B., and Carolyn F. Sargent (eds.), *Gender in Cross-Cultural Perspective*, Englewood Cliffs, New Jersey: Prentice Hall, 1993

Di Leonardo, Micaela (ed.), *Gender at the Crossroads of Knowledge: Feminist Anthropology in the Postmodern Era*, Berkeley: University of California Press, 1991

Ginsburg, Faye D., and Rayna Rapp (eds.), *Conceiving the New World Order: The Global Politics of Reproduction*, Berkeley: University of California Press, 1995

Ong, Aihwa, *Spirits of Resistance and Capitalist Discipline: Factory Women in Malaysia*, Albany: State University of New York Press, 1987

Visweswaran, Kamala, *Fictions of Feminist Ethnography*, Minneapolis and London: University of Minnesota Press, 1994

Ward, Martha C., *A World Full of Women*, Boston and London: Allyn and Bacon, 1995

In the 1970s, feminists in anthropology reexamined the anthropological literature for data and theories with which to analyze the inequalities of status and power between women and men. Their reexamination exposed a double male bias—that of the subjects and that of the anthropologists. Thus, feminist anthropology developed with field studies of women by women, with ethnographies focused on gendered power differences, and with new theories critical of ahistorical, apolitical, purely structural concepts of culture. In the 1980s, anthropologists began to question the coherence of the category "women," pointing out that there is no culture-free basis for analyzing the status of women cross-culturally. Their critique of the category "women" paralleled criticisms by ethnic and cultural studies scholars who argued that feminism was defined by white, middle-class, western women, who lacked sufficient understanding of race, class, and ethnicity in the constitution of hierarchies. In the 1990s, feminist anthropology has confronted these challenges with attention to issues of international concern to women, with experiments in writing reflexive ethnography, and with studies of the intersections of gender and other relations of power.

In her introductory text, WARD reviews many of the standard debates in feminist anthropology, but without much attention to arguments deconstructing the category: women. Ward addresses many of the issues, including violence against women, women's human rights, and the international gendered division of labor, which are important to understandings of global feminism. She writes for the non-specialist, which makes her book especially useful to anyone who wants a concise, clear overview of feminist anthropology.

BRETTELL and SARGENT's anthology makes an excellent companion work to Ward's by providing a reasonably representative set of articles, written over the 20 period of feminist anthropology, as well as accessible introductions to various topics, including sexuality, the sexual division of labor, politics, kinship, and development. The articles combine ethnographic description with theoretical analyses of gender. The editors conceptualize gender as relational and fluid, in contrast to the category: women, which has been conceived of as relatively stable and essential.

BEHAR and GORDON focus on the ways anthropology is written as ethnography. This focus is part of a postmodern critique of the traditional style of writing ethnography as objective science. The articles in this superb anthology review the writings of selected earlier female anthropologists, such as Ruth Benedict, Margaret Mead, Ruth Landes, and Zora Neale Hurston. Behar and Gordon argue that one of the reasons these writings were often disregarded by academic anthropology was their authors' refusal to write in the scientific style that authorized the ethnographies of their day. Another reason was the feminist character of some of their writings.

In *Translated Woman*, BEHAR offers a new way of writing feminist ethnography in the form of the life story of a Mexican peddler, whom Behar calls "Esperanza" (Hope), because she refused to be silenced or subdued by poverty and abuse. While life stories are not new in anthropology, the first person and dialogue style of Behar's account is, as is her frank questioning of her relatively privileged position, and her intertwining of her own life story with Esperanza's. This much-discussed work is an excellent example of the more reflexive form of writing that characterizes new feminist ethnography.

VISWESWARAN's collection of her essays takes the experiment in writing feminist ethnography one step closer to literature and to the cultural studies' supposition that it is impossible to write ethnography that is not, in some sense, fiction. That is, Visweswaran works on the idea that the author's subjectivity is always present in her writing; therefore, the "truth" value of ethnography is not that it tells something objectively true, but that it tells the author's story, a story which is historically positioned and constituted by relations of power.

DI LEONARDO's anthology represents another perspective within feminist anthropology, one that is more closely tied to history and political economy. Beginning with di Leonardo's own superb analysis of the history of feminist anthropology, the articles relate the symbolic aspects of gender to the material ones, and relate global feminism to local practices. Historical and political economic approaches are useful to conceptualize the fluid, emergent quality of culture, and to analyze the political conflicts over culture among genders, classes, races, and ethnic groups. The articles are divided into the themes of gendered discourse in colonialism and anthropology, gender as cultural politics, representation of gendered labor, and gender and reproduction.

This last theme of reproduction is the subject of GINSBURG and RAPP's anthology. The articles cover such topics as population policy, lesbian motherhood, reproduction, HIV, and adolescent pregnancy. By raising issues about reproduction, which are of vital political interest to western feminists, in ways that recognize race, class, sexual, and ethnic differences as critical factors in the potentiality of global feminist politics, Ginsburg and Rapp present examples of some of the best work being done in feminist anthropology.

In the same vein, ONG's ethnography analyzes how global expansion of multinational capitalism affects the lives of Malaysian factory women in ways the workers themselves regard as both positive and negative. Ong sees them as victims and as resisters of international gendered, ethnic, and class-based forms of subjugation, as well as agents of their own futures.

—LYNN WALTER

Anthropology: Traditional

Etienne, Mona, and Eleanor Leacock, *Women and Colonization: Anthropological Perspectives*, New York: Praeger, 1980

Evans-Pritchard, E.E., *The Position of Women in Primitive Societies and Other Essays in Social Anthropology*, London: Bedford College, 1955; New York: Free Press, 1965

Gacs, Ute (ed.), *Women Anthropologists: A Biographical Dictionary*, New York: Greenwood, 1988

Golde, Peggy (ed.), *Women in the Field: Anthropological Experiences*, Chicago: Aldine, 1970

Lowie, Robert, *The Crow Indians*, New York: Farrar and Rinehart, 1935

Mead, Margaret, *Sex and Temperament in Three Primitive Societies*, New York: Morrow, and London: George Routledge, 1935

Reiter, Rayna R. (ed.), *Toward an Anthropology of Women*, New York: Monthly Review Press, 1975

Rosaldo, Michelle, and Louise Lamphere, *Woman, Culture, and Society*, Stanford, California: Stanford University Press, 1974

Much of anthropology before the 1970s ignored women by assuming that women everywhere were housewives and mothers and that these roles were the same and uninteresting. EVANS-PRITCHARD, a leader in British anthropology, raised these assumptions to facts in his book. He asserted that men are always superior to women and women can only be discussed in terms of their roles in kinship. In the title article he demonstrates the attitude and scholarship of his day. He refers those interested in the topic to "lady" anthropologists. While he admits to disliking modern feminism and knowing little about it, he compares contemporary English gender settings with the primitive. Little of his data or conclusions would hold up today. He finds that compared to English women, primitive women are confined in the home, and have many children and no idea of romantic love. On the other hand, the sexes live largely separately and rarely "intrude" on one another. In both types of societies, men hold authority in the family and society and, he asserts, this will not change despite the hopes of feminists.

In this dismal arena some anthropologists did write about gender, although this was rarely appreciated at the time. MEAD wrote about women and gender issues throughout her long career. In 1935 she directly addressed the issue of gendered personality. She questioned the American concept of her time that women were genetically programmed to be passive and nurturing while men were born for aggression and dominance. In New Guinea she found three societies that did not fit this pattern. Among the Arapesh and Mundugumor, both genders were expected to have identical personalities. Among the Arapesh the ideal personality type for both genders was similar to that of the American woman, and among the Mundugumor to that of the American man. In the third society Mead discussed, the Tchambuli (now Chambri), the ideal personalities of men and women were different from each other but opposite to those of Americans. She asserted that this proved the importance of culture, rather than nature, in creating gendered individuals.

A contemporary of Mead's, LOWIE used traditional ethnography in an atypical way. His description of Crow culture emphasized the roles of both men and women. In his book, he showed Crow women to be active players in their society, who had freedom and respect. Their roles in religion and economics as well as the family are shown to be essential to the well-being of all Crow.

The activities and contributions of the "lady" anthropologists referred to by Evans-Pritchard are summarized in two useful anthologies. The biographical dictionary edited by GACS covers the lives and careers of 50 female anthropologists, divided into two time periods: the "First Generation" (born before 1901), and the "Second Generation" (born between 1901 and 1934). In addition to discussing the trials and challenges of pursuing a professional career as an anthropologist when this was still largely a male domain, contributors were instructed to pay special attention in their entries to early work by their subjects on gender roles and/or on the status of women (including that of female anthropologists). Each entry contains a valuable bibliography of selected works.

GOLDE's collection of fourteen first-hand accounts of female anthropologists' fieldwork experiences spans many locales and over four decades of work by female ethnographers—from the 1930s through the 1970s. In addition to an article by Margaret Mead reflecting on her forty years of work in the Pacific Islands, such pioneers as Laura Nader, Jean Briggs, Cora Du Bois, Ruth Landes, and Helen Codere write about their field experiences. The articles emphasize the personal challenges faced by the ethnographer in the field, including the experiences of culture shock and the particular challenges of negotiating the role of researcher in societies where women are defined exclusively by their domestic roles. Regardless of whether or not they had gone to the field with the intention of studying gender and the status of women, these early ethnographers frequently ended up with considerable insight into the gender systems of the peoples they were living with and studying.

Three edited collections, by Etienne and Leacock, Reiter, and Rosaldo and Lamphere mark the critical turning point when women and gender issues began to be taken seriously within the discipline of anthropology. Each represents a distinct theoretical perspective: ETIENNE and LEACOCK's framework derives from a Marxist-feminist orientation and views capitalist penetration as the culprit for undermining women's power and influence in traditional societies. The editors' introduction in especially valuable.

ROSALDO and LAMPHERE, on the other hand, assume that gender asymmetry is universal, and the articles in that collection explore the causes, permutations, and implications of that fact. In large part, the initial task of feminist anthropology was to go back over the theoretical underpinnings of the discipline and meticulously critique the male bias distorting our understanding of human cultures and societies. Landmark essays include those by Rosaldo, Ortner, Chodorow, and Collier. REITER's focus, like that of Etienne and Leacock, is Marxist-feminist. Especially important are the essays by Leibowitz, Slocum, and Rubin. These three volumes together, in their evaluation of past work and setting of agendas for the future, provide an unparalleled understanding of the issues of women and gender in traditional anthropology.

—LAURA KLEIN and ELIZABETH BRUSCO

Antifeminism

Conover, Pamela Johnston, and Virginia Gray, *Feminism and the New Rights: Conflict over the American Family,* New York: Praeger, 1983

Denfeld, Rene, *The New Victorians: A Young Woman's Challenge to the Older Feminist Order,* New York: Warner, 1995

Dworkin, Andrea, *Right-Wing Women,* London: Women's Press, and New York: Perigee, 1983

Faludi, Susan, *Backlash: The Undeclared War against Women,* New York: Crown, 1991; London: Chatto and Windus, 1992

Hewlett, Sylvia Ann, *A Lesser Life: The Myth of Women's Liberation in America,* New York: Morrow, 1986; London: Michael Joseph, 1987

Klatch, Rebecca E., *Women of the New Right,* Philadelphia: Temple University Press, 1987

Sommers, Christina Hoff, *Who Stole Feminism? How Women Have Betrayed Women,* New York and London: Simon and Schuster, 1994

Antifeminism refers to the counterassault on women's rights, which attempts to reverse the achievements of the feminist movement and to build political opposition to its goals. The initial focus on this countermovement has been joined by a generational, cultural, and largely internal critique or "backlash" against the feminist movement. Political scientists CONOVER and GRAY use public opinion polls and interviews with those attending one of the 1980 White House Conferences on the Family to examine the origins, organizations, and participants of both the feminist and antifeminist movements. They conclude that opponents of the Equal Rights Amendment (ERA) and abortion join the New Right movement out of ideological principles. Most are newly middle-class but have retained traditional working-class conservative values that view these policies as an attack on religion, family, and limited government; they reject the feminist position that women are individuals who are not necessarily subsumed in a family role. The authors find little evidence of antifeminist single-issue voting sufficient to defeat candidates, or of strong state organizations or real accomplishments. They warn, however, that the image and perception of antifeminist strength held by the media, government, and organized religion can be an adequate substitute, as can the movement's very substantial fundraising capacity.

KLATCH, an academic sociologist, provides a nuanced portrait of the women of the new conservative movement, a countermovement to feminism that is neither monolithic nor cohesive. Instead there are two distinct branches, composed of (1) social conservatives who are religiously based, and (2) laissez-faire economic conservatives who share feminism's concern for libertarianism and individualism. Through the use of interviews, participant observation, and textual analysis of New Right materials, the author provides an empathetic view of how these women rationally act to preserve traditional sex roles. The New Right, she concludes, speaks a common language in opposition to Communism and big government, but one devoid of common meaning, particularly on the role of government in social and moral issues. Social conservatives reject feminism as antifamily and immoral, whereas laissez-faire conservatives object to government advancement of feminism through subsidies and the ERA, but may be potential feminist allies on issues such as corporate day care, abortion, and gay rights.

Feminist author and journalist DWORKIN concludes that women rationally adopt a conservative ideology in hopes of protection from male violence and aggression. Women are promised structure, shelter, safety, and love by the New Right. Dworkin makes the provocative argument that right-wing women may see the oppression of women more clearly than do feminists; that is, women may be worth more in the home than in the paid labor force, where they are not sexually or economically independent of men. Christian marriage can protect from battering and rape; housework provides a buffer against economic exploitation. Pregnancy gives women some value, respect, and control over men; homosexuality could make women useless as a class. Although antifeminism is defined as a political defense of misogyny, some antifeminist views are presented as a logical accommodation to an inevitable sex-class system. Dworkin warns that feminism, a movement of the powerless against powerlessness, may be doomed to fail.

Economist HEWLETT created a furor within the feminist movement with the "losing ground" critique of the impact of the U.S. women's rights movement upon working women and their families. As indicated by the high divorce rate, large earnings gap, and lack of social services such as flextime, family leave, child care, and health care, U.S. women trail their counterparts in England, France, Italy, and Sweden. Hewlett charges the feminist movement with uncritically adopting the male competitive model and stressing formal equality on male terms, a position that aligns her with the "difference" school of feminism, which argues that women must be treated differently in order to be treated equally. She points to a number of problem areas—no-fault divorce, gender-neutral alimony, poor enforcement of child support, lack of a family allowance—and several flaws within feminism—natural childbirth, breastfeeding, nonsexist childrearing, and a general anti-male/child/motherhood orientation—that have created an even more stultifying "cult of motherhood." By concentrating almost exclusively on gaining equal rights and sexual freedom for women, the women's rights movement failed to make alliances with political parties, unions, and other groups that could have led to policies that reduced the work-family conflict for women.

Journalist FALUDI long rode the bestseller lists with her highly readable account of the backlash against feminism, a backlash rooted in the popular culture and fueled by media that uncritically accept inaccurate statistical information about women on subjects such as the man shortage, the infertility epidemic, and dangerous day care. The agents of this backlash are numerous: purveyors of high fashion, lingerie, cosmetics, and plastic surgery; television shows, movies, and self-help books featuring love-addicted single women and cocooning "mommy trackers"; the Republican New Right; male critics such as George Gilder and Robert Bly; and feminist turncoats such as Sylvia Hewlett and Betty Friedan. But the bottom line, Faludi concludes, is that women resisted much of this, as evidenced by facts such as "Murphy Brown" maintaining her popularity as a single mother by choice, and the sales of Jocky underwear outstripping that of sexy teddies.

Journalist DENFELD is typical of the so-called post-feminist generation, young women who see little need for a feminist movement to combat what they see as long-dead traditional sex-role behavior. Although the ideals of feminism are supported, the current feminist movement represents to them a return to chastity, Victorianism, and repressive anti-sexuality arising from the antipornography and date rape movements. The movement has become, to them, an extremist moral and spiritual crusade, the captive of cultural and patriarchal conspiracy theories. Denfeld regrets that issues of jobs, child care, health care, and reproductive rights have been deemphasized on the feminist agenda, or even replaced by trendier issues such as ecofeminism, animal rights, goddess worship, lesbianism, and self-esteem. The now-popular assertion that women speak in a "different voice" is viewed as a return to the old and restrictive separate sphere for women within the home. Denfeld makes a persuasive argument that the liberal feminist quest for political and economic equality was abandoned too soon.

Academic philosopher SOMMERS also mourns the demise of liberal feminism's hegemony. For Sommers, the answer to "who stole feminism?" is "women's studies scholars," who have failed to rigorously define and measure the incidence of anorexic deaths, the wage gap, sexual harassment, domestic violence, self-esteem, the demise of the nuclear family, and gender bias in education. The inability of social scientists to provide accurate measures is crucial, in that women's studies are now the primary sources for media stories about feminism. Flawed figures can also result in poor program design; she cites as an example the funding for college date rape education, when poor women are far more likely to be raped. Sommers further charges that, because of the dominance of the male-bashing critique of gender feminists, women's studies courses today too often constitute biased indoctrination that results in illiteracy in the standard canon of western civilization, and the inclusion of "filler feminism" consisting of minor female characters and events.

—JANET K. BOLES

Apartheid

Bernstein, Hilda, *For Their Triumphs and for Their Tears: Women in Apartheid South Africa*, London: International Defence and Aid Fund for Southern Africa, 1985

Cock, Jacklyn, *Women and War in South Africa*, London: Open Letters, 1992; Cleveland, Ohio: Pilgrim, 1993

Lazar, Carol, *Women of South Africa: Their Fight for Freedom*, Boston and London: Little Brown, 1993

Lipman, Beata, *We Make Freedom: Women in South Africa*, London and New York: Pandora, 1984

Magona, Sindiwe, *Forced to Grow*, Claremont, South Africa: Philip, and London: Women's Press, 1992

Russell, Diana E.H., *Lives of Courage: Women for a New South Africa*, New York: Basic, 1989; London: Virago, 1990

Walker, Cherryl, *Women and Resistance in South Africa*, London: Onyx, 1982

Apartheid means "separateness," and designates the official policy of race relations that governed South Africa between 1948, when the Afrikaner nationalist party seized power, and 1996, when Nelson Mandela's government adopted a new constitution. Under apartheid, women's lives were determined more than anything else by race; and there remains a vast difference between the lives of African women (who comprise the majority) and women of European descent. BERNSTEIN offers an excellent overview of these circumstances. Her book introduces basic features of apartheid society, examines the laws and social conditions that shape women's lives, and explores women's health, work, education, family relationships, and political struggles. For example, Bernstein explains the migrant labor system that controls women's movements and disrupts their family lives; analyzes women's work in domestic service, agriculture and manufacturing, as well as in informal occupations such as beer-brewing; and describes women's local organizations for food-sharing, savings, and resistance to apartheid. The book is equipped with photographs, sidebar excerpts from women's testimonies and official documents, an appendix that explains key terms of the language of apartheid, and a series of statistical diagrams on, for example, population, labor, marital status, and infant mortality.

WALKER's book provides a detailed assessment of the lives of women between 1910 and the early 1960s, while tracing the development of a women's movement in South Africa. It is academic in tone, influenced by Marxism, and draws on both statistical evidence and oral testimony. Arguing that women do not comprise a category that can be studied apart from society as a whole, Walker examines women's grassroots political organizations in the context of, for example, the migrant labor system, the subsistence economies of the "reserves" (where many black women were forced to live), the country's legal and educational systems, and World War II. She analyzes the role of women in the African National Congress (ANC), the South African Indian Congress (SAIC), the Communist Party, and trade unions. The book also contains an extended discussion of the establishment, growth, activities, finances, and membership structure of the Federation of South African Women (FSAW).

LAZAR's book includes photographs by Peter Magubane that chronicle the everyday lives of South African women in a series of stunning images: the hands of an illiterate washerwoman who has washed white people's clothes for 30 years; the inside of a barren matchbox house where a baby lies on the floor; a black nanny guarding a white girl who sits on a bench labeled "Europeans only"; a woman finding her home demolished; infant twins brought to court to see their mother who has been charged with treason; the funeral of a child who has died of starvation. In large format with pithy captions, the book also documents such moments as the 1956 women's march on the Union Building in Pretoria, a group of women walking to work during the bus boycotts, and the Sharpeville funeral. And it contains a number of poignant portraits: Ntsiki Biko leaving the inquest where the security police have been found innocent of her husband's brutal death; Helen Joseph peering through a bullet-shattered window; Winnie Mandela, under house arrest, looking through her gate; Nokukhanya Luthuli grieving at her husband's funeral. An introduction by Nadine Gordimer, and a brief history of apartheid by Lazar supplement Magubane's photographs.

COCK, a sociologist, is the author of two specifically focused studies of women in South Africa. The first (*Maids and Madams: A Study in the Politics of Exploitation,* 1980) concentrates on domestic workers and the women who employ them; the second (reviewed here) on women's roles in the military during the decade of the 1980s. Cock examines the way masculinity and femininity are defined and deployed by both the (white) South African Defense Force (SADF) and the ANC. Employing lengthy quotations from first-hand interviews, she analyzes the attitudes of five groups: the "protectors" (white men of the SADF), the "protected" (white women), the "resisters" (women in the military wing of the ANC and in the End Conscription Campaign), feminists, and victims. She explores, for example, how white women support militarization, both by symbolizing "home and hearth," and by working in the military, armament factories, and support organizations; how stereotypes of masculine aggressiveness and feminine vulnerability are deployed to denigrate resisters; and how legal, ideological, and social forces urge young men into military service. The book debates whether feminism should endorse or resist military service for women, and compares the roles of women in the ANC and the SADF. Walker's book is probably the best source for those interested in the attitudes of white women toward apartheid.

Two books based on interviews provide insight into the lived experience often obscured by statistics. RUSSELL's book is a compilation of interviews with women involved—in very diverse ways—in the struggle against apartheid. It is geared toward those without a knowledge of the subject, and includes a glossary, a guide to South African acronyms, a chronology of major events in South African history, a helpful bibliography, and a map that, unlike most, represents the black townships and "homelands." Introduced with a photograph and brief biography, Russell's interviewees discuss their backgrounds and political activities, as well as a variety of subjects such as the FSAW, problems of sexism in the ANC, sexual harassment of domestic workers, and tactics used to circumvent apartheid laws. The book includes interviews with a number of prominent South African women, such as Winnie Mandela, Ruth Mopati, Albertina Sisulu, and Helen Joseph.

LIPMAN's journalistic endeavor does not always provide sufficient contextual information, and may be confusing to those with little knowledge of South Africa. It is valuable nonetheless for its first-hand accounts of ordinary women's lives. It contains the testimonies of, for example, a clerk in Johannesburg, a sex worker, and a woman who organizes an agricultural cooperative; and it conveys the everyday preoccupations of many South African women: their loneliness for husbands from whom they have been separated by the migrant labor system, their humiliation at being photographed bare-headed or arrested in pajamas, their anxiety over malnourished children, and their anger over the blatant biases of school textbooks. While Lipman also includes interviews with several well-known South African women, her study is most adept at capturing the kinds of everyday details that a single nurse may take into account, but that academic studies may overlook: for example, African children often suffer severe burns because parents must leave them alone in homes lit by paraffin lamps.

MAGONA's book is the absorbing autobiography of an African woman who, deserted by her husband, becomes a teacher, pursues an education through correspondence, wins a fellowship to Columbia University, and, ultimately, acquires a post at the United Nations. Magona's narrative offers vivid insights into laws that discriminate against single mothers, the impact of local women's organizations on everyday life, the psychological consequences of daily dispossession and insult, and the simple joys of one's first bank account or a second-hand dress.

—REBECCA SAUNDERS

Arab Women

Abu-Lughod, Lila, *Veiled Sentiments: Honor and Poetry in a Bedouin Society,* Berkeley and London: University of California Press, 1986

Ahmed, Leila, *Women and Gender in Islam: Historical Roots of a Modern Debate,* New Haven, Connecticut, and London: Yale University Press, 1992

Altorki, Soraya, and Camillia Fawzi El-Solh (eds.), *Arab Women in the Field: Studying Your Own Society,* Syracuse, New York: Syracuse University Press, 1988

Baron, Beth, and Nikki R. Keddie (eds.), *Women in Middle Eastern History: Shifting Boundaries in Sex and Gender,* New Haven, Connecticut, and London: Yale University Press, 1991

Beck, Lois, and Nikki R. Keddie (eds.), *Women in the Muslim World,* Cambridge, Massachusetts: Harvard University Press, 1978

Chatty, Dawn, and Annika Rabo (eds.), *Organizing Women: Formal and Informal Women's Groups in the Middle East,* Oxford and New York: Berg, 1997

Göçek, Fatma Müge, and Shiva Balaghi (eds.), *Reconstructing Gender in the Middle East: Tradition, Identity, and Power,* New York: Columbia University Press, 1994

Kandiyoti, Deniz (ed.), *Gendering the Middle East: Emerging Perspectives*, New York: Syracuse University Press, 1996

Khoury, Nabil F., and Valentine M. Moghadam, *Gender and Development in the Arab World: Women's Economic Participation: Patterns and Policies*, London: Zed, 1995

Mernissi, Fatima: *Beyond the Veil: Male-Female Dynamics in Modern Muslim Society*, New York: Schenkman, 1975

Tucker, Judith E. (ed.), *Arab Women: Old Boundaries, New Frontiers*, Bloomington: Indiana University Press, 1993

Although studies on Arab women, or more generally on women in the Middle East, can be traced back to the 1970s, in recent years there has been a more emphatic shift to gender studies. The works mentioned here reflect research in various disciplines and cover a wide range of subjects regarding Arab women's lives, sometimes including articles on women in non-Arab Islamic countries. The books chosen provide comprehensive bibliographies leading the interested reader to works, many of a more specific nature, that could not be included, and the collections of essays familiarise the reader with well-known experts in various fields for further reference.

AHMED's book is an indispensable account of the discourses on women and gender throughout the history of the Arab Muslim Middle East, and an important contribution to the current debate on women and Islam. She outlines practices and concepts of pre-Islamic societies and their continuities with Islamic civilization, and she discusses topics of current interest such as the veil and the segregation of sexes. Ahmed then investigates Islamic discourses on women both in the classical and the modern ages, taking into account the socio-economic, political, and cultural conditions and changes in the respective societies and times. This valuable overview contributes to dismantling stereotypes and understanding changing concepts of gender in the Middle East.

ABU-LUGHOD's anthropological study of Bedouin society has become a standard in anthropology, Middle Eastern studies, and gender studies alike. She explores the social structure of this society, providing the reader with an excellent introduction to the code of honour and modesty that is important in many Arab cultures. Studying the oral lyric poetry of women and young men in an Egyptian Bedouin tribe, Abu-Lughod discusses gender ideology and the politics of sentiment. She reveals the dichotomy of discourse: the "discourse of ordinary life" as a manifestation of the ideology of honour and modesty, and the "discourse of poetry" as a sometimes defiant medium to express sentiments that violate these concepts.

MERNISSI's book is a classic among the studies on women and Islam. From the point of view of a Moroccan sociologist, she analyses the gender relations in modern Muslim societies between the constraints of traditional structures and the requirements of modernisation. Outlining a theoretical model of the traditional Muslim concept of female sexuality, she then depicts in case studies carried out in Morocco various aspects of modern male-female relations and reflects on ideas on women's liberation in Muslim countries.

One of the pioneering works on Middle Eastern women is the volume edited by BECK and KEDDIE, which brings together essays organised in four parts: general perspectives on legal and socioeconomic change; historical perspectives; anthropological studies on nomads, villagers, and town and city dwellers; and ideological, religious, and ritual systems. With its wide range of topics and various perspectives, this book is useful to those who want a broadly based coverage. Another work on gender in the Middle East from a historical perspective is that edited by BARON and KEDDIE. The introduction gives a survey of major questions in Middle Eastern women's history with an emphasis on the Muslim majority, followed by a comparative essay on Islam and patriarchy. The essays are organised in chapters on gender relations in the first Islamic centuries, the Mamluk period, Modern Turkey and Iran, and the modern Arab world. They reflect a wide range of historical sources and illustrate that gender relations in the Middle East have proven dynamic throughout history. They also analyse hitherto ignored material depicting women's views, thus revealing the gender bias of historical books.

TUCKER's collection of essays focuses on some of the dominant gender-related issues in today's Arab World: gender discourses, women's work and development, politics and power, and gender roles and relations. Some essays are of a more general nature, encompassing such issues as modern Islamic thought, feminism, and cultural authenticity; others are case studies of women in particular Arab countries and particular contexts. They link up specific historical experiences with present changes in the ideas of gender and in the realities of women's lives.

KANDIYOTI's book reflects upon the state of gender studies on the Middle East. Scholars from the fields of history, anthropology, political sociology, international relations, and literary criticism explore the extent to which gender analysis as a tool for social criticism has succeeded in both informing and challenging established views of culture, society, and literary production. This volume considers the shift from grand narratives accounting for women's subordination to detailed studies of local institutions and cultural processes through which gender hierarchies are reproduced. It both illustrates and contributes to new directions in feminist scholarship.

The essays collected by ALTORKI and FAWZI EL-SOLH discuss a hotly debated issue in the social sciences: the constraints on fieldwork resulting from the cultural backgrounds of social scientists. Examining the role of gender and indigenous status in their access to and construction of knowledge, but also touching on aspects such as class origin, education, and a complexity of other variables, this book is an impressive document of personal experience and contains useful information, not only for indigenous fieldworkers but for the field of the sociology of knowledge in general.

KHOURY and MOGHADAM focus on the aspect of the participation of women in national economic development, reflecting the increasing awareness of the necessity of intvmegrating gender aspects as an indispensable part of the process of ensuring sustainable human development. An analysis of the politico-economical background to women's employment in the Arab region, and an investigation into women as mobilisers of human resources, are complemented by case studies on the Maghreb countries, Yemen, Lebanon, Jordan, and Egypt, both highlighting the bias in underestimating women's real contribution and the limitations and inequalities of women's employment.

GÖÇEK and BALAGHI's volume came out of a conference on "Gender and Society in the Middle East." Their concern is to discuss, from an interdisciplinary perspective, the relationship between gender and three dimensions frequently used in social studies on the Middle East—tradition, identity, and power—by incorporating the voices and experiences of Middle Eastern women. This work makes an important contribution to theoretical debates in the field of gender studies.

CHATTY and RABO's volume does away with stereotypes of Middle Eastern women as either silent shadows or helpless victims of suppressive customs and traditions. The papers, given at a workshop in 1995, depict women as actors. They show the wide variety of ways in which women organize together, and the similar difficulties they face in many countries: to avoid being drawn into groups that are either approved or established by the state, and are often simply charitable organisations; and to set an agenda that will enable them to further women's aims rather than simply shoring up the existing gender hierarchy.

—KERSTIN WILSCH

See also Israeli-Palestinian Conflict

Architecture

Agrest, Diana, *Architecture from Without*, Cambridge, Massachusetts, and London: MIT Press, 1991

Bell, David, and Gill Valentine (eds.), *Mapping Desire*, London and New York: Routledge, 1994

Berkeley, Ellen Perry (ed.), *Architecture: A Place for Women*, Washington, D.C.: Smithsonian Institution Press, 1989

Colomina, Beatriz (ed.), *Sexuality and Space*, New York: Princeton Architectural Press, 1992

Hayden, Dolores, *The Grand Domestic Revolution: A History of Feminist Designs for American Homes, Neighborhoods, and Cities*, Cambridge, Massachusetts: MIT Press, 1981

MATRIX, *Making Space: Women and the Man-Made Environment*, London: Pluto Press, 1984

McCordquodale, Duncan, Katerina Rüedi, and Sarah Wigglesworth (eds.), *Desiring Practices: Architecture, Gender and the Interdisciplinary*, London: Black Dog, 1995

Torre, Susana (ed.), *Women in American Architecture: A Historic and Contemporary Perspective*, New York: Whitney Library of Design, 1977

Wilson, Elizabeth, *The Sphinx in the City: Urban Life, the Control of Disorder, and Women*, London: Virago Press, 1991; Berkeley: University of California Press, 1992

The introduction of feminism to architectural discourse was sparked by the dire situation of women within the architectural profession. Indeed, although their status has improved, women continue to be under-represented at all stages in the production of the built environment. Works tend to fall into two categories. One group deals with the recovery of the history of women as producers and consumers of architecture, and the other questions how gendered identities are constructed and reinforced through the built environment. The central role of the built environment in shaping everyday life has made it of interest to a wide range of disciplines.

A group of feminist designers, educators, builders, journalists, and mothers, MATRIX intends to subvert the man-made environment through examining the relationships between users, builders, and designers of architecture. They emphasize the need to combine the practice of architecture with theoretical analysis. Their analysis upsets the traditional dichotomy of the public/masculine and the private/feminine spheres, emphasizing that gaining control over built environment is one of the most effective forms of political action.

An important feminist endeavor has been recognizing women whose contributions to architecture have been lost or neglected by traditional architectural history. TORRE's book is based on the ground-breaking exhibition "Women in American Architecture." Looking beyond the category of "architect," this collection of essays combines an archival survey of women's contributions as critics, reformers, designers, and consumers, with an examination of those circumstances that have supported or hindered the achievement of women in American architecture.

HAYDEN's emphasis is on social and urban history. She recounts the history of the "material feminists," and the impact of their ideas on American intellectual, political, and architectural thought between the 1870s and the 1920s. Material feminists used architecture and design to create new cooperative environments, and to conceive of utopian communities to ease the burden of domestic labor on women, which they believed caused female inequality.

The essay collection by BERKELEY was published on the centenary of the first woman's acceptance into the American Institute of Architects. In describing her own experiences of discrimination, Scott Brown mixes the personal with the political. While recognizing the increase in numbers of women entering architecture, she highlights a profession dominated by a male "star system," with its power to exclude women from the status and recognition achieved by their male colleagues. Intending to inform current design in a positive way, Lobell employs a different strategy in her attempt to recover a reservoir of archetypal female imagery for architectural history. She analyzes a variety of prehistoric sites, which she believes are associated with matriarchal societies, concluding that women design differently than men because of their biological differences.

More recent works such as COLOMINA's book—based on a Princeton University symposium—stress that neither gender nor architecture is naturally or biologically determined, but that both are social constructions. For instance, Colomina, through her detailed analysis of the domestic architecture of Le Corbusier and Adolf Loos, attempts to demonstrate how the users of those spaces are positioned differently according to sex, age, and class. Her approach treats architecture not as a fixed object of art, but as a social and cultural practice, which not only reflects, but also produces power relations in society. In another essay from this collection, Bloomer draws on psychoanalysis, literary criticism, and the philosophical writings of Deleuze and Guattari. She believes that through writing, it is possible to explore a position other than the dominant one traditionally occupied by the architect—the practice of writing becomes inseparable from the practice of design.

AGREST, a practicing architect and theoretician, is concerned with blurring the dichotomy between theory and design. She feels she occupies a position that is both "between and without" the profession. She notes that western notions of architecture are founded on Renaissance principles, based on the anthropomorphism of the male body. Consequently, "woman" is assigned the negative term and repressed.

McCORQUODALE, RÜEDI, and WIGGLESWORTH bring together a variety of essays concerned with notions of gender and architecture. Ghirardo perceives post-modern feminist politics to be paralyzed by a fear of the essentialism inherent in the investigation of feminist design practices. Choosing one of many conflicting agendas that feminist design history encounters, she herself concentrates on recording the history of buildings and spaces neglected by traditional history, because of their association with women. Interpreting the notion of site to be marked as feminine, Kahn reconceptualizes the minor role site analysis plays in traditional architectural production. By expanding the boundaries of site beyond that of ownership, she considers site analysis as instrumental to the design process. Asking what feminism can do for architecture, Rendell suggests that it opens opportunities for new objects of study, as well as new criteria for their interpretation. Expanding Marxist architectural history through deconstructive strategies, she outlines a feminist methodology around the notion of use, experience, and representation.

The belief that the built environment shapes and is shaped by the individual and collective subjectivity is one of the reasons why architecture is increasingly discussed in disciplines like cultural studies, film studies, and urban and cultural geography. A good summary of these writings is found in BELL and VALENTINE's collection. Knopp, a geographer, argues that all social relations are structured around axes of difference—class, race, gender, and sexuality—which are engaged in a constant power struggle. Their continual conflict has a profound impact on the urbanization process and experience of the city, fueling the dynamics of urban life. Munt also explores the connection between urban experience and sexual identity, by focusing on its representation in literature. She likens the process of writing and reading to the activities of the flaneur, or person of leisure. The experience of strolling through the city is like a literary expedition where one can endlessly reconfigure one's own identity.

WILSON's book continues the prominent debate surrounding the nature of women's relationship with the city. In contrast to the anti-urban bias implicit in many feminists critiques, she concludes that what the modern city offers to women is a space of liberation. Constructing a history of women's representations of urban experience through a variety of female sources—including literary and journalistic ones—she works from the idea that women's experience of the city is very different from that of men.

—AMELIA GIBSON, BARBARA PENNER,
and KATHARINA VON LEDERSTEGER

Arendt, Hannah 1906–1975

German Writer

Barnouw, Dagmar, *Visible Spaces: Hannah Arendt and the German-Jewish Experience*, Baltimore: Johns Hopkins University Press, 1990

Bernauer, James W. (ed.), *Amor Mundi: Explorations in the Faith and Thought of Hannah Arendt*, Boston: Martinus Nijhoff, 1987

Hinchman, Lewis P., and Sandra K. Hinchman (eds.), *Hannah Arendt: Critical Essays,* Albany: State University of New York Press, 1994

Honig, Bonnie (ed.), *Feminist Interpretations of Hannah Arendt,* University Park: Pennsylvania State University Press, 1995

Kateb, George, *Hannah Arendt: Politics, Conscience, Evil,* Oxford: M. Robertson, and Totowa, New Jersey: Rowman and Allanheld, 1984

May, Larry, and Jerome Kohn, *Hannah Arendt: Twenty Years Later,* Cambridge, Massachusetts: MIT Press, 1996

Young-Bruehl, Elizabeth, *Hannah Arendt: For Love of the World,* New Haven, Connecticut: Yale University Press, 1982

Hannah Arendt was one of the world's major thinkers on the issue of the intersections of politics and evil. Her work on Nazis like Adolph Eichmann, and on the reality of the concentration camp, are masterpieces on the politics of terror and oppression. She raises important political issues regarding totalitarian versus democratic political regimes.

YOUNG-BRUEHL's life of Hannah Arendt is a good place to begin. Arendt praised political action and the public space but was a very private person. She grew up in East Prussia when it still belonged to Germany. East Prussia was a place of constant violence. She lived her life both in a Germany overcast with the humiliation of World War I and the coming darkness of the Nazi regime of Adolph Hitler, and in exile in the United States. Thus one can see why the issues of evil, morality, and the need to be public about one's opposition to evil, played such a large part in her personal and public life.

KATEB explores Arendt's political theories. Arendt maintained a fascination for the horrors perpetrated in the public realm by supposed democratic or liberal governments and public servants. She was particularly critical of democratic individuality. She believed that governments based on this political theory were more prone to totalitarianism and evil, because there were no constraints on the individual. These beliefs were based partly on what she saw in the democracy of the Weimar Republic in Germany, which led directly to the Nazi regime.

MAY's collection of articles views Arendt as a very eclectic thinker. She claimed not to "fit" anywhere because her political ideas were neither "left" nor right." It was impossible to peg her into any one political ideology. Such diversity of thought led to critics claiming that she did not know what she believed. But in fact her political world was very stable. She was a thinker who refused to remove thinking from the day-to-day life of the world. Her Jewishness often left her straddling both the world of the mind and the world of twentieth-century reality. Because the issues of evil and totalitarianism are such important issues of this century, and because she was a participant and not an armchair spectator to these events, her views were both eclectic and horror-filled. She wanted to believe in beauty but lived through concentration camp realities. She wanted to be a "good" Jew but was repulsed by the acts of the Israeli government. She was stuck between good and evil because her world was stuck between good and evil.

HINCHMAN's essays focus on politics, not political philosophy. We see again the eclectic flavor of her work. Arendt believed that any political reality based only on moral and ethical ideas, and not on practical political actions, is a politics doomed to failure or, worse, doomed to become the evil it wants to remove. It is not the function of politics, she believed, to promote social justice, nor should politics pretend that ethics are not important to the public. But government's job is to maintain its ability to rule. Evil comes when any government makes human beings unessential.

BARNOUW looks at Arendt as a Jew. Arendt's ideas were partly developed because she was a German Jew during the twentieth century. From the Kaiser to the Fuhrer, from the concentration camp to Israel, from pogroms to Eichmann, the Jewish reality in the twentieth century has been one fraught with problems and celebrations. Arendt's concern about evil and totalitarianism, for the need of democracy to see how it can subvert its own ideas, arose partly from the problems that Jews face in this century. Yet Arendt was attacked by Jews as well as by others because she was as concerned for the evils that Israeli officials commit as she was about those done by Arab terrorists. So she was a Jew and therefore concerned for evil. But she was also a human being concerned about evil done by other Jews.

Yet faith and ethics were critical for Arendt, and, as BERNAUER illustrates, at the center of her ideas. Arendt's faith covers the whole world, not only a portion of that world. It is an *amor mundi:* a love of the world. Arendt's work reaches out to recover that which is good about western culture. Arendt loved human activity and the promise that this activity would be fruitful and positive. Political structures that facilitate this "love" should be preserved. Political structures that preserve themselves at the cost of people should be destroyed. Arendt was a partisan, but a partisan for human existence.

HONIG suggests that Arendt's political philosophy is fundamentally feminist because it is at base an ethic of care, compassion, and connection. Honig argues that the problem of contemporary political systems is that they are based on male, that is violent and alienating, structures. The hope of the world is to connect with the feminist basis of Arendt's work. This involved-with-the-world philosophy is part of a new "canon" that must replace the older and less realistic "classical canon."

—PAUL BARTON-KRIESE

Art, Images of Women in

Banta, Martha, *Imaging American Women: Ideas and Ideals in Cultural History*, New York: Columbia University Press, 1987

Betterton, Rosemary (ed.), *Looking On: Images of Femininity in the Visual Arts and Media*, London and New York: Pandora Press, 1987

Broude, Norma, *Feminism and Art History: Questioning the Litany*, New York: Harper and Row, 1982

Broude, Norma, and Mary D. Garrard (eds.), *The Expanding Discourse: Feminism and Art History*, New York: HarperCollins, 1992

Dijkstra, Bram, *Evil Sisters: The Threat of Female Sexuality and the Cult of Manhood*, New York: Knopf, 1996

———, *Idols of Perversity: Fantasies of Feminine Evil in Turn-of-the-Century Culture*, New York and Oxford: Oxford University Press, 1986

Duby, Georges, and Michelle Perrot (eds.), *Power and Beauty: Images of Women in Art*, London: Taurus Parke, 1992

Hess, Thomas B., and Linda Nochlin (eds.), *Woman as Sex Object: Studies in Erotic Art, 1730–1970*, London: Allen Lane, and New York: Newsweek, 1972

Mullins, Edwin, *The Painted Witch: How Western Artists Have Viewed the Sexuality of Women*, New York: Carroll and Graf, 1985; as *The Painted Witch: Female Body: Male Art: How Western Artists Have Viewed the Sexuality of Women*, London: Secker and Warburg, 1985

A much more open examination of the ways women are portrayed in the visual arts began in the late 1960s as a direct result of the women's movement. Before the middle of the twentieth century, the great majority of artists were male, and those few women who worked as artists were mostly little known. For this reason, the artistic view of women was a male one, largely as sex object. A rich literature has been developed about this imagery, which can, for the most part, be reduced to a two-part set of stereotypical oppositions. The Mary-Eve dichotomy, with its subdivisions, subsumes a great part of female imagery. The "Mary" side of the dichotomy, based on ideas about Mary the mother of Jesus, portrays women as chaste, protective, and the self-sacrificing source of life. The "Eve" side portrays women as erotic, powerful, and as a threat to men. By applying this set of polar opposites, authors are able to analyze the astoundingly frequent use of the female image as an inspiration to inflame men's hearts in one of two directions, either to sin or to do good. With the exception of portraiture, and sometimes even within that genre, the Mary-Eve oppositions are very strong.

DUBY and PERROT's work is the most general and presents the Mary-Eve oppositions within a chronology of western art that simplifies and broadens the presentation of women's images. Since the authors are cultural historians rather than art historians, their view of the subject is necessarily and fruitfully tied to the daily life of past times. The reader can gain a sense of the changes and emphases that different eras gave to the images of women. They do not boil their approach down to the Mary-Eve dichotomy, but it can be understood to underlie their view. This is the only book listed that does not have an extensive bibliography.

HESS and NOCHLIN edited the first work to become a standard in the field of feminist art history studies. Unfortunately it is now out of print. The book concentrates on the images of women in art. It is a collection of essays that examines the many ways that overt and covert eroticism governs the portrayal of women in western art from the seventeenth through the twentieth centuries. Some of the images these authors explore are: bathers, slaves, vampires, pinup girls, and artists' models.

The two works by BROUDE and GARRARD are companion volumes. The format is a collection of essays by various authors ranging throughout western art, beginning with the Egyptian era. Some essays reinterpret familiar artworks in the light of new knowledge turned up through feminist investigations and correcting previous scholarship. Other essays investigate the great differences that other non-male cultural perspectives have had on images of women.

The manner in which American women were portrayed in art and literature from about 1876 to World War I is the subject of BANTA's book. The figuration of women tended to be dominated by a collection of types, two of which were new: the "all-American girl" and the "new woman." Unlike the all-American girl, who possessed a new physicality but was still virginal and embodied all that woman should aspire to, the new woman contained a mixed message. She was formidable to men because she was freer than woman had been before. But, on a positive note, she was a person of accomplishment. Banta discusses the origins of these new stereotypes and their forcefulness and endurance for the American imagination. The author is also concerned to show how typically American these types were and how often they appeared in monuments and the media.

DIJKSTRA's books, also a pair, consider images of women who symbolize a threat to men. The earlier work covers the last half of the nineteenth century and the later one the turn of the century through World War II. Because it is the image of female threat that he discusses, it is the "Eve" half of the dichotomy that is emphasized. Freudian psychology is an underlying foundation of his work. An exploration of filmmaking and other media enriches the work and allows a thorough investigation of the mid-twentieth century.

It is MULLINS's thesis that most art was made for a male audience even when the patron was a woman, as in the case of Marie de Medici's commission for Rubens to create a series of paintings about her life. He discusses the complexities of emotional response men feel toward women and which male artists have revealed in artworks. The goal of defining what makes women essentially virtuous or vicious (in terms of the Mary-Eve dichotomy) underlies the work.

BETTERTON's collection of essays by various authors covers the most recent time periods and is the most postmodern in its outlook. Cultural politics underlies all works that discuss the images of women in art, but this book is the most overt in its presentation. The ways female artists represent the female body and female sexuality are discussed. The media, its presentation of women, and the resulting change in stereotypes are central to this work. Pornography and violence in art and the media are confronted in a more direct way.

—ANN STEWART BALAKIER

Art and Gender Issues

Broude, Norma, *Feminism and Art History: Questioning the Litany*, New York: Harper and Row, 1982

Broude, Norma, and Mary D. Garrard (eds.), *The Expanding Discourse: Feminism and Art History*, New York: Icon, 1992

Chadwick, Whitney, *Women, Art and Society*, London and New York: Thames and Hudson, 1990

Harris, Ann Sutherland, and Linda Nochlin, *Women Artists: 1550–1950*, New York: Knopf, 1976

Nochlin, Linda, *Women, Art, and Power and Other Essays*, New York: Harper and Row, 1988; London: Thames and Hudson, 1989

Parker, Rozsika, and Griselda Pollock, *Old Mistresses: Women, Art, and Ideology*, London: Routledge, and New York: Pantheon, 1981

Pollock, Griselda, *Vision and Difference: Femininity, Feminism and the Histories of Art*, London and New York: Routledge, 1988

Raven, Arlene, Cassandra L. Langer, and Joanna Frueh (eds.), *Feminist Art Criticism: An Anthology*, Ann Arbor, Michigan and London: UMI Research Press, 1988

Tufts, Eleanor, *Our Hidden Heritage: Five Centuries of Women Artists*, New York and London: Paddington, 1973

While the contributions of women artists have long been recognized by their contemporaries, consideration of gender as a factor in art production—its impact on artists' access to institutions of art training, production, and exhibition—is relatively new. Since the early 1970s, when U.S. feminist art historian Linda Nochlin posed the question "Why have there been no great women artists?" numerous artists, critics, and scholars have addressed the relation of gender and art in works ranging from broad historical overviews of female artists to studies of specific female artists in particular historical circumstances. These listings can only suggest the range of works on this topic that have proliferated since the early 1970s; among the most useful sources are exhibition catalogues, and anthologies of essays by feminist art historians and critics. These general sources include extensive notes and bibliographies that will aid the interested reader in finding texts on specific artists.

The rediscovery of female artists lost or neglected by traditional art historical scholarship was the first step in examining the role of gender in art production. TUFTS and others compiled general surveys that brought the work of European and European-American artists to light; many of these artists had been well known in their time, but were subsequently written out of art history. HARRIS and NOCHLIN organized the germinal exhibition *Women Artists: 1550–1950*, which was accompanied by a catalogue containing extensive historical essays exploring ways that women's art production is shaped by social institutions and ideologies that vary with changing social and historical circumstances. Despite the limitations of their nearly exclusive emphasis on European painters and sculptors, such texts offer a useful overview of the work of these artists, and the conditions of their lives and art production.

The identification and study of neglected women artists—a necessary first step—took place within the traditional art historical framework that did not question the assumptions underlying the notion of "greatness." PARKER and POLLOCK further examined the cultural values inherent in art historical evaluation of the work of women artists. Their analysis of art as a gendered social practice, of women's historical and ideological position in relation to art education, art production, and ideology challenged the concept of greatness that underlies the discipline of art history. They also looked at the role of art in the social construction of gender difference. Parker and Pollock's recognition of art history as an ideological discourse, in which the meanings of "art" and "artist" in relation to the meaning of "woman" are assumed but often unexamined, is fundamental to subsequent examination of gender and art.

Anthologies compiled by BROUDE and GARRARD contain essays on the relation of gender and art in women's art production, and in male artists' representations of women. Their first anthology (1982) includes germinal essays that question art historical evaluative standards—whose life experiences are seen as valid for artistic representation—and look at gender in relation to the representation of the female body by female and male artists of European origin. Ten years later, their second anthology (1992) includes essays that incorporate more recent developments in feminist and poststructuralist theory, and consider artists from multiple cultures of origin. Both texts are useful for the depth of scholarship on individual artists that informs the essays, as well as the range of approaches to questions of gender and art that go beyond revealing the work of neglected artists within a standard art historical framework.

Questions of gender and art also inform writings by feminist critics on contemporary artists. RAVEN, LANGER, and FRUEH's anthology contains key texts in U.S. feminist art criticism. These explore the work of artists concerned with important issues in feminist art—the female body, the question of a female aesthetic, and the politics of women's creativity and choice of art forms, media, and imagery. This anthology is particularly valuable for the range of theoretical positions represented, from the celebration of an essential "female voice" to analysis of femaleness and its visual representation as ideologically constructed.

Building on such earlier foundational studies, more recent approaches to questions of gender and art emphasize gender difference in relation to visual representation. Informed by feminist, Marxist, and post-structural theory, POLLOCK employs what she calls "feminist interventions in the histories of art" in her re-examination of modernist art historical narratives. For example, she considers the difference in access of women and men to public spaces in late nineteenth-century France, and its impact on female and male artists' representations of these spaces, arguing for recognition of the force of gender ideology as shaping, and as shaped by, visual representation. The evolution of feminist art history from Nochlin's formative question to the critical examination of gender, art, and ideology is demonstrated by NOCHLIN's collected essays. In several of these essays, Nochlin brings feminist critical analysis to canonical subjects in nineteenth-century European art history, amply demonstrating her ongoing expansion of the boundaries of art history as she explores the connections between ideology, visual representation, and power.

CHADWICK's work brings together these various approaches to the study of gender and art. In a general survey text that introduces the reader to numerous women artists from the medieval period in Europe through the 1980s in the United States, Chadwick addresses the ongoing need for accessible information on artists excluded from, or only summarily mentioned in, standard art history texts. She also incorporates critical discussion of art historical discourse and its impact on female artists, along with references throughout the text to more theoretical approaches to questions of gender, art, and ideology. This is a valuable source of information, written in language easily understood by the general reader, that also serves as an introduction to the critical questions raised by feminist art history.

—MELANIE HERZOG

Artists: General Surveys

Chadwick, Whitney, *Women, Art, and Society,* London and New York: Thames and Hudson, 1990

Glanville, Philippa, and Jennifer Faulds Goldsborough, *Women Silversmiths, 1685–1845: Works from the Collection of the National Museum of Women in the Arts,* New York: Thames and Hudson, 1990

Heller, Nancy G., *Women Artists: An Illustrated History,* London: Virago Press, and New York: Abbeville Press, 1987

Kirker, Anne, *New Zealand Women Artists: A Survey of 150 Years,* Aukland: Reed Methuen, 1986

Parker, Rozsika, *The Subversive Stitch: Embroidery and the Making of the Feminine,* London: Women's Press, 1984; New York: Routledge, 1989

Petteys, Chris, *Dictionary of Women Artists: An International Dictionary of Women Artists Born before 1900,* Boston: G.K. Hall, 1985

Slatkin, Wendy, *Women Artists in History: From Antiquity to the Twentieth Century,* Englewood Cliffs, New Jersey: Prentice-Hall, 1985

Weidner, Marsha, *Views from Jade Terrace: Chinese Women Artists, 1300–1912,* New York: Rizzoli, 1988

Before 1986, general surveys of world art rarely included women. Even Helen Gardner, the sole female author of a major survey, only illustrated the work of a few women in her classic *Art Through the Ages: An Introduction to Its History and Significance* (1926), and by the fourth edition (revised in 1959 by Yale's art history faculty after Gardner's death), only one of eight hundred illustrations represented a woman's work. However, with the publication in 1971 of Linda Nochlin's influential article, "Why Have There Been No Great Women Artists?" and the discovery of several nineteenth-century books about the history of women in art, scholars began a serious search for more information and lost paintings and sculpture. The result has been a plethora of surveys of female artists and the first steps toward a revised understanding of world art history.

Artist surveys have taken many forms. Some authors, including PETTEYS, have provided bare-bones biographical dictionaries that present names, dates, media, education, and a few bibliographic citations for further research. By using abbreviated entries, Petteys covers over 21,000 artists, mostly European and American, but including women from other continents as well. Such sources provide an invaluable starting place for the collector, dealer, or researcher who has only a name to go on.

Other authors, such as HELLER, include fewer artists but provide a more expansive narrative. Organized by century from the Renaissance to the present, this book relates biographical information about a dozen or more western painters and sculptors per chapter, with emphasis on the former. Heller considers training, professional opportunities, reputation, subject, and style in a text that is richly illustrated in color. One of the most recent chronological surveys of this type, by CHADWICK, expands its scope still more to consider the decorative arts and issues of class, race, sexuality, spectatorship, patronage, criticism, and theory from the Middle Ages to the present. Chadwick's book provides a concise distillation of the state of feminist art historical scholarship in 1990.

Another approach to the general survey limits its subject to artists of a single country with the purpose of reevaluating that country's art history. Such surveys now exist for women of several countries. KIRKER explores painting and sculpture in New Zealand from nineteenth-century colonial British watercolors to contemporary Maori installations. In addition to biographical information, she discusses the professionalization of women's art at the turn of the century, and the women's art movement of the 1970s. While denying an essentialist position, Kirker nevertheless suggests that women focused on figures and personal relations in their art to a greater extent than men, and she believes that women tended to create in a more diverse range of media, while men specialized. She ends with a summary of the current position of women in New Zealand as art teachers, curators, critics, historians, and students.

WEIDNER wrote her beautifully illustrated text to accompany a traveling exhibit that introduced art by Chinese women to the American public. Focusing on paintings of the Ming (1368–1644) and Qing (1644–1912) dynasties, she suggests that the study of women's art can illuminate family structures and social systems of artistic production. Unlike western women, Weidner explains, Chinese women of several social classes had fairly open access to art training and could specialize in any subject. In addition, being an amateur did not carry the same stigma as in the west, for among male artists, amateurs tended to come from a higher social class than professionals and looked down on professionals as plying a trade. Chinese histories of art recognized women who pursued painting as an elite social pastime, although in smaller numbers than men and in segregated sections of the texts. Additional essays by Ellen Laing on three Ming painters, Irving Yucheng Lo on painter-poets, and Weidner on flower painting round out the book.

Other authors survey a single medium or process. One of the first such books, by PARKER, addresses a medium strongly associated with women but rarely considered art, and that is embroidery. Demonstrating that both men and women practiced embroidery professionally in the Middle Ages when it held equal status with painting and sculpture, Parker goes on to trace its evolution through the Renaissance, when major collaborative embroideries were less appreciated than individual works of "genius," and women were increasingly restricted to amateur practice; the Victorian age, when embroidery became thoroughly associated with domesticity and femininity; and the twentieth century, when artists transformed it into a medium of revolution. Throughout, Parker considers needlework as material evidence of the changing social constructions of femininity, as well as resistance to those constructions.

GLANVILLE and GOLDSBOROUGH choose a different approach in their study of women working in a medium normally gendered as masculine, silversmithing. While noting that British and Irish women filled a variety of roles from unskilled, low-paid burnishers to skilled engravers, shop managers, and designers, the authors focus on those at the top of the profession. Each object in this collection is discussed in terms of style and function, and most are illustrated in color. The authors conclude that women with registered marks (primarily widows) worked in all styles, forms, and sizes and were treated exactly as male smiths. Despite some evidence that women were paid less, nothing distinguishes their work from that of men.

All of these, and many other surveys of female artists have helped redress the absence of a significant female presence in surveys of world art. But it is SLATKIN who writes for that specific purpose. Conceived as a companion text to H.W. Janson's *History of Art* (1962) and other popular college surveys, this slender volume not only provides biographical information and black and white illustrations, but it also presents feminist interpretations of art from the era before individual female artists can be identified. For example, it examines images of women on ancient Greek vases for evidence of their activities as weavers, embroiderers, and vase painters. In addition, art education, patronage, and architecture are considered.

In time, perhaps, female artists and the issues raised by feminist perspectives will become so fully integrated in general surveys of world art as to alter the basic structures and methods of understanding the history of art. In the meantime, these and dozens of other excellent books offer insights to temper the prevailing view of world art as a history of "Old Masters."

—ANNETTE STOTT

Artists: Nineteenth Century

Burkhauser, Jude (ed.), *"Glasgow Girls": Women in Art and Design 1880–1920*, Edinburgh: Canongate, 1990; Cape May, New Jersey: Red Ochre, 1993

Callen, Anthea, *Women Artists of the Arts and Crafts Movement, 1870–1914*, New York: Pantheon, 1979

Cherry, Deborah, *Painting Women: Victorian Women Artists*, London and New York: Routledge, 1993

Garb, Tamar, *Women Impressionists*, New York: Rizzoli, and Oxford: Phaidon, 1986

———, *Sisters of the Brush: Women's Artistic Culture in Late Nineteenth-Century Paris,* New Haven and London: Yale University Press, 1994
Marsh, Jan, and Pamela Gerrish Nunn, *Women Artists and the Pre-Raphaelite Movement,* London: Virago Press, 1989
Tufts, Eleanor, *American Women Artists 1830–1930,* Washington, D.C.: National Museum of Women in the Arts, 1987

Although art historians have attempted to retrieve information about the art and lives of women from all parts of the globe, attention has focused largely on Europe and North America. Several scholars have located female artists within particular styles and movements that art history had already defined based exclusively on art by men. In the process, they are altering some basic conceptions about nineteenth-century art. In one of the first such books, CALLEN examines dozens of British, Irish, and American women who worked within the Arts and Crafts movement. Separate chapters consider design school education, ceramics, lacemaking, jewelry and metalwork, woodcarving and furniture, needlework, bookbinding, and illustration. Paying close attention to the intersection of class and gender, Callen identifies four groups of women in the movement: working-class and peasant craft workers, impoverished gentlewomen seeking to earn a genteel living, lady philanthropists who organized craft industries and patronized their products, and middle-class women associated by family and friendship to the men previously identified as Arts and Crafts leaders. Callen claims that this vast network of women was responsible for spreading Arts and Crafts ideals by allowing women to pursue activities within their traditional spheres: domestic needlecraft, charity work, interior design, and arbitration of "taste." She documents a sexual division of labor within the movement that frequently gave design roles to men and limited women to needlework, concluding that although the movement's alliance with socialism gave it some radical leanings, its patriarchal and class structures remained intact.

Inspired by Callen's inclusion of several Scottish artists, BURKHAUSER set out to illuminate the Arts and Crafts women of the Glasgow School, first with an exhibition in 1988 and then with this book. Her approach is less class-conscious and political than Callen's. Instead, she questions the dominant art historical model of elevating a few artists to the status of individual genius and suggests that a more accurate history will accommodate women and men who collaborated with one another. That collective spirit is also modeled in these essays, cooperatively authored by twenty contributing scholars. The essays describe the needlework, graphic design, metal work, and paintings of over 30 "Glasgow Girls," exploring the professional associations among them and with their male colleagues.

MARSH and NUNN investigate a movement that is commonly interpreted as images of female beauty created by men for men's visual consumption. Even the name, Pre-Raphaelite Brotherhood, seems to identify its patriarchal nature. But Marsh and Nunn document the extensive involvement of 18 female artists over a period of three generations. They posit that the disappearance of these women from history (except as mythic models and mistresses of the male Pre-Raphaelites) is not due to the Brotherhood, which originally encouraged and admired women's contributions, but to the economic, social, health, and psychological conditions of women in British society. By treating the three generations separately, Marsh and Nunn also trace the changing conditions for Pre-Raphaelite women as the century progressed and the women's movement accelerated.

Rather than survey all the female impressionists, GARB (1987) examines just four painters working in France: Berthe Morisot, Marie Bracquemond, Eva Gonzales, and Mary Cassatt. She reveals that they had stronger connections to male impressionists—Eduard Manet, Edgar Degas, and Claude Monet—than to one another, and that they never formed the self-conscious category that the term "women impressionists" implies. Their life situations, training, and art opportunities differed, but these women produced paintings (represented here by 32 color reproductions) that demonstrate their place within impressionism. In addition, Garb believes that Morisot was instrumental in organizing the impressionists' exhibitions and developing the ideals and practices of impressionism.

While other scholars recovered the female artists of individual art movements and reevaluated the assumptions upon which previous art historical interpretations had been based, CHERRY chooses to look at the social fabric of the lives of British artists. The first half of her book considers the family, social, and professional relationships upon which women's art practice was based, paying attention to issues of class and race, and offering a glimpse into the life of at least one Jewish artist. The second half examines how these women represented femininity in their art and concludes that their domestic subjects both contributed to and challenged domesticity as the prescribed feminine condition. Issues of spectatorship and art "matronage" are also addressed. The sheer number of names recorded in these pages may overwhelm the reader, but they also certify the substantial presence and activity of Victorian female artists.

GARB (1994) turns to the professional networks created by late nineteenth-century French female artists, with an emphasis on the Union des Femmes Peintres et Sculpteurs (Union of Women Painters and Sculptors) founded in 1881. She examines this all-female exhibition society, its ultimately successful attack on the all-male national Ecole des Beaux Arts, and the roles these institutions played in the professionalization of women's art.

Academic painters Mme Bertaux and Mme Demont-Breton are constants in this story that includes many now-forgotten artists. Despite their revolutionary mission, Garb shows Union members to have been steeped in conventional ideologies that caused them to cast themselves as saviors of French culture and champions of conservative, rather than impressionist and modernist, influences.

In 1987 the first museum dedicated to collecting and exhibiting art by women opened its doors with an inaugural exhibition of American painting and sculpture, for which TUFTS wrote this catalog. An essay by Wanda Corn on nineteenth-century women's buildings at the World's Fairs of 1876 and 1893 points out that the new National Museum of Women in the Arts still faces the same questions and criticisms that were prevalent in earlier attempts to display women's creative accomplishments. A second essay by Alessandra Comini examines the parallel careers of sculptors Harriet Hosmer and Elisabet Ney, both celebrated in their time. But it is Tufts's notes on the exhibited works and the 124 large-format color reproductions that document the high quality of this assemblage, including a remarkable group of self-portraits and portraits of artist-friends.

—ANNETTE STOTT

See also Artists: General Surveys

Artists: Twentieth Century

Broude, Norma, and Mary D. Garrard (eds.), *The Power of Feminist Art: The American Movement of the 1970s, History and Impact*, New York: Abrams, 1994

Chadwick, Whitney, *Women Artists and the Surrealist Movement*, Boston: Little Brown, and London: Thames and Hudson, 1985

———, *Women, Art and Society*, London and New York: Thames and Hudson, 1990

De Zegher, M. Catherine (ed.), *Inside the Visible: An Elliptical Traverse of Twentieth Century Art, in, of and from the Feminine*, Cambridge, Massachusetts, and London: MIT Press, 1996

LaDuke, Betty, *Women Artists: Multi-Cultural Visions*, Trenton, New Jersey: Red Sea Press, 1992

Lippard, Lucy R., *The Pink Glass Swan: Selected Essays on Feminist Art*, New York: New Press, 1995

Parker, Rozsika, and Griselda Pollock (eds.), *Framing Feminism: Art and the Women's Movement 1970–1985*, London and New York: Pandora Press, 1987

Rubinstein, Charlotte Streifer, *American Women Artists: From Early Indian Times to the Present*, Boston: G.K. Hall, 1982

Witzling, Mara R. (ed.), *Voicing Our Visions: Writings by Women Artists*, New York: Universe, 1991; London: Women's Press, 1992

——— (ed.), *Voicing Today's Visions: Writings by Contemporary Women Artists*, New York: Universe, 1994; London: Women's Press, 1995

While mainstream art history recognizes that women have been active as artists during the twentieth century, their role in shaping this history has often been minimized or obscured. The efforts of artists, critics, and art historians to bring to light the contributions of women to the art of this century have resulted in feminist re-evaluations of twentieth-century art. Since the 1970s, the study of twentieth-century female artists has been a focus of feminist art history and criticism; this has resulted in a proliferation of widely available publications. These include general survey texts, investigations of women's involvement in twentieth-century art movements, and monographs or other publications devoted to the lives and art of individual artists.

Many of the initial writings on female artists were essays that appeared in feminist art journals. Because the majority of these have ceased publication, and back issues are not readily accessible, compilations of feminist critical essays are a welcome source for these writings. Several of these contain what are now regarded as key texts in the field of feminist art history and criticism. LIPPARD's essays on female artists and the women's art movement are examples of feminist art criticism from the 1970s to the present. These examine key issues in the women's art movement—the question of the existence of female imagery, images of the female body, the politics of visibility, and access to institutions of art production and exhibition—and they reflect the development of feminist art criticism since its inception. More recent essays reflect Lippard's commitment to building bridges among predominantly white feminist groups and communities of color, as she examines questions of art and politics, identity, representation, and intercultural exchange. PARKER and POLLOCK's compilation of essays, reviews, and artist statements offers an overview of the diversity of critical and theoretical positions taken by feminist artists, scholars, and critics in the United Kingdom from 1970 through 1985. The range of feminisms and voices represented here makes this a particularly useful anthology.

Although the information they contain on individual artists is often only cursory, general surveys of female artists are useful for gaining an overview of general directions in art, and an important introduction to artists who have been excluded from standard art historical period surveys. Most useful are surveys that examine the work of female artists within a broader social and art historical framework. In her survey of American women artists, RUBINSTEIN examines their work in relation to social and art historical contexts. This well-researched introduction to artists of various ethnicities—some well known and others less so—will entice the interested reader into further study. Although now out of print, this remains a standard for the study of U.S. female artists. CHADWICK (1985) presents numerous female artists from the medieval period in Europe through the 1980s in the United States, and gives substantial attention to twentieth-century artists. References throughout the text and an up-to-date bibliography guide the interested reader to more in-depth scholarship on individual artists, and to the more theoretical approaches of feminist critics and art historians to the relations of women, art, and society.

Feminist art historical investigations of women's involvement in particular twentieth-century art movements have brought to light information on little-known artists, and have also resulted in new understanding of these movements. CHADWICK's (1990) re-examination of surrealism presents new information on female artists associated personally, philosophically, and artistically with this movement. Through this exemplary study, Chadwick undermines conventional definitions of surrealism, challenging art historical assumptions about gender and surrealist representation as previously understood.

Catalogues of exhibitions of the work of female artists often contain some of the most provocative and challenging writing on this subject. DE ZEGHER's catalogue for an exhibition that "bypasses the artificiality of 'oppositional thinking' while acknowledging the work of deconstructionism, feminism and poststructuralism" challenges accepted definitions and categories of twentieth-century art by "drawing on disciplines from phenomenology and psychoanalysis to art history and sociology." A multitude of recognized and "invisible" twentieth-century artists is represented here, as various authors explore issues of gender and identity, aesthetics, language, politics, and representation of the body in the art of women from Europe and the Americas, working in relation to different historical contexts. In this catalogue, a compendium of theoretically rich essays represents twentieth-century art through examination of women's creative processes and visual expression, as they converge in what de Zegher conceptualizes as recurring historical cycles—the 1930s–40s, the 1960s–70s, and the 1990s.

With a focus on the 1970s to the present, BROUDE and GARRARD bring together essays by renowned scholars, critics, and artists. These are figures who have been central to the feminist art movement in the United States; several have had an international impact. The amply illustrated compilation of essays written for this volume includes an examination of predecessors to the feminist art of the 1970s, and art by feminist artists in light of the history of twentieth-century art. It documents the rise of several of the educational programs and activist artists' organizations that were key to the growth of the feminist art movement. In addition, it explores a multiplicity of forms of visual expression that can be considered "feminist art," and considers the impact of this art for the 1970s and beyond. This is sure to become a classic text for its breadth and depth of research, as well as for the vitality of writing by women involved in various ways in the U.S. feminist art movement.

While recent scholarship has increasingly examined the artistic contributions of women of color, much of this scholarship has been published in exhibition catalogues that are not easily obtainable, and they are thus not included here. LaDUKE, an artist who is also committed to making available information on female artists of color, has conducted interviews with female artists from various parts of the world. Her book, one of only a few to take such a global approach, presents this information along with her responses to her experiences with these artists. Combining personal impressions and material derived from her interviews and previous studies, LaDuke's work points to the need for further scholarly attention to the work of female artists of color.

Recognition of the importance of writing for female artists, and the importance of female artists' writings in understanding their lives and work, has been crucial to feminist scholarship in the visual arts. In two anthologies of female artists' public and private writings, WITZLING makes the point that listening to their "voices may enable readers to 'see' the authors' visions with greater clarity." She introduces each artist with a biographical and art historical overview, and identifies themes in the artist's writing and art. A theme that recurs in many of these writings is the centrality of writing for female artists as a means of self-validation and connection to other artists. For many, writing clearly is also a means of representing their experience as female artists in terms that often challenge art historical assumptions about art and gender.

—MELANIE HERZOG

Arts and Crafts, Traditional

Berliner, Nancy Zeng, *Chinese Folk Art: The Small Skills of Carving Insects*, Boston: Little Brown, 1986

Callan, Anthea, *Women Artists of the Arts and Crafts Movement 1870–1914*, New York: Pantheon, 1979; as *Angel in the Studio: Women in the Arts and Crafts Movement 1870–1914*, London: Astragal, 1979

Coomaraswamy, Ananda K., *The Arts and Crafts of India and Ceylon*, London: T. N. Foulis, 1913; New York: Farrar, Straus, 1964

Donnell, Radka, *Quilt as Woman's Art: A Quilt Poetics*, North Vancouver, British Columbia: Gallerie, 1990

Hedges, Elaine, and Ingrid Wendt, *In Her Own Image: Women Working in the Arts*, New York: McGraw Hill, 1980

Jefferson, Louise D., *The Decorative Arts of Africa,* New York: Viking Press, 1973; London: Collins, 1974
Toneyama, Kojin, *The Popular Arts of Mexico,* translated by Richard L. Gage, New York: Weatherhill, 1974

Western society has taken renewed interest in women's traditional arts and crafts of bygone eras. In other areas of the world, however, much of the handiwork is discussed in exclusively male terms, as being passed down "from father to son." This sentiment prevents serious analysis of women's work itself, as well as discussion of the creators. As a result, some of the works discussed here do not specifically focus on women in the traditional arts, even if women do provide the creative labour force behind their production. From such books, however, one might extract enough information on the social and cultural conditions for women to use them as a basis for further research. In all the works chosen, beautiful samples of the craftswomanship are represented.

The Northern Shaanxi marriage rhyme, which opens BERLINER's book, "Give birth to a boy, you want a good one, who'll wear blue robes and a cap [of an official]; raise a girl and you want a clever [skilful] one like a pomegranate and a peony," underscores the creation of folk art as primarily a female phenomenon, considering women were excluded from traditional arenas of political and social action. Paper cuts, shadow puppets, embroidery, dye work, woodblock print—all were perpetuated by peasant farmers' wives in the rituals of marriage and childrearing in China for thousands of years. In this way, women sustained their culture's traditions and morals through their art. Berliner also discusses the more recent evolutions folk art has undergone: first, how it was reviled and burned as subversive during the cultural revolution, and then restored and praised, the female elders having saved it from certain extinction.

CALLAN's book is clearly the groundbreaking work on women in the traditional arts and crafts movement in England in the nineteenth century. The background of Callan's book is the socialist Arts and Crafts movement that railed against the industrialisation of society and embraced, in the process, women's traditional handiwork as a means of subverting mechanisation in an increasingly capitalist society. While this provided new education for women, it also, Callan points out, created new socio-economic structures that subsequently encompassed women: the working-class peasant woman, the lady philanthropist, working gentlewomen, and the arts and crafts elite. The work demonstrates how the movement for social reform took the forms of ceramics, embroidery, needlework, lacemaking, jewelry, metalwork, woodcarving, furniture-making, interior design, hand-printing, bookbinding, and illustration. It is a testament to an early organised feminist socialism, which fought capitalist oppression and sought economic emancipation for women. Callan's research documents the new manifestations of male control that simultaneously emerged, and the American response to the happenings overseas. Callan aptly shows how early feminists carried out this "male" political reform and restores the women artists who have remained unrecognised.

COOMARASWAMY considers the folk arts of sculpture, painting, architecture, metalwork, enamels, textiles, pottery, wood and ivory carving, and jewelry throughout the history of Indian society. A most interesting aspect of his work is the discussion of the philosophical and spiritual underpinnings that inspire all folk art, particularly the representations of the mystical feminine. Feminine influence, or *shakti,* is an essential component (along with its masculine counterpart) to all aspects of Hindu creation. Much of Indian folk art, therefore, represents what he calls "sexual symbolism," the interaction of male and female creative energies to achieve spiritual fulfilment. His book does not discuss the work of female craftspersons per se, but his explication of Indian philosophy regarding women, combined with depictions of folk art, provides a foundation for further inquiry.

Since art was traditionally in the eye of the (male) beholder, the female metaphor of quilt as canvas, from early civilisations up to the present, was all too often lost on critics. DONNELL, therefore, explores the symbolic energies of quilts through the application of feminist and psychoanalytic theory. In this work, the quilt is interpreted as an altar (and catalyst) of archetypal behaviour—birth, death, and sex, the physical manifestations of *eros* and *thanatos.* Such criticism also focuses on the female unconscious as it is compelled, through quilting, to binary tendencies—separation and reconnection, silence and expression—as a means of re-enacting the primal maternal relationship. Donnell considers the sublimated messages of societal oppression latent in the finished body of the quilt, as well as the cathartic healing processes of its construction. She includes interesting analyses of several cross-cultural quilts, as well as commentary on the creative powers that enact the integration of separate, often disparate, parts, to create meaning.

HEDGES and WENDT's book on women in traditional arts and crafts emerged as a response to the query as to why there were no women in the art canon. Their research not only showed that there were female artists, but also that (since they were traditionally excluded from "classical art training") they had created their own highly individualised art canon. The authors allow this canon to be recognised in its own right, and for its own unique strengths. The book is a broad collection of essays exploring different genres of the so-called domestic arts from different cultures—from Pueblo pottery to medieval tapestry. It also includes discussions of several works of fiction and poetry (for example, Alice Walker's "Everyday Use" and Charlotte Brontë's *Jane Eyre*) to show that the struggle to maintain the domestic arts and crafts lies at the intersection between heritage and duty, social change, and personal expression.

JEFFERSON analyses the arts and crafts from a somewhat intertextual perspective, that is, as they manifest themselves in various forms across the African continent while preserving certain themes. She discusses the symbols, patterns, and motifs of folk art, and how they represent both the history and the culture of the nations of Africa, from Morocco to South Africa. The important role of women in her study is implicit; in discussing the particular modes of dress, ceremonial costumes, hairstyles, textiles, body decoration, metalwork, carving, basketry, pottery, and beadwork, she reveals the spiritual and social roles women played. Jefferson also reveals the framework of the division of craft labour by gender, and how each gender fulfilled an economic and community function by producing crafts as commissioned by a village chief.

While TONEYAMA's book is not specifically on women, he nevertheless offers a depiction of the Mexican woman producing traditional arts and crafts. He demonstrates how the Mexican woman is an integral part of the crafts' cottage industries, working alongside her husband and child; in this sense he empowers women by including them in the economic sector. Women, then, become partly responsible for reproducing a blend of aboriginal Indian culture and newer Spanish influences, seen in the crafts produced for cultural events like marriages and births. An important part of Toneyama's work is the discussion of representations of women through art and custom, which involve both their strong Christian faith and a certain sense of pre-Christian magic. He traces how this continues in the iconography of arts and crafts in colour and form. Toneyama moves geographically from Nayaret to Veracruz, including several different areas. He focuses on the usual crafts media as well as rarer ones like stone, feather, wax, leather, and shells.

—ANNMARIE PHILLIPS

Asia

see Asian Women; Buddhism; Economic Development: Asia; Hinduism; Polygamy; Purdah; Sex Customs in China, Japan, and India; Sexual Slavery; Sex Tourism

Asian Women

Chipp, Sylvia, and Justin J. Green (eds.), *Asian Women in Transition,* University Park: Pennsylvania State University Press, 1980

Breitenbach, Josef, *Women of Asia,* New York: John Day, and London: Collins, 1968

Esterline, Mae Handy (ed.), *They Changed Their Worlds: Nine Women of Asia,* Lanham, Maryland: University Press of America, 1987

O'Barr, Jean F. (ed.), *Perspectives on Power: Women in Africa, Asia, and Latin America,* Durham, North Carolina: Duke University, Center for International Studies, 1982

Shah, Nasra M., *Women of the World: Asia and the Pacific,* Washington, D.C.: U.S. Department of Commerce, Bureau of the Census, 1985

The World's Women 1995: Trends and Statistics, New York: United Nations, 1995

It is difficult to discuss Asian women in a single category, because they are not a homogeneous group. Such heterogeneity is recognized by BREITENBACH's book which, although dated, still portrays a very good background of Asian women through pictures. The introductory chapter provides the reader with the rationale for this work, which is to show how the women of Asia live and work. The Asian woman is not white, and for the most part does not care to be; she is seldom a Christian and may more often than not be Hindu, Buddhist, or Muslim. She may live in a society where marriage is still arranged and in which most of the heavy work is done by women—carrying water from the well, cooking, planting rice and caring for children.

CHIPP's book contains readings on the women of east, southeast, and south Asia (these are the divisions of most of the literature on women in this region). It contains an introduction that recognizes women's changing roles and status in Asia. The studies included are based on field research, not just on the reading of government documents. It is a book useful to those doing comparative studies of women around the world and those attempting to gain a broader understanding of Asia. The editors admit that is not easy to generalize about a region where so much diversity in political, economic, cultural, and religious beliefs and practices exist. However, in general there is a growing recognition that an Asian woman is a person who has the same rights in marriage, property holding, and voting as men and is therefore entitled to education and health services. This is true even in societies that used to provide food, education, and services primarily to male members of the family.

Chipp describes some of the differences among Asian women's experiences. In the past, Asian women have been relegated to their own world and excluded from the mainstream of economic and political power. And although women may be important, powerful, or influential, in some societies they lack the recognized and culturally-valued authority that men have. Religion and political ideology seem to play a role in reinforcing the status of women. Maoism considered women to hold up their half of the sky, even though east Asian Confucianism was deemed to be patriarchical. Women in southeast Asia held a higher status because of the kinship system and ample land supply. However, the women of south Asia held a status at its lowest due to the strong patriarchal family, reinforced by caste divisions and the Hindu and Muslim religious ideals. Likewise, the total or near absence of opportunity for economic activity for women outside the home further weakened women's status.

SHAH's book provides the statistics based on census data that are relevant to understanding the women of Asia. Each of the chapters has an introduction. The material in the book shows changes that have occurred in the data needed by planners for policy making. The relevant data are based on women's access to resources in the countries of the region and they provide a picture of women's status in education, employment, marriage, fertility, mortality, age, and urban/rural residence. They indicate the various roles that women play: parental, occupational, conjugal, domestic, kinship, community, and individual roles.

Of course the importance of women in the region is reinforced by the fact that 37 percent of the world's population is in two of the largest Asian countries, China and India. Shah's book shows that in terms of literacy rates, more men in the region can read, although younger women are becoming more literate. Men are considered head of the family and most Asian women eventually marry. Their main goal is to bear children, male offspring viewed more favorably than female.

The UNITED NATIONS publication on trends and statistics about the world's women updates and reinforces Shah's data. Asian women display high participation rates when counted as part of the labor force. But this does not mean greater improvement in the status of women. Their increased role in the economy may be primarily in response to a severe economic need. Therefore rarely is it an emancipating or enhancing experience. Usually it is an additional role in conjunction with their wife-mother role. Thus, they take on the form of unpaid family workers, clustering in the agricultural, sales, and service sectors where the low-paying jobs are. These jobs are prestige-reducing rather than prestige-enhancing for women. The book concludes that in spite of the fact that in 1995, four of the world's ten female heads of state or government held office in Asia, women's representation at the highest levels of government is generally still weakest here.

ESTERLINE's book is a work that tries to close the gap in the literature on women in developing countries, and in particular on women in Asia. It emphasizes the links among women worldwide, and their common problems, goals, and achievements. However, it recognizes that there are severe challenges to women in the various regions of Asia. In Bangladesh and India, issues such as purdah restrictions, poverty, caste, and custom have left women with little decision-making power and self-esteem. In Japan and Korea, Confucian patriarchal influences have bestowed a perpetual dependency status upon women that has made them legal non-persons. Thai, Indonesian, and Philippine women (Filipinas), even though they have had more say in their family and society, have lacked the resources to do things on their own, so they have concentrated on activities that alleviated their country's general conditions of extreme poverty, malnutrition, and disease.

O'BARR's book is made up of eight papers all written by western writers. This fact points to the paucity of Asian female writers in the field, a fact acknowledged by this publication. However, this scholarly endeavor increases our knowledge of the situation of women outside North America. The relevant themes of the section on Asian women include: catching up in education, employment, and economic activity so that women can have more political power; taking cognizance of women's work and integrating that knowledge in future planning and thinking; finding out where women fit in the economic, political, and social systems; and designing programs for change that will effectively integrate them. It is recognized by the international system that there are structures in Asian societies that limit women, structures that need to be changed in order to more effectively integrate them in their societies.

—CECILIA G. MANRIQUE

See also Economic Development: Asia

Astell, Mary 1616–1731

British Writer

Hill, Bridget (ed.), *The First English Feminist: Reflections Upon Marriage and Other Writings by Mary Astell*, New York: St.Martin's Press, and Aldershot: Gower/Maurice Temple Smith, 1986

Perry, Ruth, *The Celebrated Mary Astell: An Early English Feminist*, Chicago and London: University of Chicago Press, 1986

Rogers, Katharine, *Feminism in Eighteenth Century England*, Urbana: University of Illinois Press, and Brighton: Harvester, 1982

Smith, Florence Mary, *Mary Astell*, New York: Columbia University Press, 1916

For 200 years the achievement of Mary Astell has been neglected by both literary critics and philosophers. Only in the past several decades, as modern feminism has embraced attempts at discovering its historical roots, has it located them in the work of Mary Astell. Thus this seventeenth-century philosopher, essayist, poet, and scholar acquired the reputation of the first systematic feminist thinker with enlightened views on education and matrimony.

However, the very first full-length treatment of Astell's ideas started from a purely antiquarian interest in this, at that time, obscure woman writer. SMITH's book was originally a Ph.D. dissertation at Columbia University. It provides a summary of most of Astell's published work and concentrates on her contributions in the fields of education, religion, politics, and her writings on marriage and the relations between the sexes. Because of her own historical limitation, Smith treats Astell more as a subject of purely academic enquiry and does not grasp Astell's importance as a feminist thinker. Nevertheless, this thesis remains an essential introduction for anyone concerned with Astell's life and work, and it has been admired by many feminist scholars.

All contemporary accounts of Astell's work start from the tacit assumption of Astell as primarily a feminist. However, the authors are not blind to contradictions within her system of beliefs. HILL argues that seeing Astell only in terms of a simple portrayal as a progressive feminist is a distortion that ignores her complexity and fails to see the paradoxes of her thinking. In the extended introduction to an anthology of Astell's texts, Hill presents this writer in a socio-historical context. A valuable discussion of the changing social role of women in the seventeenth century precedes the critical analysis of Astell's religious and political views and of her major texts. This study is highly informative, with a wealth of important biographical and literary detail. It can therefore be considered a most useful introduction to Astell's contribution to philosophy and literature.

ROGERS deals with Astell when she traces the history of eighteenth-century feminist ideas. She discusses her in the context of early rationalism together with the male writers, both novelists and playwrights, of the same period. After summarizing Astell's position on the issues of women's education and marriage, she compares it with those of Defoe and Swift, and discovers a certain one-sidedness in her thought, which denies women sexual expression. Rogers notices as the distinguishing features of Astell's thought her stress on education and on reforming the individual, rather than on changing social institutions or expanding career opportunities and achieving financial independence. This book is a very good survey of the various attitudes and responses to the woman question as expressed in the literature during the entire eighteenth century. It is clearly and accessibly written, intended for both the informed student of the period, as well as the general reader interested in the history of ideas about women.

PERRY's text is more than a standard biography. In the only current monographic treatment of Astell's life and works, the author combines new material from the archives with a keen sense for historical detail, and manages to reconstruct the complex world of Astell's day. Her primary aim is to reflect the public and private forces that shaped Astell's life as a woman of letters in the early eighteenth century, and that helped define her thought. For example, Perry discusses her numerous and sustaining friendships with women, the attitudes of her political allies and enemies, and her deep religious beliefs. Perry sees Astell first and foremost as an early systematic feminist thinker, but does not neglect the complexity of her ideas. She confronts the limits of Astell's convictions and arguments, noting especially how the emphasis on rationalism severed the mind from the body. In a thorough and deep analysis, Perry throws new light on Astell's texts. On a more general level, this is an investigation of the motivations and tribulations of an intellectual woman writer of the past. It is a fascinating study of the literary world of the Augustan period, and will be useful to anybody interested in the achievements of women, as well as to the eighteenth-century specialist.

—SOŇA NOVÁKOVÁ

Athletes

Cayleff, Susan E., *Babe, The Life and Legend of Babe Didrikson Zaharias*, Urbana: University of Illinois Press, 1995

Engelmann, Larry, *The Goddess and the American Girl: The Story of Suzanne Lenglen and Helen Wills*, New York: Oxford University Press, 1988

Johnson, William O., *Whatta-Gal: The Babe Didrikson Story*, Boston: Little Brown, 1977

Navratilova, Martina, and George Vecsey, *Martina*, New York: Ballantine, 1985

Stambler, Irwin, *Women in Sports*, Garden City, New York: Doubleday, 1975

Sports personalities abound in women's sports, but the literature is not as deep as the pool of players. Many of the works done on female athletes can be found in the category of children's and young adult literature instead of in categories such as nonfiction, history, and sports. A good example deals with the 1996 Olympic gymnasts, who have been discussed in a number of juvenile texts as a team and as individuals because they are role models for other young girls. Janet Guthrie, the first female driver at Indianapolis, has been examined in a juvenile text, but not in adult nonfiction. The books discussed here are not exhaustive, but simply representative of the kinds of texts that are being published for the adult level.

CAYLEFF examines the life of female sporting legend Babe Didrikson Zaharias and the many achievements of her career. Zaharias participated in a number of different sports at their most competitive level and excelled in each of them. Cayleff focuses on the strength of character Zaharias displayed and the differing perceptions the public developed of her and who she was. Zaharias was a female sports hero whose name became synonymous with greatness and excellence, while at the same time she was dealing with the problem of femininity and muscular sports. Zaharias had many personae she presented to the public, depending on the situation in which she found herself, and what she wanted to convey.

Cayleff also explains how her account differs from Zaharias's own version of her life story, because of the time during which each book was written. Cayleff's work comes at a time when women's stories are being told in a more realistic fashion rather than just reflecting what society wants to hear. She bases her account on Zaharias's own words and discussions with many who knew her and were willing to share those experiences. The book extensively examines her entire life, including the legacy that remains.

Another book about Babe Didrikson Zaharias came out in 1977, focusing on her great achievements as an athlete. JOHNSON also talks about her as a role model that some mothers did not want their daughters to admire because she was too unladylike. Johnson examines the changes she went through in her career because of the ambivalence that surrounded her, and how her marriage to George Zaharias affected newspaper accounts of her life. Focus shifted from her athletic accomplishments to her daily chores at home, especially as a cook taking care of her husband. Through it all she remained a true legend and sporting great.

ENGELMANN discusses two athletes, looking at the lives of Suzanne Lenglen and Helen Wills. Engelmann follows the careers of both tennis players as they rose to stardom in a sport that had no female celebrities until they came along. Engelmann discusses the contrasts between these two women and how they played the game. Both were introduced to the game by their fathers, but the similarity ends there. While Lenglen did not fit the image of femininity, Wills was considered a great beauty who could also dominate a sport.

Engelmann goes beyond just the importance of these two players in his examination, by introducing the reader to the larger world of sports. Lenglen and Wills are seen in the context of the international sports scene alongside many of the other famous athletes of the day. The 1920s were the "Golden Age of Sports," and Engelmann brings that idea to life through the careers of these two women. He has an extensive bibliography included for the serious researcher that also reveals the depth of sources used in constructing these stories.

VECSEY helps NAVRATILOVA tell her story. The reader is introduced to Navratilova as a person as well as a tennis player. The reader learns about all the obstacles she had to overcome, and the competitive spirit that drove her to achieve her goals. Her father's disappearance had a profound affect on her life, as did her growing up in Czechoslovakia. Navratilova set goals for herself throughout her life and managed to achieve them all, even though the road was not always easy or expected.

In this text the reader learns about the people who influenced Navratilova's life, both positively and negatively. Relationships are examined openly and honestly. Since this text is mainly autobiographical, that has to be kept in mind as one reads, but there is an honesty displayed that helps the reader feel what the athlete felt as she triumphed and failed in life. While not an objective account, the reader gains a sense of who Navratilova saw herself to be, and how she struggled with the way the world viewed her.

STAMBLER does not focus on just one athlete, but instead gives short accounts of the career highlights of 12 female sports personalities. Included in the text are famous names, such as Babe Didrikson Zaharias and Billie Jean King, as well as lesser-known athletes like jockey Robyn Smith, swimmer Melissa Belote, and diver Micki King. Each woman is depicted as a role model for young women looking for sports figures to emulate. Stambler discusses their greatest achievements and some of the difficulties they each faced because of gender.

—LESLIE HEAPHY

See also Sport and Gender; Sport, History

Atwood, Margaret 1939–

Canadian writer

Hengen, Shannon Eileen, *Margaret Atwood's Power: Mirrors, Reflections and Images in Select Fiction and Poetry,* Toronto: Second Story Press, 1993

Howells, Coral Anne, *Margaret Atwood,* Basingstoke and New York: St. Martin's Press, 1995; London: Macmillan, 1996

McCombs, Judith (ed.), *Critical Essays on Margaret Atwood,* Boston: G.K. Hall, 1988

Nicholson, Colin (ed.), *Margaret Atwood: Writing and Subjectivity,* New York: St. Martin's Press, 1994

Rao, Elenora, *Strategies for Identity: The Fiction of Margaret Atwood,* New York: Peter Lang, 1993

Rigney, Barbara Hill, *Margaret Atwood,* London: Macmillan and Totowa, New Jersey: Barnes and Noble, 1987

VanSpanckeren, Kathryn, and Jan Garden Castro (eds.), *Margaret Atwood: Vision and Forms,* Carbondale: Southern Illinois University Press, 1988

Margaret Atwood explores both Canadian subjectivity and feminine identity with the great frequency: correspondingly, many critical works on Atwood focus on either feminism or nationalism. Another widespread critical approach is to explore Atwood's appropriation of the popular genres such as romance and autobiography. Perhaps this accounts for Atwood's popularity with both the critical and popular audiences: both genre and the subversion of genre are equally present in her works. Recent studies of Atwood's poetry and novels are especially useful, because they highlight the considerable number of recurring themes within her work. One example is Atwood's subversion of fairy tales, which remains a substantial theme, yet has become more sharply ironic in the twenty-five years from *The Edible Woman* to *The Robber Bride.* Perhaps the best critical works on Atwood are the ones that do not attempt to define her as either a post-colonial or feminist writer, but appreciate that her work is inseparably bound up in both these concerns.

McCOMBS has edited in an extremely useful volume tracing the critical responses to Atwood's work, from her first acclaimed collection of poetry, *The Circle Game,* in 1966, to her 1985 *The Handmaid's Tale.* The range of this book is impressive: reviews include *Survival,* Atwood's critical study of trends in Canadian literature, as well as a focus on articles from works that are no longer in print. It is particularly interesting to note that, with the publication of *The Edible Woman,* reviewers began seriously considering the feminist aspects of her work. McCombs also provides bibliographical notes on the first full-length studies of Atwood, which were limited to her 1970s work. This is invaluable guide to the critical receptions, both positive and negative, of Atwood's prose, poetry, and criticism.

HENGEN's project is to trace, from a psychoanalytic perspective, instances of narcissism throughout the works of Margaret Atwood. This book begins by discussing Atwood's early works, which feature women defined by narcissistic men. In the mid- to late 1970s, Hengen asserts, Atwood began to critique this narcissism. In the work appearing in the 1980s and 1990s, narcissism became an aspect of both male and female characters in Atwood's works. Equally concerned with Canadian identity, this book also relates the Lacanian mirror stage to Canada's discovery of itself as uniquely different. This book is a complex psychoanalytic reading of Atwood's prose and poetry.

RIGNEY's study is perhaps the best introduction to the work of Margaret Atwood. It is a concise, but far-reaching study of some of the most important aspects of Atwood's work. Rigney provides critical readings of Atwood's prose and poetry in terms that are accessible yet thorough, providing cogent introductions to feminist and post-colonial approaches, as well as reviewing literary criticism of and by Atwood. This volume provides especially interesting sections comparing Canada with feminine "victimisation." This is an extremely useful book for anyone beginning to research on Atwood.

HOWELLS provides an introduction to the fiction of Margaret Atwood. It includes discussion of Atwood's important and recent book, *The Robber Bride,* which falls back on the familiar Atwoodian themes of storytelling and illusion. Howells groups the novels thematically rather than chronologically, including a strong chapter on the Canadian aspects of Atwood's *Surfacing, Survival,* and *Wilderness Tips,* which cover a 20-year span. This volume includes a brief biography of Atwood, locating her development as a writer in a time when Canada was becoming aware of its own literary identity. This study provides a strong feminist reading of Atwood's works, and is especially adept at relating Atwood's very early works to more contemporary ones.

RAO's book is another recent study of Margaret Atwood's fiction, which is less recent and more theoretically informed than Howell's work. Rao is particularly interested in the postmodern aspects of Atwood's fiction, specifically her appropriation of genres such as the romance and Gothic tale. This study is perhaps less approachable than other works, both because it assumes considerable critical sophistication, and because it focuses on many different critical approaches to Atwood's works, rather than providing detailed analysis of a few select works.

VanSPANCKEREN and CASTRO's collection includes an autobiographical forward by Atwood, prints of some of her early artwork, an interview with Atwood, and a transcribed talk she gave to university students. This study features an emphasis on the persona of the writer, which although highly interesting, is perhaps less critically vigorous. The remainder of the essays consider a wide range of Atwood's prose and poetry, usually with feminist overtones. Because this book has given the first and last words to Atwood herself, it creates the appearance of a degree of authority and approval on her part over the criticism.

NICHOLSON's collection of essays focuses less on gender and power than on the questions of place and power, including post-colonialism, nationalism, and so forth. It is the only work discussed in this article that does not have the primarily feminist critical approach. Particularly impressive articles in this collection deal with the issues of post-colonial subjectivity, a look at the progressive drafts of *The Circle Game,* comic deconstruction in *Lady Oracle,* and several different views of *The Handmaid's Tale.* Although this volume contains feminist essays as well, it locates Atwood firmly within the Canadian borders, and for this reason it is an especially important piece of Atwood criticism.

—ERIN STRIFF

Aung San Suu Kyi 1945–

Burmese Human-Rights Activist and Nobel Peace Prize Winner

Lintner, Bertil, *Aung San Suu Kyi and Burma's Unfinished Renaissance,* Mytholmroyd, West Yorkshire: Peacock Press, 1990

Parenteau, John, *Prisoner for Peace: Aung San Suu Kyi and Burma's Struggle for Democracy*, Greensboro, North Carolina: Morgan Reynolds, 1994

Stewart, Whitney, *Aung San Suu Kyi: Fearless Voice of Burma*, Minneapolis: Lerner, 1997

Win, Kanbawza, *A Burmese Perspective: Daw Aung San Suu Kyi, The Nobel Laureate*, Bangkok: CPDSK, 1992

Except for short biographical entries in reference works about female Nobel Prize winners, or women who have achieved greatness or changed the world, surprisingly few book-length studies are available on Aung San Suu Kyi (pronounced "awng sahn suu chee"). She was nominated for the Nobel Prize by another Nobel laureate, Czech Republic President Václav Havel, who praises her as "an outstanding example of the power of the powerless." Only two years old when her father, Aung San (1915–47), modern Burma's major national hero, was assassinated by political opponents, Aung San Suu Kyi has steadfastly, but nonviolently, opposed the military dictatorship in Burma (also called Myanmar), which initially came to power through a coup in 1962. In 1988, the repressive and corrupt military government crushed an uprising in which thousands of people were either killed, imprisoned, or exiled. In the wake of these events, Aung San Suu Kyi cofounded and is today leader of the opposition National League for Democracy (NLD). The ruling military junta placed her under house arrest that lasted six years, which resulted in, among other things, her receiving the Nobel award *in absentia*. In 1990, the NLD, with Aung Sang Suu Kyi as its leader, overwhelmingly won national parliamentary elections, which the junta has refused to recognize.

LINTNER's brief study, originally a working paper published by the Center of Southeast Asian Studies, Monash University, in Clayton, Australia, is one of the first attempts in English to contextualize Aung Sang Suu Kyi's meteoric rise to prominence in Burma's volatile and often tumultuous contemporary political scene. Lintner also discusses the preeminent role her father played in similar events a generation earlier. It should surprise no one, suggests Lintner, that the daughter has taken up where the father had left off.

WIN's study is lengthier and more detailed than Lintner's, and fills in the gaps and lacunae found in Lintner's work, offering a balanced and sometimes cautious interpretation of events and personalities. Win underscores the continuity between father and daughter in Burma's struggle to establish parliamentary democracy: first, the father's efforts during the 1940s to oust the colonialist British; and, more recently, the daughter's defiance of Burmese socialists and militarists. Win suggests that Aung Sang Suu Kyi's refusal of permanent exile from Burma, in favor of permanent house arrest there, flows from what seems to be a family tradition of fighting for justice and freedom in that country. A Burmese, Win has had the advantage of using primary sources in the Burmese language.

PARENTEAU and STEWART have both written appreciative biographies intended mainly for young readers. Based entirely on secondary source material, both works are factually accurate, and attempt, with moderate success, to make sense of the complexities and intricacies of post-World War II Burmese history and politics. Parenteau's writing is not as fluid as Stewart's, but the former's extensive bibliography and notes make up in part for this shortcoming. Neither book seems to be able to get beyond the reporting of facts and information about their subject; in the end, their subject remains elusive and somewhat enigmatic. This problem notwithstanding, both books offer sometimes inspiring, but sometimes uneasy, discussions for both youngsters and adults about one of the bravest and possibly one of the most harassed women of the twentieth century.

—CARLO COPPOLA

Austen, Jane 1775–1817

British Writer

Bush, Douglas, *Jane Austen*, London and New York: Macmillan, 1975

Evans, Mary, *Jane Austen and the State*, London and New York: Tavistock, 1987

Hardy, John, *Jane Austen's Heroines: Intimacy in Human Relationships*, London and New York: Routledge, 1984

Kirkham, Margaret, *Jane Austen, Feminism and Fiction*, Brighton: Harvester, and Totowa, New Jersey: Barnes and Noble, 1983

Monaghan, David (ed.), *Jane Austen in a Social Context*, London: Macmillan, and Totowa, New Jersey: Barnes and Noble, 1981

Weldon, Fay, *Letters to Alice on First Reading Jane Austen*, London: Michael Joseph, 1984; New York: Taplinger, 1985

Jane Austen has frequently been accused of being "a woman's writer" or "rather dull" or "very limited," generally by people who have never read her work. WELDON's witty and eclectic *jeu d'esprit* faces such charges head-on. It is both an excellent introduction to Austen's novels, and an informative background study to the social life of the late seventeenth and early eighteenth centuries. Weldon manages to create the situations of women in Austen's time almost incidentally; she insists that Austen lived with the understanding of the reality around her: the constant pregnancies, the horrors of childbirth, and the treatment of unmarried mothers, and that she wrote her own personal beliefs and morality into the novels. Weldon sets in perspective the lives of women as Austen would have perceived them, particularly of women whose financial and social standing was such that they had to rely on work or marriage in order to survive. Not written from an aggressively feminist stance, the book nevertheless places the presentation of women at its center, and suggests that Austen illuminates their problems, not by attacking men, but by showing them as they are. This showing, she says, is sufficient to involve the readers in understanding their real nature, just as much as they understand the reality of the variety of women characters offered throughout the novels.

A generally sympathetic and fairly traditional view of Austen is to be found in BUSH. His chapter on Austen's England is more concerned with the social divisions of class than with the position of women, but in a stimulating novel-by-novel analysis, he looks at the way Austen presents courtship and marriage. He suggests that the novels have a "timeless" dimension because they deal with those aspects of human nature that are essentially unchanging, and he rejects utterly the view which sees Austen as narrow and her moral values as obsolete. Bush is particularly interesting in his comments on Austen's satire and social comedy.

HARDY writes perceptively about Austen's heroines, and explores the presentation of human relationships in the novels. He devotes a chapter each to the six heroines of Austen's major novels, asserting that their individuality becomes apparent through their ability to respond to the hidden feelings of others, and thus to develop their own potential in a mutual sharing of emotions. He expresses doubts about the future of Fanny Price's marriage to Edmund because of what he sees as a failure of genuine intimacy between them; on the other hand, he strongly endorses the unions of Emma and Knightley, and of Anne Elliot and Frederick Wentworth, because he sees them as establishing a sharing that will "extend into the future." Austen's interest in sex, he asserts, allows to her heroines "both fascination and dignity."

As the title suggests, MONAGHAN's collection of essays is unified around the concept of the social context of Austen's novels. It provides an interesting survey of a variety of aspects of Austen's art, and particularly of the presentation of her contemporary women characters, living as they were in an essentially patriarchal society. Monaghan himself contributes two essays, starting his discussion of the position of women from a different standpoint from that of Weldon, in that his examination is not of women in general, but more specifically of Austen's women characters, upon whom he bases his deductions. One contributor, Leroy Smith, considers the upbringing of girls in a society dominated by stern authoritarian fathers. Another, Nina Auerbach, contests the more traditional view that Austen submitted to the limitations of her world; she explores the tensions created by Austen's apparently comfortable acceptance of the limitations imposed upon women, and her simultaneous presentation of women's lives as a kind of continuous imprisonment.

KIRKHAM is one of the more significant feminist writers on Austen. She constantly challenges traditional views of her author, suggesting that Austen's sympathies lay with the rational feminism of her age, and that her moral viewpoint is essentially feminist. She considers both Mary Wollstonecraft and Rousseau as influences upon Austen, although she looks a little cynically at Rousseau's attitude to the education of women. Like Bush, Kirkham identifies Austen's comic vision as a significant contribution to her criticism of manners and of morals. In discussing the later novels, she picks up the theme of imprisonment, explored in Monaghan, and sees Sir Thomas Bertram, slave-owner and patriarchal ruler of Mansfield Park, as enslaving his family at home. Kirkham is particularly interesting when discussing the emergence of female writers in Austen's day; she suggests that they encouraged the growth of feminism, and that in her novels Austen often reacted against the writings of her male contemporaries. This is a lively and provocative reading of Austen.

EVANS writes an excellent short study, starting from a sociological perspective. In her turn, she challenges many traditionally accepted beliefs about Austen's conservatism, her limited outlook, her romantic view of marriage, and her attitude to economic materialism. She discusses Austen's concern with the financial vulnerability of women and their apparent submission to the restrictions that govern their lives; because of their economic insecurity, they are left in a state of dependence upon a patriarchal society. In a lively discussion of *Pride and Prejudice*, we are made to think again about the relative common sense of Mr. and Mrs. Bennett: while Mr. Bennett stands cynically aloof, Mrs. Bennett has to arrange the future support of their five daughters. Evans claims that Austen condemns the sexual and moral double standards of her time, which accept one law for men and another for women. Nevertheless, despite the hardship involved, some of Austen's characters are shown to display significant feminist characteristics, in that they are willing to forego marriage and dependence upon men if such is against their own moral principles; she gives as examples Elizabeth Bennett, Elinor Dashwood, Fanny Price, and Anne Elliot. She asserts that Austen questions the patriarchal order, not only through obviously morally impaired fathers, such as Sir Walter Elliot or Mr. Price, but also through fathers such as Mr. Bennett and Sir Thomas Bertram, who abdicate their parental responsibilities.

—HILDA D. SPEAR

Aviation

Bell, Elizabeth S., *Sisters of the Wind: Voices of Early Women Aviators,* Pasadena, California: Trilogy, 1994

Cole, Jean Hascall, *Women Pilots of World War II,* Salt Lake City: University of Utah Press, 1992

Ebbert, Jean, *Crossed Currents: Navy Women from WWII to Tailhook,* Washington, D.C.: Brassey's, 1993

Lomax, Judy, *Women of the Air,* London: Murray, 1986; New York: Dodd Mead, 1987

Rich, Doris L., *Queen Bess: Daredevil Aviator,* Washington, D.C., and London: Smithsonian Institution Press, 1993

Ware, Susan, *Still Missing: Amelia Earhart and the Search for Modern Feminism,* New York: Norton, 1993

Women in aviation have historically stood as representatives of feminism, equality, and rising above the limits placed here on earth. Aviation has been one endeavor that women could use to express themselves comparably in relation to men's achievements, and it was one area in which women could match, or even better, their male counterparts. The period of early aviation was short in relation to other historical events, but rich in the contributions made by women.

LOMAX reminds us that while it was men who created aviation, women quickly adapted to the new environment. She takes the reader from Madame Thible's first balloon flight, over 200 years ago, to the early powered-flight pioneers of the 1920s and 1930s. Lomax underpins her discussions with the realization that the entertainment side of flying brought aviation to the consuming public, whereas the competition side created the evolution of manufacturing and technological improvements. These forces propelled many female pilots into the forefront of aviation history. Many do not remember that Amelia Earhart's last flight was a combination of Purdue University testing technology and a well-publicized around-the-world flight. Lomax gives a standard panorama of the early pioneers such as Amy Johnson, Amelia Earhart, Jacqueline Cochran, and Jacqueline Auriol. However, she adds insightful relevance to events and personalities as they relate to the issues of men versus women in the skies, the hearts, and the memories of the public and press. Although Lomax looks for equity in accounts such as Jeana Yeager's partnering the Voyager flight, this equity does not seem to flow naturally.

The 1920s and 1930s were eras of prosperity that fueled adventurous and innovative times. Aviation, and particularly female aviators, benefited during this early period when the technology was new and unregulated. In addition, flight captured the imagination of the public and propelled many early pioneers from obscurity to the heights of notoriety. Early female aviators saw their efforts given recognition equal to men and found themselves untethered by the usual restrictions of society. BELL discusses individual female pilots of the 1920s and 1930s. She bemoans the general inability of many early female aviators to create lasting records of their stories. The newspapers did not document the exploits of female pilots as well as they did their male counterparts. Other primary sources are limited or scarce. Bell seeks to explain the female aviators as individuals, separate from the activities and individual acts that we hold as important history.

No review of women and aviation would be complete without focusing on certain female aviators, particularly Amelia Earhart. WARE equates Earhart and feminism with the search for her remains and the continuing quest for equality. Earhart symbolized the early age of aviation and its relevance to the freedom and new possibilities for modern women. Earhart's rise to popularity has seen no abatement and perhaps, as Ware suggests, it is even greater today than in her own time. Although she was unquestionably the most famous female aviator in the world, she never could separate her achievements from comparison to Charles Lindbergh. Ware discusses Earhart in respect to Lindbergh, but points out that the benefits of this comparison generally outweighed the disadvantages. Besides their "spooky" resemblance (which even Anne Lindbergh noticed), Amelia handled the fame much better than Charles. Ware sees Earhart as representative of the loss of female heroes in every aspect of American culture, from sports to politics to entertainment.

RICH details a woman who not only conquered the skies and gender inequality, but transcended racial inequities as well. Bessie Coleman was the first African-American woman to obtain a pilot's license. She was forced to learn flying in France because no flight schools in the United States would accept her for training. Her record is sparse because she was ignored by the conventional press of the time. Rich goes to great lengths expounding on the difficulty of piecing "Queen Bess's" life together. Almost everything known about her comes from first-person accounts by those who knew her. Like Earhart, her star has grown brighter in death than in life.

Aviation was in its infancy during World War I, but government investment into this new innovation helped propel its growth and maturity. Although the natural advancement of any technology is assured through the achievements of its innovators, history has shown that military conflicts accelerate this process. Such are the reflections of COLE in her book on female pilots of World War II. This summary account of the Women's Air Force Service Pilots (WASPs) marks the expansion of women in aviation on a grand scale but also represents the governmental subjugation of women into a supporting role. World War II brought regulations and governmental control to the growth of the "sport" of aviation. Women suffered, as they always do, from male-controlled regulation, and they served secondary roles in the male-dominated aviation "industry." Even with these changes happening, women still played important roles in support of the aviation war effort. The advent of the

WASPs expanded women's role in aviation but also restricted them through segregation from the focus of aviation activity and development. The high-flying days of equality in the skies ended with regulation and regimentation. The purpose of the WASPs was to free male pilots for combat roles, while women took over towing targets, training, transport, and testing. Although a few female pilots stayed in the military after the war ended, none retained flying status.

The transition of women in the U.S. military is aptly related by EBBERT in her record of Navy women from World War II to the Tailhook scandal. Ebbert not only recounts the emergence of women in the Navy, but particularly in previously male-dominated specialties such as aviation. Slowly through bureaucratic evolution, the government finally began to accept female military pilots and female astronauts. This book follows the highs and lows, including the death of the first female carrier pilot and the Tailhook scandal. The Tailhook scandal, particularly, represents the clash between old traditions and new procedure—the painful transition into the current of change that has been evolving since women first looked to the sky for acceptance and freedom. It is ironic that while women were able to orbit in space alongside men, on earth the Tailhook scandal reflected back on old mores and norms. The more things changed, the more they remained the same.

—GARY D. CRANE

B

Barton, Clara 1821–1912

American Founder of Red Cross

Bacon-Foster, Corra, *Clara Barton, Humanitarian, from Official Records, Letters, and Contemporary Papers,* Washington, D.C.: Columbia Historical Society, 1918

Barton, William E., *The Life of Clara Barton, Founder of the American Red Cross,* 2 vols., Boston: Houghton Mifflin, 1922

Burton, David Henry, *Clara Barton: In the Service of Humanity,* Westport, Connecticut: Greenwood, 1995

Oates, Stephen B., *A Woman of Valor: Clara Barton and the Civil War,* New York: Free Press, 1994

Pryor, Elizabeth Brown, *Clara Barton: Professional Angel,* Philadelphia: University of Pennsylvania Press, 1987

Ross, Ishbel, *Angel of the Battlefield: The Life of Clara Barton,* New York: Harper, 1956

Young, Charles Sumner, *Clara Barton: A Centenary Tribute to the World's Greatest Humanitarian,* Boston: Badger, 1922

As the titles of the books listed above will demonstrate, studies of Clara Barton's life and accomplishments have tended toward hagiography, especially until the mid-1980s. Barton's pluck in the face of danger, her willingness to sidestep convention, her indomitable spirit—all true, and all admirable—bound early writers with such awe that they could not see her as a real, complex, imperfect woman. Interestingly, some of the first works to treat the more difficult sides of her personality were biographies written for young readers.

BACON-FOSTER typifies the early approach, comparing Barton to Joan of Arc, and quoting a senator who ranked her the greatest living American woman. The book gives little personal information, emphasizing instead Barton's relief efforts during the American Civil War and the Franco-Prussian War, and as founder of the American Red Cross. Readers must infer Barton's nature from her list of accomplishments and from kind things said about her work; there are no insights into her daily life, or comments from friends or family. All that emerges is a vague image of a hard-working cardboard saint. Interestingly, though, liberal quotations from letters of thanks and accounts of catastrophes averted reveal that most men who had responsibility to authorize Barton's innovative programs dealt with her simply as an accomplished organizer and worker, with neither the condescension nor the awe that one might expect.

Another early work that is fascinating in its own way is that by YOUNG, a chronological series of 103 sentimental "pen pictures" intended to "give to the boys and girls of America inspiration to loftier patriotism and higher ideals in achievement." The amount of detail is numbing: the dozens of illustrations include a photo of Barton's baby cradle and a sketch of Baba, her pet horse; hundreds of quotations include the report of a leading phrenologist who explains her fearful and sensitive nature. The author presents Barton as angel and national heroine, exaggerating her role in winning the vote for women and her influence as a vegetarian and temperance worker, but also giving important information about her work in Cuba and Turkey.

When she died, Barton left more than forty boxes of unsorted letters, clippings, and other documents; she seems never to have thrown any papers away. Her executors named a close relative and friend, William E. BARTON, to gather the materials into a new biography, emphasizing Clara's work with the Red Cross. The work presents her in an unwaveringly flattering light, telling the story the way the family wanted her to be remembered. This book is valuable for its quotations from unpublished materials, including Barton's unfinished autobiography. However, in attempting to protect the privacy of Barton and the family, the author has the frustrating habit of describing important characters but not giving their names.

ROSS's biography was the first written after the Barton papers were made available to scholars outside the family, and the first to describe Barton's struggles with depression. While sometimes melodramatic and coy by today's standards (of Barton's relationship with John Elwell, with whom she had a wartime affair, Ross says only that they shared meals and discussed battle scenes), it remains the most accessible of the complete biographies for the general reader. The photo section offers illuminating pictures of some of Barton's equipment and rooms not found elsewhere. An extensive but, of course, dated bibliography is also included.

PRYOR presents Barton as a woman whose first concern was for her appearance and reputation. She falsely reported her actions during the Civil War to enhance her importance, wrote personal letters with an ear for how they would be quoted publicly, dyed her hair, lied about her age, and resisted intimate relationships. Pryor's subtitle, *Professional Angel,* echoes the paradox of Barton's life: A woman of undeniable accomplishments, she was never satisfied with what she had done; a figure beloved by millions, she lived and died essentially alone. In reviewing Barton's accomplishments, the book looks beyond her relief efforts and includes important information about her feminism, which she embraced early, and her belief in equal rights for blacks, which came later.

BURTON's biography is the story of a woman who "was much loved but often not much liked." The author is a historian, more concerned perhaps with events than with personalities. The least expansive and interpretive of the biographies, it is also the most critical of Barton herself. Burton's strategy is to offer a central question: will we remember "the merciful Clara Barton or the dauntless seeker after notice?"—and then to present her accomplishments and her self-centeredness with studied detachment. The author gives Barton full credit for her remarkable achievements, but is the only writer to suggest that she eventually lost leadership of the Red Cross, not because of the dominance or ingratitude of others, but because in the challenge of modernizing the agency, she had finally found a task that was beyond her.

OATES, as the title suggests, deals only with Barton's experiences in the Civil War, which he sees as the defining event in her life. This is not a scholarly biography, but a work of "narrative nonfiction," with one hundred pages of notes to support the graphic images and details. Oates combines the frank treatments of sex, ego, and depression found in recent studies with the unswerving admiration of earlier ones. The author is clearly moved by—not just intellectually interested in—his compelling and tragic central character.

—CYNTHIA A. BILY

Battlefield Nursing

Bingham, Stella, *Ministering Angels,* Oradell, New Jersey: Medical Economics, and London: Osprey 1979

Leneman, Leah, *In the Service of Life: The Story of Elsie Inglis and the Scottish Women's Hospitals,* Edinburgh: Mercat Press, 1994

McBryde, Brenda, *Quiet Heroines: Nurses of the Second World War,* London: Chatto and Windus, 1985

Norman, Elizabeth, *Women at War: The Story of Fifty Military Nurses Who Served in Vietnam,* Philadelphia: University of Pennsylvania Press, 1990

Piggott, Juliet, *Queen Alexandra's Royal Army Nursing Corps,* London: Cooper, 1975

Summers, Anne, *Angels and Citizens: British Women as Military Nurses 1854–1914,* London and New York: Routledge, 1988

The field of military conflict has always been considered to be a distinctly male sphere, traditionally excluding all those who could not bear arms for their cause. Yet for centuries, women have been able to penetrate the field of battle despite their alien status, taking on a traditional role of their own: that of nurse. Since the high profile work of Florence Nightingale in the nineteenth century, there has been considerable interest in this invasion by women into an arena of male domination, but it has taken a more scholarly direction with the growth of women's studies as an academic discipline.

The studies range from those that give a broad overview of the history of battlefield nursing to more focused books that concentrate on particular organizations or specific wars. A good example of the former is BINGHAM's book, which traces the history of the nursing profession from the Middle Ages to the end of World War II and beyond, placing it within the wider battle for women's emancipation. Bingham argues that the opportunities for the development of the nursing industry were greatly enhanced by the succession of modern wars, all requiring female labor as part of the fighting process, which have affected western society since the American Civil War and the Crimean War. Bingham's history tends to be a little simplistic, generally presenting only one, rather conventional, view point, but it provides a useful guide to the importance of the battlefield in the wider development of the nursing profession.

A much more detailed and analytical study can be found in SUMMERS's book, which considers the history of military nursing from 1854 to 1914. Summers's assessment of the battlefield nursing of the Crimean War operates as an attempt to demythologize the Nightingale story, by simultaneously illustrating the work of other pioneering women, and acknowledging the relationships and the conflicts between these various nursing factions. She goes on to give a detailed history of the development of military nursing through the founding of early Nursing Corps movements, which evolved into organizations like the Queen Alexandra's Imperial Military Nursing Service (QAIMNS), the Army Nursing Service, and the Red Cross Voluntary Aid Detachments. She emphasizes the fact that all these movements were in place and functional by the time of the outbreak of World War I in 1914.

PIGGOTT's book on the origins of and development of the QAIMNS into Queen Alexandra's Royal Army Nursing Corps (QARANC) again begins with an examination of early army nursing and the subsequent consequences of the developments of the Crimean War. Piggott brings the reader relatively up-to-date by commenting on the service up to the end of the 1980s. But by focusing attention on one specific military nursing organization, she provides a different emphasis. Although clearly an admirer of QARANC, Piggott remains reasonably objective throughout, assessing the impact of the evolving organization on the development of battlefield nursing through all the major European wars since the Crimean.

For a more detailed study of the experience of battlefield nursing in one particular war, LENEMAN's book on the Scottish Women's Hospitals, which saw active service in the war zones of Serbia in World War I, provides considerably more depth. She presents a detailed account, which consolidates recent feminist interest in the expeditions headed by prominent Scottish suffragist Dr. Elsie Inglis. Leneman's book suggests that the women involved were an inspiration to their contemporaries and to the generations that followed, and provides an up-to-date study and valuable assessment of their wartime activities. She offers a step-by-step account of the setting up of the hospital units, and the adventures and experiences of those concerned, as they worked very close to the front line in war-torn Serbia. By drawing on the original source material, often in the form of the unpublished diaries and letters of the women who participated, Leneman is able to draw a convincing and informed picture of the reality of the battlefield nursing experience in World War I.

McBRYDE'S book performs a similar service for World War II, although offering a more global version of women's wartime nursing experience. She traces the position of military nurses from 1938, through mobilization and conflict, placing them within a framework of the most significant military campaigns of the war. Her approach is again based on the testimonies of individual participants. It provides a lively and interesting account, which interweaves the personal stories of military nurses in Europe, the Middle East, and the Far East, incorporating diverse records, such as the experiences of women in prisoner-of-war camps, and others who were present at important historic moments like the evacuation of Dunkirk and the liberation of Belsen. Although much of the book is presented from a British point of view, it does include the experiences of Commonwealth nurses, and its global perspective gives it many dimensions.

NORMAN's book, related from a primarily American point of view, provides a useful study. She brings the experience of battlefield nursing almost up-to-date by concentrating on the women who went to Vietnam as military nurses. Using the real-life experiences of those who nursed in Vietnam, Norman is again able to create an authentic picture. She comments on the similarity among the testimonies of all military nurses, suggesting that they experience the same emotions, regardless of the time or of the particular war in which they are involved. In addition, Norman considers the status of modern women operating in what remains a primarily male arena, and compares the experiences of women in different branches of military service, highlighting the continuing political implications of the role of the battlefield nurse. She also argues that, although like their predecessors, the trauma of the experience remained with the women long after the war was over, this time nobody said thank you.

—ANGELA K. SMITH

Beauty Pageants

Banner, Lois W., *American Beauty*, New York: Alfred A. Knopf, 1983

Cohen, Colleen Ballerino, Richard Wilk, and Beverly Stoeltje (eds.), *Beauty Queens on the Global Stage: Gender, Contests, and Power*, New York and London: Routledge, 1996

Deford, Frank, *There She Is: The Life and Times of Miss America*, New York: The Viking Press, 1971; Harmondsworth: Penguin, 1978

Dworkin, Susan, *Miss America, 1945: Bess Myerson's Own Story*, New York: Newmarket Press, 1987

Jewell, K. Sue, *From Mammy to Miss America and Beyond: Cultural Images and the Shaping of US Social Policy*, London and New York: Routledge, 1993

Riverol, A.R., *Live from Atlantic City: The History of the Miss America Pageant before, after and in Spite of Television*, Bowling Green, Ohio: Bowling Green State University Popular Press, 1992

The beauty pageant is one aspect of popular culture that has received very little scholarly treatment. Books tend to be popular histories of a particular pageant or biographies of particular pageant queens. DEFORD's popular history of the Miss America pageant is probably the standard. From the standpoint of an objective journalist, Deford uses an anecdotal approach focusing on individuals to illustrate the history of the pageant from bathing beauty contest at its inception in 1921 to scholarship vehicle for college women. Covering scandals, the influence of community politics at local competitions, the impact of sponsors, changes in judging priorities, and the Miss America year of winners, the book takes us through the 1970s. Deford shows the backstage politics, largely the efforts of Lenora Slaughter, to make the pageant "respectable" by enlisting the Jaycees to run local pageants and soliciting college scholarships. The book provides an account of the "women's lib" protests of the late 1960s, as well as some information on other pageants such as Miss Universe and those for teens, children, and married women.

RIVEROL's book is a scholarly analysis of the Miss America pageant by decades, from the 1920s through the 1980s. Focusing on one key year of each decade, Riverol analyzes minute changes in procedure, judging, and the format of the preliminary and final programs; he then summarizes other changes and continuities in the decade. The theme is the change from a community pageant to extend Atlantic City's tourist season to a nationally televised event. The book covers the "women's lib" protests, including contestants' responses and media coverage, as well as the gradual opening of the pageant to racial minorities, with some discussion of the Vanessa Williams scandal. Chapter One contains a useful annotated bibliography.

BANNER's book places the beauty pageant phenomenon in the United States within the context of a larger discussion of a social history of beauty ideals for American women. She traces the history of May Day celebrations, tournaments, and festivals through the eighteenth and nineteenth centuries, discussing everything from photographic contests sponsored by P.T. Barnum and newspapers at mid-century, to carnival contests, to the respectability of the Miss America pageant in 1921. The book discusses the issue of socioeconomic class in relation to attitudes toward nudity and propriety, as well as the changing definition of feminine beauty.

Despite its title, JEWELL's book gives only cursory treatment to the experience of African-American women in the Miss America pageant. Four African-American Miss Americas are mentioned, with most of the analysis directed toward the negative coverage of Vanessa Williams in the media. DWORKIN's book is largely the story of two women, Bess Myerson, the first and only Jewish Miss America, and Lenora Slaughter, who ran the pageant from 1935 to 1967. The book shows both women's attempts to elevate the pageant's priorities, even as they are in conflict with each other. Myerson's story is told in the context of American anti-Semitism during the contest itself and her Miss America reign, leading her to espouse a "Brotherhood" platform and uncharacteristically politicize the Miss America role.

The edited volume by COHEN, WILK, and STOELTJE illustrates that beauty pageants have become a global phenomenon. The collected essays highlight the range of beauty pageants around the world, covering pageants in Texas, Minnesota, Spain, Russia, Thailand, Polynesia, Guatemala, Liberia, Tibet, Nicaragua, and the British Virgin Islands. Two general themes emerge. Most pageants are understood not to be about physical beauty, but to reflect the values of the local community which the "beauty queen" is to represent. The second theme reflects the global consciousness and western influence that these local pageants represent but also seek to contradict through a nationalist ethos. Each essay provides a detailed analysis of the local political and cultural context in which the pageant takes place. Pageants discussed include those of drag queens and other men, as well as of women.

—ALLISON CARTER

Beauty Standards

Bordo, Susan, *Unbearable Weight: Feminism, Western Culture, and the Body,* Berkeley: University of California Press, 1993; London: 1995

Brownmiller, Susan, *Femininity,* New York: Linden Press, and London: Hamilton, 1984

Chapkis, Wendy, *Beauty Secrets: Women and the Politics of Appearance,* Boston: South End Press, 1986; London: Plicto Press, 1987

Friday, Nancy, *The Power of Beauty,* New York: HarperCollins, and London: Hutchinson, 1996

Halprin, Sara, *"Look at My Ugly Face!": Myths and Musings on Beauty and Other Perilous Obsessions with Women's Appearance,* New York: Viking, 1995

Lakoff, Robin Tolmach, and Raquel Scherr, *Face Value: The Politics of Beauty,* Boston: Routledge and Kegan Paul, 1984

Wolf, Naomi, *The Beauty Myth: How Images of Beauty Are Used against Women,* London: Chatto and Windus, 1990; New York: Morrow, 1991

In 1968, protesters gathered at the Miss America contest kicked the second wave of the U.S. feminist movement into gear. More recently, Indian feminists made the news for continuing the struggle against oppressive beauty standards. But while beauty is clearly a feminist issue, it hasn't always been acknowledged as such in feminist literature. In 1984, BROWNMILLER was one of the first authors to dedicate an entire book to the impact of beauty standards in western cultures. Her investigation of how definitions of femininity have been used through the ages to thwart women's aspirations is often considered a radical feminist classic. Brownmiller argues that standards of beauty employed to construct femininity—including hairstyles, clothing, perfume, and cosmetics—have historically served to control the female body, voice, and movement. Despite her recognition of the culturally determined nature of femininity, her attempt to link beauty standards to their biological origin has exposed her to charges of biological determinism. Brownmiller has also been criticized for her unyielding interpretation of the meaning of beauty standards—she implies that shaving one's legs and wearing pants is politically compromising—and for her tendency to focus solely on the plight of white middle-class women. Her analysis nevertheless usefully lays the groundwork for many of the issues still discussed today in feminist examinations of beauty.

In another classic work, LAKOFF and SCHERR also propose to develop a political understanding of the socio-cultural importance of beauty standards. After noting some of the paradoxes of beauty stereotypes, the authors outline the evolution of beauty representation in cultural texts from ancient art to current media. Lakoff and Scherr maintain that the development of photography and visual media has contributed to the creation of increasingly public and intrusive beauty standards. They explore the psychological impact of such a development, focusing in particular on how standards of attractiveness, and even the language used to talk about beauty, affect our image of ourselves and others. Possibly the greatest contribution of Lakoff and Scherr's work is their examination of the connection between racism and sexism in the definition of beauty. The authors argue that U.S. standards of attractiveness have been defined in opposition to nonwhite women and used to maintain an oppressive political and economic system.

Along similar lines, CHAPKIS uses the testimony of some 25 women to explore how constructions of female attractiveness interact with race, ethnicity, sexual orientation, disability, class, age, transexuality, and weight—to name a few of the topics approached in her book. By including the stories of women from varied cultural backgrounds, Chapkis shows how conceptions of attractiveness are culturally and historically grounded, and how beauty standards and cultural identity are mutually constitutive aspects of women's experience. She further uses women's testimonies as a basis for reflection on larger issues, such as the classist aspect of the dress-for-success movement and the impact of global advertising.

WOLF argues that the myth of beauty developed in the context of a backlash against women, as an insidious means to replace the "old" myth of domesticity challenged by the feminist movement. Wolf maintains that images of beauty promoted in popular culture, religion, and pornography compromise women's advancement in the workplace and result in unhealthy sexuality, eating disorders, and violence in the form of cosmetic surgery. She concludes that the problem lies not in women's desire to engage in beauty rituals, but in the intense cultural pressure to do so, and she advocates redefining beauty in noncompetitive, nonhierarchical, and nonviolent terms. Unfortunately, Wolf shares Brownmiller's tendency to focus on white middle-class women and does not address how membership in a different class, race, or ethnicity might affect women's experience of beauty.

BORDO compensates to some extent for Wolf's omissions. More philosophical and theoretically sophisticated, her collection of essays investigates the complex interactions of race, class, ethnicity, and gender in the construction of the body in western ideology. In this context, Bordo places eating disorders on a continuum of cultural constructions of femininity, relating the ideology of hunger and bodybuilding promoted in the media to different aspects of western ideology—including Christianity, the American work ethic, and the need to control the female appetite. Bordo identifies dieting as one of the most powerful means to control female sexuality and argues that beauty standards serve as a normalizing agent dedicated to making all bodies fit into a thin, white upper-class, heterosexual ideal.

In a more personal exploration of the concept of beauty, HALPRIN examines how myths of appearance have been constructed in cultural texts from fairy tales to contemporary media. Concentrating particularly on the representation of whiteness and youth, Halprin reflects on how definitions of beauty affect women's self-perception and sexuality. She concludes that beauty as it is defined today is a double bind, as women are both respected and ridiculed in their efforts to approximate the proposed ideal. In an innovative move, Halprin offers specific advice on how to heal our relationships with our bodies, and even daily exercises to perform. She also proposes that women creatively recreate myth and reinvent beauty for ourselves to reclaim its spiritual power.

Even more personal than Halprin's work is FRIDAY's psychoanalytical investigation of the power of beauty in women's lives from infancy to adulthood. Friday touches on a wide variety of topics and offers particularly useful interpretations of the impact of our society's increased focus on beauty, the role of advertising in promoting envy, the power of image in adolescence, and the association of beauty with passivity. Friday argues that feminists have wrongfully attempted to deny the importance of female competition, which she sees as a central component of the destructive effect of beauty. Unfortunately, Friday—who blames much of women's insecurities on their relationships with their mothers—falls into essentializing arguments often bearing disturbing implications. Her definition of "matriarchal" singleparent families as pathological has racist and homophobic overtones. Furthermore, while she accuses "matriarchal" feminists—from Gloria Steinem to Andrea Dworkin, Carol Gilligan, Susan Brownmiller, and Simone de Beauvoir—of male-bashing, Friday herself engages in a considerable amount of feminist-bashing. The tone of her book consistently implies that men have been wrongly accused of oppressing women by what she characterizes as "anti-male and anti-sex" feminists "sucking profit out of female victimization."

—FABIENNE DARLING-WOLF

See also Beauty Pageants; Body Image; Fashion; Femininity

Beauvoir, Simone de 1908–1986

French Writer

Brosman, Catherine Savage, *Simone de Beauvoir Revisited,* Boston: Twayne, 1991
Evans, Mary, *Simone de Beauvoir: A Feminist Mandarin,* London and New York: Tavistock, 1985
Fallaize, Elizabeth, *The Novels of Simone de Beauvoir,* London and New York: Routledge, 1988
Heath, Jane, *Simone de Beauvoir,* New York and London: Harvester Wheatsheaf, 1989
Marks, Elaine, *Critical Essays on Simone de Beauvoir,* Boston: G.K. Hall, 1987
Moi, Toril, *Simone de Beauvoir: The Making of an Intellectual Woman,* Oxford and Cambridge, Massachusetts: Blackwell, 1994
Okely, Judith, *Simone de Beauvoir: A Re-Reading,* London: Virago, and New York: Pantheon, 1986
Whitmarsh, Anne, *Simone de Beauvoir and the Limits of Commitment,* Cambridge and New York: Cambridge University Press, 1981

As a pioneering feminist and one of the few female intellectuals of the twentieth century to have achieved international fame, Simone de Beauvoir remains a widely read, popular, and highly controversial figure. It is not surprising that the existing body of critical studies on de Beauvoir's life and work is not only extensive, but also partial and biased. Of the books reviewed here, all but two have been published after de Beauvoir's death, and they represent a sampling of the strong and divided response she has evoked from contemporary feminists and critics.

In contrast to the other works reviewed here, many of which are partial in their focus on a restricted range of texts, BROSMAN succeeds in covering most of de Beauvoir's writing; she usefully reviews and critically evaluates her literary, philosophical, and other works chronologically and in generic groupings against the background of her life and career. Brosman's study provides a balanced overview of de Beauvoir's life and work. It also contains an annotated bibliography of secondary works, which should be a valuable resource for students unfamiliar with de Beauvoir scholarship in English.

The majority of full-length studies on Simone de Beauvoir divide their attention between the non-fiction and the fiction. One exception is that of FALLAIZE. Her study focuses on de Beauvoir's five novels and two collections of stories, with a view to examining their specifically formal literary qualities—narrative structure, language, character construction, and myth. The study aims to establish a relationship between the narrative strategies used in the fiction and de Beauvoir's sexual politics, a project that is contextualized in an opening chapter on the development of de Beauvoir's intellectual preoccupations.

The essays in MARKS's collection are written within different theoretical discourses and from different feminist positions. There are twenty-seven essays in all, some by friends of de Beauvoir, others by philosophers, scholars, and other specialists. These articles and reviews represent significant or outstanding textual moments in the study of Simone de Beauvoir by critics in Canada, France, Great Britain, and the United States, and their chronological arrangement—from Maurice Merleau-Ponty's text on *She Came to Stay* to Virginia Fischera's essay on *Who Shall Die*—enables the reader to note changes in theoretical, ideological, and stylistic modes of critical writing. Michèle La Doeuff's powerful and incisive analysis of de Beauvoir's difficult relationship to existentialist philosophy, which appears in expanded form in her brilliant study, *Hipparchia's Choice* (1991), is worth singling out for special attention, because it remains one of the few serious considerations of de Beauvoir by a major French feminist philosopher. That at least half of the pieces in Marks's collection are sarcastic testifies to the disproportionate hostility of much critical commentary on de Beauvoir.

This is a phenomenon MOI attempts to account for in her study of de Beauvoir as an emblematic twentieth-century intellectual woman. Moi's study is primarily focused on *She Came to Stay, The Second Sex,* and the memoirs, and it includes a useful analysis of the institutional structures and education that contributed to de Beauvoir's development as an intellectual. Moi sees the construct, "Simone de Beauvoir," as an effect of a complex network of different discourses and determinations. Hence her approach is not confined to biography and literary criticism, but also contains reception studies, sociology of culture, philosophical analysis, psychoanalytic inquiry, and feminist theory. Rather than aiming for comprehensiveness in her discussion of individual texts, Moi reads particular scenes and issues as overdetermined effects of a number of factors. For example, de Beauvoir's idealisation of men and masculinity in *The Second Sex* puts her argument about women's oppression in contradiction with itself, and this is an overdetermined effect of her position as a philosopher, her relationship to Sartre and her mother, her class position, and her metaphorical logic. While Moi's study is highly selective, its impassioned originality and theoretical sophistication will ensure its status as an important reference, not only for students of de Beauvoir, but also for those with a general interest in feminist criticism and theory.

The feminists inspired by the French feminist theory developed in the 1970s have tended either to ignore de Beauvoir or to treat her as a theoretical dinosaur. In view of this historical silence, HEATH's attempt to rescue de Beauvoir for poststructuralist feminism is of particular interest. This study begins with the recognition that de Beauvoir wrote consciously from the "masculine" position. Drawing on recent French feminist and Lacanian psychoanalytic theory, Heath examines the autobiographies and three novels—*She Came to Stay, The Mandarins,* and *Les Belles Images*—to locate stress points in the texts that mark the return of the repressed feminine against and despite the denials of femininity. The study is to be recommended for its close readings of the chosen works and for its sensitivity to issues of language and textuality.

By contrast to Moi and Heath, WHITMARSH's concerns are exclusively political and philosophical. Her study focuses upon the ethical, social, and political implications of de Beauvoir's commitment to the revolutionary Left in her work and her life. Specifically it addresses the extent to which the notion of engagement was restricted in theory and practice. She concludes that de Beauvoir was a morally committed writer with deeply held political convictions, but that the nature of these convictions restricted her range of activities and hence her possibilities for changing the world. According to the logic of this analysis, de Beauvoir's contribution is circumscribed by her commitment to a philosophy that exalts the individual and eschews the type of action usually defined as political. De Beauvoir herself was well aware of this discrepancy between theory and practice in her own life, but in view of the importance attached to the role of writer in France, she felt herself justified in choosing writing as her public solution to the obligations of engagement. Whitmarsh, however, seems to be working with a more restricted notion of political action, as when she concludes that writing was for de Beauvoir a substitute for action. In other ways, this is a balanced and meticulously researched study of de Beauoir's politics in terms of existentialist commitment.

EVANS finds de Beauvoir's political writing lacking, but unlike Whitmarsh, she does consider writing politics. Accordingly, she sets out to examine the universalist and individualist assumptions implicit in de Beauvoir's project, arguing, for example, that the existentialist concepts of autonomy, independence, and self-realisation are co-extensive with the values of imperialism and capitalism. She also argues that *The Second Sex* is fundamentally flawed by an essentialist conception of biology, a dichotomous conception of male and female, an inadequate understanding of the structures and processes of the social world, and a commitment to the existentialist belief in the possibility of absolute free choice. The debates surrounding de Beauvoir's work are complex, and Evans is not the first commentator to have drawn attention to these various lacunae in her work. Evans's study remains, however, the most provocative exposition of the theoretical differences that make de Beauvoir such a problematic figure for socialist and radical feminists.

Taking de Beauvoir's inspirational value to women as her central focus, OKELY's study sets out to map the contemporary reception of de Beauvoir's work in the 1950s and 1960s. In doing so, she provides a personal history of her own relationship to de Beauvoir's work, then and now. There is some discussion of the memoirs and selected novels, but over a third of this study is devoted to *The Second Sex.* Like Evans, Okely identifies theoretical and methodological blind spots in *The Second Sex.* She notes, for example, de Beauvoir's tendency to generalize on the basis of her limited experience of the bourgeoisie and its fringes but argues that the subjective emphasis was an important part of its appeal at the time the book first appeared. Okely claims that this limitation was paradoxically a strength; because the account was grounded in concrete experience, it was recognized not only by large numbers of white middle-class women, but also by women of different class and racial backgrounds. Although Okely's study is of limited theoretical value, it is a salutary attempt to redress the tendency of critics to judge de Beauvoir's work entirely on the basis of later standards, rather than in her own context.

—JENNIFER McDONELL

See also Feminist Theory, Formative Works

Behn, Aphra 1640–1689

British Writer

Ballaster, Ros, *Seductive Forms: Women's Amatory Fiction from 1684 to 1740,* Oxford: Clarendon Press, and New York: Oxford University Press, 1992

Cameron, William J., *New Light on Aphra Behn: An Investigation into the Facts and Fictions Surrounding Her Journey to Surinam in 1663, and Her Activities as a Spy in Flanders in 1666,* Auckland, New Zealand: University of Auckland Press, 1961; Darby, Pennsylvania: Arden, 1979

Duffy, Maureen, *The Passionate Shepherdess: Aphra Behn 1640–89,* London: Cape, and New York: Avon, 1977

Goreau, Angeline, *Reconstructing Aphra: A Social Biography of Aphra Behn,* Oxford: Oxford University Press, and New York: Dial, 1980

Hutner, Heidi (ed.), *Rereading Aphra Behn: History, Theory, and Criticism,* Charlottesville: University Press of Virginia, 1993

Link, Frederick M., *Aphra Behn,* New York: Twayne, 1968

Sackville-West, Vita, *Aphra Behn: The Incomparable Astrea,* London: Howe, 1927; New York: Viking, 1928

Woodcock, George, *The Incomparable Aphra,* London and New York: T.V. Boardman, 1948

Aphra Behn has been acknowledged as the first English-speaking professional female writer, and credited with influencing the development of both drama and the novel. However, throughout the twentieth century, critical evaluation of her work has widely varied. The following survey can only attempt to offer a partial account of some of the directions that the literature devoted to the study of Behn's life and work has taken.

An early survey, influenced by early notions of feminism, was provided by SACKVILLE-WEST, who for the first time acknowledges that Behn was the first woman to earn her living by the pen. However, in a typical conflation of the writing subject and the actual historical figure of Aphra Behn, Sackville-West substitutes the writer for her writing. Behn's importance thus lies in her very existence, in the fact that she wrote at all, not in what she wrote or its quality and influence. The book is fairly dated in its approach, but it is important as the first serious study that does not absolutely dismiss Behn, and that considers her historical, if not literary, importance.

A purely biographical study of two important events in Behn's life is the subject of CAMERON's book. He attempts to sort out the various conflicting accounts of Behn's activities in Surinam, and also provides a detailed investigation of her career as a spy in Holland.

WOODCOCK's book is an early attempt at a thorough full-length study. He discusses Behn's life and her importance as a precursor to many new themes and methods, such as the idea of the noble savage, and as a major influence on the use of realism in literature. Thus he acknowledges her innovative way of writing, and the quality of her writing.

A standard treatment of Behn comes from LINK, who offers a comprehensive evaluation of her life, works, and times. His is a useful survey of plays, poems, and novels with a great deal of critical analysis. Interestingly, Link's interpretations of some of Behn's works are somewhat different from those of earlier commentators. So, for example, Behn's most famous work, the novel *Oroonoko*, is by most critics considered to be an ironic portrait of the evil of civilized humanity in comparison with the noble savage. Link considers it a study of the reaction of a society confronted by its own ideals. However, Link's overall attitude to Behn is negative, because he finds her writing unoriginal, and concludes that she made no significant contribution to literature.

In the past twenty years, Behn has stood in the foreground of feminist critical interest as a major female writer. At the beginning, though, feminist critics also tended to read her work as an extension of her biography. Thus, at first, feminist work largely consisted of biographical research, and Behn became the subject of two critical biographies. DUFFY brings the valuable insight of a creative artist into the discussion of the biographical roots of Behn's works. GOREAU is more concerned with the social, political, and intellectual background of Behn's life. Both works are written in a readable style, and are of interest both to the general reader and the informed student looking for details about the life and works of Behn, and the historical background of the Restoration period.

Gradually, critics adopted theoretically more sophisticated approaches to the work of Aphra Behn. One such attempt is by BALLASTER, in her specialized study of the conventions in late seventeenth-century English amatory fiction by Behn, Delarivier Manley, and Eliza Haywood. In the section on Behn, Ballaster looks at how party politics and the ideology of gender were reflected in Behn's specific variety of this genre. She is interested in Behn's gendered subject positions—in both lyrics and fiction. In a constructive reworking of the theory of the gaze, Ballaster argues that the persona the female writer constructs as an erotic enigma for the reader is a part of the seductive nature of the text. This study is useful to the informed student of Behn's texts for its careful textual analysis.

Significantly, HUTNER's collection of essays claims to contain a "playful plurality" of readings and interpretations. The contributors adopt a variety of critical and theoretical perspectives—from Greimas's semiotics to new historicism—in the discussion of Behn's fiction, drama, prose, and literary criticism. The general tendency of all essays is to examine the ideological complexities in Behn's writing, and to demonstrate how these interpenetrate her work. Destabilizing traditional categories and approaches, the essays offer historically grounded interpretations of Behn's feminism, focus on the problematics of female representation, analyze the categories of race, class, and gender, examine female desire in Behn's fiction, and explore her transgressive rhetorical strategies. This is an immensely valuable contribution to recent Behn studies, and a must for all scholars of Restoration literature.

—SOŇA NOVÁKOVÁ

Benedict, Ruth 1887–1948

American Anthropologist

Caffrey, Margaret M., *Ruth Benedict: Stranger in This Land,* Austin: University of Texas Press, 1989

Goldfrank, Esther, *Notes on an Undirected Life: As One Anthropologist Tells It,* Flushing, New York: Queens College Press, 1978

Mead, Margaret, *Ruth Benedict,* New York: Columbia University Press, 1974

Modell, Judith Schachter, *Ruth Benedict: Patterns of a Life,* Philadelphia: University of Pennsylvania Press, 1983

Stocking, George (ed.), *Malinowski, Rivers, Benedict, and Others: Essays on Culture and Personality,* Madison: University of Wisconsin Press, 1986

Viking Fund, Inc., *Ruth Fulton Benedict: A Memorial,* New York: Viking Fund, 1949

Ruth Benedict was one of a few female pioneers in anthropology in the early part of the twentieth century.

MEAD was as close to Benedict personally and academically as anyone, and her biography reflects her special understanding. Using personal letters and Benedict's papers, she fondly traces Benedict's life and work. This book is for readers interested in the ins and outs of anthropological intrigue. Mead names Benedict's academic enemies and points out the restrictions on her career advancement due to gender. An interesting sideline in this book is how it inadvertently places Benedict in a negative light. Descriptions of her fieldwork practices and dislike for "broken" cultures seem horrifying through the lens of contemporary anthropology. In a more favorable way, it shows how far anthropology has come. Half of this volume is reprints of works by Benedict.

Readers hoping to get a different picture of Benedict might well look to the memoirs of GOLDFRANK. She met Benedict while the secretary of Benedict's mentor, Franz Boas. Goldfrank became an anthropologist in her own right and remained a colleague of Benedict to her death. Goldfrank's work in the pueblos brought her to disagree with Benedict's analysis, and the history of their disputes on the issue is well described. While the focus of this book is not on Benedict herself, it does show her in the context of her peers. It shows a side of Benedict that is far less romanticized than in other books. It is a view of Benedict as a woman who could be distant and self-absorbed as well as capable and brilliant.

MODELL provides the first of two detailed biographies of Benedict to be published in the 1980s. Modell describes her approach to writing this biography as "Benedictine," which means that, borrowing Benedict's preoccupation with "patterns," she searches for the basic configurations in Benedict's own life. Modell explores how Benedict's anthropological theories ultimately derived from her own emotional and psychological configurations, especially the predominant theme of "not fitting in."

CAFFREY's biography extends this psychological approach even further, asking the question of what made Benedict the woman she became. Her focus lies on Benedict's childhood, the early death of her father, and the intensive mourning of her mother. She suggests that Benedict's interest in psychology and dichotomies stemmed from this background. Caffrey asserts that Benedict was a feminist, but not a political feminist. Unfortunately feminism in this definition seems more a personal quest for freedom and a fondness for being with women rather than a philosophical stance. Caffrey also focuses more on Benedict's sexuality than the others, discussing her sexual relationships with women, including Margaret Mead, and the way that her understanding of homosexuality colored her work. This is not the book for readers searching for the weaknesses in Benedict as a woman or scholar, however.

The volume edited by the preeminent historian of anthropology, STOCKING, contains eight essays examining the development of the discipline of anthropology during the very significant period between the world wars. The essays, as well as the editor's fine introduction, are invaluable for situating Benedict's ideas within the wider context of anthropological thought during her time. Understandably, Benedict crops up as a topic in several of the pieces but is primarily discussed alongside Edward Sapir in an article by Richard Handler, "Vigorous Male and Aspiring Female: Poetry, Personality, and Culture in Edward Sapir and Ruth Benedict." Handler examines the poetry of the two anthropologists, the relationship between them, and the tension between humanistic and scientific impulses in their work.

The publication by the VIKING FUND is a record of a gathering in New York City in remembrance of Ruth Benedict two months after her death in 1948. The publication includes short eulogies by Alfred Kroeber, Cora DuBois, Erik Erikson, Clyde Kluckhohn, Robert Lynd, and Margaret Mead. Several of Benedict's poems are reprinted here, and the volume includes a useful chronology of Benedict's life as well as a comprehensive, year-by-year listing of Benedict's publications and unpublished writings.

—LAURA KLEIN and ELIZABETH BRUSCO

Bernhardt, Sarah 1844–1923

French Actor

Agate, May, *Madame Sarah*, London: Home and Van Thal, 1945; New York: Benjamin Blom, 1969

Aston, Elaine, *Sarah Bernhardt: A French Actress on the English Stage*, Oxford and New York: St. Martin's Press, 1989

Brandon, Ruth, *Being Divine: A Biography of Sarah Bernhardt*, London: Secker and Warburg, 1991

Richardson, Joanna, *Sarah Bernhardt and Her World*, London: Weidenfeld and Nicolson, and New York: Putnam, 1977

Taranow, Gerda, *Sarah Bernhardt: The Art within the Legend*, Princeton, New Jersey: Princeton University Press, 1972

Verneuil, Louis, *The Fabulous Life of Sarah Bernhardt*, translated by Ernest Boyd, New York and London: Harper and Brothers, 1942

Sarah Bernhardt, a French actor and worldwide legend at the turn of the century, inspired a great deal of literature on her life, work, dramatic technique, and public notoriety. Bernhardt elevated stage drama to a new form of artistic expression for women. An independent woman, manager of two theatre companies, actor, and mother, Bernhardt symbolized the progressive woman to her female followers. She achieved her goals without the assistance of a man—she did it all on her own. Bernhardt attained worldwide fame without the aid of television or radio—she performed around the world in person.

Verneuil and Agate provide the reader with a wealth of personal anecdotes gathered from their years of personal interaction with Bernhardt. A former pupil and longtime friend of the actor, AGATE details the private person backstage as opposed to the public persona written about in most of the other books. As a member of Bernhardt's *cours* (circle of friends), Agate's access to the actress enables the reader to get a glimpse of the "real Sarah Bernhardt." VERNEUIL's book writes adoringly of both Bernhardt and himself. A son-in-law to Sarah in her last years of life, and a playwright, Verneuil details her stage work, world tours, films, and private performances. His admiration of her very presence may make the reader wonder why he did not marry Sarah instead of her daughter, Lysianne.

ASTON describes Bernhardt's annual staged performances in England. To Victorian-era British theatregoers, the French-speaking Bernhardt represented the exotic woman who led her own life and did as she pleased with whom she pleased. Aston asserts that, unlike most actresses of the era, Bernhardt expressed herself with exuberance as opposed to constraint. Her passion, gestures, glamorous costumes, and enchanting vocal techniques attracted a popular audience. Her believable death scenes, as described various times by Aston, became her signature or her gimmick. Bernhardt believed that acting enabled women to act out their emotions in character and on stage without fear of reproach. To Bernhardt, the theatrical stage was the canvas for women's art. Aston describes the positive reaction to Bernhardt's performances of young, educated, English women who appreciated her talent and independence.

TARANOW examines the technical aspects of Sarah Bernhardt's stage performances. Unlike the other writers cited, Taranow focuses on the work of the artist, not the personality. Her thesis states that Bernhardt's dramatic training at the Comédie Française and the Paris Conservatoire strongly influenced her own technique, which would eventually catapult her to worldwide popularity. Bernhardt was unique in her vocal technique, style, stage direction, and dramatic presentation. Her voice was an instrument that transcended language barriers, while her gestures and expression mesmerized her audience. Her awareness of her visual impact made excellent costume design a priority for her portrayal of her roles and for her public image. Taranow suggests that Bernhardt's ability to bring emotion to the stage made her legendary.

RICHARDSON describes Sarah Bernhardt as an icon of her age. The author asserts that Bernhardt was the type of figure who set a new standard for women on stage and off. Richardson is one of the two authors, along with Brandon, who mentions Bernhardt's Judaism. Her unfailing strength as an independent woman is also detailed in this book. The actor freed herself from two acting companies, bought and managed two theaters, and organized her own world tours. Richardson details the people and world around the turn of the century. The extensive illustrations and photographs of the era provide the reader with the visual *mise-en-scène* of the people and places in Bernhardt's time.

BRANDON describes Bernhardt as a phenomenon and as the first "goddess of popular culture." She goes so far as to compare Bernhardt's popularity to that of Marilyn Monroe in the 1950s, and Madonna in the 1990s. Bernhardt broadened the possibilities of careers available to French women at the turn of the century, as she proved that a woman could make it on her own without the assistance of a man. Brandon discusses her hypothesis that Sarah Bernhardt was really a multiple personality who was able to assume public, private, and stage personas with relative ease. Brandon argues that the stage was really a therapy for Bernhardt, in which she was able to act out a range of emotions and personalities.

Brandon candidly discusses Bernhardt's preference for, and insistence on, strong female protagonist-centered roles in her plays. Bernhardt was always the star. Brandon contrasts the strong image of Bernhardt to the popular representation of women at the time as being sick, weak, and dying. Although Bernhardt learned her lines while lying in a coffin and was known for her trademark death scenes, she did not represent a frail woman on stage. The author appreciates the actor's ability to attract popular audiences to the theatres.

All the authors mention where Bernhardt was born, where she was buried (Père Lachaise), and her motto, *Quand même* (however done). It is clear that Bernhardt's popularity and coverage in the paper press outshone all other celebrities of the time. As Brandon states, Sarah Bernhardt was a *génie de la réclame* (advertising genius). In addition, she was a master interpreter who was able to reach her audience through emotion, gesture and voice.

—ALEXANDRA HART

Bethune, Mary McLeod 1875–1955

American Activist

Holt, Rackham, *Mary McLeod Bethune, A Biography,* New York: Doubleday, 1964

Peare, Catherine Owens, *Mary McLeod Bethune,* New York: Vanguard, 1951

Sitkoff, Harvard, *A New Deal for Blacks: The Emergence of Civil Rights as a National Issue,* New York: Oxford University Press, 1978; Oxford: Oxford University Press, 1981

Sterne, Emma Geddes, *Mary McLeod Bethune,* New York: Knopf, 1957

Mary McLeod Bethune was undoubtedly one of the most influential and respected African-Americans of the twentieth century. However, very little has been published about her since the 1980s. Overall, early works tend to be uncritical, idealized presentations of the major influences on, and events in, her life. More recently, writers have examined Bethune's leadership style during the New Deal, and the influence of religion in shaping her perception of the world, and in guiding her actions.

PEARE's work focuses on Bethune's life from her childhood in Mayesville, South Carolina to the 1940s. Peare combines recreations of dialogue with narrative in her description of Bethune's own quest for education, and her determination to create an education institution in rural Florida for African-American women. The author also examines Bethune's involvement with the National Youth Administration during the New Deal, the National Association of Colored Women, and the National Council of Negro Women. Peare's work is extremely laudatory, and, while it may provide an overview of Bethune's activities, it lacks depth in its presentation of her educational and political leadership.

STERNE's analysis of Bethune is similar to that of Peare; however, within her uncritical rendering of Bethune's activities, the reader can discern an early feminist interpretation. She presents Bethune as a woman who not only believed that she had to challenge restrictions on her rights, but who also saw the value of unifying African-American women. Sterne attributes the failure of Bethune's marriage, and her determination to vote, to the force of a personality that would not be controlled by any man. Sterne also contends that Bethune felt that the unification of women across racial lines was the only real hope for interracial harmony.

HOLT's work provides a deeper analysis of Bethune's motivations, and the strategies she utilized in her educational, social, and political activities, yet he is at times condescending on racial issues. Like Sterne and Peare, Holt sees Bethune's talent for attracting the support of wealthy whites as an important asset, and stresses her appeal as "the universal woman." Yet he suggests that it was Bethune's "masculine" qualities of clarity of thought and decisiveness of action that caused men of both races to support her. Holt's Bethune molds her behavior and physical appearance to make herself more acceptable to upper-class African-Americans and whites who could assist with her causes. But he presents a Bethune who is conservative in her goals for African-American women. For her, the purpose of women's education was not just to acquire a degree, but to learn how to create homes and make themselves "comely." Holt also contends that Bethune advocated scientific housekeeping and social work as tools for strengthening African-American communities. She was adamant in her demands for full political rights for blacks, nonpartisan in her politics, and a consensus builder in political relationships. Although Holt's book continues the laudatory pattern of Peare and Stern, it is a valuable work, particularly in its discussion of Bethune's work during the Roosevelt administrations.

SITKOFF also places Bethune's activities within the context of the Roosevelt administrations. He presents an aggressive Bethune who "masked her militancy with homespun homilies and appeals for fair play." Sitkoff describes her use of her influence and reputation to focus the administration's attention on the campaign for a federal anti-lynching law and civil rights for African-Americans. This book is valuable for its insight into the impact of New Deal programs on African-American communities, and its examination of the influence of black leaders in the 1930s.

—BEVERLY GREENE BOND

Bhutto, Benazir 1953–

Pakistani Prime Minister

Bhargava, G. S., *Benazir, Pakistan's New Hope,* Bangalore: Arnold, 1989

Bhola, P. L., *Benazir Bhutto: Opportunities and Challenges,* New Delhi: Yuvraj, 1989

Chitkara, M. G., *Benazir: A Profile,* New Delhi: A.P.H ., 1996

Jafri, Sadiq (ed.), *Benazir Bhutto on Trial,* Lahore: Jang, 1993

Lamb, Christina, *Waiting for Allah: Pakistan's Struggle for Democracy,* London: Hamish Hamilton, 1991; revised edition, as *Waiting for Allah: Benazir Bhutto and Pakistan,* London: Penguin, 1992

van Heugten, Jan, *A Taste of Power: The Uneasy Reign of Benazir Bhutto, 1988–1990,* Amsterdam: Middle East Research Associates, 1992

Zakaria, Rafiq, *Benazir Bhutto,* Bombay: Popular Prakashan, 1989; also as *The Trial of Benazir Bhutto: An Insight into the Status of Women in Islam,* Petaling Jaya, Malaysia: Pelanduk, and New York: New Horizons, 1990

Daughter of and political heir to Pakistan's Prime Minister Zulfikar Ali Bhutto (1928–1979), who was hanged by the military regime that toppled him from power in 1972, Benazir Bhutto, educated both at Harvard and Oxford universities, has served as Pakistan's prime minister twice, and has been dismissed from office both times. Her first time was from 1988 to 1990, at which point she and her government were dismissed by the president of Pakistan through devious political and legal machinations. She was then tried on charges of corruption, which, after a protracted trial, were dismissed due to lack of conclusive proof. To the surprise of many, she narrowly won reelection again in 1993 in a hotly disputed contest and served only half of this second term, until

November, 1996, when charges of corruption were again brought against not only her, but her husband, polo player-construction magnate Asif Ali Zardari. She failed to win a third bid for office in February, 1997.

Indian political scientist CHITKARA's brief and generally sympathetic profile provides much factual information succinctly stated. Published in 1996, it is the most up-to-date discussion of Bhutto, the leader of Pakistan, the country Indians perceived as their arch-enemy. In spite of fifty years of enmity, including four wars, between India and Pakistan, Bhutto is perceived more positively in India than any previous Pakistani prime minister. There she is seen as the politician who wrested control of her country from religious fundamentalists and corrupt politicians, and who restored political democracy to that beleaguered nation.

Thus, Chitkara is cautiously positive, as are the studies of BHARGAVA and BHOLA, also writing from an Indian perspective, that the mutual hatred between Pakistan and India might, under Bhutto's leadership, start to ebb. However, the matter of religion remains a major factor between these two countries. Pakistan, an overwhelmingly Muslim country, is concerned about the rise of Hindu fundamentalism in India as a threat to India's substantial Muslim minority population (about twelve percent). Bhola, perhaps more realistically than Bhargava, sees the steady rise of anti-Muslim sentiment in India as a major factor affecting the relations between the two countries. All three of these studies would have benefitted greatly from the work of a hard-nosed English-language editor and a more careful proofreading.

VAN HEUGTEN's book characterizes Bhutto's first "reign," a term used as much ironically as condescendingly, as an unsuccessful attempt to bring order and democracy to a country overrun by rabid fundamentalists and corrupt politicians, one of the latter being Bhutto's father himself. While Heugten suggests that Benazir Bhutto would continue to play a major role in Pakistani politics, he was probably surprised by her rapid return to power the year after his book was published.

JAFRI's work deals with Bhutto's inconclusive corruption trial. He has gathered a large number of public documents related to these proceedings and provides a thorough chronology and account of them, but he offers little analysis and interpretation. This book is intended for specialists. ZAKARIA seems to have changed the title of the reprint of his volume to suggest erroneously that its topic is Bhutto's corruption trial. In this context one might expect the author to address such questions as: How can a woman get a fair trial in an Islamic court where a woman's testimony is only worth half that of a man? Instead one finds a pedantic description of Bhutto's rise to political power. One might extrapolate from this study that Bhutto's position as the first prime minister of a Muslim country proves that, contrary to popular thinking, especially in the west, women are accorded high status in Muslim countries, both publically and privately. Feminists, both Muslim and non-Muslim, would contest this point.

LAMB provides the most objective, detailed, and analytical discussion of Bhutto. One refreshing aspect of this work, which is more journalistic than scholarly, is that the author does not fall into the trap of overplaying the importance of Bhutto's father's reputation and legacy, which were not always sterling, on his daughter's thinking and career. In Lamb's book, Benazir Bhutto emerges as her own person, an always deft, sometimes intemperate politician who has not only been able to make tough political decisions but who has also ably steered a successful path in a country where women are perceived as fit for the family home rather than the prime minister's palace.

—CARLO COPPOLA

Bible: General

Collins, Adela Yarbro (ed.), *Feminist Perspectives on Biblical Scholarship,* Atlanta, Georgia: Scholars Press, 1985

Fiorenza, Elizabeth Schussler, *In Memory of Her: A Feminist Theological Reconstruction of Christian Origins,* New York: Lexington, and London: S.C.M. Press, 1983

———, *Bread, Not Stone: The Challenge of Feminist Biblical Interpretation,* Boston: Beacon Press, 1984

———, *But She Said: Feminist Practices of Biblical Interpretation,* Boston: Beacon Press, 1992

———, Shelly Matthews, and Ann Brock (eds.), *Searching the Scriptures: A Feminist Commentary,* 2 vols., New York: Crossroad, 1993; London: S.C.M. Press, 1994

Hollyday, Joyce, *Clothed with the Sun: Biblical Women, Social Justice and Us,* Louisville, Kentucky: Westminster/John Knox Press, 1994

Kam, Rose Sallberg, *Their Stories, Our Stories: Women of the Bible,* New York: Continuum, 1995

Newsom, Carol A., and Sharon H. Ringe (eds.), *The Women's Bible Commentary,* Louisville, Kentucky: Westminster/John Knox Press, and London: S.C.M. Press 1992

Schneiders, Sandra M., *Women and the Word: The Gender of God in the New Testament and the Spirituality of Women,* New York: Paulist Press, 1986

———, *The Revelatory Text: Interpreting the New Testament as Sacred Scripture,* San Francisco: Harper, 1991

Stanton, Elizabeth Cady, *The Woman's Bible,* New York: European Publishing Company, 1895–1898; Boston: Northeastern University Press, 1993

Weems, Renita J., *Just a Sister Away: A Womanist Vision of Women's Relationships in the Bible,* San Diego, California: LuraMedia, 1988

An increase in the number of women who have pursued the academic study of religion, and biblical study in particular, has led to a new field: namely, feminist biblical studies. Those who pursue biblical studies using feminist methodologies differ from one another as do the monographs they have produced. STANTON's volume is now a classic. First published at the end of the last century, it represents the collected efforts of several women to single out biblical texts that portray women from a patriarchal perspective and comment on the obvious biases that have legitimated discrimination against women. FIORENZA, MATTHEWS and BROCK's edited volumes began as an effort, a century later, to produce a new woman's bible, one that would incorporate the sophisticated feminist hermeneutics that have developed since Stanton's seminal work. The new feminist commentary "transgresses canonical borders," commenting on the traditional books of the New Testament but also including for comment other contemporaneous texts—many ascribed to female authors—such as "Thunder, Perfect Mind," "Trimorphic Protennoia," and "The Sibylline Oracles."

NEWSOM and RINGE's edited volume, while more traditional, includes the contributions of forty-two female biblical scholars. In addition to providing comment on each of the books of the Hebrew Bible, the Apocrypha, and the New Testament, the volume contains an introduction, an essay on women interpreting the Bible, essays on everyday life in the periods of the Hebrew Bible and of the New Testament, and an essay on early extracanonical writings.

COLLINS' volume contains seven essays: a historical essay developing the differences as well as similarities between nineteenth- and twentieth-century feminists and their approaches to the Bible; two essays challenging the assumption of objectivity and acknowledging the role of historical conditioning and the particularity of history's purpose and audience; an essay suggesting new perspectives and a new framework for studying early Christian women; an essay proposing hermeneutical alternatives determined by women's conditioning and experience (rejectionist, loyalist, revisionist, sublimationist, and liberationist); and three essays dealing with particular texts (the Jacob cycle, and texts dealing with barren women and with deceptive women).

FIORENZA's contributions include not only an essay in Collins' volume and the edited feminist commentary but also several monographs that chronicle her struggle to develop appropriate feminist methodologies. In her 1983 volume, Fiorenza develops her understanding of the history of the Jesus movement and the early Christian missionary movement as a history of the discipleship of equals; later theology aligned the Christian mission with the patriarchal order of the household. In her 1984 volume, she asserts that all feminist theology begins with the experiences of women. Feminist interpretation of the Bible seeks to reveal both its oppressive, as well as its liberating power for women and to find ways to interpret the texts that will function to end domination and exploitation. Toward this end, she proposes four reading strategies, which she refers to as ideological suspicion, historical reconstruction, theoethical assessment, and creative imagination. In her 1992 volume, she engages in feminist interpretation of specific texts and particular biblical women; for example, Herodias, Mary and Martha, Mary of Magdala, the Syro-Phoenician woman, Prisca, and the nameless woman of Luke 13:10–17.

SCHNEIDERS's 1986 volume situates the biblical gender of God in its contemporary relation to women's spirituality. Her 1991 volume incorporates the interpretive theories of Hans Georg Gadamer and Paul Ricoeur; she asserts that not all interpretations are of equal merit and concludes that those for whom the biblical texts contain revelation—the believing communities for whom the texts are Sacred Scripture—are, in fact, privileged interpreters. Although Fiorenza and Schneiders are both considered New Testament scholars, their work, because of its methodological import, has been applied to the Old Testament/Hebrew Bible as well.

Kam's, Holliday's, and Weem's efforts are more popular than those referred to above. KAM presents portraits of no less than 35 women whose stories are told in the Old and New Testaments. Each chapter is organized in six parts: (1) background (current scholarship), (2) the story as told in the Bible, (3) reflection, (4) prayer, (5) connections to the reader's life, and (6) suggestions for further reading. HOLLYDAY treats the biblical women, not in the order in which they appear in the Bible, but according to categories: (1) women of patriarchy, (2) victims of male abuse, (3) women of treachery and guile, (4) women in relation to men of power, (5) clever and courageous heroines, (6) devoted mothers, (7) leaders and prophets, (8) faithful widows, (9) women touched by Jesus, and (10) witnesses to life and resurrection. WEEMS's selections from the Bible all deal with relationships between women; for example, Hagar and Sarah, Naomi and Ruth, Elizabeth and Mary. As an African-American biblical scholar, she is more than aware of power relations between and among women. At the conclusion to each chapter, Weems posits questions for thought that challenge the reader's appropriation of the biblical text for his or her contemporary context.

—ALICE L. LAFFEY

Bible: New Testament

Corley, Kathleen E., *Private Women Public Meals: Social Conflict in the Synoptic Tradition*, Peabody, Massachusetts: Hendrickson, 1993

Fiorenza, Elisabeth Schussler, *In Memory of Her: A Feminist Theological Reconstruction of Christian Origins*, New York: Crossroad, and London: SCM, 1983

———(ed.), *Searching the Scriptures,* 2 vols.: *A Feminist Introduction* and *A Feminist Commentary,* New York: Crossroad, 1993, and *A Feminist Commentary,* London: SCM, 1994

Kraemer, Ross Shepard, *Her Share of the Blessings: Women's Religions among Pagans, Jews, and Christians in the Greco-Roman World,* New York and Oxford: Oxford University Press, 1992

Reid, Barbara E., *Choosing the Better Part? Women in the Gospel of Luke,* Collegeville, Minnesota: Liturgical Press, 1996

Schaberg, Jane, *The Illegitimacy of Jesus: A Feminist Theological Interpretation of the Infancy Narratives,* San Francisco: Harper and Row, 1987; Sheffield: Sheffield Academic Press, 1995

Schottroff, Luise, *Lydia's Impatient Sisters: A Feminist Social History of Early Christianity,* translated by Barbara and Martin Rumscheidt, Louisville, Kentucky: Westminster John Knox Press, 1995

Wire, Antoinette Clark, *The Corinthian Women Prophets: A Reconstruction through Paul's Rhetoric,* Minneapolis: Fortress Press, 1990

A feminist approach to the Bible acknowledges that its texts were written from a perspective that supports patriarchal religious social structures. One of the first feminist studies of the Bible, Elizabeth Cady Stanton's *The Woman's Bible,* published in 1895, offered a largely nonscholarly analysis. In contrast to Stanton's volume, modern feminist biblical criticism utilizes historical, literary, sociological, and theological methods of interpretation. Feminist criticism recognizes the largely silent role of women, whose voices were either muted or eliminated from the biblical text and from religious history.

In the area of New Testament studies, FIORENZA's *In Memory of Her* has become perhaps the best known historical reconstruction of early Christianity from a feminist perspective. Using early Christian texts, this work argues that the Jesus movement (those who followed him during his lifetime) and the early churches were egalitarian, but that by the second century of the common era, the churches had become dominated by males. Fiorenza's approach is based on liberation theology, which highlights both women's oppression and women's power. Fiorenza's broad reconstruction of early Christianity has stimulated scholarly debate and refinement, as evidenced in the remaining works in this bibliography.

The two-volume work *Searching the Scriptures,* edited by FIORENZA, is a collection of essays from different religious, cultural, and geographic locations, which challenge the male-biased assumptions of modern biblical criticism. The essays concern not only issues of gender but of race, class, and other forms of oppression. Volume one includes 24 essays written by American, European, Asian, African, and Latin American women. Among them is an essay by Kwok Pui-Lan that offers 10 theses for correcting middle-class, educated, eurocentric interpretations of the Bible.

Volume two contains 40 commentaries written by feminist biblical scholars from the United States, Europe, Central America, and Australia, who represent a variety of religious backgrounds. The essays are commentaries on each book of the New Testament canon, as well as non-canonical Gnostic writings, such as the Gospel of Mary Magdalene, Jewish intertestamental texts, and later Christian writings, such as the Acts of Thecla and the Martyrdom of Perpetua and Felicity. The purpose of the essays is to expose the marginalized voices within the texts, and to broaden the notion of canon.

Recognizing the small number of written resources available for the study of women in the New Testament, KRAEMER provides a historical context for a study of women in Judaism and early Christianity, with her survey of women's religions in the Greco-Roman world. Kraemer explores women's devotion to the Greek goddess Demeter, the Egyptian goddess Isis, the gods Dionysos and Adonis, and rites of Roman matrons as well as women in Judaism and Christianity. Kraemer examines the leadership roles women played in early Christianity in an attempt to offer a sociological critique of the subordinate role of women in these religious groups.

SCHABERG offers a controversial analysis of the narratives about the birth of Jesus in Matthew and Luke. Schaberg cites early Jewish sources that support the accusation that Jesus was illegitimately conceived. According to Schaberg, virgin birth theology is a later interpretation of Mary's premarital pregnancy. She claims that Matthew and Luke intended to pass along this illegitimacy tradition and reinterpret it. She argues that what may be perceived as an illegitimate conception was absolved by the Holy Spirit, and therefore has transcendent value. Thus Schaberg claims that Mary's disgrace becomes grace, a concept that overturns patriarchal social structures.

CORLEY investigates the private/public role of women in the gospels of Matthew, Mark, and Luke, by examining their presence, absence, or behavior at public meal settings. Drawing upon a wide range of ancient sources from the Greco-Roman world, Corley concludes that the general movement in the first century was toward a liberalization of women's roles in public meals. This thesis emphasizes a commonality among Greco-Roman society, Jews, and Christians, rather than the idea that Christianity was more uniquely egalitarian in this respect. Corley investigates the meal scenes in Matthew, Mark, and Luke, and claims that Matthew is the only gospel to assert that women reclined with men at meals, and that "courtesans" were among Jesus' followers. Thus Matthew portrays a view of the early Christian community that more readily embraced diversity.

Recent feminist biblical criticism claims that the Gospel of Luke is the most "woman friendly" gospel, because it contains more narratives about women than the others. REID's analysis of the stories in Luke, including the narratives about the woman who anoints Jesus' feet, Mary and Martha, and Mary and Elizabeth in the birth story, lends support to those who challenge such a reading. According to Reid, Luke portrays women in largely silent or passive roles. For example, instead of assuming that the woman in Luke 7, who anoints Jesus' feet and wipes them with her hair, was a repentant prostitute, Reid suggests that the narrative has more to do with how one perceives the person of Jesus. According to her, this woman rightly perceived Jesus, while Simon incorrectly perceived both Jesus and her. Reid calls for an interpretation that challenges the patriarchal systems that curtail women's roles, particularly in the ministry. This work is especially recommended for preachers.

WIRE attempts to reconstruct the behavior, roles, and theology of the female prophets in the first-century Christian Church in Corinth. Wire contends that in I Corinthians, Paul is addressing female prophets who are among those in his audience at Corinth. Wire claims that the women have gained a newly acquired status as Christian prophets in the community. This status poses a threat to Paul and other males at Corinth. Wire's commentary includes an analysis of Paul's preference for celibacy rather than marriage, his discussion of headgear to be worn by female prophets, and his call for women to keep silent. Yet, the book concludes, the female prophets at Corinth appear to have practiced freedom from patriarchal authority, based on their experience as mediators of Jesus' wisdom.

SCHOTTROFF makes use of a socio-historical interpretation of the New Testament. This interpretation examines the social context of the original text, and then reads the text through the lens of modern social feminist liberation movements. In her discussion of women's work, she claims that the spectrum of women's jobs went well beyond what is mentioned in the New Testament. Women are not mentioned as workers of the land or as fishers, while both occupations were commonly performed by women, and vital to economic survival. The patriarchal nature of the biblical writing precludes mentioning women in roles unrelated to the patriarchal family structure of the times. The importance of women to the common life of the community is not mentioned, nor has traditional interpretation seen symbolic significance in women's work. Schottroff highlights the descriptions of women's work, such as bread baking and sweeping the floor, in such a way as to see a liberating transcendent value in the very ordinariness of these tasks.

—BARBARA B. MILLER

Bible: Old Testament/Hebrew Bible

Bellis, Alice Ogden, *Helpmates, Harlots and Heroes: Women's Stories in the Hebrew Bible*, Louisville, Kentucky: Westminster/John Knox Press, 1994

Bronner, Leila Leah, *From Eve to Esther: Rabbinic Reconstructions of Biblical Women*, Louisville, Kentucky: Westminster/John Knox Press, 1994

Brown, Cheryl Anne, *No Longer Be Silent: First Century Jewish Portraits of Biblical Women*, Louisville, Kentucky: Westminster/John Knox Press, 1992

Darr, Katheryn Pfisterer, *Far More Precious Than Jewels: Perspectives on Biblical Women*, Louisville, Kentucky: Westminster/John Knox Press, 1991

Exum, J. Cheryl, *Fragmented Women: Feminist (Sub)Versions of Biblical Narratives*, Valley Forge, Pennsylvania: Trinity Press International, and Sheffield: I.S.O.T. Press, 1993

Laffey, Alice L., *An Introduction to the Old Testament: A Feminist Perspective*, Philadelphia: Fortress Press, 1988

Meyers, Carol, *Discovering Eve: Ancient Israelite Women in Context*, New York: Oxford University Press, 1988

Trible, Phyllis, *God and the Rhetoric of Sexuality*, Philadelphia: Fortress Press, 1978; London: S.C.M. Press, 1992

———, *Texts of Terror: Literary-Feminist Readings of Biblical Narratives*, Philadelphia: Fortress Press, 1984; London: S.C.M. Press, 1992

MEYERS, keenly aware of how the biblical texts, especially Genesis 2 and 3, have influenced western attitudes about gender for two millennia, studies the relationship of the biblical texts dealing with women to the women of ancient Israelite society. Her work is primarily historical, with chapters devoted to the highland environment of ancient Israel, the family household, and female roles in household functions. She also traces how the female roles set forth in Genesis 2 and 3 and in 3:16 became paradigms, fully aware that as long as the Bible is quoted as justification for one or another belief or policy regarding women, the value of understanding the biblical texts involved and the social world from which they (and their later interpretations) emerged is critical.

TRIBLE's 1978 monograph was groundbreaking; it was the first to appear whose methodology was an application of rhetorical criticism from a decidedly feminist perspective. Although scattered articles had appeared previously dealing with feminist biblical hermeneutics, her work provided a sustained model. Because she approaches the texts with feminist assumptions, she is able—using a respected traditional methodology—to arrive at uncommon interpretations. She interprets Genesis 2 and 3, the Book of Ruth, and Jer. 31:15–22. In addition, she does a detailed word study of the Hebrew root *rhm*. TRIBLE's 1984 volume contains literary-feminist readings of very different biblical texts, in which women—Hagar, Tamar, the unnamed woman of Judges 19:1–30, and the daughter of Jephthah—are victimized by patriarchy.

EXUM draws on contemporary feminist literary theories—in particular, certain aspects of deconstruction and psychoanalytic literary theory—to reveal strategies by which the patriarchal biblical literature excludes, marginalizes, and subjugates women. She does this both in order to subvert the men's stories, and to construct from the women's submerged voices versions of their own stories. The essays examine Jephthah's daughter and Michal, the four women associated with Samson, the "matriarchs" as presented in Genesis, the three episodes where patriarchs present their wives as their sisters, and the rape accounts in Judges 19 and 2 Samuel 12. LAFFEY provides a survey of the books of the Old Testament—the Pentateuch, the Deuteronomistic History, the Major and Minor Prophets, and the Writings—suggesting historical and literary considerations for each section and then examining selected themes and texts from a feminist perspective.

Darr's, Brown's and Bronner's volumes are each part of a series, *Gender and the Biblical Tradition.* DARR selects several biblical women—Ruth, Sarah, Hagar, and Esther—and examines each using historical and literary criticism as well as rabbinical and feminist perspectives. BROWN selects other biblical women for examination; she compares and contrasts the depictions of Deborah, Jephthah's daughter, Hannah, and the witch of Endor in Pseudo-Philo's *Biblical Antiquities* and in Flavius Josephus's *Jewish Antiquities.* Brown concludes that the first-century Jewish portraits of the women differ from their depiction in the biblical texts and also from one another; on the whole, Pseudo-Philo depicts women in a more favorable manner than does Josephus. BRONNER's study also selects specific biblical women—Eve, Serah bat Asher, Ruth, Hannah, and Deborah—while including chapters on daughterhood and harlotry. Her focus is the portrayal of biblical women in Aggadic literature. Although she finds certain dominant attitudes toward women in the literature (for example, the extolling of modesty), she also finds that the portrayal of certain women (such as Serah bat Asher, who is hardly mentioned in the biblical text) is considerably expanded in the Aggadic materials. Hannah's prayer becomes in the rabbinic materials a model of how to pray worthily: in a low voice, with lips moving, with concentration, and not when drunk. Bronner finds that the Aggadah most commonly emphasizes in its depictions the particular characteristics attributed to specific women in the Bible.

BELLIS's work marks the next step in feminist interpretation of the Old Testament/Hebrew Bible texts. Whereas the other monographs consist of feminist interpretation of biblical texts or present interpretations of biblical women done in early Jewish and rabbinic tradition, Bellis has compiled the interpretations of many contemporary feminist biblical scholars and incorporates them into her own interpretations of the biblical women.

—ALICE L. LAFFEY

Biological Determinism

Bleier, Ruth, *Science and Gender: A Critique of Biology and Its Theories on Women,* New York: Pergamon Press, 1984

Fausto-Sterling, Anne, *Myths of Gender: Biological Theories about Women and Men,* New York: Basic Books, 1985

Haraway, Donna, *Primate Visions: Gender, Race, and Nature in the World of Modern Science,* New York: Routledge, 1989; London: Verso Press, 1992

Hubbard, Ruth, *The Politics of Woman's Biology,* New Brunswick, New Jersey: Rutgers University Press, 1990

Lewontin, R.C., Steven Rose, and Leon J. Kamin, *Not in Our Genes: Biology, Ideology, and Human Nature,* London: Penguin, and New York: Pantheon, 1984

Oudshoorn, Nelly, *Beyond the Natural Body: An Archeology of Sex Hormones,* London and New York: Routledge, 1994

Sayers, Janet, *Biological Politics: Feminist and Anti-Feminist Perspectives,* London and New York: Tavistock, 1982

Schiebinger, Londa, *Nature's Body: Gender in the Making of Modern Science,* Boston: Beacon Press, 1993

Tavris, Carol, *The Mismeasure of Woman: Why Women Are Not the Better Sex, the Inferior Sex, or the Opposite Sex,* New York: Simon and Schuster, 1992

Biological determinism is the concept that it is nature/biology (physiology, hormones, genes) that determines behavior differences, rather than nurture/culture (social and environmental influences). In the case of gender differences, biological determinism naturalizes, for example, an "essence" of femininity. Its critique questions the feasibility of isolating biology from interactions with nurture, pointing to the multiple ways in which culture influences what counts as nature, and what gets written as differently-gendered expectations.

As a medical doctor and a professor of both neurophysiology and women's studies, BLEIER challenges the simple assurances of biological determinism through her theoretically informed work, which shows a complex understanding of scientific and medical practices and their political ramifications. She argues that the ideas of biological determinism are most prevalent as explanations for inequality during periods of political, social, and economic upheaval. She shows the scientific flaws of sociobiology, the impossibility of separating biology from culture in brain development, the methodological and conceptual inadequacies of hormonal and brain lateralization studies, the problems with the "Man-the-Hunter" theory, the value of feminist anthropology, and the social construction of sexuality and its connection to the violent oppression of women. Finally she examines the promise of a feminist science that questions linear notions, binary assumptions, and traditional forms of power. This book has become a classic.

In an accessible, well-referenced book, FAUSTO-STERLING, a biologist trained in developmental genetics, rejects the validity of both biological and social determinism, discards the search for singular, fundamental causes, and, instead, argues for a robust analysis that appreciates the overlapping, multi-directional interactions between the biology of a being and its social environment. She argues that scientists, herself included, are cultural products, and that, as a result, certain blind spots appear in research design and interpretation. Her project is to examine other people's research, scientifically and politically, illuminating the unseen. Each chapter is a detailed inquisition of a multitude of claims about biological sex differences in brains, genes, hormones, and human evolution, based on scientific evidence. Updated with a chapter on brain anatomy and homosexuality, and an afterword that examines new information, this valuable book is considered a standard text by many.

SAYERS, working in psychology, engages the diverse literature on the nature-nurture debate helpfully, but perhaps too neatly. The first half presents historical and contemporaneous versions of the conservative, anti-feminist, "biology-is-destiny," scientific defense of sex differences in strength, reproduction, brain function, aggressiveness, and so on. She argues that such differences are not actually grounded in biological explanations, but in social considerations. The second half of the book claims that feminists are divided by two approaches to biology: social constructionism and biological essentialism. The former is an indirect argument stressing the mediated manner in which biology is interpreted and constructed; the latter is a direct argument for essential feminine characteristics, which need to be seen as strengths, but which, in patriarchy, are not valued. Sayers, instead, argues for a feminist recognition of biological, historical, and social contributions to the process of sexual inequality, along with a critique of social class and capitalism. While the thematic threads of this book remain very useful, the feminist theory is somewhat dated.

In a more current work, TAVRIS, a psychologist, addresses the popular debates about sex difference that spring from the confusion over whether women and men are "different but equal" or "the same," by asserting the basic premise that nothing about the nature of woman (or man) is essential or universal. She focuses her inquiry on the biological emphasis of male-as-normal and woman-as-inferior, which informs scientific examination, and underwrites the institutions and practices of daily life: law, medicine, social reforms, mental health, relationships, sexual practices, and so on. This comprehensive and helpful book is written in a style available to a general audience.

Looking through the triple filter of race, gender, and science, HARAWAY's work on the construction of nature provides a less direct, although no less important, critique of biological determinism, by its examination of the manner in which monkeys, apes, and, ultimately, all primates, inhabit the fluid border zones between nature and culture. Trained as a biologist and a philosopher of science, Haraway considers scientific practice as a form of rule-bound storytelling, where all evidence must be interpreted and all dualisms are suspect. Informed by genealogy, historical materialism, semiotics, discursive analysis, the practices of representation, and an active political awareness, she examines the consequences of the functions of sex, race, and class in the construction, limitation, and production of scientific knowledge and fact. This is an important, theoretically imposing book.

LEWONTIN, ROSE, and KAMIN, an evolutionary geneticist, a neurobiologist, and a psychologist, respond to their concern over the rise of the New Right in science—the advocacy of biological determinism and sociobiology—with a rigorous, yet readable challenge. They explore the roots of biological determinism systematically, examining its social uses and its scientific weaknesses. Offering an integrated dialectical understanding of the biological and the social, their major goal is to demonstrate the human and nonhuman flawed "world" that results from reductionism and biologism. Themes studied include: IQ presumptions, sex- and race-based ability, medicalization of political resistance, and modern sociobiology. However, they also take the discussion far enough to offer ways in which biology and psychology might work to provide a more emancipatory alternative.

In a useful collection of essays, HUBBARD, a biologist, turns her scientific eye toward the practices of science itself. She is interested in the subtle ways (institutional support, notions of objectivity, the limits of language) that political and social realities become part of biological or health descriptions. This work shares much with the critique of Lewontin, Rose, and Kamin, but Hubbard's focus is women's biology and health, specifically directed toward topics such as eugenics, evolution, and reproductive technologies. The book is divided into three parts: "How Do We Know?" "What Do We Know?" and "How Do We Use It?"

In a readable, sometimes humorous, historical approach, SCHIEBINGER explores how, in the seventeenth and eighteenth centuries, notions of gender influenced and shaped the structure, politics, descriptions, and classifications of European science. By presenting certain episodes, such as the sexualization of plants and animals, and the use of a secondary sex characteristic—the male beard—to differentiate races, she demonstrates how power relations affected the practices and priorities of science. She shows how scientists were affected by the equality notions of the Enlightenment in their search for natural biological, sex, and race differences that would, then, provide a natural basis for inequitable social conventions. The subchapter on sexual difference, and the three chapters on mammals, anatomy, and theories of gender and race may be of particular interest. The implications for modern scientific practices, and the search for biological foundations of difference today are clear.

In a different historical approach, OUDSHOORN argues that the sex/gender distinction (where sex means biological difference and gender means difference produced by socialization) does not defy the notion of a natural body; rather, it assumes biological sex difference exists, unproblematically, in a knowable body that has not changed through history. However, she argues, our perceptions of the body do change; they are mediated—often through the language of biomedical science. Her research focuses specifically on a major biological foundation of sex difference: the notion of the body as controlled by sex hormones. Using the materiality of discourse-building to investigate biomedical knowledge claims, Oudshoorn traces the scientific creation of the hormonal body, as it was informed by notions of sexual dualism and the dissonance between expectations and experimental results. Matters of sex difference are especially featured in the chapters entitled: "The Birth of Sex Hormones," "The Measuring of Sex Hormones," and "The Power of Structures That Already Exist." This is a fascinating and scholarly history of the hormonal body.

—CAROLYN DI PALMA

See also Gender as a Social Construct

Birth Control Movement

Chen, Constance M., *"The Sex Side of Life": Mary Ware Dennett's Pioneering Battle for Birth Control and Sex Education,* New York: New Press, 1996

Chesler, Ellen, *Woman of Valor: Margaret Sanger and the Birth Control Movement in America,* New York and London: Simon and Schuster, 1992

Gordon, Linda, *Woman's Body, Woman's Right: A Social History of Birth Control in America,* New York: Grossman, and Harmondsworth: Penguin, 1976

Kennedy, David M., *Birth Control in America: The Career of Margaret Sanger,* New Haven, Connecticut, and London: Yale University Press, 1970

McCann, Carole R., *Birth Control Politics in the United States, 1916–1945,* Ithaca, New York, and London: Cornell University Press, 1994

Reed, James, *From Private Vice to Public Virtue: The Birth Control Movement and American Society since 1830,* New York: Basic Books, 1978

Reynolds, Moira Davison, *Women Advocates of Reproductive Rights: Eleven Who Led the Struggle in the United States and Great Britain,* Jefferson, North Carolina, and London: McFarland, 1994

Since the 1970s, numerous social histories and individual biographies have been written about the birth control movement (primarily between 1916 and 1945). The texts overlap in useful ways and, in fact, each author provides a commentary on the strengths and problems with the earlier key texts. By reading the prefaces, especially the sections on previous studies, the reader will discern the complicated issues and perspectives surrounding the place of this movement for feminist history and social history.

GORDON represents the first social history of the American birth control movement; she provides a survey of the underlying ideas and motivations of the movement's adherents and opponents, from an explicitly (1970s) feminist point of view. Throughout, she argues that birth control has always been more a product of politics than of technological advancements or medical practices. Gordon presents the birth control movement as part of larger discussions of sexuality and women; she notes a change in emphasis and terminology—from "voluntary motherhood" to "birth control" to "planned parenthood"—as the movement progressed and the class and gender concerns of the constituents changed. Topics include the politics of reproduction (especially eugenic ideas about controlling reproduction), concerns about women's power, the movement as sexually and socially revolutionary, and the professionalization of birth control as it became family planning/planned parenthood. Gordon provides a useful overview of the movement as a whole and positions it within the context of American social history and feminist history.

McCANN also looks at the larger sociopolitical and cultural contexts that shaped and provided the meaning for much of the rhetoric underlying the birth control movement; she critically examines the language employed by the movement and by individuals within it. Specifically, she analyzes the ways in which Margaret Sanger drew on contemporary discourses of gender, race, and economics, particularly the shifting registers of meaning within early- to mid-century American political activity. She offers detailed discussions of the movement's rhetoric within several contexts: feminism, the medical profession, eugenics, and other national health care movements. McCann explains that by looking at the birth control movement in these contexts, we can see how other cultural debates and issues, as well as shifting alliances within the movement itself, caused the change in focus from feminist ideas about women's reproductive freedom to eugenic ideas about population quality and acceptable family values. McCann also outlines the chronology of events in the U.S. birth control movement.

REED provides a history of the birth control movement, not by looking at the movement as a large-scale social phenomenon as Gordon and McCann do, but by detailing the efforts of key individuals at various stages in the movement: Margaret Sanger's early crusades to establish clinics in the name of women's control over their bodies; Robert Dickinson's efforts to improve maternal health as well as his campaign to lobby physicians and organize medical research on reproduction; and Clarence Gamble's experiments in population control as an attempt to curtail the perceived over-fertility of poor women. Reed analyzes the differing methods, goals, and rationales used by each of these three individuals, including the conflicting ways each dealt with medical practitioners and changing concerns about population control and women's rights. Reed also extends his discussion into American efforts to establish worldwide birth control measures, particularly in less industrialized nations.

CHESLER focuses more fully on Margaret Sanger in her sympathetic biography of Sanger's public and private life; she draws on archival material collected by Sanger during her lifetime and by Sanger's friends and relatives, as well as correspondence between Sanger and acquaintances. She focuses on the difficulty of legitimizing birth control and issues of women's independence and power, explaining how the trajectory of Sanger's life was at least partially determined by other intellectual and political movements at the time. Chesler presents Sanger's personal and political concerns as central to the entire birth control movement; in fact, partially because of the nature of biography, Chesler positions Sanger as almost the sole determining factor in the direction, scope, and effectiveness of the movement (a position McCann and Gordon reinvestigate).

KENNEDY explores the relationship between Sanger's life and personality and the birth control movement as a whole. The focus is on her public career rather than her personal life; Kennedy outlines her efforts as well as governmental, institutional, and public responses to those efforts through World War II. Topics include nineteenth-century views of the family and feminism, Sanger's views of sexuality, feminism, and women's self-sufficiency, the biographical beginnings of the movement, debates about morality surrounding the movement, and interactions between the movement with the medical and legal establishments. This book is useful for its discussion of Sanger's leadership in the movement as well as for its discussion of the changing ideology of birth control, as publicly stated by Sanger, from a means of establishing the health and welfare of children to race- and class-based broad-ranging social programs.

REYNOLDS, as the title indicates, provides brief biographic accounts of women instrumental in the American and British birth control movements; she includes early twentieth-century American activists Emma Goldman, Mary Dennett, and Margaret Sanger as well as British activists Annie Besant and Marie Stopes, nineteenth-century American Fanny Wright, and contemporary American women such as Betty Friedan and Sarah Weddington. By presenting the key women involved in the movement in the context of other female reproductive rights activists, Reynolds considers the influences on, interconnections among, and lasting implications of the work of individuals within the birth control movement; her book is also useful since it provides some background on members of the movement besides Sanger.

CHEN presents a more extended biography of Mary Ware Dennett, a contemporary of Sanger and an advocate for both birth control and sex education; Chen explains the ways in which Dennett and Sanger clashed within the movement, particularly over the question of access to birth control information. According to Chen, Dennett was concerned with what she saw as a decline in sexual ethics and wanted to make contraceptive information and sex education available to all Americans regardless of class, gender, or profession; that is, she wanted the information disseminated broadly to all women rather than to male doctors who would then control its distribution to female patients. This text not only provides a view of the movement from a different angle than most of the other texts on the subject, but it also introduces two corresponding facets of the birth control movement: the battle for sex education and the fight to get beyond federal censorship for pamphlets detailing birth control information.

—KIMBERLY VanHOOSIER-CAREY

See also Reproductive Freedom

Bisexuality

Bisexual Anthology Collective, *Plural Desires: Writing Bisexual Women's Realities,* Toronto: Sister Vision, 1995

George, Sue, *Women and Bisexuality,* London: Scarlet, 1993

Hutchins, Loraine, and Lani Kaahumanu (eds.), *Bi Any Other Name: Bisexual People Speak Out,* Boston: Alyson, 1991

Rust, Paula C., *Bisexuality and the Challenge to Lesbian Politics: Sex, Loyalty, and Revolution,* New York: New York University Press, 1995

Tucker, Naomi (ed.), *Bisexual Politics: Theories, Queries, and Visions,* New York: Haworth, 1995

Weise, Elizabeth Reba (ed.), *Closer to Home: Bisexuality and Feminism,* Seattle, Washington: Seal Press, 1992

Despite increased academic interest in gay and lesbian lifestyles and culture over the past twenty years, bisexuality has remained a relatively unexplored area, which is just now beginning to receive serious critical attention. Several anthologies and two book-length studies examining the relationship among bisexuality, feminism, and lesbian politics have recently been published, providing visibility and voice to the growing bisexual feminist movement. GEORGE's book, which reports the findings of research based on approximately 150 bisexual women living in the United Kingdom, provides the best general overview of the subject to date. The first two chapters trace the construction of, and the confusion surrounding, bisexuality, and provide useful historical background on varying conceptions of female sexuality, homosexuality, and the role of the family. Particularly valuable are George's brief summaries of key texts concerning bisexuality. For example, in less than five pages, George concisely reviews and contextualizes Freud's contributions to understandings of bisexuality, and explains why, if one accepts Freud's conceptualization of the Oedipus complex, bisexuality appears more likely to occur in women. In a chapter on bisexuality and feminism, George reviews the various waves of feminism, and the exclusion of bisexuality from certain constructions of lesbianism and revolutionary feminism. The middle chapters of the book, which focus more closely on the views and experience of the women questioned, touch upon various aspects of bisexual living, from coming out to raising children. The last chapter explores the politics of bisexuality, and the need for the bisexual community to engage with wider political struggles. Overall, this book is an extremely useful introduction, offering readers clear and concise historical and theoretical background and personal perspectives.

RUST's work, by contrast, focuses more exclusively and comprehensively on the highly charged relationship between bisexual women and lesbians. Rust begins by tracing representations of bisexuality in a variety of gay and lesbian publications, analyzing the patterns of coverage, and the reasons why bisexuality emerged as an "issue" in the late 1980s to early 1990s. After concluding that bisexuality is an issue primarily of interest to lesbians, who view bisexuality as a threat to lesbian communities and politics, Rust's middle chapters compare and contrast lesbians' and bisexual women's perceptions of bisexuality, using findings from Rust's research of 470 lesbian and bisexual women. These chapters, and the 40 pages of charts provided in the appendix, present the most comprehensive statistical analysis available. In her last chapter, Rust questions whether the bisexual movement can find a home in the lesbian/gay movement, since by challenging a dichotomous gender-based definition of sexuality, bisexuals challenge the very essence of lesbianism.

Several anthologies designed to affirm bisexuality as a psychologically and politically viable identity category have recently appeared. HUTCHINS and KAAHUMANU's anthology is the first collection of bisexual voices to explore multiple aspects of bisexual experience. The first section, featuring more than 20 bisexual coming-out stories written by both women and men of varied races, ages, classes, and identities, challenges myths and stereotypes, while offering a number of competing visions and definitions of bisexuality. The remaining three sections of the anthology focus on "healing the splits" within individual bisexuals, and between bisexuals and exclusively heterosexual and homosexual communities. Although this anthology does not focus exclusively on women and bisexuality, more than half of the over 70 essays are written by bisexual women. Referred to as the "bi bible," this anthology remains unsurpassed in sheer diversity of voice, topic, and approach.

Another anthology, which, while not solely about women, does feature contributions mostly by bisexual women activists, and also maintains a strong feminist orientation, is TUCKER's work. This collection of essays focuses predominantly on the politics of bisexuality, and gives voice to competing visions and organizing strategies for the movement's future. Aside from several essays that challenge conventional formulations of identity politics, this anthology offers historical background on the bisexual movement, and a number of essays on the relationship among bisexuality, feminism, and lesbianism. What distinguishes this anthology from others like it is that many of the essays, while including personal experience, are not merely personal narratives; historical and theoretical contextualization helps establish connections between bisexual politics and other communities and movements.

WEISE's collection of essays by 22 bisexual women is the first book to focus exclusively on the relationship between bisexuality and feminism. The anthology maintains a comfortable balance between personal narratives and more theoretically-oriented explorations of bisexual-feminist identity and praxis. The often-strained relationship between bisexual women and the lesbian community is a recurring theme, as many of the essays work to counter lesbian perceptions of bisexuality as either merely a "phase" or a "cop-out" for women wishing to maintain heterosexual privilege. The notion that bisexual women are less committed to women's issues, since they continue to associate with men, is repeatedly challenged; instead, what emerges from this collection of disparate voices is an emphasis on the fluidity of sexuality, and a bisexual-feminist perspective that rejects attempts to dichotomize politics and desire.

The plurality of bisexual desire is creatively expressed and represented in the collection of essays and artwork published by THE BISEXUAL ANTHOLOGY COLLECTIVE. Poetry, short narratives, interviews, and cartoons by bisexual women are all featured in the anthology, which includes sections on defining bisexuality, forging a bisexual identity, and community politics and organizing. While focusing on a Canadian context, the anthology succeeds in representing the diversity of experience among bisexual women. The way in which bisexual identification intersects with, and makes an impact on, other facets of women's identity (such as race and class) is explored by several writers, as is the relationship between bisexual women and lesbians. This anthology is less theoretically and academically oriented than the previously mentioned anthologies, and tends to focus more on personal experience and creative expression. Helpful lists of bisexual organizations, resources, fiction, and non-fiction are included at the end of the book.

—SUSAN FELDMAN

Bishop, Elizabeth 1911–1979

American Writer

Goldensohn, Lorrie, *Elizabeth Bishop: The Biography of a Poetry,* New York: Columbia University Press, 1992
Harrison, Victoria, *Elizabeth Bishop's Poetics of Intimacy,* Cambridge and New York: Cambridge University Press, 1993
Kalstone, David, *Becoming a Poet: Elizabeth Bishop with Marianne Moore and Robert Lowell,* New York: Farrar, Straus and Giroux, and London: Hogarth, 1989
Lombardi, Marilyn May (ed.), *Elizabeth Bishop: The Geography of Gender,* Charlottesville: University Press of Virginia, 1993
McCabe, Susan, *Elizabeth Bishop: Her Poetics of Loss,* University Park: Pennsylvania State University Press, 1994
Parker, Robert Dale, *The Unbeliever: The Poetry of Elizabeth Bishop,* Urbana: University of Illinois Press, 1988
Schwartz, Lloyd, and Sybil Estes (eds.), *Elizabeth Bishop and Her Art,* Ann Arbor: University of Michigan Press, 1983

Elizabeth Bishop has finally begun to receive the serious critical consideration that she deserves. As these books indicate, Bishop is no longer seen as only a naturalist or a poet of impersonal, minute observation: she is now considered an important postmodern poet, whose work is informed by autobiography, gender issues, and sexual politics.

The collection of essays by SCHWARTZ and ESTES is an important contribution to the recent critical appreciation of Bishop as one of the major poetic voices of the twentieth century. The first part of the book comprises nine essays, that offer close readings of Bishop's work. The essays range from discussions of Bishop's metrics and versification to ambiguities of tone. The second section is a chronology of reviews, memoirs, and memorials, including pieces by Marianne Moore, Robert Lowell, Randall Jarrell, and James Merrill. These articles, often brief, nonetheless contain valuable literary and historical detail. The final section of the book is a chronological selection of Bishop's own "writings about writing." These colorful and self-revealing passages come from reviews, interviews, essays, and conversations. This book is an excellent introduction to understanding and appreciating Bishop's poetry.

PARKER's argument is that Bishop possessed the sense of anxiety and "unbelief in the self" that is found in much contemporary American poetry, but that her best work embraces that tension. Parker sees Bishop's oeuvre in three stages: poems of "wish" or longing; poems of "where," in response to the present; and poems of "retrospect." His approach is chronological, and his readings of Bishop's work proceed largely through comparisons with Emily Dickinson, Walt Whitman, Lowell, Robert Frost, and Wallace Stevens. Parker's essay is particularly useful in placing Bishop in context with her contemporaries.

KALSTONE is one of the most important critics of Bishop's work. This book expands his discussion of Bishop in an earlier work, *Five Temperaments* (1977); here he emphasizes more thoroughly the links between Bishop's personal life and her work. The first half of Kalstone's book is a discussion of Bishop's personal and poetic relationship with Marianne Moore. Moore was a valuable mentor to Bishop, but Bishop eventually had to move beyond Moore's influence to find her own voice. In the second half of the book, Kalstone focuses on Bishop's later relationship with friend, confidant, and fellow poet Robert Lowell; like Moore, Lowell could be both helpful and constraining. Kalstone provides a clear understanding of how Bishop assimilated and departed from these influences in establishing her own poetics.

GOLDENSOHN claims that although Bishop's work seems reticent, particularly in contrast to the self-display of her contemporaries, the confessional poets, it gradually came to include more of the directly personal. Goldensohn examines Bishop's poetry, stories, and letters; she also makes considerable use of the unpublished papers, using biography to illuminate the poetry. Bishop is generally not considered a love poet, but Goldensohn emphasizes this side of her work, providing close readings of some of the erotic works unpublished in the poet's lifetime, especially the poem, "It Is Marvelous to Wake up Together." Goldensohn discusses how Bishop's ambivalence towards her homosexuality and her relationships both informed and were disguised in her poetry. This ambivalence, which Goldensohn sees as originating in the inherent sadness of Bishop's childhood, was also seen in her attitudes to gender roles and race.

Like Goldensohn, HARRISON's book explores Bishop's unpublished writings, as well as her published work: memoirs, journals, travel pieces, letters, unfinished poems, notebooks, and drafts. In exploring this archival material, Harrison is particularly attentive to the process of Bishop's writing. Grounded in pragmatic, postmodern, and feminist theories, Harrison's book analyzes Bishop's poetry and prose as intimate but not confessional, and daily but not prosaic.

LOMBARDI's book is an excellent, wide-ranging collection of essays based on current feminist critical theory, which explore the "psychosexual tensions" in Bishop's work. Eight of the eleven essays were published previously in various books and journals, and the contributors form an impressive list of Bishop scholars. Central to the collection is Lee Edelman's essay, "The Geography of Gender: Elizabeth Bishop's 'In the Waiting Room,'" which has become a seminal essay for the consideration of gender issues in Bishop's poetry. Common to all of the essays is the point that "Bishop's gender plays a significant role in the questioning of aesthetic, ethical, and sexual boundaries that constitutes so much a part of her poetic practice." These essays discuss the ways in which Bishop's poetry challenges our prior assumptions about "women's poetry."

McCABE's aim is to show how Bishop's work reflects both her postmodernism and her feminism. The theme informing McCabe's study, as her title suggests, is how Bishop's personal experience of loss determined her poetics. Her close explications of Bishop's poetry and prose are informed by psychoanalytic theory; Bishop's sense of personal and primal loss, McCabe argues, leads to poems that are often evasive, unstable, and unsettled. The fluid and arbitrary nature that permeates Bishop's work, according to McCabe, is in keeping with feminine notions of self. McCabe concludes that Bishop is a major poet of our times, partly for her openness to ambiguity.

—JO ELDRIDGE CARNEY

Black Activism *see* Apartheid; Black Woman's Club Movement; Black Women; Race/Ethnicity and Gender; Slavery, Black

Black Woman's Club Movement

Davis, Angela Y., *Women, Race and Class,* New York: Random House, 1981; London: Women's Press, 1982

Davis, Elizabeth Lindsay, *Lifting As They Climb,* Washington, D.C.: National Association of Colored Women, 1933

Jones, Beverly Washington, *Quest for Equality: The Life and Writings of Mary Eliza Church Terrell, 1863–1954,* Brooklyn, New York: Carlson, 1990

Hine, Darlene Clark, Wilma King, and Linda Reed, *"We Specialize in the Wholly Impossible": A Reader in Black Women's History,* Brooklyn, New York: Carlson, 1995

Neverdon-Morton, Cynthia, *Afro-American Women of the South and the Advancement of the Race, 1895–1925,* Knoxville: University of Tennessee Press, 1989

Salem, Dorothy, *To Better Our World: Black Women in Organized Reform, 1890–1920,* Brooklyn, New York: Carlson, 1990

In the nineteenth century, a black woman's club movement began in the United States on both local and national levels. However, the impetus behind this movement has been a matter of debate. Stephanie Shaw's essay in HINE, KING, and REED contends that the impetus toward national organization can be found in the traditional values and relationships within the black community. Shaw points out that ideas of self-help and racial uplift were always a part of black women's activism, but the way in which this activism would be manifested changed over time.

Angela DAVIS provides an analysis of race, class, and gender in the black woman's club movement. She locates the origin of black women's organizational experiences in their pre-Civil War participation in literary and benevolent societies, particularly in their antislavery activities. Davis notes that, for the leadership of black and white woman's clubs at the turn of the century, racism in American society was a more critical concern than gender solidarity. However, while common experiences with racism tended to link middle-class black women to their working-class sisters, Davis notes the elitism of the black woman's clubs.

SALEM's book provides a valuable resource for examining the involvement of African-American women in the reforms of the late nineteenth and early twentieth centuries. She examines how and why the black woman's club movement developed during this era of reform. She explores the role of black woman's clubs and organizations in dealing with problems concerning the health, housing, education, and working conditions in their communities and identifies three stages in the development of African-American women's organizational efforts. Salem connects the earliest clubs to national issues such as temperance and suffrage and theorizes that black women developed their own national organization after they were rejected by the national organization for white women.

Elizabeth DAVIS's book was the first description of the founding of the National Association of Colored Women (NACW) and includes notes of past meetings, lists of officers and members, and accounts of the struggles, ambitions, and achievements of the organization. Davis also includes histories of NACW conferences between 1895 and 1930, and biographical sketches of key individuals in the organization's early history. Davis's work is an invaluable resource for chronicling the early years of the woman's club movement on the national level.

Mary Church Terrell, the first president of the NACW, was instrumental in establishing the direction the organization would take in its early years. In her biography of Mary Church Terrell, JONES suggests that Terrell's vision of the organization was both radical and conservative—radical in that the NACW would be controlled by black women, and conservative in that it reinforced the traditional roles of women within households. Jones examines Terrell's leadership style and the strategies and tactics she used to implement these goals. Selections from Terrell's writings are included in the second half of this book.

NEVERDON-MORTON is concerned with the development and activities of woman's clubs in the South and how these organizations worked within their communities and within the national club movement. She also examines instances of interracial cooperation between woman's clubs and the involvement of the leaders of black woman's clubs in other African-American organizations. She notes that in many cases men led the organizations while women implemented the programs. Combined with other regional studies, Neverdon-Morton's book presents a more localized picture of the woman's club movement.

—BEVERLY GREENE BOND

See also Woman's Club Movement

Black Women

Bell-Scott, Patricia (ed.), *Double Stitch: Black Women Write about Mothers and Daughters*, Boston: Beacon Press, 1991

Collins, Patricia Hill, *Black Feminist Thought: Knowledge, Consciousness and the Politics of Empowerment*, Boston: Unwin Hyman, and London: HarperCollins, 1990

Davis, Angela Y., *Women, Race and Class*, New York: Random House, 1981; London: Women's Press, 1982

hooks, bell, *Feminist Theory: From Margin to Center*, Boston: South End, 1984

Jones, Jacqueline, *Labor of Love, Labor of Sorrow: Black Women, Work, and the Family from Slavery to the Present*, New York: Basic Books, 1985

Steady, Filomina Chioma (ed.), *The Black Woman Cross-Culturally*, Cambridge, Massachusetts: Schenkman, 1981

The works cited here provide only a representative sampling of the impressive and growing body of scholarship on black women. DAVIS, one of the first to provide a comprehensive historical study of black women in the United States, examines black women's lives from slavery to World War II, with particular emphasis on the Southern antebellum and reconstruction periods. Davis covers abolition, suffrage, the club movement, and the campaign for reproductive rights in the United States. Davis is best known for her pioneering and probing investigation of racism in the feminist movement, in particular the campaign for suffrage at the turn of the century. Particularly insightful are her discussions on nineteenth-century white women's resistance to black male suffrage, and the current myth of the black rapist, expressed in some of the leading 1970s feminist writings. Written from a socialist perspective, Davis's work is also important for its argument that class must be included in an analysis of women's oppression, black and white. With her emphasis on political and social movements, Davis, however, provides only brief commentary on the personal dimensions of black women's lives, family, mothering, sexuality, and friendships.

No bibliography of black women would be complete without reference to HOOKS, who has authored many books on the subject of black women. Arguably her most influential work *Feminist Theory: From Margin to Center* explores black women's relationship to the contemporary feminist movement. Hooks argues that 1970s feminism was fashioned from the life experiences of privileged white women, and as such alienated most black women, who did not identify with the standpoint and agenda of the feminist platform. Particularly problematic for black women, hooks emphasizes, was the belief that male dominance caused women's oppression, and that this oppression was most keenly felt in the family unit. Hooks maintains that for black women, black men are more often comrades in the fight against racist oppression, and that the family is, as she describes it in a later book, a site of resistance. Particularly good are the chapters on sisterhood, men, and parenting. While the book has become somewhat dated, it nonetheless provides an informative overview of feminism and black women, and serves to remind us of the need to achieve and maintain inclusiveness in feminism.

Regarded by many as the best social history of black women in the United States, JONES's book provides an exceptionally thorough and detailed study of black women, work, and family from slavery to the present. In her nuanced explication of slavery, Reconstruction, the northern migration, the Depression, World War II, and the civil rights movement, Jones conveys the complexity, richness, and diversity of black women's lives. Particularly good are the photographs, extensive explanatory notes, bibliography, and index the book provides. More scholarly than the hooks and Davis books, Jones's work is nonetheless exceptionally readable and inspiring in the truths it imparts.

Many of the themes covered in the above works are explored from a global perspective in STEADY's extensive and lengthy edited collection. Divided into four sections: Africa, the United States, the Caribbean, and South America, the book covers topics as diverse as women's political participation in Nigeria, African women as entrepreneurs, images of black women in African-American poetry, women's roles in West Indian society, and the spread of capitalism in rural Colombia. Particularly good is Steady's introduction to the collection, where she identifies the unifying themes of the volume. These themes include the commonality of an African heritage, black women's shared experience of economic exploitation and marginalization, the self reliance and strength of black women, and the specific experience of feminism for black women, which is founded on the centrality and importance of motherhood in black culture. Though at times the volume seems quite dated, no other collection published since provides the same scope of inquiry. In this, the volume remains an essential introductory text to black women cross-culturally.

While the previous studies take a sociological perspective in their concern with black women's social, economic, and political oppression and resistance, COLLINS provides a theoretical study of what she calls black feminist thought, an independent, yet subjugated knowledge of black women's subordination. Drawing on the writings of African-American female scholars and activists, Collins identifies the essential themes that compromise the black female standpoint. Themes discussed include family, motherhood, activism, and sexual politics. The goal of the book, in Collins's words, is to "reclaim the black feminist intellectual tradition." Particularly important is Collins's study of black motherhood, where she argues that there exists a unique Afrocentric meaning and experience of mothering. Also important is her discussion of the "controlling images" of black womanhood.

The articles, stories, and poems contained in BELL-SCOTT's collection give voice to the unique experience of black mother and daughter relationships. Readers of African-American women's writing have long observed a deeply rooted matrilineal tradition in the lives of black women, whereby the daughter gains authority and authenticity through identification and connection with the mother and her motherline. The contributors include many of the best known black female writers and scholars: Karla Holloway, Sonia Sanchez, Gloria Joseph, Patricia Hill Collins, June Jordan, bell hooks, and Alice Walker. The volume is an essential contribution to the study of black women, in its comprehensive examination of a central and defining feature of black women's lives—namely the mother-daughter relationship—and in its insistence that there exists a distinct kind of black mothering that is empowering to both mothers and daughters, and that differs from that of the dominant white culture.

—ANDREA O'REILLY

Blackwell, Elizabeth 1821–1910

American Physician

Hays, Elinor Rice, *Those Extraordinary Blackwells: The Story of a Journey to a Better World*, New York: Harcourt Brace, 1967

Johnston, Malcolm Sanders, *Elizabeth Blackwell and Her Alma Mater: The Story in the Documents*, Geneva, New York: W. F. Humphrey, 1947

Ross, Ishbel, *Child of Destiny: The Life Story of the First Woman Doctor*, New York: Harper, 1949; London: Gollancz, 1950

Sahli, Nancy Ann, *Elizabeth Blackwell, M.D. (1821–1910): A Biography*, Philadelphia: University of Pennsylvania Press, 1974

Wilson, Dorothy C., *Lone Woman: The Story of Elizabeth Blackwell, the First Woman Doctor*, Boston: Little Brown, and London: Hodder and Staughton, 1970

Wright, Mary, *Elizabeth Blackwell of Bristol: The First Woman Doctor*, Bristol: Bristol Branch of the Historical Association, 1995

Elizabeth Blackwell is widely credited as "the first female doctor." In fact, women have served as doctors and healers from time immemorial. Blackwell's real accomplishment is having been the first woman to break through the previously male bastions of professionalism that had arisen in order to exclude women from medical practice, by insisting upon certain credentials and a diploma from medical schools that excluded women. Blackwell not only opened the doors to these institutions, she furthered the medical education of women by founding a women's hospital where women could train, and a women's medical college that certified women doctors.

Blackwell's life has not been considered in light of newer feminist criticism, although books exist that deal with her life in the context of the women's movement and other prominent women's movements of the time—the temperance and antislavery movements. However, to date, the biographies of Blackwell emphasize her struggle and sacrifice without examining the historical contexts of medicine and the ways in which women had been deliberately excluded by the professionalization of medicine.

HAYS provides a general background of Elizabeth Blackwell's family and the social context in which they lived. This work is a biography of the entire family of five sisters and two brothers. Emily, a sister who was five years younger than Elizabeth, followed in her sister's footsteps and became a doctor. The two brothers married important and famous suffragists, Lucy Stone and Antoinette Brown, the latter being the first woman to become an ordained minister. The book is very detailed and contains a great deal of social history and many illustrations. It has a thorough index and bibliography.

The biography by WILSON focuses exclusively on Blackwell. Wilson uses dialogue and imagined conversations between the characters. She provides an interesting historical background about the role of women in medicine throughout the ages. Wilson's overview demonstrates quite clearly that women were doctors all through the classical and medieval ages, but she does not go on to speculate about what might have happened to displace women from this profession. She also provides much useful detail about the practice of medicine in Blackwell's time, and about Blackwell's emphasis on prevention through better hygiene. Wilson portrays Blackwell's career as a noble sacrifice, suggesting that she would have liked to marry but could not imagine how she could combine marriage and medicine. The author indicates that medicine was a "higher" calling, and she goes to some length to emphasize the choice as a "struggle." The book contains an extensive bibliography and index.

ROSS provides a perceptive and interesting book that speculates more fully on Blackwell's motivations and psychology. For example, Ross grapples extensively with the problem of Blackwell's decision to become a doctor and forgo the more traditional path of wife and mother. Ross sees this conflict as a serious crisis in Blackwell's life and quotes from Blackwell's diary in which she describes how attracted she felt toward men in general and one in particular, and that she embraced the idea of a medical degree as a way of placing "an insuperable barrier between myself and those disturbing influences." Ross speculates on what this might have meant and its implications for Blackwell's determination to follow another path. This book, too, contains an extensive bibliography and index.

Wright and Johnston's books were written primarily to celebrate the importance of Bristol, England, where Blackwell was born, and Geneva, New York, where she attended medical school. WRIGHT wrote her book for the Bristol Branch of the Historical Association and provides a few facts that relate to Blackwell's importance in English history. For example, Blackwell was the first woman to have her name on the British Medical Register. Wright briefly discusses Blackwell's career in the United States and then continues with her career in England, where she lived until the end of her life. In 1870 she set up a private practice in London and helped Elizabeth Garrett, a young Englishwoman, become a doctor. In 1871 she founded the National Health Society, whose motto was "Prevention is Better than Cure."

JOHNSTON's book was written to celebrate the history of Geneva, New York, and the community's pioneering spirit. Johnston believes that it was "inevitable" that Blackwell would have been admitted to Geneva College when no other medical school would consider enrolling a woman. He quotes extensively from her autobiographical writings and refutes what he feels does not support his thesis concerning the unusual pioneering spirit of Geneva. For example, when he discusses whether Blackwell was admitted to the college as a "hoax," as Blackwell herself suggests in her writings, Johnston postulates that the administrators knew exactly what they were doing when they proposed to the other students that they must decide whether to admit her. The administrators wanted her admitted but would not have wanted her subjected to any unpleasantness had the male students objected. The "hoax," if there was one, was therefore played by the administration on the students and not the other way around. The book is an interesting account of her school days in Geneva but is biased toward displaying Geneva College in the best light.

Finally, there is SAHLI's work on Elizabeth Blackwell. This book, originally written in 1974 for Sahli's doctorate in history from the University of Pennsylvania, is the most thorough study available, with an extremely long and comprehensive bibliography of both primary and secondary sources.

—ROBIN S. LENT

Blavatsky, Helena Petrovna 1831–1891

Russian Spiritualist

Barborka, Geoffrey A., *H.P. Blavatsky, Tibet and Tulku*, Madras, India: Theosophical Publishing House, 1966

Cranston, Sylvia, *HPB: The Extraordinary Life and Influence of Helena Blavatsky, Founder of the Modern Theosophical Movement*, New York: Putnam, 1993

Meade, Marion, *Madame Blavatsky: The Woman Behind the Myth*, New York: Putnam, 1980

Murphet, Howard, *When Daylight Comes: A Biography of Helena Petrovna Blavatsky*, Wheaton, Illinois: Theosophical Publishing House, 1975

Ryan, Charles J., *H.P. Blavatsky and the Theosophical Movement: A Brief Historical Sketch*, Wheaton, Illinois: Theosophical Publishing House, 1975

Helena Petrovna Blavatsky was born in the Ukraine in 1831 and manifested a variety of extraordinary psychic abilities from an early age. Her adventures took her all over the world during the nineteenth century, always traveling in search of "higher knowledge." She is best known for having been a founder of the Theosophical Society, an organization devoted to the development of higher consciousness. A brilliant woman with little formal education, she was a master of many languages, and her psychic powers and enigmatic personality contributed to a shroud of mystery surrounding her work. While some attempted to vilify her as a charlatan and a fraud, others treated her like a saint who deserved a devout following. Neither of these extremes captures the truth about this strong-willed Russian mystic.

There are several well-written sources on Madame Blavatsky. They range from those written by members of the Theosophical Society who tended to be uncritical, to those that attempted to discredit the psychic phenomena attributed to her. Few works probe beneath the surface in order to understand the woman and the time in which she lived. Most sources have a difficult time analyzing the great complexity of this extraordinary woman.

One of the most widely read biographies, by RYAN, is not an objective treatment of the life of Madame Blavatsky. The author was an active member of the Theosophical Society, and he treats her as a "sower of the messianic seed for the coming Aquarian age." He dismisses charges that she was a charlatan and places great emphasis on her important role as a bridge between East and West. Although Ryan's book is not a definitive biography, it is a valuable source on the history of the Theosophical movement.

BARBORKA's volume describes Madame Blavatsky's spiritual accomplishments. Most of it is devoted to examining the powerful psychic phenomena manifested by Madame Blavatsky. The author connects these events to the Tibetan tradition of spiritual masters who were her influential teachers. Even though it is not really a biography, this book is valuable because it uses sources not found in other works, particularly correspondences with members of Madame Blavatsky's Russian family. Barborka places the Russian mystic in the context of Tibetan religion, stressing how she wrote her spiritual treatises as a medium in contact with a higher plane—through divine dictation, clairvoyance, or instructions from spirits.

MURPHET has written one of the best biographies of Blavatsky. He describes her early life in great detail. From a young age Helena Blavatsky displayed strong mystical tendencies. The author describes invisible playmates in childhood, an early marriage which she refused to consummate, an encounter with a mysterious Indian prince, and her extensive journeys throughout the world in search of the "philosopher's stone." Murphet draws attention to a very important event, Madame Blavatsky's meeting with Henry Olcott in Vermont, and their eventual partnership as co-founders of the Theosophical Society. The author examines the assertion of a report from the Society for Psychic Research (1885) that Madame Blavatsky's telepathic manifestations and materialization of objects were fraudulent. He rationalizes these attacks on her integrity by asserting that Madame Blavatsky threatened the materialism of the scientific community in the nineteenth century.

A more critical biography is the one by MEADE, who doubts the claims by Madame Blavatsky that she was a virgin despite two husbands, a child, and numerous lovers. The author of this book perceives the Russian mystic as an eccentric whose attempt to change the world was a failure. According to her, Theosophy did not change western materialism; it had virtually no significant effect. Despite this skepticism, Meade gives Madame Blavatsky credit for inspiring Hindus like Mohandas Gandhi to rediscover the richness of their own heritage. Also, the author points out the important influence of Madame Blavatsky on European literary figures like William Butler Yeats, James Joyce, and the "Irish Renaissance." Meade's biography is quite ambivalent. While at one level she distrusts Madame Blavatsky, at another she admires her great strength of character, describing her as being "larger than life."

The most up-to-date biography of Madame Blavatsky is by CRANSTON. This is the best overall source. The author presents a relatively unbiased and elaborate treatment of this complex and brilliant woman. Especially important is a final section with several chapters concerned with cosmic consciousness today. Cranston notes a 1986 apology by the Society for Psychic Research, for having unjustly condemned Madame Blavatsky in 1885 based on erroneous evidence. The author asserts that Blavatsky never claimed that the spiritual teachings she shared with her devotees were her own. Particularly important in this book is information about the many influences Madame Blavatsky had on the twentieth century. She inspired Jack London, E.M. Forster, D.H. Lawrence, T.S. Eliot, Thornton Wilder, Paul Gauguin, L. Frank Baum, Gustav Mahler, Jean Sibelius, Alexander Scriabin, Sigmund Freud, Carl Jung, and Joseph Campbell. She was one of the first to criticize Charles Darwin for omitting "consciousness" from his theory of evolution. Her books have been translated into all the world's languages. They were banned in both czarist and Communist Russia, where they are widely read today. Madame Blavatsky predicted the whole field of atomic science. She had enormous influence on the philosophical and scientific worlds of her time. Albert Einstein is reported to have kept a copy of her magnum opus *The Secret Doctrine* on his desk.

As the years pass Madame Blavatsky has become increasingly more relevant. She has been called the "Mother of the New Age." Her work is well known throughout the emerging worldwide community of seekers after higher consciousness and alternative life styles. The controversies surrounding her psychic powers are less interesting than her overall contribution to raising human consciousness to higher levels. She is one of the most interesting and controversial women of the nineteenth century. After her death in 1891 at the age of sixty, Madame Blavatsky has become what she predicted about herself—an influential figure more accepted in the twentieth century than in her own time.

—JAMES J. PRESTON

Bly, Nellie 1867–1922

American Journalist

Davidson, Sue, *Getting the Real Story: Nellie Bly and Ida B. Wells*, Seattle, Washington: Seal, 1992

Kroeger, Brooke, *Nellie Bly: Daredevil, Reporter, Feminist*, New York: Times Books, 1994

Marks, Jason, *Around the World in 72 Days: The Race between Pulitzer's Nellie Bly and "Cosmopolitan's" Elizabeth Bisland*, New York: Gemittarius Press, 1993

Nellie Bly (Elizabeth Seaman), the first and best of the gutsy late nineteenth-century journalists known as "girl stunt reporters," exposed the oppression of poor women and children in urban America and, at the same time, helped to move women's writing from the fashion section to the front page. Since her death in 1922, however, her sensational reporting career has attracted more attention from writers of juvenile literature than serious scholars. Only recently have more in-depth studies become available. Although the scores of young-adult books on Bly have fictionalized her life and simplified the more complicated aspects of her career, their authors deserve credit for keeping her fascinating story from being entirely forgotten.

DAVIDSON's book echoes the tone and content of other Bly books designed for young adults. Inventing dialogue and imagining scenes based on the known facts about Bly, Davidson chronicles both the high and low points of Bly's eventful career, beginning with her first job at the Pittsburgh *Dispatch*, and detailing her spectacular success writing for Joseph Pulitzer's New York *World.* Davidson portrays Bly as an ambitious, plucky young woman, imbued with a passion for social justice, suggesting strong parallels to the other reporter featured in the book, African-American anti-lynching crusader Ida B. Wells. Yet, as Davidson's introduction points out, the juxtaposition of these two women—one white, one black—also highlights how their racial identity shaped their writings.

Two recent authors have moved Bly studies beyond the juvenile literature market, offering adult readers a more nuanced and historically accurate view of her life and work. KROEGER, the first biographer determined to search beyond easily accessible, but often inaccurate, published descriptions of Bly's life, draws not only from all of Bly's voluminous writings, but also from contemporary magazine reports, census records, county and family histories, and court records and transcripts. She tells the stories behind Bly's best-known "stunts," from her first break into big city journalism—having herself committed to an insane asylum to write an exposé—to her most ambitious stunt—racing around the world faster than Jules Verne's fictional hero, Phineas Fogg.

At the same time, Kroeger relates Bly's achievements to the changing newspaper world, and the changing place of women within that world. She also uncovers details that Bly's public persona sought to obscure or downplay; for instance, she provides a context for Bly's idealized descriptions of her father (a county judge) by noting that as a teenager, Bly testified in court to help her mother obtain a divorce from the man she had married after Bly's father died. As Bly reported on the witness stand, her alcoholic stepfather had physically and verbally abused her mother. Kroeger's work stands alone as the only carefully documented book-length study of Bly. A thorough and suggestive study, it is accessible to general readers, but will also prove useful to scholars interested in giving Bly's career the sustained critical attention it warrants.

MARKS focuses on Bly's much-publicized race around the world in 1889, comparing her to Elizabeth Bisland, the challenger from a rival publication who almost—but not quite—beat Bly to the finish line. Marks retells the story of their very different trips around the world in a fictionalized account written for adult readers. Despite its embellishment of the known facts, the book creates a gripping, historically detailed narrative that offers considerable insight into Bly's most famous newspaper stunt. Quoting liberally from both Bly and Bisland's published reports, Marks explores the strengths and the weaknesses of Bly's journalistic style. He praises her attention to detail, while refusing to gloss over her often-racist reactions to the foreigners she encountered in her hasty travels. While readers more interested in Bly than her challenger may find themselves frustrated by Marks's obvious preference for Bisland's more genteel, sophisticated style, this book draws the most complete picture available of Bly's globe-trotting journey, other than Bly's own account.

—JEAN MARIE LUTES

Boadecia d. 62

British Warrior Queen

Cassius Dio, *Dio's Roman History,* translated by Earnest Cary, New York: Putnam, and London: Heinemann, 1914

Dudley, Donald R., and Graham Webster, *The Rebellion of Boudicca,* New York: Barnes and Noble, and London: Routledge, 1962

Fraser, Antonia, *The Warrior Queens,* London: Weidenfeld and Nicolson, 1988; New York: Knopf, 1989

Gildas, *The Ruin of Britain and Other Works,* edited and translated by Michael Winterbottom, London: Phillimore, and Totowa, New Jersey: Rowman and Littlefield, 1978

Spence, Lewis, *Boadicea: Warrior Queen of the Britons,* London: Hale, 1937

Tacitus, *The Agricola and the Germania,* translated by H. Mattingly, New York and London: Penguin, 1970

Webster, Graham, *Boudica: The British Revolt against Rome, AD 60,* Totowa, New Jersey: Rowman and Littlefield, and London: Batsford, 1978

Boadicea (also Boudicca, Bundicca, and Voadicea) is famous for leading the A.D. 60 rebellion that nearly defeated Roman rule in Britain. Accounts of her crusade can be found in the later histories of Raphael Holinshed, Hector Boece, and Polydore Virgil, while poetic interpretations of her performance appear in the works of Edmund Spenser, John Milton, Alfred, Lord Tennyson, and William Cowper. But all these interpretations and emendations, resulting in the accumulated body of research about her, acknowledge their debt to the primary Roman historical sources of Dio, Tacitus, and Gildas. Recently, more archaeological evidence has been brought to the fore regarding Boadicea and her tribe, the Iceni, and has allowed a more precise historical perspective.

Written around A.D. 540, most likely from South Wales, GILDAS's perspective is proudly and unwaveringly Roman, and as a result, his brief portrait of Boadicea is rather unsympathetic. For him, she exemplifies the social, cultural, and political decay of the age, and through his staunch didacticism he condemns her for what he believes is hubris, her overweening pride that refused to submit to the proper authority. While he does moralize about certain sins of the Roman population, he mostly credits them for trying to instill peace, and better the general quality of life through industry, markets, and agriculture. He speaks in biblical allegories about the obstinate and "treacherous lioness" that disturbed the fold, and promises a just reward for those who obey the will of the Romans, and therefore the will of God.

While CASSIUS DIO, like Gildas, is patriotically Roman, he seems caught up in the creation of myth, rather than the creation of a moral fable. In dramatic style, he censures both parties, the profligate Romans as well as the pagans who were susceptible at the hands of Boadicea. In order to show the "greatest shame" and ruin that was brought on by a woman, he devotes a great deal of time to the explication of her character. He is also the first to mention her name, her chariot, her lengthy speech, her dress, and her invocations to the goddess Andraste/Andarte, as well as the prophetic rabbit she pulled from the folds of her skirt. Through her own words, Cassius Dio also seems to enjoy parodying a certain Roman effeminacy, which includes wines and oils, and "sleeping with boys." Boadicea mocks Nero as a lyre-playing woman and then calls him Mistress Domitia. As did Milton for his Satan, Cassius Dio seems to want to display her eloquence for both its power and its inherent danger.

Since the purpose of TACITUS's Agricola is to eulogize his father-in-law, a Roman general in occupied Britain, his view of Boadicea is, like Gildas's and Cassius's, highly critical. When he does attribute strength to her, it is only to show, by contrast, how pathetic Roman rule (specifically Nero's) was, as well as to highlight the officious abilities of Agricola in restoring order in A.D. 78. As for the Boadicea narrative, it is brief, but telling. Tacitus quickly informs us of her royal origins, as well as of her savagery in battle. Her rousing speech is put in the mouth of a male, Calgacus, but this most likely serves as the incarnation of the theory that her daughters, not mentioned in Gildas or Cassius, were violated by Roman soldiers.

Later works have built upon these classical writings. Although SPENCE's account of Boadicea appears somewhat dated, its depth of scholarship remains impressive and relevant. Written when modern archaeological evidence was beginning to illuminate the subject, Spence attaches archaeological speculation to interpretations from classical narrative. The strength of his book lies in the background information it provides on prehistoric Britain, Iceni's lands, and the industries of its people, as well as the genealogical origins of the Iceni. Spence has also charted the progress of the Roman conquest of Britain, including a thorough catalogue of early Roman leaders, the first relationships between the Romans and the Iceni, and the ultimate Roman abuses that precipitated the revolt. He establishes the relationship between the influential Boadicea and her people, the violent revolt itself, and its disastrous outcomes. Spence theorizes about the various motivational psychologies of all involved parties.

Since WEBSTER had the advantage of at least four more decades of archaeological discoveries, his book is able to exert a more concentrated focus on the new information yielded about the specific locale of Icenia and its people through coins, pottery, and reconstruction of military forts. But Webster spends less time expositing the entire history of the life and people of Romano-Britain, as well as the classical narratives, and simply begins in 54 B.C. with the first of the invasions. Webster discusses times of relative peace that existed between 54 B.C. and A.D. 43, and the post-Augustus policies and trade that exploited the Britons. Webster elucidates the events surrounding A.D. 43—the accession of Nero, the new conquests, and the raids—that finally enraged the Britons. Webster gives solid information as to subsequent military maneuvers and routes, both Roman and Briton, that followed, including battles, as well as the destruction of several cities and temples. Oddly enough, Webster's final glimpse at Boadicea is deconstructive, and reduces her to a pawn, or "figurehead," of the religious/political fanaticism of the Druids.

DUDLEY and WEBSTER, literary scholar and historian respectively, combine their efforts to present a comprehensive portrait of Boadicea. In many ways, it seems like the rough draft for the book that Webster would publish by himself after Dudley's death, except for the compelling literary explication of the histories and myths of Boadicea that accompanies the wealth of archaeological evidence. Dudley discusses the evolution of Boadicea's image through historical narrative, poetry, and drama, from Hector Boece's Scottish history in 1536, to the analogous incarnations of Queen Elizabeth in Spenser's *Faerie Queene*, to the iconography of her statue on the Thames.

In her evocative study of feminism and patriotism, FRASER's book extricates Boadicea from the encumbrances of archaeological evidence for those who are more interested in the images, themes, and mythical incarnations of the archetypal "warrior queen." Using the name "Boudicca" to represent the historic woman and "Boadicea" to represent the various incarnations through literature and myth, Fraser first points to a duality: on the one hand the queen is sentimentalized as a brave warrior and fearless fighter, while on the other she is vilified as a vicious and dangerous woman. Then, Fraser contextualizes Boudicca/Boadicea in terms of other warrior queens (Judith, Zenobia, Maud, Tamara, Rani of Jhansi, and Jinga of Angola, among others), and reveals how historic patterns and mythic incarnations repeat themselves. As her name means "victory" and her image is one of power, she has often been appropriated by female leaders throughout history.

—ANNMARIE PHILLIPS

Body Image

Bordo, Susan, *Unbearable Weight: Feminism, Western Culture, and the Body,* Berkeley and London: University of California Press, 1993

Brownell, Kelly, and Christopher Fairburn (eds.), *Eating Disorders and Obesity: A Comprehensive Handbook,* New York: Guilford Press, 1995

Fallon, Patricia, Melanie Katzman, and Susan Wooley (eds.), *Feminist Perspectives on Eating Disorders,* New York: Guilford Press, 1994

Fisher, Seymour, *Development and Structure of the Body Image,* vol.1, Hillside, New Jersey and London: Lawrence Erlbaum Associates, 1986

Hesse-Biber, Sharlene, *Am I Thin Enough Yet? The Cult of Thinness and the Commercialization of Identity,* New York and Oxford: Oxford University Press, 1996

Northrup, Christiane, *Women's Bodies, Women's Wisdom: Creating Physical and Emotional Health and Healing,* New York, Bantam, 1994

Thompson, J. Kevin, *Body Image Disturbance: Assessment and Treatment,* New York: Pergamon Press, 1990

Vaeth, Jerome (ed.), *Body Image, Self-Esteem, and Sexuality in Cancer Patients,* Basel and New York: S. Karger, 1980

Villarosa, Linda (ed.), *Body and Soul: The Black Guide to Physical Health and Emotional Well-Being,* New York: Harper Perennial, 1994

Wilson, Deborah S., and Christine Monera Laennec (eds.), *Bodily Discursions: Genders, Representations, Technologies,* New York: State University of New York Press, 1997

The issue of female body image has been given considerable attention in recent years, especially with the advent of modern feminisms. The breadth and scope of relevant material goes far beyond the much smaller but very substantive and informative material included here. We have brought together texts that reflect the breadth and scope of the subject of women and body image by choosing sources that speak to the issue in divergent ways.

BORDO's book is a much celebrated and often-cited feminist examination of female body image and materiality as it is constructed and pathologized within cultural, historical, and postmodern contexts. She examines the cultural relationships of food, commercial media, history, and body image in our society and its gendered pathological products—eating disorders. In addition to and related to eating disorders is the medical establishment's role in reproducing and supporting unhealthy cultural and historical meanings of femininity. As a critical framework, her book aims to challenge contemporary postmodern imaginings of the body as a transcendent text inhabiting multiple meanings and perspectives along race, gender, and class lines. According to Bordo, this popular postmodern discursive strategy loses sight of the very cultural and historical contexts in which women's bodies are engaged and from which they are constructed.

BROWNELL and FAIRBURN are editors of a book that covers a broad range of topics related to body image, eating disorders, and obesity. The topics covered regarding these issues are meant to provide the reader with a comprehensive review of all aspects of these two conditions. Diverse topics such as the regulation of eating and weight, dieting, and body image, along with the history, clinical features, treatment, and pathogenesis of eating disorders and obesity are examined in 101 succinct chapters. The contributors used empirical evidence to back up their findings, and each chapter has references for further reading. It should be considered a useful resource book for anyone, but especially for clinicians and students with research questions in this area.

FALLON, KATZMAN, and WOOLEY's anthology of writings provide a feminist perspective on the etiology of eating disorders. It is a feminist perspective in that the contributors of this book examine how gender roles of women contemporaneously and throughout history predispose women toward developing dysfunctional relationships with food, which may take the shape of body dissatisfaction, anorexia, bulimia, or compulsive overeating. Further, several of the authors offer commentary on the need for political and social equality for women. The book is divided into five sections: first, a historical examination of the cultural contributions to eating disorders such as fashion is presented; next, problems that can occur for female clients and female therapists because of what their bodies represent is discussed; third, provocative treatment issues are explored from this feminist perspective; fourth, novel and varied experiences from adolescent girls and women are shared with the reader regarding their bodies; and last, preventative strategies for the epidemic problem of eating disorders are suggested not only at the individual level, but at the societal level as well.

HESSE-BIBER's work uses the metaphor of a "cult of thinness," the ritualized and preoccupying impulses of women to attain culturally idealized images of the female body, in order to delineate the delimiting and burdensome effects of negative weight consciousness and negative body imaginings. Analyses of culture and history relating to weight consciousness are covered, but the author also provides her own eight-year research in much of the book. The testimonies and results from her data attest to the pervasive pressures behind predominately female eating disorders. Hesse-Biber also examines how the "cult of thinness" affects little girls, men, and women of color. Finally, unlike many critical texts on this topic, the last chapter of her work offers liberatory possibilities for those affected by burdensome weight consciousness, by providing alternate ways for women to relate to themselves and society.

THOMPSON transforms the old notion of viewing body dissatisfaction among women as merely a symptom of an eating disorder, by providing convincing scientific evidence that the problem of body image should be viewed as an entity in and of itself. He names this process "body image disturbance." He provides an overview of body image disturbance along with theory, assessment techniques, and treatment considerations. In particular, his chapter on the assessment of body image disturbance contains several brief descriptions of psychological instruments that can be used to identify body dissatisfaction among men and women. A comprehensive examination of current psychological literature on body dissatisfaction among women is presented. This book may be particularly useful to a mental health or health practitioner who would like to have a better understanding of clinical management of body image disturbance.

FISHER's text is primarily composed of psychological reviews and analyses of body image research projects between the years 1969 and 1985. Using conventional research over the aforementioned years, his text aims to elucidate the ways various psychological profiles interpret what the body is experiencing in social environments. The author attempts to make correlations among his own research, the psychological research of others, and his own findings in other disciplines concerned with the way the body is perceived.

NORTHRUP's goal is to provide women with guidance, information, and support regarding their mental and physical well-being. The book covers three major themes. First, the author introduces the idea of inner guidance and how the mind and body are connected. The next section deals with specific parts and processes of women's bodies, such as menstruation, breasts, ovaries, and birthing. Several common health concerns regarding women's bodies are explored such as breast cancer or sexually transmitted diseases. In the last section of the book, she challenges women to create a personal plan of healing for their bodies. Throughout the book, medical information is provided in simple and understandable language, in hopes that women will take more responsibility for knowing their bodies and for healing their bodies. In addition, the author and several other women share their personal stories of how they created healthier lifestyles. This book is meant to empower women to create physically healthy bodies by integrating spiritual and emotional healing.

VILLAROSA's edited text addresses the particular needs of African-American women by offering a reservoir of information on many topics. The editor's principle goal here is to educate and inform women on the many issues and ways the body is affected by emotional and physical health. Each section of the text covers a different topic on the issue. Also provided at the end of every section is a listing of alternate resources, such as private and public organizations and books.

VAETH's book is a culmination of several papers presented at the Fourteenth Annual San Francisco Cancer Symposium in 1979. The types of papers presented are varied. That is, some are research studies, others are practical information, and some are theoretical. All papers are written in a scientific style whereby the reader is provided with several references that support empirical findings. Specifically, the papers provide information on how cancer and the management of cancer can affect body image and sexuality. In particular, a theoretical framework that examines body image, self-esteem, and sexuality of individuals with cancer is discussed. Most of this information is based on an adult framework; however one paper specifically examines some treatment approaches to body image problems among adolescents that are living with cancer. The book provides the reader with notes from the discussant, which sum up the major themes, information, and future considerations presented by the panelists.

WILSON and LAENNEC's edited collection of essays on the relationship between women's bodies and technology branches out in divergent paths to apprehend a spectrum of multiple discourses. Their book incorporates perspectives from many areas: art history, cultural studies, health politics, literary theory, psychoanalysis, rhetorical history, and social theory. As a result, the essays are unified thematically, but each one offers lucid and engaging perspectives on the ways the female body has and is contextualized, reconfigured, and represented within the matrix of technology and culture.

—TANYA E. WILLIAMSON and CECIL WALTERS

See also Beauty Standards; Eating Disorders

Bourke-White, Margaret 1904–1971

American Photographer

Callahan, Sean (ed.), *The Photographs of Margaret Bourke-White*, Greenwich, Connecticut: New York Graphic Society, 1972; London: Secker and Warburg, 1973

Goldberg, Vicki, *Margaret Bourke-White: A Biography,* New York: Harper and Row, and London: Heinemann, 1986
Rosenblum, Naomi, *A History of Women Photographers,* London and New York: Abbeville Press, 1994

Margaret Bourke-White managed to be present at many of the most significant moments in world history during her lifetime, and to record the majority of them on film. As a photographer for *Life* magazine from its inception in 1936 until 1971, Bourke-White set a standard of photography that determined how many Americans viewed themselves and their changing world during the most turbulent decades of the twentieth century. She has been of great interest to scholars of women's studies, not only as a pioneer in the field of photography, but as a strong and independent woman who carved out an impressive career in what was primarily a man's field.

GOLDBERG's text offers the definitive treatment to date of Bourke-White's career and personal life. Goldberg, a respected photography critic and art historian, provides a meticulously researched treatment of Bourke-White's family, childhood, and adolescence, with particular attention to how her parents' rather unusual political beliefs helped to shape her character and her desire to succeed at the difficult task of becoming a female photographer in the 1920s. Goldberg traces the photographer's development throughout college and the major phases of her career. She gives particular attention to Bourke-White's years with *Fortune* and then *Life* magazines, where she pioneered a style of photography that became archetypal with the rise of the major picture magazines, such as *Life* and *Look,* in the 1930s. Goldberg also provides realistic and unromanticized versions of Bourke-White's personal life. Finally, though not intended to be a photographic study, Goldberg's book provides representative photographs from all major periods of Bourke-White's work, including the industrial photographs of the 1920s and 1930s, social documentary photographs of the 1930s, the World War II concentration camp studies, and post-war photographs of India and South Africa.

A text that treats Bourke-White's photographs more exhaustively is provided by CALLAHAN. Theodore M. Brown provides a brief biographical treatment in an introductory essay, but Callahan gives great attention to the precise details behind the creation of many of Bourke-White's most memorable images. He follows her early fascination with industrial machinery, which was exploited to good advantage in *Fortune* magazine, and also provides numerous examples from the later periods of her work, including her books in collaboration with Southern writer Erskine Caldwell, her war photographs, and a good selection of her early commercial and advertising work. The book also contains a detailed annual bibliography of books and articles by Bourke-White from 1931 to 1971.

ROSENBLUM's book places Bourke-White in the context of other women working in the medium from the turn of the twentieth century into the modern era. Rosenblum discusses Bourke-White's attendance at Clarence White's school of photography in New York, which also produced the well-known female photographers Dorothea Lange, Laura Gilpin, and Doris Ullmann; she also compares and contrasts her work with that of her European contemporaries, such as Germaine Krull and Hannah Höch. Rosenblum stresses the importance of Bourke-White's presence on the *Life* photographic roster, and the influence of her social documentary photographs, primarily through this magazine. Rosenblum also examines the usefulness of Bourke-White's war correspondent photographs of World War II to the popular image of the "American century." Finally, Rosenblum offers black-and-white photographic plates showing an example from each major phase of Bourke-White's prewar and wartime career.

—VICKI A. SANDERS

See also Photography

Bradstreet, Anne 1612–1672

American Poet

Cowell, Pattie, and Ann Stanford (eds.), *Critical Essays on Anne Bradstreet,* Boston: G.K. Hall, 1983
Daly, Robert, *God's Altar: The World and the Flesh in Puritan Poetry,* Berkeley: University of California Press, 1978
Hammond, Jeffrey, *Sinful Self, Saintly Self: The Puritan Experience of Poetry,* Athens: University of Georgia Press, 1993
Martin, Wendy, *An American Triptych: Anne Bradstreet, Emily Dickinson, Adrienne Rich,* Chapel Hill: University of North Carolina Press, 1984
Piercy, Josephine, *Anne Bradstreet,* New York: Twayne, 1965
Rosenmeier, Rosamond, *Anne Bradstreet Revisited,* Boston: Twayne, 1991
Stanford, Ann, *Anne Bradstreet: The Worldly Puritan,* New York: Burt Franklin, 1974
White, Elizabeth Wade, *Anne Bradstreet: The Tenth Muse,* New York: Oxford University Press, 1971

Critical assessments of Anne Bradstreet's poetry and prose have dramatically changed in the twentieth century. In contrast to generalized appreciations in the colonial period, and nineteenth-century negative readings of Bradstreet's poetry, the twentieth century has produced a plethora of readings that reaches no consensus on her individual poems. Each of the critics, however, recognizes the profoundly intimate connection between Bradstreet's life and her art. Whether critics perceive her poetry to be a reinforcement of or a reaction to her Puritanism, most would agree that Bradstreet's piety directly effected and certainly inspired her poetry.

PIERCY's study paves the way for subsequent twentieth-century readings of America's first poet, who came to New England as a member of the Massachusetts Bay Company in 1630. Analyzing Bradstreet's poetry and prose "for their revelation of the author's spiritual growth in her own very personal struggle with orthodoxy," Piercy attends to Bradstreet's religious beliefs by offering readers a useful overview of some basic tenets of Puritanism. The biographer also traces Bradstreet's poetic career, from an "imitative apprenticeship," to what Piercy considers her maturation as a true poet in the spirit of the English romantic poets.

The first full-fledged twentieth-century biography of Anne Bradstreet, by WHITE, is based on extensive research of manuscript sources in the United States and England. White places Bradstreet fully in her English environment, before she emigrated from Lincolnshire to Salem with her family at the age of 16. White's analysis of the poetry and prose suggests that Bradstreet may have unwittingly revealed more than she intended. In particular, White's persuasive reading of one of Bradstreet's earliest poems, "A Dialogue between Old England and New," reveals a "sharply contemporary" depiction of a religious crisis in England that greatly moved "colonial counterparts," including Anne Bradstreet. White's inclusion of an appendix, with a listing of the books contained in the library of Bradstreet's father (Thomas Dudley), is highly useful, because the variety of subjects available to the poet offers another lens through which to read her poetry.

Believing that Bradstreet's work represents an ongoing struggle between visible and invisible worlds, STANFORD demonstrates how this poet's work regularly takes the form of an argument between the physical world and the heavenly hereafter. In an early poem, "The Flesh and the Spirit," Bradstreet directly presents the visible world of material comforts; but Stanford suggests that the argument between flesh and spirit reaches its climax in the later elegies, in which Bradstreet confronts the conflict within herself as she mourns the deaths of her grandchildren. Stanford adeptly shows how, during the latter part of Bradstreet's career, the invisible world won her heart and soul, but the victory was never complete. Two appendices are particularly useful: "Chronology of the Works of Anne Bradstreet," and "Books with Which Anne Bradstreet Was Acquainted;" the latter places Bradstreet in a literary and cultural milieu distinct to educated people of the early seventeenth century.

DALY responds to critics who believe that Puritanism ruined Anne Bradstreet's poetry (Moses Coit Tyler), that Bradstreet's heart rebelled at something in Puritan dogma (Stanford), and that Bradstreet anticipated the Romantics in her depiction of nature (Piercy). Diverging from each of these views, Daly instead examines what Bradstreet made of her theology, "where experientially her religion took her and where poetically she took her religion." Insisting that Bradstreet's poetry and poetics were illuminated by her Puritanism, Daly shows how the poet came to the convincing resolution of living in the world, "with weaned affections." Considered by most critics (including Daly) her finest poem, Bradstreet's "Contemplations" is an example of the poet's ability to convey the struggle involved in weaning one's affections from the physical world "without ceasing to love them." Daly includes Bradstreet, along with other Puritan poets such as Edward Taylor, in his analysis of Puritanism and poetry, thus convincingly placing Bradstreet in her religious and ideological environment.

In the tradition of Daly, HAMMOND analyzes Bradstreet alongside other Puritan poets, such as Michael Wigglesworth and Edward Taylor. Employing what he calls an anthropological approach to reading Bradstreet, Hammond emphasizes to modern readers the fact that the Puritan way of reading was not like ours. Obsessed by the question "What must I do to be saved?" (Acts 16:30), Puritan writers like Bradstreet felt it necessary and aesthetically apt to write poetry that was both didactic and conventional. Believing that Bradstreet's incorporation of Puritan models of experience included both the dogmatist and the rebel, Hammond reinforces the fact that struggle and "dark moods" were entirely acceptable to the Puritan identity. Particularly useful is Hammond's analysis of Bradstreet's ongoing concern with teaching; his reading of "The Prologue" and "The Author to Her Book" in Bradstreet's *The Tenth Muse* as didactic exercises with moral lessons enhances our reading of these early poems, without taking away their playfulness.

The collection of critical essays edited by COWELL and STANFORD is wide-ranging and informative. Featuring colonial, nineteenth-century, and twentieth-century responses to Bradstreet's work, this is the first collection ever assembled on the poet. Besides offering useful reprinted materials by early writers, such as Cotton Mather and Nathaniel Ward, the editors include 30 essays, ranging from Robert Richardson's highly informative analysis of Bradstreet's work as a poet of Puritanism, to Cheryl Walker's reading of Bradstreet as a female poet. Both early poems (the Quaternions) and later poems (the elegies) are examined in this book; Anne Hildebrand's essay on Bradstreet's Quaternions alongside "Contemplations" is an especially useful contribution to reading the poet holistically.

Examining Anne Bradstreet alongside Emily Dickinson and Adrienne Rich, MARTIN's feminist critique places each poet in the context of her particular historical period. Martin reads Bradstreet as a poet who celebrated life in the world, and demonstrated her "commitment to nurturance rather than dominance." Asserting that Bradstreet was ultimately unable fully to "accept the Puritan God," Martin is most persuasive in her reading of Bradstreet's penultimate poem, an elegy for her month-old grandson. Bradstreet's line, "Let's say he's merciful as well as just," has been subject to several interpretations which recognize the "forced resignation" in the poet's voice. Likewise, Martin contends that such lines reveal deep reservations held by Bradstreet "about the wisdom of God's decisions."

ROSENMEIER moves away from viewing Bradstreet either as an orthodox Puritan or as a seventeenth-century feminist. Choosing a developmental structure to revisit Bradstreet's life and work, Rosenmeier uses issues of role and identity as guiding principles in her analysis of Bradstreet's poetry and prose. Shying away from assumptions of a "unitary Puritanism," Rosenmeier interprets selected poems in which certain personae are employed: child/daughter, sister/wife, and mother/artist, enriching such poems with a dramatic quality. Particularly effective is Rosenmeier's analysis of Bradstreet's use of the biblical wisdom tradition, which "constitutes an important key to understanding Bradstreet's feminism." Rosenmeier's reading of Bradstreet's elegy to Queen Elizabeth highlights the poet's relationship to the wisdom tradition, as well as to a transatlantic community of women writers. In addition, it anticipates the work of the modern American poet, H.D., whose epic poem, *Trilogy,* also recreates a female figure who represents, like Elizabeth, "just and righteous uses of power."

—MARY JO BONA

Breastfeeding

Baumslag, Naomi, and Dia Michels, *Milk, Money, and Madness: The Culture and Politics of Breastfeeding,* Westport, Connecticut: Bergin and Garvey, 1995

Eiger, Marvin S., and Sally W. Olds, *The Complete Book of Breastfeeding,* New York: Workman, 1972; London: Bantam, 1973; revised edition, New York: Workman, 1987

Goldfarb, Johanna, and Edith Tibbetts, *Breastfeeding Handbook: A Practical Reference for Physicians, Nurses, and Other Health Professionals,* Hillside, New Jersey: Enslow, 1980

Helsing, Elisabet, and Felicity Savage King, *Breast-Feeding in Practice: A Manual for Health Workers,* Oxford and New York: Oxford University Press, 1983

Jelliffe, Derrick B., and E.F. Patrice Jelliffe (eds.), *Programmes to Promote Breastfeeding,* Oxford and New York: Oxford University Press, 1988

Lawrence, Ruth A., *Breastfeeding: A Guide for the Medical Professional,* St. Louis, Missouri: Mosby, 1980

Raphael, Dana, *The Tender Gift: Breastfeeding,* Englewood Cliffs, New Jersey: Prentice-Hall, 1973

The advantages of breastfeeding for the infant's physical well-being are clearly established. In developing countries, especially, where access to clean water, sufficient amounts of formula, and quality medical care are often lacking, the mother's decision to breastfeed her baby or use formula is the single best predictor of infant mortality. However, many factors combine to encourage mothers not to breastfeed.

BAUMSLAG and MICHELS's book is a comprehensive overview of breastfeeding and formula feeding practices through history and throughout the world. They summarize research documenting the health benefits of breastfeeding to the mother and infant. Detailed information on the composition and suitability of breast milk versus formulas or cow milk is presented in a format that is highly accessible and engaging. The book also explores some of the political and social barriers to breastfeeding. The practices of the makers of infant formula are exposed, and the battle by the World Health Organization and others to limit the advertising of formula and distribution of free samples is described. They also summarize the difficulties of women breastfeeding while working and discuss legislation and initiatives developed in many countries that provide adequate maternity benefits to working mothers.

RAPHAEL is an anthropologist, and her book also contains a cross-cultural perspective on breastfeeding. However, Raphael has also served as a breastfeeding mentor or doula for a large number of American women who were not having success at breastfeeding their babies, and who wanted to do so. This experience has given her a more personal perspective, upon which she draws extensively. She describes how she has been able to help women reverse their unsuccessful experiences with breastfeeding, and how, in her view, societal, familial, and individual attitudes toward breastfeeding can lead to failure for many women. Although this book would not be accurately described as a "how to breastfeed" book, Raphael does make some very specific suggestions about the need for all breastfeeding women to have a doula, a support person for a definite time period after childbirth, in order to breastfeed successfully and happily.

EIGER and OLDS's book includes findings from the most current scientific research, as well as advice from nursing mothers themselves. It also addresses a number of lifestyle issues that are increasingly important to contemporary mothers. In this guide, nursing mothers will read more about diet and fitness, breastfeeding for the working mother (including the best ways to express or pump and store breast milk), breastfeeding as a sexual passage in their lives, nursing in public, and nursing in a variety of special situations. This manual attempts to provide the nursing mother with three essential tools for successful breastfeeding: knowledge of what to do, confidence, and the determination to persist in the face of any minor setbacks.

Several books have been published for medical professionals who may be assisting nursing mothers, but many of these are written so that the interested layperson who is seeking more detailed or specific information should have no major difficulty using them. LAWRENCE's book contains a great deal of information about the physiology, anatomy, and biochemistry of lactation. It also describes medical complications and medical interventions to address these complications. The few chapters addressing psychological and social aspects of breastfeeding summarize a substantial amount of research and provide the reader with references for further information, if desired.

The purpose of HELSING and KING's manual is to make old traditions from the cultural history of women, and recent research on the practical aspects of lactation, readily available to physicians, midwives, nurses, and all interested health workers. The manual provides detailed descriptions of how to diagnose normal breastfeeding problems, how to give advice and explanations, and tips on providing sympathy and support for nursing mothers. It also provides solutions on dealing with special cases characterized by premature or mentally handicapped infants. Other concentrated topics include nutritional requirements of the mother, mechanical aids for breastfeeding, and the effects of various drugs on lactation and infants.

GOLDFARB's book attempts to be somewhat comprehensive in the enumeration of potential breastfeeding problems and approaches that the professional (nurse, physician, counselor) should take. The explicit purpose is to help the professional feel confident enough to strongly advise women who wish to breastfeed to do so, and to be able to provide assistance for physical problems that may be encountered. Although drawing upon research findings, as available, it is less directly tied to research findings and is less scholarly and academically oriented than Lawrence's book.

JELLIFFE and JELLIFFE's book is a summary of various topics related to breastfeeding. While the information presented in the book is useful and interesting to both the lay person and the professional, it is targeted toward the professional. A brief description of the benefits and barriers to breastfeeding is offered by the editors. Several chapters then describe breastfeeding programs that have been developed by institutions around the world, in both developing and developed countries. The descriptions of these programs often include details of how the programs were implemented, changes that were made in preexisting policies in order to ensure the success of the program, and outcome data. Several chapters describe national as well as grass-roots programs such as La Leche League. The book offers information on the programs and objectives of international agencies such as UNICEF and the World Health Organization. Jelliffe and Jelliffe also include chapters of concrete information on specific components of programs that have proven effective. These include specific information on relieving nipple soreness and inadequate milk production, practices such as rooming-in, or allowing the mother and infant to remain together in the hospital after birth, and a comparison of the various instruments that are used to assist in breastfeeding and the suggested use for each. The training of health professionals and specialists to promote breastfeeding is discussed, as well as the status of legislation and marketing practices that affect breastfeeding. The book concludes with an examination of the direction that program evaluation and development should take. For those wishing more information, a selected bibliography including both practical and more theoretical information on breastfeeding is supplied, as well as an annotated bibliography of works discussing the relationship between breastfeeding, bottle-feeding, and illness.

—JANE CONNOR, ANNA NG, and ROXANNE MANNING

Bride Price *see* Dowry

British Women during World War II

Byles, Joan Montgomery (ed.), *War, Women, and Poetry, 1914-1945: British and German Writers and Activists*, Newark: University of Delaware, and London: Associated University Presses, 1995

Gledhill, Christine, and Gillian Swanson (eds.), *Nationalising Femininity: Culture, Sexuality, and British Cinema in the Second World War*, Manchester and New York: Manchester University Press, 1996

Lant, Antonia, *Blackout: Reinventing Women for Wartime British Cinema*, Princeton, New Jersey: Princeton University Press, 1991

Summerfield, Penny, *Women Workers in the Second World War: Production and Patriarchy in Conflict*, London and Dover, New Hampshire: Croom Helm, 1984

Virden, Jenel, *Good-Bye Picadilly: British War Brides in America*, Urbana: University of Illinois Press, 1996

The focus of SUMMERFIELD's book is the making and implementation of official policy toward women during World War II. The Ministry of Labour and National Service is prominent, because of all government ministries it had the greatest responsibility for designing and implementing policies for the mobilization of women. Chapter Two outlines the history of women in the period before the war, concentrating on women's varied experiences in paid employment and in the home. Chapter Three looks at the problems the Ministry of Labour met in trying to move women from one type of job to another that counted as "war work." Chapter Three also looks at the efforts of the Ministry of Labour to reconcile mobilization with conventional expectations about women's roles, in the context of evidence about women's own attitudes to being mobilized. Chapters Four, Five, and Six examine the interplay between the assumptions of certain governmental groups about domestic work, and the need to mobilize women and to sustain their productivity at work, in the areas of child care, shopping, and the hours of work. Chapter Seven investigates the policy of "dilution" of male labor by female labor, which was orchestrated by the Ministry of Labour, although conducted by employers and trade unionists. Thus, the theme of this book is that the war economy placed the government in a position in which it had to make decisions about changing women's roles at work and at home.

GLEDHILL and SWANSON's collection of essays is about women, the homefront, and cultural representation during World War II. While offering a special study of the role of film in the refashioning of femininity for a wartime homefront, this book seeks to situate cinema at the crossroads of social policy and representation. This book has a three-part structure that focuses on social policy and regulation concerning women, cultural practices that address femininity and the family, and the representation of gender and sexuality in wartime British cinema. This book asks questions about the reconstruction of femininity in wartime in relation to questions of women's place in the pre-war 1930s and in the period of reconstruction in the late 1940s and 1950s. Thus, this work provides a close historical focus that warns the reader against a too general account of the effects of governmental intentions, industrial objectives, or social propaganda. Rather than attempting a definitive history, this book unearths, from a diversity of sources and documents, a multitude of social and institutional policies and practices.

Each chapter in LANT's book deals with a different perspective on the relation of gender to national identity in British wartime cinema. The first chapter examines concrete instances of the projection of national identity on the British screen. Chapter Two furthers the investigation of sexual representation in cinema, linking it to contemporary imagery in other media, and describing how the mobilization of femininity for the war effort produced highly contradictory results. Chapter Three proposes that wartime conditions emphasized the status of the cinema as a visual luxury. The purpose of Chapter Four is to investigate the temporal qualities of the homefront films, as they reinvented femininity.

BYLES's book is about European, especially British and German, women's experiences of World War I and World War II. The focus is essentially on an explanation of women's literature in relation to war, rather than on women and war in general. This book also looks at men's literary response, particularly to politics. The study is both literary and historical and seeks to interweave the historical circumstances of these two appalling wars with women's and men's literary responses. It also asks what the impact of each was upon women's lives and focuses on how female writers represented that impact in their writing. The approach to social history is not that which would be taken by a social historian, but it is a literary approach.

VIRDEN combines archival sources with firsthand accounts. Oral histories and questionnaires are presented in this book. These are not complete records, but only supplemental to other sources. The few personal recollections and memoirs of war brides included provide more information on the participants' views of events. The author did not collect or analyze the data from the questionnaires, interviews, and memoirs using sociological techniques or statistical tools. The purpose of the book was to gather information supplemental to archival material. This work contains a high incidence of quoted material. The use of these oral histories provides the researcher with the opportunity to explain history in the words of the participants. The author uses the immigration theory (conceptual assimilation). The women's responses to specific questions on the survey and their own words in the interviews serve to enhance the stories.

—SUSAN M. TAYLOR

See also Women at Work during World War II, United States

Brontë, Charlotte 1816–1855 and Emily 1818–1848

British Writers

Barker, Juliet, *The Brontës*, London: Weidenfeld and Nicolson, and New York: St. Martin's Press, 1994

Boumelha, Penny, *Charlotte Brontë*, Bloomington: Indiana University Press, and London: Harvester, 1990

Davies, Stevie, *Emily Brontë*, London, Harvester Wheatsheaf, 1988

Ewbank, Inga-Stina, *Their Proper Sphere: A Study of the Brontë Sisters as Early-Victorian Female Novelists*, London: Edward Arnold, 1966

Maynard, John, *Charlotte Brontë and Sexuality*, Cambridge and New York: Cambridge University Press, 1984

Nestor, Pauline, *Charlotte Brontë*, London: Macmillan, and Totowa, New Jersey: Barnes and Noble, 1987

Pykett, Lyn, *Emily Brontë*, London: Macmillan, and Savage, Maryland: Barnes and Noble, 1989

Stoneman, Patsy, *Brontë Transformations: The Cultural Dissemination of* Jane Eyre *and* Wuthering Heights, London: Harvester Wheatsheaf, and New York: Prentice Hall, 1996

Tayler, Irene, *Holy Ghosts: The Male Muses of Emily and Charlotte Brontë*, New York: Columbia University Press, 1990

Since their own lifetimes, a genuinely critical response to the achievements of Charlotte and Emily Brontë has been impeded by a number of factors. In the first place, the two sisters (along with the less prominent Anne) have been regularly set up by critics in a kind of evaluative competition, so that admiration for one has too frequently entailed denigration of the other. Secondly, *a priori* assumptions about the aptitudes and range possible to female writers have been allowed to obscure the radicalism of what the Brontës actually wrote. Finally, the sisters' isolated lives, passed largely in a remote Yorkshire village at the opposite end of England to the metropolitan center of literary activity, have encouraged a belief that their works bear minimal relationship to the writings of their contemporaries, that they are (as F.R. Leavis wrote of *Wuthering Heights*) "sports" of nature, inexplicably erupting in the mid-nineteenth century like some exotic biological mutation.

This last misapprehension, in particular, should have been finally dispelled by EWBANK's pioneering study. Writing of the Brontës specifically as "early-Victorian female novelists," Ewbank surveys the social and economic conditions under which women's writing was produced in the nineteenth century (her use of conduct books—guides to proper female behavior—to establish normative expectations, is especially innovative); she is thus able to assess the extent of the Brontës' affinity with, and distinctiveness from, their surrounding literary culture. She concludes that while Emily's "genius" enables her largely to transcend gender issues, Charlotte's fiction is preoccupied with them, and that indeed she consciously chose the "Woman Question" as her proper sphere.

PYKETT, while admiring Ewbank's originality, is not in full agreement with her on the nature of Emily's achievement. Her valuable introductory study offers one of the most incisive recent discussions of the poetry (a discussion centered on the female poet's difficulty in extricating an authentic voice from the conventions established by male precursors), and follows it with four excellent chapters on *Wuthering Heights*. For Pykett, Emily's novel embodies a formal transition from gothic to domestic romance, a transition that also entails an evolution from patriarchal tyranny to the companionate marriage of Hareton and the second Catherine. Although the ending of the book fails to achieve full closure (it is still haunted by the specter of Heathcliff), it at least concludes with a relationship in which the socially constructed opposition of masculine and feminine has been largely overcome.

DAVIES, whose book is almost exclusively concerned with *Wuthering Heights*, shares some ground with Pykett, but pushes her own argument to a more challenging conclusion. The literary tradition to which Emily principally belongs, Davies contends, is that of Milton and Radical Protestantism: Her fiercely independent questions to the Calvinist father-God ends in an act of rebellion in which she rejects the repressive values of the adult world (represented in the figure of Joseph). Instead, she returns to the language and passion of childhood, in which sexual difference enables self-identification rather than opposition, and which is presided over not by the patriarchal Judge of Calvinism but by maternal Nature.

Both Pykett and Davies are much concerned with Emily's self-defining response to male predecessors. Pursuing the same line of inquiry, TAYLER argues that both Emily and Charlotte seek to liberate their writing from the burden of the past by transforming the female muse of romantic poetry into a male muse (a phenomenon also noticed, in the case of Emily, by Pykett). But whereas Emily's muse signifies the female artist's fragmented condition, and embodies her need for a creative distance from human interaction, Charlotte's muse represents the artist's role as an apostle of God-the-Father, and validates her status as a public figure with a reformist social mission. Tayler's post-Freudian readings produce some striking insights, but her conclusion that Emily writes in a visionary romantic mode while Charlotte is firmly aligned with the purposeful Victorian novel, is hardly more than a restatement of conventional wisdom.

Much contemporary criticism of Charlotte's fiction seeks to qualify the kinds of sharp contrast that Tayler perceives between her work and Emily's. BOUMELHA, for example, in her important recent study, concedes that Charlotte's novels only occasionally exhibit Emily's visionary intensity. She argues, nevertheless, that her fictional closures incorporate a "core of utopian desire," and that this is generated by her attempted fusion of (female) romance plots (with marriage as the predestined happy ending) and the (male) bildungsroman, whose goal is the protagonist's moral independence. By positing for her heroines a simultaneous quest for sexual fulfillment and autonomy, Charlotte ultimately disrupts the fictional conventions within which she works.

Boumelha's concise account offers the most sophisticated formulation of what has become almost a consensus in modern criticism. MAYNARD, for example, reads Charlotte's novels as a series of acutely perceptive depictions of their heroines' initiation into sexual awareness. At the same time, they become increasingly preoccupied with the relationship between this awakening and other (sometimes conflicting) ways in which the self can develop. NESTOR, similarly, in her excellent monograph, sees Charlotte's assertive treatment of female sexuality as always coexisting with an awareness of potential threat. To enter into a relationship, for Charlotte's women, is to risk a diminution of the self by domineering men. The resultant tension, Nestor argues, is expressed in a recurrent metaphor of inner, private space, which affords a refuge for the subject, but which is always vulnerable to invasion from outside.

Ever since the publication of Elizabeth Gaskell's *Life of Charlotte* in 1857, all of the Brontës have been subjected to a dense barrage of biography, and this has tended to perpetuate myths (self-sacrificing Charlotte, mystically withdrawn Emily) which implicitly inform even the most theoretically aware criticism. BARKER has performed an invaluable service, both by producing a collective biography in which individuation (with its danger of stereotyping each sister as an isolated genius) is subordinated to the depiction of relationship, and by returning rigorously to primary sources which have been repeatedly misrepresented. She creates a complex portrait in which, for the first time, the Brontës are contextualized within the surprisingly rich cultural life of their region and, although she herself offers little in the way of critical analysis, she provides the indispensable historical materials for an informed revaluation.

STONEMAN has developed the most innovative approach to Brontë studies in recent years. Instead of seeking to retrieve a "right" meaning for *Wuthering Heights* and *Jane Eyre*, she charts their "cultural dissemination" through stage versions, film treatments, and sequels, showing how the two books have had different meanings for different audiences at different times and places. Her exciting, scholarly book not only illuminates the Brontës' novels from a range of fresh perspectives, but provides abundant evidence of their continuing vitality and relevance.

—ROBERT DINGLEY

Brooks, Gwendolyn 1917–

American Writer

Melhem, D.H., *Gwendolyn Brooks: Poetry and the Heroic Voice*, Lexington: University Press of Kentucky, 1987
Mootry, Maria K., and Gary Smith, *A Life Distilled: Gwendolyn Brooks, Her Poetry and Fiction*, Urbana: University of Illinois Press, 1987
Shaw, Harry B., *Gwendolyn Brooks*, Boston: Twayne, 1980
Wright, Stephen Caldwell (ed.), *On Gwendolyn Brooks: Reliant Contemplation*, Ann Arbor: University of Michigan Press, 1996

Poet laureate of Illinois following Carl Sandburg, Gwendolyn Brooks is known as both a militant black activist and an extremely talented poet. Brooks has worked to include her activism in her poetry and has used her unique position as a recognized and respected artist in her activism. She has written many collections of poetry, a novel, and several autobiographical works, including *Report from Part One* and *Report from Part Two*, and her work is appreciated for many reasons in many different and diverse communities.

SHAW's biography of Brooks is fairly comprehensive and covers her early life, beginning with her birth in 1917, and ends with her work up to 1978. This biography details the important and influential events in Brooks's life during these six decades, including her family life and work for civil rights, as well as her writing. Shaw pays particular attention to 1968, the year that Brooks became poet laureate of Illinois, as a year of profound change in Brooks's life. Following the clear biography, Shaw gives close readings of several poems and examines general themes in Brooks's work. These readings are all from a historical/social perspective. Shaw also devotes a chapter to detailing the general themes from *Maude Martha*. Shaw provides an excellent starting point for general scholarship on Brooks's works.

Another biographical account of Brooks's life paired with analysis of her works can be found in MELHEM's work. Melhem's biographical text is brief and focuses primarily on Brooks's home and family life. Melhem gives a very comprehensive publication history of Brooks's work and discusses each book of poetry as a coherent whole, rather than focusing on individual poems. Melhem's main objective is to place Brooks within the canon as a part of a black literary tradition. The text contains analyses of *Street in Bronzeville, Annie Allen, Maud Martha, The Bean Eaters, In the Mecca*, and some later individual poems. All Melhem's poetry analyses focus primarily on how they fit into his definition of "heroic style." This text contains some very good general information about Brooks, although the analysis is quite narrow in focus.

MOOTRY and SMITH's text examines the aesthetic and social elements of Brooks's oeuvre. The book is divided into three sections: aesthetics, poetry analysis, and a discussion of *Maude Martha*. Mootry and Smith discuss the various literary influences on Brooks's work, and they specifically focus on the dual roles she plays as artist and activist. The introduction considers the problem of attempting to place Brooks's position in the canon and traces the evolution of her work. Mootry and Smith provide an extensive biography of Brooks as a Chicago poet, again focusing on her often conflicting roles as artist and activist. Most of the book is taken up with analysis of poetry and fiction, which focus on Brooks's personal history, the social and cultural influences of being a black woman living in Chicago, and the literary influences on her work. Mootry and Smith present clear, detailed critical scholarship on Brooks's works.

WRIGHT's anthology is an excellent source for a historical perspective on the reception of Brooks's works. The anthology contains reviews and essays written about many of Brooks's works, beginning in 1945 and including works as recent as 1994. The articles were selected to demonstrate Wright's position on the evolution of Brooks's oeuvre and the social/cultural/historical influences that affected Brooks and her work. The text is made up entirely of original reviews and essays regarding Brooks's work, and it includes a diverse selection of reactions, reviews, and opinions of readers from the past five decades. Wright's anthology is an excellent place to begin any kind of historical scholarship on Brooks, as it contains clearly cataloged responses to Brooks's work from a very wide variety of sources.

—STACEY C. SHORT

Browning, Elizabeth Barrett 1806–1861

British Writer

Forster, Margaret, *Elizabeth Barrett Browning: A Biography,* London: Chatto and Windus, 1988; New York: Doubleday, 1989

Hewlett, Dorothy, *Elizabeth Barrett Browning: A Life,* New York: Knopf, 1952; London: Cassell, 1953

Leighton, Angela, *Elizabeth Barrett Browning,* Brighton: Harvester, and Bloomington: Indiana University Press, 1986

Mermin, Dorothy, *Elizabeth Barrett Browning: The Origins of a New Poetry,* Chicago and London: University of Chicago Press, 1989

Stephenson, Glennis, *Elizabeth Barrett Browning and the Poetry of Love,* Ann Arbor and London: UMI Research Press, 1989

Stone, Marjorie, *Elizabeth Barrett Browning,* London: Macmillan, and New York: St. Martin's Press, 1995

Taplin, Gardner B., *The Life of Elizabeth Barrett Browning,* London: John Murry, and New Haven, Connecticut: Yale University Press, 1957

Almost everyone knows something of the legendary life of Elizabeth Barrett Browning. Poor in health and controlled by a tyrannical father, her elopement with Robert Browning from Wimpole Street was one of Victorian England's most celebrated love stories. This romantic interest in Browning as a woman led, however, in the years following her death in 1861, to a neglect of her work in favor of idealized accounts of her life. Criticism of her work in the first half of the twentieth century, where it is not overtly hostile, is often characterized by only a brief mention, before going on to discuss the more "important" contributions of her husband to poetry and the period.

It is not surprising, then, that in her biography, HEWLETT insists that our main interest in Browning lies with her love story and with her letters. Hewlett ranks her well below her husband as a poet, and although she does not altogether avoid difficult issues, such as Edward Barrett's reliance on slavery for his wealth, the biography is marred by a sentimentalizing narrative voice that renders any assessment of the facts difficult.

TAPLIN's biography is a more extensive and authoritative work based also on Browning's letters, but since many of those used were unpublished at the time, this work offers a useful insight into the bitterness and despair engendered by Browning's father's implacable objection to her marriage. The treatment of Browning's poetry is largely descriptive, but Taplin gives a meticulous and sympathetic account of her literary life and her influence on her time.

For many years Taplin's was the standard biography, but FORSTER's was able to take advantage of the exensive work done by Philip Kelly in collecting and publishing known and previously unknown correspondence. As a consequence, Forster's biography is able to explore the childhood, adolescence, and premarriage days of Browning, presenting a far stronger portrait of the woman who at 21 had had two volumes of poetry published, enjoyed an extensive correspondence with many of the leading figures of the day, and was not beyond exploiting her apparent fragility to avoid those household duties she disliked. The Browning that emerges from Forster's work is not ideal, after the manner of early biographies, but altogether more likable.

Forster's work is part of a growing body of feminist criticism. LEIGHTON, in a strongly feminist work, argues that twentieth-century critics have paid too little attention to the poetic stature accorded Browning in her lifetime, and offers a radical reassessment of the sexual and textual politics of Browning's poetry. Leighton insists upon the presence of a conscious and reforming emphasis on the female voice in Browning's poetry as a basis for reading the work. A comprehensive discussion of the poetry considers the position of the female writer as "other," suggesting that Browning's assertion of the right to break the silence of Victorian womanhood was shaped against the "other" who was her father. Since this approach differs from the relations that govern the male poet and his muse, Browning's poetry demands a different account.

MERMIN is inclined to agree. In a largely biographical account, she endeavors to place Browning within a type of canonical construct as the originator of a new poetry; that of a first Victorian poet, and the first major woman poet in England. Mermin links her work with Tennyson's, Robert Browning's, Swinbourne's, and others. The means used by Browning to escape gendered roles is emphasized in Mermin's work, as is the political poetry, in order to demonstrate Browning's feminist ideas and feelings, despite her avoidance of any organized women's group. Browning emerges as a strongly intellectual woman whose life, as a female poet, was part of the meaning inherent in her poetry.

STEPHENSON, on the other hand, unashamedly concentrates on the love poems, and takes recent critics to task for a tendency to separate out the interests of the love poems from those of the intellectual Browning, perhaps from a fear of becoming associated with the cloying sentimentality of earlier critics. Stephenson argues that the love poems rarely indulge sentimentality, and often undermine it. Further, although asserting the satisfactions of romantic love, Browning's poems often insist on a renegotiation of the male-female relationship. Placing the poetry in the context of other nineteenth-century love poems, Stephenson considers the difficulties for a woman writer in this genre, suggesting that Browning rejected the conventional persona of romantic love in order to assert the woman's right to speak, both in the poem and in the romantic relationship.

STONE begins by focusing on the past. Drawing on nineteenth-century assessments of Browning's work, Stone asserts that Browning could easily have been incorporated into a traditional canonical construct, and was excluded only because she was a woman. This study, then, reconstructs her poetic development, not only via the conflicts inherent in being a female poet, but also in the light of the assumptions, both past and present, associated with romanticism. Stone points to the ways in which Browning's early work invokes the continuities of romanticism, rather than the discontinuities of Victorianism. In an energetic reappraisal of Browning's emancipatory strategies and her often neglected early poems, this work challenges the period paradigm on which the exclusion of her work was based.

—JAN PILDITCH

Buddhism

Allione, Tsultrim, *Women of Wisdom,* London and Boston: Routledge, 1984

Boucher, Sandy, *Turning the Wheel: American Women Creating the New Buddhism,* San Francisco: Harper and Row, 1988

Gross, Rita M., *Buddhism after Patriarchy: A Feminist History, Analysis, and Reconstruction of Buddhism,* Albany: State University of New York Press, 1993

Horner, I.B., *Women under Primitive Buddhism: Laywomen and Almswomen,* New York: Dutton, and London: Routledge, 1930

Klein, Anne Carolyn, *Meeting the Great Bliss Queen: Buddhists, Feminists and the Art of the Self,* Boston: Beacon Press, 1995

Paul, Diana Y., *Women in Buddhism: Images of the Feminine in Mahayana Tradition,* Berkeley, California: Asian Humanities Press, 1979

Shaw, Miranda, *Passionate Enlightenment: Women in Tantric Buddhism,* Princeton, New Jersey: Princeton University Press, 1994

Tsomo, Karma Lekshe, *Sakyadhita: Daughters of the Buddha,* Ithaca, New York: Snow Lion, 1988

Buddhism, which originated in India in the sixth century B.C., and spread from there to become a major religion throughout Asia, is counted among the world's most important religions. Recently it has become a religion of choice for many westerners, including many articulate, well-educated feminist women, which accounts in part for the strong international Buddhist women's movement. In its traditional forms, Buddhism, like all other major world religions, is male-dominated and disadvantageous for women. However, many contemporary women are seeking the path of post-patriarchal forms of Buddhism. In so doing, they often rely upon the more accurate historical records that some female scholars are now writing.

HORNER's book was the first, and for many decades, the only book-length account of women and Buddhism, even though, as its title indicates, it covers only the early period of Buddhist history in India. It remains an unsurpassed account of women in that period, detailing a great deal of information not found in other sources. It is especially useful on the topics of the monastic rules of discipline for women, the stories of the early nuns, and the attitudes of the historical Buddha toward women.

PAUL's book, the first on Buddhist women in many decades, was also the first example of women's studies scholarship on this topic. The book is a sophisticated commentary on important texts, many of which were newly translated for this project. It takes up many controversial topics, including the degree of misogyny in early Buddhism, whether later Mahayana forms of Buddhism are more woman-friendly, and whether traditional Buddhism includes the possibility that there could be a female Buddha. Although it does not include all forms of the religion, it is more comprehensive than many books on women and Buddhism.

TSOMO's book is the record of an international conference on Buddhist nuns held at Bodhgaya (the birthplace of Buddha) in 1987, the first worldwide gathering on this topic. True to its name, it focuses mainly on Buddhist nuns and the issues and problems they face in the modern world. It is especially useful for the information it provides on nuns in the various Buddhist countries, since the situation of nuns varies greatly in the different contemporary forms of Buddhism. Since monasticism has always been important in Buddhism, and since nuns have usually been less well supported than monks, this book provides important information on a critically important topic for Buddhist women.

GROSS's book, the first book-length feminist account of Buddhism, is concerned with retelling Buddhist history with an eye to a past that could be both accurate and usable for women, a feminist analysis of key Buddhist doctrines from all major periods of Buddhist intellectual development, and a feminist reconstruction of all major Buddhist institutions, both monastic and lay. It also takes up the question of whether women would have anything novel to add to the sum total of Buddhist teachings, which to date have been formulated by men. Written by a practicing Buddhist, the book attempts to be faithful, both to academic standards and to Buddhism as experienced by an insider. The author is especially familiar with Tibetan Buddhism, but the book also attempts to be inclusive, although East Asian Buddhism is not as fully discussed as would be ideal.

ALLIONE's book represents a woman's search for female exemplars of her chosen spiritual path. A western convert to Tibetan Vajrayana Buddhism, Allione begins her book with an autobiographical essay on being a female practitioner of Tibetan Buddhism. In Tibetan Buddhism, stories of the great teachers and practitioners of the past are an important source of inspiration, but Allione felt a great lack when presented mainly with stories about men. She knew that Tibetan Buddhism is more open to women than some other forms of Buddhism, and had heard that there were also great female teachers who were less well-known. Her task became seeking out those stories, and this book is the result of her search. Many important stories not easily available in other sources are presented in an accessible fashion in this book, although it does not include the stories of some of the more famous female exemplars of Tibetan Buddhism.

SHAW's book is a bold scholarly attempt to establish that Tantric (or Vajrayana) Buddhism was very responsive to women's spiritual and psychological needs. She claims that Tantrisms's well-known use of passion and erotic experience as a spiritual path benefited not only men, but also women, whereas previous scholarship had claimed that Tantric ritual served male needs, using females as instruments to fulfill those needs. Shaw also claims that women were partially responsible for the development of Tantrism as a religious movement, and that they were active and well-respected teachers and innovators. Because this book contradicts a great deal of established scholarly consensus, it has received mixed reviews.

KLEIN is also a specialist in Tibetan Tantric Buddhism. Her book, unlike the books just discussed, is oriented more to philosophy than to history. She brings together two very difficult bodies of thought—the Dzogschen (Great Completeness) school of Tibetan Buddhism, often considered the most advanced of all Buddhist teachings, and postmodern western feminism. She conceives of her book as a conversation on the art of the self between these two schools, carried out in the hopes that each might have something to say to the other. The reader should also be forewarned that this book is written in a difficult style on a difficult topic.

Finally, BOUCHER's book is a highly accessible account of the topic so well summarized by the book's subtitle. It is a veritable "who's who" of women who have taken leadership roles of various kinds in the development of North American Buddhism. In Boucher's estimation, North American Buddhism is also a feminist Buddhism, far more responsive to women's leadership and women's needs than any previous form of Buddhism anywhere in the world. The book represents an optimistic note on which to end this survey of the most relevant literature on the topic of Buddhism. It should also be noted that discussions of women and Buddhism are very much in their infancy, and many significant works should be forthcoming in the next decades.

—RITA M. GROSS

Bulimia *see* Eating Disorders

Burney, Frances 1752–1840

English Writer

Adelstein, Michael E., *Fanny Burney*, New York: Twayne, 1968

Cutting-Gray, Joanne, *Women as "Nobody" and the Novels of Fanny Burney*, Gainesville: University Press of Florida, 1992

Doody, Margaret Anne, *Frances Burney: The Life in the Works*, Cambridge: Cambridge University Press, and New Brunswick, New Jersey: Rutgers University Press, 1988

Epstein, Julia, *The Iron Pen: Frances Burney and the Politics of Women's Writing*, Bristol: Bristol Classical, and Madison: University of Wisconsin Press, 1989

Hemlow, Joyce, *The History of Fanny Burney*, Oxford: Clarendon Press, 1958

Rogers, Katharine, *Frances Burney: The World of "Female Difficulties,"* New York and London: Harvester Wheatsheaf, 1990

Simons, Judy, *Fanny Burney*, London: Macmillan, and New York: Barnes and Noble, 1987

Straub, Kristina, *Divided Fictions: Fanny Burney and Feminine Strategy*, Lexington, Kentucky: University Press of Kentucky, 1987

Frances (Fanny) Burney was also known as Madame d'Arblay. Biographies and critical accounts of her work are frequently polarized in their assessment of both her person and her writings. In some primarily older commentaries, her works are merely minor, with no lasting value, and her personal qualities are described as unliberated, shy, snobbish, and even prudish. More recent biographers and critics view her as an innovator who influenced literary genres and more well-known writers, such as Jane Austen, and as a commentator on gendered social conventions of her day. The most heated debates center on whether or not Burney should be considered a feminist writer.

HEMLOW's work was the standard biography for many years. Based upon primary materials that were largely unpublished at the time of Hemlow's writing, we see Burney according to her own letters, journal, and notebooks. The work is extensively indexed, with an appendix listing library holdings of Burney's manuscript materials, reproduction of a letter in manuscript, and several photo plates of the Burney family. This literary biography discusses Burney's life and works simultaneously, as well as others' perceptions of both Burney and her writings. As criticism, Hemlow's work is weak, offering mainly plot summaries and some evaluation. It is most helpful in setting a historical and biographical context for Burney's works.

As part of the Twayne's English Authors Series, ADELSTEIN's volume combines basic biography with literary study. His assessment of Burney's work is based on technical considerations, such as her lack of adherence to rule of genre, and her use of melodrama and didacticism. As a result of his critique, Adelstein places Burney in the category of a minor writer, who has many shortcomings in the writing style of her novels, plays, and diaries. He does, however, list several important and lasting contributions to literature that Burney has made, including her respected novel *Evelina*, her journals and letters that capture the age, and her influence on the novel of manners.

SIMONS's brief volume is a good beginning resource for a study of both Burney and her works. It is part of the "Women Writers Series," which seeks to reexamine and reevaluate works by female writers. The biographical chapter is very helpful, and focuses on "the many contradictions" of Burney's life. These contradictions show Burney as torn between conventional patriarchy and more independent womanhood, and render it difficult for the reader to label Burney as either feminist or traditionalist. The remainder of the book concentrates on Burney's works, primarily her novels, and sees her, while not as a liberated woman, as one developing the desire for independence as she matured.

An excellent full-length critical study of Burney, STRAUB's book employs a "feminist, revisionary view of literary history." She focuses on Burney's novels, spending the longest analysis on *Evelina*. The work examines eighteenth-century gendered social conventions, and discusses the tensions Burney experienced as a writer and a woman.

A good updated literary biography is DOODY's work, which includes a Burney family tree, photo plates, and extensive notes. Doody considers Burney "to be a true artist who made something handsome and lasting out of her discontents." She sees Burney as rebelling against the societal restrictions concerning women. Much of the book involves a combination of close analysis of her novels in particular with a special interest in the development of her own language as a female writer, and the circumstances of her life.

EPSTEIN's critical analysis of Burney's letters and novels is feminist, and she sees Burney as a feminist as well. Epstein's book probes the violence depicted in Burney's works, and ties these occurrences with incidents of pain in Burney's own life, such as her unanaesthetized mastectomy. Violence is in turn linked to the oppression Burney experienced as an eighteenth-century woman, and Epstein sees her as subversive, a woman who "wrote out of pain and anger." Her final chapter on literary critical practices is particularly thought-provoking.

In contrast to biographers and critics who portray Burney as a social reformer, ROGERS focuses on the conventional side of Burney's personality and writing. Rather than seeing her as a feminist, Rogers views her as a woman who often accepted her age's feminine ideals, bowed to her father's wishes, curtailed her career as a playwright, and reflected the idea of feminine delicacy in her writing style. Rogers does acknowledge the other, bolder side of Burney, but admonishes that to see only that side is to present a distorted view of her. The book examines each of Burney's works in a very cogent manner, and concludes that the author excels in expressing the problems of "female impotence."

Concise and compelling, CUTTING-GRAY's work compares Burney's desire for anonymity to that of Emily Dickinson. Rather than the idea of "woman as nobody," denoting a submissive female, it allows for both Burney and her heroines the freedom a patriarchal system of identity denies. Special attention is paid to gaps and silences in the texts, spaces that create "the open possibility for an ongoing, ever complete and incompletable identity." Cutting-Gray uses a combination of current critical methodologies in her analysis, including feminist, deconstructive, Lacanian, and Focauldian theories.

—CAROL BLESSING

Business and Entrepreneurship

Broussard, Cheryl D., *Sister CEO: The Black Woman's Guide to Starting Her Own Business*, New York: Viking, 1987

Carter, Sara, and Tom Cannon, *Women as Entrepreneurs: A Study of Female Business Owners, Their Motivations, Experiences, and Strategies for Success*, London and New York: Academic Press, 1992

Frenier, Carol R., *Business and the Feminine Principle: The Untapped Resource*, Boston and Oxford: Butterworth-Heinemann, 1997

Rodriguez, Cheryl Rene, *Women, Microenterprise, and the Politics of Self-Help*, London and New York: Garland, 1995

Singh, Kamla, *Women Entrepreneurs*, New Delhi: Ashish, 1992

Stevenson, Lois, *Report on Tools for Business Growth: Opportunities for Women Entrepreneurs*, Moncton, Canada: Opportunities for Women Entrepreneurs, 1993

Vinze, Medha Dubhashi, *Women Entrepreneurs in India: A Socio-Economic Study of Delhi, 1975–1985*, Delhi: Mittal Publication, 1987

______, *Women and Productivity*, Tokyo: Asian Productivity Organization, 1996

BROUSSARD's book is a practical step-by-step primer for how to start up a business. She argues that an African-American woman's best opportunity to maximize her income is self-employment. To that end, Broussard writes a motivational, easy-to-read book, which leads an interested "Sister CEO" through the necessary thinking and planning to discover the ideal start-up business. She includes an interesting, effective means to empowerment. The book has numerous checklists to use when determining whether one should pursue a particular business.

FRENIER's book applies the Jungian feminine principle—a concept that attempts to explain the universal qualities of the feminine residing in "myths, legends, and fairy tales." Frenier explains four aspects of Jung's feminine principle. First, diffuse awareness sees the total picture. Second, the quick of the moment is an existential attempt to fully appreciate the present. Third, accepting the cycles of life sees setbacks as part of the life cycle. The fourth aspect of the feminine principle is deep community—drawing sustenance from the group, and helping rather than harming one another. Frenier applies each aspect to her business and her personal life. More autobiographical than practical, this book has fewer applications than Broussard's.

RODRIGUEZ provides study of the government policy written to address the unique challenges women face when initiating their own businesses. Rodriguez spent a nine month fellowship in Washington, D.C., as a participant observer in the formulation of federal policy on microenterprise, which supports women's business attempts. This book is an anthropological feminist study. Rodriguez combines both the subjective and the objective in this ethnography, presenting her, and others', perspectives, while looking at microenterprise for low-income women. Microenterprise, a concept coined during President Bush's administration, is a service-oriented, labor-intensive small business. It usually evolves from, or resembles, informal business activities and is often begun with a very small amount of capital.

In *Women and Productivity*, the Asian Productivity Organization (APO) reports the status of productivity in the member countries. The goal of the APO is to recognize achievements of female executives and entrepreneurs, and to provide motivation for greater productivity.

Specific recommendations grew out of the three-day 1994 meeting in Manila, the Philippines. These recommendations covered areas such as future research possibilities, information availability that could help women in business, specific types of education needed, methods of financing women's business ventures, legislation/policy and support, services, and awareness-raising advocacy. Productivity is a social concept, an attitude that supports the belief that constant improvement is possible. Underdeveloped countries highlighted in Part III of the productivity study highlight child care and continued cultural resistance to women in financial leadership positions as barriers to women's increased productivity, and education and government support as the most beneficial aids.

CARTER and CANNON's study discovers why British women start their own businesses, the problems they encounter in doing so, and successful strategies employed to overcome the problems. This is a case study of sixty successful female entrepreneurs, and ten women who left their businesses. Carter and Cannon utilize a chronological approach, tracing the steps one takes when starting a new business. The authors hypothesize that women's motivation and behavior will differ from traditional models. Results show that female entrepreneurs face unique challenges, which are seen by some as gender-related. Characteristics of businesses owned by women include: different routes are taken when starting up a business; planning is especially important; challenges for continuing the business are seen as having a gender dimension; successful management is often dependent upon single-minded attention to the business, training, professionalization and networking; and domestic relationships and friendships affect the progress of the business.

As increased industrialization and technological development have come in India, women have been displaced from their previously-held jobs and have turned to entrepreneurship in order to replace the income. SINGH's research used a systems approach to investigate strategies that could encourage the growth of entrepreneurship, particularly by women. Singh's definition of the phrase "female entrepreneur" is unique because it includes the concept of adjusting one's business to dovetail with other aspects of her life. Although difficult to read because of errors in English usage, the book offers interesting information relating to entrepreneurial traits, motivations, support, and communications among Indian women. Singh concludes that primarily more privileged women have progressed in the areas studied.

Recognizing the need to create economic self-sufficiency for women of India, the government of India has sought to improve women's participation in entrepreneurship. Analyzing the experiences of female entrepreneurs in Delhi, VINZE concludes that while women have made good progress, continued support is necessary. Further training in areas such as management, assistance in financing, control of pricing of raw materials, more efficient government assistance, and making upgraded technology available to these entrepreneurs would increase their likelihood of success. The women of Delhi can make a significant contribution to the Indian economy if given stable conditions in the country's economy, politics, and social structure, and if given useful information.

STEVENSON edited the report of the 1992 Opportunities for Women Entrepreneurs, Inc. conference, which focused on issues of growth for female entrepreneurs. Workshops were taught by successful Canadian female entrepreneurs. Recommendations that came from the conference included: concentrating on helping women's businesses through helping women gain financing; improving access to information, training, and research; training in financial and marketing knowledge; and providing opportunities for networking and mentoring among women in business. The book concludes that, because women-owned businesses are growing in number and success, it is to the Canadian economy's advantage for the government to further facilitate growth of these businesses.

—DEBORAH BUSH HAFFEY

See also Management

Byron, Ada, Countess of Lovelace 1815–1852

British Mathematician

Baum, Joan, *The Calculating Passion of Ada Byron*, Hamden, Connecticut: Archon, 1986

Moore, Doris Langley, *Ada, Countess of Lovelace: Byron's Legitimate Daughter*, New York: Harper and Row, and London: J. Murray, 1977

Stein, Dorothy, *Ada: A Life and a Legacy*, Cambridge, Massachusetts, and London: MIT Press, 1985

Ada Byron, later Countess of Lovelace, has been embraced in recent years for her involvement with an early nineteenth-century British prototype of the modern computer. Byron did not invent the machine herself—the unfinished "analytical engine" was designed by Charles Babbage—but she did publish a much-read commentary on it, suggesting potential future applications, or programs, for it. This 40-page essay, together with her unusual status as an amateur female mathematician in the 1830s and 1840s, accounts for her current interest to historians. Three biographers disagree on the extent of her talents and achievements, as well as the severity of the obstacles she faced, and they have presented her life in very different ways.

MOORE, Byron's first biographer, clearly feels a great deal of sympathy for her subject. She offers a detailed discussion of Byron's complicated and unhappy family history, and the extent to which Ada Byron, as the estranged daughter of the scandal-plagued poet Lord Byron, faced public scrutiny all her life. Indeed, Byron's domineering mother and famous father sometimes seem to be more the subject of the biography than Byron herself. Moore offers lengthy quotations from letters and other primary sources on Byron's overprotected childhood, her various illnesses, her marriage, her efforts to become a mathematician, her relationship with Charles Babbage, her secret and unsuccessful gambling on horse races, and her agonizing death from uterine cancer at age 37. Yet Moore's book is also rather confusing. She does not provide any background source material to help a reader not already familiar with early nineteenth-century England, she accepts most of her material at face value, she is often imprecise about dates, and she has the habit of including every bit of information she has found, whether or not it is really relevant to her discussion. Moore's lack of technical expertise means that her discussion of Byron's mathematical work is by necessity fairly superficial. Moore paints, in general, a sympathetic portrait of Ada Byron. She attributes Byron's volatility and inconsistent commitment to her work to a nervous temperament and the medicinal use of opium and brandy, although she does so in a rather patronizing way. Overall, Moore concludes, "Ada's time was too brief, her health too brittle . . . [and] She was born a hundred years too soon," identifying her illness and her gender as the primary impediments to greater achievement.

STEIN has produced a more objective assessment of Byron's life and work, making use of additional archival sources and illustrations. She offers ample background information on social customs and expectations, suitable for a reader with no prior knowledge of this era, and organizes her work in a more comprehensible manner. In addition, Stein takes advantage of her technical background to devote much more space to analysis of Byron's work and illnesses, and offers several examples of misinterpretation by Moore. For example, Byron's "coded notes," which Moore sees as part of a secret gambling system, are given much simpler explanations, and Byron's emotional volatility is attributed to manic depression rather than "nerves" or drugs. Stein also disagrees with Moore in her overall evaluation of Byron's work. While Moore sees Byron's gender and poor health as tragic checks on the full expression of her talents, Stein takes the opposite view. She argues that Byron's talents have been overrated, and that her associations with famous men are the main reason for her fame: "At twenty-eight, in a field where important original contributions are (still) often made before the age of thirty, and after ten years of intermittent but sometimes intensive study, Ada was still a promising 'young beginner.'" Stein's analysis of Byron's essay on Babbage's machines highlights small errors and argues that her "programs," although of much interest to scientists today, were not especially interesting to Byron herself. And while Moore saw Byron's early death as cutting off her future development, Stein argues that Byron's productivity had vanished long before her cancer developed, and that other well-known thinkers with bad health overcame it and achieved much more. In conclusion, Stein deems Byron both a professional and personal failure, not only in her "almost total failure to leave behind any tangible evidence of achievement or even progress," but in her poorly-thought out arrangements for the upbringing of her three children after her death. Only Byron's persistent interest and determination, despite her limited abilities, arouse Stein's reluctant admiration.

BAUM's book, published just after Stein's and apparently without reference to it, builds upon Moore's work and is generally in agreement with it. To Baum, Byron's story illustrates "the tragic consequences of forcing native talent to symbolic purpose," and "the theme of creative energy in collision with suppressed desire." Like Moore, Baum is interested in Byron's family history and the extent to which Byron's life was influenced by it. Unlike Stein, Baum clearly admires Byron's mathematical accomplishments, calling her "a fine mathematical expositor" and noting that the programming language "ADA" has been named after her. Baum provides adequate, although not extensive, commentary on social and medical customs and scientific inquiry in early nineteenth-century Britain. Moore saw Byron's gender and illnesses as the primary restraints on her career, and Baum endorses these while noting that the customs of her social class also proved limiting. Unconvincingly, Baum attributes Byron's fluctuating enthusiasm and focus on her work neither to "nerves"(Moore) nor to manic depression (Stein), but to her mother's domination, and to the periodic receipt of new information about her father and his scandalous activities. Although her work is much shorter than Moore's or Stein's, Baum includes a lengthy discussion of the technical and mathematical aspects of Byron's work, devoting an entire chapter to a detailed analysis of her famous article on Babbage's machines, and praising it as "the first extensive explanation and illustration of how such a machine could receive, store, manipulate, and print out data given numerically, literally, and symbolically." Overall, Baum argues, Byron's "place in mathematical science, though small, is legitimate," and she deems her "the world's first computer programmer."

—NAN H. DREHER

C

Cabrini, Mother Frances 1850–1917

American Saint

Borden, Lucille Papen, *Francesca Cabrini: Without Staff or Scrip,* New York: Macmillan, 1945
Di Donato, Pietro, *Immigrant Saint: The Life of Mother Cabrini,* New York: McGraw-Hill, 1960
Lorit, Sergio C., *Frances Cabrini,* New York: New City Press, 1970
Maynard, Theodore, *Too Small a World: The Life of Francesca Cabrini,* Milwaukee, Wisconsin: Bruce, 1945; London: J. Gifford, 1947
Sullivan, Mary Louise, *Mother Cabrini: "Italian Immigrant of the Century,"* New York: Center for Migration Studies, 1992

Mother Frances Cabrini was an important figure in the settlement of Italian immigrants in the United States. Her tireless dedication to the reduction of suffering among immigrant populations has earned her the distinguished title "Italian Immigrant of the Century." This honor was bestowed on Mother Cabrini in 1952 by the American Committee on Italian Migration. In 1909, at the age of 38, Mother Cabrini migrated from Italy to the United States. After a few years she became an American citizen and spent the last half of her life as a missionary in the midst of one of the largest migrations in human history. In America she founded the Missionaries of the Sacred Heart, a religious order devoted to helping immigrants. Soon after the death of Mother Cabrini there were many reports of miracles and cures. After an extensive investigation of her cause by the Roman Catholic curia, Pope Pius XII declared her a saint in 1946. This was an extremely important event in the history of American Catholicism because Mother Cabrini was the first American citizen to be canonized. Also, she was made a saint within a mere thirty years after her death.

There has been little scholarly research on the life of Mother Cabrini. Many works have been written by admiring devotees or members of the Roman Catholic hierarchy. Most of these accounts are romantic and somewhat fanciful. They tend to be presented in the classic hagiographic style. All the virtues of the saint are articulated, with special emphasis on the heroic and extraordinary spiritual gifts of the individual. The emphasis is not on pure biography, but rather the sketching of a model of spiritual purity to be emulated by devotees. This is particularly true for early works on Mother Cabrini. In recent years the Roman Catholic Church itself has become more interested in fostering better-documented and more accurate biographical studies of the lives of saints.

Many of the earliest sources on the life of Mother Cabrini are written in Italian and are not easily accessible to English-speaking readers. For many years the standard works in English on the life of Mother Cabrini were those by MAYNARD and BORDEN. These early books have little formal documentation. They are highly romanticized and somewhat fanciful biographies.

More recently Di DONATO's life of Mother Cabrini tells the gripping story of a woman of great perseverance, courage, and profound godliness. It is easy reading and recommended as a clear and well-written introduction to her life. This volume has a good final chapter describing Mother Cabrini's beatification and canonization, and noting many miracles attributed to her intercession. It also documents the enormous response to her death in Italian immigrant communities across the United States. The biography by LORIT is less impressive. It reads like a novel but lacks the depth and detail of other works. Both of these later biographies are still part of the hagiographic tradition. Very little emphasis is placed on historical accuracy and documentation.

One source alone stands out from all the rest. That is the recent historical approach taken by SULLIVAN. She provides an extraordinarily well-researched and documented treatment of the life of Mother Cabrini. It is neither fanciful nor maudlin. Despite the fact that Sullivan is a prominent member of the Missionaries of the Sacred Heart, her biography of the founder is sophisticated and objective in its approach. She portrays Mother Cabrini as a simple, bright, well organized, and very hard-working person with a shrewd business sense and a deep spiritual life. Cabrini established a network of educational, health, and social service institutions. In 1891 she reached out to the large immigrant population of New York City of over 100,000 Italians, many of whom were hostile to the Roman Catholic Church. For them, Mother Cabrini and her religious order offered solace in a highly competitive foreign land. She built orphanages and established schools. The Missionary Sisters visited families in their homes and regularly sought out Italians in public hospitals, prisons and mines.

Sullivan's volume is an excellent contribution to women's history in the United States and the great European expansion of the nineteenth and early twentieth centuries. She describes the strong character of Mother Cabrini, whose philosophy of education for immigrants combined the need for Americanization with the equally important preservation of the Italian cultural heritage. This modern and sensible approach to cultural adaptation was way ahead of its time. Despite poor health for much of her life, Mother Cabrini had enormous energy and is to be admired as one of the great spirits of the early twentieth century. She was strong-willed, unafraid of challenges, and had a clear vision about the future. Her life work represents an ideal model for the twentieth century, both in terms of social benevolence and the spiritual life.

—JAMES J. PRESTON

Cameron, Julia Margaret 1815–1879

British Photographer

Gernsheim, Helmut, *Julia Margaret Cameron: Her Life and Photographic Work,* London: Fountain Press, and New York: Transatlantic Arts, 1948

Hamilton, Violet, *Annals of My Glass House: Photographs by Julia Margaret Cameron,* Claremont, California: Ruth Chandler Williamson Gallery, 1996

Hill, Brian, *Julia Margaret Cameron: A Victorian Family Portrait,* London: Peter Owen, and New York: St. Martin's Press, 1973

Julia Margaret Cameron, Los Angeles, California: J. Paul Getty Museum, 1996

Lukitsh, Joanne, *Julia Margaret Cameron: Her Work, Her Career,* Rochester, New York: International Museum of Photography at George Eastman House, 1986

Newhall, Beaumont, *The History of Photography from 1839 to the Present,* New York: Museum of Modern Art, 1949; London: Secker and Warburg, 1972; revised 5th edition, 1982

Weaver, Michael, *Whisper of the Muse: The Overstone Album and Other Photographs by Julia Margaret Cameron,* Santa Monica, California: J. Paul Getty Museum, 1986

Woolf, Virginia, and Roger Eliot Fry, *Victorian Photographs of Famous Men and Fair Women by Julia Margaret Cameron,* London: Leonard and Virginia Woolf, and New York: Harcourt Brace, 1926; London: Hogarth Press, and New York: Godine, 1973

In the discussions of the life and work of nineteenth-century photographer Julia Margaret Cameron, two issues related to her role as a woman in the Victorian period appear in some form or another with consistency. First is the question about her status as a photographer: should she be taken seriously as a professional pioneering in an emerging field or seen as an amateur "lady" merely dabbling inexpertly at picture-making as a kind of expensive hobby? Second is the issue of the perceived split in her work between a predominantly religious art that focused on allegorical, painter-like, staged compositions featuring women and children on the one hand, and the dramatic portraiture, primarily of men she admired (some say hero-worshipped) for their genius and greatness on the other.

GERNSHEIM's monograph contains the famous Clive Bell introductory essay that also reflects the "problem" of Cameron's use of the realistic medium to express a painter's vision. The monograph begins with a lengthy biography and then discusses her photographic work in a somewhat rambling and disconnected manner; it is, however, so crammed with both information and opinion that it is an invaluable resource. Gernsheim lists all of the Cameron exhibitions, discusses reviews of her work, and provides over one hundred plates and numerous appendices full of useful information.

NEWHALL, in the revised and expanded version, emphasizes Cameron as an artist-photographer and expresses ambivalence about the camera's ability to both capture an image in a moment and to create the desired effects of art. He compares Cameron's costume pieces to Pre-Raphaelite painting but prefers the portraits to what he considers the sentimentality of the staged pieces intended to echo paintings. Newhall presents an interesting analysis of the reciprocal relationship of painting and photography in the nineteenth century, which helps to contextualize Cameron's work.

Biographical material appears in almost all of the writings about Cameron's work, but two sources are of particular interest. HILL provides a biography of all seven daughters of James Pattle, an official of the East India Company in Bengal, with particular emphasis on Julia Margaret Cameron. The sisters were renowned in Anglo-Indian society for their intelligence, beauty, and unconventional ways. Cameron's life was very intertwined with those of her sisters and their extensive families; she used family members as models, and her series of photographs of her niece, Julia Jackson Duckworth (the mother of Virginia Woolf), is among her most striking work. Woolf's anecdotal biographical sketch of her great aunt in WOOLF and FRY's book is an amusing inside-the-family account, although the editor of the 1973 edition points out several inaccuracies in it. That monograph also contains forty-four plates of the portraits of famous men and women with a commentary on the photographs by Fry.

Some of the most valuable analysis of Cameron's work appears in monographs related to specific collections. LUKITSH discusses the holdings at the International Museum of Photography at George Eastman House in Rochester, New York. This volume includes over one hundred black-and-white photographs and a bibliography. Lukitsh is also one of the discussants in a colloquium at the J. Paul Getty Museum, the transcript of which makes up part of the JULIA MARGARET CAMERON volume published by the museum. This book features 50 plates from the Getty collection of 302 prints, with commentaries on the plates by Julian Cox, Assistant Curator of the Department of Photography, and the transcript of the colloquium featuring Lukitsh, Judy Dater, David Featherstone, Weston Naef, Pamela Roberts, and Robert Woof. The introduction by Cox takes up the issue of Cameron's so-called technical imperfections and her status as a professional; Cox discusses Cameron's use of the new Copyright Bill of 1862 to protect her work and to profit by the selling of the prints. The analysis of the prints includes discussion of the manner in which women are portrayed by Cameron, especially in the scenes in which women are shown in relation to each other. The colloquium section considers technical matters as well as the feminist issues evoked by her tendency to allegorize women (as virtues, or Biblical or mythological figures) and to present men, especially famous ones, as heroic figures. The Getty collection has as its core the Overstone album, one of more than a dozen such presentation books Cameron made up with her own inscriptions for persons she admired.

Overstone advanced (and simply gave) the Camerons money, but WEAVER suggests in his discussion of the Overstone album that such a gift was not just a way of thanking him for his patronage or a gesture of typical Cameron generosity; Weaver maintains that Cameron, as a professional photographer who wanted public recognition for her work, used such presentations to get her work into the hands of influential persons. Weaver emphasizes the spiritual aspects of Cameron's art but counters the notion that she was a wealthy amateur. Recounting the family's financial difficulties after their return to England from India, he notes the financial arrangements Cameron made with the Autotype Company and Colnaghi to sell her prints. Weaver's analysis of her photographs first breaks them into categories, which suggests a split between the portraits and what he calls "Madonna groups" and "fancy subjects for pictorial effect," but he then argues that in all three categories Cameron was striving for the same effect. The representation of the great men, he suggests, is the same kind of idealization, with a moral purpose, found in the Christian typology of the allegorical photographs. His analysis of the Magdalene-Madonna figures and his views on the dark side of the male authority figures in both the portraits and in the "fancy subjects" category are of particular interest to feminists.

The opening of the new Getty Museum and research center in Los Angeles will make a large portion of Cameron's work available to scholars; new volumes based on collections there and elsewhere are to be expected. HAMILTON also draws on the Getty material for a catalogue of an exhibition at Scripps College of Cameron's work from 1864 to 1874; Cameron's unfinished autobiography of the same title as this monograph is part of the prefatory material of this study. Hamilton's analysis of Cameron's work extends the discussion of the portrait portrayals of men both as individuals and ideal types: prophets, philosophers, geniuses; and of her representation of women typologically as legendary heroines or poetic muses. Hamilton sees this female portrayal as a way of empowering women and as a response to the conservative Victorian attitude that relegated women to the domestic sphere. A chapter is devoted to the Madonna groups and another to the "fancy subjects" pictures.

—SHARON LOCY

See also Photography

Capitalism

Barrett, Michele, *Women's Oppression Today: Problems in Marxist Feminist Encounter*, London and New York: New Left Books, 1980

Clark, Alice, *Working Life of Women in the Seventeenth Century*, London: Routledge, and New York: Dutton, 1919

Davidoff, Leonore, and Catherine Hall, *Family Fortunes: Men and Women of the English Middle Class, 1780–1850*, Chicago: University of Chicago Press, and London: Hutchinson, 1987

Engels, Frederick, *The Origin of the Family, Private Property, and the State*, Chicago: Kerr, 1902; London: Lawrence and Wishart, 1940

Enloe, Cynthia, *Bananas, Beaches, and Bases: Making Feminist Sense of International Politics*, London: Pandora Press, 1989; Berkeley: University of California Press, 1990

Mies, Maria, *Patriarchy and Accumulation on a World Scale: Women in the International Division of Labor*, London and Atlantic Highlands, New Jersey: Zed, 1986

Pinchbeck, Ivy, *Women Workers and the Industrial Revolution 1750–1850*, London: Routledge, and New York: Crofts, 1930

Tilly, Louise A., and Joan W. Scott, *Women, Work, and Family*, New York: Holt 1978; London: Methuen, 1987

These works are landmarks in the debate about capitalism's impact on the lives of women. Written from a variety of political perspectives, they characterize capitalism in diverse ways, and reach very different conclusions about its consequences for women. Drawing on outdated studies of prehistoric matriarchy, ENGELS argues that women's oppression arises with capitalism. The institution of private property requires the dependence of the bourgeois wife to ensure legitimate heirs. Idealized as a freely-entered contractual relation between equals, in reality, he says, monogamous bourgeois marriage is a form of prostitution, the woman fulfilling her role in the transmission of property in exchange for board and lodging. The conditions for realizing the ideal of "individual sex love" obtain only in proletarian marriage, in which the partners have equal status as wage laborers and no property to safeguard. For Engels, since women's oppression depends on exploitative class relations, their emancipation first requires the overthrow of capitalism.

Based on her study of women's economic activity in seventeenth-century England, CLARK takes a similarly pessimistic view of capitalism's impact on women. Clark finds ample evidence of women's engagement in economic production early in the century. In this period the home was still the central unit of production, and women played an important role in running farms, trades, and estates, enjoying a mutually supportive and relatively egalitarian relation with their husbands. But as a cash economy spread, rewarding a greater division of labor, enterprises reorganized on a capitalist basis, hiring wage labor and relocating outside the home. As a result of the separation of home and work, by century's end aristocratic and bourgeois women were confined to an idle domestic existence, and lower-class women to low-paid wage labor.

Focusing on England in the period from 1750 to 1850, PINCHBECK sees the transition from the domestic to the industrial mode of production as a more extended process, not completed until the nineteenth century. She also departs from Clark in arguing that capitalism created the conditions for women's emancipation. While admitting that capitalism had negative consequences for women of all classes in the short term, she contends that the opportunity for work outside the home created by factories eventually led to greater economic, social, and political independence for all women by the end of the nineteenth century.

In their survey of women's economic and family life in England and France from the early modern period to the present day, TILLY and SCOTT stress not the breaks, but the continuities in women's work and family experience, from the early modern to the modern period. Concentrating on the lower classes, they divide this history into three phases: the "family economy" of the pre-industrial period, when production for use still predominated and women worked chiefly in the home; the "family wage economy" of early industrialization, when the family unit depended on the collective wages of its members; and the "family consumer economy" of modern times, when the family became a site of consumption, and women moved in large numbers into retail and clerical jobs in the rapidly expanding service sector. This shift represented a redistribution of female workers into new areas, not any absolute increase in their participation in the labor force. Scholars have overgeneralized, Tilly and Scott point out, from the experience of bourgeois women in concluding that more women began working at this time. For the majority of women, work had always been a necessity.

Examining the provincial middle class in early nineteenth-century England, DAVIDOFF and HALL likewise dispute the notion of a sharp break between a domestic and an industrial mode of production, by pointing to women's active role in reproducing the middle-class family as an economic, social, and cultural unit throughout the transitional period. While acknowledging the gradual separation of home and work, and the decreasing importance of women's labor power, they show how women supported early industrial enterprises by investing capital, and by maintaining the family and social networks on which business success depended. Arguing that the Victorian polarities of public and private, masculine and feminine, were still taking shape at this time, they recover the part middle-class women played in the creation of the nineteenth-century class/gender system.

BARRETT provides a useful introduction to the complex theoretical questions concerning the relationship between capitalism and patriarchy implicitly raised by these historical studies. For her the radical feminist claim that patriarchy is a distinct system rests on an overly essentialist theory of the sexes. At the same time, she rejects as reductionist the Marxist view explaining women's oppression solely in terms of its usefulness for capitalism. She argues for a historical approach that explores the independent development of patriarchal gender relations in prior epochs, while also grasping the particular ways capitalism incorporated these preexisting sexual divisions of labor.

Enloe and Mies focus on capitalism as a world system based on an international and sexual division of labor. ENLOE argues that international politics and the global economy depend on exploitative relations between men and women, which conventional political discussions overlook as mere "private" matters. Looking beneath the surface, we find women as wives of diplomats, maids in hotels, prostitutes outside military bases, and sweatshop workers for multinational corporations. Rendering women visible in this international system exposes the gender ideology that helps reproduce it, and raises the possibility of feminist alliances across boundaries of class and nation.

MIES refers to the current world order as "capitalist patriarchy," because for her capitalism is just a manifestation of patriarchy. The latter began in prehistoric times, when males monopolized the means of violence to extract the surplus of women's productive work. Whereas for Barrett, the interconnection between capitalism and patriarchy is just a contingent historical fact, for Mies, capitalism necessarily requires the patriarchal appropriation of women's labor. The ideology that naturalizes the role of women as housewives conceals this exploitation, rendering domestic work invisible as labor. In the current international division of labor, first world women function mainly as consumers, third world women as producers. Although the former benefit from the exploitation of the latter, Mies argues that ultimately they have a shared interest in overthrowing the system of capitalist patriarchy, which denies them both control over, and recognition of, their productive work.

—JOHN DIXON

Caregiving

Abel, Emily K., and Margaret K. Nelson, *Circles of Care: Work and Identity in Women's Lives*, Albany: State University of New York Press, 1990

Baines, Carol, Patricia Evans, and Sheila Neysmith, *Women's Caring: Feminist Perspectives on Social Welfare*, Toronto: McClelland and Stewart, 1991

Bumiller, Elisabeth, *May You Be the Mother of a Hundred Sons: A Journey among the Women of India*, New York: Random House, 1990

Clement, Grace, *Care, Autonomy and Justice: Feminism and the Ethic of Care*, Boulder, Colorado: Westview Press, 1996

England, Kim, *Who Will Mind the Baby?: Geographies of Child Care and Working Mothers*, New York and London: Routledge, 1996

Finch, Janet, and Dulcie Groves, *A Labour of Love: Women, Work and Caring*, London and Boston: Routledge and Kegan Paul, 1983

Tronto, Joan C., *Moral Boundaries: A Political Argument for an Ethic of Care*, New York: Routledge, 1993

Women's caregiving has become the locus of debate and contention since the origins of the feminist movement. Resulting from this debate is a large body of feminist knowledge about the subject. This new knowledge encompasses a broad spectrum of women's caregiving issues, including unpaid care, child care, and other methods of care, as well as debates surrounding the ethic of care.

FINCH and GROVES provide us with one of the first examinations of the specific dynamics of unpaid caring. This book focuses on women who participate minimally or do not participate at all within the existing labour market. The authors examine the implicit obligation for women to be economically independent while providing the traditional care for others stipulated by women's role in a patriarchal society. This book examines avenues of social policy that promote this dichotomy while creating inherent role strain for women. The social ramifications for women are highlighted through a thorough examination of policies related to women and the caregiving experience. The authors explore the public and private costs of caregiving in order to determine whether informal caregiving is a low-cost measure. This cost/benefit analysis depends on the assumption that informal caregivers are not considered to be of financial value in our current society. However, this book illustrates that the financial, social, and emotional weight of caregiving is carried primarily by women, who are expected to cope with the designated role as the unpaid and undervalued caregiver.

ABEL and NELSON provide a broader spectrum of women's caregiving. This text crosses several population lines and policy areas. It addresses multiple avenues of women's caregiving, such as the care provided for children, the disabled, and the chronically ill, as well as caregiving for other adults. Unlike many caregiving texts, its focus is on the experience of the caregiver rather than the care beneficiary. Abel and Nelson define the changing nature of caregiving due to the shifting economic climate and labour market restructuring. They examine the implications for female caregivers during this current economic and ideological transformation. This book highlights the difficulties women experience in managing social caregiving expectations in conjunction with other demands and stresses in their lives.

BAINES, EVANS, and NEYSMITH present one of the few texts that examine the ethic of caregiving in relation to women's social welfare in Canada. Several authors collaborate to examine both the formal and informal structures of female caregiving. This book provides the reader with a detailed understanding of the definition of caregiving. Its authors attempt to illustrate the basic correlation between caregiving and issues such as poverty, abuse, neglect, and disadvantage, and their connections to the Canadian women's caregiving experience. Throughout this text, the authors examine society's underlying assumptions about women's caregiving roles. They consider how these assumptions can have a negative impact on the wellbeing of female caregivers. The authors demonstrate that there are implicit societal expectations requiring women to assume the role of the unpaid caregiver. Female caregivers forgo significant opportunities with great cost and consequence in order to fulfill this implicit caregiving role. Women's caregiving obligations are also embedded in the ideology of the existing Canadian social welfare infrastructure. The authors assert that the social welfare system stresses the need for women to provide care to others, with little or no regard to their own personal care needs.

TRONTO's examination of care diverges from the traditional studies of female caregiving. It is distinguished by its examination of the moral and philosophical aspects of care. The focus of this text is deliberately restricted to an examination of the politics related to the ethic of care within a feminist framework. Tronto argues that the historical connection commonly made between women, morality, and care is unfounded and politically imprudent. She demonstrates how those who are disadvantaged in society are more likely to engage in greater levels of caregiving. She also illustrates how the onus for care is placed primarily on the shoulders of the underprivileged. This onus is hidden in the structure of the existing political framework by those who have authority. The author asserts that this hidden agenda is used as a way to maintain power, domination, and privilege.

CLEMENT also examines the feminist ethic of care from a philosophical perspective. Her exploration differs, in that she examines the dichotomy between the ethic of justice and the ethic of care. Clement distinguishes between these two classifications and illustrates how they often challenge each other and develop in divergence from one another. She also defines the difference between these two ethical forms. Generally, the ethic of justice is abstract, essentially masculine, and concentrating on issues of equality, while the ethic of care is often contextual, and essentially feminine, centring around the maintenance of human relationships. Throughout her debate, the author attempts to illustrate how other features associated with the ethic of care, including autonomy, must be acknowledged in order to construct a feminist ethic of care. She argues that the feminist ethic of care transcends the private sphere of personal relations. In her concluding statements, she asserts that the ethic of care depends on the interplay with the ethic of justice in order to develop thoroughly the concept of moral reasoning.

ENGLAND focuses on another kind of caregiving, that between working mothers and their children. Her interest is in the geographical barriers to child care provision in Canada and the United States. This book provides a rare examination of child care policies and their geographical impact on female caregivers. It illustrates working women's struggle to provide adequate child care, and the strategies used by women to cope with the effects of added child care arrangements. It also examines women's access to government regulated child care services and non-regulated services. It provides a comparison among geographical communities to determine spatial equity issues. The author reveals the current piecemeal status of our national child care policies and the equality of access problems created by our current child care system. She also indicates how women are often held primarily responsible for ensuring that their children have adequate child care provision and transportation. In conjunction with this responsibility, women are expected to act as equal participants in the paid labour market.

In stark contrast to other texts on caregiving, BUMILLER provides the reader with a generalist understanding of the changing nature of the lives of women in India. The author is a journalist who reports on her perspective of the condition of the modern Indian women from a western perspective. This book does not specifically focus on caregiving but is a significant inquiry about aspects of women's lives in India, including their role as family caregivers. The author describes the changing nature of the middle-class Indian woman who struggles to balance her new transition into the work force, while finding adequate ways to fulfill her caregiving responsibilities. This text recounts several stories told by Indian women from all classes, providing the reader with several individualistic pictures of women's lives and positions in Indian society. While not all-inclusive, this book provides a broad example of the status of women and their multiple caregiving roles within a changing culture.

—CHRISTINE O'GRADY

See also Aging; Elder Abuse; Ethic of Care

Carr, Emily 1871–1945

Canadian Painter

Appelhof, Ruth Stevens, *The Expressionist Landscape: North American Modernist Painting, 1920–1947*, Birmingham, Alabama: Birmingham Museum of Art, 1988

Blanchard, Paula, *The Life of Emily Carr*, Vancouver: Douglas and McIntyre, and Seattle: University of Washington Press, 1987

Gowers, Ruth, *Emily Carr*, Leamington Spa and New York: Berg, 1987

Shadbolt, Doris, *Emily Carr*, Vancouver: Douglas and McIntyre, and Seattle: University of Washington Press, 1990

———, *The Art of Emily Carr*, Vancouver: Douglas and McIntyre, and Seattle: University of Washington Press, 1979

Thom, Ian M., *Emily Carr in France*, Vancouver: Vancouver Art Gallery, 1991

Tippett, Maria, *Emily Carr: A Biography*, Oxford and New York: Oxford University Press, 1979

Although long considered a national treasure by Canadians, the artist Emily Carr is little known beyond Canada's borders. One of Carr's biographers rightly attributes this ignorance to the parochialism of the American and international art communities. More troubling is the neglect of

Carr by feminist art historians. Nevertheless, scholarship has been substantial in the last three decades. In particular, Carr has proven an irresistible subject for biographers, in large part because of the wealth and richness of the artist's own writings (in the form of published journals, letters, and memoirs) on both her art and her life.

Two of the first important studies of Carr were published in 1979. TIPPETT's book is a solid, well-researched biography that focuses on the artist's life. Although she draws extensively on Carr's writings, Tippett has approached this material cautiously, and is careful to distinguish fact from fantasy. The author is also conscientious about flagging for the reader when she is interjecting her own speculation about the significance of events in Carr's life.

Whereas Tippett focuses largely on Carr's life, both of SHADBOLT's books seek to provide "a fuller appreciation" of her as an artist. Shadbolt's earlier publication (1979), replete with large, handsome color reproductions of Carr's paintings, might best be characterized as a coffee-table book, although the text is serious and enlightening. In her more recent publication (1990), Shadbolt's prolonged, attentive study of Carr's art is crystallized and given full voice in an accessible, beautifully written study that describes her artistic influences and intentions, and her conception of nature, particularly in its spiritual dimension. In both books, Shadbolt draws on Carr's own writing to elucidate the artist's paintings and her artistic stance, and to trace the development of Carr's form.

Like Shadbolt, THOM writes as an art historian, but his focus is narrow, where Shadbolt's encompasses Carr's entire oeuvre. Thom's catalogue illuminates a formative moment of Carr's artistic development. Included are color and black-and-white reproductions of both Carr's work from her French tour and that of her mentors.

Though she covers much the same material as Tippett, BLANCHARD inflects her biography of Carr with a gentle but distinct feminist viewpoint. In her introduction, Blanchard maintains that there is room for a biography such as hers, which "focuses primarily on the inner conflicts of a woman painter of Emily Carr's time and place and tries to answer once more the nagging familiar question of why one woman transcended them when others did not." In places, she presents Tippett's interpretation and analysis of particular events, and then offers her own alternative analysis, in a spirit that celebrates and acknowledges the subjectivity of the biographical endeavor, and is respectful of the reader's intelligence.

Yet another biography, by GOWERS, should be mentioned here. It is useful as a short, concise introduction to Carr's life and the major themes and methods in her art. However, as part of Berg's Women's Series, the brevity of this book and its emphasis on the trajectory of Carr's life preclude critical or contextual analysis.

APPELHOF provides the most unusual, and in some respects the most visionary study of Carr. Whereas much of the scholarship discussed to this point carries a strong nationalistic tenor, and presents Carr as a solitary artist working outside a mainstream tradition, this publication repositions Carr firmly within a North American context, as one artist among many who participated in, and contributed to, the spread of modernism on this continent. Without completely discarding the familiar model of the female artist working "beyond the fray," this catalogue tempers that stereotype by showing that Carr's "overall development had resonances in the mainstream evolution of modern art in North America. In subject matter, style, and philosophical concerns, her work proves that she was typical." In the catalogue, as in the exhibition that it accompanied, Carr is presented for the first time among—and as part of—a constellation of American and Canadian artists such as Georgia O'Keeffe, Arthur Dove, Charles Burchfield, and Lawren Harris. At the same time, however, Appelhof "features" Carr with an essay devoted solely to her (while the others are discussed collectively in two essays), and with a relatively larger number of her works represented in reproduction. Carr's art and career are highlighted not (as is usually the case) because she was an outstanding or exemplary practitioner, but presumably because she is the least known of the artists included. Appelhof's conception provides an exciting model for feminist art historians who wish to affirm and emphasize the accomplishments of individual female artists, without resorting on the one hand to a monographic approach (with its attendant dangers of ghettoization) and on the other, to the conventional group approach, from which female artists tend to emerge as "derivative" and lesser than their male counterparts.

—JO ORTEL

Carson, Rachel 1907–1964

American Writer

Brooks, Paul, *The House of Life: Rachel Carson at Work*, Boston: Houghton Mifflin, 1972; London: Allen and Unwin, 1973

Gartner, Carol B., *Rachel Carson*, New York: Ungar, 1983

Graham, Frank, *Since Silent Spring*, Boston: Houghton Mifflin, and London: Hamish Hamilton, 1970

Hynes, Patricia, *The Recurring Silent Spring*, New York: Pergamon Press, 1989

McCay, Mary, *Rachel Carson*, New York: Macmillan, 1993

Sterling, Philip, *Sea and Earth: The Life of Rachel Carson*, New York: Crowell, 1970

Although much attention has been devoted to the environmental movement, which has become one of the most significant movements of the late twentieth century, much less attention has been paid to the woman who significantly changed the way we view the world and the way we view our responsibility for the environment. Rachel Carson died in 1964, two years after *Silent Spring* (1962) was published. In the more than thirty years since her death, there have only been six serious books devoted to her life and work. She herself has, unfortunately, been neglected, yet the movement she was so instrumental in focusing and energizing has grown worldwide.

Almost a decade after *Silent Spring*, GRAHAM warned that Carson was indeed correct in her assessment of environmental damage done by pesticides. His book puts Carson's *Silent Spring* in context, and shows the enormous amount of scientific data Carson studied to buttress her case. Largely concerned with undercutting the agri-chemical companies' scurrilous personal attacks on Carson, Graham devotes a good deal of time to illustrating Carson's meticulous research and writing process.

STERLING's book focuses on Rachel Carson the person as scientist and writer. He is interested in her friendships, her family bonds, and her work colleagues. He gives excellent background on the relationship between Dorothy Freeman, the friend of Carson's later life and the guardian of Carson's nephew after her death. Not a scholarly writer, Sterling does capture Carson's personality, her dedication to family and friends, and her commitment to her work.

Ten years after the publication of *Silent Spring*, her editor at Houghton Mifflin, BROOKS, wrote a comprehensive study of Carson's life and work, focusing primarily on the process of writing. Brooks fills in information about Carson's work at the Fish and Wildlife Service, and gives a very good sense of the genesis of *Silent Spring*, a book that seemed unusual for Carson at the time. While this study is quite thorough, it is marred by Brooks's attitude toward unmarried women. He felt that Carson's life was narrowed by her failure to marry, and that attitude colors much of his biographical information.

HYNES's study of Carson argues vehemently with Brooks. More than any other study, Hynes looks at Carson's relationships with women as mentors, colleagues, and friends. Her book highlights the role of women, including Carson's mother, Mary Scott Skinker, her biology teacher at Pennsylvania College, and Dorothy Freeman, her companion during the controversy surrounding *Silent Spring*. While Hynes implies homoerotic feelings between Carson and her female friends, the real value of her book is that it strengthens the assertion that Carson's life was truly rich and full, a position that is also clearly supported by the book, *Always, Rachel: The Letters of Rachel Carson and Dorothy Freeman, 1952–1964* (1995).

Both Gartner and McCay have done critical studies of Carson's work with introductory biographies. GARTNER's study emphasizes the role of the scientist as artist, bringing a literary slant to the study. McCAY puts Carson in the context of the American naturalist tradition of John Bartram, Henry David Thoreau, John Muir, and others whose concern for the environment was linked to a sense of humanity's place in nature.

—MARY A. McCAY

See also Ecofeminism; Nature

Cassatt, Mary 1844–1926

American Painter

Bullard, E. John, *Mary Cassatt: Oils and Pastels*, New York: Watson-Guptill, 1972

Costantino, Maria, *Mary Cassatt*, New York: Barnes and Noble, and London: Bison, 1995

Dillon, Millicent, *After Egypt: Isadora Duncan and Mary Cassatt*, New York: Dutton, and London: Penguin, 1990

Hale, Nancy, *Mary Cassatt: A Biography of the Great American Painter*, New York: Doubleday, 1975; reissued with a new author's prologue, Reading, Massachusetts: Addison-Wesley, 1987

Mathews, Nancy Mowll, *Mary Cassatt: A Life*, New York: Villard, 1994

McKown, Robin, *The World of Mary Cassatt*, New York: Crowell, 1972

Pollock, Griselda, *Mary Cassatt*, New York: Harper and Row, and London: Jupiter, 1980

Sweet, Frederick Arnold, *Miss Mary Cassatt, Impressionist from Pennsylvania*, Norman: University of Oklahoma Press, 1966

Of the important female artists of the late nineteenth and early twentieth centuries, Mary Cassatt has remained one of the most consistently admired and studied. Unlike several of her contemporaries, her art has steadily received as much critical attention as her biography, and several useful examinations of the work and the life are available. Cassatt is generally regarded as a woman who succeeded in a male-dominated world, while retaining a woman-centered artistic vision. Central critical questions include the role of gender in her art, and why and how she was able to sidestep societal restrictions on her work.

POLLOCK's book is an oversized, illustrated volume, intended to introduce Cassatt to a general audience interested in learning about a forgotten woman artist, and to introduce feminist art history. In clear instructional language, the author explains the status of women painters—specifically American women painters—in the nineteenth century, the role of the independent avant-garde artist in France, and the themes of Cassatt's work. Pollock finds

Cassatt's central theme to be the phases of womanhood, presented as a cycle with maternity at its center. Eighty-five paintings and drawings by Cassatt (32 reproduced in color) are analyzed individually, and comparisons are reinforced by 15 small reproductions of the work of other artists. This book is an excellent introduction to Cassatt.

BULLARD's volume came out of a major retrospective of Cassatt at the National Gallery, and includes 32 large color plates. Each is analyzed by the author, who focuses on the technical aspects rather than on the thematic discussion offered by Pollock. The explanations are clear and instructive, intended for the nonspecialist. The introductory essay offers a brief and basic biography, again with an emphasis on technique over vision.

COSTANTINO's book is primarily a collection of gorgeous oversized color plates, but the brief introduction offers an interesting, because seldom presented, explanation for Cassatt's body of work. The author guesses that Cassatt may have directed most of her energies to painting women, not out of any conscious choice, but simply because she had no alternative: as a woman in the restrictive nineteenth century, she would have had little opportunity to observe a man's world, or to study male anatomy.

The most important biography for students of art is that by MATHEWS, which emphasizes the development of Cassatt's methods, and details the historical context for that development. Mathews is an important art historian and curator, who previously published three books on Cassatt's letters and work, and three on other art of the period. To this book she brings a clear and wide understanding of Cassatt's role in the history of art, especially her place in the impressionist movement and in shaping the Havemeyer art collection. The book stays strictly away from psychoanalytic approaches to Cassatt's life, but does give more information about her family than previous studies. This excellent volume includes over 100 photographs, and a bibliography.

Another important biography, both comprehensive and readable, is that by HALE. The author is primarily a novelist, but has written two books about her painter parents, and is well-equipped to analyze the paintings and the workings of a painter. The book traces Cassatt through the various phases of her artistic development, but unlike Mathews, the emphasis here is on the emotional development of the woman who succeeded in what was then a man's world. With a novelist's skill, Hale presents Cassatt's many triumphs; the chapters describing her blindness and old age are painful but unflinching. The black and white reproductions of Cassatt's paintings and photographs are of poor quality, but there is a useful annotated bibliography.

SWEET's book was for a decade the definitive biography, and was an important corrective for long-held and often-published errors of fact about Cassatt's life. The author was Curator of American Art at The Art Institute of Chicago, and he brings more expertise than Hale to contemplation of the art. Sweet's biography is not as complete as Hale's, and suffers from well-intentioned but ultimately sexist stereotyping, but it offers an interesting view of the role of Cassatt's family in all that she became, and includes extensive quotations and analyses of her parents' letters.

McKOWN's book, the least scholarly of the biographies, is part of the Women of America series, a collection of popular biographies of plucky rebels written for the general reader. The author relies on Sweet for much of her biographical information about Cassatt, but adds interesting and vivid descriptions of the painters whom Cassatt befriended in France. The book is most useful as an introduction to the impressionist movement, and Cassatt's role in it, presented in clear, non-technical language.

DILLON rejects the linear qualities of traditional biography, and attempts to get at a deeper, intuitive truth in an eccentric book about Cassatt and Isadora Duncan. Though the two never met, each traveled to Egypt, boated up the Nile, was changed by her experiences, and wrote about them. DILLON sets these two trips side by side in individual chapters with no unifying commentary. Alternating snippets from the two women's lives, which are presented in lyrical language and out of chronological order, the book echoes the workings of memory, with its repetitions and seeming randomness. Cassatt did not enjoy her trip to Egypt in her 66th year; she was haunted by images of sickness and death, and wanted only to return to her beloved Paris, although her negative viewpoint was altered when she was overwhelmed by the power of Egyptian art.

—CYNTHIA A. BILY

Cather, Willa 1873–1947

American Writer

Harvey, Sally Peltier, *Redefining the American Dream: The Novels of Willa Cather*, Rutherford, New Jersey: Fairleigh Dickenson University Press, and London: Associated University Press, 1995

Kaye, Frances W., *Isolation and Masquerade: Willa Cather's Women*, New York: Peter Lang, 1993

Lee, Hermione, *Willa Cather: Double Lives*, New York: Pantheon, 1989; as *Willa Cather: A Life Saved Up*, London: Virago Press, 1989

O'Brien, Sharon, *Willa Cather: The Emerging Voice*, New York and Oxford: Oxford University Press, 1987

Rosowski, Susan J. (ed.), *Approaches to Teaching Cather's "My Ántonia,"* New York: Modern Language Association of America, 1989

Urgo, Joseph R., *Willa Cather and the Myth of American Migration*, Urbana: University of Illinois Press, 1995

Wasserman, Loretta, *Willa Cather: A Study of the Short Fiction*, Boston: Twayne, 1991

Woodress, James, *Willa Cather: A Literary Life*, Lincoln, Nebraska: University of Nebraska Press, 1987

Willa Cather was first celebrated for her regional focus as a writer of the American West, whose stories portrayed the heroism of ordinary people. She remained popular during the Depression, although some reviewers complained that she ignored current social problems by setting several novels in a romanticized past. Many biographical, thematic, and stylistic studies of the Pulitzer Prize-winning writer appeared by the late 1970s. Subsequently, as gender and culture became prominent issues in literary scholarship, critics argued that Cather's fiction embodies both lesbian desire and an ambivalent attitude toward the pioneer experience. Increasingly, Cather has been discussed not as the elegist of the American West but as a modernist author receptive to international influences.

The most complete introduction to Cather's work in a biographical context is WOODRESS's book, which is a major expansion of his *Willa Cather: Her Life and Art* (1970). He supplies many details on Cather's friendships with Dorothy Canfield Fisher, Louise Pound, Isabelle McClung, Edith Lewis, and Elizabeth Shepley Sergeant. Most chapters are titled after Cather's books, and Woodress refers to hundreds of letters by Cather and her correspondents to establish the conditions of her writing, and to develop relationships between her fiction and her life. He also indicates the contemporary reception of Cather's work by citing many reviewers. Copious photographic illustrations identify models for Cather's characters; for example, Annie Pavelka, a friend of Cather's, is equated with the protagonist of *My Ántonia*. Woodress is a traditional biographer in his focus on character and on theme, such as the growth of the female artist in *The Song of the Lark* and *Lucy Gayheart*. He discusses not only Cather's 12 novels, but also her short stories and her early journalistic writing, including articles on female opera singers, and reviews of female authors.

Psychoanalytic and feminist theorists are cited frequently in O'BRIEN's influential study of Cather's long literary apprenticeship. Although O'Brien covers Cather's first 40 years in depth, she is not a good source on the later life and works, since her focus is the progression from Cather's early Jamesian stories to her discovery of her own "voice" with her depiction of a female hero in her second novel, *O Pioneers!* O'Brien argues that Cather's bonds with women—family members, authors (especially Sarah Orne Jewett), and friends (particularly Isabelle McClung)—helped her to reconcile the terms "writer" and "woman." While Woodress is extremely circumspect in his comments on Cather's sexuality, O'Brien's assumption that she defined herself as a lesbian has made a large impact on Cather scholarship of the past decade.

KAYE, for example, is indebted to O'Brien in her study of Cather's work as lesbian literature, but she challenges many of O'Brien's remarks on Cather's development and her depictions of women. Kaye agrees that Cather enjoyed close female relationships, yet she claims that Cather distrusted women as a group, and thus isolated herself from such reform societies as the Woman's Christian Temperance Union. Kaye says that Cather's fiction involves serious costs for author and reader alike, since Cather could not bring herself to portray passionate ties between women. Although Kaye's documentation is light, and her treatments of several novels are surprisingly brief, her analysis is of special interest to gay studies scholars.

Like Kaye, HARVEY views Cather's fiction in cultural context. She centers on the tension between community spirit and self-interest in four of Cather's short stories, and in all 12 novels. Stressing that Cather's vision of America is fundamentally optimistic, Harvey cites recent historians, along with George Santayana and other social commentators of the 1920s and 1930s. She suggests that Cather saw the European values of her immigrant characters as a "corrective" for American materialism, and she considers Cather unusual for opening up an idealistic version of the American dream to immigrants and to women.

A more controversial reading of Cather's migration theme appears in URGO's provocative study of 10 novels. Curiously, he omits *Alexander's Bridge* and barely mentions *My Mortal Enemy*. The homeless tramps, the missionaries, the railroads, and the trans-Atlantic crossings in Cather's fiction all reflect America's "overarching myth": the migratory experience. Urgo states that the women-centered pioneer novels—*O Pioneers!*, *My Ántonia*, and *A Lost Lady*—are saved from extreme nationalism, because Cather clearly acknowledges the personal losses and the "political costs" that migration incurs. Urgo's approach toward *One of Ours*, with his stress on America's move toward militant imperialism, should stir up debate on this World War I novel. (Ernest Hemingway scorned the book as a woman's failed effort to write about war.)

LEE, one of the few British critics to discuss Cather in a book-length study, suggests that *One of Ours* is less about battle and national chauvinism than it is about Claude Wheeler's knightly quest for redemption, when the western "pastoral," including Claude's marriage, turns to "junk." Cather's fascination with the ability of language to express the incommunicable is one of Lee's motifs. As her title implies, Lee explores many such dualities, from Cather's adoption of the male tradition of epic, to her stories of divided selves like Alexandra Bergson of *O Pioneers!* and Thea Kronborg of *The Song of the Lark*. Lee places Cather on an international modernist scene, in the company of D.H. Lawrence, Katherine Mansfield, and Virginia Woolf. An excellent survey of Cather's life and work, this book reflects contemporary critical developments in a readable, well-balanced fashion.

More specialized in scope is WASSERMAN's three-part study of Cather's short stories, a body of work that merits further research. Like Lee, Wasserman describes Cather's modernism; the "evolutionary vitalism" of Henri Bergson and William James are among the influences she discerns in such well-known stories as "Paul's Case" and "Neighbour Rosicky," and also in the less familiar "The Bohemian Girl" and "Old Mrs. Harris." Wasserman includes a section of interviews with Cather, and a gathering of five critics' reactions to specific stories. Among these is Marilyn Arnold's piece on the artist theme and the female narrator of "Uncle Valentine," reprinted form Arnold's valuable *Willa Cather's Short Fiction* (1984).

ROSOWSKI's guide to Cather's very popular fourth novel, *My Ántonia*, is part of a Modern Language Association series directed toward teachers. (Rosowski also wrote *The Voyage Perilous: Willa Cather's Romanticism*, 1986, which was one of the first studies leading to the resurgence of interest in Cather.) Students and general readers will also appreciate the wealth of information. Rosowski's "Part I: Materials" reviews critical and biographical resources. "Part Two: Approaches" brings together 25 previously unpublished essays by many notable Cather scholars. Essayists approach *My Ántonia* in the contexts of gender and sexuality, religion, plains epic, immigration, women's traditions, modernism, romanticism, the American novel, and more. Instructors can find suggestions for teaching the book in first-year writing, women's studies, and other courses. Scholars will find stimulating ideas on the novel's illustrations, inset stories, and "self-reflexivity." The long list of works consulted is a good bibliography for anyone seriously interested in Cather.

—JOAN WYLIE HALL

Catherine de Medici 1519–1589

French Queen

Heritier, Jean, *Catherine de Medici*, translated by Charlotte Haldane, New York: St. Martin's Press, 1959

Mahoney, Irene, *Madame Catherine*, New York: Coward McCann, and London: Gollancz, 1975

Neale, J.E., *The Age of Catherine de Medici*, London: Cape, 1943

Roeder, Ralph, *Catherine de' Medici and the Lost Revolution*, New York: Viking, and London: Harrap, 1937

Sichel, Edith, *Catherine de' Medici and the French Reformation*, New York: Dutton, and London: Constable, 1905

Van Dyke, Paul, *Catherine de' Medici*, 2 vols., New York: Scribner, and London: J. Murray, 1922

Weil, Rachel Judith, *The Crown Has Fallen to the Distaff: Gender and Politics in the Age of Catherine de Medici*, Princeton, New Jersey: Princeton University Press, 1985

Williamson, Hugh Ross, *Catherine de' Medici*, New York: Viking, and London: Joseph, 1973

Arguably one of the most powerful women of the Renaissance, Catherine de Medici (also spelled Catherine de' Medici, Catarina de' Medici, and Catherine de Médicis) has been long portrayed in both history and fiction as a ruthless, manipulative, superstitious queen and queen-mother, whose hunger for power and misplaced religious zeal produced one of the darkest periods of French history. The most infamous deed attributed to her was the St. Bartholomew Massacre (August 24, 1572), lasting several weeks during which an estimated 30,000 French Protestants (Huguenots) were slaughtered. Early biographies tend to repeat unsubstantiated and speculative assertions about persons and events either attributed to her, or drawn from unreliable and often biased contemporary sources. More recent twentieth-century scholarship has only started to correct these errors.

VAN DYKE's massive work, the first in English to draw on theretofore unused primary archive sources scattered throughout Europe, is a model of careful scholarship. It is possibly the best documented study of Catherine de Medici in any language, for it is cited repeatedly in other English studies, as well as French, Italian, and German works on Catherine in particular, and on sixteenth-century France in general. Detailed and meticulous, this study is intended for people who have more than a working knowledge of the times and the major personae of the period.

In contrast, NEALE's study, which uses Van Dyke as a source, benefits from conciseness, offering a clear overview of Catherine's chaotic, rapidly changing times. His lengthy discussion of religion and religious rivalry in this period is particularly enlightening. The underlying flaw in the book, however, is the author's seeming inability to view Catherine as anything other than a negative, destructive force in her times. This attitude emerges as unscholarly remarks, slurs really, such as his reference to Catherine's "unscrupulous Italianate mind," and assassination being "a pestiferous Italian custom." As a result, the scholarly tone of this book is compromised.

MAHONEY, who also uses Van Dyke as a secondary source, is a more temperate scholar, who admits that she came to writing about "the shopkeeper of Florence," one of the many epithets with which the French put down their Italian-born queen, with certain negative predispositions, but changed these in the course of her research. In this book, Mahoney attempts to present a balanced picture of Catherine, and does so successfully. HERITIER, a distinguished French journalist who tries to steer a middle ground between the picture of Catherine as "the Sinister Queen," and "the portrait [of Catherine] lost behind the lurid colors of the legend," also presents a balanced picture. In fact, Heritier submits that Catherine, whom he calls a "female incarnation of the [French] national monarchy," was not only "misunderstood," but was significantly in advance of her times in terms of *Realpolitik*.

ROEDER does an notable job of contextualizing Catherine within the complex times in which she lived and ruled, especially in terms of the decline of feudalism and the rise of capitalism, and the upheaval caused by the erosion of the power of the Roman Catholic Church and the rise of Protestantism in France. He provides the reader with useful chronologies and helpful genealogical charts. However, his work suffers from bias, as demonstrated at, among other places, the end of the book when he assigns Catherine to "the dust and the certitude of everlasting negation."

SICHEL's book, while lacking in some of the basic modern scholarly paraphernalia of full citations, attribution, and footnotes, is striking for its discussion of Catherine beyond the religious-political sphere, the grist of most studies. It is refreshing to read something about Catherine's contributions to, and support of, the arts in France, for she was, after all, a Medici, great granddaughter of Lorenzo the Magnificent (1449–92), one of the most distinguished of Europe's art patrons. Her father, another Lorenzo de Medici (1492–1519), was also the patron for whom Machiavelli wrote *Il principe* (1517). One of the arts she deeply influenced in France, the culinary arts, is overlooked by most scholars, who prefer the more dramatic aspects of her reign. When she married in 1533 at the age of fourteen, she brought to France an army of Italian cooks, who introduced the French to, among other things culinary, the fork, and a beef tenderloin dish which the French subsequently called *tournedos* (literally, "turn on [its] back"). It is from this period that the French culinary historians refer to Italian cooking as their *mère cuisine*.

WEIL views Catherine de Medici from a feminist perspective. While not an ideologue, she addresses with insightful analysis the manner in which Catherine managed, not through manipulation, but through maternal and matriarchal instincts, to consolidate the power of her sons, none of whom was particularly capable of ruling as well as she, in a period when that power was threatened religiously, politically, and economically, from both inside and outside of France. The results are lucid and informative, and function as a small palliative to the reputation Catherine seems to have suffered throughout history. It is surprising that feminist scholars, historians in particular, have not offered more of this kind of analysis of Catherine, whose worst shortcomings seem to have been shrewdness and shortsightedness, rather than the many negative characteristics heaped upon her by phallocentric historians and scholars.

WILLIAMSON offers no new understanding of Catherine or her times, but his is a particularly attractive book, generously illustrated with scores of plates, many of them in sumptuous color, which offer the reader both a mental and a visual look at Catherine and her period. The text is highly readable, and intended for the general reader; thus it is a good starting point for the beginner with an interest in Catherine or the period in which she lived.

—CARLO COPPOLA

Catherine the Great 1729–1796

Russian Empress

Alexander, John T., *Catherine the Great: Life and Legend*, New York and Oxford: Oxford University Press, 1989

De Madariaga, Isabel, *Catherine the Great: A Short History*, New Haven, Connecticut: Yale University Press, 1990

———, *Russia in the Age of Catherine the Great*, New Haven, Connecticut: Yale University Press, and London: Weidenfeld and Nicolson, 1981

Epp, George K., *The Educational Policies of Catherine II: The Era of Enlightenment in Russia*, New York: Peter Lang, 1984

Erickson, Carolly, *Great Catherine: The Life of Catherine the Great, Empress of Russia*, London: Simon and Schuster, and New York: Crown, 1994

Haslip, Joan, *Catherine the Great: A Biography*, New York: Putnam, and London: Weidenfeld and Nicolson, 1977

Mangan, J. J., *The King's Favour: Three Eighteenth Century Monarchs and the Favourites Who Ruled Them*, Stroud: Sutton, and New York: St. Martin's Press, 1991

Troyat, Henri, *Catherine the Great*, translated by Joan Pinkham, Henley-on-Thames: Ellis, 1978; New York: Dutton, 1980

Until recently, studies in English of the life and reign of Catherine the Great have tended toward the salacious, as writers were drawn as much to the stories of her sexual conquests as to her impressive military and political successes. Over the last few decades, scholars have enjoyed expanded access to Soviet and Russian archives, and have produced important studies that place Catherine more firmly in her own time, and reveal the bases for the extremes of adulation and condemnation that have always shaped her reputation.

The leading scholar on Catherine is DE MADARIAGA, and it is to a few of her many publications that one should turn first. *Russia in the Age of Catherine the Great* is a massive historical account that shows the contemporary effects and legacies of Catherine's reign throughout her empire. The emphasis is not on Catherine's private life, but on her career and on her country.

A Short History is an admirable synthesis, again from a wide-sweeping historical standpoint. Both books include helpful illustrations and maps, and comprehensive bibliographies.

EPP's monograph on Catherine's educational reforms gives valuable insight not found elsewhere about this domestic issue, which was of such great importance to Catherine. He presents in full detail the state of education at the time of Catherine's coronation, the contemporary European (particularly French) thinking about the importance of education even for the masses (and even for girls), and the hopes that public elementary schools could improve the lives of individual citizens as well as benefit the state. Epp synthesizes a great deal of eighteenth-century European educational theory and philosophy—material that Catherine studied carefully herself—and shows how educational reform increased the polarization of classes in Russia.

Several biographies of Catherine have been published in English; most of them are more commonly found in public than in scholarly libraries. The major biographies have relied on the same sources, and differ little in their presentations of verifiable information; certain scenes taken from Catherine's diaries are nearly identical in each book. The various authors do offer different interpretations, however, of her motivations and character.

ERICKSON is perhaps the most sympathetic, even admiring, of the authors, looking at Catherine with a feminist's understanding of history and domestic roles. Presenting Catherine as an emotionally battered wife, the author gives useful information about what treatment a wife might expect in this milieu, what recourse she had, and how important it was for Catherine to produce an heir—no matter who the father was. Catherine recognized a woman's place, and ignored it when she could. Erickson believes she was often bored, with few people around her as intelligent as she was or who shared her passion for reading. She may have been drawn to men as much out of yearning for educated companionship as out of sexual appetite. As a ruler, Erickson states, she increased the land holdings and the international prestige of Russia, and was generally accepted as kind and fair.

Although HASLIP acknowledges Catherine as the greatest woman of her age, she finds more problematic actions taken by the ruler that need to be "justified." Foremost among these is her betrayal of her own youthful dreams of liberating the serfs, whose numbers greatly increased during Catherine's reign. This issue clearly nags at the author as it did at Catherine, and the book returns to it again and again as Catherine discusses and worries over the serfs, as she writes her famous set of guidelines for a new legal code, and as she ultimately fails to be a woman a century ahead of her own time. If Haslip finds much to criticize in Catherine's decisions, she also places the responsibility more firmly on the general understandings of the time than on a weakness of character; Catherine would have had to be an even more remarkable woman to have acted differently.

TROYAT deals the most harshly with Catherine; of the major biographers, this author seems the least comfortable with the idea of a strong, sexually free, female ruler. The book quotes without comment several contemporary rumors about her sexual appetite, gives more detail than others about her sexual practices, and accepts contemporary assessments (including Catherine's own) that in many ways she was more like a man than like a woman. The book is most interesting for its interpretations of Peter's character, and it claims, almost uniquely, that Peter did not die a virgin, did in fact consummate his marriage, and may have believed himself to have impregnated Catherine at least twice.

MANGAN presents a Catherine controlled by her sexual desires. The author describes how she carved out a great empire, then gave much of it away piece by piece to placate cast-off lovers. When Gregory Potemkin came into her life, he assumed control of the southern empire, while the self-promoting Catherine took credit for his ideas and decisions.

ALEXANDER differs from the other biographies in focusing on the years of Catherine's reign, devoting little attention to her early life. An excellent examination of her long career, her military triumphs, and her political genius, this book succeeds as both a popular biography accessible to the general, educated reader, and as a scholarly study with new important information and insights, especially about Catherine's mental and physical health. Alexander examines Catherine's different treatments by male and female scholars, concluding that female scholars are more admiring of Catherine's achievements, while males tend to disapprove of her sexuality. He manages to downplay the significance of rumors of her sexual activities, while at the same time retelling more of those explicit rumors than other books.

—CYNTHIA A. BILY

Catt, Carrie Chapman 1859–1947

American Suffragist

Fowler, Robert B., *Carrie Catt: Feminist Politician,* Boston: Northeastern University Press, 1986

Katz, David H., *Carrie Chapman Catt and the Struggle for Peace,* Syracuse, New York: Syracuse University Press, 1973

Miller, Helen Hill, *Carrie Chapman Catt: The Power of an Idea,* Washington, D.C.: Carrie Chapman Catt Memorial Fund, 1958

Peck, Mary G., *Carrie Chapman Catt: A Biography,* New York: H.W. Wilson, 1944

Van Voris, Jacqueline, *Carrie Chapman Catt: A Public Life*, New York: Feminist Press at the City University of New York, 1987

Carrie Chapman Catt was famous in her lifetime but faded into obscurity thereafter. Her principal, although not her only, claim to importance was leading two million suffragists to victory. She succeeded Susan B. Anthony in 1900 as president of the National American Woman Suffrage Association (NAWSA), but resigned the post in 1904 because of her husband's illness. In 1915 she returned to the presidency and shifted the movement's emphasis from propaganda to political action. She was a persuasive speaker and had outstanding organizational ability. Catt's leadership helped the NAWSA increase its membership in two years from one hundred thousand to two million. From 1904 to 1923 she was also president of the International Woman Suffrage Alliance. Catt was the first international leader of the political phase of the feminist movement. With the attainment of the Nineteenth Amendment to the U.S. Constitution, which gave women the vote, she transformed the NAWSA into the League of Women Voters. With Nettie Rogers Shuler she authored, in 1923, *Woman Suffrage and Politics: The Inner Story of the Suffrage Movement.*

Catt was a modest and private person. She objected when her friend, Mary PECK, proposed to write a biography of her. Peck idolized Catt, stating that Catt looked the part of a leader. The result was a sort of official but superficial biography, not one analyzing her life and work. Catt cooperated because her devoted friend could be counted on to avoid Catt's private life, although she burned a vast number of letters (including many exchanged with Peck).

Not until the mid-1980s was there to be a serious study of Catt. Then two books appeared, both handicapped by Catt's efforts to protect her privacy by destroying evidence. FOWLER gives us a portrayal of a powerful and often contradictory leader. He adopts a reasonable tone, and a willingness to honor both sides in the debate over who deserves credit for the success of the suffrage movement. (The partisans of Catt and NAWSA and those of Alice Paul and the National Woman's Party tended to slight each other's contributions.) Fowler does not write a conventional biography. Instead it is a study of a political leader and political visionary, who had an ambivalent attitude toward politics and politicians. Catt shared the Progressives' hostility toward ordinary politics, with a distaste for corruption, ignorant immigrants, and minority groups. Yet she created a potent machine. She had an understanding of precinct organization, partly copying her organization from Tammany Hall. She undercut rivals and then adopted their ideas as her own (including campaigning for a federal amendment, lobbying Congress, and defeating opponents of women's suffrage at the polls). Fowler's Catt is a set of contradictions. She was both a reformer and a pragmatist. She was a Machiavellian politician but created the largest nonpartisan organization (the League of Women Voters) in the country. She was a tireless advocate of peace and disarmament, but she disavowed pacifism and urged support for World War I. Seemingly mild-mannered and modest, she was driven by ambitions, anger, and resentment of men.

VAN VORIS, working independently of Fowler but coming to similar conclusions, also emphasizes Catt's public life. (She does discuss Catt's romantic friendships with Peck and others.) The impact of Catt's ideas and of her organization of women continues to influence the lives of millions. She knew the importance of education and agitation and evolved from activist to leader, from nativist to internationalist. She was a compelling speaker, who inspired many. Starting with a deep suspicion of all foreigners, she dedicated the last 27 years of her life to working for peace and internationalism. These are aspects of Catt's life discussed by Van Voris.

KATZ discusses how Catt helped to form the Woman's Peace Party (WPP) in 1915 but kept apart from the pacifists' cause. In 1917 she broke with the WPP and joined the Committee for National Defense. She had only nominally involved herself in peace work. Later, after America's entry into the war, she also only nominally involved herself in war work. In the 1920s she created the National Conference on the Cause and Cure of War, an educational forum for the discussion of international issues. In the 1930s she helped to organize some of the earliest anti-Nazi protests in the United States. From 1939 on Catt supported aid to the Allies.

MILLER's work was issued to mark the centennial of Catt's birth. It gives a brief account of her career and reports on the first decade of the Carrie Chapman Catt Memorial Fund, a living memorial intended to spread the theory and practice of democracy through international exchange of persons, publications, and in-service courses.

—MARTIN GRUBERG

See also Suffrage: United States

Chaucer, Geoffrey 1342?–1400

British Writer

Crane, Susan, *Gender and Romance in Chaucer's Canterbury Tales,* New Jersey: Princeton University Press, 1994

Dinshaw, Carolyn, *Chaucer's Sexual Poetics,* Madison and London: University of Wisconsin Press, 1989

Evans, Ruth, and Lesley Johnson (eds.), *Feminist Readings in Middle English Literature: The Wife of Bath and All Her Sect,* London and New York: Routledge, 1994

Hansen, Elaine Tuttle, *Chaucer and the Fictions of Gender,* Berkeley: University of California Press, 1992

Mann, Jill, *Geoffrey Chaucer,* New York and London: Harvester Wheatsheaf, 1991

Martin, Priscilla, *Chaucer's Women: Nuns, Wives and Amazons,* Iowa City: University of Iowa Press, and London: Macmillan, 1990

Critics of all political persuasions have long observed that Chaucer's poems spoke, often directly, to topical debates concerning gender and the relationships between men and women. One task, therefore, of the now considerable body of Chaucerian feminist criticism has been to demonstrate how the standard accounts fail to address these textual representations and power relations in sufficiently critical terms. A weakness of some gender-aware Chaucerian criticism is its focus on authorial intention, promoting Chaucer as either sexist or protofeminist, and thus tending to fix a single meaning for his works. More successful are those critics who have demystified the often hidden operations of sexual politics in his writings and in their modern critical reception. Few critics, however, have proposed readings that attempt a significantly new configuration of sexual difference in the oeuvre. Feminist readings that articulate gender with class (or other categories) are lacking: the essays by Crane and Riddy (in Evans and Johnson's book) are exceptions.

DINSHAW's widely acclaimed book locates a powerful dynamic at work in the poetry: masculine desire to control the unruly feminine. Derived partly from medieval understandings of literary activity as gendered (reading, writing, translating, and interpreting as masculine activities carried out on the feminine text) and partly from modern anthropological understandings of woman as an object of exchange between men, this model yields persuasive readings of *Troilus and Criseyde*, the *Legend of Good Women*, and, from the *Canterbury Tales*, the tales of the Man of Law, Wife of Bath, Clerk, and Pardoner—and of their modern (masculinist) critics. This is a highly sophisticated, scholarly, and cogent account of the discursive structures that served to naturalize asymmetric power relations between men and women in Chaucer's texts, and thus to exclude other ways of understanding sex/gender and sexuality, traces of which are nevertheless present in the texts—and which Dinshaw hints at, notably in her discussion of the Pardoner.

MARTIN's long and rather diffuse volume challenges dominant readings of Chaucer's women as allegorical personifications of Christian vices or virtues, but it lacks an overall argument. Organized through pairs (mother and duchess, virgin and lady, nun and wife, fabliau and romance, wives and merchants, language and silence) and categories (Saints, Criseyde, medieval literary traditions, and medieval gardens), the study does not really justify this organization by reference to larger critical concerns. Although it usefully incorporates some recent textual and linguistic scholarship, its lack of focus and limited understanding of gender issues do not recommend it.

Despite announcing itself as a feminist reading, MANN's book is essentially an argument for a liberal Chaucer. She presents a strong case for attention to the feminine as that which allows the reader to recover "the full human meaning" of Chaucer's work. Written with clarity and verve, this is a scholarly reading that is responsive to literary effects. Its discussion of *Troilus and Criseyde*, *House of Fame*, *Legend of Good Women*, and several *Canterbury Tales* is arranged thematically: women and betrayal, anti-feminism, sovereignty, female suffering, and the "feminised hero," with Troilus and Theseus the chief representatives of a non-coercive masculinity: generous, noble, vulnerable, sensitive, and open to change. Typically, Mann argues that Chaucer's texts reverse the hierarchical gendered opposition between active and passive, but that this newly valued feminine passivity is something that is "actively" experienced. She addresses power relations but frequently elides their problematic aspects, arguing for example that Chaucer reveals a vision of obedience as a "spontaneous fusion of wills" rather than as a model of domination and subservience.

Arguing that "women characters and the feminine are the battleground over which [masculine] authority, selfhood and unity can be established," HANSEN's reading loosely deploys Freudian castration theory and notions of male homosocial bonding to analyse women and the female as what is excluded in Chaucer's texts. This polemical study offers useful and uncompromising insights into masculine anxiety about the feminine as it is worked out in the oeuvre, but it does not ultimately present a satisfying political reading. The book ends up being complicit with patriarchal woman-as-absence, because it does not sufficiently suggest alternative ways of reading female (or even male) figures. More textual analysis and historicising, and some recognition of the political usefulness of gender fluidity, might have strengthened the case. British readers may feel left behind by the fixation on challenging Chaucer's critical reputation for artistic and aesthetic greatness—what Hansen calls "fearing for Chaucer's good name"—which arises out of a specifically U.S. institutional matrix, although it is vitally important to recognise this institutional construction.

CRANE's careful scholarly study takes romance as the genre par excellence in which sexual difference is at stake. Using motifs from medieval romances—magic, adventure, male and female crossgendering—to organize her discussion, Crane traces effects of gender asymmetries in the tales of the Knight, Wife of Bath, Squire, and Franklin, and in the *Tale of Sir Thopas*. She argues that while romance centres on the masculine subject and treats masculine experience as universal, Chaucer's use of romance displays the capacity to resist and critique the dominant medieval sexual hierarchy. The study refers liberally to other Old French and Middle English romances, usefully contextualising and historicizing its case but also making the reading difficult at times. Especially valuable is the attention not only to gender but to other sets of power relations, notably social hierarchy, but also ethnic and political identity, with interesting discussion of magic as a manifestation of medieval orientalism, in which the feminine is associated with the exotic. However, the book does not quite realise its radical potential.

Aimed at students, EVANS and JOHNSON's anthology is not wholly devoted to Chaucer but does contain new essays on the *Franklin's Tale* (by Felicity Riddy) and *Clerk's Tale* (by Johnson), and it reprints three outstanding pieces by Carruthers, Delany, and Schibanoff that deal directly or indirectly with the Wife of Bath. A specially commissioned "Afterword" by Carruthers reviews the reception-history of her 1979 essay, providing a valuable snapshot of academic debate about feminism within medieval studies and about reading the Wife in particular. Evans and Johnson's accessible introduction uses the complex figure of the Wife of Bath as a focus for surveying feminist criticism within Middle English and Chaucer studies.

—RUTH EVANS

Chiang Ch'ing *see* Jiang Qing

Child, Lydia Maria 1802–1880

American Abolitionist

Baer, Helene G., *The Heart Is Like Heaven: The Life of Lydia Maria Child,* Philadelphia: University of Pennsylvania Press, 1964

Clifford, Deborah Pickman, *Crusader for Freedom: A Life of Lydia Maria Child,* Boston: Beacon Press, 1992

Karcher, Carolyn L., *The First Woman of the Republic: A Cultural Biography of Lydia Maria Child,* Durham, North Carolina: Duke University Press, 1994

Meltzer, Milton, *Tongue of Flame: The Life of Lydia Maria Child,* New York: Crowell, 1965

Mills, Bruce, *Cultural Reformations: Lydia Maria Child and the Literature of Reform,* Athens and London: University of Georgia Press, 1994

Osborne, William S., *Lydia Maria Child,* Boston: Twayne, 1980

Yellin, Jean Fagan, *Women and Sisters: The Antislavery Feminists in American Culture,* New Haven, Connecticut, and London: Yale University Press, 1989

A successful woman of letters and a tireless advocate for abolition, Lydia Maria Child was one of the most well-known and influential women in the nineteenth century. Child had an extensive literary career, writing novels, short stories, children's books, domestic advice books, and political tracts, as well as editing a children's magazine and an antislavery newspaper. Several recent historians and literary critics have brought her life and work to the fore of women's studies.

KARCHER has written the definitive biography on Child, a comprehensive analysis of how her life and writings reflected and shaped nineteenth-century American culture. From carefully analyzing all of Child's prolific writings on the home, the family, abolition, Indian rights, urban life, religion, and women's history, and setting Child's voice in dialogue with her contemporaries, Karcher argues that Child influenced and critiqued her culture as significantly as any other writer in the period. According to Karcher, Child's work exposes the contradictions of American society in the nineteenth century, particularly regarding the human rights of African Americans, Native Americans, the urban poor, religious minorities, and women. To study Child, Karcher concludes, means revising our notions of nineteenth-century women's authorship as far more complex than the sentimental and domestic tradition of women's writing suggests.

Like Karcher, CLIFFORD looks closely at Child's published writings and her extensive correspondence to trace the complexities of Child's character, and to reintroduce her to a central place in American history. Clifford's biography focuses on Child as an author, arguing that her life was fundamentally a struggle for recognition and respect as a whole person. Suggesting that Child worked hardest when confronted by obstacles, Clifford contends that Child's marriage to the feckless, unsuccessful David Child, whom she supported throughout their life together, may have been one of the many trials that motivated her creativity and ambition.

Both Karcher's and Clifford's biographies rely on publications of Child's manuscripts and correspondence in the 1980s. Important first steps in the recovery of information about Child include three earlier, and now somewhat outdated, biographies. The first of these is BAER's biography, which tells a sentimental, anecdotal narrative of Child's life. Baer portrays Child as a nineteenth-century "true woman," suggesting that she took up the abolition cause primarily because her husband did. In contrast, MELTZER's biography celebrates Child's own initiative, tracing her commitment to educating herself and helping others. Meltzer celebrates Child as a role model for younger adult readers, a similar audience to that which Child reached with her magazine *Juvenile Miscellany.*

OSBORNE's biography introduces Child to those unfamiliar with her by sketching out the major events in her life, by describing the context of nineteenth-century social reform movements, and by presenting interpretative readings of her major works.

Since the late 1980s, two analytical works on Child's literary significance have appeared. In his study of

Child's reform literature, MILLS argues that—even in her most radical abolitionist writings—Child worked within accepted rhetorical structures; her texts contributed to a gradual movement toward emancipation and social reform. Mills suggests that an analysis of Child's rhetoric within the context of nineteenth-century fiction, sermons, reviews, and newspaper articles provides insight into how writers of the time combined a belief in the didactic function of literature with a commitment to reforming the most pressing moral and social problems of their day. By contrasting Child's practical, earnest style with Harriet Beecher Stowe's fire and brimstone preaching, Mills contends that Child was a subtler reformer, true to the doctrines of individual reason and restraint that marked her Boston literary circle.

YELLIN examines a narrower selection of Child's texts than Mills, focusing on *An Appeal in Favor of that Class of Americans Called Africans*, her editorials in the *National Anti-Slavery Standard*, and her abolitionist fiction. In her close readings of Child's language in her nonfiction prose, Yellin identifies tensions between female supplication and confident assertion. Such tensions, Yellin suggests, indicate the contradictions involved in projecting a voice that is both political and female. Less comfortable with defending the rights of women as part of the antislavery movement than many of her abolitionist contemporaries, Child both used and subverted the conventions restricting women's discourse. Yellin praises Child's frankness in speaking out on such taboo issues as Northern prejudice and the sexual victimization of black women. However, she criticizes Child's construction of tragic mulatto heroines whose white heritage justifies their intelligence and their desire for freedom, contending that Child's conceptions of race and gender were limited by conventional attitudes.

—KIRSTEN JAMSEN

Child Custody

Crean, Susan M., *In the Name of the Fathers: The Story Behind Child Custody*, Toronto: Amanita Enterprises, 1988

Edwards, Harriet, *How Could You? Mothers without Custody of Their Children*, Freedom, California: Crossing Press, 1989

Friedman, Debra, *Towards a Structure of Indifference: The Social Origins of Maternal Custody*, New York: Aldine De Gruyter, 1995

Furstenberg, Frank F., Jr., and Andrew J. Cherlin, *Divided Families: What Happens to Children When Parents Part*, Cambridge, Massachusetts, and London: Harvard University Press, 1991

Maccoby, Eleanor E., and Robert H. Mnookin, *Dividing the Child: Social and Legal Dilemmas of Custody*, Cambridge, Massachusetts, and London: Harvard University Press, 1992

Maidment, Susan, *Child Custody and Divorce: The Law in Social Context*, London: Croom Helm, 1984

Marafiote, Richard A., *The Custody of Children: A Behavioral Assessment Model*, London and New York: Plenum Press, 1985

Weithorn, Lois A. (ed.), *Psychology and Child Custody Determinations: Knowledge, Roles, and Expertise*, Lincoln and London: University of Nebraska Press, 1987

Although many people do not go to battle over issues of child custody, the laws and psychological theories that the experts have fashioned around divorce and parenting affect everyone. Male parenting is a fairly new phenomenon, one that has relatively little backing from social institutions and the cultural attitudes that define gender roles. CREAN's book is not an argument against fathers or shared parenting or even paternal custody as such. However, it is an argument for being truthful and realistic about children, about who is really hurting, who is really carrying the load, and who really has the power over whom. The stories related in this book are true. Reading it is a kind of continuous jolt: illusion after illusion is illuminated and discarded, all in an effort to help people turn away from simplistic cure-alls.

The overall theme in WEITHORN's book is the message that, above all, humility and caution must characterize the involvement of psychologists in custody cases. The book focuses on psychological consultation in divorce custody cases, rather than in child custody cases generally or in the child protection context in which some custody cases arise. The authors do not discuss in any depth the scientific literature or professional issues relevant to psychological testimony in child abuse and neglect cases. Chapters one and two present a brief overview of relevant legal concepts that define custody adjudication. Broad judicial discretion resulting from the "best interests" standards is highlighted. Chapter two presents an analysis of the functioning of the adversary legal system in custody cases. Some of the possible effects of the custody process are identified here. Chapters three and four review that state of scientific knowledge in psychology relevant to child custody adjudication. Chapter three focuses on the "best interest" standard, while chapter four addresses the debate over the alleged superiority of joint custody. Chapters five and six focus on professional issues, common problems characterizing psychological participation in custody cases. Finally, ethical issues that arise in relation to psychologists' testimony in custody cases are discussed.

EDWARDS's book is about mothers who have given up or lost custody of their children. This book is based on the author's personal experience, on her research, and on questionnaires answered by more than three hundred women who have made the decision to leave but not lose contact with their children. How could an ordinary woman defy the dictates of custom, religion, society, a lifetime of conditioning, and a bred-into-the-bone expectation of roles and duties and choose to live apart from her children? And moreover, how can it be made to work? Questions like these are answered in this book. This is the self-revelation of the pioneer women living apart from their children, who have described fully with painful honesty the fears and guilt, the joys and rewards, the problems, the processes, and the people they have encountered on their journeys.

FURSTENBERG and CHERLIN provide a prototype of short volumes by scholars who seek the opportunity to step back from their research and communicate important conclusions by policy makers, practitioners, and the public at large. This book draws liberally from current research in many different disciplines to help the reader understand how children are affected by divorce. Research on marital instability is not summarized; rather, it is used to draw judgments about what can be done to help parents and children manage marital disruption and remarriage.

The purpose of MAIDMENT's book is to put the law of child custody in its social context. The author makes available a large body of knowledge about the social process in which the legal process plays only a small part. The author presents material for a greater social understanding of the legal process surrounding child custody. The focus of this volume is on social science evidence and findings as they relate to children, and the contribution that they can make to a greater understanding of the issues that form the subject matter of child custody legal decision-making. The emphasis is on recent research findings that are less widely known. This treatise represents not only an academic commitment, but also a search for a better legal system.

MACCOBY and MNOOKIN's publication is divided into four parts. It begins with an introduction to the study. Chapter two analyzes the tasks facing divorcing parents with respect to family functioning and provides an analytical framework for understanding the process of decision-making and divorce bargaining between spouses. Chapter three introduces the families discussed here, by describing their social and economic characteristics before they filed for divorce. It discusses changes that occur with time in the de facto arrangements for residence and visitation. The final section draws together the important themes of the book and explores the implications of the findings for making arrangements for the children of divorce.

MARAFIOTE divides his book into three major sections: background issues, areas of assessment, and assessment strategies. In the first section, important questions related to the espousal and development of the behavioral assessment model are discussed. The chapters relate to the history of child custody determinations, describe some of the current approaches to performing these evaluations, and review research relevant to the study of personality, the person-situation controversy, and the appropriateness of using many traditional trait-oriented assessment methods. The final chapter in this section provides a comparison between behavioral and traditional assessment. The last section of the book takes a detailed look at two behavioral assessment strategies that played a significant role in gathering assessment data, and the behavioral and structured behavioral observations.

FRIEDMAN begins with the proposition that adults not only fail to speak the truth, but they do not see it because their vision is obscured by the force of norms. This volume was shaped by children: their interests, encouragement, and criticisms. In chapter one the author talks about child custody in a historical context. Chapter two looks at marriage as the basis of family structure. Chapter three emphasizes motherhood and the change in maternal preference in child custody. Chapter four looks at the rising divorce rate and its causes. Chapters five and six examine the dilemma for women following divorce and the financial obligations to fathers. Finally, the author takes a hard look at the structure of indifference and proposed child custody alternatives.

—SUSAN M. TAYLOR

See also Child Support; Divorce: Present-Day

Child Sexual Abuse

Driver, Emily, and Audrey Droisen (eds.), *Child Sexual Abuse: Feminist Perspectives*, London: Macmillan Education, 1989

Ennew, Judith, *The Sexual Exploitation of Children*, Cambridge: Polity Press, and New York: St. Martin's Press, 1986

Family Secrets: Child Sexual Abuse, London: Feminist Review, 1988

Finkelhor, David, *Sexually Victimized Children*, New York: Free Press, 1979; London: Collier Macmillan, 1981

———, *Child Sexual Abuse: New Theory and Research*, New York: Free Press, 1984

Finkelhor, David, and Sharon Araji, *A Sourcebook on Child Sexual Abuse*, Beverly Hills and London: Sage, 1986

Rush, Florence, *The Best Kept Secret: Sexual Abuse of Children*, New York: McGraw-Hill, 1980

Russell, Diana E H., *Sexual Exploitation: Rape, Child Sexual Abuse, and Workplace Harassment*, Beverly Hills: Sage, 1984

Feminist work on child sexual abuse has burgeoned since the 1970s, and the new student or scholar can easily be overwhelmed by the present wealth of publications.

However, there remain some classic works in the field in terms of both political analysis and research, as well as some important updates and extensions of original concepts. RUSH's book is an early feminist classic, one of the first to argue that child sexual abuse must be seen as endemic to societies that disempower both children and women. Rush traces abusive practices and their incitement through different histories and literatures (Christian, Jewish, Greek, the Victorians), as well as in selected fairy tales, novels, films, and the mass media. As with most ground-breaking work, it is easy in retrospect to criticise aspects of this text on the grounds that its scope is so broad as to result in sweeping generalisations or in only brief attention to what have now become whole areas for research and theory in themselves. Feminist media and popular culture critiques have also developed considerably in sophistication since this book. Nevertheless, the chapter on Freud's recantation of his childhood sexual abuse thesis marks the origin of important contestations of "the truth" of psychoanalysis and related professions by feminists and children's advocates, and the book as a whole is one of the original guiding beacons for child sexual abuse survivor movements and their allies.

DRIVER and DROISEN provide a more recent British and Australian collection, which is grounded in the experiences and activism of feminist incest survivors. It includes both individual biographies and discussion of different theoretical perspectives. Perhaps most useful is the chapter discussing racism and anti-Semitism and their complex potential connections to both abuse itself and the resulting situation for the abused child, and a chapter addressed to professionals from the perspective of incest survivors.

There are several books by well-known social science researchers, which are essential to anyone embarking on a study of their own. Finkelhor and Russell have collaborated in some of their work, and both have published extensively. FINKELHOR's book (1979) is based on a study of the sexual victimisation experiences of 796 New England college students. Both women and men were given a survey questionnaire, and there was a follow-up, smaller scale, interview study. The book's prevalence findings were some of the first to be set in social science context and also to incorporate feminist ideas, and it is often still cited as the best source for data about the sexual abuse of boys.

FINKELHOR (1984) considers child sexual abuse as a social and moral problem and develops a theoretical analysis of it from a sociological and pro-feminist perspective, as well as presenting new research based on his own studies—the latter on under-researched topics like parents' attitudes to and knowledge of child sexual abuse, and what parents tell their children about it. This book includes chapters on the sexual abuse of boys and its comparison to data for girls, and on abuse by women (co-authored with Russell). It also puts forward a combination of a psychological and sociological framework for understanding sexual abuse, called the Four-Preconditions Model of Sexual Abuse, also used by Russell in her work. FINKELHOR and ARAJI's sourcebook is particularly essential background for trying to come to grips with the research field. It reviews a decade of research from a range of social science disciplines on child sexual abuse and evaluates findings, including discussing problems of methodology and offering suggestions for improving research. There are five main topic areas: prevalence, children at high risk, offenders, effects, and prevention.

RUSSELL's book is one of several based on her now classic, late 1970s feminist study, using random survey-interviews of 930 adult women in San Francisco. The study produced quantitative and qualitative data about the incidence, prevalence, and characteristics of sexual victimisation, and this book compares its findings to the considerable under-reporting of official methods such as crime reports. One of the greatest strengths is the way in which the wealth of information from the survey is used to consider various theories of causes of, and to criticise myths about, rape and child sexual abuse; and to build up a complex picture of patterns of interconnected forms of sexual exploitation in terms of both different kinds of victims and (to some extent) perpetrators. There is considerable detail on characteristics of both intra-familial and extra-familial childhood abuse, providing the background for commonly used feminist overall prevalence figures such as "between one in three and one in four" for the sexual abuse of girls. While some of the book's conclusions and arguments now deserve re-examining, and in some cases, updating, the study remains a rare large-scale feminist foray into research on this topic.

An equally rare examination by a social anthropologist of the involvement of children in prostitution, sex tourism, and pornography, ENNEW not only bases her arguments on concerns for the effects of adult power over children, and of male over female, but she also takes a more internationalist perspective. This results in the consideration of cross-cultural, racist, and class-based issues of power, making the book important reading in a contemporary climate where western assumptions about childhood and appropriate family life are often not questioned.

FAMILY SECRETS: CHILD SEXUAL ABUSE, published as a special issue of the British journal *Feminist Review,* responds to various controversies and conflicts over child sexual abuse in the 1980s. There is a particular focus on issues raised by "the Cleveland affair" in 1987, in which children suspected by a female pediatrician of having been sexually abused were taken into state care. Subsequently politicians and media tended to claim that this was a misdiagnosis and that feminists and state professionals were conducting a witch hunt against families, and fathers in particular. Various feminist contributors use the case as a marker to analyse the cultural politics of the British context, including making connections to U.S. history, investigating media constructions, and generally reasserting a non-simplistic but feminist analysis of the issue of child sexual abuse as a whole, and support for feminist workers against child sexual abuse.

—CHRIS ATMORE

See also Incest; Sexual Assault/Rape: Other

Child Support

Beller, Andrea, and John Graham, *Small Change: The Economics of Child Support,* New Haven, Connecticut: Yale University Press, 1993

Garfinkel, Irwin, Sara S. McLanahan, and Philip K. Robins (eds.), *Child Support Assurance: Design Issues, Expected Impacts, and Political Barriers as Seen from Wisconsin,* Washington, D.C.: Urban Institute Press, 1992

———(eds.), *Child Support and Child Well-Being,* Washington, D.C.: Urban Institute Press, 1994

Josephson, Jyl J., *Gender, Families, and State: Child Support Policy in the United States,* Lanham, Maryland: Rowman and Littlefield, 1997

Krause, Harry D., *Child Support in America: The Legal Perspective,* Charlottesville, Virginia: Michie, 1981

Mezey, Susan Gluck, *Children in Court: Public Policymaking and Federal Court Decisions,* Albany: State University of New York Press, 1996

United States Commission on Interstate Child Support, *Supporting Our Children: A Blueprint for Reform,* Washington, D.C.: U.S. Government Printing Office, 1992

Weitzman, Lenore, and Mavis Maclean (eds.), *Economic Consequences of Divorce: The International Perspective,* Oxford: Clarendon Press, and New York: Oxford University Press, 1991

Child support, or child maintenance, has emerged as an important component of contemporary social policy as more children worldwide spend some portion of their childhood living with only one of their parents. Since most single parents are women, and women's wages are generally lower than men's, child support policy can have a significant effect on the economic well-being of women heads of single parent families. To some extent, the study of child support is linked to related policies, such as divorce and family law, and to social policies that provide public transfer payments to families with children and/or to single parent families. Further, generalizations about child support policy must be made with some caution, given that there is a great deal of variation among nation-states in terms of the institutional structure of their child support or child maintenance policies, in systems of family and divorce law, and in the structure and generosity of social welfare policies. Studies of child support thus tend to be country-specific; further, often the best source of basic program information for a given country are reports of government commissions or administrative agencies.

WEITZMAN and MACLEAN provide a useful collection of essays on various aspects of the economic consequences of divorce, including a section that deals with child support policies in various countries. Margaret Harrison details the development of child support policy in the 1980s in Australia, especially the Child Support Act of 1988, which established administrative procedures for the enforcement of child support, as well as child support guidelines to determine the amount of support payments. Harrison also discusses some of the political controversies over the implementation of these new policies. Barbara Willenbacher and Wolfgang Voegeli detail the development of child maintenance policies in the Federal Republic of Germany (which were adopted nationwide upon unification in 1990), where the common law tradition has well-established obligations for parental support of children, and there is a 75 percent compliance rate with child support orders. Karel Maddens and Jean van Houtte report on a study conducted in Belgium of compliance with orders for child support and alimony, concluding in part that women who are most dependent on male partners—due to low educational attainment, lack of attachment to wage labor, and larger families—also have lower support awards and more difficulties with enforcement. Irwin Garfinkel provides an overview of the development of federal child support policy in the United States, including an outline of a proposed child support assurance system.

KRAUSE provides a comprehensive introduction to the child support system in the United States. Included is an extensive discussion of the politics surrounding the Social Security Amendments of 1974, as well as discussion of program implementation through the early years of the program. Krause also extensively analyzes many of the legal issues involved in child support enforcement policy, such as the use of scientific evidence in establishing paternity, and the rights of mothers and of putative fathers in the paternity establishment and support enforcement process. Krause also addresses the question of federal and state cooperation in the implementation of child support policy, and assesses the success of the policy through the first five years of federal efforts at strengthening child support enforcement in the United States.

There are two major sources of national-level data regarding child support in the United States: annual reports prepared by the federal Office of Child Support Enforcement, and data collected since 1979 by the Census Bureau. BELLER and GRAHAM use the latter to analyze the success of child support policy in the United States in the 1980s. Their study finds that child support policies have had small effects in some areas. However, the data utilized dates only through 1986, prior to major reforms of the U.S. child support system enacted in 1988. Thus, more recent data, particularly after the adoption of child support guidelines and mandatory wage withholding policies, will likely indicate greater effectiveness of state and federal laws.

GARFINKEL, MCLANAHAN, and ROBINS have edited two volumes that report findings from studies of the implementation of child support policy in Wisconsin. These studies include the most comprehensive set of data assembled from various sources on child support policy, including court records, records of child support agencies, census data, and surveys. The first volume addresses the proposed Child Support Assurance system in Wisconsin, discusses the politics that prevented its full implementation, and analyzes the effects of various specific aspects of child support policy. The second volume specifically addresses the effects of child support policy on the well-being of children, with findings indicating that, in general, the receipt of child support payments does have a positive effect on several aspects of child well-being, such as educational attainment.

MEZEY's subject is U.S. federal court decisions dealing with public policy questions that affect children. In this context, she discusses social welfare programs such as Aid to Families with Dependent Children (AFDC), Women, Infants, and Children (WIC), and Head Start, and includes a very useful chapter on U.S. child support policy. After outlining the basic structure and history of child support policy in the United States, Mezey discusses Supreme Court decisions from the 1970s through 1993 that have dealt with some aspect of child support law. Mezey concludes that most decisions have involved contests between fathers seeking to avoid support obligations and children in need of support. Not surprisingly, since the interests of the state generally converge with the interests of the child in these instances, the Court has upheld children's right to receive support from noncustodial parents.

The United States Commission on Interstate Child Support was formulated in response to a major problem in enforcement of support obligations in a federal system such as that of the United States: the problem of interstate support. One-third of all child support cases in the United States are interstate cases, and these are the most difficult to enforce. This volume is useful in part because it provides a fairly comprehensive overview of the research on child support policy through the date of publication. The Commission also proposes major changes in the child support system in the United States, and the dissenting opinions of commission members, which are also printed in the volume, highlight some of the political controversy that surrounds child support policy.

JOSEPHSON combines an analysis of federal child support policy with a more in-depth study of the implementation of child support policy in two states. The book also includes a survey of custodial and non-custodial parents, as well as individual interviews with parents regarding their experiences with the child support system, and analyzes the impact of gender roles on the structure and implementation of child support policy. The book places child support policy in the context of family law and social welfare policy, provides a feminist analysis of these policies, and more generally situates the policies as examples of family-state relations in a liberal republican polity.

—JYL JOSEPHSON

See also Child Custody; Divorce: Present-Day

Chopin, Kate 1851–1904

American Writer

Ewell, Barbara, *Kate Chopin*, New York: Ungar, 1986

Hoder-Salmon, Marilyn, *Kate Chopin's "The Awakening": Screenplay as Interpretation*, Gainesville: University Press of Florida, 1992

Koloski, Bernard (ed.), *Approaches to Teaching Chopin's "The Awakening,"* New York: Modern Language Association of America, 1988

Martin, Wendy (ed.), *New Essays on "The Awakening,"* Cambridge and New York: Cambridge University Press, 1987

Papke, Mary, *Verging on the Abyss: The Social Fiction of Kate Chopin and Edith Wharton*, New York: Greenwood, 1990

Seyersted, Per, *Kate Chopin: A Critical Biography*, Baton Rouge: Louisiana State University Press, 1969

Skaggs, Peggy, *Kate Chopin*, Boston: Twayne, 1985

Taylor, Helen, *Gender, Race, and Region in the Writings of Grace King, Ruth McEnery Stuart, and Kate Chopin*, Baton Rouge: Louisiana State University Press, 1989

Toth, Emily, *Kate Chopin*, New York: Morrow, 1990; London: Century, 1991

The recovery in the 1970s of Kate Chopin's novel *The Awakening* marked a paradigmatic moment in twentieth-century feminist criticism. Finding works of fiction whose excellence had been overlooked, essentially because of their feminist themes and female authors, defined one of the major purposes of feminist criticism, not to mention a powerful motivation for the rereading of hundreds of forgotten texts by women. The eventual restoration of Kate Chopin to the U.S. literary canon became a model of what could happen when women's work was properly appreciated. After more than a half-century of neglect, during which time her literary reputation rested on one or two local-color stories, Kate Chopin has come to be regarded as one of the most significant writers of the late nineteenth century. And while *The Awakening* has thus far garnered the bulk of critical attention, her remarkable short stories have received increasing interest, while local color as a genre has itself begun to be regarded with fresh insight.

Chief among those responsible for Chopin's recovery was the Norwegian scholar SEYERSTED, who provided not only the first complete edition of Chopin's works (*Complete Works* 1969), but also a very influential critical biography. Seyersted's biography was in fact the first important appraisal of Chopin's oeuvre, which includes some one hundred short stories, dozens of poems, various essays, and one other novel, *At Fault* (1890). Seyersted weaves together the story of Chopin's life in St. Louis and Louisiana with a thoughtful analysis of her fiction, including several previously unpublished stories. Seyersted established several important features of Chopin study: the centrality of *The Awakening* (which earlier U.S. critics had all but ignored); and the singular character of her contributions to U.S. literature, exploring "the unsparing truth about woman's submerged life" and doing so with a modern consciousness. Seyersted also helped to perpetuate the notion of Chopin as a writer "banned" and defeated by the critical rejection of her novel, a notion that added an appropriate poignancy to Chopin's role as a prototype of the recovered female writer. His biography, including a detailed bibliography of Chopin's work and good background material on her life and times, remains a standard source.

With the exception of Robert Arner's work in a special edition of the periodical *Louisiana Studies* in 1975, no further book-length study of Kate Chopin was published until the late 1980s, although critical essays began appearing in scholarly journals with increasing regularity. Skaggs's volume in the Twayne series and Ewell's monograph in Ungar's "Literature and Life" series appeared in close succession, both taking feminist perspectives and attempting to assess the whole of Chopin's work. SKAGGS stresses Chopin's increasing focus on "the special problems that women face" in achieving individuality without relinquishing their sexual and maternal desires, a focus culminating in *The Awakening*. Skaggs is interested in what she perceives as universal conditions of womanhood. However, despite this universal concern, she focuses as well on the regional context of the novel and its historical setting in the late nineteenth century. Skaggs also provides a helpfully annotated bibliography.

EWELL attempts to set the novel's achievement in the context of Chopin's short fiction, whose development also reflects her ambitions as a serious artist. She offers as well a detailed chronology, and biographical material, synopses of the stories, and information on Chopin's other work, including poetry, essays, and personal writings.

Chopin's appearance as the first woman writer in the Modern Language Association's influential series, "Approaches to Teaching World Literature," provided a further index to her meteoric rise in critical regard. The essays collected by KOLOSKI on *The Awakening* focus on teaching practices, but are also of value to the general reader because of the wide spectrum of critical approaches to the novel, as well as materials that help place the novel in terms of Chopin's cultural and literary background. Also included are a good bibliographic overview, and information about editions and film adaptations of Chopin's works.

MARTIN's collection of essays provides several thoughtful assessments of the liminality or transitional quality of the novel, highlighting its richness as a subject for critical study. These are sophisticated articles, and Elaine Showalter's is particularly interesting in delineating the literary contexts of *The Awakening*, exemplifying the difficulties in placing work by women in conventional categories. Michael T. Gilmero's essay argues that the novel provides a foreshadowing of postmodernism. Andrew Delbanco focuses on gender identities within the novel, and Christina Giorcelli specifically analyzes the liminality of Edna's character as a woman always on the border between life roles.

Similarly limiting her scope to *The Awakening*, HODER-SALMON uses an inventive methodology (rewriting the novel as a filmscript) to arrive at her engaging interpretation of the novel and its contexts. Her transformation of the text as a critical exercise puts into relief several important qualities of Chopin's fiction, particularly her deft characterizations, her resonant uses of place and material objects, and her ability to convey the interiority of her heroine.

Perhaps the most important work on Chopin, aside from Seyersted's, is that by TOTH. When Toth's biography appeared in 1990, it immediately became a definitive source. One of the earliest critics to write on Chopin, Toth invests the writer's life with a remarkable depth of detail. Her inventive detective work and analysis yield many new perspectives on Chopin, including fascinating evidence of an amorous relationship with Albert Sampite in Cloutierville, and a notable lack of evidence that Chopin was ever a "banned writer" in St. Louis. Toth's appraisal of Chopin's fiction is often closely biographical, but she is one of the liveliest and most informed of Chopin's interpreters.

Two studies (among many) that are devoted only in part to Chopin help to establish her relationship to other contemporary women writers. TAYLOR views Chopin and her fellow Louisiana local colorists, Grace King and Ruth McEnery Stuart, as popular writers whose work helped to shape the image of the South. Taylor has a strong introductory chapter, outlining the complex cultural and editorial factors that shaped Southern women's writing after the Civil War. Although Taylor finds Chopin less explicitly racist than her peers, she concludes that Chopin's conservative views had a compromising effect on the trenchant critique of Southern ladyhood that both her short stories and *The Awakening* propose.

PAPKE also argues for Chopin's revolutionary attempts to refigure the place of women in society. For Papke, both Wharton and Chopin were trying to say something about women's lives for which there was not yet any explicit language. Her brief, though provocative, analyses of several of the major short stories and both novels are fine elucidations of the deeper stories that Chopin's disturbing fictions tell.

—BARBARA EWELL

Christianity: Pre-Reformation

Brown, Peter, *The Body and Society: Men, Women and Sexual Renunciation in Early Christianity*, New York: Columbia University Press, 1988

Bynum, Caroline Walker, *Fragmentation and Redemption: Essays on Gender and the Human Body in Medieval Religion*, New York: Zone 1991

Cloke, Gillian, *"This Female Man of God": Women and Spiritual Power in the Patristic Age, AD 350–450*, London and New York: Routledge, 1995

Newman, Barbara, *From Virile Woman to Woman Christ: Studies in Medieval Religion and Literature*, Philadelphia: University of Pennsylvania Press, 1995

Ruether, Rosemary Radford (ed.), *Religion and Sexism: Images of Woman in the Jewish and Christian Traditions*, New York: Simon and Schuster, 1974

Salisbury, Joyce E., *Church Fathers, Independent Virgins*, London and New York: Verso Press, 1991

Witherington, Ben, III, *Women and the Genesis of Christianity*, Cambridge and New York: Cambridge University Press, 1990

Although the pre-Reformation Christian Church has often been presented as a decidedly masculine institution, women were active and influential members of the Christian church of late antiquity and the Middle Ages. Contemporary writers have produced a wealth of material for anyone wishing to understand the historical, theological, philosophical, and cultural contexts of Christian women before the Reformation.

CLOKE takes as her subject the spiritual power of women in the later Roman Empire, using patristic sources as a means of reconstructing the idea of "holy women" in this age. Between A.D. 350 and 450, Christianity shifted from a persecuted, radical sect to an institutionalized state religion. This shift also changed its perception of women. In the very early history of the church, the most admired women were the female martyrs who stood in opposition to the state. During the patristic age, however, such martyrs seemed too vehement for a church trying to adapt itself to the institutions and customs of the culture. In response, the church developed two modes of womanhood: woman as either the betrayer of men or as the inspiration of men. The extensive primary source bibliography is valuable for anyone interested in patristics or saints' lives.

SALISBURY explores the connections among virginity, chastity, sexuality, and gender roles from late antiquity through the Middle Ages. Because women who followed the ascetic tradition placed themselves outside cultural norms, they were not subjected to the demands of wifehood and motherhood normally placed on women. Rather, their renunciation of sexuality offered them some control over their own lives. The dilemma for the Church Fathers, however, was that while they preached female virginity, they were not in favor of female independence. The first half of Salisbury's work demonstrates how the Church Fathers managed to maintain the ideal of the virgin, while nonetheless limiting the power and independence of women. The second half of the book investigates female saints' lives and the tensions between cultural expectations of women and the definition of holy women.

BROWN also examines the ascetic tradition in his study of permanent sexual renunciation in early Christianity. Brown centers his examination on what sexual renunciation reveals about "the nature of sexuality, the relation of men and women, and the structure and meaning of society" in early Christianity. The first part of the book uses the writings of early church leaders from Paul to Anthony. Further, Brown establishes the relationship between pagan and Christian notions of celibacy. The second part of the book focuses on asceticism and society in the Eastern Empire. In this section, Brown draws on Gregory of Nyssa as a source for ideals about marriage and morality, and also offers a careful look at the life of women ascetics in the fourth century. In his final section, Brown focuses on the work of Ambrose, Jerome, and Augustine for an examination of women, men, the body, and society. Brown's book is considered a landmark study, one that should be consulted by anyone striving to understand gender, sexuality, and the role of women in the early church.

WITHERINGTON closely examines New Testament material to describe the roles of women in the first years of Christianity. He first offers an overview of the roles of women in first century Judaism, in Hellenistic society, and in Roman society, in order to provide a context for his discussion. In part two, "Jesus and Women," he uses biblical texts to uncover Jesus' attitudes toward family life, widows, and marriage, as well as to offer a picture of the roles women played in Jesus' ministry. In part three, Witherington turns to the Pauline texts, and acts as an apologist for Paul and his writings on women. Finally, in the last section, Witherington examines the texts of the evangelists for accounts of women in the ministry of Jesus, their roles in the resurrection stories, and their contributions to the primitive church.

NEWMAN argues in her study of medieval religion that women have always been a potent force in Christianity, and that therefore gender has always been "an issue" for the church. She discusses the two ideals women occupied in the medieval theological context: virago and virgo. The virago is a virile woman, one on equal footing with men because of the negation of gender made possible by Galatians 3:28. The virgo is a highly feminized ideal, and one that places women in a superior position to men. Newman connects these two poles to two poles of contemporary feminism, equality feminism and difference feminism. She draws on her extensive knowledge of saints' lives to provide illustrations for her ideas. Further, she uses the lives of Hildegard and Heloise to provide medieval models for her categories of virile woman and womanChrist.

BYNUM's work is particularly valuable to any student of gender, Christianity, and the Middle Ages. Her book is a collection of her own essays, in which she explores the connections between religious experience and the body in the Middle Ages. In this period, Christ is often described in feminine terms. Bynum argues that this is because women are associated with flesh, while men are associated with spirit; when Christ becomes "enfleshed," he enters the feminine realm. Further, Christ bleeds and gives new life, both womanly signs. In her chapter, "The Female Body and Religious Practice," Bynum demonstrates how firmly religious experience is connected to bodily manifestation in women; stigmata (or the appearance of Christ's wounds on a believer's body) is nearly always a "female miracle."

RUETHER's work is a classic collection of essays, one that provides the foundation for a number of more recent studies. She seeks in the collection to offer essays that examine the roots of cultural misogyny in the Christian tradition. Ruether makes an important distinction between women as they really are, and women as they have been represented across time by male writers. Eight of the 10 essays are concerned with either medieval or early Christian traditions. Because several of the chapters discuss Jewish as well as Christian traditions, the book is especially helpful in placing Christian attitudes within a historical and cultural context. Important essays by leading scholars cover such topics as women in medieval theology; woman as seductress and source of sin; and women and canon law. Although Ruether's volume is an older book, it remains a necessary source for students of the role of women in Christianity.

—DIANE ANDREWS HENNINGFELD

See also Church Fathers; Convents and Nuns; Saints; Virgin Mary

Christianity: Post-Reformation

Beilin, Elaine V., *Redeeming Eve: Women Writers of the English Renaissance*, Princeton, New Jersey: Princeton University Press, 1987

Coon, Lynda L., Katherine J. Haldane, and Elizabeth W. Sommer (eds.), *That Gentle Strength: Historical Perspectives on Women in Christianity*, Charlottesville and London: University Press of Virginia, 1990

Douglass, E. Jane Dempsey, *Women, Freedom, and Calvin*, Philadelphia: Westminister Press, 1985

Fiorenza, Elizabeth Schussler, *Discipleship of Equals: A Critical Feminist Ekklesia-logy of Liberation*, New York: Crossroad, and London: SCM, 1993

MacHaffie, Barbara J., *Her Story: Women In Christian Tradition*, Philadelphia: Fortress Press, 1986

Oden, Amy (ed.), *In Her Words: Women's Writings in the History of Christian Thought*, Nashville: Abingdon Press, 1994; London: SPCK, 1995

Ruether, Rosemary, and Eleanor McLaughlin (eds.), *Women of Spirit: Female Leadership in the Jewish and Christian Traditions*, New York: Simon and Schuster, 1979

Wiesner-Hanks, Merry, *Convents Confront The Reformation: Catholic and Protestant Nuns in Germany*, Milwaukee, Wisconsin: Marquette University Press, 1996

The last quarter of the twentieth century has brought increased awareness of the status, role, and contribution of women in the written history of Christianity. Before that time, the history of Christian theology gave little or no record or texts from women themselves. WIESNER-HANKS has translated the major works of the well-known Reformation scholar Roland Bainton, who turned his attention from the men who had transformed religion in the sixteenth century to the women who had assisted them and opposed them at that time and during post-Reformation times. This study of women deepens the understanding of women's experience in the past and also shows a view of major historical changes, such as the Renaissance and the post-Reformation era, in new ways. The women in these texts were or had recently been residents in a convent or other type of religious house in the years following the Reformation. During this time, professed nuns in convent residences were much more literate and better educated than laywomen, and therefore, they could leave written records of their experiences and thoughts. Wiesner-Hanks gives some insight into the understanding of women's lives and religion in early modern society, through the writings of Katherine Rem, Ursula of Munsterberg, Anna Sophia of Quedlingburg, and Martha Elizabeth Zitter as these women confronted the years after the Reformation from their own experiences.

In her desire to understand the role of women in Christianity after the Reformation, DOUGLASS questions the context of John Calvin's understanding of freedom and order. In particular she puzzles over Calvin's inclusion of women's silence in church as an "indifferent matter" among matter of order and decorum. In relation to this she raises question about the theological understanding of women's nature, and about the roles of real women in historical theology. She finds Calvin himself accountable for Protestant women's continued subordination to men in the church, because he understood the theological possibility of giving freedom to women but decided not to make any practical attempt to argue for it. However, Calvin's approach to the biblical material proves helpful as an example of exegesis by a respected theologian that can be used in support of women's ordination. He pointed to the fact that greater freedom for women in the direction of the equality of the kingdom would come someday—he was just not ready for it in his day.

BEILIN uses women's own writing after the Reformation to establish the cultural setting and tradition of women's pious writing in prose, poetry, and translation. She describes Margaret More Roper as epitomizing the humanist ideal of the learned and virtuous woman, followed by Anne Askew, whose learned and virtuous personality subverts the restrictions on women's roles. Finally, the years following the Reformation are shown to have provided women with the opportunity and the language for literary preaching that fostered a feminine image of the true Christian woman.

After presenting some early female writers, COON, HALDONE, and SOMMER share the work of other authors describing women's activity in Christianity from the fifteenth through the nineteenth centuries. The ideals and experiences among women in fifteenth- and sixteenth-century France are outlined in the religion of the *Femmeletes,* who were passionately interested in the changes of religious belief and practice introduced by the reform movement. A study of female spirituality in seventeenth-century France is portrayed in a description of the life of the nuns of Port-Royal. Other activities of women are discussed, including the relationship of women to the supernatural in late Victorian Britain, and religion in the lives of slaveholding women of the antebellum South.

ODEN's research has led her to discover that the actual body of women's writings within the history of Christianity is broad and greatly diversified. As well as discussing some early writers, she presents some of the writings of Teresa of Avila, Jane de Chantal, and Susanna Wesley written between 1500 and 1800. The section from 1800 to 1947 unveils writings by Ann Lee, Lucretia Mott, Hannah Whitall Smith, Elizabeth Cady Stanton, Georgia Harkness, and others. Each writing shows the woman's interest in and insight about doctrinal norms, theological claims, spiritual experiences, and the practical consequences of all of these for personal and ecclesial church life. Many of these writers were gripped by the engagement of transformational Christian thought with urgent cultural and social issues of their day.

The status of women in the Christian tradition is the focus of MacHAFFIE's writing, as she explores women's roles inside leadership structures, in religious ceremonies, and outside the official institutional churches and formal worship services. She looks at women and Christianity in the American colonies, describing Anne Hutchinson as the "American Jezebel." Women are shown as organizing for mission and reform through organized feminism, working for women's rights, and providing leadership in religious orders and in various Christian denominations. Changes in the world after World War II have also brought changes for the better for women in the Christian tradition. MacHaffie describes the new perspectives on ministry that develop, the situation of theological education, and the reforms in the liturgy. She points to the ongoing need for feminist theologies and for female theologians to become agents of transformation in this Christian reinterpretation process.

Female theologians have begun that process. RUETHER and McLAUGHLIN share the writings of a number of women in their collection of essays on leadership roles of women in the Jewish and Christian traditions. These essays make a contribution both toward the recovery of important aspects of women's history, and toward the charting of the paradigms of female leadership that could be possible within successive theological worldviews. In one essay Elizabeth Schussler Fiorenza looks to early Christian writings to explore the equality of women in the radical roots of the Christian traditions. Ruether herself in another essay looks to the ascetic women of the late patristic period as the early "Mothers of the Church." She depicts them as writers, thinkers, biblical scholars, and innovators, but because they were female they did not have public voice in the teaching Church. The leadership of women during other periods is addressed, including the role of the liberated American nun and women finally entering the sanctuary as officially ordained ministers with full voice to preach and teach.

FIORENZA challenges some of these past ways of discovering the role of women in the Christian tradition. Her book represents her own feminist theological struggles and reveals her attempts to reclaim and rename women's spiritual powers in very concrete situations. She claims that the women's movements in society and religion need a critical feminist analysis of patriarchal religious structures and a critical feminist theological articulation of liberation. She argues for a theological integration of biblical roots both with western notions of liberty and democracy, and with the radical egalitarian vision from the Bible of a discipleship of equals. A liberating Christian feminist theology must, then, overcome patriarchal frameworks and articulate instead a Spirit-filled vision of faith and hope in a liberating God.

Fiorenza dynamically presents this democratic feminist vision, which can give birth through the leadership of women today to a different society and a different Christian Church for the "global village" of tomorrow.

—BILLIE SALISBURY BALADOUNI

See also Clergywomen; Convents and Nuns; Fundamentalism: Christian; Saints; Spirituality, Feminist; Theology, Feminist

Christine de Pizan ca. 1364–1431

French Writer

Bornstein, Diane (ed.), *Ideals for Women in the Works of Christine de Pizan,* Detroit: Michigan Consortium for Medieval and Early Modern Studies, 1981

Brabant, Margaret (ed.), *Politics, Gender, and Genre: The Political Thought of Christine de Pizan,* Boulder, Colorado: Westview Press, 1992

Quilligan, Maureen, *The Allegory of Female Authority: Christine de Pizan's Cité des Dames,* Ithaca, New York: Cornell University Press, 1991

Willard, Charity Cannon, *Christine de Pizan: Her Life and Works,* New York: Persea, 1984

Christine de Pizan, a writer in the French court of Charles VI, was one of the first to write from what might be called a "protofeminist" perspective. Widowed at the age of twenty-five, and responsible for the support of her three children, she earned her living by writing, and several of her works seek to redress injustices against women in the literature and attitudes of the time.

BORNSTEIN provides a collection of essays on Christine de Pizan's major works and is a brief but useful introduction. Several of the essays focus specifically on her ideas regarding the roles and nature of women. Christine's portrayal of women varied according to genre. Bornstein suggests that women were seen as heroic and powerful in the imaginative works but as submissive and subservient in the realistic works. Bornstein argues that Christine's initial lack of self-confidence and vulnerability as a woman, combined with her strength as a writer, made her a strong champion for women.

QUILLIGAN's study provides an excellent analysis of Christine's most important work, *The Book of the City of Ladies*, an allegorical history of women. This was the first work of its kind in Europe to be written by a woman, and it is a response to the masculine traditions of women's history. Quilligan's approach, grounded in contemporary feminist and post-Lacanian theory, demonstrates how Christine's work critiques previous narratives by male writers such as Boccaccio and Vincent de Beauvais. She also discusses Christine's politics, arguing against feminist critics who have accused Christine of political conservatism. Although Christine was not a political revolutionary, Quilligan contends that she was one of the first women to use her writing as a means to discuss women's issues and other political concerns. Quilligan's book is an extremely important contribution to scholarship on Christine de Pizan.

WILLARD has devoted her career to the study and translation of the works of Christine. This definitive biography of France's first professional female writer is a very informative and accessible survey of Christine's life and works. Willard demonstrates how Christine's writings chronicle her inner life and her struggle for recognition and success, even though few models existed for such introspective and autobiographical writings. Christine's works also detail the late medieval French society in which she grew up. Christine vividly describes her cultural and historical milieu in her biography of the French king Charles V; in her conduct book written to advise women about how to live an honorable life; and in her last known work, a poem about Joan of Arc. This book is a superb and essential introduction to any serious consideration of Christine de Pizan.

The collection of essays edited by BRABANT focuses specifically on Christine's political theories and positions as demonstrated in her life and writings. As some of the essays point out, there are inconsistencies or paradoxes in some of Christine's political statements, but her work nonetheless reveals a concern with the issues of power, law, and justice. As Quilligan also argued, Christine was no political radical; essays in this book claim that Christine's opposition to disorder and anarchy was a result of her own politically unstable world. In her works, Christine also suggests that political and ethical action cannot be exclusive. This important collection focuses on Christine as a protofeminist figure and an early humanist, whose writings are useful in understanding medieval politics and society. This book will be particularly useful to philosophers, political scientists, and general medievalists.

—JO ELDRIDGE CARNEY

See also Feminist Theory, Formative Works

Church Fathers

Borresen, Kari Elisabeth, *Subordination and Equivalence: The Nature and Role of Women in Augustine and Thomas Aquinas,* translated by Charles H. Talbot, Washington, D.C.: University Press of America, 1981

Clark, Elizabeth A., *Ascetic Piety and Women's Faith: Essays on Late Ancient Christianity*, New York: Edwin Mellen Press, 1986
———, *Jerome, Chrysostom, and Friends: Essays and Translations*, New York: Edwin Mellen Press, 1979
LaPorte, Jean, *The Role of Women in Early Christianity*, New York: Edwin Mellen Press, 1982
Power, Kim, *Veiled Desire: Augustine on Women*, New York: Continuum, 1996
Salisbury, Joyce E., *Church Fathers, Independent Virgins*, London and New York: Verso Press, 1991

It is surprising, in light of the importance of women in the early Christian church, that there is still relatively little scholarly consideration of the ideas about women contained in the writings of the Church Fathers. One of the earliest book-length studies of the Church Fathers' attitudes toward women is that by CLARK (1979), a book that investigates the theological and social status of women in the eyes of early Christian theologians John Chrysostom and Jerome. This study is divided into two parts. In the two lengthy essays that comprise the heart of the book, Clark argues that Chrysostom and Jerome were able, in spite of their strong convictions that women were divinely ordained to be subordinate to men, to forge friendships based on a likeness of interests and inclinations, bordering on equality, with Christian women who led lives of sexual renunciation. The second part of this volume consists of translations of primary sources, each preceded by a brief comment from Clark, which provide textual support for the argument she makes in the essays. Taken as a whole, this accessibly written volume offers valuable insights into some of the conflicts between theory and practice in the lives of two Church Fathers, and it suggests the richness of opportunity for further feminist work in this field.

In a later work, CLARK (1986) turns her attention to other related issues arising from the writings of the Church Fathers. Essays in this broad-based collection range from an excellent historical overview of attitudes toward women in early Christian texts to more focussed considerations of views of the early Christian thinkers on sexuality and asceticism, and include two examinations of the Church Fathers' interpretations of biblical texts—the early chapters of Genesis and the Song of Songs—that have commanded much attention from scholars and exegetes interested in the role of women in Christian history. Again, this volume is accessible in its language and sufficiently broad in its scope to be of interest to a wide range of readers.

In another major study, POWER offers a thorough consideration of Augustine's attitudes toward women. This clear and well-argued volume, which respects the theological and socio-cultural context within which Augustine wrote, brings insights from psychology, feminist theory, and theology to bear on Augustine's texts, in order not only to explicate the actual content of those texts, but also to explore the consequences of Augustine's views for the modern age. Chapters consider such topics as women's roles in early Christianity and in the Greco-Roman world; Augustine's relationships with actual women (including, most significantly, his mother Monica); his theological understanding of women's relationship with God; and the importance of the Virgin Mary in his thought. This book, written from a decidedly feminist perspective, provides a valuable guide to the views of perhaps the most influential of the Church Fathers.

In BORRESEN's book the reader encounters an examination of Augustine's views on women that is equally feminist, equally exhaustive, and equally valuable, and is coupled with a similar analysis of the work of Thomas Aquinas. The work proceeds in three parts. Parts I and II explore such topics as women's place in the created order, original sin, the role of the feminine in salvation, and the stages of a woman's life as seen in the work of Augustine and Aquinas, respectively. Part III examines the theological anthropologies of the two thinkers and argues that the androcentric views of Augustine and Aquinas—views that encourage the subordination of women to men—will have to give way to new theological and anthropological understandings if women are to find true equivalence. While intended primarily for an academic audience, this book is extremely clearly written and should be of interest and value to any motivated reader.

The remaining volumes under consideration here offer not in-depth studies of the texts of one or two Church Fathers, but rather more panoramic views of the attitudes of the early Christian theologians toward women. LaPORTE, for example, turns to the writings of such diverse figures as Clement, Tertullian, Augustine, Jerome, Chrysostom, and Origen to examine the role of women in the early church. She considers various aspects of that role—including martyrdom, marriage, asceticism, and ministry—and also explores the symbolic place accorded to women in early Christian theology. More survey than analysis or feminist critique, this book includes extensive quotations from the sources LaPorte consults and is sufficiently general in its interests to comprise a good introduction to this still relatively unmined field of research.

SALISBURY, like LaPorte, considers the writings of a number of Church Fathers, including Cyprian, Ambrose, Jerome, Tertullian, and, most notably, Augustine; however, the focus of her study is much narrower. This is a study of early Christian ideas about virginity, chastity, and sexuality, and it juxtaposes views culled from the writings of the Church Fathers with those of ascetic Christian women in order to suggest that in asceticism women were able to find an otherwise unavailable spiritual independence. This clearly written and interesting book argues the existence of a diversity of early Christian views on sexuality that is often overlooked in the shadow of Augustine's overwhelming influence, and for this reason it makes an important contribution to the field.

—JUDITH L. POXON

See also Christianity: Pre-Reformation

Circumcision, Female *see* Female Genital Mutilation

Citizenship

Fraser, Nancy, *Unruly Practices: Power, Discourse and Gender in Contemporary Social Theory*, Minneapolis: University of Minnesota Press, and Oxford: Polity Press, 1989

Meehan, Elizabeth, and Selma Sevenhuijsen (eds.), *Equality Politics and Gender*, London and Newbury Park, California: Sage, 1991

Pateman, Carole, *The Disorder of Women: Democracy, Feminism, and Political Theory*, Cambridge: Polity Press, and Stanford, California: Stanford University Press, 1989

———, *The Sexual Contract*, Cambridge: Polity Press, and Stanford, California: Stanford University Press, 1988

Van Steenbergen, Bart (ed.), *The Condition of Citizenship*, London and Thousand Oaks, California: Sage, 1994

Yeatman, Anna, *Postmodern Revisionings of the Political*, New York and London: Routledge, 1993

The issue of gender and citizenship is fundamental to discussions of women's status in contemporary society. A number of feminist arguments have been based on the claim that as citizens, women have the same rights as men. However, feminists have also found it necessary to deconstruct the concept itself, in terms of its historical development and current usage, to interrogate the real extent of its usefulness. The books included in this entry represent some of the major trends in that deconstructive and interrogative project.

The author whose name most readily springs to mind in discussions of gender and citizenship is PATEMAN. Pateman analyses both citizenship (1989), and contract theory (1988), on which current conceptions of citizenship are predicated. She argues that citizenship is a masculinist construct that has as its subject the normative (white) male of contract theory. As a patriarchal concept/category, citizenship presents women with what Pateman refers to as the "Wollstonecraft dilemma." On the one hand, if we demand equality on the basis of shared citizenship, we perforce accept the patriarchal construction of the term, and as a consequence we become, in a sense, second-class males. On the other hand, to demand recognition and positive valuation of women as women is to claim recognition of precisely what is excluded by the dominant discourse of citizenship. In other words, since the individual of contract theory is male, women can never be incorporated in political society as anything other than subordinates. Moreover, the relationship between public and private spheres underlies the development of political society, and is fundamentally implicated in women's relationship to citizenship. The other books in this entry are in many ways extensions of, responses to, or modifications of Pateman's groundbreaking works.

YEATMAN provides an excellent overview of traditional conceptualizations of citizenship and their implications for various "others," including women. Chapters four through seven are the most relevant in this regard. Yeatman's basic point is that "the dominant discourses of modern citizenship are predicated on systemic exclusions of those who are othered by these discourses." She traces the historical roots of the concept in natural rights theories of action, which are based on a particular conception of the "individual," which is itself based on the construction of a dependent "other" who cannot hold the status of individual. This "other" is often female (or young, or a racialized minority). This is the liberal discourse of modern citizenship. Yeatman also traces republican and welfare state discourses of citizenship. While the former is participatory in nature, and the latter actually brings women under its purview, both, like liberal discourse, require a partioning off of the non-rational, the needy, the subjective, the private. Again, women are the "other" of these discourses. Yeatman's argument is that we need a fundamentally new framework for thinking about citizenship. She presents the outlines of such a new conceptualization in her discussion of the politics of difference, in which heterogeneity and what she calls "perspectival dialogism"—a form of conversation and negotiation that valorizes rather than works to subsume difference—prevail.

The collection of articles edited by VAN STEENBERGEN also explores the usefulness of the concept of citizenship in contemporary society. While all the chapters are useful, some providing an analysis of historical traditions, and others focusing on "where to next," those that focus on issues of inclusion and exclusion are particularly relevant to gender and citizenship. Adriaansens, for instance, examines the relationship between citizenship and the welfare state in a changing socioeconomic context. He focuses on the "traditional family philosophy" of male breadwinner and dependent wife as a barrier to women's participation in paid labor, which he sees as the best means of increasing participation in the community and public life, the hallmark of citizenship. Vogel also explores marriage as a "nexus of domination and subjection," which serves to exclude women from full citizenship by limiting their life chances in the public sphere.

She advocates the development of a gender-neutral form of marriage, which would have positive implications for women's citizenship status. Finally, drawing on T.H. Marshall's 1949 distinction among civil, political, and social citizenship, Fraser and Gordon provide an analysis of the tensions currently underlying the relationship between civil and social citizenship in the United States, the former concerned with individual freedom, the latter focused on the right to social provisioning and to full participation in society. The tension relates to the contract-charity/male-female binary underlying civil citizenship. Fraser and Gordon trace the historical construction of contract as the normative mode of interaction, and outline how female dependence was a necessary constituent of the (white) male "possessive individualism" required for contract exchanges. This distinction between contract and charity has negative implications for the way in which particular ("noncontributory") social provisioning for the poor—much of which is directed at women as single mothers—is viewed. Thus, as dependents on husbands or on the state, women's social citizenship is undermined. While space considerations preclude discussion of the other parts of the book, readers will also find the chapters by Falk and Turner, which address globalization and the modern/postmodern nexus, particularly useful.

The gendered nature of the concept and practice of citizenship is further outlined by FRASER. In addition to a critical examination of the concept as it is used by Habermas, Fraser presents an analysis of citizenship and gender in the context of the welfare state. Her analysis of the U.S. dual welfare system complements the analysis of contract-charity she presents with Gordon in the article described above. In short, there are two types of social welfare programs: "masculine" programs, such as worker's compensation, which uphold the civil rights of recipients; and "feminine" programs, such as Aid to Families with Dependent Children, which effectively deny citizenship rights to their recipients, rendering them "the negatives of possessive individuals." As is reflected in the dual labor market, women are constituted not as individuals, but as members of a (family) unit. Again, as outlined by others, the "citizen" is usually a (white) male, and his citizenship status is predicated on the degradation and dependence of women. This process has its fundamental basis in philosophical and political discourses outlined by Pateman and Yeatman.

While most of the books in this entry are theoretical in nature, the articles in MEEHAN and SEVENHUIJSEN discuss the deployment of concepts in feminist politics, particularly that directed at public policy. Simultaneously theoretical and practical, the book has as its project a deconstruction of the concept of equality. This entails close examination of the term as it is used in social contract theory, and in relation to citizenship. The basic point, made by authors focusing in turn on Finland, Denmark, the United States, France, Ireland, the Netherlands, and Britain, is that political concepts are gendered; thus the possibility of framing "feminist goals in the received languages of politics" is problematic. The points the authors make about citizenship are similar to those made by other authors discussed in this entry: that the normative citizen is the male "possessive individual" of contract theory, and that the public/private divide is fundamentally implicated in women's status as second-class citizens. What is particularly useful about this collection is its interrogation of the relationship between concept and practice. As such, it provides an excellent complement to primarily theoretical works.

—CATHERINE PÉLISSIER KINGFISHER

Cixous, Hélène 1937–

French Writer

Conley, Verena, *Hélène Cixous: Writing the Feminine*, Lincoln: University of Nebraska Press, 1984

———, *Hélène Cixous*, Toronto: University of Toronto Press, and London: Harvester Wheatsheaf, 1992

Sellers, Susan, *Hélène Cixous: Authorship, Autobiography and Love*, Cambridge: Polity Press, and Cambridge, Massachusetts: Blackwell, 1996

Shiach, Morag, *Hélène Cixous: A Politics of Writing*, London and New York: Routledge, 1991

Wilcox, Helen, Keith McWatters, Ann Thompson, and Linda Williams (eds.), *The Body and the Text: Hélène Cixous, Reading and Teaching*, New York: St. Martin's Press, and London: Harvester Wheatsheaf, 1990

Critical responses to Cixous's work have tended to be split between detailed and specific analyses appearing in academic journals, and introductory books designed to present Cixous's extensive oeuvre to a readership assumed to be largely unfamiliar with it. Although most articles focus upon Cixous's so-called theoretical essays, which have gained a certain notoriety in the English-speaking world, the critical books have all managed to pay more balanced attention to her theory as well as her fiction and drama.

CONLEY is a Cixous scholar of some stature, and she provided the first full-length critical study in English (1984). In order to avoid crude paraphrase of Cixous's difficult and innovative texts, Conley writes in a quasi-Cixousian manner, employing a fluid, poetic, and allusive/elusive style to convey her critical arguments. Such a technique usefully provides a sense of the flavor of Cixous's work—especially her use of myth—but at the expense of some critical distance, and the result is a book that is less accessible than some of its successors. The book concentrates largely on fictional and theoretical works, with less emphasis on Cixous's drama, and follows the trajectory of Cixous's writing career chronologically. The updated paperback edition (1991) has a new preface, bibliography, and a fascinating interview with Cixous conducted by the editors of *Hors Cadre*.

WILCOX, MCWATTERS, THOMPSON, and WILLIAMS have provided the only book on Cixous that does not aim at introduction, being a collection of critical essays from the conference on Cixous at Liverpool University in 1989. The first part of the volume is devoted to work by and about Cixous, and the subsequent sections broaden out to a more general discussion of writing, reading, and gender. There are chapters by well-known Cixous scholars Sarah Cornell, Nicole Ward Jouve, Susan Sellers, and Françoise Defromont. Cornell's essay introduces readers to the biography and thought of Cixous, and Ward Jouve analyzes the movement from inner theater to world theater in Cixous's work, as she has moved from fiction and "theory" to drama in more recent years. Critic Judith Still makes a closely theoretical analysis of Cixous's notions of a "feminine economy" of desire. The complex relationship between "feminine" and "female," and between culture, biology, and language is examined to assess the possibility of a feminine economy as "theoretical extreme or poetic utopia." Sellers explores some of the implications of *études féminines*, for reading, teaching, and the practice of criticism. Defromont's essay on metaphorical thinking in Cixous and Virginia Woolf links the techniques of the two writers together in a celebration of the textual and political effects of *écriture féminine*. Overall, the collection provides a welcome dialogue among scholars interested in debating issues raised by Cixous's work, rather than merely introducing her work at a basic level.

In contrast to Conley's study, SHIACH's volume is a model of clarity and detail. Four chapters announce themselves straightforwardly: "Politics and Writing"; "Strategies of Reading"; Writing Differently"; and "Staging History." Shiach's approach is less personal or idiosyncratic than that of Conley's first book, and is perhaps aimed more directly at student readers. All the major areas of Cixous's work are covered, clarifying its philosophical and theoretical content, and placing it in historical context. For the first time in a book-length study, Cixous's dramatic works and her collaboration with the Théâtre du Soleil are given detailed attention. Cixous as a reader—of Poe, Lispector, Freud, Hoffmann, Kleist, and Joyce—is also addressed. Unlike Conley, Shiach examines both the strengths and the shortcomings of Cixous's feminist ideas.

CONLEY's second book on Cixous (1992) appeared in a series entitled "Modern Cultural Theorists" and—much more so than her first study—provides a lucid account of Cixous's relationship to contemporary culture and literary and philosophical history. Critical poetics gives way to a more straightforward style and balanced approach, revealing how Cixous's work reflects the major intellectual currents in France in the last three decades, while in some respects remaining intriguingly anomalous.

SELLERS has provided yet another introductory book, this time focusing largely on those works that have been translated into English. Sellers presents, rather than analyzes, the philosophical ideas embodied in Cixous's literary texts, and the condensation required of an introductory study results in some simplification. Each of Cixous's texts that is examined in detail is assessed for its ability to function as (as well as describe) *écriture féminine*, or "writing the body." The book includes an extremely valuable bibliography on Cixous-related texts.

—VAL GOUGH

Class and Gender

Abbott, Pamela, and Roger Sapsford, *Women and Social Class*, London and New York: Tavistock, 1987

Crompton, Rosemary, and Michael Mann (eds.), *Gender and Stratification*, New York: Blackwell, and Cambridge: Polity, 1986

Delphy, Christine, *Close to Home: A Materialist Analysis of Women's Oppression*, translated and edited by Diana Leonard, London: Hutchinson, and Amherst: University of Massachusetts Press, 1984

Dex, Shirley, *Women's Occupational Mobility: A Lifetime Perspective*, London: Macmillan, and New York: St. Martin's Press, 1987

Martin, Jean, and Ceridwyn Roberts, *Women and Employment: A Lifetime Perspective*, London: HMSO, 1984

Payne, Geoff, and Pamela Abbott (eds.), *The Social Mobility of Women*, London and New York: Falmer, 1990

Feminists have raised strong objections to the way social class has been handled in conventional social science theorizing, resulting in a theoretical debate and empirical research to demonstrate the necessity of incorporating women into stratification and class theory. Two broad areas may be distinguished within the feminist challenge to class theory: the attempt to revise class theory to make sense of women's class relationships, and the wider attempt to recast stratification theory as a whole so that gender differences and inequalities are properly recognized within it. Many important contributions to the debate have been presented as journal articles or articles in edited collections. ABBOTT and SAPSFORD provide a useful summary of many of these, and reexamine the conventional wisdom about women's social mobility, labor market position, and class sentiment, using data from a British national survey carried out by students.

They give an overview of the key debates, and an analysis of female mobility (both intra- and intergenerational), and women's class imagery and identification, examining in detail the assumption of conventional class theory that a woman's class position is derivative from that of her husband or father.

DELPHY, from a materialist feminist perspective, argues that stratification theory should be more concerned with gender inequalities. She argues that sexual inequality is primary, and more fundamental to understanding society and social structures than occupational inequality. Women are a class exploited by men as a class. Because women are opposed as a class to men, are exploited by men, and therefore have shared interests in opposition to men, and patriarchal structures are fundamental to our form of social organization, it follows that the main axis of differentiation must be gender.

The edited collection by CROMPTON and MANN contains articles that contribute to both debates. The view that it is necessary for stratification theory to account for gender inequalities is further developed. Articles in the collection point to the need to recognize that women have two class positions—as women, and as paid workers. Other articles point to the need to recognize the ways in which women's domestic roles structure the opportunities available to them in the labor market, and therefore their social class, and others point to the inadequacies of conventional social class scales for differentiating between women's occupations.

The books by Dex, and Martin and Roberts, and the edited collection by Payne and Abbott, all focus on the question of women's occupational mobility. MARTIN and ROBERTS consider women's occupational mobility over the life course, their work orientation and commitment to the labor market, and the ways in which the labor market is segmented and segregated by gender, using data from a national British government survey. DEX uses the same survey data to develop the analysis by considering women's occupational profiles across a number of "female" occupations. She makes an important contribution to debates about core and peripheral labor markets, by demonstrating the existence of a female core labor market. The PAYNE and ABBOTT collection includes articles that contribute further to the debates about female inter- and intra-generational mobility, showing that it is necessary to incorporate women into class research in order to understand male mobility. Various articles continue the debate with conventional social class theorists, present results from major British surveys that have included women in their samples, explore differences within the household, and examine changing occupational patterns and profiles of occupational mobility.

—PAMELA ABBOTT

Cleopatra 69–30 B.C.

Egyptian Queen

Flamarion, Edith, *Cleopatra: The Life and Death of a Pharaoh*, New York: Harry N. Abrams, 1997

Grant, Michael, *Cleopatra: A Biography*, London, Weidenfeld and Nicholson, 1972; New York: Dorset Press, 1992

———, *From Alexander to Cleopatra: The Hellenistic World*, London: Weidenfeld and Nicholson, and New York: Charles Scribner's Sons, 1982

Hughes-Hallett, Lucy, *Cleopatra: Histories, Dreams, and Distortions*, London: Bloomsburg, and New York: Harper and Row, 1990

Volkmann, Hans, *Cleopatra: A Study in Politics and Propaganda*, London: Elek, and New York: Sagamore Press, 1958

Weigall, Arthur, *The Life and Times of Cleopatra, Queen of Egypt*, New York: Putnam, and London: W. Blackwood, 1914

Cleopatra has been a prominent figure in poetry, drama, and literature since her death by suicide in 30 B.C. The exaggerated portrayals of the Egyptian queen in literature, theater, and film have distorted the true character of the woman who was one of the major contenders for power in the Hellenistic world. It must be stated that although very popular and widely available, there is little historical accuracy in Shakespheare's tragedy *Anthony and Cleopatra* or George Bernard Shaw's *Caesar and Cleopatra*. It is somewhat suprising, considering the wealth of writings about Cleopatra, that so few have focused on her role as a political leader rather than as a temptress. It has only been since the 1970s that histories have emerged truly unencumbered by sexist and racist inferences.

Although it is not based on feminist theory, the standard has become GRANT's biography of Cleopatra. One of only a few books written about the queen still in print, the text was recently released in a revised edition. The author is a well-known historian and has published more than 50 books on subjects related to the Hellenistic age. Grant is critical of the "fog of fiction and vituperation" that has surrounded Cleopatra's career, promoting his text as one that tries to cut through the western myths and stereotypes. The text is a painstaking attempt at surveying available sources of information and filtering out prejudices in an effort to portray Cleopatra as she really existed. Grant relies on coins, for example, as one of several types of non-literary evidence used to develop his thesis. The bibliographical information in the revised edition is current and well organized.

GRANT also published a book on the Hellenistic world that is worthy of note. Although Cleopatra is mentioned in the title, the book only refers specifically to the queen in a few of the chapters. Most notably, however, there is an entire chapter on the Hellenistic woman that gives considerable insight into the changing societal role of women during the age of Cleopatra. The contributions of the Hellenistic Ptolemiac queens in emancipating women of their day are discussed in detail. Illustrations included with the text are a great complement. The text is full of original source material and should be viewed as a companion piece to Grant's biography of Cleopatra. Both of Grant's books mentioned here are widely available in libraries and bookstores.

HUGHES-HALLETT is concerned with the actual events of Cleopatra's life, but also with the evolution of her place in history and popular culture. She states that the view of Cleopatra through the ages has changed depending on society's view of women at the time. Many have referred to this work as a cultural history rather than a biography. Hughes-Hallett, who makes no effort to hide her feminist slant, is not a historian, but rather a former writer for *Vogue* and a televison critic. Most of the text, as a result, is devoted to the male chauvinist fantasy that has become Cleopatra. The highly touted book contains numerous illustrations of the queen from various sources, most nude.

FLAMARION's newly released English translation of her popular book, first published in France in 1993, is very brief text (slightly over 150 pages) filled with a collection of illustrations and photographs unavailable elsewhere. The book is divided into two sections, one full of text and illustrations, the other "documents" that deal with the history, myth, and literature surrounding the woman. The very colorful illustrations are pleasing to the eye and thought provoking, but the text offers no new material of consequence. The inexpensive price of Flamarion's book will aid its success in bookstores. It is not a scholarly text but is worthy of note.

VOLKMANN's book was the standard prior to Grant's work but is now to be considered outdated with a few exceptions. Factually, the information contained in the text is accurate, but the reader will find it lacking contemporary theoretical concepts. He relies heavily on the ancient literary sources. Volkmann's book is fasinating reading, especially for those interested in the evolution of historiography as it relates to the study of Cleopatra. Volkmann's bibliographic information on ancient sources is considered excellent, perhaps the most extensive ever assembled.

WEIGALL provides an acceptable alternative when the texts listed above are not available. Weigall makes use of his extensive knowledge of Egypt and its history to create a workable book. It should be noted that the original version was first published during World War I, and that much has been learned since that time. One should also keep in mind when reading the book that Weigall was greatly influenced by the prejudices of his day. This book is easy reading and a well-respected work, although outdated.

—DONALD C. SIMMONS, JR.

Clergywomen

Carroll, Jackson W., Barbara Hargrove, and Adair T. Lummis, *Women of the Cloth: A New Opportunity for the Churches,* San Francisco: Harper and Row, 1981

Chaves, Mark, *OrdainingWomen: Culture and Conflict in Religious Organizations,* Cambridge, Massachusetts: Harvard University Press, 1997

Lawless, Elaine J., *Holy Women, Wholly Women: Sharing Ministries of Wholeness Through Life Stories and Reciprocal Ethnography,* Philadelphia: University of Pennsylvania Press, 1993

Lehman, Edward C., *Women Clergy: Breaking Through Gender Barriers,* New Brunswick, New Jersey: Transaction Books, 1985

Proctor, Priscilla, and William Proctor, *Women in the Pulpit: Is God an Equal Opportunity Employer?,* Garden City, New York: Doubleday, 1976

Purvis, Sally B., *The Stained Glass Ceiling: Churches and Their Women Pastors,* Louisville, Kentucky: Westminster John Knox Press, 1995

Schmidt, Frederick W., *A Still Small Voice: Women, Ordination, and the Church,* Syracuse: Syracuse University Press, 1996

Tucker, Ruth A., and Walter Liefeld, *Daughters of the Church: Women and Ministry from New Testament Times to the Present,* Grand Rapids, Michigan: Academie Books, 1987

Wallace, Ruth A., *They Call Her Pastor: A New Role for Catholic Women,* Albany: State University of New York Press, 1992

Weidman, Judith L. (ed.), *Women Ministers: How Women Are Redefining Traditional Roles,* San Francisco: Harper and Row, 1981; expanded edition, 1985

Wessinger, Catherine (ed.), *Religious Institutions and Women's Leadership: New Roles Inside the Mainstream,* Columbia, South Carolina: University of South Carolina Press, 1996

Between 1956 and 1984, almost all mainline Protestant denominations, and both Conservative and Reform traditions in American Judaism, had officially moved to ordain women to public ministry. Only the Roman Catholic Church, Orthodox Judaism, and certain smaller and more conservative Protestant denominations persisted in their prohibition of women from the pastoral office. Each denomination has as part of its own history the story of how women came to be ordained in that church body.

The literature on clergywomen reflects the steady progress of the generation-long process by which women have integrated the previously almost exclusively male profession of public ministry. Most of the studies have been done by sociologists, although some are historical or ethnographic. The language of a quiet but ongoing revolution pervades all genres. PROCTOR and PROCTOR's book, an early text, is composed of the anecdotal accounts of several "firstwomen" rabbis and clergywomen in the United States. Persistent themes in the women's stories relate the variety of pressures, conflicts, and challenges to authority they met, whether in congregations, institutionally, or personally.

CARROLL, HARGROVE, and LUMMIS report the results of the initial cross-denominational survey of clergywomen made after the first full decade during which women entered the ministry in large numbers—the 1970s. The authors of this comparative sociological study recount stories of women's experience in seminaries, in parishes, and in the job market. Despite increasing numbers of women in professional ministry, the survey found that the persistence of both institutional and personal sexism remained the primary basis for inequality in the churches.

In another sociological study, LEHMAN provides a different perspective, describing laypersons' attitudes to women clergy. Noting that the response of the people in the pews is neither monolithic nor consistent, his findings support the "contact hypothesis," which suggests that church members' attitudes toward female clergy change once they have direct contact with either an interim or an installed clergywoman. Resistance is thereby transformed, first into receptivity, then acceptance, leading congregations generally to report the ministry of clergywomen as a positive experience.

As church members differ greatly, so do clergywomen. WEIDMAN emphasizes the diversity among women and ministries—the essays in this volume consider not only the usual tasks involved in parish leadership but also specialized areas such as prison ministry, educational ministry, marriage counseling, and health care, offering an important perspective by suggesting the multidimensional nature of ministry. Clergywomen relate firsthand accounts of both personal and professional experience in diverse cultures, denominations, and locations, highlighting the means by which female clergy bring redefinition to concepts of preaching, liturgy, church administration, the pastoral office, and spiritual formation that have long been taken for granted. In one essay, a clergy couple addresses their unique situation.

The most comprehensive historical survey from the time of the early Christian church to the present is found in TUCKER and LIEFELD's book. Offered as neither a feminist history nor a "traditionalist" interpretation, but instead pursuing an "open centrist position," the authors use changing attitudes about women to trace the course of women's leadership over time. The largely twentieth-century development of women's entry into ordained ministry would have been far more difficult without prior centuries of women's involvement in a variety of non-ordained ministries. Tucker and Liefeld maintain that women's activities have focused more on social (external) needs than on doctrinal (internal) issues, as evidenced by women's more obvious influence in ecumenical efforts. Encyclopedic in scope, particularly regarding the late twentieth century, this work is most useful for its synopses of the primary arguments of the multitude of texts used in the debate over women's ordination.

Practicing her trademark methodology of reciprocal ethnography among a group of small town and rural Midwestern clergywomen from five different denominational affiliations, LAWLESS provides ample evidence for her claim that women do ministry differently because they are women. The women's voices relate their stories of calling in a context of ecumenical dialogue. Interspersed with the women's narratives is Lawless's important discussion of the multilayered ethnographic process that forms one text of a woman's life. The author's claim—that the women's ministries must be considered holistic because they are based on connection, relation, and relatedness—affirms Carol Gilligan's notion of women's different voice.

PURVIS provides a feminist analysis of issues of power and authority in churches headed by women, specifically focusing on the case studies of two Protestant churches in Atlanta, Georgia, and their female pastors. Claiming no intent to generalize from such a limited sample, Purvis nevertheless raises important questions about female clergy's ability to transcend limited gender expectations and yet meet the often high standards expected of clergy. Therefore, clergywomen have to be both exceptional women and exceptional pastors, and in so doing, they accomplish a regendering—what happens when "conventional roles in unconventional combinations" challenge traditional gender expectations.

Still another sociological study finds SCHMIDT arguing that mainline churches that ordain women to the ministry are guilty of creating a facade—a pretense that female clergy are fully integrated into that aspect of the church, when the reality is that women are still marginalized. He relies on organizational theory to discuss the attitudes of churches to the ordination of women, using a model of bureaucratic and cultural linkages to support his claim that churches do not practice what they preach, as exemplified by the persistent presence of a "stained glass ceiling" limiting women's access to positions of bishop or judicatory leadership. Schmidt uses surveys and interviews as the raw material of his research on women in four Protestant denominations that ordain women—the Episcopal Church, the Evangelical Lutheran Church in America, the United Methodist Church, and the Southern Baptist Convention—and one church body that does not, the Roman Catholic Church.

Women in the Roman Catholic community are precluded from ordination but not from pastoral ministry. WALLACE introduces a relatively recent phenomenon in the Roman Catholic Church in the United States, the administration of priestless parishes by either nuns or laywomen. Her sociological study of twenty such parishes gives evidence of an alternative, yet practical, solution to the shortage of male priests in the face of the Vatican's refusal to allow discussion of women's ordination. While these women are not comparable in training to clergywomen, their responsibility for the total life of a parish is not unlike that of their Protestant counterparts. Concurring with Lehman, Wallace finds that Roman Catholics in parishes served by a woman they look upon as a pastor confirm the transformative process in attitude introduced by women in leadership positions.

WESSINGER offers an extensive and valuable chronology of key events in women's religious leadership in the United States and other countries in the nineteenth and twentieth centuries including, but not limited to, dates relevant to women's ordination in various denominations. This comparative study is arranged in roughly chronological order as denominations opened ministry opportunities to women. Themes of authority, separate women's institutions, resistance to women's leadership, and competing demands on women manifest themselves differently but appear in every account. Wessinger concludes that the process of women's movement into leadership positions in the churches begins with a social expectation of gender equality and continues through the development of women's consciousness of and insistence on inclusive language. The transformation of either the leadership role defined as clergy or of religious institutions themselves remains an issue for the future, as do intrafeminist tension, backlash, marginalization, and the question of gay and lesbian clergy.

In contrast to the sociologists whose work focuses on the experience of clergywomen, CHAVES studies formal denominational policy regarding women's ordination and finds loose coupling between rules and practice. Through a comparative and historical analysis of the 100 largest Christian denominations in the United States, Chaves argues that external pressures—the women's movement and ecumenical considerations—rather than internal pressures—clergy shortage, for example—have led denominations to the decision to ordain women. He uses a "new institutionalist" approach to organizational change to suggest that a denomination's formal policy on female clergy reflects that church body's position on gender equality. The ordination of women then becomes a "symbolic display" of support for gender equity and a marker of a denomination's public identity, just as its prohibition supports an antimodernist posture of denominational subcultures bounded by ideas of sacramentalism and biblical inerrancy.

—MARY TODD

See also Christianity: Post-Reformation

Clerical Work

Davies, Margery W., *Woman's Place Is at the Typewriter: Office Work and Office Workers 1870–1930,* Philadelphia: Temple University Press, 1982

Fine, Lisa M., *The Souls of the Skyscraper: Female Clerical Workers in Chicago, 1870–1930,* Philadelphia: Temple University Press, 1990

Goldberg, Roberta, *Organizing Women Office Workers: Dissatisfactions, Consciousness, and Action,* New York: Praeger, 1983

Lowe, Graham S., *Women in the Administrative Revolution: The Feminization of Clerical Work,* Toronto and Cambridge: Polity, and Buffalo, New York: University of Toronto Press, 1987

McNally, Fiona, *Women for Hire: A Study of the Female Office Worker,* New York: St. Martin's Press, and London: Macmillan, 1979

Rotella, Elyce J., *From Home to Office: U.S. Women at Work, 1897–1930,* Ann Arbor, Michigan: UMI Research Press, 1981

Clerical work is considered inherently feminine today because, as women increasingly took clerical jobs, office work was socially reconstructed to be considered a female task. FINE's book explains how women came to be clerical workers and describes the meaning that clerical employment has had for women. The author focuses on telling the story of female clerical workers in Chicago. She discusses the fact that clerical work held promise for women before 1929, although significant numbers of black and married women did not enter clerical work until after World War II. The shift of the gender association of clerical work is an important part of this book. Understanding the social construction of clerical work as a female occupation reveals the importance and plasticity of gender roles. In this book, the author focuses on four settings where the gender definition of clerical work was debated, discussed, and negotiated: the world of technical experts concerned with the clerical field and office management; the popular culture and its expression in the popular media of the day; the prescriptions and actions of reformers, politicians, and city administrators; and finally, the private worlds of clerical workers themselves.

The particular focus of McNALLY's study is research about women in routine white-collar employment. Women constitute an overwhelming majority of those employed in this sector of the labor market, and clerical work is the single most common form of occupation among women. This research was conducted among female temporary clerical workers, whose services are hired by firms from private employment agencies. The intention is not to provide information from which to generalize about all women, but to offer some insight into the diversity of factors that influence women's perceptions of their jobs. The phenomenon of temporary work illustrates the manner in which women can manipulate and actively maneuver within a structure of limited economic alternatives. This study incorporates a shift of focus away from the nature of their work situation and toward their attitudes about their jobs. Chapter One is an analysis of sociological literature that deals implicitly with the question of women's work attitudes. Chapter Two examines the existing literature concerning white-collar work. Chapter Three concentrates exclusively on female office workers. Chapter Four looks at the phenomenon of temporary labor and the role of the private employment agency. Chapter Five incorporates the findings of the research among female temporary clerical workers. Finally, the broad conclusions of this study are presented and discussed in relation to both past and present orientations in sociological literature.

Throughout U.S. history most women worked at home. ROTELLA discusses the changes from 1870 through 1930 that took women out of the home and into the workplace. This study describes and analyzes the economic changes associated with the movement of women out of the home and into the office. Since most of the growth in the female labor force in this period was due to increased participation by unmarried women, this analysis focuses on determinants of labor supply decisions by young, single women. Chapter Two describes the pace and pattern of changes in women's participation in the labor force, paying particular attention to the demographic structure and occupational distribution of female employment. Chapter Three uses a model based on standard economic theories of labor supply to analyze variation in female labor force participation in two cross-sections of American cities. Chapters Four through Seven focus on clerical work: overall clerical employment from 1870 to 1930, expansion of female employment in office work, and the causes of the change in gender composition of the clerical work force.

In most societies, people assume that women and men have proper places. This sexual division of labor is usually seen as natural. In the United States, it was often viewed that a woman's place was at the stove or with the children or at the typewriter. In discussing the feminization of clerical workers and changes in the organization of clerical work, DAVIES's book spans the late nineteenth century and the first three decades of the twentieth. During this period, the class position of office workers changed dramatically. This book illustrates how the gender organization of clerical work is historically specific, rather than ordained by nature. The major themes of this book include the enormous expansion of clerical jobs in the nineteenth century, the changing composition of the labor force, and the proletarianization of clerical employees, which transformed autonomous male clerks into female office operatives and members of the working class.

LOWE's book is a study of how clerical work was transformed from a strictly male-dominated occupation in the late nineteenth century to the leading female occupation of the twentieth century. This book is organized into seven chapters. Chapter One sets the stage for an analysis of the changing gender composition of the office work-force during the administrative revolution, by critically examining theoretical perspectives on the feminization process. In Chapter Two, the author explores the economic and organizational foundations of the administrative revolution. Chapter Three charts the growth of clerical occupations historically in Canada, showing how they have become the largest occupational group and the major source of employment for women. Chapter Four is an in-depth investigation of the circumstances surrounding the initial recruitment of women as clerks and their eventual predominance in clerical jobs. Chapters Five and Six deal with the organizational and technological dimensions of the modern office. Finally, Chapter Seven takes a close look at whether or not the factors reshaping the office led to a proletarianization of clerks as a social group. The concluding section synthesizes the various strands in the author's analysis of how clerical work came to be the leading female job ghetto.

GOLDBERG's study is an examination of the concepts of dissatisfaction and consciousness as they are experienced by female office workers who belong to a working women's organization. The author investigated the types of consciousness that women in clerical work roles experience in relation to class and gender as they participate in working women's organizations. These findings clarify the unique conditions for women, who experience specific demands in terms of family obligations and at the same time must work for wages. The author used interviews with female clerical workers. In addition to these, she recorded small group discussions that took place at general meetings organized to discuss the particular problems women face on the job, as well as their ideas to remedy these problems. A combination of participant observations, informal interviews, and standardized questions show the dynamic interplay between forces that contribute to the experiences and the attitudes of the respondents.

—SUSAN M. TAYLOR

Codependency

Beattie, Melody, *Beyond Codependency: And Getting Better All the Time*, New York: Harper and Row, 1989

———, *The Language of Letting Go: Daily Meditations for Codependents*, Center City, Minnesota: Hazelden, 1990

Greenleaf, Jael, *Co-Alcoholic, Para-Alcoholic: Who's Who and What's the Difference*, Los Angeles: J. Greenleaf, 1981

Schaef, Anne Wilson, *Co-Dependence: Misunderstood-Mistreated*, San Francisco and Cambridge: Harper and Row, 1986

———, *When Society Becomes an Addict*, San Francisco: Harper and Row, 1987; London: Thorson's, 1992

———, *Women's Reality: An Emerging Female System in the White Male Society*, Minneapolis, Minnesota: Winston Press, 1981

Van Den Bergh, Nan (ed.), *Feminist Perspectives on Addictions*, New York: Springer, 1991

Wilkinson, Sue, and Celia Kitzinger (eds.), *Women and Health: Feminist Perspectives*, London: Taylor and Francis, 1994

The array of books chosen for this essay witness by their listing that the topic of codependency demands many-faceted considerations: theoretical and practical understandings of the experience itself, social context and social implications, placement in women's whole health across the lifespan, practical advice, and support. In earlier days of speaking about codependency, addictions professionals tended to mean the effects of living with a significant other dependent upon alcohol or another drug, or the enablement provided the substance abuser by this significant other. GREENLEAF began to distinguish between the spouse/significant adult of the alcoholic and the children of that addicted person. In some sense, professionals saw the codependent person, in fact all of the family, as indirectly addicted to the substance of choice of the addict.

Beattie widened the picture through reflective, practical, and supportive considerations addressed directly to those struggling with codependency. BEATTIE (1989) places the accent on insightful information and pragmatic empowerment. She raises and deals with questions of ongoing growth in working through issues of recovery after coping with the initial pain of recognizing codependency. This book is not simply for reading, but also for doing. BEATTIE (1990) extends that approach in a book of meditations. She provides pointed reflections suitable not only for specific concerns of women in codependence recovery, but also for myriad concerns of large numbers of other women. In her 365 meditations, Beattie addresses topics such as dealing with grief, finding direction, understanding boundaries, accepting one's feelings, and claiming one's own energy.

Schaef, dealing with a larger theoretical framework, and able both to see and to say that codependency is a primary and a relational disease, presents codependency as larger than something involved with simple chemical dependency. SCHAEF (1986) presents a history and development of theories of codependence, arriving at a general dynamic that she calls the addictive process. Drawing the dynamics of the relational dysfunctions of addiction and of codependency to business, culture, and gender issues, SCHAEF (1987) provides systemic insights pertinent to wider understandings of codependency. Uncovering parallel patterns in social and political groups, she shows that systems reveal the same characteristics as individual addicts, and she points toward systemic recovery.

Changes in the understanding of codependency mirror changes in society. Recovery programs, both professional in-house treatment and 12-step self-help groups, had formerly invited family members and facilitated family work primarily for the sake of the addicted spouse. Family recovery work was primarily about keeping the substance abuser, usually male, in good recovery. In weaving through her books the connections between what SCHAEF (1981), in a book that is not primarily about addiction or codependency, but which provides a theoretical underpinning for her later anlysis of both codependency and addiction, calls the white male system and the emerging female system, she points out similarities that are key to the addictive system. Issues of honesty in relationship, and issues of women's experience, voice, and visibility are related to issues of the addicted system. A correlate conclusion, vis-à-vis women, is that some experiences labeled as "symptoms" of codependency, for example, "control," may well be modes of survival, and attempts at voice and/or visibility.

As understandings by and about women moved from typologies of woman existing to care for husband and children to woman being seen as person in her own right and with her own growth issues, some of the shorthand that codependency language had provided began to have possibilities for backfire. The terminology and understandings could easily "blame the victim" where women were concerned. As time progressed, it became clearer that naming and treating codependency well dealt with issues congruent with those of feminism, for example, interconnectedness rather than domination, new modes of social relation, and different ways of perceiving culture, pleasure, pain, and power.

WILKINSON raises a helpful distinction in speaking of a dual conception of dependency. "For women as a social group, the former definition (dependency of the addiction kind) is the unacceptable face of dependency, while the latter meaning (dependency of the subordinate thing kind) is not only the acceptable face of dependency, but also the prescribed norm." Dependency of the addiction kind interferes with all those jobs connected to dependency of the subordinate kind: male identification, the need for male approval, and congruence with the overall structure of power. Sifting of the issue of codependency made possible by this dual notion challenges traditional 12-step self-help groups at the same time that it finds them an aid in dealing with the learned helplessness of codependency.

This dual concept fits well with VAN DEN BERGH's sense of codependency. "Codependency is a form of learned helplessness consisting of family traditions and rituals taught from one generation to the next concerning how the family teaches intimacy and bonding." Van Den Bergh names four common themes in the learned helplessness she associates with codependency: no perceived control of one's environment, no task involvement, disrupted normal routines, and avoidance of social support. Three of the four themes, she points out, are built into societal development of women even before any specific impact of the addicted family. She perceives feminism as offering important tools in understanding and treating codependency.

These tools are: encouraging social support, redefining codependency, using empowerment concepts, emphasizing the codependent person's strengths and accomplishments, focusing positively on growth, and encouraging spiritual exploration. She points out that the social support of self-help groups can help to dissipate guilt and shame undergirding codependency, aiding women in breaking silence and using their own pain for their own liberation.

Ultimately, recovery is an act of the person reclaiming herself. Only secondarily is it a recovery from an addiction or dysfunction that keeps the self from the self. Many descriptions of codependency and programs for codependency recovery stress the latter. They function on male normativity, ignoring female psychological, social, and physical differences. Recovery of the female self in a society still primarily male-identified continues to require systemic change.

—FRANCES R. BELMONTE

See also Addictions

Coeducation

Chamie, Mary, *National, Institutional, and Household Factors Affecting Young Girls' School Attendance in Developing Countries*, Washington, D.C.: Agency for International Development and the International Center for Research on Women, 1983

Clifford, Geraldine Jonçich (ed.), *Lone Voyagers: Academic Women in Coeducational Universities, 1870–1937*, New York: Feminist Press, 1989

Conable, Charlotte Williams, *Women at Cornell: The Myth of Equal Education*, Ithaca, New York: Cornell University Press, 1977

Deem, Rosemary (ed.), *Co-education Reconsidered*, Milton Keynes: Open University Press, 1984

Hyde, Karin, *Gender Streaming as a Strategy for Improving Girls' Academic Performance: Evidence from Malawi*, Zomba: University of Malawi, 1993

Lasser, Carol (ed.), *Educating Men and Women Together: Coeducation in a Changing World*, Urbana: University of Illinois Press, 1987

Lever, Janet, and Pepper Schwartz, *Women at Yale: Liberating a College Campus*, New York: Bobbs-Merrill, and London: Allen Lane, 1971

Riordan, Cornelius, *Girls and Boys in School: Together or Separate?* New York: Teachers College Press, 1990

Sadker, Myra, and David Sadker, *Failing at Fairness: How America's Schools Cheat Girls*, New York: Scribner, 1994

Tyack, David, and Elisabeth Hansot, *Learning Together: A History of Coeducation in American Schools*, New Haven, Connecticut: Yale University Press, 1990

At first glance, coeducation would seem to be an essential prerequisite for equality between women and men. With disturbing consistency, however, studies of coeducation have indicated that girls and women suffer when they are educated in systems shaped by the needs, desires, and anxieties of boys and men. Nevertheless, most writers on education ignore the impact of coeducation or take it for granted. The books listed above are important exceptions to this general disinterest, and cover three topic areas: primary and secondary education in the United States and Great Britain, primary and secondary education in developing countries, and collegiate education in the United States.

TYACK and HANSOT raise important questions about the history of coeducation in the United States. They point out the oddity of coeducation becoming the typical form of childhood schooling in the early nineteenth century—a time when American society was increasingly differentiating the activities of adult women and men—and discuss the varied gender policies (formal rules) and gender practices (actual behaviors) that ostensibly coeducational systems have embodied. Their account focuses on how schools have encouraged "appropriate" gender behavior, and on the various groups that have sought to shape educational systems in order to promote their visions of gender relations.

RIORDAN, a sociologist, attempts to evaluate rigorously the outcomes, both short-term and long-term, of single-sex and mixed-sex schools. Minority girls and boys and white girls, he concludes, all benefit substantially from single-sex schooling. He attributes these disparities in outcomes to the interaction between school structures and adolescent peer cultures, which can perpetuate social stratification even when teachers and administrators do their best to eliminate it, and ends with a call for American schools to experiment with different forms of single-sex education.

SADKER and SADKER have devoted their careers to exposing the unequal treatment of girls and boys in U.S. schools. Academically-oriented girls' schools, they note in their most recent book, can provide girls a place to shine in the absence of boys and their demands upon teachers' attention. Single-sex boys' schools, on the other hand, tend to provide intense lessons in sexism and fetishization of women's bodies. The Sadkers conclude that America will continue to rely primarily on coeducational schools, so the goal should be to mitigate the effects of sexism within those schools.

DEEM's volume focuses on Great Britain, where coeducation is a mid-twentieth-century innovation, appearing along with the transition to comprehensive schools. Its essays cover a range of topics, from a history of views of coeducation in the early twentieth century to examinations of gender development in both coeducational and single-sex schools. The authors all see coeducation as detrimental to girls' academic achievement, and suggest a range of possible alternatives.

Most people writing on coeducation in developing countries focus on its effects on girls' access to education, rather than on the quality of the education they receive, and simply note in passing that coeducation has both advantages (girls receive roughly the same curriculum and physical plant as boys) and disadvantages (boys are very likely to dominate the classroom). CHAMIE argues that the effects of single-sex education depend on its purpose: if the goal of separate schools is to provide better facilities for the boys, then girls benefit from coeducation, but if single-sex schools aim to provide both sexes with opportunities for high achievement, then girls tend to perform better in girls' schools. Since communities are often unwilling to establish girls' schools, and the girls' schools that do exist often have difficulties attracting qualified faculty, Chamie concludes that coeducation is generally the preferable alternative.

HYDE has performed one of the few studies on coeducation's impact on female students in developing countries. Girls' educational performance in Malawi, she demonstrates, is significantly poorer in coeducational schools than in single-sex schools. Experiments with "gender streaming"—single-sex classes within coeducational schools—suggest that separate instruction can be effective in increasing girls' achievement at the secondary level. The most important factor depressing girls' achievement, Hyde suggests, is harassment from male peers if girls show any signs of ability. This harassment is especially effective because girls' higher drop-out rate means that they are already a minority in the schools.

The best over-all study of coeducation on a collegiate level is the volume edited by LASSER. Published on the 150th anniversary of the opening of Oberlin College, the first coeducational college in the United States, the volume is framed by two essays by Alice Rossi and Catherine Stimpson that raise thought-provoking questions about different kinds of "coeducational" structures and their variable effects on female students. Other sections of the book contain studies of historical views of women's education, the history of Oberlin College's experiment with coeducation, and the intersecting effects of gender, race, class, and sexual preference on students' experiences of "equal education."

Most studies of coeducation on the collegiate level emphasize the vast disparities in the experiences of male and female students. Although Cornell University was founded as a coeducational institution, CONABLE argues that economic and social pressures soon led its administrators to create a network of policies designed to produce "womanly women and manly men." Although some alumnae have gone on to impressive accomplishments, the hostility of many male students and the domestic orientation of the university's treatment of its female students hardly created an equitable educational atmosphere.

A century after Cornell's founding, the elite men's colleges began to convert to coeducation. LEVER and SCHWARTZ describe women's experiences during the first year that Yale University admitted female students, a year characterized by men's sexual objectification, intense tension between women's intellectual aspirations and their expectations of femininity, and a crash course in dealing with men's discomfort and hostility.

The volume edited by CLIFFORD is unusual in assessing the effects of coeducation on faculty rather than students. Educated women have long had difficulty finding professional positions, and coeducational institutions have had a notably poor track record in hiring women. The seven biographical studies collected by Clifford indicate that academic women historically found positions in coeducational colleges, both elite and non-elite, by carving out a "women's world" within the institution: supervising female students and/or developing "female departments" such as domestic science. In other words, female faculty found positions only when coeducational institutions became less coeducational.

—LORI KENSCHAFT

Colette 1873–1954

French Writer

Eisinger, Erica Mendelson, and Mari Ward McCarty (eds.), *Colette: The Woman, the Writer*, University Park: Pennsylvania State University Press, 1981

Flieger, Jerry Aline, *Colette and the Fantom Subject of Autobiography*, Ithaca, New York: Cornell University Press, 1992

Huffer, Lynne, *Another Colette: The Question of Gendered Writing*, Ann Arbor: University of Michigan Press, 1992

Jouve, Nicole Ward, *Colette*, Bloomington: Indiana University Press, and Brighton: Harvester, 1987

Richardson, Joanna, *Colette*, London: Methuen, and New York: Dell, 1983

Sarde, Michele, *Colette: Free and Fettered*, translated by Richard Miller, New York: Morrow, and London: Michael Joseph, 1980

Certainly the most famous female French writer, and possibly the most famous French writer of her time, Colette, born Gabrielle-Sidonie Colette, has fascinated biographers and literary critics alike, drawing them toward both her work and her life. Colette's works are best known as semi-autobiographical accounts. Her oeuvre covers almost all of her life, beginning with her early years in *Sido* and *My Mother's House*, and ending with *L'Etoile Vesper*, her memoirs of her latter years. Best known for her zest for life as well as her blatant sensuality, Colette was a popular example of the liberated woman in her own time and remains a model of the feminist writer today.

Colette's unique combination of creative and autobiographical fiction has persuaded some authors to infuse their biographies with extensive information and quotes from her books. JOUVE focuses her biography of Colette almost entirely upon the autobiographical elements in the writer's early novels. Jouve compares the actual events to those detailed in Colette's works. She pays particular attention to the men in Colette's life, and to refuting psychoanalytic and hierarchical readings of Colette's works. This work gives a good comparison between life and autobiographical fictions—and is excellent for providing an understanding of Colette's relations with her husbands and father.

SARDE's biography also borrows heavily from Colette's novels. Sarde includes events from the writer's mother Sido's life, as well as events from the life of her father. Sarde merges quotes from Colette's texts seamlessly with her own descriptions, so it seems as if both are telling the story of her life. Sarde provides very extensive details of Colette's family and full life, many quotes from her works, and plenty of quotes from family and friends. This biography provides psychoanalytic approaches to Colette's works, as well as important historical grounding in the literary and political movements of the time.

RICHARDSON's biography does not rely on the autobiographical elements of Colette's work but rather uses carefully researched historical facts and the descriptions of those who knew her. The result is a much less personally biased and more straightforward biography. This book also contains the best account of the last half of Colette's life, including her marriage to "the dark young man," Maurice Goudeket. While most biographies of Colette focus on her earlier life with Willy and de Jouvenal, Richardson focuses on her middle and old age, carefully chronicles her last years, including her debilitating arthritis and steady decline into immobility, and gives special attention to her death and state funeral—the first state funeral given to any French author.

The best work detailing Colette's growth as an author is the anthology edited by EISINGER and McCARTY, which forms a chronological *kunstleroman* covering Colette's artistic growth: how she came to writing, the ways and contexts in which she writes, and the production of text. All of the articles are concerned with Colette's growth as a female writer, and they explore how gender affects all areas of her writing. This work is both biographical and critical.

Because of the strong autobiographical presence in Colette's texts, autobiographical criticism is an excellent tool for understanding her works. There are two major books applying autobiography theory to Colette's texts, those by Lynne Huffer and Jerry Aline Flieger. FLIEGER's work uses theories of women's autobiography to approach several Colette novels. Flieger adds to the basic autobiographical readings a very psychoanalytic discussion of mother/daughter and father/daughter relationships in Colette's text. The introduction to this work contains a discussion of fictional autobiography and the basis behind women's autobiographical criticism. For the reader unfamiliar with those theories, this is an excellent starting place. In addition, there is an entire chapter discussing discursive sexuality in Colette's work—all within the overarching framework of fictional autobiographical criticism.

HUFFER's work uses autobiographical critical theories to examine Colette as a female writer, rather than as the subject to be read. Huffer describes earlier criticism of her oeuvre as reading the text as Colette the woman: applying theories to Colette's life and using interpretations of her life to interpret the texts. Huffer interprets the texts as texts, while keeping Colette's life in mind, but as the author, rather than the subject, of the text. Gender and sexuality, then, rather than autobiography, form the pivotal interpretive modes for Huffer. This critical interpretation is unapologetically feminist and gives a clear analysis of the texts unbiased by the actual events in the author's life.

—STACEY C. SHORT

Comedians

Ball, Lucille, *Love, Lucy*, New York: Putnam, 1996; Bath: Chivers, 1997

Banks, Morwenna, and Amanda Swift, *The Joke's on Us: Women in Comedy from Music Hall to the Present Day*, London: Pandora Press, 1987

Barreca, Regina (ed.), *New Perspectives on Women and Comedy*, Philadelphia: Gordon and Breach, 1992

Gray, Frances, *Women and Laughter*, Charlottesville: University Press of Virginia, and London: Macmillan, 1994

Martin, Linda, and Kerry Segrave, *Women in Comedy*, Secaucus, New Jersey: Citadel Press, 1986
Rowe, Kathleen, *The Unruly Woman: Gender and the Genres of Laughter*, Austin: University of Texas Press, 1995
Unterbrink, Mary, *Funny Women: American Comediennes, 1860–1985*, Jefferson, North Carolina, and London: McFarland, 1987

To the surprise of some people, women have a long and rich history in comedy on film, television, and stage. One of the most extensive books to chronicle this history in America is by UNTERBRINK. This text presents over a century of comedic performers. Starting with the days before the Civil War, Unterbrink writes eight chapters that describe vaudeville legends, women of radio, early stand-up comics, women of television, familiar and popular performers at the time of the book's publication, writers and directors, and "rising stars." Each chapter consists of several separate sections on individual women; in the later chapters, interviews with the women add to the author's own words.

MARTIN and SEGRAVE, two Canadian writers, complete a similar project. They write individual entries on several North American women and gather them together in chapters arranged by time. Although each book discusses several of the same women, they also include different women, an act that reflects the breadth of women in this field.

BANKS and SWIFT shift the focus to women in Britain. Like Unterbrink, they arrange their book by subject area, discussing women in music halls and cabarets, radio, film, writing, and television. Each section describes several women involved in that particular medium, but the real uniqueness of this book rests in the inclusion of several scripts and comedy bits that feature women's efforts in both writing and performing. An extensive chart at the end of the book lists several important historical events in the lives of British women next to the fundamental comedic happenings of the same time. This adds a social perspective to the numerous events that they mention.

BALL's book details her own life in comedy. After her death in 1989, her daughter Lucie Arnaz discovered an unpublished text written by her mother with the help of Betty Hannah Hoffman. Apparently, the book was finished in 1966 but never published. Hoffman had taped her interviews with Ball, and those tapes were also in the boxes with the manuscript. Arnaz and her brother decided to have the book published, and the final product recounts one woman's struggle to become one of the country's most famous comedic stars. Discussing family, career, friendships, and business, the book presents many larger issues women have had to contend with in their own struggles for success in comedy.

Several other books use more theoretical or contextual frameworks to analyze the relationships between women and comedy. GRAY begins her book with a more general discussion of comedy and laughter, focusing on how different scholars have defined and understood the key issues. The bulk of the book looks at situation comedy and the female stand-up comic. One chapter reports on the American sitcom from the 1950s to the 1980s and another focuses on the British version. The chapters on stand-up comedy focus on women both as performers and subject matter.

Toward the end of her book, Gray also mentions the importance of the book by BARRECA, an anthology that contains a wide range of essays. These 20 articles define "comedy" in a broad way. Several essays look at literature such as Maxine Hong Kingston's *The Woman Warrior* (1976), Charlotte Brontë's *Jane Eyre*, and the short stories of Flannery O'Connor. However, many essays look beyond the traditional academic subject matter and analyze cartoonists like Nicole Hollander, performance artists such as Karen Finley, and comics such as Roseanne and Florence Guy Seabury. Some essays are even written by comics themselves, including a piece on working as a stand-up comic by Laura Kightlinger. The pieces in the book run the gamut from personal perspectives to more theoretical considerations.

ROWE writes a more theoretical text that analyzes the representations of women in comedic films and television. She focuses on the "unruly woman" who challenges patriarchal authority and demands a voice and presence. One chapter looks in detail at Roseanne and her work in television, and her representation in other forms such as magazines and news media, and another goes into detail on the muppet, Miss Piggy. The bulk of the book centers on film, with detailed looks at *It Happened One Night*, *Bringing Up Baby*, and *The Lady Eve*, along with several other films. Special discussion is given to actresses such as Katharine Hepburn, Barbara Stanwyck, and Marilyn Monroe. Overall, Rowe's analysis shows how women have used comedy to present empowered images of themselves for all of their audiences.

—NELS P. HIGHBERG

Communication Styles and Gender

Coates, Jennifer, and Deborah Cameron (eds.), *Women in Their Speech Communities: New Perspectives on Language and Sex*, London and New York: Longman, 1988
Hall, Kira, and Mary Bucholtz (eds.), *Gender Articulated: Language and the Socially-Constructed Self*, New York and London: Routledge, 1995
Lakoff, Robin Tolmach, *Language and Woman's Place*, New York: Harper and Row, 1975
McConnell-Ginet, Sally, Ruth Borker, and Nelly Furman (eds.), *Women and Language in Literature and Society*, New York: Praeger, 1980

Philips, Susan, Susan Steele, and Christine Tanz (eds.), *Language, Gender, and Sex in Comparative Perspective*, Cambridge and New York: Cambridge University Press, 1987

Tannen, Deborah (ed.), *Gender and Conversational Interaction*, Oxford and New York: Oxford University Press, 1993

Until the 1970s, researchers paid little attention to relationships between gender and communication styles. Investigation in the area is recently burgeoning in a variety of disciplines, including anthropology, feminism, linguistics, and communication studies. LAKOFF's book is one of the most important foundational works in the study of communication styles and gender. She examines the relationship between language practices and the position of women in the United States. Based upon her own observations about women's speech practices, Lakoff argues that American women use more polite forms, use weaker expletives, and are more deferent than men. In turn, these stylistic characteristics of "women's language" are emblematic of the subordinate position of women in U.S. society. Lakoff's book provided the impetus for empirical investigations in several different disciplines.

One of the early responses to the questions raised by Lakoff is the compilation of essays edited by McCONNELL-GINET, BORKER, and FURMAN. Their book offers diverse perspectives on the relationships between women and language in literature, as well as in society, from the disciplinary perspectives of linguistics, anthropology, psychology, and literary criticism. The authors attempt to bridge the gap between studies of literary language and other uses of language by focusing on the cultural contexts that shape the production and interpretation of language. Although the essays address diverse topics, such as the use of generic masculine forms, politeness phenomena, women's speech communities, and women's writing, they are united by a common concern with notions of power, feminist analysis, and empirically-based studies.

While the aforementioned books focus upon social and cultural differences for speaking, the collection edited by PHILIPS, STEELE, and TANZ attempts to integrate analyses of biological and cultural factors that influence differences in men's and women's speech. The three sections of the book present various essays, all based upon empirical investigations by anthropologists, linguists, and psychologists. Authors in the first section address women's and men's language practices from a cross-cultural perspective, and offer examinations of speech practices in the contemporary United States, Japan, Samoa, and indigenous communities in Mexico and Panama. Section two deals with language socialization as a part of child socialization. Taken together, the essays from both sections argue that there is no isomorphic relationship between gender and communication styles, or speech practices. Men's and women's ways of speaking are shown to be heterogeneous practices. Furthermore, the essays show that what constitutes men's and women's ways of speaking is highly variable, and dependent upon gender ideologies in each community. Here the relationship between gender and language practices is complicated by other social factors, such as age and status. The final section deals with cognitive differences between men and women that are influenced by both culture and biology. The authors agree that while males and females process language in different parts of the brain, the implications of this fact remain to be investigated.

The aforementioned books are representative of a North American intellectual tradition; the COATES and CAMERON book represents a British scholarly perspective on the investigation of language practices and gender. The collection includes essays that represent quantitative as well as qualitative research by British scholars. The first section of the book examines linguistic variables in phonology, morphology, and syntax, as they are correlated with social variables, such as gender. Essays in this section challenge earlier findings that have shown women's language use to be more "careful" and conservative than men's. While they do not question this in every instance, the authors urge scholars to examine the biases and stereotypical assumptions on which much of the quantitative scholarship has been based. Also, the authors attempt to move beyond the demonstration of men's and women's differential language styles to theorize reasons why the differences exist. The essays in the second section of the book focus upon gender differences in language practices through qualitative methodology, particularly ethnographic methods. Authors are concerned both with the forms (such as tag questions, interruptions, minimal responses, hedges, topic development, and verbosity) and functions of men's and women's patterns in speech events. Two theoretical positions to explain differences between men's and women's speaking patterns are represented in these essays. The first posits that differences in men's and women's communication patterns are reflections of social dominance and subordination. The second argues that different communication patterns are reflections of different gendered subcultures.

Much of the contemporary debate about gender differences in communicative practices is between the "domination" and the "difference" theory. TANNEN's work is often most associated with the "difference" model. In this edited volume, Tannen and the other contributors attempt to challenge this dichotomy, and to integrate both the "difference" and "dominance" theories for understanding gender differences in speaking patterns. Like Cameron and Coates, Tannen is concerned with methodology in the investigation of language and gender. She advocates ethnographic methodology, and the practice of tape-recording naturally occurring speech—a feature all the research in the book has in common. The sections of the book focus on conversational speech, conflict talk, and interruption. Collectively, the contributors demonstrate that any feature of speech or way of speaking, regardless of which gender is producing it, can have multiple functions, and must be understood within the particular social context.

The interdisciplinary perspectives presented in HALL and BUCHOLTZ are less united by methodology than by a particular theoretical perspective on the relationship between language practices and gender. The authors in this book argue for, and demonstrate, that language practices are constitutive of gender—men's and women's language practices both create and reflect gendered identities. They illustrate how language use is a site for maintaining a gendered social order, as well as a site for resistance to gendered stereotypes. With this theoretical perspective, the authors in the first section of the book examine ways through which language practices maintain power, by examining discourse practices in a variety of contexts including: the Anita Hill-Clarence Thomas Hearings, the internet, household dinners, therapy sessions, and teen magazines. The following two sections address how men and women appropriate gender stereotypes, and in doing so, challenge them. Other contributors in this edited book argue that the study of gender and language cannot be separated from the study of other social identities, such as class, race, and sexual orientation.

—BRIGITTINE FRENCH

See also Language: Gender Inclusive/Exclusive

Composers

Bowers, Jane, and Judith Tick (eds.), *Women Making Music: The Western Art Tradition, 1150–1950,* London: Macmillan, and Urbana: University of Illinois Press, 1986

Cohen, Aaron I., *International Encyclopedia of Women Composers,* New York and London: R.R. Bowker, 1981

Glickman, Sylvia, and Martha Furman Schleifer (eds.), *Women Composers: Music through the Ages,* New York: G.K. Hall, 1996

Jezic, Diane Peacock, *Women Composers: The Lost Tradition Found,* New York: Feminist Press, 1988

Lepage, Jane Werner, *Women Composers, Conductors, and Musicians of the 20th Century: Selected Bibliographies,* Metuchen, New Jersey: Scarecrow Press, 1980; London: 1988

Pendle, Karin (ed.), *Women and Music: A History,* Bloomington: Indiana University Press, 1991

Sadie, Julie Anne, and Rhian Samuel (eds.), *New Grove Dictionary of Women Composers,* New York and London: Macmillan, 1994

Tick, Judith, *American Women Composers Before 1870,* Epping: R.R. Bowker, and Ann Arbor: UMI Research Press, 1983

In the canonical narrative of music history, only a few names of female composers appear. In the late 1970s and 1980s, however, books exclusively on female composers, their music, and their history began to appear in force, some attempting to publicize accomplishments of women that had been overlooked, and others scrutinizing the reasons for their absence or searching for a "feminine" voice in music. While not all-inclusive, these listings offer an overview of the type of scholarship that has been undertaken. One of the first lexicograhic works—and one that has strongly influenced the studies that followed—is that of COHEN. An international historical encyclopedia covering periods from ancient times to the present, the book provides biographical information, a works list, and a list of publications (both by the composer, and about the composer) for 5,000 female composers from nearly seventy countries. Cohen's primary goal is to make the names of these women known to a wider audience, and his book is an excellent reference tool.

Like Cohen, SADIE and SAMUEL call attention to the role of women in music history. In the last of the subject dictionaries related to the eminently useful *New Grove Dictionary of Music and Musicians,* Sadie and Samuel include articles on nearly 900 female composers writing in the western classical tradition. Although less expansive than Cohen's in scope, Sadie and Samuel's volume offers essays with much greater detail, each of which concludes with a very useful bibliography and works list. Unique to this work are the interesting introductory essays, one that briefly outlines the history of women and music, and another that examines scholarly precedent for the study of female composers.

Also encyclopedic in form, LEPAGE's work focuses exclusively on the twentieth century. In two volumes, Lepage outlines the lives and careers of 34 female musicians—many of them composers—compiling her information from newspaper articles and conversations with the composers themselves. The result is interesting and anecdotal, offering a glimpse of the society in which each woman worked. Lepage also ventures into the musical style of each composer and her individual aesthetic principles, where applicable, and provides work-lists and discographies. These volumes will be useful to those either exploring the lives of the women covered, or studying twentieth-century music more generally.

In a series that will ultimately be twelve volumes in length, GLICKMAN and SCHLEIFER seek to prove the quality of women's composition to that of men through example, offering annotated, modern performance scores from the ninth through the twentieth centuries. To aid in performance, Glickman and Schleifer include interesting essays—written by a number of specialists—

with each piece of music, along with useful bibliographies and discographies (where applicable). Although only two volumes were available at the time of writing, this series will be invaluable not only to music scholars interested in studying scores, but also to musicians desiring to perform music written by women.

JEZIC aims specifically at the paucity of women in standard textbooks on music, investigating the reasons behind the general exclusion of women. Styled as a companion to introductory music textbooks, Jezic's work presents a guide to the lives and works of 25 composers of western art music from the eleventh century to the present. Each chapter is devoted to a single composer and includes a biographical summary, a discussion of her life and work, a musical analysis of at least one composition, and a selected bibliography and discography. Rather than writing her own story of women in music, Jezic chooses to rely on the traditional paradigm of western art music in order to highlight the unique contributions and life situations of female composers. Very useful appendices—names and addresses of record companies that feature works by women, additional twentieth-century female composers born after 1920, and selected female conductors, to name a few—and a helpful bibliography conclude the volume. This work may be of particular interest to educators seeking to integrate the music of female composers into their curricula.

For those attracted to the historical survey Jezic's book offers, that edited by PENDLE may also prove to be useful. A collection of essays that surveys women's activities in composition, performance, and patronage from the ancient Greeks to the present, the book also includes popular music and jazz. The contributors to the volume cover a variety of topics, situating women as writers of music within broader social contexts. While the basic principles of traditional music surveys govern the organization of the book, it nevertheless offers a good, sweeping view of the role of women in music history.

Rather than placing women into already-existing paradigms of music history, the work edited by BOWERS and TICK moves to a more local level of inquiry, trying to understand the unique circumstances in which each female composer worked. This collection of essays, while compensating for the absence of women in traditional music history, also explores gender as a historical variable, ultimately seeking connections between socialization and creativity. The contributors cover a wide variety of topics, ranging from specific composers—Barbara Strozzi, Clara Schumann, and Ethel Smyth, to name a few—to broader discussions of musicians and musical practices. While the essays cover a vast expanse of time, the work does not attempt any sort of historical unity and may be more useful to those researching topics specifically covered in the book. The volume also offers many outstanding models for those wishing to write about music and women.

TICK takes this one step further in the first extensive study of American female composers, and attitudes toward female musicians, before 1870. Inspired by the work of Ann Douglas, Tick locates music within a larger sphere of femininity, showing connections between the social meaning of music and the social meaning of femininity in nineteenth-century America. To facilitate her exploration of cultural and musical meaning, Tick reaches far outside the bounds of traditional musical studies, examining attitudes in etiquette books, methods of music education for women, and discussions of popular female composers of the time. The thoughtful discussion that results will be useful to those interested in American culture, music, and the role of women in the arts.

—JENNIFER MORE

Computers and Cyberspace

Cherny, Lynn, and Elizabeth Reba Weise (eds.), *Wired Women: Gender and New Realities in Cyberspace*, Seattle, Washington: Seal Press, 1996

Haraway, Donna, *Simians, Cyborgs, and Women: The Reinvention of Nature*, New York: Routledge, 1991

Kramarae, Cheris (ed.), *Technology and Women's Voices: Keeping in Touch*, New York and London: Routledge and Kegan Paul, 1988

Menzies, Heather, *Whose Brave New World?: The Information Highway and the New Economy*, Toronto: Between the Lines, 1996

McCorduck, Pamela, and Nancy Ramsey, *The Futures of Women: Scenarios for the 21st Century*, Reading, Massachusetts: Addison-Wesley, 1996

Senjen, R. Rye, and Jane Guthrey, *The Internet for Women*, North Melbourne: Spinifex Press, 1996

Spender, Dale, *Nattering on the Net: Women, Power, and Cyberspace*, North Melbourne: Spinifex Press, 1995

Taylor, H. Jeanie, Cheris Kramarae, and Maureen Ebben (eds.), *Women, Information Technology, and Scholarship Colloquium*, Urbana, Illinois: Center for Advanced Studies, 1993

Writing about women in cyberspace runs along two lines: books and essay collections about women's relations to technology and books by and for women on how to use the internet. The key issues in the field are technologies' effects on agency, identity, language, voice, and social relations.

SPENDER's book presents a critique of the domination of computer culture by patriarchal values that are antithetical to women's participation in cyberculture, both on-and off-line. Spender cites well-documented research on male elitist attempts to keep women off-line.

She also points to the atmosphere of hostility toward women in most computer science labs, ranging from male macho behavior to pornography, used to exclude women from machine access. The culture she describes for women once they get on-line is equally repellent. From Spender's perspective, this is a time in which women can make a difference in the virtual world while it is still in its formative stages. She also makes her most compelling arguments for women to be involved in the new media as it becomes a viable alternative to conventional publishing. Indeed, Spender argues that these on-line technologies will reshape notions of authorship and ownership themselves, not unlike the way the printing press challenged the manuscript in the fifteenth century. There are, Spender insists, tremendous and heretofore unavailable opportunities for women to be heard despite the considerable obstacles against women's on-line participation.

The nature of women's participation on-line is well documented in the excellent collection of essays edited by CHERNY and WEISE. Written by women from many areas of computing (from magazine editors to hackers), the essays cover topics from how to use newsgroups to what happens to women once they use them and the perception of women by men and women within cyberculture.

While the growing ubiquity of the net has given the question of women's relations to technology a currency not previously seen in women's studies research prior to this attention, two collections of essays specifically consider women's relations to computing technology. In the collections edited by Kramarae and by Taylor, Kramarae, and Ebben, the new technology was marked as an area of crucial concern for feminist research. The essays edited by TAYLOR, KRAMARAE, and EBBEN present overviews of discussions on the implications for women from computing technology in the areas of research, particularly publishing. The collection also considers the effectiveness of the exchange of ideas on-line. The essays reflect the networking of networking as well as issues of agency and empathy in a virtual culture. The collection's annotated bibliography on women and information technology, compiled by Maureen Ebben and Maria Mastronardi, is an indispensable resource. The earlier collection, edited by KRAMARAE, focuses specifically on the effects of technologies, from computers to sweatshops, on women's communication and language within these interactions. The collection is especially noted for Sherry Turkle's essay "Computational Reticence: Why Women Fear the Intimate Machine."

MENZIES presents a more recent study of the impact of these technologies on women's lives. Menzies effectively challenges what she reads as the uncritical embracement of technologies that supposedly liberate women and that in reality do quite the opposite. She points to telecommunicating work as the new remote sweatshop for women; women stay home to do telephone piecework (placing pizza orders, for instance) and find that they have no time for their own home. Their phone becomes the company's surveillance device. Menzies makes a compelling argument against the rush to technologize ourselves quite literally out of meaningful social existence.

HARAWAY's view of the technologizing of the self, especially what can be marked as women's self, is radically distinct from Menzies's. While Menzies focuses on the empirical, everyday experience of those already technologically disenfranchised, those on the edge of "mattering" to the interests that embrace technology, Haraway embraces the effects of this technology in an effort to critique the postmodern conceit of self without subject. She constructs a transmogrified human identity as cyborg, a human-machine combination. Drawing from her earlier work "Cyborg's Manifesto," she uses the construct of the constructed, technologized self, not to celebrate a self that can presume/appropriate any identity, but a self that by its cyborg nature takes into account agency and power relations as identity constructs.

A more speculative view of women's relations to an increasingly technologized self and environment is presented in McCORMACK and RAMSEY. The authors present four future scenarios for women: two that see women increasingly disenfranchised from meaningful social participation in an increased backlash against women and two that see women's lives provided more opportunities in a post-backlash world of virtual communities and financial opportunities. The authors' scenarios are based on scenario planning. Their study is particularly relevant as a cautionary tale for discerning points of intervention women may engage in now to create what the authors view as more positive futures for women.

For women to engage with these technologies (in particular, the increasingly present internet), they must know how to wield the tools. To that end, an entire how-to-internet for women genre seems to have emerged. While some of these texts presume an audience of tough chicks with attitude who, in a few steps, can uuencode right up there with the boys, SENJEN and GUTHREY takes a more straightforward approach to getting on-line and making the technology work. Best of all, the text contextualizes women's historical and social relations to computer culture. It presents "Our Computing Foremothers," deals with gender issues on-line, and then proceeds to get to the "nuts and bolts" of connecting to the internet and what is available once there. It also presents an impressive 30-page section of women-oriented on-line resources.

—M.C. SCHRAEFEL

Concubinage

Alloula, Malek, *The Colonial Harem: Images of Subconscious Eroticism*, Minneapolis: University of Minnesota Press, and Manchester: Manchester University Press, 1986
Callaway, Helen, *Gender, Culture and Empire: European Women in Colonial Nigeria*, London: Macmillan, and Urbana: University of Illinois Press, 1987
hooks, bell, *Ain't I a Woman: Black Women and Feminism*, Boston: South End Press, 1981; London: Pluto Press, 1982
Kabbani, Rana, *Imperial Fictions: Europe's Myths of Orient*, London: Pandora, 1988
Kocturk, Tahire, *A Matter of Honor: Experiences of Turkish Women Immigrants*, London and Atlantic Highlands, New Jersey: Zed, 1992
Stoler, Ann Laura, *Race and the Education of Desire*, Durham, North Carolina, and London: Duke University Press, 1995

In cultures that allow men to have multiple legal sex partners, the concubine is one step below the role of wife. She is controlled by and required to be faithful to her husband, but she does not have all the social rights of a wife. The male control of Orientalised female sexuality and the eroticisation of Islamic women as odalisques and concubines are the key themes of ALLOULA's critique of the colonisation of the African Mahgreb. Through a selection of postcard images, Alloula astutely illustrates how ethnocentric observations and the manipulation of peoples created photographic "documents" of women, which then fed harem fantasies for European consumption.

CALLAWAY documents how reconstructions of colonial accounts have either made women invisible or presented them from a negative perspective. She documents the double alienation of European women as female and white in a "foreign" world, and their empathy and involvement in the lives of African women. Incisive analysis is made of the structural realignments forced by imperial cultures and administrative practices upon colonised women, as well as the ethnocentric attitudes towards Nigerian women, which shaped sexual relations across racial boundaries.

In her classic work, HOOKS locates her study of racism and feminism in the United States in an exploration of the black female slave experience. She argues that planters quickly recognised the economic gain they could accumulate by breeding black slave women and documents the traumas black women endured as they were forged to their new social condition. Hooks depicts the sexual exploitation experienced by black women within which, as the property of men, they had no legal significance, nor political or social protection.

KABBANI's work explores the representation of women in British literature during the Victorian era which, she argues, made women appear to be inferior to men. For Kabbani, such representations made Eastern women doubly inferior, because they were both women and of the Orient. In tracing the ways in which diverse male writers construct images of non-western peoples, she examines the pervasive contempt that, she argues, has been an intrinsic element of the imperial world-view. In addition, perceptions of the East as sexually despotic and capricious and as a domain to be colonised were, she asserts, complementary aspirations that reflected the strong racial biases and deep-seated misogyny of western male colonisers.

KOCTURK's book provides an understanding of the traditional restrictions on women appearing in public in Turkish society. She provides a historical perspective in order to make the behavior of Turkish immigrants comprehensible to European cultures, and to show that cultural differences can be explained. She examines the status of women through different periods of Turkish history, focusing particularly on the post-fifteenth century, when wives and concubines were relegated to harems and were constrained in their life of absolute confinement by eunuchs.

Within her conceptualization of a colonial radicalized economy of sex, STOLER investigates the evolutions of a discourse that initially condoned concubinage as a type of necessary induction for imperial men into their new surroundings, but which then identified the women as degenerate, a "betrayal" of Europeans, whose social and sexual activities were guided by "disciplined restraint." She argues that sexual morality and bourgeois conventions denigrating indigenous wives came to define those who were eligible for European status, and those "mixed" connections, who were not so eligible.

—HELEN JOHNSON

See also Polygamy

Consciousness-Raising

Browning, Genia K., *Women and Politics in the USSR: Consciousness-Raising and Soviet Women's Groups*, New York: St. Martin's Press, and Brighton: Wheatsheaf, 1987
Dreifus, Claudia, *Woman's Fate: Raps from a Feminist Consciousness-Raising Group*, New York: Bantam, 1973
Echols, Alice, *Daring to Be Bad: Radical Feminism in America, 1967–1975*, Minneapolis: University of Minnesota Press, 1989
Henry, Kristin, and Marlene Derlet, *Talking Up a Storm: Nine Women and Consciousness-Raising*, Sydney: Hale and Iremonger, 1993
Loughlin, Kathleen A., *Women's Perceptions of Transforming Learning Experiences within Consciousness-Raising*, San Francisco: Mellen Research University Press, 1993

Shreve, Anita, *Women Together, Women Alone: The Legacy of the Consciousness-Raising Movement*, New York: Viking, 1989

In popular lore, consciousness-raising often is associated with other kinds of suspect therapeutic experiments from the 1960s, such as group encounters and primal scream therapy. However, consciousness-raising, frequently called "c-r" or "rapping," was a highly effective form of systematic education for women during the early years of second-wave feminism. Its importance as a foundation for most feminist theorizing since then cannot be overstated. In c-r, women used their personal experiences as daughters, wives, mothers, lovers, students, and workers to critique larger social structures that conspired to keep them silent, miserable, and convinced that their discontent was a personal problem. Typically, in c-r groups that met between 1970 and 1974, anywhere from five to fifteen women would meet one evening a week, sit in a circle, and talk about everything including childhood traumas, work, marriage, and orgasms. The point was to bring personal experience to bear on social mythology. This process of using personal experience to test cultural ideals became a form of knowledge production that was uniquely feminist. Further, the social critique often led to organized activism. This knowledge-to-action process instituted that famous feminist slogan, "the personal is the political." In effect, consciousness-raising became the U.S. women's movement's most effective organizing tool.

To better understand the particular context of consciousness-raising's emergence in the United States, ECHOLS's book should not be missed. Her thoroughly researched and well-written account of radical feminism between 1967 and 1975 presents a nuanced and balanced record of some of the women's movement's most outrageous, yet theoretically sophisticated participants. Echols's purpose is to set the story straight about radical feminism, which she defines as a "political movement dedicated to eliminating the sex-class system." She argues that too often, however, it is lumped together with cultural feminism, which emphasized the need for "women's spaces." Cultural feminism was a "counter-culture movement" that sought to revalorize all things female in ways that came uncomfortably close to a new form of Victorianism. Echols details the histories of many radical feminist groups operating on the east coast, including New York Radical Women (NYRW), the organization that pioneered consciousness-raising. Through primary documents as well as extensive interviews with movement participants, Echols offers us a "warts-and-all" reading of radical feminism's highly influential legacy.

DREIFUS wrote her book during the peak of consciousness-raising's popularity in the United States. While working for a feminist speaker's bureau, Dreifus traveled the country, and discovered rural and small-town women's tremendous thirst for information about c-r. The book is her contribution to such women. Although the first chapters offer a brief but satisfying history of c-r within second-wave feminism and a "Do-It-Yourself Guide," the majority of the book is an edited transcript of an actual c-r group that Dreifus organized and in which she participated. Following the guidelines distributed by NYRW, the book is structured around weekly topics, such as sexuality, love and marriage, abortion, rape, and aging. Of course, this work is now a historical document, but if read in that way, it is quite enjoyable and extremely informative for those who have never experienced c-r groups firsthand.

Two more recent works look back on the history of consciousness-raising to analyze its legacy in women's lives. HENRY and DERLET's work has as its central theme the question: "where are they now?" Both authors were members of the same c-r group in suburban Melbourne, Australia, in 1972. In the late 1980s, they asked the rest of the group's members to get together and reminisce on what they discovered about themselves through c-r. Like Dreifus, the authors use an edited transcript for the bulk of the book. Although it paints intimate pictures of these women's lives, this method provides only the vaguest allusions to the historical context in which their transformations took place. This is especially problematic when the final chapter asks each member to appraise the successes, failures, and possible future of the women's movement.

SHREVE poses the same kinds of questions to former c-r members, but works from 56 interviews and a smattering of feminist theory. The structure of the book is unusual in that there are two distinct voices employed by the author: one is a narrator to the stories of "composite" characters assembled from the numerous interviews, and the other is Shreve herself, a rather savvy pop sociologist. Through these dual voices, Shreve examines the way in which consciousness-raising's success stories often have a dark side. She observes, for example, that through c-r, many women gained the confidence and sense of entitlement to be "superwomen." They went back to school, obtained professional positions, and now work to balance family and job commitments. To achieve such unprecedented success, however, they adopted many of the values they had critiqued in their c-r groups: regarding other women at work as competitors rather than allies, eschewing politics in favor of personal gain, and hiring impoverished women to do the housework and child care they no longer have time for. Although a unique approach, the composite characters too often slide into uncomfortable stereotypes and eclipse the contributions of the interviewees. The rewards of the book are found in Shreve's own voice and those of the women who shared their stories with her.

Both Browning and Loughlin use consciousness-raising as a lens through which they view prevailing assumptions in their respective academic disciplines.

BROWNING argues that previous Soviet studies theory has failed to account for the discrepancy between the lack of women's participation in formal political leadership and the informal political networks women have created. Obviously, with the break-up of the Soviet Union, Browning's analysis must be regarded more historically, but she provides a well-written analysis of the discrepancies between stated and actual equality in the history of Soviet politics. Likewise, LOUGHLIN attempts to trace the process between knowledge acquisition and political action in her interviews with 24 former c-r participants who are now feminist activists. The problem with these works is that even though they attempt contemporary applications of c-r, neither ground consciousness-raising historically within the women's movement nor theoretically within feminist epistemology. Browning, for example, never really defines c-r beyond a vague notion of all-women groups that act as informal political networks; thus, she seems to be missing opportunities for critiquing her discipline's understanding of what it means to be political. Although Loughlin defines c-r, she does not account for the vast amount of theoretical work by feminist philosophers who already have criticized the work of the few authors she uses. Because of these limitations, neither of these books would be appropriate for a general reader interested in the historical emergence of consciousness-raising or its important legacy within women's studies.

—CATHERINE M. ORR

See also Women's Liberation Movement

Contraception *see* Birth Control Movement

Convents and Nuns

Donovan, Mary Ann, *Sisterhood As Power: The Past and Passion of Ecclesial Women*, New York: Crossroad, 1989
Ewens, Mary, *The Role of the Nun in Nineteenth-Century America*, New York: Arno Press, 1978
Kenneally, James Joseph, *The History of American Catholic Women*, New York: Crossroad, 1990
McNamara, Jo Ann, *A New Song: Celibate Women in the First Three Christian Centuries*, New York: Haworth Press, 1983
McNamara, Mary Jo Kay, *Sisters in Arms: Catholic Nuns through Two Millennia*, Cambridge, Massachusetts, and London: Harvard University Press, 1996
Munley, Anne (ed.), *Threads for the Loom*, Silver Spring, Maryland: Leadership Conference of Women Religious, 1992
Schneiders, Sandra M., *New Wineskins: Re-Imaging Religious Life Today*, New York: Paulist Press, 1986
Ware, Ann Patrick, *Midwives of the Future: American Sisters Tell Their Story*, Kansas City, Missouri: Leaven Press, 1985
Wittberg, Patricia, *The Rise and Fall of Catholic Religious Orders: A Social Movement Perspective*, Albany: State University of New York Press, 1994
Wong, Mary Gilligan, *Nun: A Memoir*, New York: Harcourt Brace Jovanovich, 1983

MUNLEY's volume, commissioned by the Leadership Conference of Women Religious, develops a history of nuns structured according to the five historical periods of religious life: the period of retreat into the desert, the age of the monastics, the era of the mendicants, the rise of apostolic orders, and the development of teaching congregations. These periods were set forth by the French historian Raymond Hostie and adapted in the English volume *Shaping the Coming Age of Religious Life*, authored by Lawrence Cada and others (1979). This five-period historical structure, which had become normative for studies in religious life, unfortunately makes invisible some of the obvious achievements of women religious that "fall between the cracks."

M.J.K. McNAMARA'S scholarly volume traces the history of religious women, or more accurately, "the twin roles that women made for themselves within the Christian community: the mystic and the minister," from the first century A.D. to the present. Women pursued contemplative life but also dedicated themselves to the poor and the sick. She draws a portrait not of the dependent and weak female but of "a soldier resolutely guarding the cosmic frontier, a dragon-slaying Martha rescuing souls in peril."

Although not exclusively a history of women religious (and only dealing with North America) KENNEALLY's book situates the history of nuns in the United States within the larger history of women. He thus provides a context from which to appreciate the contributions of religious women to American history. His study is dependent on, among other sources, that of Ewens. EWENS chronicles how and why sisters were generally regarded with suspicion and hostility in the pioneering life of nineteenth-century America, until their willingness to aid and nurse the soldiers during the Civil War gained them public respect and lessened hostility toward them and the Catholic Church.

J.A. McNAMARA's study is of the earliest Christian centuries; she details the struggle of communities of consecrated women to be religiously autonomous but also to participate in the ministries of the church. Her work shows the gradual success of the clergy and the Fathers of the church in finding a formal place for the religious women in the larger institutional structure of the church.

WARE's book allows nineteen women religious to answer the question, "What have the vast changes during the years of experimentation in the post-Vatican II church meant in your life?" Contributors to the book include sisters from diverse ethnic and geographical backgrounds; they represent many communities, including Benedictines, Sisters of Mercy, Sisters of Loretto, School Sisters of Notre Dame, School Sisters of St. Francis, and Sisters for Christian Community. Several are well known, including Mary Luke Tobin, Elizabeth Carroll, Margaret Ellen Traxler, Maureen Fieldler, and Joan Chittister. SCHNEIDERS's emphasis is also contemporary. Divided into three parts, her monograph focuses on religious life in contemporary experience and reflection, the vows taken by the women, and some of the contemporary challenges to religious life. Among the challenges she includes permanent commitment, friendship, the changing shape of community life, and the place of dissent.

DONOVAN's monograph reflects on the ecclesial identity of women religious, the gifts of women for ecclesial ministry, the role of ecclesial women in the U.S. church between 1870 and 1960, ecclesial women between 1960 and 1985, the relationship between fewer numbers of religious and the emphasis on celibacy, leadership as a mutual responsibility, St. Catherine of Siena's teaching on the way of life of the ecclesial person, and valuable qualities for apostolic religious women in the late twentieth century.

WITTBERG's study of religious life as a social movement employs sociological categories to identify the multiple factors that accounted for the rise of religious life and to delineate the particular circumstances that she considers responsible for its decline. Her analysis is not dependent on traditional religious explanations (for example faith and generosity) but rather on the larger social setting out of which such a lifestyle could have emerged and been sustained. Changes in the larger social setting have quite naturally influenced religious life.

WONG's book is a personal account of her eleven years in religious life prior to Vatican II. She combines her own story with details from the stories of other women who also left the convent. The book gives an individual's rendering of experiences; it is hardly a systematized treatment of the theology of religious life. Nevertheless, for those completely unfamiliar with convent life "from the inside" before Vatican II, it gives a flavor for the potential interpretation—and misinterpretation—of many aspects of the life by those who were living it. Wong's memoir complements Wittberg's contribution, approaching religious life, as it does, from a very different angle.

—ALICE L. LAFFEY

See also Christianity: Pre-Reformation; Christianity: Post-Reformation

Criminal Punishment

Dobash, Russell P., R. Emerson, and Sue Gutteridge, *The Imprisonment of Women,* Oxford and New York: Blackwell, 1986

Glueck, Sheldon, and Eleanor Glueck, *Five Hundred Delinquent Women,* New York: Knopf, 1934

Mann, Coramae Richey, *Female Crime and Delinquency,* University: University of Alabama Press, 1984

Moyer, Imogene, *The Changing Roles of Women in the Criminal Justice System,* Prospect Heights, Illinois: Waveland, 1985

Simon, Rita James, and Jean Landis, *The Crimes Women Commit, the Punishments They Receive,* Lexington, Massachusetts: Lexington Books, 1991

Smart, Carol, *Women, Crime and Criminology: A Feminist Critique,* Boston: Routledge, 1976

Feminist examinations of women's treatment in the criminal justice system, specifically of their punishment and imprisonment, followed on the heels of feminist research about women offenders and their crimes in the 1970s. One study, which preceded this current appraisal by four decades, is considered a classic in the examination of female inmates and penal institutions in the early years of the twentieth century. The husband and wife research team of Sheldon and Eleanor GLUECK conducted a case study of "types" of delinquent women in the Massachusetts Reformatory for Women in 1934. They examined social factors such as family background, childhood and adolescence, sexual history and marriage, and past offense/arrest information in order to sketch "typical" profiles of offending women. The middle section of the book focuses on the conditions and regimen in the penal institution itself. The last part of this voluminous work examines the nature and benefits of the reformatory experience, by conducting interviews with a number of female "graduates" of the institution. Today's reader will find the book informative as a window on the world of early female penal institutions, and on the state of female criminological research at that point in history.

SMART was one of the first criminologists to link traditional theories of female crime with contemporary theories, and to call for the formation of alternate—feminist—theories. Her study of the treatment of female offenders in the United Kingdom between the 1950s and 1970s uncovered a pattern that equated criminal behavior in women with mental illness, and that treated offending women as mentally ill. This individual pathology model was employed not only by traditional theorists, who believed female criminals were biologically maladjusted, but also by more recent theorists, who saw evidence of psychological sickness in female offenders. Smart rejects the entire sickness analogy, and calls for new models and feminist theories on which to base more productive treatment of female offenders.

DOBASH and GUTTERIDGE, in their study of the imprisonment of women in Britain and North America in the late nineteenth and early twentieth centuries, find evidence of Smart's individual pathology theories in operation as early as the 1860s. In the first section, the authors trace the long history in the west of believing women offenders were mentally disturbed or mentally ill—citing examples of female penal centers in England, Scotland, and Wales, and in particular, the development of the first prison psychiatric unit at Holloway. The second section of the book compares the female prisons of the nineteenth century with modern prisons in the 1970s and 1980s, considers such topics as therapy, work, training, and educational programs, and finds evidence of a new generation of thinking about women and penal regimes.

MOYER's collection of essays employs conflict theory to explain the different treatment of women in the three areas of the criminal justice system that her book examines: women as offenders, women as victims—particularly in the crimes of rape, battery, and incest—and women professionals in the system, from police officers and prison guards to attorneys and judges. A particularly informative essay discusses critical problems faced by incarcerated women.

MANN is concerned at the lack of any theory of criminality that treats men and women the same. In her view, there is no difference between the male and female criminal, which explains why all theories about female criminality are flawed. The first section of her book disputes traditional and contemporary theories, and then moves into a case study of female juvenile offenders to illustrate specific discriminatory practices in the criminal justice system. In her final chapters, Mann critiques the correctional system in the United States, pointing to such features as disparate treatment of female inmates, poor vocational training programs and rehabilitation efforts, and lack of attention to the special needs of pregnant inmates. Her suggested reforms center around the specialized needs of female inmates.

Almost twenty years after the publication of Simon's previous book, *Women and Crime* (1975), SIMON and LANDIS have updated the statistical data and the discussion of theory contained in that ground-breaking work. The authors conducted surveys of all the women's prisons in the United States to determine what, if any, prison reforms have been implemented since the 1970s. They interviewed more than thirty criminal court judges in the Midwest for evidence of lingering paternalism in the treatment or sentencing of female offenders. They also examined federal and state court records to detect any differences in the amount or pattern of female crime between the two periods of time. More than fifty pages of tables and graphs supply statistical support for their findings and conclusions. The reader is doubly blessed with comparative knowledge of "then" and "now" in one volume.

—CHERYL KALNY

See also Female Offenders

Cult of True Womanhood

Armstrong, Nancy, *Desire and Domestic Fiction: A Political History of the Novel,* New York and Oxford: Oxford University Press, 1987

Matthews, Glenna, *"Just a Housewife": The Rise and Fall of Domesticity in America,* New York and Oxford: Oxford University Press, 1987

Motz, Marilyn Ferris, and Pat Browne (eds.), *Making the American Home: Middle-Class Women and Domestic Material Culture 1840–1940,* Bowling Green, Ohio: Bowling Green State University Popular Press, 1988

Nead, Lynda, *Myths of Sexuality: Representations of Women in Victorian Britain,* Oxford and New York: Basil Blackwell, 1988

Ryan, Mary P., *The Empire of the Mother: American Writing about Domesticity 1830–1860,* New York: Institute for Research in History and Haworth, 1982

Strickland, Charles, *Victorian Domesticity: Families in the Life and Art of Louisa May Alcott,* University: University of Alabama Press, 1985

Welter, Barbara, *Dimity Convictions: The American Woman in the Nineteenth Century,* Athens: Ohio University Press, 1976

The source of the term "cult of true womanhood," referring to nineteenth-century notions of femininity and women's roles, is from WELTER; other scholars also use the term "cult of domesticity." Welter explains that the "true woman" was one who was pious, pure, submissive, and domestic, a source of strength in the home and the community, and responsible for upholding Christian virtues and American values. Welter examines the sources of this imagery in medical and religious discourses; she also looks at the ways in which nineteenth-century female novelists represented femininity. As in most texts on the subject, Welter combines historical survey and literary analysis by looking at how the "cult of true womanhood" was transmitted and solidified through various cultural media.

MATTHEWS presents a survey of the origins and development of domestic ideology in nineteenth-century America. She looks at how changes in the world outside the home affected women's assigned sphere of influence; in particular, she analyzes the impact of industrialization and evolution on notions of domesticity. Matthews uses a broad historical approach, surveying large-scale cultural ideas rather than the lives of individual women; she draws on sources from both high culture and popular culture, including materials from Harriet Beecher Stowe, Elizabeth Cady Stanton, Ralph Waldo Emerson, and Nathaniel Hawthorne, as well as nineteenth-century cookbooks, magazines, and advice manuals. Matthews also adds a discussion of the changes in domestic ideology in the twentieth century, primarily changes that marked the devaluation of domesticity and the dismantling of the home as a separate sphere.

RYAN provides a social history of domesticity, the home, and marriage using popular literature as her primary sources; she examines the ways in which domestic advice literature and women's fiction codified notions of domesticity and "true womanhood." Ryan's work is useful in that she adds a discussion of various reform efforts that coexisted with efforts to entrench domestic ideology firmly; furthermore, she positions the "cult of domesticity" within American economic and publishing history and considers the effects of the Civil War on domestic ideology. Part of Ryan's objective is to examine the political and personal contradictions that existed within the seemingly unified vision of the American woman's domestic and social roles.

ARMSTRONG provides the standard discussion of domesticity in fiction, offering an analysis of the British version of domestic ideology that supported fixed notions of femininity and "true womanhood." Armstrong positions the rise of domestic ideology within British cultural and political history; she also analyzes the discourse and rhetoric of domestic ideology in order to consider the ways that culture works through language. Individual chapters discuss female authority in eighteenth- and nineteenth-century novels, the increasingly prominent representations of the domestic woman in the mid-nineteenth century, and the novel's rise within the context of gender ideology; she examines several authors individually, including Jane Austen, Charlotte Brontë, and Emily Brontë. Armstrong argues that the cult of domesticity in fiction (that is, representations of the ideal domestic woman) preceded the practice of it by individual women and, in fact, fiction created the space called the home within which women functioned; most of the other writers tacitly or explicitly rely on this assumption. Just as importantly, Armstrong argues that for a complete understanding of political and social events, historians must fully analyze women's history, including representations of women's place in the home and women's sexuality.

NEAD, like Armstrong, focuses on the British version of domesticity; her main argument is that norms of femininity were inherently bound up with ideas of deviancy and abnormality. She investigates how concepts of femininity and deviancy developed and shifted in Britain during the nineteenth century, first by discussing notions of women's "duty" and domestic ideology, and then by considering the primary versions of female "deviancy": the adulteress and the prostitute. Nead adds an interesting discussion of visual representations of "true and deviant" womanhood as she analyzes how visual culture helped shaped definitions of femininity and notions of female sexuality.

STRICKLAND's text is partially a biography of Louisa May Alcott, but Strickland surveys her life as a way to examine the enculturation of nineteenth-century young women through ideas about sentimentality, childhood, and domesticity. His primary focus, as the title suggests, is a discussion of families in Alcott's work; specific topics include images of young womanhood, marriage, successful (almost idealized) families, and the role of the family in society at large. Strickland points out that despite popular visions of Alcott as a young woman's novelist and a proponent of conventional notions of womanhood, her views of the family were not entirely rosy or traditional. Strickland chooses Alcott as his subject not just because of the volume of her fictional output related to the home and family, but because she both was shaped by and reshaped the prevalent ideology of domesticity; he is interested in her explorations of the significance and implications of that ideology. The book is useful in its close examination of one author's—and one woman's—interactions with a broad cultural ideal.

Rather than looking at how fiction and popular literature shaped notions of femininity, the essays edited by MOTZ and BROWNE consider how notions of domesticity shaped and were extended by material culture; the overall focus is on the ways that material consumption and domesticity overlapped and combined to shape notions of "true womanhood." Individual essays examine the physical space of the home as the "true woman's" sphere of influence, and changing notions of women's work or "domestic arts" including quilting, fancywork (lace work), tailoring, landscaping, gardening, and interior decorating. By analyzing these individual areas of work, the essays consider how the household environment served as a moral standard, indicating the success of an individual woman as an icon of domesticity.

—KIMBERLY VanHOOSIER-CAREY

See also Separate Spheres; Victorian Era

Curie, Marie 1867–1934

French Scientist

Curie, Eve, *Madame Curie,* translated by Vincent Sheean, New York: Doubleday, 1937; London: Heinemann, 1938

Giroud, Françoise, *Marie Curie: A Life,* translated by Lydia Davis, New York and London: Holmes and Meier, 1986

Pflaum, Rosalynd, *Grand Obsession: Madame Curie and Her World,* New York and London: Doubleday, 1989

Quinn, Susan, *Marie Curie: A Life,* New York: Simon and Schuster, and London: Heinemann, 1995

Reid, Robert, *Marie Curie,* New York: New American Library, and London: Collins, 1974

Marie Curie's scientific achievements include the discoveries of radioactivity and radium, which earned her Nobel prizes in 1903 and 1911. She accomplished this as one of the few female scientists of her time, and the first female professor at the Sorbonne. While Curie never became involved in the feminist movement, most of her biographers have made her gender a central focus of their work. Recent books have also focused on the questions of how to attribute the work she performed jointly with her husband, Pierre, and on the significance of a love affair she had after Pierre's death.

CURIE's biography of her mother was published shortly after Marie Curie's death. It is filled with anecdotes and personal recollections, beginning with Curie's childhood in Poland, and continuing through her journey to France, her marriage and family life, her scientific career, and finally her death from anemia. Curie announces straightforwardly that she plans to tell her mother's story "like a legend," and the book rarely returns to the level of reality. As might be expected from a biography written by a family member, it is overwhelmingly complimentary in tone. Curie is portrayed as beautiful, brilliant, self-sacrificing, and loyal, a tragic heroine; her disagreements with colleagues and her affair with Paul Langevin are barely noted. All subsequent biographers have made Curie's image of her mother a starting point for their work.

Nearly forty years passed between the publication of Curie's work and the first biography by an outsider. REID highlights the paradoxes of Curie's life. She fulfilled her dream of studying science in Paris, but did so at a time when the Sorbonne was one of the most backward scientific centers in Europe. She remained devoted to pure rather than applied science, and refused to take out a patent on radium, but spent much of her life lobbying for government support for scientific research, because she was chronically short of money. Although "her uniqueness during her creative years lay in the simple fact of her sex," she rejected the feminist movement. Finally, her belief in the power of science to solve the world's problems was dramatically disproved by her own work, which later led to the development of the atomic bomb. Reid also reveals some of the less heroic aspects of Curie's life, including a nervous breakdown as a teenager, and an abrasive and uncompromising personality, which sometimes alienated colleagues. He also discusses her affair with Paul Langevin after Pierre Curie's death.

GIROUD's book significantly adds to the reader's understanding of Curie's life, with clearly presented background information on life in Poland and France in the late nineteenth and early twentieth centuries. This context helps to illuminate the ways in which Curie's life both was and was not typical of her time. For example, Curie's much-discussed poverty as a student was somewhat voluntary; Curie was no worse off than other students, and could have remained in her sister's comfortably middle-class home if she had so desired. Giroud also notes that Curie's long hours in the lab do not stand out against the statutory eleven-hour workday for French women at that time. Although Giroud clearly admires Curie's ambition and will, she does not put her on a pedestal. On her daughter's cover-up of the Langevin affair, she argues: "When we try to turn her into a saint and a martyr, we not only falsify her but we take away another of her dimensions," and indeed, Giroud seems to view the episode as an asset rather than a liability in Curie's personality. She emphasizes Curie's continued contributions to science even in the last part of her life, when she was suffering serious problems from radiation poisoning: "She had never stopped challenging herself, and she had never stopped trying to meet that challenge."

Curie's long-term contributions to science are especially well explored in the biography by PFLAUM, which spans the period from Curie's childhood until 1958, more than twenty years after her death. Curie's daughter Irene and son-in-law Frederic Joliot, who won their own Nobel Prize for discovering artificial radioactivity, are allotted a substantial portion of the text. Pflaum's book stands apart in a second way as well, since the author argues that Curie's famous discovery of radium was due, not so much to any genius on Curie's part, as to her willingness to take on a tedious project: "If Pierre and Marie had not made their discovery when they did, someone else would have, shortly thereafter." Unlike other recent biographers, Pflaum argues that Pierre Curie was more important than Marie in their discoveries. She dismisses Marie as "an amazing, brilliant woman...[but] never the genius that Pierre was," basing this assessment on the fact that Marie's work was limited to one field, whereas Pierre made important discoveries in three separate scientific fields. Like Giroud, she offers some discussions of the historical context, stressing that while Curie's affair with Langevin would not be scandalous now, social standards were significantly different in early twentieth-century France.

The best biography of Curie is the most recent one, by QUINN, who has benefited from access to archival sources closed to earlier biographers, in particular the private diary kept by Curie after her husband's death. Armed with this information, she takes nothing for granted in the story of Curie's life. An extensive photo section complements the documentary research. Quinn's goal is to "peel back the layers of myth and idealization . . . around Marie Curie's story," and in this she succeeds. Her picture of Curie is of a more emotional, more fallible woman than those of previous biographers. Combining the attributes of Giroud and Pflaum, Quinn provides substantial historical context on both the scientific and private aspects of Curie's life. She offers a balanced discussion of the Langevin affair, finally concluding that its importance lies not in the details of the scandal, but the in fact that Curie's scientific accomplishments ultimately enabled her to transcend it.

—NAN H. DREHER

See also Scientists

Curricular Transformation

Graff, Gerald, *Beyond the Culture Wars: How Teaching the Conflicts Can Revitalize American Education*, New York and London: Norton, 1992

Miller, Casey, and Kate Swift, *The Handbook of Nonsexist Writing for Writers, Editors and Speakers*, New York: Harper and Row, 1980

Ruiz, Vicki L., and Ellen Carol DuBois, *Unequal Sisters: A Multicultural Reader in U.S. Women's History*, New York: Routledge, 1990

Simonson, Rick, and Scott Walker (eds.), *Multi-cultural Literacy: Opening the American Mind*, St. Paul, Minnesota: Graywolf, 1988

Curricular transformation has been debated intensely in the last decade, and the nuances of that far-reaching debate require some sort of methodological and disciplinary guide. Unfortunately, in a brief piece it is only possible to mention the highlights of particularly useful resources in which that sort of guidance might be located. Titles used in this regard include those specifically oriented to particular disciplines in women's studies such as history and English, as well as broader collections and volumes that provide a contextualization, and an embedded discussion of women's studies curricular transformation as part of a more general historic process of democratization in higher education.

RUIZ and DuBOIS transform the landscape of women's history as studied in classrooms dealing with women's studies in the United States by bringing together some of the best resources in feminist history. Some articles included in the second edition are on the sex role socialization of immigrant Vietnamese women, cross currents of American Indian feminine identity, development of Chicana feminist discourse, rethinking race and gender as social categories, historical analysis of the Women's Strike for Peace, and the history and study of sexuality in the lesbian community. An introduction develops the narrative of emergent multicultural women's history over intense debates about its legitimacy, both in popular culture and in academe.

MILLER and SWIFT's handbook is a vehicle for curricular transformation in that it provides guidelines for students as editors, writers, and speakers in the classroom. These guidelines can be used for transforming their own work, as well as for reevaluating the traditional work of others, and for understanding the nature of the newer works assigned in classes. In engaging students to understand the way language reflects the prejudices of the society in which it evolved, the deeper level of changes in language is explored, rather than prescribed as a new form of "correctness." Terms such as "man-hour" are explained as imprecise "at best," and examples of alternatives are given. Sports writing, sexist phrasing, figurative personification, the use of "girl" and "gal" for adult women, the misuse of "housewife" in a political context, and double standards in describing women by appearance are all examples of the kinds of discussion available in concise form. Reading this as a text in any class assigned to write papers will also elucidate the problems of traditional literature in a field.

GRAFF, writing and editing about curricular transformation, including but not exclusively with respect to women's studies, provides an essential volume in tracing the development of "culture wars" as they affect the undergraduate classroom. He advocates making use of the wars being fought over multiculturalism as part of the educational process itself. He provides a useful analysis of the widespread incoherence in education today, and practical proposals for overcoming it in universities. He proposes the idea of learning communities, brought together, not by artificial consensus, but by engaged argument. Noting that the term "common culture" is always evolving, he argues eloquently for a curriculum that includes political debate and multicultural texts. This theory is based on research into the history of American education, as well as on personal reflection about the author's own learning and teaching process. He feels that cultural studies and women's studies should be in dialogue with traditional studies, and neither separatist nor ghettoized, since the established Western curriculum is separatist in its exclusions in the first place. He points out that the concerted attack on women's studies and ethnic studies, after these programs have been in effect for 30 years, only shows that they have achieved enough power to be threatening. His argument is that defensiveness in response to such attack, in protection of hard-won turf, only leads to extended marginalization. His logic leads him to oppose the institutionalization of separate "cultural diversity" courses, since simply asking students to cover a certain number of units is an evasion of dialogue. He asserts that the curriculum was never free from politics, as conservatives maintain, but that as the curriculum has been democratized, its opponents have become more dramatic and openly political.

Similarly, SIMONSON and WALKER's collection is an important contribution in the wider context in which women's studies curricular transformation occurs. The focus of the collected articles is on the issue of cultural literacy, and on the contested arena of what body of knowledge constitutes cultural literacy. Essays by such writers as James Baldwin, Carlos Fuentes, Ishmael Reed, and Wendell Berry enlarge our perspective to include a variety of voices and heritages that contribute to the vibrant culture of the United States. In particular for women's studies transformation, Paula Gunn Allen's essay "Who Is Your Mother? Red Roots of White Feminism" brings the Laguna Pueblo question "who is your mother" to white feminism using the idiom of clan membership. Gloria Anzaldúa's contribution, *Tlilli, Tlapalli*: The Path of the Red and Black Ink," relates the telling of stories to the reading of books. She cogently discusses the ethnopoetics and performance of the shamans, who never split the artistic from the functional, the sacred from the secular, or art from everyday life. Her analysis makes one question the ethnocentrism of high art and great book literacy of western standards of creativity. Michelle Cliff's discussions of her journey into speech and her feelings of invisibility lead well into the editors' beginnings of an expanded list of essential names, phrases, dates, and concepts, which might be institutionalized into any curricular transformation project, undertaking, or program.

—BATYA WEINBAUM

See also Pedagogy, Feminist

D

Dance

Adair, Christy, *Women and Dance: Sylphs and Sirens*, New York: New York University Press, and London: Macmillan, 1992

Allen, Robert C., *Horrible Prettiness: Burlesque and American Culture*, Chapel Hill: University of North Carolina Press, 1991

Franko, Mark, *Dancing Modernism/Performing Politics*, Bloomington: Indiana University Press, 1995

Jowitt, Deborah, *Time and the Dancing Image*, Berkeley: University of California Press, 1988

Kendall, Elizabeth, *Where She Danced; The Birth of American Art-Dance*, New York: Knopf, 1979

Manning, Susan A., *Ecstasy and the Demon: Feminism and Nationalism in the Dances of Mary Wigman*, Berkeley: University of California Press, 1993

Morris, Gay (ed.), *Moving Words: Re-Writing Dance*, London and New York: Routledge, 1996

Thomas, Helen (ed.), *Dance, Gender, Culture*, London: Macmillan, and New York: St. Martin's Press, 1993

Dance studies have a complex relationship to women's studies and the field of feminist scholarship. Of all the fine arts, dance is the one in which women are most central as leading creators and participants, and as figures of representation. Consequently, historical and aesthetic studies in dance have often examined individual women's lives or emphasized the aesthetic dimensions of feminized attributes, such as beauty and grace. This traditional gendering of research has been reinforced by the mind/body dualism conventionally attributed, on the one hand (mind), to the intellectual functions of analysis and criticism, and on the other (body), to the corporeal activity of dancing. Feminist and poststructuralist approaches to knowledge have modified this terrain, and dance studies has recently become a significant focus for academic research.

One of the first books to move beyond a narrow historical or biographical focus was KENDALL's investigation of the emergence of modern American dance as a cultural phenomenon closely linked with ideas about the emancipation of women. Focusing on the pioneering figures of Ruth St. Dennis and Martha Graham, Kendall argues that these women "invented" the aesthetic aspirations and conventions of modern theatrical dancing. JOWITT's subsequent book adopts a similar approach, although it embraces women from the classical ballet as well as contemporary dancers. She regards the image of the dancer as reflective of ideas circulating within a particular cultural milieu, but given inspirational form in the body of the dancer. Both books affirm a chronology of progress for the history of modern dance, as well as asserting a dominant narrative of female authorship and authority within that choreographic history.

MANNING rejects the construction by dance critics of the Americanness of modern dance in her study of the German choreographer Mary Wigman. Utilizing ideological critique, she examines the convergence of both feminism and nationalism in Wigman's choreography. Beginning with the creation of all female ensembles freely moving in exploration of women's experience during the Weimar period, the dances became increasingly unified and anonymous representations of the folk glorified by Nazi rhetoric. However, Manning argues that *Ausdruckstanz* (German expressionist dance that continues in the work of female choreographer Pina Bausch) successfully accommodated both the avant garde and mass culture in its version of modernist aesthetics. This rich tradition centered around women cannot, however, be considered in isolation from the ideological forces shaping cultural history.

ADAIR is concerned with the sexual politics of dance as a social practice. The female dancer is considered in relation to the processes of training and the conditions of production and reception available to women in particular historical circumstances. In the nineteenth century, for instance, women tried to reform the ballet as dancers, but were largely excluded from positions of creative or administrative control. Social change through feminism has included increasing opportunities for women to participate in performances and to establish companies that do not reproduce racist and sexist stereotypes. This book includes many unique examples of women's involvement in dance from Europe, America, and England, and significantly recognizes both black dance and popular dance.

THOMAS's collection extends further into the field of social dance, and includes essays on disco dancing, the sexual politics of the musical, the position of women within classical Indian dance, and the extensive participation of women in community dance activities. By developing a more sociological approach to dance, this book argues that dance is a significant site for the rehearsal of social selves, and that the cultural significance of dance goes beyond that of the concert stage in women's lives.

Popular theatrical dancing provides both employment and pleasure for many women, and yet because of its low culture status and its ambiguous gender politics, it raises many issues for feminist or cultural studies. ALLEN's history of burlesque charts the transgressive role of female burlesque in relation to middle-class social relations, as well as the forces which sought to contain and sanitize it. With her sexual audacity and independence of spirit, the burlesque dancer threatened the moral and artistic respectability of proper "feminine" behavior in the nineteenth century. Her voice was silenced, and her freedom restricted, by an increasing emphasis on bodily display within the genre of popular entertainment. The detailed historical evidence of this book highlights the contradiction within dance of an emphasis on showing the pleasures of the body and the social constraints placed upon women who appear within the public domain.

Some of the more vocal criticism of gender bias in dance research has come from male writers such as Phillip Auslander, Roger Copeland, and Mark Franko. FRANKO argues against the restriction of modern dance to pure movement, and considers lesser known figures of American dance, including left-wing dancers. He also reexamines Martha Graham as a figure, not unlike Mary Wigman, variously interpolated by both feminism and American nationalism. Utilizing theories of spectatorship and textual criticism of written statements about dance, as well as movement analysis, this book argues for a more complex and historicized approach to the aesthetic and gendered emphasis on the expression of emotion in dance history.

MORRIS's collection reflects the proliferation of topics covered by dance studies, and an increasing theoretical sophistication in relation to aesthetic, cultural, and political ideas about the body, culture, and artistic practice. Her contributors use recent theory to disrupt categories that have previously defined genres and modes of representation. Several essays address gender and the body in the choreography of contemporary dancers, while others reevaluate familiar dances, such as the ballet of Coppelia, through feminist and psychoanalytic critique. Another reconstruction of history examines the physical culture of Delsarte and its influence upon the ideals of nobility adopted by the early feminist movement. This book provides a useful overview of the complex debates circulating within the field of dance studies that have made it critically relevant to disciplines such as women's studies.

—RACHEL FENSHAM

Davis, Angela Y. 1944–

American Activist and Writer

Aptheker, Bettina, *The Morning Breaks: The Trial of Angela Davis*, New York: International Publications, 1975

Ashman, Charles, *The People vs. Angela Davis*, New York: Pinnacle, 1972

Major, Reginald, *Justice in the Round: The Trial of Angela Davis*, New York: Third Press, 1973

Nadelson, Regina, *Who Is Angela Davis? The Biography of a Revolutionary*, New York: P. H. Wyden, 1972

Parker, J. A., *Angela Davis: The Making of A Revolutionary*, New Rochelle, New York: Arlington Press, 1973

Timothy, Mary, *Jury Woman: The Story of the Trial of Angela Davis*, Palo Alto, California: Emty, 1974

The 1972 murder/conspiracy trial of Angela Davis focused the attention of the American public not only on the life of this already well-known critic and activist, but on the combination of political and judicial systems working in tandem to suppress dissent. Most of the books written on Davis appeared soon after the trial and focused more on how and why she became a Communist and the conduct of her trial than on who she was. These works have become standard for any examination of academic freedom, political resistance, and the workings of the American judicial system.

NADELSON's book focuses on the roots of Davis's activism. The author suggests that Davis's philosophical beliefs and actions were grounded in a consciousness of American racism and her association with friends and teachers like Herbert Marcuse. Critics of Nadelson's book charged, however, that the author's decision to interview only Davis's white friends and teachers seriously limited the perspective of her work.

ASHMAN begins his work with a description of the events in Davis's life and education that politicized her, her involvement with the Community Party, and the confrontations with the California Board of Regents, which led to her dismissal from a position at the University of California Los Angeles. The author then turns his attention to Davis's murder trial, providing descriptions of the setting and the characters involved. From that point his work is a day-by-day account of the forty-nine-day trial, responses to Davis's acquittal, and an analysis of the impact of the jury's decision. This book's principal value is the insight it provides into the workings of the American judicial system.

TIMOTHY furnishes an account of the trial from the perspective of the forewoman of the jury. The author describes the process of jury selection, the conduct of the trial, the way in which evidence was analyzed, how the jury reached its verdict, and the reactions in the courtroom when that verdict was read. She also includes a "Bill of Rights for Jurors," which she contends could strengthen the jury system. Timothy's book is a fascinating account of Davis's trial from the point of view of those asked to weigh the evidence and form a reasonable, just verdict. However, its focus is less on Davis than on the racism, sexism, and general weaknesses of the American jury system.

APTHEKER describes the sequence of events from the courtroom killings in 1970 to Davis's acquittal. The author examines the charges against Davis, the evidence of police abuse of power, and the complicity of the judicial system, the media, and political leaders in Davis's prosecution. Aptheker also discusses the role of American Communists and other groups in Davis's defense and in the campaign to have her released on bail during the trial. Although the author does not critically evaluate trial strategy or the factors that combined to produce a defense victory, the book gives an excellent description of the details surrounding the trial.

MAJOR sees the Davis trial as political, and as he leads the reader through an analysis of the charges against Davis, the individuals involved in the trial, and the trial itself, he continually directs attention to the political implications. He concludes that Davis was not on trial for her alleged criminal actions, but for her beliefs. He notes that for the prosection (i.e., the dominant political system) the central goal of trials like Davis's is not to determine the guilt or innocence of the accused, but to reinforce public awareness of the power of the state. Major also presents a powerful analysis of the intertwining of race, class, and the judicial system as well as the manipulation of and by the media that occurred during Davis's trial.

PARKER supplies a less sympathetic perspective than any of the other works. The author is an African-American conservative who believes that change can be achieved by working through the system rather than by attacking it, and that Marxism is a poor alternative for black Americans. He attempts to explain how and why Davis turned to the Communist Party, but his explanation is always grounded in the belief that her decision was ill-conceived. The principal value of this work lies in the challenge it presents to other, more supportive, views of Davis.

—BEVERLY GREENE BOND

Day, Dorothy 1897–1980

American Activist

Coles, Robert, *Dorothy Day: A Radical Devotion,* Reading, Massachusetts: Addison-Wesley, 1987

McNeal, Patricia, *Harder than War: Catholic Peacemaking in Twentieth-Century America,* New Brunswick, New Jersey: Rutgers University Press, 1992

Merriman, Brigid O'Shea, O.S.F., *Searching for Christ: The Spirituality of Dorothy Day,* Notre Dame, Indiana: University of Notre Dame Press, 1994

Miller, William D., *Dorothy Day: A Biography,* New York: Harper, 1982

Piehl, Mel, *Breaking Bread: The Catholic Worker and the Origins of Catholic Radicalism in America,* Philadelphia: Temple University Press, 1982

Dorothy M. Day was the cofounder of the Catholic Worker movement, a lay apostolate in service of the poor. Day embraced a lifestyle of voluntary poverty and the daily practice of the Gospel's corporal works of mercy. She focused her attention on economic and social changes that were consistent with the goals of Christian personalism. She was most noted for her commitment to the poor, economic and social justice for the worker and minorities, and pacifism.

Although Dorothy Day was a journalist and a prolific writer, her books are not well-known. The first book that she wrote was a novel, yet partially autobiographical. Her next five books contain elements of reportage, moral reflection, political analysis, and autobiography pertaining to the Catholic Worker movement. *The Long Loneliness* (1952) is her autobiography. Her journalism covered a span of 50 years, with most other columns appearing in the *Catholic Worker,* a penny a copy newspaper, which she edited from 1933 until her death in 1980.

MILLER has written the one major biography on Dorothy Day. After he wrote a comprehensive account of the entire Catholic Worker tradition, Day designated Miller to be her official biographer, and opened to him all her materials, which she had placed in the Marquette University Archives. Although the biography has become the standard work on Dorothy Day, Miller refused to provide documentation of his sources in the work.

PIEHL provides the most comprehensive and documented history of the Catholic Worker: a movement, a radical newspaper, "houses of hospitality," and farms for the poor. And he has also provided the most thorough biographical information on Dorothy Day, specifically on her life before her conversion to Catholicism. Piehl did not keep from readers the truth of Day's abortion and suicide attempts during those years. Most importantly, Piehl placed the Catholic Worker movement and the thought and actions of its founders, Dorothy Day and Peter Maurin, within the broad historical context of European Catholicism and the American Social Gospel. Piehl contends that the Catholic Worker movement presented the dilemma of combining personal commitment to social change with religious faith, which enabled its members to be a conscience to the church and to American society.

MERRIMAN attempts to identify the religious influences at work within Dorothy Day's spirituality. Merriman establishes the following categories: literary, monastic, retreats, friends, and spiritual guides. These influences are analyzed to provide an integrated perspective into the religious experience of Dorothy Day's life.

McNEAL's work establishes Dorothy Day as the mother of American Catholic pacifism. Day first proclaimed Catholic pacifism during the Spanish Civil War. During World War II, she maintained her pacifist position, and the Catholic Worker movement was the only Catholic group to support Catholic conscientious objectors. After the war, she added an activist dimension, by integrating nonviolence into her pacifism. Day and the Catholic Worker were the heart of the American Catholic peace movement during the Vietnam War, and assisted in the formation of other groups, such as the American Pax Association, the Catholic Peace Fellowship, and Pax Christ USA.

COLES, a research psychiatrist and friend and admirer of Dorothy Day, brings new insights and dimensions into why and how this woman of faith could work for almost 50 years with such courage, determination, sacrifice, and love. Coles's writing is sensitive and inspirational.

—PATRICIA McNEAL

de Beauvoir, Simone *see* Beauvoir, Simone de

Depression

Formanek, Ruth, and Anita Gurian (eds.), *Women and Depression: A Lifetime Perspective*, New York: Springer, 1987

Jack, Dana Crowley, *Silencing the Self: Women and Depression*, Cambridge, Massachusetts: Harvard University Press, 1991

McGrath, Ellen (ed.), *Women and Depression: Risk Factors and Treatment Issues: Final Report of the American Psychological Association's National Task Force on Women and Depression*, Washington, D.C.: American Psychological Association, 1990

Nolen-Hoeksema, Susan, *Sex Differences in Depression*, Stanford, California: Stanford University Press, 1990

Seeman, Mary Violette (ed.), *Gender and Psychopathology*, Washington, D.C.: American Psychiatric Press, 1995

Silverstein, Brett, and Deborah Perlick, *The Cost of Competence: Why Inequality Causes Depression, Eating Disorders, and Illness in Women*, New York and Oxford: Oxford University Press, 1995

Wenegrat, Brant, *Illness and Power: Women's Mental Disorders and the Battle between the Sexes*, New York: New York University Press, 1995

Depression is experienced by more than 6 million American women during any given six-month period. Approximately one-quarter of women experience depression at a clinical level during their lives. Women's risk for depression exceeds that of men by a ratio of more than two to one. The significant impact of depression on women has produced several books on women and depression. The book edited by FORMANEK and GURIAN explores the relationship between gender and depression throughout the lifespan. Theories of depression in women are described by experts with varied theoretical orientations. Contributors discuss issues that influence depression in females during childhood, adolescence, adulthood, and later life. This book emphasizes the complex interaction of psychological, socioeconomic, and cultural factors that places a woman at risk for depression throughout her life.

The book edited by McGRATH summarizes and synthesizes theories and research on women and depression. The three major sections in this volume cover risk factors, treatment issues, and depression in specific female populations. Contributors examine six areas that may contribute to women's high rate of depression: reproductive events, personality and other psychological factors, family roles and intimate relationships, work roles, victimization, and poverty. Diagnostic and treatment issues for depressed women are also discussed. The overview of the treatment research includes gender differences in the efficacy of antidepressant medications, and the specifics of interpersonal therapy, feminist therapy, and cognitive-behavioral therapy with depressed women. The book describes the needs, experiences, and treatment issues of specific subgroups of women at risk for depression, such as women who are members of ethnic minorities, adolescents, professional women, lesbians, older women, substance abusers, women with eating disorders, women of low socioeconomic status, and physically abused women.

The book edited by SEEMAN considers gender differences in the prevalence, symptomatology, course and treatment of depression and bipolar depression (manic depression). Contributors review biological, characterological, and social factors that may cause women to be more vulnerable to depression than men. Chapters examine the relationship between depression and the physiological changes that occur in women prior to menstruation and after childbirth. Other chapters examine how dependence in relationships, lack of assertion, and victimization may influence women's greater vulnerability to depression.

NOLEN-HOEKSEMA initially addresses the validity and persuasiveness of gender differences in depression. She examines whether women experience depression more than men across cultures, age groups, and socioeconomic classes. The author critically reviews evidence supporting biological, social, and psychological theories of women's increased vulnerability to depression. Concluding that there is little empirical support for theories of women's greater incidence of depression, Nolen-Hoeksema advances her theory that differences in how women and men respond to potentially depressing life events influence the greater incidence of depression in women. According to the author, while men limit the duration and impact of their depression by cutting off their depressive thoughts and feelings, women exacerbate their depression by focusing on their depressive thoughts and feelings.

JACK offers an interesting perspective on the vulnerability of women to depression. While the author addresses traditional factors such as anger and dependence in the development of depression in women, she emphasizes the influence of "silencing the self." According to Jack, in order to cultivate and maintain intimate relationships, women devalue their thoughts and achievements and repress their feelings. The author uses the words of depressed women, myths, and fairy tales to illustrate her arguments.

Some authors assert that social factors primarily determine the greater incidence of depression in women. SILVERSTEIN and PERLICK examine the social biases that cause many women to experience depression and/or eating disorders. Debunking beliefs that the combination of depression and eating disorder in women is a modern phenomenon, the authors trace evidence as far back as the times of the ancient Greek republic. The authors argue that times of social change, especially times of significant advancement for women, lead to an increase in the prevalence of depression, eating disorders, and headache in women. They argue that society-wide gender biases cause women who define themselves nontraditionally and aspire to achieve in areas typically reserved for men to be particularly susceptible to these symptoms.

WENEGRAT offers an interesting perspective on the greater incidence of depression, anxiety, and eating disorders in women. The author contends that women's lack of social power significantly influences the higher incidence of these emotional problems in women. The book examines women's social power from evolutionary and cross-cultural perspectives. Wenegrat details the way in which societal organization influences the greater incidence of emotional problems in women.

—MARK SERGI

See also Mental Health

Depression, Great *see* Great Depression

de Staël, Madame *see* Staël, Madame de, Anne-Louise-Germaine

Dickinson, Emily 1830–1886

American Writer

Barker, Wendy, *Lunacy of Light: Emily Dickinson and the Experience of Metaphor,* Carbondale: Southern Illinois University Press, 1987

Bennett, Paula, *Emily Dickinson: Woman Poet,* Hempstead: Harvester Wheatsheaf, and Iowa City: University of Iowa Press, 1990

Dobson, Joanne, *Dickinson and the Strategies of Reticence: The Woman Writer in Nineteenth-Century America,* Bloomington: Indiana University Press, 1989

Farr, Judith, *The Passion of Emily Dickinson,* Cambridge, Massachusetts, and London: Harvard University Press, 1992

Lease, Benjamin, *Emily Dickinson's Reading of Men and Books: Sacred Soundings,* London: Macmillan, and New York: St. Martin's Press, 1990

Miller, Cristanne, *Emily Dickinson: A Poet's Grammar,* Cambridge, Massachusetts, and London: Harvard University Press, 1987

Sewall, Richard B., *The Life of Emily Dickinson,* 2 vols., New York: Farrar, Straus and Giroux, 1974; London: Faber, 1976

Ward, Theodora, *The Capsule of the Mind: Chapters in the Life of Emily Dickinson,* Cambridge, Massachusetts: Belknap Press of Harvard University Press, 1961

Emily Dickinson has presented something of an enigma to twentieth-century criticism, and feminist criticism is no exception. On the one hand the recluse of Amherst, cloistered in her father's house, would seem to suggest the very epitome of the nineteenth-century female poet. On the other hand her work, with its stylistic compression and indirection, and its startling subject matter, anticipates many twentieth-century aesthetic and thematic preoccupations. To reconcile the life and the poetry within a coherent approach has proved difficult.

WARD's book has six essays, divided into two parts, and it sets out to explain something of the origins of Dickinson's poetry by a consideration of her emotional life. "Part One" deals with the general emotional tenor of Dickinson's life, and, in the second essay, it argues strongly that a severe psychological crisis precipitated Dickinson into transforming and ordering her inner turmoil into poetry. Ward goes on to suggest that this period, between the ages of twenty-nine and thirty-six, were

Dickinson's most creative. In "Part Two," Ward discusses the three friendships represented by the bulk of the surviving letters—those to the Hollands, to Samual Bowles and his wife, and to Thomas Wentworth Higginson—in order to consider the varying facets of mind represented by each of these friendships, and their part in the poetry.

Ward does not attempt biography, and the more definitive work of that type is the two-volume edition by SEWALL, which was able to draw upon the earlier work of Ward, Thomas H. Johnson, and Millicent Todd Bingham. Sewall begins by admitting the difficulties of his subject but goes on to present a complex picture of the poet who stayed at home because it was the place in which she could best work and live the intense inner life with which her poetry is synonymous.

MILLER's work on Dickinson's poetry takes a different direction. She insists that one difficulty for the modern reader is that of reconciling Dickinson's obvious desire to speak to an audience with her elliptical and often puzzling poetry. In a careful explication of the grammar of the poetry, Miller argues that Dickinson's sense of herself, as a poet and as a woman, was intrinsic to her poetic method. In one reading, by conflating the nineteenth-century conception of women as essentially ministering and selfless beings with the romantic conception of the poet as sensitive and suffering, Miller marks a connection between the romantic act of creating poetry and the woman's life. Sacrificial suffering reduces earthly concerns until the woman/poet becomes essential soul, which is then distilled to beautify existence. In this way Miller demonstrates Dickinson's anticipation of twentieth-century feminist metaphors for creativity.

BARKER, similarly concerned with female metaphor, points to Dickinson's concern with the gender-related metaphors of sunlight and shadow. Using other nineteenth-century women writers as a backdrop—the Brontës, George Eliot, Elizabeth Barrett Browning, and Elizabeth Gaskell—Barker concludes that sun and light imagery as a repressive force on female energy is present also in Dickinson's poetry. To understand these common metaphoric threads is to add depth to one's reading of the work. DOBSON also considers Dickinson as an essentially nineteenth-century female writer, but one caught in the conflict between her need to express her womanhood in traditional terms, and at the same time to deny this stereotyped notion. Dobson sees Dickinson's idiosyncratic restructuring of received female imagery, and her linguistic explorations, as symptomatic of both assent and dissent to the role assigned to her by society.

BENNETT's challenging perception of Dickinson, while drawing on other feminist criticism that places her work firmly in a nineteenth-century context, finds homoeroticism central to an understanding of Dickinson's poetry. An over-emphasis on Dickinson's relations with "Master" have distorted our readings of the poetry, she asserts. Thus, while Bennett's work functions primarily as an introduction to Dickinson as a female poet, her relationship to men, and the masculinised concepts of God and death within the poetry, are seen in the light of Dickinson's homoeroticism. LEASE, on the other hand, seeks to illuminate the poetry by demonstrating the creative response Dickinson made to men and books, transforming their message into something uniquely her own. Dealing only with poems that can be accurately dated, and considering the effects of the Civil War and the growth of Christian Spiritualism, Lease discovers a Dickinson passionately involved with family and friends, and one who was a legatee of cultural unorthodoxy.

Although not a biography, FARR's book attempts an ambitious synthesis of the poet's life and work. Reading the poetry in its nineteenth-century contexts, personal and public, Farr demonstrates a Dickinson who knew far more about her artistic contemporaries than had hitherto been thought. Further, by concentrating on the poetry of the 1860s and 1870s, she argues that much of it is difficult because it is encoded to protect the private passion she felt for a married man and woman. Like Bennett, Farr finds that Dickinson's love for the woman she called "My Sue" was central to her emotional life, but Farr suggests that her love went equally to "Master." It is, Farr asserts, the larger questions of God and eternity that ultimately form Dickinson's central themes.

—JAN PILDITCH

Dinesen, Isak 1885–1962

Danish Writer

Aiken, Susan Hardy, *Isak Dinesen and the Engendering of Narrative,* Chicago: University of Chicago Press, 1990

Horton, Susan, *Difficult Women, Artful Lives: Olive Schreiner and Isak Dinesen, In and Out of Africa,* Baltimore: Johns Hopkins University Press, 1995

Juhl, Marianne, and Bo Hakon Jørgensen, *Diana's Revenge: Two Lines in Isak Dinesen's Authorship,* translated by Anne Born, Odense: Odense University Press, 1985

Langbaum, Robert, *Isak Dinesen's Art: The Gayety of Vision,* Chicago: University of Chicago Press, 1975; as *The Gayety of Vision, A Study in Isak Dinesen's Art,* London: Chatto and Windus 1964; Random House, 1965

Stambaugh, Sara, *The Witch and the Goddess in the Stories of Isak Dinesen: A Feminist Reading,* Ann Arbor, Michigan: UMI Research Press, 1988

Thurman, Judith, *Isak Dinesen: The Life of a Storyteller,* New York: St. Martin's Press, 1982

The name of Isak Dinesen signals a body of writings almost invariably pursued by the shadow of division. In itself a double, being as it is the best-known pseudonym by which the Danish author Karen Blixen is known outside her native country, Isak Dinesen names an authorship precariously balancing between Denmark and the English-speaking world, between two languages and two sets of critical responses. In a move that further reinforces this duplicity of critical engagement, American feminists rediscovered Dinesen's short fiction in the 1980s, providing it with a second lease on a now world-famous life, after a period of relative obscurity following her triumphant invasion of the American literary scene in the 1960s.

LANGBAUM may be singled out as addressing the principal concerns of that first wave of predominantly male-centered criticism, which strove to secure Dinesen's canonical legitimation as "serious" writing. Langbaum's study is especially concerned with exploring her relationship to modernism and romanticism, emphasizing her use of symbolism, the artifice of her style, her preoccupation with the issues of personal identity, and the relativity of truth as signs of a modern imaginative vision, akin to those of Mann and Yeats. Discussing Dinesen's writings in terms of collections of tales, each organized around a central theme, Langbaum succeeds in underlining the unity he reads as structuring her philosophy on art and life. If Dinesen makes a statement on artistic creation, as Langbaum seems to argue, this is art that obeys and reproduces a design, a vision of order deemed comic for ultimately eliminating conflict through the reconciliation of opposites. Langbaum's study is informative, and although in some respects theoretically dated, it still remains a reference point, which later critical formulations, not least the more recent feminist ones, would more or less explicitly measure themselves against.

Published in the early 1980s, THURMAN's book is considered today by many to be the standard Dinesen biography, and a rich source of information regarding the historical moment, the social spaces, and the literary vocabularies that inform her fiction. Drawing often on archival material not available in English, it structures itself along the chronological path of Dinesen's life, veering with frequency off its stated course to offer life-based readings of her tales. Thurman's text reads well as a biography, and can prove immensely useful in building contexts around Dinesen's writings. Her attempts, however, at producing a literary criticism that can systematically read Dinesen's life into her literary texts lack a rigorous theoretical framework, preventing its obvious awareness of gender issues from developing into a full-blown feminist critique.

Working within the feminist theoretical climate of the seventies, JUHL and JØRGENSEN seek to locate Dinesen's feminist gesture in her textual demand for women's freedom, the freedom of erotic love, and the freedom to be a human being. Theirs is one of the first attempts to systematically investigate the inscription of gender in Dinesen's tales, pointing to the gender roots of her attack on bourgeois morality, and her concomitant valorization of the sensual. Their book is divided into two parts. The first explores, through a reading of *Seven Gothic Tales*, feminine consciousness as a site written into by a potent desire for revenge against men, while the second focuses on *Winter's Tales*, and deals with Dinesen the storyteller and her artistic techniques.

From a self-proclaimed new critical standpoint, STAMBAUGH sets out to identify Dinesen's critique of patriarchy as a twofold gesture: her attack on the middle-class idealization of female chastity, and her rejection of Protestant Christianity. What is Dinesen's most effective weapon in this transgressive assault, Stambaugh suggests, is her association of "woman" with a pre-Christian natural world, and her identification with the mythical figure of a mother-goddess. In an argument weaving itself across a series of chapters thematically organized around "glorified" images of women, Stambaugh singles out the bayadère-witch, as that Nietzschean descendant who counters the misogynism of patriarchal convention, and speaks the word of Dinesen's feminism. Stambaugh's book is an important contribution to the feminist rereading of Dinesen, although the author is unwilling as yet to challenge the legacy of Langbaum's emphasis on the seamless unity of her fiction.

Departing from this preoccupation with continuities, AIKEN's study appears primarily concerned with the discursive practices, and the discontinuities and rifts that came to undermine the neat and orderly structure of Dinesen's tales. Drawing mostly on French feminist theories, Aiken introduces into the debate surrounding Dinesen post-structuralist concerns regarding the text, its gendering, and specifically its engendering. The principal issue addressed is the intricate relationship between sexual difference and representation. In a series of close textual analyses, which limit themselves to *Seven Gothic Tales* and *Out of Africa*, Aiken explores the question of how Dinesen "engenders" her narratives—both in the sense of giving birth to them within male-oriented discourses, and of simultaneously opening up the question of gender in relation to writing—and follows the (feminine) textual strategies of resistance that her texts deploy in order to challenge the androcentric languages they are often accused of uncritically reproducing. Aiken's study is elegant and incisive, and signals a major turn in Dinesen criticism, toward an engagement with contemporary theories of femininity, textuality, and culture.

HORTON contributes to this reoriented approach by producing a cultural reading of Dinesen's "life-works" along those of Olive Schreiner. Her project forms part of a recent move to uncover the complexities underwriting the concept of an "invisible" whiteness, by drawing attention to the unstable positionings of the white woman writer and the white critic vis-à-vis a racial alterity. Reading Dinesen's African tales, and viewing her photographs and psychic landscapes, Horton attempts to trace the racial and gender identifications to which Dinesen resorts, in order to formulate subject positions that will guarantee her a surviving self. Helped by Walter Benjamin's philosophical theses, and art history, as well as feminist and (post-)colonial discourse theories, Horton identifies Dinesen's chief survival strategy as being one of oscillation between absolutes of gender, race, and nationality. This is a form of resistance to the solid structures of white masculinity, which Dinesen learns from the Africans, thus confounding racial allegiances and complicating gender affiliations. Horton's study is innovative, and can prove helpful to those interested in the intricate interrelation of gender and race.

—EFFIE YIANNOPOULOU

Disability Issues

Driedger, Diane Lynn, and Susan Gray (eds.), *Imprinting Our Image: An International Anthology by Women with Disabilities,* Charlottetown, Canada: Gynergy, 1992

Driedger, Diane, Irene Feika, and Eileen Giron Batres (eds.), *Across Borders: Women with Disabilities Working Together,* Charlottetown, Canada: Gynergy, 1996

Jamison, Kay Redfield, *An Unquiet Mind: A Memoir of Moods and Madness,* London: Picador, and New York: Knopf, 1995

Morris, Jenny, *Pride against Prejudice: Transforming Attitudes to Disability,* London: Women's Press, and Philadelphia: New Society, 1991

Thomson, Rosemarie, *Extraordinary Bodies: Figuring Physical Disability in American Culture and Literature,* New York: Columbia University Press, 1997

Tremain, Shelley (ed.), *Pushing the Limits: Disabled Dykes Produce Culture,* Toronto, Canada: Women's Press, 1996

Wendell, Susan, *The Rejected Body: Feminist Philosophical Reflections on Disability,* New York: Routledge, 1996

Willmuth, Mary E., and Lillian Holcomb (eds.), *Women with Disabilities: Found Voices,* New York: Haworth, 1993

Women with disabilities are now articulating their challenge for inclusion of their perspectives in mainstream feminist thought, just as women of color and lesbians have done before them. Women with disabilities feel they are objectified, stereotyped, and devalued by nondisabled women. It is an exciting time in disability studies, with a recent influx of books incorporating perspectives on women with different disabilities, written in personal and academic forms to further the feminist agenda of theory and practice.

JAMISON provides an important example of why both the personal and academic perspectives are important in understanding women with disabilities. Jamison herself is the foremost expert on bipolar disorder (also called manic-depressive disorder) and has the disorder herself. This book challenges the reality that mental illness is frequently ignored and stigmatized in our society. Through rich prose and readable technical explanation, Jamison outlines the benefits she acquired from bipolar disorder—energy, creativity, and expansive moods—as well as the frightful hallucinations and psychosis. By sharing this perspective, Jamison provides insights into why medicating bipolar individuals is difficult—because there are losses not evident to those without the disorder.

Morris and Wendell blend their personal experience of disability into their books, which attempt to critique society from a feminist perspective and offer strategies for change. MORRIS, a British activist who uses a wheelchair, writes from her own experience, as well as interviews from eight women with different disabilities and different ethnic and sexual orientation backgrounds. She begins with a discussion of prejudice, then critiques what she sees as nondisabled people's assumption that disabled people's lives are not worth living—evident in the increase in prenatal testing and physician-assisted suicide. She examines images of disability in popular culture and critiques institutionalization, community care, and feminist research on both. Lastly, she calls for the collective organization of people with disabilities.

WENDELL's book is also catalyzed by her disability, myalgic encephalomyelitis, or chronic fatigue immune dysfunction syndrome. Wendell, a feminist philosopher in Canada, begins by examining definitions of disability. She then analyzes the social and cultural factors—including the authority of scientific western medicine to describe bodies—that, upon interaction with biological difference, create disability. She suggests the possibility that disability could be regarded as a neutral form of difference. Wendell, too, critiques images of disability in popular culture, arguing that they help people embrace the myth that the body can be controlled. Similar to Morris, Wendell argues for the integration of this disability perspective into the project of feminist ethics, especially the attempt to develop an ethics of care. Lastly, she shares her strategies for living with pain and physical limitation and suggests a feminist understanding of transcendence with the body.

Most anthologies make a self-conscious effort to incorporate the experiences of different disabilities with interlocking issues of identity (for example, race, ethnicity, class, and sexual orientation), while highlighting a variety of expressive forms along a certain theme. WILLMUTH and HOLOCOMB's book is actually also a special edition of the journal *Women and Therapy,* on women with disabilities in therapy. There are academic literature reviews and studies on disability and therapy, as well as the blending of personal perspectives on issues such as commonalities and differences among women, including older women and women with disabilities; coming out as lesbian with a disability; and the experiences of an interracial couple with disabilities navigating the adoption process.

Two fine international anthologies on disability collect essays, reports, poetry, and art from activists across the world, from countries such as Bangladesh, Brazil, Germany, and Zaire. Writings in DRIEDGER and GRAY's anthology delve into the complex cultural factors playing into disability, such as ethnicity, religion, laws, and disability rights organizations in each author's country. The book is broken into five sections: constraints in the family, images in the community, "imprinting" through art and careers, challenges to societal expectations of beauty and sexuality, and the growth of worldwide disabled peoples' movements.

DRIEDGER, FEIKA, and BATRES's book also discusses these factors, but more specifically focuses on organizations for women with disabilities in particular countries and their attempts to build international ties in promoting education/literacy, vocational training, and health care. Dispersed throughout the book are "Snapshots from Beijing": interviews of women with disabilities from the 1995 Fourth World Conference on Women in Beijing.

TREMAIN's anthology specifically presents the works of "disabled dykes." The book is divided into sections that suggest a progression toward a political consciousness of each writer as a disabled dyke. Tremain's introduction is powerful in its critique of feminists and lesbians for exclusive language and attitudes toward lesbians with disabilities, which erase the possibility that they are sexual, active women, and which therefore naturalize stereotypical ideas about ability and disability.

THOMSON offers an excellent and important model for a feminist cultural studies approach to disability, discussing literature that transcends mere discussion of stereotypes. She offers the study of the "disabled figure" and its counterpart, "the normate": the latter is the unmarked, assumed societal norm, which can be revealed through scrutinizing "the social processes and discourses that constitute physical and cultural otherness." Thomson analyzes crucial cultural discourses that define the normate and disability, as well as the female and racialized body: stigma theory, impurity, Michel Foucault's idea of "docile bodies," and liberal individualism. She then takes this theoretical framework and examines disability in a historical context. She begins with freak shows in which those on display—dwarfs, tribal non-westerners, fat people, hermaphrodites, and so forth—were alike only in their physical difference from the audience. Next, she discusses a "compensation model" of disability—in which disability is shown as a lack that must be compensated for by the generosity of white women. She uncovers this model through her analysis of the social protest novels of nineteenth-century middle-class white women that construct gendered and racialized disabled figures (for example, Harriet Beecher Stowe's *Uncle Tom's Cabin*) "to spotlight the conflict between social justice and individual freedom inherent in the American liberal tradition." Lastly, she discusses twentieth-century woman-centered African-American liberatory novels (for example, Audre Lorde's *Zami*) that use the disabled figure to celebrate physical difference—representative of what she calls a contemporary "accommodation model."

—CATHERINE L. MARSTON

Division of Labor by Sex

Baron, Ava (ed.), *Work Engendered: Toward a New History of American Labor*, Ithaca, New York: Cornell University Press, 1991

Bergmann, Barbara, *The Economic Emergence of Women*, New York: Basic Books, 1986

Blaxall, Martha, and Barbara Benton Reagan (eds.), *Women and the Workplace: The Implications of Occupational Segregation*, Chicago: University of Chicago Press, 1976

Goldin, Claudia D., *Understanding the Gender Gap: An Economic History of American Women*, New York: Oxford University Press, 1990; Oxford: Oxford University Press, 1992

Jacobs, Jerry A., *Revolving Doors: Sex Segregation and Women's Careers*, Stanford, California: Stanford University Press, 1989

Matthaei, Julie A., *An Economic History of Women in America: Women's Work, the Sexual Division of Labor, and the Development of Capitalism*, Brighton: Harvester, and New York: Schocken, 1982

Rhode, Deborah L., *Speaking of Sex: The Denial of Gender Inequality*, Cambridge, Massashusetts, and London: Harvard University Press, 1997

Tang, Joyce, and Earl Smith, *Women and Minorities in American Professions*, Albany: State University of New York Press, 1996

Tinker, Irene, *Persistent Inequalities: Women and World Development*, New York: Oxford University Press, 1990

Williams, Christine L., *Still a Man's World: Men Who Do "Women's Work,"* Berkeley: University of California Press, 1995

The division of labor by sex, or occupational segregation, occurs when certain occupations are culturally, or even legally, designated as men's work while others are deemed to be women's work. In varying degrees, occupational segregation is evident in various periods within one nation as well as across divergent cultures. Male-dominated professions tend to have higher status and higher wages and include administrators, executives, managers, professional specialists, and skilled blue-collar workers. Female-dominated professions tend to have lower status and lower wages and include clerical workers, domestics, school teachers, nurses, and retail workers. The explanations for men and women holding distinct kinds of jobs range from the benign to the sinister. The reason may be benign if, for example, the absence of women in a particular occupation is due to the desire of women to choose more flexible jobs, but sinister if women are systematically excluded from certain types of jobs because of overt discrimination or statutory bans.

JACOBS provides a comprehensive analysis of the sexual division of labor and the economic and social mechanisms that help sustain it. Using an impressive and extensive array of empirical data, Jacobs's book outlines the scope and conditions of occupational segregation in the United States. It presents comparative information to analyze the continuation, as well as the transformation, of the sexual division of labor. Jacobs concludes that despite its prevalence and persistence, occupational segregation and other sex-typing attitudes are socially constructed and thus adaptable.

BERGMANN provides a thorough and incisive inquiry into the origins and alteration of gender roles in the American economy. Bias and the division of labor by gender are identified in her book as the basis of a great many of the disadvantages faced by women in the United States. Times and conditions have changed to some extent, but as Bergmann's study illustrates, long-standing habits and customs are resistant to change and thus demand mindful and meaningful policies.

Since occupational segregation is neither a unique nor recent situation, it is best understood in its historical and cultural context. GOLDIN provides an authoritative history of the economic position of women, which discusses gender differences in employment and wages in the American workplace. This thorough study documents the division of labor and its relative impact on the wage gap between men and women by occupations, industries, and economic sectors. Since Goldin's book explains changes in occupational segregation over such a long time span, it illustrates how market conditions and cultural forces have interacted to affect the lives of American women and the performance of the American economy.

MATTHAEI's work is a nontraditional analysis, which examines the impact and the connection between the sexual division of labor and the evolution of capitalism. Matthaei uses a radical feminist position to explain the process of social development and as such offers an alternative perspective to Goldin's book. Nevertheless, Matthaei's analysis is consistent with other studies that illustrate that the sexual of division of labor is neither a recent nor a confined phenomenon, and that it has widespread economic and social consequences.

Since workplaces have economic as well as social meanings, it is helpful to examine occupational segregation from various political and intellectual perspectives. BLAXALL and REAGAN offer a collection of papers from a number of eminent economists and policy-makers that examine the institutional, social, and economic aspects of occupational segregation. These papers analyze the structure and historical origins of segregated labor markets, along with policies designed to counteract occupational segregation. BARON provides a compilation of gender-based histories of American labor markets. These are labor histories that investigate the range of opportunities and workplace conditions of workers and the communities in which they live.

A comparative review of the relative economic position of women can be found in the book by TINKER. It is a volume of contributed essays that examine the role of women and economic change in the industrial and developing world, with the explicit aim to explain persistent inequalities. Tinker's book demonstrates that in order to understand the relative economic and political position of women within a particular culture, it helps to investigate that nation's record on the sexual division of labor.

TANG and SMITH provide a collection of essays that examine the role of women within eight professional occupations. These essays demonstrate that even though the number of women employed in professions ranging from management to military service has expanded, there are enduring gender distinctions in access, career advancement, and earnings. Tang and Smith's book examines some of the institutional constraints within professions that contribute to these gender inequalities.

RHODE's book is a discerning legal and social history of the patterns of gender inequality in the United States. By examining such issues as media images, family values, and political movements, Rhode's book clarifies some of the origins and repercussions of gender differences. Even within occupations that employ both women and men, there are often strict culturally defined standards of behavior that are different for women and men. Gender-based stereotypes and standards (such as women ought to be nurturing while men strong and aggressive) affect opportunities for employment and career advancement. The origins of gender roles and sexual stereotyping are deeply ingrained, pervasive, and difficult to undo. Even the sexual division of labor within the model of a traditional family culturally imparts distinct levels of status and compensation. Women for example are more likely to carry the burden of childrearing, and this typically holds much less prestige than does the employment of men in a market-based labor market.

WILLIAMS uses extensive interviews from diverse locales to investigate how culture and the sexual division of labor has affected those males employed in occupations that are predominantly female. Williams's book illustrates that rather than being disadvantaged in those occupations, such as elementary school teaching, nursing and social work, men have advanced to positions of authority in disproportionate numbers. Williams concludes that genuine equality in the workplace will not be reached until occupational segregation is diminished or abolished.

—TIMOTHY E. SULLIVAN

See also Dual Career Families; Dual Labor Market; Earnings Gap; Glass Ceiling

Divorce: History

Chused, Richard H., *Private Acts in Public Places: A Social History of Divorce in the Formative Era of American Family Law,* Philadelphia: University of Pennsylvania Press, 1994

Griswold, Robert L., *Family and Divorce in California, 1850–1890: Victorian Illusions and Everyday Realities,* Albany: State University of New York Press, 1982

Kingdon, Robert M., *Adultery and Divorce in Calvin's Geneva,* Cambridge, Massachusetts: Harvard University Press, 1994; London: Harvard University Press, 1995

May, Elaine Tyler, *Great Expectations: Marriage and Divorce in Post-Victorian America,* Chicago: University of Chicago Press, 1980

Phillips, Roderick, *Putting Asunder: A History of Divorce in Western Society,* Cambridge and New York: Cambridge University Press, 1988

Riley, Glenda, *Divorce: An American Tradition,* New York and Oxford: Oxford University Press, 1991

Stone, Lawrence, *Road to Divorce: England 1530–1987,* Oxford and New York: Oxford University Press, 1990

Three trends have made the history of divorce a newly invigorated study in the 1980s and 1990s: the attempt to find the history of women in legal records, the new emphasis on the history of everyday life and ordinary people, and the evolution of the history of the family. All of the authors below exemplify these recent trends. The history of divorce in the western tradition can be summarized briefly by noting that the major events in that history were the Roman Catholic suppression of divorce, the sixteenth-century inroads made on the Roman Catholic doctrine by the Protestant Reformation, the increasing availability of divorce through legislative bills, the liberalization of divorce laws in response to the feminist movement of the nineteenth century, the raised expectations of marriage in the early twentieth century, and the advent of no-fault divorce toward the end of the twentieth century.

Most ambitious of the works on divorce is PHILLIPS's book, which examines divorce in the western tradition, from the Roman Catholic belief in the "indissolubility" of marriage that allowed only for annulment or separation, to the no-fault divorce of the modern era. Whereas divorce had been possible in some ancient and medieval traditions, by the 1500s the Roman Catholic Church had achieved uniformity of the legal codes of western Europe, allowing no dissolution of marriage. The Protestant Reformation, in its rebellion against Roman Catholic tradition, overturned the tradition of indissolubility and allowed divorce, particularly in cases of adultery. England was the exception to this general Protestant acceptance of divorce by its continuation of the Catholic prohibition against divorce in the Anglican church. Phillips continues his survey of divorce history through the twentieth century in Europe as well as the United States. For an overall view of the history of divorce in the western tradition, his is a most useful work.

STONE focuses on England from 1530–1987. Part One is really a treatment of marriage and the permutations of that institution. Part Two discusses the "road to divorce," which proceeded from "desertion, elopement, and wife-sale" through private separation, judicial separation, and parliamentary divorce to the eventual passage of a divorce reform act in 1857. Stone concludes his discussion of divorce with a description of the dramatic changes of the twentieth century. His is an invaluable work on the unique aspects of divorce in England.

Whereas both Phillips's and Stone's works give us the macrocosm of divorce history, KINGDON provides a microcosm. He places the origins of modern divorce in sixteenth-century Geneva, Switzerland among the followers of John Calvin. Here in three case studies we see the working out of the Protestant belief that marriage was dissoluble. Full divorce with dispensation to remarry was allowed on two grounds—adultery and desertion. Men and women who were divorced could remarry. Divorce was granted upon petition to the Consistory, or governing council of Geneva. The petitioners were more often male than female and were influential or well-to-do. Often the dower property brought to the marriage by the wife was at issue. The guilty party in the case of adultery could be sentenced to death by drowning for women and by decapitation for men. Kingdon's cases indicate that men were benefiting more from this new possibility of divorce than were women, but he attributes this to the general inferior position of women in society.

There have been a number of recent works on divorce history in the United States. RILEY chronicles divorce in the United States from colonial times to the present, showing that divorce is an American institution. One of the major motivations to colonize the present-day United States was to practice Calvinism, so it stands to reason that the United States would be fertile ground in which the practice of divorce might grow.

Riley reveals the course of divorce from the colonial period to the increase in divorce after the American Revolution; she shows the progressive easing of restraints upon divorce in the nineteenth century and the explosion of divorce in the twentieth, but her thesis is that dissatisfied spouses will find a way out of marriage no matter the legal strictures.

CHUSED focuses on the colony and state of Maryland. He details the important changeover from legislative divorce to judicial divorce in the late eighteenth and early nineteenth centuries. Chused analyzes divorce by legislative petition, and the difficult transition to judicial divorce, and he attributes the cause of the rise of judicial divorce to the economic difficulties experienced by married women during the Panic of 1837. Chused's work is a detailed legal study of one state's transition from legislative to judicial divorce. From the general divorce act's passage in 1841, it remained virtually the same until 1937.

GRISWOLD presents the unique case of California, which became a state almost overnight after the 1849 Gold Rush, and which quickly instituted a divorce law in 1851. Griswold's purpose is not so much to reveal the history of divorce as it is to use divorce records to give us insights into women's history. He believes that as early as the period between 1850 and 1890 a new companionate marriage was the ideal that women sought. Most petitioners were women, and it is clear that women were the beneficiaries of divorce to the extent that they were able to extricate themselves from difficult, and sometimes dangerous, marriages.

MAY would place the date when "expectations" of marriage went beyond the most basic duties of husband and wife to those of a more inchoate standard of "personal fulfillment" at the turn of the twentieth century. She compares divorce cases in the 1880s to divorce cases in the 1920s. In the 1880s, petitioners seemed to want the traditional husband or wife, but by the 1920s, divorce rates were soaring and the causes for divorce appeared to be less clear and convincing, giving evidence of a desire for domestic satisfaction that was elusive. She believes that a revolution in expectations of marriage had taken place, and that it was these new, higher, and undefined expectations that caused the divorce rates to take off exponentially.

At this point there are good overviews of the history of divorce in Europe and the United States and a number of focused works that show us in detail the workings of marriage and divorce in more specific places such as Geneva, Maryland, and California. With the exception of Griswold's book, we do not, however, have a divorce history that puts women at the center and uses divorce to explicate women's history.

—BONNIE L. FORD

Divorce: Present-Day

Dingwall, Robert, and John Eekelaar, *Divorce Mediation and the Legal Process,* Oxford: Clarendon Press, and New York: Oxford University Press, 1988

Fineman, Martha Albertson, *The Illusion of Equality: The Rhetoric and Reality of Divorce Reform,* Chicago: University of Chicago Press, 1991

Glendon, Mary Ann, *The Transformation of Family Law: State, Law, and Family in the United States and Western Europe,* Chicago: University of Chicago Press, 1989

Goode, William, *World Changes in Divorce Patterns,* New Haven, Connecticut: Yale University Press, 1993

Kay, Herma Hill and Steven Sugarman (eds.), *Divorce Reform at the Crossroads,* New Haven, Connecticut: Yale University Press, 1990

Kurz, Demie, *For Richer, for Poorer: Mothers Confront Divorce,* New York: Routledge, 1995

Maccoby, Eleanor E., and Robert H. Mnookin, *Dividing the Child: Social and Legal Dilemmas of Custody,* Cambridge, Massachusetts, and London: Harvard University Press, 1992

Weitzman, Lenore, *The Divorce Revolution: The Unexpected Social and Economic Consequences for Women and Children in America,* New York: Free Press, and London: Collier Macmillan, 1985

Weitzman, Lenore, and Mavis Maclean (eds.), *Economic Consequences of Divorce: The International Perspective,* Oxford: Clarendon Press, and New York: Oxford University Press, 1991

The increasing rates of divorce in most industrialized democracies in the late twentieth century have fostered a great deal of debate about the meaning, functions, and future of family life, as well as about the consequences of divorce for the parties affected (although it should be noted for the record that divorce rates in the United States peaked in 1981). Thus, research on divorce ranges from large-scale statistical analyses of data on the economic consequences of divorce, or the social, psychological, and developmental effects of divorce on children, to studies of particular legal issues such as the determinants of child custody decisions, to studies that explore the meanings that people affected by divorce create for their familial experiences. One ongoing concern is the extent to which women and their dependent children may be made economically and socially vulnerable by divorce.

One study that has had a significant impact on public policy, as well as on popular understandings of the consequences of divorce, is WEITZMAN's book. In 1970, California became the first state in the United States to adopt "no-fault" divorce laws, which ended the requirement that one party be found "at fault" before a divorce could be granted. With no-fault divorce laws, a couple can divorce by mutual consent. Weitzman studied the effect of this law by drawing court case samples from the San Francisco and Los Angeles area in 1968,

1972, and 1977, interviewing family law judges and attorneys, and divorced men and women. Her findings with respect to the economic consequences of divorce, in particular, are widely cited: Weitzman found that men's economic status after divorce, on average, increases, while women's economic status declines significantly. Weitzman argued that this was partly due to judges' failures to award alimony, based on assumptions about women's ability to support themselves and their children economically that were unrealistic at best, and biased at worst. Although Weitzman's findings have since been criticized as painting a somewhat inaccurate picture of the extent of post-divorce inequality, the study remains significant and useful.

Parallel developments in the liberalization of divorce law internationally, and the empirical research that has been conducted by many scholars to determine the effects of these new policies, are brought together in WEITZMAN and MACLEAN's volume. Indeed, most of the scholars whose work is discussed here are also represented in this book, making it extremely valuable. William J. Goode's essay provides an overview and sociological analysis of recent changes in patterns of divorce in Western countries, contrasted with such patterns in traditionally high-divorce societies such as Japan, China, and Malaysia. The book contains a section that discusses changes in divorce law, one on developments in marital property law, and a section on income support—both alimony and child support—in a number of industrialized democracies. Also included are essays that address societal consequences of divorce, and specific aspects of divorce law in a number of countries. The book concludes with a set of policy recommendations by Weitzman and Maclean based on the findings in the volume. While the book contains the usual strengths of an edited volume, making available in one place information otherwise more difficult to locate, it also contains some of the concomitant flaws, such as great variety in the approaches and quality of the essays.

GLENDON, a legal scholar, offers a comparative analysis of the structure of family law systems in the United States and western Europe, and the legal changes in family law in these countries in the last several decades. The primary focus is on four countries: France, West Germany, England, and the United States, although Glendon also refers to other nations, most prominently Sweden. The book begins by outlining the emergence of marriage as a legal institution in the western world, and summarizes each nation's laws with respect to the formation of marriage and relations within the legal marital union. Glendon then discusses the law of divorce in each nation, each of which reformed its divorce laws in the late 1960s or early 1970s. Glendon also addresses the legal effects of divorce, as well as the trend away from legal regulation of marital relationships. As a guide to the development of contemporary divorce laws in the countries studied, this is a valuable and important reference.

GOODE provides a highly useful look at changes in divorce patterns in many regions of the world. Partly due to availability of data, the analysis of Europe is the most thorough. However, the book also includes information on divorce patterns in Latin America, northern Africa and the Middle East, Japan, China, Taiwan, Indonesia, and Malaysia. One significant contribution of the book is Goode's analysis of what he terms "stable high-divorce-rate systems" in Japan and Malaysia. Both societies had relatively high divorce rates prior to the mid-twentieth century, sustained in part by high rates of remarriage, and kinship systems that helped to sustain divorced women's social support. Both have had declining rates of divorce in the latter half of the twentieth century, in contrast to trends elsewhere. Goode is also concerned with the consequences of divorce, most especially for women and children, and concludes by offering some policy proposals for improving social supports for divorced women and their dependent children.

DINGWALL and EEKELAAR provide a look at one aspect of contemporary divorce law: mediation. Many scholars in the United States have been concerned that mediation may sometimes harm the less powerful party, therefore making women more vulnerable in the divorce process. Although the book focuses primarily on mediation practices in England and the United States, also included are chapters on mediation in Japanese family courts, and on informal family mediation among the Bakwena people of Botswana. The editors conclude that the effects of mediation are not well known, and require further research.

A great deal of research has been done on contemporary no-fault divorce in the United States and its consequences. One volume that summarizes some of this research is that by KAY and SUGARMAN. Several chapters address various questions related to the economic consequences of divorce. David L. Chambers provides a useful essay on the legal role of stepparents in post-divorce families. The book concludes with an excellent chapter by Deborah L. Rhode and Martha Minow that provides a feminist analysis of divorce law.

FINEMAN's book also provides a feminist approach to the analysis of no-fault divorce and its effects. Fineman is very critical of equality-based approaches to family law, especially to the division of property upon divorce, and the provision of income support after divorce. The book provides a case study of the adoption of divorce reforms in Wisconsin, which used an equality-based approach. Fineman also analyzes the implications of equality-based rules for child custody decisions, and the uses and abuses of social science research in these decisions. Fineman concludes by offering alternative rules for guiding such decisions, especially the use of a primary caretaker standard in determining child custody decisions upon divorce.

KURZ provides an alternative approach to understanding divorce, by actually listening to women's voices: her study is based on interviews of a random sample of more than one hundred divorced women in the Philadelphia area. Kurz begins by discussing the work of those who see divorce as evidence of family breakdown and social decline, and offers an analysis that considers the roles of gender, race, and class in both marriage and divorce. She then proceeds to discuss the data gathered in her study, including how marriages end, and the role of violence in these women's relationships, how women cope with separation and divorce, and the nature of negotiations over custody, visitation, and resources. Kurz concludes by discussing policy changes that would help provide support for divorced women and their children.

MACCOBY and MNOOKIN's book provides one of the most comprehensive studies of child custody decisions. Many previous studies were based on case studies or non-representative samples; the authors here sought to provide reliable evidence based on a sample of 1,100 families in two counties in California who filed for divorce in 1984 to 1985. The study was longitudinal, and included both interviews with the adults involved as well as study of the court records. Maccoby and Mnookin discuss the effects of California's laws regarding support, visitation, and custody on outcomes, and found that most families in their sample did not have high-conflict divorces. The majority of custody arrangements were traditional, with mothers receiving custody, and even in those cases where there was joint legal custody, mothers usually had primary physical custody.

—JYL JOSEPHSON

See also Child Custody, Child Support

Dix, Dorothea 1802–1887

American Social Reformer

Baker, Rachel, *Angel of Mercy: The Story of Dorothea Lynde Dix*, New York: Julian Messner, 1955

Gollaher, David, *Voice for the Mad: The Life of Dorothea Dix*, New York: Free Press, 1995

Schlaifer, Charles, and Lucy Freeman, *Heart's Work: Civil War Heroine and Champion of the Mentally Ill, Dorothea Lynde Dix*, New York: Paragon House, 1991

Tiffany, Francis, *Life of Dorothea Lynde Dix*, Boston and New York: Houghton Mifflin, 1890; and Cambridge: Riverside Press, 1891

Wilson, Dorothy C., *Stranger and Traveler: The Story of Dorothea Dix, American Reformer*, Boston: Little Brown, 1975

TIFFANY is the initial biographer of Dix, who wanted the world to know about her remarkable life. The sources for this book are letters written by Dix, letters from Anne Heath and from associates, and newspaper articles. In the first five chapters Tiffany discusses her unhappy childhood, which caused Dorothea to realize that at an early age she had to face the world alone and fight her way on her own resources. To be independent, the only respectable position for any young girl then was teaching. This would satisfy her thirst for knowledge and help her exert moral influence on others. Tiffany relates that Dix believed knowledge could be used to teach habits of introspection, and that knowledge serves humanity. While caring for her younger brothers and teaching her pupils, Dix developed a sense of pitying compassion for the ignorant, the degraded, and the suffering. Tiffany describes her as a person full of passion, heartbreak, poetic enthusiasm, and religious exaltation.

Dix's state-by-state gathering of information on the treatment of the insane, and her lobbying of state legislatures, are presented in the next six chapters. Tiffany describes her method as taking close quarters with politicians and working their sensibility and reason. Tiffany writes that her campaign came at an opportune time because New England was then experiencing the "New Awakening." There were men in the United States who had enlightened ideas about the treatment of the insane but lacked the inspiration and fire to crusade against ignorance, superstition, and apathy. Dix was the one who had both. This fire would cause her to neglect her health. In spite of it, she led an unsuccessful campaign, as described in the middle chapters, to get the national government to sell land and use the proceeds for perpetual care of the insane. Between 1853 and 1858 Dix went to Europe for a much needed rest but found herself in a campaign against poor treatment of the insane throughout Europe and Turkey, as described in most of the second half of the book. Tiffany describes Dix as a servant to her own virtues of goodness and self sacrifice in the care of the poor outcasts.

BAKER writes simply and chronologically about a woman who had an idea and who, with passion and compassion, single-handedly brought about a complete revolution in the care of the mentally ill. In the first four chapters Baker highlights the childhood events of Dorothea's life and how she developed her interest in the treatment of the insane. A theme that runs continuously throughout the book is her love for humankind. Chapters four through 12 describe the detailed surveys by Dix of how the insane were treated in the United States and foreign countries, and how she sought the aid of caring and respectable reformers in the community to convince local and state politicians and national governments to appropriate money for mental institutions and better care of the insane. The book describes her efforts to get the government to train nurses for the United States Army during the Civil War, and it ends with her struggles with the army to provide clean hospitals, proper diet for the sick and wounded, and humane treatment.

WILSON relies on collections of historical societies in the communities in which Dix lived and on information gathered from university personnel, directors of state special hospitals founded by Dix, and collections departments at various New England libraries. She portrays Dix as coming from a background of oppression and poverty. Because of her mother's illness, Dix became responsible for the household chores and for the care of her younger brothers. The family lived off the income her father made tending another man's land, and later from his scant earnings from his itinerant preaching and from the sales of his printed sermons. This necessitated frequent moves from town to town. Because of this lifestyle, at the age of 12 Dix ran away to live with her grandmother in Boston. She wanted to be educated, and it was here that she later first established a school for the poor.

In Boston Dix had many relatives for companionship, and she took advantage of her grandfather's library. Wilson writes that Dix had no desire for social pleasures. She saw them as transitory delights. Reading, however, was her pleasure, and it helped her achieve two great loves, literature and art. Wilson writes that while in Boston, the Unitarian Minister William Ellery Channing influenced her religious thought. She learned that God was good, just, merciful, and loving. She learned from Channing to be concerned with social problems such as housing for the poor and economic help for the immigrants. Later in life she would say that her work with the insane was the result of a simple obedience to the voice of God. Up to her mid-40s, schools and church activities consumed her whole time. Most of Wilson's book describes Dix's national and international campaign to improve the treatment of the insane. One chapter is devoted to Dix's training of nurses during the Civil War.

SCHLAIFER and FREEMAN devote a chapter on the early years in order to show how Dorothea's childhood of desperation and emotional pain influenced her life's works. They rely heavily on letters between Dix and her acquaintances and friends, and on Tiffany's biography. In a richly detailed book, the authors present Dix as a driven person who was hiding a childhood rage that she had buried in order to gain her parents' love. The unhappy family situation gave her an unhappy portrait of marriage; therefore, Dix rejected marriage and remained a spinster.

Dix's mother was ill and not available to give loving care to her children. It fell upon Dorothea to be in charge of house chores and care for her younger brothers. Because of this and her father's alcoholism, Dorothea grew up feeling that she had to be the savior of the family. Schlaifer and Freeman render a detailed narrative, showing how Dix proved she could go it alone. This book also discusses her teaching career, and her later work to establish hospitals for the mentally ill in the United States and Europe. In her painstaking work, Dix gave to others loving care, the very thing she lacked as a child.

GOLLAHER criticizes earlier biographers of Dix because they used unreliable sources. He wanted to set the record straight, and he was fortunate to have available original manuscripts. He relied on the Houghton Library of Harvard University, which holds the original letters, diaries, journals, and newspapers clippings on Dix. The detailed first three and a half chapters of the book describe the factors that influenced Dix by her mid-40s to champion the cause of the insane. Gollaher describes how living at home and later with her grandmother, Dix was surrounded by sorrow. She grew up with anger; therefore, she wiped her parents from her past. This void would remain until she moved to live with her great aunt Sarah, whose home was frequented by guests. Unable to adjust to the new life of socializing, Dix preoccupied herself with work. She started a school, which reaffirmed her sense of independence. By this time, Dix saw herself as being an orphan and homeless. While living with her aunt Sarah, Dix met her life-long friend and confidant, Anne Heath, who would provide her with much love and support.

It was in Boston, writes Gollaher, that Dix met several Unitarian ministers, including Channing, who was a genius of liberal Christianity. From discussions with them she envisioned herself as an apostle of Christ serving his children. She learned life had a purpose and Christians had a social obligation. She learned to view Jesus as one who sought and saved those who were lost. Dix came to believe that the essence of Christianity was feeding the poor and comforting the sick. Coupled with her belief of being an orphan, Dix could identify with the mad and insane who were the homeless and abandoned of America. To overcome the resistance of the politicians, Gollaher writes, Dix interjected her personal anger at how the insane were treated and depicted her own interactions with the insane. This book shows that Dix was different from other early nineteenth-century female reformers because she drafted legislation, built major institutions around the country, and directed the Civil War Army nurses.

—BILL MANIKAS

Doctors

Drachman, Virginia G., *Hospital with a Heart: Women Doctors and Separatism at the New England Hospital, 1862–1969*, Ithaca, New York: Cornell University Press, 1984

Glazer, Penina Migdal, and Miriam Slater, *Unequal Colleagues: The Entrance of Women into the Professions, 1890–1940*, New Brunswick, New Jersey: Rutgers University Press, 1987

Lorber, Judith, *Women Physicians: Career, Status and Power*, New York: Tavistock, 1984

Morantz-Sanchez, Regina Markell, *Sympathy and Science: Women Physicians in American Medicine*, New York: Oxford University Press, 1985

Walsh, Mary Rothe, *"Doctors Wanted: No Women Need Apply": Sexual Barriers in the Medical Profession, 1835–1975*, New Haven, Connecticut and London: Yale University Press, 1977

Women's entry into the field of medicine as physicians is fairly well-documented. As GLAZER and SLATER illustrate, entrance of women into medicine was part of a larger professionalization process that occurred in that period. These authors show the reader that women's early involvement with the medical profession, similar to other professions, was very different than that of men. Although also writing about women in social work, scientific research, and academic careers, these authors spend a good portion of their time focusing on the first generation of women to attend medical schools and receive modern medical training. This focus allows Glazer and Slater to examine women's entrance into a profession that was male-dominated, that was attempting to control membership, and that was increasingly unfriendly to outsiders. These authors document the difficulty women had in being token females within the medical profession. To succeed in medical schools with men, women often chose the strategy of super-performance. Other women attended women's medical schools, taking a separatist approach. Glazer and Slater also emphasize that since medicine required long hours and unusual amounts of energy, marriage represented a special problem for these women. Male colleagues could choose whether or not to marry, but women who remained single were considered deviant. Nonetheless, Glazer and Slater state that at least in this early period of modern medicine, most female physicians remained single.

WALSH documents the specific ways in which American society has historically tried to keep women out of the medical profession in large numbers. Rather than studying career patterns of female doctors, this author explains why there are so few careers to study. Walsh records sexual discrimination during the second half of the nineteenth century and until recent years in medical school acceptances, within medical school classrooms, and in subsequent hiring practices. Walsh makes the point that women are the major consumers of American health care, accounting for an estimated two-thirds of patient visits and for 87 percent of the health workers in this country. Despite these statistics, however, most women have not been able to break the sexual barriers that prevent them from practicing medicine on their own. Although she writes generally about the discrimination against female doctors, Walsh also looks at the socialization of women and men, in order to pinpoint the exact reason why women have only just begun to enter medical school in large numbers.

MORANTZ-SANCHEZ gives a much fuller historical analysis of women's entrance into the medical profession than the first two sources, and carries her history through to the present situation of female physicians. Morantz-Sanchez's work is especially helpful in detailing the separatism of female physicians, but also the pressures on women to assimilate during certain periods of American history. The author concludes that in many ways, women and men are still not integrated within the medical profession, or rather, are integrated in name only. Morantz-Sanchez, like other researchers, documents the extreme pressures on women to marry and be respectable wives and mothers. Female doctors are expected to be "ladies" despite their primary interests in fulfilling medical careers. Morantz-Sanchez does well in paralleling the advances in feminism, describing how it influenced female physicians as they tried to secure a stable base for themselves within a male-dominated profession.

DRACHMAN's work is a case-study of one all-female medical institution in the United States, and the book complements other histories that have been written on female physicians. This book essentially tells the story of female doctors at the New England Hospital during a century of separatism. Drachman's study is the first historical study of any all-female medical institution in this country, and it thus presents an interesting in-depth analysis of women's place within the medical profession. Built upon a foundation of nineteenth century separatism, the New England Hospital offered women professional opportunites apart from those of men. However, with the turn of the century, all-male medical institutions began opening their doors to women. Drachman finds that the opportunity to work with male physicians represented a major step forward for female doctors. At the same time, this transition threatened the very existence of all-female medical institutions. Drachman thus emphasizes a paradox: whereas separatism originally laid a path for women's equality within the medical profession, gradually integration became a competing route to professional equality, challenging the separatist tradition of female doctors.

Drachman also describes three contexts in which to think about the history of female physicians: sexual discrimination, sisterhood, and professionalism. The reader of this book will do well to compare and contrast these perspectives, for one or more of these interpretations appear in most secondary sources on this topic. Although Drachman discusses these three perspectives in detail, she attempts to form her own interpretation of female doctors, describing them both as women and as doctors, and she interprets New England Hospital both as an all-female institution and as a medical institution. This work presents an interesting feminist analysis of female doctors, separatism, and the institution in question.

LORBER takes a unique approach, in that she intertwines historical material with current qualitative research on female doctors. After interviewing a sample of sixty-four female and male physicians, Lorber analyzes the differences between the career patterns of each sex. Lorber finds that female physicians, who achieved just as highly as males in medical school, lag behind men by mid-career. This researcher hypothesizes that limited sponsorship for women after their early career stages, and taken-for-granted inequality in the family division of labor, were the major reasons for lack of success as physicians. She discusses the obstacles that women face in their professional lives as well as in their family lives. Lorber urges the reader to see female physicians as similar to other highly qualified professional women who try to attain equal status in a male-dominated work world. She concentrates on female physicians' struggles to secure and maintain some sort of power or status in a profession that has still not completely accepted women.

Although there is a plethora of articles on female doctors, there are relatively few recent books written solely on this subject. Furthermore, now that women have entered medical schools in large numbers, more research is needed to understand the situation of women in medicine. For other sources on this subject, the reader should consult medical and social science journals, or more general works on the professionalization of women.

—HEATHER DILLAWAY

Domestic Service

Chaney, Elsa M., and Mary Garcia Castro (eds.), *Muchachas No More: Household Workers in Latin America and the Caribbean*, Philadelphia: Temple University Press, 1989

Cock, Jaclyn, *Maids and Madams: Domestic Workers under Apartheid*, London: Women's Press, 1989

Dill, Bonnie Thornton, *Across the Boundaries of Race and Class: An Exploration of Work and Family among Black Female Domestic Servants*, New York: Garland, 1994

Fairchilds, Cissie, *Domestic Enemies: Servants and Their Masters in Old Regime France*, Baltimore, Maryland: Johns Hopkins University Press, 1984

Glenn, Evelyn Nakano, *Issei, Nisei, War Bride: Three Generations of Japanese-American Women in Domestic Service*, Philadelphia: Temple University Press, 1986

Gregson, Nicky, and Michelle Lowe, *Servicing the Middle Class: Class, Gender and Waged Domestic Labour in Contemporary Britain*, New York: Routledge, 1994

Heyzer, Noeleen, Geertje Lycklama a Nijehold, and Nedrea Weerakoon (eds.), *The Trade in Domestic Workers: Causes, Mechanisms and Consequences of International Migration*, London: Zed, 1992

Katzman, David, *Seven Days a Week: Women and Domestic Service in Industrializing America*, New York: Oxford University Press, 1978

Palmer, Phyllis, *Domesticity and Dirt: Housewives and Domestic Servants in the United States, 1920–1945*, Philadelphia: Temple University Press, 1990

Romero, Mary, *Maid in the USA*, London and New York: Routledge, 1992

Until the second wave of the feminist movement, little consistent questioning about the lives of domestic workers, or domestic service itself, appeared in academic literature. Those studies that were made are best documented in the books by Katzman and Chaney and Castro. KATZMAN begins his discussion with Lucy Maynard Salmon's 1897 work, *Domestic Service*, and proceeds from this starting point back and forth to other periods and approaches. Other chapters in his work highlight "the voices of domestics and mistresses," conditions of work, African-American servants, immigrant servants, technology, domestic-service reform, guidebooks, and vice. He also includes a brief exploration of domestic workers in England, France, and Canada. By using the voices of servants themselves in his analysis of U.S. industrialization, Katzman gives readers both a historical and a sociological viewpoint. His source notation traces the publishing record of monographs, government documents, and articles on domestic service.

CHANEY and CASTRO investigate domestic service in Latin America. With chapters by a number of authors, their work complements Katzman's in several important ways, notably in providing a more extensive historical treatment (from 1492 to the present), and by including references to television shows and other works of popular culture. The most focused essays consider conditions in Jamaica, the Dominican Republic, Cuba, and other parts of the Caribbean as well as Brazil, Colombia, and Peru. Four articles deal with the organization of workers in labor unions or self-help groups and their interaction with government.

GLENN looks at another group of workers, Japanese-American women of the period from 1900 to 1970, the transformation of the economy of northern California and the process of labor migration. Although her work overlaps some of the period covered by Katzman, she bases her work more closely on oral interviews. And, unlike other authors, she compares generations of workers by looking at their relationships with their own families and with their employers. In so doing, she shows how their lives remained the same, noting, for example, that a domestic of the nisei (second generation) had options almost as restricted as that of her immigrant mother.

Reaching farther back in time, the work of FAIRCHILDS is clearly informed by the emergence of the Annales school, the history of the family, and the history of popular culture. Using quantitative and qualitative methods, she considers domestic service through a study of tax rolls, marriage contracts, and household account books. She concentrates on urban servants in southwestern France and broadens her coverage through interpretation of letters, memoirs, household manuals, cookbooks, architectural handbooks, and religious treatises. The servants of her study clearly played a part in creating French domesticity and family life. Fairchilds's work, therefore, is one of the broadest studies, connecting domestic work to attitudes toward children, sexual relationships, household management, and consumption patterns.

For a contemporary work about the relationship of domestics and their employers, COCK provides a study of a group of women who in 1979 represented one million black women in South Africa. Perhaps because she began her study during the early part of the second wave of feminism, Cock draws upon feminist theory more self-consciously than do later authors. However, her work pioneered the exploration of contemporary thought by asking about the cost of domestic service to the worker's family and the ways in which both white and black women are subject to patriarchy. Other chapters explore self-image and the resolutions adopted by the domestic workers' labor union in 1986.

Like Cock, Palmer, Romero, and Dill approach their subject from a feminist standpoint—acknowledging even more their own confrontations with domestic responsibilities. PALMER begins where Katzman ends but instead builds her analysis around the employing family, the housewife in a modern marriage, the businessman's working wife, and education for the vocation of housework. She also notes that sex, dirt, housework, and badness are linked in the western unconscious. White middle-class women, she claims, sought to transcend these associations by demonstrating their sexual purity and their pristine domesticity. An afterword looks at the period from 1945–80.

ROMERO turns her attention specifically to employers. She designates six categories of American employers: bosses, utopian feminists, dodgers and duckers, common victims, maternalists, and contractors. Her strongest chapters, however, analyze the daily activities of Chicana household workers. In these chapters, she helpfully interweaves an exploration of earlier studies dating from the nineteenth century, drawing special attention to conditions that have not changed during the twentieth century. She sees domestic workers themselves as striving to change many of the inequities of their work.

DILL also devotes attention to such changes as she explores the dynamics of the employer-employee relationships through workers' stories. Dill concentrates on three case studies and through them seeks to understand the structure and nature of domestic work, its relationship to family, and the role of race, ethnicity, culture, and immigration. Her book is more focused than others on African-American workers engaged in both live-in and "day work" in urban U.S. cities. She also presents information on child rearing and upward mobility among the families of domestic workers.

GREGSON and LOWE extend the feminist consideration of housework and discuss in depth the impotance of considering housework as a form of work exhibiting the social relations of both wage labor and kinship. They investigate the demand by middle-class families for domestic labor and the reappearance of a transformed "servant" class in Britain in the 1980s. As geographers, they discuss the global considerations of supply and demand for nannies and cleaners, and the theoretical and political ramifications of such economics. In addition, they consider the role of automobiles and public transportation as a policy consideration and as an indicator of the way class relates to social reproduction. They also provide lengthy theoretical comparisons of gender and class inequalities and supply maps and charts that reveal much about life in England during the 1980s.

HEYZER, NIJEHOLD, and WEERAKOON expand this view of the changing world of domestic service even further as they identify and discuss issues concerned with migration, profits of agents, and the indebtedness of workers. In chapters devoted to domestic workers from Sri Lanka, Indonesia, the Philippines, and Bangladesh, the authors note that the employment of housekeepers is now big business. The countries that employ these housekeepers—Malaysia, Hong Kong, Singapore, and the Gulf nations—are fifteen times richer than the countries the workers come from, and this inequity alone adds to many harsh conditions in the lives of domestic workers.

—SUSAN TUCKER

Domestic Violence

Berry, Dawn Bradley, *The Domestic Violence Sourcebook: Everything You Need to Know,* Los Angeles: Lowell House, and Chicago: Contemporary Books, 1995

Counts, Dorothy Ayers, Judith K. Brown, and Jacquelyn C. Campbell (eds.), *Sanctions and Sanctuary: Cultural Perspectives on the Beating of Wives,* Boulder, Colorado: Westview Press, 1992

Edwards, Susan S.M., *Policing "Domestic" Violence: Women, the Law, and the State,* London: Sage, 1989

Maracek, Mary, *Breaking Free from Partner Abuse: Voices of Battered Women Caught in the Cycle of Domestic Violence,* Buena Park, California: Morning Glory Press, 1993

Martin, Del, *Battered Wives,* San Francisco: Glide, 1976; revised ed., San Francisco: Volcano Press, 1981
Sipe, Beth, and Evelyn J. Hall, *I Am Not Your Victim: Anatomy of Domestic Violence,* Thousand Oaks, California: Sage, 1996

Feminist thinking has transformed society's ideas about domestic violence. Traditionally it was considered a husband's right, even his responsibility, to physically "discipline" his wife to some extent at least, and until the resurgence of the women's movement at the end of the twentieth century, women were routinely blamed for their own abuse, and law enforcement agencies considered acts of domestic violence to be private matters of family conflict. Now, although it still occurs on a large scale, it is more and more taken seriously, and the perpetrators are charged with violent acts.

In her desire to make society aware of the impact domestic abuse has not just on its individual victims but on society as a whole, BERRY provides a comprehensive sourcebook that includes the history of domestic violence and the psychological, legal, and familial issues that surround it. Prevention, awareness, and improvement programs are discussed, as are emergency treatment shelters and programs. In addition to the extensive bibliography, numerous relevant organizations are listed.

COUNTS, BROWN, and CAMPBELL have edited a collection of essays that focus on anthropological research into domestic violence in a number of different cultures. Communities in Papua New Guinea, Belize, Iran, India, and Taiwan, among others, are examined in various ways, from societies that effectively eliminate domestic violence to those in which physical violence forms a large part of interaction among domestic couples to those (such as the United States) in which women are often trapped in abusive situations. As Campbell suggests in her conclusion to the volume, systematic study of the cultural factors that produce domestic violence is the best way to transform those cultural factors and eliminate violence against women.

By studying the response of police in England to cases of domestic violence, EDWARDS demonstrates that these cases are treated differently than other crimes by both law enforcement agencies and society in general. Through her analysis of reported crimes of various types in addition to those involving violence against women, Edwards demonstrates that women are not adequately represented in cases of domestic violence. Edwards concludes with a description of current programs for prevention and consideration of what additional programs and legislation are necessary.

MARTIN stresses the underacknowledged nature of the problem of domestic violence by pointing out the lack of statistics available, largely due to law enforcement's reluctance to get involved in family matters. Through interviews with wives of violent husbands, social and psychological professionals, and examination of studies of the problem in England, Martin analyses the causes of domestic violence and looks at possible solutions.

SIPE and HALL are victim and therapist to the victim, respectively, in an 18-year case of domestic violence. Unlike the other titles discussed here, this book is a personal account of a specific case of abuse. Not for the faint of heart, Sipe's story is a graphic retelling of the horrific events of her marriage and the self-defense murder of her husband. The book contains an extensive appendix in which authors representing the medical and legal professions as well as social work and academia comment on Sipe's story and its larger implications for society.

—ELEANOR B. AMICO

Doolittle, Hilda (H.D.) 1886–1961

American Writer

Buck, Claire, *H.D. and Freud: Bisexuality and a Feminine Discourse,* New York: St. Martin's Press, and London: Harvester Wheatsheaf, 1991
Burnett, Gary Dean, *H.D. Between Image and Epic: The Mysteries of Her Poetics,* Ann Arbor, Michigan: UMI Research Press, 1989
Chisholm, Dianne, *H.D.'s Freudian Poetics: Psychoanalysis in Translation,* Ithaca, New York, and London: Cornell University Press, 1992
Edmunds, Susan, *Out of Line: History, Psychoanalysis, and Montage in H.D.'s Long Poems,* Stanford, California: Stanford University Press, 1994
Friedman, Susan Stanford, *Psyche Reborn: The Emergence of H.D.,* Bloomington: Indiana University Press, 1981
———, *Penelope's Web: Gender, Modernity, H.D.'s Fiction,* Cambridge and New York: Cambridge University Press, 1990
———, and Rachel Blau DuPlessis (eds.), *Signets: Reading H.D,* Madison: University of Wisconsin Press, 1990
Guest, Barbara, *Herself Defined: The Poet H.D. and Her World,* New York: Doubleday, 1984; London: Collins, 1985
King, Michael (ed.), *H.D.: Woman and Poet,* Orono, Maine: National Poetry Foundation, 1986

The work of H.D., the American expatriate writer, soon outstripped the straitjacket of early modernist theories and forged a characteristic style shaped by a variety of influences: classical Greek poetry, Freudian psychoanalysis, the burgeoning European film industry, the study of a range of religious and occult experiences, the impact of two world wars, and avant garde modernist ideas and their practitioners. Initially well received by contemporary critics, after a period of writer's block in the 1930s followed by mental breakdown after World War II, her writing was dismissed and neglected by critics until the 1970s, when second-wave feminist poets and scholars rediscovered her work and reassessed its importance. This has resulted in a wealth of scholarship on H.D.'s life and writing, as well as publications of her previously unpublished and out-of-print texts.

Feminist criticism has rescued H.D.'s texts from the narrow prescriptions of early modernism and later dismissive critics. Friedman's two books are comprehensive, provocative and illuminating investigations of the textual strategies that enabled H.D. to claim authority as a writer. Aware of H.D. as both exponent of modernism and precursor of postmodernism, Friedman grounds her arguments in English and French feminist theories as well as poststructural contexts. FRIEDMAN (1981) considers H.D.'s poetry through the spectrum of artistic, intellectual, political, and spiritual influences, which she brought to bear on her language and its quest for alternative meanings. For H.D. this involved responding to the dominant patriarchal imperatives with narratives of the female subject, which included the lesbian erotic, in a woman-centred mythmaking. FRIEDMAN (1990) considers H.D.'s place in the remapping of modernism, examining her discourse in relation to gender, genre, and history, and illuminating her contributions to the theory and practice of a women's poetic tradition.

BURNETT chronologically surveys the poems H.D. wrote after her celebrated imagist period and preceding her first long epic, *Trilogy,* written in response to World War II. He reads the poems within the framework of the volumes of which they form a part and sets them against and within the contexts of her life, the world wars, her research into the Eleusinian mysteries, and the avant-garde traditions of the period. Burnett regards H.D.'s oeuvre as one diverse, discontinuous text and argues that each volume of poetry is part of a single complex and interconnected whole, glossed by the exploratory poetics of her contemporaneous prose.

In the 1930s H.D. became an analysand of Sigmund Freud. This experience proved a crucial juncture not just in her life, but in the structure and discourse of her subsequent work. CHISHOLM demonstrates the fundamental importance of Freudian psychoanalysis in the figures and structures of much of H.D.'s prose and epic verse narratives. Chisholm's intertextual methodology regards H.D. and Freud not as doctor and patient but as collaborative and contesting colleagues, whose "intertexts" reveal the differences between her poetic discourse and his psychoanalytic one. Chisholm sees H.D. appropriating for her own discourse Freudian concepts such as translation, fantasy, melancholia, and catharsis. She investigates the way in which the politics, aesthetics, and therapeutics of H.D.'s acts of "translation" subvert many of Freud's exclusionary, misogynist ideas, allowing H.D. to articulate desires and aspirations of her own. Chisholm includes H.D. along with Melanie Klein, Julia Kristeva, Hélène Cixous, Catherine Clement and Luce Irigaray in her group of leading feminist revisionists who continue the transformation of Freudian psychoanalysis.

BUCK traces the similarities and differences between models of representation and how they relate to H.D.'s construction of the female self in narratives where Freud is central. Buck starts with the implications of the Lacanian process, by which a "lack" is supposedly assigned to "Woman." She then draws on the challenge Cixous and Irigaray make to Freud's account of phallic dominance and especially bisexuality, which has a privileged place in H.D.'s writing, where it creates an alternative economy of difference and desire. While Buck finds a variety of psychoanalytical models useful for exploring the themes of subjectivity, sexual difference, language, their shifting relationships, and the implications of each shift for reading the self as feminine, she discovers that resistance to such theoretical interpretation is also a strategy in H.D.'s writing.

EDMUNDS's psychoanalytic readings of H.D.'s late long poems exercise the same ambivalence and self-reflexiveness she finds in H.D.'s meditations on sexuality, gender, and writing. Moving beyond the earlier feminist project of recuperation, she centres on the contemporary psychoanalytic and film theories, as well as the social conflicts that informed H.D.'s work at the time it was written, revealing how H.D.'s revisionary solutions nevertheless reveal their own political bias, ambivalence, and incoherence. Through a rhetorical positioning of the two contradictory bodies she reads in H.D.'s work—"the twisted body of history and narrative and the radiant body of epiphany"—she traces the controversies surrounding Melanie Klein's ideas and practices, the film theory and practice of Sergei Eisenstein, and the concept of art as revolution in the African independence movements of the 1950s and 1960s.

The volume edited by KING reveals the variety of responses to H.D.'s work, exploring her influence as modernist, poet, novelist, translator, memoirist, critic, essayist, correspondent, actor, and filmmaker. It covers a spectrum of reading and writing practices, with a predominant feminist emphasis on gender, and includes biographical, contextual, textual, and psychoanalytic argument. Also included is an annotated bibliography of criticism devoted to H.D.'s work spanning 1969–85. A complementary volume edited by FRIEDMAN and DUPLESSIS combines with King's work to offer a wide range of critical and biographical coverage of H.D.'s life and work. Also included in Friedman and DuPlessis's book are a photobiography, a selected biography, and chronologies of both H.D.'s life and the production and publication of her work.

GUEST's chronological biography of H.D. offers an interpretation of the life of a modernist woman of letters disciplined and dedicated to her gift. Guest traces H.D.'s preoccupation with penetrating the self in order to define it through texts that are themselves autobiographies of an intense inner life. Guest examines H.D.'s chosen life of exile and shows the development of the writer's poetics from the influences of psychoanalysis, film, and modernist theories.

—JENNIFER R. MOORE

Dowry

Diwan, Paras, *Dowry and Protection to Married Women*, New Delhi: Deep and Deep Publications, 1987

Kaplan, Marion A. (ed.), *The Marriage Bargain: Women and Dowries in European History*, New York: Harrington Park Press, 1985

Nazzari, Muriel, *Disappearance of the Dowry: Women, Families, and Social Change in Sao Paulo, Brazil (1600–1900)*, Stanford, California: Stanford University Press, 1991

Thankappan Nair, P., *Marriage and Dowry in India*, Columbia, Montana.: South Asia Books, 1978

Dowry can be defined as the wealth a woman brings to a marriage partnership. It may constitute either a small amount of money or property, or it may be quite substantial, such as large quantities of money, land, or movable property. In recent years, particularly in India where it remains widely practiced, dowry may include houses, cars, and other forms of modern technology.

The literature on dowry is surprisingly weak. It is rare to find whole books about dowry, although chapters in more general books about marriage customs will be devoted to the topic. Most frequently dowry is treated in particular societies—European, South Asian, or South American. Also, many sources spend little time exploring the psychological and experiential impact of dowry on women. The majority of literature on dowry is focused on this custom in the Indian subcontinent where it is most widely practiced today.

KAPLAN's volume on dowry in European history is an excellent collection inspired by the Women's History Research Group. While love is the main ingredient of contemporary marriages, for most of human history economic factors like dowry constituted the glue that held a couple together. Dowry was a significant factor in a young woman's marriageability, and it affected her future. The articles in Kaplan's book span a thousand years of western history. They focus on the institution of the dowry in the Mediterranean cities of the eleventh and twelfth centuries, the middle and upper classes of Siena, the Sicilian peasantry of the nineteenth century, the Imperial German bourgeoisie, and Greek workers and farmers today. These studies raise the question about the rise, decline, or persistence of the dowry in different periods of history. Kaplan's collection is an excellent source on the institution of the dowry from a woman's perspective.

THANKAPPAN NAIR's book on marriage in India surveys a wide variety of tribal customs in various parts of the subcontinent. Only a few portions of the volume focus particularly on the dowry system. Among tribal peoples bride price—where a man or his family pays a woman's family to be married to her—is a more frequent economic arrangement. Dowry is mostly found among Hindus.

More valuable as a source on dowry in India is the volume by DIWAN. It is an excellent source on legal dimensions of the Indian dowry system. The Dowry Prohibition Act of 1961 (amended in 1985 and 1986) has had little effect on preventing this widely practiced custom. Dowry deaths involving "bride burnings" have rapidly increased in recent years. Diwan documents many cases, citing numerous court decisions. In this volume there is a summary of the law, illustrations of dowry offences, punishments determined by the courts, and an argument that there is a strong need for Dowry Prohibition Officers to enforce the law. There is an excellent discussion of the history of women's property rights. Also there are several important chapters concerned with dowry deaths and the protection of battered wives. While Diwan's book is a good technical source, it is not particularly sensitive to the social and emotional impact of the Indian dowry system on women.

NAZZARI's book is a fascinating study of the disappearance of dowry from Brazilian society in the nineteenth century. The Portuguese brought the dowry custom to Brazil in the sixteenth century. Daughters of upper-class families were given large amounts of land, cattle, agricultural tools and even Indian slaves. According to the author, dowry was among the many institutions that disappeared with the worldwide spread of industrial capitalism. Brazil changed from a hierarchical patron-client society to a more individualistic society in which contract and the market reigned. In the nineteenth century a new concept of private property developed. The family changed from being the locus of both production and consumption to being mainly the locus of consumption. Nazzari asserts that the disappearance of dowry had a negative effect on women in Brazil. It made the bride's position within the marriage worse, since she no longer contributed to the couple's support. This volume is an excellent source with a sophisticated theoretical section.

The lack of studies of the impact of dowry on women is due to scattered data, lack of interest on the part of male scholars, and the inaccessibility of some of this information to men who, until recently, dominated this field of study. It is clear that dowry needs much more probing study from a variety of disciplinary perspectives.

—JAMES J. PRESTON

Dowry Murder/Bride Burning

Hawley, John Stratton, and Donna Marie Wulff (eds.), *Devi: Goddesses of India*, Berkeley: University of California Press, 1996

Kishwar, Madhu, and Ruth Vanita (eds.), *In Search of Answers: Indian Women's Voices from Manushi*, London: Zed, 1984

Kumari, Ranjana, *Brides Are Not for Burning: Dowry Victims in India*, New Delhi: Radiant Publishers, and London: Sangam, 1989

Minturn, Leigh, *Sita's Daughters: Coming Out of Purdah: The Rajput Women of Khalapur Revisited*, New York: Oxford University Press, 1993

Mitter, Sara, *Dharma's Daughters: Contemporary Indian Women and Hindu Culture*, New Brunswick, New Jersey: Rutgers University Press, 1991

Sunder Rajan, Rajeswari, *Real and Imagined Women: Gender, Culture, and Postcolonialism*, London and New York: Routledge, 1993

A variety of works dealing with the issues of dowry murder and bride burning generate important theoretical questions and, at the same time, explore the ways in which stereotyped and sensationalist images of the "Third World woman" as victim can be critiqued. In a work that combines textual analysis and intensive fieldwork, HAWLEY and WULFF edit a collection of essays that explore the feminine dimension in religious experience in India. A major essay on *satī* explores the important and widely shared assumptions that attend the concept of the *satī*, that is, the "good woman." The authors examine the tensions and perspectives embraced by the concept as well as mythological narratives but do not address the sexual politics of contemporary women's lives.

KISHWAR and VANITA collate illuminating and moving articles that have appeared in *Manushi*, India's leading radical women's journal. A selection focus particularly on the diverse struggles of women enmeshed in caste and class expectations, and the injuries perpetrated against them by police and family members. Using field workers' reports, and letters from victims' families, they examine the implications of wife-murder and rape. Their powerful analysis of the endeavours and exertions of rural and urban women against contemporary family structures critiques relations of power that are designed to ensure the subordination and exploitation of women.

KUMARI's book is a broad study that inquires into the types, forms and incidence of dowry giving and its violent consequences for women. The author sets out to determine the socioeconomic background of dowry murder victims, to evaluate the impact of recent legislation against dowry giving, and to suggest proposals to eradicate its practice. Focusing on Delhi, Kumari provides a sociologically based survey and case studies to argue for legal and social policy changes, as well as psychosocial change.

The ethnographic detail in MINTURN's account of field work in Uttar Pradesh attempts to counter the sensationalism that pervades representations of dowry giving. It is a book that is written for both Indian and western audiences, with descriptions of the roles and customs that shape women's lives. Minturn defends some traditional customs, arguing that feminist ideas would impose inappropriate interpretations on her informants' accounts. The work covers a broad range of topics and describes the transition of women from daughters to wives, the customary beliefs supporting purdah, and the economic basis for dowry gifts, which makes the distinction that women are killed for land rather than dowry goods, as well as the role of and restrictions on widows.

An accessible, descriptive account that focuses on urban manifestations of dowry giving, MITTER's colloquial reporting style reflects the observations, encounters, and rapport she has constructed over many visits to families in Calcutta. Mitter adds perceptive zest to the dry, yet grim statistics of women's dowry deaths by focusing on sociopolitical understandings of women's inferior status.

SUNDER RAJAN's endeavour is a classic work, designed for scholars and researchers. She offers a sociopolitical commentary and literary analysis, which reconstitutes female subjectivity in the interests of feminist practice. Using a comparative perspective in a self-conscious reflection upon female subjectivity, she moves between examinations of western perspectives and explorations of gendered subaltern consciousness. Her investigation of the "historically victimised" critiques the traditional construction of the subjectivity of widows who "choose" to die upon the husband's funeral pyre. She emphasises a consideration of embodied subjects who experience pain, as well as historical representations of the widow who "chooses" to live.

—HELEN JOHNSON

See also Dowry; Sati

Dual Career Families

Bernasco, Wim, *Coupled Careers: The Effect of Spouse's Resources on Success at Work*, Amsterdam: Thesis Publishers, 1994

Ferber, Marianne A., Brigid O'Farrell, and LaRue Allen, *Work and Family: Policies in a Changing Work Force*, Washington, D.C.: National Academy Press, 1991

Frankel, Judith (ed.), *Families of Employed Mothers: An International Perspective*, New York and London: Garland, 1997

Hochschild, Arlie Russell, *The Time Bind; When Work Becomes Home and Home Becomes Work,* New York: Metropolitan, 1997

Lewis, Suzan, Dafna N. Izraeli, and Helen Hootsmans (eds.), *Dual-Earner Families: International Perspectives,* London and Newbury Park, California: Sage, 1992

Rapoport, Robert, Rhona Rapoport, and Janice Bumstead, *Working Couples,* New York: Harper and Row; and London: Routledge and Kegan Paul, 1978

Schwartz, Felice N., *Breaking with Tradition: Women and Work, the New Facts of Life,* New York: Warner, 1992

Stanfield, Jacqueline Bloom, *Married with Careers: Coping with Role Strain,* Aldershot and Brookfield, Vermont: Avebury, 1996

RAPOPORT, RAPOPORT, and BUMSTEAD conducted the initial research on dual career families. The problems dual career families face include stress connected with changing their lifestyle from the traditional pattern, social resistance toward a couple who deviates from the norm, and maintaining relationships within the family. The book looks at western and Soviet couples. It lists many areas of adjustment couples must make: finding two jobs that are equally attractive; working out interpersonal agreements that seem fair to both; handling competition between resources, prestige, or power; choosing child care resources that will be best for the children; and balancing work and fulfilling domestic obligations.

HOCHSCHILD, a widely recognized researcher in the area of dual career couples, employs the case study method to describe how working couples use their time, balancing family life with work. Working couples interviewed said they were in a "time bind" that robbed them of life and relationships they wanted at home. Hochschild's "third shift" is the task of helping children adjust emotionally to an increasingly industrialized, mechanized home life. Finding more time becomes the answer. While there are individual alternatives to the time bind, Hochschild prefers collective action for a movement that would limit the length of the workday, in order to allow more time for the family. This is necessary for the sake of children who most feel the effects of the time bind. This movement must be based outside the corporation and must challenge prevailing opinions of our present work world. She offers the Swedish model and some U.S. experiments as methods that could be copied in a time movement.

LEWIS, IZRAELI, and HOOTSMANS focus on international differences among working families in Europe, Asia, and the United States, dual careers' effects on the family, and policy implications for organizations. The chapters address specific issues concerning dual-earner families, and how distinct cultural societies meet the needs of family members. In all the societies discussed, responsibilities for family care requiring relational skills fell to women, even if the mother worked outside the home, and even if the particular society approved hiring domestic help (again, female). Some degree of gender inequality was universally present. Sweden, Hungary, Israel, Singapore, Britain, the United States, and Japan differ in how they view gender responsibility for childcare, but the result in each case is that women are in a "secondary position in the workplace, as in the family." To date, all adjustment has been done by families, especially women. Cook, in the final chapter, proposes organizational changes that could help women. Throughout the book, a systems approach is recommended, with corporations and governments taking more of the lead to improve the situation for families.

Having been influenced by the Rapoports' research on the dual career family, STANFIELD's work is an outgrowth of her Ph.D. dissertation. She presents a descriptive, sociological study of how couples cope with role strain. Role strain includes the conflicting obligations that occur simultaneously, forcing the individual to meet one responsibility at the expense of another. Family role strain occurs in the areas of medical/psychiatric emergencies, conflict with the community, disaster, and family crises (departure, desertion, death, divorce). Two styles of coping are described: flexible style, which includes a flexible work schedule, a high degree of planning, and low work-to-home role compartmentalization (taking care of home needs during work hours); the rigid style demonstrates low flexibility of work schedule—at the office during work hours, "regardless of other obligations."

SCHWARTZ created a stir with an article about women in management, and became associated with the term "mommy track." She wrote this book in order to answer the fever her 1989 *Harvard Business Review* article created. She calls for another step for the women's movement, this time in the corporate world. She presents the problem of a pattern of silence in the professions. The silence is created by the recognition that women will usually marry and have families, but their employers cannot broach this subject during the hiring process. This book is primarily Schwartz's personal conclusions about women facing work and family.

Having previously studied the effect of the employed mother on the U.S. family, FRANKEL here turns to maternal employment and the family internationally. The themes emerging internationally mirror those seen in the United States. Women across cultures must prioritize and choose between traditional and modern values. Major themes all authors discuss are the needs for adequate substitute child care, and ways to face the conflict and stress accompanying dual roles. These issues contribute to the life satisfaction of the employed mother. Thus changes are needed in how male and female family roles are valued, in the family structure, and in the roles assigned to primarily one gender.

After reviewing assumptions concerning support of an individual entering the work force, BERNASCO examines the extent to which the resources of a spouse positively or negatively affect an individual's success at work. He looks specifically at the areas of education, promotion, level of earnings, and employability. Bernasco suggests that the interrelationship and support between spouses differs from other social networks. He concludes that informational resources are more useful to the spouse than financial resources, and the more resourceful a spouse, the greater likelihood of success an individual has. Husbands' resources affect wives more than wives' resources affect husbands. The book includes detailed summaries of previous research addressing spousal effects and social inequality in the Netherlands, the United States, and Canada.

The shift of women to the workforce has social implications only now being measured for the worker with less time at home, the dependents who have less support, and employers whose workers' attention is divided. FERBER, O'FARRELL, and ALLEN present the conclusions of a study by the National Research Council's Committee on Women's Employment and Related Social Issues. The panel of 12 experts from relevant fields synthesized and evaluated the research on working families and employer policy, discussed policy alternatives, and suggested additional research. Extensive references prior to 1990 are included. The panel calls for further consideration by labor and government about how to benefit workers and business alike, including paid and unpaid family sick leave, and more flexibility in work hour options.

—DEBORAH BUSH HAFFEY

See also Dual Labor Market; Earnings Gap

Dual Labor Markets

Amott, Teresa L., and Julie Matthaei, *Race, Gender, and Work: A Multicultural Economic History of Women in the United States*, Boston: South End Press, 1991

Blau, Francine D., and Marianne A. Ferber, *The Economics of Women, Men, and Work*, Englewood Cliffs, New Jersey: Prentice-Hall, 1986

Lloyd, Cynthia B., and Beth T. Niemi, *The Economics of Sex Differentials*, New York: Columbia University Press, 1979

Roos, Patricia A., *Gender and Work: A Comparative Analysis of Industrial Societies*, Albany: State University of New York Press, 1985

Attempting to explain gender-based occupational segregation has long been a cottage industry among economists and sociologists. Dual labor market theory is part of the institutional approach to this problem. Closely related to segmented labor market theory and internal labor market theory, the notion of dual labor markets argues that productivity differences between workers are at least partially explained by the characteristics and nature of the workers' jobs. This is in direct contrast to the human capital approach, which argues that individual workers' characteristics are the primary cause of productivity differences. More simply put: Are women's wages low because women aren't productive enough, or are women's wages low because women are confined to jobs that are unproductive?

The human capital model, at present, is the most popular model among neo-classical economists, who dominate this field of study; thus, full-length treatments of dual labor market analysis of women's work are rare. LLOYD and NIEMI's text provides an overview of the various approaches to understanding the economics of the earnings gap and occupational segregation. Their explanation of segmented labor market theory includes a good discussion of dual labor markets. Another, more up-to-date, overview of current work on occupational segregation is included in BLAU and FERBER's book. This text, with its excellent set of references, will guide the interested reader to more work on occupational segregation.

ROOS's book is an interesting attempt to test which theory performs best in explaining occupational segregation in twelve industrialized countries. She contrasts the human capital approach with the institutional explanations. While she finds that human capital theory explains only a small part of the observed differences in the labor market behavior of men and women, she is unable to completely test the institutional hypotheses because of data limitations. Indeed, the difficulty of quantifying the impact of institutional restraints may be one reason the theory is less popular than the easily testable human capital theory.

Perhaps the best application, to date, of institutional explanations for women's low wages and segregation into female-dominated jobs is AMOTT and MATTHAEI's economic history of American women. Written from a Marxist-feminist perspective, Amott and Matthaei divide the labor market into three sectors: primary, secondary and tertiary. They analyze the impact of not only gender, but also race and ethnicity, on the employment of women. Written as a textbook, it is very accessible to the general reader. It is also well-referenced, and can serve as a guide to more work on the economic history of various groups of women, and to more work on economic explanations for wage and occupational differences.

—PAMELA J. NICKLESS

See also Division of Labor by Sex; Earnings Gap; Glass Ceiling

Duncan, Isadora 1877–1927

American Dancer

Blair, Fredrika, *Isadora: Portrait of the Artist as a Woman*, New York: McGraw-Hill, 1986; Wellingborough: Equation, 1987

Dillon, Millicent, *After Egypt: Isadora Duncan and Mary Cassatt*, New York: Dutton, and London: Penguin, 1990

Duncan, Dorée, Carol Pratl, and Cynthia Splatt (eds.), *Life into Art: Isadora Duncan and Her World*, New York and London: Norton, 1993

Loewenthal, Lillian, *The Search for Isadora: The Legend and Legacy of Isadora Duncan*, Pennington, New Jersey: Princeton Book, 1993

Schneider, Ila Ilich, *Isadora Duncan: The Russian Years*, translated by David Magarshack, London: Macdonald, 1968; New York: Harcourt, 1969

Terry, Walter, *Isadora Duncan: Her Life, Her Art, Her Legacy*, New York: Dodd Mead, 1963

As modern critics often lament, Isadora Duncan performed her remarkable transformation of dance before the age of motion pictures; even still photography required the subject to hold a pose for minutes. This has made it difficult for recent scholars to study the dances themselves, although choreographic records of some pieces do exist, and some works are still performed. For this reason if no other, criticism of Duncan has tended to focus on her fascinating life, and on the contemporary reception of her work; there is little technical or critical analysis of the work itself.

LOEWENTHAL's book is a study of Duncan's legacy as a dancer. The first section describes as accurately as possible the costumes, stage design, music, and choreography of some of Duncan's most important dance compositions. The second section focuses on Duncan's dance academies, her methods of instruction, major performances by her students, and the inevitable conflicts between the teacher and the students she had trained to be independent and free. Each of the Isadora Duncan Dancers is given a brief biography, including insightful analysis of these dancers' own contributions to the dance. The final section addresses Duncan's "Legend and Legacy," especially her reception in France, her influence on sculptors and graphic artists, and the survival of her choreographies and methods through the decades. An extensive bibliography (unfortunately not annotated) and chronology are included.

Although somewhat outdated, TERRY's book is another study that focuses on Duncan's work, although the first section of the book is structured as a brief biography. Terry was for many years an influential dance critic, and his book demonstrates how Duncan's contributions helped shape the state of dance in the 1960s, when this book first appeared. Writing so long ago, Terry was able to interview many people who remembered Isadora Duncan, and he includes previously unpublished material from her contemporaries, including comments about the Greek ideal, the use of music, and the relationship between sculpture and the dance.

The most comprehensive of the biographies is that of BLAIR, who went so far in her extensive research as to study Duncan Dance for two years. Blair skims over Duncan's relationships with her students and the Russian years, as they are covered well in other books, but gives a full story of the other important periods of Duncan's life, emphasizing her evolving philosophy of dance centered on natural movement. This book includes several contemporary dance reviews to show how the dance was received in Duncan's time, and also analyzes its influence since her death. Most important for students of the biography, it attempts to sort out various episodes that had been recounted rather subjectively in the memoirs written by Duncan's friends and students. This is a very readable yet solid study, insightful about Duncan's art as well as her personal life.

DUNCAN's volume is a feminist biography focusing on Duncan's roles as artist, mother, and independent woman. Through her enormous contributions to the dance as an art form, she also worked to reeducate men and women about women's bodies and minds in their natural state, freed from male-created restraints. Dividing the life into three sections, "Lyrical," "Dramatic," and "Heroic," this book presents Duncan as a hard-working and generous woman. She worked well with men, but did not form strong romantic ties with them; her love was for the dance, for her students, and for her children. The book contains many important photographs and sketches not previously published. Agnes de Mille contributes a foreword, in which she proclaims Duncan an unpretentious and heroic dancer, and a true revolutionary.

SCHNEIDER shared a home with Duncan during her years in Russia, and acted as her manager, librettist, lighting designer, and friend; when she left Russia, he continued for twenty years as principal of the Isadora Duncan School. This biography is shaped equally by the author's adoration of his subject, his professional understanding of dance and theater, and his intimate knowledge of Duncan's thoughts and intentions as she created new productions and developed methods of instruction. Schneider perhaps overestimates his reader's interest in Duncan's love affair with Sergei Esenin, which he describes in close detail, and his tone is sometimes patronizing. But as a record of how one man who knew her well faced her brilliant but erratic personality, this book is valuable.

DILLON rejects the linear qualities of traditional biography, and attempts to get at a deeper, intuitive truth in an eccentric book about Duncan and Mary Cassatt. Although the two never met, each traveled to

Egypt, boated up the Nile, and wrote about her experiences. Dillon juxtaposes these two trips, narrating them in individual chapters with no unifying commentary. With alternating snippets from the two women's lives, presented in lyrical language and out of chronological order, the book echoes the workings of memory, with its repetitions and seeming randomness. In her travels to Egypt, Dillon seems to say, Duncan confirmed her connections to the ancients, (which she achieved through dance) and, because she was pregnant, contemplated the future as well.

—CYNTHIA A. BILY

Duras, Marguerite 1914–1996

French Writer

Cohen, Susan D., *Women and Discourse in the Fiction of Marguerite Duras: Love, Legend, Language,* London: Macmillan, and Amherst: University of Massachusetts Press, 1983

Glassman, Deborah N., *Marguerite Duras: Fascinating Vision and Narrative Cure,* Rutherford, Maryland: Fairleigh Dickinson University Press, and London: Associated University Presses, 1991

Hill, Leslie, *Marguerite Duras: Apocalyptic Desires,* London and New York: Routledge, 1993

Hofmann, Carol, *Forgetting and Marguerite Duras,* Niwot: University Press of Colorado, 1991

Schuster, Marilyn R., *Marguerite Duras Revisited,* New York: Twayne, 1993

Selous, Trista, *The Other Woman: Feminism and Femininity in the Work of Marguerite Duras,* New Haven, Connecticut, and London: Yale University Press, 1988

Vircondelet, Alain, *Duras: A Biography,* translated by Thomas Buckley, Normal, Illinois: Dalkey Archive Press, 1994

Willis, Sharon, *Marguerite Duras: Writing on the Body,* Urbana: University of Illinois Press, 1987

French author Marguerite Duras was a prolific novelist, playwright, and filmmaker, as well as a journalist, political activist, and media icon. Many of her works feature women protagonists, and treat themes of mourning, desire, and sexual relationships. As a result, her oeuvre has often been studied from both psychoanalytic and feminist perspectives. The first major work about Duras in English was WILLIS's book, which appeared at the moment when Duras was acquiring international recognition for her autobiographical novel, *The Lover.* Willis explores the relationships among writing, the body, pleasure, and power, and assumes that readers have some knowledge of post-structuralist theory. She organizes her study around readings of four central texts: *Hiroshima Mon Amour, The Ravishing of Lol Stein, The Vice-Consul,* and *L'Amour.* She explores hysteria as a figure for Duras's language in these texts, and interprets the cries of the beggarwoman as emblematic of a larger disruption of dominant discourse She analyzes Duras's transgressions of literary genre, and, in light of Freud's theory of the repetition compulsion, the texts' linguistic and thematic repetitions.

SELOUS's book appeared shortly after Willis's, and is a standard text of Durassian criticism. It is a good introduction to feminist and psychoanalytic interpretation of Duras, and provides an overview of Durassian criticism in French. The book is divided into two parts. The first assesses the numerous difficulties of theorizing "femininity," describes the psychoanalytic theories of Jacques Lacan, and articulates the relationships among femaleness, femininity, and feminism. The second part of the book explores the "blanks" in Duras's texts and their relation to femininity. Selous is concerned, for example, with gaps in plot, silences in dialogue, "disappearing" narrators, and Duras's use of the French indefinite personal pronoun "*on.*" Selous concentrates on Duras's novels, and traces in them a transformation in the way women characters are portrayed: from women who are active subjects, to women who thematize their own desire as enigma, to women who, without desire themselves, function as objects of men's desire.

The sole existing biography of Duras in English is by VIRCONDELET. The book argues that customary biographical techniques are inappropriate to Duras's life, the "events" of which were often rescripted by Duras herself. The volume affords basic information about Duras's life, although it is more a work of worship than of scholarship, and is largely comprised of speculation about what Duras might have been thinking or feeling at particular moments. The book will be informative for those entirely unacquainted with Duras, and entertaining for those who relish pulp fiction. It also contains a series of evocative photographs, previously unavailable in an English-language text, of Duras in Indochina, on the sets of her plays and films, and with friends such as François Mitterand and Yann Andréa.

Several general works about Duras also contain biographical information, as well as textual analyses. SCHUSTER's book—The Twayne World Authors series' second pass at "summing up" Duras—begins with a helpful chronology of Duras's life and career. The book argues that a woman is always at the center of Duras's narratives, and that her oeuvre dramatizes the struggle inherent in telling a woman's story. Schuster describes Duras's female characters as split subjects, objects of desire, agents of resistance, and bearers of both life and death. While the book's periodization of Duras's work is perhaps deceptively tidy, it nonetheless provides a good overview of the progression of her novelistic and cinematic work. Schuster contends that Duras's novels of the 1940s and 1950s are parodies of realism, which explore the semiconscious and emphasize their own fictionality. She interprets Duras's turn to film in the 1970s as resulting from stylistic impasses encountered in writing, and argues that it is the new narrative strategies developed through film that subtend Duras's erotic and autobiographical texts of the 1980s.

GLASSMAN's book is also a good source for biographical background, critical reception history, and analyses of Duras's work in multiple genres. Glassman situates Duras's novels among French New Novelists, explores the intertextuality of Duras's oeuvre—her reuse of characters, contexts, and themes—and identifies a thematic unity in the texts' concerns with adultery, remembered love affairs, family relationships, and mourning. The book also analyzes Duras's films in relation to new wave cinema, and introduces feminist and semiotic theories of film. Glassman's book is primarily comprised of close readings, although it also makes reference to psychoanalysis, and pursues the argument that Duras's characters are unable to find "narrative cures"—unable to understand and reconcile the past through narrative.

The most extensive discussion of the social context of Duras's writing is to be found in HILL's book. In this work, the author provides biographical and historical material on Duras's childhood in Indochina, her relationships with Robert Antelme and Dionys Mascolo, her journalistic writings, and her involvement with the Resistance, the French Communist Party, and the student revolts of May 1968. Hill explores the ways in which Duras has framed her own work in interviews and journalistic essays, and assesses the sites at which Duras's work has intersected with the women's movement in France. The book also contains analyses of a wide range of written texts and technically sophisticated discussions of the films. Hill argues for a fundamental relationship between writing and disaster in Duras's work. This "apocalyptic mode" of writing does not seek to represent the world, but to push experience to the limits at which meaning falters; it resists progressive interpretations of history, and appeals to myth. Hill also investigates Duras's fascination with agents that transgress social order and challenge representation—particularly Jews, mad people, and women.

Two books that continue Selous's work on the "blanks" in Duras's texts are those by Cohen and Hofmann. While COHEN covers a wide range of issues, she focuses much of her discussion on the presence of "ignorance" in Duras's texts: for example, the reader's lack of knowledge about who is speaking, the narrator's ignorance of the textual implications of his or her own utterances, or the uncertainty created by shifts in point of view or intertextual discrepancies. Cohen argues that Duras's language exposes the exclusion and denigration of women by, and within, dominant discourse. She contends that Duras's approach to erotic discourse deconstructs stereotypes, and exposes the customary complicity of (male) reader, author, and hero in pornography. Cohen also examines the ritual or ceremonial atmosphere created by Duras's textual repetitions, parataxis, and unnamed characters.

HOFMANN identifies two modes of "forgetting" in Duras's texts. The first is "forgetting-as-repression," in which traumatic memories remain intact but do not accede to consciousness. The second is "forgetting-as-remembering," in which memories, through the phenomenon of repetition, come to consciousness where they can then be genuinely forgotten. Hofmann's argument is informed by Melanie Klein's theory of mourning, and Freud's theory of the repetition compulsion. On the basis of analyses of *The Ravishing of Lol Stein*, *Agatha*, *The Vice-Consul*, and *Hiroshima Mon Amour*, Hill concludes that Durassian characters, while they do some of the work of mourning, rarely move beyond it. This book assumes a knowledge of French (quotations are not translated), but offers lucid explanations of complex psychoanalytic concepts.

—REBECCA SAUNDERS

Dyer, Mary 1591?–1660

American Quaker

Crawford, Deborah, *Four Women in a Violent Time*, New York: Crown, 1970

Plimpton, Ruth Talbot, *Mary Dyer: Biography of a Rebel Quaker*, Boston: Branden, 1994

Rogers, Horatio, *Mary Dyer of Rhode Island: The Quaker Martyr*, Providence, Rhode Island: Preston and Rounds, 1896

White, Ethel, *Bear His Mild Yoke: The Story of Mary Dyer, a Quaker Martyr in Early New England*, New York: Abingdon, 1966

Mary Dyer, a member of the Religious Society of Friends (Quakers), was hanged on Boston Commons in 1660 as an example of early attempts for freedom of religion, speech, and assembly. She is an example of how religion and politics often mix. Dyer believed that governments are ruled by individuals under God's guidance, placed upon each person. Dyer is a role model for those who fight to overcome religious and political oppression. And, while there is not much current material on Dyer, her life is worth exploring, especially in regard to topics such as colonial America, social and political change in the United States, and the politics of gender relations.

CRAWFORD illustrates that Dyer was one of several very visible and effective female pioneers in the American colonies. Along with others such as Anne Hutchinson, Deborah Moody, and Penelope Stout, Dyer used her speaking and writing abilities to argue for individual and group rights, believing that institutions and offices should be created by the people, and not forced upon then from above by secular or ecclesiastical authority. Crawford suggests that women came under special oppression as they were not only challenging accepted political and religious doctrines, but also very rigid gender roles.

WHITE provides a personal view of Dyer, using many of her own writings and journal entries to weave a view of a strong and dedicated freedom fighter. White follows Dyer from her modest background in Britain to her involvement with the Quakers after she journeyed to the New England colony with her husband. Dyer's political activity was a response to the brutality of the Massachusetts Bay Colony's treatment of its citizens, not from some deep-seated ideological position. It was after this radicalizing experience and then her meetings with George Fox, one of the founders of the Quaker movement, that she began her political protest against intolerance in the colony. Here is a story of one woman's willingness to die for freedom of speech and assembly.

ROGERS shows us Dyer's religious side. Mary Dyer is portrayed as a deeply religious person, who believed in a God who had provided each individual with a "divine spark," which allows individuals the right and obligation to make up their own minds. All political or religious oppression was foreign to Dyer's idea of God and government. She believed, as did most Quakers, that governments were developed and administered of, by, and for the people, including the men, women, and children. She likewise believed that religious institutions also rested on the will of God, which flowed from God directly to the believer. No intermediaries in the guise of the church or state were either needed or wanted. These two sets of political and religious views were bound to conflict. And thus Mary Dyer found herself in the middle between the monarchs' view of the world and her inner beliefs. For her the choice was a simple one.

PLIMPTON's book clearly shows the political impact of Dyer's ideas. Plimpton writes of how the intolerance showed against Mary Dyer was simply the first in a long list of intolerant acts by a male-dominated society. The Puritans, often seen as apostles of freedom, were, in New England, as oppressive as any monarch. Mary Dyer's struggle for individual freedom of belief and assembly is fundamental to a democracy. Dyer was a champion for freedom of choice, as well as a role model for women who refuse to allow men to dominate their lives and dictate their fortunes.

—PAUL BARTON-KRIESE

E

Earhart, Amelia 1897–1937

American Aviator

Briand, Paul L., Jr., *Daughter of the Sky: The Story of Amelia Earhart*, New York: Duell, Sloan, and Pearce, 1960
Goerner, Fred G., *The Search for Amelia Earhart*, London: Bodley Head, and Garden City, New York: Doubleday, 1966
Klaas, Joe, *Amelia Earhart Lives: A Trip through Intrigue to Find America's First Lady of Mystery*, New York: McGraw-Hill, 1970
Loomis, Vincent V., and Jeffrey L. Ethell, *Amelia Earhart: The Final Story*, New York: Random House, 1985
Lovell, Mary S., *The Sound of Wings: The Life of Amelia Earhart*, New York: St. Martin's Press, 1989
Pellegrano, Ann Holtgren, *World Flight: The Earhart Trail*, Ames: Iowa State University Press, 1971
Putnam, George Palmer, *Soaring Wings: A Biography of Amelia Earhart*, New York: Harcourt Brace, 1939; London: Harrap, 1940
Rich, Doris L., *Amelia Earhart: A Biography*, Washington, D.C.: Smithsonian Institution, 1989

Amelia Earhart is probably the most well-known female aviator, and the puzzle of her disappearance on a round-the-world flight has continued to fascinate many. Earhart broke aviation records throughout her career and constantly spoke for equality between men and women in all fields.

RICH's biography describes Earhart as a feminist, whose celebrated feats were done in part in order to show that women could do as much as men. She also had what her sister called a "questing spirit" that led her to pursue her many accomplishments. She believed that women could combine careers and home life, and that men could share household work, an idea radical for her time. She also participated in activism for an early version of the Equal Rights Amendment. During a time of teaching at Purdue University, she encouraged women to enter nontraditional fields such as engineering, science, medicine, and business.

According to LOVELL, Earhart was reluctant to marry because of a fear that marriage would stifle her freedom to be active in aviation and other areas (although she did ultimately marry). Her desire for adventure is illustrated by her speeches before and after her record-breaking flights. Lovell recounts Earhart's positive influence on young women of her day, as she encouraged them to succeed in any field.

Earlier books on Earhart are less straightforwardly factual and biographical and more focused on the question of her disappearance, which has never been solved. PUTNAM, who was her husband, wrote the first of these books by making (what have turned out to be erroneous) assumptions about where she crashed. His biography of Earhart is, of course, slanted by his relationship to her, but it does provide information about her from someone who knew her well.

BRIAND concentrates mostly on Earhart's career as an aviator, including the questions concerning her disappearance. He relates the testimony of a Pacific islander who contends that Earhart and her navigator Fred Noonan wandered off course and ended up in Japanese territory, where they were summarily executed as spies. GOERNER, in his investigation of the disappearance mystery, concludes that they were indeed acting as spies and that they probably died after interrogation by the Japanese who found them when they crashed in the Marshall Islands.

KLAAS also believes Earhart and Noonan were agents of the U.S. government, that they crashed in Japanese territory, and that Earhart may have escaped Japan in disguise. His consipiracy theory has Earhart found alive 30 years later but escaping from the investigator who found her. PELLEGRANO, herself an aviator, writes about her own trip in a similar aircraft over the same route Earhart followed.

A more detailed study, not just of the final flight but of Earhart's personality and life, is provided by LOOMIS. He describes the aviator as a woman plagued by poor health, emotional instability, overconfidence, and poor judgment in stressful situations. Further, he says, she was technically ill-equipped to handle the navigation and radio communication tasks so necessary to her flights. Agreeing with the theory that Earhart and Noonan were captured by the Japanese as spies and that they eventually died in captivity, he nevertheless disagrees that the pacifist Earhart would in truth have acted as a spy.

—ELEANOR B. AMICO

See also Aviation

Earnings Gap

Afshar, Helen (ed.), *Women, Work and Ideology in the Third World,* London and New York: Tavistock, 1985

Goldin, Claudia D., *Understanding the Gender Gap: An Economic History of American Women,* New York: Oxford University Press, 1990; Oxford: Oxford University Press, 1992

Jacobs, Jerry A. (ed.), *Gender Inequality at Work,* Thousand Oaks, California: Sage, 1995

Kessler-Harris, Alice, *A Woman's Wage: Historical Meanings and Social Consequences,* Lexington: University of Kentucky Press, 1990

Safa, Helen I., *The Myth of the Male Breadwinner: Women and Industrialization in the Caribbean,* Boulder, Colorado: Westview Press, 1995

Stichter, Sharon, and Jane L. Parpart (eds.), *Women, Employment and the Family in the International Division of Labor,* Philadelphia: Temple University Press, and London: Macmillan, 1990

Although women have long been active in the paid workforce, women's wages have always fallen, on the average, well below those of men, and this has held true even when such factors as women's frequently shorter overall time in the job market, women's greater likelihood of working part-time, and women's tendency to cluster in lower-paying jobs are considered. A number of books analyze and attempt to explain this differential.

GOLDIN's work is a neoclassical economics approach to the history of the gender gap in wages in the United States. She focuses on the experience and characteristics of individual women in the labor market. Her work is primarily concerned with the role of market forces in determining relative wages; thus she devotes little attention to social and cultural constraints. One exception is her excellent discussion of marriage bars—rules restricting or forbidding the hiring of married women. Her book, which is the result of years of archival research, contains much new data on women in the paid labor force. It is already a classic work in economic history.

KESSLER-HARRIS's book takes a different approach to the determination of women's wages, focusing on the social context within which wages are determined. Her book of essays raises different, more philosophical questions about the role of family and ideology in determining women's wages and the role of women in the paid labor force. Gender is seen as determining wages through social and cultural constraints, and as being deeply embedded in the institutions of the labor market. This volume makes a good companion piece to Goldin's book.

JACOBS's book is a collection of work by social scientists on wage determination. Focusing on occupational segregation as well as differences in compensation, the book offers a sampling of approaches from the social sciences, as well as across careers and industries. A fine introductory essay frames the articles and helps explain the diverse approaches to discussion of the earnings gap.

The great bulk of the literature on the earnings gap is concerned exclusively with the industrial countries. Although the gap between women's and men's earnings appears to be cross-cultural, the work on the developing countries is usually more concerned with the gender definitions of work and the gender division of labor than with the gap between men's and women's wages. STICHTER and PARPART's anthology is primarily concerned with the gender division of labor, but it does contain some articles specifically about the earnings gap. Readers will find this work more concerned with the social and cultural meaning of work than is typical of the work of economists and other social scientists on the U.S. earnings gap.

AFSHAR's anthology also presents work on the gender division of labor and relative wages for women in the Third World. Most articles specifically address the role of ideology in determining the evaluation of women's work. Several authors focus on the role of religion, specifically Islam, in preventing or hampering women from acquiring skills and education. In some countries, work is redefined as men's work when the process of modernization moves the site of work from the home to the factory. The focus on ideology in shaping not only the work women do but the wage they are paid makes this anthology an interesting contrast to Jacobs's anthology.

SAFA's book provides a comparative study of female industrial workers in Puerto Rico, the Dominican Republic, and Cuba. In all three countries, she finds an earnings gap, with women confined to low wage jobs. Interestingly, female workers in these countries have been more successful in overcoming or moderating subordination in the home than they have in the workplace or the political arena. This is in sharp contrast to the conclusions often reached about the source of women's low wages in more developed countries, where domestic constraints are often cited as more important than workplace or political constraints.

—PAMELA J. NICKLESS

See also Division of Labor by Sex; Dual Labor Market; Glass Ceiling

Eating Disorders

Bordo, Susan, *Unbearable Weight: Feminism, Western Culture and the Body,* Berkeley: University of California Press, 1993
Bruch, Hilde, *The Golden Cage: The Enigma of Anorexia Nervosa,* New York: Vintage, and London: Open Books, 1978
Brumberg, Joan Jacobs, *Fasting Girls: The Emergence of Anorexia Nervosa as a Modern Disease,* Cambridge, Massachusetts: Harvard University Press, 1988
Chernin, Kim, *The Hungry Self: Women, Eating and Identity,* New York: Times, 1985; London: Virago Press, 1986
Fallon, Patricia, Melanie A. Katzman, and Susan C. Wooley (eds.), *Feminist Perspectives on Eating Disorders,* New York: Guilford, 1994
Hesse-Biber, Sharlene, *Am I Thin Enough Yet? The Cult of Thinness and the Commercialization of Identity,* New York and Oxford: Oxford University Press, 1996
Silverstein, Brett, and Deoborah Perlick, *The Cost of Competence: Why Inequality Causes Depression, Eating Disorders and Illness in Women,* New York and Oxford: Oxford University Press, 1995

Over the past twenty years, there has been an explosion in the number of publications on the connections between eating disorders and women. In general, these publications are concerned with anorexia nervosa and bulimia nervosa, although some also include discussions of morbid obesity and pica. Many books examine the cultural, social, and psychological contexts of eating disorders. Often, books in this category make explicit the connection between gender and troubled relationships with food.

BRUCH, a medical doctor, is acknowledged as the clinician who most influenced the way later researchers thought of eating disorders in general and anorexia in particular. She identifies the roots of anorexia in the adolescent's struggle to establish selfhood, and characterizes the pre-illness phase of anorexia as one in which the subject's body image is grossly distorted, her hunger cues are interpreted incorrectly, and her sense of control in her life is non-existent. The purpose behind Bruch's book is to help people recognize and understand the pre-illness behaviors before these behaviors become unchangeable.

BRUMBERG provides the historical background of anorexia nervosa, tracing its incidence from the medieval period through the Victorian era to the present day epidemic. She carefully discusses three ways of understanding the condition: the medical model, which views anorexia as a disease of the body that must be treated with drugs; the psychological model, which views anorexia as a struggle for separation and autonomy coupled with anxiety over sexuality; and the cultural/social model, which sees anorexia as a response to a cultural privileging of thinness. Brumberg's driving question as a social historian is this: why do certain diseases manifest themselves more in one historical period than in another? She chooses to examine the complicated interactions of social and cultural forces, both in the past and in the present, as she attempts to answer her question. The book is meticulously researched, and is a valuable resource for anyone attempting to place anorexia within the context of women's history.

CHERNIN, a psychoanalytically trained therapist, connects eating disorders with women's struggle for identity in the contemporary world. Further, she argues that disordered eating is the primary way in which the problems of being female manifest themselves. Obsession with food is an incomplete rite of passage, in that it fails to move the woman on to the next level of selfhood. Chernin suggests that there are three stages of understanding eating disorders. First, an eating disorder will often disguise a woman's problem with self-identity. She notes that this is particularly true in a culture which is reconstructing the very idea of "woman." Next, the problem with identity is rooted in an unresolved mother-daughter relationship, in which the daughter is expected to surpass her mother. Finally, the only way that the mother-daughter relationship can be resolved is for the daughter to return to childhood to sort out conflicting messages about food, separation, and identity.

BORDO opens her book with a discussion of the Western dualistic notion of the body, a cultural tradition that associates women with the passive body, a receptacle for the life-giving male energy in reproduction. Bordo continues throughout the opening section to trace the most influential ideas about the female body in Western culture. In the middle section, Bordo identifies anorexia as the representative psychopathology of Western culture. In the final section, Bordo employs postmodernist feminist theory to critique representations of gender in contemporary Western culture. Although Bordo's book is highly theoretical, it is nonetheless accessible, and offers an important link between the study of eating disorders and postmodernism.

FALLON, KATZMAN, and WOOLEY offer a collection of essays written by feminist psychologists, social workers, therapists, and professors. The selected essays share some or all of these criteria: they are based on the psychology of women; they demonstrate the importance of women's equality; and they offer a reassessment of available therapy based on the recognition of the gender of the patient and the therapist. The book has five sections. In the first, "A Gendered Disorder: Lessons from History," the essays examine the history of fashion and the historical occurrence of specifically female maladies. The second section, "A Place for the Female Body," includes essays which discuss problems of the body and of body image among women. The third section, "Treatment Issues: A Feminist Reanalysis," studies a range of topics including the link between sexual abuse and eating disorders; the role of medication and hospitalization in the treatment of eating disorders; and the representation of mother-daughter relationships in the literature of eating disorders. The fourth section of the book, "Reconstructing the Female Text," offers narrations by women of their own eating disorders. The final section, "Possibilities," examines the current state of feminist studies of eating disorders and feminist therapies, and points to routes the field may take in the future. The book offers the advantage of many minds in one collection, and is a valuable resource for anyone wishing to study eating disorders from an explicitly feminist perspective.

SILVERSTEIN and PERLICK argue that ambitious young women who grow up during times of changing gender roles often exhibit psychosomatic illnesses, including depression and eating disorders. The authors examine the connections between families and female achievement, discussing at length the way fathers are idealized and mothers are devalued. Much of the gender ambivalence found in eating disordered women has its roots in adolescence, as the young woman attempts to define herself as a woman. The writers assert that this is particularly true during periods when gender roles undergo significant change in a culture.

HESSE-BIBER argues that in western culture, fatness represents moral failure. On the basis of extensive surveys of young men and women, Hesse-Biber asserts that the "quest for thinness" is a "cultic behavior, replete with ritual and obsession." She demonstrates the ways that women distort their body images and come to identify their own value with how much they weigh. Perhaps the most important contribution of Hesse-Biber's book is the connection she draws between women's weight obsessions and the multimillion dollar industry that supports these obsessions. She is alarmed at the way that disordered eating behaviors are spreading to younger and younger children as well as to young men. The book closes with an examination of available therapies and support systems for women. This is a readily accessible book that offers important information for the reader interested in the connections between a woman's development of selfhood and the consumer society in which she finds herself.

—DIANE ANDREWS HENNINGFELD

See also Body Image

Ecofeminism

Bigwood, Carol, *Earth Muse: Feminism, Nature, and Art*, Philadelphia: Temple University Press, 1993

Diamond, Irene, and Gloria Feman Orenstein (eds.), *Reweaving the World: The Emergence of Ecofeminism*, San Francisco: Sierra Club, 1990

Gaard, Greta (ed.), *Ecofeminism: Women, Animals, Nature*, Philadelphia: Temple University Press, 1993

Merchant, Carolyn, *Earthcare: Women and the Environment*, New York: Routledge, 1996

Mies, Maria, and Vandana Shiva, *Ecofeminism*, London and Atlantic Highlands, New Jersey: Zed, 1993

Plant, Judith (ed.), *Healing the Wounds: The Promise of Ecofeminism*, Philadelphia, Pennsylvania: New Society, and London: Green Print,1989

Ruether, Rosemary Radford, *Women Healing Earth: Third World Women on Ecology, Feminism and Religion*, Maryknoll, New York: Orbis, and London: S.C.M. Press,1996

Warren, Karen J. (ed.), *Ecological Feminist Philosophies*, Bloomington: Indiana University Press, 1996

Feminist theories that emphasise the interdependence of all living things and the relationship between social oppression and ecological domination are called ecofeminism. A major strand of feminism and an important environmental movement, ecofeminism is a feminist response to the global environmental crisis. Ecofeminists work toward the improvement of women's situation and the environment, viewing these as interconnected. Merging ecology, feminism, and the peace movement, the term was first used in the mid-1970s and has developed critically in the 1990s. Although the strength of the philosophical argument relating the oppression of women to the mistreatment of the earth has come under attack, there can be no doubt that the issues discussed by ecofeminism are important. Ecofeminist positions usually derive from critiques of male-centered frameworks of knowing. Their aims are utopian, for a society based on ecological and feminist principles. Ecofeminists are critical of dualisms such as those that separate people from nature and thought from feeling. The 1992 United Nations Conference on Environment and Development in Rio de Janeiro was a major event for many of these writers, highlighting the importance of their environmental activism for earth's ecological future.

There are many books on this topic—mainly edited volumes—and only a selection are discussed here, varying in degrees of complexity. These books are centrally concerned with ecofeminism as a movement, not just women and the environment, although the latter is what ecofeminism is principally about. Two streams of ecofeminism are identifiable. Cultural ecofeminism emphasizes women's "essential" features such as empathy and caring. The representation of woman as a symbol of nature is employed. Social ecofeminism is based on recognition of the social construction of gender and is rooted in social ecology and focused on social change.

One of the early standard ecofeminist texts is edited by PLANT. It is more descriptive than analytic, providing a straightforward and accessible introduction to ecofeminism. Essays, stories, poetry, and invocation make up this text, which emphasizes the spiritual as well as the political. It is one of the earliest ecofeminist anthologies, promoting a vision of the world free of nuclear weapons, sexism, racism, violence, and repression. Aiming for a nonviolent and ecological-feminist transformation of social structures, the contributors to this book focus on the United States and the Third World. Unity in diversity is an important theme, as is thinking globally and acting locally. Feeling the life of the other is a starting point for decision making. Plant's cultural ecofeminist text is easily criticized for essentialism, for accepting an innate connection between women and nature, when in reality that connection is based on myth and metaphor. However, this collection is useful to show the fundamental ideas associated with ecofeminism.

In another founding anthology, DIAMOND and ORENSTEIN point out that ecofeminism is not a monolithic homogeneous ideology. The diversity of ecofeminism, they argue, is what makes it such a promising catalyst for change. Strong cases are made for the urgency of environmental action. Boundaries between academic and creative writing are crossed in this collection of essays. Mythical foundations of ecofeminism are examined in an account of the Eleusinian Mysteries of Demeter and Persephone, symbolizing cyclic renewal and regeneration. The politics of ecofeminism are discussed in relation to deep ecology and bioregionalism. One contributor states that the discovery of goddess religions led to an understanding of the divine as immanent and around us. Other paths to ecofeminism are identified as politics and environmentalism.

WARREN edits an analytical and scholarly text with an overview of the issues involved in ecological feminist philosophies. The introduction to this advanced collection examines ecofeminist arguments as historical and causal, conceptual, empirical and experiential, epistemological, symbolic, ethical, theoretical, and political. The essays are philosophical in their pursuit of connections between feminism and environmentalism.

RUETHER—a theologian—edits a text composed of essays by women from Latin America, Asia, and Africa. Race, religion, and spirituality are additional important themes. The state of the environment is often of crucial importance to the daily survival of these women. Impoverishment of women and the earth is more clearly interconnected in the Third World, where ecofeminism is an effective movement to highlight this and work for change. This text demonstrates an epistemological point often made by ecofeminists, that claims to knowledge depend on the values of the culture from which they arise.

MERCHANT's text is very readable and insightful. The first part looks at the theory of ecofeminism and the age-old historical associations of women and nature. The Greek Gaia, the Christian Eve, and the Egyptian Isis are female symbols of nature with differing implications for ecofeminist practice. These images of nature as female are inspirational, yet overall the author argues that gendering nature is too problematic to take as a central focus of today's emancipatory social movements. The second part of this text is historical, arguing that organic societies in England and America had female imagery as core components, and that they gave way to industrial capitalism and mechanistic science. The third part concerns the practice of ecofeminist activists and green politics in First World countries. Ultimately a partnership ethics—between people and nature—is encouraged. Representations of the world reflected in metaphors and myths are deemed important because they convey social values.

In contrast to the mainly theoretical approaches of the other texts, with perhaps the exception of Plant's, MIES and SHIVA write from their participation in the women's and ecology movements, rather than as academics. The authors seek common ground for feminism and environmentalism in countries of the capitalist north, such as Europe and America, and the countries of the exploited south, such as India. Topics include an account of new reproductive technologies as sexist, racist and fascist, and an engagement with the Chipko women's concept of freedom. Mies and Shiva propose a concrete utopia called the subsistence or survival perspective, a self-supporting way of living on basic necessities. Examples of subsistence-oriented initiatives are provided.

GAARD's text is important for bringing non-human animals into ecofeminist politics. The purpose of this collection of essays is to contribute to the debate among feminists, ecofeminists, animal liberationists, deep ecologists, and social ecologists. The relationships among human beings, the natural environment, and non-human animals are examined. Bibliographic references in this text are useful for locating further important ecofeminist texts. The conclusion replies to some arguments made by authors in the collection, incorporating criticisms made of ecofeminism, and providing a balanced critique.

BIGWOOD writes at the intersection of continental philosophy and ecofeminism, highlighting the philosophy of the feminine. The author categorizes her writing as ecofeminist, postmodern art-philosophy. Ecofeminism is linked to a critique of phallocentricism and the phallus as a unitary mark of presence. In the first part of the book the oppressive traditional association of the feminine with the body and earth is reconstructed to allow for female experience, desire, and subjectivity. The second part works toward an ecofeminist description of the situation of the human being. A caretaker and cultivator model of being human is proposed.

—BRIDGET HOLLAND

See also Nature

Economic Development: Africa

Bay, Edna (ed.), *Women and Work in Africa,* Boulder, Colorado: Westview Press, 1982

Boserup, Ester, *Woman's Role in Economic Development,* New York: St. Martin's Press, and London: Allen and Unwin, 1970

Davison, Jean (ed.), *Agriculture, Women, and Land: The African Experience,* Boulder, Colorado: Westview Press, 1988

Gladwin, Christina (ed.), *Structural Adjustment and African Women Farmers,* Gainesville: University of Florida Press, 1991

Nelson, Nici (ed.), *African Women in the Development Process,* London and Totowa, New Jersey: Frank Cass, 1981

Palmer, Ingrid, *Gender and Population in the Adjustment of African Economies: Planning for Change,* Geneva: International Labour Office, 1991

Snyder, Margaret C., and Mary Tadesse, *African Women and Development: A History,* London and Atlantic Highlands, New Jersey: Zed, 1995

Women and work in Africa has been one of the most well-developed topics of women's and gender studies in all areas of the world. In particular, African female farmers have begun to make gender central to the study of agricultural development. In a continent that depends heavily on agriculture for food subsistence and export production, attention to African women gave rise to the field of women in development, now increasingly known as gender and development, a field that insists on linking scholarly research to practice.

The founding mother of this research is Danish economist BOSERUP, whose book analyzes Africa as a "female farming system." The promotion of "modern" agriculture, first by colonial and then independent governments, puts resources and opportunities in men's hands, leaving women with unpaid work in agriculture and increasing gender disparities. Land reforms undermine women's control over major means of production in agricultural society. Boserup set the research agenda, increasingly contextualized on a country-by-country basis.

With approximately fifty countries on the continent, a series of rich field research results have been published in various edited collections. Publishers have seemed to think that few of these many African countries would generate enough commercial interest to justify single-country studies (unlike other world regions, with books on women in Mexico, Peru, India, and China).

NELSON edited the first of these collections, drawing on chapters about Lesotho, Zambia, Tanzania, Nigeria, and the Gambia. Gambian female rice farmers in particular have become famous because of the way multilateral aid projects have consistently ignored their work and incentives for labor, ultimately tied to the ability to control the income generated by that labor. Whether donors are from Britain, the United States, Taiwan, or the People's Republic of China, they assumed that men were the major economic development players, and gave them resources and control over land. Several chapters also analyze the ways contemporary census methodologies underestimate women's activities, along with the implications of those distortions for effective development planning.

BAY's collection expands the effort even more widely, with fourteen chapters covering Sierre Leone, Nigeria, Zambia, Zaire, Upper Volta (now called Burkina Faso), Tanzania, Kenya, Ghana, the Ivory Coast, and the Gambia. This collection delves even more deeply into the implications of research findings for development programming and women's collective action. Three themes in particular would capture the imagination of subsequent researchers and practitioners: agricultural extension programs, which routinely ignore women farmers; land reform, which puts control in men's hands; and government resettlement programs, which limit and control women, all in the name of benevolent and rational planning.

Later collections develop these subthemes even more. DAVISON's book focuses almost entirely on women's dependence on land for production, and the ways that (men in) official institutions undermine their ability to share or to control these major means of production. Chapters cover Guinea-Bissau, Nigeria, Cameroon, Zaire, Sudan, Kenya, Swaziland, Zimbabwe, Mozambique, and the Gambia. Once again, in the tiny Gambia, readers are told of officials' inability to learn from previous research. Simply put, programs and projects do not work unless gender interests are taken into account.

In GLADWIN's collection, field researchers have begun to set their work into globally macro frameworks, more macro than the colonialism and international donor ideological frameworks of earlier collections. At the instigation of international banks, many African countries were compelled to downsize government and social programs (paltry as they were), and concentrate instead on the market and export trade. Contributors to this collection analyze how women farmers fare in both continent-wide chapters and those that are country focused, such as Nigeria, Zaire, Tanzania, Malawi, Cameroon, Ghana, and

Kenya. A particularly interesting debate was published between a leading mainstream thinker whose work routinely ignores gender, and another thinker who studies gender in the household context. While many chapters sound alarms about the effects of structural adjustment on consumers and support for farmers, few discuss opportunities that might be associated with eliminating male appropriation of surplus (whether government marketing boards or husbands who collect payments on the crops wives produce).

PALMER turns the question around, and asks not what structural adjustment does, but what gender does to structural adjustment results. Her work with the International Labor Office shows the continuing interest of this long-time United Nations affiliate in moving analytic thinking forward in understanding gender. Palmer has heretofore been responsible for organizing a series of gender-rich monographs that the Kumarian Press published in 1985. One is a composite profile of a disastrous resettlement scheme (the "Nemow" case [spell it backwards!]), and others are on Kenya and Nigeria.

An apt close for this review is found in the book by SNYDER and TADESSE, who chronicle the history of the African Center for Women, which is part of the United Nations Economic Commission for Africa. They tell the story of struggles with the bureaucracy to put women in development ideas into practice with an African-driven agenda.

—KATHLEEN STAUDT

Economic Development: Asia

Black, Naomi, and Ann Baker Cottrell, *Women and World Change,* Beverly Hills, California: Sage, 1981

Boserup, Ester, *Women's Role in Economic Development,* New York: St. Martin's Press, and London: Allen and Unwin, 1970

Bray, Francesca, *The Rice Economies: Technology and Development in Asian Societies,* Oxford and New York: Blackwell, 1986

Charlton, Sue Ellen M., *Women in Third World Development,* Boulder, Colorado: Westview Press, 1984

Fawcett, James T., Siew-Ean Khoo, and Peter C. Smith (eds.), *Women in the Cities of Asia,* Boulder, Colorado: Westview Press, 1984

Goldschmidt-Clermont, Luisella, *Economic Evaluations of Unpaid Household Work: Africa, Asia, Latin America and Oceania,* Geneva: International Labour Organization, 1987

Nelson, Nici, *Why Has Development Neglected Rural Women? A Review of the South Asian Literature,* New York and Oxford: Pergamon, 1979

Books on economic development abound. But not many of them focus on the role that women play, let alone emphasize women's role in economic development in a specific part of the world like Asia. The lack of attention can be attributed to many factors. In the past, women's contributions to development were considered negligible, because of views that assumed that only men were economic contributors. Women's work was deemed not calculable, and therefore it did not find its way into national product valuations. Not many women were educated enough to protest this situation. And national and international institutions perpetuated this neglect by the lack of data-gathering activities that might have enlightened us.

BOSERUP's classic work has served as the basis of much of the writing about women and the issue of development. Although the book discusses women and economic development in general, it places special emphasis upon the Asian pattern of women's high level of activity, in both village and town, which contrasts with other parts of the world. In Asia, employment opportunities for educated women are high. Boserup cites three factors that have changed women's roles in economic development. One is the combination of increased education for both men and women, and the growing ability of an economy to provide opportunities in rural areas so that people will remain there, rather than migrating to the cities and contributing to unemloyment, crime, and crowding. The second factor is the advent of birth control, and its connection to women's increased employment. The third factor is the mechanization of much of their domestic work, which has contributed to the ability to devote time and energy to other endeavors.

Despite the need to consider women's vital role in economic development, NELSON decries the fact that development has neglected rural women. Nelson's book places emphasis on South Asian women and those from Indonesia. The fact that women have been neglected in rural development programs is attributed to the lack of attention by researchers, administrators, planners, and aid-giving agencies to women and the roles that women play in rural societies that are in the process of change. The book begins with a review of the literature in this field, and comes up with some of the major common conclusions that past studies (village studies, development studies, women's studies) have drawn. Women are not a homogeneous group, but Nelson identifies them as a disadvantaged group. Part of the disadvantage stems from having been excluded from education for various reasons: financial loss to family in terms of dowry, the fact that their household labor was considered more important than education, and the belief that education was undesirable because it "spoiled" women. There is an acknowledgment that women in rural villages work very hard, sometimes harder than men. Nelson calls for greater knowledge through research about women, so that they can be more action-oriented and contribute further to development.

From the early 1980s, the tone of writings shifts toward whether or not women benefit from development and modernization. BLACK's book is a set of readings that deals with the internationalization of the issue of women and development. It begins by presenting the traditional notion that women are objects rather than agents of change, coping rather than initiating, by-standers rather than participants, and are acted upon rather than actors in the development drama. The book argues that the emphasis of development should be equity especially for women, that women as agents of change should be recognized, and that the absence of women in groups planning for change should be remedied. The book takes a look at domestic values in Asia such as the extended family, within which women are constantly adapting to change while their basic values and preferences remain the same. The focus of the book is on three main shared characteristics of women: their persistent disadvantage in treatment and well-being, their minimal access to authority and influence in planning for change, and their dependence upon other women. This would pave the way for discussions of women's groups and organizations (for example, non-governmental organizations) and their roles. These would serve as instruments of social mobilization for their members, who could share problems and goals.

CHARLTON reinforces these concepts by stating that women are politically dependent at the local, national, and international levels, and thus have little say in development policymaking. The book further indicates that development often hurts Third World women, rather than helping them. Inadequate information and data make it difficult to ascertain the extent of the problem. The issues of women and children's nutrition, educational opportunities, and the decision to seek paid employment, are major areas covered in this book as case studies on the green revolution, cash crops, and the infant formula debate. The book concludes that development by and for women is the direction in which to go.

The FAWCETT work looks at the increase in female mobility from village to city in Asia. Along with this movement come new roles for women, new problems associated with city living, and prospects of radical change in status. The readings in this book cover the various crosscurrents of ideas in analyzing the situation in different countries.

Later works have focused on providing more data about women in various sectors. The BRAY book looks at women in Asian rice cultivation, and concludes that they play a major role in all facets of rice production, from planting and transplanting to weeding, harvesting, and threshing. However, direct seeding methods and mechanized threshing have led to decreased demand for women's labor. The GOLDSCHMIDT-CLEMONT book is part of a series examining women, work, and development, contracted by the International Labor Organization. Through 40 studies in Asia, Africa, Latin America, and Oceania, which look at the invisible contributions of women, the study concludes that there is irrefutable evidence about the importance and value of unpaid domestic and household work. If the economic value of unpaid household activities is taken into account, national income estimates would be increased by 25 to 50 percent for developing countries.

Based on these works, some conclusions can be drawn about women and economic development in Asia. Asian women are not homogenous, they belong to different societies with varying levels of development status. Women can be found in agriculture engaged in the cultivation of cash crops. They can be found in industry providing low wage labor, especially in the newly industrializing countries. One of the major concerns for Asian women is the level of education. There is a realization that without education there can be no improvement. But educated women migrate and exacerbate the rural/urban dichotomy. Solutions to this problem will therefore need to be developed.

—CECILIA G. MANRIQUE

Economic Development: Latin America

Babb, Florence E., *Between Field and Cooking Pot: The Political Economy of Marketwomen in Peru,* Austin: University of Texas Press, 1989

Bose, Christine, and Edna Acosta-Belen (eds.), *Women in the Latin American Development Process,* Philadelphia: Temple University Press, 1995

Bourque, Susan C., and Kay Barbara Warren, *Women of the Andes: Patriarchy and Social Change in Two Peruvian Towns,* Ann Arbor: University of Michigan Press, 1981

Chaney, Elsa M., and Mary Garcia Castro, *Muchachas No More: Household Workers in Latin America and the Caribbean,* Philadelphia, Pennsylvania: Temple University Press, 1989

Chant, Sylvia, *Women and Survival in Mexican Cities: Perspectives on Gender, Labour Markets and Low-Income Households,* Manchester: Manchester University Press, 1990; New York: St. Martin's Press, 1991

Deere, Carmen Diana, and Magdalena Leon, *Rural Women and State Policy: Feminist Perspectives on Latin American Agricultural Development,* Boulder, Colorado: Westview Press, 1987

Fernandez-Kelly, Maria Patricia, *For We Are Sold, I and My People: Women and Industry on Mexico's Frontier,* Albany: State University of New York Press, 1983

Ruiz, Vicki L., and Susan Tiano, *Women on the U.S.-Mexico Border: Responses to Change,* Boston: Allen and Unwyn, 1987

Once one has confronted the loaded terminology "economic development," it is necessary to inquire about the type of development, the ways it is measured, and the visibility of women's work therein. Latin Americanists do as much field research as those in other world regions, but they are especially preoccupied with theoretical frameworks that distinguish capitalist from socialist strategies, and that contextualize Latin America in the global economy. From that vantage point, Latin America has been viewed as dependent, and/or pushed into neoliberal structural adjustment. Who pushes? International banks like the World Bank, with some collaborative help from their own political and economic elite who would profit therefrom.

Field researchers have focused on women's varied work activities that add value to the economy, even if mainstream economists rarely recognized them as such. Women are overrepresented among informals, or those whose work tends to be unregulated and uncounted in traditional census machinery. Two key occupational groups include sellers and maids. BABB analyzes market vendors in a central Peruvian highland town, often berated as premodern predators. Vendors combine their productive and reproductive work in ways modern planners and middle-class consumers would like to destroy.

CHANEY and CASTRO bring together 22 chapters, plus an extended bibliography, on the quintessential informals: domestic workers who account for nearly a quarter of the female labor force in many Latin American countries. A particularly rich and inspiring section offers workers' testimonies of their struggles to organize and to improve working conditions in Brazil, Colombia, Peru, and Venezuela, along with pictures of posters, resolutions, and bulletins.

Women also contribute to the household and agricultural economies, however unrecognized in mainstream studies. CHANT focuses on women's movement into and out of the labor force during Mexico's 1980s crisis in three cities. She offers particularly rich and contextualized analyses of different urban economies over the decade of crisis. BOURQUE and WARREN compare two towns in Peru, illuminating the special constraints of indigenous women in the rural highlands. DEERE and LEON edit a volume of 12 chapters which make women's agricultural work visible, even as state policy ignores or undermines women's ability to control land and income therefrom. Many chapters are set in the theoretical contexts that critique neoliberal models, and state land and agricultural reform, which leave class relations relatively untouched.

If borders have increasingly become metaphors for transitional zones of change, then we must focus on these spaces for insights and forecasts for change. FERNANDEZ-KELLY's now classic book on Mexico's Border Industrialization Program uses multiple methods to analyze the predominant female-majority workers in foreign export-assembly plants. Transnational corporations have spread this model throughout the globe, including the gender demographics and consequent hierarchy. Her book has become a model for comprehensive research on the topic. RUIZ and TIANO look at women on both sides of the Mexican border in more holistic ways, from factory workers to maids, from subordinate work with meager wages to collective strategies for resisting workplace exploitation and/or fostering change in the wider society.

BOSE and ACOSTA-BELEN edit a collection of new and reprinted articles on the wide range of women's work, from micro-enterprise to industrial labor, and women's empowerment strategies. Of special interest in this book is the effort to link North with Central and South America, including the Caribbean (and Puerto Rico). Women in the United States are not immune from global strategies to cheapen their labor, and this collection integrates them into its study, adding to its value. Women's work increases, as does its value to "economic development," now subsumed within triumphant global capitalism. The real question is: Will women benefit from that increased work?

—KATHLEEN STAUDT

Eddy, Mary Baker 1821–1910

American, Founder of Christian Science

Cather, Willa, and Georgine Milmine, *The Life of Mary Baker Eddy and the History of Christian Science,* New York: S.S. McClure, 1908

Dakin, Edwin Franden, *Mrs. Eddy: The Biography of a Virginal Mind,* New York and London: Scribner, 1929

Gardner, Martin, *The Healing Revelations of Mary Baker Eddy: The Rise and Fall of Christian Science,* Buffalo, New York: Prometheus, 1993

Knee, Stuart E., *Christian Science in the Age of Mary Baker Eddy,* Westport, Connecticut: Greenwood, 1994

Peel, Robert, *Mary Baker Eddy,* 3 vols., New York: Holt, Rinehart and Winston, 1966–1977

Silberger, Julius, *Mary Baker Eddy: An Interpretative Biography of the Founder of Christian Science,* Boston: Little Brown, 1980

Thomas, Robert Davis, *"With Bleeding Footsteps": Mary Baker Eddy's Path to Religious Leadership,* New York: Knopf, 1994

Twain, Mark, *Christian Science,* New York and London: Harper and Brothers, 1907

Wilbur, Sibyl, *The Life of Mary Baker Eddy,* Boston: Christian Science Publishing Society, 1907

The founder of the Christian Science Church was one of the most visible and well-known women of her day, and the life of Mary Baker Eddy has continued to fascinate writers throughout the twentieth century. This fascination can be attributed to both the widespread influence that Eddy's teachings carried, and to the various ambiguities and contradictions of her life. As the Christian Science Church—and Eddy herself, most notably in her autobiography *Retrospection and Introspection*—promoted an official but narrow version of Eddy's life, it was perhaps inevitable that controversies arose as to this version's accuracy. It is thus useful to follow the trajectory of changing perspectives on Eddy and her church by considering notable and representative volumes. Whether written by defenders, detractors, or more neutral scholars, these accounts frequently reveal how much there was at stake in discussing a woman whose life became inextricable from the myths surrounding it.

Early narratives of Eddy's life and the Christian Science Church initiated interpretive controversies and laid the groundwork for later scholarship. One of the first and most vociferous critics of Eddy, TWAIN published a scathing volume that sarcastically attacked Christian Science and Eddy for what he saw as her hypocrisy, her hunger for power, and her false sense of self-importance. Presumably in response to such assaults, especially by a prominent figure like Twain, the Christian Science Church authorized WILBUR's hagiographical narrative of Eddy's life. In it, Wilbur critiques "exaggerated" and "dramatic" accounts. Instead, she follows "the methods of St. Mark" and concerns herself "only to report the truth." Wilbur's "truth" is detailed but also idealized and filled with romantic generalizations. Embraced by the church, this biography was reprinted numerous times throughout the century. Many unauthorized biographies were suppressed in favor of such accepted versions, the only ones available at most Christian Science Reading Rooms.

Less partial—but suppressed by the Christian Science Church nonetheless—CATHER and MILMINE's biography, originally published as a series of sensationalistic articles in *McClure's* magazine, removed Eddy's life from the realm of myth by citing documents and reminiscences that describe the major events of her life from a variety of perspectives. Cather and Milmine portray Eddy as a practical genius and compelling personality who successfully adapted accepted truths to a new era. They celebrate her intellectual innovations, while cautioning against what they consider the potential for harmful excess in strict adherence to her ideas. This account is especially important as it has served as the primary source of material for all later unauthorized biographies. It is helpful to note, however, that—since Cather's central role in the writing and editing of this text has been proven only recently—most writers referring to this work cite Milmine, under whose name it was originally published.

While Wilbur opened the door for similarly idealized accounts, like those of Lyman Powell (1930) and Norman Beasley (1963), Cather and Milmine prefigured more qualified versions of Eddy's life, like those of Fleta Campbell Springer (1930) and Ernest Sutherland Bates and John Dittemore (1932). On the whole, the latter are more useful to scholars, as they tend to be balanced, highly detailed, and quite thorough. DAKIN's narrative is perhaps best representative of this group, significant for his self-conscious evenhandedness and his attempts to reconcile opposing images of Eddy by arguing that her failings and limitations were part of her greatness. Dakin also includes an extensive biography of early twentieth-century books and articles on Eddy and Christian Science.

Recent scholarship has widened the field of inquiry surrounding Eddy, asking new questions and exploring new directions. GARDNER gives a useful overview of the controversies surrounding Eddy's life by organizing his biography around major points of dispute (in conjunction with which he provides a useful schemata of previous "favorable" and "critical" accounts). Gardner sides with the skeptics, presenting the logical and practical—although not particularly thorough—observations regarding what he considers credible and valuable in Eddy's teachings and what he rejects. He also draws on critiques forwarded by Eddy's contemporaries and associates, most notably Adam Dickey (Eddy's secretary from 1908–10), to imply that the eventual decline of Christian Science was inevitable, considering its—and Eddy's—inherent contradictions. Gardner concludes with a discussion of Eddy's relationship to Ella Wheeler Wilcox and the "New Thought" movement and draws interesting parallels to contemporary New Age movements.

PEEL, a Christian Scientist himself, draws extensively on previously untapped material to present Eddy in a positive light without simplistic idealization. The most thorough and detailed of Eddy's defenders, his monumental, three-volume biography focuses on the development of her ideas rather than on her personality. Interestingly, Peel seeks to ignore controversies completely by confining discussions of conflicting evidence and questions of reliability to his notes. He also includes useful chronologies of important events in Eddy's life.

Two recent works consider Eddy from a psychoanalytical perspective. THOMAS's biography works to avoid well-worn debates by concentrating on Eddy's personality rather than on her role in the institution she founded. Thomas preserves the complexities and inconsistencies of Eddy's life in exploring who she was and why her life generated so much debate. He takes Eddy and even her most absurd-sounding ideas seriously, asking why she often did and said such contradictory things. Thomas theorizes finally that her appeal was more complex than simple charisma; rather, her life and her church had profound symbolic resonance, especially for women who embraced a kind of empowerment more acceptable than the women's rights movement. SILBERGER's otherwise traditional narrative of Eddy's life also seeks to understand the development of Eddy's personality—her "strength" and "ingenuity" as well as her ambiguity—in psychoanalytical terms, while ultimately suggesting that she embodied the contradictions of her era. He also draws interesting parallels between the Christian Science Church and the field of psychoanalysis itself.

KNEE considers Eddy's life in a broader context, investigating the cultural climate during the period in which Eddy and Christian Science gained prominence and popularity. He argues that Christian Science was a "manifestation of the unrest gripping the United States after the Civil War," a period in which it found an especially receptive audience. This scholarly account draws on cultural theory, reading contemporaneous documents and newspaper articles and addressing how Eddy and Christian Science were viewed and talked about in American society, suggesting that ultimately Christian Science remained too closely tied to the individual personality of Eddy to survive.

—CAROL E. DICKSON

Elder Abuse

Aitken, Lynda, and Gabriele Griffin, *Gender Issues in Elder Abuse,* London: Sage, 1996
Eastman, Mervyn, *Old Age Abuse,* Mitcham: Age Concern, England, 1984
Kosberg, Jordan I. (ed.), *Abuse and Maltreatment of the Elderly,* Boston: John Wright, 1983
McCreadie, Claudine, *Elder Abuse: New Findings and Policy Guidelines,* London: Age Concern, 1993
Pillemer, Karl A., and Rosalie S. Wolf, *Elder Abuse: Conflict in the Family,* Dover, Massachusetts: Auburn House, 1986
Steinmetz, Suzanne K., *Duty Bound: Elder Abuse and Family Care,* Newbury Park, California, and London: Sage, 1988

Discussion about domestic violence, child abuse, and elder abuse obscures the gendered specificities of that abuse, and despite much research confirming that the majority of cases of abuse in all three instances involve women or female children being abused by men, this recognition has not as a matter of course self-consciously informed writings on such abuses, especially in the case of elder abuse. In the United States, elder abuse has been a fairly widely researched phenomenon in the last twenty years or so, but there has been very little discussion of its gendered dimension. The "discovery" of elder abuse followed in the wake of concern about wife battering and baby bashing and, like the latter two, suffered degenderization through a change in terminology from the 1970s to the 1980s.

KOSBERG was one of the earliest writers on the issue; his work centered on elder abuse as an expression of the dysfunctional family. Family violence theorists have had a powerful influence on discussions of elder abuse in the United States, partly because the identification of the family as the source and site of violence moves issues of abuse into the private domain, and partly because such a move deflects from the structural and economic inequalities which differentiate women's and men's lives, and propagate the abuse of women by men. Family violence theorists indicated older women as the objects of abuse by men, but did not draw gender-conscious conclusions from this.

STEINMETZ's work honed in on the characteristics of the victims of abuse. Like Kosberg, her focus is on the family and potential cycles of violence within the family. This has subsequently been shown to be insufficient to account for all kinds of elder abuse, as much abuse occurs not only in domestic, but also in institutional settings. A significant number of older women are also abused by non-relatives, both in their own homes and in institutions.

PILLEMER and WOLF focused on the traits of the abuser rather than on the abused, suggesting that these were more important in promoting elder abuse than the relative vulnerability or dependence of the older person. Again, little was drawn by way of gendered conclusions, although their view was that the abuser is likely to be a male relative, possibly a son, living with the abused person and having a history of difficulties including alcohol and drug abuse. Their work has been important in shaping debates about elder abuse in the United States, and in shifting them away from regarding the abused person's characteristics as indicative of the likelihood of their being abused, a stance which can amount to victim blaming, and which is familiar from the context of sexual abuse of women.

EASTMAN is the best-known early writer on elder abuse in the United Kingdom; as a social worker who came across elder abuse in the context of care-giving situations, and due to the way in which he sought informants through women's magazines, he was crucial in developing the idea that being in the situation of having to care for an older dependent person is instrumental in promoting abuse. The image he constructed of the typical abuser was that of a stressed middle-aged female, for whom caring for an older relative was just another burden on top of her daily chores. Despite the gender specificity of the abuser—female—which correlated with Steinmetz's findings, Eastman did not discuss this as a surprising phenomenon; the fact that a rationale for the abuse, namely stress and having to care for someone, was offered seemed to obviate the necessity to consider its gender implications. Eastman's work has been important, because in the context of the new care-in-the-community policies that have come to dominate the United Kingdom in the late 1980s and 1990s, the issue of who is responsible for looking after people who need care has become a significant political debate. To this day, care is largely provided by females. Among elders, however, there is also an increasing number of older spouses looking after each other.

McCREADIE provides a brief but comprehensive and up-to-date overview of research on elder abuse, predominantly though not exclusively in the United States and the United Kingdom, including a discussion of the changing definitions of that abuse and what it entails (for example, physical, psychological, sexual, financial, and emotional abuse as well as neglect). McCreadie presents summaries of the research on the prevalence of elder abuse, as well as a summary of the different kinds of interventions which have been made, ranging from non-intervention to mandatory reporting in the United States. She also provides a description of the state of development of policy guidelines by health authorities and social services departments in the United Kingdom. This text is a very useful introduction to the topic of elder abuse, and while it offers no gender-specific reading of the issue, it indicates the gendered dimensions of the phenomenon by highlighting the debates about who are the abusers and who are the abused.

AITKEN and GRIFFIN follow their analysis of the absence of gender considerations in the history of research on elder abuse with a discussion of the gender implications in abusive situations, both in the home and in institutional settings. In particular they highlight that elder abuse predominantly affects older women, and that as a disenfranchised group in western society, these women's rights are a low priority on public agendas, hence the generally low level of interest in the phenomenon, especially in the United Kingdom. They emphasize the impact of shifting household patterns on patterns of abuse, suggesting that increasingly, older women will be abused by non-relatives. They also focus on the fact that elder abuse in an institutional context is predominantly abuse between women, an area that remains under-researched. Similarly under-researched is the question of elder abuse among groups from diverse ethnic backgrounds, which, especially in the United Kingdom, is becoming more of an issue.

—GABRIELE GRIFFIN

See also Aging; Caregiving

Eleanor of Aquitaine 1122?–1204

French and English Queen

Kelly, Amy, *Eleanor of Aquitaine and the Four Kings*, Cambridge, Massachusetts: Harvard University Press, 1950; London: Cassell, 1952

Kibler, William W. (ed.), *Eleanor of Aquitaine: Patron and Politician*, Austin: University of Texas Press, 1976

Owen, D.D.R., *Eleanor of Aquitaine: Queen and Legend*, Oxford and Cambridge, Massachusetts: Blackwell, 1993

Pernoud, Régine, *Eleanor of Aquitaine*, translated by Peter Wiles, London: Collins, 1967; originally published in French as *Alienore d'Aquitaine*, Paris: A. Michel, 1965

Walker, Curtis Howe, *Eleanor of Aquitaine*, Chapel Hill: University of North Carolina Press, 1950

Eleanor of Aquitaine was the queen of France as wife of Louis VII, and then, after marrying Henry II of England, she became queen consort of England as well. In addition, she was duchess of Aquitaine, a large, independent duchy that is now part of France. She also was one of the few women to venture on a Crusade to the Holy Land, and she was mother of the famed English king Richard the Lion-Hearted.

KELLY's biography begins with Eleanor's early life and her court at Aquitaine as well as her independent attitudes toward her role as ruler of that land, which was then larger than France itself. When left as regent of England by her son Richard when he went on his Crusade, she also ruled that country gladly, taking the reins of government with great skill.

WALKER's biography tells less about court life and gives fewer historical details than other biographies, but it is an easier to follow assessment of Eleanor's life. Because of a lack of detailed historical information about Eleanor, most scholars must sort between what is known for sure and what may be myth, a line that is fuzzier in Walker's portrayal than in Kelly's. Walker admits that he has filled in his story and that much of what he has written is necessarily "probable" because of the difficulty of ensuring historical accuracy (since much that is known about her comes from such sources as the songs of minstrels). In addition, he has constructed dialogue, and he tells her life as a story.

PERNOUD focuses more on Eleanor's personality, portraying her as a woman of great intelligence and keen governing skill, energy, persuasiveness, and eloquence. The book includes photos of places and historical materials. Pernoud, in addition to the usual biographical information, had access to and used letters and charters of Eleanor of Aquitaine to provide more factual detail and a better understanding of the queen's thinking.

OWEN's work, the most recent, also includes plates showing photos of places, illuminated texts, effigies of the royal figures from their tombs, and seals. This book differs from the usual biographies because the study of the queen is divided thematically into Eleanor's lineage, her life, her legend, and the literature about her. It also includes as an appendix to the book a lengthy and detailed chronology of her life.

KIBLER's collection of essays is based on a symposium on Eleanor of Aquitaine held at the University of Texas. It includes articles on poetry, music, and painting in twelfth-century England and France as well as a discussion of her roles as the mother of kings, queen consort of two countries, duchess of her own land, and patron of the arts.

—ELEANOR B. AMICO

Eliot, George 1819–1880

British Writer

Barrett, Dorothea, *Vocation and Desire: George Eliot's Heroines*, London and New York: Routledge, 1989

Beer, Gillian, *George Eliot*, Brighton: Harvester, and Bloomington: Indiana University Press, 1986

Dentith, Simon, *George Eliot*, Brighton: Harvester, and Atlantic Highlands, New Jersey: Humanities Press, 1986

Shuttleworth, Sally, *George Eliot and Nineteenth-Century Science: The Make-Believe of a Beginning*, Cambridge and New York: Cambridge University Press, 1984

Smith, Anne (ed.), *George Eliot: Centenary Essays and an Unpublished Fragment*, London: Vision, and Totowa, New Jersey: Barnes and Noble, 1980

Uglow, Jennifer, *George Eliot*, New York: Pantheon, and London: Virago Press, 1987

George Eliot poses serious problems for feminist criticism. While she was acutely aware of the restrictions that her culture imposed on women's lives, she nevertheless distanced herself from many of the radical objectives of the emerging women's movement. Although she persistently questions the essentialist presuppositions that underlie the ideology of the "separate spheres," she never wholly abandons them, and in her fictional explorations of the ethic of renunciation, it is largely her female characters who are called upon to do the renouncing.

If, however, Eliot's novels provide women readers with no triumphant examples of feminine self-determination, that in itself may constitute a large part of their continuing relevance. BEER, in what is probably the single most important recent study, contends forcefully that Eliot's deliberate concern is not with the careers of exceptional women (like herself), but with the typicality of her characters' situations, with their need to recognize both their own limitations and those of the shaping environments they can never wholly transcend. Their desire for autonomy is at last compelled to adjust itself to the ethical imperative of social interdependence. However, the very effort of that adjustment, Beer argues, sets up a disruptive tension between the formal closures of Eliot's narratives, and the incompleteness, the imperfect fulfillment, of her protagonists' lives.

Beer's account sets Eliot against a dense range of historical and literary contexts in order to evaluate her distinctiveness, and that is also a central project in other recent studies. SHUTTLEWORTH's scholarly and closely argued treatment of Eliot's preoccupation with organicist scientific and social theory, for example, describes a gradual transition in her novels. In them, she moves from an unquestioning endorsement of stable, pastoral communities to a radical doubt (culminating in *Daniel Deronda*) about whether organic coherence is ever fully realizable. That growing intellectual uncertainty, moreover, entails both a disruption of realist conventions based on the unity of the text, and an increasing tendency to emphasize and explore the careers of female characters like Dorothea Brooke in *Middlemarch*, and Gwendolen Harleth in *Daniel Deronda*, whose hopes and desires cannot readily be reconciled with inclusive ideals of organic order.

A differently nuanced but complementary approach is offered in DENTITH's serviceable introductory study. Dentith argues that Eliot's early fiction comfortably synthesizes an aesthetic of realism with a belief in human progress, but that this balance is disturbed in the 1860s by a general crisis in liberal thought. The result for Eliot's fiction is a developing skepticism about the possibility of homogeneous resolution for complex problems. Dentith exemplifies Eliot's increasing openness to ambiguity and contradiction in a detailed discussion of the representation of women in *Daniel Deronda*. If, he concludes, Eliot's definition of femininity remains a broadly conservative one, she nevertheless uses it to underwrite a radical critique of her (male-oriented) culture.

Beer, Shuttleworth, and Dentith all argue for revisionist readings of *Daniel Deronda*, Eliot's final novel, whose unevennesses they see, not as an aesthetic failure, but as symptomatic of a bold experimental purpose. This is also the view of Bonnie Zimmerman, whose "Gwendolen Harleth and 'The Girl of the Period'" is one of the most stimulating of the 10 essays collected in SMITH's centenary volume (another is Janet K. Gezari's reassessment of the neglected *Romola*). Zimmerman sees the characterization of Gwendolen both as the culmination of Eliot's fictional enquiry into feminine roles, and as part of the topical controversy over the "new woman," which took place in Britain in the late 1860s and 1870s. Gwendolen, uninterested in sex, egotistical, and ambitious, represents much that Eliot deplored in the emancipated "Girl of the Period," but her inevitable chastening is not accompanied by a reversion to marriage and motherhood, the conventional agenda of "Women's Mission." Her future is uncertain, and that, Zimmerman concludes, is a measure of Eliot's responsiveness to a transitional moment in women's history.

The apparent contradiction between Eliot's sometimes reactionary public statements on women and her own financial, intellectual, and sexual independence has inevitably attracted the attention of biographical critics. UGLOW combines a sensitive account of Eliot's life with a perceptive commentary on the fiction, but she has not always been able to integrate the two as fully as she sets out to do. Even so, her account offers some valuable insights: she is, for example, perceptive on *Felix Holt* and its relationship to the contemporary vogue of the "sensation" novel, and she includes a detailed and informative chapter on Eliot and the "Woman Question" in the 1850s.

Unlike Uglow, BARRETT offers less a sequential biography than a critical study, which is based largely on biographical and psychoanalytic procedures, and which makes a fruitful working distinction between "Marian Lewes," who was not a feminist, and "George Eliot," who was. The prevailing critical emphasis, Barrett believes, on the intellectual (implicitly masculine) agenda of the novels has tended to suppress the radicalism with which they explore the varieties of desire. This radicalism disrupts the coherence of Eliot's fiction at the levels both of form and of content. Barrett sees in the development of Eliot's fiction an increasing polyphony in which conflicting voices can be accommodated, and in which full narrative closure becomes a trap to be avoided rather than a goal to be achieved. Any resolution that the novels provide, Barrett concludes, is exemplified in the sane balance of Eliot's own narrative voice, which provides, in its openness and lucidity, both a counterbalance to the conflicts it defines and a lastingly valuable exemplar for feminist writing.

—ROBERT DINGLEY

Elizabeth I 1533–1603

British Queen

Bassnett, Susan, *Elizabeth I: A Feminist Perspective,* Oxford: Berg, and New York: St. Martin's Press, 1988
Doran, Susan, *Monarchy and Matrimony: The Courtships of Elizabeth I,* London and New York: Routledge, 1996
Frye, Susan, *Elizabeth I: The Competition for Representation,* New York: Oxford University Press, 1993
Haigh, Christopher, *Elizabeth I,* London and New York: Longman, 1988
Levin, Carole, *The Heart and Stomach of a King: Elizabeth I and the Politics of Sex and Power,* Philadelphia: University of Pennsylvania Press, 1994
MacCaffrey, Wallace, *Elizabeth I,* New York and London: E. Arnold, 1993
Somerset, Anne, *Elizabeth I,* New York: Knopf, and London: Weidenfeld and Nicolson, 1991

Elizabeth I is one of the most famous women in history. In the last century there have been close to a hundred biographies of her. She has also been the subject of many films and novels. Elizabeth comes to us surrounded by myth, and each age refashions her image according to its own cultural needs and beliefs. There are a number of recent biographies of Elizabeth as well as more specialized studies. Two very fine recent ones with similar perspectives are those by Somerset and MacCaffrey. Somerset discusses more the private elements of Elizabeth's life, while MacCaffrey focuses more on her public persona. Somerset's study has a wealth of detail but is not as heavily analytical as MacCaffrey's. They both present Elizabeth for the most part as successful, especially in the creation of a national Church.

Somerset also argues that Elizabeth, except for Ireland, left a nation that was fundamentally stable and united. While some of this success was due to luck, Somerset asserts it would be absurd to dismiss Elizabeth's achievement as mere good fortune. She chose her advisors well. Though she had no intention of marrying, she used her marriage negotiations with foreign powers to England's advantage. Somerset argues that Elizabeth's success as a ruler was very much a personal triumph.

MacCaffrey shows the difficulties of the final years, but he too presents a mostly successful Elizabeth, who triumphantly disproved men's doubts about a woman's rule, who imposed her will as effectively as Henry VIII ever did, except he ruled by fear and she by winning her people's devotion. MacCaffrey believes that Elizabeth had more personal popularity than any other ruler, but he argues that where Elizabeth was least successful was at keeping England at peace. For the first two decades of her reign she was able to manage it, but by the late 1570s, events moved beyond her control, and she could not contain the drift toward war, which became more acute by 1585. After 1585 her deficiencies as a ruler became more apparent, especially her reluctance to make decisions. And Ireland was a poisoned legacy that she left her successors. Yet MacCaffrey is convinced that Elizabeth will be remembered more for her successes than her failures.

BASSNETT's feminist study is also positive, though much briefer and more idiosyncratic. She sees Elizabeth as a woman of energy and cunning, of intelligence and determination to survive, constantly on her guard, shrewd, with a sense of humor. She appointed men around her in whom she had absolute trust. She was unpredictable, and she kept ultimate power in her own hands. She was a powerful woman who wanted to stay in control. Bassnett sees Elizabeth's virginity not as some sexual or psychological inadequacy, but as a political statement—that it gave her a special position. Bassnett's Elizabeth is a woman who struggled against anti-feminist prejudice and who remained a symbol of active female assertiveness for future generations.

A perspective that strongly counters the positive view of Elizabeth is presented by HAIGH in a thematic book with chapters on the queen and her throne, the church, the nobility, the council, the court, the parliament, the military, and the people. The book is very colloquially written, and very hostile about Elizabeth, describing her variously as bullying, emotional, and acting like a lovesick teenager in the Alençon marriage negotiations of the late 1570s and early 1580s. He sees Elizabeth as a failure, arguing that she did not have much power and really did not care about the welfare of her people. He claims Elizabeth died unloved and almost unlamented.

Other recent studies are more specialized. DORAN's book focuses on the marriage negotiations, placing these courtships within the context of court politics, religious developments, and international diplomacy in order to assess their historical significance. Doran argues that Elizabeth was far more sincere in these negotiations than is traditionally believed, and that she truly wished to marry Robert Dudley in 1560 and the Duke of Anjou (Alençon) in 1581, but her Council did not support either marriage. Doran also suggests that had there not been division in her Council in the 1560s, Elizabeth would have agreed to marry the Archduke Charles. Doran believes that the marriage negotiations demonstrate Elizabeth's great strength as a ruler; she listened to her Council and refused to make a divisive marriage.

The books by Frye and Levin complement each other. FRYE's work is a semiotic analysis of Elizabeth's strategies as queen. She focuses on three moments in Elizabeth's reign, though on the first two much more concretely than on the last. Frye analyzes Elizabeth's coronation entry of 1559, the Kenilworth entertainments of 1575 devised by Robert Dudley for the queen, and the events and literature of the 1590s that preceded the rebellion led by the Earl of Essex in 1601. Frye is concerned with a rhetorical analysis of Elizabeth's agency in presenting herself. Frye's work is thought provoking, although the technical language makes it less accessible for non-specialists.

LEVIN's study examines how Elizabeth I presented herself as an unmarried woman in power, and the different ways people responded to her. Chapters deal thematically with Elizabeth as a religious figure, her courtships, rumors about her sexual behavior, rumors about her brother Edward VI's survival, other attempts to suggest that she was not the true monarch, and responses to her at the end of her reign, culminating in the Essex rebellion. Although rumors and gossip do not provide us with factual information about Elizabeth's life, they do tell us a great deal about the social-psychological response to Elizabeth's reign.

—CAROLE LEVIN

Entrepreneurship *see* Business and Entrepreneurship

Ethic of Care

Chodorow, Nancy, *The Reproduction of Mothering: Psychoanalysis and the Sociology of Gender*, Berkeley: University of California Press, 1978; London: University of California Press, 1979

Gilligan, Carol, *In a Different Voice: Psychological Theory and Women's Development*, Cambridge, Massachusetts: Harvard University Press, 1982

Noddings, Nel, *Caring: A Feminine Approach to Ethics and Moral Education*, Berkeley: University of California Press, 1984

Ruddick, Sara, *Maternal Thinking: Toward a Politics of Peace*, Boston: Beacon Press, 1989; London: Women's Press, 1990

Tronto, Joan C., *Moral Boundaries: A Political Argument for an Ethic of Care*, New York: Routledge, 1993

West, Robin, *Caring for Justice*, New York: New York University Press, 1997

The idea of an ethic of care, in all its various dimensions and manifestations, has since the early 1980s spawned a veritable cottage industry of academic writings covering it from the perspectives of the social sciences, law, history, and philosophy. The earliest explorations of this feminist concept focused primarily on its gendered nature and origins, while more recently there has been an emphasis on determining how such an ethic can be used in practice to promote a more just and humane society—to realize, that is, its progressive potential.

CHODOROW advances a psychological rationale for why women bear disproportionately the burden of motherhood across generations. She argues that motherhood gets reproduced for women and not for men because little girls, as they begin to form their identities, look to their mothers for role models, and so develop attachments to others and an appreciation for the maintenance of relationships that is continuous and powerful. Little boys, conversely, push the mother away as they struggle to locate their identity and so develop a strong sense of otherness and individuation, along with the rejection of mothering skills as inappropriate for their gender. Chodorow is concerned that this gendered differentiation causes harm to both sexes. Men are hurt by their psychologically induced inability to form strong emotional attachments to others, including their children, while women, with their disproportionate commitment to mothering, are put at a disadvantage in the workplace. She argues for a more equal division of parenting labor between men and women.

GILLIGAN articulates perhaps the single most influential argument concerning an ethic of care. It is her book that kicked off the intense debate over an ethic of care within the academic community. Gilligan advances the argument that there exist two kinds of moral reasoning. Lawrence Kohlberg had earlier created a scale of moral reasoning based on a study of 84 boys. He argued that the very highest levels of morality are characterized by abstract thought, a strong commitment to individuality, and a hierarchy of rights. This scale disproportionately excluded women from achieving the highest stages of moral development. Gilligan in response posits the existence of an alternative mode of moral reasoning that seemed, at least in her studies, to emerge from girls rather than boys. This "different voice," she argues, is characterized by a commitment to the preservation of relationships, responsibility to care for, and empathize with, others, and careful attention to context. Gilligan refrains from arguing that this voice is gendered, although the overall thrust of her work seems to lead ineluctably in just this direction.

NODDINGS argues that a feminist ethic of care deserves careful and thorough analysis, given the tendency of (masculine) philosophical theorists to dismiss such an ethic as marginal. She believes that an ethic of care, contrary to the implicit claims of those who advocate an ethics based on objectivity, abstraction, and scientific reasoning, requires that its practitioners possess and practice courage, patience, sacrifice, and the ability to make difficult decisions. An ethic of care, furthermore, recognizes and implements the social fact that we only exist as an interconnected community of caregivers and care-receivers. She also notes that such an ethic finds its highest and best expression as a practice rather than an abstract principle, and so she provides throughout the book examples of effective caring in practice. Noddings argues that if we are to make caring central in our society, there must be an ongoing dialogue about who should be cared for, who should do the caring, how much care should be provided, and so forth.

WEST provides a stirring, unapologetic defense of cultural feminism's take on an ethic of care—that this moral stance grows largely out of women's experiences, both biological and social, and that it can be successfully defended as such. She argues that recognizing and affirming women's role in creating and fostering this moral position does not necessarily undercut feminists' attempts to make an ethic of care a central element of both the public (workplace and politics) and private spheres of life. West also asserts that an ethic of care must be integrated with an ethic of justice—one without the other, she argues, results in the impoverishment of each. West concludes that the law, as well as society at large, must take seriously the difficult project of combining these two ethics if we are to create and sustain a just and caring future.

RUDDICK advocates the use of an ethic of care informed by women's experiences as mothers to resist the masculine practice of war. She characterizes maternal thinking as marked by subjectivity, attachment, and context. Ruddick is concerned that such a morality has been marginalized by the enthronement of scientific reasoning. She endorses the kind of moral reasoning that can emerge from the extended practice of caring for children, a task that falls disproportionately to women. Ruddick recognizes that mothers can be violent, and that men are not inherently violent. She finds, nonetheless, that traditionally masculine values tend to condone violence, while the feminine practices attached to child-rearing are oriented toward the practice of peace. She believes that we must apply this ethic to the political realm in order to advance an agenda of nonviolent social change. She advocates a feminist politics of peace that requires an engaged resistance to the tyranny and violence of war.

TRONTO sets forth an ambitious set of arguments designed to make an ethic of care a core part of democratic theory and practice. She fears that such feminist theorists as Gilligan and Noddings, while ably conceptualizing and encouraging an ethic of care, have made a sort of "add care and stir" argument that threatens to leave such an ethic permanently marginal. Tronto also argues that identifying an ethic of care as feminine risks keeping it forever in a gendered box. She thus points out, at some length, the care-oriented arguments set forth by such eighteenth-century Scottish Enlightenment (male) thinkers as Adam Smith and David Hume. Tronto also undertakes the more ambitious task of erasing the traditional boundaries between morality and politics, whereby moral considerations are made central to the theory and practice of politics. She also advocates a rethinking of morality that takes into serious account the value of engaged and subjective attention to context rather than abstract, objective, and disengaged reasoning. Finally, Tronto argues for reconceptualizing the traditional boundary between public and private, whereby an ethic of care is made critical in not just the latter sphere, but also the former. She attempts, in short, to make an ethic of care a central part of democratic politics.

—FRANCIS CARLETON

F

Family

Abbott, Pamela, and Claire Wallace, *The Family and the New Right*, London and Boulder, Colorado: Pluto Press, 1992

Bernard, Jessie, *The Future of Marriage*, New York: World, 1972; London: Penguin, 1973

Barrett, Michele, and Mary Mackintosh, *The Anti-Social Family*, London and New York: Verso, 1982

Chodorow, Nancy, *The Reproduction of Mothering: Psychoanalysis and the Sociology of Gender*, Berkeley: University of California Press, 1978; London: University of California Press, 1979

Delphy, Christine, and Diana Leonard, *Familiar Exploitation: A New Analysis of Marriage in Contemporary Western Societies*, Cambridge, Cambridgeshire, and Cambridge, Massachusetts: Polity Press, 1992

DeVault, Marjorie, *Feeding the Family*, Chicago: University of Chicago Press, 1991

Finch, Janet, *Married to the Job: Wives' Incorporation in Men's Work*, London and Boston: Allen and Unwin, 1983

———, *Family Obligations and Social Change*, Cambridge: Polity Press, 1989

Gittins, Diana, *The Family in Question: Changing Households and Familial Ideologies*, London: Macmillan, 1985; Atlantic Highlands, New Jersey: Humanities Press, 1986

Oakley, Anne, *Housewife*, London: Allen Lane, 1974; New York: Penguin, 1976

Rich, Adrienne, *Of Woman Born: Motherhood as Experience and Institution*, New York: Norton, 1976; London: Virago Press, 1977

Thorne, Barrie (ed.), *Rethinking the Family: Some Feminist Questions*, New York: Longman, 1982

Feminists have seen the family as central to women's subordination and exploitation. They have argued that there are two interlocking structures of subordination in the family: women's position as wives and mothers, and socialisation processes in the family in which children internalise male and female attitudes and transmit them to their own children, thus perpetuating male domination and female subordination. What is transmitted is familial ideology—that is, that the nuclear family is natural and universal, and that a sexual division of labour that results in women being economically dependent on men is biologically (naturally) determined.

BARRETT and MACKINTOSH provide a Marxist feminist analysis of the family, arguing that the patriarchal nuclear family serves the interests of capitalism by ensuring the reproduction of the relations of production, as well as serving the means of men. DELPHY and LEONARD reject the Marxist feminist analysis, and provide a theoretical analysis of their own from the materialist feminist perspective. They argue that the family is an economic system—a system of labour relations in which men benefit from and exploit the work of women. In modern western society, they indicate, the family is the main site for the reproduction of patriarchy.

The collection edited by THORNE contributes to the political debate surrounding the family. The articles develop analysis around four key feminist issues about the family: familial ideology; the family as an area of study; women's experience of the family life; and the challenge to the view that the family is a private sphere. GITTINS provides a feminist historical study of the family in western societies. She challenges the notion that "the family" exists, arguing that there have always been and continue to be a variety of kinship forms and relationships. She points to the difference between ideology of the family and the lived reality, and to the ways in which the bourgeois nuclear family has been socially and politically constructed.

ABBOTT and WALLACE contribute to the feminist analysis of the political debates surrounding "the family" by uncovering the ideologies underpinning New Right views of it. They demonstrate that pro-family economic and social policies do not always advantage the bourgeois nuclear family, and that they reinforce the subordinate position of women and women's exploitation in contemporary Britain and the United States of America.

BERNARD examines relationships in marriage, arguing that there is "her marriage" and "his marriage," and that women are exploited in marital relationships. OAKLEY examines housework as work, indicating that it is the work of a real and demanding nature. DeVAULT further contributes to the housework debate by demonstrating the real emotional and physical labour involved in feeding the family.

Feminists have been considerably concerned about the ways in which women provide, and are expected to provide, physical and emotional care for kin, which place a large (and unacceptable) burden on women, who are expected to care "naturally"—both in the sense of being prepared to do so and of having the skill to do so. FINCH (1989), following on from this analyses the basis of family obligation, and argues that gender is the key element in understanding the variations in patterns of support between kin. Women's lack of financial resources, the domestic division of labour, and the ways in which men's and women's lives are so differentially ordered means that women have more time to provide assistance, which requires the input of time and domestic labour. Furthermore, women are seen as more suitable, as caregivers. FINCH (1983) provides an analysis of the ways in which many men depend on a wife to support them in carrying out their occupational roles. In doing so, the wives of men in a wide range of jobs are providing unpaid labour for employers

A major role that women play in the family is as mothers, and women's role in caring for children is central to their subordination. RICH argues that motherhood as an institution is controlled by men under patriarchy. She argues that women have to challenge men and recover the power of the mother, which patriarchal history has suppressed. CHODOROW also examines the psychological meanings and consequences of women's mothering. Unlike most other feminists, she argues that women's mothering is a central feature in the reproduction of gender inequality.

—PAMELA ABBOTT

See also Marriage; Mother-Daughter Relationships; Motherhood; Sisterhood

Fashion

Ash, Juliet, and Elizabeth Wilson (eds.), *Chic Thrills: A Fashion Reader,* London: Pandora Press, 1992

Craik, Jennifer, *The Face of Fashion: Cultural Studies in Fashion,* Berkeley: University of California Press, and London: Routledge, 1992

Hollander, Anne, *Seeing Through Clothes,* New York: Viking, 1978

———, *Sex and Suits: The Evolution of Modern Dress,* New York: Knopf, 1994

Steele, Valerie, *Fashion and Eroticism: Ideals of Feminine Beauty from the Victorian Era to the Jazz Age,* New York: Oxford University Press, 1985

Wilson, Elizabeth, *Adorned in Dreams: Fashion and Modernity,* London: Virago Press, 1985; Berkeley: University of California Press, 1987

These works, as well as others not cited, confirm one salient fact about the scholarly discourse on fashion: namely, that it is a multi-disciplinary, and sometimes even an interdisciplinary endeavor. Fashion is amenable to a variety of perspectives, derived from such widely divergent disciplines as art history, social history, sociology, cultural studies, women's studies, psychology, semiotics, and aesthetics. Given that women's studies, semiotics, and cultural studies tend already to be the sites of intense interdisciplinary collaboration, fashion's resistance to location within predictable parameters becomes more remarkable. In eluding containment within disciplinary boundaries, the discourse on fashion exemplifies the disdain for fixity that fashion itself demonstrates in its relentless pursuit of change. Lately, fashion's fondness for change has affected even the long-held understanding of what constitutes fashion, calling into question the sanctioned dichotomies between fashion and costume, and between western and non-western dress. However, before considering this dissolution of the authorized frames for the study of fashion, it is best to plot some of the recent significant moments in a predominantly Eurocentric discourse on fashion. Some of the reiterated assumptions of this discourse are: that fashion is distinguished from costume by the former's dedicated pursuit of change, that fashion commenced some time in the late Middle Ages, and finally that fashion is allied to mercantile capitalism and the consumerist ethos it has inaugurated.

Such assumptions underpin HOLLANDER's first work (1978), although her analysis of how clothes function in works of art both includes and extends beyond the contributions of fashion. Hollander perceives western clothing as analogous to figurative art, in that neither conveys "direct social and aesthetic messages," in that both are expressions of forms of "self-perpetuating visual fiction[s]." Not surprisingly, the clothing that she discusses is to be found in painting and sculpture. In separate chapters, she examines the evolving symbolism of drapery in visual art, and the variations in the idealized representations of the nude body produced by changes in fashion. Next, she surveys the conventions surrounding theatrical costume and stage design, and their connection with the conventions of figurative art. From theatrical costume, she passes to the consideration of dress itself, for which she claims an independent history. She attributes changes in dress style or fashion to the desire for a new look, which then becomes the visual ideal for a time. She examines the contributions of fashion plates, painting, photography, and cinematography in transmitting vestmentary styles, and influencing the sense of the visually desirable in fashion. In her final chapter, Hollander moves beyond the depiction of fashion in art and cinema to literary representations of clothes and fashion. She maintains, then, that the history of dress is a history of its images.

STEELE deals with a very specific period in fashion, namely, the Victorian Age, which, for her purposes, stretches from 1820 to 1910, between the two manifestations of the Empire Style. She argues for a symbiotic relationship between changing concepts of the erotic, translated into ideals of beauty and changes in fashion, although she concedes that this is not a sufficient explanation for the evolution of fashion, which is also motivated by its own internal currents. In trying to define the concept of the erotic, she dispenses with simplistic explanations based on the fetishistic significance of clothing, or on a "shifting erogenous zone." According to her, the erotic significance of clothes terminates in a more general, idealized, and even unconscious interplay between concealment and display, aimed at approximating prevailing conceptions of beauty. Although the ideal of beauty has an erotic origin, the goal of achieving beauty is not explicitly sexual. She rejects reductive equations between the constrictions of Victorian fashion and the presumption of a repressed, masochistic female sexuality. Steele concludes her book with attention to the end of the Victorian ideal of beauty, and the inauguration of the "look" that characterized the 1920s.

WILSON'S work provides a more extended foray into fashion's negotiations with modernity. Although she is attentive to fashion's affinity with the postmodern aesthetic, particularly evident in the pluralistic nature of the discourse inhabiting the field of fashion, as well as in fashion's own predilection for the ephemeral, the novel, and the superficial, her primary interest in this work lies in etching fashion's connection with the locale, the media, the institutions, and the cultural politics of modernity. In fashion's ambivalent gestures in the directions of both individual style and congruity with prevailing codes, she suggests that it offers an antidote to the depersonalization experienced in mass society. She explores how the modes of mass communication, and changes in the fashion industry and in cultural practices, have popularized fashion and produced new styles. Fashion has also been the target of reform by various groups. In her final chapter, she examines the feminist agenda for dress reform, and questions the plausibility of the feminist pursuit of "authenticity" and freedom in dress. Like Hollander, Wilson sees fashion as an art form, and additionally as a "symbolic social system" and a place for the play of fantasy.

WILSON and ASH's book is an anthology of essays, which by its collaborative nature defies reduction to any single theme or perspective. Wilson's article, "Fashion and the Postmodern Body," sets the tone for the first section of the book, entitled "Imagery and Language." Subsequent articles explore fashion photography, masculine fashions, and the dress of the lesbian couple, besides attempting a theory of fashion. The second section investigates the relationship between design and ethnicity through reference to three ethnic groups. Asian Women's Dress, Dress in the Celtic Revival of 1880 to 1910, and Black Street Style are examined by Naseem Khan, Hilary O'Kelly, and Carol Tullock respectively. The third section of the book discusses the contrasts and continuities between haute couture and popular style. General articles on the Manufacture of Fashion, Paris Couture, Popular Fashion, and Sportswear by Ellen Leopold, Lou Taylor, Angela Partington, and Judy Rumbold respectively are situated next to more specific studies on Chanel and Vivienne Westwood by Valerie Steele and Juliet Ash respectively. The final and fourth section explores Utopian and Alternative Dress through articles by Sheila Rowbothan, Kate Luck, Linda Coleing, and Aileen Ribeiro.

CRAIK's unorthodox approach to fashion identifies fashion as body decoration, mediating the relationship between the body and its social milieu. As a technique of the body, it is culturally transmitted and modified over time by a complex of utilitarian, aesthetic, moral, and political factors. Craik's major contribution to the existing discourse on fashion is the insistence upon the universal practice of fashion, even while conceding the cultural and historical specificity of local practices. Thus, she discusses the body enhancement practices of the Hageners of Papua New Guinea, as well as the influences upon indigenous dress from colonial or western contact in Nigeria, India, and Korea. Such influences have not been unilateral, inasmuch as exotic impulses have also modified western fashion techniques. Although the dominant emphasis of her work is on techniques of constructing the feminine, she includes a chapter on fashioning masculinity. This work takes the intellectual debate on fashion substantially further, particularly through its deliberate rejection of fashion as being solely a western phenomenon, and through a rhetoric that locates fashion within the spectrum of the social and technological production of the self.

In contrast to Craik's attempt to technologize fashion, and the resultant production of the social body, HOLLANDER's latest book (1995) invokes the aesthetic appreciation of the human form, which she sees most vividly articulated in the suit. She rejects J.C. Flugel's view that fashion has been the "Great Masculine Renunciation" of the last two centuries. Rather, she claims that fashions for men and women have evolved on different principles since the middle of the eighteenth century. While women's fashion has continued to insist on display and volume, male fashion has veered towards coherence of form, appropriate fit, precise cut, and a distinct scheme of color and texture. According to her, only in the twentieth century has women's fashion come to emulate the formal virtues of the male suit. Thus she sees the suit as epitomizing the ideal toward which fashion has been evolving for over 200 years. From this survey, it can be seen that the discourse on fashion is engaged in intense revaluations across the frontiers of gender, ethnicity, and class, besides interrogating the claims to privilege that it has erected for fashion.

—DOREEN D'CRUZ

See also Beauty Standards

Female Genital Mutilation

Abdalla, Raqiya Haji Dualeh, *Sisters in Affliction: Circumcision and Infibulation of Women in Africa,* London, and Westport, Connecticut: Zed, 1982

ad-Darir, Asma, *Woman, Why Do You Weep?: Circumcision and Its Consequences,* London: Zed, 1982

Dorkenoo, Efua, *Cutting the Rose: Female Genital Mutilation: The Practice and Its Prevention,* London: Minority Rights Group, 1994

Hicks, Esther K., *Infibulation: Female Mutilation in Islamic Northeastern Africa,* New Brunswick, New Jersey: Transaction, 1993

Toubia, Nahid, *Female Genital Mutilation: A Call for Global Action,* New York: Women, Ink., 1993

Walker, Alice, and Pratibha Parmar, *Warrior Marks: Female Genital Mutilation and the Sexual Blindings of Women,* New York: Harcourt Brace, 1993

Female Genital Mutilation (FGM) generally refers to an array of surgeries carried out on women worldwide and the accompanying rituals and ceremonies. The practice is especially frequent in parts of sub-Saharan and east Africa and the Middle East, as well as in Egypt, and it is also called female circumcision or pharaonic circumcision. Specific procedures entail various degrees of cutting or removal of the clitoris (clitoridectomy), labia minora, and labia majora, and may also include infibulation, the closing of the vaginal opening except for a small opening to allow urination and menstrual flow.

The practice has sparked much controversy. Western feminist activists view it purely as a case of violence against women and/or child abuse. African and other non-western female writers and activists have taken offense at the ethnocentric bias of some of these critiques and attempts at reform. The reader should take care with sources that examine the practice without contextualizing it within the details of the lives of women in societies where it occurs.

TOUBIA is an Egyptian-trained physician who was born in the Sudan. She now lives and works in New York City, and serves as an advisor for the World Health Organization, UNICEF, and the United Nations Development Programme (UNDP). This book is primarily a call to action and grows out of Rainbow (Research, Action Information Network for Bodily Integrity of Women), the organization Toubia leads. The text is a valuable source of information on the subject and includes clear color illustrations and photographs. There are useful chapters on the distribution of the practice in Africa, on the cultural significance of FGM, and on FGM and children's rights. Toubia recognizes that the ethnocentric condemnation of this practice as a custom of inferior societies is not going to bring about change but will merely promote resentment. In the concluding chapter, "A Global Call to Action," an excellent summary of international and regional human rights conventions and declarations relating to FGM is provided. Also noteworthy is the author's sensitivity to the tension between parental rights and state responsibilities to protect citizens from harm. A good list of recommendations for actions on many levels to stop the practice of FGM is included.

DORKENOO, who was born in Ghana, is the director of the Foundation for Women's Health, Research, and Development in England. This non-governmental organization promotes the health of African women and children and deals primarily with immigrant populations in the United Kingdom. This book covers, in somewhat more detail, many of the same issues as Toubia's book. It also includes an interesting chronology of individual initiatives to bring attention to the practice of female circumcision, from the early work of Fran Hosken in 1973 through the publication in 1992 by Alice Walker of *Possessing the Secret of Joy,* a best-selling novel that brought the theme of female mutilation to the attention of a large audience of readers in the United States. Case studies contextualizing the practice of female circumcision in the Sudan and Egypt are helpful and are supplemented by a survey of variation in the practice in a wide range of African countries. The author also covers FGM in the western world and includes a consideration of the problems of racism as they relate to regulation of the practice. Dorkenoo's attention to issues of culture, class, race politics, and gender oppression, as well as her recognition that white liberal guilt has influenced the discourse on this subject, is to be commended. A well-conceptualized concluding chapter offers point-by-point suggestions for activist goals, appropriate to African countries, western countries, international organizations, and grass roots organizations. The appendix includes the names and addresses of contact organizations and advocacy groups, along with brief descriptions of their main concerns and activities.

HICKS has reviewed some of the ethnographic material on the subject, placing the practice of infibulation within the context of cultural beliefs and practices in Ethiopia, Somalia, and the Sudan. Central here is the monogenetic theory of procreation common to the area, and the way in which the closing up of women defines them as physically and ritually ready for marriage. Her work is based on information from 26 populations that are known to practice infibulation, as well as a control group of 20 that do not. The goal of this cross-cultural analysis is to identify societal variables associated with FGM. A good deal of quantitative data is presented showing the correlations that were identified, including low position of women, high bride-price, Islam, and exogamy.

The film, "Warrior Marks," by PARMAR and WALKER, is a documentary about the practice of FGM and about activist efforts to put an end to it. It premiered in the United States in 1993. The book by the same name is an account of the filmmaking project and includes additional information about the practice.

AD-DARIR, who is herself circumcised, is a physician who works for the Ministry of Health in the Sudan. Her book is a report on a four-year project funded by the World Health Organization in the late 1970s to study the prevalence of female circumcision in the Sudan and resulting health problems in women, as well as to document existing cultural and religious attitudes toward the practice. The stated goal of the project was to lead to eradication of FGM. A questionnaire was administered to over 3,000 women and over 1,500 men in five provinces of northern Sudan. The book provides a wealth of detail that merits further analysis. Ad-Darir reports that over 80 percent of the women interviewed favored continuation of the practice, and she explains this attitude in terms of religious, social, and cultural factors. The book also contains an interesting chapter on the history of efforts to abolish FGM in the Sudan, beginning with the British colonial administration.

ABDALLA was Director of Culture in the Somali Ministry of Culture at the time of publication of this study of the practice of female circumcision in Somalia. Introductory chapters explain the practice and its distribution. The practice is then analyzed in terms of the value system of traditional Somali society, including its relationship to Islamic attitudes toward women. Also included is a chapter reporting on the results of a small community study, examining the attitudes of 70 women and 40 men toward the practice in 1980, from which she concludes that it leads to physical and psychological complications. She also concludes from the evidence collected that the economic importance of FGM is related to the customs of bride-price and control of men over women. Appendices include three short first-person narratives describing the experience of female circumcision.

—ELIZABETH BRUSCO

Female Infanticide

Afshar, Haleh (ed.), *Women, State and Ideology: Studies from Africa and Asia*, Albany: State University of New York Press, and London: Macmillan, 1987

Kuhse, Helga, and Peter Singer, *Should the Baby Live?: The Problem of Handicapped Infants*, Oxford and New York: Oxford University Press, 1985

Lyon, Jeff, *Playing God in the Nursery*, New York and London: Norton, 1985

Miller, Barbara D., *The Endangered Sex: Neglect of Female Children in Rural North India*, Ithaca, New York, and London: Cornell University Press, 1981

Panigrahi, Lalita, *British Social Policy and Female Infanticide in India*, New Delhi: Munshiram Manoharlal, 1972

In a number of cultures, both past and present, the practice of infanticide occurs, often tolerated even if illegal, and usually it is female babies who are killed. Works on female infanticide are relatively rare, as social scientists have only recently focused on the diversity of beliefs and practices that can be encompassed by this term.

AFSHAR's edited collection investigates the general themes of women's social condition, gender, and the population policies in developing countries. Papers examine the role of women, anchoring viewpoints in particular in China's single-child family policy, and exploring its special implications for women, as well as the ways in which women's lives are shaped and/or limited by government policies. Explorations of son-preference, the perception that male offspring are regarded as better potential supporters, and traditional concerns with continuing the family line support statistical evidence to substantiate claims regarding the reappearance of female infanticide.

In a work that ranges broadly to amass contentious arguments for the killing of some infants with severe disabilities, KUHSE and SINGER present an overview of cultures in which infanticide is an acceptable practice. They present cross-cultural examples of communities that rely primarily on female infanticide for this purpose, in order to argue that the doctrine of the sanctity of life is not always appropriate. They contend that female infanticide is a rational action to maintain a sex ratio among adults, to provide adequately for surviving children, and to control population in areas of limited arable land. The authors then compare modern-day anthropological cases with stories of infanticide in classical European traditions, tracing the Christianised transition to contemporary western thought.

Couched in a work addressing the appropriate medical treatment for severely disabled children, LYON proffers only a gender-neutral stance when discussing infanticide in European and non-European cultures. Touching upon the ignorance and bigotry that has marked women who have borne disabled children, the work analyses the array of ethical issues emerging in western societies due to advances in technology, as well as the questions that arise in contemporary medicine relating to the care of newborns. From a standpoint of sympathy and critical enquiry, he examines the financial and emotional pressures, the feelings of guilt and frustration, and the potential for neglect and abuse that can affect the care of the severely disabled child.

MILLER's seminal study researches the ways in which culture both shapes family attitudes toward children and enfolds the power to determine how children are treated differently depending upon their sex. Miller analyses the powerful relationship between culture and mortality, discussing those beliefs and practices that produce the preponderance of males over females in India and determine which gender is targeted for death. The contemporary condition of female neglect and discrimination is examined through a historical perspective that explores unconditional female infanticide during the nineteenth century. Yet an investigation of the three factors of allocation of food, of medical care, and of love suggests to Miller a linkage with the low participation of women in agricultural production, particularly in the north. However, her study does not neglect the subjective aspects of the phenomenon of female infanticide, manifested in preference for sons, the need for heirs, desired economic support of aged parents, ritual needs, and distress concerning marriage costs.

Tracing the practice of female infanticide to the institutions of caste and marriage in Hindu society, PANIGRAHI charts the anxiety that the birth of a daughter brought to parents, as well as the perceived linkages with the social difficulties experienced by families who have fallen in caste and class status. The author cites the forces of pride, poverty, contempt for the female sex, the complicated entanglement and rigidity of the ranked caste system, and difficulties in finding suitable bridegrooms as contributing factors toward the occurrence of female infanticide. She contends that the combination of authoritarianism and paternalism of British social policy from 1870 onward was instrumental in aiding the protection of female infant life and the lessening of concomitant practices such as the sale of girls, prostitution, and polyandry. In tracing whether preventative and persuasive measures were expedient in the northwestern provinces, she illuminates a significant aspect of nineteenth-century Indian social history and the plight of female being.

—HELEN JOHNSON

Female Offenders

Adler, Freda, *Sisters in Crime: The Rise of the New Female Criminal,* New York: McGraw-Hill, 1975

Brodsky, Annette, *The Female Offender,* Beverly Hills, California: Sage, 1974

Crites, Laura, *The Female Offender,* Lexington, Massachusetts: Heath, 1976

Heidensohn, Frances, *Women and Crime,* London: Macmillan, and New York: New York University Press, 1985

Hull, N.E.H., *Female Felons: Women and Serious Crime in Colonial Massachusetts,* Urbana: University of Illinois Press, 1987

Jones, Ann, *Women Who Kill,* Boston: Beacon Press, 1980; London: Gollancz, 1991

Worrall, Anne, *Offending Women: Female Lawbreakers and the Criminal Justice System,* London and New York: Routledge, 1990

Until the 1970s, the study and interpretation of female criminality had long been the domain of male researchers, from Cesare Lombroso and his biological determinism at the beginning of the twentieth century, to Otto Pollack and his psychological theories at mid-century. One of the first feminist approaches to female crime was ADLER's book. Examining the effects the women's liberation movement had on women, namely creating more assertive, less inhibited women, Adler predicted a rise in female crime, especially violent crime. Now, she predicted, women would increasingly participate in the traditionally more masculine and violent crimes of assault, armed robbery, and murder.

JONES's work directly challenges this cause-and-effect relationship between feminism and female criminality, while refuting claims of any significant increases in female violent crime. Her book follows a historical timeline from the American colonial period to the present day, spotlighting famous cases along the way, such as those of Lizzie Borden, Bonnie Parker, and Jennifer Patri. In addition, she examines crimes typical to each period, including, for instance, infanticide cases and those of battered women who kill. Jones contends that both feminism and female criminality alarm society, and that, historically, the first has always prompted a reactive fear of the second. From a sociological context, knowing whom women kill, why, and how the community reacts sheds light on the society.

Two other sociological approaches to female crime are Hull's and Heidensohn's books. Both examine women's deviance in terms of their social and sexual roles. HULL's study focuses on seventeenth- and eighteenth-century court records from New England, looking for evidence of sex discrimination against female defendants in the male-dominated judicial system, tracking cases through the justice system, from the reporting of crimes and the trials, through the sentencing and punishment phases. While acknowledging the existence of a duality in attitudes toward women in the Bay Colony (women being considered as "both saintlier and more sinful than men," in Hull's words), she finds surprisingly little evidence of legal bias. HEIDENSOHN broadens the study of female deviance to encompass images of offending women, starting with Eve, the original earth-mother turned temptress who brought about the fall of all humankind, leading to images of deviant women, including witches in the sixteenth century, and prostitutes in contemporary society. Her chapters examining traditional as well as feminist criminological theories in Britain and North America are the heart of the book.

Two early collections of essays, one by Brodsky and the other by Crites, are noteworthy on several levels. In BRODSKY's book, Francine Goyer-Michaud's article provides an international bibliography of more than 200 sources related to adult female offenders, while Eileen N. Slack's essay is one of the first to focus on delinquent girls and their treatment in the criminal justice system. Brodsky makes a strong case in the final essay for the decriminalization of nonvictim status offenses, which statistically represent the largest percentage of female crime. At the same time, she calls for penal reforms which would acknowledge the "female" as well as the "offender" by providing more training programs and family contact.

The essays in CRITES are divided into four areas of study: female offenders, laws and the court system, women's prisons in the United States, and prostitution. Crites's book encompasses a broad range of contributors and their perspectives, ranging from social workers, newspaper reporters, and attorneys to professors and doctoral candidates. Both Brodsky's and Crites's books are excellent sources on early feminist debate and research on this topic.

WORRALL employs a case study approach to call into question the literature accumulated over the past two decades about female offenders. She challenges standard assumptions about the boundaries between law-abiding and law-breaking women, and suggests alternate approaches to the study of women and crime. According to Worrall, the criminal justice system deals with women in categories of criminal behavior identified as domesticity, sexuality, or pathology, and attempts to "manage" them according to these definitions. Her interviews with 15 representative female offenders in Britain, as well as interviews with probation officers, judges, and psychiatrists, are cross-referenced and used as evidence to illustrate her contention that many female offenders do not fit into these standard classifications, and, indeed, cannot be stereotyped for the purpose of "treatment." This is an important study of resistance to social controls, and the many forms that resistance can take.

—CHERYL KALNY

See also Criminal Punishment

Feminine Archetypal Theory

Bolen, Jean Shinoda, *Goddesses in Everywoman: A New Psychology of Women*, San Francisco: Harper and Row, 1984

Johnson, Robert A., *Lying with the Heavenly Woman: Understanding and Integrating the Feminine Archetypes in Men's Lives*, San Francisco: HarperSanFrancisco, 1994

Lauter, Estella, and Carol Rupprecht (eds.), *Feminist Archetypal Theory: Interdisciplinary Re-visions of Jungian Thought*, Knoxville: University of Tennessee Press, 1985

Lichtman, Susan A., *Life Stages of Woman's Heroic Journey: A Study of the Origins of the Great Goddess Archetype*, Lewiston, New York; Edwin Mellen Press, 1991

Neumann, Erich, *The Great Mother: An Analysis of an Archetype*, translated by Ralph Manheim, London: Routledge and Kegan Paul, and New York: Pantheon, 1955

Preston, James J. (ed.), *Mother Worship: Theme and Variations*, Chapel Hill: University of North Carolina Press, 1982

Reis, Patricia, *Through the Goddess: A Woman's Way of Healing*, New York: Continuum, 1991

The idea of the presence of a feminine principal operating in the human psyche has received ambivalent responses in western scholarly circles. This is not the case in the East, where the feminine is an important focal point of divinity. In Hinduism and Taoism the feminine constitutes a central part of all being. Female deities are widespread and deeply ingrained theologically. While goddesses are significant in the religions of the ancient Middle East, the emergence of radical monotheism banished the feminine or at least suppressed it dramatically.

In the twentieth century, Carl Jung sought to correct for this imbalance by postulating a feminine archetype at the root of the human psyche. This notion has generated heavy debate and many studies of female goddess symbolism. The literature in this field ranges from Jungian psychologists who seek insights into psychological wholeness through the goddess, to social scientists who are skeptical about such generalizations, and feminists who find something therapeutic as well as liberating about rediscovering the feminine archetype.

The great classic work in this field is the pioneering and monumental *magnum opus* of NEUMANN. In this volume the author does a structural analysis of the feminine archetype using the primordial image of the Great Mother in ritual, mythology, and the art of early human populations. Neumann carries on the work of his mentor and friend Jung. First the structure of the archetype is examined, revealing the two characters of the feminine—the Good Mother and the Terrible Mother. The central symbol is the "vessel." It represents the essence of the feminine, a protected space like the womb or sheltering cave for nurturance of new life. The feminine archetype has enormous transformative potential for the integration of the psyche and the achievement of wholeness. Thus, according to Neumann the feminine archetype places one in touch with the primordial mysteries of preservation, nourishment, and transformation. The images of various deities are examined as different manifestations of the feminine archetype. In Neumann's words: "The Great Goddess...is the incarnation of the Feminine Self that unfolds in the history of mankind as in the history of every individual woman."

In a similar vein, BOLEN investigates feminine archetypes, personified as the goddesses of ancient Greece, as models for women living under patriarchy. This volume is written by a feminist psychiatrist interested in exploring goddesses as inner images or archetypes of women. By invoking these inner archetypes, women can develop profound insights into themselves. The author attacks both Sigmund Freud's and Jung's approaches to women's psychology.

A collection of excellent articles edited by LAUTER and RUPPRECHT explores Jung's concept of the archetype by rethinking it in a feminist perspective. Here there is an attempt to revise Jung's theories by drawing on studies of religion, art, mythology, neurophysiology, analytical psychology, and archetypal theory. This is an excellent and thoroughly scholarly work with articles on women's dreams, religious dimensions of the feminine archetype, and the use of mythology in therapy. The concluding chapter proposes a "feminist archetypal theory." This revision of Jung's concept is done with great respect for his approach to psychology.

LICHTMAN's book investigates the life stages of women, using archetypal imagery as a model for the hero's quest among women. It is a collection of short essays that explore literary, psychological, and mythical dimensions of the feminine archetype. There is an attempt to provide strong, positive female images as inspiration for women during various phases of their psychological development.

REIS places emphasis on the healing powers of female sacred imagery. She proposes that the female psyche can be revealed through a journey back in time provided by the study of archaeology and mythology. Reis wants to reform Jung's notion of the feminine. She attempts a "feminist corrective, a revisioning and amplification of archetypal concepts from a woman-centered perspective." The focus in the book is on healing, with particular emphasis on the role of the feminine archetype as an important source of integration and wholeness.

The volume by JOHNSON is a refreshing discussion of feminine archetypes in men. While this book is not presented in a scholarly fashion, it is thoughtful and sensitive. The author reviews the principal elements that make up a man's feminine nature including the mother, sister, anima, wife, daughter, Sophia and homoerotic parts. He demonstrates how these feminine aspects of a man's psyche can be the cause of mental problems. A man needs to have a good relationship with his internal feminine, according to this book, in order to have good mental health.

PRESTON questions the validity of a feminine archetype at the root of goddess worship. His collection of articles reviews goddess symbolism in the major world religions. Particularly useful is the final chapter, which surveys early theories about female deities. Here Preston observes that Jung's concept of a feminine archetype ignores cultural contexts. Jung treats symbols as though they were floating, disconnected entities separated from sociocultural realities. Preston asserts that although there are some common patterns of female symbolism in the world, these commonalities do not necessarily suggest the existence of a feminine archetype. Also, he notes that goddess imagery is often overinterpreted by Jungian scholars who pay attention to similarities and ignore differences. The presence of a particular type of goddess figure in a society, for instance, does not mean the same thing in all the cultural contexts where it is found.

There can be no question about the powerful stimulant provided by Jung's notion of a feminine archetype. It has produced a flood of intriguing speculative works, particularly among some feminists who find it a focus for identity and a source of healing. Others have been critical of Jung's generalizations about feminine psychology. Only a few studies have questioned the validity of the feminine archetype as a tool for understanding female sacred imagery.

—JAMES J. PRESTON

Femininity

Chodorow, Nancy, *Femininities, Masculinities, Sexualities: Freud and Beyond*, Lexington: University of Kentucky Press, and London: Free Association, 1994

Freeman, Barbara Claire, *The Feminine Sublime: Gender and Excess in Women's Fiction*, Berkeley and London: University of California Press, 1995

Irigaray, Luce, *Sexes and Genealogies*, New York: Columbia University Press, 1993

Mitchell, Juliet, *Women: The Longest Revolution*, Boston: New England Free Press, 1966; London: Virago Press, 1984

Morell, Carolyn Mackelcan, *Unwomanly Conduct: The Challenges of Intentional Childlessness*, New York: Routledge, 1994

Root, Jane, *Pictures of Women: Sexuality*, London and Boston: Pandora Press, 1984

Singh, Nikky-Guninder Kaur, *The Feminine Principle in the Sikh Vision of the Transcendent*, Cambridge: Cambridge University Press, 1993

Wikan, Unni, *Managing Turbulent Hears: A Balinese Formula for Living*, Chicago: University of Chicago Press, 1990

Recent studies have illustrated the difficulties in conceptualising feminity and the unfixed significations of the term. The following listings provide a necessarily limited introduction to the blossoming number of works that research the concept and the relational analysis it proposes.

The collection of lectures in her book enables CHODOROW to examine the role that variation between individuals plays in an understanding of psychoanalytic theory about sexuality. She revisits Freudian pronouncements upon femininity to explore the normalising status of heterosexuality in psychoanalysis, its role in pathologising alternative sexualities as abnormal, and the universalising power of gender theories. Placing formations of femininity and masculinity within an understanding of varied and contradictory cultural repertoires, Chodorow argues for a sensitive and comprehensive exploration of the pluralistic forms of gendered sexuality.

FREEMAN's work explores the feminine "sublime," to make explicit the female subject's encounter with, and response to, an alterity that exceeds, limits, and defines a woman's subjectivity. Anchoring her argument in the notion that the feminine sublime is a domain of experience that resists categorisation as it enters into relations with otherness, the author examines the role that gender plays in the articulation of theories of the sublime. Tracing the philosophical histories of such notions, she then examines how "feminine" subjects are constituted through experience, exemplifying her theory through American and British female twentieth-century fiction.

In a collection of lectures that addresses the issue of ethics governing relationships between the sexes, IRIGARAY traces the genealogies of notions of gender. The work distinguishes power relations and epistemological productions that oppress women. Critiquing constitutions of femininity that relate only to women's social function, rather than to female identities and autonomy, Irigaray scrutinises notions of sexual difference that contrive "femininity" and argues for a nondeterminism that allows women the authority to affirm and fulfill themselves.

In a diverse selection of essays and lectures shaped by political, literary, and psychoanalytical interests, MITCHELL engages with meanings generated by the term "women" through a range of political perspectives that also incorporates ideas of women's bodily capacities. Her acute psychoanalytical understandings examine the close association of femininity with hysteria, to analyse the social constructions that define women's supposed emotionality against men's rationality. Aesthetic issues are keenly problematised through explorations of literary representations, then given depth by research into the enculturation of "femininity" through signifying terms and the symbolic order.

In a provocative study that presents the voices of women whose decision not to become mothers challenges social constructions of "femininity" in many cultures, MORELL argues that the experiences of not-mothering women are untheorised. The author proposes that such women's reproductive difference is erased by pro-natal imperatives that do not consider the politics of not-mothering. Women's voices illustrate a text that, while empathetic, retains an intensely analytical core.

An entertaining, yet astute consideration of women, their relationship to sexual practices, and social constructs of femininity permeate ROOT's critical investigation of the presence and absence of sex in British society. Through an examination of sexual ideas created in pornography and advertising, connections between sex and work made through prostitution, and assumptions permeating Britain's legal system, the work elucidates debates around femininity and sexuality developed throughout the past decade.

SINGH explores the feminine dimension of Sikh sacred and secular literature, examining the appearance and absence of the feminine in metaphysical, ethical, and ritual systems. Extending a western-educated feminist consciousness to a reevaluation of Sikh tradition and culture, the work revalidates a literature that abounds with feminine symbols and imagery. The approach enables a reconsideration and restructuring of "traditional" ideas and a concomitant celebration of feminine spirituality.

WIKAN's classic ethnography enacts a "confessional approach," which attends to the ways in which Balinese women interpret themselves and each other through discourse and in the events of their lives. Through her exploration of their formula for living, she explores the ways in which a young Balinese woman conceptualises and engages with deep existential dilemmas using Balinese notions of femininity, and the sociocultural outcomes of these concepts upon the challenges and pleasures of her individual existence.

—HELEN JOHNSON

Feminism, Black *see* Womanism

Feminism: Cultural

Daly, Mary, *Gyn/Ecology: The Metaethics of Radical Feminism,* Boston: Beacon Press, 1978; London: Women's Press, 1984

Echols, Alice, *Daring to Be Bad: Radical Feminism in America, 1967–1975,* Minneapolis: University of Minnesota Press, 1989

Edwalds, Loraine, and Midge Stocker (eds.), *The Woman-Centered Economy: Ideals, Reality, and the Space in Between,* Chicago: Third Side Press, 1995

Eisenstein, Hester, *Contemporary Feminist Thought*, Boston: G.K. Hall, 1983; London: Allen and Unwin, 1984
Griffin, Susan, *Woman and Nature: The Roaring inside Her*, New York: Harper and Row, 1978; London: Women's Press, 1984
Kimball, Gayle (ed.), *Women's Culture: The Women's Renaissance of the Seventies*, Metuchen, New Jersey: Scarecrow Press, 1981
Rich, Adrienne, *Of Woman Born: Motherhood as Experience and Institution*, New York: Norton, 1976; London: Virago Press, 1977
Spretnak, Charlene (ed.), *The Politics of Women's Spirituality: Essays on the Rise of Spiritual Power within the Feminist Movement*, Garden City, New York: Anchor, 1982

Cultural feminism, one of the major developments in American feminism in the 1970s, is for the purposes of this essay understood as the attempt to create a specifically women's culture, based on a celebration of femaleness and entailing the undoing of the dominant cultural valorization of the male. The books considered here fall into two categories: five can be seen as expressions of the cultural feminist ethos, while the remaining two offer both historical contextualization and critical evaluation of that ethos.

An example from the first category—one that serves as an excellent introduction to the wide range of issues and concerns of the cultural feminist movement—is KIMBALL's anthology of essays and interviews. This book opens with two short texts that outline the theoretical parameters of the movement; subsequent sections explore cultural feminist expressions within the visual arts, music, literature and drama, religion, and political and social organizations. Contributors to the volume—including such noted feminists as Robin Morgan, Marge Piercy, and Z. Budapest—provide a good introduction to, for example, the gynocentric art of Judy Chicago, goddess imagery in feminist wicca, and the history and significance of women's health centers.

RICH's exploration of the double aspect of motherhood—as women's experience and as patriarchal institution—is one of the classic texts of cultural feminism. In it Rich argues for the necessity of overturning the institution of motherhood, with its legacy of masculine control, in favor of a liberation of the female power implicit, for Rich, in women's experience of maternity. She documents the institutionalization of motherhood in its religious, political, legal, social, medical, and economic aspects, making constant reference to the women's culture whose suppressed history she wants to chronicle and whose (re)emergence she hopes to foster.

Another classic articulation of the cultural feminist ethos is found in the book by DALY. This book, which is divided into three sections (called "passages" in reference to Daly's view that the creation of women's culture entails a voyaging beyond patriarchy), moves from a stringent critique of masculine culture and values to an extensive documentation of the atrocities perpetrated against women throughout history—including Chinese footbinding, African genital mutilation, and practices of the American gynecological establishment—and concludes with a spirited and poetic vision of what a culture based on deep bonds among women might be.

In GRIFFIN's book the reader will find an admittedly unconventional and intuitive, rather than scholarly, elaboration of women's oppression under patriarchy, as well as a view of the process whereby women may reclaim the power that is, for Griffin, their ancient birthright. In its alignment of woman with nature as victims of patriarchal dominance and exploitation, this volume explores important concerns of the ecofeminist movement that emerged in the late 1970s.

The essays contained in the volume by EDWALDS and STOCKER take a more pragmatic—and for that reason especially valuable—approach to the cultural feminist desire to create a gynocentric culture. Edwalds's introductory essay suggests that the collective wager of the contributors is that women's power is linked to economic power. Other essays and interviews explore various aspects of what contributors see as an emerging woman-centered economy, including the relation of that economy to the larger global economy, the use of resources within the feminist and lesbian communities, the role of business within women's culture, and the nuts-and-bolts realities of trying to run a woman-centered business.

The many essays collected in SPRETNAK's book offer differing views of the spiritual dimensions of cultural feminism. Spretnak's introductory essay suggests that feminists need to honor the religious or spiritual elements of life in order to be able to give full expression to the inherent interrelatedness of all living beings, and—sounding an ecofeminist note—argues that an explicitly feminist spirituality is essential to an adequate recognition of the sacred nature of the earth itself. Other contributions—from Merlin Stone, Starhawk, Mary Daly, Adrienne Rich, and Robin Morgan, among many others—explore ancient goddess traditions, reinterpret patriarchal mythologies, imagine a new feminist spirituality, and argue the necessity of a spiritually informed vision of feminist politics.

EISENSTEIN provides a view of cultural feminism from the outside, as it were. This book presents a historical/critical reading of feminist thought in the United States; it reviews the upsurge of feminist thought in the early 1970s and traces the emergence, during the middle and late 1970s, of the woman-centered perspective that marks cultural feminism. While the text makes explicit the author's fundamental perspective—that feminism ought to be primarily a force of progressive social change, and that feminists should be wary of what Eisenstein sees as a cultural feminist tendency to advance a new essentialism based on an assertion of the natural superiority of women—it nevertheless finds much in cultural feminism to applaud.

While ECHOLS offers primarily a history of radical feminism (which Echols, like Eisenstein, is careful to distinguish from cultural feminism, noting radical feminism's roots in the male-dominated leftist politics of the late 1960s and early 1970s), it is worth considering here because it offers such an excellent view of the rise of cultural feminism as the dominant American feminist paradigm of the middle 1970s. Echols traces the roots of cultural feminism in radical feminism, observing that cultural feminism was able to supplant radical feminism because it promised to resolve the conflicts between heterosexual and lesbian feminists. On the whole, though, Echols takes a negative view of cultural feminism and looks in her epilogue to a renewal of feminist activism informed by an increased sensitivity to the differences among women.

—JUDITH L. POXON

Feminism: Liberal

Burrell, Barbara C., *A Woman's Place Is in the House: Campaigning for Congress in the Feminist Era*, Ann Arbor: University of Michigan Press, 1994

Falco, Maria J. (ed.), *Feminist Interpretations of Mary Wollstonecraft*, University Park: Pennsylvania State University Press, 1996

Kelber, Mim (ed.), *Women and Government: New Ways to Political Power*, Westport, Connecticut: Praeger, 1994

Okin, Susan Moller, *Justice, Gender and the Family*, New York: Basic Books, 1989

Pateman, Carole, *The Disorder of Women: Democracy, Feminism, and Political Theory*, Cambridge: Polity Press, and Stanford, California: Stanford University Press, 1989

Tulloch, Gail, *Mill and Sexual Equality*, Hertfordshire: Harvester Wheatsheaf, and Boulder, Colorado: Lynne Riener, 1989

Liberal feminism combines a theoretical and a practical commitment to extending to women the liberal values of personal freedom and social equality traditionally accorded to men. On the theoretical level, the most comprehensive liberal feminist arguments against sexual inequality are still those developed in the seventeenth and nineteenth centuries respectively, by such thinkers as Mary Wollstonecraft and John Stuart Mill. Devoted to the work of the former, FALCO's collection of essays includes nine contributions from researchers in a variety of fields. Although they focus on different aspects of Wollstonecraft's life and work, including the development of her liberal feminist ideas, the discussion takes place in the context of a general agreement that Wollstonecraft's arguments in support of the political, social, and economic equality of women continue to be relevant and are worthy of study today.

Similarly, TULLOCH offers a comprehensive exposition of Mill's liberal feminist argument against sexual inequality, and defends its continued relevance. This treatment of Mill's argument emphasizes that, in addition to challenging the legitimacy of women's unequal legal and political status, Mill's approach revealed how women's social subordination had been naturalized, and was able to be reinforced and perpetuated, through the institution of the family. Part of the book is devoted to an extensive review of Mill's essay, *The Subjection of Women*, which explores the implications of some tensions in a number of Mill's claims about women, especially in marriage, and argues that Mill is best understood as relying on an androgynous, developmental conception of the nature of human beings. Mill's essay on women is also linked to his other works, which elaborate liberal political principles of freedom and individuality. The final part of the book considers the important question of how Millian liberal feminist principles might be applied today in the context of current debates about the concepts of equality, equal opportunity, and discrimination.

For BURRELL, the theoretical rationale underlying the struggle to achieve women's political equality is the liberal feminist belief in women's ability to make important contributions to the policy-making agenda. The book focuses on feminist activism in the United States, which, since the formation in 1966 of the National Organization for Women (NOW), has aimed at increasing women's political participation at all levels. It provides useful statistics on women's participation in the Senate and House of Representatives, as well as in local government and political parties. There is a useful review of the available research on women in public office. In addition, the author identifies trends in public attitudes toward women in public office, and evaluates the efforts of newly formed organizations created to promote women's candidacies.

KELBER's book is focused on women's struggle to achieve sexual equality in political leadership and government on an international scale. It brings together very useful information on the current status of a number of national struggles to increase women's political participation. In addition to presenting a brief overview of the current state of affairs as regards women's political inequality around the world, the book contains separate chapters on six northern European countries and the United States. It details the uses of both official and unofficial strategies for bringing about women's political equality, and the experiences of women taking up government positions. Of particular interest is the discussion of uses of quota systems aimed at raising the number of women in government. There are also some recommendations concerning strategies for further increasing women's political power.

Notwithstanding the importance accorded by liberal feminist activists to the achievement of women's equal access to public office, PATEMAN develops some of the most serious objections to liberal theory, arguing that liberal ideals are inevitably patriarchal and, therefore, antithetical to the realization of feminism's goals. The essays in this book challenge a number of different aspects of liberal thought, including its most fundamental assumptions about individuals and society. Pateman argues that the notion of individuality at the heart of liberalism is not sex-neutral, but contains an inherent masculine bias. The notions of freedom, rationality, and equality that are attributed to individuals reflect the experiences of men, rather than of human beings in general. Relatedly, the liberal division of society into public and private domains governed by different principles inevitably works to exclude women and female difference from the public sphere, as well as to naturalize, and remove from critical view, domestic activity in which women are involved.

In light of the seriousness of objections such as Pateman's, liberal feminist theorists, such as OKIN, have had to reconceptualize the public and private domains. The author agrees with feminist critiques of liberal theory, which argue that it has failed to address the conceptual problems generated by its insistence on the division of the social world into separate public and private spheres regulated by different norms and principles. She argues that the exclusion of women from the public sphere, and of the domestic sphere from public political discourse, have emerged from an unjustified historical and, therefore, contingent association of women and femininity with the family. In other words, she does not think that there is an inherent conflict between the liberal conceptions of privateness and publicness, domestic and civil life, civil and political life, or individual and society. What she singles out as the source of the problem is the "gender structure" of the family. By this she means not just the organization of responsibilities, opportunities, and activity within the domestic sphere on the basis of gender, but also that such organization results in unfair or unequal distributions—for example, of power, of paid and unpaid labor, of leisure time—to the detriment of women. The focus of her attention has thus been the degendering of the domestic and public spheres in liberal theory. She thinks that this degendering process can be achieved by rethinking questions about freedom, equality, and justice from the perspective of women's lives. The book defends a "fully humanist theory of justice" that acknowledges and deals with the effects of the gender-structured family referred to above.

—TOULA NICOLACOPOULOS

Feminism: Marxist/Socialist

Barrett, Michele, *Women's Oppression Today: Problems in Marxist/Feminist Encounter*, London and New York: New Left Books, 1980

Eisenstein, Zillah, *Capitalist Patriarchy and the Case for Socialist Feminism*, New York and London: Monthly Review Press, 1978

Hartsock, Nancy, *Money, Sex and Power: Toward a Feminist Historical Materialism*, Boston: Northeastern University Press, 1983

Kuhn, Annette, and Anne-Marie Wolpe (eds.), *Feminism and Materialism*, Boston and London: Routledge, 1978

Mitchell, Juliet, *Psychoanalysis and Feminism*, London: Allen Lane, and New York: Pantheon, 1974

Rowbotham, Sheila, *Hidden from History: Rediscovering Women in History from the 17th Century to the Present*, London: Pluto Press, and New York: Pantheon, 1973

Saffioti, Heleieth, *Women in Class Society*, New York and London: Monthly Review Press, 1978

Sargent, Lydia (ed.), *Women and Revolution: A Discussion of the Unhappy Marriage of Marxism and Feminism*, London: Pluto Press, and Boston: South End Press, 1981

Vogel, Lise, *Marxism and the Oppression of Women: Toward a Unitary Theory*, New Brunswick, New Jersey: Rutgers University Press, and London: Pluto Press, 1983

Feminist theories are concerned with helping us to understand how and why women are subordinated—in analyzing the economic, social, and cultural processes through which women's subordination is perpetuated. Marxist feminists use the concepts and methodology of Marxism to theorize the situation of women. However, there is considerable debate as to whether the subordination of women can be explained within Marxist theory, or whether it is necessary to develop the theory further to explain the situation of women under capitalism. A central debate concerns the relationship between capitalism and patriarchy—between those who see capitalism as a material base and patriarchy as ideology (that is, as determined by the material base) and those who see capitalism and patriarchy as two systems.

ROWBOTHAM, from a Marxist feminist perspective, provides a history of women's oppression and struggle in Britain from the Puritan Revolution of the seventeenth century to the 1930s. She argues that the rise of capitalism, the growth of a market economy, and the increasingly complex division of labor resulted in the marginalization of women from productive roles, and their subordination in the private sphere.

SAFFIOTI provides a detailed study of women's oppression and the perpetuation of class relations in Brazil. She argues that the economic marginalization of women in capitalist society, the inability of capitalist economies to employ all workers, and the role of women in the family, which leads to their function as a reserve army of labor, together explain the continuing subordination and exploitation of women.

The collection edited by KUHN and WOLPE contains articles that provide a materialist analysis of women's oppression in contemporary capitalism by analyzing the structure of the family and the labor process. Central arguments are that gender inequalities are determined by capitalism, and that the state in capitalist societies plays a pivotal role in the oppression of women by supporting a form of household—the bourgeois nuclear family—in which women provide unpaid domestic services for men and children, so ensuring the reproduction of the relations of production and their own availability as reserve army of labor. VOGEL, in a theoretical analysis, argues that Marxist theory can be extended to address all the concerns of women's liberation. Capitalism is the material base of women's oppression, which can be explained in terms of social reproduction and the reproduction of labor power.

MITCHELL develops a feminist version of Marxism, in which she emphasizes the importance of patriarchal ideology in the subordination and exploitation of women. She argues that there are four structures—reproduction, production, the socialization of children, and sexuality—that are interdependent and combine in the family, and that form the material basis of women's subordination. Patriarchy, she suggests, is an ideological phenomenon that underpins the cultural construction of masculinity and femininity. Women's liberation will come only from the overthrow of capitalism and the psychic transformation of patriarchy.

BARRETT provides a materialist analysis, but sees patriarchy and capitalism as distinct "systems" in alliance—as having common interests. Women's subordination under capitalism is explained as the outcome of a specific historical struggle, in which men often act collectively against women's interests. Processes of production and reproduction explain women's subordination. The institution of the nuclear family enables men to dominate women—the family/household system controls women's access to paid employment because of their role as reproducers. The institution of the family creates and constructs a sexist gender ideology, making inevitable the sexual division of labor, because women's roles in the home and in paid employment reinforce each other.

The edited collections by Eisenstein and Sargent contain articles that explore the relationship between capitalism and patriarchy. EISENSTEIN argues for a synthesis between Marxist analysis and feminist theory. An understanding of dynamics of power requires an analysis of both class relations and the sexual hierarchy. Capitalist patriarchy, she suggests, is one system—patriarchy is the system of control, law, and order, and capitalism is an economic system in pursuit of profit. Changes in one part of the capitalist/patriarchy system result in changes in another.

The essays in the collection by SARGENT conduct a debate with the lead essay by Heidi Hartmann, which is an analysis of the problems of combining Marxism and feminism. She argues that it is necessary to develop an understanding of the interdependence of Marxism and capitalism. Women have to struggle against both men and capitalism, since men's position in capitalism and patriarchy prevents them from recognizing the need for a non-patriarchal, as well as a non-capitalist society, if it is to meet the needs for nurturance, sharing, and growth.

HARTSOCK moves further from Marxist theory by developing a feminist historical materialism based on Marxist epistemology. She offers a methodology that analyzes all dimensions of social life in terms of the development of the material goods necessary to secure human existence. Material life shapes consciousness; all knowledge is an ideological construct. Women's subordination in the private sphere and in reproduction results in a way of knowing that enables them to distinguish reality from false appearance. Women's standpoint enables them to uncover the real relations of male domination (which is analogous to the classic Marxist argument that the position of the proletariat in capitalism enables them to uncover the real relations of bourgeois domination in capitalist society).

—PAMELA ABBOTT

Feminism: Postmodern

Ferguson, Margaret W., and Jennifer Wicke (eds.), *Feminism and Postmodernism,* Durham, North Carolina, and London: Duke University Press, 1992

Hekman, Susan J., *Gender and Knowledge: Elements of a Postmodern Feminism,* Boston: Northeastern University Press, and Cambridge: Polity Press, 1990

Jardine, Alice, *Gynesis: Configurations of Women and Modernity,* Ithaca, New York: Cornell University Press, 1986

Marchand, Marianne H., and Jane L. Parpart, *Feminism/Postmodernism/Development,* New York and London: Routledge, 1994

Moi, Toril, *Sexual/Textual Politics: Feminist Literary Theory,* London and New York: Methuen, 1985

Nicholson, Linda J. (ed.), *Feminism/Postmodernism,* New York and London: Routledge, 1990

Postmodern feminism is a result of the intersection of two contemporary theoretical currents, feminism and postmodernism. Since the 1960s, postmodern theories in diverse forms and disciplines, most notably in the French post-structuralist work of Jacques Derrida and Jacques Lacan and the cultural theories of Jean François Lyotard, Michel Foucault, Gilles Deleuze, Félix Guattari, and Jean

Baudrillard, have presented a radical critique of traditional, particularly modernist, conceptions of western philosophy, language, culture and subjectivity. French feminist theoreticians, especially Julia Kristeva, Hélène Cixous, and Luce Irigaray, whose writings were available in English translations by 1980, directed postmodern theories toward a feminist critique of patriarchal culture and phallocentric language.

MOI's book was the first full study of feminist literary theory published in English to include an analysis of French postmodern feminist theory. She makes an important distinction between Anglo-American feminist theory, which tended to rely on liberal-humanist philosophy, and French feminist theory, which looked to post-structuralism to explore theoretical problems raised by feminism. She points out that although works by Gayatri Spivak, Shoshana Felman, and Jane Gallop were drawing on the theories of Derrida and Lacan by the mid-1980s, the majority of Anglo-American feminist critics depended largely on traditional, male-centered critical approaches and methods, practicing an analysis of sexual politics that remained entangled with insufficiently politicized theoretical paradigms. Her investigation thus served to open Anglo-American feminist thought to French postmodern theory. Moi's book remains one of the most useful volumes for those seeking an overview of feminist literary theory in addition to an introduction to French postmodern feminist thought.

Although Anglo-American feminists found the work of the French feminists of interest, generally they distanced themselves from post-structuralism as articulated by French male theorists. JARDINE was among the first to question this disregard and to analyze extensively the male post-structuralists in relation to postmodernity ("modernity" in France) and Anglo-American feminist theory and practice. To explore the commonalities and conflicts between post-structuralism and feminism, Jardine focuses on "gynesis," the theorized "feminine" of post-structuralism, directing her study toward analyzing and interrogating the relation between gynesis and feminism. Do they overlap and reveal one another? Or do the post-structuralist texts reintroduce traditional representations of women? How might post-structural theories open the radical insights of feminism to the large questions facing postmodern culture? Finally, if postmodernism and feminism are not mutually exclusive, and if feminism is to remain political viable, what new strategies must be devised? This book raises significant issues that scholars have continued to explore in evaluating the complex and uneasy relationship between feminism and postmodern theory.

HEKMAN focuses her study of the interrelationship of feminist and postmodern theory on the critique of Enlightenment epistemology, the move effecting a postmodern shift from foundational philosophy to theories of discourse, a crucial issue in contemporary theoretical inquiry. Hekman maintains that feminist thought, as well as postmodernist theories, have challenged the hierarchical dualism of Enlightenment thought. She organizes her discussion around a comparative examination of their rejection of fundamental dualisms: rational/irrational, subject/object, and culture/nature. Assessing the writings of postmodern theorists Hans Georg Gadamer, Foucault, and Derrida, she argues for the relevance of their work to feminist theory. She also analyzes and attempts to refute feminist criticisms of postmodernist thought, considering charges of relativism, nihilism, and, most importantly, political inactivity. She seeks in this book to promote a "conversation" between the two theories and to present, not a conflation of the theories, but rather "a postmodern approach to feminism."

NICHOLSON's book, perhaps the most useful single volume, brings together essays by feminist scholars in a number of disciplines speaking to the major theoretical issues confronting postmodernism and feminism. Nicholson frames the encounter between the two theories by calling attention to the complementary strengths and weaknesses of postmodernist and feminist theories, the former providing persuasive criticisms of foundationalism and essentialism but weak social criticism, the latter offering strong approaches to social criticism but tending to lapse into essentialism. This volume is intended to proceed toward a postmodernist feminism by staging mutually beneficial and corrective critical encounters between the two theories. An important and widely referenced essay by Nicholson and Nancy Fraser initiates the critique and concludes by proposing the incipient theoretical conditions of a "postmodern feminism." The collection includes influential essays by Seyla Benhabib on post-modern epistemologies, Jane Flax on postmodernism and feminist theory, Nancy Hartsock on Foucault's theories of power and their relation to feminism, Sandra Harding on feminism and science, Donna Haraway on postmodern cyborgs, and Judith Butler on feminist theory and psychoanalytic discourse. These scholars have written extensively on feminist theory and postmodernism and have books treating the topic in greater detail.

Another useful collection of essays is edited by FERGUSON and WICKE. In their introduction, subtitled "the way we live now," the editors present feminism and postmodernism as discourses attuned to contemporary culture, stretching across disciplinary and geographical boundaries, struggling to account for the new texts and contexts of the world as it appears now. Previous investigations of the intersection of postmodernism and feminism allow the editors to make certain assumptions regarding the possibilities of a postmodern feminist theory and practice. In seeking to understand the transformations of postmodernity, feminist theory and practice now require an understanding of the philosophical and cultural critiques of postmodern theory; and postmodernism requires the historical, material specificity of feminist theory and politics. The editors organize the volume around the task of reading one theory's discourse through the terms of the other, putting each theory under pressure across disciplinary and political lines. The result is a collection of broadly defined postmodern feminist essays that not only offer theoretical insights but also address a variety of multidisciplinary and multicultural texts and cultural productions. This book reveals the current trajectory of postmodern theory as it has come into contact with feminist theory and practice and become more self-consciously directed toward social and political criticism; and it marks the current phase of a dynamic, purposely open postmodern feminist theory and practice capable of addressing a wide range of contemporary issues.

The volume edited by MARCHAND and PARPART takes an important step in the elaboration of postmodern feminism, interrogating the theory in a global context and putting it to a practical test in assessing and addressing contemporary gender issues in developing countries. The editors situate this collection in the context of the ongoing debate between postmodernist and feminist theory initiated by Nicholson and Fraser. Positing a postmodern feminism that combines postmodernist incredulity toward meta-narratives and the social-critical power of feminism, they direct the volume toward an exploration of the relevance of this theory to development issues. The collection brings together the thinking of a number of specialists on gender and development, focusing it on the potential of a more politicized and accessible version of postmodern feminism to address the problems facing women in developing countries and women of color globally. Essays in the first and second parts of the book engage theoretical issues; the following essays locate their analyses in a particular vantage point or locale and apply the theory to practical problems of gender and development. The volume does not impose fixed answers to the questions posed; rather, it provides the context for an expanded confrontation between postmodernism and feminism and opens the critical discussion to the different but interrelated problems and prospects facing women in the contemporary world.

—GWEN RAABERG

Feminism: Radical

Burstow, Bonnie, *Radical Feminist Therapy: Working in the Context of Violence,* Newbury Park, California, and London: Sage, 1992

Echols, Alice, *Daring to Be Bad: Radical Feminism in America 1967–1975,* Minneapolis: University of Minnesota Press, 1989

Eisenstein, Zillah R., *The Radical Future of Liberal Feminism,* New York and London: Longman, 1981

Klein, E.R., *Feminism under Fire,* Amherst, New York: Prometheus, 1996

Radical feminism, which arose out of the "new left" of the late 1960s, has as its major proposition the belief that nothing but the elimination of patriarchy will ever sufficiently achieve the aims of the feminist movement, since attempting to raise the position of women within patriarchal structures can only perpetuate systems of domination and inequality. ECHOLS documents the rise of radical feminism as a political force and its subsequent disappearance into mainstream liberalism. Abortion rights provided the platform for radical feminists to take center stage within the female countercultural movement. This evolved into "sexual politics," putting women's historical roles, established in law and tradition, into a modern social context. The author notes that feminism may be more noted for inspiring adversarial groups than for motivating its own followers. She views the result of radical feminism as the subversion of traditional values and destabilization of the family. The resultant economic independence of women has contributed to instability of marriage in general. Feminism has generated less social pressure for marriage, social acceptance of children out of wedlock, and open antagonism between the sexes. Since the birth of radical feminism in the late 1960s, expectations have waned in the face of society's recalcitrant structures inhibiting this "revolution." The legacy of radical feminism lies in the subtle changes that have been made in everyday society and those that continue, albeit slowly, to change our everyday lives.

EISENSTEIN feels it is imperative for feminists to reconcile the radicalism within mainstream feminism. She expresses that egalitarianism and sexual ideology must step beyond liberalism, especially as American society moves politically more to the right. The author struggles with the contradiction of radical theory and the actual practice of "mainstream" liberal feminism. Independence and individualism are historical elements of bourgeois ideology dominant in western society. The patriarchal bias of modern liberalism reinforces the limits of feminism as a radical force. The antithetical ideology of patriarchal liberalism establishes the theoretical basis of sexual class consciousness that defines radical feminism. Women are sexually distinguished from men, but such selective recognition allows, not sharing of power, but collective subjugation in its place. This sexual class differentiation is based on patriarchal oppression, designed to manipulate women's capacities. Therefore, an antithesis results from the concepts of women as biological entities and women as political entities. The rise of the bourgeois, capitalistic economy has created a middle-class woman, fully conscious of her potential, but also of the subsequent struggles inherent within the relationship of historical liberalism and the development of radical feminism.

BURSTOW focuses on the aspect of therapy as an integral and important part of carrying on the fight for feminism. However, feminists see traditional psychiatry as a male-dominated, sexist, and oppressive institution that subjugates females. Humanist orientation was found by most to be an inadequate representation of the vulgarities women are subjected to on a universal basis. Radical feminism is a response to the mental and, more particularly, the physical violence wreaked against women. Burstow outlines the foundation of radical feminism and defines the basis of the conceptual orientations of therapy and its meaning and purpose. She also presents the positions of oppression and the objectification and exploitation of women by the male power elite. These exploitations have many faces, but all are focused toward different systematic male self-gratifications that result in eventual "rape" of the body of woman.

KLEIN introduces many variances of feminism, from radical lesbianism to Marxism. Problematic to her epistemological quest is the analysis of differences among feminist philosophy, nonfeminist philosophy, and feminist nonphilosophy. Traditionally, philosophy as a science has been exclusively developed, she suggests, by men to oppress women. Knowledge, or the search for truth, as it relates to the philosophy of women, must be reevaluated through the unbiased analysis of women and their place in the universe. Klein concludes that reason itself has no gender, and thus, this renders any opposition to philosophy as moot to the question of validity, when understanding the feminist agenda and purpose.

—GARY D. CRANE

Feminist Activism

Cantarow, Ellen, Susan Gushee O'Malley, and Sharon Hartman Strom, *Moving the Mountain: Women Working for Social Change,* Old Westbury, New York: Feminist Press, 1980

Echols, Alice, *Daring to Be Bad: Radical Feminism in America, 1967–1975,* Minneapolis: University of Minnesota Press, 1989

Griffin, Gabriele (ed.), *Feminist Activism in the 1990s,* London: Taylor and Francis, 1995

Kosambi, Meera (ed.), *Woman's Oppression in the Public Gaze: An Analysis of Newspaper Coverage, State Action and Activist Response,* Bombay: Research Centre for Women's University, 1994

Moghadan, Valentine M. (ed.), *Identity Politics and Women: Cultural Reassertions and Feminism in International Perspective,* Boulder, Colorado: Westview Press, 1994

Radcliffe, Sarah A., and Sallie Westwood, *"Viva": Women and Popular Protest in Latin America,* New York and London: Routledge, 1993

Rowbotham, Sheila, *Women and Movement: Feminism and Social Action,* New York and London: Routledge, 1992

For many, feminist activism implies a bygone era of mass mobilization, street marches, and public spectacles in the name of women's suffrage or women's liberation. Yet limiting activism to such visible agitations in the nostalgic past denies the extent and effects of women's organized struggles throughout history. Feminist activism, in other words, includes a variety of activities undertaken to improve various conditions for women across the globe. Distilling this broad category into a few basic books is, at best, arbitrary. Thus, the attempt here is to demonstrate the multiplicity of approaches to understanding activism as it relates to women.

ROWBOTHAM's book is a good place to start. Designed as "an historical introduction to the ideas, organizations, and activities" of women in emancipatory movements since the eighteenth century, Rowbotham illustrates the sweep of women's activism across many western and non-western cultures and political movements. This is a huge task, and the work, at times, strains under the sheer volume of history it attempts to incorporate. Its brief chapters cover everything from women in the French, Russian, and Chinese Revolutions to consciousness-raising in the United States. More than providing mere snippets of history as the social backdrop for contemporary feminisms, though, Rowbotham constantly works to draw parallels, note influences, and highlight contradictions within and among the various movements in which women agitated for social change. It is an accessible text, in that there are discussion questions at the beginning of each of the major sections, and a list of further readings for each chapter, complete with difficulty ratings.

ECHOL's history works within much more narrow parameters. This thoroughly-researched and well-written account of radical feminism in the United States between 1967 and 1975 presents a nuanced and balanced record of some of the women's movement's most outrageous, yet theoretically sophisticated, activists. Her purpose is to set the story straight about radical feminism, which she defines as a "political movement dedicated to eliminating the sex-class system." She argues that too often, however, it is lumped together with cultural feminism, which emphasized the need for "women's spaces." Cultural feminism was a "countercultural movement" that sought to revalorize all things female in ways that came uncomfortably close to the new form of Victorianism. This book offers a very complex reading of what many consider to be the peak of activism, and illustrates how nostalgia can smooth over some very rough and uncomfortable rifts among feminist activists during this very exciting time.

CANTAROW presents a different kind of history, in recounting the lives of three women activists: suffragist agitator, Florence Luscomb; civil rights organizer, Ella Baker; and farm labor movement veteran, Jessie Lopez de la Cruz. Originally part of the Feminist Press's mission to provide alternatives to sexist teaching tools, this trilogy is very accessible and well-researched example of oral history. In each of the three chapters, the women's own tellings of their stories are weaved through historical contexts, biographical summaries, and documentary photographs. It is the generous amount of space turned over to the activists' own words that makes this work so pleasurable. Each of these women orients her activism within very personal life-lessons, and in doing so offers herself as a role model.

GRIFFIN makes the argument that feminist activism is not just historical, but is alive and well and all around us. She is convinced that women's movement veterans now housed in women's studies departments, who lament feminist activism's demise, are isolated and unaware of what is going on outside their particular sphere of activity. Concentrating on various organized women's groups in and around the United Kingdom, each of the chapters is authored by one or more members of the respective organizations. As the reader moves from one chapter to another, the fragmentation and contradictions among these activists become palpable. For example, both Rights of Women (ROW), a group of feminist legal advocates, and Justice for Women, a grassroots feminist organization, focus on domestic homicides. Whereas ROW's goal is legal reform, however, the members of Justice for Women argue that such approaches construct women as victims, dependent on the legal system to wage their battles. Instead, Justice for Women organizes "zap" actions that raise public awareness. If diversity is strength when it comes to current activism, then this work is an inspiration.

Representation, the social process of making meaning, is the key issue in many recent books that consider women's activism in a transnational context. A number of the contributors to RADCLIFFE and WESTWOOD's book concern themselves with the representation of women in nationalist discourses. This anthology offers several interesting case studies of women's activism throughout Latin America. Through the exploration of local movements, such as the Comadres of El Salvador, which organizes on the basis of very traditional women's roles, the editors attempt to make a case for the more complex understandings of women's political practices.

MOGHADAM concentrates on the women's relationships to discourses and movements organized around questions of religious, ethnic, and national identities. Many of the essays explore "woman" as a cultural symbol of the community's purity and integrity. One contributor, for example, draws on Hitler's state-sponsored "Aryan" copulation in 1930s Germany, Khomeini's mandatory *hijab* (modest dress for women) in contemporary Iran, and in the U.S. Religious Right's obsession with abortion, to argue that in times of increased nationalism, political battles are played out literally on the bodies of women. Overall, the anthology is a rich collection of essays that reorient "women's issues" into current global political movements. Although less geographically focused than Radcliffe and Westwood's book, Moghadam's anthology is conceptually tighter and more provocative in its challenges to feminist understandings of politics.

KOSAMBI offers yet another anthology that concerns itself with the representation of women, but it is very different from the previous two. Focusing on newspaper reports of specific acts of violence, including infanticide, widow immolation (sati), rape as a political weapon, and sexual assaults by the police in and around Bombay, India, the authors document and analyze the combined effects of the media and feminist activism on state policy. Although very uneven in analytical quality, several chapters form a useful and unique model for the study of the ways meanings are constructed in journalistic accounts of violence against women, and of subsequent feminist activism.

—CATHERINE M. ORR

See also Feminist Movements: Global; Feminist Movements: Nineteenth Century; Feminist Movements: Twentieth Century; National Woman's Party, United States; Suffrage: British; Suffrage: United States; Suffrage: Worldwide

Feminist Movement, Abolitionist Origins of

DuBois, Ellen Carol, *Feminism and Suffrage: The Emergence of an Independent Women's Movement in America, 1848–1869*, Ithaca and London: Cornell University Press, 1978

Eckhardt, Celia Morris, *Fanny Wright: Rebel in America*, Cambridge, Mass.: Harvard University Press, 1984

Gurko, Miriam, *The Ladies of Seneca Falls: The Birth of the Woman's Rights Movement*, New York: Macmillan Publishing, 1974

Lerner, Gerda, *The Grimké Sisters from South Carolina: Rebels Against Slavery*, Boston: Houghton Mifflin, 1967

Lumpkin, Katharine Du Pre, *The Emancipation of Angelina Grimké*, Chapel Hill: University of North Carolina Press, 1974

Lutz, Alma, *Crusade for Freedom: Women of the Antislavery Movement*, Boston: Beacon Press, 1968

Taylor, Clare, *Women of the Anti-Slavery Movement: The Weston Sisters*, New York: St. Martin's Press, 1995

Yee, Shirley J. *Black Women Abolitionists: A Study in Activism, 1828–1860*, Knoxville: University of Tennessee Press, 1992

Politics is possibly the most popular subfield of women's history and a great number of pages have been devoted to the first feminist movement. With the emergence of the women's liberation movement in the 1960s, many politically-conscious scholars, struck by the absence of women in history textbooks, vowed to uncover the hidden past of half the population. Since many of these researchers had moved from activism in the civil rights movement to participation in the feminist movement, they expected to find evidence of other women who had completed a similar journey. This second wave of feminists knew from experience that participation in reform movements teaches women the skills and confidence to offer political leadership to other women. Feminists found their foremothers in the nineteenth century, in the abolition and women's rights movements. This listing, which includes several classic works, is only able to scratch the surface of an extensive body of literature.

LERNER, the grande dame of women's history, launched her career with a study that traces the impact of the Grimkés, two sisters born to a slaveholding aristocratic South Carolina family. Although rather long, this book explains the status of women in the early nineteenth century and situates the Grimkés in the middle of the conflict over women's roles. The first female antislavery agents, Sarah and Angelina shocked much of the American citizenry by daring to defy public opinion and, in 1837, to speak in public. Not content to simply voice their opinions about the antislavery movement, the sisters often offended the sensibilities of their audiences by bringing up the place of women in society. Many of the key figures in the struggle for women's rights, Lerner argues, were personally inspired by the Grimké sisters.

LUMPKIN focuses on the life of Angelina, the bolder of the two Grimkés. Angelina accepted slavery until she was well into her twenties. Then, she passionately challenged the very foundation of the society in which she had been raised. Like many of the women active in abolition and feminism, Angelina belonged to the Society of Friends, better known as the Quakers. Converted to Quakerism by Sarah, Angelina renounced slavery because she had been taught by the Friends that it was sin to support human oppression. LUMPKIN explores Angelina's disgust with the practice of slavery and explains why her religious awakening led her to break with the slaveholders of the South. A comprehensive bibliography of materials that focus on the Grimké sisters completes the book.

Fanny Wright, a Scottish-born predecessor of the Grimké sisters, spent her life promoting equality between the sexes and races. She is most famed for establishing a utopian settlement in Tennessee to help newly emancipated slaves adjust to freedom. In 1825, Wright became the first woman in America to act publicly to oppose slavery and, in 1828, the first to argue in public that women were men's equals and must be granted an equal role in all the business of public life. ECKHARDT has produced the best biography of Wright, a book that is both well-written and extensively researched.

YEE takes a rare look at the lives of African-American abolitionists. She explores free black women's participation in the struggle to end slavery in the United States between 1828 and 1860. YEE's book is important in many ways. Historians have acknowledged the activities of individual black women abolitionists, most notably Harriet Tubman and Sojourner Truth, but they have devoted little attention to the collective role of black women in the movement. Yee argues that black women abolitionists laid the groundwork for a distinct pattern of black female activism that would become important a century later in the struggle for civil rights.

TAYLOR sketches the lives of the abolitionist Weston sisters of Massachusetts and their place in the emerging feminist movement. Although the Westons worked primarily in the New England area, they also campaigned for abolition among the liberals of Britain and Europe. Taylor's book is particularly strong for its examination of the Boston Female Anti-Slavery Society and its focus on abolitionist sentiment in Europe. Some of Taylor's claims, such as the allegation that organized anti-slavery activity in the United States declined after 1840, are highly debatable and her writing style is occasionally marred by odd phrasing. Nevertheless, this remains as one of the few books to attempt a comparative history of abolition.

Designed for a popular audience, LUTZ's book serves as a good introduction to women in public reform movements. Written in the style of a novel, this is a highly enjoyable bit of light reading. The endnotes are far too brief, but the bibliography is surprisingly extensive and may prove useful to researchers.

A perennially popular book, GURKO is now beginning to show its age. This book is a study of the women who united at the 1848 Seneca Falls Convention to protest the social, civil, and religious conditions and rights of women, but it also takes a broader look at the feminist movement in antebellum America. Since Gurko's publication, feminist scholars have extensively analyzed the motivations of female reformers, while others have uncovered the history of African-Americans. None of this new scholarship is reflected by Gurko and, except for mentions of African-Americans as the objects of antislavery agitation, her great neglect of black women is a serious fault. Gurko reprints the Declaration of Sentiments and Resolutions and includes a chronology of the (white) feminist movement to 1920.

DuBOIS offers a sophisticated study of the woman suffrage movement, focusing on how the vote generated a movement of increasing strength and vitality. In a book which has become required reading for every historian of women, DuBOIS shows how the beginnings of the demand for women's suffrage lie in the antislavery movement.

With crisp writing, she argues that the development of feminism before the Civil War was restrained by the organizational connection of its leaders with the abolition movement and how this bind kept activists from mobilizing women around a primary commitment to their own rights.

—CARYN E. NEUMANN

See also Women's Rights Convention, Seneca Falls, New York

Feminist Movements: Global

Basu, Amrita (ed.), *The Challenge of Local Feminisms: Women's Movements in Global Perspective,* Boulder, Colorado: Westview Press, 1995

Bulbeck, Chilla, *One World Women's Movement,* London: Pluto, and Winchester, Massachusetts: Unwin Hyman, 1988

Davies, Miranda (ed.), *Third World, Second Sex: Women's Struggles and National Liberation,* 2 vols., London and Atlantic Highlands, New Jersey: Zed Press, 1983–87

Mies, Maria, *Patriarchy and Accumulation on a World Scale: Women in the International Division of Labor,* London and Atlantic Highlands, New Jersey: Zed, 1986

Miles, Angela, *Integrative Feminisms: Building Global Visions, 1960s–1990s,* New York: Routledge, 1996

Morgan, Robin (ed.), *Sisterhood Is Global: The International Women's Movement Anthology,* Garden City, New York: Anchor Press/Doubleday, 1984; Harmondsworth: Penguin, 1985

Russell, Diana, and Nicole Van de Ven (eds.), *Crimes Against Women: Proceedings of the International Tribunal,* Millbrae, California: Les Femmes, 1976

Schuler, Margaret (ed.), *Empowerment and the Law: Strategies of Third World Women,* Washington, D.C.: OEF International, 1986

———, *Women, Law, and Development: Action for Change,* Washington, D.C.: OEF International, 1990

———, *Freedom from Violence: Women's Strategies from Around the World,* New York: OEF International, U.N. Development Fund for Women, 1992

Sen, Gita, and Caren Grown, *Development, Crises, and Alternative Visions: Third World Women's Perspectives,* New York: Monthly Review Press, 1987; London: Earthscan, 1988

Shiva, Vandana, *Staying Alive: Women, Ecology and Development,* London: Zed, 1988

Stienstra, Deborah, *Women's Movements and International Organizations,* London: Macmillan, and New York: St. Martin's Press, 1994

In the last few decades, feminism has developed into a truly global movement, shaped by and reflecting the interests of women in every region of the world. All over the world, women are engaged in feminist environmental, economic, health, housing, social justice, human rights, peace, anti-debt, pro-democracy, anti-violence, and anti-fundamentalist struggles of major proportions (to name only a few). The most current information about this is in the newsletters, manifestos, and other publications of the groups themselves. However, MORGAN provides over 800 pages of valuable accounts of women's condition and feminist history and movement in 68 countries, written by feminists from each country, and arranged alphabetically from Afghanistan to Zimbabwe. DAVIES has compiled two volumes of important interviews and articles, including group manifestos and statements, from Third World women and women's groups around such issues as women's political organization, the relation of women's struggles to national liberation movements, women's role in armed struggle, women's fate "after the revolution," and women's organizing against violence against women, around health and at work.

SCHULER presents three volumes of articles, including many case studies, from groups and individuals around the world, especially the Third World, on their strategic approaches to overcoming legal constraints (volume I), transforming development (volume II), and resisting violence against women (volume III). The material in these volumes supports Schuler's proposals for the systematic comparative global study of women's activism. BASU provides a collection of articles by scholar-activists invited to assess the distinctive characteristics, priorities, and achievements of the women's movements in their countries and to draw lessons of general significance. Articles are grouped regionally, four each from Asia, Africa, and Latin America, three from Europe, and one each from the Middle East and the United States. All these collections reveal the exciting variety of women's cultures and conditions, and their diverse strategic priorities, as well as the common interests and perspectives that underlie their commitment to global solidarity.

STIENSTRA provides a historical overview of the varied institutional forms of this solidarity, and the increasing diversity of the women involved, from the 1840s, when women organized at the World Anti-Slavery Convention in London, through women's organizing for suffrage, for peace, and for the establishment of the League of Nations in the early years of this century, to the most recent formative involvement of women from every region of the world in United Nations conferences and autonomous global networks.

More detailed information about global feminist analyses and visions, and the international dialogue that is forging them, is found in the manifestos, statements, journals, and reports of these conferences and global networks. Some of the work of these networks and conferences is published in books. For instance, the proceedings of the International Tribunal of Crimes Against Women in 1976 appear in RUSSELL and VAN DE VEN's work. The Tribunal brought together 2,000 women from 40 countries in one of the first international conferences of the second wave of feminism. The book reproduces the powerful testimonies that hundreds of diverse women made to the tribunal, as well as the resolutions and proposals for change, and debates that emerged. A number of long-term initiatives came out of this gathering, including the International Feminist Network, an action network that women in any country can call on for quick international support around urgent local issues.

The Third World women's network, Development Alternatives with Women for a New Era (DAWN), launched in Bangalore, India in 1984, grew partly out of these gatherings. SEN and GROWN appear as authors of what is actually a manifesto of the group, criticizing existing modes of "development" and offering alternative feminist visions. The book was disseminated and discussed widely by feminists in many regions and many networks, and made a formative contribution to global feminist analysis, particularly at the World Women's Congress in Nairobi in 1985, which closed the United Nations Decade for Women.

Burgeoning international dialogue has resulted in an emerging global feminist consensus around alternative, holistic, life-centred values and visions. MIES, in a feminist transmutation of Marxist theory, reveals the parallels between violent and expropriative colonization in the Third World and what she calls "housewifization" in the industrial world, highlighting the value of women's life-producing work in home and community, and women's historic resistance to these violent processes. SHIVA, influenced by Mohandas Gandhi, shows that "development," inspired and legitimized by a dualistic and destructive western scientific world view, has involved the colonization of nature as well as women, workers, and traditional cultures and communities. She presents feminism as an essentially holistic and ecological defense of all of human and non-human life, which links indigenous, anti-colonial, and women's struggles.

MILES provides a political and theoretical account of the development of global feminist perspectives and practices in both northern and southern hemispheres, emphasizing the transformative, women-centred nature of these feminisms, and their struggles not only to win women's equality, but to put women-associated work and concerns for all of life at the center of global priorities, and to build solidarity through the honouring of diversity. BULBECK outlines the challenges presented by this project and documents tensions stemming from the different perceptions and priorities of feminists in northern and southern hemispheres. She reports specifically on debates around the nature of patriarchy, the relation of race and gender oppression, and the critical understanding of colonialism, imperialism, and development. Both volumes have large and useful bibliographies.

—ANGELA MILES

See also Suffrage: Worldwide

Feminist Movements: Nineteenth Century

Behnke, Donna A., *Religious Issues in Nineteenth-Century Feminism*, Troy, New York: Whitston, 1982

Blair, Karen J., *The Clubwoman as Feminist: True Womanhood Redefined, 1868–1914*, New York and London: Holmes and Meier, 1980

Bolt, Christine, *The Women's Movements in the United States and Britain from the 1790s to the 1920s*, Amherst: University of Massachusetts Press, and London: Harvester, 1993

Epstein, Barbara Leslie, *The Politics of Domesticity: Women, Evangelicalism, and Temperance in Nineteenth-Century America*, Middletown, Connecticut: Wesleyan University Press, 1981

Gleadle, Kathryn, *The Early Feminists: Radical Unitarians and the Emergence of the Women's Rights Movement, 1831–1851*, New York: St. Martin's Press, and London: Macmillan, 1995

Hersh, Blanche Glassman, *The Slavery of Sex: Feminist-Abolitionists in America*, Urbana: University of Illinois Press, 1978

Kraditor, Aileen S., *The Ideas of the Woman Suffrage Movement, 1890–1920*, New York: Columbia University Press, 1965

Leach, William, *True Love and Perfect Union: The Feminist Reform of Sex and Society*, New York: Basic Books, 1980

Rendall, Jane, *The Origins of Modern Feminism: Women in Britain, France, and the United States, 1780–1860*, New York: Schocken, 1984; London: Macmillan, 1985

Wheeler, Marjorie Spruill, *New Women of the New South: The Leaders of the Woman Suffrage Movement in the Southern States*, New York: Oxford University Press, 1993

The word "feminism" entered the English language in the 1910s to describe women's seemingly new desire to break down, rather than simply expand the bounds of, a women's sphere. To use the word "feminism" to refer to nineteenth-century women's movements is, therefore, somewhat anachronistic. Nevertheless, as the above titles show, it is common for twentieth-century writers and readers to perceive certain nineteenth-century individuals and movements as direct ancestors to twentieth-century feminism. Whether they would have accepted the label or not, these nineteenth-century "feminists" were the more radical of the innumerable nineteenth-century women who sought to improve women's lives: they did not simply form mothers' societies, moral reform societies, or benevolent societies, but in some way or other sought to change the ground rules that women and men lived by. The books listed here are some of the more recent and comprehensive contributions to the ample literature on nineteenth-century women's movements. Together they illustrate the ongoing debates about the relation between the rise of specifically "feminist" ideas and other efforts to change the organization of society.

In the United States, organizations for women's rights emerged first among abolitionist women and a few of their male allies. These women discovered the depth of their political impotence when they sought to aid other women and men in an unpopular cause, and their increasing awareness of the civil and social position of the slave gave them a new analogy for thinking about their own condition. HERSH focuses on how the general moral idealism of the abolitionist movement, and its belief that social change can be accomplished through concerted effort and organization, enabled a cohort of women to insist on their right as women to determine the boundaries of their sphere of action for themselves. While they did not directly affect more than a small circle of women and men, Hersh concludes, these women's efforts to achieve equality not only in public arenas, but also in their marriages, make them inspiring foremothers.

GLEADLE similarly locates the origins of British feminism in a social reform movement: the "radical Unitarians" who broke off from mainstream Unitarianism to articulate a social, political, and cultural, as well as theological, critique of British society. At the heart of their movement, she suggests, was an awareness of the historical subordination of women to men and a commitment to establishing equality between the sexes. They did not, however, simply want women to be able to act like men, but also hoped that a reaffirmation of women's traditional values and priorities would contribute to a broader new vision of society.

RENDALL takes a cross-cultural perspective—examining the rise of women's organizations in Britain, France, and the United States—and argues that the early nineteenth-century drives for female autonomy and female association arose out of the mainstream of western cultural development, not from marginal groups. Her story begins with the Enlightenment, the American and French Revolutions, and the ideal of republican citizenship, all of which led to the idea that women, as mothers of citizens, must be educated and elevated if a republic based on reason and equality were to survive. She then turns to the evangelical movement, with its exaltation of submission and other feminine virtues, which gave women a privileged position within the church, and the church a privileged position within society. Subsequent chapters explore how these twin roots played themselves out in education, work, homes, and politics.

KRADITOR's book is one of the most influential in the field of nineteenth-century women's history, and deserves the status of a classic. Her central thesis is that while mid-century arguments for women's suffrage were based on claims of justice for a common humanity, later in the century, "expedient" arguments about the good that women (specifically white, middle-class, educated women) would do with the vote came to prevail. Women's suffrage became a popular movement among white, middle-class women only once it was divorced from other movements for social justice for blacks, immigrants, and the poor.

WHEELER takes this analysis several steps further in her study of southern suffragists, who claimed that women's suffrage, appropriately limited, could solve the "Negro problem" by reestablishing white supremacy without overtly disenfranchising blacks. The national leadership of the National American Woman Suffrage Association tacitly endorsed such arguments, although conflicts between northern and southern suffragists continued as the northerners turned toward a federal amendment, and the southerners resented both the amendment's abrogation of states' rights and the (correct) assumption that their states would not ratify the amendment.

BOLT's purposes are more comprehensively descriptive than schematically analytical. She is very wary of any oversimplification of the British and American women's movements, and her conclusions are carefully nuanced. Her comparative approach allows her to analyze the strengths and weaknesses of various strategies, and to identify which pitfalls might have been avoided and which were intrinsic to the historical situation. Her work is useful for anyone who wants a thorough overview of British and American women's movements through the 1920s.

Behnke and Leach both focus on specific aspects of feminist thought: Behnke on women's critical engagement with theology, and Leach on women's attempts to restructure sexuality and family life. The theological arguments over the nature of biblical authority, human nature, and the roots of women's subordination that BEHNKE chronicles may seem obscure to many late twentieth-century readers, but were vitally important in a society perfused by religious ideas. LEACH sometimes plays fast and loose with his category of "feminists," whom he never really defines, but he provides an interesting introduction to nineteenth-century thinking about sex and the body. These topics have produced much historical controversy, and much work has been done since Leach's book was published, but it remains a thought-provoking survey.

Epstein and Blair both discuss the meaning of widespread changes in ideas about women's proper place. EPSTEIN argues that antebellum women's religious experiences produced an increasingly explicit antagonism toward men, which led to moral crusades against certain forms of women's oppression. While the Woman's Christian Temperance Union came to endorse suffrage and various other feminist causes, Epstein concludes that its primary loyalty to the nuclear family ultimately blunted its attacks on male supremacy.

BLAIR describes the women's club movement as empowering women and leading them to a successful expansion of women's sphere far beyond its previous boundaries. While most club women used the ideology of women's sphere to support their claims for autonomy, their moderate "domestic feminism" raised a generation of daughters who were far more overtly rebellious. Both books provide useful reminders of the complex relation between "feminist" ideas and more mainstream efforts to improve women's lives.

—LORI KENSCHAFT

See also Feminist Movement, Abolitionist Origins of; Suffrage: Britain and Ireland; Suffrage: United States; Women's Rights Convention, Seneca Falls, New York

Feminist Movements: Twentieth Century

Badran, Margot, *Feminists, Islam, and the Nation: Gender and the Making of Modern Egypt*, Princeton, New Jersey: Princeton University Press, 1995

Cott, Nancy F., *The Grounding of Modern Feminism*, New Haven, Connecticut: Yale University Press, 1987

Echols, Alice, *Daring to Be Bad: Radical Feminism in America, 1967–1975*, Minneapolis: University of Minnesota Press, 1989

Kaplan, Gisela, *Contemporary Western European Feminism*, New York: New York University Press, 1992

Miller, Francesca, *Latin American Women and the Search for Social Justice*, Hanover, New Hampshire: University Press of New England, 1991

Rupp, Leila J., and Verta Taylor, *Survival in the Doldrums: The American Women's Rights Movement, 1945 to the 1960s*, New York: Oxford University Press, 1987

Stites, Richard, *The Women's Liberation Movement in Russia: Feminism, Nihilism, and Bolshevism, 1860–1930*, Princeton, New Jersey: Princeton University Press, 1977

Wieringa, Saskia (ed.), *Subversive Women: Women's Movements in Africa, Asia, Latin America, and the Caribbean*, New Delhi: Kali for Women, 1995

A global definition of feminism simply does not exist, for the reason that women's movements have never spoken with a single voice. From Indonesia to the United States, women have consistently defined liberation in widely differing ways. Yet most scholars do agree on a working description of feminism, as an awareness of women's oppression on domestic, social, economic, and political levels, accompanied by a willingness to struggle against such subjugation. However, what may be called "feminist" in one historical period, or in one particular political setting, is not necessarily denoted as feminist in another. The works considered in this essay contain definitions of feminism specific to the places and time periods that they address. The twentieth century has witnessed the flourishing of a number of feminisms. Far more than any other era, it has been the century of women's liberation.

As COTT writes, the word "feminism" only came into wide usage in the United States about 1910. She argues, in a fascinating book that has since become essential reading for historians of politics, that women's efforts in the 1910s and 1920s laid the groundwork and exposed the fault lines of modern feminism. Cott's history of the western definitions of feminism, part of the introduction, is worth the price of the book itself.

In another book that is widely judged to be a classic, RUPP and TAYLOR pick up the story of American feminism in the 1950s, exploring the persistence of the women's rights movement in a period generally considered devoid of feminist activism. This blend of history and sociology shows the ways in which the more radical women's movement of the 1960s was influenced by the successes and failures of the 1950s.

A work of social and intellectual history, ECHOLS's book explores the radical wing of the feminist movement from its emergence in the 1960s to its overshadowing by cultural feminism in the mid-1970s. Elements of radical feminism, such as the concepts of sexism and sexual politics, can be found in all branches of the second wave of the women's movement. Echols argues that radical feminists succeeded in pushing liberal feminists to the left, and leftists towards feminism.

STITES's book is an intellectual history of the women's movement in Russia, of which feminism was only a component. Russia had a deeply embedded antifeminist value system until the Soviet revolution. Stites's focus is on the Communist variety of women's liberation in Russia. In the second half of his book, he explores the impact of industrialization and urbanization upon women, and upon the shape of the women's movements that emerged at the opening of the twentieth century. This part assesses the limits of female equality achieved by Russian women up to about 1930, and relates the sexual revolution of the 1920s and its outcome to the larger question of women's roles in Soviet society. The section interpreting the Soviet liberation of women and its self-styled resolution of the woman question in the light of prerevolutionary dreams, achievements and failures, is particularly helpful in understanding the debates between feminists and Marxists.

Although BADRAN's work focuses on Egypt, its discovery of links between Islam and nationalism make it useful to explanations of all Middle Eastern women's movements. Badran argues that Middle Eastern feminist women, of the middle and upper classes, reconstructed Islam and nationalism to include a liberated role for women. As Egypt experienced increasing western economic and political intrusions, like so many other states in the region, Islamic modernists called upon Muslims to reexamine Islam in terms of contemporary realities. Women took up this challenge to rescue religion from narrow and incorrect interpretations, and made Islam a vital force in the Egyptian feminist movement. Nationalism involved a collective self-review as part of a national independence project. To this day, Egyptian feminism continues to affirm its Islamic and nationalist dimensions. Like Wieringa, Badran proves that feminism is not solely a western product.

MILLER's work is the first comprehensive history of women in Latin America, showing their role in the national liberation, democratic, and international feminist movements. She argues that a belief in women's different mission lies at the heart of feminist movements in Latin America, a conclusion supported by many other historians, and differentiates these movements from the form of feminism that developed in the United States and England. The book is particularly strong in its history of feminism in the Southern Cone countries (Argentina, Chile, and Uruguay). Miller's look at the women leaders of the Latin American grass roots movements of the 1980s is also quite good.

KAPLAN's survey provides an overview of the character and development of western European feminism in the post-World War II era. The emphasis of the book is on breadth and general trends rather than on in-depth analyses. Kaplan addresses the status and employment of women as affected by changes in education, technology, labor, and politics. The histories and contexts, strategies, structures, and cultures of women's movements in West Germany, Austria, Switzerland, France, Italy, Greece, Spain, Portugal, the Netherlands, Sweden, Norway, Denmark, Finland, and Iceland are outlined. Kaplan's 24-page bibliography will be particularly useful to anyone interested in locating more detailed studies about European women.

WIERINGA has edited an anthology of feminist writings from Peru, Trinidad and Tobago, Jamaica, Somalia, India, Indonesia, and the Sudan. This collection offers historical analyses of experiences of women involved in women's movements in their own countries in the final third of the twentieth century. Its central argument is that feminism is not a western concept only applicable to the struggles of western, white, middle-class women. The accounts of the women's movements in Indonesia, Somalia, and the Sudan all demonstrate the involvement of feminist women in nationalist causes. Wieringa's work also contains a challenge to traditional historical periodization. The decades generally categorized as those of the doldrums for feminist movements in the west, those years from 1920–60, saw feminism in Indonesia and the Sudan going through its most vigorous and subversive stages.

—CARYN E. NEUMANN

See also Feminist Movements: Global; National Woman's Party, United States; Suffrage: Britain and Ireland; Suffrage: United States; Suffrage: Worldwide; Women's Liberation Movement

Feminist Theory

see **Ecofeminism; Feminine Archetypal Theory; Feminism: Cultural; Feminism: Liberal; Feminism: Marxist/Socialist; Feminism: Postmodern; Feminism: Radical; Feminist Theory, Formative Works; Lesbian Studies; Literary Criticism, Feminist; Matriarchal Theory; Queer Theory; Womanism**

Feminist Theory, Formative Works

Beauvoir, Simone de, *The Second Sex,* 1949, translated by H.M. Parshley, New York: Knopf, 1952; London: Cape, 1953; originally published as *Le Dieuxième Sexe,* Paris: Gallimard, 1949

Christine de Pizan, *The Book of the City of Ladies,* 1405, translated by Earl Jeffrey Richards, New York: Persea, 1982; London: Pan, 1983

Friedan, Betty, *The Feminine Mystique,* New York: Norton, and London: V. Gollancz, 1963

Greer, Germaine, *The Female Eunuch,* London: McGibbon and Kee, 1970; New York: McGraw-Hill, 1971

Millett, Kate, *Sexual Politics,* New York: Doubleday, 1970; London: Hart-Davies, 1972

Wollstonecraft, Mary, *A Vindication of the Rights of Woman,* London: J. Johnson, and Boston: Thomas and Andrews, 1792; edited by Miriam Brody, Harmondsworth: Penguin, 1992

Woolf, Virginia, *A Room of One's Own,* London: Hogarth Press, and New York: Fountain Press, 1929

This is a selective listing of works that have had an impact on English speakers and that point to a series of "founding moments," rather than to a single, original moment in feminist history. Written before critiques of the unitary category of "woman" by lesbians and women of colour imposed themselves, these texts largely see women as an undifferentiated group. Although no longer cutting edge, these books are emphatically not to be relegated to the role of naïve antecedents: their theorising has made possible many current postmodern feminist concerns.

Although CHRISTINE's medieval text cannot be called "feminist" without considerable historical negotiation of the term, it has nevertheless become important for feminist readers of this century, especially those interested in the long history of protofeminist thought. Describing the building of a mythical *polis*, the City of Ladies, as a bulwark against misogyny, Christine contests misogyny's view of women's "natural" inferiority. Although she does this in equally problematic, essentialist ways, by pointing to the "natural" superiority of outstanding historical and mythical women, the framing of the text as the narrator's experience of misogyny opens it up to more complicated readings, anticipating later feminist concerns with the question of objective truth.

A work of philosophy, WOLLSTONECRAFT's book is a feminist intervention in the debates about citizenship and subjectivity stirred up by the French Revolution. This is the classic statement of women's rights as rational, human subjects. Although Wollstonecraft repudiates her own sex by excoriating women for their defects—their softness, feminine wiles, and lack of ambition—she nevertheless relentlessly questions stereotypes of female behaviour, proposing sexual difference as a man-made, not natural, distinction. Arguing that women should be subject to justice, not charity, and adamant that they take responsibility for their own lives, Wollstonecraft delivers a powerful critique of the social effects of excluding women from proper education and of denying them rationality.

WOOLF's elegant book is a minor tour de force, addressing the importance of economic and artistic autonomy for women's literary production, the difference of women's writing, and the need to record ordinary women's lives. The work, originally a series of lectures, puts style firmly on the agenda for feminists, recognising the impossibility of getting at a transparent "truth" about the situation of women. Although its twin ideals of the private room and androgyny have been criticised as sterile, the book can be seen as fruitfully exploring these ideals in terms of women's relationship to modernism and futures for feminism.

De BEAUVOIR's erudite, philosophical study is essential reading. "Book One" adapts G.W.F. Hegel's master-slave dialectic to argue that woman is man's "Other," pursuing this thesis across a range of disciplinary fields, including biology, history, and psychoanalysis. "Book Two" presents the study's other famous thesis, that gender is not natural but constructed: "One is not born, but rather becomes, a woman." The extent of the volume's debt to Sartrean existentialism, sometimes obscured in Parshley's translation, is no slavish copying—de Beauvoir's exposition of women as immanent and men as transcendent, and of true freedom as consisting in having an authentic "project," distinctly complicates Sartre's ontology by implicating the social and historical. De Beauvoir's considerable wit and irony are sometimes missed, as well as the fact that she does not set out to formulate a politics of identity, but to analyse sexual power relations. This remains the most incisive and wide-ranging twentieth-century feminist analysis of women's situation.

Although not a work of theory, FRIEDAN's charting of U.S. women's dissatisfaction with the ideal of "homemaking" in the late 1950s does at some level understand as ideological the myth of femininity promoted during that decade by advertising and women's magazines. Still useful for its critique of conservative functionalism in cultural anthropology and sociology, its mix of interviews and interpretation exemplifies a politically committed, feminist sociology. A conservative reformist, not a radical, Friedan believes strongly in women's equality and right to self-fulfilment.

MILLET's book is responsible for coining the term "sexual politics" to describe the unequal power relations between the sexes. Deliberately polemical, it argues that literary texts are political, and that literary criticism can be political too. Although challenged by some feminists for its totalising of "women" and "patriarchy," its humanist literary values, and its hostility toward Sigmund Freud, the book remains a landmark classic for demolishing the pieties of literary criticism and the novels of D.H. Lawrence in particular. Millett convincingly shows that in terms of literature, at least, the so-called sexual revolution of the 1960s was far from being a liberating event for women.

GREER's classic blueprint for women's liberation argues that all women are eunuchs in patriarchal society, castrated by their efforts to achieve a culturally determined ideal of femininity. Sharp, stylish, and unsentimental, the book debunks a number of middle-class values, including romance, romantic fiction, marriage and the family, arguing that traditional structures will have to change radically if there is to be any change in women's position. Freud gets short shrift (psychoanalysis is "a farrago of moralism and fantasy unilluminated by any shaft of commonsense"), but Greer does not ignore women's desires and sexual energy. Her revolutionary future of strong, independent femininity would be founded on women's understanding of their condition, sisterhood, and a sense of fun. Greer accepts the open-endedness and political risks of a feminist future. This book is an invaluable definition of the mood of a specific generation of feminism.

—RUTH EVANS

Feminization of Poverty

Buvinic, Mayra, Margaret Lycette, and William Paul McGreevey (eds.), *Women and Poverty in the Third World*, Baltimore: Johns Hopkins University Press, 1983
Glendinning, Caroline, and Jane Millar (eds.), *Women and Poverty in Britain: The 1990s*, New York and London: Harvester Wheatsheaf, 1992
Goldberg, Gertrude Schaffner, and Eleanor Kremen (eds.), *The Feminization of Poverty: Only in America?*, New York: Praeger, 1990
Scott, Hilda, *Working Your Way to the Bottom: The Feminization of Poverty*, London and Boston: Pandora Press, 1984
Zopf, Paul E., *American Women in Poverty*, New York: Greenwood, 1989

The feminization of poverty refers to a worldwide trend of women, and families supported by them, constituting the majority of the world's poor. More broadly, the concept refers to the complex forces that systematically keep women economically vulnerable. In her cross-national study, SCOTT argues that the singular nature of women's poverty derives from two facts. First, women have primary responsibility for child-rearing and domestic labor, activities that are classified as "unproductive work" by mainstream economics and hence receive no remuneration. Second, occupational segregation, sex discrimination, and sexual harassment limit women's income and economic mobility. Scott calls for a revisioning of society in a way that would transcend the division between the personal and the political, paid and unpaid work, monetized and nonmonetized values. According to Scott, the solution to the phenomenon of the feminization of poverty lies in such a fundamental transformation of society. Scott's readable and cogent work is among the very first books on an issue that was first "named" by Diana Pearce in an article in 1978.

In another cross-national study, edited by GOLDBERG and KREMEN, the focus is on the industrialized world, specifically Canada, Japan, France, Sweden, Poland, the former Soviet Union, and the United States. The authors use a four-factor framework, comprising labor-market factors that affect women's employment, policies that seek to promote the labor-market equality of women, social-welfare benefits or government income transfers, and demographic factors that contribute to the prevalence of single motherhood, for their analysis. The feminization of poverty is found to be most pronounced in the United States, especially among women of color, but it is present in the other countries to varying degrees. Rosenthal's chapter on Sweden shows that the low rate of women in poverty is primarily due to progressive legislation. Axinn's study of Japan reveals an absence of the feminization of poverty because of the general rarity of single-parent motherhood, although the potential for women's poverty remains high, given the social and economic discrimination women face. This book is an extremely useful and important study and has become a standard text.

BUVINIC, LYCETTE, and McGREEVEY examine issues of poverty facing women in the Third World. They argue that it is the Third World poor women's double roles of having to look after the household and contribute to the family income that makes poverty a women's issue. Women spend longer hours than men working, receive less pay for their work, and have more limited access to education than men, all of which result in a loss of women's productivity and contribution to the development process. Although a useful source of information on women in specific Third World countries, the book reflects an unquestioning acceptance of "development" as defined by mainstream economics, without an acknowledgment of the fact that it is this skewed vision of development as economic growth that is responsible for the increasing economic marginalization of poor Third World women. There is little awareness, too, of the fact that poverty is a phenomenon that affects women in the industrialized world as well.

In a systematic study of the feminization of poverty in the United States, ZOPF offers demographic and sociological analyses of statistical data on the U.S. population, differentiated by age, race, ethnicity, farm and nonfarm residence, and urban and nonurban residence. Zopf points to an economy that denies women equity in job and wage opportunities, and to inadequate governmental financial support that together are responsible for and exacerbate the poverty that women and children face. According to Zopf, poverty in the United States disproportionately affects women and children largely because of the increasing number of female-headed households in which there is no husband present (because men's median income is significantly higher than women's) and that have much smaller incomes than married-couple families (where in a majority of cases both spouses work for wages). The presence of dependent children also contributes to high poverty rates in female-headed families, both because children cost money to raise, and because their presence restricts women's ability to get full-time employment, especially in the absence of affordable childcare. When couples divorce, on average, the men's economic status is unaffected or may improve, whereas women's economic well-being deteriorates drastically. In this significant contribution to the scholarship of the feminization of poverty, Zopf argues for a sounder, more effective welfare system that can help keep people out of poverty and off welfare at the same time. Zopf also makes a persuasive case for structural changes in the "occupational-industrial complex" that would ensure decent wages and the elimination of gender discrimination. The work is useful to scholars, policy analysts, and activists interested in social policy in general and the issue of the feminization of poverty in particular.

Offering an analysis of the causes, extent, and consequences of women's poverty in Britain, GLENDINNING and MILLAR argue that the gender division of labor, which relegates women's primary role to the home and men's primary role to the labor market, is fundamentally responsible for women's increasing poverty. Women receive no pay for their work at home and low pay for the work they do outside of the home—a pattern that legitimates the assumption that women's economic dependence on men is desirable. Two chapters in the book, by Juliet Cook and Shantu Watt, and by Hilary Graham, focus on the significance of race in the phenomenon of poverty. Racism and sexism permeate social policy in Britain, and black women have been unable to rely on state support to fight poverty. Jane Lewis and David Pachud, through a historical analysis of the prevalence of poverty, contend that the feminization of poverty is not a recent phenomenon—women have always constituted a majority of the poor in the last century, although the composition of female poverty has changed. Whereas married women were the largest group of women in poverty in the early part of this century, single women, especially among the elderly, are at highest risk today. The book as a whole also points to the increased risk of poverty and economic handicap that women with children face. A significant contribution to the scholarship on the feminization of poverty, this book is a critical resource for anyone with an interest in social policy.

—PRIYA A. KURIAN

See also Poverty; Welfare

Film, Images of Women in

Cook, Pam, and Dodd Philip (eds.), *Women and Film: A Sight and Sound Reader*, London: Scarlet Press, and Philadelphia: Temple University Press, 1993

De Lauretis, Teresa, *Alice Doesn't: Feminism, Semiotics, Cinema*, Bloomington: Indiana University Press, and London: Macmillan Press, 1984

Haskell, Molly, *From Reverence to Rape: The Treatment of Women in the Movies*, Harmondsworth and New York: Penguin, 1973; revised edition, Chicago and London: University of Chicago Press, 1987

Kuhn, Annette, *Women's Pictures: Feminism and Cinema*, Boston and London: Routledge and Kegan Paul, 1982

Mulvey, Laura, *Visual and Other Pleasures*, Bloomington: Indiana University Press, and London: Macmillan, 1989

Tasker, Yvonne, *Spectacular Bodies: Gender, Genre and the Action Cinema*, London and New York: Routledge, 1993

Feminist film criticism first appeared in the 1970s, having emerged out of the women's movement. Initial investigations focused on defining and identifying positive and negative portrayals of women, critiquing the stereotyping of female characters, and theorising the lack of semblance between film images of women and the actuality of women's experiences. First published in 1973 and extended in its second edition, HASKELL's descriptive survey of a vast number of films is typical of this approach. Concentrating mainly on Hollywood films (although including some discussions of European productions), Haskell assesses the changing nature of cinematic images of women from the 1920s through to the 1980s. She argues that women were idealised in films of the 1920s and 1930s, but by the 1960s they were increasingly subjected to violent attack and victimisation on screen. During the 1970s and 1980s, when the male action genre predominated, women were, according to Haskell, practically invisible. Haskell argues that the way in which women have been represented on screen is largely a reflection of male fantasy and misogyny.

As the 1970s progressed and feminist film criticism moved to consider psychoanalytic and semiotic theories of the text, the function that "woman" performed in film narrative as a "sign," along with how film spectators were encouraged to look at this "woman-as-sign," became of central analytical concern. Chapter Three of MULVEY's book reproduces the extremely influential article that set this debate in motion. Drawing on Freudian theory, Mulvey argues that the female figure within classic Hollywood film is constructed as an erotic spectacle "to-be-looked-at" by both the central male character and the male cinema spectator. Thus, the cinematic gaze is theorised as being male. Iconographically, the woman's image represents sexual difference, but her lack of a penis has the potential to arouse unpleasurable castration anxiety in the unconscious of the male spectator. Therefore, according to Mulvey, the female character is treated as a guilty object to be voyeuristically punished and/or fetishised by the camera.

DE LAURETIS also uses psychoanalytic and semiotic theories in her analysis of film representations of women. Yet she challenges the hierarchical assumptions of these analytical tools and therefore presents a feminist rereading of them in developing her theory of film. De Lauretis argues that cinema, in servicing male subjectivity, constructs "woman" as an object and contains her within the signs of femininity. She also argues that women as historical subjects are not represented in the cinema. Consequently, female film viewers are theorised as only able to gain pleasure from popular mainstream movies by denying the contradictions between their historical experiences of patriarchy and cinema's privileging of feminine subjectivity. This is a seminal text in feminist film criticism, which includes analyses of Nicholas Roeg's film *Bad Timing* and Michael Snow's avant-garde project *Presents*.

KUHN assesses various links between feminism and cinema. Her methodology is contextual in approach, and she therefore includes a useful explanation of what constitutes "dominant cinema" in terms of social, historical, and economic contexts, and structures of production, distribution, and exhibition. There follows an explanation of how images of women in film can be analysed in relation to a film's textual characteristics, and how Lacanian psychoanalysis and theories of ideology inform feminist analyses of woman as a signifier in cinema. Kuhn then considers how film can reflect feminist interests and desires and examines various images of women and spectator-text relationships in "New Hollywood" and social realist cinemas, feminist documentary films, and deconstructive cinema. This book provides a lucid explanation of the premises of feminist film theory and offers an excellent demonstration of how film images of women can be considered in relation to contexts of production, distribution, and reception.

TASKER's analysis of gender representations in the action movie genre provides a detailed critique of films that place the female hero at the centre of the narrative. Tasker argues that in portraying women as aggressive and very often muscular, films such as *Terminator 2*, *Aliens*, and *Thelma and Louise* suggest a potential challenge to traditional masculine/feminine binary oppositions. Yet the action movie never realises this potential, because the female body is portrayed as vulnerable to violent penetration, if not in the form of actual rape, then in its symbolic representation. The book also includes analyses of film images of black women, with a particular focus on Whoopi Goldberg's detective character in *Fatal Beauty*. Tasker's text-based arguments are underpinned by contemporary theories of the body and gender, and also film genre criticism.

COOK and DODD's edited collection provides insight into both the breadth and depth of recent writing on women and film. All originally published in the *Sight and Sound* film magazine since 1990, the articles cover issues such as female stars and their film characters; film representations of black and white women, lesbians, queers, and daughters; femininity; female filmmakers; and a variety of film genres. Cook's introductory chapter summarises many focal points of feminist film criticism, and in its entirety this book demonstrates the complex relationship that women have with the cinema, and the variety of ways in which that relationship can be discussed. Largely because it avoids the theoretical terminology of much feminist film theorising, and because it reflects a certain enthusiasm for the medium, this book provides an ideal starting point for those beginning to investigate how women have been imagined in and by the cinema from its beginnings to the present day.

—C. KAY WEAVER

Filmmaking

Acker, Ally, *Reel Women: Pioneers of the Cinema, 1896 to the Present*, London: Batsford, and New York: Continuum, 1991

Attwood, Lynne (ed.), *Red Women on the Silver Screen: Soviet Women and Cinema from the Beginning to the End of the Communist Era*, London: Pandora Press, 1993

Foster, Gwendolyn Audrey, *Women Film Directors: An International Bio-critical Dictionary*, Westport, Connecticut: Greenwood, 1995

Frieden, Sandra (ed.), *Gender and German Cinema: Feminist Interventions*, 2 vols., Providence, Rhode Island, and Oxford: Berg, 1993

Heck-Rabi, Louise, *Women Filmmakers: A Critical Reception*, Metuchen, New Jersey: Scarecrow Press, 1984

Kuhn, Annette, and Susannah Radstone (eds.), *Women in Film: An International Guide*, London and New York: Fawcett Columbine, 1991

Rosenberg, Jan, *Women's Reflections: The Feminist Film Movement*, Ann Arbor, Michigan: UMI Press, and Epping: Bowker, 1983

Sullivan, Kaye, *Films for, by, and about Women*, Metuchen, New Jersey: Scarecrow Press, 1980

The general historical impression of the film industry is that it has been a man's industry, that women's overall involvement with the filmmaking process during the industry's first century was limited to acting, costuming, and assisting with scripts—but ultimately to buying the tickets and viewing. Another general historical impression is that female filmmakers came into existence in the early to mid-1970s. Both impressions are misleading. Since the 1970s, these notions have been challenged. Women have been in key filmmaking roles (writing, directing, producing, distributing, and even studio ownership) since the birth of film in the 1890s. Women, in fact, have been a part of all facets of the movie industry, from acting to directing; they have been a part of it always.

This has been as true for the United States as it has been for Europe and the former Soviet Union. However, it has not been true for Germany, as FRIEDEN's two volumes testify. While the emphasis is on films by women, she neatly ties the close connection between masculinity and femininity in German film. The text has a Marxist as well as feminist bent, and this too emphasizes the historical exclusion of female filmmakers from the industry until the 1960s. Politically, the former Soviet Union had a completely different attitude toward women in its claim to be the first country to publicly embrace men and women as equal, and this supposedly included filmmakers.

ATTWOOD has compiled a book that was only truly possible since the ending of the Cold War. Attwood covers a large scope, from the treatment of women in Soviet history to interviews of Soviet female filmmakers. The book is, unfortunately, limited, perhaps because it tries to cover too much—too many years covered, too many types of women (from directors to critics) interviewed, and too many over-generalizations made. The book is an excellent start, but it is only just a start, which has inspired more in-depth research and writing.

The same could said of other earlier works. HECKRABI's work is also limited, but an excellent start. She covers eleven filmmakers from all over the world, mostly from the earlier part of the twentieth century. Her intention seems to be to emphasize that female filmmakers have always existed, but she also seems to be attempting to define the "true" feminist filmmaker. She even makes a list of characteristics that include looks and marital status.

ROSENBERG provides a more detailed portrayal of feminist filmmakers. She covers more depth in time, quality, and number. Her approach is more overtly political and logical. SULLIVAN seemed to recognize the limitations of one book, but her approach is also limited. She does not so much attempt a historical or critical narrative as she does a kind of high quality encyclopedia—the films are listed in alphabetical order.

ACKER recognizes that her single volume is incomplete, and she intends to generate a second book. The book's table of contents is more resourceful than any of the earlier works, recognizing the multiple roles of filmmakers and the permutation of female influence and impact throughout the entire industry's history. She covers both the obvious as well as lesser-known female filmmakers—pointing out such significant historical markers as the fact that the first film director was a woman and that women practically controlled the industry during the silent era. This is an excellent history.

Another excellent text, although more an encyclopedia than a history text, is KUHN and RADSTONE'S international guide, which provides over six hundred biographical and critical entries. It is, however, much more than an encyclopedia, attempting to cover film movements, festivals, terminology, studios, and theory. Contributors include filmmakers, critics, and scholars from all over the world; contributors frequently add a list for further reading. Full of some great photographs and bits of trivia, the book is one of the most comprehensive.

FOSTER also provides a text with an international focus, although limited to just directors. The limitation, in this case, is useful since it allows Foster to go into greater depth on the history and nature of female film directors from all over the world. While the text is biased toward western film directors and is incomplete in its coverage of minorities, it is still a very comprehensive survey, containing both biographical and critical entries.

—CAROL L. ROBINSON

Flaubert, Gustave 1821–1880

French Writer

Culler, Jonathan, *Flaubert: The Uses of Uncertainty*, London: P. Elek, and Ithaca, New York: Cornell University Press, 1974

Diamond, Marie J., *Flaubert: The Problem of Aesthetic Discontinuity*, Port Washington, New York, and London: Kennikat Press, 1975

Donato, Eugenio, *The Script of Decadence: Essays on the Fictions of Flaubert and the Poetics of Romanticism*, Oxford: Oxford University Press, 1992; New York: Oxford University Press, 1993

Gervais, David, *Flaubert and Henry James: A Study in Contrasts*, London: Macmillan, and New York: Barnes and Noble, 1978

Ramazani, Vaheed K., *The Free Indirect Mode: Flaubert and the Poetics of Irony*, Charlottesville: University Press of Virginia, 1988

To date there has not yet appeared a monograph devoted solely to the question of how Gustave Flaubert portrayed women in his nineteenth-century novels. Yet, this issue has been addressed by Flaubert analysts in conjunction with other literary questions involving language and style. All literary analysts assume an excellent knowledge on the part of their readers of Flaubert's life and times.

The CULLER book provides the biographical background essential for English readers to know Flaubert and his works as translated from French. This book should allow an appreciation for other books, which go beyond to larger issues of aestheticism, style, the uses of language and voice, the uses of history, and the characterizations within Flaubert's novels. Culler establishes Flaubert in the honorable position of having established the autonomy of the novel. As a romantic, Flaubert defied certain romantic conventions used by other writers in the nineteenth century, and by defying convention, or experimentally moving beyond them, in many ways Flaubert was a pioneer in the movement toward the development of realism in the novel. Gustave Flaubert was born in Rouen, France, and his father was Chief Surgeon of L'Hotel Dieu. In 1842 Flaubert went to Paris to study law, where he began writing *Education Sentimentale,* which was later published in 1869, but he failed his exams. He continued his writing and began in 1848 *The Temptation of Saint Anthony.* He traveled with his friend Du Camp to Italy, Greece, and the Middle East for eighteen months, and returned to write *Madame Bovary,* later published in the *Reve de Paris* in 1856. Also in 1856 he revised *The Temptation of Saint Anthony* and parts were published, later to be published in full in 1874. In 1857 he was brought to trial for writing *Madame Bovary* but was acquitted of immorality and heresy by the courts. In 1858 Flaubert traveled to Tunis and the site of Carthage and completed *Salammbo* which was published in 1862. He enjoyed a wide reputation and was prominent in French society, being named Chevalier de la Legion d' Honneur in 1866. Flaubert began *Bouvard et Pecuchet,* and it was published after his death at Croisset in 1880. What Culler presents as a first-rate biography acts as a foundation for other Flaubert studies.

DIAMOND best examines Flaubert the artist and the development of his female character Madame Bovary. Diamond also best addresses the issue of aesthetic discontinuity in Flaubert's writing, or the appearance of Flaubert's idealism in some scenes paralleled by contemptuous materialism in others. It is perhaps in the tension or movement between these two worldviews that the reader can best appreciate the transition between romanticism and realism or modernism in Flaubert's works. Diamond explains the maturation of Flaubert's aestheicism by examining his writings in chronological order, and she is more interested in explaining his representation of female characters such as Marie in *Novembre,* which was somewhat autobiographical. Marie had early in the story been portrayed as a madonna figure, sainted and sacred; then later in the work Marie became an enchantress dressed in black satin with malevolent eyes, her embrace likened to that of a wild animal. Flaubert's characterization of Marie, suggests Diamond, was based on his early experiences with Elisa Schlesinger, with whom he fell in love as an adolescent on a Tourville beach. Flaubert often cast his female heroines as ideals and then destroyed them in a classical tragic sense.

One of the first critics of Flaubert was Henry James, and the GERVAIS volume interprets the contrasting styles between these two famed writers. Several sections are significant, such as James's reading of *Madame Bovary,* Emma Bovary in Her World, and Flaubert's Art: Beauty versus Tragedy? James confronted Flaubert essentially on the differences in their philosophies and the Gervais book attempts to analyze their variant beliefs and views of tragedy in novels, especially *Madame Bovary.*

RAMAZANI examines Flaubert's style and explains his use of verbal irony and situational irony, free indirect discourse, and free indirect mode, which were used as different voices or means of communicating between the novel's characters and the reader. Ramazani offers the famous bedroom mirror scene in *Madame Bovary* as an example of verbal irony. Emma Bovary is married, yet she rejoices in her first adulterous affair; she is a romantic lusting after romantic love, only to ultimately find melancholy disenchantment and death.

DONATO's book is based on a general discussion of several of Flaubert's works, including *Bouvard and Pecuchet, The Temptation of Saint Anthony,* and *Madame Bovary,* and it offers an analysis of Flaubert's characters, many of the most famous of whom were women. The opening chapter titled "Flaubert and the Quest for Fiction" includes Flaubert's own view of the Queen of Sheba. This woman, as drawn by Flaubert's pen, was powerful as a ruler, a controller of wealth and position, but also a seductress and temptress. The Queen of Sheba represented, for Flaubert, all women could possibly desire in fiction or fact, dream or reality. Women for Flaubert often represented the passions of the romantics—love, beauty and refinement. They also represented the coming of realism in literature, as Madame Bovary was at first enthralled by passionate romantic desire for a lover and later became disenchanted and disillusioned by the reality of her situation.

Flaubert was powerfully drawn to the historical past and to exotic places for many of his characters, as he was drawn to Carthage and used this site as the backdrop for his female character in *Salammbo,* which is discussed by Donato in chapter two. Throughout Donato's volume, references are made to the correspondence Flaubert had with many female friends, such as Madame Regnier, Louise Colet, and George Sand, and this correspondence reveals Flaubert's desire to achieve stylistic perfection in his fiction, as he searched for *le mot juste* (right word). Donato suggests that Flaubert was too complex in his motives, and his characters too heterogeneous, for simple answers to questions of style and theme. Flaubert was also too complex for his motives to be simplified in regard to women, as he was at the same time attracted to both the sacredness and lustfulness of his feminine characters and to the women in his personal life.

—BARBARA BENNETT PETERSON

Fonteyn, Margot 1919–1991

British Dancer

Anthony, Gordon, *Ballerina: Further Stories of Margot Fonteyn,* London: Home and Van Thal, 1945

Bland, Alexander, *Fonteyn and Nureyev: The Story of a Partnership,* London: Orbis, and New York: Times, 1979

Chappell, William, *Fonteyn: Impressions of a Ballerina,* London: Springbooks, and New York: Macmillan, 1951

Fisher, Hugh, *Margot Fonteyn,* London: Adam and Charles Black, 1952

Money, Keith, *The Art of Margot Fonteyn,* London: M. Joseph, and New York: Reynal, 1965

———, *Fonteyn: The Making of a Legend,* London: Collins, 1973; New York: Reynal, 1974

———, *Fonteyn and Nureyev: The Great Years,* London: Harvill, and New York: HarperCollins, 1994

The ballerina is the figure who is traditionally the pinnacle of the ballet. One of the female soloists who earned the title "ballerina" was Margot Fonteyn. MONEY (1966) writes about the roles most satisfying for Margot Fonteyn. He uses many quotes and dialogue that give the reader some clue to Fonteyn's mental approach, as well as to her reaction to such profoundly beautiful works as "Symphonic Variations." This book not only takes the reader on a journey of Fonteyn's greatest roles, but leads the reader progressively through the multiple images of Fonteyn in each role. Throughout the book, Money interjects random comments that reflect a subtle emphasis, a suggestion of her particular development.

MONEY's book (1974) provides a guide path to an astonishing life. The milestones of Margot Fonteyn's life are clearly marked, not only by the pictorial index of roles at the end of the book, but also by the numerous photographs throughout. Some of the photographs may appear familiar to the reader; however, a high proportion actually made their debut in this book. The author gives the reader a somewhat comprehensive view of Margot Fonteyn's life. This work has validity both historically and as an inspiration to younger generations.

MONEY (1994) tries to do three things: to tell the story of this great partnership much more completely than has been done before, to describe Fonteyn and Nureyev's way of working on stage and off, and to give his own assessment of their gifts and achievements. Money also adds some comments and opinions from some dancers, choreographers, and others who have worked with the pair. He tries to give the reader a glimpse of the extraordinary magic of Fonteyn and Nureyev's performances.

Partnering in dance is a form of pair-bonding, like marriage (although somewhat more ephemeral). BLAND writes about a partnership of two dancers, Margot Fonteyn and Rudolf Nureyev, that was harmonious, fruitful, and famous. Their presence together on the dance scene was immediately electrifying and lastingly dominant. This book is a tribute to (and to some extent a record of) that elusive phenomenon. The account of its development can only be partial, because a complete account of the activities of Fonteyn and Nureyev would require an international research team to compile and more space than this volume to write down. This narrative serves only as a kind of temporal skeleton supporting a rich and varied succession of performances in many parts of the world. In Bland's accounts of the 26 dance pieces, varying from full-length classics to brief duets, which Fonteyn and Nureyev have performed together, he has used quotations from articles written by many critics who were present at their performances. This is especially good, because the view of a single writer is less illuminating than a chorus of mixed voices.

ANTHONY pays tribute to the dancer. He not only discusses her relationship with the company, but also paints a picture of Fonteyn in the classroom, in the unglamorous testing atmosphere of rehearsals. He writes about her sense of order, the organization of her day, her punctuality, the arrangement of her dressing room, the darning and patching of her tights, and her fastidious and original taste in clothes. The reader gets a great deal of insight into the ballerina.

The reader who looks to CHAPPELL's work for a biography of Margot Fonteyn will be disappointed. The subtitle describes the book as a study of Fonteyn rather than a biography. By this study the reader can become aware of the immense complexity of the art of ballet and its exponent, as well as the ballerina herself. The book is filled with photographs that give a true, harmonious, and compelling visual rendering of the beauty of a ballerina and the immediate decor of her life in her work. The assistance of the photographs gives the reader an in-depth look at Margot Fonteyn.

FISHER's book captures how Margot Fonteyn became a ballerina of international fame and reputation. Fisher tells of her early years with the Vic-Wells Ballet. He illustrates the progress she showed with each season and the powers of expression and feeling she brought to her art. The strongest part of this book is the discussion of the range of parts Fonteyn has danced throughout her career. The reader gets a sense of the impeccable technique, sincerity, and beauty Fonteyn brought to her art.

—SUSAN M. TAYLOR

Frame, Janet 1924–

New Zealand Writer

Dalziel, Margaret, *Janet Frame,* Wellington: Oxford University Press, 1980

Delbaere-Garant, Jeanne (ed.), *Bird, Hawk, Bogie: Essays on Janet Frame,* Aarhus: Dangaroo, 1978

——— (ed.), *The Ring of Fire: Essays on Janet Frame,* Sydney: Dangaroo, 1992

Evans, Patrick, *Janet Frame,* Boston: Twayne, 1977

Mercer, Gina, *Janet Frame: Subversive Fictions,* Dunedin: University of Otago Press, 1994

Panny, Judith Dell, *I Have What I Gave: The Fiction of Janet Frame,* Wellington: Brasell, 1992; New York: Braziller, 1993

Although Janet Frame is one of New Zealand's most celebrated authors, there have been few books written about her work. Most Frame scholarship consists of articles and essays found in literary journals, newspapers, and magazines. Some critics have attributed this dearth of book material to the level of difficulty of Frame's oeuvre, arguing that few have understood the full scope of her work; others suggest that she is difficult to place in the contemporary literary scene because she writes "against" literary tradition.

EVANS was the first to produce an extended analysis of Frame's work in book form. Although biographical information on Frame was limited at the time Evans's book was published, he presents particular phases in her life as a backdrop to her writings. He discusses her fiction (up to 1972, including *Daughter Buffalo)* chronologically, arguing that themes in her early fiction are further developed in her later work. He comments on Frame's "literary development" since her first publication, and highlights the influence her overseas experience has had upon her later work. The book ends with a discussion of Frame's place in the New Zealand literary tradition and in the wider context of post-war society. Evans has also produced a student guide to Frame's novels entitled *An Inward Sun: The Novels of Janet Frame* (not listed here). This booklet provides short plot summaries, character descriptions, and lists of questions to prompt discussion and critical thinking.

DALZIEL undertakes a formalist and thematic study of Frame's writings. She analyses Frame's fiction in chronological order from *The Lagoon* to *Living in the Maniototo*, arguing that themes from her earliest work can be traced throughout her fiction. These themes include the lives of various members of society, with a particular focus on children, the "deranged," the "solitary," and the "unsuccessful;" the experience of the writer is another early theme developed further in Frame's later work. The book is divided into three sections: the first deals with action and character, the second with language, and the third focuses on Frame's critical "vision" of society. Although Dalziel argues that characters often become mouthpieces for Frame's own views on culture and social identity, she also suggests that Frame, like T.S. Eliot, believes that a work of art creates its own "self subsistent world" rather than reflecting the artist's personal experience.

DELBAERE-GARANT has edited two collections of essays on Frame's writings. In the first collection, *Bird, Hawk, Bogie*, the majority of these contributions focus on individual Frame novels, and are arranged in chronological order according to each novel's date of publication. There are also two more general essays, and an introduction in which Delbaere summarizes each essay and comments on particular aspects of Frame's work. Delbaere highlights the dual nature of Frame's vision of society, focusing on her opposition of "this world" and "that world:" the world of conformists and the world of outcasts, visionaries and artists. Delbaere suggests that all contributors have recognized the tension between Frame's "passionate longing for oneness" and her conviction that the "limited vision" characteristic of contemporary western society precludes any kind of lasting unity. Delbaere's later collection of essays, *The Ring of Fire*, includes all the essays and the introduction from the previous volume, but adds a number of new essays discussing Frame's novels produced since *Bird, Hawk, Bogie* was first published. Articles on *Living in the Maniototo*, *The Carpathians* and the autobiographical novels are thus added to the original list. Delbaere argues that we can find in Frame's later work traces of the "new confidence" she has gained since becoming one of New Zealand's most celebrated authors. This volume also contains an extensive annotated bibliography, which is a useful starting point for anyone interested in Frame and her writings.

PANNY aims to offer a new perspective on Frame's fiction, arguing that there is extensive allegorical patterning in Frame's work. Panny claims that in Frame's prose fiction, there are clues linking plot, situation, and character to earlier books, myths, and concepts. Thus, for example, in *The Edge of the Alphabet*, Toby Withers's trip to London and back is patterned on Orpheus's descent into the underworld. Further, Panny argues that Frame often parodies these earlier texts and stories through exaggeration and inversion. Panny analyses Frame's eleven novels and her short story "Snowman, Snowman," firstly in terms of the "literal significance" of each text, with attention to key words and images, and secondly by considering the "figurative implications," revealing the allegorical aspects of each work. She claims that while many previous critics have recognized Frame's "linguistic virtuosity," they have overlooked the "humor and subtle irony" that emerges through an allegorical reading of her work.

MERCER presents a feminist angle on Frame's writing, arguing that Frame writes from the position of "other," of those who are "marginalized" in contemporary western culture. Mercer claims that Frame writes against the patterns of domination and exclusion enforced by patriarchal society. She suggests that Frame subverts these patterns by writing about taboo subjects and drawing attention to language as a weapon that reinforces oppositions between the powerful and the powerless. Frame overcomes the "problem of language" by constructing new languages or even removing language altogether, as is the case in *The Carpathians.* Mercer also applies Irigaray's theories on female sexuality and identity to Frame's work, arguing that multiplicity, fluidity, and dynamism are central to Frame's writing. Mercer claims that one of the reasons why Frame has received little critical attention is because she defies and subverts literary conventions, "playing games" with her readers. Mercer's approach is refreshingly inventive: her chapter on *Living in the Maniototo*, for example, is presented as a dramatic dialogue between herself, Frame's characters, and various well-known literary figures. Her comments on the cryptic nature of Frame's writings serve as a challenge to other critics who may wish to unlock further meanings and associations within Frame's work.

—MICHELLE KEOWN

Franklin, Rosalind, 1920–1958 and the DNA Controversy

British Biophysicist

Baldwin, Joyce, *DNA Pioneer: James Watson and the Double Helix,* New York: Walker, 1994

Crick, Francis, *What Mad Pursuit: A Personal View of Scientific Discovery,* New York: Basic Books, 1988

Judson, Horace Freeland: *The Eighth Day of Creation: Makers of the Revolution in Biology,* New York: Simon and Schuster, 1969

Newton, David E., *James Watson and Francis Crick: Discovering the Double Helix and Beyond,* New York: Facts on File, 1992

Olby, Robert C., *The Path to the Double Helix,* London: Macmillan, and Seattle: University of Washington Press, 1974

Portugal, Franklin H., and Jack S. Cohen, *A Century of DNA: A History of the Discovery of the Structure and Function of the Genetic Substance,* Cambridge, Massachusetts: MIT Press, 1977

Sayre, Anne, *Rosalind Franklin and DNA,* New York: Norton, 1975

Watson, James D., *The Double Helix: a Personal Account of the Discovery of the DNA Molecule: Commentary, Reviews, Original Papers,* edited by Gunther S. Stent, London: Weidenfeld and Nicholson, 1981

Discovery of DNA's molecular structure opened the way to direct manipulation of processes of heredity, that is, modern molecular biology. Many historians of science rate this discovery second only in importance to Charles Darwin's theory of evolution. Rosalind Franklin, along with Francis Crick, James Watson, and Maurice Wilkins, made the discovery, communicating with one another, but hardly working in cooperation. Crick and Watson formally published the structure of the DNA molecule in 1953.

In 1962 Crick, Watson, and Wilkins received the Nobel Prize in "physiology or medicine" for the discovery, but Franklin was never so honored. Her receiving a Nobel Prize jointly with the others would have violated the Nobel rule prohibiting the sharing of an individual prize by more than three persons. Also she could not receive a prize after her death in 1958, because Nobel Prizes are not granted posthumously. Her personal conflict with Wilkins and Watson's portrayal of her in *The Double Helix* has generated controversy over her contribution to the DNA project. This, in addition to the treatment of women in British scientific research establishments at the time, has made her a feminist icon.

WATSON's uninhibited account of how he and Francis Crick outmaneuvered Maurice Wilkins and Rosalind Franklin is an enduring classic in both the history and psychology of science. Watson's highly colored version of scientific and personal interchanges is unrestrained and was offensive to most of those mentioned in the text. Rosalind Franklin is painted as a narrow, unimaginative experimentalist and the butt of all jokes. The plots and counter plots of scientists competing for credit and glory are laid bare. The book also is the source of most of the controversy over Rosalind Franklin's role in the DNA discovery, and as to whether she suffered discrimination.

Gunther Stent's 1981 edition of Watson's book includes essays by Stent, Francis Crick, and Linus Pauling. Crick reviews initial reactions to his and Watson's two papers advancing the double helix model, and to contemporary work by Pauling, Wilkins and Franklin. He concludes that, without Watson, he could not have created the model, but that Pauling probably soon would have. Also, in his opinion, Franklin was only two steps away from the solution when she left the project in 1954 to work on the Tobacco Mosaic Virus. He also refers to Watson's book as a vivid autobiographical fragment rather than a scholarly historical account. Pauling reviews his own attempts to develop a "triple helix" model for nucleic acids. He acknowledges that, had he begun work on the double helix rather than the triple helix model, he might have succeeded. He also states that he might have thought of the Watson-Crick structure within a few weeks of seeing Wilkins's X-ray diffraction photographs of DNA. Pauling finally concludes that without Watson and Crick's persistent effort, with advice from Jerry Donohue on nitrogen bases and hydrogen bonds and with access to the Wilkins photographs, the discovery of the double helix might have been delayed several years. Aaron Klug summarizes not only Franklin's publicly known ideas and observations on DNA structure but her unpublished papers and notebooks. These show that her reputed rejection of a helical structure of the molecule resulted from careful consideration of all possible structures for the molecule. She felt that the solution would come only from further experimental analysis. Her notebooks show her very close to elucidating the structure presented by Watson and Crick. Stent also reprints 13 contemporary reviews of *The Double Helix,* ranging from superficial to profound and from favorable to condemnatory.

SAYRE's avowedly partisan biography of Rosalind Franklin, written largely to counter Watson's image of her, is the only book-length biography of Franklin. Although not herself a scientist, Sayre was the wife of one of Crick and Watson's fellow scientists at Cambridge. She was a personal friend of Rosalind Franklin. Her book is the best source of information on Franklin's childhood and family associations, and about her career before and after her tenure at Kings College. Sayre defends Franklin's personality and describes problems and discrimination she faced as a female scientist in a male-dominated institution.

In his book, CRICK reminisces 35 years later about his experiences between the elucidation of the DNA molecule in the 1950s and the first "cracking" of the genetic code in about 1966. As a friend and former colleague, he has much to say about Rosalind Franklin and her contributions. His discussion of the TV documentary *Life Story*, or, in the United States, *Double Helix*, includes a frank commentary on the depiction of social life and exposes other inaccuracies in the documentary.

OLBY is a historian of science, and his book is a scholarly account of research from 1900 to 1953 leading to elucidation of the DNA molecule. He concentrates on X-ray diffraction applications, Franklin's specialty, and her place in the story is thoroughly and dispassionately presented. Francis Crick brings his impressions up-to-date in the foreword to the book.

PORTUGAL and COHEN place the Watson-Crick-Wilkins-Franklin investigations in the context of an entire history of DNA research, from Miescher's discovery of nuclein in 1869 through the solution of the genetic code in the 1960s. Franklin's work and her conflicts with Wilkins and Watson are evaluated. Reactions to *The Double Helix* on the part of many reviewers are summarized.

JUDSON's thoroughly documented account of the DNA, RNA, and protein discoveries is largely based on extensive interviews with the principals. Written for the general public, it most emphatically is not a review of scientific details. He describes the DNA discovery as a high comedy of intellect in which the grasshoppers defeated the ants, leaving the ants still disgruntled 26 years after the fact. Franklin is cast as the archetypical ant, but by no means in Watson's terms. Although her problems arising from being a woman in science are acknowledged, her personal difficulties are ascribed more to her "prickly" personality, an initial misunderstanding with Wilkins, and the conflict between experimentalists and theoreticians.

NEWTON's and BALDWIN's books, although intended for "young adults," will be very helpful to adult readers not able to follow detailed scientific arguments. Essentials of the science are well presented in understandable form. Personality conflicts and rivalries, including Rosalind Franklin's role, are given neutral treatment. Both polemics and complex language are absent.

—RALPH L. LANGENHEIM, JR.

Freud, Anna 1895–1982

Austrian Psychoanalyst

Coles, Robert, *Anna Freud: The Dream of Psychoanalysis*, Reading, Massachusetts: Addison-Wesley, 1992

Malcolm, Janet, *In the Freud Archives*, New York: Knopf, and London: Cape, 1984

Peltzman, Barbara R., *Anna Freud: A Guide to Research*, New York: Garland, 1990

Peters, Uwe Henrik, *Anna Freud: A Life Dedicated to Children*, New York: Schocken 1984; London: Weidenfeld and Nicolson, 1985

Sayers, Janet, *Mothering Psychoanalysis: Helene Deutsch, Karen Horney, Anna Freud, and Melanie Klein*, London: Hamish Hamilton, 1991; as *Mothers of Psychoanalysis*, New York: Norton, 1991

Young-Bruehl, Elisabeth, *Anna Freud: A Biography*, New York: Summit, 1988; London: Macmillan, 1991

It was probably difficult to come into one's own as the youngest daughter of Sigmund Freud. However, Anna Freud, whom Freud himself dubbed "Anna Antigone," devoted most of her life to her father and his work, and made distinguished contributions to psychoanalysis, especially that of children.

Psychoanalytically trained YOUNG-BRUEHL has written this authorized and authoritative biography. Using primary-source materials from the Freud Archives, which include not only correspondence and manuscripts, but poetry and dream interpretations as well, Young-Bruehl presents Anna Freud as a gifted, formal, modest woman who played an important part in developing theories and strategies for child psychoanalysis in the early formative years of the field. Of particular interest to some might be Young-Bruehl's frank and unabashed discussion of Anna Freud's sexuality, long a topic of gossip and speculation, especially by the detractors of psychoanalysis and its revisionists. Young-Bruehl concludes that Anna Freud remained a virgin throughout her life and, very importantly it seems, that she was not a lesbian.

PELTZMAN has written an excellent, thorough bibliographical study of both primary- and secondary-source materials related to Anna Freud. Not merely a list, the volume provides helpful, succinct remarks about works. One appreciates the way in which the author has been able to separate out and distinguish materials on Anna Freud from those on her illustrious father. This volume is helpful to the generalist who wants to understand Anna Freud, and to the specialist needing specific references as well.

PETERS's book is a respectful study of Anna Freud, whose perusal and blessing it received in manuscript form. The author is best when discussing her innovative work in developing her theories and strategies related to child psychoanalysis. Peters includes some materials that are available to English-language readers for the first time, notably letters to the Russian-German psychoanalyst, Lou Andreas-Salomé, who had psychoanalyzed Anna Freud. If one is interested in more personal aspects of Anna Freud's life, one will have to look elsewhere. Peters does not seem to get beyond presenting her as she was generally perceived: serious, self-effacing, laconic, the watchdog of her father's intellectual legacy.

COLES, a friend and associate of Anna Freud, and a biographer of Erik Erikson, presents his subject with warmth and affection in this straightforward, chronological study. Although hardly objective in its intent or tone, Coles does give Anna Freud her due in terms of her work in the field of psychoanalysis, not only in its early developing years, but after Sigmund Freud's death as well. Coles tends to play down Anna Freud's fierce and impassioned rivalry with Melanie Klein, as well as her various efforts to suppress innovative applications of her father's techniques by second- and even third-generation psychoanalysts.

The books by Appignanesi and Forrester, and by Sayers, treat the various women important in Sigmund Freud's life. All three authors agree that Freud attracted some of the most intelligent women of his day. APPIGNANESI and FORRESTER offer biographical studies and analyses of nineteen individuals, including several from his family—his mother, his wife, and his daughter Anna—as well as a number of colleagues, patients, and students. The list is not complete, of course. For example, the authors discuss the independent-minded Melanie Klein only in relationship to her disagreement with Anna Freud over issues of child psychoanalysis. The last section of the book, "The Question of Femininity," addresses many of Freud's controversial assertions about women. The subsection "Feminism and Psychoanalysis" within this last section is a subtly argued, and at times convincing, attempt at reconciling the two. Sayers's book presents an integrated study of the four women mentioned in the title. Using the mothering metaphor, Sayers shows how all four women literally "mothered" psychoanalysis to its second phase, and went on to make their own distinctive contributions to psychoanalytic theory and practice. Sayers's view of Anna Freud is pretty standard: she was both Freud's dutiful daughter, and an innovator in her own right. Taken together, these two volumes, although covering much of the same territory, amply demonstrate the importance of women's contributions to this field.

MALCOLM's brief book profiles Jeffrey M. Masson, a Toronto-trained psychoanalyst whom Anna Freud appointed as Director of the Freud Archives, and the ensuing conflict between them because, according to Masson, she had suppressed the publication of certain of her father's letters relating to his abandonment of the seduction theory, which held that mental illness comes from children having been seduced by a parent, in favor of his Oedipal theory and the concept of infantile sexuality. Over and above this feud with the Freud establishment, Masson subsequently sued Malcolm for allegedly fabricating quotes for this book, and the case went all the way to the Supreme Court (Masson lost on appeal). This affair, which some have described as Byzantine, caused a major stir in the psychoanalytic community, and underscored the extent to which Anna Freud and those close to her defended Freudian orthodoxy.

—CARLO COPPOLA

See also Psychological Theories about Women: Pre-Feminist

Freud, Sigmund 1856–1939

Austrian Founder of Psychoanalysis

Chodorow, Nancy, *Femininities, Masculinities, Sexualities: Freud and Beyond,* London: Free Association, and Lexington: University of Kentucky Press, 1994

Gay, Peter, *Freud: A Life for Our Times,* London: Dent, and New York: Norton, 1988

Gilman, Sander L., *Freud, Race, and Gender,* Princeton, New Jersey: Princeton University Press, 1993

Jones, Ernest, *The Life and Work of Sigmund Freud,* 3 vols., New York: Basic, and London: Hogarth, 1953–57

Krüll, Marianne, *Freud and His Father,* New York: Norton, 1986; London: Hutchinson, 1987

Kurzweil, Edith, *Freudians and Feminists,* Boulder, Colorado: Westview Press, 1995

Robinson, Paul A., *Freud and His Critics,* Berkeley: University of California Press, 1993

Webster, Richard, *Why Freud Was Wrong: Sin, Science and Psychoanalysis,* London: HarperCollins, and New York: Basic Books, 1995

One of the intellectual colossi of the twentieth century, Sigmund Freud had, even during his lifetime, those who boldly championed or vehemently debunked him and his theories. Studies of Freud, especially biographies, tend to fall into two such camps. His various pronouncements on and ideas about women—for example, anatomy is destiny, penis envy, and "What do women want?"—have become part of mainline western cultural thinking about women. These, and others of his views, have come under attack, often by feminists, and have either been rejected, modified, or revised by many scholars.

JONES's study of Freud, written to coincide with the centenary celebrations of Freud's birth, is the most complete biography in English. Jones had the advantage of being a member of Freud's trusted inner circle, thereby allowing him personal insights and recollections, as well as access to primary source materials in the Freud Archives. Some critics suggest that he engages more in hagiography than biography. An orthodox Freudian, Jones sometimes either glosses over or simply ignores problems Freud had both with his theories and with other people. A one-volume condensation of this monumental study has also been published.

Distinguished Yale historian and psychoanalytically trained GAY has produced a biography that, like Jones's, intends to reveal the total Freud, but does not. It is, however, different from Jones's both in emphasis and attitude. Gay's is generally more objective than Jones's, especially since the former seems willing to take on some (but not all, certainly) of the embarrassing or sensitive issues ignored by the latter, which might show Freud in a less-than-favorable light. Moreover, Gay's prose, infused with wit and irony, is more readable than Jones's, which tends to be stuffy and stiff. Of particular value in Gay's book is the long bibliographical essay at the end, which is helpful in sorting out the plethora of material written about Freud.

GILMAN investigates the effects contemporaneous writings on race and gender about Jews, much of it from medical literature, may have had on Freud's theories, by addressing three interrelated points: the Jewish body, the Jewish psyche, and Jewish illnesses. Gilman argues that in the anti-Semitic atmosphere of *fin de siècle* Europe in general, and Vienna in particular, Jewish males were viewed as disease-ridden, feminized, and prone to psychopathology. He further hypothesizes that Freud displaced this kind of internalized Jewishness, shaped by such hostile contemporary thinking about Jews, on to his image of women.

Psychoanalytically trained feminist sociologist CHODOROW concisely indicates in the three lectures that constitute this book that, first, on carefully reconsidering Freud, one will find that his views on women are, in fact, more empathetic, diverse, and nuanced than some critics, especially some of the more radical feminists, have thought; that because various kinds of heterosexualities, homosexualities, femininities and masculinities exist, psychoanalysts should not abandon this diversity in favor of only one—heterosexuality—which, she suggests, might be viewed as "a set of defensive solutions" to certain kinds of psychological problems found among all people at all times, "not better or worse than any other kind of sexual preference"; and, finally, that human beings love in as many different ways as there are human beings; these differences should be celebrated, not denigrated.

KURZWEIL, a sociologist by training, and editor of *The Partisan Review*, investigates the intersection of psychoanalysis and feminism over the past sixty years, and the differences in response to Freud based on national and disciplinary approaches. She distinguishes between the "First Wave" theorists such as Horney, Deutsch, and Klein, whose feminism she describes as modernist and empirical; and the "Second Wave," such as Kristeva, Irigary, and Cixous, whom she characterizes as postmodernist and Lacanian. The value of this book is the description, analysis, comparison, and contrast of the thinking of these various figures. Her treatment of the earlier group favors them over the postmodernists, whose major contribution, Kurzweil suggests, is to have popularized Freud in the literary classroom.

KRÜLL investigates Freud's abandonment of the seduction theory—that mental illness results from children having been seduced by a parent—in favor of the Oedipal complex and infantile sexuality. She argues that this significant development was the result of Freud's unconscious fear of revealing this kind of sexual misconduct by his father, Jacob. While this meticulously researched book makes fascinating reading, it seems to arbitrarily preclude other reasons, some of them much less dramatic than the possibility of Jacob Freud's sins, for shifting, modifying, or abandoning a theory, one of them simply being: it didn't work.

Of the many books that attack Freud, WEBSTER's is one of the most accessible to non-specialists. Webster, who refers to psychoanalysis as "pseudo-science," argues without stridency that Freud's personality, even from childhood, was deeply religious, and because of his parents' high expectations of him, he allowed his "messianic" dreams to formulate the "science" he created. Because Freud's ideas are essentially religious doctrines in scientific disguise, claims Webster, they were safe from attack by science "precisely because they were not science."

Intellectual historian ROBINSON treats three major, and well-publicized, contemporary critics of Freud: Frank J. Sulloway, the distinguished historian of science, who views Freud as little more than an early sociobiologist; Jeffrey M. Masson, a former Sanskritist, former psychoanalyst, and, for a brief period, Director of the Freud Archives, who attacks Freud because of his abandonment of the seduction theory in favor of the theory of infantile sexuality; and Adolf Grünbaum, the venerable philosopher of science, who insists that the cornerstone of Freudian thinking, the unconscious, is scientifically unprovable. Robinson argues that these critiques appear in the wake of political feminism, as well as the "neopositive intellectual backlash of the 1980s," which demands certitude, and rejects the kind of ambiguity inherent in psychoanalysis. Though he fully presents the cases of each of these individuals, Robinson concludes that Freud will survive these critics and others like them. Unfortunately, Robinson has not included in this study any female critics of Freud. One wonders why.

—CARLO COPPOLA

See also Psychological Theories about Women: Pre-Feminist

Friendship

Brain, Robert, *Friends and Lovers*, London: Hart-Davis MacGibbon, and New York: Basic Books, 1976
Block, Joel D., and Diane Greenburg, *Women and Friendship*, New York: Franklin Watts, 1985
Eichenbaum, Luise, and Susie Orbach, *Between Women: Love, Envy, and Competition in Women's Friendships*, New York: Viking, 1988; London: Arrow, 1994
Raymond, Janice G., *A Passion for Friends: Toward a Philosophy of Female Affection*, London: Women's Press, and Boston: Beacon Press, 1989
Oliker, Stacey J., *Best Friends and Marriage: Exchange among Women*, Berkeley: University of California Press, 1989
O'Connor, Pat, *Friendships between Women: A Critical Review*, London: Harvester Wheatsheaf, 1991; New York: Guilford Press, 1992
Gouldner, Helen, and Mary Symons Strong, *Speaking of Friendship: Middle-Class Women and Their Friends*, New York: Greenwood, 1987

Friendship between women has a long history, but scholarship on women's friendship is a relatively new field, which began to appear in major book forms in the early 1980s. O'CONNOR's critical review of friendship between women brings together British, Canadian, and American literature on women's friendship. The book devotes one chapter to theoretical perspectives; one each to friendships among married women, single women, and elderly women; one to a comparison of female friendship with kin relationships, work-based friendships, and lesbian relationships, and a last chapter on directions for future research. Each chapter contains detailed vignettes and concludes with a useful starting point for new research. This book is written in a dense academic style and is appropriate for advanced undergraduate and graduate students, faculty, and anyone looking for fruitful research topics regarding female friendship, marriage, and family from a feminist perspective.

RAYMOND provides another theoretical account of female friendships. The author presents her philosophy as a theory of women's empowerment, an account of possibilities of women's sustaining relations with women. Throughout the book, three concepts: *Gyn/affection*, *hetero-relations*, and *hetero-reality* are used consistently to express her theoretical assumption that "the empowering of female friendship can create the conditions for a feminist politics in which the personal is most passionately political." To express her conviction that "the political is personal," Raymond traces the genealogy of female friendships of a particular group of women: women who have resisted *hetero-reality*—an institution that confers social and political status only on hetero-relations (women-to-men relationships). Toward this end, the author devotes one chapter to nuns, who were regarded as "loose women" because of their virginity representing female independence from men, and another to the Chinese marriage resisters during the late nineteenth to the early twentieth centuries. This is an important book on female friendships viewed from a feminist perspective. The book uses many feminist terminologies and may be hard to read for readers who are unfamiliar with feminist scholarship.

Based on their personal experiences and psychoanalytic work in therapy centers in London and New York, EICHENBAUM and ORBACH explore feelings of envy, competition, anger, betrayal, and abandonment experienced by close female friends. The discussions and examples of the emotional and psychological dynamics between women friends mostly reflect the lives of well-educated, middle-class women in the 1980s, although they are not limited to this particular group—included are also experiences of women who come from a wide range of backgrounds, differing political persuasions, and sexual orientations. Written in a conversational style and a loosely psychoanalytic framework, the book is suitable for general readers.

GOULDNER and STRONG introduce the reader to information concerning the beginnings of friendship, the types of relationships formed, and the breakdowns or endings of friendships among middle-class American women. This is a qualitative investigation based on interviews conducted with seventy-five women, aged 30 to 65, who were selected through the "snowball" method of sampling. The book provides important insights into the life-cycle processes of friendships among middle-and upper-middle-class women. Lacking a formal theoretical framework, this highly readable and informative book is suitable for general readers.

BLOCK and GREENBERG discuss how historically women's friendships have been viewed as trivial and on the whole inferior to men's. In contrast, the authors' research shows that women have more satisfying relationships than their male counterparts. Many women enjoy close female friendships because of their capacity to be open with one another. This ability to reveal one's inner feelings facilitates the development of intimacy and allows women to experience much support and comfort from one another throughout their lives. The discussion of the mentor-protégé relationship is especially informative for women who seek female friends who not only share their common interests, but who can also give encouragement and guidance to their career aspirations.

OLIKER's book is based on interviews with middle- and working-class California women. The book offers insights into the relationships between female friends, including friendships between lesbians, and their impact on family relationships and gender roles. The author has touched upon some sensitive topics and left some theoretically open questions: If gender roles were equalized, would women have no need of marriage? How are lesbian friendships different from those of male-centered women? Do professional women use friendship to help them accommodate to marriage? This book is also intellectually daring—it challenges traditional views of marriage in which the family is seen as the major boundary of the emotional lives of women and men. Oliker's study probes into a relatively unacknowledged area and adds substantially to the understandings of family, gender, friendship, and community.

Although not directly addressing friendship between women, BRAIN's book provides a view of friendship that goes beyond narrow boundaries of western tradition and rigid divisions of gendered friendship. It is a classic study of friendship from a cross-cultural perspective. Drawing from cultures as diverse as the ancient Israelites, Mayan Indians, Trobriand Islanders, and the Bangwa of the Cameroon (where the author conducted his fieldwork), Brain examines a number of non-kin, nonsexual relationships including blood friends—friends whose bonds of affection are sanctioned by "blood ceremony," trading partners, same-sex friends, and same-sex marriage. Brain is probably the first anthropologist who attacks the racist and sexist view that women are incapable of making true friends, by providing evidence of female friendship and solidarity from non-western sources. Based on his own fieldwork in Bangwa, Brain demonstrates that women not only form strong friendship ties among themselves, but they also make lasting friendships with men without sex in any way disturbing it. One of the central themes of this book is that love and friendship are as important, if not more important, than aggression in ensuring personal well-being and the survival of culture. This is a book celebrating friendship in its most splendid form: friendships that transcend age, social status, gender, and sexual orientation.

—JIAN LI

Fuller, Margaret 1810–1850

American Reformer

Allen, Margaret Vanderhaar, *The Achievement of Margaret Fuller*, University Park: Pennsylvania State University Press, 1979

Blanchard, Paula, *Margaret Fuller: From Transcendentalism to Revolution*, New York: Delacorte Press/Seymour Lawrence, 1978

Capper, Charles, *Margaret Fuller: An American Romantic Life*, vol. 1, New York and Oxford: Oxford University Press, 1992

Chevigny, Bell Gale, *The Woman and the Myth: Margaret Fuller's Life and Writings*, Old Westbury, New York: Feminist Press, 1976

Dickenson, Donna, *Margaret Fuller: Writing a Woman's Life*, London: Macmillan, and New York: St. Martin's Press, 1993

Higginson, Thomas Wentworth, *Margaret Fuller Ossoli*, Boston: Houghton Mifflin, 1884

Von Mehren, Joan, *Minerva and the Muse: A Life of Margaret Fuller*, Amherst: University of Massachusetts Press, 1994

Zwarg, Christina, *Feminist Conversations: Fuller, Emerson, and the Play of Reading*, Ithaca, New York, and London: Cornell University Press, 1995

While Margaret Fuller's place as a notable nineteenth-century figure has remained relatively secure in the century and a half since her death, and many biographies have been written about her, her reputation suffered from negative statements made by early biographers who were scandalized by the sensational aspects of her personal life, and from inaccuracies in her biographical record owing to difficulties with source material. Following the publication of several important works on Fuller in the 1970s, however, recent biographers and scholars, armed with new approaches, have begun to re-examine Fuller's life and writings, assisted by the first-time publication of her letters and journals, and the reprinting of her essays, books, and newspaper writings.

The first attempt to improve Fuller's reputation began with the biography by HIGGINSON. Writing three decades after her death, Higginson, who knew Fuller personally, claims to approach Fuller's life and work objectively. Higginson, in contrast to earlier biographers, chooses to dwell on Fuller's intellectual and literary work rather than her personal life. In addition, Higginson returns to original source materials, drawing his conclusions from written evidence, even when it means countering the opinions of earlier biographers. Higginson also emphasizes Fuller's efforts to combine thought and action in her life, especially in her later years.

Feminist scholars rediscovered Fuller more than a century after her death. Three works published in the 1970s were especially important in initiating the current interest in Fuller. The ground-breaking anthology edited by CHEVIGNY made a broad range of Fuller's writings widely available for the first time. In her introductory essays to the primary source material, Chevigny argues that examining Fuller is helpful both in understanding the difficulty Americans had developing social or political ideas, as well as the problematic status of middle-class American women. Chevigny organizes her anthology around Fuller's perception of the problem of identity and vocation, and the various identities—friend, transcendentalist, feminist, social critic, and radical—she assumed in her efforts to resolve this struggle. Chevigny pairs Fuller's own writings with writings by contemporaries about Fuller in order to capture a sense of the combination of Fuller's lived presence and her work.

One of the first biographers to reevaluate Fuller's life in the light of feminism, BLANCHARD counters Fuller's negative public image and the bluestocking myth that surrounded her. Blanchard emphasizes the development of Fuller's political consciousness by showing how she bridges the gap between transcendentalism and social activism. She also considers Fuller's education, isolation, and emotional life.

ALLEN is the first to consider Fuller as a great intellectual and moral leader, placing her on a level with Emerson and Thoreau. Less concerned with Fuller's life than with her ideas and where they led her, Allen explores Fuller's achievement and the reasons for the neglect and negative reputation she suffered after her death. Together, these three works—one an anthology, one a biography, and one an analysis of Fuller's ideas—set the stage for the flurry of Fuller scholarship to come.

Recent scholars have continued the themes established earlier: feminist analysis, close attention to original source materials, and emphasis on Fuller's intellectual and literary activity. DICKENSON's biography is informed by feminist theories put forth by Sandra Gilbert and Susan Gubar, Elaine Showalter, Carol Gilligan, and Carolyn Heilbrun, which explain the denigration of Fuller's life by male writers. Dickenson contrasts the details of Fuller's life with her posthumous reputation by focusing on the ways the "Margaret myth" developed through the efforts of various male writers such as Ralph Waldo Emerson, Nathaniel Hawthorne, and Henry James. By not writing a traditional chronological biography, Dickenson highlights the differences between the legend and the life.

CAPPER offers the first of his planned two-volume biography of Fuller as an act of historical recovery. Capper returns to the original source materials in order to correct the inaccuracies of earlier biographies, fully acknowledge Fuller's complexity, and create what he calls a social biography, by depicting Fuller in relation to the people and socio-political movements that surrounded her. Capper's first volume focuses on Fuller's early life, leading to her transformation into a public figure, while his second volume, when completed, will examine her position as the preeminent female intellectual of her day.

In contrast to the broad social context delineated by Capper, VON MEHREN closely focuses on Fuller herself. Von Mehren considers the growth of Fuller's character, her negotiations between private and public life, her initiation of a new narrative for women's lives, and how her private life shaped her political beliefs and actions. Von Mehren writes in the form and style of nineteenth-century women's biographies, but utilizes insights gained a century later.

ZWARG argues that Fuller's most important achievement was her persistent attempt to provide a radical theory of reading, one which did not focus on the text alone, but on the interplay between the text and reader, and especially on the power structure within that relationship. Zwarg considers Fuller's theory of reading within the context of her relationship with Emerson, showing how both writers used their written conversations with each other to develop their feminist thinking. In addition, Zwarg sees Fuller scholarship as a means to bridge the schism in feminist criticism between a focus on women's life experience, and a concern with the theoretical underpinnings of gender. Zwarg herself draws heavily on recent feminist theories, especially those by Alice Jardine and Gayatri Chakravorty Spivak. Invaluable to literary historians for the first in-depth analysis of Fuller's correspondence with Emerson, Zwarg also provides readings of Fuller's early translations, major works, *New York Daily Tribune* writings, and dispatches from Italy.

—THERESA STROUTH GAUL

Fundamentalism: Christian

Bendroth, Margaret Lamberts, *Fundamentalism and Gender: 1875 to the Present*, New Haven, Connecticut: Yale University Press, 1993

Brink, Judy, and Joan P. Mencher (eds.), *Mixed Blessings: Gender and Religious Fundamentalism Cross Culturally*, New York: Routledge, 1997

DeBerg, Betty A., *Ungodly Women: Gender and the First Wave of American Fundamentalism*, Minneapolis: Fortress Press, 1990

Gerami, Shahin, *Women and Fundamentalism: Islam and Christianity*, New York: Garland, 1996

Hawley, John Stratton (ed.), *Fundamentalism and Gender*, New York: Oxford University Press, 1994

Klatch, Rebecca E., *Women of the New Right*, Philadelphia: Temple University Press, 1987

Stacey, Judith, *Brave New Families: Stories of Domestic Upheaval in Late Twentieth Century America*, New York: Basic Books, 1990

Weaver, Mary Jo, and R. Scott Appleby (eds.), *Being Right: Conservative Catholics in America*, Bloomington: Indiana University Press, 1995

Often misunderstood and even more often misrepresented by the media, Christian fundamentalism is a twentieth-century phenomenon whose goal is for its followers to live by a literal interpretation of the Bible. Gender is central to the fundamentalist agenda, for women's place in church, family, and society is the most visible evidence of its insistence on an inerrant scripture. Christian fundamentalists tend to be firm believers in gender difference and its concomitant construct of separate spheres, which emphasizes domesticity and limits women's public roles. Concern over women's behavior and sexuality leads fundamentalists to be anxious over the blurring of gender roles they understand to be inherent in feminism, thus fueling the antifeminist aspect of their conservative religious values. Fundamentalism is often conflated with, but remains distinct from, evangelicalism, a conservative Christianity that rarely engages in either the political activism or separatism that are frequent hallmarks of fundamentalism.

In large measure a reaction to modernism and the late nineteenth-century embrace of science, fundamentalism spread across various Protestant denominational boundaries. It continues to challenge church bodies marked by liberal and conservative divisions. BENDROTH presents the only comprehensive narrative account of the uneasy relationship between gender and Protestant fundamentalism since its origins in the United States. She argues that central to the early growth of fundamentalism was a stress on masculinity and male leadership, despite women's participation as Bible students and teachers during the first wave (1880–1925). Bendroth locates the theological roots of fundamentalism in Calvinism and its belief in a hierarchical created order. This reliance on a scriptural order of creation has become the most distinctive feature of late twentieth-century fundamentalism, which insists on male headship and female subordination and submission.

DeBERG's study of first-wave fundamentalism focuses on fundamentalists' efforts to reclaim the Victorian gender ideology of separate spheres, in particular the "glorification of motherhood," as both biblical and essential to a well-ordered society. Fundamentalists understood the Christian home as not only the locus of character formation and moral development but, as such, the heart of a Christian nation. The revolution in manners and morals of the 1910s and 1920s was to them clear evidence of spreading moral decay that could only be stopped by strict application of biblical principles. Appeal to an inerrant scripture and its absolute truth thus became the first fundamental.

Aside from Bendroth and DeBerg's histories of gender and Protestant fundamentalism, the primary genre of the literature is ethnography, and the focus is on the late twentieth-century resurgence of fundamentalism globally. Although she does not specifically use the term "fundamentalist," KLATCH uses the term "social conservatives" for those right-wing women who hold a religiously-informed worldview, one based on the hierarchical chain of authority and command considered essential to social and family structure.

Several texts are comparative in nature. HAWLEY's book is a collection of case studies on fundamentalisms, important because of the common threads shared by the fundamentalist worldview, even as it is manifested differently among disparate religious traditions. Those tendencies include reliance on selective authoritative texts, militance against modern culture, an either/or posturing that precludes compromise on matters of morality and doctrine, desire for the restoration of an ideal past (in the context of American Protestant fundamentalism, a nineteenth-century femininity), a defined enemy, and "a conservative ideology of gender." Because fundamentalists perceive the world as out of control, they seek order through the control of women, their bodies, and their sexuality. In fundamentalists' thinking, woman uncontrolled is both the result of sociocultural disorder and its cause.

In contrast to Hawley, BRINK and MENCHER declare their collection to be the first that considers fundamentalisms from a feminist perspective. Critical of the absence of women in most studies of fundamentalism, the essays stress women's agency, while not denying their frequent victimization. The authors argue that absolutism needs to be emphasized less and the complexity of fundamentalism more, and the fact that "it does not uniformly result in less power for women." When women use their attraction to fundamentalism to convert the men in their lives or to escape male domination, fundamentalism can be a positive force. Written primarily by anthropologists, the essays consider the influence of fundamentalisms cross-culturally, seeking to understand women's attraction to the phenomenon, as well as the restrictions it imposes on them. Vastly disparate circumstances and cultures contribute to the authors' assessment that fundamentalisms bring to women "mixed blessings."

GERAMI compares Christian and Islamic fundamentalisms through women's perceptions of their place and role within that religious context. In surveying a sample of midwestern American women, Gerami found dissonance between the religious fundamentalist ideology of what she calls the New Christian Right and the women's perceptions of their reality. The women in Gerami's survey neither identified themselves solely by gender and family nor upheld strict gender role segregation.

STACEY also found a curious mix of feminism and fundamentalism in her study of California's Silicon Valley in the 1980s. Struggling to understand the attraction of fundamentalist Christianity and its influence on women's attitudes toward and behavior in marriage, she discusses the notion of mutual submission under a male headship model, and the hybrid church that taught this. Stacey found that women who self-consciously chose this marriage model felt not only a sense of order in their lives, but at the same time expressed a "postfeminist" egalitarian gender ideology she calls "patriarchy in the last instance."

While fundamentalist is not a term ordinarily applied to Roman Catholics, those within Catholicism who identify with a conservative position on matters of doctrine and practice (in particular the church's teachings on abortion, birth control, and women) are referred to as traditionalists. The volume edited by WEAVER and APPLEBY contains various voices of conservative Catholicism, including the group Women for Faith and Family, which expressly rejects Catholic feminist claims to speak for all Catholic women in their discontent with the church.

—MARY TODD

Fundamentalism: Islamic

Brink, Judy, and Joan P. Mencher (eds.), *Mixed Blessings: Gender and Religious Fundamentalism Cross Culturally*, New York and London: Routledge, 1997

Callaway, Barbara, and Lucy C. Creevey, *The Heritage of Islam: Women, Religion, and Politics in West Africa*, Boulder, Colorado, and London: Lynne Reinner, 1994

Choueiri, Youssef M., *Islamic Fundamentalism*, London: Pinter, and Boston: Twayne, 1990

El-Solh, Camillia Fawzi, and Judy Mabro (eds.), *Muslim Women's Choices: Religious Beliefs and Social Reality*, Oxford and Providence, Rhode Island: Berg, 1994

Hawley, John Stratton (ed.), *Fundamentalism and Gender*, New York: Oxford University Press, 1994

Kandiyoti, Deniz (ed.), *Women, Islam and the State*, Philadelphia: Temple University Press, and London: Macmillan, 1991

Tucker, Judith E. (ed.), *Arab Women: Old Boundaries, New Frontiers*, Bloomington: Indiana University Press, 1993

Islamic fundamentalism is a relatively new phenomenon, emerging in the Muslim world in the 1970s. In part it seems to be a reaction to the continuing political, economic, and cultural influence that the west has exerted over the independent Muslim nation-states. Recently studies have moved on from treating Islamic fundamentalism as a unified political ideology, and from concern with its global political impact. Employing anthropology, ethnography, and multi-disciplinary feminist studies, the focus is now on one of Islamic fundamentalism's core elements—women. This has served to articulate the diversity within the phenomenon and its varied role in the lives and understandings of Muslim women.

CHOUEIRI's volume is a general book, which usefully traces the emergence of Islamic fundamentalism from its nineteenth-century roots. He presents a study of two of modern fundamentalism's founding ideologues, Qutb (1906–66) and Mawdudi (1903–79), and the centrality that women and the family played in their vision of Islam's future. It is the role accorded to women in nurturing children within the family that makes them pivotal: the source of hope for the future and the possible route through which irreparable damage will enter Islam. In this analysis Choueiri begins to account for the ways in which notions of control, ambiguity, and danger attend understandings of women in Islamic fundamentalism.

Reacting against treatments of Islam as a unified phenomenon detached from history and geo-political contexts, KANDIYOTI seeks to establish the ways in which states and Islam are engaged in complex exchanges and interrelations that produce differing patternings of "woman." While not focused exclusively on fundamentalism, the book's concerns with both the state and women enable the voices of traditionalist, modernist, and fundamentalist Islam to be heard, encouraging the reader to form an understanding of the boundaries and differing intonations of these voices. Kandiyoti presents histories relating to the construction of women's identities in Turkey, Pakistan, India, Iran, Iraq, Lebanon, Bangladesh, Egypt, and Yemen. These provide an understanding of the dynamism and variety of Islam, and also of the way in which women have been actively involved in their definition of self, whether that has been in support of, or in opposition to, Islamic fundamentalism.

CALLAWAY and CREEVEY's volume seeks to determine the potential influence that Islam and Islamic fundamentalism will exert in Senegal and Nigeria. This work is valuable as a study of Muslim women in three West African countries. In these countries there is a complex interface between Christianity, Islam, and indigenous religious traditions, and also between African, Arab, and European cultures. The authors explore the layers of identity and cultural resources that women possess, and the ways in which Islam has affected them differently. The book's political and social histories of Senegal and Nigeria present an interesting comparative study of the ways in which fundamentalism has worked and the uneasy alliances it has formed with both nationalists and Muslim traditionalists. It points to the economic and political pressures that are bringing women into the public space, and to the cultural resources that West African women possess. It is these that might facilitate the emergence of an indigenous feminism working within, rather than against, the fundamentals of Islam.

TUCKER gives a clear understanding of the differences between modernists, conservatives, and fundamentalists in Islam. This book shows the ways in which these groups use the Qur'an, the *hadith* (sayings) of Prophet Muhammad, and hagiographical and historical traditions to justify their positions with regard to women. These models of how Islam is formulated usefully illustrate its capacity for sustaining different social visions. Through studies conducted in six Muslim countries, Tucker shows the ways in which women participate in their societies and play an active role in shaping the worlds of work, politics, and gender relations. Women are depicted engaging with fundamentalism and working to empower themselves in contexts that have real political, economic, and ideological strains.

EL-SOLH and MABRO aim to move the analysis of Muslim women away from a male, western perspective. They do this through deconstructing such terms as "fundamentalism" and "Islam," seeing these as monolithic constructs of a western ideology, and moving toward fine-grained studies of Muslim women as human beings exercising real-world choices. This humanisation of Muslim women, which sees infinite variety across age, culture, and social class, serves to show how the west has employed a notion of Muslim woman as passive victim of an unyielding Islam. The studies span many contexts, including South Africa and the former USSR. They show women as negotiators of their gender roles. This text is invaluable in marking a transition to women-sourced, more fully ethnographic, studies.

HAWLEY's text is the first to dedicate itself exclusively to gender and fundamentalism. Although concerned with fundamentalism across several religions, it usefully establishes a set of family resemblances between fundamentalisms and shows the centrality of women and the family in the articulation of fundamentalist visions. Working with concepts from the social and psychological sciences, it attempts to account for the importance fundamentalism places on the control of women. This analysis directs the reader beyond the various religions to the human, and in particular, male, psychologies that fashion fundamentalist ideologies. The chapter on Islamic fundamentalism provides in-depth analysis of India's Shah Bano affair of the 1980s. This case-study illustrates the way in which a Muslim minority, mobilised by a small group of fundamentalists, challenged the Indian constitution and established itself as a separate community subject, in circumstances often relating to women, to Shari'ah (Islamic Law) rather than Indian Civil and Criminal Codes.

In extending the work of Hawley, BRINK and MENCHER also look at fundamentalism across a range of religious cultures, but this time from the perspective of women in those cultures. This ethnographic approach leaves behind Hawley's "male" perspectives and focuses. Indeed, the authors suggest that "fundamentalism" is largely a male concept: one that is defined by external features and by political, public activity. Although a cross-cultural study, the chapters on Islam are substantial enough to provide detailed insights into differing understandings of fundamentalism in Middle Eastern, Asian, and African contexts. Its treatment reveals a new, women's dimension to fundamentalism, suggests positive reasons for women's active support of Islamic fundamentalism, and shows how, in some situations, women have gained from fundamentalist movements.

—ANDREW CLUTTERBUCK

G

Gandhi, Indira 1917–1984

Indian Prime Minister

Abbas, Khwaja Ahmad, *Indira Gandhi: Return of the Red Rose*, Delhi: Hind Pocket, 1966
Ali, Tariq, *An Indian Dynasty: The Story of the Nehru-Gandhi Family*, New York: Putnam, 1985
Carras, Mary C., *Indira Gandhi: In the Crucible of Leadership, Political Biography*, Boston: Beacon Press, and Bombay: Jaico, 1979
Drieberg, Trevor, *Indira Gandhi: A Profile in Courage*, Delhi: Vikas, 1972
Jayakar, Pupul, *Indira Gandhi: A Biography*, New Delhi: Viking, 1992
Malhotra, Inder, *Indira Gandhi: A Personal and Political Biography*, London: Hodder and Stoughton, and New Delhi: Arnold, 1989; Boston: Northeastern University Press, 1991
Moraes, Dom, *Mrs. Gandhi*, New Delhi: Vikas, and London: Cape, 1980
Sahgal, Nayantara, *Indira Gandhi's Emergence and Style*, Durham, North Carolina: Carolina Academic Press, 1978; New Delhi: Vikas, 1979
Singh, Khushwant, *Indira Gandhi Returns*, New Delhi: Vision, 1979

Most biographies are based on interviews with Gandhi, information gathered from people who knew her, and the autobiographies of her father, Jawaharlal Nehru, and her aunts, Vijayalakshmi Pandit and Krishna Hutheesing. The focus is on her assuming dictatorial power in 1976, rather than on the significance of a woman's coming to power. All of them recount the main incidents: her birth as the first grandchild of Motilal Nehru, the patriarch who changed his luxurious lifestyle late in life when the call of Mahatma Gandhi drew him and his son Jawaharlal into the nationalist movement; Indira's childhood, when she organized the *Vanar Sena*, a children's brigade that imitated the nationalist movement of the elders; the death of her mother Kamala when Indira was nineteen; her marriage to Feroze Gandhi against the wishes of Nehru; the slow disintegration of the marriage, precipitated by Indira's leaving their home in Lucknow to keep house for Nehru in Delhi when he became Prime Minister; and her entry into politics. She became uncrowned queen of India in 1971, but declared a national Emergency and postponed elections in 1975. She lost the elections she called in 1977, but came back to power in 1980.

JAYAKAR comes nearest to an authorized biography; she claims that Indira Gandhi herself had broached the topic, and Jayakar has four hours of interviews tape-recorded in 1984, just a fortnight before Gandhi's unforeseen death, assassinated by her own Sikh security guards. Jayakar is a family friend, who had known Gandhi from 1930. She reveals Gandhi's isolation after the death of her husband Feroze, the "growing sycophancy around her" after she came to power, and the way she turned to religious leaders like Dhirendra Brahmachari, or the less notorious Ma Anandmayee, her mother's *guru*. She claims that Gandhi's surprising decision to lift the Emergency was prompted by her meeting with J. Krishnamurthi, the religious thinker.

ABBAS's book is a better guide to the early years, for she was writing when events were still fresh in her memory. Jawaharlal Nehru used to wear a red rose in his buttonhole; Abbas projects Gandhi as Nehru's daughter, inheriting his concern for democracy, and her election as the culmination of the historical process of the empowerment of women in India.

DRIEBERG provides a detailed and scrupulously fair account of the events on the Indian subcontinent in 1971. But he accepts Gandhi's versions of earlier events unquestioningly: her childhood heroism, the "sacrifices" she made to stay by Prime Minister Nehru's side for the sake of the country, and her sufferings in prison. It is left to Abbas and Sahgal to set the record straight, for Sahgal's mother, Vijayalakshmi Pandit, and sister Chandralekha, shared the same prison.

SAHGAL writes as an insider: Jawaharlal Nehru was her maternal uncle. She had spent much of her childhood in the Nehru's ancestral home in Allahabad, and reveals the especially privileged childhood Indira enjoyed. To her, Gandhi's actions in the 1960s clearly revealed the autocratic behavior that led her to impose the Emergency in 1975. Gandhi's style represents a clear departure from the political values and behavior of her predecessors. In her first political position as minister for information and broadcasting in 1964, she had attempted to muzzle the radio. Sahgal recounts many dubious actions: the Congress split, which she maneuvered for grabbing power; populist measures like nationalization of banks taken up against the express advice of the finance ministry; using government machinery for electioneering; and the "Nagarwala Case" (1971), where a cashier of the State Bank of India handed over six million rupees in cash on the basis of a phone call supposedly from Gandhi. Sahgal gives credit where it is due, in hailing Gandhi's handling of the crisis in East Pakistan, but concludes that "No crisis but that of Mrs. Gandhi's own political survival necessitated the Emergency in 1975."

CARRAS, a political scientist, looks to psychology for the explanation of political actions. She analyzes Gandhi's personality, her motivations, and her characteristic way of dealing with conflict. She argues that the imposition of the Emergency in 1975 was virtually inevitable, considering the near anarchy in India. Carras gives an unbiased account of both sides in the conflict. She shows the weaknesses of the opposition "J.P. Narayan Movement," as well as Gandhi's fatal leadership flaws.

MORAES, an established poet, provides the most readable narrative. With a beautiful narrative style, he covers her years in and out of power, prefaced with an artistic recreation of her ancestors in nineteenth-century India. His book is full of interesting anecdotes featuring the author and his encounters with Indians who knew Gandhi, who are invariably shown in a poor light, speaking comic Indian English.

Everyone holds Gandhi's younger son, Sanjay, responsible for her unpopularity; the exception is SINGH, the novelist, who feels that the imposition of the Emergency was justified. His book, predicting her return to power a year before the event, presents Sanjay as a young man in a hurry to serve India, and rejects all allegations of his grabbing power or interfering in the administration. Like Carras, Singh ends with a long interview with Gandhi.

The personal and the political are finely balanced in MALHOTRA's biography, which presents all the facts, and other information, some uncorroborated in his opinion. His closeness to Feroze Gandhi provides him special insight into Indira Gandhi's earlier years and their failed marriage. He reveals the "shortcut to supremacy" taken by Gandhi in ignoring democratic norms. He briefly considers the problems, some quite hilarious, arising from the fact of her being a woman.

ALI presents a concise account of India's first family, with sections on Nehru, Indira, and "The Brothers Gandhi" (which discusses the role of Sanjay and his wife Maneka from 1974–80, and the accession of Rajiv Gandhi in 1984). Salman Rushdie's introduction is a valuable analysis of the myths surrounding leaders in India. The high drama of Indira Gandhi's life, and her dynastic succession in the world's largest democracy, still attract the attention of political analysts. S.S. Gill's *The Dynasty: A Political Biography of the Premier Ruling Family of Modern India* (1996) is the latest of such books.

—SHYAMALA A. NARAYAN

Gaskell, Elizabeth 1810–1865

British Writer

Duthie, Enid L., *The Themes of Elizabeth Gaskell,* London: Macmillan, and Totowa, New Jersey: Barnes and Noble, 1980

Lansbury, Coral, *Elizabeth Gaskell: The Novel of Social Crisis,* London: Paul Elek, and New York: Barnes and Noble, 1975

Schor, Hilary M., *Scheherazade in the Marketplace: Elizabeth Gaskell and the Victorian Novel,* New York and Oxford: Oxford University Press, 1992

Stoneman, Patsy, *Elizabeth Gaskell,* Brighton: Harvester Press, and Bloomington: Indiana University Press, 1987

Uglow, Jenny, *Elizabeth Gaskell: A Habit of Stories,* London: Faber, and New York: Farrar Straus, 1993

Elizabeth Gaskell has long been one of the most critically misrepresented of the major women novelists of nineteenth-century Britain. After decades of patronage by the male academic establishment (Lord David Cecil's influential *Early Victorian Novelists* [1934] depicted her as a charming miniaturist who got sadly out of her depth when she tried to tackle "big" questions), Gaskell's reassessment began in the 1950s with historicist critics like Arnold Kettle and Raymond Williams, who respected her willingness to address momentous social issues, but who deprecated what they saw as her simplistic or evasive solutions to complex political problems. In all of this earlier commentary there is little willingness to address Gaskell as, specifically, a female writer, or to examine the role played by gender issues in her work. In addition, until very recently, women themselves have found it difficult to see beyond the prescriptive limits imposed by their male precursors.

DUTHIE, for example, provides a serviceable descriptive analysis of Gaskell's writing, arranged under standard thematic headings like "The Individual" and "The Social Scene." But while this procedure helpfully categorizes a wide range of material, the categories themselves are derived from the expectations of liberal humanist criticism. They therefore preclude any focused discussion of Gaskell's treatment of gender (although there are some useful pages on her attitudes to women's education) and, for that matter, any real sense of her development as a writer over nearly twenty years of a productive career.

If Duthie's book presents an image of Gaskell that Lord David Cecil would have recognized and endorsed, LANSBURY's study argues that Gaskell's central achievement lies in her perceptive critique of the English social structure, and in her sympathetic portrayal of working-class life. Lansbury, however, foreshadows later feminist criticism in her sensitive response to Gaskell's treatment of her female characters, and in her particular emphasis on their developing sexual awareness. She also briefly discusses the way Gaskell implicitly encouraged an erosion of stereotypical gender roles, as well as the way she radically questioned the politics of the family.

Insights of this kind remain subordinated, in Lansbury's account, to an exploration of Gaskell's brand of Christian Socialism, but in the work of STONEMAN they move decisively from the periphery to the centre of attention. Stoneman's book opens with a useful overview of the history of Gaskell criticism. She argues that previous feminist scholars neglected Gaskell because of her apparent readiness to conform to the conventions of domestic realism and to the ideology of separate spheres. Stoneman concedes some truth to this position, but contends that Gaskell worked to establish positive ideals of familial nurturance, which could then be extended outward into the public realm. Applying the theories of radical feminist thinkers like Dorothy Dinnerstein and Nancy Chodorow to Gaskell's fiction enables Stoneman to produce a series of persuasive and stimulating analyses of individual texts, which build toward a coherent thesis about her development as a writer. Gaskell, Stoneman suggests, consistently explored ways in which paternal authority could be modified and even transformed by maternal care, at the levels both of the individual family and, by extension, of the political state. In this way, the fictions of provincial life and the novels of social crisis, which earlier critics saw as generically discrete, can be seen to be united in a common questioning of patriarchal values.

While Stoneman sees Gaskell as working within existing conventions to extend the possibilities of female agency, SCHOR believes that Gaskell's narratives revise the conventions themselves. The trajectory of the "woman's plot" through romance to marriage becomes increasingly destabilized as Gaskell's writing matures, and as the novels become both more self-reflexive and more uneasy with the implications of fictional closure. Moreover, just as the desires and aspirations of her heroines make the restrictively inevitable sequence of romantic narrative problematic, so Gaskell herself exhibits a growing restiveness with the limited and limiting possibilities assigned to the female novelist. The novels thus become, to an extent, allegories of Gaskell's own creative evolution, so that, for example, Mary Barton's gradual acquisition of an independent public voice echoes her creator's discovery of the expressive power of fiction, and *Cranford* seeks to define the role of the female writer in relation to an antecedent masculine tradition (represented in this case by Dickens' *Pickwick Papers*).

In the books of Stoneman and Schor, Gaskell has at last begun to attract the kinds of criticism that her complex fiction demands; in UGLOW, she has found an ideal biographer. Uglow's long, sympathetic book is a mine of information, not only about Gaskell herself, but about her enabling intellectual and literary contexts. There are, moreover, chapters of sustained descriptive analysis on each of the novels and, although these lack the theoretical consistency of Stoneman and Schor, Uglow is nevertheless exceptionally responsive to the nuances of textual detail, and to the implications of Gaskell's figurative language. Each of these three writers, indeed, has helped to lay a firm foundation for Gaskell's critical reappraisal, and to render unthinkable any return to the misunderstanding and condescension of the past.

—ROBERT DINGLEY

Gender as a Social Construct

Basow, Susan A., *Gender: Stereotypes and Roles,* Pacific Grove, California: Brooks/Cole, 1992

Bem, Sandra Lipsitz, *The Lenses of Gender,* New Haven, Connecticut: Yale University Press, 1993

Carver, Terrell, *Gender is Not a Synonym for Women,* Boulder, Colorado: Lynne Rienner, 1996

Lorber, Judith, *Paradoxes of Gender,* New Haven, Connecticut: Yale University Press, 1994

Lorber, Judith, and Susan A. Farrell (eds.), *The Social Construction of Gender,* Newbury Park, California: Sage, 1991

Peterson, Spike V., and Anne Sisson Runyan, *Global Gender Issues,* Boulder, Colorado: Westview Press, 1993

Schaum, Melita, and Connie Flanagan (eds.), *Gender Images,* Boston: Houghton Mifflin, 1992

The study of gender as a social construct is a new field, growing largely out of feminist research in the 1970s and 1980s on the ways in which our roles are defined and prescribed in society. The literature reflects a broad range of analyses of the ways in which gender is constructed in our society, of the socialization process, and of the institutionalization of gender-prescribed roles and behaviors.

LORBER and FARRELL have collected a diverse range of essays drawn from the journal *Gender and Society,* which analyze how gender is built into our society on different levels, from economic and political to social and religious. The early essays focus on gender construction in nineteenth-century family life, and on how a gendered workplace keeps women poor. The middle section of this book contains essays which examine the intersection of race, class, and gender in the lives of Asian-American and Chicana women, and examines the infamous 1983 New Bedford gang rape case from the perspectives of ethnic community identification and victim-blaming. Strategies for change are explored in the final section, with the Israeli kibbutz model used to suggest ways of reorganizing work and family along nongendered lines.

The founding editor of *Gender and Society*, LORBER draws on twenty years of teaching and writing about gender issues to discuss the understanding of gender as a social institution rather than a biological imperative. The author divides her book into three sections entitled: "Producing Gender," in which the social, biological and cultural construction of gender is outlined in separate chapters; "Gender in Practice," which looks at how deeply embedded gender is in our society, particularly in our families, workplaces and relationships; and "The Politics of Gender," which examines how macro- and micro-politics are related as outgrowths of the construction and practices of gender. Lorber raises important questions highlighting the many paradoxes of institutionalized gender in our society and, in her last chapter, calls for the deconstruction of gender

BEM, writing as a psychologist, explores the institutional, ideological, and psychological mechanisms that keep women powerless in our society. The author identifies what she terms three "gender lenses" embedded in our culture, and examines each of these lenses in separate chapters on gender polarization, biological essentialism, and androcentrism. After analyzing the insights and shortcomings of four of the major theoretical perspectives on the social construction of gender over the last 50 years, Bem proposes a new model—gender depolarization—in which biological sex would no longer be the core of human identity.

CARVER's book is a collection of his essays on political theories of gender construction, or, as the author states, "the ways that sex and sexuality become power relations in society." He calls into question issues such as gender categorization, gender/sex identity, and postmodernist theories of what constitutes maleness and femaleness, and calls for a gender-critical theory "to liberate people from gender and its constraints." Several essays explore Marx and Engel's theorization of family, but the most compelling example of gender politics is his examination of the Hill-Thomas judicial confirmation hearings from the perspective of how sex and power are related.

PETERSON and RUNYAN bring an international perspective to gender issues. They analyze the social construction of gender, also using the metaphor of a lens, which they focus on global political issues such as power, labor, violence, and resistance. The authors provide a valuable link between "women's issues" and "global issues" by asking a series of seemingly simple but compelling questions. How does one get access to power? Why do so few women make it to the top? What are the worldwide gender implications of women in power? With its pages of tables, graphs and photographs, as well as lists of discussion questions for each chapter, this is an excellent primer on global gender politics.

Also valuable as study texts on gender are those by Schaum and Flanagan, and Basow. BASOW organizes her book by chapters addressing a series of questions, from how gender roles are established, transmitted and maintained, to how these gender roles affect us in our society. Separate chapters explore familial and social relationships, the gendered labor force, and the uses and abuses of power. In her final section, the author suggests various possibilities for change, and for moving beyond gender stereotypes. SCHAUM and FLANAGAN have gathered a large selection of essays addressing such gender issues as defining gender and roles, language, popular culture, media and advertising, work, and violence. Essays are written from the male perspective as well as the female. The section on popular culture, which contains essays exploring images of women in fairy tales, while male images are viewed through the world of sports, is a particularly interesting reflection of our gendered society. The diversity of thought and perspective represented in these essays is stimulating and challenging—certainly useful to spark discussion.

—CHERYL KALNY

See also Biological Determinism

Gender Bias in Education

Davies, Bronwym, *Shards of Glass: Children Reading and Writing beyond Gendered Identities*, Cresskill, New Jersey: Hampton Press, 1993

Gaskell, Jane, and John Willinsky (eds.), *Gender In/forms Curriculum: From Enrichment to Transformation*, New York: Teachers College Press, 1995

Lomotey, Kofi (ed.), *Sailing against the Wind: African Americans and Women in U.S. Education,* Albany: State University of New York Press, 1997

Mac an Ghaill, Mairtin, *The Making of Men: Masculinities, Sexualities, and Schooling*, Philadelphia and Buckingham: Open University Press, 1994

Sadker, Myra, and David Sadker, *Failing at Fairness: How America's Schools Cheat Girls*, New York: Scribner, 1994

Stitt, Beverly, *Building Gender Fairness in Schools*, Carbondale: Southern Illinois University Press, 1988

Streitmatter, Janice, *Toward Gender Equity in the Classroom: Everyday Teachers' Beliefs and Practices*, Albany: State University of New York Press, 1994

Wrigley, Julia (ed.), *Education and Gender Equality*, Washington, D.C. and London: Falmer Press, 1992

There is rapidly expanding feminist scholarship on education, particularly concerning gender bias. Instead of a theoretical approach as often is the case with feminist scholarship, current writing on this topic seems replete with determination to see the theory into practice. The most well-known writers to tackle this agenda are SADKER and SADKER. Their work discusses 20 years of research showing that gender bias in schools makes it impossible for girls to receive an education equal to boys. Based on classroom observations from elementary through higher education, they describe how sexism sabotages girls at school—that female students are still invisible members of classrooms. Parts of this book are written to be read by boys and girls in school, as well as by their parents and teachers. The book includes strategies for nonsexist education that have been developed and field-tested all over the United States. Other sections include a history of women's education, the self-esteem slide, the cold climate of higher education, the miseducation of boys, and the value of single-sex education. Because of their long years of observation and reporting of what happens in the classroom at various educational levels, most researchers interested in gender bias in education use the Sadker material as a base, and then focus more clearly on one of the areas of their concern.

STITT has adapted parts of the Sadker material and developed other topics into a set of readings that were a summary of the foundation research in the 1970s and 1980s. These readings focus on gender bias, sexism, interactions between students and teachers, bias in instructional materials, language bias, and parental influence. The second half of the book includes units of instruction on gender-fair teaching competencies. Each unit contains a stated competency performance objective and learning activities suitable for classes of pre-service teachers or in-service workshops. The units range from developing an awareness of the effects of gender bias, and identifying personal gender bias, to developing gender fair verbal and nonverbal interactions with students. There are also units on developing curriculum materials, recruitment and retention of nontraditional students, and effecting societal change. A gender-fair rating sheet is included that summarizes all the competencies outlined in the units of instruction.

Another book directed toward teacher education and based on the Sadker research was written by STREITMATTER. This work is primarily composed of conversations with and observations of eight teachers. There are a great number of quotations from articles written in the 1970s and 1980s when gender bias was first exposed to the light of day. The author uses the information from the eight teachers to highlight student participation by gender, teaching methods, teacher interactions with students by gender, curriculum and instructional materials, and teachers' language.

GASKELL and WILLINSKY focus on of the significance of recent developments in research on gender, and on what it means for the school curriculum—from art education to technology studies. Their premise regarding art is that discipline-based art education would "defeminize" art, that women's work is undervalued and misconstrued in the workplace, and that this points to a need for development of progressive vocational programs. Other sections consider women's ways of caring and knowing, feminist developments in literary theory, and music composition. They propose the transformation of science teaching to include gender issues, and encourage antidomesticity, transforming family studies, improving social studies curriculum through relevant professional organizations, and providing gender-sensitive physical education programming aimed at fitness and well-being. Other areas of curriculum are also included.

DAVIES proposes applying theory to practice by describing the results of a primary school study. The project was to locate the ways in which post-structuralist theory might be made available to primary school children in such a way that they could develop deconstructive/reconstructive skills. This book is based on the premise that versions of male-female dualism are found within and across class and cultural boundaries. Generally studies about gender bias focus on girls; however, boys were included in this study and considered in relation to each other. The work includes personal primary school stories of the author, who read feminist stories to children and asked them questions as she went along about their hearing of each story.

With full focus on boys in school, MAC AN GHAILL writes from the premise that masculine perspectives are pervasively dominant in secondary schools, but masculinity tends to be absent from mainstream educational research. The work presents the findings of a three-year study to investigate the social construction and regulation of masculinities in a state secondary school in England. The author examines the interplay of schooling, masculinity, and sexuality and views schools as complex gendered and heterosexual arenas. The work looks at school institutional material, social and discursive practices, student selection, subject allocation and stratification, disciplinary modes of authority, instruments of surveillance and control, and gendered and sexual student-teacher and teacher-student relations. The author searches for the specific conditions under which schools construct relations of domination and subordination and the particular impact this may have for the homosexual male student.

A recent book by LOMOTEY provides a learning tool for educators and members of the educational community, who must engage the fact that two enormous barriers, specifically racism and sexism, are not only active constructs in schools, but also exist at every level of education. The book includes ethnographic studies, case studies, and conceptual pieces. It goes beyond the reporting of data to include personal collection and interpretation of data. The book is divided into four parts: multiculturalism (including African Americans, other women, and those with limited physical ability and performance expectations), African-American students in secondary schools, women in higher education, and African-American students in higher education. The focus is on the significance of culturally relevant curricula and social outlets, and of cultural representation among teachers, staff, and peers.

Lomotey recommends restructuring teacher education programs so that they efficiently prepare prospective teachers to work with students of color in communities of color, by implementing culturally relevant curricula into pedagogy and practice; providing mentors and role models of color to support and guide students of color; and using textbooks and supplemental learning materials that represent the histories and lives of the whole community. Concerning women in higher education, Lomotey finds that socially defined gender roles virtually immobilize women in the advancement of their careers. He encourages women to take risks and confront sexism head on, and for African-American women in particular, to do so with both racism and sexism.

WRIGLEY looks at the gender bias in education issue from a larger perspective. The author examines the bridge between the public world of occupations and the private world of families, which are linked by the schools. This bridge is described by looking at four topic areas. One is an analysis of gender and education from a comparative and historical perspective, with particular attention to the role of the state. This includes welfare, national economic development, and the subordinate role of women in types of schooling women seek. A second is gender and social relations with schools and universities, including interaction of race and gender in the schooling of African-American and white girls, gender segregation in elementary school, student differences in social class, feminist knowledge, and sexual orientation. A third area is the social context of learning. Issues discussed include why women do well in school, differences in notions of intelligence measured in terms of academic achievement, and socially influenced math scores. The fourth area is families and schools—the link conditioned by social class and gender. Special focus is placed on working-class and middle-class mothers' roles in managing their children's educational careers.

—BEVERLY STITT

See also Pedagogy, Feminist; Sexual Harassment in Education

Gender-Role Socialization

Devor, Holly, *Gender Blending: Confronting the Limits of Duality,* Bloomington: University of Indiana Press, 1989

Golombok, Susan, and Robyn Fivush, *Gender Development,* New York: Cambridge University Press, 1994

Howard, Judith, *Gendered Situations, Gendered Selves: A Gender Lens on Social Psychology,* Thousand Oaks, California: Sage, 1997

Leaper, Campbell, and William Damon, *Childhood Gender Segregation: Causes and Consequences,* San Francisco: Jossey-Bass, 1994

Lorber, Judith, *Paradoxes of Gender,* New Haven, Connecticut: Yale University Press, 1994

Richardson, Laurel Walum, *The Dynamics of Sex and Gender: A Sociological Perspective,* Chicago: Rand McNally, 1977

Thorne, Barrie, *Gender Play: Girls and Boys in School,* Buckingham: Open University Press, and New Brunswick, New Jersey: Rutgers University Press, 1993

Scholarly work in the area of gender-role socialization has been most strongly influenced by research in the areas of social psychology and sociology. Social psychologists have examined how interaction shapes development while sociologists have examined the more structural forces behind gender-role development. GOLOMBOK and FIVUSH's book addresses the changing nature of women's role socialization through the past four decades. This book examines how shifting family structures, expanding job opportunities and new reproductive issues influence the process of gender socialization for women. Writing from a developmental psychology perspective, the authors argue that scholars of gender-role development must begin to look beyond parent/family socialization. Instead, gender roles are developed through a complex pattern of interaction between individuals and their wider social environment.

HOWARD explores more specific theoretical questions about the relationship between social psychology and gender role socialization. Essentialist, social construction, socialization, and structural approaches and theories about gender development are nicely described and analyzed in the first section of this book. Howard also examines the emergence of social exchange theory, behaviorism, and social learning theories on our understanding of gender-role development. This book is a vital resource for gaining a theoretical background of social psychological approaches to gender-role socialization.

The study of gender socialization in early childhood development is a well-established area in both women's studies and social psychology. LEAPER and DAMON offer a rich edited volume containing important current research on gender socialization in the field of developmental psychology. The authors combine works from a variety of authors to uncover the physiological, emotional, and behavioral correlates of forced and voluntary gender segregation for small children. By examining the emergence of gender segregation in toddler play groups, the authors offer an important understanding on early stages of gender socialization. The book explores the consequences of gender segregation on children's interpersonal relationships and cognitive abilities.

THORNE's research on grade school children successfully combines social psychological and structural perspectives on gender-role socialization. The author conducts extensive qualitative field observation of grade school children over an extended period and examines how the structure of schools, set-up of classrooms, and discipline of teachers effects gender-role socialization in children. Unlike other studies that examine gender-role socialization as a static process, Thorne depicts gender socialization as a process mediated with different tactics and results depending on the race or class of young children.

Through interviews with fifteen gender-blending females, DEVOR explores how gender roles are developed in individuals with ambiguous biological sexual characteristics. This book successfully addresses the debate between biological and social explanations for gender-specific behavior. Interviewees talk candidly about their experiences defining their gender through learning cues from social interaction, parents, teachers, and medical professionals. This book is critical for understanding the importance of the medical community in defining and shaping the gender roles of a biologically sexually ambiguous individual.

RICHARDSON provides an older, yet extremely comprehensive, analysis of both social psychological and structural underpinnings for gender-role development. She examines the relationship between biology and language, arguing that how humans communicate about gender is critical in shaping gender-specific behaviors and roles of the individual. It is through this process of communicating, naming, and reacting that children are shaped into masculine or feminine personalities. Additionally, she explores how the social sciences, psychological theories and therapies, law, and religion work to create social understandings of appropriate gendered roles and action. According to Richardson, sexual inequality has been structured into our social understandings of appropriate gender-role development. This process is illuminated through the book as Richardson examines gender roles in occupational structures, politics, industrial economics, and the family.

Using a postmodern deconstruction of gender roles, LORBER explores and critiques the structural, medical, and social processes of gender socialization. Lorber argues that gender roles are not biologically or naturally derived. Instead, gender roles are social constructions designed and motivated by power and social stratification. This book is a good overview of the arguments of many poststructuralist and postmodernist gender theorists who argue that gender-role socialization cannot be changed to advance the position of women; rather, gender should become obsolete as a social category. Lorber's work is theoretical in nature and slightly utopian in content, but it is an extremely important work in the field of postmodern gender socialization theory.

—AMY S. FARRELL

Gender Stereotyping

Elfenbein, Anna Shannon, *Women on the Color Line: Evolving Stereotypes and the Writings of George Washington Cable, Grace King, Kate Chopin*, Charlottesville: University Press of Virginia, 1989

Fuss, Diana, *Essentially Speaking: Feminism, Nature and Difference*, New York and London: Routledge, 1989

Garner, Helen, *The First Stone: Some Questions about Sex and Power*, Sydney: Picador, 1995; New York: Free Press, 1997

Hall, Catherine, *White, Male, and Middle Class: Explorations in Feminism and History*, New York: Routledge, and Cambridge: Polity, 1992

hooks, bell, *Black Looks: Race and Representation*, Boston: South End Press, and London: Turnaround, 1992

Kennedy, Helena, *Eve Was Framed: Women and British Justice*, London: Chatto and Windus, 1992

Kloppenborg, Ria, and Wouter J. Hanegraaff (eds.), *Female Stereotypes in Religious Traditions*, Leiden and New York: E.J. Brill, 1995

Lewis, Reina, *Gendering Orientalism: Race, Femininity and Representation*, London and New York: Routledge, 1996

Ranging from examinations of concepts of gender in the law to religious perceptions of women and to the intricate and ambiguous power relations inherent in allegations of sexual harassment, a broad array of works is available for research into gender stereotyping. Authors have explored notions of "essential" biological sexual characteristics and the ways in which they shape social and cultural preceptions of women.

KLOPPENBORG and HANEGRAAFF edit a collection of contributions that testify to the endurance and potential universality of various stereotypes of women in different religious traditions. The contributions examine stereotypes of widowhood, women's unbridled sexuality, female ignorance and emotionality, "Great Mother" symbolism, and images of witches, to elucidate the generalisations and the fears that emerge in male-controlled society when challenged by women who confront male authority.

In contrast to many cultural histories of imperialism that analyse Orientalist images of rather than by women, LEWIS's work explores the ways in which women contributed to Orientalist discourse. Lewis contests masculinist assumptions in relation to the consistency and homogeneity of the Orientalist gaze, proposing that her chosen authors used their experience as women and their gendered access to female experience in the Orient to challenge stereotypes. Consequently, women's relationships to the shifting meanings of race, nation, and gender produced positions from which female writers and artists could express alternative representations of gendered, classed and racialised difference propagated through stereotypes.

A revisioning of the rhetorical power of essentialism, the idea that people innately hold certain stereotypical characteristics, moves FUSS to examine the motivations for the deployment of essentialist texts, and to analyse the political and textual effects of essentialism in particular sets of discourses. Arguing that there is no essence to essentialism, she rethinks constructionism, the idea that characteristics are culturally constructed, as a sophisticated form of essentialism, in order to question the stability and impermeability of the essentialist/constructionist binarism. A profound theoretical analysis of sexual difference prefaces the debates in which she addresses notions of "sex" and "race" as empirical categories.

HALL's work surveys the development of feminist history to demonstrate the theoretical evolutions that have shaped many historians' efforts in the recent past. The essays examine the construction of middle-class gendered identities within the imperialist past of England. The work questions constructs of gender and class from a perspective of race, ethnicity, and difference in order to decentre the fixed meanings attached to the categories "man" or "woman," and to engage in a dynamic relation to the political world that shapes such categories.

HOOKS addresses the stereotyping that represents African-Americans in the mass media. She challenges readers to rethink the internalised racism that maintains the connection between mass media as a system of knowledge and power and the negative aspects of black representation. A variety of arguments are proposed to emphasise the concept of non-white subjectivity as a radical critique of race and of the sexual politics of black women and men.

KENNEDY examines the ways in which the British legal system disregards, denigrates, and discriminates against women. She scrutinises the stereotypes of the young, the working-class, the immigrant, the Irish, and the black woman, which permeate and construct negative images of women, and deny their experience in order to maintain male power. Her powerful analysis demonstrates the insensitivities of a masculinist criminal justice system that lacks mechanisms for self-reflexivity.

In writing about the color line after the American Civil War, ELFENBEIN's work treats three authors who were aware of the plight of those barred by gender, race, or class from determining their own destinies. She argues that they attempted to understand the disintegration of the Southern world through fiction that deploys the prewar stereotype of the "tragic octoroon." Elfenbein examines the ways in which this fantasy continues in the transhistorical stereotype of liminal femininity. In exploring the power of the stereotyped woman in manacles she argues that it displays an extreme version of the sexualisation of powerlessness, and of the black woman as a servant of the oppressive ideology that neutralises women's chances for freedom and fulfilment.

A personalised and journalistic reconstruction of the complexities and ambiguities surrounding an incident of alleged sexual harassment at an Australian university, GARNER's lucid account rewrites the parameters for discussing this topical issue. Her propositions that understandings of eros should be factored into modern feminism drive a narrative that distinguishes elder feminists from those of the younger "priggish, disingenuous, unforgiving" generation. This is an unsettling account of the gender stereotypes constructed for men and women, as well as the intergenerational divisions evolving between women.

—HELEN JOHNSON

Geography

Hanson, Susan, and Geraldine Pratt, *Gender, Work, and Space*, London and New York: Routledge, 1995

Massey, Doreen, *Space, Place, and Gender*, Minneapolis: University of Minnesota Press, and Cambridge: Polity Press, 1994

Norwood, Vera, and Janice Monk, *The Desert Is No Lady: Southwestern Landscapes in Women's Writing and Art*, New Haven, Connecticut, and London: Yale University Press, 1987

Rose, Gillian, *Feminism and Geography: The Limits of Geographical Knowledge*, Minneapolis: University of Minnesota Press, and Cambridge: Polity Press, 1993

Seager, Joni, *Earth Follies: Coming to Terms with the Global Environmental Crisis*, New York: Routledge; as *Earth Follies: Feminism, Politics and the Environment*, London: Earthscan, 1993

Townsend, Janet, *Women's Voices from the Rainforest*, London and New York: Routledge, 1995

In recent years, feminist geography has transformed the scope of the field. Contemporary writings critique traditional geography for its male bias and severe under-representation of women. In response to traditional geography, which focuses on men's interpretations of landscape, NORWOOD and MONK's classic text describes women's interactions with the environment, as well as interpretations and reactions to a changing landscape. Norwood and Monk focus on women's literary and artistic interpretations of southwestern landscapes and the role of gender in environmental perception. The text also illustrates a more recent concern with women's communities of various cultures.

In a textbook that sets a foundation for feminist critical geography, ROSE discusses the limitations of masculinist scientific traditions in geography. In her book, Rose reveals the gendered thinking ingrained in traditional geographical work. Feminist critique of geography often focuses on methodology, revealing the problems with "objective" (or positivist) scientific methods. A white, male "gaze" is the traditional way of both seeing and obtaining knowledge and "truth." A rational, objective male gaze in science holds a feminine object as "other." This gaze is the dominant mode of analyzing landscapes and of obtaining knowledge of other cultures through imperialism. Rose seeks to deconstruct the unexamined subject position and the same/other dichotomy of masculinist geographical discourse. Many basic theories and concerns of feminist geography are presented in this book and are expanded in other geographers' writings. Rose reveals the inherent power in looking at landscapes, and the similar positioning of women and landscape, using sexual psychoanalytical analyses. The female subject can challenge the duality in geographical academic tradition and dominant discourses of identity. There is also an introduction to concepts of Marxist critique in feminist geography. This branch of writing concerns connections among space, labor, and class.

Marxist geographers emphasize the significance of class as a determinant of women's position in society. This analysis is integral to the new emphasis on Third World women's geographies. Marxist geography examines spaces of women's oppression, distinguishing between women of different class and color. HANSON and PRATT's book examines the construction of gender differences and their spatial expression using a case study in Worcester, Massachusetts. Hanson and Pratt combine theory and ethnographic research, a popular technique of feminist geography, to focus on women's labor patterns in the city. The authors acknowledge their own subjectivity and positioning, an integral step of feminist research. Hanson and Pratt assume the inseparability of economic and social spheres and include a Marxist analysis of factors that shape women's work, including community, household geographies, labor relations, work patterns, distance and commuting, and local labor processes. An analysis of gendered geographies explains why women who live in different parts of the city have access to different types of employment. The authors find strong links between domestic responsibilities and employment situations of women, as well as between position in the home and position in the labor market. A household's residential location is found to influence women's access to employment more than men's. Distance is found to help constitute gender divisions of labor.

MASSEY also works from a Marxist perspective in her book, which deals with space and place concepts of social relations. Included are analyses of class and work relations, the role of geography in the construction of gender relations, interrelations of space, place, and gender, and a conceptualization of the spatial. Massey uses British examples from different time periods to analyze and illustrate the industrial milieu and women's situation within specific industrial geographies. Much recent feminist geographical work concerns finding the place of women in postmodern geography and globalization, both of which are topics that Massey introduces.

SEAGER's book is a crucial contribution to feminist environmental geography. A unique perspective on the global environmental crisis suggests that institutions operated by men are primarily responsible for destroying the earth. Seager shocks readers with details of environmental destruction by war, a male activity. Corporate culture is compared to masculinist positivist science in which people are detached from the "truth" and seek to control nature. Seager reveals the global politics that cause environmental inequality and "dumping on the poor." Even seemingly innocent environmental philosophies and activism contain inherent sexism. This book is riveting and effective in weaving theories of gender and geography with examples. Seager ties Marxist critique and philosophies of scientific reason and gender to the roots of environmental degradation. It is a necessary book for feminist geographers.

New thresholds in geography move from a rigid, structuralist, essentialist perspective to a poststructural (or postmodern) geography, which acknowledges difference and diversity among people and validates their voices and experiences. Poststructuralist geography offers more flexible perspectives on gender, race, and class. As an example, TOWNSEND explores the lives of female pioneers in Latin America, focusing on Mexican case studies. A main focus of the study is women's production and community. A new focus on representation and allowing the voices of marginalized women to be heard is exemplified by presenting four full uncut interviews with women at the end of this book. Townsend presents the findings of a team of researchers who are described and positioned in relation to the research. Their agenda is socialist and feminist. Townsend clearly defines their own biases and translational problems arising from language differences. Not only are the communities and problems of female pioneers documented, but the researchers also devised possible solutions with the women. Community, government, and private actions could all improve the lives of female pioneers.

—SHARÓN GORDON

Gilman, Charlotte Perkins 1860–1935

American Writer

Allen, Polly Wynn, *Building Domestic Liberty: Charlotte Perkins Gilman's Architectural Feminism*, Amherst: University of Massachusetts Press, 1988

Golden, Catherine (ed.), *The Captive Imagination: A Casebook on the Yellow Wallpaper*, New York: Feminist Press, 1992

Hill, Mary A., *Charlotte Perkins Gilman: The Making of a Radical Feminist, 1890–1896*, Philadelphia: Temple University Press, 1980

Karpinski, Joanne B. (ed.), *Critical Essays on Charlotte Perkins Gilman*, New York: G.K. Hall, 1992

Kessler, Carol Farley, *Charlotte Perkins Gilman: Her Progress toward Utopia with Selected Writings*, Syracuse, New York: Syracuse University Press, and Liverpool: Liverpool University Press, 1995

Lane, Ann J., *To Herland and Beyond: The Life and Work of Charlotte Perkins Gilman*, New York: Pantheon, 1990

Meyering, Sheryl L. (ed.), *Charlotte Perkins Gilman: The Woman and Her Work*, Ann Arbor, Michigan: UMI Research Press, 1989

Scharnhorst, Gary, *Charlotte Perkins Gilman*, Boston: Twayne, 1985

Although she gained an international reputation among late nineteenth- and early twentieth-century theorists and commentators, Charlotte Perkins Gilman's writings were out-of-print by the time of her death in 1935. Not until the resurgence of American feminism in the 1960s and 1970s did Gilman's life and work experience a happy resurgence. Along with her pioneering study *Women and Economics*, works such as *Herland* and the widely anthologized and critiqued story "The Yellow Wallpaper" have become staples of abiding interest to historians and literary critics alike.

In the first volume-length biography of Gilman, HILL explores the distinction between Gilman's public image and private self. Hill declares that Gilman's theories stem not only from her devotion and commitment to public reforms, but from her personal needs as a woman who struggled to find satisfying human relationships. Convincingly tracing the origins of Gilman's feminist convictions to her family history—the illustrious Beecher clan, including great aunts Catharine Beecher and Harriet Beecher Stowe—Hill offers a thorough introduction to the early and sustaining influences on Gilman's life. Hill's analyses of the early short stories, such as "The Test Case," do a good job of providing clues to Gilman's private struggles, and her anger with social norms that upheld a double standard regarding male and female behavior.

SCHARNHORST has written a literary biography that focuses less on Gilman's private life, and more on the body of her written work. Attempting to move away from reading Gilman's imaginative work as thinly disguised memoir, Scharnhorst suggests that the overarching purpose of Gilman's canon is didactic; the poetry and fiction thus anticipate and amplify this purpose. Particularly useful is Scharnhorst's chapter on Gilman's seven-year stint as sole editor, writer, and publisher of 86 issues of the *Forerunner*, which included nonfiction pieces on issues of social concern (e.g., white slavery, noise pollution), editorials, poems, fiction, sermons, and book reviews. Gilman's debt to a kind of reform Darwinism put her at odds with contemporary literary naturalists such as Theodore Dreiser and Jack London. According to Scharnhorst, however, Gilman's "reform naturalism...enabled her to transcend the contradiction of design and purpose inherent in conventional naturalism."

Focusing on Gilman's architectural analysis of the work and home place, ALLEN persuasively argues that Gilman's writings on the relationship between spatial design and gender relationships are a vital precursor to emerging fields of contemporary urban and women's studies. Inspired by the ideas of communitarian socialists such as Charles Fourier, Gilman strongly believed that central to the perpetuation of sexual inequality was the "exploitation of women's domestic labor." Allen's analysis of Gilman's "indictment against the organization of the home" provides a succinct and helpful overview of the anachronistic "evils of the unevolved home." To reinforce Gilman's extraordinary efforts in the field of spatial reformation, Allen also examines the many articles and speeches written, the sketches made, and the photographs taken by Gilman to spell out her architectural vision to urban planners, developers, builders, and consumers.

Providing the first edition of critical essays on Gilman, MEYERING includes Carl Degler's seminal essay on Gilman's feminism, along with more recent articles on "The Yellow Wallpaper," *Herland* and *What Diantha Did*. Meyering's introduction adeptly places Gilman's life and works in a historical and cultural context, providing important connections to both nineteenth- and twentieth-century women writers, including such figures as Harriet Jacobs and Sylvia Plath.

LANE'S full-length biography complements both Hill and Scharnhorst's earlier work, by analyzing the major relationships that formulated Gilman's personality and her prodigious output of writings. Lane analyzes the influence not only of family, friends, and Gilman's first and second husbands, but the crucial, if not damaging, influence of the foremost nineteenth-century neurologist, Silas Weir Mitchell. Particularly revealing is Lane's chapter on Katharine, Gilman's only child, who was 93 years old when Lane interviewed her. Lane's lengthy chapters on Gilman's work illuminate the integral relationship between Gilman's private and public selves.

Focusing solely on Gilman's famous short story, "The Yellow Wallpaper," GOLDEN's collection amply provides both the historical backgrounds of women's political, medical, and social situation in nineteenth-century Victorian America, and a plethora of twentieth-century critical articles on the story itself. Throughout the first section, Golden includes selections from S. Weir Mitchell's analysis of women's nervous conditions, Gilman's article on why she wrote the story, and more recent analyses of upper-middle-class white women's "fashionable diseases." Golden provides useful and succinct introductory commentary before each article. The second section offers theoretical breadth, including feminist, psychoanalytical, linguistic, and historical analyses of this widely canonized story.

In her collection of essays on Gilman, KARPINSKY has brought together reviews, contemporary comments, and modern criticism. Particularly excellent is Carol Ruth Berkin's "Private Woman, Public Woman: The Contradictions of Charlotte Perkins Gilman," which functions as a biographical introduction to Gilman's life and personal confrontation with feminism. Also included are assessments of Gilman by writers personally acquainted with the author. In the section on modern criticism, Karpinsky includes good essays illustrating the breadth and depth of Gilman's prolific writing career. Gilman is also analyzed alongside other English and American writers, such as Jonathan Swift, Olive Schreiner, and William Dean Howells.

In her book, KESSLER presents the first full-length genre study based on Gilman's utopian fiction. Providing a superb analysis of utopian writing as "cultural work," Kessler recasts Gilman as a social activist who used her writing as a method of social action. Illustrating in the first four chapters how Gilman subscribed to a literature that self-consciously sought to effect social change, Kessler collects 14 reprinted selections from Gilman's utopian writing that support and explicate Gilman's literary didacticism and hopeful vision. Kessler includes an extensive and highly useful bibliography on utopian fiction and cultural studies.

—MARY JO BONA

Girlhood

Belotti, Elena, *What are Little Girls Made Of?: The Roots of Feminine Stereotypes*, New York: Schocken, 1976

Bingham, Mindy, Sandy Stryker, and Susan Allstetter (eds.), *Things Will Be Different for My Daughter: A Practical Guide to Building Her Self-Esteem and Self-Reliance*, New York: Penguin, 1995

Grossman, Herbert, and Suzanne H. Grossman, *Gender Issues in Education*, Boston: Alwyn and Bacon, 1994

Rivers, Caryl, Rosalind Barnett, and Grace Baruch, *Beyond Sugar and Spice: How Women Grow, Learn, and Thrive*, Putnam, 1979

Thorne, Barrie, *Gender Play: Girls and Boys in School*, Buckingham: Open University Press, and New Brunswick, New Jersey: Rutgers University Press, 1993

Verma, K.K., Rajan Verma, and Saboohi Kazim, *Towards Gender Equality: An Experiment in Development Education*, New Delhi: Commonwealth, 1995

While books on many issues could be included in a discussion of "girlhood," the following books were chosen because of their emphasis on gender differences, whether differences in how girls are raised, in the school experience, or in boys' play versus that of girls. The collection of books, while not extensive, illustrates that experiences for girls are similar from one decade to another and from one country to another.

BINGHAM and STRYKER's book is intended as a manual for the mothers of girls, but it is a theoretical reference as well as a "how-to." It covers the range of issues affecting a girl's life from infancy through adolescence. Topics discussed range from how to give and take criticism, to the meanings of nursery rhymes and fairy tales. The book is a good reference for parents and teachers, who will appreciate the suggestions for action sprinkled throughout, and for academics, who will appreciate the summaries of much of the research relating to girls and growing up.

GROSSMAN and GROSSMAN's book is more focused than Bingham and Stryker's, in that it looks at sex differences in education, and in that its discussions and recommendations are confined to academic issues. The authors are thorough, however, in their chapters on the origins and development of gender differences, gender equity, accommodating gender differences, and reducing gender-specific behavior. For example, as areas on which to focus with girls, the authors include stereotypical language patterns, cooperation versus competition, self-confidence, and male dominance in groups. Although the book is most useful to educators, parents too can benefit from the suggestions for action, and researchers have in one volume much of the information available on gender issues in education.

THORNE's book is similar to Grossman and Grossman's in that it is an examination of the school experience and the ways in which it differs for girls and boys. It is a more personal account, however, including the author's observations of her own children—from which she concludes that gender is socially constructed—and her use of fieldwork for the book. She spent time in fourth- and fifth-grade classrooms as an observer but also spent time with the children on the playground and in the cafeteria to find out what they were like in venues beyond the classroom. The book is not restricted to her field notes; as a sociologist, Thorne also injects theory and research into her accounts. As do other authors, she has advice for educators that includes grouping students in ways other than by gender, reinforcing cooperation among all children, facilitating access to all activities for all children, and actively intervening to challenge the dynamics of stereotyping and power.

Two books from the 1970s sound depressingly relevant in the 1990s. RIVERS, BARNETT, and BARUCH mix history, psychology, anthropology, and child development into discussions of treatment of girl babies versus that of boy babies, working mothers versus stay-at-home mothers, the trials and tribulations of girls and team sports, academic issues, and relationships of girls with their mothers and fathers. Their chapter on educational experiences is reminiscent of later books, and their complaints about the treatment of female athletes compared with their male counterparts were still valid 20 years later.

BELOTTI's findings do not differ from those of other researchers, even though she was writing about the Italian experience of raising girls. Her basic theme is that home, toys, books, school, and the media all contribute to stereotypes that prevent girls from growing up with the choices boys have. She says that despite legal equality and acceptance into most professions, most females will not be able to have access to these rights until the psychological structures that prevent them from wanting and appropriating these rights are modified.

In India, historically one of the least progressive countries for girls and women, researchers experimented with a media campaign designed to teach gender sensitization, and the results of this campaign are described in VERMA, VERMA, and KAZIM'S book. Sponsored by the Indian government, the project was designed to present a positive image of the girl child as a start toward gender equality. Areas of the country identified as the most backward in terms of gender equality were chosen for the experiment. Evaluation at the end of the project indicated that there had been "some" change in attitude, and the authors conclude that with changes in the structure of the campaign there would be much more.

—KATE PEIRCE

See also Adolescence

Girls' Organizations

Fedder, Ruth, *Guidance through Club Activities,* New York: Teachers College Press, 1965

Knupfer, Anne Meis, *Toward a Tenderer Humanity and a Nobler Womanhood: African-American Women's Clubs in Turn-of-the-Century Chicago,* New York: New York University Press, 1996

McLaughlin, Milbrey Wallin, *Urban Sanctuaries: Neighborhood Organizations in the Lives and Futures of Inner City Youth,* San Francisco: Jossey-Bass, 1994

Soto, Carolyn, *The Girl Scouts,* New York: Exeter, 1987

Girls' organizations typically help to foster a sense of identity and self-worth in a group setting. FEDDER's book gives insight into the theory of adolescent group process. There are descriptions of the ways in which actual clubs and their activities can be used for the guidance of club members. She shows how certain specific clubs were formed, and how and why the leaders worked with them for the guidance purposes the leaders held. She intersperses the realistic accounts of these real clubs and their activities with explanations of why the activities were guided as they were, and why the experiences that the members had in their clubs affected them as they did. This book is divided into four parts. Part one deals with the significance of group experience and the roles of the leader. Part two specifically discusses a girls' leadership council and how it is organized. Part three looks at the sponsor's responsibility and the development of a hobby program. And finally, part four sums up the value of girls' organizations to the members, the leaders, and society in general. Although Fedder's book was published in 1965, it remains an informative and accurate account of club organization.

Changing focus slightly, McLAUGHLIN writes about organizations in terms of inner-city youth. The disintegration of community and of the sense of community is quite evident throughout the world, but it is even more obvious in the inner city. Young people need community. If they cannot find it in conventional settings, gangs offer a grim alternative. The author addresses this need and underscores some basic realities. One such reality is the importance and vitality of activities for boys and girls that are firmly rooted in the local community and are shaped by local knowledge. Another reality is that young people become more deeply involved in and committed to the activities in which they have a shaping role. The sense of personal control engendered in youth by their participation is another reality, and this is an important ingredient in the discipline and respect for rules stressed in this book. The young girls and boys described here want to work hard in some challenging and worthwhile activity. They want to be seen as respected and trusted contributors to the common venture. They want to be valued members of society, and this is true whether or not the child (boy or girl) is from the inner city.

KNUPFER narrows the focus to African-American girls in Chicago at the turn of the century. Looking at the social life and customs, she discusses the roles of clubs for African-American girls. The idea of these clubs was to give the girls a cultural bond, shared values, and a sense of belonging. She explores the significance of ethnicity for these clubs and finds that their activities supported community spirit, social concern, and philanthropic involvement. Knupfer shows how such clubs turned young girls' problems into hope and created environments that treated young African-American women as resources to be encouraged, instead of problems to be managed. This book is also about this city's social compact with its young African-American women.

SOTO's book discusses how far Girl Scouting has come in merely 80 years. The organization is pictured as an upward- and outward-looking source of inspiration, learning, and sisterhood for the girls and young women who are (or were) involved in it. This book demonstrates that contemporary activities from camping to career exploration further the challenge of modern girls' Scouting experiences. The author also shows how the girls' participation in that challenge helps to prepare them for their own best future. The book looks at Girl Scouts and Girl Guides in the United States, the United Kingdom, and Canada.

—SUSAN M. TAYLOR

Glasgow, Ellen 1873–1945

American Writer

Ekman, Barbro, *The End of a Legend: Ellen Glasgow's History of Southern Women,* Stockholm: Uppsala, 1979

Godbold, E. Stanley, *Ellen Glasgow and the Woman Within,* Baton Rouge: Louisiana State University Press, 1972

Matthews, Pamela R., *Ellen Glasgow and A Woman's Tradition,* Charlottesville: University Press of Virginia, 1994

McDowell, Frederick P.W., *Ellen Glasgow and the Ironic Art of Fiction,* Madison: University of Wisconsin Press, 1960

Raper, Julius Rowan, *Without Shelter: The Early Career of Ellen Glasgow,* Baton Rouge: Louisiana State University Press, 1971

———, *From the Sunken Garden: The Fiction of Ellen Glasgow, 1916–1945,* Baton Rouge: Louisiana State University Press, 1980

Richards, Marion K., *Ellen Glasgow's Development as a Novelist,* The Hague: Mouton, 1971

Santas, Joan Foster, *Ellen Glasgow's American Dream,* Charlottesville: University Press of Virginia, 1965

Wagner-Martin, Linda, *Ellen Glasgow: Beyond Convention,* Austin: University of Texas Press, 1982

Ellen Glasgow's 19 novels function as a social history of Virginia from antebellum days through her own lifetime and of the universality of human experience. In the critical community, she was defined as the first Southern realist writer, one of the outstanding female writers between World War I and World War II, and one of the few American authors of her period to satirize the foibles of Southern society. Many of Glasgow's books were best-sellers, and she received numerous awards, including the Pulitzer Prize for fiction in 1942 with *In This Our Lives.* In spite of this acclaim, her works were neglected after her death in 1945 until a critical revival took place in the 1960s and 1970s. Until recently, critics have too often approached her works through the limits of her gender and her position as a Southern upper-class woman, asserting that she worked out her own life experiences, particularly her emotional life, through her fiction.

McDOWELL traces both Glasgow's life and literary development. His book was the first full-length critical study of the author and established her place in American literature. McDowell links Glasgow to the current literary use of modified naturalism through her ability to combine realism with irony (which he perceived as her retreat from actuality), reflecting her belief in a modified determinism that operates in human lives.

SANTAS is the first of several critics to link Glasgow's interest in Darwinian theories with her literary development of the evolution of moral values. While critiquing the hypocrisy and decay of the Southern chivalric code of behavior, which resulted in tragedies of frustration and wasted lives through maladjustment to post-plantation life, Glasgow's work expresses her belief in the upward evolution of virtue, and an internally civilized world, resulting in a society of blessed individuals who manifest the primary, but long forgotten, real chivalric virtues: truth, justice, courage, loyalty, and compassion.

Somewhat similarly, RAPER (1971) correlates the Darwinian influence on Glasgow's first 10 novels with her search for those human values that she believed were universal and enduring in the face of the changing values and dying traditions of the post-Civil War South.

In his second book (1980), RAPER studies the second half of Glasgow's writing career, addressing her concern with the evolution of the spirit, heredity, and her use of traditional literary devices such as the foil, the double, and projection to create the psychologically rich inner lives of her most enduring characters.

RICHARDS traces the consistencies and changes in Glasgow's literary development from her first published novel, *The Descendent* (1897), to *Barren Ground* (1925), her first major critical success, which reveals "her full grasp of her craft." Richards is the first to point out how thoroughly Glasgow's personal and literary rebellion against the Virginia tradition of "evasive idealism" (escapist gentility) negatively affected women; her central female characters achieve triumph only by defying intricate and too often corrupt traditions.

In GODBOLD's biography (which he took up after the initial biographer Marjorie Kinnan Rawlings died), he too facilely relates Glasgow's life experiences to her fiction. He asserts that she vacillated between the roles of an old-fashioned Southern girl and the modern intellectual, the latter of which incorporated a code for living that drained both Glasgow and her heroic women characters of their humanity, even as she critiqued such wavering in her characters.

EKMAN describes the 12 novels that made up the 1938 Virginia edition of Glasgow's work as a social history of women's lives in the South, expressive of Glasgow's personality and her own struggles to strike a balance among three possible roles for women. These roles were (1) the woman of the Southern romantic tradition, which made aristocratic women victims of the code of chivalry, (2) the liberated woman, who, because of her "vein of iron," learned to live without love, and (3) the new woman, who, with no respect for old traditions, believed she had the right to happiness.

WAGNER-MARTIN refutes earlier critics' contentions that Glasgow's writing was immediately and consistently affected and informed by her personal life experiences and emotions. Wagner-Martin contends that Glasgow combined experience, observation, reflection, and learning about women with a hard-fought sense of confidence as woman and artist to create her later, more mature fiction.

MATTHEWS, Glasgow's most feminist critic, defends her from the persistent critical and social bias that denigrated her for being a woman trying to find a place in a man's world. This traditional bias forces female writers into a split existence of writing for acceptance in a patriarchal social and literary world and for themselves as individuals. Matthews critiques this bias that praised Glasgow when she wrote in a "masculine" way and then criticized her for being too unfeminine, for writing too much about women's lives and concerns, for believing that her life must be the basis for her art, and for allowing her own life and love experiences to overly inform her writing. Matthews also questions earlier critics' attempts to fix Glasgow squarely in heterosexuality and thus explain the marriage plot both in her life and her art. Matthews reevaluates Glasgow's position on women's friendships, redefining the evolution of virtue and Glasgow's use of women's communities.

—JANET M. LABRIE

Glass Ceiling

Amott, Teresa L., and Julie A. Matthaei, *Race, Gender, and Work: A Multicultural Economic History of Women in the United States*, Boston: South End Press, 1991

Davidson, Marilyn J., and Cary L. Cooper, *Shattering the Glass Ceiling: The Woman Manager*, London: Paul Chapman, 1992

Goldin, Claudia D., *Understanding the Gender Gap: An Economic History of American Women*, New York: Oxford University Press, 1990; Oxford: Oxford University Press, 1992

Morrison, Ann M., *The New Leaders: Guidelines on Leadership Diversity in America*, San Francisco: Jossey-Bass, 1992

Rhode, Deborah L., *Speaking of Sex: The Denial of Gender Inequality*, Cambridge, Massachusetts, and London: Harvard University Press, 1997

Rosener, Judith, *America's Competitive Secret: Utilizing Women as a Management Strategy*, New York: Oxford University Press, 1995

U.S. Department of Labor, *A Report on the Glass Ceiling Initiative*, Washington, D.C.: U.S. Government Printing Office, 1991

Walsh, Mary Roth (ed.), *Women, Men, and Gender: Ongoing Debates*, New Haven, Connecticut: Yale University Press, 1997

"Glass ceiling" is a phrase that originated in 1986, which metaphorically describes an invisible barrier that delays or precludes the promotion of capable women, and minorities, from positions of top management or authority. This is a discriminatory barrier that can be particularly frustrating due in part to the transparent property of glass—you can clearly see the upper level but are prevented from reaching it. As a result of various civil rights legislation and affirmative action programs, women and minorities have begun and continue to achieve some measure of success in breaking through the barrier of the glass ceiling. The degree to which the glass ceiling has been cracked, shattered, or endures intact remains a matter of some debate. However, as is the case with other forms of labor market discrimination, measuring the relative burden of the glass ceiling remains problematic, since documenting the actual reasons for not being promoted can be quite difficult. As a form of discrimination, a glass ceiling differs from the so-called and more prevalent "sticky floor." A glass ceiling bars a person, on the basis of race or gender, from rising to the top, while a sticky floor keeps that person in an entry-level, dead-end, and low-paying job.

Historical perspective allows a more comprehensive understanding of the changing conditions and long-term trends of the gender differences in employment opportunities and earnings. GOLDIN provides a substantial and thoughtful economic history of the female labor force in the United States. Goldin's study uses useful statistical information to examine the market and institutional forces that have inspired not only the changes, but also some constancies in the economic and social lives of American women over the course of a century or more.

AMOTT and MATTHAEI offer a more radical feminist economic and social history of the gender-based differences in occupations and wages across the United States. Amott and Matthaei examine social customs and institutions in diverse racial-ethnic and class hierarchies and by that provide an expansive and perceptive economic history, a history that extends and deepens our understanding of the multicultural similarities and differences in the workplace.

An account and comparison of the role of female managers in western Europe, Australia, and the United States is outlined in the book by DAVIDSON and COOPER. Their study demonstrates by examples that despite the fact that women have made progress in obtaining more managerial jobs, they remain disproportionately concentrated in the traditionally female industries. Since Davidson and Cooper's book offers comparative statistics and examples from a variety of industrialized nations, their study encourages the investigation of the relative impact, and timing, of contrasting public and private policies. Inasmuch as a glass ceiling is an obstacle to the promotion of qualified women and minorities, there is also an economic and social cost to the under-utilization of barred individuals. An inquiry into the effectiveness of strategies designed to help corporations in their efforts to increase managerial diversity can be found in MORRISON's study, which argues that among the most destructive barriers to managerial advancement are biases that regard racial and gender differences as weaknesses, and hostile and unsupportive work environments.

ROSENER examines the relative effects of underutilization of women and contends that the ability of corporate executives to recognize labor force and managerial diversity as an economic resource will produce a competitive advantage. Rosener's study reveals, among other things, that while women are reasonably represented in middle-management positions, they are still infrequently promoted to be the top executives within their firms. Moreover, the ratio of female top executives to middle managers is similar, although clearly not identical, in the United States, Britain, Japan, and across western Europe.

The U.S. DEPARTMENT OF LABOR's report is a concise summary of a commission that investigated why the glass ceiling exists within America's largest corporations and how the Department of Labor planned to work with public and private groups to do away with unnatural workplace barriers, which impede and diminish not only the economic progress of barred individuals but also of society in general. Thus, society has a self-interest in promoting sufficient career advancement opportunities and eliminating labor market obstacles.

WALSH provides an overview of opposing and interdisciplinary opinions on a number of meaningful gender-based issues. These are alternative and opposing opinions that provide general readers with some understanding and perspective on the cultural, psychological, biological, legal, and economic conditions of gender-related topics. Like many other works, this volume of collected essays investigates the differences and similarities of attitudes, social values, and decisions based upon gender. Despite the many over-simplifications and pitfalls of using simple gender as the basis of study, gender remains a significant and easy method of classification.

Despite persistent statistical and anecdotal evidence that gender inequality remains a substantial problem, there are those who doubt the degree to which the glass ceiling continues to obstruct the advancement of capable women and minorities. These people believe that such significant and sufficient progress has already been achieved that barriers to career advancement have ceased to be a problem, or that, even if the glass ceiling continues to exist, it will collapse of its own heavy-handiness soon enough, and without the need for any active intervention. RHODE's book examines the ways in which society denies or discounts the persistence of gender inequities. It explains how the cultural and social forces that help to perpetuate workplace inequalities are deeply rooted and sadly all too often unrecognized. Rhode's thoughtful study suggests that the enduring problems of gender-based inequality can never really be resolved until society not only acknowledges the true extent of the problems but finds the necessary determination to confront them.

—TIMOTHY E. SULLIVAN

See also Earnings Gap; Division of Labor by Sex; Dual Labor Market

Goddesses

Baring, Anne, and Jules Cashford, *The Myth of the Goddess: Evolution of an Image,* London and New York: Viking, 1991

Christ, Carol P., *Laughter of Aphrodite: Reflections on a Journey to the Goddess,* San Francisco: Harper and Row, 1987

Downing, Christine, *The Goddess: Mythological Images of the Feminine,* New York: Crossroad, 1981

Eller, Cynthia, *Living in the Lap of the Goddess: The Feminist Spirituality Movement in America,* New York: Crossroad, 1993

Hawley, John Stratton, and Donna Marie Wulff (eds.), *Devi: Goddesses of India,* Berkeley: University of California Press, 1996

Johnson, Elizabeth A., *She Who Is: The Mystery of God in Feminist Theological Discourse,* New York: Crossroad, 1992

Kinsley, David, *Hindu Goddesses: Visions of the Divine Feminine in Hindu Religious Tradition,* Berkeley: University of California Press, 1986

Olson, Carl (ed.), *The Book of the Goddess: Past and Present,* New York: Crossroad, 1983

Starhawk, *The Spiral Dance: A Rebirth of the Ancient Religion of the Goddess,* San Francisco: Harper and Row, 1979

Wolkstein, Diane, and Samuel Noah Kramer, *Inanna: Queen of Heaven and Earth—Her Stories and Poems from Sumer*, New York: Harper and Row, 1983; London: Rider, 1984

The difficulty with this crowded field is not finding books, but separating those containing reliable information from those filled with wish-fulfillment, fantasy, and projection. In no area of religious studies is popular writing more out of touch with accurate scholarly information and interpretation. This situation is unfortunate, because the topic of goddesses is centrally important to the feminist project of creating religions that are more responsive to women, and that treat them with dignity and respect. Many feminists would agree that symbolizing deities only as males cannot work for women, and that religions which have traditionally done so are in need of serious and thoroughgoing reform. Many other feminists would argue that religions of male monotheism cannot change quickly or thoroughly enough to be able to meet women's emotional and spiritual needs, and that non-mainstream religions are more appropriate. This selection of literature surveys some reliable books that encompass the broad range of topics relevant to scholarship on goddesses.

The most basic type of book on goddesses would be cross-cultural surveys that provide information on a wide variety of goddesses, past and present, from the array of world cultures. Unfortunately, this essential type of book is seriously under-represented in scholarship on goddesses. The best of the lot is OLSON's edited volume, written by a number of experts on different cultures and historical epochs. Especially recommended within this book is Barstow's extremely balanced and influential article on the prehistoric goddesses.

Goddesses of the ancient world have become very popular in feminist writings, and great care must be exercised in selecting from a vast array of books. As a whole, this literature is Eurocentrically one-sided, in that goddesses are important in all known ancient cultures, but those of pre-western antiquity are highlighted. A common tactic is a chapter by chapter chronological survey of such ancient goddesses, beginning with paleolithic figurines and ending with the Virgin Mary. An especially comprehensive and representative offering of this type is BARING and CASHFORD's survey, which includes numerous illustrations and some intriguing interpretations. More detailed discussions of a single goddess are less common, but one such book stands out. WOLKSTEIN and KRAMER's book on the goddess Inanna represents the cooperative effort of a major Sumerologist and a storyteller. The result is a compelling account of one of the most enduring goddess myths, and a vivid translation of some of the world's most stirring erotic poetry.

A central category of goddess literature involves contemporary appropriations, reconstructions, and interpretations of ancient deities. Such literature is concerned not only with accurate representations of these ancient deities, but also with how contemporary people might improve their spiritual and emotional lives by venerating such deities, newly interpreted in feminist fashion. Four innovative books represent the best of this literature, as well as the variety of approaches taken by those concerned with contemporary religiously useful interpretations of ancient deities.

The feminist spirituality movement is one of the major innovations in the world of contemporary spirituality. It claims to be "a rebirth of the ancient religion of the great goddess," to quote the subtitle of STARHAWK's book. Although the historical accuracy of that claim is disputed, the movement is unquestionably life-giving to many contemporary practitioners. Starhawk's manual is one of the earliest, most comprehensive, and evocative books of its type. ELLER's book is highly recommended as a sympathetic anthropological study on this new religious movement.

The second type of contemporary appropriation of ancient goddesses is represented by DOWNING's learned and provocative reflection on Greek goddesses. Her method involves using the ancient mythologies as a "myth-mirror" upon which to reflect and understand her own life, and to offer the resulting insights to others as helpful reflections for their spiritual development and self-understanding. Equally proficient as a scholarly account of Greek goddesses and as a suggestion regarding contemporary religious possibilities, this book is highly recommended.

Feminist theologian CHRIST's book is a sustained, systematic, autobiographical reflection on why religiously sensitive contemporary women might move away from traditional male monotheism to veneration of "the goddess." Trained in academic theology, and deeply loyal to traditional western monotheism at one point in her life, Christ grew increasingly aware of, and frustrated with, the systematic exclusion and demeaning of women in such religions. Her book represents the best internal conversation on the issues involved in a religious journey such as hers—a "journey to the goddess."

The final type of contemporary interpretation of ancient deities is represented by JOHNSON's book. Thinkers such as Johnson believe that male monotheism can be reconceptualized so that the monotheistic deity is now symbolized as both female and male, rather than male only. Such an approach is extremely widespread among Jewish and Christian feminists. Johnson's book is one of the more thorough-going of such reconceptualizations. She works within a very traditional Catholic model of Trinitarian theology, but she radically re-images that model, always referring to the deity in female terms. She suggests such language, not as an eternal linguistic style, but as a relevant, much needed contemporary corrective.

The final type of goddess literature is much underutilized by religious feminists. The only contemporary traditional goddess-worshipping religion is Hinduism, but Hindu goddesses have either been overlooked because Hindu society is male-dominated, or romantically and inaccurately portrayed in popular goddess literature. Nevertheless, accurate portrayals of Hindu goddesses have much to offer religious feminists, and many high quality books on Hindu goddesses have recently been published by specialists on Hinduism. The two included here are surveys of the broad range of Hindu goddesses, rather than more specialized accounts of individual goddesses. KINSLEY's book is a thorough discussion of many well-known and important Hindu goddesses, including accounts of both historical origins and contemporary practices for each goddess. HAWLEY and WULFF's edited volume includes discussions of some of the same goddesses as Kinsley's book, as well as much recent scholarship by younger scholars of Hinduism. Many of the articles discuss goddesses of recent origin, or goddesses who are less well known to English-speaking audiences.

—RITA M. GROSS

Goldman, Emma 1869–1940

American Activist

Chalberg, John, *Emma Goldman: American Individualist,* New York: HarperCollins, 1991

Drinnon, Richard, *Rebel in Paradise: A Biography of Emma Goldman,* Chicago: University of Chicago Press, 1961; London: University of Chicago Press, 1982

Falk, Candace, *Love, Anarchy, and Emma Goldman,* New York: Holt, Rinehart and Winston, 1984; London: Rutgers University Press, 1990

Ganguli, B.N., *Emma Goldman: Portrait of a Rebel Woman,* New Delhi: Allied, 1979

Haaland, Bonnie, *Emma Goldman: Sexuality and the Impurity of the State,* Montreal and New York: Black Rose, 1993

Morton, Marian J., *Emma Goldman and the American Left: "Nowhere at Home,"* New York: Twayne, 1992

Solomon, Martha, *Emma Goldman,* Boston: Twayne, 1987

Wexler, Alice, *Emma Goldman in Exile: From the Russian Revolution to the Spanish Civil War,* Boston: Beacon Press, 1989

A Russian immigrant to the United States, Emma Goldman is best known for her radical political beliefs. A leader of the American anarchist movement, "Red Emma" repeatedly denigrated capitalism, and these attacks triggered her numerous encounters with the police, eventually leading to Goldman's deportation from the United States. In an era of Communist scares, Goldman managed to frighten all manner and all number of American officials and citizens. Besides her work as anarchism's premier promoter, Goldman lectured for birth control and sexual liberty, against a military draft, and in favor of free speech. A few calmer contemporaries recognized Goldman's sharp wit and her feminist attitude, and it is for these qualities that Goldman has been immortalized by radical feminists. When the women's liberationists of the 1970s looked into the past for a feminist role model, they found Goldman. The liberationists detected a link between their radicalism and Goldman's politically provocative behavior and her determined refusal, in the face of all forms of coercion, to bow to conservative pressure. As befits a feminist icon, Goldman has been the subject of a great variety of studies. This listing only covers the tip of the Goldman iceberg.

DRINNON's book remains the classic biography of Goldman. This critical volume provides an excellent summary of Goldman's life, and it is essential reading for all scholars of the anarchist movement she led. Drinnon argues that Goldman confronted Americans with an archetypal rebel who challenged their social, intellectual, and political convictions. He suggests that the reactions of American citizens and the state show the changing capacities to accept an open society in which there could be true disagreement. Relying heavily on the revealing personal and political letters exchanged by Goldman and her anarchist comrade-in-arms and former lover, Alexander Berkman, Drinnon is particularly strong on political context. This lively book offers the best analysis of the legal complexities of the trial and the deportation of Goldman and Berkman.

A brief study of Goldman's life, GANGULI's book is drawn from a series of lectures about "Red Emma" that were delivered in India in 1977. It is an examination of how a female anarchist tried to solve her own specific existential problems. Ganguli argues that to Goldman, women's freedom came to have nuances that were not acceptable to conventional thought, but that were entirely consistent with anarchism as she understood it. This work is marred by heavy use of jargon and poor editing. The year of Goldman's death is reported incorrectly, not once but twice.

CHALBERG provides a biography of Goldman that is designed for an undergraduate audience. In this easy-to-read work, the author shows how Goldman's career reveals a great deal about the texture of American radicalism at the turn of the nineteenth century. A bibliographical essay completes the book.

WEXLER gives a full and fascinating account of Goldman's life after her 1919 deportation to Russia. This sequel to her *Emma Goldman in America* (1984) is heavily psychologically oriented, however, and in a controversial turn, Wexler suggests that Goldman's fervent anti-communism stemmed from her emotional stress and psychological disorientation, rather than from her reasoned political assesssment. The psychological and political dimensions of Goldman's life are far too closely intertwined for the comfort of most historians.

FALK, the editor of the *Emma Goldman Papers* (1990), is perhaps the foremost Goldman scholar in the world. Her sympathetic account is based upon a cache of letters discovered in 1975 that were written by Goldman to her manager and lover, Ben Reitman. It focuses on Goldman's relationship with Reitman between 1908 and 1918. Falk juxtaposes Goldman's erotic and romantic dependence on Reitman against her fiercely independent public persona.

MORTON examines Goldman's place within the American left. Goldman often found her home inside the political left and to many people, she personified this political orientation. Morton explores why anarchism, a response to the growing size and power of the economic and political institutions that accompanied nineteenth-century industrialization, proved so appealing to people who felt that their individuality was threatened with being dwarfed and stifled. More of a history of a political movement than a biography, Morton's book provides a sophisticated contribution to the body of work that focuses on Goldman. An excellent bibliographical essay and an annotated bibliography conclude this superb book.

SOLOMON explores Goldman's writing and speaking styles, examining Goldman's *Anarchism and Other Essays, The Social Significance of Modern Drama, Living My Life, My Disillusionment in Russia,* and *Mother Earth* in order to analyze her literary style and rhetorical strategies. In choosing to focus on the public Goldman, Solomon neglects the private one and, unlike Falk, does not examine the contradictions between the two. HAALAND's book opens with a superb yet brief sketch of Goldman's life and a review of the available Goldman literature. This book focuses on the ideas of Goldman as they relate to the centrality of sexuality and reproduction within her anarchist theory. Haaland analyzes Goldman's theories in light of contemporary feminist thought and the "sex wars" of second-wave feminism, which focus on the extent to which women's sexuality can be viewed as a liberatory force.

—CARYN E. NEUMANN

Gordimer, Nadine 1923–

South African Writer

Clingman, Stephen, *The Novels of Nadine Gordimer: History from the Inside,* Boston and London: Allen and Unwin, 1986

Cooke, John, *The Novels of Nadine Gordimer: Private Lives/Public Landscapes,* Baton Rouge and London: Louisiana State University Press, 1985

Ettin, Andrew Vogel, *Betrayals of the Body Politic: The Literary Commitments of Nadine Gordimer,* Charlottesville and London: University Press of Virginia, 1993

Haugh, Robert F., *Nadine Gordimer,* New York: Twayne, 1974

Heywood, Christopher, *Nadine Gordimer,* Windsor, England: Profile Books, 1983

King, Bruce (ed.), *The Later Fiction of Nadine Gordimer,* New York: St. Martin's Press, and London: Macmillan, 1993

Smith, Rowland (ed.), *Critical Essays on Nadine Gordimer,* Boston: G.K. Hall, 1990

Wagner, Kathrin, *Rereading Nadine Gordimer,* Bloomington: Indiana University Press, 1994

The career of novelist, essayist, and short story writer Nadine Gordimer, winner of the 1991 Nobel Prize for Literature, is inseparable from her lifelong residence in South Africa during the period of dramatic changes from colonialized white control through the horrors of the Nationalist government policy of apartheid to a cautious hope for a multiracial democracy ruled by a majority of its citizens. Her writing reflects a commitment to chronicle, through artistic fiction, the distinctive realities of South African life for both white and black citizens. Characteristically, her novels use the *bildungsroman* (apprenticeship) format, usually with female protagonists.

HAUGH, who wrote the initial book about Gordimer, introduces her writings with a topically organized first half focused on her short stories, and a chronologically structured second half about her first five novels. Haugh details Gordimer's literary debts to predecessors like Gustave Flaubert, Guy de Maupassant, Antonin Chekov, and Katherine Mansfield. He praises her short stories for their brilliant style and focus on personal love, while faulting the novels for weaknesses in point of view and structure, and for failure to handle racial confrontations well, advocating that she avoid political issues. He believes Gordimer's polemical, idealized view of black South Africans precludes complex character development; yet he admits that *Guest of Honor* has some merit. Haugh's rather superficial and impressionistic analysis limits its usefulness and renders his work outdated.

HEYWOOD surveys in 47 pages the contours of Gordimer's development as writer and social commentator in her first six novels and the short story collection *Some Monday for Sure* (1976). He asserts that the short stories signal significant shifts in the fictional techniques and goals that Gordimer will fully realize in the novels that follow. He discusses the prevalence of sexual and landscape symbols as mirrors of both individual and cultural values. He finds pervasive irony as Gordimer shifts from an emphasis in the first three novels on the centrality of personal relationships to pessimism in the second trio about the tragic social fractures resulting from apartheid. Heywood traces Gordimer's waning dependence on European literary and political models in favor of indigenous, revolutionary black cultural values and analyzes her exploration of mythic regeneration from the matrix of social disorder, especially in *The Conservatist.*

COOKE discusses three stages in Gordimer's personal, political, and artistic maturation through her first eight novels, demonstrated by her deepening vision of South African culture. These stages employ distinctive literary influences, styles, and philosophical perspectives. Her earliest novels from the 1950s derive inspiration from European literature and theory—particularly E.M. Forster's liberal humanism—and focus on personal relationships, affirming that individual connections between blacks and whites can heal South Africa's fractured society. A persistent metaphor for social liberation is the release of daughters from domineering mothers. Brutal political repression in the 1960s eroded this optimism; Gordimer shifted her settings from urban to veldt, espoused ironic detachment, and became more overtly political. She absorbed black African literary models, emphasizing the impassible gulf between black and white cultures. In the third stage—the late 1970s and early 1980s—Gordimer's characters become actively engaged with their broken society despite the high personal cost. A fragmentary style without transitions, a third-person point of view, and larger, more diverse perspectives control the construction of these novels. Landscape imagery is essential to Gordimer's novels and shifts from detailed surface documentation in earlier novels to more symbolic landscapes to convey South Africa's inner vitality. Here Gordimer expresses a double vision of simultaneous detachment from and engagement with her society.

CLINGMAN offers the deepest and broadest insight into Gordimer's artistry and historical significance. He integrates the author's personal, psychological, and political development with her artistic reflection of the radical changes in modern South African history. He indicates how her art delicately counterpoises the perspective of a white African woman with the objective documentation of a society fractured by class and race. He shows how her novels both crystallize historical "truth" uncompromised by ideological bias and at the same time project her "vision" of South Africa, which metamorphoses in tandem with crucial historical events from liberal optimism to ironic cynicism to revolutionary black consciousness. Clingman places Gordimer in the context both of other African writers and influential European writers and theorists such as Forster and Gyorgy Lukács. Clingman's impeccable research, brilliant analysis, and sophisticated scholarship make his book essential to understanding Gordimer's novels.

Of the two edited essay collections by various writers, King's is better written and more insightful than Smith's. SMITH uses previously published articles concerning Gordimer's major works dating from 1952 to 1987 to indicate the historical development of criticism. Just one essay focuses on short stories. His organization is chronological, and some articles address general issues while others focus on specific works. Four essays concern feminist issues such as the ability to synthesize masculine and feminine perspectives, the possible genesis of colonialism and racism from sexual insecurity, women's greater moral sensitivity to political issues, and the link between racism and sexism.

Both Smith and KING address major critical debates: personal versus political motives; tension between art and social documentation; the special dilemma of a white, female writer; and Gordimer's radical shifts in political philosophy. Five essays in King's book address general issues; seven concern novels from *The Conservationist* through *My Son's Story*; three focus on short stories since 1972. These essays frequently center on feminist issues, and many depend on modern critical theory, some using it judiciously while others are clogged with jargon.

ETTIN's gracefully written book offers no fresh interpretations or insights. Instead, with lengthy, nuanced explications of selected novels and short stories, he highlights Gordimer's persistent issues and their corresponding literary strategies. He explores Gordimer's practical feminism and sexual themes; the painful personal/political distortions caused by secrets, lies, and self-delusion; racism's pandemic destructiveness; and the ways apartheid exacerbates inherent human alienation.

WAGNER's highly polemical critique faults Gordimer's unconscious enthrallment to colonial values and her use of fiction to exorcize guilt about her own privileged life. Wagner dislikes Gordimer's dual stereotypes of blacks as either primitive "others" or idealized revolutionaries; her persistent, romantic propaganda for the African National Congress; and her failure to provide a proper feminist view. Wagner reprimands Gordimer for not producing fiction in a mode congruent with contemporary literary critical theory and for failing to supply "solutions" for South Africa's problems. Wagner analyzes Gordimer's fiction more as political ideology and psychoanalytical case history than symbolic literary art. Ironically, Wagner chastizes Gordimer for being a product of the culture that produced her but fails to apply the same scalpel to her own critical perspectives.

—SUZANNE H. MacRAE

Graham, Martha 1894–1991

American Dancer

Armitage, Merle (ed.), *Martha Graham*, New York: Dance Horizons, 1966
De Mille, Agnes, *Martha: The Life and Work of Martha Graham*, New York: Random, 1991; London: Hutchinson, 1992
Horosko, Marian (ed.), *Martha Graham: The Evolution of Her Dance Theory and Training, 1926–1991*, Chicago: A Cappella Books, 1991
Leatherman, LeRoy, and Martha Swope, *Martha Graham: Portrait of the Lady as an Artist*, New York: Knopf, 1966
McDonagh, Don, *Martha Graham: A Biography*, New York: Praeger, 1973; Newton Abbot: David and Charles, 1974
Stodelle, Ernestine, *Deep Song: The Dance Story of Martha Graham*, New York: Schirmer, and London: Collier Macmillan, 1984
Terry, Walter, *Frontiers of Dance: The Life of Martha Graham*, New York: Crowell, 1975

Without question, Martha Graham was one of the most important pioneers in twentieth-century American art. Her name is practically synonymous with modern dance; her legacy includes nearly two hundred choreographic works, a school and company based in New York, several generations of dancers, choreographers, and teachers, and a rigorous, comprehensive dance technique. Graham was one of a handful of women whose radical innovations indelibly changed the face of serious dance, which had for centuries been dominated by classical ballet. Of these great artists—including Isadora Duncan, Ruth St. Denis, and Doris Humphrey—Graham is arguably the most prolific and widely renowned. Her autobiography, titled *Blood Memory*, was published the year Graham died.

A number of biographers have attempted to capture the long life and career of this phenomenal woman, who performed through her mid-seventies and continued to teach and choreograph thereafter. TERRY guides readers on a quick journey through the key events in Graham's life and career: from childhood, to her studies at Denishawn, performing and teaching in New York, forming her own company, and on through her many decades of dancing and touring the world. This book offers a good layperson's account of basic Graham technique; Terry also provides brief descriptions of some of her major dance works.

The biography penned by McDONAGH is longer and more detailed; this author carefully situates Graham's life in a larger cultural context, considering both the influences on and the impact of her work. McDonagh writes thorough descriptions of many of Graham's choreographed pieces. The bulk of STODELLE's book is made up of lengthy accounts of Graham's plot-heavy works—those based on real life characters (for example, Emily Dickinson and the Brontë sisters) and Greek mythology—constitute the bulk of STODELLE's book. These descriptions tend more toward the theatrical: the author focuses more on story line, costume, and set design than on the quality of the movement itself. Stodelle offers sketchy background information on Graham's life.

Of the biographies listed here, De MILLE's is the most intimate and insightful. As a dancer and choreographer, and as a friend and confidante of both Graham and Louis Horst (Graham's long-time composer, critic, and friend), De Mille is uniquely able to weave her own technical knowledge and inside experience into Graham's story. While her narrative occasionally meanders through somewhat tangential events, De Mille nevertheless paints a vivid portrait of the pain and glory of an artist's life, including Graham's deep and often stormy relationships, her violent temper, and her battles with alcohol and illness upon retiring from the stage. De Mille also provides an excellent explanation of Graham's technique, particularly by comparing it with classical ballet (in which De Mille was schooled): ballet is light, airy, pictorial, and generally aims to delight and impress, whereas Graham's modern technique is grounded, weighty, deeply emotional, and seeks to stimulate and provoke. Graham technique focuses on the pelvis and spine: the basis of every movement in this dance vocabulary is the contraction, a subtle but powerful movement deep in the lower torso. While ballet technique features a stable, upright torso, Graham technique requires the torso to contract, release, and spiral.

All of the above books include photographs of Graham, as well as appendices chronologically listing her choreographic works. The best collection of photographs, taken by official Graham photographer Martha SWOPE, appear together with text written by LEATHERMAN. Swope's stunning photographs record Graham's major performances in the late 1950s and early 1960s, capturing the drama of these works as fully as is possible in a print format. Leatherman, who served as Graham's manager for a time, records a detailed slice of her life work, focusing on that same time period; he includes mini-biographies of the company members dancing with Graham in the mid-1960s. Of particular interest is his explication of Graham's creative process, including her choreographic struggles and triumphs, and her collaborations with sculptor Isamu Noguchi and lighting designer Jean Rosenthal.

The earliest book published about Graham—one thousand copies were first printed by the author in 1937—is a collection of excerpts and short essays compiled by ARMITAGE, a long-time friend and financial supporter of Graham's. These commentaries by critics, composers, and artists date from the early part of Graham's career; they reveal the innovative, often controversial nature of Graham's performances, and connect her work to the cultural, technological, and aesthetic milieu of the early twentieth century. Armitage also includes a section of statements by Graham, titled "Affirmations 1926–37"; these are eloquent, concise articulations of Graham's understanding of human movement and emotion, her perspectives on American art, and her philosophy of dance.

Graham's pedagogical prowess and dance technique are elicited in HOROSKO's book, through the compiled reflections of many students and company members who studied with Graham over the years. Company dancers recall their own experiences in Graham classes, noting the utter dedication demanded of them in both rehearsal and performance. Actors describe learning not only how to move more dramatically, but how to create emotion from movement, and enhance vocal delivery by using the Graham contraction. This volume traces the evolution of Graham technique through the minds and bodies of those who danced it. Horosko includes as appendices a full syllabus of the Graham technique class, and a list of the dancers in the Martha Graham Dance Company from 1926.

—MARILYN BORDWELL

Grandma Moses 1860–1961

American Painter

Kallir, Jane, *Grandma Moses: The Artist Behind the Myth,* New York: C.N. Potter, 1982

Kallir, Otto, *Grandma Moses, American Primitive,* New York: Dryden Press, 1946

———, *Grandma Moses,* New York: Harper, 1948

Ketchum, William C., Jr., *Grandma Moses: An American Original,* New York: Smithmark, 1996

When the paintings of Anna Mary Robertson Moses, a farmer's wife in her 80s, first came to the attention of the American public, many articles about her began to appear in newspapers and magazines. Rather than dealing with her art, these pieces tended to present Moses as a phenomenon of survival from a bygone world of rural peacefulness and self-contentment. The first comprehensive publication gathering all that was known about the painter and her craft is the work of OTTO KALLIR (1946), the art dealer who had done the most to promote Moses since 1940. By defining a primitive painter as one who is not academically trained, who in her work maintains a childlike quality, and who tends to represent aspects of her life and experience, Kallir set the main lines of all future studies. Grandma Moses was thereby confirmed as the artist of rural America, inspired by the work and leisure times of farmers as they evolved in Moses's life span in the section of New York State that borders on Vermont. The painter's artistic development is presented in parallel line with the story of her life and professional success, and a history of her painting emerges, from her early decorated objects and paintings, influenced by postcard reproduction and needlework, to the paintings that display full mastery of color and composition. Kallir's essay is followed by a sketch of her life by the artist herself and forty reproductions, each one with comments also by her.

OTTO KALLIR's 1948 volume is the catalog *raisonné* (descriptive catalogue) of Moses's work, which contains 347 plate illustrations, many in color. The first half of the book analyses Moses's work and career and is organized in four parts, each one followed by a set of illustrations. Part one is concerned with Moses's beginning at painting and her first successes; part two with the growing public recognition of her, and subsequent confrontation with the American and European art world; and part three with her fame and with her declining years. The fourth, more analytical, section considers the full range of Grandma Moses's art with respect to themes, narrative elements, variations of interior scenes and landscapes, and color scheme. The second half of the volume is the documentary section, which contains a biographical outline, a complete catalog of the works, a selected bibliography, and a list of exhibitions, as well as excerpts from *My Life's History* by the painter and Edward R. Murrow's interview with her.

JANE KALLIR places Grandma Moses in the American tradition of folk painters and suggests the possible reasons for her extraordinary popularity by juxtaposing the optimism and serenity of her scenes with the existential anxiety that had brought forth the work of contemporary abstract expressionists. She then appraises the painter's art with a detailed analysis of her technique. She points out recurring images and motifs: houses, barns, people, and animals are combined differently in each painting for different functions. She illustrates Moses's approach to composition, which was achieved by sketching fields and buildings directly on the panel and disposing around them groups of figures engaged in a variety of tasks and leisure activities. She then examines the artist's coloring procedures, which combined areas of flat pure color with sections of multi-layered hues. Finally Kallir describes the realism prevalent in the representation of nature, and the degree of abstraction that Moses achieves in the depiction of people and animals.

Prefacing his commentary with the statement that understanding Grandma Moses's life is essential to appreciate her art, KETCHUM illustrates each work with a discussion of the aspect or event of the painter's experience that is depicted in the painting. This anecdotal approach allows the reader to enter the process by which Moses arrived at her scenes of farm and village, most famous among them her landscapes. This was done by creating a patterned background of brown hills, green valleys, and distant blue mountains, and establishing in the foreground a variety of human activities, for which recurring sets of human figures were frequently used. Ketchum's presentation also considers Moses's painting techniques, as well as to the influence exercised on them by "women's work" of embroidery and quilting. A historical sketch of folk art in the United States precedes the discussion of Moses's art. Ketchum, a scholar in this field, distinguishes a line of folk, or untrained, painters, who made art for a living and catered to that section of the public who could not afford the services of trained artists, from the "Sunday painters" who worked for pleasure rather than for profit. The first group, the most popular being Matthew Prior and Edward Hicks, came to an end in the second half of the nineteenth century, when the use of the camera became popular and new techniques of representation were developed. The "Sunday painters," on the other hand—among them many women and men who started to paint at an advanced age—continued to prosper, often attaining a degree of fame, as did John Kane, Joseph Pickett and Horace Pippin. Grandma Moses is an eminent exemplar of the latter American tradition.

—RINALDINA RUSSELL

Great Depression

Blackwelder, Julia Kirk, *Women of the Depression: Caste and Culture in San Antonio, 1929–1939,* College Station: Texas A and M University Press, 1984

Hapke, Laura, *Daughters of the Great Depression: Women, Work, and Fiction in the American 1930s,* Athens: University of Georgia Press, 1995

Low, Ann Marie, *Dust Bowl Diary,* Lincoln: University of Nebraska Press, 1984

Nelson, Paula M., *The Prairie Winnows Out Its Own: The West River Country of South Dakota in the Years of Depression and Dust,* Iowa City: University of Iowa Press, 1996

Scharf, Lois, *To Work and to Wed: Female Employment, Feminism, and the Great Depression,* Westport, Connecticut: Greenwood, 1980

Westin, Jeane, *Making Do: How Women Survived the '30s,* Chicago: Follett, 1976

The Great Depression killed the hopes, dreams, and lives of millions of people. This economic disaster evolved into a wide-ranging social catastrophe, and, along with adding reinforcement to demands that women remain in traditional female roles, the effects of the Depression ultimately changed the way that people throughout the world viewed the role of government. The welfare state, a development that has largely benefitted women, arose out of the ashes of the Depression, but this decade is perhaps more notable for the setbacks it delivered to the feminist movement. When jobs became scarce, women in most countries faced severe attacks for taking away the breadwinning role of men, with the ultimate result that many single women could not find work, and many married women were forced out of the workplace both by employment regulations and by social pressure.

Given all this, it is particularly surprising that there is such a dearth of books about women in the Great Depression. The few available English-language books focus entirely on Americans, and most of these books ignore the lives of minority women. Canadian and British women occasionally warrant a chapter in books that purport to provide a complete history of the 1930s. German women are no better served. The Depression in Germany began earlier as a result of the ravages of World War I, and it has been argued that the dismal German economic situation was a large factor in the rise of Nazism, yet the major work on Fascist German women devotes only a small portion of its text to the Depression. Perhaps reflecting the infant status of women's studies in developing nations, there are no studies of Depression-era women in Third World countries. This listing reflects the available literature, and, as such, it is unavoidably devoted to the United States.

LOW provides a story of the Dust Bowl years of a young woman who lived on a large stock farm in North Dakota. The Depression struck the farm belt several years before the stock market crashed, when an interminable drought sent farmers and ranchers into bankruptcy, and North Dakota was one of the states most affected by the environmental disaster. Low tells the story of her coming to maturity under frustrating family circumstances, and hampered by the restrictions that society placed upon the young. This book is drawn from a diary that Low kept from 1927 to 1937, and, because the tale is so personalized, this work serves as an engaging introduction to the ravages of the Depression. Low's account of the effect of the drought, the Depression, and subsequent government aid programs upon her family and neighbors adds substantially to the body of 1930s-era literature.

The crash of the agricultural economy in the 1920s United States initiated a trend of regional decline amidst national prosperity and cultural change. NELSON tells of relentless drought, clouds of grain-devouring grasshoppers, and blowing dust. In a heavily researched study of gender history, she explores how women carried out their traditional duties as the processors and preparers of food, as the manufacturers of clothing, and as housewives and mothers. Many of the details of everyday life are drawn from reports of federal relief workers. Relief prevented actual starvation, but as Nelson reports, malnutrition and other suffering was widespread, since the

Depression knocked the bottom out of the agricultural market and made it impossible for farm families to acquire the goods and services that they needed. This is another good introduction to the Depression, a book that will hold the attention of students.

Unlike Nelson and Low, WESTIN focuses exclusively upon women. By 1932, over a million American wives had been deserted by out-of-work men. Millions of other women sought to bolster the egos of their faithful but unemployed husbands—men who felt that the Depression was their personal failure. Westin explores how these women survived the Depression. An interesting work, this book nonetheless gives short shrift to the millions of struggling unmarried women.

HAPKE analyzes literary and cultural descriptions, not only of the domestic woman, but also of her breadwinning counterpart, the female wage earner. For sources, Hapke relies upon best-selling fiction of the time. This well-written work explores how the Depression inherited, combatted, and transfigured a decades-old American debate about women's suitability for paid work outside the home. It is a study of attitudes and representations of the working woman of the 1930s, but it locates her within a Depression-era context by using fiction as a reflector and reshaper of American attitudes. Each chapter includes a substantial historical section and extensive notes in an effort to aid the reader.

SCHARF tells how the Depression affected working women, their ideals, and their place in history. Women's employment rose during this era, but Scharf argues that this gain was accompanied by a loss of status by women in professional occupations, an increase in discrimination against working wives, and a near-abandonment of the feminist ideology that had seemed so strong just a few years before. Although somewhat dated, this remains an excellent source and a classic work of feminist history.

One of the rare authors to examine class and ethnicity in the 1930s, BLACKWELDER uses qualitative and quantitative sources to examine the lives of San Antonio, Texas women. The hardships that Depression-era women faced and the avenues of escape open to them, Blackwelder concludes, depended not only on their economic circumstances, but also on their ethnic identification as black, Anglo, or Mexican-American.

—CARYN E. NEUMANN

Greenham Common Women's Peace Camp

Blackwood, Caroline, *On the Perimeter,* London: Heineman, and New York: Penguin, 1984

Brown, Wilmette, *Black Women and the Peace Movement,* Bristol: Falling Wall Press, 1984

Cook, Alice, and Gwyn Kirk, *Greenham Women Everywhere: Dreams, Ideas and Action from the Women's Peace Movement,* London: Pluto Press, and Boston: South End Press, 1983

Feminism and Nonviolence Study Group, *Piecing It Together: Feminism and Nonviolence,* Devon, England: Feminism Nonviolent Study Group, 1983

Jones, Lynne (ed.), *Keeping the Peace,* London: Women's Press, 1983

Harford, Barbara, and Sarah Hopkins (eds.), *Greenham Common: Women at the Wire,* London: Women's Press, 1984

Liddington, Jill, *The Road to Greenham Common: Feminism and Anti-Militarism in Britain since 1820,* London: Virago Press, 1989, and Syracuse, New York: Syracuse University Press, 1991

On August 27, 1981, in response to a North Atlantic Treaty Organization (NATO) decision to deploy Cruise missiles in Britain, a group of 36 women calling themselves "Women for Life on Earth" walked 120 miles from Cardiff, Wales, to an air force base outside of Newbury, England. Upon arrival they demanded a televised debate with Margaret Thatcher's government on the risks of nuclear war. As a sign of their urgency, four women chained themselves to the fence around the base. No debate took place and the women decided to stay; Greenham Common Women's Peace Camp was born. In 1982 the camp became women-only. Arrests, evictions, and imprisonments increased, and on December 12, over 30,000 women responded to a plea to come to Greenham, join hands and "embrace the base." The action immediately made Greenham the most powerful symbol of women's anti-nuclear resistance. Over the course of the next decade, women from all over the world would travel to Greenham to support the encampment and share their ideas and visions.

The literature on Greenham is almost exclusively historical and testimonial in nature. Drawing on handwritten diaries, autobiographies, hard-to-find books, and life-story interviews with peace activists, LIDDINGTON presents Greenham Common as part of a long history of resistance, with roots in the tradition of British and American white women's political movements, such as the Olive Leaf Women, Women's International League For Peace and Freedom (WILPF), Citizens for Nuclear Disarmament (CND), and women's protests against H-bomb tests in the late 1950s. Focusing on women's anti-militarism work in Britain since 1820, Liddington offers historical accounts of early feminist pacifist movements (1820–1916), twentieth-century movements sparked by World War I (1915–1970), and the peace camp movements of the 1970s and 1980s. The last section will be of particular interest to readers looking for behind-the-scenes accounts of early organizers and more visible figures at the camp.

BROWN's account is at once historical and autobiographical. As an African-American woman living and working with the peace movement in Britain, she sketches the links between racism, education, immigration, and poverty as "wider" issues which are inseparable from peace." From the point of view of women of color, Brown argues that the threat of nuclear power and war is inseparable from day-to-day military industrial oppression. The book also addresses black women's autonomy, black herstory, and black and white organizing. The second half of the book contains Brown's 1984 "Across the Divide of Race, Nation and Poverty" speech.

Like Brown's account, the monograph published by the Feminism and Nonviolence Group is a grassroots feminist publication. It is designed to introduce the lay reader to the basic issues of feminist anti-militarist organizing during the 1980s. It raises and answers a number of questions: Do women have a special contribution to make to the struggle for disarmament? And, what insights can feminists bring to theories of nonviolent social change? This publication will be a valuable resource for scholars interested in documents coming out of women's anti-nuclear grassroots organizing. Rare photos of actions are included.

BLACKWOOD's book is the Ulster writer's account of the daily lives, fears, and prejudices of persons living at and around Greenham. Having been asked by an American magazine to write on the defeat of the women's peace movement, Blackwood went to Greenham only to quickly find herself sympathetically drawn into the cause. This book is unique in that it focuses not only on the lives and ideas of women at the camp, but also on responses of the wider Newbury community. Interviewing Greenham women, local shopkeepers, bystanders, Newbury landowners opposed to the encampment, policemen, and visitors to the camp, Blackwood describes the violent evictions, sexual abuse of women by paratroopers, and the court cases of women tried for trespass.

COOK and KIRK's chronicle is the most widely read account of the ideas and actions of the movement. The book is a rich mixture of peace movement history, including excerpts from interviews, photographs, memos, news clippings, documents, and press releases. Of particular use are chapters covering why the movement became women-only, the importance of non-violent strategies, and struggles with Newbury District Court over eviction orders.

A similar approach is taken by HARFORD and HOPKINS, who use the writings of over fifty women, personal photographs, letters, diaries, press releases, and memos to the District Council of Newbury, to address daily life, law, political actions, and non-violent philosophies of encampment. The book has an indispensable Greenham history timeline and a map of the United States Air Force Greenham Common and the surrounding peace camp.

Although not exclusively about Greenham, JONES's edited collection is an indispensable resource for understanding the breadth of the women's peace movement in the 1980s. In addition to her essay on Greenham, the collection includes essays on grassroots women's organizing in Germany, the Women's Pentagon Action, Oxford Mothers for Nuclear Disarmament, the Shibokusa Women of Kita Fuji, and Families Against the Bomb. The appendix and resource section offer useful examples of campaigning, networking, and non-violent organizing strategies used by the women's anti-nuclear movement.

—ALISON BAILEY

See also Peace Movement

Grimké, Angelina 1805–1879 and Sarah 1792–1873

American Activists

Bartlett, Elizabeth Ann, *Liberty, Equality, Sorority: The Origins and Interpretations of American Feminist Thought—Frances Wright, Sarah Grimke, and Margaret Fuller,* Brooklyn, New York: Carlson, 1994

Birney, Catherine H., *The Grimke Sisters: Sarah and Angelina Grimke, The First American Women Advocates of Abolition and Women's Rights,* Boston: Lee and Shepherd, 1885

Lerner, Gerda, *The Grimke Sisters from South Carolina: Pioneers for Woman's Rights and Abolition,* New York: Schocken, 1971

Lumpkin, Katharine Du Pre, *The Emancipation of Angelina Grimké,* Chapel Hill: University of North Carolina Press, 1974

Sterne, Emma Gelders, *They Took Their Stand,* New York: Crowell-Collier Press, 1968

Yellin, Jean Fagan, *Women and Sisters: The Antislavery Feminists in American Culture,* New Haven, Connecticut, and London: Yale University Press, 1989

Daughters of a prominent South Carolina slaveholding family, Angelina and Sarah Grimké moved to the North in the 1820s and became public advocates for abolition and women's rights. The Grimké sisters were recognized as influential female reformers during their lives. BIRNEY's major biography, written within a decade of their deaths, describes their influence. Birney, the daughter-in-law of abolitionist James Birney, draws on her own relationship with the sisters, and her access to their letters and diaries, to present a detailed narrative of their lives and achievements that is admiring but not sentimental. The Grimkés, however were largely forgotten in the twentieth century, like many other nineteenth-century feminists, until feminist historians in the 1960s and 1970s recovered their writings, speeches, and correspondence. More recently, scholars have closely analyzed the rhetoric of the Grimkés to present arguments about their race and gender politics and their influence on feminist thought.

In the most complete biography of these remarkable reformers, LERNER analyzes the Grimké family history and the sisters' private and public writings within the social, political, and religious context of the mid-nineteenth century. Lerner examines how both sisters resisted the limited roles of southern belle and plantation mistress within the patriarchal slave system. She argues that the Grimkés' own sense of injustice and restriction based on sex made it possible for them to identify with their oppressed slaves, implying that an early feminism inspired their abolitionism. While charting both sisters' losses of faith, of family, and of romantic attachments in their search for justice, Lerner suggests that they approached reform as a mission—meaningful work that would fulfill their ambitions. While acknowledging the sisters' doubts and insecurities, Lerner celebrates both their bravery in facing hostile audiences and their open and frank discussion of Northern race prejudice among reformers.

Like Lerner, YELLIN examines the connections between the Grimkés' feminism and their abolitionism through an analysis of their rhetoric. Although she focuses primarily on Angelina, Yellin suggests that both sisters experienced a complex identification with black slaves that enabled them to describe their own development from enchained victims to empowered, free women. Yellin analyzes the politics of such identification in her close readings of Angelina's private and public writings, suggesting that Angelina invoked images of her own bondage to create ties of sisterhood with both black slave women and Northern white women. Both sisters used the language of bondage to describe the condition of women, asserting that a woman can achieve her own liberation by acting to liberate others. Yellin also examines responses to Angelina's speeches and writing, dividing up her audience into admirers who saw her as a superhuman angel, and critics who branded her as sinful and loose—"Devil-ina." The admirers won out, Yellin contends, because Angelina's descriptions of shared bondage and sisterhood across race lines have endured and influenced future generations of female reformers.

LUMPKIN's biography also concentrates on Angelina, who was more visible than her sister as a result of her eloquent public speeches and her pamphlet debate with Catharine Beecher. LUMPKIN's biography of Angelina focuses on her lifetime commitment to the emancipation of both slaves and women. By examining Angelina's struggles against the restrictions placed on her by her family, her husband, her church, and the various factions of the antislavery movement, Lumpkin celebrates Angelina's resilience in the face of controversy and criticism.

In her study of white Southerners who spoke out for African Americans from the 1750s to the 1960s, STERNE offers an anecdotal narrative of Angelina's transformation from Charleston belle to exile abolitionist. Sterne recreates scenes of Angelina's speeches for the American Antislavery Society, and of her courtship with abolitionist Theodore Weld. Unlike other biographers who are troubled by Angelina's relative silence after her marriage, Sterne suggests that Angelina found fulfillment in both her own activism and her marriage to a fellow reformer.

Although Angelina is often remembered as the more publicly influential sister, one study focuses exclusively on Sarah Grimké's contributions to feminism. In her intellectual history of the origins of nineteenth-century feminist thought, BARTLETT argues that Sarah's *Letters on the Equality of Sexes* was the first compelling philosophical treatise on the condition of women in the United States. Bartlett contends that Sarah's *Letters* skillfully interprets the Bible to make a case for the moral autonomy of women, asserting convincingly that women deserve the same educational and social opportunities as men to develop their individual potential. Like other Grimké scholars, Bartlett suggests that Sarah's feminism developed out of her own resentment toward men for denying her dreams of education and legal practice. However, Bartlett identifies an evolution in Sarah's thinking away from anger toward men to an affirmation of sisterhood and the potential of women.

—KIRSTEN JAMSEN

See also Feminist Movement, Abolitionist Origins of

Gynecology, History and Development of

Eccles, Audrey, *Obstetrics and Gynaecology in Tudor and Stuart England*, Kent, Ohio: Kent State University Press, and London: Croom Helm, 1982

Kerr, John Martin Munro (ed.), *Historical Review of British Obstetrics and Gynaecology, 1880–1950*, Edinburgh: E. and S. Livingstone, 1954

McGregor, Deborah Kuhn, *Sexual Surgery and the Origins of Gynecology: J. Marion Sims, His Hospital, and His Patients*, New York and London: Garland, 1989

Moscucci, Ornella, *The Science of Woman: Gynaecology and Gender in England, 1800–1929*, Cambridge and New York: Cambridge University Press, 1990

Ricci, James V., *The Genealogy of Gynaecology: History of the Development of Gynaecology throughout the Ages, 2000 B.C.–1800 A.D.*, Philadelphia: Blakiston, 1943; 2nd edition, Philadelphia: Blakiston, 1950

Speert, Harold, *Obstetrics and Gynecology in America: A History*, Chicago: American College of Obstetricians and Gynecologists, 1980

The term gynecology was first used to characterize a discrete branch of women's medicine in the 1840s. Until that point, most of what we now think of as gynecology was subsumed under obstetrics or midwifery; in other words, concerns about the health of women's reproductive systems primarily arose in relation to childbirth. Consequently, most histories of gynecology also discuss the history of obstetrics. The range of histories in this field is fairly broad, including histories of gynecological practice and histories of key individuals, as well as analyses of the ideological factors at work in changing perceptions of both the patients and the practitioners of gynecology.

RICCI reviews the history and development of gynecology from the Egyptians and Babylonians through the Greco-Roman, Byzantine, Arabic, and medieval European periods to the end of the eighteenth century. His sources are extant manuscripts and other written documents from various "classic" civilizations; he includes folklore and popular opinions on the subject as well as the writings of prominent researchers or practitioners. Ricci attempts to reconstruct various societies' perspectives on gynecology, physiology, pathology, and overall women's health, although he also includes an overview of the technological advances and practical developments within the field such as new methods, instruments, and procedures. This text is useful for its comprehensive discussion of gynecology prior to the nineteenth century; it also shows the ways in which gynecology overlapped with other medical fields and advances.

ECCLES examines what changes and development in ideas about gynecology and gynecological practices meant for practitioners in the sixteenth through the eighteenth centuries. Her concern is not discoveries and developments per se, but how new discoveries gained acceptance and how practices based on new and outdated ideas overlapped, especially during this period when male medical practitioners began to eclipse female health-care workers. Her sources include early obstetrical textbooks as well as books and tracts produced by midwives, anatomists, physiologists, medical researchers such as William Harvey, and other authors on gynecology. Topics include ideas about the female reproductive system, menstruation, sexuality and conception, childbirth, pregnancy, contraception, and obstetric surgery.

MOSCUCCI provides a history of the development of gynecology in the eighteenth and nineteenth centuries in England; she traces the evolution of the profession from male-midwives and the "obstetric revolution" in the eighteenth century through various professional controversies in the nineteenth century to the Royal College of Obstetricians and Gynaecologists established in 1929. She includes separate sections on the rise of women's hospitals and increasingly specialized medical procedures designed to treat what Moscucci calls the "pathology of femininity." Moscucci also analyzes the cultural and political factors influencing the professionalization of gynecology, including views of nature, notions of sexual differentiation, Enlightenment political concepts, concerns about population control, and nineteenth-century evolutionary and anthropological theory. Throughout the history, she analyzes the gender politics involved in the rise of gynecology by positioning the theories and practices of gynecology firmly within contemporaneous views of femininity, women's sexuality, and notions of normality and disease.

SPEERT discusses the development of gynecology as a specialty in the nineteenth century, as Moscucci does, but he concentrates on the work of individual American (primarily male) doctors and researchers. Speert details the beginnings of the American Gynecological Society in the 1870s and includes a discussion of the societies, journals, and textbooks that helped consolidate gynecology into a specialized field of professional medical practice. Speert also provides a larger history of gynecological practice in America, including colonial midwifery, Native American gynecological and birth practices, and other early versions of gynecology, as well as the history of obstetric nursing through the twentieth century. This text is useful in its presentation of the origins of gynecology as a specialty in America and in its sections on specific advances such as anesthesia, prenatal care, contraception, hospitals for women, and new therapies, and its discussions of individual "trailblazers" in female physiology and pathology.

KERR edits a collection of essays written by professors of gynecology and obstetrics from various English and Scottish universities and practicing doctors from British hospitals. The essays review the treatments and perceptions of female anatomy, hormones, and physiological abnormalities, as well as the increasing acceptance (and success) of surgery in gynecology and obstetrics. More specific topics include advances such as anesthesia, analgesia, and radiography in relation to gynecology and obstetrics. Like Moscucci and Speert, Kerr provides an overview of the professionalization of gynecology; the essays detail the rise of medical schools and instruction in gynecology and midwifery (which had become standard courses by the mid-nineteenth century) and the corresponding rise in medical journals and societies devoted to gynecology and obstetrics during the nineteenth century. This book, although written in the 1950s, is useful for a particular view of the professionalization of gynecology, that of male practitioners and professors who were optimistic about the ability of gynecologists to solve women's health problems through increasing technology and physiological research.

McGREGOR analyzes the development of gynecology as a specialty through the biography of J. Marion Sims, a nineteenth-century American surgeon and gynecological researcher who created many influential surgical techniques and tools. The author examines in detail the emergence of procedures and treatments for several conditions, including vesico-vaginal fistulas, sterility, dysmennorhea, and ovarian cysts and tumors. Rather than writing a social history of gynecology or simply a biography of one influential figure, McGregor offers a more complex picture of the development of gynecological practice and ideas; she examines the interrelations between cultural ideology and medical practice, specifically the ways in which notions of gender, sexuality, race, and class influenced the course and parameters of nineteenth-century medicine. An especially significant addition to the history of gynecology is McGregor's consideration of the implications of medical research for the women who were the subjects of that research, primarily slave women from South Carolina in Sims's case.

—KIMBERLY VanHOOSIER-CAREY

H

Hall, Radclyffe 1886–1943

British Writer

Baker, Michael, *Our Three Selves: A Life of Radclyffe Hall,* London: Hamish Hamilton, and New York: Morrow, 1985
Brittain, Vera, *Radclyffe Hall: A Case of Obscenity?,* London: Femina, 1968; South Brunswick, New York: A.S. Barnes, 1969
Franks, Claudia Stillman, *Beyond the Well of Lonelinesss: The Fiction of Radclyffe Hall,* Amersham: Avebury,1982
O'Rourke, Rebecca, *Reflecting on The Well of Loneliness,* London and New York: Routledge, 1989
Troubridge, Una, *The Life and Death of Radclyffe Hall,* London: Hammond and Hammond, 1961

Radclyffe Hall has been most well known for the trials for obscenity based on her fourth novel, *The Well of Loneliness,* in England in 1928, and in the United States in 1929. Although the novel achieved notoriety as a banned book, this was not the desired effect of its author. Hall had an established profile as the author of three novels when she deliberately and courageously sought to write about "sexual inversion," knowing that it might end her writing career. The strength of Hall's commitment to representing the lesbian in a detailed and sympathetic manner in the novel derived from her own experience as a lesbian, as a Roman Catholic, and as a white, English upper-class woman. In the event, devastating as the trial was, particularly to Hall and her lover, Una, Lady Troubridge, it did not see the end of Hall's career as a writer. The effects of the London trial have been far-reaching, marking a legislative landmark in lesbian history. The effects of the representation of lesbian characters in Hall's novel have also been significant. A lesbian identity was brought into public (heterosexual) debate, but its declared biological and pathological basis has provided a controversial and deeply ambiguous legacy for subsequent lesbian readers.

TROUBRIDGE's biography of Hall does not engage in special pleading, and is determined to emphasize Hall's work as a writer, not as a legislative footnote. It was written in early 1945 but was not published until 1961. The book is written in the form of a letter to the reader. It is selective, particularly with respect to Hall's relationship in later years with Evgenia Souline, but Una, Lady Troubridge, courageously writes about her relationship with Hall in emphatically unapologetic terms.

BAKER's biography appropriately narrates the lives of the women most significant to Hall, Mabel Batten (Ladye), as well as Una Troubridge. It dispenses with the narrow lens of legislation, and assesses the totality of Hall's life and writings. Thus, *The Well of Loneliness* and its trial are decentred in Hall's life, and Baker enables the reader to contextualize Hall's writings in the lesbian cultural milieu of her social life.

The title of BRITTAIN's book demonstrates the way in which Radclyffe Hall, rather than her novel *The Well of Loneliness,* has been remembered as the defendant in the 1928 London trial for obscenity. The lesbian identity that Hall self-consciously represented in the novel endorsed current theorizing about lesbianism as a biological abnormality. While Hall's motivation was to render the lesbian visible, and to promote tolerance, this project was double-edged: addressed as it was to a heterosexual, Christian audience, it positioned the lesbian as victimized object of pity. In her testament, Brittain acts as court reporter, recording the London trial (which she attended as one of the witnesses for the defence) and the important later New York trial, which found in favor of the novel. Brittain had favourably reviewed the novel before it was charged; her book about the trials bears witness to the novel but re-emphasizes its plea for tolerance.

FRANKS's study focuses on the fiction of Radclyffe Hall, emphasizing its literary perspective, and arguing for a consistency in its thematic patterns. Nevertheless, the close readings of Hall's novels are bound by the circularity of biographical criticism, whereby an author's life is found in her writings but not recognized as a product of the theoretical perspective of the reading. Most interesting is Franks's study of Stephen Gordon (protagonist of *The Well of Loneliness*) associating her development as a writer with her identity as a lesbian. The strength of Franks's study, as O'Rourke suggests, is the contextualizing of Hall's writing in women's writing, while the prioritizing of the aesthetic over sexuality produces an ambiguous effect.

O'ROURKE has charted the controversies arising from Hall's fourth novel, providing a comprehensive critical analysis of readings of *The Well of Loneliness* and its protagonist. Readers' responses to the novel and to Stephen are assessed through two surveys, one conducted by the Lesbian Herstory Archives in New York, the other circulated by O'Rourke in Britain. O'Rourke's study, part of Routledge's "Heroines" series, explores the ambivalence of many readers to *The Well of Loneliness.* The novel's representation of the lesbian as not only fundamentally lonely, but also castigated and exiled, romanticized the struggle against homophobia through the appropriation of a heroic martyrdom. It also appealed to the sympathy and tolerance of presumed heterosexual readers. Although Hall's representation in *The Well of Loneliness* raised awareness generally about the existence of lesbians, this was in terms which were ultimately disempowering. Nevertheless, O'Rourke's reader-response survey provides evidence of the differing interpretations of the novel, which for some readers provided an (ambivalent) point of identification.

—KATHERINE COCKIN

Hatshepsut c.1505–1470 B.C.

Egyptian Pharaoh

Gedge, Pauline, *Child of the Morning*, London: Raven, and New York: Dial Press, 1977

Tyldesley, Joyce, *Hatshepsut: The Female Pharaoh*, London and New York: Viking, 1996

Wells, Evelyn, *Hatshepsut*, Garden City, New York: Doubleday, 1969

Whitman, Ruth, *Hatshepsut, Speak to Me*, Detroit, Michigan: Wayne State University Press, 1992

Women in ancient Egypt possessed a favorable position compared to other women of the ancient Near East. Several women acted as rulers, including Queen Nitokerty at the end of the Old Kingdom, Queen Sobeknofru at the end of the Middle Kingdom, and Queen Twosret at the end of the New Kingdom period. Hatshepsut, however, stands out as the only woman known to have vaulted from the status of the "God's Wife of Amun" to the position of pharaoh, complete with the pharonic beard. Her position varied from co-regent with her father Thutmose I to queen of her effeminate husband and half-brother Thutmose II to regent for her stepson and son-in-law Thutmose III. During her regency she actually ruled as pharaoh for more than a decade, until Thutmose III reasserted his power and Hatshepsut disappeared into Egypt's long history, helped by Thutmose III's careful eradication of all of his predecessor's monuments and stelae. The challenge of Hatshepsut is recreating her life from a historical viewpoint at a distance of four millenia.

The most comprehensive and current work is that written by TYLDESLEY, who pursues Hatshepsut and her story from the vantage point of an archaeologist and classical scholar. Tyldesley introduces the archaeological background of classical Egyptology in the aggregate and the history of the Eighteenth Dynasty in particular. She leads the reader on an archaeological discovery of Hatshepsut, with careful detail to both her historical and religious antecendents. The work is well-researched with copious notes and a careful attention to detail, but the scholarly style may sidetrack novices to the study of ancient Egypt. Although not a feminist study per se, Tyldesley's work carefully examines the issues of Hatshepsut's cross dressing and the issues of kingship versus queenship in Egypt. She makes a strong effort to compare Hatshepsut to other female leaders in history, including women like Cleopatra in the Egyptian tradition and Joan of Arc and Marianne of France in the western tradition. Tyldesley's careful research does differ substantially from other works in her treatment of Hatshepsut's architect and love interest, Senenmut, her discussion of Hatshepsut's death from natural causes and her balanced portrait of Thutmose III as a reasonable, rather than mother-in-law obsessed, leader.

The other primary biography of Hatshepsut takes a decidedly different approach in WELLS's portrayal of the pharaoh and her cohorts. As a journalist, Wells takes the reader on a scavenger hunt through a museum and Egyptian history looking for Hatshepsut. Her reader-friendly and chatty version is grounded in the genealogical background of the eighteenth dynasty, but the overall tone is an effort to recreate a personality, somewhat like a newspaper feature story. Wells does not cite any sources and tells the reader what Hatshepsut is doing and feeling, a risky technique for a scholarly inquiry. The work predates the advent of feminist history with remarks that are downright sexist, for example, the idea that Hatshepsut "doubtless hated arithmetic, as most girls do." The monograph is a fun read, but the personalization of the subject makes this book more fiction than fact.

GEDGE, on the other hand, opts strictly for fiction in her exploration of Hatshepsut. She begins the novel at the end of Hatshepsut's career as Thutmose III sends his mother-in-law her final draught of poison. The book is entertaining and well-written, with a careful attention to the history behind the story, but the somewhat sensationalized plot relegates this work to the status of a romance novel rather than a historical biography.

Finally, WHITMAN frames her introspective book of poetry on her own life within the context of Hatshepsut's life. With many and varied references to Hatshepsut and her historical experiences, this short volume nevertheless has only peripheral significance to the understanding of its Egyptian pharaoh namesake.

—MICHAELA CRAWFORD REAVES

H.D. *see* Doolittle, Hilda (H.D.)

Head, Bessie 1937–1984

South African Writer

Abrahams, Cecil (ed.), *The Tragic Life: Bessie Head and Literature in Southern Africa,* Trenton, New Jersey: Africa World Press, 1990

Eilersen, Gillian Stead, *Bessie Head: Thunder behind Her Ears: Her Life and Writing,* Portsmouth, New Hampshire: Heinemann, and London: Currey, 1995

MacKenzie, Craig, *Bessie Head: An Introduction,* Grahamstown, South Africa: National English Literary Museum, 1989

Ola, Virginia Uzoma, *The Life and Works of Bessie Head,* Lewiston, New York: Edwin Mellen, 1994

Bessie Head was born in 1937 in South Africa to a white mother and an unknown African father. After her mother died in the mental asylum where she gave birth, the little girl was immediately given up for adoption with only her mother's name, Bessie Amelia Emery, to take with her. Bessie's childhood with her foster family, and her young adolescence in a mission, were followed by her marriage to Harold Head, the birth of their son Howard, and her departure from South Africa. Possibly because of a brief period of involvement with the Pan-African Congress, Head left South Africa not with a passport, but with an exit visa that stripped her of citizenship rights and left her only refugee status. She settled in Botswana (then Bechuanaland), and there fulfilled the literary promise that had first shown itself when she was still in school in South Africa.

MacKENZIE's book usefully adopts Arthur Ravenscroft's division of Head's literary oeuvre into two trilogies. The first contains the introspective and autobiographical early novels, *When Rain Clouds Gather, Maru,* and *A Question of Power.* The second begins with Head's collection of short stories, *The Collector of Treasures and Other Botswana Village Tales,* and includes her oral history of *Serowe, Village of the Rain Wind* and her historical novel, *A Bewitched Crossroad.* Opening with a biographical note, this volume is, as its title states, a useful if very brief introduction to Head.

In her overview, OLA pursues what she calls a "quaint" form of criticism, "which considers the writer's mind and life of vital importance" to a complete understanding of the written works. Such an approach is well suited to Head's own vision of the integration of physical and mental or spiritual activity as essential for a fulfilled life. Accessible to the general reader, and with chapters that focus on good and evil, the role of women, and nature, the volume is nonetheless flawed. To be fair, without much information available about Head's life, Ola's task was virtually impossible. The book has also had poor editing: in one case a quotation and its analysis are repeated verbatim less than 20 pages later, and there are numerous typographic and punctuation errors. More to the point, the separate topics have not come apart easily, leading to repetition, and much of the material is devoted to synopsis rather than extended analysis. Ola does try to locate Head's work in larger contexts: in the light of postcolonial and African literature, and in the light of other African women's writing. The short bibliography confirms that Head's works have here been defined in a limited fashion; Ola discusses only Head's fictional work—the three early novels and *The Collector*—not all of her published writing (one novel, one story collection, and two works of non-fiction).

A similar focus on the fiction is shared by the twelve essays collected and edited by ABRAHAMS. The collection includes an essay by Head herself, and a few general essays on the political pressure of writing in Southern Africa. Femi Ojo-Ade and Ezenwa-Ohaeto study the oral and imagistic components of Head's stories, and argue that they best suit her foci. Predominant are articles on *A Question of Power,* regarded by most as Head's masterpiece. Carol Davison and Roger Berger take contrasting slants on madness, and Ola's chapter on good and evil reappears here. Most intriguing is Nancy Bazin's article. While acknowledging the sometimes disconcertingly homophobic and patriarchal language of the novel, Bazin argues that Head here focuses on sexism, rather than racism, in order to force her readers to acknowledge the inextricability of all these forms of power-based oppression.

EILERSEN's biography, the first full-length investigation into the rumors and legends surrounding Bessie Head's background in the racially-charged atmosphere of South Africa, is the most recent, and certainly the most comprehensive overview of Head's life to appear so far. Although not analyzing the written work as such, Eilersen does more successfully what Ola set out to do, and weaves the writing into the fabric of Head's own life. This illuminates the early work, with its admittedly autobiographical components, particularly well; it also accounts for the development of Head's interest in local history. Eilersen's thorough research has led her to uncover and publish a collection of Head's work, *Tales of Tenderness and Power,* posthumously; understandably, this is the only work of the four here reviewed that looks at such recently gathered material. Eilersen takes an admirably moderate tone toward her subject throughout. In so doing, she rescues Head from the encrustations of legend that have made her a symbol for all that was outcast and alienated during the days of South African apartheid, and has restored to us a lively, rambunctious, and temperamental woman, whose faith in her work carried her past obstacles that would have stopped most people in their tracks. The neutral account of Head's life makes her death from hepatitis in 1984 show up all the more starkly as a great loss for her friends and readers.

—VICTORIA CARCHIDI

Healers and Herbalism

Achterberg, Jeanne, *Woman as Healer*, Boston and Shaftesbury: Shambhala, 1990

Apple, Rima (ed.), *Women, Health and Medicine in America: A Historical Handbook*, New York: Garland, 1990

Chamberlain, Mary, *Old Wives Tales: Their History, Remedies, and Spells*, London: Virago Press, 1981

Ehrenreich, Barbara, and Deidre English, *Witches, Midwives, and Nurses: A History of Women Healers*, Old Westbury, New York: Feminist Press, 1973; London: Compendium, 1974

Hughes, Muriel, *Women Healers in Medieval Life and Literature*, Freeport, New York: Kings Crown Press, 1943

McClain, Carol Shepherd (ed.), *Women as Healers: Cross-Cultural Perspectives*, New Brunswick, New Jersey: Rutgers University Press, 1989

Perrone, Bobette, H. Henrietta Stockel, and Victoria Krueger, *Medicine Women, Curanderas, and Women Doctors*, Norman and London: University of Oklahoma Press, 1989

St. Pierre, Mark, and Tilda Long Soldier, *Walking in the Sacred Manner: Healers, Dreamers, and Pipe Carriers: Medicine Women of the Plains Indians*, New York: Simon and Schuster, 1995

Although an avalanche of new works about women as healers has been produced in the last 25 years, some of the better books for the general reader appeared early in that period; most are still in print. The varieties of female healers through history embrace the goddesses of ancient cultures, which believed that medicine was the prerogative of women, and the modern herbalist, offering alternative treatments for an assortment of ailments. This complex classification also entails witches, wise women, midwives, and old wives. The small book by EHRENREICH and ENGLISH affords a thoughtful starting point, dealing with witchcraft and medicine in the Middle Ages before segueing into an examination of women and the rise of the American medical profession.

CHAMBERLAIN renders an excellent, entertaining overview of the role of women as healers throughout history. Using a wealth of primary sources, she begins with the wise women of the ancient world before focusing on the medieval sorceress, pointing out that the use of women-created home remedies transcended class distinctions until the seventeenth century. Because the church and associations of physicians, many of them clerics, proscribed women from legitimate health-care activities, female healers were labeled charlatans rather than medical experts. Nevertheless, ill people appreciated the humane, non-interventionist approach of old wives and patronized them instead of expensive, aloof licensed doctors. For the sick poor, the female healer remained a necessary alternative. The recipes and advice of wise women were even employed by university-trained physicians; indeed, many old-fashioned concoctions are still used in modern households for minor ailments. Chamberlain appends 65 pages of herbal remedies common to old wives; unfortunately, the book is now out of print.

Similar in range but benefiting from an active decade of research on female healers, ACHTERBERG sketches the trajectory of medicine women from the shamanic practices of the ancient world to an apogee of activity in early Christian times. She argues persuasively that wherever a culture encouraged an androgynous image of its deities, women could function as autonomous healers. However, medieval Christian theology alleged the masculinity of the Trinity, while simultaneously saddling women with the consequences of original sin. Charges of devil worship led to the persecution and slaughter of female healers. Achterberg notes the appearance of a few, glittering female healers in the Middle Ages, such as Trotula of Salerno, but charts the decline of female healers from the thirteenth century when they were excluded from the beginnings of scientific experimentation and professional licensing. The collapse of feminine wisdom was completed when Enlightenment scientists developed a methodology that lauded the masculine attributes of reason and objectivity. Achterberg concludes her book by musing over the market-driven renaissance at the end of the twentieth century for female healers as nurses, midwives, and physicians. Her notes and bibliography are exemplary, making this the ideal text in the field.

An earlier, but still useful analysis of factual and fictional European female healers can be found in the book by HUGHES. Originally published in 1943, it investigates the plight of lay women as healers, midwives, and nurses by analyzing literary evidence from the later Middle Ages and early Renaissance. Among the authors explicated are Héloise, Hildegarde von Bingen, Christine de Pisan, and Geoffrey Chaucer. The glossary of herbs is particularly helpful, but the listing of authentic female practitioners (barbers, surgeons, nurses, and empirics) between 1100 and 1500 needs significant updating in light of more recent scholarship.

PERRONE, STOCKEL, and KRUEGER have collaborated to probe the special effects of Native American and Hispanic societies on medicine and healing. The authors spotlight Navajo, Apache, and Cherokee medicine women and their various restorative practices. Hispanic female healers, *curanderas*, resist amalgamation into American healing folkways and employ contrasting Spanish colonial traditions depending on regional differences. However, they share a great religious faith as the source of their talents and rely on their strength to escape cultural roles reserved for women in Hispanic life. The authors interviewed several female physicians in the southwest for a chapter on female doctors and included their own separate musings on the value of the comfort-producing rituals associated with female medicine.

Focusing on Native American protocols associated with medicine women of the Great Plains, ST. PIERRE and LONG SOLDIER, over a two-year period, interviewed holy women and their families for insights on female participation in sacred Indian traditions. Healers, dreamers, and pipe carriers, these women and those whom they touched spoke of their voices, dreams, and experiences. The authors found that regardless of tribe, Lakota, Cheyenne, Crow, or Assiniboine, medicine women were "ordinary" women. St. Pierre and Long Soldier contend that to the detriment of these tribes, the patriarchal bias in the Judeo-Christian tradition has reduced the spiritual status of Indian medicine women and distorted their actual relationships with their people.

The international scope of women's healing roles is dramatically apparent in the diverse articles edited by McCLAIN, who provides a fine overview of recent scholarship in her introduction to the collection. Andean and Sri Lankan women acting as informal healers in their cultures are examined, as is healing accomplished with characteristic female metaphors found in Serbian conjuring and Jamaican "Balm." Other articles deal with the ritual specialties of a Korean shaman, a Puerto Rican *espiritista,* and a Zulu mystic, and their reluctance to assume public healing roles. A final section addresses the impact of cultural change on female healers, manifest equally in the rural-urban conflict of Benin and in the professionalization of midwifery in the United States. This assortment of essays is particularly important for those interested in the relatively new fields of medical anthropology and the anthropology of women.

Lastly, APPLE has edited and provided an excellent summary introduction to an eclectic collection of historically based articles, which range from American women's life-cycle issues to female pharmacists. A unifying theme of the book is the role of women's agency in health care matters, although some of the essays veer from our topic. Particularly germane to healing and herbalism are the chapters on the patent medicine business, charismatic women and health, sectarian medicine, and women's experiences with toxic environments. Scholarly notes and bibliography fully complement the essays.

—ELIZABETH LANE FURDELL

See also Medical History

Health: Gender Politics of

Bayne-Smith, Marcia (ed.), *Race, Gender and Health,* Thousand Oaks, California, and London: Sage, 1996

Boston Women's Health Book Collective, *The New Our Bodies Ourselves,* New York: Simon and Schuster, 1984; revised edition, 1992

Doyal, Lesley, *What Makes Women Sick: Gender and the Political Economy of Health,* New Brunswick, New Jersey: Rutgers University Press, and London: Macmillan, 1995

Dreifus, Claudia (ed.), *Seizing Our Bodies: The Politics of Women's Health,* New York: Vintage, 1977

Ehrenreich, Barbara, and Deirdre English, *For Her Own Good: 150 Years of the Experts' Advice to Women,* New York: Anchor, 1978; London: Pluto Press, 1979

Fee, Elizabeth, and Nancy Krieger (eds.), *Women's Health, Politics and Power: Essays on Sex/Gender, Medicine, and Public Health,* Amityville, New York: Baywood, 1994

Koblinsky, Marjorie, Judith Timyan, and Jill Gay (eds.), *The Health of Women: A Global Perspective,* Boulder, Colorado: Westview Press, 1993

Rosser, Sue V., *Women's Health—Missing from U.S. Medicine,* Bloomington: Indiana University Press, 1994

Whelehan, Patricia, et al., *Women and Health: Cross-Cultural Perspectives,* New York: Bergin and Garvey/Greenwood, 1988

White, Evelyn C. (ed.), *The Black Women's Health Book: Speaking for Ourselves,* Seattle, Washington: Seal Press, 1990, revised edition, 1994; London: Airlift, 1994

Worcester, Nancy, and Mariamne H. Whatley (eds.), *Women's Health: Readings on Social, Economic, and Political Issues,* Dubuque, Iowa: Kendall/Hunt, 1988; second edition, 1994

Gender politics, in this context, refers to the many ways in which power is mobilized along a path marked by the awareness, recognition, and concerns of women's daily lives, as represented in the practices, science, and service of women's health. In this vein, the work of the BOSTON WOMEN'S HEALTH BOOK COLLECTIVE has become both a classic women's health text and a standard for woman-centered health activism. This comprehensive large format work contains over 700 pages written in plain talk, from an inclusive, self-help point of view that mixes health and diagnostic facts with multiple first-person accounts and provocative pictures, to political analyses, exhaustive bibliographies, and resource lists. If only one book can be chosen from this list, this is it.

EHRENREICH and ENGLISH address the gendered politics of health from a historical perspective. This theoretically rich book examines the political motivation of the persecution of witches as midwives and female healers, the resultant rise of male professionalism, the male perspective of and the deference to male expertise in science, medicine, psychiatry, and psychology, and the economic practices of capitalism. This examination is a nuanced critique of the detrimental manifestations of these events for women's health, as seen in: the sexual politics of sickness, the manufacturing of housework as a hygienic domestic science, the changing notions of childhood and child-rearing, the pathological and masochistic notions of motherhood, and the marketing of female sexuality.

Although DREIFUS's book is out of print, it remains available in many libraries; and, it, too, is a classic. This collection of works from the 1970s documents the pioneering spirit of those fomenting social revolution through a feminist critique of health care. Several of the selections were extracted from book-length commentaries, while others were, later, further developed into book-length analyses—many of these by authors who are, today, well known for their influential work. Following a useful introduction, the concise and politically powerful essays are divided into five sections, addressing issues of history, reproduction, institutionalized (male) practices, women working in the health industry, and the women's health movement.

WORCESTER and WHATLEY have assembled over 100 "classic" and current popular and scholarly readings covering a wide range of women's health topics, with an eye to maintaining an anti-racist, anti-heterosexist, cross-cultural perspective. This useful and politically informed work is designed for a first-year college-level women's health course. The selections, chosen to be provocative and to stimulate discussion, are divided into 13 sections, such as gender roles, stereotypes, mental health, sexuality, violence against women, the politics of disease, fertility, body image, aging, and menstruation. Each section has its own introduction and thought-provoking worksheet.

WHITE's book contains 52 selections written by black women and assembled in the spirit of the National Black Women's Health Project: recognizing and changing the health crisis in the African-American community while celebrating the creativity, affirmation, and comfort black women can bring to each other. This collection reflects courage, suffering, love, and struggle, and is written as interviews, scholarly assessments, poetry, statistical analyses, autobiography, policy statements, and excerpts from novels. It addresses a wide scope of black women's experiences, understandings, and fears about matters of health. The topics covered range from teenage pregnancy, obesity, sickle cell anemia, AIDS, cancer, substance abuse, and hypertension, to the use of medicinal roots and other practices of non-western healing, and the experiences of medical training, nursing, and dentistry.

In a somewhat dry but thorough overview of the health status of minority women in the United States, BAYNE-SMITH's contributors examine the confluence of health, race, and gender in four specific groups of women: African-American, Latino, Asian/Pacific Islander, and Native American/Alaskan Native. This is a well-organized and scholarly reference work, which analyzes health care reform in contrast to social and welfare reform. It ends by asserting that the move toward managed competition in health care will not improve the health of women of color, and it explores the possibilities for a new, more robust, definition of health.

Looking to practices within the United States that have left women out of most health research, ROSSER makes the medical model itself more inclusive by bringing women to its center. Beginning with a critique of the androcentric focus of clinical research and practice, especially in the fields of internal medicine, psychiatry, and obstetrics and gynecology, Rosser discusses the issue of ignoring diversity among women in research and practice, pointing to the fact that almost no research acknowledges minority women, lesbians, or elderly women. She concludes this scholarly work with a four-chapter argument for inclusion of women in medical education. Combining feminist methodologies and an insider's understanding of research and policy with a complex understanding of feminism, she looks for solutions in pedagogical, methodological, curricular, and evaluation changes. She argues that an emphasis on women's medical education means inclusive training for both male and female physicians, as well as mainstreaming women's health, resulting in improved health care for all. Each chapter has a thorough and useful list of references.

Approaching the biomedical model as far too limited, DOYAL looks cross-culturally at the economic, social, and cultural ways in which women's lives can make them sick. The gendered division of labor dividing all societies has, she argues, profound ramifications for the health of women. Mobilizing an exhaustive bibliography with the voices of women from many cultures, Doyal intriguingly and helpfully examines not only the ways in which patterns of health and illness point to inequalities between men and women, but how they point to important ways in which women differ from each other. And, finally, she examines the ways in which women act on their own behalf to address health issues.

WHELEHAN's anthropologically based, extraordinarily diverse, cross-cultural and holistically focused collection mixes participant observation and interviews with theory and specific health concerns. A few of the topics covered include: health in a Newfoundland fishing community, midwifery in a Mayan village, menopause in Peru, health in Turkish women in Berlin, suicide in Sri Lanka, stress in Brunei, Vietnam and in a British mining town, and depression in Andean Ecuador. This book centers its attention on the common themes and similar strategies which emerge from a broad range of samples: the rational activism of women recognizing their own concern for health matters, the stress of changing gender-role expectations, and the merging of western and traditional medical practices and beliefs. The strength of this book is the scope of its diversity, combined with its emphasis on the similarity of women's coping strategies.

FEE and KRIEGER have thematically assembled interdisciplinary essays on issues concerning the women's health movement during the last 15 years, from the *International Journal of Health Services.* Like Doyal, they argue that the biomedical model is not sufficient, and that new kinds of research must be explored in order to address the differences and similarities between the health of women and men, as well as the inequalities between and among various women. This is a somewhat uneven, yet useful collection of cross-cultural case studies and experiences—from the United States and England as well as Asia, Africa, and Latin America—which addresses traditional topics along with those of women as health professionals, politicians, and community activists. The emphasis is on public health policy and policy makers.

Basing their book on work presented at "Women's Health: The Action Agenda," the 1991 National Council for International Health's Conference, KOBLINSKY, TIMYAN, and GAY take a global perspective in addressing improvements for the context of women's lives and their health. The contributors work in development, as anthropologists, epidemiologists, nutritionists, public health specialists, health care workers, and policy consultants. The focus is, therefore, on the politics of bureaucracies, and the book is heavily weighted in the direction of concrete suggestions for development policy and program concerns. The center section contains photographs of women in a variety of urban, rural, clinic, home, and work settings.

—CAROLYN DIPALMA

Health: General Works

Boston Women's Health Book Collective, *Our Bodies, Ourselves: A Book by and for Women,* New York: Simon and Schuster, 1973; British edition edited by Angela Phillips and Jill Rakusen, Harmondsworth: Penguin, 1978; 25th anniversary edition, 1996

Dan, Alice (ed.), *Reframing Women's Health: Multidisciplinary Research and Practice,* Thousand Oaks, California: Sage, 1994

Doyal, Lesley, *What Makes Women Sick: Gender and the Political Economy of Health,* London: Macmillan, and New Brunswick, New Jersey: Rutgers University Press, 1995

Foster, Peggy, *Women and the Health Care Industry: An Unhealthy Relationship?,* Buckingham and Bristol, Pennsylvania: Open University Press, 1995

Koblinsky, Marjorie, Judith Timyan, and Jill Gay (eds.), *The Health of Women: A Global Perspective,* Boulder, Colorado: Westview Press, 1993

Rosser, Sue V., *Women's Health—Missing from U.S. Medicine,* Bloomington: Indiana University Press, 1994

Sherwin, Susan, *No Longer Patient: Feminist Ethics and Health Care,* Philadelphia: Temple University Press, 1992

Wilson, Melba (ed.), *Healthy and Wise: The Essential Handbook for Black Women,* London: Virago Press, 1994

The issue of women's health was among the first and most well-explored concerns of second-wave feminism. The enthusiasm generated at that time has invigorated the whole area of study and produced a growing recognition, even within the mainstream, that women are far more than their reproductive systems. Nonetheless, even within feminist texts, the focus on reproduction and its associated demands remains strong, albeit with greater attention given to the different health concerns of women in other areas.

The BOSTON WOMEN'S HEALTH BOOK COLLECTIVE was one of the first to move outside traditional concerns and to publish a general compendium on women's health. Their groundbreaking work introduced the idea that by understanding their own bodies more fully, women could take a real part in controlling their own lives in both health and illness. The main educational purpose of the book is greatly helped by the lavish use of both line drawings and photographic material, which creates a confident hands-on approach to self-help. The work also carefully guides readers through health concerns that require professional intervention. The book has been through several editions, including a special British edition—edited by PHILLIPS and RAKUSEN—and remains highly influential. Revisions made since its first appearance cover new developments and areas of concern and update existing concerns.

A less optimistic approach to health issues, but one that gives an extensive overview of the generally poor health of women worldwide, is provided by KOBLINSKY, TIMYAN, and GAY. The book outlines the health consequences of poverty, malnutrition, inadequate access to medical resources, and gender discrimination in social—including health-care—practices. In addition to the material about reproduction, the book contains useful chapters on mental health and violence against women. Nonetheless, the authors generally recommend reallocation of resources rather than any rethinking of gender values. Equally surprising, in the context of its claims to global significance, is the overall lack of contributions from writers from developing countries.

The imperative to be sensitive to the different health needs and experiences of diverse groups of women is well represented, however, in a variety of texts published since the 1980s. Lesbians, disabled women, and women of color are among those for whom the everyday maintenance of health demands special attention. WILSON's book, for example, speaks directly to and for black women about a wide range of issues including stress, sickle-cell disorders, sexual abuse, aging, lupus, cancer, and AIDS. The book has an impressive list of transatlantic contributors, including Alice Walker, Angela Davis, Jenny Douglas, Pro Torkington, and Audre Lorde, who integrate a practical, political, and personal approach to health care.

Since the early 1970s, feminist interests have resulted in many works that take a multidisciplinary approach, which enables a fuller inquiry into the social and political context of health care, as well as its more clinical aspects. DAN's collection is exemplary in this respect in covering not only social/medical issues such as sexuality, reproduction, and violence, but also health-care reform, legal perspectives, and the nature of provider-patient relationships. The book also directly addresses the health-care concerns of lesbians and of women in developing countries.

Two books that largely dispense with the biomedical approach are those of Foster, who writes about Britain, and Rosser, who refers specifically to the United States. Both, however, make points that have relevance for the western model of health-care provision. FOSTER takes a strong view that health care is intrinsically more harmful to women than it is beneficial, and she argues that commercial interests have led to the unnecessary medicalization of women's bodies. In her assessment of expensive high-tech medicine and preventive screening services for safety, effectiveness, and potential for social control, Foster found all these services inadequate. In contrast, ROSSER analyzes the neglect of women's health issues within the medical establishment. She identifies an androcentric bias in clinical research that results in the underdiagnosis of female ill health in general, unless such illness is associated with reproductive and heterosexual activity. Rosser then identifies the even greater neglect experienced by older women, lesbians, and women of colour. Her solution is to overcome bias by means of far-reaching changes in the methodologies and curricula of medical education and by making women's health care a more accepted specialty.

In a similar way, DOYAL highlights male bias in research and extends her argument to show that traditional medical models lack sufficient understanding of women's health status worldwide. Her book is less about medicine per se than it is about the external factors that affect health. Accordingly, she looks both at the ways in which women's experiences and activity—such as sexuality, work patterns, fertility control, and exposure to violence—give rise to health problems, and at how such threats to well-being might be countered.

Finally, SHERWIN takes on the ethical concerns that always mediate health-care encounters. She insists that biomedical interventions are always influenced by gender, and that conventional bioethics fails to address the relationships of dominance because they are obscured by neutral terms such as "patient," "parent," or "the elderly." She argues that not only are many health-care practices bad for individual women, but that the institution of medicine as a whole reinforces patriarchal structures. Sherwin's concern is to bring feminist ethics to bear on specifically clinical issues like abortion, advanced reproductive technologies, and doctor-patient relationships in order to suggest what would constitute morally acceptable health care.

—MARGRIT SHILDRICK

Health: Women's Health Movement

Adams, Diane, *Health Issues for Women of Colour: A Cultural Diversity Perspective,* Thousand Oaks, California, and London: Sage, 1995

Boston Women's Health Book Collective, *The New Our Bodies Ourselves,* New York: Simon and Schuster, 1984; revised edition, 1992

Crook, Marion, *My Body: Women Speak Out about Their Health Care,* New York and London: Plenum Press, 1995

Dan, Alice J. (ed.), *Reframing Women's Health: Multi-Disciplinary Research and Practice,* Thousand Oaks, California, and London: Sage, 1994

Davis, Flora, *Moving the Mountain: The Woman's Movement in America since 1960,* New York: Simon and Schuster, 1991

Friedman, Emily (ed.), *An Unfinished Revolution: Women and Health Care in America,* New York: United Hospital Fund of New York, 1994

Smyke, Patricia, *Women and Health,* London and Atlantic Highlands, New Jersey: Zed, 1991

Whatley, Mariamne, and Nancy Worcester, *Women's Health: Readings in Social, Economic, and Political Issues,* Dubuque, Iowa: Kendall/Hunt, 1988; second edition, 1994

In the landmark book *The Second Sex* (1952), Simone de Beauvoir chronicled the history of thousands of years of women's subjugation that survived, and thrived, in the suspicions and superstitions promulgated because of their physical "otherness;" for years after this book was published, a woman's biology indeed appeared to be her destiny. More importantly, her "biological destiny" continued to be the province of male speculation. In the late 1960s, women finally revolted against their "destiny" and demanded rights and information long withheld from them, thus commencing the women's health movement, which continues to evolve as it incorporates new issues, and has effectively positioned itself at the fore of political rhetoric and debate.

The BOSTON WOMEN'S HEALTH BOOK COLLECTIVE's original book, *Our Bodies, Ourselves* (1973), was born out of the roots of the movement in the early 1970s, beginning as a revelation of women's previously unshared experiences; it culminated in a comprehensive collection of culturally-diverse literature aimed to inform women about their bodies, and thus empower their status as patients in the male-dominated medical professions. Now, the Boston Women's Health Book Collective's newest manual has added some up-to-date information on AIDS, new birth control methods, and women's disorders to its already tremendous compilation, in order to reflect the changing issues in women's health care. It does not address the historic and political machinations of the women's movement per se, but instead persists in its original aim of declassifying medical information and ending patient exploitation.

WORCESTER and WHATLEY's compendium is not a manual for physical self-knowledge, like the *New Our Bodies Ourselves* collection, but instead involves the same issues as they have evolved into cross-cultural debates politicized in a public forum. The essays represent authors from different ideologies, political opinions, and popular theories on a variety of universal topics: women and their health care systems, women and age, ethnic diversity and stereotypes, mental health, violence against women, the politics of disease, body image and food, menstruation, fertility and reproduction, and tobacco, alcohol, and drugs, among others. Gleaned from a variety of women's periodicals and magazines, this lively dialectic covers the treatment of women in these arenas. Worcester and Whatley provide the historical backgrounds that contextualize the discussions.

The section entitled "The Women's Health Movement" in DAVIS's book is a comprehensive look at the social and cultural situations that precipitated the women's health movement. Davis discusses the inherent fear of women's bodily functions (menstruation, childbirth) and how this fear over time embedded itself in the medical institutions, a process that took the woman as healer/midwife and reduced her to a helpless and endangered patient. One of the most interesting aspects of her research is her analysis of the financial and political underpinnings of pharmaceutical companies and medical associations, which allowed unsafe practices to continue despite knowledge of their unsafe nature (i.e., the Dalkon Shield). She also details specific leaders and grassroots organizations that were instrumental in creating change for women's reproductive health.

FRIEDMAN's book is a compilation of essays that spans several areas of the relationship between women and health care, from their roles as users of health services, informal caregivers, health care providers, and health care leaders. In particular, Andrea Boroff Eagan's essay "The Woman's Health Movement and Its Lasting Impact" shows, in an accessible and cursory history of the movement, how awareness of these roles was made possible. She discusses the surge of activism that dedicated itself to reforming the system by disseminating information on issues that had been previously suppressed, like abortion, natural childbirth, unsafe yet accepted practices and prescriptions (i.e., DES and the Dalkon Shield), breast cancer, and the essentially powerless role of female patients. She also shows how the movement's impact is seen in the entrance of more women into the medical profession, and the increased number of women's health centers.

The women's health movement that began in the 1960s largely ameliorated health conditions for white women only, ADAMS contends, while women of color were still made to suffer through conditions and treatments that, even to this day, have changed very little for them. Adams rallies for the continuation of the women's health movement on behalf of women of color, including American Indians, Alaskan Natives, Asians, Pacific Islanders, and Hispanics and Latinas. Her urgent work considers the environmental, economic, and social factors that have heretofore hindered their treatments, and then discusses variables that have gone unexplored, such as the differences among ethnic groups regarding disease and death, as well as these rates for men and women within a certain ethnicity. She offers in-depth data and descriptions, as well as her own prescriptions for certain policies, programs, and intervention strategies.

A project of the United Nations/Nongovernmental Organizational Group on Women and Development, SMYKE's book uniquely focuses on health issues that face women in Third World and developing countries. Ten years after her first edition, Smyke's evidence concludes, astonishingly enough, that health care continued to decline for this particular group of women, who, because of their low status as females, particularly in developing countries, are left to fend for themselves in deplorable conditions. Smyke details not only the tragic conditions endemic in such countries (poverty, lack of family planning, scarcity of resources, absence of health care, no education, environmental deterioration), but also shows how poor health practices are passed from mother to daughter, diminishing hope for improvement, leaving generations of women and entire countries in chronic ill health.

DAN's book rides the sophisticated cusp of the women's health movement's aim in the 1990s to systematize itself into mainstream, but independent, academic discourse. Its approach to pedagogy is interdisciplinary, and it involves the interweaving of anthropology, psychology, sociology, social work, and the legal system; for Dan, all disciplines contribute to a definition of women's healing and women's health. The underlying premise of her collection of essays is the application of various philosophies in order to change the medical establishment. Dan's curricular and educational paradigms liberate themselves from the western stereotypical models, generalizations, and abstractions that have heretofore prevented clear discussion on women's health. The essays in her book address involvement at the individual, community, and national levels in order to solve international concerns.

—ANNMARIE PHILLIPS

Hellman, Lillian 1905–1984

American Writer

Adler, Jacob H., *Lillian Hellman,* Austin, Texas: Steck-Vaughn, 1969

Bryer, Jackson R., *Conversations with Lillian Hellman,* Jackson: University Press of Mississippi, 1986

Estrin, Mark W. (ed.), *Critical Essays on Lillian Hellman,* Boston: G.K. Hall, 1989

Falk, Doris V., *Lillian Hellman,* New York: Frederick Ungar, 1978

Feibleman, Peter S., *Lilly: Reminiscences of Lillian Hellman,* New York: Morrow, 1988; London: Chatto and Windus, 1989

Lederer, Katherine, *Lillian Hellman,* Boston: Twayne, 1979

Moody, Richard, *Lillian Hellman, Playwright,* New York: Pegasus, 1972

Rollyson, Carl E., *Lillian Hellman: Her Legend and Her Legacy,* New York: St. Martin's Press, 1988

Wright, William, *Lillian Hellman: The Image, The Woman,* New York: Simon and Schuster, 1986; London: Sidgwick and Jackson, 1987

Since the grand success of her first play, *The Children's Hour,* in 1934, Lillian Hellman has been among the most notable of U.S. female playwrights. Her life, more than her dramatic work, received enormous attention with the publication of her three volumes of memoirs—*An Unfinished Woman* (1969), *Pentimento* (1973), and *Scoundrel Time* (1976)—and with the sustained controversy that followed the film *Julia* (1977), based on a section in *Pentimento.* Throughout the late 1970s and the 1980s, critical and biographical discussion has centered on the truthfulness (or lack thereof) of Hellman's self-characterizations, in her memoirs and in her later plays as well.

The swirling controversy culminated in the two definitive biographies by Rollyson and Wright. WRIGHT began his biography during Hellman's lifetime, and near death Hellman asked friends not to speak to him. Although his is the first major biography, some critics have found it flawed and biased by lack of information from Hellman's intimates, who obeyed her injunction. Wright sees Hellman as composed of antithetical qualities and urges, rocking between her love for a luxurious lifestyle and her passion for politics. He traces Hellman's developing persona and obsessions very deliberately through the chronology of her life, giving full attention to the relatives, friends, husbands, lovers, acquaintances, and enemies. He also dispassionately considers the honesty of Hellman's claims in her memoirs, some of which credited her with achievements and involvements in U.S. and world affairs that strained her credibility even with supporters.

ROLLYSON tracks the honesty controversy through Hellman's three memoirs, looking for corroborating evidence through other sources—public records, correspondence, archives, and interviews with those people named in the books and those who knew them. While not finally landing on the side of those, like Mary McCarthy, who claimed Hellman falsified her life in self-glorification, Rollyson finds Hellman's autobiographical efforts at best "authentic," but sometimes fictionalized renderings of emotional memory, although sometimes fairly accurate in their portraits.

MOODY writes before the Hellman controversy became the fodder of talk shows, indictments, and rebuttals. His is a now atypical view of a Hellman who compartmentalized her life, whose plays had few autobiographical elements, and whose career was a rather inexorable march to higher levels of greatness. Replete with extensive summaries of Hellman's works, Moody's treatment is dated in both methodology and conclusions.

LEDERER sticks to the format of the Twayne authors series in which her work appears and so her book contains minimal biography and very little comparative analysis. Lederer's claim is that Hellman is unique among American playwrights, especially in her use of irony in a "moral, not political" vision. BRYER compiles various articles on and interviews with Hellman, providing a closer resource for readers to judge whether Hellman indeed loved to talk about herself and rewrote her life to emphasize her own heroics. More of the book is about the theater than some of the narrative biographies.

ESTRIN brings together the widest ranging and most comprehensive collection of critical essays on Hellman, from articles on individual plays—and, of course, the memoirs—to those attempting to place Hellman in the dramatic traditions of Ibsen and Chekhov. Perhaps inevitably, Estrin concludes with a selection of pieces on "The Hellman Persona" from those who knew—or knew of—Hellman, so that finally this book offers critical essays in both senses of criticism.

FEIBLEMAN responds to all the controversy with a most positive, most sympathetic, reminiscence of Lillian Hellman as, and when, he knew her. Hellman's companion in her late years and her principal heir, Feibleman protects her image while compassionately recounting the travails of her later years and illnesses. His book provides an antidote to all those who criticized Hellman's persona as well as her achievements.

FALK brings many fewer resources to her relatively slight work than do Wright and Rollyson, and she is surprisingly dispassionate about the surging controversies around Hellman. Her chapters track through the plays and the memoirs, often in very deliberate summary. Her assessment of critical reception lies in counting positive reviews, and she tracks reaction to *Scoundrel Time* by looking to letters in the *Times* and reviews and magazine articles.

ADLER writes before the *Julia* controversy and within the format constraints of the "Southern Writers Series" author volumes. He is rather melodramatic about Hellman's life (he speaks of her near starvation before her first play) and seems principally concerned with placing her plays within standard dramatic categories, such as the well-made play and the comedy of manners. Adler's book is primarily useful for brief, easily read coverage of the traditional canonical opinion of Hellman's work.

—CAROL KLIMICK CYGANOWSKI

Herbalism *see* Healers and Herbalism

Heterosexism *see* Homophobia and Heterosexism

Heterosexuality

Brownmiller, Susan, *Against Our Will: Men, Women, and Rape*, London: Secker and Warburg, and New York: Simon and Schuster, 1975

Butler, Judith, *Gender Trouble: Feminism and the Subversion of Identity*, New York and London: Routledge, 1990

Dworkin, Andrea, *Intercourse*, London: Secker and Warburg, and New York: Free Press, 1987

Ehrenreich, Barbara, Elizabeth Hess, and Gloria Jacobs, *Re-Making Love: The Feminization of Sex*, New York: Doubleday, 1986; London: Fontana, 1987

Foucault, Michel, *The History of Sexuality: An Introduction*, translated by Robert Hurley, New York: Pantheon, 1978; London: Lane, 1979

Hite, Shere, *The Hite Report: A Nationwide Survey of Female Sexuality*, New York: Macmillan, 1976; London: Macmillan, 1977

Jackson, Stevi, and Sue Scott (eds.), *Feminism and Sexuality: A Reader*, New York: Columbia University Press, 1996

Katz, Jonathan Ned, *The Invention of Heterosexuality*, New York: Dutton, 1995

Millet, Kate, *Sexual Politics*, New York: Doubleday, 1970; London: Hart-Davies, 1972

Richardson, Diane (ed.), *Theorising Heterosexuality: Telling It Straight*, Philadelphia and Buckingham: Open University Press, 1996

Wilkinson, Sue, and Celia Kitzinger (eds.), *Heterosexuality: A Feminism and Psychology Reader*, London and Newbury Park, California: Sage, 1993

Wittig, Monique, *The Straight Mind and Other Essays*, Boston: Beacon Press, New York and London: Harvester Wheatsheaf, 1992

EHRENREICH, HESS, and JACOBS assert that although the "sexual revolution" effected little actual change in beliefs and practices of heterosexual men, women began to claim *their* sexual rights. Betty Friedan's research for *The Feminine Mystique* (1963) revealed dissatisfied housewives unwilling to accept lack of sexual fulfillment. Single, urban, working women's economic and marital independence set the stage for greater sexual independence. As women began speaking openly about oral sex and demanding "orgasm equity," traditional marriage manuals were supplanted by such books as Helen Gurley Brown's *Sex and the Single Girl* (1962) and Terry Garrity's *The Sensuous Woman* (1969). Christian women such as Mirabelle Morgan, while advising women to maintain their traditional roles, contributed their own visions to the sexual revolution and urged wives to use costumes and fantasies to increase their own sexual satisfaction—and to produce more indulgent husbands.

The focus on woman's ownership and use of her body was encouraged by HITE's extensive analysis, which presented interviews and data gathered from over 3,000 women nationwide. This was a first: a comprehensive study in which women discussed their sexuality in their own terms, rather than having it defined (and thus controlled) by male experts. MILLET was one of the first theoretical critics of heterosexuality and what she calls the coercive political power of "heterosexual orthodoxy." She says normative heterosexuality, "postured" by men in order to prove their manhood, is based on violent domination and requires that women be construed as both different and inferior—although usefully reflective and complementary.

Brownmiller and Dworkin each have critiqued intercourse as inherently violative. BROWNMILLER argues that throughout history the physical act of penetrative sex has privileged and empowered men while subordinating women, and that social custom, politics, and law all reflect this intercourse-based inequality. DWORKIN states that because "[i]intercourse occurs in a context of power relations that is pervasive and incontrovertible" we live in a society in which (hetero)sexuality is enacted as 'woman hating.'"

WITTIG looks closely at language's impact on institutionalized power and class. She asserts that the gender categories of man and woman are not organic but are based on the "political regime" of patriarchal heterosexuality. These difference-focused categories are both products of and reinforcement for a class system that oppresses women. To fight society's deeply embedded sexism, feminists must refuse the label "woman," which reflects an identity of subordinate status in heteropatriarchy.

FOUCAULT documents nineteenth-century social scientists' medicalizing and pathologizing of human sexuality. Their new terminology and studies focused on identifying not just sexual practices, but the practitioners themselves, as either "normal" (heterosexuals) or "deviant" (thus in need of containment and/or treatment). Although Foucault deals only minimally with women's sexuality, his historical work and corollary argument, that (hetero)sexuality is not merely regulated through social custom and law but is actually produced through cutural actions and discourse, have greatly influenced feminist theorists.

BUTLER extends the Foucauldian argument, stating that although society views heterosexuality as the hegemonic and stable norm of "natural," biologically determined sexual behavior, actually the heterosexual repeatedly (re)constructs sexual identity through socially prescribed performances. Even non-heterosexual identities are not natural or independently developed but are performed as reactions to heterosexual scripts.

KATZ's overview, covering primarily the past two hundred years, is rich in examples and quotations. Of particular interest are Chapter Six, discussing early critiques pairing heterosexuality and women's oppression, and Chapter Seven, describing the complex and divisive contemporary arguments over ways sexuality and desire are conceived and enacted.

Noting that the nineteenth-century women's movement generally tended to avoid the subject of female (hetero)sexuality, JACKSON and SCOTT have collected excerpts from twentieth-century feminists. Adrienne Rich's groundbreaking essay questions whether women ever freely choose their sexuality, given their lifelong, overt, and subtle instruction in conformity. Most women are not even aware that there is an alternative to "compulsory heterosexuality," since women-loving women have systematically been erased from recorded history. Yet, she suggests, even heterosexual women can locate themselves on a "lesbian continuum" by being woman- (rather than man-) identified. Anne Koedt's "Myth of the Vaginal Orgasm" argues that this widely accepted belief has led men—and women themselves—to pathologize those who don't achieve vaginal orgasm (or even pleasure) through intercourse. In privileging the man (and the phallus), it has denied women's rights to their bodies' true mode of sexual pleasure, that is, clitoral orgasm. Stating, "Sexuality is to feminism what work is to marxism: that which is most one's own, yet most taken away," Catharine MacKinnon analyzes how the power/desire connection in both definitions and practices of heterosexuality reinforce the "class system" between men and women. Feminist textual analysis and psychoanalytical theory inform Luce Irigaray's critique of patriarchal versions of sexuality. She argues that the phallocentrism of most psychological and medical descriptions of sex deny the power of woman's bodily difference, and thus her very being.

RICHARDSON discusses feminists' analyses that challenge "heteronormativity," by uncovering ways in which dominant discourses affect how we see, use, and symbolically understand our bodies. She also explores concepts of a non-oppressive heterosexuality. One contributor, Wendy Hollway, applies a feminist perspective to object relations theory and Lacanian psychoanalytical theory of desire. In contrast to these theories' "eroticisation of gendered power difference," she sees (heterosexual) desire arising from shared recognition between lovers of similar psychological and physical needs. Other key theorists are included, such as Sheila Jeffries, Stevi Jackson, and Carol Smart.

In WILKINSON and KITZINGER's book, thirty-eight lesbian and heterosexual theorists explore the nature of heterosexuality, asking, "How does heterosexual activity affect the whole of a woman's life, her sense of self, her relationships with other women, and her political engagements?" Many wrestle with the apparent "paradoxical identity" of being heterosexual and feminist, while others resist being labeled at all. Yet, as Kitzinger and Wilkinson state, under heteropatriarchy, such a denial of labels is only possible for heterosexuals, since lesbians' and bisexuals' lives are much affected by others' labeling. One contributor, Kadiatu Kanneh, suggests that identity politics, including the politics of heterosexuality, need to be reconceptualized as fluid, sexual identity being only one facet of identity, not necessarily excluding other (for example, feminist) identities.

—H. ELIZABETH RENFRO

Higher Education

Aisenberg, Nadya, and Mona Harrington, *Women of Academe: Outsiders in the Sacred Grove*, London and Amherst: University of Massachusetts Press, 1988

Clifford, Geraldine J. (ed.), *Lone Voyagers: Academic Women in Coeducational Universities, 1870–1937*, New York: Feminist Press, 1989

Holland, Dorothy C., and Margaret A. Eisenhart, *Educated in Romance: Women, Achievement, and College Culture*, Chicago: University of Chicago Press, 1990

Horowitz, Helen Lefkowitz, *Alma Mater: Design and Experience in the Women's Colleges from Their Nineteenth-Century Beginnings to the 1930s*, New York: Knopf, 1984

Levine, Susan, *Degrees of Equality: The American Association of University Women and the Challenge of Twentieth-Century Feminism*, Philadelphia: Temple University Press, 1995

Lewis, Magda Gere, *Without a Word: Teaching beyond Women's Silence*, New York: Routledge, 1993

Morley, Louise (ed.), *Feminist Academics: Creative Agents for Change*, London and Bristol, Pennsylvania: Taylor and Francis, 1995

Seller, Maxine Schwartz (ed.), *Women Educators in the United States, 1820–1993: A Bio-Bibliographical Sourcebook*, Westport, Connecticut: Greenwood, 1994

Solomon, Barbara Miller, *In the Company of Educated Women: A History of Women and Higher Education in America*, New Haven, Connecticut, and London: Yale University Press, 1985

Subbarao, K. (ed.), *Women in Higher Education: Progress, Constraints, and Promising Initiatives*, Washington, D.C.: World Bank, 1994

Excitement about the more visible roles of women in higher education can be contextualized by the knowledge that while vast gains are taking place, historically, some women have always equipped themselves with solid intellectual training. Much of the progress we celebrate is in solid numbers of women enrolling in undergraduate programs, undertaking many graduate programs, although there are fewer in the sciences, and working at the lower levels of higher education as faculty and administrators. While women are today very visible as faculty on our campuses, they are not present in classrooms proportionately with their female students, and they are not always reimbursed or promoted equally with their male peers. Yet many of these same female professors attained their credentials at a time when admission to many of the most elite colleges and universities was denied them on the basis of gender. Put in that light, women's advances in the last 25 years are remarkable. Yet, when one looks at statistics about women who have been promoted to full professorship in major research institutions, or especially when one directs one's curiosity toward the status of women in education in the Third World, one sees less cause for optimism.

Several book-length studies published in the last decade remain unreplaced in their excellence as introductions to the study of women in higher education in the United States. SOLOMON's readable and comprehensive study investigates anxiety about the impact of education on women's—and men's—traditional roles. This issue continues to rankle segments of contemporary society, but Solomon reminds the reader that in colonial times the barriers to widely available public education were insurmountable. She explores what the impact of larger social forces has had in shaping women's options for education and what effect education has had on women's life choices.

Complementing Solomon's work, HOROWITZ explores the so-called seven sister elite eastern women's colleges. She looks at their individual histories and describes how they changed in response to societal reexamination of women's roles, moving from a goal of sheltering women to one of emboldening them. Her study suggests how these institutions' efforts to serve their privileged students provided ideological leadership for offering liberal arts education free of gender stereotypes to women everywhere.

CLIFFORD focuses on individual female faculty, rather than institutions, to examine the challenges to academic women seeking careers in coeducational institutions in the late nineteenth and early twentieth centuries. Often confined to lower-status institutions, these women generally labored alone. Perhaps radicalized by their struggle, they recorded their frustrations in autobiographical accounts, which Clifford quotes extensively. Her work illustrates the historical role of female faculty; her focus is on the individual women whose stories she tells rather than on generalizations about higher education.

While Clifford tells of the struggles of female faculty born in the nineteenth century, AISENBERG and HARRINGTON offer startling parallels of contemporary women's often thwarted or compromised efforts to carve out academic careers. Aisenberg and Harrington focus on familial attitudes toward professional career goals and pressures to conform, even within the academy, to traditional roles and established areas of research. They offer suggestions for professional survival.

Surviving higher education even as an undergraduate takes pluck. HOLLAND and EISENHART provide extensive research that suggests that for female students, academic culture takes a distinct second place to an intense emphasis on sustaining peer culture: nurturing friendships, pursuing romantic relationships, and socializing. Even bright women often manage to embody practices during college life that contribute to derailing their expectations for success as breadwinners and to sustaining their subordinate status in the workplace.

Seeking to ameliorate such subordinate roles, LEWIS theorizes about the reasons for women's silence in intellectual debate. Her study, based on observation of British classroom dynamics, suggests that silence is both an expression of women's oppression and of their revolt. This study will inspire anyone seeking to create more gender balance in education. MORLEY and WALSH offer an edited collection describing the transformative possibilities of feminism as an oppositional discourse in British higher education. A strength of this collection is its focus on race and class as sources of negation of intelligence.

SELLER offers profiles of 66 women in a broad range of roles. Along with biographical information about women working at every level of education, helpful bibliographies follow each entry. She includes profiles of women of color and women working in nontraditional educational settings. When the biographies are read as a group, the book becomes a history of women's achievements as both creators and beneficiaries of expanded educational opportunity.

An excellent overview of trends in higher education in global perspective, including helpful tables and charts, makes up the book by SUBBARAO. Here the reader can see what challenges face contemporary women in Africa, Latin America, and elsewhere in the world. As with most comparative studies, not only is this global context informative in itself, but the analyses that accompany the statistical studies also provide insight about the role of economics and gender that the western world is still addressing in seeking to educate women.

Finally, LEVINE asks what happens to women once they complete their formal educations. Her historical study of the American Association of University Women, their impact on fostering educational opportunity for women, and the effectiveness of their efforts to raise consciousness not only among educators, but also political leaders and opinion makers, testifies that achieving opportunities for women requires the active support of women and men beyond the academy.

—VIVIAN FOSS

Hildegard of Bingen 1098–1179

German Abbess, Mystic, and Composer

Bobko, Jane (ed.), *Vision: The Life and Music of Hildegard von Bingen*, New York: Penguin, 1995

Dronke, Peter, *Women Writers of the Middle Ages: A Critical Study of Texts from Perpetua to Marguerite Porete*, Cambridge and New York: Cambridge University Press, 1984

Flanagan, Sabina, *Hildegard of Bingen, 1098–1179: A Visionary Life*, London and New York: Routledge, 1989

Newman, Barbara, *Sister of Wisdom: St. Hildegard's Theology of the Feminine*, Berkeley: University of California Press, and Aldershot: Scolar, 1987

BOBKO's book is an excellent introduction to the remarkable life this twelfth-century abbess, healer, composer, and writer who wrote nine books on theology, medicine, science, and physiology. The book is divided into three parts: a brief biography; an interpretation of Hildegard's visions, including 12 superb reproductions of the visions from the illuminated manuscripts; and an analysis of Hildegard's music that considers her compositions in the context of medieval music. Scholar Barbara Newman and theologian Matthew Fox provide commentary on Hildegard's work.

In her more in-depth study of Hildegard, NEWMAN argues that she should not be examined as part of the tradition of female mysticism, because that category is too broad to provide a context for Hildegard's special gifts of vision and prophecy. Newman's study considers Hildegard in terms of what she calls the "sapiential tradition," the school of thought that focuses on such themes as divine beauty, the feminine aspect of God, and the moral and aesthetic ideal of virginity. Feminine imagery for the Holy Spirit, the Church, and the cosmos are prominent in the sapiential tradition. Through close readings of the various works, Newman demonstrates how important Hildegard was in the development of this tradition. Newman also discusses how Hildegard was successful in combining her symbolic thinking with practical application. This work is solidly grounded in the theology of the feminine, but it is a very useful study for all readers.

FLANAGAN's excellent biography is a sensitive but balanced consideration of Hildegard's life and writings. Flanagan's comprehensive study examines Hildegard as visionary, mystic, musician, theologian, healer, and poet. Her focus is on Hildegard's unique writing, specifically on how Hildegard came to produce her works and have them accepted in a world where few women wrote at all. Flanagan's book is especially useful in explaining how Hildegard managed the opportunities for, as well as the constraints against, writing. Several chapters provide thorough descriptions of Hildegard's various writings; Flanagan also explores the interrelations of theories and ideas within Hildegard's own oeuvre, rather than placing her within her contemporary literary context.

DRONKE's book is a study of several female writers of the medieval period, but the largest chapter and selection of texts is devoted to Hildegard. Dronke's work on Hildegard is critical to any complete understanding of the Hildegard scholarship. In this book, he begins with a biographical approach, by focusing on 12 autobiographical selections from the *Vita* and several passages from her letters. Dronke demonstrates how Hildegard's unique understanding of the allegorical tradition is also evident in these letters. He also examines the work known as *Causae et curae*, a book of medical lore that covers subjects such as sexual intercourse, conception, childbirth, and a variety of diseases. Dronke concludes that while Hildegard is clearly mystical in disposition, her medical writings are grounded in a practical and realistic attempt to understand the physical nature of human existence.

—JO ELDRIDGE CARNEY

Hill, Anita 1956–

American Lawyer

Brock, David, *The Real Anita Hill: The Untold Story*, New York and Oxford: Free Press, 1993
Chrisman, Robert, and Robert L. Allen (eds.), *Court of Appeal: The Black Community Speaks Out on the Racial and Sexual Politics of Clarence Thomas vs. Anita Hill*, New York: Ballantine, 1992
Mayer, Jane, and Jill Abramson, *Strange Justice: The Selling of Clarence Thomas*, Boston: Houghton Mifflin, 1994
Miller, Anita, *United States Congress, Senate Committee of the Judiciary, The Complete Transcripts of the Clarence Thomas-Anita Hill Hearings: October 11, 12 and 13, 1991*, Chicago: Academy Chicago Publishers, 1994
Phelps, Timothy M., and Helen Winternitz, *Capitol Games: Clarence Thomas, Anita Hill, and the Story of a Supreme Court Nomination*, New York: Hyperion, 1992
Ragan, Sandra, *The Lynching of Language: Gender, Politics and Power in the Hill-Thomas Hearings*, Urbana: University of Illinois Press, 1996
Smitherman, Geneva (ed.), *African American Women Speak Out on Anita Hill-Clarence Thomas*, Detroit, Michigan: Wayne State University Press, 1995

Few events in the United States have created the firestorm of national debate generated by the confirmation hearings of the Supreme Court Justice Clarence Thomas. Yet, with all the intense media coverage, one aspect seemed continually side-stepped: the response of America to this televised investigation of race, gender, sexuality, and especially the black psyche and intra-racial politics. CHRISMAN assembles all the material relevant to understanding the Thomas hearings: a complete chronology of the confirmation process, the statements of both Hill and Thomas, the position statements of the major black organizations that testified, and the essays by prominent African-Americans. This collection examines such issues as how African-Americans perceive their interests, and the disturbing sexual backlash against Hill and what it says about the position of black females. This book represents voices from every part of the political spectrum and reaffirms that the black community is the final "court of appeal" in this debate.

The press has characterized the Anita Hill-Clarence Thomas confrontation as an impenetrable mystery whose truth can never really be known. BROCK dissents from this conclusion. His book is at odds with the myth of Anita Hill. He corrects numerous misconceptions and introduces new factual evidence. This book is not about whether or not Thomas should have been confirmed to the Supreme Court. Nor does it seek to question whether sexual harassment is a serious offense. Rather, it seeks to establish whether sexual harassment occurred in the Hill-Thomas case. Hill remains Thomas's sole accuser, and so Brock's inquiry focuses on which of the two was the more reliable witness. The evidence put forth in this book argues that Hill misrepresented or suppressed various facts pertaining to her relationship with Thomas, contracts with the Senate staff during the nomination proceedings, and her background, beliefs, and possible motives. Brock's cumulative portrait argues that Hill does not deserve the credence that she continues to be granted.

SMITHERMAN's book is structured to give voice to African-American women. It provides an avenue for articulating the impact and meaning of the Hill-Thomas case on the African-American community. This work captures the poignancy and immediacy of that historical moment both for black women and for other groups. This critique demands that the reader deplore the assault upon Hill's dignity and the racist, sexist treatment accorded her as an African-American woman who refused to continue her silence about gender subordination and sexual harassment. The reader gets to know Hill as an African-American, as a person with origins in poverty, and as a woman. Unlike other journal collections and books on Hill-Thomas, this book has neither male nor European-American women as contributors. This design is to focus on the historically silenced voice of black women in the United States. The voices presented are those of activists, writers, journalists, and scholars across many disciplines. There are 20 African-American women speaking on the Hill-Thomas case and its meaning and significance for African-American women and the nation.

RAGAN's work stands out from most of the discussions of sexual harassment. This book extends prior research and theorizing by posing questions and suggesting answers that are intelligent and original. It has a complexly layered analysis of events and issues that have been too often reduced to one-dimensional, simplistic accounts. On one level, it focuses on the dispute between Hill and Thomas about the events in the 1980s. On the second level, this book extends what others have previously noticed about the hearings and their meaning. A distinctive contributiion of this book is its attention to the role of discourse, or language, in reproducing or contesting prevailing ideologies. This focus on communication sheds light on the radical transformation that occurred early in the hearings. The book enhances understanding of how discourse creates the meaning of issues and identities in both public and private settings. These essays show that Hill began as the plaintiff and Thomas the defendant who must refute charges against him or justify his actions. The tables quickly turned and Anita Hill became the defendant who was on trial to defend herself against not only Thomas's claims that she was lying in claiming he harassed her, but also a deluge of other charges that impugned her professional competence, personal integrity, sanity, and sexual normalcy. These essays provide sophisticated and often subtle insights, not only into the Hill-Thomas hearings, but also into Anita Hill on a more personal level, both of which enlarge understanding of the ways in which cultural consciousness is shaped.

MILLER published a complete transcript of the Hill-Thomas hearings, and the important exhibits that were submitted. This work allows the audience an opportunity to read Anita Hill's closed door testimony, the hearings, the affidavits about character and lack of it, and it finally lets the reader decide what it all means. A complete list of the submitted material is included in Appendix B, separated into categories of general interest, support, and opposition. Telephone logs submitted by Senator Hatch are also included. There are three indices. The first is an alphabetical list of witnesses with page numbers of their testimony. The second, called "colloquy," identifies page numbers of each senator's questioning of each witness. The third locates names mentioned in the text apart from testimony.

MAYER's book illustrates how Thomas's ascension to the Supreme Court goes far beyond what emerged during the hearings. Through interviews, including the first on-the-record interview with Anita Hill, readers learn who Clarence Thomas and Anita Hill are and how both were treated unfairly by the Washington establishment. A volatile mix of issues—race, sex, and the politics of the High Court—made the Thomas nomination a watershed event. This book tells the full story of one of the most troubling episodes of our time. The reader learns about Clarence Thomas's campaign for the Supreme Court and the doubts about him that haunted the White House. The book shows profound cycnicism behind the administration's campaign for Thomas.

PHELPS presents a chronological listing of the events in Washington in the lives of Clarence Thomas and Anita Hill leading up to the hearings. The reader is taken behind the scenes in this piece of investigative reporting. This book outlines the divisions in the black community and shows the leader of an influential civil rights organization secretly cooperating with the White House, thereby crippling the anti-Thomas coalition. It also reveals why certain key senators allowed the hearings to unravel into a televised fiasco and why initial elements of the story, such as the testimony of the "second" women (Angela Wright) were held back. Special detailed focus is given to Anita Hill in Chapter Fourteen. The author delves into her personal and professional life in order to shed more light on the woman behind the hearings.

—SUSAN M. TAYLOR

Hinduism

Erndl, Kathleen, *Victory to the Mother: The Hindu Goddess of Northwest India in Myth, Ritual, and Symbol,* New York: Oxford University Press, 1993

Falk, Nancy Auer, *Women and Religion in India: An Annotated Bibliography of Sources in English, 1975–92,* Kalamazoo, Michigan: New Issues Press, 1994

Harlan, Lindsey, and Paul B. Courtright (eds.), *From the Margins of Hindu Marriage: Essays on Gender, Religion, and Culture,* New York: Oxford University Press, 1995

Kinsley, David, *Hindu Goddesses: Visions of the Divine Feminine in the Hindu Religious Tradition,* Berkeley: University of California Press, 1986

Leslie, Julia, *Roles and Rituals for Hindu Women,* London: Pinter, and Rutherford, Pennsylvania: Fairleigh Dickinson University Press, 1991; Delhi: Motilal Barnasidass, 1992

Marglin, Frederique Apffel, *Wives of the God-King: The Rituals of the Devadasis of Puri,* New York and Delhi: Oxford University Press, 1985

Raheja, Gloria Goodwin, and Ann Grodzins Gold, *Listen to the Heron's Words: Reimagining Gender and Kinship in North India,* Berkeley: University of California Press, 1994

Roy, Anisha, *Bengali Women,* Chicago: University of Chicago Press, 1975

Sangari, Kumkum, and Vaid Sudesh, *Recasting Women: Essays in Indian Colonial History,* New Brunswick, New Jersey: Rutgers University Press, 1990

Sax, William S., *Mountain Goddess: Gender and Politics in a Himalayan Pilgrimage,* New York: Oxford University Press, 1991

Hinduism may be the world's most variegated, internally diverse religion; it certainly is one of the most difficult for outsiders to comprehend. Hinduism is also the only living major world religion with an active practice of goddess worship that is central to the religion. Socially, Hinduism is formally male-dominated, but, because men's and women's religious lives are quite distinctive and separate, Hinduism also demonstrates significant religious complementarity. Women have an extensive religious life practiced largely without male guidance or participation. In recent years, western scholars have begun to become aware of this dimension of Hinduism, which had been largely hidden to male researchers of earlier generations who had no interest in or ability to study women's religious lives.

Unfortunately, there is no reliable book-length survey of women's religious and social lives and roles within the Hindu context. However, a reliable and useful survey of Hindu goddesses can be found in KINSLEY's book. A chapter-by-chapter survey of the various goddesses, it is recommended as the single best volume on the topic and a good place to find other sources for additional research.

For the lives and roles of Hindu women, students at all levels of the study of Hinduism are indebted to FALK for her bibliography. Containing 1,015 entries, this bibliography is quite complete. It is especially useful because it includes numerous books published in English by Indian presses. One can hardly do scholarship on India without utilizing publications from the English-language Indian presses, but these books often go unnoticed in the United States; hence the usefulness of this bibliography.

Two anthologies serve as the best available substitutes for a survey of women in Hinduism. LESLIE's collection of articles is especially helpful in demonstrating the diversity of ritual roles for Hindu women. It includes both women's numerous domestic rituals and women's extra-domestic religious pursuits—much more rare in the Hindu context—as well as an illuminating section on the ritual of women's dance. SANGARI and SUDESH's volume presents a much needed corrective to the models of Hinduism and Hindu women perpetrated by colonial and androcentric scholarship about Hinduism. Several articles reconstruct a number of topics important to western understandings of Hinduism.

The richest and fastest-growing literature on women in Hinduism is found in the in-depth, fieldwork-based accounts of specific regions of India, authored by women who are either academically trained natives of India or western women with considerable experience of life in India. The oldest of this genre, written by a Bengali woman, is ROY's book. With its detailed account of everyday life and "religion on the ground," this book represented a fresh perspective in Hindu studies when it was first published. Ostensibly about Bengali women's social lives, the way in which society and religion are intertwined in Hindu culture means that much information about religion is also contained in this book.

MARGLIN's book about the women who serve as ritual dancers at one of Hinduism's most famous temples has significant implications for understanding gender in Hinduism. She finds that such women, and women in general, although classified as "impure" on the "pure-impure" scale, are nevertheless also classified as "auspicious"—an equally important term in Hindu religious values. This clarification is an important corrective to androcentric views of Hindu women based only on considerations of ritual purity and impurity, in which men are always more pure than women.

HARLAN and COURTRIGHT's edited volume continues the theme of looking beyond the more public androcentric and normative traditions of Hinduism to what stories and songs of the oral tradition and everyday life reveal about women's experiences of marriage. This book contains many refreshing perspectives beyond the idealized accounts of marriage so often encountered in western discussions of Hindu marriage. RAHEJA and GOLD's book is an important discussion of Indian women's dissent to dominant patriarchal cultural norms, as evidenced in the oral tradition of women's songs and narratives. These songs and narratives demonstrate that women have not completely internalized oppressive cultural norms and stereotypes but have methods of self-affirmation in their own women's culture.

Finally, two books begin discussions of the difficult and important topic of the relationships between goddesses and women in Hinduism. Many have noted the paradox of strong, important goddesses in a patriarchal religion, but as the books listed above have begun to demonstrate, there is more to the story of women in Hinduism than public, formal male dominance. Erndl's and Sax's books explore the relationship between a goddess and her devotees as expressed in rituals, songs, pilgrimage, and everyday life. SAX's book discusses a Hindu pilgrimage in which the goddess journeys to her deity-husband's home as projection and parallel of women's journeys between their natal and marital homes. ERNDL's book focuses on pilgrimages and rituals to the goddess of northwest India, as well as on how the goddess is understood in both textual and popular traditions. Her book is especially illuminating on how the goddess enters into the lives of women living in a male-dominated social setting and enriches those lives.

—RITA M. GROSS

See also Goddesses

History: American

DuBois, Ellen Carol, and Vicki L. Ruiz (eds.), *Unequal Sisters: A Multicultural Reader in U.S. Women's History*, New York and London: Routledge, 1990

Giddings, Paula, *Where and When I Enter: The Impact of Black Women on Race and Sex in America*, New York: Morrow, 1984

Kessler-Harris, Alice, *Women Have Always Worked: A Historical Overview*, Old Westbury, New York: Feminist Press, 1981

——, *Out to Work: A History of Wage-Earning Women in the United States*, Oxford and New York: Oxford University Press, 1982

Lerner, Gerda, *The Majority Finds Its Past: Placing Women in History*, New York and Oxford: Oxford University Press, 1979

Matthews, Glenna, *The Rise of Public Woman: Woman's Power and Woman's Place in the United States, 1630–1970*, Oxford and New York: Oxford University Press, 1992

Norton, Mary Beth, *Major Problems in American Women's History*, Lexington, Massachusetts: D.C. Heath, 1989

Ruether, Rosemary Radford, and Rosemary Skinner Keller (eds.), *Women and Religion in America*, 3 vols., New York: Harper and Row, 1981–86

Scott, Anne Firor, *Making the Invisible Woman Visible*, Urbana: University of Illinois Press, 1984

Strasser, Susan, *Never Done: A History of American Housework*, New York: Pantheon, 1982

Woloch, Nancy, *Women and the American Experience*, New York: McGraw-Hill, 1984

The literature of U.S. women's history is enormous. The books above have been selected as well-written introductions to the field that can provide a curious reader with a framework for thinking about the large scope of the topic.

For a general overview, WOLOCH's book is the place to begin. Woloch alternates chapters that describe one person or episode in detail—Sarah Josepha Hale and her contribution to the emerging cult of domesticity, for example—with narrative chapters that provide a broad introduction to women's history from colonial settlement until the 1990s. Woloch is thorough but never tedious, and her alternating structure allows her to provide both a sense of the variety of women's lives, and a feeling for what it would have been like to live in each of the time periods she discusses.

NORTON's volume is very helpful for anyone who wants either to teach U.S. women's history or to study it thoughtfully. Each chapter focuses on an area of controversy among historians, and contains a variety of primary sources, followed by two or three essays by notable historians presenting contrary interpretations of the era. The goal of the book is to enable readers to come to their own conclusions about each topic. The book requires active reading, and is well worth the effort.

The collections of essays by LERNER and by SCOTT, both of whom helped create the field of women's history, provide a different type of introduction to the field. Lerner's essays focus around issues of race, class, and the emergence of feminism, while Scott explores women's biography, voluntary associations, and women in the South. Their autobiographical essays shed light on the history of women's history itself.

GIDDINGS provides a comprehensive narrative of U.S. black women's history. The goal of this classic work is clearly compensatory: to acquaint modern readers with a lost history both of notable individuals and of a multitude of "ordinary" women who have shaped the history of their race in the face of enormous obstacles. While much additional work on black women's history has been done since this book was published, the framework presented by Giddings remains a valuable introduction to the varied history of black women in America.

Some of this new scholarship is contained in the anthology edited by DuBOIS and RUIZ, which also contains articles on Asian-American, Native American, Hispanic-American, and Euro-American women of all classes, and brings together much of the most interesting work done in the last 20 years. The articles are in the original forms in which they were published, and were generally written for an audience of historians, so the language can seem a bit formal to those not accustomed to reading academic journals. The authors do, however, avoid the obscurity of much academic prose, and are genuinely concerned with making their discoveries accessible to a general reader. Any reader interested in the diversity of U.S. women's history will find at least some of the essays in this volume fascinating.

Each of the remaining books listed focuses on some aspect of women's lives. MATTHEWS is concerned with the public dimensions of women's experience: both their political power and their access, literally, to public space. Beginning with the seventeenth century, and drawing on an extensive and high quality monographic literature, Matthews writes insightfully about the ironies as well as achievements of women's entry into public life.

The two books by KESSLER-HARRIS are closely related to each other: *Out to Work* is the more scholarly of the pair, while *Women Have Always Worked* is aimed at a more general audience. *Out to Work* traces the economic, cultural, and political factors affecting women's paid work from the colonial period to the postwar era, men's frequent opposition to the independence that women can gain through wage work, and women's efforts to shape the circumstances of their work. Only 150 pages, *Women Have Always Worked* includes five photo essays, and focuses on the changing meanings of work, both paid and unpaid, in women's lives.

STRASSER's goal is to produce a greater understanding and appreciation of women's generally unpaid household labor. Each chapter of her book is devoted to a necessary household function—getting water, providing heat for cooking, or clothing a family—and describes how the means of achieving these goals have changed as a result of changes in technology and social organization. To a large degree her narrative is one of progress away from unceasing drudgery, but she is not unaware of the occasional ironies of household technology: the rising standards that mean women often spend more time on housework after they acquire "labor-saving" tools, or the dehumanization that can result from the movement of the commercial market into previously non-commercial domains.

The three volumes edited by RUETHER and KELLER are also notable for their breadth of coverage. Each chapter is written by a specialist in a certain field, for example, women and religion in colonial Spanish America, and is followed by a carefully edited selection of primary sources. Together these essays explore the history of American women's religious experience in its racial, cultural, and regional diversity. The result is an enormously useful work that lacks a overall narrative thread, but provides an unmatched introduction to women's experiences in the broad range of America's religions.

—LORI KENSCHAFT

History: British

Bennett, Judith M., *Women in the Medieval English Countryside: Gender and Household in Brigstock before the Plague*, New York: Oxford University Press, 1987

Bland, Lucy, *Banishing the Beast: English Feminism and Sexual Morality, 1885–1914*, New York: New Press, and London: Penguin, 1995

Charles, Lindsey, and Lorna Duffin (eds.), *Women and Work in Pre-Industrial England*, London: Croom Helm, 1985

Clark, Anna, *The Struggles for Breeches: Gender and the Making of the British Working Class*, London: River Oram Press, and Berkeley: University of California Press, 1995

Fulford, Roger, *Votes for Women: The Story of a Struggle*, London: Faber, 1957

Malmgreen, Gail (ed.), *Religion in the Lives of English Women*, London: Croom Helm, 1986

McCrone, Kathleen E., *Playing the Game: Sport and the Physical Emancipation of English Women, 1870–1914*, Lexington: University of Kentucky Press, 1988

Peterson, M. Jeanne, *Family, Love, and Work in the Lives of Victorian Gentlewomen*, Bloomington: Indiana University Press, 1989

Prior, Mary (ed.), *Women in English Society, 1500–1800*, London and New York: Methuen, 1985

Stenton, Doris Mary, *The English Woman in History*, New York: Macmillan, and London: Allen and Unwin, 1957

Stone, Lawrence, *The Family, Sex, and Marriage in England, 1500–1800*, New York: Harper, and London: Weidenfeld and Nicolson, 1977

The subject of women and their role in British society was largely ignored by social scholars until FULFORD and STENTON's works were published in 1957. Since that time, beginning in the 1960s, a wealth of publications have emerged that focus on many aspects of the topic. Unfortunately, however, for those in search of a reliable general survey text on the history of women in England, no such work exists. The subject is still a relatively new field, and much still needs to be addressed. Most of the research done continues to focus on the women of the nineteenth century. While many more excellent works exist on a number of topics related to the field of study, the following are a good starting point.

STONE's pioneering book was one of the first adequately to explore the role of English women during the Renaissance. Well written and researched, the text is a must for those interested in the topic. Stone's conclusions have been challenged in recent years by feminist historians, but it is still considered by many to be an excellent text. It is a very useful work and available in many university libraries. The illustrative material is worthy of note.

Among the existing studies of English medieval women, the premier work is that by BENNETT. The author's extensive knowledge and careful research is evident throughout the text. Bennett's thesis is that the status and role of women in society was greatly influenced by the ever-changing world in which they lived. For example, according to Bennett, wives behaved and interacted in ways very different from widows. She also argues that the public activities of women were influenced by the economic circumstances of the day. The book adds a unique and valuable perspective to the study of the history of women in general.

PETERSON challenges the traditional view that upper-middle-class gentlewomen were passive members of society in Victorian England. She supports her thesis by making use of sources available from the Paget clan, an entrepreneurial family in the early nineteenth century. According to Peterson, the well-educated and resourceful Paget women were unencumbered by many of the societal gender constraints that limited other women of their age and thus made substantial contributions as partners in their husbands' business enterprises. Peterson has been criticized by some as "optimistic," but others argue that perhaps the Pagets were representative of the changing role of women in society.

McCRONE states that the social and political emancipation of women could not have been accomplished without physical emancipation through sport. The female athlete, a nontraditional role for women according to the author, broke the gender barrier and dispelled the idea that women were by nature weak and frail beings. McCrone describes the growth of intercollegiate sports in women's colleges, as well as competitive sports in girls' schools, and how that phenomenon influenced the women's movement. The text is well-written and very informative. This book is a must for those interested in the evolution of women's sports.

MALMGREEN brings together essays addressing the role of religion in the lives of English women. Most are specific to the nineteenth century and much is ignored. It should be noted, however, that very little research has focused on this field of study, and the included essays reflect the recent trends. This book is hardly an adequate statement on the subject for a specialist, but for the novice it is a substantial introduction.

CHARLES and DUFFIN's collection of essays are to be commended for their excellent use of primary sources. Much study of custom and common law was employed by the authors in their effort to explore the role of women in England's pre-industrial economy. For anyone interested in the history of pre-industrial England, this book deserves to be read and pondered. The essays are a useful contribution to the literature and a very interesting collection to read. The collection of essays by PRIOR explores the life of the average English woman during the time period. As a collection, the text adds much to the study of the role of women in English society, but more research is needed to test the assumptions presented.

CLARK's insightful work on the struggle of the British working class challenges traditional English labor historiography. Her thesis on the role of gender antagonism in undermining the potential of labor to achieve its goals is well documented. Clark blames the "sexual crisis" within the working-class family for the failures of the early British labor movement. She has been criticized by some for over-simplifying the issues, focusing too heavily on the role of women in her thesis.

The often contradictory and confusing rhetoric on sex by feminists at the turn of the century is addressed by BLAND in her excellent book. Focusing on the feminist campaigns that transformed late Victorian England, the author is to be commended for her analysis of the conflicting moral dilemmas faced by feminists trying to achieve their goals without compromising principles. The book is well-crafted and informative, synthesizing material taken from case histories to formulate the thesis. A welcome addition to the analysis of the evolution of feminist thought, it is hard to imagine a future work that would displace Bland's as the standard for the issues she addresses.

—DONALD C. SIMMONS, JR.

History: Medieval

Berman, Constance H., Charles W. Connell, and Judith Rice Rothschild (eds.), *The Worlds of Medieval Women: Creativity, Influence, Imagination*, Morgantown: West Virginia University Press, 1985

Bornstein, Diane, *The Lady in the Tower: Medieval Courtesy Literature for Women*, Hamden, Connecticut: Archon, 1983

Ennen, Edith, *The Medieval Woman*, translated by Edmund Jephcott, Oxford: Basil Blackwell, 1989

Erler, Mary, and Maryanne Kowaleski (eds.), *Women and Power in the Middle Ages*, Athens: University of Georgia Press, 1988

Hanawalt, Barbara A. (ed.), *Women and Work in Preindustrial Europe*, Bloomington: Indiana University Press, 1986

Harksen, Sibylle, *Women in the Middle Ages*, New York and London: Schram, 1975

Howell, Martha C., *Women, Production, and Patriarchy in Late Medieval Cities*, Chicago and London: University of Chicago Press, 1986

Jewell, Helen M., *Women in Medieval England*, Manchester and New York: Manchester University Press, 1996

Lucas, Angela M., *Women in the Middle Ages: Religion, Marriage and Letters*, Brighton: Harvester, 1983

Mirrer, Louise (ed.), *Upon My Husband's Death: Widows in the Literature and Histories of Medieval Europe*, Ann Arbor: University of Michigan Press, 1992

Power, Eileen, *Medieval Women*, Cambridge and New York: Cambridge University Press, 1975

Shahar, Shulamith, *The Fourth Estate: A History of Women in the Middle Ages*, translated by Chaya Galai, London and New York: Methuen, 1983

Although the history of medieval women had been a topic of interest among scholars since the early nineteenth century, and historical research until the 1950s occasionally dealt with the biographies of medieval women, modern research on the actual conditions of women's life in the Middle Ages did not develop before the late 1960s, when feminist activism began to influence academia. POWER's articles, posthumously edited and published as a book in 1973, represent, however, the best scholarship on this topic, as she pays close attention to the medieval sources, and gives full credit to those women whose voices can be heard in the literary and historical documents. Since the 1970s, we have witnessed a growing body of critical studies on the culture and economic conditions of medieval women.

SHAHAR explicitly objects to a medieval history written only from a male perspective, and argues for a balanced view of that time, taking the various social and professional groups of women into account. In her monograph she focuses on public and legal rights, on the lives of nuns, noble women, urban women, peasant women, and women on the margins of society, such as witches and heretics. The particular strength of her study rests on her deliberate effort to analyze the available historical documents, whereas her greatest weaknesses consist in the selective use of documents to confirm her argument, and the disregard for distinctive historical epochs and social class differences.

ENNEN, rather critical of Shahar because of her tendency to exclude the early Middle Ages, and because of her ignorance of constitutional aspects affecting the lives of women, studies medieval women in a chronological sequence, analyzing women's lives from the early Middle Ages through the late Middle Ages. In each chapter, she considers the considerable range of social stratification of medieval women and resorts to the always useful interpretation of specific historical sources pertaining to individuals and their lives.

Very often, historical research must first determine the type and quality of its sources, and this also applies to the subject of medieval women. BORNSTEIN primarily focuses on courtesy books, didactic treatises, and instruction manuals for and by women. With this material in hand, she fathoms the common images medieval society had of women, but she is limited by the prescriptive nature of these texts. Nevertheless, her book serves well as a complimentary study to those of a purely historical orientation.

In LUCAS's monograph, many different aspects pertaining to the life and culture of medieval women are combined to paint a lively and well-stratified picture. The kaleidoscopic approach is instructive, in conjunction with more detailed examinations of specific social classes, but it also loses some of its strength by discussing too many different types of documents produced by a wide variety of people. Lucas offers a little of everything, whether it be marriage in the early Middle Ages, or nunneries and female patronage in later centuries.

HARKSEN realizes that our understanding of medieval women cannot be solely based on historical and literary sources, but also requires the visual elements. In the first half of her book, she discusses the various aspects of women's lives during the Middle Ages, summarizing the current stage of research of women. She considers medieval law, life in the city, working women, religious women, political women, and female artists and musicians. Her examination of female writers, however, is basically limited to views developed by medieval male writers, and is primarily influenced by the writings of the French author Christine de Pizan. The outstanding quality of Harksen's work, however, consists of the rich body of medieval depictions of women in stone and ivory carvings, book illustrations, sculptures, embroidery, and other mediums.

HOWELL argues convincingly that medieval women enjoyed a considerably higher degree of economic independence than previously assumed. Through a careful analysis of available documents from the cities of Leyden and Cologne, she is able to demonstrate that women were fully entitled to enter many professions, and even to run businesses and workshops far into the late fifteenth century. With the increasing transformation of family based firms to money-based companies, together with the deep-cutting effects of the Protestant Reformation, women were quickly forced out of the public spheres and limited to private lives. Howell makes valuable observations, but she cannot fully apply her conclusions, drawn from the analysis of these city documents, to the economic situation of medieval women in other areas of late-medieval Europe. To compensate for this shortcoming, MIRRER has put together a valuable anthology of articles treating the economic, social, and cultural lives of medieval widows, who often achieved, after their husbands' deaths, the highest level of power and recognition possible for a medieval woman.

Considering the complexity of the material, often such efforts to synthesize the history of medieval women, covering a time period of about 1,000 years, quickly lead to dangerous generalizations and distortions, reflecting more the author's personal perceptions and ideals than the historical reality. In this respect, collections of individual articles tend to serve the reader better, as in the case of the anthology edited by BERMAN, CONNELL, and ROTHSCHILD. In the first section, the contributors examine creative contributions by women to medieval literature; in the second, they discuss the role women enjoyed in public; and in the third, they include articles dealing with literary projections of women.

A similarly productive collaboration is the anthology published by ERLER and KOWALESKI. The editors provided even more specific guidelines to their authors, using the aspect of women's public power as the primary focal point for all articles assembled here. The individual contributors outline a chronological development, from the early through the late Middle Ages. These are all case studies, and as such their arguments are well-knit and thoroughly researched on the basis of rich manuscript resources. The contributors to HANAWALT's collection also add important information about medieval peasant women, slaves and servants, wet nurses and midwives, business women in the cities, and, finally, the economic decline of women at the turn of the fifteenth century.

One of the latest attempts to summarize the present body of information about medieval women is presented by JEWELL. Although her interest primarily rests on medieval England, her conclusions, based on extensive readings of the relevant research literature, can easily be applied to other areas of European history. In her study she discusses women from the medieval countryside, women in medieval urban communities, women in the aristocracy, and religious women. Jewell examines poll tax records and other legal documents as a basis for far-reaching conclusions about women's social, economic, and political conditions during the medieval period. Jewell also emphasizes the powerful impact of modern feminism on medieval research.

—ALBRECHT CLASSEN

See also Literature: Medieval

History: Prehistory

Barber, Elizabeth Wayland, *Women's Work: The First 20,000 Years: Women, Cloth, and Society in Early Times*, New York: Norton, 1994

Dahlberg, Francis, *Woman the Gatherer*, New Haven, Connecticut: Yale University Press, 1981

Ehrenberg, Margaret, *Women in Prehistory*, Norman: University of Oklahoma Press, and London: British Museum, 1989

Gero, Joan M., and Margaret W. Conkey (eds.)., *Engendering Archaeology: Women and Prehistory*, Oxford and Cambridge, Massachusetts: Blackwell, 1991

Gimbutas, Marija, *The Civilization of the Goddess*, San Francisco: Harper San Francisco, 1991

Walde, Dale, and Noreen D. Willows (eds.),*The Archaeology of Gender*, Calgary: University of Calgary Archaeological Association, 1991

There is wide popular interest in the role of women in prehistory, as evidenced by the huge sales of Jean Auel's novels following the adventures of a Paleolithic heroine (beginning with *The Clan of the Cave Bear* 1980) and the frequent references in feminist magazines and discussion groups to Riane Eisler's non-fiction account of women's early religions, *The Chalice and the Blade: Our History, Our Future* (1987). This has not been accompanied by a parallel academic interest. Many archaeologists and historians exploring the earliest millenia of human history note that their fields have lagged behind other related social science fields, such as anthropology, in incorporating feminist theory, and in developing an explicit focus on women or gender. In part this is because the sources available—physical remnants such as bones, stones, marks on the landscape where there were once buildings and fields, pieces of pottery, a few drawings, and carvings—are so difficult to interpret. It is also the result of what had been until about 20 years ago the prevailing view of early human development, which focused on "man the hunter," and viewed hunting meat as the most important catalyst for human intellectual, physical, and social development.

DAHLBERG was one of the first to challenge this model explicitly, and her stress on the importance of gathered foods to the diet of early humans has now been confirmed by sophisticated methods, such as analysis of the wear patterns on stone tools (termed microwear analysis), chemical analysis of human bones which reveal the relative amounts of animal and plant foods eaten (termed stable isotopic analysis), analysis of the food remains in fossilized human feces, and analysis of cooked and uncooked food remains, primarily bones. Such analysis indicates that the majority of hunter-gatherers' diets comes from plants, and that much of the animal protein in their diet came from foods gathered or scavenged rather than hunted directly. In these activities women were most likely more active than men, although this "man the hunter/woman the gatherer" dichotomy has also been challenged, based primarily on evidence from contemporary hunter/gatherer societies.

Women have thus emerged in recent scholarship as more active players in the development of early human capabilities and skills, a good example of which is speculation that the first human tool may have been a sling of some sort for carrying children, rather than a hand-ax or weapon. Scholars are also exploring the role of women in the development of horticulture, the production of art, the organization of families and clan groups, and many other areas. GERO and CONKEY provide a collection of articles by anthropologists and archaeologists that discuss both physical and social issues in a sophisticated manner, including considerations of space (what did households look like? where were men and women likely to be in the course of a day?), food production in shellfishing, crop-raising and the processing of gathered foods such as acorns, women's role in tool and pottery production, and gender relations indicated by artistic evidence. The contributors discuss the ways in which sources reveal aspects of gender that anthropologists—often including themselves—had not seen earlier, providing examples of the impact of feminist theory in a field that has been reluctant to accept it.

WALDE and WILLOWS offer an extensive series of papers from a single conference, which address a range of issues, including the evolution of gender in primates, gender differentiation among hunter-gatherers, the role of women in the origins of agriculture, and gendered analyses of artistic and materials remains. The book includes brief papers by many of the major scholars in the field, and is a good introduction to theoretical and practical issues, and to the range of cultures and questions that are currently being explored. Several of the essays in Walde and Willows note that objects from the lives of men, such as stone hunting tools and animal bones, are more likely to remain, while those from the lives of women, such as plant remains and wooden tools, are more likely to have disappeared, thus biasing the record even before interpretations bias it further.

EHRENBERG's book is a relatively brief survey that could be used in an upper-division classroom, and covers women in prehistoric Europe from the earliest human settlements through the Celtic Iron Age. It is nicely illustrated, and includes extensive discussion of how various types of sources have led to scholarly disagreement, although the main thrust of the book is the relationship between the role of women and economic production. BARBER traces one particular type of economic production, that of textiles, from Paleolithic string-making through textiles of Bronze-Age Mesopotamia, Egypt, and Greece. The author is an established authority on prehistoric textiles and also a weaver herself, and she combs all types of ancient sources—pottery, grave goods, statuary, marriage contracts, literature—for what their depictions of or references to textiles reveal about women's lives. She notes the difficulties encountered in the study of textiles because of their perishability, a problem that, as Walde and Willows point out, applies to other objects as well.

One archaeologist in particular has been accused of biasing her interpretations, asserting a prominent role for women in some prehistoric cultures in which the record is more ambiguous. Over a 30-year career, GIMBUTAS has consistently argued that Europe was originally inhabited by peaceful, gynocentric, egalitarian, art-loving people—what she calls the "Civilization of Old Europe"—and that this society was destroyed by patriarchal, hierarchical, and war-loving Indo-Europeans invading from the east. This idea was taken up by Eisler in *The Chalice and the Blade*, and has gained wide popular acceptance, although many archaeologists and prehistorians regard Gimbutas's theory as idiosyncratic and idealistic. Gimbutas provides an extensive discussion of her findings and conclusions, discussing all aspects of European Neolithic culture. This is a large-format book, very well illustrated with photographs, drawings, maps, and reconstructions; these and the text can provide a vast amount of information even if one does not accept Gimbutas's conclusions.

—MERRY WIESNER-HANKS

History: Renaissance

Benson, Pamela Joseph, *The Invention of the Renaissance Woman: The Challenge of Female Independence in the Literature and Thought of Italy and England*, University Park: Pennsylvania State University Press, 1992

Brink, Jean R. (ed.), *Privileging Gender in Early Modern England*, Kirksville, Missouri: Sixteenth Century Journal Publishers, 1993

Davis, Natalie Zemon, and Arlette Farge (eds.), *A History of Women in the West*, vol. 3, *Renaissance and Enlightenment Paradoxes*, Cambridge, Massachusetts, and London: Belknap Press of Harvard University Press, 1993

Henderson, Katherine Usher, and Barbara F. McManus, *Half Humankind: Contexts and Texts of the Controversy about Women in England, 1540–1640*, Urbana: University of Illinois Press, 1985

Hull, Suzanne W., *Women According to Men: The World of Tudor-Stuart Women*, Walnut Creek, California, and London: AltaMira, 1996

Maclean, Ian, *The Renaissance Notion of Women: A Study in the Fortunes of Scholasticism and Medical Science in European Life*, Cambridge and New York: Cambridge University Press, 1980

Prior, Mary (ed.), *Women in English Society, 1500–1800*, London and New York: Methuen, 1985

Rose, Mary Beth (ed.), *Women in the Middle Ages and the Renaissance: Literary and Historical Perspectives*, Syracuse, New York: Syracuse University Press, 1986

Stone, Lawrence, *The Family, Sex, and Marriage in England, 1500–1800*, New York: Harper, and London: Weidenfeld and Nicolson, 1977

The history of Renaissance women is a relatively new field, which began to flower in the late 1970s and 1980s; these listings only scratch the surface of works written on the subject during that time. However, several have become standards. They range from broad historical overviews to considerations of specific women in specific circumstances. One of the first to become a standard is STONE's book. Although it is not based on feminist theory, it does deal with such subjects as patriarchy and the patriarchal nuclear family, and analyses of marriage and sexual behavior. Recently, Stone's conclusions have been challenged, but the work is still useful as an overview of attitudes about issues central to women of the English Renaissance.

MACLEAN's book, although presently out of print, is another extremely useful work. This volume considers the bases for Renaissance concepts of women in specific areas, including law, medicine, and religion. This work is a casebook of original source material. For example, Maclean brings together medical ideas about women from works by Hippocrates and Galen, as well as others, in the section on medical concepts; in the section considering women and the law, he lists laws which restrict women's ownership of property, their rights to their children—indeed their very identities. This very useful work is still available in many university libraries.

HENDERSON and McMANUS bring together works specific to the *querrelle des femmes*, the ongoing controversy about the nature of women. The first half of the book has a useful discussion of distinctive stereotypes about women, such as the seductress and the shrew. The second half contains selections from Renaissance works that were part of the *querrelle des femmes*, including Jane Anger's response to misogynistic attack. This book has become a standard for those interested in the *querrelle*, as well as for those looking for compilations of primary sources.

PRIOR's collection of essays focuses on specific groups of women during the time period, including nursing mothers, widows, urban women, wives of Tudor bishops, and women writers. The purpose of the collection is to begin to examine the histories of ordinary English women. While not broad enough to be considered a standard, the collection is very useful for those interested in the lives of women not usually considered in traditional works of history.

ROSE's book is another that considers the effects of patriarchy on the lives and work of Renaissance women. This collection of essays came out of the Newberry Library's conference on "Changing Perspectives on Women in the Renaissance." As the title of the book suggests, the essays in this collection fall under two headings. Topics covered in the historical group include such diverse issues as the difficulties of women who had public lives, the very real effects of men's concepts about women, and the queenship of Elizabeth I. The second grouping of essays discusses women in the world of literature. Topics include the recovery of lost female voices, revealed purpose in the work of the Countess of Pembroke, and women's feelings of alienation from the literary tradition.

BENSON examines what she considers to be profeminism in the literature of the time. She considers works by such authors as Boccaccio, Sir Thomas More, Sir Thomas Elyot, Juan Luis Vives, Baldesar Castiglione, Ludovico Ariosto, and Edmund Spenser. Her main focus is on Spenser's *Faerie Queene* and Ariosto's *Orlando Furioso*. These two influential works are not generally considered to contain controversial concepts of women. Benson, however, believes that they do alter received notions, although stopping short of suggesting political reform.

For this reason, she calls them "profeminist" works. Benson's book presents interesting and challenging ideas about the subversive effects of literature on concepts of women.

A work that covers a broad range of topics concerning women in the Renaissance is that edited by DAVIS and FARGE. In this volume, the editors reexamine the sources used to construct concepts about Renaissance women, and place them within the contexts of the discourse about women at the time. There are essays on many topics, including women and work, ideals of female beauty, education, women in politics, witches, criminals, and protesters. The last section deals with specific women. Several of the essays have been translated from French, and have certainly been influenced by French feminist theory. The series as a whole will unquestionably become a standard text, and this volume contains a great deal of useful and informative material.

BRINK is concerned with interpretations of the construction of gender based on texts by and about women. The topics covered are diverse, encompassing such issues as women as readers, women as translators of religious texts, concepts of sexual difference, Shakespeare and patriarchy, and the private (and public) boundaries of women's lives. Several of the contributors to this book of essays approach their topics through examination of specific women, such as the Fettyplace sisters, Anne Vaughn Lok, Mary Sidney Herbert, The Countess of Pembroke, Elizabeth Tanfield Cary, and Margaret Fell Fox. The essays are interesting and informative, but the collection as a whole is not unified along thematic lines, and may be more useful to those who wish to examine specific figures than to those who want broadly-based coverage.

HULL's work will be universally useful. This book examines original texts from the period about women and their activities. Hull notes that men wrote and printed the books that instructed women in every facet of their everyday lives. These books, which were reflections of patriarchal society, instructed women over and over again about women's inferiority and men's appropriate dominance. The introduction places the reader in the general context of Renaissance society; Hull then considers instructions for women in various domestic situations, addressing marriage, health, conception and childraising, food preparation, and fashion. Each chapter contains several lengthy quotations from primary sources, along with commentary, and includes several attractive illustrations taken from the author's extensive source material. This work will be very useful as the introduction Hull intends it to be, but it will also be sought for its extensive bibliography.

—KATHERINE ROBERTS

Hodgkin, Dorothy Mary Crowfoot

1910–1994

British Chemist

Abir-Am, Pnina G., and Dorinda Outram (eds.), *Uneasy Careers and Intimate Lives: Women in Science, 1789–1979,* New Brunswick, New Jersey: Rutgers University Press, 1987

Dodson, Guy, Jenny P. Glusker, and David Sayre (eds.), *Structural Studies on Molecules of Biological Interest: A Volume in Honour of Professor Dorothy Hodgkin,* Oxford: Clarendon Press, and New York: Oxford University Press, 1981

Kass-Simon, G., and Patricia Farnes (eds.), *Women of Science: Righting the Record,* Bloomington: Indiana University Press, 1990

Opfell, Olga S., *The Lady Laureates: Women Who Have Won the Nobel Prize,* Metuchen, New Jersey: Scarecrow Press, 1978

By analyzing the patterns generated by X-rays after they passed through crystals, Dorothy Crowfoot Hodgkin determined the detailed arrangements of atoms in such compounds of medical significance as penicillin, vitamin B_{12}, and insulin. For this work on the structures of important biochemical substances she was awarded the 1964 Nobel Prize in Chemistry. This placed her in a very select group, since among the previous hundred winners of the prize there had been only two other women: Marie Curie and her daughter Irène Joliot-Curie. Feminist critics have often commented on the small number of women in the ranks of the Nobel laureates in all fields, but especially in the physical sciences. Even male critics have noticed how sexism has characterized at least some of the choices of the Nobel Committee. With regard to Hodgkin's selection, for example, Max Perutz (who, with John Kendrew, won the Nobel Prize in 1962) states that he felt "embarrassed" when he was given the prize before Hodgkin, whose great discoveries had actually preceded his own work on hemoglobin. It is conceivable that, without the ardent lobbying of Perutz and others, Hodgkin might never have received her richly deserved award.

In her book OPFELL examines the lives and accomplishments of the small number of women who have won Nobel Prizes, including Hodgkin, Curie, and Joliot-Curie. In the course of her analysis she proposes answers to the question of why so few women have been honored with Nobel Prizes. Prejudice that women were incapable of such "male" virtues as intelligence, creativity, and objective thinking was one of the factors responsible for the second-class status of women in science. Opfell's book was written at a time when the women's movement was starting to achieve some understanding of the problems of the institutionalized exclusion and subordination of women in various intellectual fields, and her book contains some preliminary probing, both sociological and ethical, of the origin, nature, and possible solutions to these problems.

In her career Dorothy Crowfoot Hodgkin was one of the exceptional women who challenged these limitations on what she could accomplish. In the festschrift edited by DODSON, GLUSKER, and SAYRE and dedicated to Hodgkin by her colleagues on her 70th birthday, her former students and fellow crystallographers delineate how she played a pivotal role in the determination of structures of complex organic molecules, thus making this field an important part of modern science. Furthermore, these structures helped scientists understand the biological and medical functions of these molecules. As the authors of several papers in this collection point out, Hodgkin's achievements are now inextricably integrated into the history of X-ray crystallography. Through her students she has also become essential to the future of X-ray analysis, and many new studies on protein structure, some of which are described in this book, were started in her Oxford laboratory.

As the introduction and several articles in the historical section of Dodson, Glusker, and Sayre's book bring out, Hodgkin's family and her own determination to pursue a career in chemistry helped her to overcome the barriers then hampering women who were interested in devoting their lives to science. Her first X-ray studies of crystals were carried out in Oxford while she was an undergraduate at Somerville College. She was able to develop her interest in X-ray crystallography under the tutelage of J.D. Bernal at Cambridge University. Her work in his laboratory on the digestive enzyme pepsin and on cholesteryl iodide determined the direction that the rest of her scientific career would follow: the X-ray analysis of the structures of complex organic substances.

Hodgkin was appointed a research fellow of Somerville College, Oxford, in 1933, and the rest of her life centered on her teaching and research there. Some of the articles in Dodson, Glusker, and Sayre's book contain analyses of her principal achievements in X-ray crystallography. Although these articles are not written from a feminist perspective, some of them make clear that, as a woman, she was barred from full participation in academic life. According to one of her students, Oxford in the 1930s was "a masculine stronghold and the science faculties even more so." The number of women in various colleges were limited by statute, and they were segregated from the men (for example, female medical students had separate dissection rooms). Dorothy Crowfoot was ineligible for membership in the Alembic Club, the association that was supposed to unite all chemists in the university. Despite these obstacles, she was ultimately able to better her situation by means of very successful and influential work. For example, penicillin, an antibiotic widely used in World War II, was obviously an important substance, but chemists had conflicting evidence about its structure. By using new electronic computers and other techniques Hodgkin, working in secret, was able to determine penicillin's three-dimensional structure, which she made public in 1949.

Even before completing her work on penicillin, Hodgkin began her structural analysis of vitamin B_{12}, an enormously complex compound of over 180 atoms, which was crucial in the treatment of the blood disease pernicious anemia. By using advanced X-ray techniques and improved electronic computers, she worked out vitamin B_{12}'s three-dimensional structure, which included a hitherto undiscovered ring system. She then applied her new methods to insulin, a hormone containing nearly 800 atoms.

A different picture of the community of crystallogaphers is presented in Maureen M. Julian's major section of the KASS-SIMON and FARNES's book, whose purpose is to make the academic community aware that female scientists have achieved much more than is commonly recognized. Julian found that many male scientists had formed the opinion that crystallography had become, in the post-World War II period, a disciplne "overrun with women." She decided to gather data about the actual numbers of female crystallographers. Using standard reference works, she discovered that fewer than ten percent of crystallographers were women. These data left her with the question of why such a small percentage of women seemed so large to their male colleagues. One of her answers is that such outstanding crystallographers as Kathleen Lonsdale, Rosalind Franklin, and Dorothy Hodgkin had achieved so much that these accomplishments served to multiply the actual number of female crystallographers in the minds of certain men.

The feminist movement became much more influential and diverse in the 1980s than it had been earlier, and the articles in the ABIR-AM and OUTRAM collection reflect this increasing complexity. In finding ways to combine intensive work with their family lives, female scientists have adopted different lifestyles and attitudes. These new perspectives also inform how new feminists perform historical analyses. Abir-Am's own article in this collection, which centers on the career of the mathematical biologist Dorothy Wrinch, shows how different the views of Wrinch and Hodgkin were. In the late 1930s, Wrinch proposed a theory of protein structure called the "cyclol theory," which was criticized by Hodgkin, who found the ideas of Linus Pauling on protein structures much more compelling. Linus and Ava Helen Pauling were good friends of Thomas and Dorothy Hodgkin, and Pauling and Hodgkin not only shared scientific views but political ones as well (both Pauling and Hodgkin were denied passports in the 1950s because of their leftist political ideas and activities). Hodgkin's scientific views on protein structure led to a weakening of her friendship with Wrinch. Abir-Am uses this story to reveal that the interactions between science and gender have now become so complex that they resist reduction to facile theories. These case studies also show that pluralism in science can be exciting and instructive to investigate. Rather than discouraging scholars, this revelation of complexity should lead to more sophisticated and probing studies than in the past, and the results of such studies will help scholars to build a truer, more human, and more relevant history of science.

—ROBERT J. PARADOWSKI

Holocaust

Bridenthal, Renate, Atina Grossmann, and Marion Kaplan (eds.), *When Biology Became Destiny: Women in Weimar and Nazi Germany,* New York: Monthly Review Press, 1984

Delbo, Charlotte, *Auschwitz and After,* translated by Rosette C. Lamont, New Haven, Connecticut: Yale University Press, 1995; originally published as *Auschwitz et Après,* Paris: Editions de Minuit, 1970

Felstiner, Mary Lowenthal, *To Paint Her Life: Charlotte Salomon in the Nazi Era,* New York: HarperCollins, 1994

Heinemann, Marlene E., *Gender and Destiny: Women Writers and the Holocaust,* New York: Greenwood, 1986

Katz, Esther, and Joan Miriam Ringelheim (eds.), *Proceedings of the Conference on Women Surviving the Holocaust,* New York: Institute for Research in History, 1983

Koonz, Claudia, *Mothers in the Fatherland: Women, the Family and Nazi Politics,* New York: St. Martin's Press, and London: Jonathan Cape, 1987

Laska, Vera, *Women in the Resistance and in the Holocaust: The Voices of Eyewitnesses,* Westport, Connecticut: Greenwood, 1983

Linden, Robin Ruth, *Making Stories, Making Selves: Feminist Reflections on the Holocaust,* Columbus: Ohio State University Press, 1993

Nomberg-Przytyk, Sara, *Auschwitz: True Tales from a Grotesque Land,* Chapel Hill: University of North Carolina Press, 1985

Schwertfeger, Ruth, *Women of Theresienstadt: Voices from a Concentration Camp,* Oxford and New York: St. Martin's Press, 1988

Focusing on women in the Holocaust is a relatively new approach to understanding Nazi genocide and is still considered controversial by most historians and others in Holocaust studies. This new area of inquiry examines the experiences of women during the war (whether in ghettos, in hiding, in concentration camps, or in the resistance) as well as the lives and memories of female Holocaust survivors.

KATZ and RINGELHEIM actively seek to recover the lost or neglected stories of women during the Holocaust and to utilize feminist theory in order to better understand women's experience during the period of Nazi genocide. The editors hypothesize a theory that has become central (although by no means uncontested) in the study of women and the Holocaust: bonding. The theory of bonding suggests that women supported rather than competed with one another in the struggle to survive in the camps by forming surrogate families, while men competed aggressively for individual survival.

The few studies on women and the Holocaust to emerge since Katz and Ringelheim's follow one of two approaches. The first approach asserts the equality of men and women—as victims, as resistance fighters, as sufferers, and as survivors of Nazi atrocity. In this view, the events of the Holocaust undermine notions of sexism, because men and women alike were genocidal victims. Thus, LASKA focuses on women's activities in the resistance to refute the general misconception that such contributions were exclusively made by men. In addition to fighting alongside male resisters, women engaged in daring acts of sabotage and smuggling, relying on the traditional image of the passive woman to allay suspicion. Tracing individual stories of women resisting Nazi occupation in diverse countries, German women's resistance to Nazism, and Jewish women's resistance in ghettos and camps, the book encompasses a wide range of women's activities during the war.

Similarly, SCHWERTFEGER uses the vehicle of women's art to examine the experiences of women during the Holocaust. In Theresienstadt, a camp established for Jewish artists and musicians—most of whom were eventually murdered in Auschwitz—women's art and writing exemplifies what has been referred to as inner or spiritual resistance to the dehumanized force of Nazi atrocity. In almost every case, the art outlives the artist, leaving a trace of the individual's life and suffering.

The second approach seeks to distinguish women's lives and deaths from those of men and to bring into view uniquely female experiences. HEINEMANN sees women as having a special vulnerability by virtue of their gender, experiencing different conditions than men in the labor camps and death camps, which were segregated by gender. Central themes of her study include the humiliating initiation into concentration camps as a form of sexual assault (for example, nakedness in the presence of strange men, shaving of genital hair), pregnancy as a predicament endangering women, anxiety about menstruation or amenorrhea, prostitution and rape as forms of exploitation and domination, and bonding as a means of escape. One methodological problem of this approach is the undifferentiated use of memoirs and fiction by women as documentary evidence.

What made "decent" German women abet a regime of racism and atrocity? Beginning with an analysis of reactions to feminism in the pre-Nazi, Weimar republic, KOONZ offers a complex analysis of German women in the Third Reich. The contradictory Nazi image of the ideal Aryan woman was powerful, but only by virtue of her submission to the masculine domination of the Reich. Previously unexplored archival documents reveal that both ordinary and high-placed women evoked ideals of motherhood, purity, and femininity to facilitate the enactment of Nazi ideology. Topics in Koonz's study include the reproductive component of Nazi ideology, female resisters, Catholic, Protestant, and civic women's groups, and Jewish women. In exploring Nazi attitudes toward women as "'objects' of . . . social policy," Koonz's work opens up the dangerous possibility of equalizing women and Jews—the one group consisting of compatriots and the other of victims of genocide.

BRIDENTHAL examines the socioeconomic and political condition of women in Weimar and Nazi Germany. The collection of essays focuses first on the external struggles and internal dynamics of the women's movement in the Weimar era, then looks at the belief in biological determinism that supported both sexism and racism during the Third Reich. Topics include forced sterilization and control of women's reproductive capacities, the ideal of Aryan motherhood, and eugenics.

A larger body of work shedding light on women's experience during and after the Holocaust includes a plethora of memoirs by female survivors. In addition to presenting an author's individual experiences during the war, some memoirs offer a broader perspective, because the author played a particular role during the war, the writing encompasses others, or the author offers a special understanding of her life and times. Most notable among these, DELBO presents the memories and post-war reflections of a member of the French resistance who was captured and sent to several camps, including Auschwitz. Written in stunningly evocative language, the book wonders about the very ability of a survivor to transmit the essence of the extremities of human suffering to those who did not share them at the same time that it vividly describes the daily assault of Nazi atrocity, the different women in the camps, survival strategies, and post-traumatic stress. Similarly, NOMBERG-PRZYTYK details the daily enactment of atrocity for women in Auschwitz and the different responses to unimaginable cruelty. Central issues of her memoirs include hidden pregnancies, abortions, infanticide in a regime where pregnancy consigned a woman to death, and the heroic altruism of some women.

In a biography of "a Jewish artist with no place to go," FELSTINER places the life of Charlotte Salomon in the context of the Nazi era, which deemed her a nonhuman. Salomon's unusual art form, which combines graphics and language through transparent overlays, is made to testify both to the artist's own life and to the brutal conditions that curtailed first her academic possibilities and finally her right to life itself.

In LINDEN's sociological study of several female survivors, the author intersperses her own reflections on the human dimension of sociological research, her attitude toward the women she interviews, and her own position as an American Jewish ethnographer spared the extreme experiences she documents. Central to the study is the sense that the Holocaust disrupted conventional ways of constructing and representing knowledge, and thus calls for changes in conceptualization.

—SARA R. HOROWITZ

Home-Based Work

Beneria, Lourdes, and Martha Roldan, *The Crossroads of Class and Gender: Industrial Homework, Subcontracting, and Housing Dynamics in Mexico City,* Chicago: University of Chicago Press, 1987

Boris, Eileen, and Elisabeth Prugl (eds.), *Homework in Global Perspective,* London: Routledge, 1996

Buvinic, Mayra, and Margaruite Berger (eds.), *Women's Ventures: Assistance to the Informal Sector in Latin America,* West Hartford, Connecticut: Kumarian Press, 1989

Dixon-Mueller, Ruth, *Women's Work in Third World Agriculture,* Geneva: International Labour Organisation, 1985

Illo, Jeanne Frances, and Cynthia Veneracion, *Women and Men in Rainfed Farming Systems,* Quezon City: Institute of Philippine Culture, Ateneo de Manila University, 1988

Jahan, Rounaq, and Hanna Papanek (eds.), *Women and Development: Perspectives from South and Southeast Asia,* Dacca: Bangladesh Institute of Law and International Affairs, 1979

Leonard, Ann (ed.,), *Seeds 2: Supporting Women's Work around the World,* New York: Feminist Press, 1995

Romero, Mary, *Maid in the U.S.A.,* London and New York: Routledge, 1992

Staudt, Kathleen, *Globalization, Political Community, and Informal Economies at the United States-Mexican Border,* Philadelphia: Temple University Press, 1997

The study of home-based work has flourished in international women's studies. Much of it is based on women's work in agriculture, in the so-called "informal economy," and/or in neighborhood-based communities. Home-based work is not necessarily done in isolation from other people; however, home-based workers produce goods and provide services outside of formal workplaces, unregulated by the state for compliance with wage, hour, and benefit laws. Needless to say, the work is frequently unpaid, or meagerly paid.

Not only is home-based work unregulated, but it is also unevenly counted (if counted at all). Government census machineries frequently incorporate ideologies about what is genuine work, and the ways in which to solicit information about work. Historically, these ideologies have assumed that women's work at home is classifiable in the "housewife" category, that is not official work worth counting. Moreover, these ideologies frequently transfer work categories developed in so-called modern industrialized countries to the majority of the world's population located in the "south" (Africa, Asia, and Latin America).

The International Labour Organisation (ILO), the oldest United Nations affiliate, founded in 1919, has pioneered in research that examines all kinds of women's work and the value it reaps. In one of these pioneering studies, DIXON-MUELLER takes on the mismeasurement and misinterpretation of women's work in the agricultural labor force, thoroughly institutionalized in census and mainstream research. In many countries, homes are on small farm plots, where crops are grown and animals are reared for home consumption and for sale. She first documents women's extensive involvement in agriculture, then goes on to analyze the merits of "time-use" studies as a methodological approach, makes the case for investment in improving women's productivity, documents the under-representation of women's agricultural labor in national and international studies, and makes recommendations for policy.

ILLO and VENERACION put their study of women and men in the context of household survival strategies. (More and more, women's difference from and relation to men are the focus of gender studies, rather than studies of women separate from men.) They find flexibility in the division of labor and women's control of "surplus" earnings, after men have met their needs. National studies like these point to the need for contextualizing research in national and cultural terms. In many countries, women work separately from men in a rigid division of labor, their earnings appropriated by men.

JAHAN and PAPANEK edit a huge volume with 21 chapters on women's work in Asia, the most populous world region. Several chapters analyze the methodological complexities of this research. Ela Bhatt's chapter on the Self-Employed Women's Association (SEWA), an organization of home- and street-based workers who acquire credit, discusses the community bank model now made famous with the Grameen Bank of Bangladesh, which has been replicated in many world regions, including North America.

Women who do home- or street-based work can organize for collective action in politics, credit acquisition, and other self-determined goals. LEONARD'S second edition of *Seeds* contains seven cases of such organizations, plus afterwords on implications for policy and teaching. Women documented here worked out of homes in microenterprise, childcare, and tree-planting, collectively improving their income and strengthening their power. Added to the nine cases in the first edition, readers find 16 different readable analyses from most world regions.

Home-based work is frequently grim, isolated, and poorly paid, located in low-income communities under highly exploitative conditions. BENERIA and ROLDAN analyze in-depth interviews from a sizable sample of women who do piecework production in their homes, connected to a global chain of cheapened industrial production. With meager options, women jump at the chance for this work, for they acquire money and bargaining leverage in household relations. Based on empirical data, the authors draw conclusions about the proportional income contributions that give women leverage to tip the household authority balance in their favor.

From ROMERO, we get a picture of home-based work that women do in other homes besides their own. Maids are one of the most common occupational groups for women world-wide; working conditions are perfect examples of the unregulated, personalistic relationships in which women are engulfed. Romero's slim sample focuses on Latina maids in Denver, Colorado, doing work chosen by those with few options.

STAUDT focuses on the sizable amount of informal work on both sides of the U.S.-Mexico border, in Ciudad Juarez and El Paso, including totally a third of households in a sizable research sample. Women work informally, out of the homes (or in other people's homes as maids), acquiring earnings that are meager in U.S. terms, but two to three times the official minimum wage in Mexico. The border offers women the comparative advantage of crossing to maximize earnings and profits for their buying and reselling businesses. Informality is linked to a global economy that cheapens all labor, formal and informal.

What, then, should be done about home-based work that offers meager earnings on the whole? Two collections offer international studies and prescriptions for change: BUVINIC and BERGER support credit for microentrepreneurs, while BORIS and PRUGL favor increased government regulation in formalized occupations. Most other writers tie research findings to action, whether in policy change, program support, or collective organization to strengthen the self-employed or to promote political transformation.

—KATHLEEN STAUDT

Home Economics

Attar, Dena, *Wasting Girls' Time: The History and Politics of Home Economics*, London: Virago Press, 1990

Brown, Marjorie, *Philosophical Studies in Home Economics in the United States: Our Practical-Intellectual Heritage*, 2 vols., East Lansing: College of Human Ecology, Michigan State University, 1985

East, Marjorie, *Home Economics: Past, Present, and Future*, Boston: Allyn and Bacon, 1980
Peterat, Linda, and Mary Leah DeZwart, *An Education for Women: The Founding of Home Economics Education in Canadian Public Schools*, Charlottetown, Canada: Home Economics Publishing Collective, 1995
Thompson, Patricia, *Bringing Feminism Home: Home Economics and the Hestian Connection*, Charlottetown, Canada: Home Economics Publishing Collective, 1992

Home economics has an intertwined and long-standing relationship with women's studies. Since its emergence as a field of study in the late 1800s, home economics has been the most basic form of study for women and for the efforts to make women's work equal to men's work. At the same time, by including the word "home" in its description, home economics has assumed all the devaluation and disregard attributed to home issues by outside patriarchal forces.

The most comprehensive examination of the history of intellectual thought in home economics is contained in the two volumes by BROWN. She focuses her analysis on the history and evolution of thought in the United States, although the founding conferences that initially defined the field of study and profession drew representation from women of Britain and Canada. She argues that concepts of home economics in the mid- to late 1800s accepted the position of women in the home, and families as paternalistic structures. She contends that anti-feminist social thought was exploited to some extent in establishing home economics as a discipline of study in educational institutions. In the mid-twentieth century, she sees a convergence of views among feminists and home economists regarding women's roles and families. While Brown addresses feminism in relation to home economics, she regards the oppression of women in society as only one oppressive force among others, including scientism, anti-intellectualism, consumerism, and individualism, which have influenced and constrained the thought and practice of home economics this century.

In contrast to Brown, EAST claims that home economics is inescapably a female-identified discipline, and that this to a large extent influences many of its characteristics. East is concerned about women's differences and draws on sociological and psychological theories to query the differences inherent in a female-dominated discipline and profession. East's analysis moves through reviews of past home economists, a profile of present participants, and perennial concerns of the discipline and its nature, in projecting alternate futures.

ATTAR observes home economics as an outsider in the context of British schools and finds that it lacks relevance to women's lives and experiences. She asks how girls can secure access to educations in ways other than through home economics, and which are not geared to their subordination. In a brief historical analysis, she concedes that home economics came about originally because women could not find a place in the scientific community of the late 1800s. She questions whether home economics should continue to be taught, or if it is in fact detrimental to women's current educational efforts.

PETERAT and DeZWART trace the development of home economics in Canada through the writings of practitioners, proponents, and opponents. A wide collection of viewpoints show those in the field of home economics as a human, struggling community. Beginning with home economics as women's work and ending with gender equity in home economics curricula, the authors show the evolution from women's past roles as supportive and home-centered to a current call for a gender-sensitive and gender-balanced perspective that does not support patriarchy.

An attempt to integrate feminism and home economics is undertaken by THOMPSON. She uses the metaphors of Hestia, goddess of the hearth, to describe the private household/family/domestic domain, and Hermes, god of public spaces, bridges, commerce, and communication, to describe public government/state and civic domain. Hestia stands for material essentials of everyday life, embodied in home economics with its focus on the perennial problems of everyday life. According to Thompson, current discourse is organized on a male or Hermean basis, and an extra-patriarchal grounding is needed for feminist thought. Because women and men live in both the private Hestian domain and the public Hermean domain, they must learn to use their intelligence to function effectively in both. Rather than being anti-feminist and devalued, home economics has commonalties with many themes from feminist theory. Thompson seeks to broaden gender-based behaviours by adding the terms Hestian and Hermean to our vocabulary and accepting both men and women as victims of patriarchy.

LINDA PETERAT and MARY LEAH DeZWART

Homemaking and Housework

Beasley, Chris, *Sexual Economyths: Conceiving a Feminist Economics*, Sydney: Allen and Unwin, and New York: St. Martin's Press, 1994
Delphy, Christine, translated and edited by Diana Leonard, *Close to Home: A Materialist Analysis of Women's Oppression*, London: Hutchinson, and Amherst: University of Massachusetts Press, 1984
Fraad, Harriet, Stephen A. Resnick, and Richard D. Wolff, *Bringing It All Back Home: Class, Gender, and Power in the Modern Household*, London and Boulder, Colorado: Pluto Press, 1994
Hochschild, Arlie Russell, and Anne Machung, *The Second Shift: Working Parents and the Revolution at Home*, New York: Viking, 1989; London: Piatkus, 1990

Malos, Ellen (ed.), *The Politics of Housework,* London: Allison and Busby, 1980

Oakley, Ann, *The Sociology of Housework,* London: Martin Robertson, and New York: Pantheon, 1974

Waring, Marilyn, *Counting for Nothing: What Men Value and What Women Are Worth,* Wellington, New Zealand: Allen and Unwin, 1988; published as *If Women Counted: A New Feminist Economics,* San Francisco: Harper and Row, and London: Macmillan, 1988

A central goal of feminist research and activism has been to make visible and give value to women's unpaid domestic work. In doing so, a range of views about the reasons why it is women who are responsible for homemaking and housework have been put forward. Perhaps the most spirited debates took place during the early years of second wave feminism—the late 1960s and the 1970s. Many of the key papers from this period appear in the edited collection by MALOS. These papers argue that work in the home, including childrearing, fulfills capitalism's requirement for healthy and ready workers, and for future workers. There is, however, considerable disagreement about whether domestic work should be regarded as an integral part of the capitalist system, or as adjunct to it. According to the first position, housework produces workers as a commodity for capitalism, and housewives are, like the working class, directly exploited by capitalism. One political strategy based on this position was the Wages for Housework campaign, initiated in England in 1972, which several papers in the collection debate. The alternative position agrees that housework contributes to the functioning of capitalism through the production of workers but refutes that this work is part of the capitalist mode of production. Most of the papers in the collection date from this heady period; however, the inclusion of an extract from Charlotte Perkins Gilman's *The Home: Its Work and Influence* (1903) serves as a reminder that feminists have long been concerned with women's responsibility for homemaking and housework.

A different intervention in the debates of the 1960s and 1970s is provided by the French feminist DELPHY. Although identifying as a radical feminist, Delphy uses the tools of Marxism to explicate a domestic mode of production, which exists alongside an industrial mode. Just as workers in the industrial mode are subject to capitalist exploitation, Delphy argues, in the domestic mode of production women are subject to patriarchal exploitation. Women and men are positioned by Delphy as two antagonistic classes. The argument that patriarchy—and not capitalism—is the key determinant of women's domestic exploitation and oppression was criticised by socialist and Marxist feminists. Several of Delphy's responses to these critiques are included in her volume. Taken together, the books of Malos and Delphy provide an exposition of the debate that continues to set the terms of engagement for more recent work.

The anti-essentialist Marxist feminists FRAAD, RESNICK, and WOLFF attempt a rewriting of domestic work by opposing the essentialism of the earlier debates. They argue that factors like patriarchal power relations and capitalist class processes, as well as a host of other economic, cultural, political, and natural processes mutually determine domestic work arrangements, and that no one factor can be isolated as more important than any other. Class is also redefined in this book as a process of producing, appropriating, and distributing surplus labor, a definition that enables the authors to identify a range of domestic class processes. They argue that there is a transition in households in the United States from an exploitative feudal domestic class process to a non-exploitative communist domestic class process. The narrative of domestic transformation that the authors present is a powerful vision of social revolution. But the vision is not uncontested. Included in the book is an interchange between the authors and six other feminists, and an introduction by Gayatri Chakravorty Spivak that spells out the cross-cultural implications of the analysis, making this a lively and provocative work.

BEASLEY embarks on a different project of attempting to develop a specifically feminist economics. Central to this project is a re-evaluation of the earlier debates, as well as the household work studies of mainstream economics. Beasley argues that both feminist and mainstream efforts to deal with women's unpaid domestic work are infected by the assumptions of market-based economics, and that a feminist economics needs to consider the domestic economy on its own terms. This would involve, she proposes, working from a recognition of the emotion-laden nature of homemaking and housework. Beasley's book is an important contribution to the nascent field of feminist economics.

Women's experiences of homemaking and housework in different parts of the globe are addressed by WARING. She is particularly concerned with the absence of women's unpaid domestic work from the Systems of National Accounts—the system used by the United Nations for assessing aid programs and World Bank funding, and by individual nations and companies for developing their own economic policies. Waring advocates that women's unpaid domestic work—whether it be baking a cake for a child's birthday party in Canada or walking five hours to collect water for drinking, cooking, and washing in Zimbabwe—should be given a monetary value and included in the accounts of nations. This would have an immediate affect, argues Waring, on aid programs, funding priorities, and so on, and also a long-term affect on our understanding of terms such as dependency, welfare, and value.

Alongside theoretical debates about domestic work, feminists have also conducted empirical studies into homemaking and housework. One of the earliest was OAKLEY's study of 40 full-time housewives in London. Oakley outlines the range of activities involved in homemaking and housework, and the housewives' attitudes to their work and the role of housewife. Differences between working-class and middle-class housewives are considered. The book concludes with a discussion of strategies for making housewives aware of their oppression. Although expressed in slightly different terms today, the notion that women need to be liberated from homemaking and housework still underlies many studies.

In a more recent study of 50 families with both partners in paid employment in the United States, HOCHSCHILD documents women's "double day" of full-time paid work and housework. Hochschild finds that, despite awareness of the burden of domestic work, and, in some cases, commitment to an egalitarian marriage, the majority of men do not share domestic work. She argues that the industrial revolution brought about the most change in the lives of men, whereas the large-scale entry of women into paid work is a second industrial revolution that has dramatically changed the lives of women, with men being left behind. The upheaval that this recent revolution has wrought on domestic relationships and domestic work arrangements suggests that theoretical and empirical explorations by feminists into homemaking and housework will continue well into the future.

—JENNY CAMERON

Homophobia and Heterosexism

Berzon, Betty, *Setting Them Straight: You Can Do Something about Bigotry and Homophobia in Your Life*, New York: Penguin, 1996

Blumenfeld, Warren J. (ed.), *Homophobia: How We All Pay the Price*, Boston: Beacon Press, 1992

De Cecco, John P. (ed.), *Bashers, Baiters, and Bigots: Homophobia in American Society*, Binghamton, New York: Harrington Park Press, 1985

Jung, Patricia Beattie, and Ralph F. Smith, *Heterosexism: An Ethical Challenge*, Albany: State University of New York Press, 1993

Kirk, Marshall, and Hunter Madsen, *After the Ball: How America Will Conquer Its Fear and Hatred of Gays in the 90s*, New York: Doubleday, 1989

McNaron, Toni A.H., *Poisoned Ivy: Lesbian and Gay Academics Confronting Homophobia*, Philadelphia: Temple University Press, 1997

Nichols, Jack, *The Gay Agenda: Talking Back to the Fundamentalists*, Amherst, New York: Prometheus, 1996

Oikawa, Mona, Dionne Falconer, and Ann Decter (eds.), *Resist: Essays against a Homophobic Culture*, Toronto: Women's Press, 1994

Peterson, K. Jean (ed.), *Health Care for Lesbians and Gay Men: Confronting Homophobia and Heterosexism*, Binghamton, New York: Harrington Park Press, 1996

Sears, James T., and Walter L. Williams, *Overcoming Heterosexism and Homophobia: Stategies that Work*, New York: Columbia University Press, 1997

Heterosexism is defined as the belief that heterosexuality is the only type of intimate relationship that people do or should have. It is generally institutionalized by society in law, custom, and unwritten, unquestioned rules and assumptions about behavior. Some of the economic and social privileges of married people include being able to file joint tax returns, to visit each other in the hospital during "restricted" hours, and to inherit from each other with favorable tax consequences. Homophobia, a term coined by George Weinberg in 1972, refers generally to an individual's rejection, dislike, hatred, or fear of gay, lesbian, and/or bisexual persons. It may also refer to the feelings of self-hatred and contempt that a gay, lesbian, or bisexual person has about himself or herself as a result of internalizing negative societal attitudes.

OIKAWA, FALCONER, and DECTER's book contains a number of relatively brief, personal essays addressing different aspects of the contemporary experience of gay, lesbian, and bisexual persons. These include parenting, being a teacher, public displays of affection, passing as a straight person, and sexuality. They are easy to read and represent a wide variety of perspectives.

BLUMENFELD begins his collection of essays with an excellent outline of different aspects of homophobia and a summary of the ways in which all people are restricted and limited by homophobia. The subsequent essays address these issues in greater detail. The negative effects of homophobia that are discussed include how homophobia limits the knowledge and relationships of heterosexual persons with persons of minority sexual orientation (often incuding close family members), how it encourages persons being "squeezed into gender envelopes" for fear of being labeled gay, how homophobia inhibits the development of close intimate relationships with people of the same gender, how it can silence straight people who may be perceived as gay, and how it can foster premature sexual involvement as a way of "proving" one's heterosexuality. This book of essays has been well-received by a wide variety of readers; it is informative, easy to read, and at times very moving.

PETERSON's collection of eight articles (simultaneously published as an issue of the *Journal of Gay and Lesbian Social Sevices*) includes essays addressing the specific health needs of gay men, lesbians, gay and lesbian youth, and older lesbians and gay men, and how homophobia and heterosexism affect both the quality and the quantity of health care services that they receive. The issues of substance abuse among gay men and lesbians, as well as legal aspects of health care for this population, are also addressed. The essays are clearly written and well-referenced, although not extemely long or detailed.

SEARS and WILLIAMS have collected 33 well-referenced essays, which describe theoretical perspectives, empirical research, and personal and professional experience, with strategies designed to reduce homophobia and heterosexism. Techniques and approaches suitable for interventions with a wide variety of groups are described, including techniques for working with social workers, college students, teachers, coaches, and members of the clergy.

De CECCO, one of the leading authorities in the field, has edited a collection that was also published as a volume of the *Journal of Homosexuality* (Fall, 1984), and which includes two excellent, theoretical essays describing a social psychological perspective on homophobia and misconceptions of homophobia. The collection also includes six empirically-based chapters describing the relationship between homophobic attitudes and other attitudes, experiences, cognitions, and behaviors. The final chapter is a comprehensive bibliography of all publications by the federal government related to homosexuality (legislative actions, speeches, hearings, and reports) before 1983. It is noted that no mention of homosexuality was found in federal records prior to 1920, sporadic references were found until 1970, and there has been a sharp increase in discussion, both positive and negative, since 1975.

NICHOLS is one of the long-time pioneers in the gay rights movement, and his book is a coherent and cogent critique of the methods, ideas, and approaches taken by fundamentalist religious leaders to attack gay persons and the gay rights movement. He describes how such leaders have told both blatant and subtle lies about homosexuality and linked homosexuality to every perceived evil in American society, as part of a deliberate plan to increase dislike of and disrespect toward lesbians and gays. Integrating material from psychology, economics, sociology, and history, Nichols also outlines a pragmatic vision of the future.

In 1964 there were virtually no openly gay college professors. McNARON's book describes how higher education has changed since then, drawing upon the experiences of the author and 300 gay and lesbian academics who have had at least 15 years experience in academia. The author describes the changes that started taking place in the 1970s with the rise of ethnic studies and women's studies, and the first courses to focus on gay and lesbian issues. She describes the impact of being closeted on the wide range of activities in which professors engage, from ordering new books for the library to being available to advise gay and lesbian students. A wide range of contemporary issues relevant to the lives of both gay and straight members of the academic community are discussed.

JUNG and SMITH are two teachers at a Lutheran seminary, whose book examines scriptural passages and interpretations related to heterosexism in a thoughtful and scholarly way. They define heterosexism as a "reasoned system of bias regarding sexual orientation." By this they mean that heterosexism is a set of cognitions or beliefs concerning the superiority of heterosexuality to homosexuality or bisexuality, cognitions which may or may not co-occur with emotions of hate and fear toward homosexuals. They make a biblical case for eliminating heterosexism. Jung and Smith also describe the fears that maintain heterosexism, and the kinds of changes that they view as desirable and necessary to eliminate heterosexism in the church. In their view, a whole new sexual ethic is needed, one that includes heterosexism as a sin. This book is especially useful for persons wishing to understand and work toward change in the institutionalized relationship between the church and homosexuality.

The first six chapters of BERZON's easy-to-read book describe the causes and effects of anti-gay sentiment and why it must be addressed directly. The last eight chapters discuss different ways that people can confront bigoted remarks by friends, family, co-workers, strangers, and acquaintances as well as prejudicial content in the media.

KIRK and MADSEN analyze homophobic behavior from a political and societal perspective. Drawing upon a great deal of personal experience, they describe a large number of practical approaches, strategies, and tactics for changing laws and institutions with the goal of reducing homophobia and heterosexism. Their discussion should have great relevance for persons wishing to see social change and will, undoubtedly, have relevance well into the future.

—JANE CONNOR and ALISON THOMAS-COTTINGHAM

Horney, Karen 1885–1952

German Psychoanalyst

Kelman, Harold, *Helping People: Karen Horney's Psychoanalytic Approach*, New York: Science House, 1971

Lerner, Harriet Goldhor, *Women in Therapy*, Northvale, New Jersey, and London: Jason Aronson, 1988

Paris, Bernard J., *Karen Horney: A Psychoanalyst's Search for Self-Understanding*, New Haven, Connecticut: Yale University Press, 1994

Quinn, Susan, *A Mind of Her Own: The Life of Karen Horney*, New York: Summit, and London: Macmillan, 1987

Rubins, Jack L., *Karen Horney: Gentle Rebel of Psychoanalysis*, New York: Dial Press, 1978; London: Weidenfeld and Nicolson, 1979

Sayers, Janet, *Mothering Psychoanalysis: Helene Deutsch, Karen Horney, Anna Freud, and Melanie Klein*, London, Hamish Hamilton, 1991; as *Mothers of Psychoanalysis:*

Helene Deutsch, Karen Horney, Anna Freud, and Melanie Klein, New York: Norton, 1991

Westkott, Marcia, *The Feminist Legacy of Karen Horney,* New Haven, Connecticut and London: Yale University Press, 1986

Rejecting the orthodox Freudian notion of biological determinism, especially as it relates to women, Karen Horney developed an approach to psychoanalysis that stressed social and cultural factors, such as environment, social mores, and interpersonal relationships, as the basis for anxiety and alienation—and hence—neuroses—in the individual. Disqualified from the orthodox Freudian New York Psychoanalytic Institute in 1941, Horney, together with other associates, eventually developed what has come to be known as the neo-Freudian school of psychoanalysis.

KELMAN, an associate of Horney's, provides one of the first full-length studies of her in English and one of the most complete. His account of her early life and her struggle for recognition within her family, and even for permission to become a doctor, are particularly notable. He explicates Horney's psychoanalytic principles, delineating where she diverges from Freud and where, indeed, she agrees with him, a point often missed by many of her Freudian critics. The portrait of Horney that emerges from this study is that of a complex woman with a remarkable capacity for common-sense thinking.

RUBINS's book builds on Kelman's study. Using many of the same primary sources as Kelman, as well as Horney's published works, Rubins presents a sympathetic portrait of a woman destined to rebellion, because of her relationship not only with an oppressive father, but with other patriarchal figures, such as her husband, Oskar, and her psychoanalysts, Karl Abraham and Hans Sachs, both members of Freud's inner circle. The use of the word "gentle" in the title is misleading, for what emerges from Rubin's portrayal of Horney is an independent-minded woman, secure in her intellect, although not without contradictions and insecurities in other areas of her life. Rubins does not discuss what some have called Horney's rather tyrannical nature at her American Institute of Psychoanalysis. Perhaps this omission is the result of trying to show his subject as "gentle."

SAYERS uses the mothering metaphor to show how all four women mentioned in the title not only nurtured psychoanalysis in its infancy, but went on to make their own distinctive contributions to its development. Sayers views Horney as the first true feminist psychoanalyst and underscores the particular difficulties she faced as a woman not only in her repressive home, but in medical school and in the early psychoanalytic community as well. In discussing the major features of Horney's theories, Sayers seems indirect, perhaps even diffident, as she discusses the differences Horney had with Sigmund Freud and other members of his group. However, Sayers's comparison and contrast of the theories of these four women are helpful in understanding the history of psychoanalysis and the rich legacy women have offered to it.

LERNER presents a general overview of Horney's theories and how they differ from orthodox Freudian thinking, then proceeds to discuss women's issues and themes in psychoanalysis and psychotherapy based on Horney's theories: for example, work inhibition. Here Lerner suggests that many women basically fear success because they feel they will be punished for their accomplishments. As a result, these women are not willing to succeed because success may, first, jeopardize important interpersonal relationships, and, second, promote fears that they are unfeminine, success being a masculine quality. Thus, many women feel it necessary to apologize for their success and often sabotage it. The neuroses to emerge from this type of thinking, like so many others related to women, are not the result of women's biological destiny, as Freud insisted, but are, according to Horney, the effects of societal conditioning and expectations.

PARIS, a professor of English and founder of the International Karen Horney Society, attempts to show in his study the manner in which Horney's theories and insights evolved from her own personal inner struggles throughout her life. For example, the psychological abuse she suffered from her dour sea-captain father, among other pressures, gave rise to Horney's idea of denigration as a factor in causing anxiety, one of the fundamental bases of mental illness. Notable for its discussion of Horney's later mature theories, this study draws on new primary sources, especially Horney's letters to her daughters; as such, it expands on other earlier biographies.

QUINN's study is a highly readable and candid biography of Horney, offering an abundance of colorful details about her difficult relationship with her fundamentalist father, her unhappy marriage and divorce, and her near suicide in 1923 while on a family vacation. It is especially helpful in its discussion of how Horney broke into the male-dominated, Freudian circle of Berlin, and the dislocation she experienced when she immigrated to the United States to become Associate Director of the Chicago Psychoanalytic Institute in 1932. Quinn offers a highly nuanced account of Horney's move from Chicago to New York in 1934, when she became a training analyst at the New York Psychoanalytic Institute. It was there that the clash began between her revisionist views and the orthodox thinking of her colleagues, which led to her eventual disqualification from that organization. Quinn effectively conveys the enormity of the price Horney paid—professionally and personally—for having had "a mind of her own."

WESTKOTT wishes to present "a social psychological theory that . . . explain[s] women's personality development as a consequence of growing up in a social setting in which they are devalued." To do so, the author turns first to Horney's early theories on the psychology of women, and then, showing the limitations of these early hypotheses, addresses the larger, more complete theory of personality that has emerged, not only in Horney's later writings, but in the work of her followers as well. Westkott is understandably harsh in her analysis of Freud's pronouncements about women and savors Horney's concept of the fully evolved "female hero." This is one of the best-integrated and most up-to-date feminist studies of Horney and post-Horney psychology available.

—CARLO COPPOLA

See also Psychological Theories about Women: Pre-Feminist

Howe, Julia Ward 1819–1910

American Writer and Activist

Clifford, Deborah Pickman, *Mine Eyes Have Seen the Glory: A Biography of Julia Ward Howe,* Boston: Little Brown, 1979

Elliot, Maude Howe, *The Eleventh Hour in the Life of Julia Ward Howe,* Boston: Little Brown, 1911

Grant, Mary H., *Private Woman, Public Person: An Account of the Life of Julia Ward Howe from 1819–1868,* Brooklyn, New York: Carlson, 1994

Hall, Florence Howe, *The Story of the Battle Hymn of the Republic,* New York and London: Harper and Brothers, 1916

Richards, Laura Elizabeth Howe, *Two Noble Lives: Samuel Gridley Howe, and Julia Ward Howe,* Boston: Dana Estes, 1911

Richards, Laura Elizabeth Howe, and Maude Howe Elliot, *Julia Ward Howe, 1819–1910,* Boston: Houghton Mifflin, 1915

Tharp, Louise Hall, *Three Saints and a Sinner: Julia Ward Howe, Louisa, Annie, and Sam Ward,* Boston: Little Brown, 1956

Best known for penning the Civil War anthem, "The Battle Hymn of the Republic," Julia Ward Howe dedicated her life to social reform—most notably abolition and women's rights—as a writer, poet, and public speaker. Her literary production was considerable: she edited the anti-slavery newspaper *Boston Commonwealth* with her husband Samuel Gridley Howe, and she wrote a number of books, including social tracts (*Sex and Education, Modern Society*), biography (*Margaret Fuller*) and collections of poetry.

Early accounts of Howe's life were written primarily by her daughters, Laura E. Richards, Maude Howe Elliot, and Florence Howe Hall (a fitting tribute for the woman who also invented Mother's Day). These versions draw heavily on both the writers' personal experience with their mother and Howe's own *Reminiscences.* Furthermore, written shortly after Howe's death, they are characterized by tones of unqualified admiration. HALL's brief volume, for example, examines Howe's most enduring legacy "The Battle Hymn of the Republic," in order to convey the "fervor and ferment" and "the exaltation of the spirit" that characterized the Howe household. Focusing on the factors that led to the Civil War, and how these events affected their family, Hall describes the context for the creation of the "Battle Hymn." She addresses the significance of the verse in Howe's life, bestowing upon her both honor and fame, and its inspirational influence in American culture.

RICHARDS's (1911) short, first-person narrative of the lives of her parents is anecdotal and aims primarily to engage the admiration of children. Her treatment centers on Julia and the death of Samuel. ELLIOT's admittedly "slight and hasty account" looks at Howe's years after 1906. It too is anecdotal and highly personal, celebrating the ways in which Howe maintained an energetic focus on living even in her waning years.

RICHARDS and ELLIOT's lengthy and detailed biography gives the most complete early account of Howe's life. In this conventionally chronological account, Richards and Elliot offer what they suggest is an objective "record" of Howe's life and public career. Indeed, within a framework of family history, they dutifully outline all of the major personal and public events in her life, emphasizing her connections with members of the intellectual and political elite in working toward political reform. Their work concludes with a chapter entitled "The Battle Hymn of the Republic," whose influence they posit as a metaphor for legacy.

Little scholarly attention was paid to Howe mid-century. The exception is THARP's group biography in which she treats Howe's life alongside that of her siblings, Samuel Ward, Jr., Louisa Ward Crawford Terry, and Annie Ward Mailliard. Concentrating on her early years, Tharp considers the ways in which Howe's upbringing and relationship with her brother and sisters influenced her own career. Although Howe is the centerpiece of this account, in-depth examination is sacrificed to broad observations of the family's involvement in social movements of the day.

Two recent treatments of Howe look at the relationship between her family life and her public career. CLIFFORD updates Howe's biography through a somewhat more scholarly account, which emphasizes Howe's role within the social and literary milieu of mid-nineteenth-century New England. She also devotes significant attention to the tensions between Howe's marriage and her involvement in social organizations.

As its title indicates, GRANT's biography focuses even more pointedly on Howe's negotiation between her private experiences and her public voice. In the most scholarly work of the group, Grant draws on contemporary feminist research to analyze Howe's 1868 "conversion" to public advocacy of woman suffrage, which marked the beginning of her influential public career as leader and speaker on behalf of social reform. Examining her life previous to this point, Grant argues that Howe's earlier, more private experience—her marriage to a domineering husband, in particular—actually prepared her well for a later career as a public figure. By concentrating on Howe's personal and intellectual development rather than simply her relationship with her family and the social reform community, this account endows Howe with a greater sense of individuality and agency than most previous works.

—CAROL E. DICKSON

Hunting/Gathering Cultures

Brock, Peggy, *Women, Rites, and Sites: Aboriginal Women's Cultural Knowledge*, Sydney and Boston: Allen and Unwin, 1989

Burbank, Victoria K., *Fighting Women: Anger and Aggression in Aboriginal Australia*, Berkeley: University of California Press, 1994

Burch, Ernest S., Jr., and Linda J. Ellanna (eds.), *Key Issues in Hunter-Gatherer Research*, Oxford and Providence, Rhode Island: Berg, 1994

Goodale, Jane C., *Tiwi Wives: A Study of the Women of Melville Island, North Australia*, Seattle: University of Washington Press, 1971

Hamilton, Annette, *Nature and Nurture: Aboriginal Child-Rearing in North-Central Arnhem Land*, Canberra: Australian Institute of Aboriginal Studies, and Atlantic Highlands, New Jersey: Humanities Press, 1981

Shostak, Marjorie, *Nisa: The Life and Words of a !Kung Woman*, Cambridge, Massachusetts: Harvard University Press, 1981; London: Allen Lane, 1982

Despite a broad range of works available on hunter-gatherer cultures, relatively few studies focus specifically upon women. Beginning in the 1970s, however, some works have appeared, as female and feminist anthropologists returned to the field to "re-write" the genre and make women, their life experiences, their contributions, and their rituals, visible. In a collection of essays that examine the diversity of Aboriginal peoples, the range and variety of female cultural authority and the role of women, and the extensive music and song that emanate from a cultural life that is maintained separately to men's ceremonial life, BROCK groups a variety of contributions that deconstruct perceptions of Aboriginal male dominance imposed by white social percepts, as well as the common assumptions that Aboriginal women's roles carry as little power and authority as in western society.

BURBANK's emic analysis of Aboriginal women and aggression is a fine review of gendered sociality in a mission town populated by Aboriginal residents who had once lived in the surrounding countryside as gatherer-hunters. Its structural analysis provides a rich appreciation of Aboriginal social orginisation, in which women are presented as aggressors and only secondarily as victims. Arguing that women's overt aggression can be a positive, enhancing act, Burbank asserts that aggressive acts can provide an angle into the prisms of Aboriginal femininity as lived experience. Aboriginal women's interest in aggressive behaviour, its centre for conversations, the use of "fight stories," and the importance of fighting in a woman's self-image substantiate an exploration of western theories, metaphors, and stereotypes of female aggression and victimisation and frame broader understandings of gender relations.

BURCH and ELLANNA's compilation of papers clarify the importance of women's gathering tasks as the major contribution to gatherer-hunter food supplies, continuing to challenge the perception that hunting and maleness are important factors in explaining human evolution, and demonstrating the variety and nature of women's involvement in the food quest. Through a series of fascinating encounters, readers fall under the spell of a remarkable gallery of women and men. What emerges is a close-up portrait of women's knowledge, as well as their contributions to, and their moral dilemmas in, promoting discourses of sacredness in the face of unbalanced culture contacts.

GOODALE's seminal work observing a northern Australian Aboriginal group concentrates on the cultural role of women. From observations of the *kulama*—the initiation ceremony for Tiwi males—Goodale asserts that women played special roles, were not prevented from seeing what was going on, and were initiated at the same ceremony. In addition, Tiwi women played an important role in the funeral ceremonies of the community and, Goodale proposes, a dominant economic role. Using the life cycle of women as a frame for discussing both Melville Island culture and women's rites of passage, she details and clarifies Tiwi social organisation in a powerful descriptive analysis that presents Tiwi culture as a consistently fluid, flexible, and structurally changeable entity.

A classic investigation of the life practices of the Gidjingali peoples, many of whom have achieved a longing to return in small groups to their traditional territories and look after the land and its sacred sites, HAMILTON's work focuses upon the women and children of the community. Despite European contact altering the ecosystem, Hamilton argues that people's social relationships remain, and ritual life, far from disappearing, has intensified. From her observations she proposes that women contribute more "bush foods" to the community's diet than men. Proceeding to an analysis of interpersonal relationships in the raising of children through an examination of perceptions of Aboriginal people's "indulgence" of children, charting unselfish behaviour, the foolishness of violence, and the induction of meaning of life through sexed segregation and ritual, which models child behaviour, she provides a rich representation of the specificities of life in this gatherer-hunter community.

Through a subjective perspective on field research with the !Kung people, SHOSTAK describes the ways in which she learned about women's lives, their views about being women, and the events they considered important in their lives. As Nisa, a gifted storyteller, impressed the author favourably with her ability to describe her experience through careful articulation, she flavours the work with a vivid emotional content that deepens understandings of her people.

—HELEN JOHNSON

See also Aboriginal Women; Matrifocal Cultures

Hurston, Zora Neale 1901–1960

American Writer

Glassman, Steve, and Kathryn Lee Seidel (eds.), *Zora in Florida*, Orlando: University of Central Florida Press, 1991

Hill, Lynda Marion, *Social Rituals and the Verbal Art of Zora Neale Hurston*, Washington, D.C.: Howard University Press, 1996

Hollowly, Karla F.C., *The Character of the World: The Texts of Zora Neale Hurston*, New York: Greenwood, 1987

Howard, Lillie P., *Zora Neale Hurston*, Boston: Twayne, 1980

Nathiri, N.Y., *Zora!: Zora Neale Hurston, a Woman and Her Community*, Orlando, Florida: Sentinel Books, 1991

Plant, Deborah G., *Every Tub Must Sit on Its Own Bottom: The Philosophy and Politics of Zora Neale Hurston*, Urbana: University of Illinois Press, 1995

Zora Neale Hurston, one of the first African-American writers to honor the richness of black vernacular, to record black folk tales and oral cultural traditions, and to incorporate both into novels, plays, and nonfiction, for too long has been ignored and overlooked. Recently her talents have been given the recognition they deserve. Different types of approaches are taken by scholars of Hurston. The most common approach argues for Hurston's place in the literary tradition as a great American writer. HOWARD offers this type of traditional approach, presenting her book as a critical analysis of Hurston's life and work. Beginning with a discussion of Hurston's life, Howard illustrates the experiences that led her to become a writer. She focuses most heavily on Hurston's fiction, dedicating four chapters to her longest pieces: *Jonah's Gourd Vine, Their Eyes Were Watching God, Moses Man of the Mountain,* and *Serpah on the Suwanee.* Howard also spends one chapter discussing Hurston's nonfiction. This book is a good overview of Hurston's major pieces of fiction and her life. Howard's analysis demonstrates Hurston's important place in American literary history.

HOLLOWLY also mixes biographical details and literary analysis to explore the importance of Hurston's life and works, but she moves her study of Hurston beyond simple textual analysis. Combining sociolinguistics, feminism, and Afrocentric perspective, Hollowly discusses Hurston's innovative use of the narrative voice in her texts. While illuminating her literary talents, Hollowly argues that Hurston's literary genius, and her struggle as a black woman to be heard in the male-dominated black community and the white, male-dominated anthropological community, still need to be fully appreciated. She argues that Hurston's ethnographic research, particular into Hoodoo communities, was an origin of her unique and powerful use of language. Focusing on the use of black dialect and folk culture in Hurston's work, Hollowly concludes that Hurston is an important author in the continuation of the legacy of African-American oral tradition.

While Howard and Hollowly discuss Hurston's work as a writer and anthropologist, HILL discusses her playwrighting, directing, dancing, and singing. She argues that when Hurston began putting her energy into writing instead of theater it was not because her theatrical drive was exhausted. Instead, her energy was diverted into writing. Moreover, Hurston's "printed page becomes the stage upon which dramatized folk tales, games, sermons, jokes, hexes, songs, and even dances are enacted." Hill discusses how Hurston, despite her anthropological training, was able to unlearn academic language and create a performative language in her fiction and nonfiction. Hill also demonstrates how Hurston's ethnography and theories of theater are invaluable to classes on black theater. This book presents a unique view of Hurston, one of her drive for theater and her use of dramatic literary technique.

Feminists and African-American scholars have not only given Hurston's novels, folk-writing, and plays the recognition they deserve, but they have also discredited the myth that Hurston's work was devoid of political content. Hurston had been criticized by her contemporaries because she wrote about African-American culture and self-discovery, when most writers and scholars believed black authors should concentrate on themes of black struggle with the white majority. Therefore, they considered her a nonpolitical writer. PLANT reveals how Hurston believed cultural survival and affirmation to be the necessary tools for African-American liberation. According to Plant, Hurston understood that the strategies for resistance rest within African-American culture. These strategies of the folk—storytelling, humor, signification—all can be found in Hurston's work. Plant argues that Hurston is a model of resistance for black women and an example of black women's intellectual accomplishments. She examines Hurston's struggle to survive and resist the constraints placed on her as a black woman, to succeed on her own terms, and to gain self-empowerment. She argues that the intellectual perspective with which Hurston intertwined her academic training, and her experiences of life in Eatonville, form the basis for her individualist philosophy and are indispensable aspects of her resistance and survival strategies. Plant presents Hurston, a model of empowerment, as an inspirational black woman with a strong political philosophy.

Another book that diverges from the traditional examination of Hurston's life and work in order to examine her less-known works and her politics is the compilation of essays edited by GLASSMAN and SEIDEL. The core of this collection focuses on the influence of central Florida in Hurston's life and writings. This collection also serves to demystify Hurston and make evident the political content of her work. Included are two essays on Hurston's first novel *Jonah's Gourd Vine,* which is set almost entirely in Florida. Other Florida-based works such as *Mules and Men,* and her autobiography *Dust Tracks on a Road,* are also subjects of essays, as are the Floridian elements in all her works. Yet other chapters in the collection discuss the environment and the conditions Hurston confronted in Florida and her home town of Eatonville. Each chapter in the collection gives attention to aspects of Hurston's life and work that have been minimally discussed or completely neglected.

In contrast to all of the above mentioned authors, NATHIRI strays from the traditional academic path by compiling a warm, touching, and enlightening commemoration honoring Hurston. Nathiri's family has lived for four generations in Eatonville, and she weaves into the compilation her family's story of discovering the works of Hurston. Nathiri also includes color photographs and an extensive interview with Hurston's friends and relatives, which broaden Hurston's image. Also included are Alice Walker's, "Anything We Love Can Be Saved: The Resurrection of Zora Neale Hurston," and an essay by John Hicks, a former writer for the *Orlando Sentinel.* Helpful for those new to Hurston's writings are the annotations of Hurston's seven books, a brief essay on the use of dialect, and the essay by Eleanor Manson Ramsey and Everette L. Fly on the development and importance of "race colonies" or black American townships such as Eatonville. This collection is the much needed celebration of the life of Zora Neale Hurston, one of America's most important folklorist-writers.

—JULIE JOHNSTON

Hutchinson, Anne 1591–1643

American Religious Dissident

Battis, Emery, *Saints and Sectaries: Anne Hutchinson and the Antinomian Controversy in the Massachusetts Bay Colony,* Chapel Hill: University of North Carolina Press, 1962

Bolton, Reginald Pelham, *A Woman Misunderstood: Anne, Wife of William Hutchinson,* New York: Schoen Printing Company, 1931

Huber, Elaine C., *Women and the Authority of Inspiration: A Reexamination of Two Prophetic Movements from a Contemporary Feminist Perspective,* Lanham, Maryland: University Press of America, 1985

Lang, Amy Schrager, *Prophetic Women: Anne Hutchinson and the Problem of Dissent in the Literature of New England,* Berkeley: University of California Press, 1987

Rugg, Winnifred King, *Unafraid: A Life of Anne Hutchinson,* Boston: Houghton Mifflin, 1930

Williams, Selma R., *Divine Rebel: The Life of Anne Marbury Hutchinson,* New York: Holt, Rinhart and Winston, 1981

As her biographies attest, Anne Hutchinson was not only a wife, mother, midwife, and religious rebel, but a feminist before her time. Most historians agree in this regard. Although existing biographies chronicle her life in England and in the Massachusetts Bay Colony, her rise as a social leader, her exile to Rhode Island, and her unfortunate death, each work varies in focus. BOLTON's work is the most basic in terms of discussion or analysis. His account of Hutchinson's life is one of the very first to be written, and its purpose is simply to expand upon what historians knew and understood about this woman. Bolton documents numerous instances in which Hutchinson's actions were misinterpreted. He attempts to show that the reader of history can only understand Hutchinson's life in the context of her religious beliefs and background.

RUGG shapes her work on Hutchinson in such a way as to highlight her role as a social leader. Rugg, like other biographers, explores how Hutchinson had been a student of Reverend John Cotton's while still in England and felt compelled to follow him to New England once he fled there for fear of imprisonment. Rugg describes how once in New England, Hutchinson stood out against the background of Puritanism, believing that there was opposition between an individual's obedience to the law and the Holy Spirit. This author spends most of her time informing the reader about Hutchinson's position as the female leader of the powerful Antinomian faction in the Massachusetts Bay Colony. Rugg emphasizes that Hutchinson was never afraid of others, and this set her apart from other early leaders (in particular, female leaders). Others, being afraid of her and her beliefs, persecuted her. Rugg concludes that fear, coupled with power, leads to intolerance.

BATTIS, coming from a psychological perspective, writes mostly of Hutchinson's personal character and the circumstances that led her to act or speak in certain ways. Battis also attempts to understand why certain people were drawn to Hutchinson's teachings and took up her cause with such passion and loyalty. This biographer states that Hutchinson's religious views and her determination to carry them out were not the product of intellectualization; rather, they were a part of the specific psychological response to a complex set of emotional pressures. Emphasizing her possible motivations for certain actions and documenting her personal health, Battis aims to decipher what her emotional pressures were, as well as her exact responses to certain stimuli. Despite the fact that he is dealing with the same basic biographical information, Battis constructs a very different biography than most historians, and a very different person that is supposedly Anne Hutchinson.

Writing her biography much later, WILLIAMS organizes her work as a feminist critique of Hutchinson's life and death, as well as a scathing revision of the other, earlier biographies. Wiliams deems Hutchinson an ardent feminist trying to survive in a patriarchal society. This biographer shows that besides being a religious struggle, the Antinomian controversy in New England was partially in response to a group of women clamoring for rights in the face of powerful men. Williams notes that Hutchinson's chief opponents were often heard complaining that her behavior was "not fitting for her sex." Williams dcuments that although the primary charges against Hutchinson were "Antinomian" (a pejorative term meaning defiance of the laws on which a society is based), the Puritan society was also rebelling against any power that women had acquired via Hutchinson and her religious teachings. This book presents a needed contemporary feminist analysis of a key event and important figure in American history.

Huber frames her analysis of Anne Hutchinson in a slightly different light, as she concentrates on why some groups have the ability to question institutional authority. Specifically looking at the Antinomian movement in the Massachusetts Bay Colony, Huber describes how "authority of inspiration" gave Anne Hutchinson the courage to protest against the larger Puritan community. The Antinomian movement, because of its stress on the freedom of the Spirit to enliven the hearts of all believers, offered unique opportunities for women to participate fully and to assume positions of leadership in a religious sphere. Huber focuses on Anne Hutchinson's ability to question history as a woman in colonial times, and she develops her concept of the "authority of inspiration" in order to understand fully the importance of women's leadership within historical situations like this one.

LANG offers quite another viewpoint on Anne Hutchinson and Antinomianism by analyzing the paradoxical nature of dissent during the Antinomian movement in New England. Hutchinson supposedly possessed a direct line to God and thus acted according to how God desired. Thus, the religious knowledge that Hutchinson claimed respected no authority other than itself and also could not be proven. By its very nature, then, Antinomianism disliked authority. Nonetheless, the Massachusetts Bay group still required or adopted Hutchinson as a leader. Herein lies the paradox for Lang. This author concludes that, in various periods throughout history, American culture has simultaneously celebrated and feared authority of individuals. Using this theoretical perspective, Lang discusses two religious movements that involved dissent and the rise of authority figures from the margins and explores how mainstream society sought to deal with these movements and their leaders. In addition, Lang is concerned by the gender-specific problem of powerful female figures in her analysis. In the case of Hutchinson, however, individual autonomy and authority are particularly problematic since she was female. Thus, Lang suggests the fact that Anne Hutchinson was a woman compounds and complicates her heresy. This work represents a very different analysis of religious dissent and female empowerment than is provided by any other work cited.

—HEATHER DILLAWAY

Hypatia 370?–415 and Early Philosophers

Egyptian Philosopher

Alic, Margaret, *Hypatia's Heritage: A History of Women in Science from Antiquity to the Late Nineteenth Century*, London: Women's Press, and Boston: Beacon Press, 1986
Dzielska, Maria, *Hypatia of Alexandria*, Cambridge, Massachusetts, and London: Harvard University Press, 1995
Grinstein, Louise S. (ed.), *Women of Mathematics: A Biobibliographic Sourcebook*, New York: Greenwood, 1987
Osen, Lynn M., *Women in Mathematics*, Cambridge, Massachusetts, and London: MIT Press, 1974
Waithe, Mary Ellen (ed.), *A History of Women Philosophers*, vol. 1, *Ancient Women Philosophers, 600 B.C.–500 A.D.*, Dordrecht, Netherlands, and Boston: Martinus Nijhoff, 1987

Women's roles in philosophic and scientific areas often have been unknown, ignored, or misunderstood. Recent studies, however, have brought to light the significant contributions of many early female thinkers to traditionally male spheres of intellectual inquiry. One of the most important and ambitious of these modern projects to restore women's contributions to our shared intellectual heritage has been the four-volume series on the history of female philosophers. This series has collected an impressive amount of scholarship, including meticulous documenting of sources, careful translations of original writings by these women, and critical analysis of the findings. For scholars, philosophers, educators, or any serious readers of women's histories, these volumes are indispensable. WAITHE, the editor, starts off volume one with an informed discussion of five early Pythagoreans, all of whom, except possibly Themistoclea, were women in Pythagoras' family who played a central role in developing the early philosophy. In the next two chapters, she discusses the intellectual context and translates some of the works of later Pythagoreans, notably Aesata of Lucania, Phintys of Sparta, and Perictione I and II, as well as Theano I and II and Aspasia of Miletus, the well-known rhetorician and member of the Periclean philosophical circle. She then considers in a balanced and scholarly way all sides of the controversy on the historicity or fictitious creation of Diotima of Mantinea, characterized as a philosopher in Platonic dialogues. After considering at length the differences between the doctrines of Plato and Socrates as opposed to Diotiman views, Waithe concludes that received opinion about Diotima as a fiction is flimsy at best. The next two chapters are devoted to Julia Domna, the empress who used her imperial power to encourage philosophy and allowed it to flourish, and Makrina, sister to Gregory, Bishop of Nyssa, who wrote profoundly and knowledgeably on the nature of women's souls, showing her understanding of both Platonic and Aristotelian ideas.

Chief among the early female philosophers, however, is the fourth-century pagan Hypatia, a distinguished mathematician and teacher in Alexandria, who was known as the greatest philosopher in her own time and whose famous commentary on Ptolemy remained the standard until Copernicus, eleven centuries later. Unfortunately, however, none of her works appears to have survived to modern times. Nonetheless, it is generally agreed by scholars that her work included commentary on the following: on *Almagest*, on Diophantus, the Astronomical Table, and on Apollonius of Pergaeus's *Conic Sections*. She evidently also invented two scientific devices: an astrolabe or planisphere as well as a hydroscope. For such an extraordinary person, Hypatia has remained a mystery, and her brutal murder became the stuff of legend. Little studied by historians of science or other scholars, Hypatia and her life have been shrouded in legend and fictionalized in novels so that it has been difficult to separate out what is fact and what is fiction. The sensationalism of her death has often obscured the real accomplishments of her rich intellectual life.

There is only one modern text in English devoted solely to Hypatia, and that is the 1995 translation of the Polish text written by DZIELSKA. This rather slim volume of 157 pages attempts to sift through the legend to present the known facts of the historical woman. Dzielska divides her book into three parts, with the first being a separating out of the literary legend of Hypatia, before she moves on to reconstruct the facts about her life and death and the philosophical circle of Alexandria at the time. The conclusion briefly states what the author believes to be true about Hypatia's life, philosophy, chief intellectual pursuits, and her death. Dzielska goes against conventional wisdom with two claims, one the date of her birth and second the cause of her death. She claims Hypatia was born in 355, not 370, and that her murder had nothing to do with Cyril's anti-pagan campaign. As the first attempt to present a scholarly and accurate sense of Hypatia, this volume is critically important for any modern reader.

The six-page entry on Hypatia in the recent biobibliographic sourcebook, edited by GRINSTEIN and CAMPBELL, is another attempt to present known facts about her. This sourcebook fills a gap by presenting 43 female mathematicians and their family backgrounds, education, careers, and the significance of their work. Each entry, alphabetically organized, is divided into three sections: biography, work, and bibliography. Hypatia is the only early mathematician, as the next chronological entry skips to the eighteenth-century Gabrielle-Emilie le Tonnelier de Breteuil. To a reader interested in women's contributions to mathematics through the ages, this is an extremely useful bibliographic source, a starting point for further research.

OSEN, in a much different kind of book, also tries to trace the impact women had on mathematical thought by profiling the lives of eight extraordinary female mathematicians with a historical frame and concluding chapters on the golden age of math and the "feminine mathtique." This is a delightful and lively book unabashedly addressed to general readers in order to pique their interest in the lives and accomplishments of these outstanding women. As a popular account that unfortunately relies heavily on an outdated 1908 text by Elbert Hubbard, Osen's short history of Hypatia will spark the curiosity of any reader, who will probably read through all eight lives, captivated by the richly complex personalities of these influential women in mathematics.

ALIC traces the history of women in science from prehistoric times to the last decade of the nineteenth century, just before Marie Curie's uncovering of the mysteries of radioactivity. Broader in scope than some of the other histories of women, this one is less technical and less detailed in its coverage than the Waithe volume. It deals less with the specific scientific and philosophical content of the contributions of these female scientists and instead sketches the background of the times and gives essential facts and chronology in their lives. It is useful as a broad backdrop, but not for an in-depth, comprehensive, or focused study of each figure. Presented as fact are some hypotheses or assumptions that are being called into question now by experts in the field. Serious students and scholars should consult the Waithe history and the Grinstein and Campbell sourcebook for a discussion of current concerns or controversies, for reliable and accurate information, and for complete and primary sources, and not rely on the sweeping and necessarily inaccurate generalities that cannot be avoided in such a vast and broad overview.

All of these works point to the necessity of recovering a lost or incomplete history of women's significant contributions to fields of study assumed closed to women, some of whom became leading thinkers and practitioners with their own disciples and spheres of influence.

—JOANNE A. CHARBONNEAU

I

Incest

Bell, Vikki, *Interrogating Incest: Feminism, Foucault and the Law*, London and New York: Routledge, 1993

Butler, Sandra, *Conspiracy of Silence: The Trauma of Incest*, San Francisco: New Glide, 1978; revised edition, San Francisco: Volcano Press, 1985

Gordon, Linda, *Heroes of Their Own Lives: The Politics and History of Family Violence: Boston 1880–1960*, New York: Viking, 1988; London: Virago Press, 1989

Herman, Judith Lewis, *Trauma and Recovery*, New York: Basic Books, 1992

Herman, Judith Lewis, and Lisa Hirschman, *Father-Daughter Incest*, Cambridge, Massachusetts, and London: Harvard University Press, 1981

McNaron, Toni A.H., and Yarrow Morgan (eds.), *Voices in the Night: Women Speaking about Incest*, Pittsburgh, Pennsylvania: Cleis Press, 1982

Russell, Diana, *The Secret Trauma: Incest in the Lives of Girls and Women*, New York: Basic Books, 1986

Incest emerged as an important women's issue in the 1970s, and since then published contributions have been diverse. McNARON and MORGAN provide a collection of writings by incest survivors, which produce feminist challenges to conservative political analyses and an important validation of the experiences and strength of many women and children. This work is often particularly powerful due to its emphasis on personal stories and the use of genres such as poetry. Other similar collections have also appeared.

Dissatisfied with the prevailing patriarchal orthodoxy, women have also increasingly conducted their own social research and various forms of therapeutic intervention and prevention. BUTLER's book was one of the first to publicise incest as a widespread problem connected to male domination in families and in societies more generally. Butler's research draws extensively on interviews with victims, and to a lesser extent with perpetrators and mothers, and uses this background to criticise common myths, the lack of appropriate services, and the general low level of awareness, if not downright dangerous attitudes and practices, of professionals.

In an early feminist classic that remains a key reference on the topic, HERMAN and HIRSCHMAN draw on their experiences as clinical therapists to provide a resource for women who have experienced incestuous abuse, and to challenge the dominant myths in the professional stance towards incest survivors. Part One develops its analysis drawing on, and often taking issue with, sources as diverse as Freudian theory, Kinsey, clinical material, anthropology, popular literature, and pornography. Herman argues that incest is a common occurrence and is harmful, that the perpetrator is to blame, and that father-daughter incest typically occurs in rigidly patriarchal families. Part Two discusses the results of Herman and Hirschman's clinical study of forty victims whose words are frequently used to illustrate themes such as the long-term impact of incest. One of the most interesting and unusual aspects of the study is the inclusion of a second group of women whose fathers were not overtly incestuous but were described as "seductive," and whose experiences are analysed as being on a continuum with those of incest survivors. Part Three reviews the available formal social responses to incest, including treatment centres, crisis intervention, various therapies, self-help groups, and prosecution. While obviously dated now, this is still a helpful reminder of the origins of such services and the kinds of typologies that are still commonly in use.

RUSSELL's book is one of several based on her classic feminist study, consisting of random survey-interviews of 930 adult women in San Francisco in the late 1970s. The study produced quantitative and qualitative data about the incidence, prevalence, and characteristics of sexual victimisation. Here Russell focuses on the all-too-rich data related to incestuous abuse, which she uses to present a detailed picture of themes such as the long-term effects of incest, whether incest can ever be non-abusive, the relationship between being an incest survivor and further victimisation, social factors in the occurrence of incestuous abuse, portraits of victims and perpetrators, and the role of mothers. This is also a particularly helpful study for its statistical documentation of the enormous difference between official reporting figures and the incidence and prevalence found in the Russell survey, and for its careful approach to issues such as the different kinds of incest and how they can be understood and explained in the context of the overall domination of women by men, and children by adults. Russell also includes more documentation of the study methodology than found in her earlier publications.

A very rich and nuanced work by a leading feminist historian, GORDON's book merits inclusion here for its important insights about incest as a feature of family life in the nineteenth century rather than being unique to our own time. Even more importantly, the research documents how incest, along with other social problems, came to public attention well before its "discovery" in the 1970s and then became submerged from view with the decline of feminist influence. One of the most significant aspects of Gordon's argument concerns the way in which "family violence" and responses to it must always be understood with reference to its own specific cultural and historical setting. This is also a relevant book for its investigation of the complexities of power at work in the case histories of multiply disadvantaged families, in the diverse experiences of their disparately positioned members, and in their often fraught but not necessarily one-sided engagements with welfare workers.

The last two works give the reader an insight into the kinds of contemporary feminist work being undertaken. BELL's book is an example of a recent turn by some feminists working against sexual violence to concepts provided by postmodernist and post-structuralist theorists. Bell argues that feminists have subsumed incest within a discussion of sexual violence, thereby tending to elide other ways of understanding it. She turns to the work of Michel Foucault to suggest that his analysis of sexuality and power can be played off against the useful insights of feminist theory in order to better understand the complexities of the ways in which incest is defined in British law, in social prohibitions, and in the feminist sense of coercive sexual practices. The book's complex arguments include important critiques of the phallocentrism of Foucault's theories, but they also suggest that critically using Foucauldian concepts can produce challenges to improve feminist analysis, and ultimately to better understand incest as implicated in various technologies of power.

HERMAN's work is an example of recent feminist literature that attempts to make connections between the kinds of private abuses suffered by women and children and the more public forms of violence most commonly labeled as terrorism and as issues of human rights. The book makes these links, not by suggesting that all forms of trauma are the same, but by arguing that different forms of trauma have similarities, both in terms of their effects and the possibilities for healing and recovery. Herman draws on her own clinical work with survivors of incest as well as drawing on accounts of trauma due to war and political terror. The book's spare prose and its respectful use of survivors' testimony make it a moving and accessible resource for a broad spectrum of readers. It includes chapters on the development of psychiatric interest in the different types of trauma, and a timely discussion of the links between controversial diagnoses like borderline personality disorder and childhood abuse.

—CHRIS ATMORE

See also Child Sexual Abuse

India *see* Asian Women; Dowry; Dowry Murder/Bride Burning; Economic Development: Asia; Hinduism; Purdah; Sati; Sex Customs in China, Japan, and India

Industrial Revolution

Berg, Maxine, *The Age of Manufactures: Industry, Innovation, and Work in Britain, 1700–1820,* London: Fontana, and Totowa, New Jersey: Barnes and Noble, 1985

Blewett, Mary, *Men, Women, and Work: Class, Gender, and Protest in the New England Shoe Industry, 1780–1910,* Urbana: University of Illinois Press, 1988

Clark, Anna, *The Struggle for the Breeches: Gender and the Making of the British Working Class,* London: Rivers Oram Press, and Berkeley: University of California Press, 1995

Davidoff, Leonore, and Catherine Hall, *Family Fortunes: Men and Women of the English Middle Class, 1780–1850,* London: Hutchinson, and Chicago, University of Chicago Press, 1987

Dublin, Thomas, *Transforming Women's Work: New England Lives in the Industrial Revolution,* Ithaca, New York: Cornell University Press, 1994

Lown, Judy, *Women and Industrialization: Gender at Work in Nineteenth-Century England,* Cambridge: Polity, and Minneapolis: University of Minnesota Press, 1990

Pinchbeck, Ivy, *Women Workers and the Industrial Revolution, 1750–1850,* London: Routledge, and New York: Crofts, 1930

Rendall, Jane, *Women in an Industrializing Society: England, 1750–1880,* Oxford and Cambridge, Massachusetts: B. Blackwell, 1991

Industrial revolutions have taken place in all parts of the globe at various points over the course of the last two hundred years. However, the classical locus for the original "Industrial Revolution" is Britain in the period between 1760 and 1820. Traditionally, this metamorphosis from a primarily rural, agrarian economy to an economy centred on urban, industrial capitalism is understood as a traumatic, rapid transformation precipitating monumental changes in the social and political fabric of Britain. Recent scholarship has begun to revise this view. There is now more of an emphasis upon a slower pace of change, which allows continuities with the pre-industrial past to be recognized. Both of these interpretations retain adherents, and both are evident in works on women's relationship to the "Industrial Revolution."

PINCHBECK's book, an early example of scholarship in women's history, and worth reading for this alone, focuses upon the positive advantages industrialisation gave to women. Seeing the "Industrial Revolution" as a set of dramatic changes, Pinchbeck demonstrates how unmarried women gained independence through waged work and relocation to urbanised areas. While ignoring the problem of the division of men's and women's lives into the "separate spheres" of work and home, she does lay emphasis upon the importance of women's work prior to industrialisation. This pioneering book contains a wealth of information on women's experiences in all fields of labour, from the agrarian and domestic systems of the eighteenth century through to the incorporation of women into textile factory work and heavy industry (mining and metalworking), and the expansion of female business and trade opportunities.

Pinchbeck's positive interpretation of women's industrialising experience is problematic, but her introduction of women into analyses of the "Industrial Revolution" provides opportunities to reassess the meaning of processes associated with it. BERG offers an interpretation that focuses upon the processes of production, rather than the big, generalised sectors of the economy like agriculture and industry. Her emphasis upon the productive roles of artisans and outworkers deemphasises the factory system, which was traditionally understood as the centre of modernising industrialisation, when in fact such a system was slow in emerging. Consequently Berg stresses continuity, albeit a progressive one. Her interpretation shows that female workers were the target of new manufacturing processes that were incorporated into their ways of life. Berg's study is also notable for its examination of areas of decline within Britain, challenging once again the often triumphalist view of the birth of modernity.

RENDALL's book is an ideal short summary text that seeks to challenge Pinchbeck's views, and draws upon scholarship stressing continuity. In a clearly organised way, Rendall reassesses the close connections between an industrial economy and private domestic worlds. Instead of assessing whether industrialisation was good or bad for women, she focuses upon the historical forces that were shaping women's lives in this period. Her aim is to raise, and explore, questions such as the effect of the extension of male power to the workplace, and the changing definitions of male/female, home/workplace separations. She links such questions to a further understanding of today's work practices, and the possible consequences for industrialisation in the developing world.

An important aspect of industrialisation is its effect upon class formation and gender relations within classes. A modern classic on this topic is DAVIDOFF and HALL's book. Their analysis stresses the ways class and gender operate together to form an ideology that kept middle-class women within a clearly defined sphere. They connect the family/household with population size and the economy. For the middle classes, a wife was ideally non-productive economically. This expectation of dependency meant men married later and cautiously but then had large families. This study contrasts urban Birmingham and rural Essex and Suffolk, and explores religious and ideological ideas, economic structures, education, and family relations.

In a similar vein, but without the depth of analysis, LOWN offers a local study of women in the Courtauld silk mills of Essex. She demonstrates the role played by patriarchy, in the form of Victorian paternalism, in the molding of gender relations within this industry. Women sought to integrate their domestic and working lives and to maintain a strong identity in the community, although they were subordinated in the workplace. This is a useful book amidst the increasing number of texts with localised focuses.

CLARK's work challenges E.P. Thompson's seminal study, *The Making of the English Working Class* (1968) by incorporating into her analysis gender and the Scottish textile industry. Like Davidoff and Hall, she sees the changing definitions of gender relations as fundamental in understanding class formation. She examines work, community, culture, and class consciousness. The middle-class ideology of separate spheres allowed men to come together as political equals in the public sphere, while working-class men were denied the possibility of doing this through the sheer necessity of female wage-earning. Clark argues that working-class men who were politically radical sought the expansion of this gender ideology in order for them to ensure political and social status. The Industrial Revolution saw skilled men replaced by the cheap labour of women; thus women were seen as unskilled, and men sought to keep them out of the workplace. Clark also shows the changes in sexual relations within working-class communities, which wrought tensions of their own. Clark sees all of these developments as offering a range of "makings" and possible results in the formation of working-class identity through the transformations of industrialisation.

Studies on the process of industrialisation in the United States have largely focused upon the development of the factory system in New England. Two important studies connecting this development to women's lives are those by Dublin and Blewett. DUBLIN's work builds on his earlier ground-breaking study of female workers in Lowell, Massachusetts. He examines, in a chronological form, what he understands to be the eventual loss of female independence through the developing importance of women's wages to the family economy. This process is broken down into a movement from rural outworkers producing palm-hats, whose wages supplemented family income, through the mill "girls" of Lowell and their economic autonomy and freedom from family incorporation, to an assessment that by 1900 this fragile liberty had been eroded and women's wages once more were familial.

Although Dublin's conclusions may be critiqued for claiming generalisations from the highly specific communities he studies, this book offers an immense amount of demographic detail about female workers and their families. He offers a good example of the use of statistical data and the methodology involved in the use of official statistical material, such as the United States census, and the skill of "record linkage" whereby women's life experiences can be recreated.

BLEWETT's work focuses upon women in the shoemaking industry in New England. Her work offers a more nuanced gender analysis of the implication of the sexual division of labor in manufacturing production and its effects upon female labor activism. She traces the transformations in shoe manufacture that divided the female work force into rural outworkers that were largely married women and dependent daughters, and single factory workers. She demonstrates how both used the moral suasion inherent in "true womanhood" to defend their positions. Her analysis of the 1860 strike in Essex County reveals the tensions among female workers, and the implications for female activism. Outworkers tended to align with male shoemakers, while female factory workers increasingly drew on the rhetoric of equal rights and were most likely to lead strike action and be involved in other political activities. Blewett demonstrates the importance of situating female work experience in relation to that of men in order to recognise a female tradition of autonomous organisation and self-direction in defending their interests. She also urges a recognition for the need to differentiate working women and to understand the consequences of this for our generalisations about industrialisation in the United States.

—STEPHANIE OXENDALE

Infertility

Alden, Paulette Bates, *Crossing the Moon: A Journey through Infertility*, St. Paul, Minnesota: Hungry Mind Press, 1996

Anton, Linda Hunt, *Never to Be a Mother: A Guide for All Women Who Didn't—or Couldn't—Have Children*, San Francisco: Harper San Francisco, 1992

Salzer, Linda P., *Infertility: How Couples Can Cope*, Boston: G.K. Hall, 1986

Sandelowski, Margarete, *With Child in Mind: Studies of the Personal Encounter with Infertility*, Philadelphia: University of Pennsylvania Press, 1993

Silber, Sherman J., *How to Get Pregnant with the New Technology*, New York: Warner, 1991

Treiser, Susan, and Robin K. Levinson, *A Woman Doctor's Guide to Infertility*, New York: Hyperion, 1994

Dealing with infertility is perhaps one of the most stressful crises one can experience. It is painful for both men and women; however, women especially are affected in a deep, emotional, self-identifying way that is unique to their gender.

ALDEN's work takes the reader through a painful yet enlightening journey through her own infertility. She began infertility therapy at age 39 and brought it to closure at age 43. There is some technological discussion, but hers is more a personal story dealing with ambivalence, conflict, desire, disappointment, and resolution surrounding the struggle through infertility and motherhood. She moves through the turning points in life, discussing her infertility in conjunction with her career choice and passion as a writer. The two eloquently go hand in hand in her story. Alden explores her childhood, adolescence, and young adulthood, and how that caused her to make the choices and hold the opinions she has surrounding the decision to have a child, and how choosing always means giving something up. Her early choice to postpone or even refuse the notion of motherhood in the face of societal norms, dealing with the issue of sense of self in relation to motherhood, and the ultimate devastation in the resolution that motherhood was not a possibility for her, gives a feminist personal perspective. Alden shows us the intimate side of her relationship with her husband and how their perceptions and deep feelings of dealing with infertility differ based on gender. She gives a glimpse of the group Resolve, a nationwide layperson organization for people dealing with infertility, and the love and support of special people in her life. Any woman dealing with infertility can surely deeply relate to her story and know that through it all, one will survive.

SALZER's book focuses on coping skills in surviving the grind of infertility therapy. She discusses the physical and especially the emotional side of the struggle. Discussion of the stages that infertile couples go through is helpful in understanding what is normal, from shock and denial to the grieving process. Although heterosexual couples are predominately addressed, Salzer acknowledges that the struggle is more intense for lesbian couples, based on societal prejudice. She also delves into religion in regard to infertility, and how a woman can experience, at the very least, feelings of disillusionment. Salzer and her husband went through painful years struggling with infertility. With the adoption of their son, the pain lessened but never disappeared. Salzer emphasizes that resolution is emotional and not physical. She likens resolution of infertility to death; that is, something you live with even if you do deliver a baby or adopt a child. Her book includes a guide to discovering whether a patient is ready to give up on treatment or not and gives details on choosing childfree living or adoption. Although in vitro fertilization has made some technological advances since the publication of Salzer's book, the emotional aspects remain the same.

According to SILBER, for those beginning the infertility process, it is advisable to arm oneself with as much relevant technical and medical knowledge as possible, as well as financial resources, so as to avoid wasting precious time, especially for women over 35. Silber gives hope to all who wish to have a child, providing they have an open mind. His work explains in a detailed, comprehensive, yet easy to understand way how infertility treatment through the new technology of the 1990s works. He helps educate the reader on low-tech procedures such as basal body temperature charts, when to have intercourse, and clomid and other like procedures, as well as hi-tech procedures such as GIFT (gamete intra fallopian transfer), IVF (in vitro fertilization), ZIFT (zygote intra fallopian transfer), egg donation, sperm donation, and surrogate uterus. Silber takes the reader through the history of traditional infertility therapies from the 1980s and traditional diagnoses and helps dispel many of the myths. He is sympathetic to the emotional and financial cost of treatment and discusses in depth the politics of infertility. He discusses congressional apathy and inefficient government bureaucracy involved with the treatment of infertility. He served on a U.S. Congressional Advisory Panel during 1987 and 1988 and has many factual insights into the political side of infertility as it relates to who pays or does not pay, and why. Silber discusses the legitimate health risks associated with the tragedy of infertility that 25 percent of couples in their 30s share. In his explanations, he gives many case studies of varied situations to support his research. He discusses how long one should go through which treatments and why, and when to escalate to the next level of treatment. Silber gets right to the point in a factual, sympathetic manner and points couples dealing with infertility down the right path with education as their guide.

TREISER and LEVINSON also give a comprehensive guide to dealing with infertility from a medical as well as empathetic standpoint. Their point of view is definitely that of the woman and they address the issue of how to deal with the heartbreaking crisis of infertility. Every chapter gives caring advice on how to deal with situations surrounding friends, family, co-workers and the like. The book is very comforting, at the same time giving adequate medical facts. The last three chapters are dedicated to three personal stories of women who have survived infertility therapy. There is one woman in her 20s, one in her 30s, and one in her 40s. The ages and ultimate results of the therapy are broad enough to help anyone going through the struggle of infertility relate personally.

SANDELOWSKI's work is a feminist, academic approach to infertility. Her focus, rooted in statistical and technological research, is more on the meaning of infertility. She examines the historical perceptions of infertility and how during the nineteenth century, infertility (or sterility as it was then called) was thought to relate directly to women's pursuit of equality. The popular belief was that infertility could be blamed directly on the rising occupational and educational opportunities for women. There was also concern that this was a syndrome indicative of the possible decline of the white race. According to Sandelowski, residuals of this kind of thinking still remain today to a certain degree. Sandelowski goes into detail about the perceptions of infertility in the 1990s. She deals with cultural and societal expectations and how they affect a woman's feelings about her own potential infertility. She details how new technologies have dramatically changed the meaning of infertility from one of deficit to one of potentiality. Sandelowski retells the stories of individual women and couples dealing with infertility. She spends much time in discussing adoption and the cultural ramifications that the people in her study have had to deal with. Sandelowski is a nurse by trade and follows up her research with a look into a caregiver's responsibility and challenge in dealing with infertile patients. She analyzes differences between a visible, predominantly male-centered curing versus the invisible predominantly female-centered caring.

ANTON's work is geared toward women who want to have children but ultimately cannot for various reasons. Written by a woman who has gone through the process herself, this book's purpose is specifically to explore women's experience of loss. Many women were interviewed for her book; in fact, Anton includes the extensive questionnaire used for her research at the end of her book. She explores the many paths to childlessness from single, married, and lesbian women. Her book includes a chapter on the unique challenges lesbian women deal with in confronting infertility. Her extensive 10-step program moves from acknowledging and experiencing the loss to enhancing the quest for feminine wholeness. Different reactions from different women are exposed, from hopeless despair to disappointment. Anton explores the women's movement's effect and subsequent enlightenment of paternalistic societal pressures faced by women through this century. This is a very comprehensive self-help book on turning childlessness into childfree living.

—CARLA A. STONER

See also Reproductive Technologies

Intentional Communities

Cheney, Joyce, *Lesbian Land,* Minneapolis, Minnesota: Word Weavers, 1985

Chmielewski, Wendy E., Louis J. Kern, and Marlyn Klee-Hartzell (eds.), *Women in Spiritual and Communitarian Societies in the United States,* Syracuse, New York: Syracuse University Press, 1993

Foster, Lawrence, *Women, Family, and Utopia: Communal Experiments of the Shakers, the Oneida Community, and the Mormons,* Syracuse, New York: Syracuse University Press, 1991

Kitch, Sally L., *This Strange Society of Women: Reading the Letters and Lives of the Woman's Commonwealth,* Columbus: Ohio State University Press, 1993

Kolmerten, Carol A., *Women in Utopia: The Ideology of Gender in the American Owenite Communities,* Bloomington: Indiana University Press, 1990

Palgi, Michal, *Sexual Equality: The Israeli Kibbutz Tests the Theories,* Norwood, Pennsylvania: Norwood Editions, 1983

Rohrlich, Ruby, and Elaine Hoffman Baruch (eds.), *Women in Search of Utopia: Mavericks and Mythmakers,* New York: Shocken, 1984

Wagner, Jon, *Sex Roles in Contemporary American Communes,* Bloomington: Indiana University Press, 1982

The inhabitants of intentional communities have often experimented with gender roles that differed from the rest of society. These experiments sometimes offered women an expanded range of lifestyles. The role of women in intentional communities has often been overlooked in the literature published on this topic. Women's studies in history, sociology, and anthropology have revitalized the investigation of these communities and the experience of women who participate in them. The books included here are some of the works that examine women's roles in historic and contemporary intentional communities.

KOLMERTEN has written a history of the secular communities founded in the United States primarily in the 1820s and 1830s based on the principles of Scottish philanthropist Robert Owen. She views these communities from the perspective of the women who lived in them. Although equality of the sexes was promised to the inhabitants who formed these communities, Kolmerten contends that it was never attained. She also asserts that this failure led to the eventual collapse of the communities. By examining women's voices and experiences, Kolmerten gives the reader an understanding of how women's needs must be included in successful blueprints for organizing social experiments.

FOSTER covers the role of women and the family in the three well-known religious nineteenth-century communal experiments: the Shakers, the Oneida Community, and the Mormons. Foster focuses on the social, sexual, and religious practices of these communities. The words of the women who participated in these communities are used throughout the book. Foster examines each experimental society, asking questions about gender equality, power relationships, the experiences of women, and family structure. He concludes that while these intentional experiments all consciously tried to expand women's roles, ultimately women's needs were subordinated to the survival of each community.

KITCH's book is a history of an all-women's community that began in nineteenth-century Texas. Kitch centers her book on the letters written between the mothers who formed the Woman's Commonwealth in the late 1860s and the daughters who grew up in the community. Using the backdrop of this community experiment, Kitch focuses on how these women's lives were similar or different from their contemporaries in mainstream society. The intergenerational relationships between the women also constitute a major focus of the book.

CHMIELEWSKI, KERN, and KLEE-HARTZELL have edited a volume of essays on the experiences of women who lived in some of the intentional communities formed in both the nineteenth and twentieth centuries. The book includes essays on Shakers, women from Owenite communities, Catholic religious women, Mormons, women from The Farm in Tennessee, and from Twin Oaks, among others. The introduction to the book sets these essays within a feminist framework, describing the place women have had with the communitarian movement and the scholarship still needed in this area.

ROHRLICH and BARUCH have edited a volume of pieces that range from histories of particular communities to literary visions of utopia. Starting with the premise that women's experiences have been missing from the literature on intentional communities and visions of alternative societies, these editors include writings on women's visions of how to create society. Different sections treat past experiments, contemporary communities, and visions of utopia. This volume includes multicultural voices.

PALGI has gathered writings covering the history of the Israeli kibbutz movement and the role of women in contemporary communities. The authors in this volume examine women's work, education, family life, gender relations, and the social structure of kibbutz society. In the introduction, Palgi acknowledges that the kibbutz movement began with a basic premise of freeing women from economic and social inequality, but that this has not been achieved. Some of the authors claim that this failure to reach equality is proof of natural gender differences. Others turn to cultural, social, and economic explanations for the lack of equality. Some authors believe that contemporary feminism will revitalize the examination of women's role in the kibbutz movement.

CHENEY has edited a volume of articles from women who began forming intentional communities for women only in the 1970s. These communities are based on the feminist theories and practices that rose out of the women's, lesbian feminist, and ecofeminist movements of the 1970s and 1980s. The stories included in this book trace the joy of creating new societies with like-minded women and the pain when some of the communities fail or women leave in anger. Cheney sought a variety of voices in this volume.

WAGNER's volume of essays was one of the first books to attempt an overview of the question of gender relations in contemporary U.S. intentional communities. He and the other authors in this volume found a complex variety of sex roles for women in the communities they investigated. The communities range from the extreme patriarchy of the "Haran" commune, in which women were completely subordinate to men, to Twin Oaks, where egalitarian behavior was expected and practiced. The essays included in this volume closely analyze the role of women in each community under study, but also demonstrate how much work still needs to be done on this topic.

—WENDY E. CHMIELEWSKI

See also Lesbian Separatism

Inventors

Altman, Linda Jacobs, *Women Inventors,* New York: Facts on File, 1997

Macdonald, Anne L., *Feminine Ingenuity: Women and Invention in America,* New York: Ballantine, 1992

Panabaker, Janet, *Inventing Women: Profiles of Women Inventors,* Waterloo, Ontario: The Women Inventors Project, 1991

Vare, Ethlie Ann, and Greg Ptacek, *Mothers of Invention: From the Bra to the Bomb: Forgotten Women and Their Unforgettable Ideas,* New York: William Morrow, 1988

Books on female inventors represent the popular side of the soaring interest in women in science in the last 20 years. Emblematic biographies, stories of inventions solving problems and inventors overcoming adversity, are the mainstays of these books. Simultaneously reclaiming honor and attention for women whose achievements have been lost in the history of science, all of these works—but especially those oriented to a juvenile audience—exhort their readers to see themselves as potential inventors.

VARE and PTACEK engaged public attention with their first book, arguing that women had been inventors—and important inventors—from the beginning of recorded history. Covering the gamut from scientific invention and discovery (medicine, nuclear fission, calculus, and kevlar) to celebrity inventors and the inventions of everyday necessities and fun products, Vare and Ptacek mapped the territory that other writers followed. Their historical and geographic range, as well as inclusion of a number of pathbreaking inventions and discoveries, opened eyes and doors to the achievements of female inventors.

MACDONALD followed with a far more focused work on U.S. female inventors, organized in roughly chronological chapters, some with a thematic focus (for example, "Patenting Dress Reform"). With more of a sustained narrative than any of the other books in this list, Macdonald provides historical framework, makes connections, and traces legacies, including the effect on women of nineteenth-century popular works on female inventors. A useful antidote to the lonely genius effect of most compilations of inventor biographies, Macdonald shows the context and sometimes collaboration of invention, and the effect of public efforts like fairs and expositions.

ALTMAN writes in the "Facts on File American Profiles" series and follows the standard format of approximately 12-page treatments of nine selected female inventors: Amanda Theodocia Jones, Carrie Everson, Sara Josephine Baker, M.D., Madam C.J. Walker, Ida Rosenthal, Katharine Blodgett, Elizabeth Hazen, Rachel Brown, Bette Graham, and Ruth Handler. These longer treatments allow her to establish historical, social, and biographical context, and to take readers through each inventor's process of problematizing, inventing, and solving production difficulties.

PANABAKER offers a book focusing on Canadian female inventors, from the famous, like Dr. Rosalyn Yallow, who won a 1977 Nobel Prize, to girls who have won Canadian invention contests. Individual biographies and descriptions of inventions and their significance are arranged by the beneficiary of the inventions; for example, as agents of technological change, for women, for use in childcare, for everybody. This is a highly readable compilation with some unexpected entries and interesting explanations of the technical problems to be solved.

—CAROL KLIMICK CYGANOWSKI

Irigaray, Luce 1930–

French Writer

Burke, Carolyn, Naomi Schor, and Margaret Whitford (eds.), *Engaging with Irigaray: Feminist Philosophy and Modern European Thought,* New York: Columbia University Press, 1994

Gallop, Jane, *Feminism and Psychoanalysis: The Daughter's Seduction,* Ithaca, New York: Cornell University Press, and London: Macmillan, 1982

Grosz, Elizabeth, *Sexual Subversions: Three French Feminists*, Boston: Allen and Unwin, 1989

Kim, C.W. Maggie, Susan M. St. Ville, and Susan M. Simonaitis (eds.), *Transfigurations: Theology and the French Feminists*, Minneapolis: Fortress Press, 1993

Moi, Toril, *Sexual/Textual Politics: Feminist Literary Theory*, London and New York: Methuen, 1985

Whitford, Margaret, *Luce Irigaray: Philosophy in the Feminine*, London and New York: Routledge, 1991

Luce Irigaray was quickly embraced by feminists, philosophers, and literary critics alike in the mid-1970s, but then just as quickly, she was rejected by an audience who expected their ascendant star to provide them with all the answers to a women's movement that was burgeoning but momentarily lacking direction. The early literature on Irigaray is overly laudatory and uncritical, while the second wave of Irigaray scholarship is too readily dismissive. What followed in the 1980s was a large-scale rejection of Irigaray's writings that continued until the early 1990s. Except for a few academic studies, Irigaray's work has been victim to appalling mistranslations and misrepresentations. Subsequent readers have attributed this confusion to a largely Anglo-American audience, unfamiliar with Irigaray's complex linguistic and psychoanalytic background, and, relying on translations, incognizant of her playful, poetic writing style.

There are, however, a few texts that, early on, detailed the importance of Irigaray's project. Texts by Moi and Grosz were instrumental in making Irigaray's difficult writings accessible to the average academic. GROSZ places Irigaray's writings in relation to two other contemporary French philosophers: Julia Kristeva and Michèle Le Doeuff. Grosz's lucid prose clarifies some of the more difficult concepts in Irigaray's texts: sexual difference, alterity, and mimesis. Irigaray's relation to Emmanuel Levinas and her ensuing ethical system, both civil and spiritual, is Grosz's main focal point. Similarly, MOI's text places Irigaray's work alongside that of Kristeva and Hélène Cixous to understand fully her feminist project. Moi believes Irigaray is highly influenced by the method of deconstruction delineated by Jacques Derrida, and she spends some time outlining this alliance. While careful to synthesize Irigaray's various concepts, and highlight their importance for a feminist understanding, Moi (a Marxist) also takes Irigaray to task for neglecting to take into account the specific historical nature and economic motivations of diverse patriarchal structures. The studies by Grosz and Moi, though now slightly dated, are still considered standard texts for Irigaray scholarship.

GALLOP's text constitutes the most extensive study of Irigaray from a psychoanalytic perspective. In an engaging and humorous account of the relationship between feminism and psychoanalysis, Gallop psychoanalyses the analysts themselves. She examines the father-daughter imagery in Irigaray's writing, and probes Irigaray's complex relation to Sigmund Freud and Jacques Lacan. In a close textual reading of Irigaray's major writings, Gallop uncovers Irigaray's method, and brings to the fore the "seduction" of psychoanalytic texts generally. This book also situates Irigaray's position in regard to two other leading psychoanalysts, Eugénie Lemoine-Luccioni and Kristeva, while at the same time tracing the troubled connection between psychoanalysis and politics in their respective writings. Gallop's text remains one of the most careful and intelligent volumes of the literature on Irigaray, but it is not an easy book to read for those uninitiated in psychoanalytic history and terminology.

Some of the most important secondary material on Irigaray has been written by scholars in the field of religious studies. Theologians and philosophers of religion come together in KIM, ST. VILLE, and SIMONAITIS's anthology to discuss Irigaray's understanding of "divinity," alongside essays on her contemporaries, Cixous and Kristeva. Important for scholars of religion is Irigaray's supposition that a (female) subject can only come into being through the divination of a love relationship in which she is represented. This radical proposition—the underlying logic of Irigaray's call for the deification of the mother-daughter relationship—is thoroughly and thoughtfully assessed in many of the essays in this volume.

WHITFORD's book is the first exhaustive study of Irigaray's philosophical and feminist project. It provides, in clear and accessible language, a detailed background of Irigaray's training and influences, as well as her aims and agenda. She makes neither a star nor a demon of Irigaray, but contextualizes her writings in the French intellectual world in which they were written. Whitford depicts Irigaray as a radical "philosopher of change," who, as a psychoanalyst, uncovers the structures that have buttressed the subordination of women, and as an activist, aims to establish the means for making change possible. Whitford conclusively dismisses those critics of Irigaray who accuse her of an uncritical alliance with Lacan, and similarly, those critics who accuse her of misrepresenting Lacan. Whitford traces Irigaray's concept of the "imaginary"—a concept which provides the substratum for much of her theoretical work—and demonstrates that Irigaray's writings constitute a thorough critique of the Lacanian project that has yet to be fully understood or taken seriously by feminist scholars.

BURKE, SCHOR, and WHITFORD's anthology is the ideal companion volume to Whitford's text. A wide range of essays from a number of important feminist writers—Rosi Braidotti, Judith Butler, Elizabeth Grosz—are collected here to outline overlapping philosophic, psychoanalytic, and feminist topics related to Irigaray's work. Irigaray's relation to thinkers such as Martin Heidegger, Friedrich Nietzsche, Lacan, Gilles Deleuze, and G.W.F. Hegel, her development of a female genealogy and a feminine symbolic, her ethical system, and her literary style are all detailed in this anthology.

Throughout her own book, Whitford calls for an active "engagement" with Irigaray's writings as a means to break the inclination to either embrace or discard her philosophical works. It is no surprise then to find that Burke, Schor, and Whitford's volume is entitled *Engaging with Irigaray.* This title marks the current spirit of Irigaray scholarship, and will likely frame the proliferation of studies to come.

—KATHLEEN O'GRADY

Isabella I 1451–1504

Spanish Queen

Fernández-Armesto, Felipe, *Ferdinand and Isabella*, London: Weidenfeld and Nicolson, and New York: Taplinger 1975
Liss, Peggy K., *Isabel the Queen: Life and Times*, Oxford and New York: Oxford University Press, 1992
Mariejol, Jean Hippolyte, *The Spain of Ferdinand and Isabella*, translated by Benjamin Keen, New Brunswick, New Jersey: Rutgers University Press, 1961
Miller, Townsend, *The Castles and the Crown: Spain: 1451–1555*, London: Victor Gallanz, and New York: Coward-McCann, 1963
Rubin, Nancy, *Isabella of Castile: The First Renaissance Queen*, New York: St. Martin's Press, 1991

In the wake of the 1992 celebration of the quincentennial of the *encuentro*, or cultural encounter between Old World and New, brought about by Columbus's 1492 voyage to the west in search of a passage to the Far East, much discussion has been generated about the benefit and, conversely, the detriment of Spanish exploration and imperialism to the Americas. While much of the debate has centered upon Columbus and his disastrous pioneering of the exploitation of the indigenous peoples, no doubt attention must also be directed to Isabella of Castile, whose sponsorship made the voyage possible, and whose other, domestic policies arguably altered the course of western history and civilization in Spain and Europe, as well as in the New World. While there is no doubt as to the impact of her reign with Ferdinand of Aragon upon her country and foreign powers, debate still flourishes as to whether her legacy is that of a good and just queen, or of a religious zealot who irreparably damaged the peninsula she sought to unite through religious and cultural purity.

Based on studies authored in Spanish by scholars of the earlier twentieth century, FERNÁNDEZ-ARMESTO's book does not aim to be a source for learned scholars so much as a casual perusal of history for the less-informed reader. The year of publication is significant, because Fernández-Armesto rebukes justification for the efforts underway to declare Isabella a saint in the last years of Franco's Fascist regime. Indeed, one of the major premises that underlie his study is the consummate humanity of the monarchs, their human flaws contrasted sharply against the apotheosizing tendencies of their chroniclers and biographers. Fernández-Armesto likewise denies that Isabella and Ferdinand succeeded in the unification of the various Iberian kingdoms to form what is modern-day Spain, pointing out instead that the respective kingdoms of Castile and Aragon were allied during their reign without being integrated. Nor does he hold them to be creators of a modern state, as many historians contend. According to Fernández-Armesto, Isabella and Ferdinand imposed a centralist, absolutist monarchy, which delayed for centuries the establishment of a parliamentary government in Spain. The book is informative in its perusal of such details as the content of the queen's library as a basis for her humanist education, but it appears ultimately biased against Isabella. For example, the author's persistent ordering of the monarchs names, with Isabella after Ferdinand, seems to ignore the widely recognized fact that the monarchs were of equal stature during their reign, and that Isabella alone inherited the throne of Castile, while Ferdinand served for over thirty years as her king-consort.

On the other hand, RUBIN relegates Ferdinand to his historically accepted role as consort, while her history concentrates more on Isabella's profile and prominence in matters of state, beginning with the difficult struggle she underwent to prove not only the legitimacy of her claim to the crown of Castile, but also that of her marriage to Ferdinand. Rubin goes into much detail about Isabella's possible state of mind, and therefore her justification for the establishment of the Inquisition in Spain, the final campaign against the Moors in Granada, the expulsion of the Jews from Spain, the reform of religious orders in Spain, and her financing of Columbus in his voyage to the New World. Dynastic worries that beset Isabella and Ferdinand upon the death of their only son and their eldest daughter are covered as well, from the perspective of the queen's suffering and psychological state, based on letters and records of her chroniclers. Indeed, Rubin leads the reader through a fascinating maze of political intrigue and personal triumph followed by grief, and her extensive footnotes and excellent bibliography of primary and secondary sources provide ample evidence of the point she makes: that Isabella was indeed the first Renaissance queen of Europe.

LISS is exhaustively thorough in her depiction of Isabella, her life, and her times. Whereas Rubin seems to rely heavily on accepted lore about Isabella's political and personal circumstances, Liss provides enormously useful background on political climate and maneuvering, which lend greater depth and objectivity to her biography. In such politically intricate details as the preparations for the campaign against the Moors in Granada, and the rivalries and injustices perpetrated by the presence of the Inquisition, Liss is unrivaled in her illumination of a complicated dynamic. Liss's extensive documentation of her work is particularly useful to the serious scholar of historical, political, social, and biographical information pertaining to the life and times of Isabella the Queen.

In discussing the travails that overcame the queen toward the end of her reign, when her demented daughter Juana la Loca was to inherit the Castilian crown, Liss is careful to maintain a balanced narrative that excludes a kind of judgmental and gossipy tone found in writers such as MILLER. While there can be little question that the machinations of the Spanish court in the last half of the fifteenth century provide excellent grist for such a treatment, Miller's repeated references to politically unpopular characters such as Enrique IV, Isabella's half-brother and predecessor, and Juana, La Beltraneja, his presumably illegitimate daughter, in the negative terms legend has assigned them undermines the scholarship in his work.

It is interesting to note that Keen translated MARIEJOL's study a full 70 years after its initial Spanish publication in 1892, the fourth centenary of Isabella's expulsion of the Jews from Spain and her defeat of the Moors at Granada. One of the points that may have led to Keen's translation is the very question of the legitimacy of Isabella's ascendancy to the throne, a question that is glossed over in favor of Isabella in every other biography of the woman whose steadfastness and singularity of purpose wrought enormous change throughout the world. The debate lingers, even in biographies favorable to Isabella, as to whether the change was as righteous as her chroniclers contended when they first recorded significant events of the queen's life.

—HELENA ANTOLIN COCHRANE

Islam *see* Arab Women; Fundamentalism: Islamic

Israeli-Palestinian Conflict

Falbel, Rita, Irena Klepfisz, and Donna Nevel (eds.), *Jewish Women's Call for Peace: A Handbook for Jewish Women on the Israeli/Palestinian Conflict*, Ithaca, New York: Firebrand, 1990

Hassan, Sana, *Enemy in the Promised Land: An Egyptian Woman's Journey into Israel*, New York: Schocken, 1986

Lipman, Beata, *Israel, The Embattled Land: Jewish and Palestinian Women Talk about Their Lives*, London: Pandora Press, 1988

Sharoni, Simona, *Gender and the Israeli-Palestinian Conflict: The Politics of Women's Resistance*, Syracuse, New York: Syracuse University Press, 1995

Stern, Geraldine, *Israeli Women Speak Out*, Philadelphia: Lippincott, 1979

Swirski, Barbara, and Marilyn P. Safir (eds.), *Calling the Equality Bluff: Women in Israel*, New York: Pergamon Press, 1991

Weinbaum, Batya, *D'ot shel'nasheem b'Israel: Voices of Women in Dialogue on Politics, Religion and Culture in Israel*, Northampton, Massachusetts: YPS, 1990

The participation of women in the Israeli-Palestinian conflict has received significant attention, particularly since the outbreak of the *Intifada*, the popular uprising of Palestinians against the Israeli occupation of the West Bank and Gaza Strip, which began in December 1987 and led to an increase in women's grass-roots activism both locally and internationally. However, it is useful to read some resources that predate the outbreak of that particular moment of the historic conflict. STERN's collection of interviews with Israeli women was inspired by her first visit in 1949. Golda Meir, Shulamit Aloni, Marcia Freedman, and other female "stars" in the male-dominated constellation of political actors speak in these chatty interviews conducted in the mid-1970s. The Aloni interview charts the emergence of the Citizens Rights Party, which later played a great role in championing the cause of the Palestinians during the *Intifada* and beyond. The Freedman interview lays the basis for understanding the later activism of the peace group Women in Black, as Freedman, a daughter of a Zionist who emigrated from New Jersey, explains the rationale for founding a women's political party and for serving in the *Knesset*, to champion women's rights and to place gender issues on the national agenda.

SWIRSKI and SAFIR wrote and collected in this volume essays on such topics as national, religious, and ethnic implications of living in a Jewish state, the concept of equality in a Jewish state, challenging the roots of religious patriarchy, tradition in religion and public policy, change and mate selection among Palestinian women in Israel, women of the kibbutz and moshav movements, Israeli cinema, Israeli feminism, women and work, women in the defense force, and political participation of women beyond Golda Meir. More theoretical, sociological, and far-reaching than the personable interviews in Stern's book, the collection still provides a smattering of personal dimensions, such as a personal discussion of one woman's experience of motherhood in an early kibbutz experiment, alongside more far-reaching and critical articles. Of particular interest for those aiming to understand difficulties in resolving the Israeli-Palestinian dispute from a gender perspective and on the grass-roots level, are Judith Pope's case study of *Na'Amat*, and Hannah Herzog's profile of a female candidate for local office.

HASSAN, who has written with Israeli author Amos Elon, traveled into Israel breaking social taboos as a twenty-five-year-old Harvard graduate student three years before President Anwar Sadat made his historic journey to Jerusalem. Billed as "the first portrait of Israel through Arab eyes," this moving account, which includes interviews with Shimon Peres, Menachem Begin and Ariel Sharon documents life in the back alleys of the Tel Aviv underworld, trips to radical kibbutzim and right wing settlements, and anecdotal stories of everyday lives of rabbis, cabdrivers, prime ministers, prostitutes, and Palestinians struggling to survive in the Jewish state. From a humanistic "inside view," as the young Egyptian poses and passes moving through Israel, this volume documents the criticism the young author got from the Egyptian press, as well as the heralding by the *New York Times*, *Jerusalem Post*, and *Le Monde* for her self-declared, self-styled "peace mission," aimed at building understandings between peoples beyond the wars of their states. The personable anecdotal account is laced with insight and compassion for "the enemy," and thus it can help build bridges in exploration of "the other."

FALBEL, KLEPFISZ and NEVEL bring together women's voices from within the women's peace movement, such as those of Gila Svirsky and Rachel Ostrowitz, discussing the deep fears triggered within Israeli women by the uprising in the Occupied Territories. Women's protest groups are profiled. Facts, fears, and administrative policies are detailed to clarify realities about administrative detention and its applications. Some testimony made at women's conferences is also included, such as speeches by key organizers Dalia Sachs and Nabila Espanioli.

SHARONI is an Israeli feminist and peace activist who teaches peace and conflict resolution. Begun in October 1990, much of her book derives from a scholarly dissertation. She begins with a discussion of the outbreak of the *Intifada*, which served as a major catalyst in women's activism and visibility, both within Israel and in Palestinian territories. She discusses women's sensitivity to being "studied," and quotes extensively from her own primary interviews. She discovered that many female peace activists in Israel admitted that their own activism was prompted by the high visibility of Palestinian women's political involvement in the early stages of the *Intifada*. The volume includes photography, art, and theoretical discussion of the relationship between nationalism, gender, and the Israeli-Palestinian conflict.

LIPMAN is a Jewish feminist, a refugee from Germany who grew up in South Africa where she lived and worked for thirty years. As a journalist, she collected interviews in Hebron and on the West Bank with Geula Cohen, Shoshana Mageri, Miriam Levenger, and other Jewish settlers in the heart of an Arab population. She also explores the army and militarism, Jerusalem, marriage and divorce in religious societies, work, the concept of the pioneer, and a particular kibbutz (Barkai). She ends with "a voice of reason"—a discussion of Peace Now, a call to influence Israeli public opinion to overcome super-nationalism, chauvinism, racism, and Kahanism.

WEINBAUM collected a two-volume series of interviews during the *Intifada*, documenting a cross section of attitudes of women in Israel, expressing a range of public opinion. The voices are of women in dialogue with each other—not only the activists who conducted the Women in Black vigils against the occupation, but also the voices of women who organized counterdemonstrations on the other side of the highway in rural areas, or around the plaza in Jerusalem. The interviewees range in age from women in their early twenties to early seventies, and include life histories, for example, of pioneer kibbutzniks from early socialist families who were standing with Women in Black, as well as of women working in Rape Crisis Centers and the Haifa Women's Center *Isha l'Isha*. Palestinian leader Zahira Kamal describes grass-roots work with women in the territories.

—BATYA WEINBAUM

J

Jewish Women

Baskin, Judith R. (ed.), *Jewish Women in Historical Perspective,* Detroit: Wayne State University Press, 1991

——— (ed.), *Women of the Word: Jewish Women and Jewish Writing,* Detroit: Wayne State University Press, 1994

Bernstein, Deborah (ed.), *Pioneers and Homemakers: Jewish Women in Pre-State Israel,* Albany: State University of New York Press, 1992

Davidman, Lynn, and Shelly Tenenbaum (eds.), *Feminist Perspectives on Jewish Studies,* New Haven, Connecticut, and London: Yale University Press, 1994

Fishman, Sylvia Barack, *A Breath of Life: Feminism in the American Jewish Community,* New York: Free Press, 1993

Hyman, Paula, *Gender and Assimilation in Modern Jewish History: The Roles and Representations of Women,* Seattle: University of Washington Press, 1995

Kaplan, Marion, *The Making of the Jewish Middle Class: Women, Family, and Identity in Imperial Germany,* New York and Oxford: Oxford University Press, 1991

Kuzmack, Linda Gordon, *Woman's Cause: The Jewish Woman's Movement in England and the United States, 1881–1933,* Columbus: Ohio State University Press, 1990

The feminist critiques of traditional understandings of Jewish societies, religion, and culture, which have emerged during the last two decades, are primarily the work of the increasing numbers of women who have entered various fields of Jewish scholarship in recent years, and reflect their receptivity to the concurrent growth of women's studies scholarship. The analytical essays in DAVIDMAN and TENENBAUM, which are rich in bibliography, examine the impact of these feminist perspectives, so far, on such Jewish studies specialties as biblical studies, rabbinics, theology, philosophy, history, sociology, anthropology, and literature, and find mixed results. Despite significant advances in several fields, authors suggest that a continuing lack of integration of feminist perspectives in such areas as rabbinics, Jewish philosophy, and sociology has to do with the conservative and almost hermetic nature of these specialties, as well as with traditionally negative Jewish attitudes toward women's involvement in intellectual pursuits.

Historical studies, on the other hand, has been a particularly rich area of research on Jewish women. BASKIN's pioneering collection of 12 essays (1991), which range from the biblical period to the Holocaust and the contemporary United States, provides amply substantiated investigations by major scholars of the lives and experiences of Jewish women, in a format accessible to undergraduates and general readers. The essays, most of which were written specifically for the volume, provide overviews of the periods in question, and go on to explore the general situations of Jewish women and their activities in the Jewish community, as well as in the larger non-Jewish cultural environment. BERNSTEIN's anthology collects essays on the neglected topic of the lives of Jewish women who joined the Zionist movement of the late nineteenth and early twentieth centuries. These essays detail the efforts of these women to participate in establishing an economically viable Jewish political entity, despite overwhelming physical hardships and constant gender discrimination.

KAPLAN's volume is a significant contribution to Jewish historiography. While previous scholarship has chronicled German Jews in the period between 1871 and World War I, a crucial chapter in Western Jewry's continuing confrontation with the conflicting demands of modernity and tradition, Kaplan is the first to consider closely the distinctive parts women played in the painful acculturation process. Utilizing memoirs, contemporary journalism, popular literature, cookbooks, and interviews, alongside more traditional historical sources, she demonstrates that German Jewish women defined their identities in domestically centered religious and ethnic terms, while the men in their lives were striving for political and economic integration into German society. Kaplan divides her study into two parts, the first of which centers on female activities in the home, the center of Jewish bourgeois aspirations. The second half discusses Jewish women's confrontation with academia and the workplace, where sexism was often as problematic as anti-Semitism, and also details Jewish women's involvement in charitable and social welfare organizations.

In an important and provocative study including western and central Europe, eastern Europe, and the United States, HYMAN, a leading scholar of Jewish women's history, examines how varying conceptions of gender have shaped Jewish responses to the socioeconomic and ideological challenges of modernity over the past 150 years. Arguing the centrality of women's experiences to any understanding of Jewish accommodations to modernity, Hyman persuasively shows that the processes of acculturation and assimilation have been quite different for women and men in the various Jewish milieus under consideration, and argues that modern Jewish identity has been wrought, as well, on the battleground of internal sexual politics.

KUZMACK's volume compares and contrasts Jewish feminist movements and their leaders in England and the United States between 1881 and 1933, emphasizing those women whose feminist activities directly affected the Jewish community in such areas as social reform, feminist trade unionism, women's suffrage, welfare activities, and agitation for religious change. As Kaplan also observes, Jewish women's organizations were a way of transforming religious values into social service, and they ultimately moved middle-class women toward feminist politics and a voice in the public arena in eras before they had the vote.

The 16 chapters in BASKIN's collection (1994), like several essays in Davidman and Tenenbaum's book, testify to the impact of feminist literary theory on analyses of prose and poetic literature by or about Jewish women, in languages including English, Yiddish, Hebrew, and Spanish. A number of authors in Baskin's collection concentrate special attention on literary depictions of mother/daughter relationships, female adolescence and sexuality, and the negative consequences of male domination for female expression, as well as on women's assumption of the prophetic voice. Several essays point to the painful choices forced on writers living in Jewish cultures hostile to female literary aspirations, who experienced the double alienation of being Jews in inhospitable cultural environments, a recurring subtext in writing by and about Jewish women.

FISHMAN presents a comprehensive and accessible assessment of the impact of feminism on the contemporary American Jewish community, drawing on interviews, demographic data, scholarly studies, literature, and popular culture. The first half of her book is concerned with the repercussions of the revolutionary changes in technology, social attitudes, and economic expectations since World War II, which affect virtually all women, feminists or not. The issue for Jewish feminists, according to Fishman, is how feminism can help the American Jewish community respond meaningfully to a society that is in a seemingly continuous state of flux. The second half of Fishman's well-documented study addresses more directly the impact of feminism on Jewish religious practice, and in Jewish communal organizations, describing the radical transformations being wrought by a broad range of Jewish women, who have begun to seek equal participation and access in a tradition that has rarely considered women as central figures in its history, thought, religious practice, or communal life.

—JUDITH R. BASKIN

See also Holocaust; Israeli-Palestinian Conflict

Jhabvala, Ruth Prawer 1927–

Indian Writer

Agarwal, Ramlal G., *Ruth Prawer Jhabvala: A Study of Her Fiction,* New York: Envoy, 1990

Crane, Ralph J., *Ruth Prawer Jhabvala,* New York: Twayne, 1992

———(ed.), *Passages to Ruth Prawer Jhabvala,* New Delhi: Sterling, 1991

Gooneratne, Yasmine, *Silence, Exile and Cunning: The Fiction of Ruth Prawer Jhabvala,* London: Sangam, 1983; New Delhi: Orient Longman, 1991

Jha, Rekha, *The Novels of Kamala Markandaya and Ruth Jhabvala,* New Delhi: Prestige, 1990

Shahane, Vasant A., *Ruth Prawer Jhabvala,* New Delhi: Arnold-Heinemann, 1976

Sucher, Laurie, *The Fiction of Ruth Prawer Jhabvala: The Politics of Passion,* London: Macmillan, and New York: St. Martin's Press, 1989

Williams, Haydn Moore, *The Fiction of Ruth Prawer Jhabvala,* Calcutta: Writers Workshop, 1973

Ruth Prawer Jhabvala's work has been the subject of a great deal of critical attention both in India and elsewhere. The listings here are representative only of the range of books in the field, and it should be noted that much of the finest critical work on Jhabvala has appeared in the form of journal articles. What is evident in the journals but not in the books is the way Indian critics seem to be divided into two camps: those who view Jhabvala's work positively (as do all those who have written book-length studies) and those who see her presentation of India as monstrously distorting. In the west, however, no such polarity is apparent, and critical attention paid to Jhabvala's work has generally been favorable.

WILLIAMS's short book is one of the earliest serious studies of Jhabvala's fiction. Though now over 20 years old, it remains a useful early introduction to Jhabvala's first six novels. Approaching the novels chronologically, Williams draws attention to such recurring themes as the joint-family, marriage, and the expatriate in India, and highlights the influence of Jane Austen on her writing. SHAHANE's book, the first full-length critical study of Jhabvala's work, is useful on an introductory level, and provides an early Indian assessment of Jhabvala's fiction, where Williams's study provides a western one.

AGARWAL's book, though published in 1990, makes no use of scholarship after 1976, and is thus best considered alongside the earlier studies by Williams and Shahane. Overall it is a disappointing survey, which tends to discuss Jhabvala's work up to *Heat and Dust* on the basis of plot summaries. However, the appendices include an important early interview with Jhabvala, originally published in *Quest* in 1974, in which she talks about literary influences and her attitude to India.

GOONERATNE is one of the best known and most respected critics of Jhabvala's work. This excellent chronological survey, now published in a revised second edition, is the most comprehensive study to date of Jhabvala's fiction and her writing for the cinema, and promises to be the classic critical assessment of her work. The book begins with a detailed exploration of Jhabvala's unusual background and her position as an insider/outsider in India. This identity is used to demonstrate how, rather than presenting a negative portrait of India in her fiction (as she has been accused of doing by various Indian critics), Jhabvala is frequently the object of her own ironic analysis. In particular, Gooneratne's chapter on Jhabvala's writing for film is interesting for the way it reveals the symbiotic relationship that exists between her fiction writing and screenplays, perhaps most perfectly realized in the novel *Heat and Dust*.

SUCHER's book is another valuable contribution to Jhabvala studies, and one that diverges from the more common chronological approaches to Jhabvala's work. Sucher offers a close reading of four novels—*A New Dominion*, *Heat and Dust*, *In Search of Love and Beauty*, and *Three Continents*—and a number of related stories that she sees as the maturest statements of Jhabvala's preferred themes: the tragi-comedies of self-deception, and the loss and shedding of illusions. Approaching the fiction from a clear feminist perspective, Sucher highlights the way Jhabvala's fiction focuses on the lives of isolated young women who are frequently engaged in a quest for love and beauty. The connection Jhabvala makes between wandering and the Gothic sense of sexuality, Sucher believes, makes her, despite her Austenish irony, a direct literary descendent of Charlotte Brontë.

JHA's solid thematic study examines various manifestations of the East-West encounter in the works of Ruth Prawer Jhabvala and Kamala Markandaya. Although not by any measure a feminist study, Jha's book does include considerable discussion of the female characters in Jhabvala's fiction. The impact of western culture on Indian women is explored, as is the impact of India on the western heroines of her fiction. And implicit in the study as a whole is an interest in the roles of daughter, wife, mother, daughter-in-law, and mother-in-law in the Indian context.

CRANE (1992) provides a clear introduction to Jhabvala's fiction up to *Three Continents*. He begins his study with a biographical overview that places considerable weight on Jhabvala's complex triple heritage, and goes on to examine in separate chapters the early, middle, and late Indian novels, the short stories, and the American novels, before concluding with a chapter on critical responses to Jhabvala's work.

CRANE has also edited a collection of 10 critical essays (1991) that treat the range of Jhabvala's writing to *Three Continents* from a variety of perspectives. While most of the essays are celebratory, they are not uncritically so. Joanne Tompkins, for example, argues that the Eurocentrism in Jhabvala's work constantly sabotages her writing, and leaves her vulnerable to accusations of being anti-Indian. And in her essay on *Three Continents*, Feroza Jussawalla argues that Jhabvala's representation of Indians is so shocking and outrageous that one must question it in the strongest possible terms. Paul Sharrad, on the other hand, in a very strong essay on *A Backward Place*, cautions against such negative judgments, arguing instead for the ambiguity in Jhabvala's work. He suggests that in *A Backward Place*, the backward place of the title may not be India itself, but the expatriate enclave at the heart of the novel. Elsewhere in the collection Jhabvala is seen as a novelist in the Austen tradition, a writer who writes in the manner of E.M. Forster, and an author who shares themes in common with Saul Bellow. The range of opinions represented here makes this is a noteworthy contribution to the body of Jhabvala criticism.

—RALPH J. CRANE

Jiang Qing 1914–1991

Chinese Political Leader

Li Zhisui, *The Private Life of Chairman Mao*, London: Chatto and Windus, and New York: Random House, 1994

Terrill, Ross, *Madame Mao: The White-Boned Demon*, London: Heinnemann, and New York: Morrow, 1984; revised edition, New York: Simon and Schuster, 1992

Witke, Roxane, *Comrade Chiang Ch'ing*, Boston: Little Brown, 1972; London: Weidenfeld and Nicolson, 1977

As the wife of China's Chairman Mao Zedong and a "leading comrade" of the Chinese Communist Party, Jiang Qing (also known as Chiang Ch'ing) once stood at the pinnacle of power in the world's most populous nation. Despite her position, little was known in the west of her life and career until after Mao's death in 1976. The books discussed here provide varying images of a woman whose role remains contentious, just as her relationship to her powerful husband remains the focus of considerable speculation.

Among the few English-language sources available today is WITKE's book, unique among all sources on Jiang Qing in that it is based on a week-long series of personal interviews conducted at Jiang Qing's own request in 1972. Witke allows us to hear Jiang interpret Mao's vision of China, as well as to follow Jiang's account of her difficult early life and her rise to a position of great influence in China by 1966.

Her story was revealed in pieces to Witke, who sought to reconstruct Jiang Qing's life in chronological order. Many of the basic facts of her life are here. Born in 1914 in Shandong province, Jiang and her mother did not find favor in the extended household of her father, Li Dewen, and the two left when Jiang Qing—then known as Li Yunhe—was still a child. Forced to rely on their own limited resources, Jiang Qing only attended school intermittently, learning early that females without male protection paid heavily in China's still strongly patriarchal society. By age fifteen, she began training as an actor, gravitating to the theater world of Shanghai, where she began her acting career. In 1933, she joined the Communist Party, a move that, according to her own account, finally led her to the Communist base at Yanan in 1937. Her story as related to Witke provides little detail on her life at Yanan or on her meeting with and subsequent marriage to Mao. Instead, she emphasized her own struggle to learn through experience and her participation in events that led to the Communist victory in 1949.

Equally self-serving is her account of her career after 1949. Ill for much of the 1950s and periodically in Moscow for treatment, she emerged into the limelight in the 1960s when, again according to the version given to Witke, she began working as a fighter for Mao's ideas, "defying the masculine dominance of history." Her now-infamous role in China's Great Proletarian Revolution from 1966 to 1976 was still in progress at the time Witke interviewed her and, as Witke is clearly aware, colored much of Jiang's account of her life and activities.

At the end of the lengthy text (478 pages in all), Witke raises one of the most important questions about Jiang: Was it because of her marriage to Mao that she was in a position of power, or had she in fact won the right to be called a "leading comrade" through her own efforts? Witke suggests that Jiang Qing not only attained her status through her own struggle, but also that she came close to attaining ultimate power, only to be out-maneuvered by the opposition at the eleventh hour.

Although Witke's book was the most authoritative source when it was first published, other aspects of this complex woman's life were missing. TERRILL seeks to provide new details that place Jiang Qing and her career in quite a different light. Unlike Witke's scholarly account, Terrill writes for a broader audience. His style incorporates reconstructed incidents and dialogue as well as thoughts ascribed to Jiang Qing. There are no footnotes, itself an indication that this is not intended as a scholarly work. However, the 1992 edition includes a bibliographic note identifying many of the sources for his study; additional sources are indicated in the reference notes at the end of the text. Terrill clearly owes a great deal to Witke, whose book is the un-named source of many of the incidents in his account.

Terrill's original version drew a good deal of criticism for its erotic content. The most lurid examples are in the section on Jiang's life before Mao, when Jiang Qing, then known as Lan Ping, was an aspiring actor in Shanghai. Originally discounted by many scholars, some of his assertions about her private life are now considered to be accurate. For example, Jiang entered into a short-lived but well-publicized marriage to Tang Na, an important art critic in Shanghai. Terrill's source was revealed only in the 1992 edition of his book and proved to be Tang Na himself, adding credence to Terrill's other assertions about her early life, including her two other marriages and numerous affairs.

Terrill's portrayal of Jiang Qing after 1949 continues to mix gossip and rumor with documentable events. Jiang emerges as a quarrelsome hypochondriac, increasingly distanced from her husband who, according to Terrill, turned to a series of younger women, "nurses" and private secretaries, who displaced her. Far from being a strong political leader of China's revolution, Mao's wife of 38 years is depicted by Terrill as greedy for power denied her and anxious that she not be cast aside by her aging lothario husband. Only her embrace of the violent Cultural Revolution and her alliance with Mao's closest followers gave her temporary power, which, in Terrill's view, was doomed to end with her husband's death. Unrepentant and defiant to the end, her 1991 suicide in a Beijing prison hospital barely made the Chinese newspapers, signaling to some her ultimate insignificance.

The most damning portrait of Jiang Qing, however, appeared with the publication of the autobiographical account of Mao's personal physician, LI. This remarkable, lengthy book (649 pages) was written in the United States, by a man in self-imposed exile. Dr. Li was a bitter man, still burdened by the demands imposed on him over many years of service in a cause he increasingly despised—preserving the life of a man he came to loath. Likewise, he came to hate Mao's wife, variously depicting her as petty, conniving, tyrannical, cowardly, whining, manipulative, and ultimately, vengeful and cruel. Dr. Li confirmed that Mao and his wife had little to do with each other in the 1950s, and that she was, indeed, replaced by younger women who catered to Mao's sexual needs despite the chairman's deteriorating health and advancing age. Although Jiang Qing finally emerged as a "leading comrade" after 1966, observers like Dr. Li who hated and feared her credit her with no achievements other than snaring Mao as a husband and thereby assuring herself a life of privilege and luxury as well as access to power.

Was Jiang Qing more than the sum of these partial accounts? Certainly her power between 1966 and 1976 was vast, and all three authors concur that as Mao lay dying she was marshalling her supporters in a probable bid for leadership. Thus, whatever the truth of her Shanghai years and her relationship with Mao, she was a person of consequence in the history of revolutionary China.

—LINDA BENSON

Joan of Arc 1412–1431

French National Heroine and Saint

Barstow, Anne Llewellyn, *Joan of Arc: Heretic, Mystic, Shaman,* Lewiston, New York: Edwin Mellen Press, 1986

Berents, Dirk Arend (ed.), *Joan of Arc: Reality and Myth,* Hilversum: Verloren, 1994

Guillemin, Henri, *Joan, Maid of Orleans,* translated by Harold J. Salemson, New York: Saturday Review Press, 1973

Margolis, Nadia, *Joan of Arc in History, Literature, and Film: A Select, Annotated Bibliography,* New York: Garland, 1990

Scott, Walter Sidney, *Jeanne d'Arc: Her Life, Her Death, and the Myth,* New York: Barnes and Noble, 1974

Warner, Marina, *Joan of Arc: The Image of Female Heroism,* New York: Knopf, and London: Weidenfeld and Nicolson, 1981

Wheeler, Bonnie, and Charles T. Wood (eds.), *Fresh Verdicts on Joan of Arc,* New York: Garland, 1996

Wooster, Nora, *The Real Joan of Arc?* Sussex: Book Guild, 1992

Literally thousands of scholarly and popular studies have been written on Joan of Arc over the centuries, as she has been labeled a saint and a witch, a heroine and a lunatic, and an example of the best of "masculine" and "feminine" traits. Joan has been both an attractive and repugnant character to feminist scholars, who admire her life and integrity but shy away from her militarism and her "voices."

MARGOLIS has done an admirable job of sorting out the most reliable sources—and pointing out the most revealing of the decidedly unreliable. Although no longer up-to-date, Margolis's book is a wide-ranging and helpfully annotated bibliography, covering more than 1,400 sources in many languages on history, literature, and cinema. The section on "Feminist Perspectives, Women's History" includes feminist treatments of Joan of Arc from that of the medieval Christine de Pizan to that of Andrea Dworkin. "Special/Controversial Topics" include the bastardy theory and studies of witchcraft. There is also a chronology, an extensive cross-listing, and a brief summary of the issue covered by each section. This volume is an excellent beginning point for what is called "Johannic studies."

The best study of the entire Joan of Arc phenomenon, including the biography and Joan's significance through the ages, is the book by WARNER. With a thorough text supplemented by a chronology, a map of France during Joan's military campaigns, and dozens of color and black-and-white illustrations, Warner illuminates Joan of Arc's objective biography and mythic legacy. For Warner, Joan of Arc fascinates because she obtained immortality as a woman operating in spheres not normally open to women, and because the ways she has been interpreted through the ages reveal much about the ages themselves.

Another important biography is the objective and highly readable one by GUILLEMIN. The author carefully dissects the legends of Joan and attempt to find the true story of her life. He believes that Joan was manipulated by a French court that exploited her and then cast her aside when her zeal for battle was no longer useful, arguing that Joan's "voices," although she sincerely believed in their divine origin, were hallucinations produced by her youth and brilliance.

SCOTT provides an excellent biography with several illustrations and maps that make Joan's fifteenth-century world accessible to the nonhistorian. Like the other major biographers, Scott tells the story of Joan from birth to death, and on through her rehabilitation from heretic to saint. Much of the account is based on original documents. While little in this volume is startling or controversial, the study is solid, reliable, and scholarly.

Among the most engaging of the many alternative biographies of Joan is that by WOOSTER, a frankly subjective and enthusiastic tribute. Wooster, whose background is in crystallography, resurrects the theories that Joan's voices were hallucinations caused by a tuberculoma near her brain, and that Joan and Charles VII were brother and sister.

A decade after Warner's book was published, the author and three colleagues revisited the ideas of the book in a symposium; BERENTS's collection is the resulting volume, comprising four illustrated essays of historical criticism. Dick de Boer examines depictions of Joan in comic books and plays to show the extent of her hold on the popular imagination, Jan van Herwaarden shows the significance of contemporary accounts of Joan's appearance, and Dick Berents compares the real Joan with Claude des Armoises, a Joan pretender. Finally, in "Joan of Arc: A Gender Myth," Warner examines Joan's connections to witchcraft and the supernatural, and her cross-dressing, observing efforts, even by her admirers, to "reform" her.

WHEELER and WOOD provide a collection of 18 essays, covering the central controversies including Joan's voices and visions, her understanding of her own life, her use of language, her physical health, and her dressing in men's clothing. Of particular note are Susan Schibanoff's "True Lies: Transvestism and Idolatry in the Trial of Joan of Arc," which traces Joan's rehabilitation as an object suitable for male heterosexual desire in the twentieth century, and Deborah Fraioli's "Why Joan of Arc Never became an Amazon," refuting the recent claims that popularity of the Amazons in medieval France was an asset to Joan.

Part of the series of "Studies in Women and Religion," BARSTOW offers the first full-length feminist study that is primarily historical, not biographical. After a helpful introduction to late medieval popular religion, specifically mysticism, Barstow considers Joan as a mystic, as a shaman, as a heretic, and as a witch. An important reason for feminists' difficulty with her story, she concludes, is that the central lesson of Joan's life is that women should ignore their inner voices and listen to male authority instead.

—CYNTHIA A. BILY

Jordan, Barbara 1936–1996

American Politician

Bryant, Ira, *Barbara Charline Jordan: From the Ghetto to the Capitol,* Houston: Armstrong, 1977

Jeffrey, Laura S., *Barbara Jordan: Congresswoma:, Lawyer, Educator,* Springfield: Enslow, 1997

Johnson, Linda Carlson, *Barbara Jordan: Congresswoman,* Woodbridge, Connecticut: Blackbirch Press, 1990

Barbara Charline Jordan is an example of how excellence rises to the top. Jordan, born in a poor, all-black Houston, Texas, ghetto, is most known for her role in the impeachment hearings against President Richard Nixon. Jordan was also a lawyer and constitutional scholar, friend of legendary Texas politicians Sam Rayburn, Lyndon Johnson, and Ann Richards (who were Speaker of the United States House of Representatives, President of the United States, and Governor of Texas, respectively), and one of the most powerful African-American female (or male) politicians of the twentieth century.

BRYANT suggests that Barbara Jordan's rise to prominence was even more amazing than usual because of who she was and from where she came. Jordan was born only four years after blacks were allowed to vote in Texas (1932), grew up using textbooks 10 or more years behind the times (not being allowed to use public library or other educational advantages), and went to an all black and inferior undergraduate college. These barriers had kept many other qualified people of color from succeeding. Bryant believes that Jordan's rise is a story for all people as well as for people of color. In Texas, Jordan won the admiration of some of the most difficult and narow white men in power. Through her self-confidence and her belief that the political system of her state and nation could be made to serve all people, she stands as a role model for many in difficult circumstances.

JOHNSON argues that Jordan early learned that as a black and as a woman, she had two barriers to scale. But on her way to removing these barriers she also knew how to have fun. Jordan liked to dance and sing. She liked to play the guitar and go out with friends to the movies. Her solid family and relational base, along with firm rootage in the Baptist Church, provided her with the balance she did not often have in her public life. She wanted everyone who met her to know that Barbara Jordan was a lady. Jordan believed that she could get what she wanted and not have to give up her femininity or ethical base. Jordan as a politician and as a professor remembered to be strong and gracious. This gentle strength was at the very core of her political and public strength.

JEFFREY focuses on young readers. Jeffrey believes that one of Jordan's legacies is as a positive model for young people. Jeffrey wants younger people to develop the profound belief in democracy that Jordan kept all of her life. This desire is particularly important for African-American youth, because Jordan came from the same environment as many of these young people. Jordan's accomplishments include achieving the Presidential Medal of Freedom (1994), serving as an advisor to governors and presidents, and having a well-known school at the University of Texas named after her.

—PAUL BARTON-KRIESE

Judaism

Biale, Rachel, *Women and Jewish Law: An Exploration of Women's Issues in Halakhic Sources,* New York: Schocken, 1984

Boyarin, Daniel, *Carnal Israel: Reading Sex in Talmudic Culture,* Berkeley: University of California Press, 1993

Frankiel, Tamar, *The Voice of Sarah: Feminine Spirituality and Traditional Judaism,* San Francisco: Harper, 1990

Grossman, Susan, and Rivka Haut (eds.), *Daughters of the King: Women and the Synagogue,* Philadelphia: Jewish Publication Society, 1992

Heschel, Susannah (ed.), *On Being a Jewish Feminist: A Reader,* New York: Schocken, 1983

Plaskow, Judith, *Standing Again at Sinai: Judaism from a Feminist Perspective,* San Francisco: Harper and Row, 1990

Rudavsky, Tamar M. (ed.), *Gender and Judaism: The Transformation of Tradition*, New York: New York University Press, 1995

Sered, Susan, *Women as Ritual Experts: The Religious Lives of Elderly Jewish Women in Jerusalem*, New York and Oxford: Oxford University Press, 1992

Most past Jewish societies have followed the principles of rabbinic Judaism, an all-encompassing way of life mandating separate and unequal roles and responsibilities for men and women. This male-centered system offered protection and respect to women who complied with its customs, but put women at a legal disadvantage in a number of crucial personal status areas. Over the past 200 years, as Western Jewry has confronted modernity, more adaptive, liberal forms of Judaism have also developed, which have eliminated or moderated traditional Judaism's biases against women in legal, religious, communal, and intellectual domains.

BIALE's well-documented volume is an excellent introduction to women's position in traditional rabbinic (Orthodox) Judaism as it has evolved over time. Biale examines marriage, divorce, marital relations, menstruation, sexuality outside of marriage, procreation and contraception, abortion, and rape, the issues in which women primarily figure in rabbinic jurisprudence; she also includes a chapter on women's legal and religious obligations as human beings. Biale believes that traditional Jewish law has shown many historical adaptations to new realities, and hopes that Jewish women who become adept in its complexities will be able to play a part in ameliorating women's position in Orthodox communities today.

BOYARIN's influential examination of the ideology of sexuality, gender, and the body in rabbinic Judaism is also written with an eye toward the feminist restructuring of sex and gender in contemporary Judaism. Situating his scholarship at the nexus of rabbinic textuality and critical discourse, Boyarin reads the delineations of the body and sexuality in the rabbinic Judaism of late antiquity against the formulations of Christianity, arguing that Judaism invested significance in the body, while Christianity privileged the soul. Resisting designations of formative Judaism as misogynistic, Boyarin suggests that its androcentric interpreters accepted the body, whether male or female, as an essential human feature, but found it necessary to impose and maintain a social hierarchy based on male dominance to meet social needs for sexual expression, progeny of clear lineage, and provision of household services.

GROSSMAN and HAUT concentrate their useful collection of essays on the role of the synagogue in Jewish women's lives. The volume is divided into three parts, which explore what is known about the history of Jewish women's participation in communal worship from ancient times to the modern period; the legal issues and practices connected with women and public prayer in Orthodox Judaism, and their revision in more liberal forms of Jewish practice (Conservative, Reform, and Reconstructionist); and the contemporary realities of late twentieth-century Jewish life as they affect women's roles in the synagogue. The book's final section is enhanced by a series of personal vignettes from a wide variety of women, including rabbis and cantors, whose professions have been available for women only in recent decades.

SERED's important anthropological study deals with the Judaism of elderly, Middle Eastern women, primarily illiterate and impoverished widows, now living in Jerusalem. She portrays her subjects as part of a long female-oriented tradition that developed ways to sacralize and enrich women's lives religiously, despite their exclusion from male participation in synagogue ritual and Jewish learning. This "women's" Judaism, which Sered calls the "little" tradition, as opposed to the "great" tradition of normative, male-centered Judaism, is primarily oriented to human relationships, and Sered demonstrates how women become expert at filling the everyday female sphere with sacred meaning.

Jewish feminism has brought both religious renewal and bitter controversy to contemporary Judaism. HESCHEL's reader is a central document of the continuing struggle for egalitarianism in Jewish religious and communal life. Divided into three parts, the essays by influential scholars and activists explore traditional images of women in the Jewish past, describe contemporary women's efforts to forge new identities in a number of Jewish settings, and chronicle ongoing efforts to create a feminist theology of Judaism.

PLASKOW is the central figure in Jewish feminist theology. Her provocative book insists that feminists must move beyond their study of women's status in Jewish law and their demands for legal and institutional equality in Judaism as presently constituted. Rather, she calls for an exposure of the origins of women's oppression in the core of Judaism itself, arguing that the otherness of women is a presupposition embedded in Judaism in countless ways, not least in the identification of God with "masculine" attributes. For Plaskow, the future of Judaism demands transformations of the basic Jewish theological concepts—God, divine revelation, and the believing community—in directions that recognize the full and equal humanity of all Jews, that reflect and voice the female experience, and that reintegrate the female aspects of the divine into Jewish conceptions of the Godhead.

Not all Jewish women have embraced a feminist Judaism. FRANKIEL offers an eloquent defense of the spiritual benefits of women's role in traditional Judaism, which she believes has always recognized and celebrated inherent male-female differences in perception, abilities, and contributions. In her view, Orthodox Judaism nurtures these gender-based distinctions by prescribing domestic roles for women that emphasize female qualities of connection, relationship, and responsibility. Although she is convinced of the validity of traditional Jewish law, Frankiel looks toward a future where women's Jewish education will be of the same quality as men's, and where women's spiritual impact will be recognized and appreciated.

The essays in RUDAVSKY's lively collection are divided into four general categories based on disciplinary approach: theoretical concerns, emphasizing gendered critiques of traditional Jewish texts and practice; historical investigations of women and Judaism from a variety of times and locales from the early modern period to the present; literary studies of female Jewish writers and of female imagery in Jewish mysticism; and social scientific analyses of such topics as Jewish feminism as a geopolitical movement, the role of women in the rabbinate, the complexities of modern Jewish women's lives, and images of Jewish masculinity in popular culture. These essays offer an engaging introduction to the transformative impact of feminism and gender studies on Judaism and Jewish studies scholarship.

—JUDITH R. BASKIN

See also Jewish Women

Julian of Norwich 1343–1416?

English Anchoress, Mystic, and Writer

Baker, Denise Nowakowski, *Julian of Norwich's "Showings" from Vision to Book,* Princeton, New Jersey: Princeton University Press, 1994

Heimmel, Jennifer P., *"God is Our Mother": Julian of Norwich and the Medieval Image of Christian Feminine Divinity,* Salzburg: Institut für Anglistik und Amerikanistik, 1982

Jantzen, Grace, *Julian of Norwich: Mystic and Theologian,* London: S.P.C.K., 1987; New York: Paulist Press, 1988

Llewelyn, Robert (ed.), *Julian: Woman of Our Day,* London: Darton, Longman and Todd, 1985; Mystic, Connecticut: Twenty-Third Publications, 1987

Pelphrey, Brant, *"Love Was His Meaning": The Theology and Mysticism of Julian of Norwich,* Salzburg: Institut für Anglistik und Amerikanistik, 1982

Vinje, Patricia, *An Understanding of Love According to the Anchoress Julian of Norwich,* Salzburg: Institut für Anglistik und Amerikanistik, 1982

Although a woman of the Middle Ages, Julian of Norwich has been increasingly studied in recent times. Current focus on feminist theology, on female ways of seeing and having a relationship with the divine, has caused theologians, literary scholars, and laypersons alike to investigate the writings of this woman who wrote only two works, both based upon one 12-hour period of visions she experienced following a near-fatal illness. These works are variously entitled the shorter and longer versions of *A Book of Showings, Divine Revelations,* or *Revelations of Divine Love.* Julian is most famous for her portrayal of Christ as a nurturant female. The following book-length sources do not include several that discuss Julian along with other mystics, or critical editions of her writing that include extensive introductory materials. Those that are listed here all treat Julian very positively but differ in their portrayal of her, as either a simple vessel of God, or as a literary sophisticate with a strong education in Christian writings.

PELPHREY's volume was originally his doctoral thesis, and it was one of the first full-length critical studies of Julian. He provides good biography and historical background, places Julian's visions and writings into their religious context, and analyzes extensively her *Revelations* themselves. The quotations from Julian's works are in Middle English, as are all of those in the Salzburg series. The author presents the two possibilities, either that Julian was well-educated or that she was illiterate, although he does argue that, in either case, her works were based on knowledge of the Scriptures, whether gained through study or by hearing them read.

HEIMMEL's work is a shorter, more focused volume, examining primarily the tradition of seeing the feminine attributes of God. Thus, for Heimmel, Julian's writings are not radical in portraying God as female and Christ as mother but draw upon biblical, patristic, and mystical writings for their genesis. According to the author, the theme of the feminine divine unifies Julian's works. The study is scholarly but quite accessible and presents Julian as a self-aware literary artist. Of the three theses from Salzburg, this is the most valuable volume.

Another work in the Salzburg University series, VINJE's study asserts that love is the unifying theme of Julian's work, although it is a theme closely related to motherhood. The author, like Heimmel, discusses Julian's sources but spends less time on them and more on a close reading of Julian's works, particularly her imagery. Vinje sees Julian's brilliance as lying in her simplicity, in the ability to relate lofty concepts in laypersons' terms.

LLEWELYN provides a collection of essays written for laypersons by male and female Catholic clergy, with the chief end of seeing Julian's religion as a model for contemporary spirituality. The essay "Guide for the Inexpert Mystic" is particularly helpful as a starting place for understanding what a mystic is, and why Julian chose the life of an anchoress. The essay also summarizes the basic ideas of her *Revelations* and seems especially geared toward the non-Catholic general reader. The other essays discuss the ways in which Julian conveys a positive message of God's love to her readers.

Written from the point of view of a philosopher of religion, JANTZEN's more academic book is an exhaustive study of Julian's life, doctrine, sources, and writings. Jantzen's quotations from Julian are in modernized English. The author sees Julian as having received at least a limited education and explores especially her theology and mysticism. This well-researched and written volume aims not only at discussing Julian's work in her fourteenth-century context, but also at seeing her views as providing spiritual insight for the twentieth century. Any serious student of Julian needs to consult this study.

BAKER's volume focuses more fully on the literary aspect of Julian's work than any of the other books listed here, as well as probing the tenets of her beliefs. Emphasizing Julian as the first female English writer, as well as the major contributor to the canon of medieval prose, the author views Julian as maturing from a "visionary to a theologian" in the 20-year period that separated the two versions of *A Book of Showings*. The anchoress is presented as a careful thinker and educated person, at many points in her work both influenced by and at odds with Augustine's writings, particularly concerning sin and punishment. This very scholarly study includes an account of Julian's life and the circumstances of her writing, is heavily annotated, and helpfully prints quotations from Julian in both Middle and modern English.

—CAROL BLESSING

Jurisprudence, Feminist

Becker, Mary, Cynthia Grant Bowman, and Morrison Torrey, *Cases and Materials on Feminist Jurisprudence: Taking Women Seriously*, St. Paul, Minnesota: West, 1993

Duggan, Lisa, and Nan D. Hunter, *Sex Wars: Sexual Dissent and Political Culture*, New York: Routledge, 1995

Estrich, Susan, *Real Rape: How the Legal System Victimizes Women Who Say No*, Cambridge, Massachusetts: Harvard University Press, 1987

Fineman, Martha Albertson, *The Neutered Mother, the Sexual Family and Other Twentieth Century Tragedies*, New York: Routledge, 1995

Frug, Mary Joe, *Women and the Law*, Westbury, New York: Foundation Press, 1992

MacKinnon, Catherine, *Feminism Unmodified: Discourses on Life and Law*, Cambridge, Massachusetts: Harvard University Press, 1987

Robson, Ruthann, *Lesbian (Out)law: Survival Under the Rule of Law*, Ithaca, New York: Firebrand, 1992

Weisberg, D. Kelly, *Applications of Feminist Legal Theory to Women's Lives*, Philadelphia: Temple University Press, 1996

Williams, Patricia, *The Alchemy of Race and Rights*, Cambridge, Massachusetts: Harvard University Press, 1991; London: Virago Press, 1993

In recent years, feminist jurisprudence has gained a foothold in law schools and in legal practice. Generally speaking, feminist scholars have critiqued traditional jurisprudence on the grounds that it unselfconsciously developed an abstract, putatively objective, male approach to the law, which rather unobjectively overlooks or distorts practical legal issues that specifically concern women, such as sexual harassment and rape. Feminist jurisprudence seeks to address these omissions and distortions by creating legal theory that takes seriously the concrete experience of women, and that takes into account the political and social realities of sexism.

Several fine overviews of the field are currently in print, including works by Becker, Bowman, and Torrey, Frug, and Weisberg. Each of these works includes detailed discussions of feminist theory, female sexuality, rape, domestic violence, prostitution, pornography, reproductive rights, racism, heterosexism, family matters, work, and the legal profession. BECKER's volume distinguishes itself by offering separate chapters on the history of the women's movement. FRUG's work is structured around four models of feminist theory at the outset (cultural feminism, liberal feminism, radical feminism, and postmodern feminism) and their application to three general areas (work, family, and bodies). WEISBERG uses sex, violence, work, and reproduction as organizing themes.

The work of ESTRICH is a leading example of a feminist challenge to a seemingly settled area of the law, the law that addresses rape. Estrich exposes various ways in which male perspectives regarding sexuality inform rape law. She argues that current legal classifications allow for only certain kinds of rape to be regarded as "real," thus categorizing other rapes as unreal, however real they might seem to women subject to such assault. Estrich's frank discussion of her own rape and her subsequent experience with the legal system inform her critique of the law.

Similarly, MacKINNON was one of the first to challenge the law's male approach to sexual harassment, by devising a theoretical approach that evaluated claims of sexual harassment from the perspective of the "reasonable woman" (rather than the "reasonable man," as was previously the case). Practically speaking, MacKinnon's approach has gained some currency in federal courts in the United States. MacKinnon includes discussions of sexual harassment, rape, abortion, women in sports, and pornography in this volume. Asserting that pornography is harmful to women, MacKinnon argues that affected women should be able to sue for civil damages, regardless of the "chilling effect" that this may have on free speech and press.

Many feminist legal scholars seem to be less than enamored with MacKinnon's approach to pornography and freedom of speech. DUGGAN and HUNTER disagree sharply with her on this issue. They argue that MacKinnon's approach places far too much faith in the courts, amounting to censorship in the name of feminism, and that it creates "sex panics," which serve to repress other forms of sexual dissidence that are worthy of protection, such as lesbian erotica. Charging that anti-pornography feminists such as MacKinnon have inappropriately created an unholy alliance with the radical right rather than with local feminists, Duggan and Hunter argue that alliances should be made with sexual dissenters of all stripes under the banner of "queer." Rejecting an essentialist understanding of both sexuality and gender, they argue that the law constructs and represses homosexuals and women in a manner that makes political and legal alliances across these categories both possible and desirable.

Rejecting the broad-based coalition approach of Duggan and Hunter, on the grounds that accommodation often leads to colonization of lesbians by heterosexual men and women, as well as by gay men, ROBSON offers a book devoted specifically to lesbian legal theory and practice, claiming to be the first such book of its kind. For Robson, the rule of law is equivalent to the rule of men, and lesbians fall under it. Robson discusses legal theories and strategies for lesbians to manipulate the law as successfully to their advantage as possible, without being destroyed by the law in the process. Topics include sexual privacy, discrimination, the military, immigration, prison, children, violence, and lesbians in the legal profession.

A leader in critical race theory and feminist jurisprudence, WILLIAMS addresses intersections of race, gender, and class in the context of a self-conscious use of a subjective, first-person perspective, which rejects the white, male myth of legal objectivity. Williams discusses various contemporary issues and personalities, including affirmative action, hate speech, and the cases of Tawana Brawley and Bernhard Goetz, in an effort to deconstruct the signs and significations of race, gender, and class in everyday life, thereby revealing the deep-seated bias that informs the law, despite the insistence of white, male, legal experts who continue to insist that the law applies equally to all.

Finally, FINEMAN challenges current legal constructions of the family from a feminist perspective. She argues that the dominant legal representation of family is gendered and heterosexual. Arguing that the law is inherently conservative, Fineman offers a "utopian vision" as an alternative to advocates of both the dominant model and would-be reformers of it (who might try to gain recognition of, for example, same-sex marriage). She argues that legal support for marriage ought to be abolished, thus rendering dependents and the unique contributions of motherhood more visible. She hopes that this will disentangle sexuality from intimacy, equalize sexual relations, and lead to stronger legal support for the basic nurturing unit in this culture, the mother-child dyad.

—SUSAN BURGESS

See also Lawyers

K

Kahlo, Frida 1910–1954

Mexican Painter

Chadwick, Whitney, *Women Artists and the Surrealist Movement,* Boston: Little Brown, and London: Thames and Hudson, 1985
Drucker, Malka, *Frida Kahlo: Torment and Triumph in Her Life and Art,* New York: Bantam, 1991
Franco, Jean, *Plotting Women: Gender and Representation in Mexico,* London: Verso, and New York: Columbia University Press, 1989
Herrera, Hayden, *Frida: A Biography of Frida Kahlo,* New York: Harper and Row, 1983; London: Bloomsbury, 1989
———, *Frida Kahlo: The Paintings,* New York: HarperCollins, and London: Bloomsbury, 1991
Lowe, Sarah M., *Frida Kahlo,* New York: Universe, 1991

One of the fascinating tidbits of Kahlo lore that one learns in reading the books like those in the list above is that Kahlo's painting, "My Birth"—a graphic portrait of Kahlo's adult head emerging from between the legs of a female figure whose head is covered—hangs in the entryway of Madonna's California home. This location for one of Kahlo's most unsettling works makes materially manifest themes that are consistent and unanswered in Kahlo feminist scholarship. What are the effects of making the body's pain the centerpiece of women's experience? Does Kahlo's self-representation (like Madonna's) parody conventional images of women or reinforce them? To what extent has Kahlo's fame been a function of her appropriation by mainstream popular culture?

Many of these questions begin with HERRERA's works. Herrera's eminently readable biography (1983) reintroduced Kahlo to a contemporary audience. Herrera argues that Kahlo's treatment of subjects such as her miscarriages, her birth and the pain of the body—things usually outside of the stuff of art—sets Kahlo apart. Herrera uses the close link between these topics and the details of Kahlo's life to justify her book's psychoanalytic framework, but in doing so fails to take into account the degree of artifice in Kahlo's paintings and in her self-creation. HERRERA's later work (1991) concentrates on the paintings, but retains the premise that Kahlo's work and her art cannot be separated, and that the details of Kahlo's life are facts and not themselves creations.

Herrera's study with its psychoanalytic bent tends to place more emphasis on Kahlo's art as a unique expression of her life experience, and less on her art and personality as continuous with her culture and times. LOWE's book, by contrast, analyzes Kahlo's art in the context of art history, Mexican nationalism, and Aztec and Roman Catholic traditions. Obscure imagery in Kahlo sometimes becomes less exotic (and psychotic) when linked to its referent in Aztec mythology and iconography. The insistence on physical suffering is mitigated when read within the Roman Catholic traditions of the retablo and hagiography—both of which have the convention of graphic suffering. Lowe also places Kahlo's art as part of Mexican nationalism, alongside the murals of her husband, Diego Rivera, and as continuous with surrealism, with its female visionaries.

CHADWICK's book is an interesting study of this final category: Kahlo's relation to the European art movement, surrealism. Chadwick's study is in two parts. The first classifies Kahlo as a surrealist, the second compares her to her female contemporaries also classified as surrealists. The argument classifying Kahlo as a surrealist is weak. Kahlo herself is quoted in Chadwick's book as rejecting this classification: "[Breton may have] thought I was a Surrealist, but I wasn't. I never painted a dream. I painted my own reality." The second half of the analysis—Kahlo's relation to the other female surrealists—is much more interesting in that it discovers motifs common to these (otherwise vastly) different women: the use of the self as model, splitting of self (particularly between inner and outer, watched and watcher), pregnancy, use of animals as familiars, and relation of the female body and nature.

FRANCO's study emphasizes yet another matrix critical to understanding Kahlo: her Mexican heritage. Rather than reading Kahlo strictly through the lens of Mexican nationalism, however, Franco reads her as the last of a number of remarkable Mexican women, each of whom expresses herself vis-à-vis the dominant discourse of her time. This transhistorical study begins with a seventeenth-century nun who presents herself in the discourse of Roman Catholicism and ends with Kahlo, whose discourse is of course, nationalism. Franco notes that nationalism (like Roman Catholicism) relies almost exclusively on masculine iconography. Franco charts Kahlo's use of nationalism's discourse, by comparing Kahlo's early work with Diego Rivera's large murals, and then reading Kahlo's "Moses (the birth of the Hero)." Franco argues that in her early paintings, Kahlo reveals the suffering of the body that has been caused by nationalism. But in her later paintings, particularly in "Moses," Kahlo deletes the figure of the mother and traces the history of the hero through (almost) exclusively male figures, an indication that Kahlo has been captured by the prevailing terms of nationalism, and fails to effectively revise them to express her female experience.

DRUCKER's biography has all the earmarks of an early feminist study: it frames Kahlo as a lost mother for feminist artists; details the wrongs done to her by her culture, her loves, the art world; and catalogues her triumphs. But the work lacks subtlety and lapses into annoying fictionalizations, such as this narrative of what Kahlo called "the first major accident" of her life, the bus crash: "the [bus] drivers were macho and careless, but teenaged Frida, believing she was invincible, never worried about safety." Yet side-by-side with these clichéd readings of Kahlo are others that are complex and insightful. Drucker suggests, for instance, that Kahlo's mixture of independence and disobedience was due to her fear of her mother's iron will, her mother's rejection of Kahlo's two half-sisters, her early polio, and, finally, the bus accident. Often these complex readings are left undeveloped. For example, Drucker cites Kahlo's complex childhood relation to her mother, and in particular her early weaning, as a partial explanation for Kahlo's reworking of the madonna motif in her art.

Continuing interest in Kahlo's work will lead to more investigation into the questions with which this summary began. In particular, new scholarship on Kahlo's homoerotic relationships, the mixed media in her journal, and her relationship with her mother may provide keys to understanding Kahlo's complexities.

—PAMELA SMILEY

Kauffmann, Angelica 1741–1807

Swiss Painter

Hartcup, Adeline, *Angelica: The Portrait of an Eighteenth-Century Artist,* London: William Heinemann, 1954

Manners, Victoria, and G.C. Williamson, *Angelica Kauffmann, R.A., Her Life and Works,* London: John Lane, and New York: Brentano's, 1924

Mayer, Dorothy Moulton Piper, *Angelica Kauffmann, R.A., 1741–1807,* Gerrards Cross, Buckinghamshire: Colin Smythe, 1972

Roworth, Wendy Wassyng (ed.), *Angelica Kauffmann: A Continental Artist in Georgian England,* London: Reaktion, 1992

The literature on Angelica Kauffmann is thin and unfortunately, the scholarship (at least in published book form) tends to be repetitive. The most exciting scholarship on this artist is currently being conducted in shorter, journal-length articles. With the exception of Roworth's exhibition catalogue, the books discussed here are generally disappointing. But insofar as they span the twentieth century, these books chart the changing tastes and attitudes toward the creative production of women artists.

The pretext for MANNERS and WILLIAMSON's biography is the authors' discovery of a manuscript written by the artist herself. In the document, Kauffmann accounts for pictures she painted beginning in 1781, when she left her adopted home of England (where, arguably, she achieved her greatest fame and recognition), until her death in Italy in 1807. The authors contend that with this manuscript, a more accurate record of Kauffmann's oeuvre can be established than heretofore was possible. Thus, within a biographical framework, their project is largely connoisseurial; Manners and Williamson distinguish the works of art they believe are definitely by Kauffmann from copies after Kauffmann's time.

Such a project, which fetishizes originality and authenticity, indicates that the artist/subject is considered important from the perspective of art history. And indeed, the authors go to great lengths to establish for their readers Kauffmann's reknown during her lifetime as well as her enduring fame (for example, they note that her name has become a household word). Tellingly, though, the reasons they give for this are inextricably tied to gender, in such a way that the artist becomes the exception that proves the rule: other female artists (such as Sophonisba Anguisciola [sic], Artemisia Gentileschi, and Elisabetta Sirani) are named and discounted by the authors as forgettable or undeserving of a place in art history. Kauffmann, by contrast, has made her mark. The authors attribute her popularity during her lifetime to her "complete acquiescence in the artistic taste of her own period," to the "refinement and delicacy" of her painting, and to the "essentially feminine note" she struck in her art. Further, they suggest that her personal charm and femininity contributed to her celebrity. All these factors, they contend, created a demand for reproductions—copies—of her art, which in turn assured Kauffmann a place in the annals of art history, whereas other women artists could claim none.

Over a quarter of a century later, HARTCUP finds weaknesses in Kauffmann's art. In fact, she dismisses her history paintings as dead and concludes that Kauffmann was an artist with "small-scale" talent. Hartcup's primary interest is in Kauffmann the person. Writing as if she had been a witness to what she describes, Hartcup capitalizes on her subject's dramatic, soap-operatic personal life. Not surprisingly, perhaps, the patronizing tone the author sets in titling her book informs the entire biography. Like her dismissive manner toward the art, it is indicative of prevailing attitudes toward female artists at mid-century.

Writing in the early 1970s, MAYER achieves a better balance between discussions of the art and the artist. The author seems to have set for herself an unstated but palpable goal of reforming her subject's reputation as a spoiled coquette. Thus, throughout the book, Mayer gives voice to unsubstantiated gossip about Kauffmann's various personal relationships, but she works equally hard to persuade her readers of their falsity. To her credit, Mayer conveys a sense of the celebrity status Kauffmann achieved during her lifetime, and she paints a vivid (if somewhat speculative) picture of the artist's friendships and associations (including with Goethe).

The essays in the exhibition catalogue edited by ROWORTH employ a variety of methodologies to discuss and interpret Kauffmann's artistic production. Here, the person of the artist falls away, and the art is given priority. The shift is significant, for it stands as testament to the reassessment of female artists generally in the last decades of the twentieth century, and to approaches that consider seriously the artistic contributions of women.

Roworth's essay, for example, provides measured, insightful feminist interpretations of selected paintings. The author also delineates the significance of history painting as a genre (with particular attention to its significance in the history of English painting), summarizes the reasons why it was difficult for women to excel in this genre, and then suggests why Kauffmann was in a position to succeed. The reasons include her continental background and training, her study of antique sculpture, her acquaintance with J. J. Winckelmann, and her timely arrival in England just as Joshua Reynolds was promoting the genre of history painting there. Finally, Roworth discusses the critical reception of Kauffmann's paintings, including the perceived "effeminacy" of her male characters, and she offers several explanations for the response Kauffmann's works elicited.

The second essay in Roworth's catalogue, by Angela Rosenthal, surveys Kauffmann's portrait paintings, describing the artist's most characteristic modes, her prices, and the sizes of these works. The third essay, by Malise Forbes Adam and Mary Mauchline, is a connoisseurial, corrective study of Kauffmann's decorative compositions. The essay looks at interiors, furniture, and porcelain pieces that feature Kauffmann's designs and attempts to establish those executed by the artist and those made by copyists based on her designs.

The final essay, on "Kauffmann and the Print Market in Eighteenth-Century England," brings us full circle, back to a thread woven into Manners and Williamson's story. The differences are significant, however. David Alexander begins with a brief history of the reproductive print, and then focuses on Kauffmann's relationship with printmakers and the extent to which demands for prints influenced her artistic production. Thus, in Alexander's essay, Kauffmann is given agency. Far from being the result of what Manners and Williamson called her "acquiescence in the artistic tastes of her own period" (a characterization that constructs Kauffmann as passive), her artistic success is presented by Alexander, writing nearly seventy years later, as a manifestation of the artist's very astute professional acumen and intelligence.

—JO ORTEL

Keller, Helen 1880–1962

American Activist

Brooks, Van Wyck, *Helen Keller: Sketch for a Portrait,* New York: Dutton, and London: J.M. Dent, 1956

Einhorn, Lois J., *Helen Keller, Public Speaker: Sightless but Seen, Deaf but Heard,* Westport, Connecticut: Greenwood, 1996

Harrity, Richard, and Ralph G. Martin, *The Three Lives of Helen Keller,* Garden City, New York: Doubleday, 1962; London: Hodder and Stoughton, 1964

Several major problems face any biographer or critic of Helen Adams Keller. First, Keller herself has written several remarkably eloquent, inspiring autobiographical pieces, notably *The Story of My Life* (1902), *The World I Live In* (1908), and *Helen Keller's Journal* (1938), the reading of which is more rewarding than any biography written about her thus far. Second, because of the dramatic, heartwarming nature of Keller's many Herculean struggles and accomplishments, it is difficult to avoid sentimentality in relating her story. And, finally, the highly popular Pulitzer Prize-winning play, *The Miracle Worker* (1959) by William Gibson, and the award-winning film (1962) made from the play tend to blur those essential lines between life and art, objectivity and subjectivity, making identification of the "real" Helen Keller difficult. Works on Keller tend to fall into two or three general categories: the few written for adult readers, the many produced for young readers, and those written for persons, adult and/or children, with physical handicaps.

The distinguished veteran American literary critic and biographer BROOKS has produced a highly readable volume that contains detailed information not found in Keller's own writing, this material probably drawn from personal interviews with Keller. In spite of what the title implies, Brooks gives a rather comprehensive and compelling account of Keller's life up to the 1950s, stressing the enlightened, well-to-do, Southern background from which Keller came, which, in part, explains the type of person into which she developed. This volume is an excellent, balanced introduction to Keller's life and work.

The book by HARRITY and MARTIN, no doubt intent on capitalizing on the wildly successful reception of *The Miracle Worker*, is a readable, predictable account of Keller's life. This work draws heavily from Keller's own writings, although Harrity and Martin include information made available in the work of John Albert Macy, husband of Keller's determined teacher, Annie Sullivan (1866–1936), who devoted much of her life to teaching Keller and later functioned as Keller's constant companion until her marriage to Macy. Little new light is shed on Keller's personality or behavior in this study, however.

It might seem ironic at first glance to note that EINHORN's volume, so intriguingly titled, is one in a series entitled "Great American Orators." Much of Keller's ability to communicate was based on hand spelling, but also on her touching the vocal bands of the person speaking. Because most people found her own voice difficult to understand, Keller, when addressing an audience, which often consisted of thousands, "spoke" through an interpreter, who would vocalize what she was stating quietly at the podium. Einhorn demonstrates how the content of Keller's speeches, rather than the manner of their delivery, places Keller among the great American orators. This volume manages to be inspiring without being cloying.

Surprisingly, no biographer has pointed out, much less elaborated upon, the impact Annie Sullivan's work with Keller has had on psychology, psychotherapy, and psychoanalysis; for example, Bruno Bettelheim's "milieu therapy" with autistic children, an influence to which Bettelheim himself readily admits in his *Freud's Vienna and Other Essays* (1990). Similarly, no biographer has made much of Keller's early flirtation with socialism, possibly because it does not fit with her all-American image.

—CARLO COPPOLA

Kelley, Florence 1859–1932

American Reformer

Blumberg, Dorothy Rose, *Florence Kelley: The Making of a Social Pioneer*, New York: Augustus M. Kelley, 1966

Goldmark, Josephine, *Impatient Crusader: Florence Kelley's Life Story*, Urbana: University of Illinois Press, 1953

Sklar, Kathryn Kish, *Florence Kelley and the Nation's Work: The Rise of Women's Political Culture, 1830–1900*, New Haven, Connecticut, and London: Yale University Press, 1995

Florence Kelley did much to shape modern America. A tireless advocate of child welfare and economic reform, she worked to remove many of the abuses encouraged by rapid industrialization. Much of her work found fruit in the New Deal. Franklin Roosevelt's legislation establishing the welfare state did not spring full-blown from the minds of his political aides. Many of the laws established at Roosevelt's behest originated with Florence Kelley during the Progressive era. Kelley bears much credit for establishing a minimum wage, for setting maximum working hours, and for demanding laws to protect women and children from harsh labor practices and unsafe working conditions. Most of the child labor laws on the books can be attributed to Kelley. However, like many other early twentieth-century female activists, Kelley has largely been forgotten by scholars. While the books that she authored can still be found on library shelves some 80-odd years after their publication, just three full-length biographies of Kelley have been produced, and only one of these is a particularly strong historical study. Two of these books address only the first half of Kelley's long and distinguished life.

Although seriously dated, GOLDMARK's book is the sole study of Kelley's entire life. This is a pioneering work, and it suffers from all the difficulties of being one of the first in a field. Writing nearly a quarter of a century before the study of women's history began to flourish, Goldmark had no foundation of scholarship on which to build. As a result, her study is not particularly analytical, and it is completely uninformed by the insights of gender history. More seriously, it is not an objective study. The book is largely a study of Kelley's career as General Secretary of the National Consumers League (1899–1932). Goldmark was a close associate, friend, and fellow worker of Kelley in the National Consumer's League. As a Kelley intimate, she was privileged to receive much information that a more distanced researcher might have been unable to obtain. Specifically, Goldmark was privy to the behind-the-scenes thinking of the leaders of the Consumers League and had personal knowledge of the role played by Kelley in the policy establishment and strategic planning of the organization. She spoke with many of Kelley's acquaintances before they died and, most importantly for the historical record, managed to garner important pieces of research that later biographers would be incapable of accessing. Goldmark's study has been a landmark work for nearly half a century. The first half of the book has been rendered obsolete by Sklar's book and, with the publication of the second volume of Sklar's study, Goldmark's book will no longer be the standard reference on Kelley.

SKLAR's lengthy and superbly researched book is an excellent biography. In this volume, the first of two and the only one in publication, Sklar explores the decades between 1830 and 1900. After analyzing how earlier generations set the stage for women's political centrality in the 1890s, Sklar depicts the first 40 years of Kelley's life. She tells of the reformer's childhood as a member of an elite Philadelphia family, her graduation from Cornell University in 1882, her immersion in European socialism, her search for a meaningful place within American political culture, and her rise to great public power in Chicago as a resident of Jane Addams's Hull House. This is an amazingly insightful study. Following the trait of all classic biographies, Sklar does much more than focus on one individual. This book serves as a political history of the United States during a period of transforming change when women worked to end the abuses of unregulated industrial capitalism. Sklar shows how changes in women's public culture combined with changes in men's public culture to produce results that neither could have achieved alone. She makes gender central to the history of the Progressive era by exploring the merger of public and private themes as a fundamental feature of Progressive reform.

BLUMBERG's book pales in comparison to Sklar's. This book uses Kelley's writings to examine the first half of her life. Blumberg examines Kelley's background and the early influences and experiences that turned her into a reformer. Much of the book is in Kelley's own words, with Blumberg making heavy use of the reformer's speeches and letters. Contrary to the tendency of biographers to grow to hate their subjects, Blumberg has apparently fallen in love with hers and describes Kelley in glowing terms. This is not an objective work, and besides being marred by sloppy editing, it sheds little light on the world that Kelley inhabited.

—CARYN E. NEUMANN

Kempe, Margery b. ca. 1373

British Mystic

Atkinson, Clarissa W., *Mystic and Pilgrim: The Book and World of Margery Kempe*, Ithaca, New York: Cornell University Press, 1983

Lochrie, Karma, *Margery Kempe and Translations of the Flesh*, Philadelphia: University of Pennsylvania Press, 1991

McEntire, Sandra, *Margery Kempe: A Book of Essays*, New York: Garland, 1992

Staley, Lynn, *Margery Kempe's Dissenting Fictions*, University Park: Pennsylvania State University Press, 1994

Stone, Robert Karl, *Middle English Prose Style: Margery Kempe and Julian of Norwich*, The Hague: Moulton, 1970

The Book of Margery Kempe, a lively account of a medieval woman's life as a pilgrim and mystic, is considered the first extant autobiography in English. Although Margery dictated her story to scribes in 1434, the manuscript was lost for another five centuries. The first modernization of her narrative was not printed until 1936; most serious critical response to Kempe has been even more recent.

STONE's book is a close linguistic analysis of the prose style of both *The Book of Margery Kempe* and Julian of Norwich's *Revelations*, although his emphasis is on Kempe's work. Stone's argument is that while the prose techniques of both writers have certain elements in common, their styles differ according to their individual personalities. According to Stone, Kempe's narrative is "flamboyant, careless, unrestrained," but these qualities make for a lively and colorful work of work. Stone focuses very specifically on how Kempe employs syntax, sentence structure, alliteration, dialogue, imagery, and a particular vocabulary to attain her unique style. Even though she had the help of a scribe in writing her book, Stone argues, it is still very much a work of art created by Kempe herself.

ATKINSON was one of the first to provide a strong, comprehensive consideration of Margery Kempe's life and her work within her particular historical context. This study focuses on the nature of Kempe's spiritual calling; her relationship with the church and clergy; and Kempe's place within her family and her community. Since Kempe has suffered considerable criticism for her allegedly excessive or hysterical manifestations of faith, Atkinson's discussion of her in the context of the tradition of affective piety in medieval female religious experience is particularly helpful. Atkinson argues that Kempe was neither hypocritical nor hysterical, but a woman who attained autonomy and power within a culture that valued religious enthusiasm. She concludes with a general overview of the critical reception of Kempe's book. Atkinson's book is considered the starting point for any further critical consideration of Margery Kempe.

Continuing in this vein of considering Kempe in her social, historical, and religious context, the collection of essays edited by McENTIRE examines in further detail many of the issues raised by Atkinson. The first section of the book deals with Kempe herself, as both married woman and spiritual seeker; the recurrent point of these essays is that Kempe's dual vocation as both wife and mystic, as well as her often unconventional demonstrations of piety, resulted in conflicts that Kempe ultimately resolved as she achieved a sense of wholeness. The essays in the second part of the collection focus on the content and the literary merits of the autobiography itself; these authors discuss the narrative structure of *The Book of Margery Kempe* in light of psychoanalytical and French feminist literary theory, and argue that Kempe's work should not be read using the same tools as those used for male literary texts. The final section of the book discusses Margery Kempe's relationship to her community, and to St. Bridget of Sweden, Marguerite de'Oingt, Elizabeth of Hungary, and Julian of Norwich. Each essay argues that there were stronger influences and correspondences between Margery and these women than has been hitherto recognized.

LOCHRIE, on the other hand, does not focus on Kempe's place in the tradition of medieval mystics, because she argues that such an approach has marginalized Kempe. Lochrie's aim is to contextualize Kempe, using the theoretical framework of the body in medieval theology. The female body, Lochrie explains, was seen as a disruptive, "taboo-laden construct," and Kempe, as a woman writer, brings this sense of disruption into her text. Lochrie discusses Kempe's unconventional manner of writing, and her hysterical laughter and weeping, as ways in which Kempe subverted the barriers imposed by cultural and religious standards. Lochrie's book also provides a critique of modern scholarly approaches to Kempe that have contributed to her continuing marginalization. Lochrie concludes with a helpful discussion of the issues involved in teaching Kempe in a literature survey course.

STALEY argues for the necessity of examining *The Book of Margery Kempe* as a literary work of fiction, not as a straightforward spiritual autobiography of a medieval woman. Kempe, Staley claims, purposely employed narrative strategies similar to those of Geoffrey Chaucer and William Langland, in order to differentiate between herself as "author" and Margery as "subject." In consciously expanding conventional generic categories, Kempe created a work that opens itself to a variety of opposing readings. Staley also describes the various ways in which the scribe functions in Kempe's work, particularly as a means of masking the author's criticism of the church and her social community. Staley demonstrates how, instead of simply "writing like a woman," Kempe exploits the rhetoric of gender and her understanding of the conventions of sacred biography, to question secular and religious authority. In her book, Kempe repeatedly situates her subject, that is, herself, in scenes that describe her confrontation with civil or ecclesiastical institutions; in so doing, she is able to discuss her relationship to Lollard views, to mercantile life, to issues of nationalism, and to officially sanctioned language. Like Lochrie, Staley makes a strong, convincing case for seeing Margery Kempe as both a medieval woman who was entirely conscious of the restrictions she was subjected to by society, and as an author who was entirely conscious of how to challenge these restrictions in her work.

—JO ELDRIDGE CARNEY

Klein, Melanie 1882–1960

Austrian Psychoanalyst

Grosskurth, Phyllis, *Melanie Klein: Her World and Her Work*, New York: Knopf, and London: Hodder and Stoughton, 1986

Hughes, Judith M., *Reshaping the Psychoanalytic Domain: The Work of Melanie Klein, W.R.D. Fairbairn, and D.W. Winnicott*, Berkeley: University of California Press, 1989

Limentani, Adam, *Between Freud and Klein: The Psychoanalytic Quest for Knowledge and Truth*, London: Free Association, 1989

Pétot, Jean-Michel, *Melanie Klein*, 2 vols., Paris: Dunod, 1979; Madison, Connecticut: International Universities Press, 1990

Rustin, Michael, *The Good Society and the Inner World: Psychoanalysis, Politics, and Culture*, London and New York: Verso Press, 1991

Sayers, Janet, *Mothering Psychoanalysis: Helene Deutsch, Karen Horney, Anna Freud, and Melanie Klein*, London: Hamish Hamilton, 1991; as *Mothers of Psychoanalysis: Helene Deutsch, Karen Horney, Anna Freud and Melanie Klein*, New York: Norton, 1991

Segal, Hanna, *Introduction to the Work of Melanie Klein*, New York: Basic Books, and London: Heinemann, 1964; new enlarged edition, London: Hogarth Press, 1973

Solomon, Irving, *A Primer of Kleinian Therapy*, Northvale, New Jersey: Jason Aronson, 1995

Based on her early interest in children and her brief analysis with Sigmund Freud's associate Karl Abraham, who had done pioneering work on early stages of infantile development, Melanie Klein devised strategies for the analysis of children, notably the idea of free play, in which she treated play much the same way free association is used in adult psychoanalysis. From this point, she developed various psychoanalytic theories about children and adults that differed significantly from Freud's.

Several introductory studies of Klein and her theories have been published; among these, those by Segal and Solomon are notable. SEGAL's book is a basic, layperson's introduction, offering a brief discussion of Klein's life, including her initial exposure to psychoanalysis in Budapest, later in Vienna and Berlin, and finally in London, and a brief description of her theories, both as they conform to and differ from Freud's. SOLOMON's book is not intended for neophytes but assumes a rather sophisticated understanding of Freudian psychoanalytic theory. Solomon's exposition of such Kleinian notions as manic-depressive states, projective identification, and her controversial theory of envy are set forth with clarity and elegance.

SAYERS treats the four most important female followers of Freud named in the title. In discussing Klein, Sayers highlights the difficulties she faced in the late 1930s when many of Vienna's most distinguished psychoanalysts, including Freud himself and Anna Freud, immigrated to London. In addition, this was also the same time that Klein's son died. Sayers tends to downplay the considerable antagonism that developed between Klein and Anna Freud, perhaps in an attempt to be evenhanded and neutral. However, the importance of this comparative study of four analysts is the many insights it offers into the development of psychoanalysis and the significant roles women have played in it.

PÉTOT's study is the most exhaustive to date. The first volume is devoted to Klein's initial work and its preliminary systematization from 1919 to 1932; the second treats her work on the ego and the good object from 1932 to 1960. Pétot provides both facts and insight into Klein's early life, notably her lifelong regret that she did not follow her desire to become a doctor, her difficult, and eventually failed, marriage, her children, with whom she had stormy relationships, her association with Karen Horney (Klein psychoanalyzed two of Horney's three children), and her considerable efforts to establish herself in London as a psychoanalyst. Pétot's use of both primary archival and secondary sources is well-synthesized and nuanced.

As complete and detailed as Pétot's book is, GROSSKURTH's is the most riveting and accessible study of Klein to date. A professor of English at the University of Toronto, Grosskurth writes warmly and respectfully of her subject but does not hesitate to acknowledge the dark, tormented sides of Klein's personality, including her tendency to be provocative, intolerant, childish, and even dishonest, the latter shown by her failure to acknowledge that she used her own children as subjects in her early studies. The most distinctive feature of this biography is its lavish use of many unpublished, primary source materials: papers, correspondences (including various drafts of important letters, which were extensively reworked before finally being sent) and, most important of all, Klein's unpublished autobiography. If one were to read only one study of Klein, this should be it.

LIMENTANI presents an important contrastive, rather technical study of Klein's theories of child analysis and those of Anna Freud. This work requires a sophisticated understanding, not only of basic Freudian psychoanalytic theory, but the elaborations on it made by Anna Freud and, of course, Klein's divergences from it. Klein's stress on play therapy and spontaneous communication as supplements to conventional Freudian techniques is evenly explained. The author also shows how and why the Freudian community was shocked by Klein's idea that some specific states in infants are, in fact, related to adult psychotic processes. Anna Freud's theories orthodoxly stress the importance of phallic and genital stages of development in children and require that one must analyze children's fantasies and dreams, rather than relying on play therapy for information about children's anxieties and fears. Even though Klein's theories did have an important impact on child analysis, Anna Freud's were the ones that ultimately prevailed.

HUGHES successfully attempts to place Melanie Klein into the larger context of the British object-relations school of psychoanalysis. She first gives a full explication of Freudian theory that forms the basis of this group, then moves on to a thorough discussion of the theories of Klein, Fairbairn, and Winnicott. The way Hughes compares and contrasts the thinking of these three theorists, first with Freud and then with each other, is detailed, clearheaded, and remarkably unjargonized. Hughes aids the reader in appreciating the kind of intellectual acumen and personal strength of character these three individuals, especially Klein, possessed, showing how they reshaped and reconfigured some of what Freud had wrought.

Although many would argue that psychoanalytic theory does not translate well into ideas about large-scale social change, a number of books, mostly by sociologists, have turned to Melanie Klein seeking possible solutions to social problems. RUSTIN, a sociologist by training and a socialist by choice, has written an attractive, successful collection of essays that attempt to apply Kleinian theory to large social questions posed by aesthetics and the philosophy of science, but especially politics. Basically, Rustin argues that an increased awareness and sensitivity to psychological issues as defined and explained by Melanie Klein would not only increase our understanding of society but would actually assist in changing society as well.

—CARLO COPPOLA

See also Psychological Theories about Women: Pre-Feminist

Kollwitz, Käthe Schmidt 1867–1945

German Artist

Kearns, Martha, *Käthe Kollwitz: Woman and Artist*, Old Westbury, New York: Feminist Press, 1976

Klein, Mina C., and H. Arthur Klein, *Käthe Kollwitz: Life in Art*, New York: Holt Rinehart, 1972

Nagel, Otto, *Käthe Kollwitz*, translated by Stella Humphries, London: Studio Vista, and Greenwich, Connecticut: New York Graphic Society, 1971

Prelinger, Elizabeth, *Käthe Kollwitz*, Washington, D.C.: National Gallery of Art, and New Haven, Connecticut, and London: Yale University Press, 1992

There are few studies in English of Kollwitz's art and journals, perhaps because she wrote so much herself about her work. The studies that have been done tend to emphasize the social content of the political posters and prints, or the gender issues raised by Kollwitz's life as a woman working in a male-dominated art world. There is a need for more examination of the technical and artistic qualities of her work, and for serious study of the journals.

PRELINGER's volume is the only major assessment in English of Kollwitz as an artist. The longest essay in the book, Prelinger's "Kollwitz Reconsidered," examines the technical aspects of Kollwitz's developing art, and declares her a master of the craft of printmaking. The artist's debt to Max Klinger is detailed, especially in her use of monochromatic graphic techniques and in her decision to create cycles or series of prints. Working from Kollwitz's preparatory sketches and completed prints, Prelinger traces the artist's thematic conceptions, and the technical decisions she made at various steps along the way before producing her final images. The author gives brief attention to Kollwitz's perception of her own role as an activist and artist. Prelinger also includes an essay by Alessandra Comini, "Kollwitz in Context: The Formative Years," an evocative look at the artist's life in Berlin between the wars, and Hildegard Bachert's study of the critical reception, "Collecting the Art of Käthe Kollwitz: A Survey of Collections, Collectors, and Public Response in Germany and the United States." Serving as the catalogue for a major exhibition at the National Gallery of Art in Washington, D.C., the richly illustrated book includes a detailed chronology and an extensively annotated checklist.

NAGEL's volume is primarily an oversized book of plates accompanied by a long "biographical critique," presented by a friend of Kollwitz's who was also a graphic artist and curator. The writing is highly personal—it has been called patriarchal—relying in large part on the author's memories and on letters in his possession, and his admiration and affection for Kollwitz are never far beneath the surface. But the author writes with authority on the art. Describing the series "The Weavers," he examines each of the six pictures, explaining why the composition and light effects required for each called for different printing media. The intended audience knows something about etching and lithography, but the general reader with little background in the graphic arts will be able to follow the main argument—especially if the plate of each print is examined as it is described. Nagel was responsible for several exhibitions of Kollwitz's work in Russia, and the information about the critical reception there is unavailable elsewhere.

KLEIN and KLEIN's book was the first English-language biography of Kollwitz, and the only one attempting to be comprehensive. Written for nonspecialists, it is intended as an introduction to Kollwitz's life and, especially, her art. The book presents Kollwitz as an exemplar of the creative and liberated woman, but also acknowledges the artist's debt to several men in her life: her father, who always encouraged her to have a career in art; her literary inspirations Émile Zola, Henrik Ibsen, and others; her first mentor, Max Klinger; and her loyal husband who respected her independence, Karl Kollwitz. Over her lifetime, Kollwitz nurtured interests in feminism, socialism, and pacifism, and she had a successful career as an artist while maintaining a fairly typical home life as a wife and mother. The book shows that her ability to draw on all these sources and experiences is what makes her art so expressive. A chapter on the banishment of Kollwitz's art by the Third Reich is fascinating and moving.

KEARNS's book is an eccentric feminist biography. The author's background is not in graphic art, but in education and activism, and she presents Kollwitz as first and foremost a revolutionary. She relies most heavily on Kollwitz's diaries for chronology, on Beate Bonus-Jeep's German memoir for insight into the artist's sexuality, and on Muriel Rukeyser's poem "Käthe Kollwitz" (which is included) for psychological insight. The artist emerges as a frustrated bisexual struggling in a marriage of respect but not of love, held back by the demands of motherhood and by her own moodiness. She is a joyless woman, according to Kearn, but one who finds satisfaction in her work, and in supporting the cause of socialism. She produces a body or work showing strong women—women who do not flinch in war or poverty or servitude, women who overcome. The book includes an annotated bibliography, brief chronology, and illustrations.

—CYNTHIA A. BILY

L

Labor Unions

Balser, Diane, *Sisterhood and Solidarity: Feminism and Labor in Modern Times,* Boston: South End Press, 1987

Cook, Alice Hanson, Val R. Lorwin, and Arlene Kaplan Daniels (eds.), *Women and Trade Unions in Eleven Industrialized Countries,* Philadelphia: Temple University Press, 1984

Foner, Philip, *Women and the American Labor Movement: From World War I to the Present,* New York: Free Press, 1980

Mashinini, Emma, *Strikes Have Followed Me All My Life: A South African Biography,* London: Women's Press, 1989; New York: Routledge, 1991

Milkman Ruth (ed.), *Women, Work and Protest: A Century of U.S. Women's Labor History,* Boston: Routledge and Kegan Paul, 1985; London: Routledge and Kegan Paul, 1987

Nash, June C., and María Patricia Fernández-Kelly (eds.), *Women, Men and the International Division of Labor,* Albany: State University of New York Press, 1983

Ortiz, Altagracia (ed.), *Puerto Rican Women and Work: Bridges in Transnational Labor,* Philadelphia: Temple University Press, 1996

Rowbotham, Sheila, and Swasti Mitter (eds.), *Dignity and Daily Bread: New Forms of Economic Organizing among Poor Women in the Third World and the First,* New York and London: Routledge, 1994

The role of women in unions has surfaced at the center of debates about the revitalized international labor movement, as well as in the fields of labor history and political economy. One early text participating in both organizational and academic debates is the volume of essays collected by NASH and FERNÁNDEZ-KELLY. These groundbreaking essays discuss intersections between the consolidation of multinational corporations, changing labor practices, and gender. Essays such as Helen I. Safa's "Women, Production and Reproduction in Industrial Capitalism: A Comparison of Brazilian and U.S. Factory Workers" set up important distinctions between the character of rural and urban workers in unions' efforts to build global solidarity.

ROWBOTHAM and MITTER continue this trajectory in their volume of essays discussing new strategies devised by unions and extra-union organizations to better represent female workers in Malaysian, Filipino, and Sri Lankan Free Trade Zones. ORTIZ collects essays that provide a historical understanding of how Puerto Rico's colonial relationship to the United States produces the need for labor unions to span the range of women's work. Several of the essays address the conditions of exploitation, which severely hamper efforts to unionize Puerto Rican women working in the United States and Puerto Rico.

COOK, LORWIN, and DANIELS provide an overview of European countries' labor movements and women, primarily in formal work sectors. Each essay focuses on one country and provides a history of the labor movement, as well as efforts to transform unions to represent women's specific demands and to build women's leadership in unions overall.

MASHININI describes through her own experiences the difficulty of building workers' solidarity in a country governed by a system of racial apartheid. She describes in riveting prose black workers' struggles, first for political recognition, and only then for their rights as workers. She allows for an understanding of psychological as well as economic and political factors that affect women's experiences in union organizing.

FONER provides both detailed case studies of particular unions and a general overview of the political conditions facing the American labor movement in the twentieth century. In addition, he outlines the intertwined relationships between the first- and second-wave women's movements, women's associations, and women's roles in unions. Foner complicates our understanding of sexism in unions through discussions of the political landscape, including the anti-immigrant hysteria of the 1910s and 1920s and the anti-communist witch hunt that devastated pro-women unions in the 1950s.

MILKMAN collects vital essays that both substantiate and diversify Foner's narrative. Rosalyn Terborg-Penn documents African-American women's embattled history for recognition by men and white women in unions. Her essay describes strategies devised to confront problems of racism and sexism. Alice Kessler-Harris tries to untangle the contradictory policies and practices of trade union leadership in the 1920s which recognized the importance of building solidarity between men and women, even while refusing to grant women equal status within unions. The volume includes some of the most insightful case studies of the American labor movement.

BALSER includes nineteenth-century working women's associations in her history of women in the U.S. labor movement, but her most comprehensive chapters outline the history of two union-based women's groups created in the 1970s. Her discussion of these groups provides an illuminating understanding of how the second-wave women's movement pushed feminism in the American labor movement, and how unionized women enriched the women's movement.

—ELISABETH ARMSTRONG

Language, Gender Inclusive/Exclusive

Cameron, Deborah (ed.), *The Feminist Critique of Language: A Reader,* London and New York: Routledge, 1990

Crawford, Mary, *Talking Difference: On Gender and Language,* Thousand Oaks, California, and London: Sage, 1995

Graddol, David, and Joan Swann, *Gender Voices,* Oxford and New York: Basil Blackwell, 1989

Miller, Casey, and Kate Swift, *The Handbook of Nonsexist Writing,* New York: Lippincott and Crowell, 1980

———, *Words and Women,* Garden City, New York: Anchor, 1976; London: Gollancz, 1997; 2nd edition, New York: HarperCollins, 1991

Spender, Dale, *Man Made Language,* London and Boston: Routledge, 1980

Thorne, Barrie, Cheris Kramarae, and Nancy Henley, *Language, Gender and Society,* Rowley, Massachusetts, and London: Newbury House, 1983

Vetterling-Braggin, Mary (ed.), *Sexist Language: A Modern Philosophical Analysis,* Totowa, New Jersey: Rowman and Littlefield, 1981

Feminists of the 1960s and 70s recognized that the very language they were using to construct their arguments for equality was biased toward males. This bias included the grammatical convention of using male pronouns and nouns to represent both genders, such as men, mankind, he, him, and his. As a result, feminist linguists, communicators, literary experts, and sociologists began to study language, looking for bias, some to see if it really was masculinist, some to expose inequities, and some to propose new ways of using language. The issue of language exclusivity/inclusivity continues to be researched, and has yielded many interesting general and academic studies.

SPENDER's work is a classic in the area of language research, and any study of the topic should start with her work. She very clearly outlines the problem of sexism in our language and communication system. Spender disputes traditional research on differences between male and female speakers, and makes use of feminist studies. Her chapters on "Language and Reality" and "The Politics of Naming" in particular talk about inclusive versus exclusive language. In the former, Spender critiques patriarchal grammatical rules requiring the use of he/man to refer to either sex, and advocates breaking those rules as a means of starting to change society. In the latter, the author discusses the paucity of terms to capture women's experience equal to the male; for example, virile is applied to a sexually healthy male, but no equivalent positive term exists for the female. Her bibliography lists a number of articles from the 1960s and 1970s that were ground-breaking work in sexism and communication.

MILLER and SWIFT's *Handbook* (1980) is another classic in the field of inclusive/exclusive language. It presents a very practical way of avoiding bias in language, and has strongly influenced written communication to the extent that now almost no writer can unthinkingly use masculine pronouns to refer to all people. The writers provide a history of the words and phrases they view as masculinist, a discussion of current usage, and most importantly, suggestions for substituting different terms.

VETTERLING-BRAGGIN's collection of essays by various academics discusses the ethical problems of using traditional language or popular slang to refer to women. Although some of the contemporary jargon the essayists discuss is now dated, the work is good at presenting the sexism in our linguistic system, and the implications of that sexism from a logical perspective. Several essays aptly probe parallels between racism and sexism in language.

The volume edited by THORNE, KRAMARAE, and HENLEY presents the studies of sociologists and psychologists on the ways in which language is practiced and the effect that has on maintaining sexism. The work uses case and clinical studies as its basis, and so is somewhat technical in its terminology and approach, but is helpful in presenting data to the skeptic who might trivialize the extent of sexism in language. There is an extensive annotated bibliography of scholarly studies on the topic.

Linguists GRADDOL and SWANN discuss the intersections of gender, class, and language. The book is an introductory look at the issue from various disciplines, including linguistics, psychology, and feminist theory. The authors argue with Spender's assumption that males alone were the creators of language, hypothesizing that the process involved women as well as men. Their implications seem to be that women were and possibly still are complicit in the societal sexism that language reflects. They conclude that to focus overly on language is self-defeating, that we should be concerned with changing society, and then language will reflect that change.

CAMERON'S reader would be an excellent teaching resource for neophytes to the topic of gender inclusive/exclusive language, as well as more advanced scholars. It is a potpourri of essays on language issues, some of which are now considered classics, and some that are not currently easily attained in print. Authors range from Virginia Woolf to Tillie Olson, from Luce Irigaray to Kramarae. Cameron provides a general introduction which sets in context the subject of gender and language, as well as helpful overview introductions to each of the three sections of the volume, "Speech and Silence," "'Naming' and Representation," and "Dominance and Difference in Women's Linguistic Behavior."

Another classic, now updated, is MILLER and SWIFT's 1991 work. Aimed at the general reader, it discusses examples of sexist language from traditional dictionaries and usage guides to literature, religion, and the media. By providing information on origins of language, the authors hope to make transparent the gender bias inherent in culture, and to change attitudes by changing our words.

A very recent work, available in paperback, is CRAWFORD's study. This book carefully critiques many of the other works listed in this entry, along with other studies of gender and language. Some of the problems she sees with earlier studies include the exclusion of race and class considerations in the discussion of language used by men and women, the tendency to treat "woman" as an essential person, and the treatment of male as the norm and female as the exception. She concludes that feminist methods, particularly in her field of psychology, provide the best means of studying language and communication because they reject the idea of "dominant meanings."

—CAROL BLESSING

See also Communication Styles and Gender

Latin America *see* Economic Development: Latin America; Latin American Women

Latin American Women

Castillo, Debra A., *Talking Back: Toward a Latin American Feminist Literary Criticism,* Ithaca, New York: Cornell University Press, 1992

Deere, Carmen Diana, and Magdalena Leon de Leal (eds.), *Rural Women and State Policy: Feminist Perspectives on Latin American Agricultural Development,* Boulder, Colorado: Westview Press, 1987

Jaquette, Jane S. (ed.), *The Women's Movement in Latin America: Feminism and the Transition to Democracy,* Boulder, Colorado: Westview Press, 1987

Lavrin, Asuncion (ed.), *Latin American Women: Historical Perspectives,* Westport, Connecticut: Greenwood, 1978

——— (ed.), *Sexuality and Marriage in Colonial Latin America,* Lincoln: University of Nebraska Press, 1989

Nash, June C., and Helen Icken Safa (eds.), *Women and Change in Latin America,* South Hadley, Massachusetts: Bergin and Garvey, 1985

Pescatello, Ann M. (ed.), *Female and Male in Latin America,* Pittsburgh: University of Pittsburgh Press, 1973

Stoner, K. Lynn, *Latinas of the Americas: A Source Book,* New York: Garland, 1989

Tamez, Elsa (ed.), *Through Her Eyes: Women's Theology from Latin America,* Maryknoll, New York: Orbis, 1989

The study of women in Latin America developed in the early 1970s within the larger movements of women's studies and social history. Among the pioneering works on women in Latin America is the book edited by PESCATELLO. Contributors to this volume analyze both literary images of females and the history of women in several countries including Cuba, Argentina, Chile, and Peru. The volume provides an important source for understanding images of Latin American women. Especially useful is Evelyn Steven's essay on marianismo and machismo.

A second early and important work is LAVRIN's (1978) edited volume on the history of Latin American women. This collection focuses primarily on women's roles within colonial and nineteenth-century Latin America. It contains 11 chapters, including overviews of women in colonial Mexico and Brazil, and a final chapter that catalogues the broad changes in gender ideology and opportunities for women over the past 400 years. This collection is particularly important because much of the work on women in Latin America focuses on the twentieth century. This work continues to be useful in Latin American history courses because it analyzes the changes in women's roles over a significant time span.

STONER provides an excellent overview of the state of research in the field of Latin American women's studies in the introduction to her sourcebook. The body of the book contains 3,071 entries divided into 15 categories: anthologies, bibliographies, biography, demography, education, feminist studies, health, history, household and family studies, literature, political science, religion, rural development, urban development, and law/miscellaneous. Each category contains an introductory essay, and all categories contain both published and unpublished works—including dissertations and conference papers. This reference work, although somewhat dated, is still the best single source covering the breadth of research on Latin American women.

Some of the most successful studies of women in Latin America focus on women and development. One of the best sources is DEERE and LEON's study of rural women and development in several countries. The contributors to this volume argue that state policy and agrarian reform in Latin America, with the exceptions of Cuba and Nicaragua, have not benefited women. To prove their point, the authors analyze income-generating as well as subsistence projects in several countries. This collection is vital for understanding rural development in Latin America, and especially the role of gender in development.

Complementing Deere and Leon's work, NASH and SAFA study the effects of economic crisis on women's lives, and women's strategies for change in an urban context in Latin America. The book begins by discussing theoretical and methodological progress in Latin American women's history and then analyzes production and reproduction within the contexts of industrial and agricultural development and rural to urban migration. The final section describes women's political action in relation to the state. The book's strength lies in its consideration of women's part in the substantial rural to urban migration that has characterized twentieth-century urban development in Latin America.

Many works on Latin American women examine women's activism in political and cultural contexts. JAQUETTE's edited volume investigates the women's movement in the early 1980s. Jaquette covers three major themes: women's human rights groups, feminist groups, and neighborhood-based organizations of poor women. The book presents a valuable comparison of women's activism in Brazil, Uruguay, Argentina, Chile, and Peru. The articles also critically assess the result of women's political action and question whether the movements can now sustain themselves in new democratic climates. This book is useful for those interested in political culture and social movements in Latin America, and gender's role in both areas.

The collection edited by TAMEZ provides an important initial statement on women and religion in Latin America. While the book is uneven in quality, the essays do address a variety of topics, including pre-Columbian myths, Brazilian Candomblé, and liberation theology. All of the writers live and teach in Latin America and are affiliated with either the Catholic or Methodist church. As a result, each author attempts to connect women's daily experience—especially that of poor women—with theology. This book is an important source for understanding the role of women in Latin American liberation theology.

In the last decade scholars have begun to write about such previously neglected topics as the history of sexuality and feminist literary criticism from a Latin American theoretical perspective. In one of the first books to deal systematically with the issues of sexuality in Latin America, LAVRIN (1989) explores the laws and church regulations surrounding courtship, marriage, and the family in colonial Latin America. The book focuses on Mexico and illuminates the centrality of the Catholic Church to feminist scholarship on sexuality, race, and class. The nine essays cover both church and secular regulations of sexuality and shed new light on colonial family life. This book is very important for those interested in the role of sexuality in the gender hierarchy in Latin America.

CASTILLO examines literary and critical texts by Latin American women and proposes theoretical ways to read these texts while being sensitive to the translation of western theory into Latin America. She explores the construction of Hispanic feminisms through strategies of silence, appropriation, excavation, surfacing, negation, and marginalization, which characterize Latin American feminist literary practice. Castillo argues that Latin American feminisms are anti-hegemonic, multi-directional, and unique in relation to Anglo-European feminisms. The work contributes to feminist criticism and is a very valuable source for people in the field of Latin American women's studies.

—GINA HAMES

Laurence, Margaret 1926–1987

Canadian Writer

Buss, Helen M., *Mother and Daughter Relationships in the Manawaka Works of Margaret Laurence,* Victoria: English Literary Studies, University of Victoria, 1985

Coger, Greta M. (ed.), *New Perspectives on Margaret Laurence: Poetic Narrative, Multiculturalism, and Feminism,* Westport, Connecticut, and London: Greenwood, 1996

Morley, Patricia A., *Margaret Laurence,* Boston: Twayne, 1981

New, William H. (ed.), *Margaret Laurence,* Toronto: McGraw-Hill Ryerson, 1977

Nicholson, Colin (ed.), *Critical Approaches to the Fiction of Margaret Laurence,* Vancouver: University of British Columbia Press, 1990

Sparrow, Fiona, *Into Africa with Margaret Laurence,* Toronto: ECW Press, 1992

Thomas, Clara, *Margaret Laurence,* Toronto: McClelland and Stewart, 1969

Verduyn, Christl (ed.), *Margaret Laurence: An Appreciation,* Peterborough: Broadview Press, 1988

COGER has organized an invaluable set of 18 essays under four rubrics: Language, Theme, and Image in Laurence; Narrative Structure in Laurence; Multiculturalism in Laurence, and Feminist Perspectives in Laurence. These articles focus in various ways on Laurence as a novelist and poet who uses concrete language and rich imagery in celebrating life rather than viewing humans as victims. Many of the authors specify her themes of aging and facing death; the tension between a character's inner and outer lives or subjective and objective realities; the roles of ancestors, freedom, self-knowledge, love, and community; the difference between childhood and adult awareness; and biblical resonances, especially exodus and the struggle of the outsider. Critic Wes McAmmond even suggests Laurence invented "multiculturalism" in her exploration of her Scottish roots; the importance of Scottish history as it mingled with French and English history in Canada; her understanding of Métis (Indian and French) history, and her use and appreciation of African storytelling strategies. Three essays discuss the importance of oral traditions in Laurence's work, whereas the feminist perspectives focus on aging as self-alienation from the perspective of Karen Horney's basic patterns of neurotic behavior; the subversive voice in *Fire-Dwellers* and the inner conflicting voices of Rachel Cameron as she tries to break free from male-controlled language; and the career woman in *The Diviners.* As a sampling of modern theoretical approaches, these essays represent a critically important stance toward Laurence as an author with contemporary concerns, as the title of the collection suggests.

MORLEY, in her 171-page study, compares Laurence to two male literary giants: first to Tolstoy in her epic range and her ability to give symbolic form to social life, and then to Proust in her sophisticated use of time past and present. Morley divides her book into three parts: Laurence's own life, her work based on her African experience, and the Manawaka cycle. The main themes discussed are the mythic overtones and the archetypal underpinnings of Laurence's novels, as well as her use of religious imagery, stories, and names to connect the prairie life of western Canada with the universal human themes of bondage and freedom, searching for truth, failures, abandonment, miscommunications, survival, and finally the importance of place and land. This work, written in the tradition of Lionel Trilling, is oriented to thematic, mythic, and archetypal patterns.

NICHOLSON has brought together a varied collection of 15 essays beginning with Clara Thomas's overview of Laurence's position as a woman writing against traditional male fiction as analogous to the position of Canada vis-a-vis the United States: a position of resistance and identity formation against a dominant tradition. Another essay focuses on Laurence's Manawaka as a Canadian version of William Faulkner's Yoknapatawpha. Two essays discuss Laurence's relationship to other countries, namely Africa and Scotland, pointing to her life-long and intense interest in experiences outside her native Neepawa. Three essays on *Stone Angel* deal with memory, the stone angel as signifier with patterns of angelism and petrification converging in this single image; and a comparison with Tillie Olsen in terms of attitudes toward class, fate, politics, and place. On *The Diviners,* the articles range from consolation to the reworking of the myth of the fall. The collection also includes a piece on the importance of doubling in *Jest of God,* one on identity in *Fire-Dwellers,* one on women's narratives in both *Jest of God* and *Fire-Dwellers,* and one on the discourse of the "(M)Other." Many of the essays focus on Laurence's themes of finding one's authentic voice and language; the importance of storytelling, myth, connections to the past, and sense of place; and the movement toward reconciliation and forgiveness and finally peace. The collection offers important insights into the many facets of Laurence's art and contributes to an understanding of the depth and complexity of her artistic vision.

THOMAS, in a slim volume of 54 pages of text, includes five chapters on Laurence's work up to *A Jest of God* and the Vanessa MacLeod stories published through 1967. It is a sensitive commentary on Laurence's artistry, focusing on her empathy, insight, and double vision in her early work. NEW has collected a cross-section of 34 reviews and critical responses to the work of Margaret Laurence (as well as four pieces by Laurence) published between 1960 and 1975, divided into three categories: Roots and Continuities, From Africa to Canada, and Out from Manawaka. He has included pieces from such diverse sources as *Saturday Review, New York Times Review of Books,* and *New Republic,* with several longer pieces from scholarly journals such as *Canadian Literature, Studies in the Novel,* and *The Centennial Review.* Many of the pieces are short but insightful two-to-three-page views of her work, offering a range of perspectives as her work was received by the reading public at the time. He includes well-known authors such as Margaret Atwood, Robertson Davies, Granville Hicks, Barry Callaghan, and Marge Piercy. As a sampling of perspectives from a broad range of publications from popular to scholarly, this collection gives the reader a broad overview of attitudes current at the time her work was published.

BUSS examines the Manawaka novels through an archetypal approach, focusing on the ways the Demeter-Kore myth informs Laurence's work. She sees the reunion of mother and daughter as the iconographic moment at the heart of her fiction and the theme that unifies the Manawaka novels. Although archetypal, the study also focuses on psychological concerns as well as the relationship between maternality and creativity and between female values and literary techniques. She begins with Hagar, the dispossessed in *Stone Angel,* discusses Rachel and Stacey's voiceless vision in the sister novels of *Jest of God* and *Fire-Dwellers,* and concludes with Vanessa, Morag, and the creative spirit in *A Bird in the House* and *The Diviners.* This work is a clear, insightful analysis of this set of novels as Laurence's increasingly complex sense of the feminine and the need to reconnect with ancient feminine principles.

SPARROW has written an important work devoted to a less-known aspect of Laurence's life in and work on Africa. She divides her book into three parts: Margaret Laurence of Hargeisa, The West African Fiction, and The

Novelist as Critic. For readers who know Laurence primarily as a Canadian writer, this text will illuminate her significant contribution to an understanding of African storytelling in the western world. It gives detailed information on Laurence's life in Africa, her reading and research of African life, and analysis of the five works on Africa that Laurence wrote. Sparrow writes in an informed way about the diaries that Laurence kept of her experiences in Somaliland, which were later transformed into her memoir *The Prophet's Camel Bell* (1963), and of Laurence's first published book, *A Tree for Poverty: Somali Poetry and Prose* (1954), published in Nairobi, a highly esteemed anthology collected and translated into English by Laurence. Sparrow also illuminates Laurence's achievement as an empathetic outsider in her collection of West African stories and her study of Nigerian writers of the 1950s and 1960s.

VERDUYN's collection is a celebration and commemoration of Laurence's long association with Trent University and the *Journal of Canadian Studies* in which most of the 16 essays first appeared. Since the issue of the journal quickly sold out, these articles are again accessible to readers, as well as several previously unpublished articles and Laurence's two speeches, including her nearly legendary "My Final Hour," read to the Trent Philosophical Society in March 1983. Arranged to show the evolution of Laurence's artistry, the volume begins with her earlier African writings and then moves to her novels set in Canada, with essays that point to her concerns with human religious and spiritual aspirations, as well as the life and experiences of women, and the reality and fictions of human identity and the female body. In the essays on the Manawaka cycle, the mythic dimensions of her work are analyzed, especially the interweaving of history and myth with apocalyptic and biblical overtones. The last essays are overviews of her work with commentaries on her vision as a writer whose strong female characters offer the possibility of redeeming human tragedy.

—JOANNE A. CHARBONNEAU

Lawyers

Chester, Ronald, *Unequal Access: Women Lawyers in a Changing America,* South Hadley, Massachusetts: Bergin and Garvey, 1985

Epstein, Cynthia Fuchs, *Women in Law,* New York: Basic Books, 1981; revised edition, 1993

Harrington, Mona, *Women Lawyers: Rewriting the Rules,* New York: Knopf, 1993

Martin, Susan Ehrlich, and Nancy Jurik, *Doing Justice, Doing Gender,* Thousand Oaks, California, and London: Sage, 1996

Morello, K.B., *The Invisible Bar: The Woman Lawyer in America 1638 to the Present,* New York: Random House, 1986

In one of the best known general books on the experience of women as lawyers, EPSTEIN describes and analyzes the challenges female attorneys face from their colleagues, superiors, and families. Having interviewed female attorneys, judges, and law professors since 1960, the author presents a rich picture of the complexities of women's entry into the legal profession. This book provides a comprehensive examination of female lawyers from practice in small private firms to high-powered corporate law. Updated in 1993, Epstein deals with emerging issues affecting female lawyers, including the debate over the Anita Hill sexual harassment testimony. This book is particularly important because it illuminates the ideological conflicts that exist among different types of female lawyers. Epstein fully examines how these divergent ideologies have burgeoned into various tactics and practical strategies in the practice of law.

The study of women as lawyers is predominately divided into two areas: the history of female lawyers, and how women have challenged or changed the field of law. Using oral histories to study the lives of early American women in the legal profession, CHESTER uncovers the experience of women attending law school in the 1920s and 1930s. The author found that during the 1920s, women took advantage of the success of suffrage and increased access to the professions to enter the legal field in larger numbers. However, the 1930s and the onset of the Depression brought large setbacks to women's entry into the profession of law. Chester found that female lawyers did not experience another increase in numbers until the progressive movement of the late 1960s.

MORELLO offers a comprehensive history of women's experience in the legal profession in the United States. Morello's book stands out for its success in combining a history of women's experiences entering law school, practicing law, gaining access to major firms, and working as judges. Unlike other histories of women in law, Morello's work also includes an examination of the double impairment of black female lawyers. The author documents the challenges and experiences of early black female lawyers as they attempted to gain access to schools and later to the profession.

To examine how women's entry into the legal profession has challenged and changed the field of law, HARRINGTON interviewed over one hundred female lawyers between 1989 and 1991. From recent graduates to women who broke into the legal profession in the 1950s, she addresses what has been happening to the law and its practice. By examining the rules of law (Socratic method, ethics) this work addresses what prevents equal professional authority for female lawyers. Additionally, Harrington explores how female lawyers use the professional authority they have achieved to advance the equality of women in general.

ERLICH and JURIK explore women's role in the legal profession within the context of women's expanding role in the criminal justice system as a whole. The authors examine the changing roles of women in the criminal justice system over the past 25 years, focusing three chapters on women's entry into the practice of law. By addressing social, legal, and political changes that led to women's entry into the criminal justice system, the authors address how female lawyers have changed the type and nature of the legal profession. Erlich and Jurick argue that as women entered the legal profession in increasing numbers, they challenged the organizational logic of a gendered legal world. Additionally, the authors identify barriers and biases faced by female police officers, correctional officers, and judges. Subsequently, she examines how these challenges have brought about change and raised new questions on the place of women in the whole system of law enforcement and criminal justice.

—AMY S. FARRELL

See also Jurisprudence, Feminist

Leadership

Adler, Nancy J., and Dafna N. Izraeli (eds.), *Women in Management Worldwide*, Armonk, New York: M.E. Sharpe, 1987

Barber, James E., and Barbara Kellerman (eds.), *Women Leaders in American Politics*, Englewood Cliffs, New Jersey: Prentice-Hall, 1986

Cantor, Dorothy W., and Toni Bernay, *Women in Power: The Secrets of Leadership*, Boston: Houghton Mifflin, 1992

Duerst-Lahti, Georgia, and Rita Mae Kelly, *Gender Power, Leadership, and Governance*, Ann Arbor: University of Michigan Press, 1995

Genovese, Michael A. (ed.), *Women as National Leaders*, Newbury Park, California: Sage, 1993

Helgesen, Sally, *The Female Advantage: Women's Ways of Leadership*, New York: Doubleday, 1990

Jamieson, Kathleen Hall, *Beyond the Double Bind: Women and Leadership*, New York: Oxford University Press, 1995

LeVeness, Frank P., and Jane P. Sweeney, *Women Leaders in Contemporary American Politics*, Boulder, Colorado: Lynne Reinner, 1987

Rosener, Judith, *America's Competitive Secret: Utilizing Women as a Management Strategy*, New York: Oxford University Press, 1995

Although a relatively new field, the subject of women and leadership has been increasingly studied. Isolated examples of articles and books may be found prior to 1980, but in the late 1980s and 1990s, numerous books and articles have addressed issues of women, leadership, and leadership skills in business, government, education, and other areas. The literature falls into several categories: biographies and analyses of female leaders, including case studies of successful and unsuccessful leadership; dilemmas, advice, pitfalls, and obstacles for aspiring leaders; and works discussing the distinctiveness of women's leadership. Most of the books are written by political scientists, psychologists, business analysts, or journalists.

Two important works, which focus on the problems and dilemmas women face even in the aftermath of a successful feminist movement and greater acceptance of women in public roles in society, are those by Duerst-Lahti and Kelly, and Jamieson. Although different in style and presentation, these works share the message that women face great obstacles in their desire to be accepted as leaders. DUERST-LAHTI and KELLY focus on the concept of gender power in their analysis of leadership. The definition of leadership, they argue, is based on masculine norms, which results in de facto gendered power. Their work includes case studies and analytical articles written by a variety of scholars, which illustrate their hypothesis about gender power.

JAMIESON, on the other hand, looks at historic and contemporary examples of double binds that women face, such as notions of the womb-brain, aging and invisibility, and so on. She chooses Hillary Rodham Clinton as a focal case study, since she has endured many of the double binds that women face. Jamieson documents examples of success and progress historically, but she also leaves the reader with the distinct impression that new double binds arise to replace those that are overcome. This, however, is an important book by one of the most influential professors of journalism in the United States.

Several works focus on successful women in politics, using case study approaches. What emerges from almost every book in this category is the importance of family support at an early age, and childhood socialization. Young women who were told they could do anything and be anyone they wanted are more likely to become successful political leaders than young women who received mixed signals about their goals and aspirations. Parental support, especially the support of their fathers, appears to be especially important in shaping their aspirations to become political leaders. The political scientists LeVeness and Sweeney and the psychologists Cantor and Bernay chronicle the lives of successful women in politics. LeVENESS and SWEENEY provide a good source for reviewing the lives of prominent women in American politics of recent decades in a factual, relatively uncritical way. CANTOR and BERNAY did extensive interviewing and then created a composite figure of the successful woman in politics, and one of the unsuccessful woman. They also include brief biographies of some of the women whom they interviewed.

BARBER and KELLERMAN's anthology treats female leaders in various contexts from local activism to national politics. These are essays on prominent individuals such as Eleanor Roosevelt, Harriet Beecher Stowe, and Sandra Day O'Connor. Several essays are written by well-known female leaders including Gloria Steinem, Bella Abzug, and Patricia Derian.

On the international level, GENOVESE's work has many similarities. Genovese examines the lives and careers of women who have served as heads of government. The findings suggest that women who became national leaders in some instances had privileged childhoods, but in virtually all instances they received support and encouragement at home as the first step to their future careers. Genovese tries to establish more of a research model than some of the other works, but the findings about the personal attributes of female leaders bear similarities to others discussed.

Some newer books attempt to address whether women have distinctive leadership styles. This is especially true of studies of women in business, for which HELGESEN's work provides a basic point of departure. A journalist and commentator who did case studies on selected female leaders, replicating a well-known study of male business leaders, Helgesen's work presents examples of women's distinctive leadership style, which she has labeled the web of inclusion, a model contrasted with the more traditional hierarchical style of leadership.

ROSENER has also done extensive work on women and leadership in business, arguing that women demonstrate a more inclusive, consultative approach to leadership, which is less hierarchical than the traditional command and control style of leadership favored by men. In this book, Rosener attempts to document the impact that women managers are having on business in the United States. ADLER and IZRAELI explore the roles of female managers and women's leadership in business in developed countries on every continent. The work focuses on women's changing roles in the individual societies discussed.

—NORMA C. NOONAN

League of Women Voters

Black, Naomi, *Social Feminism*, Ithaca, New York: Cornell University Press, 1989

Brumbaugh, Sara B., *Democratic Experience and Education in the National League of Women Voters*, New York: Teachers College, Columbia University, 1946

Lall, Betty, *The Foreign Policy Program of the League of Women Voters of the United States*, Minneapolis, 1967

Lemons, J. Stanley, *The Woman Citizen: Social Feminism in the 1920s*, Urbana: University of Illinois Press, 1973

Stone, Mary, Marlene Cohn, and Matthew Freeman, *The Women's Vote: Beyond the Nineteenth Amendment*, Washington, D.C.: League of Women Voters Education Fund, 1983

Survey Research Center, University of Michigan, *A Study of the League of Women Voters of the United States*, Ann Arbor, Michigan, 1956

Watrous, Hilda R., *In League with Eleanor: Eleanor Roosevelt and the League of Women Voters, 1921–1962*, New York: Foundation for Citizen Education, 1984

Young, Louise M., *In the Public Interest: The League of Women Voters: 1920–1970*, New York and London: Greenwood, 1989

Histories of the League of Women Voters are sorely lacking. Mostly what is available are studies produced by state and local Leagues. The League of Women Voters was founded by the National American Woman Suffrage Association in 1919. It was supposed to be a temporary organization, to compensate for women's inferior political experience and knowledge. The purposes—voter education, a voice for women in politics, and governmental reform—have remained the main aims of the League, along with the later goal of improving the electorate in general. Its agenda is no longer limited to issues involving women's rights, but involves national political and social concerns. Despite its name, men have been welcomed as members since 1974. Its more than 1,200 state and local chapters conduct studies, inform the public on candidates and issues, run voter registration drives, and take stands on pending issues. It is nonpartisan. The League of Women Voters campaigned for civil service reform. It supported a number of amendments to the U.S. Constitution, while opposing others. It was the major citizen organization to campaign for the Tennessee Valley Authority. It was in the lead in campaigning for legislative redistricting. It was the school for politics for many women who later ran for office.

LEMONS argues that while social feminist reformism of the League of Women Voters and other groups was slowed in the 1920s, it neither failed nor was destroyed. The agenda included support for the Cable Act (dealing with citizenship and naturalization), the Sheppard-Towner Act (maternity assistance), disarmament, consumer protection, and employment benefits (including protective legislation). However, it was a time of retrenchment from progressivism, and women's organizations were in a defensive mode. By the early 1930s, the League had only about 100,000 members.

BRUMBAUGH looks at the League as an experiment in political education. She examines its ideas and procedures. She is concerned with those factors in the League that advanced or retarded individual growth in democratic attitudes and abilities. She studies the League's emphasis on grass roots chapter organizations. One of her concerns is that the League is a middle-class organization, and that it pays a price for its homogeneity of membership. It is little known among women of the working class. Brumbaugh advocated that the League become co-educational. League leaders at the time disagreed.

In the 1950s, the League of Women Voters commissioned the SURVEY RESEARCH CENTER of the University of Michigan to analyze its performance. Five reports were prepared, documenting how League members viewed the League, community attitudes toward the League, some problems of League membership, factors in League funding, and factors in League effectiveness. The questionnaires led to reports on satisfactions and dissatisfactions, extent of knowledge of League purposes and procedures, attitudes and experiences regarding fund-raising, the problem of becoming more representative of the community, and characteristics of local Leagues.

BLACK, a political scientist, compares the League of Women Voters with women's organizations in the United Kingdom and France (Women's Co-operative Guild and Union féminine civique et sociale). She writes in the first person, using her own experiences, in a lively style. She attempts to develop a definition of feminism that applies to those seeking to change the position of women in society. Black visited and consulted documents at the headquarters of each of the organizations studied. All three groups studied had mainly white and middle-aged membership with middle-class leadership. None had shown much policy interest in issues of sexual orientation. All three had a view of women as valuable because different. Black shows how each group developed political awareness and progressiveness. For the League of Women Voters, she focuses on its nonpartisanship and its change of view on the Equal Rights Amendment.

In 1950, YOUNG authored a book for women entitled *Understanding Politics.* In 1953, she prepared a report to the International Political Science Association on *The Political Role of Women in the United States.* In 1970, she missed her publisher's deadline for completing her history of the League in time for the organization's fiftieth anniversary, but eventually, with the aid of her historian son, the book was published. Young, a professor emerita from American University, had played a major role in the depositing of the League's records with the Library of Congress. She mined this repository for her book. She discusses the evolution of the League, its leadership, and changes in policy from its inception until about 1970. There is little attempt made at analysis or evaluation.

Two examples of the League's own contribution to women's studies scholarship are the publications of Watrous and Stone, Cohn, and Freeman. WATROUS gives a year-by-year account of Eleanor Roosevelt's League activities from 1921 to 1934, with a cursory report of the 1935–62 period. STONE, COHN, and FREEMAN summarizes the key research findings presented at a conference convened by the League of Women Voters in June, 1983, on the Women's Vote. This was precipitated by the media attention in the 1980s to the "gender gap." LALL did a specialized study of the League's foreign policy agenda. She discusses its methods of influencing government action, including effects on public opinion, and she evaluates the results of League programs.

—MARTIN GRUBERG

Lee, Ann, Mother 1736–1784

British, Founder of the Shakers

Campion, Nardi Reeder, *Mother Ann Lee: Morning Star of the Shakers,* Hanover, New Hampshire: University Press of New England, 1990

Humez, Jean M., *Mother's First Born Daughters: Early Shaker Writings on Women and Religion,* Bloomington: Indiana University Press, 1993

Stein, Stephen, *The Shaker Experience in America: A History of the United Society of Believers,* New Haven, Connecticut: Yale University Press, 1992

By the late nineteenth century, the United Society of Believers in Christ's Second Appearing (known as Shakers) advocated perfect equality of the sexes. They made these views known in church periodicals, interviews with the world's press, and on broadsides. Church spokespeople believed that their commitment to spiritual, social, and political equality for women began with their founder, Mother Ann Lee. Attempts to construct the historical Ann Lee have been hampered by a lack of documentary evidence; thus CAMPION's biography with its reliance on recollections of church members is the only full-length biography of Mother Ann. The story of Mother Ann is told as it was recorded by her disciples over 30 years after her death. Mother Ann in this tradition was not only the female Christ, but "the founder of women's liberation" in the United States. Many of the unique aspects of Shaker communal living are attributed to Mother Ann, including dual-sex government and union meetings (routine, formalized, social gatherings between sisters and brothers). Campion's unfootnoted book is of limited use to serious scholars, but does present a spiritual portrait of Mother Ann.

STEIN's book gives the best scholarly treatment of the forming of the group called Shakers in Manchester, England, and their subsequent migration to the United States. He clearly delineates what historians know of Ann Lee (the historical person), and what is church tradition about Mother Ann (the spiritual leader). Those interested in the role of women in the Shaker church will find Stein a good starting place. Most serious scholars of Shakerism have rejected the notion that Ann Lee preached equality for women, and it is clear from church records that the form of Shaker community was developed after Ann Lee's death. Mother Lucy Wright was the first appointed Eldress after Ann Lee's death, and an influential leader. Stein describes her contribution to the church in some detail. Wright struggled to establish and maintain her authority within the church, facing challenges from male Elders and Trustees.

HUMEZ's book contains the best summary of the diverse literature on Mother Ann, Mother Lucy, and the role of the Shaker sisters in the church from its beginnings until the 1840s. In recent years feminist scholars and others have questioned the alleged feminism of Ann Lee, as well as her role in creating the distinctive characteristics of Shaker communal living. Humez's and Stein's fine bibliographies will guide the interested feminist reader to the lively discussion, largely contained in scholarly articles, on the role of Ann Lee, Lucy Wright, and Shaker sisters.

—PAMELA J. NICKLESS

Legislation *see* Protective Legislation; Property Rights; Workplace Equality Legislation

Le Guin, Ursula K. 1929–

American Writer

Bloom, Harold (ed.), *Ursula K. Le Guin,* New York: Chelsea House, 1986
Bucknall, Barbara J., *Ursula K. Le Guin,* New York: Ungar, 1981
Cummins, Elizabeth, *Understanding Ursula K. Le Guin,* Columbia: University of South Carolina Press, 1990
Olander, Joseph D., and Martin Harry Greenberg (eds.), *Ursula K. Le Guin,* New York: Taplinger, 1974; Edingburgh: Harris, 1979
Selinger, Bernard, *Le Guin and Identity in Contemporary Fiction,* Ann Arbor, Michigan: UMI Research Press, 1988
Slusser, George Edgar, *The Farthest Shores of Ursula K. Le Guin,* San Bernardino, California: Borgo Press, 1976

Ursula K. Le Guin has received a great deal of critical attention, as the many-time winner of literary tributes, including the Hugo and Nebula awards, and as a much-loved author of both science fiction and "mainstream" fiction. Scholarly discussion of her work tends to pivot around two premises: firstly, that fantasy, science fiction, and children's literature (the genres in which she specializes) are not "real" or "high" literature, and secondly, that there is an overarching "pattern" in her writing. Features of her writing which do not fit into received notions of literary criticism, such as her political agenda, her poetry, and the so-called popular nature of the genres in which she often expresses herself, are frequently ignored.

SLUSSER, the earliest critic to consider Le Guin worthy of a book-length study, has, unfortunately, only written on early Le Guin works (his slim but very erudite study was published in 1976). He gives a vital outline of Le Guin's recurring themes, particularly the trope of the encounter with alien cultures that forms the basis for her early writings. He focuses largely on patterns of opposition and synthesis, especially in his analysis of *Rocannon's World, Planet of Exile,* and *City of Illusions,* noting also the difficulties inherent in creative patterning when it becomes an overriding concern. His accounts of *The Left Hand of Darkness* and *The Dispossessed* are masterly examinations of the problems of sexuality and political consciousness in those works. He ends by mentioning some of the short stories in *The Wind's Twelve Quarters,* and speculating on what the author might write in the future.

OLANDER and GREENBERG perform an indispensable service to Le Guin scholars, by collecting some of the best essays written up to 1979. While some have become dated—particularly in scope—they include classic pieces on *The Earthsea Trilogy, The Left Hand of Darkness,* and *The Dispossessed.* Peter S. Alterman's essay on "Ursula K. Le Guin: Damsel with a Dulcimer," which examines representations of nature in, among others, *The Word for World Is Forest* and "Vaster than Empires and More Slow," is a timeless examination of Le Guin's debt to the great tradition of nature writing in literature. Similarly, Thomas J. Remington's discussion of "Anarchism and Utopian Tradition in *The Dispossessed*" examines the history of anarchist thought and its traces in that novel, giving it a deserved place in the tradition of serious political writing. The volume ends with an invaluable bibliography of Le Guin's works, collected by Marshall B. Tymn.

BUCKNALL's volume is more a tribute to the author than a reasoned or scholarly evaluation of her work. Bucknall states at the outset that she has always loved fantasy and that Le Guin is one of her favorite authors. She goes on to discuss Le Guin's writings in a fairly untheoretical way. At times she lapses into plot summary, instead of examining the issues or techniques of the fiction, and her desire to rhapsodize about Le Guin's mastery of writing does mitigate the usefulness of her insights at some points. Nevertheless, she provides the reader with helpful biographical information, which is not readily available elsewhere.

The prolific BLOOM has updated Olander and Greenberg's work by collecting later essays on Le Guin in his book. A comparison of the two volumes is suggestive of shifts in Le Guin criticism in the seven years between their dates of publication. Bloom includes some justly famous articles, such as Fredric Jameson's "World-Reduction in Le Guin: The Emergence of Utopian Narrative," which gives a rare Marxist reading of *The Left Hand of Darkness* and *The Dispossessed.* Also present is Ian Watson's excellent "The Forest as Metaphor for Mind: *The Word for World Is Forest* and 'Vaster than Empires and More Slow'," a companion piece for the essay by Alterman in Olander and Greenberg's anthology. Almost all the authors in Bloom's collection are well-known science-fiction critics: for example, David Ketterer, Robert Scholes, and Eric S. Rabkin. That notwithstanding, the articles still articulate a largely untheorized view of Le Guin's fiction as "given" and "whole," not as produced within a particular historical context and part of an ongoing corpus of philosophically informed discourses. That is to say, despite the insights they offer, the authors of these articles read Le Guin from within a ghetto of so-called popular writing, and not as part of an ongoing literary tradition.

CUMMINS's major concern is Le Guin's evocation of place. She believes that to understand Le Guin, one must grasp the significance of the author's representation of locations. She also concentrates on Le Guin's desire to find an imaginative "home" within her created realms. Cummins gives a convincing argument for the preeminence of place in *The Earthsea Trilogy,* the Hainish novels, the Orsinian fictions, and *Always Coming Home.* She shows how Le Guin thematizes her characters' degree of sympathy with their surroundings. The life-affirming and inimical characteristics of each fictional domain are scrutinized as parts of a complex whole. One of the book's virtues is that she provides an early discussion of *Always Coming Home,* which has not received much critical attention. Cummins's angle is original, and certainly Le Guin's evocation of alternative worlds is part of her enduring appeal. Nevertheless, the centrality she accords to this theme, at times, appears disproportionate.

SELINGER provides the most theoretically informed work on Le Guin to date. He adopts a psychoanalytical framework for his analysis of the artist-figure in the fiction, and its relation to ongoing issues of identity. His reading focuses on the relation between language and the unconscious. This forms the starting point for speculating on what Le Guin's own identity concerns may be, as an artist who, in her own words, communicates best in writing. His chapter on *The Left Hand of Darkness,* where sexuality and identity conjoin most intimately, is one of the most sophisticated readings of this complex work. His volume is indispensable for Le Guin scholars who wish to engage with contemporary thought.

—DEIRDRE BYRNE

Lesbian Community

Allen, Jeffner (ed.), *Lesbian Philosophies and Cultures,* Albany: State University of New York Press, 1990
Anderson, Shelley, *Out in the World: International Lesbian Organizing,* Ithaca, New York: Firebrand, 1991
Card, Claudia, *Lesbian Choices,* New York: Columbia University Press, 1995
Faderman, Lillian, *Odd Girls and Twilight Lovers: A History of Lesbian Life in Twentieth-Century America,* New York: Columbia University Press, 1991; London: Penguin, 1992
Jeffreys, Sheila, *The Lesbian Heresy: A Feminist Perspective on the Lesbian Sexual Revolution,* London: Women's Press, 1994
Johnston, Jill, *Lesbian Nation: The Feminist Solution,* New York: Simon and Schuster, 1973
Lorde, Audre, *I Am Your Sister: Black Women Organizing across Sexualities,* New York: Kitchen Table, Women of Color Press, 1985
Penelope, Julia, *Call Me Lesbian: Lesbian Lives, Lesbian Theory,* Freedom, California: Crossing Press, 1992
Ross, Becki L., *The House That Jill Built: A Lesbian Nation in Formation,* Toronto, Buffalo, and London: University of Toronto Press, 1995
Stein, Arlene (ed.), *Sisters, Sexperts, Queers: Beyond the Lesbian Nation,* New York: Penguin/Plume, 1993
Wolf, Deborah Goleman, *The Lesbian Community,* Berkeley and London: University of California Press, 1979

The question of whether lesbian identity has so far been able to define anything that might accurately be called a lesbian community (or perhaps a lesbian culture) is still a matter of some debate. JOHNSTON, writing in the early 1970s, proposed lesbianism as "the solution" to the "massive complaint" that is feminism, arguing that a true feminist political revolution will not have occurred "until all women are lesbians." PENELOPE, however, writing twenty years later, reports that although lesbian identities and the lesbian perspective are identifiable, lesbians are still hard at work trying to build community even among themselves. Given the tendency of even most lesbians to see their lesbianism from a liberal-humanist perspective as a "life-style choice" or as a matter of personal sexual attraction, the idea that lesbianism is primarily a revolutionary political action is a long way from being accepted even as a basis for lesbian unity, let alone as a solution that might potentially unite all women.

That lesbian unity is elusive is well known to ALLEN, whose volume has at its heart sensitivity to differences among lesbians and women. Allen proceeds from the view that imposing a false unity is just another form of oppression, requiring recognition that there is not a single lesbian community but instead that plurality is inseparable from "lesbian cultures," each lesbian herself inhabiting multiple cultures, with no necessary point of convergence. The book's strength is in its own diversity, offering various authors' exploration—from numerous, often contradictory perspectives—of what lesbian culture might mean as well as of the problems of trying to bring about such a thing in a manner that does not impose a self-negating illusion of sameness on what is in fact a plurality.

CARD offers a series of essays exploring, from a perspective rooted in the practical world of politics, the philosophical problems inherent in conceiving lesbian culture. Beginning from a consideration of how lesbian culture might be defined, she also discusses what it means to say that one has "chosen" lesbianism, as well as offering a helpful review of the literature on lesbian ethics. What makes the book singular, however, is its thoughtful, nuanced, personal collection of essays dealing with current issues directly affecting lesbians (such as relationships, violence, homophobia, and "outing") that begin to give form to a notion of lesbian community in the world of practice.

WOLF has written a very different sort of book, a book that does not concern itself with the theoretical question of whether or not how lesbians live together should be called "community" or "communities," "culture" or "cultures." Instead, this heterosexual anthropologist—who makes a virtue of her heterosexuality as confirmation of her scientific objectivity—assumes the existence of a lesbian community as the basis for her study of San Francisco lesbians in the early 1970s. What results—despite Wolf's claim that her view of "the lesbian world . . . may serve as a model for small, self-sustaining urban communities of the future, whatever the affectional preferences of their members"—is a descriptive account of only one impression of lesbian life at the time, making the book today primarily a rather limited historical document.

ROSS proceeds in somewhat the same vein (although with a different consciousness), aiming to redress with "a full-scale, original case-study of lesbian-feminist nation-building in Toronto . . . between 1976 and 1980" the often "perfunctory treatment [given] to lesbian-feminist organizing" in extant scholarship. By limiting her focus to the community-building efforts of a particular, politically conscious, subset of all lesbians—lesbian feminists—Ross gives her study a radical political dimension lacking in Wolf's work. Along with providing an extensive bibliography that should prove very useful to anyone doing research on this topic, Ross offers a critical, insider's view of lesbian-feminist organizing at one particular place and time, and she is able to provide larger lessons for such organizing in the future.

FADERMAN moves the story onto a larger stage, tracing historically the twentieth-century development of "lesbian subcultures" in America. Conducting 186 unstructured interviews with a diverse group of lesbians, she sought to uncover not only how they saw themselves, but "how they related (or did not relate) to the subcultures." These interviews she integrates into a fascinating broader picture (supplemented by some equally fascinating photographs) of the evolution of contemporary lesbian life, of the important ways in which that life is different from the "romantic friendships" of earlier times, and of the social changes that have enabled such difference.

Jeffreys and Stein offer very different views of the changes that have rocked lesbian life since the "lesbian sexual revolution" of the 1980s. STEIN (in line with Allen) celebrates the diversity of "lesbian cultures," offering a collection of essays that often nonjudgmentally describe and support differences without seeing or seeking any convergence among the contending points of view. JEFFREYS, on the other hand, has produced a stinging, unapologetically value-driven, lesbian-feminist condemnation of the embrace of male supremacy, of racism, and of the crassest of commercialism that she sees undergirding some currently fashionable lesbian sexual practices and lifestyles. Her critique—seeking to restore lesbian-feminist consciousness to the center of lesbian meaning—is a far-ranging and bracing challenge to the easy, anything goes attitude of lesbian inclusiveness that presently reigns in lesbian thought and life.

LORDE's slim volume offers a view of lesbian diversity from the perspective of the black community. Lorde addresses the problems blacks have in organizing together due to homophobia in the black community, which divides black women and is often used by black men to shame them into silence. She points out that black lesbians and gay men have contributed to the struggle for black liberation (although they have often been invisible as gays and lesbians) and calls on black people to confront politically the homophobic prejudices that continue to keep them from uniting across sexualities.

ANDERSON has produced a useful pamphlet aimed at helping lesbians connect globally. Ignoring lesbian groups inside the United States, her guide provides a listing of lesbian (or mixed gay and lesbian) groups in quite a number of the world's countries. She also includes some helpful national and world-regional facts about lesbian political movements and life (including whether lesbian sexuality is criminalized in a given country). This book is likely to be especially of use to lesbians traveling internationally.

—EILEEN BRESNAHAN

Lesbian History

Berube, Allan, *Coming Out under Fire: The History of Gay Men and Women in World War Two*, New York: Free Press, 1990

Donoghue, Emma, *Passions Between Women: British Lesbian Culture 1668–1801*, London: Scarlet Press, 1993; New York: HarperCollins, 1995

Faderman, Lillian, *Scotch Verdict: Miss Pirie and Miss Woods v. Dame Cumming Gordon*, New York: Morrow, 1983; London: Quartet, 1985

———, *Surpassing the Love of Men: Romantic Friendship and Love Between Women from the Renaissance to the Present*, New York: William Morrow, and London: Junction, 1981

Kennedy, Elizabeth Lapovsky, and Madeline D. Davis, *Boots of Leather, Slippers of Gold: The History of a Lesbian Community*, New York: Routledge, 1993

Mavor, Elizabeth, *The Ladies of Llangollen: A Study in Romantic Friendship*, London: Joseph, 1971; New York: Penguin Books, 1973

Newton, Esther, *Cherry Grove, Fire Island: Sixty Years in America's First Gay and Lesbian Town*, Boston: Beacon Press, 1993

Until quite recently, the span of time between the collapse of ancient Greek civilization and the rise of the nineteenth-century gay subcultures has been regarded as a sort of queer Dark Ages. Women possibly did something of a Sapphic nature with one another, but historians stymied by a lack of reliable sources found it quite difficult to reconstruct the lives of male or female homosexuals during these centuries. The first scholars of the history of sexuality, viewing homosexual subcultures as outgrowths of both urbanization and the widely spread theories of the sexologists, considered the creation of a uniquely gay identity to be a late nineteenth-century development. The bulk of literature on lesbians focuses on the United States in the decades following the 1870s, with a only a few books venturing into other countries and other eras.

DONOGHUE is one of the few scholars to examine the early modern period, with an examination of the full range of representations of lesbian culture in British print during the eighteenth century. A scholar of literature, she uses pamphlets, novels, biographies, medical treatises, and printed gossip to prove that eroticism between women was not as silent and invisible as some scholars have claimed, nor as widely berated as others have argued. Donoghue finds representations of much more than asexual "romantic friendship" between women. Through looking at the images of women, she argues, the attitudes formed by lesbians toward their sexual identities can be discovered. Her synthesis of the arguments of other historians is excellent. Unfortunately, she is dismissive of earlier scholarship, while offering few explanations of her own to account for general attitudes toward passions between women.

The history of same-sex sexuality is a field characterized by ignorance about its defining core. Although a few people have left evidence for posterity about their sexual behavior, most have preferred, for a variety of reasons, to take these facts about their lives to the grave. MAVOR examines the speculation surrounding the Ladies of Llangollen, two women who lived together for fifty years in Wales. The friendship of Eleanor Butler and Sarah Ponsonby, two aristocratic spinsters, began in 1778. Ten years later, the two ladies eloped to a cottage in Llangollen where, amid scenes of scandal and havoc, their generous way of living became a legend. Many of the most celebrated figures of the age visited them, but the question of their probable lesbianism was never answered. Mavor's biography provides a detailed account of the two women, but classes their relationship as romantic friendship instead of one with sexual aspects.

For much of history, women were thought to lack sexual desire. Passionate and sensual pronouncements of love between women were defined through the centuries as romantic friendships, chaste "practice relationships" that prepared women for marriage. FADERMAN (1981) examines these loves and concludes that most did not have sexual aspects. Her pioneering work contains the assumption that intimate female friendships of the past, far from being a problematic category, were straightforwardly valued and encouraged by the societies in which they were found. The phenomenon did not become threatening until women had economic independence.

The story of Jane Pirie and Marianne Woods lies right on the threshold between the eras of romantic friendship and sexual revolution. FADERMAN (1993) adds historical context to this case of two Scottish schoolteachers who were accused of having a sexual relationship, a tale that formed the basis for Lillian Hellman's play *The Children's Hour.* Faderman's book reads like a novel, and it has been used in classrooms to spark discussions about the nature and history of homosexuality. While the question of whether or not the two women were lovers remains unresolved (although Faderman offers some intriguing guesses), the evidence of public knowledge of lesbianism in 1810s Scotland is an important discovery. The witnesses and judges in this case clearly understood that women could be sexual together, yet they found this information so threatening that they determinedly attempted to disbelieve what they knew could occur.

No full-length studies of lesbians in the early twentieth century as yet exist, but much work has been completed on women during World War II. Concurrent with the expanding public debate about the military's exclusion of homosexuals, a body of literature has developed that examines the government's treatment of "deviant" soldiers and sailors. BERUBE uses oral histories to portray the lives of gay and lesbian soldiers while also examining the complex relationship between sexual discourses and state power. She provides a description of "dangerous women," namely masculine-styled butches, also focusing upon deviance from gender norms. However, suspected lesbians did not pose such a danger as men did. The power of women lay in their ability to sexually corrupt men; therefore lesbians could not harm military capability since women were believed to have little martial value. A point of particular interest is that none of the military reports located by Berube indicate that the performance records of homosexual soldiers justified their exclusion as individuals unsuitable for military service, or as security risks.

In a groundbreaking oral history, KENNEDY and DAVIS examine the self-identified lesbians of the working-class community from the 1930s through the 1950s in Buffalo, New York. Using interviews with 45 people, the majority of whom are white "butches," they provide evidence that the categories of "butch" and "femme" served as a method of organizing both lesbian eroticism and resistance. Kennedy and Davis suggest that lesbians in Buffalo not only created a community whose members supported one another in their mutual fight for survival in an extremely negative and punitive environment, but that they also challenged and helped to change social life and morals in the United States. While this latter claim is suspect, the existence of a culture of resistance is well documented. Butch and femme lesbians came together to build a public community that affirmed the value and importance of lesbian women.

NEWTON examines the development of a gay and lesbian mecca in New York from the 1930s to the 1980s. Gay resorts, like Cherry Grove, are the only places where lesbians can socialize and assemble without fear of hostile straight society. The initial migration of gays to Cherry Grove in the 1930s, Newton argues, is one of the clearest proofs we have that sexual preference was becoming the basis for a complete social identity.

—CARYN E. NEUMANN

Lesbian Identity

Birkby, Phyllis, Bertha Harris, Jill Johnston, Esther Newton, and Jane O'Wyatt (eds.), *Amazon Expedition: A Lesbian Feminist Anthology,* Washington, New Jersey: Times Change Press, 1973

Cornwell, Anita, *Black Lesbian in White America,* Tallahassee, Florida: Naiad Press, 1983

Curb, Rosemary, and Nancy Manahan, *Lesbian Nuns: Breaking Silence,* Tallahassee, Florida: Naiad Press, and London: Columbus, 1985

Ettorre, E.M., *Lesbians, Women and Society,* London and Boston: Routledge and Kegan Paul, 1980

Johnston, Jill, *Lesbian Nation: The Feminist Solution,* New York: Simon and Schuster, 1973

Kitzinger, Celia, *The Social Construction of Lesbianism,* London and Newbury Park, California: Sage, 1987

Lorde, Audre, *Sister Outsider: Essays and Speeches,* Trumansburg, New York: Crossing Press, 1984

Martin, Del, and Phyllis Lyon, *Lesbian/Woman,* San Francisco: Glide, and London: Bantam, 1972; revised edition, Volcano, California: Volcano Press, 1991

Mason-John, Valerie, and Ann Khambatta, *Making Black Waves: Lesbians Talk,* London: Scarlet Press, 1993

Penelope, Julia, *Call Me Lesbian: Lesbian Lives, Lesbian Theory, Freedom,* California: Crossing Press, 1992

Rothblum, Esther D., and Kathleen A. Brehony, *Boston Marriages: Romantic but Asexual Relationships among Contemporary Lesbians,* Amherst: University of Massachusetts Press, 1993

Lesbianism existed long before radical feminism's emergence, but within this movement, lesbianism took on a new meaning, both in women's self-definition as "woman-identified" women, and as a practice of refusal and resistance against the patriarchal, male-dominant organization of compulsory heterosexuality. Accepting Alix Dobkin's lyric that "any woman can be a lesbian"—or that all women exist somewhere on a "lesbian continuum," as Adrienne Rich put it—women who had never before acknowledged a sexual attraction to other women "came out" as lesbians, or even as lesbian separatists (who worked politically and lived not only apart from men but from heterosexual women as well), embracing "lesbian" as a political identity. Along with this developing consciousness—which also fueled and benefited from growing militancy and self-acceptance by women who had discovered their lesbianism apart from politics, and of pro lesbian organizations (such as the Daughters of Bilitis), which had long worked to end discrimination and to give lesbians a place to belong—came books that departed from the until-then hegemonic view of lesbianism as pathology and of lesbians as sexually depraved predators or pitiful sufferers. These works instead accepted and even celebrated lesbianism as a sane, healthy—and, indeed, political—orientation toward life.

Among the earliest was MARTIN and LYON's book, which, although seen by many lesbian feminists as woefully lacking in apprehending the political dimension of lesbianism (the 1991 edition contains an "Update" that briefly addresses this without accepting it, along with providing a recent history of lesbian activism), nevertheless helped to "demystify" lesbianism and make it visible as a valid alternate way of being in the world. Martin and Lyon's focus is on the everyday experience of lesbian life from the perspective of lesbians who are comfortable with their lesbianism and self-accepting of that identity. Taking lesbianism to be the choice of a woman to live the whole of her life with another woman—to which sexual practice (so often the focus of earlier work) is only one (private and, in their liberal-humanist view, marginally significant) aspect—they demonstrate that most lesbians are less concerned about or harmed by their sexual orientation than by the constant threat to their well-being posed by legally sanctioned discrimination, the fear or reality of social and familial ostracism, and the possibility of physical violence. While some of the book today seems dated, it is remarkable (and perhaps a bit sad) how well it has retained its usefulness as a down-to-earth introduction to some of the basic facts of everyday lesbian life.

The book by BIRKBY, HARRIS, JOHNSTON, NEWTON, and O'WYATT, on the other hand, is an uncompromising representative of the radical view, offering essays that, although written from a self-consciously radical lesbian feminist perspective, address many topics beyond the political significance of lesbian identity (though this topic is prominent throughout). As such, this anthology provides valuable examples of the application of lesbian feminist political consciousness to other issues, illustrating the breadth and depth of their concerns. Especially interesting are two essays by Jill Johnston, perhaps the best-known lesbian feminist writer of the time.

In her own book, JOHNSTON provides a series of intensely personal essays that—besides offering a fascinating and critical account of the sort of chilly reception radical lesbians received in the "counter-cultural" and liberal feminist circles of the 1970s—also offers her defense of "Gay/Feminism" as the "proper sexual-political stance for the revolutionary woman." Johnston, among the first to publicly and unapologetically assert a self-affirming lesbian identity, went so far as to audaciously insist that all women are lesbians. Her book—many of whose essays were taken from her widely read *Village Voice* column—was enormously influential among women who were at the time active radical feminists, to whom a self-affirming lesbian consciousness was often integral; it remains an important document of the spirit of that movement—and of the perspective that animated many of its participants—as well as of the times of which it was born.

Building on the radical view, ETTORRE sees lesbianism as a type of feminist consciousness that, by rejecting women's traditional dependence on the male wage, and by defying traditional sexual ideology, both challenges women's position in society and questions power relations. This view forms the basis for her sociological study of a group of urban lesbians, through which Ettorre documents the historical emergence of what she calls "social lesbianism," a new form of "public" (or "out") lesbian consciousness that she sees as a stage in the development of a group identity. She argues that social lesbianism builds toward an ideological/political stage of lesbian feminism, which has the potential to disrupt all forms of social oppression.

KITZINGER directly critiques what she calls a "gay affirmative" view of lesbianism (such as is presented by Martin and Lyon) on the grounds that in conceiving of lesbianism in liberal-humanistic terms—as just another alternative lifestyle and route to personal fulfillment—this view actually oppresses lesbians by offering a depoliticized construction and emphasizing individual choices and personal relationships that systematically undermine radical feminist theories of lesbianism. Kitzinger argues that because the patriarchal institution of compulsory heterosexuality is fundamental to women's oppression, lesbianism should be viewed as representing women's "refusal to collaborate" in their own betrayal. This work, offering an extensive review of the literature of social science research on lesbianism besides the author's own research, is a rare example of a book-length, radical lesbian feminist critique of the dominant social science view of lesbianism.

In the radical vein as well, PENELOPE's nuanced and thoughtful work offers essays exploring and critiquing not only patriarchal culture, but feminism and the lesbian community as well. A lesbian who "came out" in the 1950s, outside of political movements, Penelope accepts that radical feminism can help lesbians make sense of the patriarchal order but also criticizes feminism and women's studies for being too often concerned with heterosexual women's problems with men and with how those relationships can be improved and too little concerned with women's oppression and how women resist this oppression. She argues that although lesbian identities and a specific lesbian perspective on the world already exist, it is only by working together as lesbians that this becomes the lesbian "consensus reality"—the lesbian-centered view of the world—necessary to build true community.

MASON-JOHN and KHAMBATTA's brief book is a preliminary attempt to specify a British black lesbian identity. Using interviews and questionnaires as well as various histories, the authors explore what the identity "lesbian" means to various black women and discuss the controversies current in their community and the impact of racism on their lives. Feminism, however, is barely even mentioned in the book (apparently due to its perceived identity with western colonialism)—a dismissal not at all true of the books by CORNWELL and LORDE, each a collection of essays that explores the conflicts of strongly identifying oneself as a black lesbian feminist. Both authors were radical movement activists, who produced many of their works in direct response to practical politics; both combine the personal and the political in examining the complexities of the marginalization of lesbians and feminists in the black community and of black women in the women's movement. Each has produced a distinct account of the sources of strength in each passionately embraced aspect of their complicated identities, not the least of which was their self-identification as lesbians and woman-identified women.

Another book to explore conflicting identities is that by CURB and MANAHAN, which offers narratives by forty-nine former and present nuns who identify themselves as lesbians. This work—which was motivated in part by Curb's desire to answer the question of how many women of her generation had become nuns because they were already lesbians (although they might not yet have realized it)—broke centuries of public silence on women-loving-women within religious orders (that this silence was not total, however, is demonstrated by the helpful bibliography of additional readings). The book created a major national stir on its publication and remains a valuable source of insight into the fearsome pressures and limited options with which society has traditionally confronted women who wish to live their lives independent of men.

If one wants more confirmation that lesbian identity has little to do with sexual practice, the book by ROTHBLUM and BREHONY may be able to settle the question. They seek to throw light on the little-discussed presence within the lesbian community of couples who have only briefly—or even never—had genital sex with one another, although they continue to see one another as more than friends or ex-lovers, and who live together in committed and often extremely long-term relationships. Adding more evidence to the frequent observation that lesbians and gay males are fundamentally different sexually, this book explores in a fascinating way the question of what it means to identify as a lesbian.

—EILEEN BRESNAHAN

Lesbianism *see* Homophobia and Heterosexism; Lesbian Community; Lesbian History; Lesbian Identity; Lesbian Separatism; Lesbian Studies; Literature: Lesbian; Queer Theory

Lesbian Separatism

Douglas, Carol Anne, *Love and Politics: Radical Feminist and Lesbian Theories,* San Francisco: Ism Press, 1990

Hoagland, Sarah Lucia, *Lesbian Ethics: Toward New Value,* Palo Alto, California: Institute of Lesbian Studies, 1988

Morgan, Robin (ed.), *Sisterhood Is Powerful: An Anthology of Writings from the Women's Liberation Movement,* New York: Vintage, 1970

Phelan, Shane, *Identity Politics: Lesbian Feminism and the Limits of Community,* Philadelphia: Temple University Press, 1989

Shugar, Dana R., *Separatism and Women's Community,* Lincoln and London: University of Nebraska Press, 1995

Trebilcot, Joyce, *Dyke Ideas: Process, Politics, Daily Life,* New York: State University of New York Press, 1994

Wolf, Deborah Goleman, *The Lesbian Community,* Berkeley and London: University of California Press, 1979

A significant amount of energy has been spent debating the issues surrounding lesbian separatism. Women who have separated personally and professionally from men were excited by the prospect of doing so but often utopianized collective life. Many women believed that once they separated from men, problems such as racism and classism would vanish as well. This proved not to be the case, and separatist women were not always fully prepared for confronting issues, such as racism and classism, which they had thought they would automatically lose when they formed collectives.

SHUGAR's text focuses around three main elements in women's separatism: separatist theory from the late 1960s through the 1970s, historical narratives by the women in various separatist collectives, and a discussion of utopian separatist novels. Shugar makes numerous references to an incredibly diverse group of women, discussing the theories of Robin Morgan, Ti-Grace Atkinson, and the Radicalesbians, among others, and she includes experiences from varied groups including the Gutter Dyke Collective, Cell 16, and the Bloodroot Collective. Shugar aims to go beyond the surface debate of whether or not separatism is effective, something collectives faced in addressing their own issues, and provides a detailed examination of how texts, especially utopian separatist texts, can function within and contribute to separatist and feminist collectives.

In contrast, TREBILCOT's text is much more rooted in practice and experience than in theoretical debates. She deliberately eschews "academic" writing, constructing a book in which readers are encouraged to create and develop their own ideas and contributions to what separatism means. The text includes a variety of writing forms, including dialogue, essays, and poetry, focusing around themes important to women, such as sex, guilt, and competition. Trebilcot's point is dual: to create a book in which the author is not telling the readers what to believe (encouraging them to decide for themselves), and at the same time, to explore topics common to women in a manner that is both accessible and beneficial toward a women's culture.

In 1972, WOLF undertook an anthropological study of lesbians and separatism, focusing on the lesbian-feminist community in San Francisco. She found that her own sexual orientation, heterosexual, presented difficulties. On the other hand, she states, at the time many separatists felt that it was too risky for a lesbian to conduct research in the lesbian community, wanting to avoid the possibility of accusations of bias. Wolf's text makes numerous references to texts then commonly considered highly influential and includes extensive discussion of organizations (such as the Daughters of Bilitis), community projects (coffeehouses, bookstores, community centers), lesbian mothers, and a conclusion discussing her findings regarding the struggle of separatism and feminism to overcome issues such as racism and classism, within both the separatist community and the larger whole of feminist activity. Wolf also includes an extensive bibliography, which is an excellent way to discover what was being written when separatism was gaining popularity and political sway.

HOAGLAND, on the other hand, directly states that she is writing primarily from her experience as a lesbian. She makes it clear that she is writing, as a lesbian, to lesbians in order to create dialogue and discussion among lesbians interested in issues unique to lesbians. She states that even though there have been shortcomings within separatism, such as the short lifespan of organized separatist groups and communities, there remains one large collective of lesbians, that is, lesbians as a whole, who, she urges, can indeed create a revolution. This lesbian collective, in Hoagland's eyes, needs to become truly visible, and her book is an effort to describe and promote one way in which lesbians can move together and end oppression. This is what Hoagland means by lesbian ethics.

Hoagland makes many references to other works, but often to that by MORGAN, whose anthology includes over 50 essays about various issues of interest to women, not only lesbian separatists, although separatism is directly addressed. Morgan states that the book itself is a political act created and produced by women. It includes poetry, personal testimony, historical documents such as the NOW Bill of Rights and the Redstocking Manifesto, as well as discussions of racism, classism, birth control, abortion, prostitution, the media, sexual repression, and self-defense, among others. As an anthology, it contains a little bit of everything, whetting the reader's appetite for further reading while providing an impressive overview of sisterhood and issues of importance to women.

PHELAN argues against liberalism, assimilation, and essentialism, discussing difficulties against which lesbian separatism struggled, such as economic problems and the failure to celebrate the differences among a collective's members. Phelan's call is for women to resist total and complete separatism and instead direct their energies toward working to create improved conditions and communities for all women. Otherness will not vanish, Phelan posits, nor should it, and the acceptance of otherness, not the ignorance or avoidance of it, must be the base upon which future politics stands. Her text includes discussion of liberalism, medical discourse, definition, pornography and violence, feminism and sadomasochism, and the construction of identity.

DOUGLAS's text, like Shugar's, presents an extensive and detailed discussion of issues within feminist theory, of which separatism is a section. Douglas attempts to clarify radical feminist theory and lesbian feminist theory, identify what assumptions are at work in these theories, and show how these theories can work with, not against, one another. Her text centers around American feminism, with discussion of some influential French feminist work. Like Phelan's book, the emphasis is on recognizing and respecting differences within communities. There is also some reference to socialist feminism, although that is not Douglas's main focus. She discusses self-definition, the range of radical and lesbian feminists' views on love and sexuality, and activism. Douglas works to call attention to both the similarities and differences within two groups who are often polarized, and she does so, like many other authors, to create and foster discussion among groups in order to strengthen women's community.

—ANNE N. THALHEIMER

See also Intentional Communities

Lesbian Studies

Abelove, Henry, Michele Aina Barale, and David M. Halperin (eds.), *The Lesbian and Gay Studies Reader,* New York and London: Routledge, 1993

Beemyn, Brett, and Mickey Eliason (eds.), *Queer Studies: A Lesbian, Gay, Bisexual, and Transgender Anthology,* New York and London: New York University Press, 1996

Card, Claudia (ed.), *Adventures in Lesbian Philosophy,* Bloomington: Indiana University Press, 1994

Hoagland, Sarah Lucia, *Lesbian Ethics: Toward New Value,* Palo Alto, California: Institute of Lesbian Studies, 1988

Vicinus, Martha (ed.), *Lesbian Subjects: A Feminist Studies Reader,* Bloomington: Indiana University Press, 1996

Wilton, Tamsin, *Lesbian Studies: Setting an Agenda,* London and New York: Routledge, 1995

Zimmerman, Bonnie, and Toni A.H. McNaron, *The New Lesbian Studies: Into the Twenty-First Century,* New York: Feminist Press, 1996

Lesbian studies, originally classified with the more established category of gay studies, has begun in recent years to break away from umbrella-like categories of research, even though some important and influential lesbian studies works can be found within current queer studies and feminist studies anthologies.

"Queer" is a problematic term about which scholars remain divided; some are invigorated by reclaiming a once-derogatory term and enjoy the wordplay of "queer," while others refuse the term, stating that it trivializes and assimilates. Some authors call for a specifically defined lesbian studies, distinct from queer or gay studies, because there are issues unique to lesbian studies, such as sexism, which must be discussed separately. Gay and lesbian studies share common elements but are not identical and should not be discussed or theorized as such. However, there has been a marked increase in studying gay and lesbian (and bisexual, and transgender) topics and theories at the university level, leading to an increased number of anthologies.

ABELOVE, BARALE, and HALPERIN's text was developed in order to meet curricular needs, and it consciously omits highly developed genres such as poetry, testimony, fiction, and art (specifically comics and photographic essays). It includes cross-disciplinary essays addressing topics such as philosophy, history, anthropology, politics, and psychology, as well as African-American, ethnic, literary, and cultural studies. The wide range is because Abelove, Barale, and Halperin posit that the history of gay and lesbian studies has not yet been written (because it is relatively new) and cannot be defined simply by subject, research, practitioners, methods, or themes. This text is one of the most comprehensive collections in the field, and it conveys the intricacy of recent academic work on and in lesbian (and gay) studies.

BEEMYN and ELIASON also developed their text to meet curricular needs because, despite the recent rush of publications of queer studies materials, few focused on sexual and gender identities. The aim was also to produce a general academic text accessible to all readers, not just those familiar with theory, and to address sexual identity in a wider manner than just from within the categories of gay and lesbian. The text emphasizes diversity, investigates sexual identity, and specifically addresses queer theory. The essays included are non-assimilationist and are written for an audience familiar with non-heterosexuality (not written for a skeptical heterosexual reader, like some other anthologies). This text and the one by Abelove, Barale, and Halperin complement each other.

ZIMMERMAN and McNARON, on the other hand, emphasize that queer studies and lesbian studies are two different things. The authors of this book want to advance and promote an individually defined lesbian studies, while recognizing the importance of texts that include lesbian, gay, bisexual, and transgender work, because lesbian studies, in their eyes, entails questions and issues specific to the lesbian experience. The text includes an amazingly wide range of work, addressing a great number of issues, including global perspectives on lesbian studies, culture, pedagogy, academia, and theory (postmodern queer theory), race, class, and literature. Also included is an excellent list of influential texts, including works of poetry, fiction, drama, memoir, and auto/biography, which serves to direct the reader in specialized, specific directions depending upon individual interests.

WILTON's text functions similarly, working to create an agenda for lesbian studies while providing an academic approach to gender and the erotic for anyone interested in gender studies, sociology, and cultural studies. Wilton identifies the effects of heterosexism upon lesbian studies and deals specifically with lesbian roles and visibility in cultural studies, film theory, history, feminism, politics and social policy, and psychology. Wilton calls attention, as do Zimmerman and McNaron, to the inadequacy of queer theory and feminism to fully represent lesbian studies, and attempts to create a cross-disciplinary awareness of lesbianness (terming "lesbianism" as inherently pathological-sounding), because lesbianness appears within other disciplines, of course, but must be recognized and theorized in a specific lesbian studies. She also makes reference to lesbian philosophy, including a lengthy bibliography, urging readers to look at other texts as well.

One of these texts is CARD's. She states that lesbian philosophy is an essential part of lesbian studies, but addresses the difficulty of defining the term "lesbian." Her text is organized around five main themes: creativity and seeking knowledge, controversial attitudes and practices of sexual behavior (such as pornography and sadomasochism), constructing a meaning of "lesbian," the lesbian community, and discovering (as well as "discovering") a lesbian past. Within these five themes, many issues, such as racism, sadomasochism, exclusion, the challenge of bisexuality to lesbian ethics, and abuse are discussed. There is also an extremely focused selected bibliography of lesbian philosophy and related works included in this text, providing an excellent groundwork for further reading about lesbian philosophy and its connections to other areas of study.

HOAGLAND dedicates her book to creating a strong lesbian community based on respecting, rather than destroying, differences. She proposes new ways of thinking about ethics, because traditional ethics are problematic. Choices are based in traditional ethics, she states, which use blame as a motivator, making choices overly simplistic. Her contribution to lesbian studies is interesting; she resists defining "lesbian" as well as the limits of lesbian community. What she urges is a rethinking of established boundaries and ethics, applying not only to lesbians, but to all people. Part of the strength of lesbian community, she implies, can be located within the ability to find diversity both within and outside of the community.

VICINUS's text functions as a historical document, rooted in theory, in that it collects essays originally published in the journal *Feminist Studies* between 1980 and 1995 dealing with lesbian studies and lesbian roles. She calls for a fuller picture of lesbian studies rooted in respecting differences among women and their individual constructions of identity. The text does not start from initial uncertainty and move into concrete answers as lesbian studies progressed and developed, but rather it calls attention to issues that permeate lesbian studies as a whole, such as identity and lesbian subjects. She also makes the case that lesbian studies is important not only to lesbians, but to both men and heterosexual women, because lesbianism, she states, is central to the western sexual imagination. Vicinus's introduction also provides an excellent theoretical framework to contextualize the essays that make up the text, referring to influential theorists such as Judith Butler and Eve Kosofsky Sedgwick.

—ANNE N. THALHEIMER

See also Queer Theory

Lessing, Doris 1919–

British Writer

Knapp, Mona, *Doris Lessing,* New York: Frederick Ungar, 1984

Rowe, Margaret Moan, *Doris Lessing,* London: Macmillan, and New York: St. Martin's Press, 1994

Rubenstein, Roberta, *The Novelistic Vision of Doris Lessing: Breaking the Forms of Consciousness,* Urbana: University of Illinois Press, 1944

Sage, Lorna, *Doris Lessing,* London and New York: Methuen, 1983

Schlueter, Paul, *The Novels of Doris Lessing,* London: Feffer and Simons, and Carbondale: Southern Illinois University Press, 1973

Singleton, Mary Ann, *The City and the Veld: The Fiction of Doris Lessing,* London: Associated University Presses, and Lewisburg, Pennsylvania: Bucknell University Press, 1977

Sprague, Clair, *Rereading Doris Lessing: Narrative Patterns of Doubling and Repetition,* Chapel Hill and London: University of North Carolina Press, 1987

Thorpe, Michael, *Doris Lessing's Africa,* London: Evans Brothers, and New York: Africana, 1978

Whittaker, Ruth, *Doris Lessing,* London: Macmillan, and New York: St. Martin's Press, 1988

Doris Lessing's critical reputation has remained strong since the publication of her first novel *The Grass Is Singing* in 1950. RUBENSTEIN's study of the early novels identifies Lessing's abiding theme as that of the social conventions that shape and determine private experience. That feminist concerns might form some part of those social conventions and thus offer an entrance to the canon, Rubenstein agrees. However, although she places Martha Quest and Anna Wulf as central figures in the tapestry of twentieth-century female protagonists, Rubenstein ultimately offers the more universal image of a mind discovering, interpreting, and finally shaping its own reality as the common factor in Lessing's fiction. Lessing's texts, she argues, come replete with characters who create their identities despite society's pressures, but these identities suffer a bivalent or abnormal consciousness that seeks reconciliation within the text.

For SCHLUETER, this reconciliation comes in the form of commitment. Lessing's concern with the question of what it means to be an emancipated woman in a complex and male-ordered society is noted, but Schlueter's thematic analysis discovers commitment, be it to racial equality, political parties, love, marriage, or to the act of writing itself, as a crucial factor. This last, the act of writing, is a means of finding equilibrium in a chaotic universe, and a means of achieving the most significant commitment, that is to personal freedom.

The universalising character of much Lessing criticism determines her appearance in many of the major "writer series" available. KNAPP's book provides a general introduction to Lessing's work, grouped by genre, together with a chronology as far as the most recent publication and a bibliography. Interpretation in this volume clarifies content, without becoming tediously descriptive, for readers unfamiliar with the work.

A more selective approach is taken by WHITTAKER in the Modern Novelists series, by considering Lessing in relation to influence, theme, and style. A chapter on Lessing's background and influences gives way to a chapter on the colonial legacy in the work, in which Whittaker identifies an ambiguity in Lessing's treatment of Africa. While, throughout her fiction, Lessing acknowledges the African right to Africa, in her nonfictional writings there is little doubt that it is her Africa that is being written about. Whittaker goes on to discuss other Lessing themes: politics, women, the nature of art, insanity, dream, and prophecy. She marks Lessing's movement from her acute analyses of contemporary culture to her increasingly apocalyptic view of the planet, and her role as prophet.

SAGE's survey similarly identifies Lessing's fiction with an obsession with cultural change but also credits Lessing with significantly broadening the scope of the novel, by questioning a realist tradition imbued with social beliefs about sexuality, self, and authority. For Sage, Lessing's later work validates the margins of official culture, while THORPE, in the Modern African Writers series, deals with Lessing specifically as an African colonial writer with all that such a condition might entail. Using Virginia Woolf as his point of comparison, he notes that while Woolf was aware of literary tradition and heritage, for Lessing there were no such bearings. Nevertheless, he identifies Lessing's intensely African stories as a source of wider insight into a general human condition, before going on to delineate Lessing's Africa in terms of dream and reality.

For SINGLETON, the African veld accrues specific symbolic meaning. She marks Lessing's main concern as that of the creation of a more highly developed consciousness, characterised by a balance of intellect, imagination, emotion, and responsibility, as a means of creating the unified individual in a harmonious society. Singleton demonstrates her thesis via an exploration of three dominant motifs in Lessing's fiction: the unregenerate city, the ideal city, and the natural and primitive associated with the African veld. These motifs are associated with stylistic change, symbolic for the veld and realistic for the city, which utilises the panoply of civilised symbols associated with myth, tradition, and religion. For Singleton, this variety of style illuminates Lessing's main theme by balancing intellectual and emotional responses. This psychoanalytic approach to Lessing's work indicates that unification of the individual is achieved when unconscious elements are acknowledged by the consciousness. Singleton identifies the *Children of Violence* epic as demonstrating the Jungian concept of an entire society in the grip of an identity crisis, and therefore, suicidal.

The notion of balance suggests an underlying, and commonly held, assumption that Lessing's dialectic refers to a conflict between opposites. SPRAGUE challenges this view, suggesting that, in the term "doubling," one should assume a multiplication beyond twoness. She sees Lessing's characters portrayed against multiple mirrors: women against other women, against men, against the environment. Detecting naming and number games in the novels, which modify a straightforward surface, Sprague presents these games as a perfect correlative for Lessing's well-known perception of the complexity and contradictions in human experience. They indicate disruption in the formation of identity and the private social concerns.

ROWE, in her study of Lessing's works, from *The Grass Is Singing* to *The Fifth Child*, discovers some feminist interest in Lessing's view of the large realistic novel, that it is essentially male while the novel of emotion is female or at least androgynous. This work traces the influence of Lessing's Rhodesian childhood, before considering the novels in relation to the sex war, the problem of constructed appearance as a threat to inner space, and gendered text as a way of approaching history. The exploration of a variety of Lessing's literary and cultural negations concludes interestingly by considering Lessing's tendency to preface or end her novels with an adjustment to an imagined critical perspective on the part of her readers, which circumscribes the way in which the novel should be read.

—JAN PILDITCH

Literary Criticism, Feminist

Boone, Joseph A., and Michael Cadden (eds.), *Engendering Men: The Question of Male Feminist Criticism*, New York and London: Routledge, 1990

Broe, Mary Lynn, and Angela Ingram (eds.), *Women's Writing in Exile*, Chapel Hill: University of North Carolina Press, 1989

Davies, Carole Boyce, *Black Women, Writing and Identity: Migrations of the Subject*, New York and London: Routledge, 1994

Gilbert, Sandra M., and Susan Gubar, *The Madwoman in the Attic: The Woman Writer and the Nineteenth-Century Literary Imagination*, New Haven, Connecticut, and London: Yale University Press, 1979

Hirsch, Marianne, *The Mother/Daughter Plot: Narrative, Psychoanalysis, Feminism*, Bloomington: Indiana University Press, 1989

McClintock, Anne, *Imperial Leather: Race, Gender and Sexuality in the Colonial Context*, New York and London: Routledge, 1995

Smith, Sidonie, *A Poetics of Women's Autobiography: Marginality and the Fictions of Self-Representation*, Bloomington: Indiana University Press, 1987

Spivak, Gayatri Chakravorty, *In Other Worlds: Essays in Cultural Politics*, New York and London: Methuen, 1987

To cover almost four decades of feminist literary criticism in a single entry is to leave vast areas of it uncovered. The range of feminist literary criticism encompasses frameworks such as Anglo-American, Ecriture Feminine, psychoanalytic, deconstruction, Marxist, queer, black, Third World, and postcolonial, to name just a few. Incorporated within this term are analyses of writing by women and/or about women, focusing on sexualizing of the text, construction of the female reader, gay and lesbian writing, men using a feminist framework, and nonwhite women's writing. Added to this are traditional genres such as the autobiography, the novel, and poetry as reread through the lens of feminist literary criticism. Each entry in this sampler can, in turn, lead the reader to entire shelves of books and articles.

No entry on feminist literary criticism is complete without this classic text by GILBERT and GUBAR. Though much criticized for their occlusions of matters of race, colonialism, and class from their analysis, this text is among the best introductions for undergraduate and entry-level graduate students of literary studies, not only for its sheer readability, but also in its close attention to textual details and their interpretation. This book is usefully read along with their comprehensive three volume *No Man's Land* (1987–94).

BOONE and CADDEN's work is a collection of 17 pieces, all of which are by men using a feminist framework. The book is divided into four sections, with Part I dealing with the profession of literary criticism. Part II deals with "the anxieties that attend the process of acculturation" undergone by men in a patriarchal society. Particularly readable is Andrew Ross's essay on the construction of masculinity in pop culture in shows like *Bonanza* and Steven Spielberg's films. Part III deals with gender issues as experienced by gay men. The last section deals with male critics reading women writers through a feminist framework.

BROE and INGRAM's edited volume contains 17 essays that deal with the notion of exile in women's writing. Further included are three extra chapters that deal with the same theme in a wider context. The theme of exile is traced not only from home and nation, but also from creative places. The work includes essays on intellectual, creative, and emotional expatriation. The pieces by Annette Kolodny, Esther Fuchs, and Sneja Gunew and Gayatri Spivak suggest that women critics and theorists in the present day can still undergo exile within academia.

SMITH's systematic work should be required reading for advanced undergraduate and beginning graduate students working with autobiographies. The first chapter surveys autobiographical theories, and situates women's autobiographies within the context of their exclusion from mainstream male autobiographies. Using a post-structuralist framework, Smith comes up with a poetics of women's autobiography. There are chapters on Margery Kempe, Margaret Cavendish, Charlotte Charke, Harriet Martineau, and Maxine Hong Kingston.

The mother/daughter relationship has been the focus of a number of feminist and literary critics within the psychoanalytic framework, given that the mother has been the blind-spot in much of Freud's work. In Freud, the central mother figure is sidelined in favor of the father and the threat of castration. A number of feminist critics in the 1970s and 1980s attempted to reinscribe the occluded mother, and reinstate her within psychoanalytic discourse. HIRSCH's work thoroughly and systematically resituates the Freudian family romance. She posits the Demeter/Persephone myth as an alternative to that of Oedipus, which underpins Freud's theory. She then rereads works by Jane Austen, the Brontë sisters, George Sand, Kate Chopin, George Eliot, Edith Wharton, Margaret Atwood, Toni Morrison, and Alice Walker, to name a few.

DAVIES shifts the way "black" is read predominantly in the United States by including in the term African, Afro-Caribbean, and Third World postcolonial women. She sees the urgency of making such inclusions because of the "exclusionary nature of U.S. constructions of Black feminisms" which causes black women from outside the United States to locate their identities only within the context of U.S. hegemony. The subject of the work is thus black women and their writings, in their multiple identities and in their multiple meanings. There are chapters on theorizing black feminist writing, on Ama Ata Aidoo's play *Anowa*, on the relationship between postcolonial representation and theories of black women writing, and on Afro-Caribbean women as well as on black women's writing in the United States.

SPIVAK's work is an awkward selection, in that her pieces most pertinent to this entry, such as "Three Women's Texts and the Critique of Imperialism," and "Imperialism and Sexual Difference" have appeared as articles in collections or journals. This text by Spivak, however, contains several essays which reveal her literary framework—an intersection of Marxism, deconstruction, feminism, psychoanalysis, and critiques of colonialism—in her reading of literary works. Of particular note is Spivak's translation of a short story, "Breast-Giver," by Bengali writer Mahasweta Devi, and a reading of this story. Spivak is always difficult, but once understood, always takes the reader to an advanced plane of understanding texts, literary and cultural.

Much of the mainstream feminist literary criticism written in the United States and the United Kingdom in the 1970s and 1980s only deals with issues of gender. Cultural, racial, and class differences hardly feature in the analysis. McCLINTOCK's work, however, thoroughly analyzes a variety of texts within a framework that braids discourses of race, class, gender, sexuality, colonialism, nationalism, and imperialism. Furthermore, it enmeshes psychoanalytic semiotic, socialist, postcolonial, and deconstructionist frameworks as well. It brilliantly shows the need to bring together all these various strands of feminist thought. The three chapters that deal with the story of the Munby-Cullwick relationship should be read alongside selected chapters of Sander Gilman's *Freud, Race, and Gender*, to examine how the addition of class, race, and sexuality further resituates our reading of Freud. The chapter on black women's autobiography is outstanding. This work, which has redefined 1990s feminist literary criticism, is destined to be a classic.

—RADHIKA MOHANRAM

Literature: Biography and Autobiography

Alpern, Sara, Joyce Antler, Elizabeth Israels Perry, and Ingrid Wintner Scobie (eds.), *The Challenge of Feminist Biography: Writing the Lives of Modern American Women*, Urbana: University of Illinois Press, 1992

Benstock, Shari (ed.), *The Private Self: Theory and Practice of Women's Autobiographical Writings*, London: Routledge, and Chapel Hill: University of North Carolina Press, 1988

Heilbrun, Carolyn, *Writing a Woman's Life*, New York: Norton, 1988; London: Women's Press, 1989

Iles, Teresa (ed.), *All Sides of the Subject: Women and Biography*, Oxford: Pergamon, 1991; New York: Teachers' College Press 1992

Jelinek, Estelle (ed.), *Women's Autobiography: Essays in Criticism*, Bloomington and London: Indiana University Press, 1980

Stanley, Liz, *The Auto/biographical I: The Theory and Practice of Feminist Auto/biography*, Manchester: Manchester University Press, and New York: St. Martin's Press, 1992

Stanton, Domna C. (ed.), *The Female Autograph: Theory and Practice of Autobiography from the Tenth to the Twentieth Century*, Chicago and London: University of Chicago Press, 1987

Steedman, Carolyn, *Past Tenses: Essays on Writing Autobiography and History*, London: Rivers Oram Press, and Concord, Massachusetts: Paul, 1992

Swindells, Julia (ed.), *The Uses of Autobiography*, London: Taylor and Francis, 1995

Women's writing—about ourselves and other women—provides the knowledge base of women's studies. Writing and reading narratives of self-representation have therefore seen much feminist work: in affirming the value of women's experiences; and in theorizing the ideological, psychological, and socio-historical forms and means of representation. In literary studies, that autobiography and biography have been marginalized genres relative to the novel is partly a function of enforcing the fact/fiction dichotomy. The difficulties of defining autobiography and biography as distinct genres have beset many critics. However, feminist critics, alert to the exceptions of outmoded rules, have tended to be more concerned with gender in relation to authorship, the reader, tradition, and history than with merely identifying formal characteristics of narratives.

JELINEK argues that female-authored autobiographies are distinctive and constitute a female literary tradition of writings—often formally episodic or fragmentary—representing the self at a distance, rather than in a directly revelatory fashion. The 14 essays in Jelinek's anthology concentrate on autobiographies as literary texts, ranging from the seventeenth to the twentieth centuries.

STANTON's anthology consists of little-known autobiographical texts, as well as critical essays. Its stance is emphatically interdisciplinary. In coining the term "autogynography," Stanton argues against simplistic, referential readings of narratives as simply stories of lives and against the gendered private/public dichotomy that has restricted many analyses of female-authored autobiographies. Instead, she argues that in autogynography, stages conflict, dramatizing the alterity consigned to women by the male-centered system. The female subject writes herself into language that simultaneously defines her as object. The "private self" is interrogated in BENSTOCK's anthology. The separate examination of theories and practices of autobiography is a rhetorical move, based on the contention that the autobiographical writings under discussion demand new theoretical frameworks.

Accessibility is a priority for HEILBRUN, who successfully introduces the implications of the decentering of the author, and the grounding of subjectivity in language, for writing women's lives. This broad, critical summary of the issues in the field of women's biographies and autobiographies draws on Heilbrun's story as author both of academic discourse and (under the pseudonym of Amanda Cross) of detective novels.

For STEEDMAN, self and writing are reflexively produced through language in history. Autobiographical writings are narratives given shape, even restrained, by specific historical contexts that in turn constitute the writing self. The final chapter, "Writing History," closely addresses the problems of women's biography as embedded in a romance of history, arguing that women's history tends to produce narratives about individual women, perpetuating a melancholy sense of women's consignment to absence, isolation, and interiority.

In ALPERN, ANTLER, PERRY and SCOBIE's anthology, feminist biographers of modern American women write about various problematic aspects of writing biography in the context of women's history. By contrast, ILES's anthology takes a wider focus on women's biography as a genre, doing justice to its title, exploring "all sides of the subject." Unusual issues are explored, such as copyright restrictions on writing biography, and the consumption of women's biography by reviewers and from the booksellers' perspective.

The diacritical mark in the neologism "auto/biography" is used by STANLEY to deny a simple distinction between writing about self and other. This moves the debate forward, from surveys of "is" to explorations of auto/biographical "ought." Feminist auto/biography, she says, is anti-realist, addressing an active reader through a text that is self-consciously open to its ideological framework, representing individuals as fully and inextricably social beings. For Stanley, the appropriate metaphor for biography is that of kaleidoscope rather than microscope.

SWINDELLS's interdisciplinary anthology explores the uses of the autobiographical mode, charting the dynamics of autobiographical production and consumption. The autobiographical tradition is read in terms of tensions between the "egoists," for whom autobiography endorses individualism and historical empiricism, and the "interlopers," whose use of literacy and narrative is a means of finding a voice whereby the dispossessed may challenge and eradicate social inequalities. Like many of the anthologies on the subject, this book originated from a conference and has the associated virtue of representing the breadth of contemporary work in the field. Its range of exemplifying texts, including slave narratives, letters, and suffragist autobiography, is not restricted by narrowly literary limits. The emphasis on the uses of autobiography grounds the debate in the social context and allows exploration of, for instance, performance art and the uses of life stories in an educational context.

—KATHERINE COCKIN

Literature: Diaries and Journals

Begos, Jane DuPree (ed.), *A Woman's Diaries: Miscellany*, Weston, Connecticut: Magic Circle Press, 1989

Blodgett, Harriet, *Centuries of Female Days: Englishwomen's Private Diaries*, New Brunswick, New Jersey, and London: Rutgers University Press, 1988

Bunkers, Suzanne L., and Cynthia A. Huff (eds.), *Inscribing the Daily: Critical Essays on Women's Diaries*, Amherst: University of Massachusetts Press, 1996

Cline, Cheryl, *Women's Diaries, Journals, and Letters: An Annotated Bibliography*, New York: Garland, 1989

Goodfriend, Joyce D., *The Published Diaries and Letters of American Women: An Annotated Bibliography*, Boston: G.K. Hall, 1987

Schlissel, Lillian, *Women's Diaries of the Westward Journey*, New York: Schocken, 1981

Simons, Judy, *Diaries and Journals of Literary Women from Fanny Burney to Virginia Woolf*, Iowa City: University of Iowa Press, and London: Macmillan, 1990

Within the last two decades, three interrelated trends have drawn attention to women's diaries and journals: the breakdown of the literary canon, the recovery of women's writings, and the challenge to humanism's concept of self. The breakdown of the canon has prompted interest in "quasi-literary" genres such as journals and diaries, which, in turn, feeds into the recovery of women's writing, since non-canonical genres have been favored by women. Furthermore, the study of women's diaries and journals is useful in challenging humanism's assumptions about selfhood, because these personal writings offer insights about the subjectivity of a marginalized group. Although the common distinction between diaries and journals is that diaries contain more frequent but less introspective entries than do journals, most critics use the terms interchangeably, as do many diary or journal writers themselves. This flexibility of genre boundaries, which is characteristic of non-canonical genres on the whole, has prompted literary critics to group biography, autobiography, letters, diaries, and journals in a category simply called life writing. As a result, much of the seminal work on women's diaries and journals is found in books that treat other types of life writing as well; however, there are a number of books devoted exclusively to women's journals and diaries.

Among them is a collection of essays compiled by BEGOS and envisioned as a "sampler." The essays were originally printed in or intended for future issues of *Women's Diaries*, a quarterly newsletter, published by Begos between 1983 and 1986. They are divided according to whether they contribute to a history of the genre, illuminate individual diarists, or suggest practical applications (for example, how to keep a writer's journal). In each of her three divisions, Begos has aimed for as wide a range as possible. For example, the essays on individual diaries include an artist's diary, a prison diary, and travel diaries, as well as diaries that reflect different life stages, races, and professions. An attractive added feature is the "Book Reviews" section, which contains reviews of books that correspond to the main sections' essays.

BUNKERS and HUFF have also brought together a number of essays on women's diaries and journals; however, the essays in their collection focus solely on providing a critical framework for the genre. The first section contains essays that locate the genre within current debates about feminism, canon formation, narrative, and historicism. The essays of the second section place women's diaries within cultural matrices, highlighting the diary's ability both to illuminate and to contribute to cultural assumptions. The third section focuses on self-construction and women diarists' techniques.

In addition to essay collections, there are several single-authored texts on the subject. BLODGETT's book is the most inclusive in terms of time, covering journals written between 1599 and 1939. Her reading of 69 English and Welsh women's diaries leads her to conclude that women's lives changed very little over three and a half centuries. Consistent with this conclusion that women are the same throughout the time studied, she refers to diaries from widely divergent historical periods within each of the book's major divisions: reasons for writing, degree of accommodation to or rebellion against patriarchy, marriage, motherhood, and daughterhood.

SCHLISSEL, on the other hand, arranges her book chronologically, with one section for each of the decades it covers. Although its scope, diaries of women crossing the continental United States between 1840 and 1870, is narrower than Blodgett's, Schlissel's subject is an important one. The overland journey produced more journals and diaries than any other nineteenth-century U.S. event except the Civil War. Schlissel's aim is to "correct" the history of this migration, which so far had been constructed mainly from male journals. For example, women's diaries reveal anguish over the move and frequently describe Native Americans as helpful, whereas men's emphasize a sense of adventure and frequently depict Native Americans as enemies. Schlissel examines 96 diaries and memoirs, including several written by African-American women. The book's main section is followed by four sample diaries and a useful chart that shows major content areas of each of the 96 diaries analyzed.

SIMONS's scope, the mid-eighteenth through the early-twentieth centuries, is larger chronologically than Schlissel's, but Simons limits her study to journals of literary women, assigning a separate chapter each to the journals of Fanny Burney, Dorothy Wordsworth, Mary Shelley, Elizabeth Barrett Browning, Louisa May Alcott, Edith Wharton, Katherine Mansfield, and Virginia Woolf. Because they heighten a dichotomy frequently found in women's diaries, that is, the dichotomy between public and private realms; because they reveal methods of writing and publishing; and most of all because they are literary pieces in their own right, Simons believes that the journals of these women deserve more attention than they previously have had as mere footnotes to their authors' more canonical work.

Two annotated bibliographies are included in this entry, because they contain useful information for readers interested in locating particular journals or diaries or simply interested in seeing the sheer number of as well as range of female diarists. CLINE's bibliography is valuable precisely because of its range: it covers the period from the eighteenth century up to 1987 and contains 2,600 entries that annotate both unpublished and published journals, as well as critical works, anthologies, and other bibliographies. Although it contains a strong emphasis on United States diarists, it also annotates diaries from other countries.

While GOODFRIEND's bibliography has even a wider chronological range than Cline's (1669–1980), it covers only published American diaries. As Goodfriend herself notes, the majority of the diaries listed were written by women of privilege, in other words, women of English Protestant background, since they and their families were more likely to have access to publishing. However, every life stage as well as every marital status is represented, and the range of diarists includes housewives, farm women, factory workers, and professional women. What makes this bibliography especially valuable is the length and content of the annotations.

—ERNA KELLY

Literature: Childrens' *see* Literature: Modern Childrens'

Literature: Drama

Berney, K.A. (ed.), *Contemporary Women Dramatists,* Detroit, Michigan, and London: St. James Press, 1994

Brater, Enoch (ed.), *Feminine Focus: The New Women Playwrights,* New York and Oxford, Oxford University Press, 1989

Brown-Guillory, Elizabeth, *Their Place on the Stage: Black Women Playwrights in America,* New York: Greenwood, 1988

Cerasano, S.P., and Marion Wynne-Davies, *Renaissance Drama by Women: Texts and Documents,* New York and London: Routledge, 1996

Donkin, Ellen, *Getting into the Act: Women Playwrights in London, 1776–1829,* London and New York: Routledge, 1995

Gale, Maggie B., *West End Women: Women and the London Stage, 1918–1962,* London and New York: Routledge, 1996

Lamar, Celita, *Our Voices, Ourselves: Women Writing for the French Theatre,* New York: Peter Lang, 1991

Laughlin, Karen, and Catherine Schuler (ed.), *Theatre and Feminist Aesthetics,* Madison, New Jersey, and London: Fairleigh Dickinson University Press, 1995

Quinsey, Katherine M. (ed.), *Broken Boundaries: Women and Feminism in Restoration Drama,* Lexington: University Press of Kentucky, 1996

Schroeder, Patricia R., *The Feminist Possibilities of Dramatic Realism,* Madison, New Jersey: Fairleigh Dickinson University Press, 1996

Stoll, Anita K., and Dawn L. Smith (ed.), *The Perception of Women in Spanish Theatre of the Golden Age,* Lewisburg, Pennsylvania and London: Bucknell University Press, 1990

Stowell, Sheila, *A Stage of Their Own: Feminist Playwrights of the Suffrage Era,* Manchester: Manchester University Press, and Ann Arbor, University of Michigan Press, 1992

Within the larger frameworks of feminist literary criticism, a resurgence of interest in drama by women throughout place and time has also arisen. Most authors begin their study with the English Renaissance, like CERASANO and WYNNE-DAVIES. In addition to including a few actual plays written by women such as Elizabeth I and Mary Wroth, the unique substance of the book rests in a section marked "Documents." Here, the authors gather several materials from the sixteenth and seventeenth centuries that describe such areas as women's attendance at plays, women as spectators, women as performers, and women in theatrical affairs. These texts add to understandings of what women actually experienced in this theatrical community.

QUINSEY collects 12 contemporary essays in her anthology that analyze various aspects of women's involvement in theatre during the Restoration. Most of the book focuses on plays written by women, especially those by Aphra Behn. Other articles focus on women in plays by men and discussions of the history of performance. The entire book reflects an interest in connecting literature to its social context; here, the authors focus on the ideology of England during this historical time of change.

DONKIN looks at a somewhat later time in English history. She focuses on seven playwrights including Frances Burney and Hannah Cowley. These women experienced different degrees of success while still creating a large percentage of the plays by women that reached the London stage in the latter half of the eighteenth century. The book also looks at the larger system of theatrical production, including a discussion of theatre managers and the economic operations that affected the performing process.

While extending the focus to other European countries, other authors take charge of similar projects. STOLL and SMITH focus their anthology on Spanish theatre of the Golden Age, the sixteenth and seventeenth centuries. The 15 articles include a wide range of subjects, but several focus on plays by authors such as Ana Caro, Sor Juana Inés de la Cruz, and María de Zayas. The book analyzes the representation of highly personal and political issues, including rape and women's social position. Looking at women in contemporary France, LAMAR examines 16 women ranging from Marguerite Duras to Hélène Cixous. She intends for her work to introduce a largely unfamiliar American audience to these women and present a panoramic view of the ways that these women look at their lives.

GALE divides her study of women in the London theatre during the first half of the twentieth century into various subject areas. After a few chapters of overview and historical context, she looks at how authors wrote plays to represent working women, motherhood, and women without men. One real value of this book is an extensive appendix that lists each play staged in London from 1917 to 1959 that was written by a woman. She provides the play, author, theatre, dates of performance, and number of performances; this catalogue includes single performances and extended runs. Looking at America during the same time period, STOWELL centers her analysis on four women who created plays that directly addressed women's fight for voting rights. Considering at the work of Elizabeth Rollins, Cicely Hamilton, Elizabeth Baker, and Githa Sowerby, Stowell examines the connections between politics and literary expression.

BROWN-GUILLORY writes one of the first and most important analyses of plays by African-American women. A playwright herself, she begins with a look at the Harlem Renaissance, a foundational period in the development of African-American literature generally and women's playwrighting in particular. The bulk of the book highlights the work of Alice Childress, Lorraine Hansberry, and Ntozake Shange. Brown-Guillory looks at the theatrical form, the tradition of African-American storytelling, and images of African-American people and culture.

SCHROEDER deals with topical areas similar to those of both Stowell and Brown-Guillory. Like Stowell, she dedicates one chapter to white women writing in the early twentieth century, and she uses another chapter to discuss the Harlem Renaissance much like Brown-Guillory. A later chapter examines more contemporary playwrights. Throughout the book, Schroeder examines the meanings of theoretical concepts such as "realism" and "feminism," and how the words intersect in discussions of plays by women, thus creating a more theoretical outlook than the others mentioned here.

LAUGHLIN and SCHULER also deal with theoretical issues in women's dramatic writing, questioning what a feminist aesthetic is and how it might affect plays by women. This anthology collects 15 essays that scrutinize work by a variety of women, including playwrights from Russia and South America in addition to American and English women. Overall, the book examines how women have altered theatre, revising the traditions and creating their own form of expression. BRATER's anthology also looks at contemporary women from a multitude of cultural perspectives including French, American, and English. The 15 essays utilize a variety of critical frameworks but are united in a common need to examine how women demand their presence in current theatrical practice.

One of the fundamental reference works in the field is the one created by BERNEY. The book lists, in alphabetical order, over 80 women writing in the English language. The women are either still active today or have died since 1950 after creating work that still exerts a contemporary influence. Each entry consists of a biography, a complete list of published and/or produced plays, other published books, a list of critical sources, and an essay that discusses the general themes and style of each author. A final section lists over 20 of the most powerful and influential plays by contemporary women, with an essay for each that presents the play's importance and power.

—NELS P. HIGHBERG

See also Theater: Women's Activity in

Literature: Fiction

Christine de Pisan, *The Book of the City of Ladies,* translated by Earl Jeffrey Richards, New York: Persea, 1982; London: Picador, 1983

Gilbert, Sandra M., and Susan Gubar, *The Madwoman in the Attic: The Woman Writer and the Nineteenth-Century Literary Imagination,* New Haven, Connecticut, and London: Yale University Press, 1979

Greene, Gayle, *Changing the Story: Feminist Fiction and the Tradition,* Bloomington: Indiana University Press, 1991

Kahane, Claire, *Passion of the Voice: Hysteria, Narrative, and the Figure of the Speaking Woman, 1850–1915,* Baltimore and London: Johns Hopkins University Press, 1995

Smith, Barbara, *Toward a Black Feminist Criticism,* Brooklyn, New York: Out and Out, 1977

Woolf, Virginia, *A Room of One's Own,* London: Hogarth Press, and New York: Fountain Press, 1929

The task of contemporary feminist theorists and critics of fiction has been a task of reenvisioning the tradition—of reforging stories and remaking ideas about stories. Many of those theorists suggest that a work of fiction, when written or even read by women, makes for a radically different point of view based on their experiences as women within patriarchy. The poet Adrienne Rich has called that reenvisioning "more than a chapter in cultural history: it is an act of survival."

Perhaps the grandmother of reimagining the relationship between feminine fictions and historical women is CHRISTINE DE PISAN (c. 1364–1431). Known as the first professional female writer, she countered the misogynistic moral tradition from *The Romance of the Rose,* and particularly the satirical portraits by Boccaccio in *On Famous Women.* Her "feminist" refutation and defense, *The Book of the City of Ladies (Le livre de la cité des dames),* is itself a fictional work, presented as a world history and offered as critique of the assumed condition and character of women. Her imaginatively revised narratives of classical, biblical, and historical figures, and the literary city she invented for her famous women, are inherently ways of rereading women from the past, as well as mythical, feminine figures. She represented old stories about women simply by changing perspective on them. This is the radical—as in both "root" and "revolutionary"—strategy of all readers of women and fiction who have followed after her.

WOOLF is a key twentieth-century literary figure, as well as a transitional voice between what are called first-wave and second-wave feminisms. Woolf's novels shift the parameters of gender and voice, but she made perhaps the most famous claim in twentieth-century feminism in her most accessible work, this classic essay about gender and art. Her answer to what women require in order to be able to write fiction is this: "A woman must have money and a room of her own." The book discusses women in patriarchal culture, that women play the role of looking-glasses reflecting the figure of man at twice his size. Woolf also created a fictional Judith, Shakespeare's wonderfully gifted sister and victim of tragic suicide, in order to suggest how female genius has been thwarted and wasted.

One of the most influential works for academic feminism, literary criticism in particular, is GILBERT and GUBAR's study that asks the question, how will women write if the stories they know are patriarchal? The authors examine the work and lives of nineteenth-century female writers, laying bare the patriarchal assumptions that are woven into narrative and culture. Their work is literary theory and social criticism, demonstrating how the female writer (and reader) must deconstruct and reconstruct images of femininity. The nineteenth-century answer to the patriarchal feminine image is both to succumb to it and to revise it, by the duplicitous creation of "the madwoman in the attic."

SMITH's provocative and innovative work has proposed a black feminist aesthetic that would draw upon political implications as well as contribute to the black feminist movement; it would overturn assumptions about a work, as she has, in describing Toni Morrison's *Sula;* and it would fly in the face of white patriarchal culture by portraying the black lesbian character. Smith defines lesbians as women who are central figures, who are positively described, and who have significant relationships with one another.

GREENE explores metafiction in contemporary writers, particularly Doris Lessing, Margaret Drabble, Margaret Atwood, and Margaret Laurence. Metafiction—fiction that internally comments on its own narrative—is another way, Greene suggests, of challenging inherited cultural and literary tradition. Implicity she makes an unfinished narrative of her own insightful book about "postfeminist" narrative (that is, writing after the hope of social change borne of revisiting the past has been exhausted). She concludes her book tentatively, echoing Drabble's distopic, *The Radiant Way,* that the search for the past is no longer revitalizing; yet she affirms that changes are even now making a new beginning.

KAHANE is one of a number of psychoanalytic theorists who bring premises of psychoanalysis to the understanding of literary texts. She begins with Sigmund Freud's unfinished and unsuccessful case history of "Dora," reading it as fiction, as a way of reading fiction, and as a way of reading the psyche. She suggests that the fictional and historical woman's voice is a hysterical voice within an unstable narrative in crisis. Her theoretical discourse is, she says, a "psycho-poetics of hysteria." All of these theorists and critics are polemical and original; they demand that readers look again, look both at text and context, and learn to read the politics, the sexuality, and the language of fiction.

—LYNDA SEXSON

See also Literature: Lesbian; Literature: Modern Childrens'; Literature: Mysteries and Crime Fiction; Literature: Romance; Literature: Utopian and Science Fiction

Literature: Folklore and Fairy Tales

Chinen, Allan B., *Waking the World: Classic Tales of Women and the Heroic Feminine,* New York: Jeremy P. Tarcher, 1996

Estes, Clarissa Pinkola, *Women Who Run with the Wolves: Myths and Stories of the Wild Woman Archetype,* New York, Ballantine, 1992

Jordan, Rosan A., and Susan J. Kalcik (eds.), *Women's Folklore, Women's Culture,* Philadelphia: University of Pennsylvania Press, 1985

Kolbenschlag, Madonna, *Kiss Sleeping Beauty Good-Bye: Breaking the Spell of Feminine Myths and Models,* Garden City, New York: Doubleday, 1979

Rusch-Feja, Diann, *Portrayal of the Maturation Process of Girl Figures in Selected Tales of the Brothers Grimm,* Frankfurt am Main and New York: Peter Lang, 1995

Von Franz, Marie-Louise, *Problems of the Feminine in Fairytales,* Dallas, Texas: Spring, and Shaftesbury: Element, 1972

Warner, Marina, *From the Beast to the Blonde: On Fairy Tales and Their Tellers,* New York: Farrar, Straus and Giroux, and London: Chatto and Windus, 1994

Zipes, Jack (ed.), *Don't Bet on the Prince: Contemporary Feminist Fairy Tales in North America and England,* New York: Methuen, and Aldershot: Gower, 1986

Folklore and fairy tales hold a strange attraction; they engage us in stories of human nature told in fantastic terms with magical resolutions, with the line between good and evil clearly marked. The study of folklore and fairy tales has become closely linked with women's studies because these texts and oral performances are transmitted primarily by women and usually include women as protagonists. Since the traditional audience of these tales is children, it is often debated as to whether such stories might influence a child's perception of gender in a positive or negative manner. Jungian approaches also discuss how adults relate to aspects of gender presented in folk and fairy tales. However, some scholars argue for more historic and ethnographic studies of these texts, stressing the importance of the context as well as the message.

In a lengthy introduction, ZIPES argues for a feminist re-reading of fairy tales, stressing the need to recognize their harmful portrayals of women and the negative effects these portrayals may have on young readers. As an alternative, he offers several contemporary feminist fairy tales by different authors; these new tales present both male and female characters in a positive light while retaining classic fairy-tale structures and archetypes. These new tales expand on ancient motifs such as the wise old woman and the journey to prove self-sufficiency; they also offer inversions of the typical fairy tale such as beautiful young witches and princes who must be rescued. Essays after the stories note that while several traditional fairy tales do have active and positive female protagonists, the problem is that the tales most repeated and remembered in western society are those that value the woman who is young, beautiful, passive, and victimized.

In an example of feminist writing that leans toward the self-help genre, KOLBENSCHLAG uses the images of Sleeping Beauty, Snow White, Cinderella, Goldilocks, Beauty and the Beast, and the Frog Prince to illustrate problems in women's psychological development. She explains that the largely passive roles in these stories continue to be reenacted by women because western society, for the most part, expects women to exist in a state of arrested emotional development, waiting on the "prince" who will give them meaning instead of working toward self-actualization. It is her hope that women will start to transform themselves into active and fulfilled adults by abandoning the passive behaviors and attitudes exemplified in fairy-tale women.

However, it is important to distinguish between the tales themselves and the perceptions we have of them, as illustrated by RUSCH-FEJA's study of the first seven editions of the Grimm brothers' stories. She found that the Grimms carefully changed and censored later editions of their collection to eliminate references to the budding sexuality of female characters, such as premarital pregnancy and incest. Thus, although these changes were made to accommodate the social mores of the time, the focus of maturation in these tales becomes one of emotional, rather than physical, development; for these heroines, a period of isolation spent on hard work, reflection, and piety is rewarded. The emphasis on marriage as the ultimate goal for Grimm heroines, Rusch-Feja asserts, is a reflection on nineteenth-century Germany, and not necessarily an ideal to be internalized today.

Often involving heavy-handed symbolism and obvious morals, fairy and folk tales are heavily influenced by archetype, making them a favorite subject of Jungian psychologists. Their interpretations attempt to realize how particular archetypal features of these stories may have an effect on the lives of present-day women. In this vein, ESTES presents Jungian explications and retellings of folk tales from many cultures that explore the "wild woman" as an archetype. She argues that contemporary women may consciously employ these stories in their lives in order to empower and heal themselves psychologically; by realizing that many examples of powerful women exist in fairy tale, myth, and folklore, women are provided with an alternative to passive feminine roles in both fiction and reality.

Similarly, CHINEN recounts 12 fairy and folk tales from diverse cultures, each with a female protagonist who triumphs through asserting herself. He presents extensive analyses of the characters, plots, and symbols of each to illustrate the similar ways in which women relate and respond to issues of power, wisdom, and relationships with nature, with men, and with each other. His work with these tales reveals their utopian yearnings; in his view, their ultimate message is a hope for a world in which masculine and feminine principles achieve balance in both the individual and society.

In a series of 12 printed lectures originally delivered in the late 1950s, Jungian analyst VON FRANZ explores the anima, or the feminine dimension, of men, as it is treated in many fairy and folk tales, comparing and contrasting it with the way the genre treats actual women; some stories can be interpreted through either approach. These tales are used as templates to illustrate the problems of psychological adjustment that occur in a patriarchal society where men and, ironically, women, are taught to deny or refuse to develop "feminine" aspects of themselves such as intuition in favor of "masculine" traits such as rationality.

Taking a historical approach, WARNER provides an extensive study of the fairy tale by focusing on the tellers, who were predominately women. The messages, typical plots, and stock characters, she asserts, can give us an idea of the way relationships between women worked in the historical periods from which the tales emerged. She notes that while men in these tales usually prevail by force, women most often use their voices or purposely remain silent in order to succeed.

The oral performances of women are also the focus of the collection of essays edited by JORDAN and KALCIK. This expansive grouping works with varying approaches to all kinds of women's folklore, from fairy tales and family histories to jokes and CB radio handles.

The editors stress that women's folklore is inherently different from that of men and therefore should be studied in the same manner as the folklore of an ethnic group—from both inside and outside perspectives—in order to understand it fully.

—TRIA AIRHEART-MARTIN

Literature: Journals *see* Literature: Diaries and Journals

Literature: Lesbian

Faderman, Lillian, *Surpassing the Love of Men: Romantic Friendship and Love between Women from the Renaissance to the Present,* New York: Morrow, and London: Junction, 1986
Foster, Jeannette H., *Sex Variant Women in Literature,* New York: Vantage, 1956
Grier, Barbara, *The Lesbian in Literature,* Reno, Nevada: Ladder, 1967
Griffin, Gabriele, *Heavenly Love? Lesbian Images in Twentieth-Century Women's Writing,* Manchester: Manchester University Press, and New York: St.Martin's Press, 1993
Jay, Karla, and Joanna Glasgow (eds.), *Lesbian Texts and Contexts: Radical Revisions,* New York: New York University Press, 1990; London: Only Women, 1992
Munt, Sally (ed.), *New Lesbian Criticism: Literary and Cultural Readings,* New York and London: Harvester Wheatsheaf, 1992
Rule, Jane, *Lesbian Images,* Garden City, New York: Doubleday, 1975; London: Davis, 1976
Zimmerman, Bonnie, *The Safe Sea of Women: Lesbian Fiction 1969–1989,* Boston: Beacon Press, 1990; London: Only Women, 1992

Since the 1970s, there has been a burgeoning of critical lesbian writing, meaning both critical writing by lesbian authors and critical writing about lesbian characters. The former has been promoted by an increase in the visibility of lesbians, associated in the United States and in the United Kingdom with the emergence and activities of the women's liberation movement, the civil rights movements, the lesbian and gay movements and, most recently, the "queer" movement. The political impact of these various movements has been paralleled in the publishing world by the setting up of women-only and lesbian presses and in academe by the establishment of women's studies, gender studies, lesbian and gay studies, black studies, and other such disciplines, which have resulted in lesbian texts being increasingly (re)produced, circulated, and discussed.

FOSTER produced one of the earliest surveys of writings about what she—in tune with the 1950s—called "sex variant women." Her work ranges from the classical Greek poetry of Sappho to the post-World War II period, with its major focus being on twentieth-century writing. Foster's interpretive plot summaries of numerous texts offer a useful introduction, both to writings about lesbians through 2,000 years, and to perceptions of such writings in the 1950s.

RULE provides three contextualizing chapters on lesbian writing, indicating the shifts from viewing lesbianism as a sin to regarding it as a sickness, which occurred from the late nineteenth into the early twentieth centuries. The main part of her work is taken up with biographical and interpretive portraits of 12 lesbian writers, predominantly from the early twentieth century (for example Radclyffe Hall, Gertrude Stein, and Violette Leduc, but also including May Sarton and Maureen Duffy). This writing forms part of the Anglo-American feminist tradition of uncovering authors and texts, in this instance lesbian ones, previously lost from history.

This tradition is carried on by FADERMAN, who, like Foster, offers an interpretive survey of lesbian writing from the Renaissance to the present, not just concerning western writing, but also with respect to, for example, Chinese texts. Her main argument, that women's relations with each other may be seen as romantic friendships that do not necessarily include sexual relations, has subsequently been strongly critiqued by lesbian writers who regard the sexual component of lesbian relationships as a central and defining characteristic of women identifying as lesbians.

ZIMMERMAN focuses on lesbian fiction of the 1980s and 1990s, discussing how the construction of the lesbian in fiction has changed during that time, specifically in relation to the idea of a lesbian community, which, from the notion of a "lesbian nation," has moved to a recognition of differences among lesbians that suggest fragmentation rather than cohesion. The issue of the relationship of author, text, and reader, and the ways in which material reality and textuality interrelate, become a prominent concern here in the assertion that texts both reflect and construct their contexts.

GRIFFIN centers her work on lesbian images in twentieth-century women's writing, discussing fiction as well as non-fiction, poetry, and plays. In seven roughly chronologically ordered chapters, she details the construction of the lesbian as inhabiting a twilight world in the 1950s, the claims for separatism as expressed in lesbian feminist science fiction in the 1970s, the idea of a new romanticism in the 1980s, the emergence of sexually focused writings and lesbian porn/erotica in the 1990s, and the representation of older women in lesbian writing, the latter a topic rarely addressed.

GRIER has a special place in lesbian criticism, in that she provides an extremely useful tool for tracing representations of lesbians in literature in her briefly annotated bibliography. Grier does not restrict her bibliography to writing by women or to writing sympathetic to lesbians. Her volume ranges very widely, including all kinds of genres, such as pulp fiction, and also sexological writings and biographies. It is a very useful source book.

JAY and GLASGOW's edited collection is indicative of the ways lesbian criticism and scholarship have moved forward in the 1980s and 1990s. It is divided into three sections. The first one is devoted to lesbian writers commenting on their work and on what it means to write as a lesbian, thus raising the question of a specifically lesbian aesthetic. The second section looks at how lesbians have encoded themselves in texts in a context where being lesbian could not or would not be spoken about. And the final section contains a range of essays on lesbian themes and sources, such as the "Queen B" figure in black literature, mother-daughter relationships in lesbian plays, and so forth. The volume seeks to represent the diversity of lesbian identities recognized by and informed by lesbian writing of the late 1980s and of the 1990s.

MUNT's project is not dissimilar to Jay and Glasgow's, with essays focusing on either specific authors such as Audre Lorde, on particular texts like *Oranges Are Not the Only Fruit,* by Jeanette Winterson, or on particular genres such as lesbian utopian writing or lesbian pornography. The essays in this volume are strongly informed by contemporary theoretical concerns, such as postmodernism and various kinds of critical theory. As such, they represent literary criticism as it is currently evolving and practiced within mainstream literary studies. This in itself is indicative of the advent of scholarly lesbian writing.

—GABRIELE GRIFFIN

Literature: Letters

Altman, Janet Gurkin, *Epistolarity: Approaches to a Form,* Columbus: Ohio State University Press, 1982

Cherewatuk, Karen, and Ulrike Wiethaus (eds.), *Dear Sister: Medieval Women and the Epistolary Genre,* Philadelphia: University of Pennsylvania Press, 1993

Goldsmith, Elizabeth (ed.), *Writing the Female Voice: Essays on Epistolary Literature,* Boston: Northeastern University Press, and London: Pinter, 1989

Kauffman, Linda, *Discourses of Desire: Gender, Genre, and Epistolary Fictions,* Ithaca, New York: Cornell University Press, 1986

Schweik, Susan, *A Gulf So Deeply Cut: American Women Poets and the Second World War,* Madison: University of Wisconsin Press, 1991

The art of letter writing, or *ars dictaminis,* was the first clearly defined art form to appear in western Europe. In 1087 Alberic of Monte Cassino wrote the first surviving handbook, detailing the letter's five-part structure: salutation, introduction, narration, petition, and conclusion. With the collapse of the Roman empire in the fifth century and the subsequent lowering of educational requirements, letter writing nearly ceased.

Without a formal education, women of the sixth century wrote letters, usually following Alberic's five-part structure. ALTMAN offers this background information and then studies the rhetorical relationship between the letter writer and the writer's intended audience. Without regard for their station in life, women sought self-definition and information, examined their emotions, and communicated with others, often detailing their personal, political, religious, and social thoughts. As a result, says the author, the literature of letters, the only genre common to both religious and secular women, became more vernacular, more closely associated with women. Less dependent upon masculine power systems, these letters offered authors an unusual flexibility of topics, form, voice, and style. Because correspondence creates a dialogue, the sharing of information between and among readers, Altman posits that the intended reader often determines the writer's persona. For example, the writer may honestly reveal her own voice, or she may erect a barrier between herself and her reader. Whether or not the writer adheres to epistolary conventions depends on the letter's intentions. Altman also writes on the Third-World epistolarian in Goldsmith's book.

An important work in women's epistolary theory, KAUFFMAN examines the content, form, and characteristics of feminine discourse as they relate to the love letter genre. A jilted, abandoned woman often reveals her desires in the absence of her beloved. As both a victim and a sufferer, the letter writer depends upon style, tone, and dialogue. In order to examine the artistic constructions of gender and the accompanying underlying assumptions, the author examines the dialogues and stereotypes of both masculine and feminine epistolary writing, beginning with Ovid's *Heroides* and ending with twentieth-century writings. She explores whether or not men and women write with the same tone, with the same style, and for the same reasons. Beginning with the eighteenth century, she states, internal and external texts become interspersed with multiple subplots and dialogues, myriad correspondents, a variety of letter writing topics, and multiple addresses. The protagonist in *Clarissa Harlowe,* Kauffman declares, does not act out of her Puritan beliefs, as critics have generally believed, but, instead, out of pathos and the epistolary writer's preoccupation with letters and death.

CHEREWATUCK and WIETHAUS edit a collection of essays that offer a general overview and excellent bibliography of women's contributions to letter writing in western Europe from the sixth to the sixteenth centuries.

The various contributors introduce the extant letters of many medieval female writers, including Radegund and Hildegard of Bingen. The romance of Héloïse and Abelard is examined, not as a love story but as a theory in self-definition. The writings of Catherine of Siena, the Paston Women, Christine de Pizan, and Maria de Hout reveal early praise of women, of their religious beliefs, and of their household duties. The authors examine the relationship between women's writings and those of traditional male models.

As novels, the epistolary genre reveals an extraordinarily wide range of subject matter, style, form, and content. GOLDSMITH edits a collection of essays that discusses the origins of letter writing in France and Italy, then concludes with Alice Walker's *The Color Purple.* Because of its wide range of topics, because of its examination of the female voice in writings by both genders, and because of its extensive comparison of both female and male epistolary writers, this text is important. Several contributors challenge the seventeenth-century theory that epistolary writing is mostly a female activity. Some authors reveal that men can write like women but that women cannot write like men, and that when women do write, it is mostly a letter or novel of love. The epistolary novel takes many forms: one letter may permeate the novel's theme, an exchange of letters may occur between two people, or one person may write several letters to various recipients. Always, the novelist reaches beyond the merely personal and introspective. The eighteenth century was a hallmark of epistolary writing in both fiction and non-fiction; therefore, one entire section is devoted to the female epistolary voice, including the writings of Jane Austen, Fanny Burney, and Susannah Gunning. One contributor discusses the female voice in the writings of Restoration and eighteenth-century male authors like William Wycherley, William Congreve, Ned Ward, and Samuel Richardson. The work concludes with a chapter on gender and the epistolary form in modern society. In this section, Kauffman examines Margaret Atwood's *The Handmaid's Tale,* explaining the epistolary connection despite a technological setting which, at first, appears to belie the tradition. Kauffman posits that tape recorders and computers may redefine the characteristics of letter writing and epistolary literature.

SCHWEIK interprets the role of gender in American epistolary war poems and letters written during World War II. Writers like Louise Bogan, Marianne Moore, H.D., Gwendolyn Brooks, Hisaye Yamamoto, and Muriel Rukeyser, many with family members fighting, attempted, through their texts and subtexts, to define life and death. The exchange of letters between an absent soldier and his family or friends is examined. These letters, transcending time and space, speak of abandonment, fear, isolation, and love. The author compares the female voice to the voices of many male writers, such as Wallace Stevens, Ezra Pound, Wilfred Owen, Ernest Hemingway, and Karl Shapiro. Understandably, both sexes were anxious and uncertain in this time, and both challenged accepted gender stereotypes.

—BETTE ADAMS REAGAN

Literature: Modern Children's

Dyer, Carolyn Stewart, and Nancy Tillman Romalov (eds.), *Rediscovering Nancy Drew,* Iowa City: University of Iowa Press, 1995

Foster, Shirley, and Judy Simons, *What Katy Read: Feminist Re-Readings of "Classic" Stories for Girls,* Iowa City: University of Iowa Press, 1995

Mason, Bobbie Ann, *The Girl Sleuth: A Feminist Guide,* Old Westbury, New York: Feminist Press, 1975

McGillis, Roderick, *A Little Princess: Gender and Empire,* London: Prentice Hall, and New York: Twayne, 1996

Trites, Roberta Seelinger, *Waking Sleeping Beauty: Feminist Voices in Children's Novels,* Iowa City: University of Iowa Press, 1997

Vandergrift, Kay E., *Ways of Knowing: Literature and the Intellectual Life of Children,* Lanham, Maryland: Scarecrow Press, 1996

Recent theoretical work in literary and cultural studies, along with new models of psychological growth and development, have brought fresh attention to children's literature and increasingly to feminist concerns about the literature. Virtually all general studies of children's literature now include some discussion of gender stereotypes, and most go further, devoting a chapter to discussing feminist criticism as it applies to children's literature.

New readings of classic works for girls demonstrate the benefits of these approaches. Along with enduring best sellers, such as *Little Women, The Secret Garden,* and *Anne of Green Gables,* FOSTER and SIMONS turn to popular works from 1850 to 1920, such as *The Daisy Chain, The Railway Children, The Madcap of the School,* and *The Wide, Wide World,* to find a productive site for determining attitudes toward girlhood. Arguing for a gendered reader response that reads in the gaps or silences of the narratives, they provide fresh readings of the novels that both illuminate the then contemporary culture and offer new insights into women's narrative practice. Edith Nesbit's *Railway Children* books, for example, invite girls to adopt "a creative subject position" in relation to the stories' models of the feminine, offering imaginative and political possibilities within a reassuringly conventional framework. Foster and Simons consider as well the extent to which demands from male publishers dictated the artistic and behavioral limits afforded both protagonists and authors.

McGILLIS's study of *A Little Princess* contends that the novel gives contemporary readers the opportunity to compare current constructions of gender, race, and class with those at the turn of the century, as readers consider Sara's stereotypically feminine traits as a sensitive and graceful princess, her more progressive willingness to stand up to misplaced authority, and yet her acceptance without irony of the respectful salaams of Ram Dass. Part of the Twayne Masterworks series, McGillis's book gathers valuable materials for future study, providing background about Burnett's earlier play from which the novel derives, along with discussion of images offered on books covers, film adaptations of the work, and teaching approaches.

With the boundaries around literature for children broadening beyond traditional folk and fairy tales and approved work by canonical writers from the so called "golden age" of children's literature, much important work has begun in recovering for serious attention frankly popular writing written especially for girls. While noting Nancy Drew's flaws in her discussion of the girl sleuth, MASON explores why readers so love these series books, which librarians, teachers, children's literature historians, and critics have largely ignored. In addition to readings that assess the kinds of role models girls found in the Nancy Drew, Judy Bolton, and Cherry Ames series, Mason sketches a valuable overview of these early series explicitly about girls who do things, a shift from the popular Pollyanna and Little Purdy models from the late nineteenth century.

DYER and ROMALOV's collection of essays and interviews records a Nancy Drew Conference held in 1993. The conference's keynote speaker, Carolyn Heilburn, writes in the book's introduction that despite her flaws, Nancy Drew—the original 1930 to 1959 16-year-old Nancy Drew—marked "a moment in the history of feminism." Her blue roadster, lack of a female mentor from the patriarchy, and sheer will to step up and act offered girls new options at a moment in time when they needed them. Other essays address issues of race and culture in Nancy's white world. Also included are useful essays to spur further research, including guidance for archival and manuscript work.

VANDERGRIFT defines children's literature most broadly to include imaginative and informational narratives in all formats and media. According to Vandergrift, the academics, classroom teachers, and librarians who contributed essays to this collection all believe in "a multicultural, gender-fair, and nonhierarchical view" of children's literature. Several chapters focus on the importance of literature in the aesthetic growth of children, including links between books or storytelling and dance, quilt-making, art, and museum-going. More explicitly feminist concerns are addressed in essays such as Anne Lundin's piece revisioning the late Victorian author and illustrator, Kate Greenway, and describing feminist aesthetics of picture books. Other chapters discuss ways that literature can address gaps in curriculum, giving voice to women in history, for example, or providing a context for physical education that promotes more positive views of body image and physical activity among girls.

TRITES's new study looks at popular fiction for children published in English since the resurgence of the women's movement in the 1960s, to explore how feminism and childhood intersect in children's novels. She is most interested in reaching educators, especially in providing them with clearly articulated theory to inform feminist practice in the classroom. Trites defines a "feminist children's novel" as one whose main characters, regardless of gender, ultimately triumph over obstacles by recognizing and using their own power. Unlike Jo March, Anne of Green Gables, or Laura Ingalls, who grow from forthright children into mature self-silencing young women, the protagonists Trites studies awaken to the power of their own agency and voice and call readers to do likewise. Each chapter begins with a summary of theory relevant to the chapter's topic, followed by interpretations of individual novels. Topics discussed include subjectivity as a gender issue, female interdependency, and metafiction and the politics of identity. In providing close readings of texts to support her thesis, Trites makes clear that she does not seek to establish an approved canon, but she also makes a special effort to include texts that reflect the experiences of children of color as well as those of white children.

—SUSAN K. AHERN

See also Literature: Folklore and Fairy Tales

Literature: Mysteries and Crime Fiction

Bird, Delys (ed.), *Killing Women: Rewriting Detective Fiction,* Sydney: Angus and Robertson, 1993

Irons, Glenwood (ed.), *Feminism in Women's Detective Fiction,* Toronto, Buffalo, and London: University of Toronto Press, 1995

Klein, Kathleen Gregory, *The Woman Detective: Gender and Genre,* Urbana: University of Illinois Press, 1988

———(ed.), *Great Women Mystery Writers: Classic to Contemporary,* Westport, Connecticut: Greenwood, 1994

Munt, Sally R., *Murder by the Book?: Feminism and the Crime Novel,* New York and London: Routledge, 1994

Swanson, Jean, and Dean James, *By a Woman's Hand: A Guide to Mystery Fiction by Women,* New York: Berkeley, 1996

Although the first American female-authored mystery novel was published fairly early in the development of the genre (Anna Katherine Greene's *The Leavenworth*

Case: A Lawyer's Story, 1878), few female writers achieved prominence in mystery writing. Those who did confined their plots to stereotypically feminine settings and crimes or to male detectives rescuing women, perhaps part of the reason why women's mystery fiction received so little critical attention. However, women's mystery fiction has changed considerably in the last 30 years, most strikingly in the number of women writing and solving mysteries. Equally striking, female writers and mysteries have entered the world of mean streets, hard-boiled detectives, professional women, and lesbians, a complete opposite to the more acceptable feminine locations, communities, and puzzles found in the works of the previous generation of female mystery writers.

Partly because of the explosion in the women's mystery fiction genre, women's mystery fiction criticism is fairly recent and limited. Although female crime writers have often been ignored or undervalued by critics, more women have also entered the field of mystery fiction criticism. Contemporary critical issues include whether or in what ways women are suitable for the detecting job, how women's issues become part of the plot, and in what ways the authors and their detective figures subvert a tradition and conventional ideology that significantly discounts them.

For a useful overview of recent female-authored mysteries, SWANSON and JAMES provide an alphabetical listing of works, with descriptions of the authors' styles, series characters, important characteristics, analyses of their appeal for certain readers, and lists of awards for over two hundred English-language works since 1977. They also refer the reader to authors similar in basic characteristics to the author under discussion.

KLEIN's *Great Women Mystery Writers: Classic to Contemporary*, a critical biographical dictionary, contains 117 four- or five-page interpretive and evaluative essays by expert scholars who describe the lives and over 1,000 novels of British and American female writers who have "created, molded and altered" the detective genre from Catherine Aird to Margaret Yorke and from the nineteenth century to the mid-1990s.

In one of the earliest full-length assessments of women's detective novels, KLEIN (1988) examines women's crime fiction from 1864, the historical point at which feminism had begun to be seriously incorporated, to 1978. Klein states that despite the differences in the detectives and societies in over 300 novels she surveyed, the requirements of the underlying plot and the conservative genre itself have so far denied the protagonists validity as detectives and as women, and that the mystery novel will remain innately masculine unless women writers "rethink it, re-formalize it, re-vision it."

MUNT's book rebuts Klein's negative contentions by providing a close examination of the diversity of more current crime novels (up to 1993). Munt asserts that they challenge the belief that crime fiction is an intrinsically masculine and innately conservative literary form that automatically excludes women as writers and detectives, except in the form of parody. Specifically, Munt provides discussions of mainstream female crime writers, liberal and socialist feminist crime fictions, race politics, lesbianism, psychoanalysis, and postmodernism in crime fiction.

IRONS's collection of critical essays about British and American mystery writers also examines the challenge of fictional female detectives to the traditional male detective (who operates, of necessity, outside of society), the suitability of women for the job, the fairly recent development of British women detectives who are not models of convention, the focus on women's issues, the issue of how gender and language within these novels subvert patriarchy and assert feminine autonomy, and, as a central theme, "the seemingly contradictory place of women detectives in the ideological [male-dominated] order, which [male detectives] are working to restore."

BIRD provides an introduction to Australian women's crime fiction as a historical, sociopolitical, and theoretical context with six critical essays by women crime writers about their own genre.

—JANET M. LaBRIE

Literature: Mythology

Baring, Anne, and Jules Cashford, *The Myth of the Goddess: Evolution of an Image*, London and New York: Viking, 1991

Goodrich, Norma Lorre, *Heroines: Demigoddess, Prima Donna, Movie Star*, New York: HarperCollins, 1993

Harding, Mary Esther, *Woman's Mysteries Ancient and Modern: A Psychological Interpretation of the Feminine Principle as Portrayed in Myth, Story, and Dreams*, London and New York: Longmans Green, 1935

Knapp, Bettina L., *Women in Myth*, New York: State University of New York Press, 1997

Larrington, Carolyne (ed.), *The Feminist Companion to Mythology*, London: Pandora, 1992

Lyons, Deborah, *Gender and Immortality: Heroines in Ancient Greek Myth and Cult*, Princeton, New Jersey: Princeton University Press, 1997

Spretnak, Charlene, *Lost Goddesses of Early Greece: A Collection of Pre-Hellenic Myths*, Berkeley, California: Moon Books, 1978

Stone, Merlin, *When God Was a Woman*, London: Virago, and San Diego, California: Harcourt Brace Jovanovich, 1976

Weigle, Marta, *Spiders and Spinsters: Women and Mythology*, Albuquerque: University of New Mexico Press, 1982

Mythology is a pervasive force in literature, art, and life. By mapping and reinforcing the basic patterns of its culture, a society's myth systems—however ancient—have a profound influence on the worldview and actions of its members. Although the term "mythology" is most often used in western culture to refer specifically to the myths of ancient Greece, it is important to realize that every society in the world has its own equally rich and significant myth system. Therefore, the books listed here offer studies of women in both Greek and world mythology.

By studying the rituals of ancient Greek cults, LYONS sheds light on the role heroines played in Greek myth, and the ways in which this role differed from that of the hero. She finds that heroines were more likely to blur the line between mortals and divinity by acting as mediators in prayer and ritual, by being resurrected from the dead, or by becoming goddesses themselves. Heroines were also more subject to anthropomorphic transformations. An extensive appendix lists ancient heroines, with brief discussions of their myths.

In her study of heroines, GOODRICH makes connections between heroic women in ancient Greek myth and those later portrayed in opera, literature, and film. She begins each section with a retelling and explication of a Greek myth about a particular heroine, then presents several examples of characters from literature, opera, or film that have been inspired by the myth. Following each section is a list of suggested readings, and appendices include lists of heroines of grand opera, names of legendary demigoddesses, select authors who feature myth-based heroines in their work, modern literary heroines, and actresses featured as heroines in film.

Through exploring the story of Adam and Eve, STONE demonstrates the links between theology, mythology, politics, and oppression. This often-cited work looks at ancient western goddess-oriented religious systems and attempts to document the repression and reinterpretation of their myths as the people who practiced them were conquered by patriarchal cultures. She seeks to demonstrate that the older goddess myths reflect societies in which women held influential roles, and that these roles were diminished and suppressed when male-centered religions took over.

BARING and CASHFORD present an expansive study of the continuity of goddess images in ancient western myth and religion. These images in art, artifact, and text are traced from Paleolithic and Neolithic times through their supplantation by images of male gods in the current era. The authors argue that in western society, rejection of the goddess, which represents the unity of all life, in favor of the god, which represents a spiritual existence outside of an earthly one, has been accompanied by the prevalence of a worldview that denigrates nature in favor of human will. Similarly, SPRETNAK delves into pre-Hellenic times in an attempt to recover goddess myths as they existed before being transformed by patriarchy. She retells several of the myths, which, when restored, offer a more positive view of women than the "classical" versions with which we are familiar.

LARRINGTON argues for a non-reductive view of women's mythology and women's roles in mythology, thus presenting a variety of approaches to the myth systems of several cultures. She offers a comprehensive collection of feminist studies of the mythology of the Near East, Europe, Asia, Oceania, and the Americas. This scholarly anthology also offers discussions of myth as it is used in the religion of Wicca, as it is appropriated by feminist activists, and as it is invoked by female writers.

Focusing on the mythology of women rather than on women's roles in men's mythology, WEIGLE presents a scholarly collage of myths, rituals, commentary, interpretation, illustrations, and extensive notes. Her work with western and Native American myth revives the power of archetypal figures such as the spider, the wise woman, the moon, and the heroine. HARDING, a student of Jung, approaches the psychology of women from an archetypal standpoint based on moon-related mythology. The introduction to this work, in fact, was written by Jung himself. Although Harding's work is somewhat dated and does not take a feminist approach, it provides an interesting overview of the myths of many cultures that relate the moon to women, and it furnishes a valuable insight into the way Jungian psychology appropriates myths in its treatment of women.

KNAPP approaches women in the mythology of several cultures through Jungian methods. Her introduction includes a clear explanation of these methods for those not familiar with the use of archetype in psychology. Offering both an ectypal and archetypal analysis of each myth, Knapp attempts to reveal how women were treated in the societies that told these myths. Additionally, she encourages contemporary women to use these myths to work toward understanding themselves.

—TRIA AIRHEART-MARTIN

Literature: Poetry

Erkkila, Betsy, *The Wicked Sisters: Women Poets, Literary History and Discord,* New York and Oxford: Oxford University Press, 1992

Gilbert, Sandra M., and Susan Gubar (eds.), *Shakespeare's Sisters: Feminist Essays on Women Poets,* Bloomington: Indiana University Press, 1979

Greer, Germaine, *Slip-Shod Sibyls: Recognition, Rejection and the Woman Poet,* London: Viking, 1995

Montefiore, Jan, *Feminism and Poetry: Language, Experience and Identity in Women's Writing,* London and New York: Pandora, 1987

Ostriker, Alicia Suskin, *Stealing the Language: The Emergence of Women's Poetry in America,* Boston: Beacon, 1986; London: Women's Press, 1987

Yorke, Liz, *Impertinent Voices: Subversive Strategies in Contemporary Women's Poetry*, London and New York: Routledge, 1991

Women and poetry are often regarded as having a difficult and even dangerous relationship. Western culture is haunted by suggestive images of Sappho's fatal leap in the sixth century B.C., the hypothetical Judith Shakespeare resorting to suicide and, in more recent times, Sylvia Plath taking her own life while at the height of her literary powers. In the past, some implied that women are too frail to withstand the supposedly turbulent passions and terrifying clarities of poetic inspiration. The ironic narrator of Virginia Woolf's *A Room of One's Own* asks, "Who shall measure the heat and violence of the poet's heart when caught and tangled in a woman's body?"

However, from the viewpoint of the reader of poetry, what difference does it make that the author is a woman? What, if anything, differentiates the style and subject matter of male and female poets? Is it women's writing that is "different" or is it the ways in which women's writing is read? Are female poets a distinct and homogeneous group? Should they be treated as such? Is there a "women's poetic tradition"? What of the manifold differences between female poets and between poems by women? What of the interactive and interrogative relationships between women's poetry and men's poetry?

These are the types of questions that reoccur in criticism on the subject, although with marked differences in phrasing, emphasis, and conclusions. The collection of essays edited and introduced by GILBERT and GUBAR represents an early and influential bid to stake out a critical arena in which present and future discussions of previously neglected material might take place. The title and introduction consider Virginia Woolf's story of Judith Shakespeare, William's "wonderfully gifted" but ultimately doomed hypothetical sister. Gilbert and Gubar point out that "of course Shakespeare did—and does—have many sisters." The stated aim of the anthology as a whole is to recover these lost poets and lost poems, to trace "a vigorous and victorious matrilineal heritage"—and thus to revise the official, patriarchal version of the history of literature in English. The essays collected by Gilbert and Gubar exhibit both the strengths and the limitations of 1970s Anglo-American feminist criticism. This was certainly pioneering work; however, the tendency to read poetry as little more than an elaborate transcription of personal experience often leads to what may seem an artlessly biographical approach.

The premise of OSTRIKER's book is that female poets, writing in a culture and a language which seek to deny them authoritative expression, have developed a range of poetic strategies and motifs to resist and overcome disempowerment. The project of the book is to provide a detailed survey and analysis of these strategies and motifs, in work by poets such as Emily Dickinson, H.D., Plath, Maxine Kumin, Audre Lorde, and Margaret Atwood. Ostriker denies any theoretical affiliation, but in general terms her work can be seen as representing one stage in the evolution of the Anglo-American feminist tradition.

In contrast, MONTEFIORE's book is an explicit attempt to theorize the debates that have comprised the field of feminism and poetry. Conversant with both French theory and Anglo-American criticism, Montefiore provides useful evaluations of the strengths and shortcomings of a range of approaches and attitudes to women's poetry. In particular, this book represents an invaluable and sustained critique of the still widespread assumption that women's poetry is the authentic and transparent expression of the essentially female experience, and of the identity of the poet. Poetry, Montefiore argues, is not autobiography; it is a literary form of specifically linguistic intensity. Thus, she suggests that we should ask of poetry, not what experience it expresses, but instead how it engages with, conforms to, or transforms poetic conventions and inherited definitions. The feminist power of poetry, she concludes, lies in its ability to shift or even to transfigure the meanings of women's lives.

YORKE's book is an odd hybrid, working in what it terms "the difficult margin" between French feminist theory and Anglo-American feminist criticism, and using the vocabularies and the strategies of both. At best these very different idioms question each other; at worst they jar against one another. For example, Yorke emphasizes the crucial interdependence of the tasks of "retrieval" (of that which has been suppressed) and "reinscription" (of old narratives, scripts and mythologies)—but also, in her enthusiasm for synthesis, at times she seems to collapse the history and multiplicity of feminism into a singular and homogeneous "global movement."

GREER's book surveys and reappraises the "curious group" of successful western female poets of the past, from Sappho to Christina Rossetti. However, this is not a straightforward reclamation and celebration of a line of feminist heroines. It is, in Greer's own words, "a rather jaundiced account"—iconoclastic, acerbic, and deeply suspicious of many of the traditional pieties of feminist criticism. She deplores self-pity and sentimentality, both in women's poetry and in readings of women's poetry, and writes off the romantic conception of blazing inspiration and spontaneous creation as an unhelpful myth promoting undigested "gush." The bracing epilogue takes the reader through the end of the twentieth century, heralding the emergence of women's poetry, which—having abandoned "the rhetoric of petulance" and the aesthetic of martyrdom—is free to be sane, poised, complex, witty, and stylish.

ERKKILA is also suspicious of certain aspects of the feminist criticism that have preceded her work, although for somewhat different reasons. While many previous feminist critics have represented themselves as excavating a suppressed history of women's poetry, Erkkila makes the vital point that this history is not simply there to be reclaimed: it is actively (re)constructed in each new account, and mobilized to serve a specific set of interests. Whose history is feminist literary history? she asks. Very often, Erkkila argues, it is the history of relatively privileged white women. Innocent celebrations of idyllic sisterhood and benevolent influence among the female poets of the past have the danger of becoming more important than differences of race, class, sexuality, and history. Erkkila's case against the tendency to "romanticize, maternalize, essentialize and eternalize" female poets and their writing is persuasive, and her insistence on the importance of difference and struggle is, ultimately, productive and empowering, pointing to a difficult but exhilarating way forward for work in this area.

—ANNA TRIPP

Literature: Renaissance

Benson, Pamela, *The Invention of the Renaissance Woman: The Challenge of Female Independence in the Literature and Thought of Italy and England,* University Park: Pennsylvania State University Press, 1992

Farrell, Kirby, Elizabeth H. Hageman, and Arthur F. Kinney (eds.), *Women in the Renaissance: Selections from English Literary Renaissance,* Amherst: University of Massachusetts Press, 1990

Fitzmaurice, James, *Major Women Writers of Seventeenth-Century England,* Ann Arbor: University of Michigan Press, 1997

Haselkorn, Anne M., and Betty S. Travitsky (eds.), *The Renaissance Englishwoman in Print: Counterbalancing the Canon,* Amherst: University of Massachusetts Press, 1990

Hendricks, Margo, and Patricia A. Parker (eds.), *Women, "Race," and Writing in the Early Modern Period,* London and New York: Routledge, 1994

Jankowski, Theodora A., *Women in Power in the Early Modern Drama,* Urbana: University of Illinois Press, 1992

Jordan, Constance, *Renaissance Feminism: Literary Texts and Political Models,* Ithaca, New York: Cornell University Press, 1990

Kehler, Dorothea, and Susan Baker, *In Another Country: Feminist Perspectives on Renaissance Drama,* Metuchen, New Jersey: Scarecrow Press, 1991

Lewalski, Barbara Kiefer, *Writing Women in Jacobean England,* Cambridge, Massachusetts: Harvard University Press, 1993

Newman, Karen, *Fashioning Femininity and English Renaissance Drama,* Chicago: University of Chicago Press, 1991

Wayne, Valerie (ed.), *The Matter of Difference: Materialist Feminist Criticism of Shakespeare,* Ithaca, New York: Cornell University Press, 1991

Woodbridge, Linda, *Women and the English Renaissance: Literature and the Nature of Womankind, 1540–1620,* Urbana: University of Illinois Press, 1984

In the 1990s, discussion of the role of women in medieval and Renaissance drama has evolved along with new theoretical approaches. This discussion focuses mainly on drama, but it also calls attention to texts that provide historical and cultural background, and it highlights several new collections of female writers from the Renaissance. The bibliography in these areas is large and growing rapidly; the following texts are excellent starting points for further study.

Refashioning the discussion of gender in the Renaissance, NEWMAN shows how the ideologies of femininity—her emphasis is on this concept, rather than "women"—was constructed in early modern London. Newman shows continuity in the messages of domestic handbooks, court cases, and sermons, as well as drama. The excitement and spectacle of the theater provided, she argues, a particularly useful locus for examining how attitudes toward women and femininity reflected emerging cultural anxiety about an unstable political and economic climate. Efforts to direct and restrict acceptable public manifestations of womanhood illustrate concern for challenges to patriarchy.

HENDRICKS and PARKER take an interdisciplinary approach, drawing on cultural studies and anthropology as well as women's studies, literature, and history, to explore perceptions of women during a period of European imperial expansion. They examine the cultural conditions that tended to hide women's writing. They look at the problem of female authorship, and they explore how contemporary critics reconcile or, on the other hand, find tension between the study of women and questions of race and colonialism as women strive to find voice. The 17 essays explore women's concerns from several continents and offer critical readings of several female writers from the Renaissance period, including Elizabeth Cary, Lady Mary Wroth, and Aphra Behn.

LEWALSKI examines a series of important seventeenth-century female writers and places them in the context of history, culture, and economic upheaval. Many of these writers are relatively new to the feminist canon, and this study offers a broad range and richness of detail. Many of them made it their business to challenge and subvert the repressive patriarchy of the Jacobean world.

Another text that provides primary texts is that by FITZMAURICE. This is an excellent and wide-ranging collection that is suitable for the general reader and yet would be an excellent classroom text. Ten female writers are represented.

JANKOWSKI's study examines poetry and prose as well as drama. Her concern is for publicly visible power and authority. She usefully juxtaposes a range of medieval and Renaissance texts to give context to an analysis of female ruler characters. She explores the potential disruption of gender identity that occurs when a woman is placed in a traditionally masculine position and still is characterized as female. Jankowski focuses on the subversions that occur when women simultaneously embody multiple roles that result in characters who celebrate, for example, both virginity and leadership.

FARREL, HAGEMAN, and KINNEY not only provide critical essays on the depiction of women in masques and the construction of feminine identity in Lady Mary Wroth and Arbella Stuart, but offers 100 pages of annotated bibliography of writings by and about seventeenth-century women. JORDAN studies a wide range of Renaissance works of nonfiction, asserting that feminism emerged as a mode of thought in the fifteenth century in Italy, and that arguments for equality of the sexes were common as early as a hundred years later. While taking her questions from present-day feminist perspectives, she provides access to many European texts. She provides insights about views on gender in terms of marriage, education, and literary characterization. Jordan's work is an essential resource in intellectual history.

WOODBRIDGE offers a stimulating study of the historical forces of the time, which serves as a reference to the range of cultural attitudes brought to bear on women in life and literature. She takes a particular interest in popular literature, including chapters on the controversy over women's roles that made for pamphleteering from the early Tudor period through the 1620s, the attitudes toward hermaphrodite behavior, including gossiping and public impudence, and the willingness of the public to purchase misogynist literature.

BENSON's study is provocative because she juxtaposes the literary strategies used to call attention to the abilities of women who managed to distance themselves from male authority. She also looks at the subtlety and effectiveness with which other writers discounted women's political challenge and restrained their moral and political intellectual independence. Looking at both Italy and England, Benson's study investigates non-dramatic texts as sites for discourse on intellectual history.

HASELKORN and TRAVITSKY have created an important text by bringing together critical examinations of some of the female writers of the seventeenth century who are emerging as central figures for study. This book offers 18 essays, which explore how women are represented in both the traditional canon and in women's own writings. The collection looks at the female ruler and her authority as well as her limitations and reveals competing texts on the repression of women as subjects of writing and as authors. Here too there is a good annotated bibliography for exploring the newly emergent seventeenth-century female writers, now frequently the focus for academic study by female scholars.

KEHLER and BAKER offer another collection of essays that embody new historicism and feminist analysis in 15 essays on the role of female characters in Renaissance drama. The book also includes excellent bibliographies of recent criticism on individual writers.

WAYNE's collection of essays on materialist feminist criticism takes as its main focus Shakespeare, but as is true for any student of the drama of this period, the ideologies and insights voiced here embolden readings of other drama. Here questions of class, patrimony, and patriarchal power remind the reader that feminist discussions of the literature began several decades ago in a political movement that advocates social change. Written by both British and American critics, these essays affirm that whatever contemporary insight we may hope to derive from historical texts, we must see that challenging hierarchy and oppression depends on combined and integrated studies of gender, class, and ethnicity.

—VIVIAN FOSS

Literature: Romance Fiction

Christian-Smith, Linda K., *Becoming a Woman through Romance,* New York: Routledge, 1990

——— (ed.), *Texts of Desire: Essays on Fiction, Femininity and Schooling,* London: Falmer Press, 1993

Jensen, Margaret, *Love's Sweet Return,* Bowling Green, Ohio: Bowling Green State University Popular Press, 1984

Modleski, Tania, *Loving with a Vengeance: Mass-Produced Fantasies for Women,* Hamden, Connecticut: Archon, and London: Methuen, 1982

Pearce, Lyane, and Jackie Stacey (eds.), *Romance Revisited,* London: Lawrence and Wishart, and New York: New York University Press, 1995

Radway, Janice, *Reading the Romance,* Chapel Hill: University of North Carolina Press, 1984, London: Verso, 1987

Thurston, Carol, *The Romance Revolution,* Urbana: University of Illinois Press, 1987

Despite immense reader popularity, romance fiction was long dismissed as trivial and even pernicious until recently. The interest in critically analyzing romance fiction stems from the women's movement beginning in the 1960s, which focused on the impact of culture on the formation of women's gender identities and their life expectations. Early on, fiction reading was identified as an important part of these processes. Scholars in lesbian, social class, and race and ethnic studies have also turned their attention to romance fiction.

MODLESKI was one of the first to move beyond the dismissive attitude of early romance-fiction critics and to identify the contradictory qualities for this fiction and its key role in women's consciousness formation. In maintaining that romance fiction's popularity stems from its ability to describe the real problems and dilemmas in women's lives, Modleski's textual analysis of a sample of romance novels documents the complexity of this fiction. For example, one type of romance novel, the gothic, not only helps women reflect on psychic conflicts with important people in their own lives, but also protests against women's lack of power. However, Modleski does not find romance fiction entirely positive, because male dominance in society and the institutions of family and marriage are not questioned. Rather, she suggests that romance fiction actually desensitizes readers to the evils of sexist society. The importance of Modleski's analysis lies in these findings and in the framework the book provides for subsequent studies of romance fiction.

RADWAY's book is acknowledged as a key study of traditional adult romance fiction aimed at "average" readers, defined as heterosexual and of European descent. These were "sweet" romances in which sexuality was less overt. Radway's sections on marketing provide invaluable information on the many facets of the romance publishing industry. Radway also interviewed and surveyed a group of sixteen Midwestern women, who read non-series romance fiction written by individual authors. This aspect of the study provides a rich description of the complexity of readers' responses. All readers discriminated in their book choices, preferring books with intelligent, strong, independent heroines, and empathetic, vulnerable men. From these interviews, Radway concluded that adult female romance readers gained respite from the demands of home and work responsibilities while learning about distant places and times. Radway's central finding is that romance-fiction reading is a mild form of social protest against women's devalued position, through which women claim their rights to pleasure and fantasy. Despite this, reading romances actually forestalls demands for change in the real world. This landmark study furthers understandings of the importance of fantasy in women's lives, and the use of romance fiction to mediate everyday tensions and conflicts.

JENSEN's book is a thorough examination of Canada's Harlequin Enterprises, the international leader in romance-fiction publishing. The book contains an insightful study of the genre's readers, based on letters written to Harlequin Enterprises and interviews of 30 romance readers. Jensen also skillfully traces the history of Harlequin Enterprises, its corporate operation, relations with writers, and the development of the series romance novel. The discussion of romance fiction's appeal despite the feminist movement illustrates how the romance industry is able to incorporate the notion of the new, independent woman with more traditional views of women as predominantly girlfriends, wives, and mothers.

For THURSTON, erotic romances, in which sexuality is a prominent feature, chronicle the evolution of the "liberated" American woman. Heroines who are both good and sexual, with strong tendencies toward lifestyles beyond the domestic (heroines with careers outside the home), are important departures from traditional characters. These changes have been forced on publishers by female readers and critics. As the only full-scale study of erotic romances with a national sample of 600 readers, Thurston presents compelling evidence that the changing interests and challenges of today's more independent women are reflected in erotic romance fiction. As such, these stories provide a vehicle for women to examine their evolving social positions, and the circumstances that continue to limit their life possibilities.

PEARCE and STACEY considerably advance understanding of romance fiction through essays that demonstrate how traditional narratives of love, based on heterosexuality and aimed at white middle-class readers, are being reworked today. This is largely due to diverse sexual practices and perceptions of romantic love, stemming from differences of social class, race, ethnicity, and sexuality, which have altered the meanings of romance and how romance fiction is interpreted. The discussions of romance based in lesbian and race and ethnic studies are especially strong. This book is invaluable for those searching for the most provocative current scholarship on the topic. The bibliography is especially helpful.

Romance fiction is not limited to adult readers. In two books, CHRISTIAN-SMITH examines the double-edged qualities of romance fiction written for teenagers. The 1990 book represents a textual analysis of teen romance novels, and includes an ethnography of 23 young women who initially did not like to read, along with their reading teachers. They came from diverse social class and racial backgrounds, and three urban Midwestern middle level schools. These readers chose books that were easily read and interesting, and that had intelligent, physically attractive characters. Christian-Smith's findings indicate that reading romance fiction afforded time to relax and escape home and academic problems, and provided advice on how to negotiate romantic relationships with boys. Despite readers' rich interpretations, teachers' disapproval of romance fiction worked to solidify the students' identities as academically marginal. Christian-Smith further maintains that the books' traditional focus, on domesticity and attracting boys, reconciles young women to their social subordination. Readers found these books so seductive that they read little else. When the teenage readers substituted romance fiction for textbooks, they unwittingly limited their education and work possibilities, and funneled themselves toward domestic futures.

CHRISTIAN-SMITH's 1993 book represents an international perspective on teen romance fiction in English-speaking countries. The essays contain insightful discussions of the ways desire, fantasy, politics, and economics are intertwined with literacy, femininity, and schooling. A central finding is the similarity across international boundaries regarding teen romance fiction's influences on how young female readers think of themselves and their futures. Teen romance fiction is a means for young women's incorporation into patriarchal and profit-driven social structures, but at the same time it is a potential means for them to resist traditional places in these structures. The essays show, however, that despite these criticisms, teen romance novels create new possibilities in adolescent fiction for young female readers through their focus on fantasy and pleasure.

—LINDA K. CHRISTIAN-SMITH

Literature: Science Fiction *see* Literature: Utopian and Science Fiction

Literature: Travel Writing

Behar, Ruth, and Deborah A. Gordon (eds.), *Women Writing Culture*, Berkeley: University of California Press, 1995

Davis, Gwen, and Beverly A. Joyce (eds.), *Personal Writings by Women to 1900: A Bibliography of American and British Writers*, Norman: University of Oklahoma Press, 1989

Frawley, Maria H., *A Wider Range: Travel Writing by Women in Victorian England*, London and Rutherford, New Jersey: Fairleigh Dickinson University Press, 1994

Mills, Sara, *Discourses of Difference: An Analysis of Women's Travel Writing and Colonialism*, London and New York: Routledge, 1991

Robinson, Jane, *Wayward Women: A Guide to Women Travellers*, Oxford and New York: Oxford University Press, 1990

Schlissel, Lillian (ed.), *Women's Diaries of the Westward Journey*, New York: Schocken, 1982

Stevenson, Catherine Barnes, *Victorian Women Travel Writers in Africa*, Boston: Twayne, 1982

For women, traveling became an early act toward emancipation and new perspectives. ROBINSON's account details the writings of more than 300 female travelers, mostly British or American, and examines the nearly 1,000 books they produced. Spanning sixteen centuries, this historical perspective is full of insight and wit as it examines the narrative persona and seeks to encourage further scholarship on female travelers. The serious student of travel writing will take advantage of DAVIS and JOYCE's bibliography of 5,000 works by British and American women published before 1900. The works included in this bibliography are diaries, autobiographies, letters, and travel narratives.

In the seventeenth century, Mary Rowlandson became the first female travel writer in North America when she wrote of her Indian captivity. Between 1840 and 1870, more than 100 women described their journeys over the Overland Trail from Missouri to Oregon or California. SCHLISSEL believes that although these women accomplished unusual tasks for women, they remained true to their traditional roles and beliefs. The author also challenges the belief that both men and women looked upon their long journeys with similar points of view. Citing overwhelming sacrifices by women, these diaries and journals describe several events that differ from the men's descriptions: Indian relationships and battles, constant sickness and death, opposition to the trip, hardships of the widows and abandoned women, and other daily routines. This text creates a new vision of this important historical period.

Introducing several earlier travel writers as well as Victorian writers in Africa, STEVENSON, including a bibliography of primary sources, names the reasons that these women felt compelled to travel. For instance, many desired to escape the confines of restrictive Victorian living. Their new environments allowed autonomy as well as physical and psychological freedoms. These new surroundings encouraged the female writers to surrender to their experiences and offer new possibilities rather than, like men, to schematize and judge them. The author identifies recurring literary themes and techniques shared by many of these early "new women." The writer's success depends upon her ability to describe her journey, and to create powerful metaphors and plots.

Offering an extensive listing of primary and secondary sources, FRAWLEY covers the Victorian female writers who traveled outside England and the effects of these writings on Victorian culture. The essence of her study is to determine the ways in which writing and travel functioned together to expand physical, intellectual, and metaphorical borders. She suggests that travel became a narrative vehicle in order to place the story of adventure and control outside of England. The introduction of steam locomotives and railways offered travelers new freedoms and new ways to create a wider range of interests. MILLS integrates the writings, the personae, and the experiences of Victorian female travel writers. She notes that many travel writers were connected in some way to England's imperial interests, and these lands, therefore, were the subjects of their literature.

BEHAR and GORDON discuss the multi-voiced travel writings by twentieth-century female anthropologists traveling in Egypt, Africa, India, and other countries. These sojourners, writing both fiction and nonfiction, discuss their travels among many cultures. The contributors view these feminine writings as liberating rather than imitative, writings that describe not only other lands but also homesickness, identity, and shared intimacies, often within a community of women.

—BETTE ADAMS REAGAN

Literature: Utopian and Science Fiction

Armitt, Lucie (ed.), *Where No Man Has Gone Before: Women and Science Fiction,* London and New York: Routledge, 1991
Barr, Marleen S., *Lost in Space: Probing Feminist Science Fiction and Beyond,* Chapel Hill and London: University of North Carolina Press, 1993
——— (ed.), *Future Females: A Critical Anthology,* Bowling Green, Ohio: Bowling Green University Popular Press, 1981
Jones, Libby Falk, and Sarah McKim Webster Goodwin (eds.), *Feminism, Utopia, and Narrative,* Knoxville: University of Tennessee Press, 1990
Lefanu, Sarah, *In the Chinks of the World Machine: Feminism and Science Fiction,* London: Women's Press, 1988; as *Feminism and Science Fiction,* Bloomington: Indiana University Press, 1989
Rosinsky, Natalie M., *Feminist Futures: Contemporary Women's Speculative Fiction,* Ann Arbor, Michigan: UMI Research Press, and Epping: Bowker, 1984
Staicar, Tom (ed.), *The Feminine Eye: Science Fiction and the Women Who Write It,* New York: Frederick Unger, 1982

The 1970s saw a revival of feminist utopias written by eminent female science fiction authors, or by mainstream fiction authors who saw such books as a way to comment on current conditions of oppression.

BARR's (1981) anthology begins with a look at female characters in science fiction before the 1970s, especially contrasting the scientific male with the irrational female character. Feminist utopias are discussed throughout the book, with brief attention given to the most popular authors and nineteenth-century British utopian novels. Suzy McKee Charnas discusses her difficulty in introducing an all-female science fiction novel to the publishing world. A eulogy to Ursula K. LeGuin and a discussion of *Star Trek's* "Turnabout Intruder" round out the book.

STAICAR introduces the reader to the most influential women in science fiction, beginning with the space adventure fiction of Catherine L. Moore in the 1930s and Leigh Brackett in the 1940s. Despite the limitations of the time, Moore wrote extensively about a female heroine, Jirel of Joiry, while Brackett wrote critically acclaimed screenplays and politically sophisticated science fiction novels. Staicar continues with well-known feminist science fiction authors such as James Tiptree, Jr. (Alice Hastings Sheldon), best known for a few hard-hitting short stories such as "The Women Men Don't See;" Suzy McKee Charnas, author of *The Vampire Tapestry;* and Suzette Haden Elgin, author of *Native Tongue* and creator of the female nonhierarchical language Láadan.

ROSINSKY's book is a scholarly work that discusses themes common to much of women's speculative fiction. Rosinsky begins with a look at the propensity for metamorphosis in Lois Gold's *A Sea Change* (1976), Rhoda Lerman's *Call Me Ishtar* (1973), Angela Carter's *The Passion of New Eve* (1971), and June Arnold's *Applesauce* (1966). Metamorphosis usually devolves into at least one character changing sex, either literally or in the character's perhaps psychotic imagination, making these four novels blatant commentary on the double standard. One chapter is devoted to the rarely discussed Dorothy Bryant's *The Kin of Ata Are Waiting for You* (1976) and Mary Staton's *From the Legend of Biel* (1976), in which feminist utopia is either a real place or a place created by the mind of a female child. Rosinsky concludes her published thesis with a look at the more concrete future feminist utopias of Suzy McKee Charnas, Joanna Russ, Sally Miller Gearhart, and Marge Piercy.

LEFANU begins the shift from concentrating on female science fiction to specifically relating feminism to the genre. Lefanu explores whether the representation of women in science fiction narrative has ever come across as plausible and realistic. Are strong women in fictional matriarchies merely a repetition of male rule? Does speculative fiction typically grant female characters more freedom than can be seen in contemporary society? Lefanu discusses both utopias and dystopias and concludes with a discussion of four female science fiction authors she believes to be worthy of analysis: James Tiptree, Jr., Ursula LeGuin, Suzy McKee Charnas, and Joanna Russ.

JONES and GOODWIN take a broader view in their wide-ranging anthology about feminine language and narrative in various utopian documents. Authors range from Jane Austen to Charlotte Brontë, Isaak Dinesen, Olive Schreiner (*Gloriana,* 1890), and Doris Lessing (*The Marriage Between Zones Three, Four, and Five,* 1980). A chapter dedicated to the utopias of Harriet Beecher Stowe and Charlotte Perkins Gilman, as well as a chapter on those of Marion Zimmer Bradley (*The Ruins of Isis,* 1978) and Marge Piercy, contrast with a chapter dedicated to Margaret Atwood's dystopian *The Handmaid's Tale* (1985) and Ursula LeGuin's anti-utopian *Always Coming Home* (1985).

ARMITT's anthology focuses on the more popular forms of science fiction. The first part deals with individual works, such as the dystopian patriarchies described in Charlotte Haldane's *Man's World* (1926) and Katherine Burdekin's *Swastika Night* (1937). Other chapters give a general overview of Catherine L. Moore,

Ursula LeGuin, and Doris Lessing. The second part takes up the theme of metamorphosis in Mary Shelley's *Frankenstein* and lesser known works. Recent films such as *Short Circuit* (1986), *Tron* (1983), *Starman* (1984), and *Blade Runner* (1982) are analyzed. The last two maintain male domination through demeaning language. The third part of the book ranges from the discussion of the depiction of female adolescents in Alexei Panshin's *Rite of Passage* (1968) and Madeleine L'Engle's *A Wrinkle in Time* (1962) to Josephine Saxton's disgust with the way science fiction continues to marginalize women.

BARR (1993) takes feminism within science fiction into the postmodern society. Not content merely to discuss feminist utopian authors, depictions of female and male characters in various science fiction works, and female authors' attempts to expose the patriarchy in such classic works as Joanna Russ's "When It Changed," Barr relates feminist science fiction to the broader world of postmodern literary analysis. In one chapter, Barr makes clear that fictional dystopian societies that manipulate or mutilate women for various bizarre means of reproduction are very close to today's truth, not science fiction. Another chapter explains that Ursula LeGuin's "Sur" (1985) deconstructs the male adventure story and male geography through a multicultural women's trip to the South Pole.

—ROSE SECREST

Lowell, Amy 1874–1925

American Writer

Benvenuto, Richard, *Amy Lowell,* Boston: Twayne, 1985
Damon, S. Foster, *Amy Lowell: A Chronicle, with Extracts from her Correspondence,* Boston: Houghton Mifflin, 1935
Flint, F. Cudworth, *Amy Lowell,* Minneapolis: University of Minnesota Press, 1969
Gould, Jean, *American Women Poets: Pioneers of Modern Poetry,* New York: Dodd Mead, 1980
———, *Amy: The World of Amy Lowell and the Imagist Movement,* New York: Dodd Mead, 1975
Gregory, Horace, *Amy Lowell: Portrait of the Poet in Her Time,* New York: Thomas Nelson and Sons, 1958
Heymann, C. David, *American Aristocracy: The Lives and Times of James Russell, Amy, and Robert Lowell,* New York: Dodd Mead, 1980
Ruihley, Glenn Richard, *The Thorn of a Rose: Amy Lowell Reconsidered,* Hamden, Connecticut: Archon, 1975
Wood, Clement, *Amy Lowell,* New York: Harold Vinal, 1926

When she died in 1925 at the age of 51, Amy Lowell was at the peak of a brief but brilliant career. For 13 years she had blazed like a comet on the literary scene. At the time of her death her monumental two-volume biography of Keats had just been published, and in 1926 her posthumous collection of poems, *What's O'Clock?,* was awarded a Pulitzer prize. Then for almost 10 years, until the publication of the Damon biography, the primary American spokesperson for The New Poetry—Imagism—was seemingly forgotten. She suffered another 20 years of relative neglect until the *Complete Poetical Works of Amy Lowell,* edited by Louis Untermeyer and prefaced with his admiring "Memoir," appeared in 1955. Since that time her literary reputation has been periodically revived with the publication of several other biographies, some of them critical, and inclusion of her work in anthologies, usually as a representation of the short-lived but influential Imagist Movement, which she was so responsible for organizing and proselytizing in the United States. None of her 10 volumes of poetry is currently in print. Modern poetry owes a debt to Amy Lowell—a literary progenitor to all who follow her, poetic descendants who have evolved into a different species entirely and bear little resemblance to their famous ancestor. With a few exceptions, critics today give her a kind of grudging homage, acknowledging her exceptional life and her obvious contributions to modern poetry, usually while slighting her work.

Because of the force of her personality and her indefatigable efforts on behalf of the Imagists, much of what has been written about Lowell is biographical. DAMON's indispensable biography is the chief source of information about Lowell and is the book upon which subsequent critics are still drawing. This massive work, sympathetic to Lowell, focuses on her development as a poet, the process of her writing, the critical reception of her work, and her role as the prime mover of the American Imagist movement, as well as her connections and support of contemporaries in and outside of her literary circle. Damon includes a list of Lowell's publications—individual poems, prose essays, and collections—year by year, and interweaves selected letters from Lowell's extensive correspondence throughout his text. While he makes references to and summarizes many of the poems, this biography is not a critical analysis. Damon's book is a painstaking reconstruction of what seems to be every event of Lowell's life, but the inner drama reflected in the poetry is largely missing. This is interesting in light of Lowell's own biographical writing, the Keats book in particular; she found it impossible to separate the life from the work, the narrative from the poetic criticism; yet this is largely the pattern found in most of the biographical writing on Lowell herself.

Even the more modern biography by GOULD (1975), although it contains some material not available to Damon, relies heavily upon that first major biography of Lowell and confines itself primarily to the events of her life. The full-length Gould biography is followed by a shortened version of this life in GOULD (1980), a collection of biographical sketches that includes a Lowell chapter among chapters on Emily Dickinson, Gertrude Stein, Sara Teasdale, Elinor Wylie, H.D., Marianne Moore, Edna St. Vincent Millay, Louise Bogan, and Babette Deutsch. The juxtaposition of Lowell with these other female poets provides an interesting way of seeing her particular gifts and is the closest to a feminist treatment on Lowell one gets, again not in the analysis of her work particularly, but in regard to the activities of her professional life. The avowed purpose of Gould's study is to show the role played by these poets in the evolution of modern poetry, with an emphasis on "the struggle [they] waged . . . for equality of treatment in the arts."

HEYMANN offers a comparative look at Lowell in the triple biography of Amy Lowell and two of her equally illustrious relatives, James Russell and Robert Lowell. The remarkable Lowell family and its influence on three generations of poets is the focus of this work. Amy Lowell's poetic goals were shaped in part by her desire not only to emulate her famous older second cousin, James Russell Lowell, but to surpass him and be taken as seriously as he was. The family influence—the wealth, the social position, and the value placed on intellectual development and service—were part of Lowell's inheritance and a factor in the formation of her personality and her career as a poet.

Perhaps because her public persona was so unorthodox, reaction to Amy Lowell was rarely neutral; the same can be said of the critical writing about her work. Several of the earliest book-length studies of Lowell are hostile but worthy of mention because they explain in part the current neglect on the part of critics. A work published a year after her death, WOOD's book is one of these hostile, disparaging studies. The primary value in the Wood study is an indication of the strong dislike Lowell could engender. GREGORY similarly reflects these notions and considers Lowell's literary work to be negligible; like other critiques that put emphasis on her life rather than her work, this study provides insight into the literary milieu, but the antipathy to Lowell's own work is so clear and so marked as to make the objectivity of the whole work suspect.

The three most serious and useful critical analyses of the work of Amy Lowell are those by Flint, Ruihley, and Benvenuto. FLINT's book, a brief study that is one of the University of Minnesota series on American writers, is a good introduction to Lowell's poetry and also provides some analysis of her critical lectures and writing; while disagreeing with most of Lowell's critical assessments, especially in regard to the French Symbolists and other modern poets, Flint provides a well-balanced critique and a good descriptive summary.

RUIHLEY attempts to reassess Lowell, to reverse the denigration of her work. This denigration he attributes to the failure to winnow out the really fine poetry from that of lesser quality, a process that, he maintains, usually naturally occurs over time in the evaluation of any author who has produced as much as Lowell did—but that did not happen in Lowell's case, since other views of poetry (especially those of Ezra Pound and T.S. Eliot) took precedence after her death. Ruihley's first chapter is the obligatory "life," which is followed by a chronological discussion of the major work; of particular interest is the third chapter, a discussion of the influence of Zen Buddhism on the formation of Imagist poetics and the transcendental qualities of Lowell's work.

BENVENUTO also begins with a short biographical chapter, acknowledged to be derived from Damon, but he then discusses Lowell's work by theme and genre rather than chronologically. The chapter on the critical prose combines discussion of Lowell's responses to attacks on the new theories of poetry with clear and useful discussions of *vers libre* and Lowell's "polyphonic prose." Benvenuto divides the discussion of the poetry into chapters on the narrative poems (with emphasis on Lowell's use of the dramatic monologue, history, and myth) and on the lyrics; he also undertakes to address the issue of her failings as a poet, as well as her contributions to the development of a modern poetic. In the concluding chapter, Benvenuto notes that with Ruihley's book there is a beginning of a reassessment of Lowell and states that the feminist critics are beginning to notice her. It is of interest, however, that there is no full-length study of Lowell that can be called feminist in today's terms, and that seems a serious omission, given both her public role as a spokesperson for an innovative movement in American poetry and her poetry itself, the best of which explores issues of gender and sexuality in ways quite remarkable for her time.

—SHARON LOCY

Luce, Clare Boothe 1903–1987

American Diplomat

Fearnow, Mark, *Clare Boothe Luce: A Research and Production Sourcebook,* Westport, Connecticut: Greenwood, 1995

Hatch, Alden, *Ambassador Extraordinary: Clare Boothe Luce,* New York: Holt, 1956

Lyons, Joseph, *Clare Boothe Luce,* New York: Chelsea House, 1989

Martin, Ralph G., *Henry and Clare: An Intimate Portrait of the Luces,* New York: Putnam, 1991

Shadegg, Stephen C., *Clare Boothe Luce: A Biography,* New York: Simon and Schuster, 1970; London: Frewin, 1973

Sheed, Wilfrid, *Clare Boothe Luce,* New York: Dutton, 1982

It was said of Clare Boothe Luce that she had *Time, Life,* and *Fortune*—and Henry Luce! It was a set of double entendres that tells an incomplete story. She succeeded as a magazine editor, playwright, journalist, war correspondent, politician, and diplomat. In 1956 she was ranked the second most admired woman in the world in a Gallup poll. Yet behind the glitter was a high cost. Her first husband was a spouse batterer. Her daughter died young. She was the junior partner in her second marriage. (Both partners had extramarital affairs.) She was the press's darling but the butt of snide rumors. She was known for her satiric sense of humor, authoring plays with sharp dialogue and delivering political speeches that had sarcastic characterizations. (Her foes replied in kind.)

Three of Luce's biographers were friends of long standing. Their books give her the benefit of any doubt, and disseminate myths that Luce invented about her life and accomplishments. SHADEGG's effort presents a simple reflection of Luce as she saw herself and as others saw her. Yet if it is not critical, neither is it worshipful. The story catches her excitement and vitality. Luce is portrayed as challenging, brilliant, vexing, inconsistent, charitable, and complex. There is no attempt to explain her dramatic shifts from liberalism to conservatism, from critic to partisan. In the book she plays various roles, delivering a convincing performance before audiences generally skeptical. The author has a tendency to overdramatize both the tragedies and the triumphs of her life.

SHEED, a successful novelist and critic, and a friend of Luce's for more than 30 years, is awestruck by the fascinating woman he first met when he was 18. His parents, Frank Sheed and Maisie Ward, ran a publishing house for books on Catholicism. Luce had become a convert to the faith after the death of her only child in an automobile accident. Sheed regards her as "good at just about everything." Luce cooperated with the author, the result being less a biography than "notes on a career," an appreciation by a loyal friend. The author avoids making an assessment of her life.

HATCH, a writer who specialized in biographies of popular political figures, had a nearly 30 year acquaintance with his subject. He tells the story of someone who is brilliant but often foolish, idealistic yet cynical, possessing masculine thinking but feminine instincts. In this book, Luce scintillates in her roles as a glittery society woman, a sophisticated editor, a clever playwright, an accomplished politician, a devout religious convert, and a surprising ambassador. She has a talent for making friends as well as enemies. The Ambassador to Italy had a number of strikes against her: her gender, her religion, her husband, and her capacity for giving and receiving malicious salvos. Yet Luce turned out to do well in Rome.

A different kind of treatment is that of LYONS. He was not a Luce intimate, nor was his work intended for a general audience. Yet it captured a lot of Luce's sparkle. Lyons's account was written for young adults as part of a 50-volume "American Women of Achievement" series. It is a life-and-times treatment, with many photographs.

MARTIN, author of many other profiles of nineteenth- and twentieth-century figures, presents a study of an embattled, competitive couple, two forceful domineering individuals. Henry was the son of missionary parents who became a press baron, the behind-the-scenes confidante of many world leaders. Clare grew up in poverty, abandoned by her father at an early age, pushed by her stage-struck mother to be a child actress. She grew up to be worldly and sophisticated. They both wanted the same things: power, fame and riches. Both were brilliant, disciplined workers, lovers of ideas, opinionated talkers, Republicans, used to moving in lofty circles. Their marriage lasted 31 years. Martin presents but does not make excuses for their flaws.

FEARNOW concentrates on Luce's career as a playwright. His book is part of a research series on modern dramatists. He provides descriptions and evaluations of all her plays, including many that are unpublished and completely unknown. Fearnow states that comedy of language was Luce's natural and personal style of voice in the theater, but that she had mixed feelings about this gift throughout her life, often rejecting the comic mode and attempting work of a more "serious," responsible, and pious nature. She had a simultaneous fascination with and loathing of America's wealthy classes.

—MARTIN GRUBERG

Luxemburg, Rosa 1871–1919

German Activist

Abraham, Richard, *Rosa Luxemburg: A Life for the International,* Oxford: Berg, and New York: St. Martin's Press, 1988

Dunayevskaya, Raya, *Rosa Luxemburg, Women's Liberation, and Marx's Philosophy of Revolution,* Atlantic Highlands, New Jersey: Humanities Press, 1982

Ettinger, Elzbieta, *Rosa Luxemburg: A Life,* Boston: Beacon Press, 1986; London: Harrap, 1987

Florence, Ronald, *Marx's Daughters: Eleanor Marx, Rosa Luxemburg, Angelica Balabanoff,* New York: Dial, 1975

Frölich, Paul, *Rosa Luxemburg: Her Life and Work,* London: V. Gollancz, 1940; New York: H. Fertig, 1969

Nettl, J.P., *Rosa Luxemburg,* 2 vols., London and New York: Oxford University Press, 1966

Nye, Andrea, *Philosophia: The Thought of Rosa Luxemburg, Simone Weil, and Hannah Arendt,* London and New York: Routledge, 1994

Abraham and Florence both provide excellent introductory works to "Red Rosa" Luxemburg's life and thinking. ABRAHAM's book is concise, readable, and nonscholarly. Based on material that is drawn primarily from her writings and other studies, Abraham presents an accurate, engaging picture of Luxemburg's public and private lives and passion. FLORENCE's book is notable for its avoidance of jargon, no mean task in attempting to discuss the refined intricacies of Marxist economic, political, and social theory that Luxemburg addressed in her writings. By discussing Luxemburg in the context of other radical political activists, Florence contextualizes Luxemburg's ideas and politics in a way that shows the true dimensions of her radicalism. He also emphasizes Luxemburg's broad humanistic elements, which, today, might make her seem less of a radical than she really was. Of the two, Abraham's is the more up-to-date work; thus, it benefits from research on Luxemburg based on Polish-language sources published since the appearance of Florence's work. NYE, like Florence, looks at Luxemburg comparatively, the former providing the more scholarly, academic work that would appeal to specialists rather than the general reader. Nye stresses Luxemburg as a leftist theoretician rather than as an activist, and explores the place Judaism may have played in the intellectual development of all three women.

DUNAYEVSKAYA's book is written from a committed Marxist point of view, stressing Luxemburg's development as a feminist. One of the most commanding assertions of this book is that Luxemburg became her most intellectually acute and creative after 1905 and 1906, when she ended her sexual relationship with her mentor-lover Leo Jogiches (1867–1919), a fellow Marxist and organizer who, in spite of their earlier relationship, remained a close political ally throughout her life. While thoughtful and provocative, this work may suffer from ideological overcommitment.

Similarly, FRÖLICH is a prolific author and polemicist who was once a German Communist and post-World War II Social Democrat. His own political stance and ideological agenda show through this study, which tends toward hagiography in its glorification of Luxemburg as a political heroine and socialist martyr, whose tireless organizational efforts eventually led to the establishment of the Communist Party of Germany. Fröhlich is particularly poignant in his description of the so-called Spartacist Insurrection of 1919, spearheaded by Luxemburg, and the manner in which she was murdered and her body thrown into a Berlin canal by right-wing German soldiers. Its zeal aside, this book contains a great deal of valuable information about its subject.

ETTINGER was able to utilize then newly available Polish sources for her intimate, close-up study of Luxemburg, especially material that shed light on her relationship with her mentor-lover Leo Jogiches. This study concentrates on Luxemburg's personal life, stressing her passionate and often contradictory nature, which sometimes manifested itself in her theoretical thinking and public behavior as well as her private life. For example, while she abhorred direct contact with the daily lives of the *Lumpenproletariat*, Luxemburg nevertheless championed their cause with unflagging support, especially in the form of the mass strike, the backbone of her political activism. The book offers a detailed portrait of Luxemburg as a woman rather than as a revolutionary, noting, for example, that she always regretted Jogiches's refusal to allow her to bear children, as a compensation for which she was excessively attentive to her cat, Mimi. Written with a heightened sense of the tragic overtones of Luxemburg's life, especially its end, this is an excellent complement to Nettl's exhaustive biography.

NETTL provides the first thorough, scholarly study of Luxemburg's life and work. Rather daunting in size and scope, this book remains a *sine qua non* for anyone interested not only in Luxemburg herself, but in the development of Socialist and Communist thought in the first decades of the twentieth century. While his discussion of Luxemburg's influence on German politics is meticulous and accurate, Nettl is not as successful in his treatment of Luxemburg's activities in Poland, due to the fact that Polish sources were not readily available to him when he wrote this book. This one flaw is somewhat ameliorated with the appearance of Ettinger's study. The one-volume abridgement of this work is recommended for non-specialists.

—CARLO COPPOLA

M

Magazines and Periodicals

Adburgham, Alison, *Women in Print: Writing Women and Women's Magazines from the Restoration to the Accession of Queen Victoria,* London: Allen and Unwin, 1972

Ballaster, Rosalind, Margaret Beetham, Elizabeth Frazer, and Sandra Hebron, *Women's Worlds: Ideology, Femininity and the Woman's Magazine,* London: Macmillan, 1991

Ferguson, Marjorie, *Forever Feminine: Women's Magazines and the Cult of Femininity,* Aldershot: Gower, 1983

Mitchell, Sally, *The Fallen Angel: Chastity, Class and Women's Reading 1835–1880,* Bowling Green, Ohio: Bowling Green University Popular Press, 1981

Shevelow, Kathryn, *Women in Print Culture: The Construction of Femininity in the Early Periodical,* London and New York: Routledge, 1989

Winship, Janice, *Inside Women's Magazines,* London and New York: Pandora, 1987

Periodicals have been central to popular reading in the twentieth century. Whether investigated as a social institution and ideological tool, dismissed as debilitating reading matter, or hailed as a source of pleasure, the periodical genre of the magazine has continued to attract scholars in a range of disciplines, from cultural and media studies to women's studies and literary history. Among the many types of this genre, the greatest attention has inevitably been given to the women's magazine.

One of the first to deal with magazines for women from a feminist perspective, and simultaneously to adopt a rigorous theoretical approach, was FERGUSON. In her perceptive analysis of the social role of women's magazines, she shows how women's views of themselves and society's views of women are shaped by the subject matter of the magazine. In other words, she looks at the ways women's magazines create a "cult" of femininity. She identifies the dominant themes of the magazines' messages, basing her conclusions on the contents of the three most read British women's weeklies—*Woman*, *Woman's Own*, and *Woman's Weekly,* and making comparisons with *Cosmopolitan*, *Ms*, other American women's periodicals, and several youth magazines. According to her argument, the magazine fulfills a normative function through its gender specialization, telling women who to be and what to know. This message comes about implicitly through the material selected, and is thus conveyed by the editors, whom she calls the "high priestesses" of the cult. Ferguson draws on a range of methods, from personal experience to content analysis, statistical data, and extensive interviews. Though somewhat dated in its conception of popular culture and of the audience's approach to it, this study has become a standard text. It will be valuable to any reader interested in this field.

If Ferguson condemned the traditional woman's magazine as constraining for women, WINSHIP adopts a more careful and discriminating attitude. Setting out to explain the appeal of women's magazines, she analyzes the contents of a variety of British weeklies and monthlies. She talks of the magazine as reflecting a commitment to ideologies that construct contradictory femininities, but sees that readers' responses can be various, and the magazine need not be understood as only restrictive. She argues that magazines appeal to readers by means of a combination of entertainment and useful advice. This appeal is organized around a range of fictions, which sell the myth of successful and pleasurable womanhood. Winship's book is simultaneously a chronological survey and a set of fascinating case studies devoted to the magazines *Woman's Own*, *Cosmopolitan,* and the feminist *Spare Rib.* By now it has become a standard text in the study of culture and the representation of women. The wealth of Winship's original scholarship will make her book indispensable for scholars, while her accessible style will appeal to any reader interested in the history of popular reading.

Not only the contemporary scene has interested the feminist critic. The history of the magazine, its role in the construction of femininity, and the development of the magazine's familiar elements have not been neglected. One of the first attempts at a survey of this cultural phenomenon was undertaken by ADBURHAM. She puts magazines in the context of other popular genres read and written by women from the Restoration to the 1830s. An example of the early rescue work undertaken by feminists in the 1970s, her book suffers from the lack of a clear unifying methodology, but it is valuable for its immense wealth of detail and breadth of scope.

The very beginnings of periodical literature are at the center of SHEVELOW's interest. Looking at the seventeenth- and eighteenth-century periodicals published for and by both men and women, she notices how this genre helped shape, and in turn was itself shaped by, the dominant period conceptions of femininity. The magazine, as did all popular literary forms, played a key role in the process of allowing women to participate in the public world of print culture, while, at the same time the representational practices of that culture increasingly restricted them within the private sphere of the home. Thus the ideal of the so-called Victorian woman actually emerged much earlier, already in the post-Restoration period. An impressive and original study, this book is an invaluable contribution to the ongoing literary debates surrounding this genre. It is intended for all interested in popular culture, eighteenth-century literary studies, and the history of women.

The later development of the magazine is the topic for MITCHELL. She discusses the British penny weekly family magazine of the 1840s to the 1870s in the context of genres written for various audiences, such as the Victorian middle-class novel and the sensation novel. She traces the image of woman's role as reflected in the motif of pure woman and the fallen angel, and its importance for the consolidation of Victorian family values. Well-argued, original, and bringing much factual information, it will be of interest to the specialist and informed student of nineteenth-century literature and history.

Those looking for a combination of historical survey with an application of contemporary theories and attitudes to popular culture will find the work of BALLASTER, BEETHAM, FRAZER, and HEBRON immensely valuable. A collective work, in which each section is written by a well-established specialist in the field, this book charts the history of the women's magazine in England from the beginnings to the contemporary scene. At the center of the authors' attention lie changes within the form, and the shifts and similarities in the shaping of the idea of femininity. This is a most helpful book for anybody desiring an accessible guide to the complexities of attitudes and interpretations of this genre.

—SOŇA NOVÁKOVÁ

Management

Chaney, Elsa M., *Supermadre: Women in Politics in Latin America*, Austin: University of Texas Press, 1979

Ferguson, Kathy E., *The Feminist Case against Bureaucracy*, Philadelphia: Temple University Press, 1984

Grogan, Margaret, *Voices of Women Aspiring to the Superintendency*, Albany: State University of New York Press, 1996

Guy, Mary E. (ed.), *Women and Men of the States: Public Administrators at the State Level*, Armonk, New York: Sharpe, 1992

Jahan, Rounaq, *The Elusive Agenda: Mainstreaming Women in Development*, London and Atlantic Highlands, New Jersey: Zed, 1995

Kanter, Rosabeth, *Men and Women of the Corporation*, New York: Basic Books, 1977

Staudt, Kathleen, *Women, Foreign Assistance, and Advocacy Administration*, New York: Praeger, 1985

———(ed.), *Women, International Development, and Politics: The Bureaucratic Mire*, Philadelphia: Temple University Press, 1990

Studies of women in management take two approaches. The first examines traditional personnel matters: recruitment, performance, and mobility. It is particularly interested in the demographics of gender (im)balance. The second approach examines the difference women make in what management does, both inside the bureaucracy and in interaction with its missions and constituencies.

At the highest levels, management is monopolized by men. Traditional personnel (renamed "human resources") texts report this, and even U.S. government agencies count and agonize over a "glass ceiling" women face. In explanations about imbalance, mainstream texts have focused on women's (limited) human capital (personality, expertise, aspirations).

KANTER's now classic analysis, written before the word gender studies was in vogue, focuses on institutional structures of expectations: women are frequently tracked into positions constructed to limit aspiration, and to oversee routine low-level management (thus, the stereotype: women bosses who micromanage).

Kanter provides theoretically illuminating and researchable frameworks that have spawned numerous studies; one framework posits that the proportion of underrepresented people (dominant, token, skewed, tilted, and balanced) affect institutional processes and outcomes. She also offers prescriptions for institutional change. Kanter assumes that men and women are basically the same; what differs is the work structures into which they are recruited.

Underlying GUY's collection is a similar conception of men and women. She organized a volume in which contributors report on empirical research about public managers from six states within the United States. On the whole, women's experiences are similar to men's, with the major exception of sexual harassment. Of course, the pool of women who comprise contemporary management is relatively narrow, compared to that of men.

The popular media are filled with advice books, "how-to" manuals, and tips on do's and don'ts for female upward mobility. To all this, FERGUSON reacts with her theoretic classic of management literature. According to Ferguson, bureaucracies "feminize" their occupants—male and female alike—into subordinates in relations of domination and control. Bureaucracies, she says, are incompatible with feminism. Hers is a breathtaking critique, enough to give pause to those who do not problematize hierarchy. So where does this leave feminists (admittedly, a diverse group within the United States, and even more so in global contexts)?

Are women (or at least, feminists) different, potentially infusing and transforming institutions with behavior and commitments? CHANEY's seemingly dated study rings true today, and not just for Peru and Chile, where she conducted sizable numbers of interviews. In public and private management, women are viewed as "supermothers," who are honest and less corrupt, bringing presumably "feminine" characteristics into the workplace. What is feminine varies in different cultural and national contexts.

More recently, analysts have examined what difference women would make for management process and outcome. Public schools are a good place to start, for elementary schools are a veritable world of women, including women managers (principals). At the highest level, however, women comprise less than a tenth of school superintendents. GROGAN deftly analyzes a small sample of women who aspire to the superintendency in the Pacific northwest of the United States, using what she calls a "post-structuralist" theoretical framework and qualitative interviewing. Women, she suggests, would make some difference in management.

As a bridge to a wider and more global scale, STAUDT (1985) analyzes the women who manage the Women in Development (WID) office of the U.S. Agency for International Development (USAID). WIDs mandate is not affirmative action for U.S. employees, but rather the integration of women into programs and projects from the many countries where USAID spends money. This case study identifies personalized resistance, but also WID managers' ongoing struggles to build coalitions within the agency and with outside political constituencies.

JAHAN compares four development assistance organizations (the World Bank, the United Nations Development Program, and the aid agencies of Canada and Norway), for the extent to which their missions have been integrated and transformed in gender terms. Focusing strictly on female managers, Norway has begun to transform its aid agenda, in part with critical-mass numbers of female staff (tilted to balanced, in Kanter's terms).

The comparisons extend further in STAUDT's (1990) edited collection on the bureaucratic mire in which women's/gendered programming is stuck. An introductory theoretical overview examines the conditions for change in terms of institutions, managerial demographics, and constituency relations. Contributors analyze organizations, and national and international agencies. The updated and expanded second edition (1997) offers more room for optimism, with the increasing strength from women's organizations and from managerial/policy leverage.

—KATHLEEN STAUDT

See also Business and Entrepreneurship; Leadership

Mandela, Winnie 1936–

South African Activist

Gilbey, Emma, *The Lady: The Life and Times of Winnie Mandela*, London: Cape, 1994
Haskins, Jim, *Winnie Mandela: Life of Struggle*, New York: Putnam, 1988
Hoobler, Dorothy, and Thomas Hoobler, *Nelson and Winnie Mandela*, New York: Franklin Watts, 1987
Meltzer, Milton, *Winnie Mandela: The Soul of South Africa*, New York: Viking, 1986

Winnie Mandela has spent most of her life in the shadow of her more famous husband, Nelson. Nelson was the leader of the African National Congress (ANC) and was imprisoned for 27 years by the apartheid-based South African government. Yet one might argue that it was Winnie, who led the campaign all those years to free Nelson, and was most responsible for Nelson's release, who in the process of that 27 years developed her own political style. Winnie is an excellent illustration of the critical nature of women in the struggle for freedom from apartheid in South Africa. Many women, black, white, and Indian, stood tall in this movement, but Winnie Mandela is perhaps more visible than most.

HASKINS portrays Mandela's life against the backdrop of a nation where to be black was to have no rights to anything. And for a black woman in South Africa to challenge the system, the costs and the rewards have been equally remarkable. Mandela's father was a teacher who believed in teaching his students, and his daughter, the history of the black race in South Africa. Mandela grew up proud of being a colored South African and became involved in political activity early. Thus when she met Nelson, the match seemed perfect. When Nelson was jailed for life on false charges of advocating violence to overthrow the government, Winnie began her 27-year campaign to obtain Nelson's release from jail. Winnie had been jailed, put under house arrest, and not allowed to speak to the press or to talk to people without government agents in the same room. But she continued to raise international awareness until her husband was finally released.

GILBEY looks at the trial of Winnie Mandela over her alleged participation in the slaughter of a young black South African boy. The boy had been viciously slain and dropped into some weeds where his partly decomposed body was later found. While Mandela was not formally charged with the crime, the circumstantial evidence was sufficient to cast a pall over the woman who for over 27 years had been the "soul" of South Africa. The trial was held shortly after Nelson's release from jail and his ascendancy to the presidency of South Africa. Some argued that Nelson was not sufficiently supportive of his wife in this trial. While her reputation has been hurt, she continues to work for a just and free South Africa, but now without her husband, who has since divorced her.

MELTZER's short political biography lets the reader see the political and social issues that helped to make Mandela the person she came to be. It was not until she was in her teenage years that the apartheid system was put into place. She was thus able to see how her nation worked before and after apartheid. This awareness was at the bottom of her disagreement with the government's discriminatory policies. Some of the teachers in her school encouraged her to think for herself and to make her own decisions. They also instilled in her the belief that it was possible to win a struggle if one was willing to do what was needed to win. After she went to Johannesburg, she became involved in the fight for South African freedom. She became involved in the ANC and eventually married its leader, Nelson. It was her refusal to allow Nelson to be forgotten in jail that immeasurably aided the ANC movement to succeed over the many years of her husband's imprisonment.

HOOBLER looks at the lives of Winnie and Nelson to see where they came together and why they eventually became the well-known couple they were. Both Nelson and Winnie had humble beginnings. They both early became involved in the revolutionary movements in their nation. They both were born before apartheid became dominant and lived to fight against the system. While Nelson was to spend 27 years in jail, the fact that they had such common goals helped them not only to persevere, but to be seen as the reason to continue the struggle.

—PAUL BARTON-KRIESE

See also Apartheid

Mankiller, Wilma *see* Native American Women

Mansfield, Katherine 1888–1923

New Zealand Writer

Burgan, Mary, *Illness, Gender and Writing: The Case of Katherine Mansfield,* Baltimore and London: Johns Hopkins University Press, 1994

Fullbrook, Kate, *Katherine Mansfield,* Brighton: Harvester, and Bloomington: Indiana University Press, 1986

Hankin, Cherry, *Katherine Mansfield and Her Confessional Stories,* New York: St. Martin's Press, and London: Macmillan, 1983

Kaplan, Sydney Janet, *Katherine Mansfield and the Origins of Modernist Fiction,* Ithaca, New York, and London: Cornell University Press, 1991

Michel, P., and M. Dupuis, *The Fine Instrument: Essays on Katherine Mansfield,* Sydney: Dangaroo Press, 1989

Morrow, Patrick D., *Katherine Mansfield's Fiction,* Bowling Green, Ohio: Bowling Green State University Popular Press, 1993

Nathan, Rhoda B., *Katherine Mansfield,* New York: Continuum, 1988

Ricketts, Harry (ed.), *The Worlds of Katherine Mansfield,* Palmerston North, New Zealand: Nagare Press, 1991

Robinson, Roger, *Katherine Mansfield: In from the Margin,* Baton Rouge and London: Louisiana State University Press, 1994

Van Gunsteren-Viersen, Julia, *Katherine Mansfield and Literary Impressionism,* Amsterdam and Atlanta, Georgia: Rodopi, 1990

Critical responses to the life and work of Katherine Mansfield cover a broad spectrum, with more recent work introducing questions of sexuality, gender, and national identity into the field of modernist aesthetics in which Mansfield is usually located. The classic work by HANKIN reads the stories thematically and ties them to biographical concerns through a consideration of influences and intentions. MORROW follows in this tradition by providing careful readings of "representative" stories from each collection, with the aim of producing a certain thematic and technical coherence throughout Mansfield's oeuvre. The emphasis on narratological questions provides a useful new focus, while the reader is also directed to the great biographers for more detailed commentary on aspects of Mansfield's life.

FULLBROOK engages more explicitly with the traditions and conventions of feminist literary critical projects, suggesting that there might not be a straight continuum between feminist politics and feminist literary criticism. In particular, she distances her work from postructuralist feminist analysis on the grounds that those theories are "censored," by having determined the limits of women's being from the start. She suggests that the modernist paradigm is more productive in reading Mansfield, because it provides the clear critical focus for considering "new" ideas about the self, time, and perception, which are central to the work of writers like Mansfield.

VAN GUNSTEREN-VIERSTEN develops this question of context more explicitly and in an intensely focused way, arguing that Mansfield needs to be read in light of the role impressionist aesthetics had in her work. The argument traces Mansfield's stated views on art and aesthetics from her journals and reviews to provide a basis for the discussion of the style and technique of her fiction, rather than her thematic concerns. This idiosyncratic but careful and scholarly discussion provides a more sustained attention to stylistic concerns that are often glossed over in mystifying references to Mansfield's literary sensitivity.

KAPLAN examines Mansfield's role in the development of British modernism. Her concern is to rethink the concept of modernism beyond the conventional exclusion of questions of gender and sexuality. Kaplan argues that women and, to a lesser extent, feminist imperatives were at the center of modernism, rather than peripheral to it, inflecting, for instance, other more familiar modernist concerns such as genre. The issue of literary associations is also rethought, with the more usual Mansfield connections (for instance, with Virginia Woolf), set in the context of Mansfield's literary, stylistic, and formal relations with other figures of the period such as Oscar Wilde. Kaplan also isolates and discusses the central modernist concern with urban life in relation to Mansfield's biography and fiction, providing an important specificity to questions of her literary locations. The larger question of aesthetics is approached via a consideration of Mansfield's literal and literary practices of impersonation.

BURGAN reads Mansfield's biography and her fiction together under the linked signs of illness and gender. She argues that the social, psychological, and experiential dimensions of diseases suffered by Mansfield—tuberculosis and venereal disease—can be and need to be considered as related to conditions such as pregnancy, miscarriage and abortion, and all of these should be considered within the broader alienation manifested in Mansfield's bisexuality. Rather than providing another biography and defence of the weight of Mansfield's writing, Burgan reads the stories in view of particular experiences of illness and death in Mansfield's life, which are in turn framed within the larger context of medical and aesthetic discourses of early modernism and the family narratives that order gender and identity. This is a significant contribution to the question of how to conceive the relation between Mansfield's life and work.

Several collections of essays provide essential reading on Mansfield. NATHAN's book is a wide-ranging collection that aims to critically reproduce Mansfield's stated intention to convey "the diversity of life" to her readers. It includes a selection of essays on Mansfield's "New Zealand experience," addressing biographical material and also placing it in context of the fiction. Nathan includes Bridget Orr's important discussion of colonial desire and differences in a range of readings of Mansfield. Linda Hardy's critical account of the question of authorial identity within the problematics of nationalist discourse reads Mansfield alongside and against Shakespeare and more recent invocations of both Mansfield and Shakespeare in New Zealand literature. A section on "the craft of the story" places a 1923 review alongside Judith Neaman's discussion of symbolic allusions to the Bible and Shakespeare in "Bliss." A final section on "the artist in context" includes writing by Middleton Murray, Clare Hanson's introduction to her 1987 edition of Mansfield's critical essays, and a piece on the relationship with Virginia Woolf from Alpers' 1980 biography. The range and connections are impressive and indeed necessary, as they provide a historical and geographical context for reading Mansfield and give a sense of the scope and depth of the scholarship, while offering many fine individual discussions of her work.

ROBINSON's work collects papers from two centenary conferences, articulating such conferences as sites for finally recognising Mansfield's literary status, and thus reclaiming her from her traditional literary fate of having died before achieving greatness. Again, there are important individual essays here, including Vincent O'Sullivan's 1988 lecture marking the early attempts to think through the postcolonial implications and contexts of Mansfield's work, and other essays on questions of location and notions of "home." MICHEL and DUPUIS provide an interesting take on the question of location and memory. As might be expected from a centenary publication, this collection focuses critically on questions of biography, as well as providing some new literary analysis. Some essays are based on readings of the stories in translation, while others read Mansfield alongside French authors within a specifically French, rather than a more generalized, modernist context. Collectively, these essays prompt a reconsideration of the processes and positionalities of reading, as well as of the literary and cultural location of a major writer. These questions also provide the starting point for RICKETTS's book, which contains essays on the publication of Mansfield's notebooks, more detail on her personal and literary career, and essays examining her literary relationship with, and references to, Anton Chekhov and the symbolists.

—BRIGITTA OLUBAS

Marie Antoinette 1755–1793

French Queen

Bernier, Olivier, *Secrets of Marie Antoinette,* Garden City, New York: Doubleday, 1985
Castelot, André, *Queen of France: A Biography of Marie Antoinette,* London: Vallentine Mitchell, and New York: Harper, 1957
Dunlop, Ian, *Marie-Antoinette: A Portrait,* London: Sinclair-Stevenson, 1993
Erickson, Carolly, *To the Scaffold: The Life of Marie Antoinette,* New York: William Morrow, 1991; London: Robson, 1992
Haslip, Joan, *Marie Antoinette,* London and New York: Weidenfeld and Nicolson, 1988
Hearsey, John E.N., *Marie Antoinette,* London: Heron, 1969; New York: Dutton, 1972
Hunt, Lynn Avery, *The Family Romance of the French Revolution,* Berkeley: University of California Press, and London: Routledge, 1992
Zweig, Stefan, *Marie Antoinette: The Portrait of an Average Woman,* Garden City, New York: Garden City Publishing, 1932; London: Cassell, 1933

Recent biographies of Marie Antoinette, who was Queen of France from 1774 through 1792, have generally owed a debt to Zweig and Castelot. ZWEIG's authoritative biography, based primarily upon eyewitness accounts and archival records both in Vienna and Paris, set a standard of well-written and well-researched scholarship. Zweig, who was neither in the royalist camp of hagiographers nor in the nineteenth-century camp of revolutionary detractors, viewed Marie Antoinette as a marriageable Hapsburg whose emergence on the stage of history came at a complex and difficult period. According to Zweig's analysis, there was nothing visible in the early behaviors and character of Marie Antoinette that would have led a viewer to believe that she might become a "tragic heroine" of the French Revolution.

CASTELOT's readable, equally well-researched and sympathetic treatment of Marie Antoinette focuses on the queen's metamorphosis. Treating her as a queen among many other easily forgettable queens of France, Castelot briefly traces her early, flighty years and then concentrates on her relationship to the French Revolution of 1789. Using archival, eyewitness, and published works that had previously been ignored, Castelot provides the account of a woman who needed more education, more maturity, and more sensitivity. Compellingly written by a master French biographer, this study of Marie Antoinette also contains an excellent annotated bibliography and discussion of primary sources.

Any literature search will provide ample evidence that Marie Antoinette remains one of the more popular subjects of biography. At least one new biography appears each year. This has been particularly true from the period of the 1970s until the 200th anniversary of the death of the former queen of France in 1993. The quality and focus of biographical treatments of Marie Antoinette also vary. HEARSEY's biography attempted, according to its preface, to bring a balanced view of Marie Antoinette to the readership. Hearsey's out-of-touch and out-of-time Marie Antoinette, however, ended up a "victim of a cruel and unavoidable fate." In the end, Hearsey was drawn to the queen's understated charm, turning it into a metaphor for the tarnished dazzle of the eighteenth century.

The 1980s and 1990s have provided several other directions for studies of Marie Antoinette. Renewed interest in the queen, which began just prior to the bicentennial of the French Revolution, includes works, in particular, by Haslip, Bernier, and Dunlop. HASLIP's portrayal is framed more by the youth of the future queen than by her difficult last years. Breaking Marie Antoinette's life into two sections, bisected by the infamous Diamond Necklace Affair, which became the subject of a Dumas novel, Haslip turned Zweig's assertions inside out. If Marie Antoinette were only an ordinary woman, what would she have been if her education had been better? Who would she have been if her husband had been a king with more character? What would she have been if the calumnious assaults on her had not been so virulent shortly after her arrival in France? Still a standard biography in spite of its occasional speculative nature, Haslip's focus on Marie Antoinette's early years provides a somewhat different view from other works.

Turning to Marie Antoinette's letters and correspondence, BERNIER's biography places the timing of the Revolution of 1789 squarely on the queen's shoulders. Her influence on the king, her contempt for the National Constituent Assembly, and her reactionary politics made the revolution unavoidable when coupled with France's serious economic difficulties and pressures for change. Perhaps overstating his thesis, Bernier attempts to justify biographies of "great men and women" like his study of Marie Antoinette by suggesting that Marxist analyses of the French Revolution are lacking in humanity; they only educate the reader with charts, graphs, and economic analyses. To Bernier, Marie Antoinette's accomplishments were her sponsorship of the decorative arts and patronage of musicians. She was, after all, a tragic figure.

As thousands of French citizens gathered in Paris to remember Marie Antoinette on the anniversary of her death, DUNLOP's biography of the queen appeared. Unnuanced on politics and occasionally lacking in historical context, Dunlop's work is nonetheless interesting for its surprisingly different treatment of Marie Antoinette. As an author of works on French royal palaces, Dunlop situates the queen architecturally and spacially at the end of the eighteenth century and at the end of her life. There are few extended discussions of intrigue, and almost nothing is said of the alleged scandals that prejudiced public opinion; yet, there are compelling and wonderfully descriptive scenes of a decaying monarchy.

Not necessarily less sympathetic to her fate, HUNT, along with other current historians, has focused on the body of the queen in its relationship to the desacralized French monarchy. From Austrian hag, to emasculator of the king, to debauched lesbian mother and whore, Marie Antoinette became the subject of a scurrilous pamphlet literature that ranged from libelous to pornographic. There is nothing to say that her fate in 1793 would have been different, but recent studies show that French revolutionary misogyny and xenophobia should not be ignored in future studies of Marie Antoinette.

—SUSAN P. CONNER

Marie de France 12th Century

French Writer

Boland, Margaret M., *Architectural Structure in the* Lais *of Marie de France,* New York: Peter Lang, 1995

Burgess, Glyn S., *The* Lais *of Marie de France: Text and Context,* Manchester: Manchester University Press, and Athens: University of Georgia Press, 1987

Clifford, Paula, *Marie de France:* Lais, London: Grant and Cutler, 1982

Maréchal, Chantal A. (ed.), *In Quest of Marie de France: A Twelfth-Century Poet,* Lampeter, Wales, and Lewiston, New York: Edwin Mellen Press, 1992

Mickel, Emanuel J., *Marie de France,* New York: Twayne, 1974

Rothschild, Judith Rice, *Narrative Technique in the* Lais *of Marie de France: Themes and Variations,* Chapel Hill: University of North Carolina Department of Romance Languages, 1974

Marie de France has long been considered one of the most important and best-known writers of the twelfth century, a surprising historical fact since only 12 *lais* (short poems usually with a love theme and with elements of the supernatural, exotic, or fantastic), a collection of fables, and one Latin saint's life are ascribed to her. For a writer of Marie de France's standing, feminist interpretations have been late in coming, with only a handful of scholarly articles published during the mid-1980s. There is still no book-length study of Marie's *lais* from a feminist, Lacanian, or post-modernist perspective, although critics have begun to examine her feminine poetics, the role of women, female narrators, feminine *translatio,* and the power of sisterhood in individual *lais.*

In 1982, CLIFFORD published a slim volume of 80 pages of commentary breaking no new ground, but rather offering a beginner's guide to a reading of Marie de France's *lais.* Her main focus is on the theme of love in Marie's tales, with fidelity and loyalty in both feudal and love relationships as the center of Marie's ethical code, a code that Clifford believes is at the heart of the literary achievement of this twelfth-century writer. Although there is little theoretical background or contextualization of the *lais,* this text is a clear and well-written exploration of Marie's variations on the theme of love.

Another general background, more thorough and far-reaching in scope, is the earlier work by MICKEL. Although still a modest volume, Mickel's work treats the intellectual background of the twelfth century, the identity of Marie de France and her milieu, and the genres she used. He includes sources and plots of Marie's *lais* and explores various narrative techniques such as her use of prologues and epilogues, the unifying patterns in her tales, the intermingling of the marvelous and realistic, her use of irony, and the different concepts and paths of love in the tales. He also devotes one chapter each to her fables and her saint's life *Espurgatoire Saint Patriz.* The book has a good select bibliography, although Glyn S. Burgess's Marie de France: *An Analytical Bibliography* (1977, with a supplement in 1986) supercedes it. As an introduction to Marie's art and work, this volume is an extremely useful starting point for the general reader.

ROTHSCHILD's work is another good starting point, but limited in its scope to half the known *lais* (*Equitan, Fresne, Bisclavret, Deus Amanz, Yonec,* and *Milun*). Her study focuses on the artistry of Marie de France in terms of her carefully crafted structural devices (often bipartite or tripartite) and her narrative techniques, which include a linear progression in each tale, a complex plot, a highly developed sense of place, and use of sensuous detail and development of character through revelation. The most valuable aspect of this book is its close reading of the individual *lais* with detailed observations and insights in an ongoing commentary. She moves linearly through the text by quoting the Old French original and then following with a close literary analysis. Her observations are clear, insightful, focused, and jargon-free.

Continuing in this tradition of close textual analysis in terms of thematic elements, especially chivalry and prowess in love, BURGESS examines the ways that characters and situations in the *lais* reflect the twelfth-century feudal or courtly worlds. The strength of this work is its close literary analysis of Marie's love vocabulary and treatment of love, especially its investigation of difficult passages in which he explores the ambiguities of meaning in the Old French and offers plausible and alternative interpretations when the words themselves or their contexts are ambiguous. He explores the ways that Marie described the love between men and women, men and men, and men and God in feudal terms (service, loyalty, fidelity, and honor). He does not explore the rich territory of love between women (mother-daughter, sister-sister, mistress-servant, two women in love with the same man, etc.), areas that Marie herself investigated.

BOLAND takes a different stance on Marie's artistry, not by close textual reading, but by an elaborate scheme in which she argues for an intricate structural patterning based on architectural principles at work in Marie's own time, notably the Gothic cathedrals of the twelfth century. In this structural study, she posits a deliberate patterning that Marie superimposed on the 12 *lais* to form an interlaced, interlocking, and circular structure that reflects the creation of the kingdom of God in history. She suggests a parallel structure between the first six *lais* and the last six in terms of events, characters, and vocabulary; she further sees an alternating pattern of joy and sorrow, life and death between odd and even numbered *lais*, and a tripartite structure that interlocks the *lais* in yet another way, in which the first five *lais* highlight human deficiencies, and the last four *lais* celebrate fidelity, devotion, love, and charity, with the central three *lais* as a kind of trinity at the heart of the whole collection with Yonec as a Christ figure, the nightingale as symbol of the Holy Ghost, and the mountain of God. This study is the only one that investigates Marie as a serious and pointedly Christian writer with a deliberate agenda of structuring her collection of tales to reflect her deep understanding of Old and New Testament theology.

The collection of 15 essays edited by MARÉCHAL is one of the most valuable volumes on Marie de France in terms of offering a breadth of interpretative stances to Marie's art, including feminist perspectives. Maréchal's introduction, which traces the reception and transmission of Marie's work from the twelfth century to our own times, is extremely valuable as an overview of approaches tied to the changing currents of literary criticism. In this collection are thought-provoking and new approaches to Marie's work, which are illuminating in their range from more traditional approaches such as the Celtic origins of the chess symbolism, Christian allusions and divine justice in *Yonec*, and love and envy in the *lais*. In addition the essays explore contemporary and feminist concerns such as sexual and textual politics, desire and social reproduction, and the revenge of the female storyteller. In some of these articles, critics have explored Marie's awareness of the masculine, public world of chivalry and politics versus the feminine, private world of desire, and the means by which she tries to give women the power of speech, denied them in their society, or a space for their own stories and discourses. In these ways, Marie was profoundly interested in the politics of male-female relationships, the importance of speech and silence, gesture and sign, and the exploiting of a feminine genre for exploring female desire and gender roles.

—JOANNE A. CHARBONNEAU

Marriage

Delphy, Christine, and Diana Leonard, *Familiar Exploitation: A New Analysis of Marriage in Contemporary Western Societies*, Cambridge, Massachusetts: Polity Press, 1992

Fleming, Jennifer Baker, and Carolyn Washburne, *For Better, for Worse: A Feminist Handbook on Marriage and Other Options*, New York: Scribner, 1977

Hopson, Derek S., and Darlene Powell Hopson, *Friends, Lovers, and Soul Mates: A Guide to Better Relationships between Black Men and Women*, New York: Simon and Schuster, 1994

Hydén, Margareta, *Woman Battering as Marital Act: The Construction of a Violent Marriage*, Oslo: Scandinavian University Press, and Oxford and New York: Oxford University Press, 1994

Oliker, Stacey J., *Best Friends and Marriage: Exchange among Women*, Berkeley: University of California Press, 1989

Smart, Carol, *The Ties That Bind: Law, Marriage, and the Reproduction of Patriarchal Relations*, London and Boston: Routledge and Kegan Paul, 1984

Marriage is one of the most pervasive institutions in human society and has been so since the beginning of recorded history. While the laws, customs, and expectations surrounding marriage vary from culture to culture and from one historical period to another, most people experience marriage at least at some point in their lives. One of the goals of feminist thinking has been to analyze this institution and its affect on women.

FLEMING and WASHBURNE's volume from the late 1970s attacks marriage as a patriarchal institution developed for the benefit of men, and it illustrates the kind of radical feminist thinking that was common during this time. The topics examined include romance, legal issues, motherhood, abuse, lesbianism, open marriage, group marriage, and so forth. While Fleming and Washburne propose numerous alternatives to traditional marriage, they do not overlook the disadvantages and problems of each. Although much of the discussion and conclusions were and still are controversial, the book remains of value for its strongly feminist approach to the subject.

SMART's study also focuses on the predominantly patriarchal nature of marriage and of women's relationships to men. By recounting various legal precedents in England from the end of World War II to the present, Smart demonstrates the ways in which, despite considerable change in the various laws surrounding family and divorce (many of which, Smart is quick to point out, have benefited women), society has maintained a patriarchal attitude toward marriage and family. This attitude is particularly evident in divorce cases, in which women continue to be considered financially dependent upon men, and their economic recourse is limited to the point that divorced women often are left little alternative other than remarriage, a cycle that perpetuates the subordinate role of women in marriages. Smart's solution is that women need to be able to work at jobs that compensate them at an acceptable rate, and that affordable, reliable child care should be available. It is through economic equality, she argues, that the institution of marriage will shed its patriarchal foundation.

Another feminist analysis of the institution of marriage from an economic perspective is that offered by DELPHY and LEONARD. Focusing on western cultures, the authors argue that marriage and family in capitalist societies are primarily economic systems. The book is carefully argued, and it includes bibliographic references.

HYDÉN's book concerns, as its title states, woman battering, but from the perspective of marriage. Based on official police reports and interviews with couples involved in violent relationships (that is, women abused by their husbands), Hydén effectively uncovers the various viewpoints of both men and women involved in violent marriages and their complicated relations to one another. Not surprisingly, Hydén concludes that the solution to changing violent marriages is within society: she suggests that by holding men accountable for their actions and offering women recourse, women in violent marriages will be able to transcend the role of victim.

HOPSON and HOPSON provide a self-help book from a psychotherapy perspective rather than a historical or scholarly approach to marriage between African-American men and women. Included in their discussion are the roles that fear of intimacy and uncertainty about ethnic identity play in many marriages. They focus on the importance of black culture and empowerment as means toward improved self-esteem and identity, the main ingredients of successful and fulfilling marriages.

OLIKER focuses on the role of female friendships in shaping and defining marriages. Rather than the traditional marriage and family as the center of emotional life for women, Oliker sees friendships between women as fulfilling this role, in large part because the issue of sexual identity does not form part of these relationships. In addition, friendship between women is seen as a means of strengthening marriages.

—ELEANOR B. AMICO

Martineau, Harriet 1802–1876

British Writer

David, Deirdre, *Intellectual Women and Victorian Patriarchy*, Ithaca, New York: Cornell University Press, and London: Macmillan, 1987

Pichanick, Valerie Kossew, *Harriet Martineau: The Woman and Her Work, 1802–76*, Ann Arbor: University of Michigan Press, 1980

Sanders, Valerie, *Reason Over Passion: Harriet Martineau and the Victorian Novel*, Sussex: Harvester, and New York: St. Martin's Press, 1986

Thomas, Gillian, *Harriet Martineau*, Boston: Twayne, 1985

As accurately forecast by its title, DAVID's study focuses on Martineau's career as an intellectual in the context of nineteenth-century life. Although David's discussion of Martineau comprises only a third of the study, it is included here because it is by far the most theoretically sophisticated account of Martineau's work to have appeared to date. David's analysis of Martineau's position as an intellectual is theoretically informed by Antonio Gramsci's writings on the social function of intellectuals, by theoretical and contemporary views of Victorian intellectual activity, and by contemporary views of woman's "mind" and her higher education in the Victorian period. David's introductory chapter analyzes theories and representations of intellectuals, only to conclude that most of the major theories cannot account for intellectual women writing in the Victorian period. Although Gramsci finds no place in his theory for women, David argues that Martineau fits his category of "the organic intellectual" in that she gave awareness and homogeneity to an increasingly powerful liberal English middle class and elaborated the influential ideologies of that class. Since women were considered second-class intellectual citizens, the role of Victorian female intellectuals was inevitably a burdened and conflictive one. The Victorian attitude toward intellectuals as service figures, instructors, and moral counselors was legitimized by the presence of female intellectuals because it was consistent with the conventional representation of women as morally superior beings and as ancillary guides and companions to men. Hence, David convincingly argues that Martineau's role as a Victorian intellectual was one of auxiliary usefulness to a male-dominated culture, and that this model informs her popular writing about women, political economy, slavery, English history, the working class, and Eastern travel.

David further elaborates Martineau's position as a female intellectual in terms of her filial relation as a follower of male economists and politicians who constructed the shapes and dominant ideas of her discourse. This is not to deny that Martineau welcomed her own agency and legitimation; indeed she defined herself as a fluent writer in a variety of popular forms and embraced her subordinated status, aligning it with her forthright feminism. Nonetheless it remains the case that from her initial success as a populariser of Bethamite political economy to her last autobiographical writings, she performed the work of auxiliary usefulness with vigor, never uneasy about the service she rendered the male middle-class establishment of her time. David admirably succeeds in achieving a balance between identifying Martineau's complicit ratification and resistant subversion to

Victorian patriarchy, and the value of the study is strengthened by the comparisons she is able to make between Martineau's career and the careers of Elizabeth Barrett Browning and George Eliot.

Like David, SANDERS sees Martineau's career as marked by divided sympathies and contradictory ideals. Consequently, the study is thematically organized by her interest in the debate between reason and passion, which Martineau explores in her autobiography. The conflict between passion and reason, and its variant pairings, personal and impersonal, solitude and society, imagination and discipline, principle and duty develops, Sanders argues, into a battle between repression and fulfillment. This conflict takes many forms; for example, Martineau felt the need to write but could only justify imaginative indulgence when directed to practical ends such as devotion to God or improvement in society; she questions, yet reinforces, the prescribed codes for women, and her reflections on religious life revealed the coexistence of conventional Christianity and radical skepticism. Sanders argues that this divided response of resistance and complicity speaks of the times, but also of Martineau's own limitations. The conflicts Sanders identifies are indisputably a defining feature of Martineau's life and works.

In her attempt to assess Martineau's literary achievement Sanders examines her importance in the development of the English novel. She discusses such novels as *A Manchester Strike, Sowers Not Reapers,* and *Deerbrook* as part of an enduring domestic tradition. Likewise, the history and travel books are discussed with a view to their novelistic techniques and their thematic links with the tales and the autobiography. In this respect the study is also valuable for its exploration of a pattern of affinities linking Martineau's fiction with that of other Victorian novelists. This study is to be recommended for its clear-sighted assessment of Martineau's literary achievement in the multiple genres she attempted.

PICHANICK's biography of Martineau is well researched and is of interest here for its critical reevaluation of Martineau as a historical figure. It counters some of the unsound arguments found in R.K. Webb's earlier biography, *Harriet Martineau: A Radical Victorian* (1960). Like Sanders and Thomas, Pichanick aims to provide a balanced approach to Martineau's work; she avoids the extremes represented by earlier biographies, which have tended to be either uncritically adulatory or hostile, and strikes instead a middle way. This work will be sought after for its detailed notes and useful appendix on sources. It is essential reading for those who wish to gain a fuller understanding of Martineau and her historical contexts.

Whereas Pichanick concentrates on Martineau's historical writings and her political influence, THOMAS evaluates her significance in the context of the nineteenth-century literary world. There are individual chapters on Martineau's autobiographical, travel, and political writings, and a concluding chapter on the author's critical reputation, past and present. Thomas usefully places the political journalism of such works as *Illustrations of Political Economy, Household Education and Health, Husbandry and Handicraft,* popular histories such as *The History of Peace* and *British Rule in India,* and Martineau's journalistic contributions to the *Quarterly Review* and Dickens' popular journal *Household Words* in the tradition of popular educative literature of the early nineteenth century. The chapter on Martineau's fiction is worth special mention, for it not only deals with her two full-length novels for adult readers but also contains a detailed discussion of her numerous children's stories. Thomas identifies Martineau's major weakness as a fiction writer in her reliance on exposition and didacticism in place of dramatization. She concludes that the children's books, *The Crofton Boys* and *The Playfellow Stories,* alone among her fiction, can be read for their literary merit rather than their historical significance. This study is a good general introduction to Martineau's life and work and will be particularly useful to those with a special interest in her literary achievement. Thomas also provides an annotated bibliography, a valuable resource for students new to Martineau scholarship.

—JENNIFER McDONELL

Mary I 1553–1588

British Queen

Erickson, Carrolly, *Bloody Mary,* New York: Doubleday, and London: Dent, 1978

Loades, David M., *Mary Tudor: A Life,* Oxford and New York: Blackwell, 1989

Marshall, Rosalind Kay, *Mary I,* London: HMSO, 1993

Prescott, Hilda F.M., *Mary Tudor,* London: Eyre and Spottiswoode, 1952; New York: Macmillan, 1953

Ridley, Jasper, *The Life and Times of Mary Tudor,* London: Weidenfeld and Nicolson, 1973

Though Mary I ruled for only five years, she is well known in history as "Bloody Mary," because she ordered the burning of 300 Protestants. For a long time the classic biography of Mary was PRESCOTT's.

This book is solidly documented, though it would appear rather naive to readers today, and is strongly marked by pro-Mary religious sensibilities. Though Prescott describes the burning of Protestants as a ghastly and mistaken policy, she also tries to justify it as almost inevitable given the reality of the danger they posed to the social order, a highly questionable idea. Prescott describes Mary as brave and committed, but without a keen and searching intellect, and argues that Mary would have been happy and successful in private life, but lacked the qualities necessary to be a successful queen.

RIDLEY also presents Mary as someone who was ill-treated by fate and was in no sense fitted for the role of queen, because she lacked both worldly wisdom and political judgment. His book is gorgeously illustrated, and includes a bibliography but no notes. His study has more on the Protestant martyrs and other aspects of her reign, including trade with Russia in the 1550s. Ridley describes Mary as neurotic and often living in a world of unreality because the Catholic religion was the center of her life. Ridley argues that by nature she was kind and considerate; however, because religion was so fundamental to her she earned the name "Bloody Mary."

This appellation is the title for ERICKSON's scholarly but also very lively and accessible biography, and she argues that while the memory of the martyrs looms large in any appraisal of Mary, there are other themes as well. Erickson sees Mary as a survivor, whose conscience was the highest guide to her behavior. She argues that Mary ruled with a full measure of Tudor majesty, and met a number of challenges: severe economic crises, rebellion, religious upheaval. Erickson is especially valuable in her discussion of what it meant for a woman to rule in the mid-sixteenth century.

MARSHALL is also sympathetic to Mary, wanting to examine the real Mary behind the image of the villainous queen. Marshall is thoughtful on questions of Mary's childhood and her health problems as an adult. Another strength is the discussion of the marriage negotiations with Philip of Spain. The book is weaker on Mary's treatment of heretics. Like Ridley's, this book is also beautifully illustrated but lacks notes. It also has some small inaccuracies.

The most scholarly and analytical study of Mary is by LOADES. He argues that Mary's limitations as a ruler were largely imposed by her sex. Even though Mary was well-educated, and as intelligent and strong minded as many of the male nobility, she was also profoundly conventional, and accepted the view that women should be dependent. This made her ill-adapted to cope with the stresses imposed by royal rank. While Loades sees Mary's reign as having more successes than did earlier scholars, he is also more critical of her personally. Not only was she unable to acquire an objective political vision, but, he argues, the records do not support the view of Mary as the mildest and most merciful of the Tudors. Most of the generous gestures of the reign came at the beginning, and her government got harsher as it progressed. And, because of the dictates of her conscience, she zealously and vindictively pursued the burning of heretics. Loades describes a number of achievements of Mary's reign: sound administration, sensible financial policies, and a practical approach to ecclesiastical reconstruction. But there were bad harvests and epidemics, and she died before her work had any chance to take root. Moreover, Loades argues, even if Mary had had more time, she faced a number of problems, and her success with dealing with them was uneven.

There is no sign that the English were any more reconciled to the Spanish connection in 1558 than they were in 1554. Philip was even less popular, and it is possible that if Mary had lived he would have dissolved the marriage. Loades doubts that Mary could have survived such a debacle. The persecution neither stamped out nor silenced the Protestants during the three and a half years in which it was applied. As Mary's reign progressed, there was more and more danger of a Protestant insurrection. All recent scholars see an element of tragedy in Mary's life.

—CAROLE LEVIN

Mary Stuart 1542–1587

Scottish Queen

Cowan, Ian B. (ed.), *The Enigma of Mary Stuart,* London: V. Gollancz, 1971

Donaldson, Gordon, *The First Trial of Mary Queen of Scots,* New York: Stein and Day, and London: Botsford, 1969

———, *Mary Queen of Scots,* London: English Universities Press, 1974

Fraser, Antonia, *Mary Queen of Scots,* New York: Delacorte Press, and London: Weidenfeld and Nicolson, 1969

MacNalty, Sir Arthur Salusbury, *Mary, Queen of Scots: The Daughter of Debate,* London: C. Johnson, 1960; New York: Ungar, 1961

Morrison, N. Brysson, *Mary Queen of Scots,* London: Vista, and New York: Vanguard Press, 1960

Plaidy, Jean, *Mary Queen of Scots: The Fair Devil of Scotland,* New York: Putnam, and London: R. Hale, 1975

Thomson, George Malcom, *The Crime of Mary Stuart,* London: Hutchinson, and New York: Dutton, 1967

It seems almost impossible for historians and biographers to be neutral about Mary Stuart, more commonly known as Mary, Queen of Scots. The mother of James I of England (James VI of Scotland) and cousin to Elizabeth I, Mary lived her adult life surrounded by accusations of murder and treason, spent 19 years in prison, was beheaded in the heat of controversy, and still provokes strong feelings in those writing about her. Some view her as an innocent martyr, steadfast through the end, guiltless of the charges of murder of her second husband and treason against Elizabeth that were leveled against her. Others see her as a scarlet woman, an adulterer and murderer, dangerous also for her insistence on remaining a Catholic in a Protestant England, and for the perceived threat she posed to Elizabeth's throne.

Although some of the sources listed here attempt a more objective view of Mary, others noticeably side with either her guilt or innocence; therefore, a reading of more than one perspective will help the reader gain balance.

MacNALTY's biography takes a unique approach in its study of Mary—it is from a "medical viewpoint," as the author uses Mary's physical maladies to explain her behavior and show her character in the midst of difficulties. Mary's conditions included a bleeding stomach ulcer, mental breakdowns (which made her not responsible, according to the author, for some of her behavior), severe arthritis, and dropsy, and she is portrayed here as heroic in her struggle to deal with these problems. MacNalty does admit Mary's lack of political acumen but feels that she was guileless and inwardly noble. One appendix details her medical history; another holds the partial contents of the "Casket Letters," correspondence allegedly written from Mary to her lover the Earl of Bothwell.

The biography by MORRISON, one of the few Americans who has produced a book-length study of Mary, is somewhat brief and written as an easy-to-follow narrative for a general audience; it includes black and white portraits of Mary and other royalty in her life. Morrison's assessment of Mary seems mainly to be that she was unlucky, although Morrison does believe that Mary was complicit in her husband Darnley's murder. Regarding the "Casket Letters," written during her marriage to Darnley, Morrison believes Mary wrote them, and that they were not forgeries as some believe, further providing motive for the murder of her husband.

THOMSON's volume presents a clear bias toward Mary's guilt, feeling that she initiated an adulterous affair with Bothwell, that she wrote the "Casket Letters," that she and Bothwell were both implicated in the murder of her second husband, and that she married Bothwell imprudently, based on her passions. The author states early in his account that even as a girl, Mary "was no innocent," as she had been raised viewing tortures and being schooled by her relatives the Guises and the Medicis "in bloodshed and fanaticism." This study focuses mainly on the period of Mary's life around the time of Darnley's murder, the so-called Kirk O'Field Crime, and includes a detailed analysis of the "Casket Letters."

DONALDSON's work (1969) also concentrates on whether or not Mary was involved in the Darnley murder, although the first two chapters provide more background on Mary's life up to that event. There is well-researched, extensive information on the evidence and investigation of the murder. Donaldson views the affair as primarily political in its consequences; it was not Mary's guilt and punishment for murder that was to be decided as much as the question of whether she would continue to rule as Queen of Scotland. This study tries to remain neutral, presenting the information without drawing many conclusions in the case of Darnley's murder. Because of losing her throne and freedom, however, Mary is seen as plotting and welcoming assistance from Catholics for the assassination of Elizabeth, the second major crime of which she was accused. Black and white plates of the nobles involved in Mary's life are included.

The most complete work ever written on Mary is by FRASER, an exhaustive volume of over six hundred pages, for which the author learned sixteenth-century Scottish. Fraser very clearly empathizes with Mary Stuart and does her best to present her as a beautiful and tragic heroine wronged in her own day and by history. Especially moving is the chapter that details to the last drop of blood Mary's beheading. The biography provides genealogies, plates of portraits, and engravings of people, places, and documents involved. The extensiveness and careful research in this work (including hundreds of primary and secondary sources) make it suitable for a scholarly audience; the somewhat romanticized account makes it lively reading for a general audience. An appendix presents the "Long Casket Letter" (the most significant piece of evidence that Mary wanted her second husband murdered) in both English and Scottish.

COWAN's work is concerned mainly with presenting varying points of view of Mary throughout history, seeing those biases as reflecting much of the spirit of the ages in which they were written. It is actually an anthology containing excerpts of literary treatments of Mary, first hand accounts, and secondary sources on Mary from the sixteenth century through 1969. The author is more interested in commenting on the chastisers and adulators of Mary than in deciding her guilt or innocence, as he feels that the latter assessment can never be reached. The resource includes the words of John Knox, Edmund Spenser, Algernon Swinburne, and many others, but it would be more helpful if an index were included.

DONALDSON's second work on Mary (1974), which this time includes all of Mary's life, tries to avoid "partisanship." The editor's forward notes that the author is a credentialed Scottish historian, rather than a general biographer or a British scholar, who might present a more biased view of the Scottish Queen. Donaldson does not draw conclusions about Darnley's murder but does state that Mary's subsequent marriage to her third husband Bothwell showed she was in favor of her second husband's murder. The clear writing and lack of extraneous details in this study make this an excellent beginning source on Mary Stuart. Most helpful is the final chapter, "The Continuing Debate," which summarizes the treatment of Mary by later writers and laments the lack of a full-length "satisfactory biography" that is scholarly, error-free, and objective.

PLAIDY has compiled a general work on Mary that is delightful in its wealth of color and black-and-white plates. In fact, this volume is as helpful a pictorial account of the art, architecture, and costumes of Scotland and England of the sixteenth century as it is a study of Mary's life. A photograph of the silver casket that held the famed letters, and even a snapshot of the mummified remains of Bothwell are included. The author's assessment of Mary is that she is a fascinating figure, one who is both "a saint and a sinner," who is "weak and foolish but not a criminal woman."

—CAROL BLESSING

Masculinity

Brod, Harry (ed.), *The Making of Masculinities: The New Men's Studies,* Boston and London: Allen and Unwin, 1987

Brod, Harry, and Michael Kaufman (eds.), *Theorizing Masculinities,* Thousand Oaks, California, and London: Sage, 1994

Connell, R.W., *Masculinities,* Berkeley: University of California Press, and Cambridge: Polity Press, 1995

Ehrenreich, Barbara, *The Hearts of Men: American Dreams and the Flight from Commitment,* New York: Anchor/ Doubleday, and London: Pluto Press, 1983

Kimmel, Michael, *Manhood in America: A Cultural History,* New York and London: Free Press, 1996

Kimmel, Michael, and Michael A. Messner (eds.), *Men's Lives,* London: Collier Macmillan, and New York: Macmillan, 1989

Morton, Donald (ed.), *The Material Queer: A LesBiGay Cultural Studies Reader,* Boulder, Colorado: Westview Press, 1996

Stoltenberg, John, *Refusing to Be a Man: Essays on Sex and Justice,* Portland, Oregon: Breitenbush, 1989; London: Fontana, 1990

BROD was the first to attempt to delineate a new field of "men's studies," using a variety of generally social constructionist perspectives. An opening theoretical section includes essays by philosopher Brod, psychologist Joseph Pleck, and sociologist Bob Connell followed by, among others, Peter Filene on men's history, Michael Kimmel on the historical "crisis" of masculinity, Clyde Franklin on the institutional decimation (meant literally, i.e., one out of 10 killed) of black males, Michael Messner on sports and male identity development, Drury Sherrod, Dorothy Hammond, and Alta Jablow on men's friendships, and Louis Crompton on Byron and homosexualities.

CONNELL further develops his concept of "hegemonic masculinity," very effectively and influentially deployed in his earlier *Gender and Power.* It extends the analysis of the earlier volume in its engagements with theories of masculinity from psychoanalysis, social science, and political economy, and also engages with the experiential dimension more than the earlier book, presenting ethnographic class conscious accounts of the constructions of various gay and straight masculinities.

EHRENREICH's book is a creative recounting of post-war U.S. popular culture, which synthesizes *Playboy,* the Beats, cardiology, men's liberation, and the consumer and counter cultures. She molds all these into a persuasive tale of men's flight from breadwinner responsibilities, and their rebellion against feminism before the latest feminist movement even began. Ehrenreich concludes that this male behavior was more responsible for the anti-feminist backlash than feminism itself.

KIMMEL offers a broad cultural history of the development of mostly mainstream masculinities in the United States, from the colonial period to the present. Kimmel sees men's roles in a homosocial world of work that systematically excludes women and minority men as a central factor in the construction of masculine identities. Models of masculinity range from the self-made man of the beginning of the new nation through a succession of men's competitive travails against other men as captains of industry, sports and war heroes, organization men, and contemporary weekend warriors.

KIMMEL and MESSNER's collection, probably the most widely used text in "men's studies" courses throughout the United States, provides an excellent overview of current analyses of masculinities. Shaped by the editors' social constructionist and life course perspectives, the various topical sections each contain essays examining diverse men's lives, especially along the axes of sexual orientation, race, and class. Issues discussed include theoretical perspectives, the journey from boyhood to manhood, sports and war as rites of passage, work, health, intimacy and power, friendships, sexualities, families, and the future.

BROD and KAUFMAN attempt to capture the current state of the art in the project of theorizing masculinities. In addition to the editors, essays by Connell, Kimmel, Messner, Coltrane, Hearn, and Collinson critically examine various social science perspectives on masculinities. Other contributors, namely Morgan, Mac An Ghail, Messner, Hondagneu-Sotelo, Gutterman, and Flannigan-Saint-Aubin look at the military, black English masculinities, the "New Man," Mexican immigrant men in the United States, postmodernism, literary metaphors of the male body, and the new men's movement.

MORTON is the editor of the first LesBiGay Cultural Studies reader with an explicitly materialist orientation. It includes such standard thinkers as Freud, Marcuse, Lacan, Derrida, Foucault, Wittig, Irigaray, and Butler, as well as essays probing ethnic, racial, gender, and class diversity in constructions and representations of queer identities and politics.

STOLTENBERG articulates the most radical feminist stance of men associated with profeminist perspectives.

Much indebted in particular to the work of Andrea Dworkin, the book's core essay is "How Men Have (a) Sex," which argues that men perform their sexuality in order to maintain patriarchal identity. Other essays critique the pornography industry, violence in the father-son relationship and in men's lives in general, men's identification with the fetus in their anti-reproductive rights politics, and rapist versus moral sexual ethics.

—HARRY BROD

See also Men's Movements; Men and Feminism

Mathematics: General

Dick, Auguste, *Emmy Noether,* Basel: Birkhäuser, 1970; Boston: Birkhäuser, 1981

Grinstein, Louise, and Paul Campbell (eds.), *Women of Mathematics: A Bibliographic Sourcebook,* New York: Greenwood, 1987

Koblitz, Ann Hibner, *A Convergence of Lives: Sofia Kovalevskaia: Scientist, Writer, Revolutionary,* Boston: Birkhäuser, 1983

Parker, Marla (ed.), *She Does Math! Real-Life Problems from Women on the Job,* Washington, D.C.: Mathematical Association of America, 1995

Reid, Constance, *Julia: A Life in Mathematics,* Washington, D.C.: Mathematical Association of America, 1996

Until recently, women in mathematics were simply ignored. DICK's biography of Emmy Noether (1882–1935), the founder of modern algebra, was one of the first books about female mathematicians, but at first it was available only in its original German. It chronicles a relatively uneventful personal life, but a life of kindness, creativity, and prodigious influence. Mathematicians came from China and Japan, as well as from all over the western world to study under Noether at the University of Göttingen in Germany during the 1920s. She gave invited speeches at two International Congresses of Mathematicians in 1928 and 1932. When Hitler dismissed all German Jews from their jobs in 1933, the worldwide mathematics community searched for a safe place, and she obtained a joint appointment at the Institute of Advanced Study in Princeton and Bryn Mawr College. Just as she was establishing a following in the United States, she died unexpectedly after an operation.

Another important female mathematician was Sofia Kovalevskaia (1850–91), whose life is documented in KOBLITZ's biography. In 1868 Kovalevskaia contracted a "fictitious" marriage to escape Czarist Russia so that she and her husband would have the freedom to go to western Europe to study. Living in different cities but corresponding regularly, they both succeeded in earning doctorates, and Kovalevskaia's was the first in modern times for a woman in any subject. After they returned to Russia, they produced a daughter, but the innovative new father had great trouble earning money. After Kovalevskaia returned to western Europe to continue serious mathematics, her husband committed suicide. As a widow, she was in the best position for a nineteenth-century woman to pursue a career, and she became the first woman in modern times to attain a regular university faculty position—at the University of Stockholm. She published poetry and fiction as well as research mathematics and then won the highest prize in the world for a paper in research mathematics. She became editor of the journal *Acta Mathematica,* and people wrote to her from all over the world asking her for advice. She died of pneumonia at the age of forty-one. Koblitz's book is the most readable and erudite biography of Kovalevskaia, although there are several others well worth reading. Koblitz documented Kovalevskaia's fascinating life after reading letters by, to, and about Kovalevskaia in their original language. Despite frequent scholarly footnotes, the book reads like a novel.

REID's book is much lighter, full of photographs and other memorabilia found by a loving sister after Julia Robinson's death. Constance Reid and Julia Robinson (1919–85) were the only children of their parents, and after they were both accomplished professionals, Reid decided to use her access to the mathematical world in her writing. She was already well established as one of the leading writers about mathematicians when she wrote "The Autobiography of Julia Robinson" during Robinson's last month of life, checking it with her sister almost daily. This long article is the backbone of *Julia,* but three other pieces by mathematicians about Robinson's work are included. Robinson worked in some of the most fundamental areas of mathematics, on the border between logic and number theory, was the first female mathematician in the National Academy of Sciences, and the first female president of the American Mathematical Society. Her stable, loving marriage was in contrast to Kovalevskaia's troubled marriage and Noether's apparent obliviousness to romance. Like both of them, however, she worked hard to include formerly excluded groups in the mathematical community, and to promote peace and justice in the wider world.

GRINSTEIN and CAMPBELL offer 43 biographies of women mathematicians, no more than two written by any one author. Many of the authors are themselves female mathematicians, excluded because the editors did not include any living people born after 1925. Each entry is accompanied by two bibliographies, one of the woman's own writing and the other of writing about her. The book has a brief introduction and two charts, one depicting the lives on a timeline, and the other summarizing the "origin," adult residence, education, and specialized mathematical field of each subject.

PARKER provides yet another genre. It brings the mathematical drama alive by describing how dozens of living women use math professionally. It includes short biographies and photographs of each. This may be the first book to demonstrate how satisfying it can be for many types of women to have careers in mathematics. The previous books focused on women with a strong passion for research. Parker shows how math pervades many aspects of our society, and how women enjoy a variety of fascinating career paths after studying mathematics. It would be a welcome gift for any young person (female or male) who enjoys math but wonders what careers it offers. There are many, and Parker demonstrates the breadth of opportunity.

—PATRICIA CLARK KENSCHAFT

Mathematics: Teaching to Women

American Association of University Women (AAUW), *How Schools Shortchange Girls*, Washington, D.C.: AAUW Educational Foundation, 1992

Chipman, Susan F., Lorelei R. Brush, and Donna M. Wilson (eds.), *Women and Mathematics: Balancing the Equation*, Hillsdale, New Jersey: Lawrence Erlbaum Associates, 1985

Fennema, Elizabeth, and Gilah Leder (eds.), *Mathematics and Gender*, New York: Teachers' College Press, 1990

Hanna, Gila (ed.), *Towards Gender Equity in Mathematics Education*, Dordrecht, Netherlands and Boston: Kluwer Academic Publishing, 1996

Kenschaft, Patricia Clark (ed.), *Winning Women into Mathematics*, Washington, D.C.: Mathematical Association of America, 1991

Sadker, Myra, and David Sadker, *Failing at Fairness: How America's Schools Cheat Girls*, New York: Scribner, 1994

Tobias, Shelia, *Overcoming Math Anxiety*, New York: Norton, 1978

Zaslavsky, Claudia, *Fear of Math: How to Get Over It and Get On with Your Life*, New Brunswick, New Jersey: Rutgers University Press, 1994

The 1990s were ripe for a proliferation of good books exploring both the cultural habits that prevent girls and women from enjoying their fair share of mathematical delights, and also potential remedies. Although some women throughout recorded history have brought attention to these issues, modern academic study of associated problems may have begun with Lucy Sell's coining the term "critical filter" for mathematics' effect on girls and women in the early 1970s. Soon there was an abundance of papers documenting both the many ways that girls are deflected from mathematical competence and confidence, and the extent to which mathematical inadequacies affect women financially, socially, and personally.

Both CHIPMAN, BRUSH, and WILSON's book and that by FENNEMA and LEDER include entire papers from established authors about research on girls and mathematics. They explore, for example, how teachers tend to reward girls for neatness and obedience, and boys for imagination and risk-taking, and how this affects math achievement. Expecting quick answers and calling more often on boys also dampens girls' budding math abilities. The authors consider the ways that the traditional games of each sex affect both mathematical knowledge and the social skills needed for later classroom achievement, and how both self-perception and perceptions about career opportunities motivate students to continue taking math courses. Influences of counselors, teachers, parents, and peers are studied. The decreasing mathematical enthusiasm of U.S. females as they progress through our school system is well documented. A multitude of cultural reasons for the difference between adult male and female participation in mathematically based careers are investigated. Also a variety of intervention programs are studied and evaluated.

A list of "Fifty-five Cultural Reasons Why Too Few Women Win at Mathematics," which summarizes the outcomes of such research before 1990, became a pivotal chapter in KENSCHAFT's book. Written by a committee of nine female and four male mathematicians from 11 different states, this book gives a view from inside the mathematical community. It lists programs that promote change, and suggestions for both individuals and groups who want to help. It also presents statistics, cartoons, a history, three extensive bibliographies, and over 50 photographs of female mathematicians. Scripts of the first skits about microinequities (individually small events that cumulatively are like drops of water on a rock wearing away at women's achievement) are included, depicting actual incidents reported by women in mathematics. These were the first of six sets of such skits that were performed by the committee that wrote the book.

Women's preparation in mathematics, because it so drastically affects their economic and political options, has become a worldwide concern. Cross-cultural studies are available in HANNA's collection, which was based on a 1993 international conference. It verifies that mathematical participation and achievement vary widely from culture to culture, making U.S. discussions about the extent to which male math ability is "biological" increasingly ludicrous. In some cultures there are no measurable differences between the sexes mathematically, and in a few women outpace men.

Meanwhile a popular literature has appeared on these topics. TOBIAS's publication in 1978 was publicized by a full-length article in *Ms.*, and the book has become a classic. Ostensibly not specifically about or for women, it has been viewed as serving primarily women and as identifying a predominantly female problem, "math anxiety." ZASLAVSKY has a similar theme. Written by a retired mathematics teacher and based on many interviews with mathematicians and math educators, it is regarded by the math community as more valid and helpful. However, it appeared shortly after the second edition of Tobias's book, and has not yet received the recognition it deserves.

Two of the most widely available books of this list are not specifically about mathematics, but their emphasis on mathematical inequities has brought considerable public attention to these problems. THE AMERICAN ASSOCIATION OF UNIVERSITY WOMEN (AAUW) report synthesizes many studies. Despite public perceptions, "Gender differences in mathematics achievement are small and declining," but the differences in scores in the Scholastic Achievement Tests (SAT) in math are still large, although they too are declining. The AAUW report notes that tests can be biased against either sex, and there is little accountability in testing. Too often, math tests appear to be biased against girls, although it is hard to distinguish between test bias and genuine societal and education biases being reflected in test scores. For example, the disparity in SAT scores is often seen as both a result and a cause of gender differences in taking math courses, but there is also evidence of bias in the test itself.

The AAUW report provides ample evidence that girls and boys in the same classroom can have very different mathematical experiences, and it makes a strong appeal to equalize opportunities. Widespread publicity has been given to the AAUW's statement: "Girls must be educated and encouraged to understand that mathematics and the sciences are important and relevant to their lives. Girls must be actively supported in pursuing education and employment in these areas." To fulfill these goals, the AAUW also sells a video, an eight-page summary with recommendations for educators and policy-makers, a 17-page summary with charts and graphs, and a 500-page full-data report.

SADKER and SADKER's book is a highly readable but chilling expose by two of the major authors of the report by the AAUW. It recounts 25 years of research by a wife-husband team, including both statistical and anecdotal evidence of favoritism in the classroom. Many stories enliven the stark facts. Math classes are repeatedly cited as especially discriminatory, although the entire U.S. educational system receives a scathing indictment. Much of the damaging behavior is unconscious: often it seems so familiar that readers do not notice how discriminatory it is until the Sadkers point it out. Because of the human tendency not to notice patterns that are everywhere around us, it seems likely that the study of the discrimination that keeps girls and women away from mathematics is in its infancy.

—PATRICIA CLARK KENSCHAFT

See also Pedagogy, Feminist

Matriarchal Theory

Bachofen, Johann Jakob, *Myth, Religion, and Mother Right: Selected Writings of J.J. Bachofen*, translated by Ralph Manheim, London: Routledge and Kegan Paul, and Princeton, New Jersey: Princeton University Press, 1967

Briffault, Robert, *The Mothers: A Study of the Origins of Sentiment and Institutions*, London: G. Allen and Unwin, and New York: Macmillan, 1927

Gottner-Abendroth, Heide, *The Dancing Goddess: Principles of a Matriarchal Aesthetic*, translated by Maureen T. Krause, Boston: Beacon Press, 1991

Motz, Lotte, *The Faces of the Goddess*, Oxford: Oxford University Press, 1997

Neumann, Erich, *The Great Mother: An Analysis of the Archetype*, translated by Ralph Manheim, London: Routledge and Kegan Paul, and New York: Pantheon, 1955

Preston, James J. (ed.), *Mother Worship: Theme and Variations*, Chapel Hill: University of North Carolina Press, 1982

There have been mixed responses to the idea of a previous period of matriarchy. One group of scholars argues that there is no scientific evidence for a period of matriarchy in human history. Others continue to believe that there was such a stage in human evolution, insisting on a more speculative approach to history. Indeed, for the last 20 years an extensive literature on feminine psychology and female deities has emerged based on the notion of a previous matriarchal phase of history.

Late nineteenth-century scholars interested in reconstructing human history searched for grand schemes to explain the origin of social institutions. One of these speculative histories was proposed by BACHOFEN, whose thesis on mother right and the origin of religion became famous for postulating an early matriarchal social order. Bachofen was interested in speculative history rather than scientific or fact-based human history. His emphasis was on the analysis of myths to reveal the contours of early stages of history. To him legends and myths preserve the collective memory of people, and become a living expression of the stages in a people's development, and " . . . for the skillful observer, a faithful reflection of all the periods in the life of that people."

A similar thesis was advanced by BRIFFAULT, who asserted the former universal existence of a primitive matriarchy that preceded patriarchy. However, unlike Bachofen, he did not define matriarchy in terms of mother-rule or inheritance through the mother line. To him matriarchy was a period when women were socially predominant. Briffault argued that primitive matriarchy was a universal stage in prehistory, and marriage was originally matrilocal. He used various forms of indirect evidence to support his thesis.

The works of these nineteenth-century scholars were revitalized in the twentieth century by Jungians, particularly in their analysis of goddess symbols. Especially noteworthy here is the massive study of female sacred imagery by NEUMANN. His volume relies heavily on the theories of Bachofen and Briffault to construct an understanding of goddess symbolism based on its supposed origins in a matriarchal period of history. Neumann's book stands as a major cornerstone for a large body of work that depends on the validity of matriarchy as a phase of human history.

GOTTNER-ABENDROTH believes that art in ancient goddess-centered societies was an inseparable part of daily life. According to her, patriarchal societies created a false sense of separation by removing art from life. She attempts to correct for this split by bringing back the "matriarchal art" that was lost with the rise of patriarchy. Gottner-Abendroth maintains that matriarchal societies did not recognize hierarchies, nor did they split consciousness into "art," "science," "religion," "economics," and "politics." "Matriarchal art" is intended to bring about a healing of the split created by patriarchy. The attempt here is to bring about matriarchal spirituality by reaching into the past to regain those early rituals that were lost.

Unlike popular writers, most social scientists in the twentieth century are universally opposed to the idea of a matriarchal period in cultural evolution. The idea has been universally discredited. According to PRESTON there is no evidence to support such a claim. Humans evolved for millions of years in small bands, stressing equality among members, and with no emphasis on hierarchy. This is not a period marked by the dominance of either gender over the other. It is, however, a time before the emergence of complex societies demarcated by hierarchical structures. There is no need to invoke terms like matriarchy or patriarchy to explain the normal structural changes that occur as social systems become more complex.

MOTZ attacks the idea that the Great Goddess emerged out of a matriarchal, prepatriarchal social milieu. She argues that there is no evidence in modern anthropology of a stage of development ruled by women. As a consequence, Motz asserts that the idea of a single archetypal Great Mother is erroneous. There were many goddesses, all from different origins; they were not all mothers; some were ancestors, others animal protectors or other divinities. Rather than stemming from a common goddess rooted in a matriarchal period, each female deity must be understood in its sociocultural context.

At first it might seem difficult to understand why the idea of a matriarchal period of history persists in some circles as a meaningful interpretive frame when it has been so widely discredited. However, it becomes more plausible to believe if one moves from the concrete, factual level to the realm of psychological constellations. In other words, if matriarchy is conceived, not as history, but as a model for understanding psychological processes, it might be a useful idea. If by matriarchy one means an earlier time when women were unfettered by purely patriarchal demands and agendas, then this kind of imaginative history, if not taken or presented literally, provides a platform for a new way of thinking about gender and power. Thus, for some scholars the notion of matriarchy as imaginative or intuitive history continues its appeal.

—JAMES J. PRESTON

See also Ancient Egalitarian Cultures; Hunting/Gathering Cultures; Matriliny

Matrifocal Cultures

Amadiume, Ifi, *Male Daughters, Female Husbands: Gender and Sex in an African Society*, London and Atlantic Highland, New Jersey: Zed, 1987

Chiñas, Beverly L., *The Isthmus Zapotecs: A Matrifocal Culture of Mexico*, New York: Harcourt Brace College, 1992; previously published as *The Isthmus Zapotecs: Women's Roles in Cultural Context*, New York: Holt, Rinehart and Winston, 1973

Smith, Raymond T., *The Negro Family in British Guiana: Family Structure and Social Status in the Villages*, London and New York: Routledge and Kegan Paul, 1956

———, *The Matrifocal Family: Power, Pluralism, and Politics*, New York and London: Routledge, 1996

Stack, Carol B, *All Our Kin: Strategies for Survival in a Black Community*, New York: Harper and Row, 1974

The concept of matrifocal society was first introduced to the literature by SMITH, an anthropologist, in his book (1956). Based on his extended fieldwork between 1951 and 1955 in Guiana, a British colony lying on the northeast shoulder of South America, Smith proposed that the household structure in Guiana could be best conceptualized as a matrifocal system. In this system, the mother was usually *de facto* leader of the household, although the husband-father (if present) was *de jure* head of the household group. The man was usually marginal to the complex internal relationships of the group, since he associated relatively infrequently with the other members of the group and maintained a rather loose tie with members of the household. Smith also made an attempt to examine the applicability of the matrifocal household to black communities all over the western hemisphere, including the United States. This is a pioneer work on matrifocality and is intended for readers with some anthropological or sociological background. Although this book has long been out of print, one of the most important chapters on matrifocality is reprinted in Smith's later book.

SMITH's (1995) collection of essays bring together his works on Caribbean ethnography and its relevance to urban problems in the United States. The first part of the book focuses on kinship and family structure in Caribbean societies characterized by their distinctive matrifocal organizations. The second part of the book examines the race and class conflicts that followed the ending of colonial rule in the British Caribbean. One of the themes running throughout the essays is Smith's conviction that matrifocal structures provide strong and stable environments for bringing up children in Caribbean societies and many African-American communities. This is best illustrated in chapter four, "Matrifocal Family," in which Smith questions the idea that the "nuclear" or "elementary" family of a man, his legal wife, and their legitimate children is either a universal or necessary human social institution. The matrifocal family—defined as women in their role as mothers being the focus of relationships, represents a rich and viable system in its own right. Although his major fieldwork is done in Caribbean societies, Smith also shows that many of his arguments are relevant to contemporary discussions of African-American kinship in the United States. This book provides some thought-provoking theories on family, kinship, and their relationships with regard to race and class in the best of anthropological traditions.

CHINAS's book is one of the case studies in a cultural anthropology series designed to bring students insights into the richness and complexity of human life as it is lived in different ways and in different places. This case study emphasizes sex roles in the context of a wide-ranging analysis of salient features of the Isthmus Zapotec culture of Mexico. In this new edition, Chiñas stresses the matrifocality of Isthmus Zapotec culture. Following Nancy Tanner's definition of a matrifocal culture, Chiñas demonstrates that the mother is not only structurally, culturally, and affectively central to the Isthmus Zapotecs, but that such centrality is also viewed as culturally legitimate by the society as a whole. Furthermore, Zapotec women exercise strong economic, social, and kin-related power and authority, and relations between husband and wife tend to be strongly egalitarian. Two new chapters are added to the new edition of this book. One describes *muxe* (a "man-women person"), a third gender role between men and women; and a new last chapter on changes between 1967 and 1990 concludes this study. This book is rich in ethnographic details on matrifocality and presents valuable theoretical insights to factors affecting women's social status in a society.

Based on her three years of intensive fieldwork in a black neighborhood of a midwestern city, STACK, an anthropologist, examines the role kinship played in providing daily support among the black urban poor. Although the concept of matrifocality as an analytical unit is not consciously applied in the book, Stack argues persuasively that mother-centered households among the black urban poor provide an effective network of support in which meager resources (food, housing, child care) are shared and effectively utilized. This book has become a classic for understanding rich complexities of African-American kinship, as well as the resourcefulness and resilience of female-headed households under conditions of perpetual poverty.

AMADIUME is an African anthropologist who studied her own culture—Igbo women of Nnobi in Eastern Nigeria. This book documents the conditions that led to the decline of the sociopolitical and economic power of Igbo women from the nineteenth century through the colonial period to the post-independence period. Before the nineteenth century, Nnobi culture exhibited a strong matricentric/matrifocal principle in household organization; mothers and children formed distinct, economically self-sufficient sub-compound units. Females' perseverance and industriousness were celebrated in Igbo myth and daily lives. The flexible gender system created the institution of "male daughters"—daughters who inherited father's property and a lineage name, and "female husbands"—as in "woman to woman marriage." Thus the system permitted women to assume position, power, and authority, which under strict gender definition would have been the preserve of men. After the British colonial rule, women's relatively high social status was effectively suppressed by the introduction of western systems of religion, education, and government based on patriarchal principles. Amadiume's well-researched book is important on two accounts. First, the book provides empirical data of the matricentric/matrifocal system of Zapotec culture and illustrates the process of marginalization of women's social status since the imposition of western colonial rule. Second, the author challenges the ethnocentrism of western social anthropology and the imperial arrogance of western feminism implicit in its studies of the social conditions of African women.

—JIAN LI

See also Ancient Egalitarian Cultures; Hunting/Gathering Cultures: Matriliny

Matriliny

Bachofen, Johann Jakob, *Myth, Religion, and Mother Right; Selected Writings of J. J. Bachofen*, translated by Ralph Manheim, London: Routledge and Kegan Paul, and Princeton, New Jersey: Princeton University Press, 1967

Kato, Tsuyoshi, *Matriliny and Migration: Evolving Minangkabau Trading in Indonesia*, Ithaca, New York: Cornell University Press, 1982

Lepowsky, Maria, *Fruit of the Motherland: Gender in an Egalitarian Society*, New York: Columbia University Press, 1993

Poewe, Karla O., *Matrilineal Ideology: Male-Female Dynamics in Luapula, Zambia*, London and New York: Academic Press, 1981

Raha, Manis Kumar, *Matriliny to Patriliny: A Study of the Rabha Society*, New Dehli: Gian Publishing House, 1989
Schlegel, Alice, *Male Dominance and Female Autonomy*, New Haven, Connecticut: HRAF Press, 1972
Schneider, David M., and Kathleen Gough (eds.), *Matrilineal Kinship*, Berkeley: University of California Press, 1961
Schönenberger, Regula Trenkwalder, *Lenape Women, Matriliny, and the Colonial Encounter: Resistence and Erosion of Power (c. 1660–1876): An Excursus in Feminist Anthropology*, New York: Peter Lang, 1991
Stivens, Maila, *Matriliny and Modernity: Sexual Politics and Social Change in Rural Malaysia*, St. Leonards, Australia: Allen and Unwin, 1996

Matriliny, or matrilineal kinship, is a descent system in which children are born into the kinship group of their mothers. Their fathers can be an important part of their lives but are not kin. Mother's brother is the closest senior kinsman to children. Since this system is so different from the bilateral system of Europe and seems to give social priority to women, it has long been studied as exotic and somewhat primitive.

BACHOFEN, a German cultural evolutionist, wrote *Das Mutterrecht* in 1861, excerpts of which were translated into English in 1967. In this book, he argued that matriliny with matriarchy was an early human system that was overthrown with the advent of patriliny and patriarchy. In this theory, patrilineal systems are more evolved than matrilineal, and male domination of women is also an evolved state. Of course, this theory and the connection of matriliny with matriarchy has been roundly rejected by scholars, but it is still occasionally repeated as fact in non-scholarly writing.

The classic text on matriliny is by SCHNEIDER and GOUGH. This hefty volume describes the matrilineal systems of nine cultures from North America, India, Africa, and the Pacific in solid detail. The theoretical orientation of the book questions the logic of the systems, which seem to mandate that both brothers and husbands have some authority over the same women and children. Previously labeled the "matrilineal puzzle," this thesis disregards women's authority. Men are the center of inquiry. This dates the book, but it remains a necessary volume for anyone interested in the topic.

SCHLEGEL's book takes a different approach to the matrilineal puzzle. Using a sample of 66 matrilineal societies from the ethnographic atlas, she searches for variations and trends. Having worked with the Hopi, she is aware that women can have considerable influence in societies, and that women in matrilineal societies do not have to be pawns of husbands and brothers. She hypothesizes that women should have the most autonomy when husbands and brothers had equal authority over them, and her data substantiates this. While the methodology might not appeal to all, the concept of matriliny is well-framed in this book.

LEPOWSKY's ethnography of the people of Vanatinai, an island southeast of New Guinea, attacks the matrilineal puzzle in another way. Lepowsky describes this culture as a sexually egalitarian society that has no ideology of male superiority. At all levels of society, both men and women are respected and have overlapping roles. Men's nurture of their own children takes time and energy away from their own clans, and these clans are compensated after their deaths. In this matrilineal society no adult has authority over another, and the matrilineal puzzle disappears. This is an important example of an existing egalitarian society that employs matriliny to maintain that equality.

The place of matriliny in the modern developing world is an issue widely discussed. If it is a primitive form, as some believe, it should disappear with modernization. STIVENS addresses this issue among the Minangkabau of Rembau, a Malaysian state. She finds cultural reconstitution a part of the adaptation to the contemporary world there. Matriliny has become modern with reinvention. Further, in Rembau, women are important in domestic affairs and are primary property owners. Stivens demonstrates that development can only be fully understood when gender is considered.

KATO looks at the same issues among the Minangkabau, but those living in west central Sumatra. He also sees the preservation of matriliny in times of change. The matrilineal system is not stagnant. Over the years, the residence pattern has changed from one of duolocality, where women own the houses and husbands visit, to one where couples live together and the couple jointly runs the house. This society successfully blends matriliny with migration and Islam. Unfortunately, gender is not directly addressed in the book, but the wealth of data includes descriptions of the lives of men and women.

RAHA also addresses development and matriliny, but, in this case, in western Bengal. Studying two communities, one traditional in the forest and one a developing village, Raha shows that the village is moving away from matriliny to patriliny. With the growth of a cash and market economy in the village, men became more individualistic and became property owners. In the forest community, on the other hand, women remained property owners, and the communal aspects of the matrilineal system remained intact.

POEWE places gender at the center of her discussion of matriliny among contemporary Luapulans. She rejects the concept of universal male dominance and asserts that matriliny in Zambia creates a concept of egalitarian genders. Women defend matriliny for the advantages they see in the system. Some men, however, who are active in the capitalistic market system, prefer the individualistic and patricentric life advocated by Protestant churches. The aims of women and men are not the same, and development programs are criticized for not recognizing women's concerns. This book offers a gendered analysis of a complex but common situation.

SCHÖNENBERGER presents an ethnohistorical look at the changes in matriliny. Originally a dissertation, this data-filled volume describes the loss of matriliny and reciprocal egalitarian sex roles under colonial pressures. By the early nineteenth century, individual concerns had overthrown the obligations of kinship and changed the relationships between the genders. The strength of the book is the depth of both the history presented and the data employed.

—LAURA KLEIN

See also Ancient Egalitarian Cultures; Matrifocal Cultures

Mead, Margaret 1901–1978

American Anthropologist

Bateson, Catherine Mary, *With a Daughter's Eye: A Memoir of Margaret Mead and Gregory Bateson,* New York: Morrow, 1984

Cassidy, Robert, *Margaret Mead: A Voice for the Century,* New York: Universe, 1982

Foerstel, Lenora, and Angela Gilliam (eds.), *Confronting the Margaret Mead Legacy: Scholarship, Empire, and the South Pacific,* Philadelphia: Temple University Press, 1992

Freeman, Derek, *Margaret Mead and Samoa: The Making and Unmaking of an Anthropological Myth,* Cambridge: Harvard University Press, 1983; Harmondsworth: Penguin, 1984

Grosskurth, Phyllis, *Margaret Mead: A Life of Controversy,* London and New York: Penguin, 1988

Howard, Jane, *Margaret Mead: A Life,* London: Harvill, and New York: Simon and Schuster, 1984

Margaret Mead was a scholar in American anthropology who, as a woman with unique research interests, was often unappreciated by her colleagues and, as a woman, often passed over for academic honors. As an outspoken social critic, however, she became one of the most famous female scientists in the United States. A number of biographies describing her complex life appeared shortly after her death. HOWARD's book is a journalistic biography of a famous woman. It is written for the general reader who admires Mead and takes the reader through the details of her life with emphasis on her marriages, friendships, and family. This is not a critique of her life or work. Unfortunately, her scholarly work, which is the core of her heritage, is largely ignored. The otherwise well-written book describes Mead as an American woman who became very famous.

A more complete biography is that of BATESON, Margaret Mead's daughter. She has written an important book about her parents, Mead and Gregory Bateson. Written from a daughter's perspective, rather than scholarly research, it has insights unavailable in other books. Despite her devotion to her subjects, this book is remarkably reasonable. Mead and her second husband appear as extraordinary but fallible people. Catherine Bateson, who, like her parents, is an anthropologist, writes with an understanding of the scholarly world that other books lack. Hers is the first book openly to discuss Mead's bisexuality and her sexual relationship with Ruth Benedict, which Bateson discovered after her mother's death.

A short but interesting book written shortly after Mead's death focuses on her as a social critic who made important contributions to contemporary issues. CASSIDY defines her as a humanist and a scientist but focuses on the former category. He assumes that readers have no prior knowledge of Mead's works or anthropology, and he describes the contents of important works. He focuses on her work on education, community, feminist causes, race, and ecology, which were known from her *Redbook Magazine* column and public speeches. A chapter on feminism is particularly interesting as it acknowledges a great contradiction in Mead. Her life was, as Cassidy puts it, "a living example of woman's liberation," but she found the feminist movement "anti-male," and feminism was not one of her myriad of causes. A weakness in this book is the description of anthropology and anthropological work, which, in several places, appears naive. This useful work highlights Mead's role in American social life as well as her role as a media star.

A short biography by GROSSKURTH is rather unusual, especially as a part of a "lives of modern women series," since it defines Mead using a remarkably unfeminist perspective. Although the book covers the basic facts of her life, it presents Mead's motivations in a simplistic and, perhaps, crass manner. Mead is said to have admired her mentor, Franz Boas, for his dashing looks, and to have divorced her husband, Rio Fortune, because he would not make a good father. Grosskurth asserts that Mead's marriages failed because her personality was too dominating, and that her goal in life was fame. None of this quite fits with the more complex Mead of the other biographies. There is little appreciation of her scholarship. In fact, Grosskurth uses many pages in defense of Derek Freeman and suggests that, despite the fact that her life work was discredited, Mead was a success because she was famous.

More serious critiques of Margaret Mead were leveled by FREEMAN, who harshly attacked her early work in American Samoa. He charged that Mead went to Samoa looking for a society free of adolescent stress and claimed, without good data, to find that freedom among the Samoan girls. Freeman, who studied in western Samoa, claimed that Samoans were, in fact, far more violent and disturbed than Mead described. He asserted that

Mead, in her insistence that culture was more powerful than biology, created a romantic view of Samoa that never existed. Freeman has been heavily criticized, in and out of anthropology, for this book and his attacks on Mead. The fact that the book was published only after her death when she could not defend herself was broadly condemned. The fact that he studied a different part of Samoa at a different time than Mead and that his own bias toward biology was equal to Mead's toward culture, diluted the power of his argument. While his conclusions are not widely accepted, this book did open up Mead's work for general scrutiny.

FOERSTEL and GILLIAM pursue such a critique in their collection of articles that question Mead's scholarship and ethics in her work in the South Pacific. Mead is accused of sensationalizing, and perhaps romanticizing, the region in a way that American readers would accept. Her American bias led her to promote westernization and capitalism among the people she studied. This book does not, however, support Freeman, who is treated more harshly than Mead. It asks whether Margaret Mead improved the lives of the people she studied. This is an important book that raises issues that do not appear in the general biographies.

—LAURA KLEIN

See also Anthropology: Traditional

Medical History

Achterberg, Jeanne, *Woman as Healer*, Boston: Shambhala, 1990

Backhouse, Constance, and David Flaherty (eds.), *Challenging Times: The Women's Movement in Canada and the United States*, Montreal: McGill-Queen's University Press, 1992

Dally, Ann G., *Women under the Knife: A History of Surgery*, London: Radius, and New York: Routledge, 1991

Dan, Alice J. (ed.), *Reframing Women's Health: Multidisciplinary Research and Practice*, Thousand Oaks, California: Sage, 1994

Doyal, Lesley, *What Makes Women Sick: Gender and the Political Economy of Health*, New Brunswick, New Jersey: Rutgers University Press, and London: Macmillan, 1995

Ehrenreich, Barbara, and Deirdre English, *Witches, Midwives and Nurses: A History of Women Healers*, New York: Feminist Press, 1973; London: Compendium, 1974

———, *For Her Own Good: 150 Years of the Experts' Advice to Women*, London: Pluto Press, and Garden City, New York: Anchor Press, 1979

Legato, Marianne, and Carol Colman, *The Female Heart: The Truth about Women and Coronary Artery Disease*, New York: Simon and Schuster, 1991

Rosser, Sue V., *Women's Health—Missing from U.S. Medicine*, Bloomington: Indiana University Press, 1994

A good amount of medical history, and more specifically women's medical history, is written in the lives of the health care providers. This essay, however, focuses more on trends and issues. The books listed have been chosen because each speaks, directly or indirectly, to such an approach, each has a global component, and all taken together provide some chronological understanding. Each bibliographical entry conveys the importance of the womens' movement for recapturing and for writing the history of women in medicine as well as integrating that history with women's experience and with specific medical questions.

ACHTERBERG's eminently readable approach to the history of women as healers presents four divisions of this history and includes women across the healing professions. Creating a helpful context for raising pertinent questions, she also provides a bibliography that can connect the reader to other medical histories. By placing the question in the role of healing rather than in what most would now consider a narrow meaning of the term "medical," Achterberg is able to recover women's story in broader medical history. She highlights the connections between cosmologies and healing, as well as between the birth of science and the persecution of female healers. She indicates the ties among the healing professions, specifically those developed by women. She observes the contemporary era, projecting the future of women in the healing professions and encouraging the use of historical reclamation to dream a new future.

Ehrenreich and English, their work preceding that of Achterberg, provide a breakthrough, not only by recovering segments of women's medical history, but also by uncovering sociological, political, religious, and economic reasons for their exclusion both from medicine and from medical history. EHRENREICH and ENGLISH (1973), by recapturing medieval as well as nineteenth century history and asking twentieth century questions, are able to encourage historical reclamation as well as to discourage former distinctions between health care givers and receivers. They draw a clear set of distinctions between professionalism and expertise. By tracing the professionalization of health care in the United States, EHRENREICH and ENGLISH (1979) highlight the problems of the scientific mystique and the cult of experts, arguing that such experts usurped women's traditional healing skills even as they presented themselves as sole authorities prescribing women's proper behavior.

BACKHOUSE and FLAHERTY present contemporary medical history in the context of the women's movement in both the United States and Canada. The concerns of this book are contextualized in new anthropologies, new psychologies, and new social constructs impinging upon women making medical history. The contributors to this volume provide evidence and encouragement of new integrations: of activists and academics; of economic, political, and social considerations; of medical curricula. All of these are important issues in the ongoing development of medical history, as well as the trajectories it could take to include women's health as a substantive consideration.

DALLY provides a challenging study in the history of obstetrics and gynecology written in view of the unbalanced social contract between physician and patient, pointing up the inseparability of politics and medicine. Her study shows the personal costs incurred by women in the research that eventually became the field of gynecology. The continuing costs, both in terms of unnecessary surgery, and in terms of presuming that gynecology is synonymous with women's health, are not yet over. The study does not end in gynecology. Rather it can be seen as a case study of some of the issues that concern women in the larger field of medicine.

DOYAL questions both doctors and biomedicine. She broadens the realm of women's health to those considerations external to the body of any individual woman by showing the economic, social, and cultural influences, and the gender questions keeping women from access to optimal wellness, questions related to a longstanding structured gender inequality in mainstream medical histories. LEGATO and COLMAN, while specifically addressing cardioarterial concerns, deal with beliefs and research priorities, body-mind considerations, and alternative approaches as they question the fact that women are not being taken as seriously as men with regard to cardiac symptoms. Their style itself is also a part of changing medical history, both in its clarity and its readability.

Two of the books listed, that by Rosser and that by Dan, provide heuristic models for considering more recent medical history with regard to women, as well as lenses through which to see the sweep of that history. ROSSER offers a model for a transformation of medical studies, which can be applied specifically to women's health. In her treatment of the historical, the medical, and the ethical, Rosser honors women's diversity and indicates women's contribution to medical history.

Combining the medical and the philosophical, the practical and the proactive, the contributors to DAN's book work across disciplines in the development of the new field of women's health. Dan provides a historical account of women's health scholarship, which can also be seen as a subset of women's studies, in terms of practice and theoretical developments. She describes the sweep of this history as beginning with critique and ending in assertion. This making of current history can be seen in the treatments of health curricula, specific medical issues, differing needs of diverse women, approaches of health care professionals such as nurse practitioners, and the posing of challenging questions into the next century.

Now that the field of medicine, more narrowly speaking, is coming to appreciate more fully a wholistic approach in the science and art of healing, women's approaches to medical history as broader than invasive procedures, as being concerned with whole health across the lifespan, and as being bio-psycho-socio-spiritual, can be better appreciated and more directly employed in ongoing medical history.

—FRANCES R. BELMONTE

See also Healers and Herbalism

Meir, Golda 1898–1978

Israeli Prime Minister

Agres, Elijahu, *Golda Meir: Portrait of a Prime Minister*, New York: Sabra, 1969
Mann, Peggy, *Golda: The Life of Israel's Prime Minister*, New York: Coward, McCann and Geoghegan, and London: Vallentine, Mitchell, 1972
Martin, Ralph G., *Golda: The Romantic Years*, New York: Ivy, 1988; London: Piatkus, 1989
Meir, Menahem, *My Mother, Golda Meir: A Son's Evocation of Life with Golda Meir*, New York: Arbor House, 1983
Slater, Robert, *Golda, The Uncrowned Queen of Israel: A Pictorial Biography*, Middle Village, New York: J. David, 1981
Syrkin, Marie, *Golda Meir: Woman with a Cause*, New York: Putnam, and London: Gollancz, 1963; revised as *Golda Meir: Israel's Leader*, New York: Putnam, 1969

Much, if not all, of what has been written about Golda Meir (originally Meyerson, or Myerson) in English cannot be termed objective and tends to be colored with political and/or religious bias. That is, most books on her take a markedly pro-Zionist, pro-Israel stance, which, on the one hand, lends to lionizing the subject, often to mythic proportions, and, on the other, results quite often, if not directly then by implication, in the denigration of Israel's Arab neighbors. Thus, one's political and/or religious views may influence the way in which one reacts to books on Golda Meir.

Agres, Mann and Syrkin all fall into the category of uncritical adulation of Meir. All three are journalistic, rather than scholarly, in their approach. Many famous anecdotes about Meir are repeated in all three volumes; for example, her arrival to the United States in 1948 to raise funds for Israel, a few dollars for taxi fare in her pocket, and her triumphant return home with over 50 million dollars in pledges; and the quip by Israel's first Prime Minister David Ben-Gurion that, because of Meir's staunch support for his policy of immediate retaliation against Arabs, she was "the only man in my Cabinet." SYRKIN, a distinguished and prolific American writer on Jewish subjects and a poet, provides the best-documented of these three biographies, for hers is based on extensive personal interviews with Meir. Israeli journalist AGRES's book is concise but only takes the reader up to 1969, the heady year Meir became prime minister. MANN's study was written during Meir's tenure as Prime Minister of Israel, and the updated edition ends with the aftermath of the disastrous 1973 Yom Kippur War, which cost Meir and her Labour government much popular support. None of these volumes treat the last few years of Meir's life when she and Israel witnessed the rise of the conservative Likud government.

MARTIN offers probably the most authoritative biography of Meir to date. The word "romantic" in the title is misleading. If one expects to read about Meir's "romantic" escapades, one will be disappointed. Instead, "romantic" here refers to the times in which Meir worked tirelessly in the 1920s through 1940s as a Zionist organizer and leader. In fact, the word *tireless* might be a more appropriate term in the title. From this book, Meir emerges as a remarkably competent, forceful leader, who was able to go toe-to-toe with such world leaders as Winston Churchill and Harry Truman in some instances, outsmarting them on issues vital to Israel's establishment and survival. On the other hand, she is the same prime minister who came to cabinet meetings with chicken soup she herself had made for her aides. If one were to read only one biography of Meir, it should be Martin's.

MEIR is the older of Golda Meir's two children, a cellist and protégé of Pablo Casals. His reminiscences of life with his mother come deep from the heart of a son who loved but perhaps did not see as much of his busy, celebrity parent as he had wished. While the book does treat major public events in Meir's life and in that of Zionist Palestine before it became Israel, its unique quality is the rare, intimate glimpses of Meir in informal situations, at home in the kitchen or at the seaside on vacation, unguarded and candid, sometimes humorous and animated, sometimes ironic and sad. SLATER's book, with its many photographs and plates, complements Menahem Meir's memoir. Here one is treated to photographs of many of the people who were important in Golda Meir's private life and in the nascent national life of Israel. The use of the word "queen" in the title is unfortunate although it amply suggests the basic tone of the text.

—CARLO COPPOLA

Men and Feminism

Clatterbaugh, Kenneth, *Contemporary Perspectives on Masculinity: Men, Women, and Politics in Modern Society,* Boulder, Colorado: Westview Press, 1990; revised edition, 1997

Hagan, Kay Leigh (ed.), *Women Respond to the Men's Movement: A Feminist Collection,* San Francisco: Harper, 1992

Jardine, Alice, and Paul Smith (eds.), *Men in Feminism,* New York and London: Methuen, 1987

Kimmel, Michael S. (ed.), *The Politics of Manhood: Profeminist Men Respond to the Mythopoetic Men's Movement (and the Mythopoetic Leaders Answer),* Philadelphia: Temple University Press, 1995

Kimmel, Michael S., and Thomas E. Mosmiller (eds.), *Against the Tide: Pro-Feminist Men in the United States, 1776–1990,* Boston: Beacon Press, 1992

Schwalbe, Michael, *Unlocking the Iron Cage: The Men's Movement, Gender Politics, and American Culture,* New York and Oxford: Oxford University Press, 1996

Snodgrass, Jon (ed.), *For Men against Sexism: A Book of Readings,* Albion, California: Times Change Press, 1977

Strauss, Sylvia, *"Traitors to the Masculine Cause": The Men's Campaigns for Women's Rights,* Westport, Connecticut, and London: Greenwood, 1982

If feminism is a theory and practice of gender relations, in one sense all of women's studies can be construed as concerning itself at least in part with the subject of men and feminism. The specific topic of "Men and Feminism," however, is usually taken to be about the more or less explicit stances men have taken in regard to women and feminist movements. Since men's standard enactments of, and complicity in, patriarchy are the patriarchal "norms," and therefore seem in a sense unremarkable to women's studies, however, these standard bahaviors typically stand outside the rubric of "men and feminism." This topic therefore marks the "other" men under patriarchy, principally those standing against patriarchal domination, and in support of feminism, but also those who self-consciously and explicitly articulate their identities and activities vis-à-vis feminism, whether positively or negatively.

Two books, those by Kimmel and Mosmiller and by Strauss, survey men's support of the cause of women in England and the United States. STRAUSS analyzes more than a century of male moralists and reformers, focusing on the ideas of such men as George Jacob Holyoake, Robert Owen, William Thompson, John Stuart Mill, George Bernard Shaw, and Floyd Dell.

KIMMEL and MOSMILLER's volume contains a wide and well-researched array of U.S. men's profeminist writings, using these texts to chart social and intellectual trends ranging from the eighteenth-century egalitarianism of Thomas Paine and nineteenth-century abolitionist men, to the twentieth-century Greenwich Village radicals and the contemporary profeminist men's movement. Included are the words of such figures as John Dewey, Ralph Waldo Emerson, Walt Whitman, Eugene Debs, W.E.B. DuBois, Herbert Marcuse, Jesse Jackson, and Alan Alda (as well as the lyrics to Joe

Hill's "The Rebel Girl," Woody Guthrie's "Union Maid," and James Oppenheim and Caroline Kohlsaat's "Bread and Roses").

SNODGRASS has produced one of the earliest collections for men against sexism. Much of it calls men to conscience and to conscientious activism, while at the same time remaining highly skeptical about the positive potential for anything calling itself a "men's movement." With an editorial perspective coming out of the "male left" and radical feminism, the book's sections are on male sexuality (beginning with Jack Litewka's influential "The Socialized Penis"), male supremacy (in two of the book's three essays by John Stoltenberg), anti-sexist practice (for example, men's consciousness-raising groups, anti-Playboy activism, childcare, "The Effeminist Manifesto"), criticisms of "men's liberation" (including the book's only essays by women), and sections on gay, working-class, and Third World men.

JARDINE and SMITH's collection takes on the vexing question of academic men's involvement with feminist literary criticism. The tone and terms are set by Stephen Heath's "Male Feminism," with its opening declaration that "Men's relation to feminism is an impossible one." This is followed 75 pages later by Elizabeth Weed's contribution, which adds women to this impossible relationship to feminism. Much of the book criticizes men's appropriations of feminism for their own material gain and their attempts to ventriloquize and speak as if they understood women's subjective positions.

CLATTERBAUGH maps out the theoretical terrain traversed by contemporary men's movements, guided by four feminist analytical questions about men's social reality in American society, what maintains and explains it, and how a better reality could be achieved. He then responds to these questions from the viewpoint of a variety of groups. The first edition covers the perspectives of conservative, profeminist, men's rights, spiritual, socialist, gay, and black men. The second edition updates the analyses, and adds more on mythopoetic men, as well as such more recent phenomena as the Promise Keepers and the Million Man March.

When HAGAN uses the term "men's movement," she means almost exclusively the mythopoetic men's movement, epitomized by the work of Robert Bly. This particular focus is also the concern of the following two books to be discussed here. The essays in Hagan's book are for the most part critical, some highly so. Some, however, are hopeful for this movement's potential, and a few even praise its current realities. Essays include perspectives from literature, spirituality, politics, religion, art, and academia.

KIMMEL gathers many of the leading figures of the profeminist men's academic and political worlds to respond, mostly very critically, to the mythopoetic men's movement in a volume that also includes a few responses, including one from Bly. Recurrent themes include assessments of this movement's gender politics, which range from deeming it naive to malevolent. The essays also address its relative inattention to the needs of gay men and men of color, its misleading or false representation of historical and anthropological data, and its reliance on patriarchal imagery and an overly static Jungian archetypal theory.

SCHWALBE's book is a sociological participant-observer study of a mythopoetic men's group. It is both accessible and scholarly, both sympathetic to the mostly white, middle-class, heterosexual men themselves, especially regarding the emotional and spiritual needs they are trying to fill, and critical of their theories and practices, demonstrating how many of them reinforce male dominance.

—HARRY BROD

See also Masculinity; Men's Movement

Menopause

Asso, Doreen, *The Real Menstrual Cycle,* Chichester and New York: John Wiley and Sons, 1983

Beckham, Nancy, *Menopause: A Positive Approach Using Natural Therapies,* Ringwood, Australia: Viking Penguin, 1995

Beyene, Yewoubdar, *From Menarche to Menopause: Reproductive Lives of Peasant Women in Two Cultures,* Albany: State University of New York Press, 1989

Friedan, Betty, *The Fountain of Age,* London: Jonathon Cape, and New York: Simon and Schuster, 1993

Greer, Germaine, *The Change: Women, Aging, and the Menopause,* London: Hamish Hamilton, 1991; New York: Knopf, 1992

Lock, Margaret, *Encounters with Aging: Mythologies of Menopause in Japan and North America,* Berkeley: University of California Press, 1993

McCain, Marian Van Eyk, *Transformation through Menopause,* New York: Bergin and Garvey, 1991

Sheehy, Gail, *The Silent Passage: Menopause,* New York: Random House, 1992; London: HarperCollins, 1993

An absence of material from the perspective of women, combined with androcentric western biomedical interpretations of menopause as a "deficiency disease," have resulted in a flawed body of literature on this important subject. It is only since female scholars from a variety of disciplines, but especially from anthropology, biology, psychology, and sociology, have undertaken critical research on menopause, that vital and substantive new insights about the diversity of women's menopausal experiences and perceptions have emerged.

ASSO produced one of the first contemporary texts—as distinct from journal articles or chapters, of which there are many—about women's experience of menopause. Concentrating on the cycle of menstruation, she describes typical physiological menopausal symptoms, such as the cessation of menstruation, hot flashes, night sweats, dizziness, depression, anxiety, and irritability. Asso focuses on the negative aspects of physiological symptoms only. Menopause is described as a "problem" to which women around 50 years of age will have to succumb and adapt, possibly with assistance from estrogen therapy. Asso's discussion presents interesting background material but is marred by the emphasis on biological determinism.

Other feminists, such as FRIEDAN, discuss how biomedicine, in the United States of America and Great Britain at least, continues to dominate the diagnosis and treatment of menopause. She claims that menopausal women are automatically regarded as "deficient" and in need of chemical hormones to cope with reduced estrogen levels. Friedan stresses that the response of too many male (and some female) medical doctors is to recommend increased usage of Hormone Replacement Therapy (HRT). This system rarely benefits women, who can become dependent on "hormone pills" or suffer disastous side-effects, but it does economically benefit pharmaceutical multinationals. Friedan's engaging work considers menopause within the wider context of gender and aging in western settings.

BECKHAM also contests the use of HRT. Focusing on Australia, Great Britain, and the United States of America, she suggests that most women have a choice between the hegemonic pressures of advertising and medicine, and alternative approaches to menopause: women can ignore the unitary approach of biomedicine and select a variety of means to cope with individual menopausal experiences (by changing their diet, for example, and undertaking regular exercise and relaxation). Although theoretically limited, and devoid of attention to difference, Beckham provides useful discussion on the potential power and agency of women, and on alternative approaches to menopause.

McCAIN refers to the work of psychologist Carl Jung (on ideas associated with different stages, or "functions," in life), and anthropologist Arnold Van Gennep (on "rites of passage"), to contextualize and explain her discussion of menopause as central to a process of transition. GREER also argues that menopause holds great transformative possibilities for women. Greer contributes a wealth of creative material from the humanities, social sciences, and women's studies to critique male-biased biomedical analyses, and to inform the claim that the experience and consequence of menopause (also discussed as the "climacteric" and the "change") can enhance the lives of older women.

SHEEHY writes directly from her own personal and embodied experience of menopause, including a trial of HRT, to suggest that an increase in the population of aging women has resulted in a whole different era for the analysis and treatment of menopause. Like Greer and McCain, Sheehy claims that women are not powerless when it comes to menopause: it should, and can be, a time of empowerment. The work of Greer, McCain, and Sheehy is important and often inspirational, but limited by a failure to address adequately the social inequality and sexual diversity of women, and the impact of physiological change.

Cross-cultural research has revealed that women in a variety of circumstances have diverse experiences of, and understandings about, menopause. Many findings exemplify "positive" associations with menopause, a response often underestimated by those who adopt universal views of women (and men). BEYENE, for example, undertook a comparative study on two peasant cultures in Mexico and Greece. She noted a variety of menopausal experiences and perceptions such as that some women achieved prestige once menopause had occurred, a position not always possible prior to menopause. Adopting a "bio-cultural" approach to the study of menopause, Beyene provides constructive insights on methodologies pertaining to data collection, comparison, and analysis.

LOCK, one of the most well-known feminist scholars in the field of menopause, concentrates mostly on Japan, but also on North America. Lock's findings include the view that whereas Japanese women regard menopause as an affirming aspect of the aging process, most North American women do not. Lock makes available a comprehensive and comparative account of some of the "myths" and realities surrounding menopause. Situating her discussion within the context of the gendered politics of aging, Lock also considers the power of language to define menopausal women. Lock highlights the significant point that any disucssion of menopause raises complex questions that require complex responses. Lock's excellent and discursive text, which contains a detailed and extensive bibliography, is invaluable reading for those interested in the study of menopause.

Despite many gains, it is still the case that comprehensive acknowledgement of the heterogeneity of women—class position (self-identified or ascribed), culture, ethnicity, religious heritage, sexual orientation—in relation to menopause, continues to take second place to western biomedical models of thought and practice. Perhaps this is because an entrenched androcentric history has markedly influenced the study of menopause, but it may also be due to ongoing analytical problems for feminists and others concerning the relationship between the social construct of gender and the reality of biological sex.

—SANDY TOUSSAINT

Men's Movements

Clatterbaugh, Kenneth, *Contemporary Perspectives on Masculinity: Men, Women, and Politics in Modern Society,* Boulder, Colorado: Westview Press, 1990

Hagen, Kay Leigh (ed.), *Women Respond to the Men's Movement: A Feminist Collection,* San Francisco: Harper, 1992

Harding, Christopher (ed.), *Wingspan: Inside the Men's Movement,* New York: St. Martin's Press, 1992

Kimmel, Michael S. (ed.), *The Politics of Manhood: Profeminist Men Respond to the Mythopoetic Men's Movement (and the Mythopoetic Leaders Answer),* Philadelphia, Temple University Press, 1995

Kimmel, Michael S., and Thomas E. Mosmiller (eds.), *Against the Tide: Pro-Feminist Men in the United States, 1776–1990,* Boston: Beacon Press, 1992

Schwalbe, Michael, *Unlocking the Iron Cage: The Men's Movement, Gender Politics, and American Culture,* New York and Oxford: Oxford University Press, 1996

In the last 20 years, a network of activities has arisen in response to feminism, including men's support groups, men's ritual healing groups, therapy groups for violent men, men's health programs, fathers' rights groups, and profeminist men's social action groups. As the following brief reviews will demonstrate, it is a misnomer to talk of these diverse men's activities as a homogeneous men's movement. Some men's groups embrace feminist analyses and publicly support women's struggles, others ignore women's issues, while still others articulate explicitly anti-feminist views.

CLATTERBAUGH provides a useful introduction to six different theoretical premises about masculinity, which underlie the diversity of men's collective responses to modern feminist movements. These six perspectives are: conservative, profeminist, men's rights, spiritual, socialist, and group-specific, which includes black and gay rights activists. The strengths and weaknesses of each perspective are investigated in the context of their description, explanation, and assessment of the reality of men's lives and their vision and strategies for change. This is an invaluable introductory text on the diversity of men's movements, and it provides an excellent guide to the literature, although it needs revision to incorporate more recent postmodern interrogations of men's practices.

The anthology edited by HARDING provides a more in-depth exploration of the mythopoetical strand of the spiritual perspective in the words of its proponents. The majority of the articles are drawn from *Wingspan: Journal of the Male Spirit,* and with the exception of a profeminist critique by Harry Brod, all of the collected articles celebrate men's exploration of male community, mythology, male archetypes, and ceremony and ritual, with attention to men's violence and to institutionalized gender inequality. Nevertheless, the anthology provides a useful introduction to the main writers and activists in the mythopoetic men's movement through their own words, and grounding for the critiques that follow.

The collection of essays edited by HAGEN could be more accurately entitled *Women Respond to the Mythopoetic Men's Movement,* as all of the essays are concerned with Robert Bly (the most well-known voice of the movement) and his followers. This anthology gives voice to the disquiet and distrust that many feminist women (and profeminist men) have felt about the mythopoetic men's movement. While the feminist writers here acknowledge men's isolation and pain, they locate these experiences within the wider socio-political context of men's lives, and they articulate the kind of men's movement that they would like to see: one that is more concerned with challenging men's violence and abuse and forming alliances and partnerships with women. The essays offer important challenges to men, and provide women with useful tools for analyzing the involvement of men in the mythopoetic movement.

SCHWALBE's book provides a more in-depth participant-observer study of the mythopoetic men's movement by a profeminist activist. The book aims to make sense of what rank-and-file members of this movement are doing and why they are doing it. Through an examination of the men's search for community, their attempts to recreate their moral identity as men, and their involvement in rituals, Schwalbe identifies the role that mythopoetics provides in helping men feel better about being men. He also convincingly demonstrates how the mythopoetic perspective is blind to institutional power, and how these men's practices reproduce gender dominance, whether they mean to or not. While never losing sight of feminist concerns, this ethnographic study of mythopoetic men provides insight into why this movement has been so popular with men, and examines the potential and limitations of its becoming a progressive rather than a reactionary force in gender politics.

Profeminist men's practices that challenge men's violence against women, pornography, sexual discrimination, and gender power inequality provide an important contrast to, and predate, the mythopoetic men's movement. The documentary history of profeminist men in the United States edited by KIMMEL and MOSMILLER demonstrates that men have been allies of women in their struggle for equality for over 200 years. A compilation of over 100 documents, including excerpts from speeches, songs, poems, books, plays, political pamphlets, diaries, and letters shows men's support for women's equality in such areas as suffrage, the Equal Rights Amendment, equal wages, the right to higher education, and social and sexual relations. This anthology provides substance to the belief that men can and will change in the direction of social and sexual equality.

The collection edited by KIMMEL provides both a detailed profeminist men's response to the mythopoetic men's movement, and mythopoetic responses to the profeminist critique. While Kimmel says that the essays began as a rejection of mythopoetics, he hopes that they will provide a dialogue that will explore common ground between the two movements. Most of the essays provide little basis for dialogue, however, as many of the mythopoetic responses are defensive and fail to address the specific criticisms that are directed at them. The profeminists challenge the mythopoetics for their antifeminist statements, expose the essentialist premises underlying their philosophical and psychological assumptions, and interrogate the patriarchal bases of their myths and archetypes. A minority of contributors from both sides plead for synthesis and alliances, and identify what each has to offer the other, but the essays indicate the boundaries between the different men's movements more clearly than they expand the common ground. This book is a valuable contribution to understanding the tension in men's politics between men's personal lives and challenging men's social dominance.

—BOB PEASE

See also Masculinity; Men and Feminism

Menstruation

Armstrong, Liz, and Adrienne Scott, *Whitewash: Exposing the Health and Environmental Dangers of Women's Sanitary Products and Disposable Diapers,* Toronto: HarperCollins, 1992

Buckley, Thomas, and Alma Gottlieb, *Blood Magic: The Anthropology of Menstruation,* Berkeley: University of California Press, 1988

Costello, Alison, *The Sanitary Protection Scandal,* London: Women's Environmental Network, 1989

Gardner-Loulan, Joann, Bonnie Lopez, and Marcia Quackenbush, *Period,* Volcano, California: Volcano Press, 1979

Golub, Sharon (ed.), *Lifting the Curse of Menstruation: A Feminist Appraisal of the Influence of Menstruation on Women's Lives,* New York: Harrington Park Press, 1983

Lander, Louise, *Images of Bleeding: Menstruation as Ideology,* New York: Orlando Press, 1988

Lark, Susan M., *Dr. Susan Lark's Menstrual Cramps Self Help Book,* Berkeley, California: Celestial Arts, 1995

Martin, Emily, *The Woman in the Body: A Cultural Analysis of Reproduction,* Boston: Beacon Press, and Milton Keynes: Open University Press, 1987

O'Grady, Kathleen, and Paula Wansbrough, *Sweet Secrets: Menstruation Stories,* Toronto: Second Story Press, 1997

Shuttle, Penelope, and Peter Redgrove, *The Wise Wound: Menstruation and Everywoman,* London: Gollanz, and New York: Richard Marek, 1978

Feminist scholarship on the topic of menstruation is vast and varied, but much remains to be done, as the current proliferation of studies indicates. It was not until the early 1970s that menstruation as a topic in itself was taken seriously. Prior to this time menstruation was rarely the focus of study, and it was primarily consigned to health books, where it was described in negative and moralistic terms as an illness or disease, and portrayed as the "woman's burden." Much of the emerging feminist scholarship has focused on redefining menstruation in positive terms and retrieving the social and cultural history (ethnographic accounts, rites of passage, traditional knowledge) that has long been silenced. The most recent studies on menstruation can be divided into three general categories: health and environmental issues, the politics of menstruation, and cultural history.

It has been recognized by writers of early educational health resources that a girl's experience of menstruation is intertwined with her self-image. GARDENER-LOULAN, LOPEZ, and QUACKENBUSH present one of the earliest attempts to transform menstruation from an experience that evokes shame and disgust to a natural and self-affirming occurrence. Written in simple language and generously illustrated, their text moves beyond traditional medical descriptions to include a wide spectrum of associated emotions and physical sensations that occur during the time of menarche. O'GRADY and WANSBROUGH similarly relate important health information for girls in positive and active language. Their text portrays the diversity of menarchal experiences with short "coming-of-age" stories from a variety of perspectives. Both of these resources for adolescents emphasize the important link between body-knowledge and awareness, and self-esteem. Menstrual health resources for adults stress preventative, holistic, and woman-centered health care through education. General health resources, such as the excellent handbook by the BOSTON WOMEN'S HEALTH BOOK COLLECTIVE, provide detailed biological information, personal care tips, and a listing of available treatments for menstrual related complications.

LARK has a number of books that focus primarily on menstrual complications and advocate a self-help strategy. The one listed here is on cramps. Charts and descriptions assist the reader to evaluate her symptoms, and they help her to chose from a variety of treatment schedules that include options such as diet, yoga, herbology, reflexology, and traditional medications. The plethora of information in this and similar texts demonstrates the diversity of women's perspectives on health and their personal experiences with menstruation.

The essays in GOLUB's text employ a mixture of medical and social scientific methodology to examine the interplay between physiology, individual psychology, and social views on women's experiences with their menstrual cycles. Contributors to Golub's collection examine such topics as the life stages of menarche and menopause, mental health issues, menstrual cycle influence on cognitive and physiological responses, and current research on premenstrual syndrome.

The texts by Armstrong and Scott, and Costello are more accessible and specifically activist in their agenda, each discussing the health and environmental risks of using chlorine-bleached sanitary pads and tampons. Both multinational corporations and government agencies are implicated in the discussions on Toxic Shock Syndrome. ARMSTRONG and SCOTT provide a North American account (specifically Canadian), while COSTELLO provides a British study of the shocking lack of restrictions and regulations surrounding the testing of sanitary products.

Texts that focus on the politics of menstruation have taken medical "objective" language as their point of departure. Martin and Lander both aim to expose the ideology that underlies scientific language, an ideology that functions to perpetuate the negative image of the menstrual process, and by extension, a subordinate and biologically determined female body. MARTIN notes that menstrual terminology is imbued with metaphors of production that bind the menstrual process to a single purpose, that of conception. The seemingly objective definitions of menstruation provided by the medical establishment are, in fact, framed by the concept that menstruation is only the failure to conceive, since it does not produce anything as such. Menstruation is therefore described as either "unnatural" (unproductive) or as an "excretory" process. LANDER details the last three centuries of medical research and theory on menstruation, finding that the medical model has been used as a tool to control the behavior of women. Her text demonstrates the way in which a culture's definition of menstruation reflects the position of women in that society.

SHUTTLE and REDGROVE's book was one of the first to recognize the paucity of good scholarship on menstruation—labeling it "the missing topic"—and thus noted the proclivity of studies on menstruation that focus on the negative aspects of the process. To balance the scholarship, they discuss the many positive attributes of menstruation, using psychological, mythological, spiritual, and ethnographic accounts, the increased feelings of creativity, self-awareness, erotic sexuality, heightened sensitivity, and power that come with each cycle. Their text is probably the most highly cited and important of the early literature on menstruation, putting together medical information, and mythical and ritual knowledge, as part of women's experiences of themselves and their bodies. This book has been the inspiration for many authors who aim to unite women's corporeality with a woman-centered spirituality.

Early feminist scholarship and anthropological research was too quick to declare that every culture maintains a negative view of menstruation through an intricate system of taboos and prohibitions that function to keep women subordinate. BUCKLEY and GOTTLIEB's collection challenges this widely held view by examining the rites and customs that surround menstruation in disparate cultural settings. Their studies conclude that attitudes to menstruation are highly variant, nuanced, and part of a complex system of gender and social relations that is not unilaterally oppressive to women. This text provides a great step toward recording, in all its depth and diversity, the menstrual symbolism of women across cultures and ages.

—PAULA WANSBROUGH and KATHLEEN O'GRADY

Mental Health

Ballou, Mary B., Nancy W. Gabalac, and David Kelley, *A Feminist Position on Mental Health*, Springfield, Illinois: Charles C. Thomas, 1985

Gilligan, Carol, *In a Different Voice: Psychological Theory and Women's Development*, Cambridge, Massachusetts: Harvard University Press, 1982

Lerman, Hannah, *Pigeonholing Women's Misery: A History and Critical Analysis of the Psychodiagnosis of Women in the Twentieth Century*, New York: Basic Books, 1996

Mark, Mary Ellen, and Karen Folger Jacobs, *Ward 81*, New York: Simon and Schuster, 1979

Miller, Jean Baker, *Toward a New Psychology of Women*, 2nd edition, Boston: Beacon Press, 1986

Russell, Denise, *Women, Madness, and Medicine*, Oxford: Polity Press, 1995

Silverstein, Brett, and Deborah Perlick, *The Cost of Competence: Why Inequality Causes Depression, Eating Disorders, and Illness in Women*, New York and Oxford: Oxford University Press, 1995

The social construct of "mental health" as a medical/scientific concern did not appear until the eighteenth century; prior to this, insanity was usually regarded as a sign that a person had been in collusion with the devil or other evil spirits, and thus the issue fell within the purview of the church. Of interest to the feminist perspective is how mental health issues were redefined as medical problems, and the mechanisms by which the medical system defined "appropriate" standards of mental health for women. Feminist writings on the subject first begin to appear in the 1970s. These writings, of which only a sample are reviewed here, address the use of these standards to control women, and they reflect the struggle of women to obtain the power to define mental health for themselves.

GILLIGAN's work is one of the first books to criticize existing paradigms of "normal" psychological development as biased toward males. Further, she seeks to define "normal" psychological development for women by examining the different ways of thinking, identity, and concepts of self and morality between men and women. Gilligan combines previous literature with findings of her own to make very interesting comparisons and to point out differences between males and females. The need for listening to the voice of women and the distinctly different human experiences of women is particularly well defined.

MILLER's book is one of the landmark efforts by psychologists to define female psychological development within a feminist framework. Her model is based upon a general understanding of how dominant and subordinate groups in a culture relate to one another. In particular, she discusses how women, as a subordinate group, tend to develop psychological traits pleasing to the dominant group, and how women who do not do this are often labeled as abnormal. Also discussed are the strengths of women's psychological profiles, and the sources of discontent for many women. Finally, Miller suggests a path for women to take to develop and fully "become themselves." This path involves taking risks, being creative, developing power and self-determination, confronting fears of power, and reclaiming and using conflict to eliminate the submissive/dominant hierarchy of western culture.

The work of MARK and JACOBS is an extremely valuable piece, as it brings the issue of mental illness to a personal level. The authors spent 36 days in the women's locked ward of a state mental hospital; they document this time with both photographs and conversations with the women who live on the ward. The pictures are both graphic and moving. An observation made by ward residents, that after living on the ward the authors had begun to dress and act like the residents themselves, helped the authors to realize that these are the women that any woman might have been and the women that any woman might one day become.

RUSSELL provides an excellent overview of the relationship between women's mental health and the medical/scientific community from the Middle Ages to modern times. This book details the development of the asylum and provides an in-depth examination of how laws and definitions of mental illness are used to control and corral women whose "freedom is harmful to society." This book explores the focus that both early and modern-day psychology places upon psychiatric classification and provides a strong critique of how current diagnostic schemes may harm women (depression, eating disorders, PMS, and schizophrenia are used as illustrative examples). Finally, this book provides a brief overview of early feminist thinking about mental illness and of the links between madness and creativity.

LERMAN explores the historical and current U.S. classification systems of mental illness. She provides a brief history of classification attempts, but the strength of this book is its thorough description and feminist critique of the development and subsequent revisions of the Diagnostic and Statistical Manual of the American Psychiatric Association (DSM-I to DSM-IV). Lerman discusses the relevance to women of the diagnostic criteria for a number of disorders, including depression, schizophrenia, dissociative disorders, and eating disorders. Further, she discusses both the strengths and weaknesses of using this diagnostic system and presents some suggestions for alternative systems.

SILVERSTEIN and PERLICK support their main thesis, that women who are caught in times of changing social gender roles are the most likely to be affected by psychological and somatic symptoms, both with a wealth of historical evidence and with findings from a recent study of 2,000 female students. In particular, they discuss how women who are successful are more likely to suffer from eating disorders, anxiety symptoms, and depression than are other women, or men who are successful. They also employ biographies of famous women to examine how success and achievement affect women differently from the way they affect men.

BALLOU and GABALAC provide a useful model of feminist therapy for assisting women with mental health problems. Its primary assumption is that patriarchy, social attitudes, economic discrimination, and oppression interact to disempower women in society. Oppression and disempowerment are viewed as the primary cause of women's pathology and mental illness (that is, mental illness is viewed as having primarily external, social causes). Feminist therapy provides a process of helping women to unlearn beliefs and behaviors that they develop as a response to oppression and to restore a woman's mental health through empowerment. Specifically, this means assisting the woman in self-discovery, the defining of her own needs and goals, the movement to self-responsibility and psychological autonomy, and the perception of herself as strong, skilled, and competent. Additionally, it encourages the woman to form interdependent working relationships with other women and to learn how to confront existing power systems.

—STACEY B. PLICHTA

See also Body Image; Psychological Theories about Women: Pre-Feminist; Psychological Theories about Women: Feminist; Psychotherapy, Feminist

Mentoring

Center for Sex Equity, *Hand in Hand: Mentoring Young Women*, Portland, Oregon: Northwest Regional Educational Laboratory, 1988

Collins, Nancy W., *Professional Women and Their Mentors: A Practical Guide to Mentoring for the Woman Who Wants to Get Ahead*, Englewood Cliffs, New Jersey: Prentice-Hall, 1983

Freedman, Mark, *The Kindness of Strangers: Adult Mentors, Urban Youth, and the New Voluntarism*, San Francisco: Jossey-Bass, 1993
Jeruchim, Joan, and Pat Shapiro, *Women, Mentors and Success*, New York: Fawcett Columbine, 1992

The term mentor has been synonymous in western thought with one who is a wise, trusted teacher, a guide and a friend. In Homer's *Odyssey*, the main character Odysseus had a friend and loyal counselor named Mentor to whom he entrusted the education of his son while he was away in the Trojan War. Of those who have made great accomplishments in their lives, the majority have had mentors. Traditionally, particularly in the workplace, women have not had these relationships available and therefore have lacked these role models in many areas of their lives. Due to the nature of the mentoring relationship and its recent surge in popularity, women are beginning to explore more fully the opportunities presented in these relationships. However, because of the relatively recent surge in popularity of mentoring as a concept, there have been few resources published where women can learn and understand this relationship more thoroughly, particularly as it relates to women-to-women relationships.

The CENTER FOR SEX EQUITY provides a three-volume set, including a step-by-step guide for mentors, that is now used by a wide range of counselors in at-risk and career exploration programs. With detailed program and logistic mentoring information, this text was originally field tested to train career women of color to be effective mentors for high school girls of color. The Center for Sex Equity's book has been adapted into a number of new settings, including nursing and corporate new employee programs.

COLLINS offers a glimpse of mentoring in the workplace and the lack of role models for women due to the traditional structure of male-dominated professions. Collins utilizes examples to explain the important role that having a mentor can play in professional enhancement. A nationally recognized expert on mentoring young people in poverty, FREEDMAN provides an exceptional overview of the benefits and challenges of mentoring as a concept in American society. With interviews from participants from all aspects of mentoring: mentors, young people, scholars, and youth workers, Freedman puts together the story of the surge in the early 1990s for mentoring and its resulting implications for education and social policy. While it does not focus specifically on women, this book provides an important look at mentoring as a concept in our society, particularly with young people. Freedman's book will appeal to anyone who is really interested in what is needed to help people at a community level.

JERUCHIM and SHAPIRO utilize examples from eight professions to illustrate that traditionally white male mentoring relationships have led to male success, and that the lack of mentoring for women of this fundamental element has affected their career success. They propose a new model of mentoring based on female development and new strategies for every woman who strives for professional achievement. Describing both woman-to-woman and man-to-woman mentoring relationships, they emphasize the importance of establishing what they call "a misunderstood and under-utilized relationship" that offers women power and intimacy. Presenting a wide cross-section of mentoring relationship examples involving a myriad of alliances, Jeruchim and Shapiro also present the importance of establishing different kinds of mentoring relationships at different phases in life.

—MELISSA HELLSTERN

Middle Ages *see* History: Medieval; Literature: Medieval

Middle East *see* Ancient Near East; Arab Women; Israeli-Palestinian Conflict; Jewish Women

Midwifery

Donegan, Jane B., *Women and Men Midwives: Medicine, Morality, and Misogyny in Early America*, Westport, Connecticut: Greenwood, 1978
Litoff, Judy Barrett, *American Midwives: 1860 to the Present*, Westport, Connecticut: Greenwood, 1978
———, *The American Midwife Debate: A Sourcebook on Its Modern Origins*, New York: Greenwood, 1986
Oakley, Ann, and Susanne Houd, *Helpers in Childbirth: Midwifery Today*, New York: Hemisphere, 1990
Robinson, Sarah, and Ann M. Thomson (eds.), *Midwives, Research and Childbirth*, London: Chapman and Hall, 1991
Ulrich, Laurel Thatcher, *A Midwife's Tale: The Life of Martha Ballard, Based on Her Diary, 1785–1812*, New York: Knopf, 1990

Although a reader can gain an understanding of midwifery from basic histories or analyses of childbirth practices, this essay seeks to highlight sources that are devoted solely to the study of midwifery. Most existing works on American midwifery tend to be historical in nature, due to the fact that traditional midwifery has only recently had a comeback in the United States. The sources discussed below dealing with American midwifery clearly illustrate this fact. European midwifery has faced less opposition over time, however, and has met with continued success in countries such as Great Britain. Due to midwifery's greater prevalence and acceptance there, feminist scholars in Britain have researched this topic in depth, touching on issues that American researchers may not have emphasized in the same depth.

Litoff details the practice and decline of midwifery in the United States over the past century and a half, as well as the recent resurgence in its use. LITOFF (1978) documents the history of midwifery in the United States, from colonial times to the present. She decribes midwives as the primary attendants at births well through the early decades of the nineteenth century. It was not until the development of obstetrics and the rise of hospitals as respectable medical institutions that midwives began to be displaced by physicians. Yet Litoff describes how by the turn of the twentieth century, midwives were "forgotten women." In addition, midwives were seen by many as "dirty" and "ignorant," lacking the skills needed for monitoring normal, low-risk birth experiences. Strict regulations were developed in many states in the early 1900s so that midwives could not practice without extensive certification and supervision. As these state laws were enacted, more and more births were attended by physicians in hospitals.

LITOFF (1986) shows that midwifery is again on the rise with the development of the nurse-midwife as a doctor's helper and with the impact of feminism on childbirth practices. In other words, the existence of the nurse-midwife during the twentieth century has led to a gradual re-acceptance of midwifery. This author's second work exists as a collection of articles on midwifery in various communities across the United States as she analyzes the historical debate about the value of midwifery care. A reader of this book acquires a grasp of both sides of the debate, finding that the medical community and the field of obstetrics remain determined to stamp out midwifery on one side, while midwives defending their tradition and public officials concerned about infant mortality and women's desires stand on the other.

DONEGAN also records a history of American midwifery but concentrates on the specific transition from female to male midwives. Along with this transition, she notes the parallel change from minimal medical intervention to an excess of technology and instrumentation during the actual birthing experience. In a sense, Donegan traces the change from a woman-centered, female-attended birth experience to one that was attended by males and controlled with medical technology. This author, along with other feminist historians, proposes that the development of male midwifery was the precursor to physicians stepping in to take charge of the birth process. Donegan discusses the resistance that midwives and birthing women often offered in the face of the intrusion of males, misogyny, and formal medicine into their birthing rooms. A few women even became physicians themselves in order to maintain a female-centered birthing experience.

Written for the annual meeting of the European Region of the World Health Organization (WHO) in 1979, OAKLEY and HOUD's book is the result of a research project designed to delineate the true nature and importance of midwifery. Thus, these authors present a comprehensive discussion of the history of midwifery as well as childbirth today in European countries. Oakley and Houd detail the reasons why women seek alternative birth experiences, how midwives deal with risk in childbirth, what a midwife is and should be, the key dimensions of midwifery practice, and the future of midwives. As the book is summary in nature, Oakley and Houd attempt to cover as many issues as possible that have arisen concerning European midwifery. For a reader who is not familiar with midwifery, this book proves to be an excellent resource, particularly because it assumes that the reader knows very little about the subject.

There has been even more recent research completed on issues of midwifery in Britain, however. ROBINSON and THOMSON have edited a three-volume series on midwives and the current research that exists in Britain concerning midwife-attended births and prenatal/postnatal care offered by midwives. This second volume, like the first and third, is a collection of current research rather than a historical piece. Specifically looking at issues of prenatal education, continuity of care for birthing mothers, and policy-making in the area of midwifery, this volume complements previous historical research. It is clear that these edited volumes are not only for those interested in women's studies and reproduction, but also for the education and interest of midwives themselves.

Finally, ULRICH's book stands out from the rest of midwifery research, for this work is a historical analysis of one midwife's diary and her daily experience as a birth attendant in the late 1700s and early 1800s. Ulrich does a wonderful job of integrating Martha Ballard's diary with her analysis of midwifery, giving the reader a true picture of what this midwife's life was like at the same time as providing the necessary historical commentary needed for young readers. This book would be an excellent addition to any course on women's professions or an introduction to women's history, or one interested in the history and/or sociology of reproduction.

—HEATHER DILLAWAY

See also Pregnancy and Childbirth

Migrant Labor

Chant, Sylvia (ed.), *Gender and Migration in Developing Countries*, London and New York: Belhaven Press, 1992

Nash, June C., and María P. Fernández-Kelly (eds.), *Women, Men and the International Division of Labor*, Albany: State University of New York Press, 1983

Phizacklea, Annie (ed.), *One Way Ticket: Migration and Female Labour*, London and Boston: Routledge and Kegan Paul, 1983

Schenk-Sandbergen, Loes (ed.), *Women and Seasonal Labour Migration*, Thousand Oaks, California and London: Sage, 1995

Simon, Rita James, and Caroline B. Brettell (eds.), *International Migration: The Female Experience*, Totowa, New Jersey: Rowman and Allanheld, 1986

Swaisland, Cecillie, *Servants and Gentlewomen to the Golden Land: The Emigration of Single Women from Britain to Southern Africa, 1820–1939*, Oxford and Providence: Berg, 1993

UNESCO, *Living in Two Cultures: The Socio-Cultural Situation of Migrant Workers and Their Families*, Aldershot: Gower, 1982

For centuries, female migrant workers have carried on their shoulders a burden of oppression and exploitation that is compounded on the grounds of their sex, class, and "alien" status, yet scholars in both labor studies and migration studies have historically neglected them. It was not until the 1980s that migrant women were seen as a distinct analytical category for research. The volume edited by PHIZACKLEA, which goes a long way in recognizing, documenting, and seeking solutions to the problems of the "triple oppression" of migrant women in the labor force, is an important contribution to this research. The introduction by the editor sets the tone of the book by highlighting the plight of those who belong to a "fractionalized class," and the seven chapters in the book by different authors examine various theoretical perspectives on the issue of female migration and labor. The chapters reflect a wide range of topics, from an analysis by Karen Stone of the relationship among work, motherhood, and ethnicity to a cross-cultural study by Mary Hancock on how transnational corporations target women as a cheap labor force.

The theme of transnational industry and female workers, many of whom are inevitably migrants, is discussed in great detail in the compendium of papers edited by NASH and FERNANDEZ-KELLY. While studying the dynamics of the work force in the new world of global manufacturing operations, the papers show how the changing international division of labor has been sharpening inequalities between men and women and between dominant local communities and immigrants. Fernandez-Kelly's chapter on "Mexican Border Industrialization, Female Labor Force Participation and Migration" is particularly significant, as the author looks into what she describes as the "crucial connections among gender, class, family structure, and occupational alternatives for both men and women" while she studies the thriving electronics industry along the border between Mexico and the United States and its impact on different sections of workers.

SIMON and BRETTELL put together a set of essays that attempt to direct the spotlight on female migrant workers so as to make them visible in the world of international migration studies. Although the volume edited by these two scholars is a broad exploration of the social, political, and economic dimensions of female immigration, it has a major section of six comprehensive pieces on the relationship between female migrants and work. These chapters include specific case studies involving migrant female workers in North America and western Europe. What makes the book important is its weaving together of sociological, political, anthropological, and other diverse approaches to the subject. It brings a rare degree of scholarship to an otherwise grossly underresearched area.

The UNESCO-sponsored volume on migrant workers is essentially a collection of studies on the social and cultural aspects of the lives of new immigrants in the United States and Europe, but the second half of the book deals exclusively with the special problems of female migrant workers. There are specific case analyses of the strategies used by Yugoslav, Turkish, and Algerian female migrants working in Europe "to sustain or restructure their values in carrying out their productive and reproductive functions." One interesting finding of these studies is that there are times when female migrant workers develop the necessary skills and make suitable adaptations to their personal lifestyles to survive in the country of employment but are forced to go back to the normative patterns of their home country whenever they return, leading to what the contributors call a "forward and backward process of change."

Contributors to the volume edited by CHANT provide empirical evidence to show how the mobility patterns of male and female workers are different because of the blatant gender inequality in the destination labor markets. As women do not have the same range of job opportunities as men, their mobility has a different pattern. As the introduction to the volume points out, "gender-differentiated population movement acts as a mirror for the way in which sexual divisions of labor are incorporated into spatially uneven processes of economic development" on the one hand, and on the other, it "sets a template for subsequent social and economic evolution in developing societies." The volume includes case studies from Latin America, the Caribbean, Africa, and Asia.

In many parts of rural India, labor migration is a seasonal phenomenon. It is this phenomenon that provides the focal point for the book edited by SCHENK-SANDBERGEN. A team of female anthropologists and sociologists, including the editor, study in great detail the gender-specific causes and consequences of seasonal rural labor migration, described by the contributors as "survival" migration, in the Indian states of Orissa, Kerala, Gujarat, and Maharashtra. The case studies report on a wide range of female migrants, including married and unmarried women, women abandoned by their families, and some tribal women who choose to stay behind while the men migrate. That these distinctions are important is borne out by the case studies. If, as one study shows, married women migrate with their households for "reasons of sheer survival," unmarried women, according to another study, do so, rather ironically, to raise funds for their dowries and for the educations of their brothers. The effects of "survival" migration are usually devastating for female migrants, no matter which category they belong to, because most of them are left economically and socially impoverished. The only hope for these women, Schenk-Sandbergen says, lies in the reduction of seasonal "survival" migration. She supports her argument by presenting a case study of a women's grassroots project in the Indian state of Gujarat that has succeeded in achieving economic empowerment of women by cutting back seasonal labor migration.

SWAISLAND's book is very different from the rest. It is a sociohistorical piece that looks at the emigration of single women from Britain to Southern Africa in the nineteenth and early twentieth centuries. One of the reasons for this emigration was the demand for female labor in South Africa, initially for unskilled domestic and farm labor and later for skilled and professional women. Given that the emigration of single women has not been adequately studied, despite being widespread during the era of British colonization, this book fills a major gap. It not only examines the issue of the emigration of single women in general, but also documents the experiences of such women in adapting to the workplace in a place far away from home.

—PRIYA A. KURIAN

Migration

Alexander, Meena, *The Shock of Arrival: Reflections on Postcolonial Experience*, Boston: South End Press, 1996

Findley, Sally E., and Lindy Williams, *Women Who Go and Women Who Stay: Reflections of Family Migration Processes in a Changing World*, Geneva: International Labour Office, 1991

Jones, Gavin W., *The Role of Female Migration in Development*, Canberra: Australian National University, 1992

Schiller, Nina Glick, Linda Basch, and Christina Blanc-Szanton (eds.), *Towards a Transnational Perspective on Migration: Race, Class, Ethnicity and Nationalism Reconsidered*, New York: New York Academy of Sciences, 1992

Simon, Rita James, and Caroline B. Brettell (eds.), *International Migration: The Female Experience*, Totowa, New Jersey: Rowman and Allanheld, 1986

UNESCO, *Situation and Role of Migrant Women: Specific Adaptation and Integration Problems*, Aldershot: Gower, 1982

Traditionally, women have been perceived as reluctant pioneers and immigrants, subordinated followers whose decisions to go or stay have been based on their family responsibilities and the decisions of their fathers or husbands. However, these studies show that their decision-making, while indeed affected by their childbearing and rearing, is based on a number of factors that include the kinds of jobs available, the problems of their homeland situation, and their own goals. Equally significant is how class, race, gender, and education affect their success in the migration process.

UNESCO's report contains papers prepared by experts on women's migration and immigration worldwide in English, French, and Spanish. Topics include immigrant women in host countries as workers, women not gainfully employed and their social advancement, migrant women staying in or returning to their home countries, undocumented migrant women, and refugee women.

JONES examines female roles, status, and migration patterns in the various regions of the world, determining that needs, education, opportunity, individual experience, developmental policies, and attitudes about women determine the degree of autonomy and success of women in migration. He also considers their ability to facilitate change in developing an area and in their own lives.

SIMON and BRETTELL look at the experiences of immigrating women worldwide since World War II, delineating and analyzing the "social, economic, political and cultural characteristics that influence female migrants both as immigrants and as women." Their findings oppose the traditional perception of immigrant women as passive participants moving because of their spouses. The authors consider the various labor market needs, combined with the political or policy vacuum, that enable women to migrate.

SCHILLER, BASCH, and BLANC-SZANTON have included gender in much of their study of the relationship among global capitalism, transnationalism, and neocolonialism from a perspective that includes historical, social, class, and identity issues. They also consider the future of transnationalism, its effects, and its possible challenges.

FINDLEY and WILLIAMS's study of migrating women and women who stay behind is a World Employment Programme Research report, created for the International Labour Office. It brings together research about the reasons for and consequences of migration and of remaining behind for women. Although their study acknowledges that family considerations often have greater importance for women than for men, they refute the traditional view that for women, migration is determined by marriage considerations alone, and they demonstrate that women migrate for the same reasons as men: "employment, education and the city lights."

ALEXANDER's book is an example of the personal experience narrative about immigration. She writes about the history of memory, language, shame, exile, home, childbirth, the Indian experience in America, and the postcolonial Third World, using prose and poetry to confront the stereotypes and explore the challenges facing postcolonial immigrants in America.

—JANET M. LaBRIE

Military

Binkin, Martin, and Shirley J. Bach, *Women and the Military*, Washington, D.C.: Brookings Institution, 1977

Elshtain, Jean Bethke, and Sheila Tobias (eds.), *Women, Militarism, and War*, Savage, Maryland: Rowman and Littlefield, 1990

Francke, Linda Bird, *Ground Zero: The Gender Wars in the Military*, New York: Simon and Schuster, 1997

Holm, Jeanne, *Women in the Military: An Unfinished Revolution*, revised edition, Novato, California: Presidio Press, 1992

Mitchell, Brian, *Weak Link: The Feminization of the American Military*, Washington, D.C., and New York: Regnery Gateway, 1989

Rogan, Helen, *Mixed Company: Women in the Modern Army*, New York: Putnam, 1981

Shilts, Randy, *Conduct Unbecoming: Gays and Lesbians in the U.S. Military*, New York: St. Martin's Press, 1993

Zimmerman, Jean, *Tailspin: Women and War in the Wake of Tailhook*, New York: Doubleday, 1995

The issue of the role and appropriateness of women in the military is an ancient one. Perhaps the classic discussion of the role of women in the military is found in Plato's *Republic*. Plato suggests (perhaps ironically) that if there are no essential or natural differences between men and women, then both sexes should be subject to the same screening processes and physical training to prepare for roles as Guardians in his utopian city. Theoretical and literary works aside, however, the history of warfare and hence the military is essentially a male history until modern times. Although women have often had active roles in unconventional warfare and have served as auxiliaries, "camp-followers," and nurses, the idea of women in active military roles has been seen by most cultures throughout history as an unacceptable notion. Myths like the legends of the ancient Amazons and occasional stories of women who served in combat while dressed as men are the exceptions that serve to illustrate this historical reality. It was the mass mobilizations of the two world wars of the twentieth century that introduced women to military service on a significant scale. After World War II was over, most nations again drastically reduced the number of women's units in their armed services. Social and political pressures made the United States an exception to this trend. From a global perspective, the United States has assumed the lead in the integration of women in the military. Studies of women in the American military have generally focused (often polemically) on the proper roles of women and the problems such as harassment and career limitations within the various branches of the armed services.

BINKIN and BACH note in their classic work that the question of women's participation in the modern military cannot be avoided. They argue that there are complex ideological and emotional elements that cannot be separated from this issue. The key tension is the disparity between deeply rooted traditional values and the quest for equal rights. Using various and non-ideological perspectives, including cost/benefit analysis, the authors explore the issues of the effectiveness of a gender-integrated military and its policy implications as well as the psychological and institutional resistance encountered when women confront a traditionally all-male culture. This work includes a very useful (if slightly dated) appendix, which summarizes the place of women in the militaries of 25 selected countries of Europe, Asia, and the Middle East. Binkin and Bach have set the tone and terms of the debate over women in the military for many subsequent studies.

HOLM has written what is perhaps the best survey of the history of women in the American military. It is authoritative and comprehensive. Holm deals with women from the American Revolution through the founding of women's branches of the military, stressing the many contributions women have made. She provides solid documentation of the support and obstacles that have defined and limited the roles women have had open to them. The book is well-argued and succeeds in making the case that women have been and will remain a positive presence in the armed services.

ELSHTAIN and TOBIAS have gathered a fine selection of articles by noted feminist scholars from a number of disciplines, which explore not only the role of women in the military, but within the broader context of the history and culture of militarism. Two sections of this excellent work are of special note. Part II raises the issue of citizenship and soldiering from historical and legal perspectives. This is critical for a comprehensive view of the cultural context that determines the place of women, not only within the military but in the polity itself. Part III continues this theme by showing how the trauma of war has affected various peace movements as well as the practice of practical and electoral politics. Elshtain and Tobias's work is essential to an understanding of the impact of feminist scholarship on military service, war, and diplomacy.

Perhaps the most infamous of the public scandals involving sexual harassment in the military has been the "Tailhook" (an association of navy pilots) scandal. This incident, revealing the depth of the all-male mindset of the military establishment, involved a gathering of Navy pilots who exhibited inappropriate, unethical, and illegal behavior toward female aviators. ZIMMERMAN's book is a definitive account of this scandal (which has had analogs in other branches) that changed military rules across all of the armed services. The focus is on the problems of professionalism, gender, and institutions that have not responded well prior to the Tailhook incident to the challenge of the inclusion of women.

An inescapable issue in the sexual politics of the military is the place and role of gays and lesbians. SHILTS has authored an important account of how anti-gay policies have affected military personnel and contributed to a specifically heterosexual military culture. Shilts offers a comprehensive account of this matter by focusing on the official regulations and accompanying attitudes that determine the military's policies regarding sexual orientation. It is a major contribution to understanding the military culture as it confronts those who have been traditionally excluded.

ROGAN brings a journalist's eye and ear to women's experience in the military. This enables her to give voice to the women actually serving. Her book chronicles a cycle of basic training, a visit to West Point, and wide travels to military bases. Her conclusion is that women can serve well, and that the inevitable problems are caused not by the physical or mental inadequacy of women, but by the deep-seated resistance of the military establishment. It is a solid work, especially for the general reader. FRANCKE updates Rogan's earlier work, paying special (albeit more polemical) attention to the conscious and unconscious efforts to reverse the process of women's increased participation in the military services.

A good example of a dissenting view from that of Rogan and Francke is MITCHELL's argument. He believes that there are fundamental physical differences that prevent the complete integration of women into the military, especially in combat units. It is clearly argued, often polemical, and rich in data. Taken in conjunction with Francke, the general reader can assess both the tone and assumptions that motivate both sides of this public policy issue. It is reasonable to conclude that the definitive word on the feasibility and success of the integration of women is yet to come. More time and testing in combat situations is needed for scholarship to render a final verdict.

—MELVIN A. KULBICKI

Millay, Edna St. Vincent 1892–1950

American Writer

Brittin, Norman A., *Edna St. Vincent Millay,* Boston: Twayne, 1967

Cheney, Anne, *Millay in Greenwich Village,* University: University of Alabama Press, 1975

Dash, Joan, *A Life of One's Own: Three Gifted Women and the Men they Married,* New York: Harper and Row, 1973

Freedman, Diane P. (ed.), *Millay at 100: A Critical Reappraisal,* Carbondale: Southern Illinois University Press, 1995

Gould, Jean, *The Poet and Her Book: A Biography of Edna St. Vincent Millay,* New York: Dodd Mead, 1969

Nierman, Judith, *Edna St. Vincent Millay: A Reference Guide,* Boston: G.K. Hall, 1977

Thesing, William B. (ed.), *Critical Essays on Edna St. Vincent Millay,* New York: G.K. Hall, 1993

Although very popular and well-respected during most of her lifetime, and especially so during the 1920s, Edna St. Vincent Millay fell out of favor before her death. This was due in part to her adherence to conventional verse forms, in part to the sentiment and emotionalism of her work, and in part to her pacifist politics and the propaganda poems of World War II. Although her artistic accomplishments were undervalued, interest in her unconventional life never flagged, however, and biographical material continued to appear. In the late 1970s, feminist scholars initiated a revival of critical interest in her poetry and dramatic works, although serious study of her versification still remains to be done.

Two essential book-length collections of criticism are those by Freedman and Thesing. FREEDMAN's book is published as part of the "Critical Essays on American Literature" series, and does not disappoint with its careful selection of contemporary book reviews. By themselves, the reviews trace Millay's increasing acclaim before World War II, and its gradual waning thereafter. The section of articles and essays includes insightful appreciations by Louis Untermeyer, Edmund Wilson and others, as well as influential later attacks by Marshall McLuhan and John Ciardi. More recent feminist criticism is well-represented by Elizabeth Perlmutter Frank's essay on Millay and Louise Bogan, Jane Stanbrough on Millay's language of vulnerability, Debra Fried on the sonnets, and seven other essays, including two written especially for this volume. The collection is indexed, and includes a brief list of other worthwhile articles.

THESING's collection, part of the "Ad Feminam: Women and Literature" series edited by Sandra M. Gilbert, offers a dozen additional critical essays originally presented at a Skidmore College conference celebrating Millay's 100th birthday. Several of the essays examine definitions of modernism and Millay's place in that movement; one section of the book deals with the important issue of masquerade or role-playing. With Lisa Myers's psychoanalytic study of Millay's passion for her mother, and Holly Peppe's essay on Millay's profile of the woman lover, this collection helps restore Millay's critical reputation as a poet of vision and power. The book includes an index and an extensive list of works cited.

A useful overview of the life and works is BRITTIN's volume. Many libraries still contain only the original 1967 edition, which focuses on the poetry in a straightforward and conventional manner, but is an excellent introduction to what are still considered the major works. The author describes Millay's versatility as a writer, actor, and musician, and traces her career as a poet, a humanist, and a radical. The revised edition of 1982 gives less space to the biography, and includes instead a discussion of the prose writings, and a new chapter on Millay and feminism. However, the author's awareness of a new interest in feminism and in Millay as a feminist is not enough to overcome his own stereotypical expectations for a woman writer, as he occasionally reveals. The extensive bibliography is annotated, and Brittin also includes a chronology and suggestions for Millay work still to be done.

Biographical studies of Millay tend to focus, not unexpectedly, on the more salacious details of her life, and to offer little insight into the poems. DASH admits in her introduction that she is ill-equipped to take on literary criticism, but her psychoanalytic approach to Millay's marriage to Eugen Jan Boissevain is compelling. Dash finds Boissevain "beguiling," a long-suffering devoted helpmate to a brilliant but neurotic and demanding poet. She examines closely the role of his demands and expectations, and those of Millay's mother, in the poet's formation and transformation. Most have found this book to be unduly harsh, but nevertheless fascinating.

CHENEY also focuses on only a short period of Millay's life, a time between the repression of childhood and the bonds of marriage, using quotations from the poems and plays to create a psychological profile. Her first chapter, on childhood and youth, opens an important discussion of Millay's lesbianism, especially as it informs the play *The Lamp and the Bell,* but the theme is soon dropped in favor of a discussion of Millay's relationships with male writers as she evolves as a poet, a feminist, and a pacifist. Cheney bases her interpretations of Millay's various relationships on poems written to and about her, and her poems about others. Interesting photographs, a chronology, and a lengthy but outdated bibliography are included in this book.

GOULD examines the whole of Millay's life, and finds in her a pioneer in poetry, in free love, and in social activism. Although it seems dated now, Gould's biography was the first to appear in an era of expanded acceptance of what came to be called "lifestyles;" the author is able to discuss sexuality—at least, heterosexuality—without raising her eyebrows. Her admiration for Millay's talent and hard work, and for her strong political stances, are clearly and warmly explained. The book is illustrated with 27 photographs that help demonstrate the role Millay's physical beauty played in her public persona.

Although it covers only works published through 1973, NIERMAN's bibliography is an excellent annotated guide to hundreds of books and articles about Millay. The index helpfully lists authors, titles of Millay's works, and general subjects.

—CYNTHIA A. BILY

Milton, John 1608–1674

British Writer

Belsey, Catherine, *John Milton: Language, Gender, Power,* Oxford and New York: Basil Blackwell, 1988

Davies, Stevie, *The Feminine Reclaimed: The Idea of Woman in Spenser, Shakespeare, and Milton,* Brighton: Harvester, and Lexington: University of Kentucky Press, 1986

Gallagher, Philip, *Milton, the Bible, and Misogyny,* Columbia: University of Missouri Press, 1990

Gilbert, Sandra M., and Susan Gubar, *The Madwoman in the Attic: The Woman Writer and the Nineteenth-Century Literary Imagination,* New Haven, Connecticut, and London: Yale University Press, 1979

Graves, Robert, *Wife to Mr. Milton: The Story of Marie Powell,* London: Cassell, 1943; New York: Noonday Press, 1944

McColley, Diane Kelsey, *Milton's Eve,* Urbana: University of Illinois Press, 1983

Walker, Julia M. (ed.), *Milton and the Idea of Women,* Urbana: University of Illinois Press, 1988

Willis, Gladys J., *The Penalty of Eve: John Milton and Divorce,* New York: Peter Lang, 1984

Wittreich, Joseph Anthony, *Feminist Milton,* Ithaca, New York: Cornell University Press, 1987

In his *Life of Milton* (1779), Samuel Johnson mentions Milton's "Turkish dislike of women." Thus, for more than two centuries, critics have been interested in Milton's misogyny—or at least his attitudes toward women. Not only have they scrutinized his female characters, such as Eve in *Paradise Lost* (1667) and Dalila in *Samson Agonistes* (1671), and mulled over his divorce tracts (1643–45), but they have also researched and even fictionalized his personal relationships with women. GRAVES's novel, for example, tells the story of Milton's first marriage from the point of view of his wife. The response to Milton's misogyny became more hostile over the years, reaching a nadir in the 1960s and 1970s when several feminist critics condemned Milton as a "bogey" or worse. Since the early 1980s, however, critics have sought mainly to reconcile Milton's sexism with his poetic achievement and reputation. Two critics have even proclaimed him a feminist.

Milton is anything but a feminist to GILBERT and GUBAR. The third section of their book is titled "How Are We Fal'n?: Milton's Daughters" and contains chapters on "Milton's Bogey," Mary Shelley, and Emily Brontë, respectively. The title of the first chapter is an allusion to Virginia Woolf's cryptic reference to "Milton's bogey" in her essay "A Room of One's Own" (1929). Gilbert and Gubar speculate that the bogey may be Adam, Eve, or even Milton himself—an inhibitor of epic proportions that keeps women, especially literary women, from seeing and realizing their full potential. According to Gilbert and Gubar, Milton's bogey darkens the pages of both Shelley's *Frankenstein* (1818) and Brontë's *Wuthering Heights* (1847). Whereas Shelley recapitulates Milton's misogyny, Brontë reshapes and subverts it. Gilbert and Gubar's book has made a lasting contribution to Milton studies by galvanizing the debate over Milton's misogyny and putting many Miltonists on the defensive.

McCOLLEY defends Milton's Eve against critics, including Gilbert, who view her as weak and frail before the Fall. According to McColley, Eve is not spiritually weak or sinful in her prelapsarian state; rather she is a dynamic character, whose prelapsarian vitality foreshadows the inevitable rebirth of humankind. McColley argues that Milton was not perpetuating the misogynistic stereotype of Eve found in the Bible and elsewhere; he was in fact attempting to liberate her from a reductive tradition in art and literature. Therefore, Milton's Eve is subversive. McColley's book is essential reading because it challenges assumptions that have reduced Eve's value as a literary character. McColley opened many avenues of inquiry for further study of *Paradise Lost* and Milton's treatment of women.

Offering an "objective" reading of the divorce tracts, WILLIS argues that Milton's sexism must be viewed in the context of his culture and the Bible. She finds parallels between Milton's musings on divorce and Augustine's exegesis of charity. These parallels suggest that Milton was not unorthodox in his views on the rule of charity, which superseded even the bonds of matrimony, and if violated could constitute grounds for divorce. According to Willis, Milton was sincere in his belief that a husband should be able to divorce his wife if she hindered his relationship with God; he was not, as some critics allege, motivated by an unhappy marriage to Mary Powell. Most intriguing is Willis' suggestion that *Paradise Lost* and *Samson Agonistes* are narratives illustrating propositions in the divorce tracts.

DAVIES portrays Milton as a feminist in a special sense—not as one who advocated equality for women, but one as who participated in the Renaissance reclamation of the "feminine." Sixteenth-century authors, such as Spenser and Shakespeare, entertained the dream of androgyny in their writing. Their interest in the powerful nature of woman was sparked partly by a rediscovery of classical mythology and iconography, which offered numerous examples of Venus subduing Mars. It was nurtured, during the Tudor period, by the reign of a female monarch and sustained long after by the myth of Elizabeth. Davies argues that Milton's misogyny is a manifestation of a disappointed idealism in the feminine. The feminine ideal, however, is embodied in prelapsarian Eve and the Garden of Eden.

WITTREICH attempts to show that Milton was a feminist. He points to the numerous female readers, including Lady Mary Wortley Montagu, Mary Wollstonecraft, and Mary Shelley, who regarded Milton as "an ally in their cause." Although men often used Milton's writing to foster obedience in women, female readers used Milton's poetry just as often to combat patriarchal authority. In the eighteenth century, *Paradise Lost* came to be regarded as a women's book because it offered "new gender paradigms" for women. To read Milton properly, one must understand how Milton was read historically. This is the crux of Wittreich's argument. Wittreich's book offers valuable insights into the history of female readers' responses to Milton, but it falls short of establishing Milton as a feminist.

WALKER's important collection of essays does not deny or excuse Milton's misogyny; it examines it from many angles. The reader should note that the book is not titled *Milton's Idea of Women.* The "and" in the book's title displaces the possessive in a tradition of criticism that has long subjugated women to Milton's idea of them. In addition to Walker's introduction, this volume contains 12 essays: two general studies framing 10 studies of individual works. Among the essays is Leah Marcus's intriguing reading of *Comus* (1634) as a criticism of public officials for mishandling the rape of a 14-year-old girl in 1631. Walker suggests that Milton's knowledge of women came from reading, not intuiting, and thus lacks the truth of experience.

In her excellent chapter on gender, BELSEY reads three of Milton's works from a feminist perspective, although she is careful not to deny or excuse Milton's sexism. She marvels at the feminist motif of female rescuing female in *Comus*, but she warns that *Samson Agonistes*, in its patriarchal commentary on marriage, should dispel any suggestion that Milton was a feminist. Belsey describes Graves's *Wife to Mr. Milton* as an attack on Milton's sexism and compares Marie Powell to Milton's Eve in *Paradise Lost.* In her discussion of the latter work, Belsey notes the "sexual plurality" of the angels, who have the ability to change sexes or become both sexes simultaneously. This concept intrigues her as potentially liberating.

The affinity between GALLAGHER and Wittreich is partly the result of collaboration: the two men read each other's work in progress. Like Wittreich, Gallagher defends Milton against charges of misogyny, but he does so even more vehemently and overtly. He argues that Milton strips Genesis of its antifeminism and subverts "the misogynistic tradition" in biblical exegesis. Because her fall is sinless, Eve is less guilty than Adam. This proposition, inherent in *Paradise Lost*, suggests that Milton was not a misogynist, but a feminist. Gallagher's spirited attempt to paint Milton as "the first great feminist in Western culture" is less convincing than his attempt to demonstrate Milton's rejection of the Bible's literal inerrancy.

—EDWARD A. MALONE

Ministry *see* Clergywomen

Misogyny

Blamires, Alcuin, Karen Pratt, and C.W. Marx, *Woman Defamed and Woman Defended: An Anthology of Medieval Texts*, Oxford: Clarendon Press, and New York: Oxford University Press, 1992

Bloch, R. Howard, *Medieval Misogyny and the Invention of Western Romantic Love*, Chicago: University of Chicago Press, 1991

Coole, Diana H., *Women in Political Theory: From Ancient Misogyny to Contemporary Feminism*, Brighton: Harvester, and Boulder, Colorado: L. Rienner, 1988

Elam, Diane, and Robyn Wiegman (eds.), *Feminism Beside Itself*, London and New York: Routledge, 1995

Faludi, Susan, *Backlash: The Undeclared War against Women*, New York: Crown, 1991; London: Chatto and Windus, 1992

Smith, Joan, *Misogynies*, London: Faber, 1989; New York: Fawcett Columbine, 1991

Misogyny derives from the Greek words meaning "hatred of women," but that fails to encompass the varied cultural forms that such hatred has taken. It is important to distinguish between misogyny's overtly blatant manifestations (such as the late second-century Tertullian's "You are the gateway of the devil") and its more insidious ones (such as the beliefs about female inferiority inscribed in Aristotle's judgement that in animal procreation "the male provides the 'form', . . . the female provides the body, . . . the material"). However, misogynist thinking, permeating a variety of discourses from religion and theology to medicine and literature, can appear remarkably hackneyed and monolithic. As Christine de Pizan pointed out about the male authors who made up the anti-feminist canon of the late Middle Ages: "it seems that they all speak from one and the same mouth." Feminist analyses stress the omnipresence of misogyny in western cultural history, but there have been two periods when misogyny has been particularly strong: one stretching from roughly the beginning of Christianity to the end of the Middle Ages, and the other the late twentieth century. Both periods are characterised by notable cultural movements in which misogyny has been implicated as origin and effect: the rise and consolidation of Christianity, with its demand for clerical celibacy; and the emergence of organized feminism. Because misogyny takes "woman" as its subject, making of her at worst an object of fear and loathing, and at best a talking-point, any writer on the subject can find him or herself complicit with the very problem, caught up in the logic of what is a specific form of "trafficking in women."

BLAMIRES, PRATT, and MARX edit an anthology of texts from Ovid (43 B.C.–A.D. 18) to Christine de Pizan (1365–c.1430). This is an indispensable and standard collection for its range and comprehensiveness, with new translations of Latin and Old French texts, and useful factual headnotes. The organisation and choice of extracts not only demonstrates the long history of misogyny and its appearance across a variety of discourses (and European languages), but also acknowledges that not every post-classical or medieval man (or woman) was a misogynist.

BLOCH's erudite poststructuralist study is a book-length version of an earlier essay that sparked enormous feminist controversy because of its thesis that antifeminism is a "citational mode" (i.e., something textual), which refuses the (problematic) gesture of moving beyond the text to the historical situation of women. Copiously illustrated and attentive to chronological change, the volume's main focus is Old French literary texts, but it takes in a swathe of cultural history, from Greek and early Christian writings to asceticism, virginity, and courtliness, addressing a number of founding misogynist topics: woman as riot and liar, the negative link between the feminine and speech, woman as embodiment and (paradoxically) as the figural, woman as text. The volume proposes a dialectical relationship between misogyny and "courtly love." Although lucid about the contradictions of antifeminism, Bloch never pushes them to their logical conclusion by allowing them to unsettle the texts in which they appear.

SMITH has written a collection of accessible, sometimes controversial, journalistic essays on woman-hating in contemporary popular culture, mostly drawing on examples from the 1970s and 1980s in Britain as reported in both the tabloid and quality press. The essay on the "Yorkshire Ripper" murders is the best. Written from a feminist perspective on the left, Smith's account nevertheless does not consider alternative feminist readings of the cultural phenomena she labels "misogynist." In form and title the book is reminiscent of Roland Barthes's *Mythologies* (1957), but where Barthes's agenda was the semiotic analysis of the politics of the sign, Smith's is justice for women.

Written in response to the so-called backlash against feminism, FALUDI's polemical book sets out to prove that women are the victims of a renewed antifeminist campaign inspired by male fear that women might achieve what they want. Despite occasional references to Britain, this is largely a U.S.-oriented study. Extensively researched, it covers the impact of feminism and the "backlash" within contemporary "popular" culture and across medical, legal and socio-economic territories, offering a relentless condemnation of the culture industry's exploitation of women. Its appeal to "truth," via the authority of statistics, case studies, and press reports, is very strong. Faludi's anger is powerful, but the effect of her attack is dissipated through the sheer volume of examples and the failure to address questions of representation and desire in more theorised terms. The volume offers no political remedies and adopts a crusading tone: its final sentence reads: "no one can ever take from women the justness of their cause."

Misogyny is not confined to men. ELAM and WIEGMAN's excellent collection includes a stylish essay by Susan Gubar that poses provocative questions. Through examination of Mary Wollstonecraft's writings, Gubar demonstrates that "feminist expository prose inevitably embeds itself in the misogynist tradition it seeks to address and redress." In constructing their identity, feminists are inevitably caught up in an uncanny logic that "repeatedly links feminist polemicists to their rivals and antagonists." In the same volume, Friedman's thoughtful essay on feminist historiography implicitly engages with the same problem, arguing that feminists get caught up in structures that remarkably mime misogyny, in order to promote structural narratives of "progress" or of opposition between feminisms.

COOLE's book, narrower in scope than others reviewed here, argues that western philosophy inscribed theories of the state and citizenship with a misogynist dualism that placed women as a threat to political order, making problematic their place within it. This lucid, compact history surveys the role of women and the feminine in a number of key thinkers on political theory from Plato and Aristotle to the present day. The second edition includes a stimulating new chapter on feminism and postmodernism.

—RUTH EVANS

Moore, Marianne 1887–1972

American Writer

Erickson, Darlene Williams, *Illusion Is More Precise than Precision: The Poetry of Marianne Moore*, Tuscaloosa and London: The University of Alabama Press, 1992

Goodridge, Celeste, *Hints and Disguises: Marianne Moore and Her Contemporaries*, Iowa City: University of Iowa Press, 1989

Heuving, Jeanne, *Omissions Are Not Accidents: Gender in the Art of Marianne Moore*, Detroit, Michigan: Wayne State University Press, 1992

Leavell, Linda, *Marianne Moore and the Visual Arts: Prismatic Color*, Baton Rouge and London: Louisiana State University Press, 1995

Martin, Taffy, *Marianne Moore: Subversive Modernist*, Austin: University of Texas Press, 1986

Miller, Cristianne, *Marianne Moore: Questions of Authority*, Cambridge, Massachusetts and London: Harvard University Press, 1995

Marianne Moore's poetry was long the subject of mostly New Critical readings, which characteristically saw her as a poet's poet among the American High Modernists, difficult and abstruse. Only very recently have feminist critics begun to come to terms with her work, using the tools of post-structuralism in particular to facilitate new readings of her poetry. Many such new readings see a critique of gender operating in Moore's work in terms of its innovative forms and techniques. MARTIN, for example, wants to reclaim Moore's work for a more subversive poetic than it has hitherto been granted, placing Moore at the cutting edge of American modernism. Arguing that while many features of Moore's poetry have been read as defensive strategies for dealing with the chaos of modernity, they should, on the contrary, be read as more positively engaging with and promoting the indeterminacy and radical ambiguity that are the trademarks of postmodernism.

GOODRIDGE also presents a more complex version of Moore than the defensive, self-effacing spinster that characterized her public image. Based around a study of Moore's book reviews and critical essays, Goodridge elucidates the poet's relationships with her major male contemporaries. In separate chapters devoted to each, Goodridge focuses on Moore's response to the work of Wallace Stevens, Ezra Pound, William Carlos Williams, and T.S. Eliot, whose careers Moore charted in essays and reviews spanning decades. Against this published record, Goodridge juxtaposes the views on her fellow poets that Moore expressed in private letters and notes. She finds that in public Moore tends to mask criticism of these contemporaries in order to promote a collective modernist enterprise. At the same time, close examination of Moore's critical prose along with the private record reveals both Moore's self-positioning in terms of a dialectic of self-revelation and self-preservation, and a modernist aesthetic privileging fragmentation, improvisation, shifting voice, and perspective. Consequently, Goodridge aligns Moore with Stevens and Pound over against Williams (with whom she is conventionally paired) and Eliot.

ERICKSON also regards Moore's poetic as subversive, but especially in its representation of a gendered worldview. Each chapter introduces a specific preoccupation of the poetry—time (with particular reference to Henri Bergson's ideas), the visual arts, quotations as *objets trouvés*, figures of amoring—followed by a detailed discussion of specific poems. For Erickson, the key image of Moore's poetic identity is that of the magician, and the key feature of her work its emphasis on the magic of words and the power of intuitive (over logical) connections between words-as-things.

HEUVING begins from a position similar to Erickson—that while Moore's poetry does not deal explicitly with gender issues, gender nonetheless fundamentally structures her work—but presents her case more consistently. Using Luce Irigaray's idea of the specularity of discourse, Heuving argues that Moore's poetry counters the "specular poetics" of the masculine lyric tradition through its formal innovations, especially its use of the twin modes of "contrariety" and the fantastic. Heuving traces the development of the poetry chronologically to argue that Moore's early work is characterized by an implied "I," which paradoxically attempts to represent both female selfhood and male universality, and which is more subversive than the later poetry's prevalent generalized "we," which upholds more conventional symbolic values.

LEAVELL's study is the first book-length discussion of the importance of the visual arts to Moore's work, seeing her poetic practice as deeply indebted to modernist experimentation in painting and sculpture, a fact long acknowledged by commentators but not treated in depth. The book contextualizes the development of Moore's modernism in terms of her early exposure to the arts and crafts movement and its ideology, and then of the period from 1915 to 1929, when she moved in the circle of artists associated with Alfred Steiglitz's 291 gallery. Leavell makes good use of unpublished material from the Moore papers in the Rosenbach Museum and Library, establishing the importance of visual and plastic arts influences to Moore's thinking about art. She builds on this biographical base in chapters demonstrating how the poetry offers formal experiments in analytic cubism and techniques of collage. Later chapters consider the ethical implications of Moore's poetic practice and her affinity with precisionist painters and photographers, who refused to see science and technology as a threat to artistic expression.

While concurring with feminist critics, such as Heuving, who see gender as a structuring feature of Moore's poetry, MILLER does not believe that the feminine is a privileged category in her work. In particular, Moore sought to avoid the poetic voice of romantic sentimentalism identified with the figure of the "poetess," yet she also rejected the masculine romantic role of poet-hierophant and its egoistic self-authorizing strategies. Rather, Moore attempted to create a non-essentializing gender-neutral poetic, combining features coded both masculine and feminine, the experimental form of her poetic being intrinsically linked to this gender-neutral ideal. Miller's study has some interesting biographical discussion, which historicizes Moore's attitudes to sex and gender. In a chapter devoted to the treatment of "race" in the poems, Miller argues that as a white, middle-class, Protestant Moore had the cultural authority to address issues of race and cultural diversity more freely than those of gender. While Moore rejects the poetic authority claimed by a "masculist" romantic lyric tradition, her poems assert a different kind of authority in their pluralist inclusiveness, which does not claim universal knowledge but multiple and partial truths.

—SUSAN CONLEY

Morisot, Berthe 1841–1895

French Painter

Adler, Kathleen, and Tamar Garb, *Berthe Morisot*, Oxford: Phaidon, and Ithaca, New York: Cornell University Press, 1987

Edelstein, T. J. (ed.), *Perspectives on Morisot*, New York: Hudson Hills Press, 1990

Higonnet, Anne, *Berthe Morisot*, New York: Harper and Row, and London: Collins, 1990

———, *Berthe Morisot's Images of Women*, Cambridge, Massachusetts: Harvard University Press, 1992; London: Harvard University Press, 1994

Stuckey, Charles F., William P. Scott, and Suzanne G. Lindsay, *Berthe Morisot, Impressionist*, New York: Hudson Hills Press, and London: Sotheby's, 1987

In some important respects, the literature on the French painter Berthe Morisot encapsulates the best methodological developments in feminist art historical scholarship of the past decade.

Although not a feminist work per se, the large traveling exhibition STUCKEY, SCOTT, and LINDSAY put together in 1987 was part of a wider reassessment of Morisot's contribution to late nineteenth-century painting generally, and to impressionism in particular. The accompanying catalogue features a thorough, well-documented essay by Stuckey, a highly respected art historian whose expertise on impressionism is brought to bear in this study of one of its foremost (albeit under-recognized) practitioners. His essay is a chronological survey of the artist's life and art, mapping the central formative events (and professional contacts) in Morisot's career, and the overriding themes and concerns in her art. A smaller companion essay on the artist's style and technique, written by William P. Scott, underscores the essentially conservative, but careful methodological approach taken in the entire study. The abundant, excellent reproductions (both color and black-and-white) are another significant contribution of this catalogue to Morisot scholarship.

A symposium on Morisot was held in conjunction with the 1987 exhibition, and the papers presented there were subsequently collected in an anthology edited by EDELSTEIN. Whereas the exhibit targeted a more mainstream, general audience, the symposium was largely intended for those already familiar with the topography of Morisot studies. The contributors include all the authors discussed here, along with lesser-known art historians. Each essay examines some fact of the critical issues that confronted Morisot as a woman and as a female artist. Narrow in focus, these essays nevertheless place Morisot within contexts broader than any previously considered. Thus, for example, Adler examines "the space of everyday life" in Morisot's art and in her home life; Beatrice Farwell explores Edouard Manet's portraits of his friend in an essay entitled "Manet, Morisot, and Propriety"; and Garb dissects the "feminizing" of impressionism. This collection makes an ideal complement to Stuckey's book, expanding and developing themes and observations merely hinted at in the exhibition catalogue essay.

ADLER and GARB, two of the most exciting feminists presently working in the field of art history, sought to make up for what was then a lack of scholarship in English on Morisot, and specifically, to redress prevailing imbalances and inaccuracies about Morisot and her art. Adler and Garb are unapologetic in asserting their overarching theme and goal: they are interested in Morisot's identity as a woman, and they hope with this study to make explicit the situation of one woman who wanted to become a professional painter at a particular point in time. The authors explore the ways in which class and gender placed certain constraints on the artist, while simultaneously enabling her to establish and develop her artistic career. The study suggests how Morisot reconciled the private world of the feminine sphere with the public world of artistic practice. As such, it goes a long way in dispelling the notion that Morisot painted as she did because it was somehow "natural" or bio-genetically prescribed for her as a woman.

HIGONNET has written both a biography of Morisot, which emphasizes the artist's life, and a study of her images of women, which emphasizes her art. The two books complement each other nicely. The territory covered in the biography (1990) is not significantly different from that covered by Stuckey, although the biographical format and Higonnet's unobtrusive writing style make this book accessible to a different, and possibly wider audience; it has surely introduced Morisot to some readers who might not otherwise set foot in an art museum.

In the preface to her biography, Higonnet states her bias, explaining her fascination with the way in which Morisot refused to compromise her art or sacrifice her social position in order to appease convention; sustained attention to this matter is what gives this book its feminist inflection. The biography delineates the cultural, gender-specific pressures exerted upon a woman of Morisot's class and social milieu. Throughout the study, Higonnet deftly compares Morisot's choices with other of her male and female contemporaries to support her thesis that Morisot "chose safely feminine themes, which made it possible to cling to an extremely daring unfeminine career while making minimal personal sacrifices."

HIGONNET's more recent book (1994) on Morisot's images of women is a risky, forward-looking work of feminist scholarship on Morisot. Informed by current feminist and postmodern theoretical concerns, and grounded in solid, extensive, and original research, this study covers new, fresh territory. Specifically, the study ranges beyond the traditional scope of modernist art historical studies—studies that seal art in a vacuum and render non-high art influences invisible (and invalid or unacceptable). Higonnet's work not only situates Morisot's art within art historical contexts, but also within the much broader rubric of "feminine visual culture." This strategy allows the author to consider, for example, the relationship of Morisot's images to nineteenth-century women's amateur art (which counted among the feminine accomplishments that could attract "suitable husbands" for upper-class and middle-class women), and to contemporary fashion illustrations, to mention only two. What makes this approach particularly refreshing is that Higonnet does not seem to hold any illusions about comprehensivity. Her decision to focus solely on the artist's images of women is only one of the ways she has purposely narrowed her study. This study has far-reaching implications, both for future Morisot studies, and for feminist art historical scholarship generally. It should prove to be a useful model.

—JO ORTEL

Mormonism

Anderson, Lavina Fielding, and Maureen Ursenbach Beecher, *Sisters in Spirit: Mormon Women in Historical and Cultural Perspective,* Urbana: University of Illinois Press, 1987

Bahr, H. M., S.J. Condie, and K.L. Goodman, *Life in Large Families: Views of Mormon Women,* Washington, D.C.: University Press of America, 1982

Bartholomew, Rebecca, *Audacious Women: Early British Mormon Immigrants,* Salt Lake City: Signature, 1995

Foster, Lawrence, *Religion and Sexuality: Three American Communal Experiments of the Nineteenth Century,* New York and Oxford: Oxford University Press, 1981

Shipps, Jan, *Mormonism: The Story of a New Religious Tradition*, Urbana: University of Illinois Press, 1985
Warenski, Marilyn, *Patriarchs and Politics: The Plight of the Mormon Woman*, New York: McGraw-Hill, 1978

Since its foundation in upstate New York in the 1830s, the Church of Jesus Christ of the Latter-Day Saints has provoked much attention, in relationship particularly to its family organisation and its doctrinal bases. Early persecution of the Mormons drove them into Utah, where Brigham Young established a new "American Zion," drawing to it converts from Europe as well as the United States. Here the church strengthened its institutions and developed its doctrines. Missionary activity since that time ensured that Mormonism became a truly global religion. To understand the church's contemporary position, it is necessary to comprehend its historical development.

SHIPPS's book offers an interpretation of Mormonism as the development of a separate religious tradition, as different from Christianity as Christianity is from Judaism. She provides a useful narrative of the early development of the church, but her focus is on examining the processes involved in the creation of a new religion, and perhaps more importantly, on how such processes allowed Mormonism to sustain and transform itself into a major religion of the twentieth century. Although not dealing with women specifically, Shipps's argument does address the central controversy of nineteenth-century Mormonism, polygamy.

This doctrine of "Celestial Marriage" is examined in detail by FOSTER. His book places the birth of Mormonism within its historical and cultural context. His examination also offers comparisons with other "utopian" groups, the Shakers and the Oneidas, which sought to challenge social relations at their very basis, namely sexuality and gender. For Mormons, salvation depended upon marital status. A woman could only be saved through marriage, and for men, the more wives they had, the greater would be their position in the afterlife. Foster details the horror that such a doctrine evoked to "Gentile" Americans but also sympathetically demonstrates how these groups, often understood as oddities and as subversive elements on the fringe of American society, reflected and manipulated the mainstream into their own unique, transformative vision of the future. The scorn placed upon such groups in many ways came from the fact that their very existence reflected deep anxieties within that society, especially concerning the roles and position of women.

Mormons are expected by the church to record their witness of the "latter-days." Consequently, their archives are rich in testimonies by women. BARTHOLOMEW draws upon such sources to examine those women converted in Britain, who then chose to make the long trek to Utah. She examines the stereotypes of these women as portrayed by popular writers such as Mark Twain and Charles Dickens, and then proceeds to assess how true or not these portraits were. She explores who these female converts were, their backgrounds and experiences in Britain prior to emigration, and the adaptations they had to undertake in the unfamiliar territory of Utah. Bartholomew provides a useful bibliography of her primary sources and where these are housed, which are important data for continuing research. She explores, through these primary texts, women's responses to polygamy, although as many Mormon historians do, she emphasizes its rarity compared to monogamous unions. Although the book is somewhat hagiographical at times, it is an important addition to the under-researched field of non-American Mormon women in the early history of the church.

The question of the position of women in Mormonism did not end with the outlawing of polygamy in the 1890s. Mormon opposition to the Equal Rights Amendment in the 1970s once again brought this question to the public eye, and caused consternation within the church itself. WARENSKI examines an apparent paradox in the history of Mormon women. Although early Utah allowed women's suffrage and the opening of various professions to women, seeming thus to be favorable to women's issues, the modern church appears antifeminist and wholly patriarchal, oppressive to women in its demands for marriage and large families. Warenski argues that the church was always patriarchal, and that women are manipulated within it toward its own doctrinal goals. This book is a scathing feminist critique of the church from a Mormon woman.

To temper her argument, ANDERSON and BEECHER have collected a number of essays on various historical, cultural, and theological issues of concern to women in Mormonism. Their principle is for Mormon women to build on structures already in place, and to draw strength from their past instead of iconoclastically attacking the church. Two essays explore the themes highlighted here. Balif-Peterson's essay draws on discussions with eight women in auxiliary positions in the church concerning the existence of an all-male priesthood, and thus a male-controlled church that allows women no real role in deciding church policy. Their differing responses reveal a flexibility in response to doctrine. Raynes's essay comparing Mormon marriages to those of mainstream Americans reveals more similarities than differences, although there is more of a concern with "sexual sin" within Mormon marriages than otherwise.

BAHR, CONDIE, and GOODMAN's book contains the results of their study of 41 Mormon women with more than seven children each. Although this study is circumscribed by location and by class, it provides a wealth of material on the lived experience of many contemporary Mormon women fulfilling the church's prescriptions toward motherhood. It examines the reasons that they give for such large families, primarily religious ones, but it then also highlights the consequences for family organisation in these cases. Interviews with the participants reveal the women's conceptions of themselves, their husbands, their marriages, and a variety of "women's issues." Such a source provides a chance to assess modern Mormon women in the light of their specific historical and religious experiences.

—STEPHANIE OXENDALE

See also Polygamy, Mormon

Morrison, Toni 1931–

American Writer

Bjork, Patrick Bryce, *The Novels of Toni Morrison: The Search for Self and Place within the Community,* New York: Peter Lang, 1992

Bloom, Harold (ed.), *Toni Morrison,* New York: Chelsea House, 1990

Coser, Stela Maris, *Bridging the Americas—The Literature of Toni Morrison, Paule Marshall and Gayl Jones,* Philadelphia: Temple University Press, 1995

Gates, Henry Louis, Jr., and Anthony Appiah (eds.), *Toni Morrison: Critical Perspectives Past and Present,* New York: Armistad, 1993

Heinze, Denise, *The Dilemma of "Double-Consciousness": Toni Morrison's Novels,* Athens and London: University of Georgia Press, 1993

Holloway, Karla F.C., and Stephanie A. Demetrakopoulos, *New Dimensions of Spirituality: A Biracial and Bicultural Reading of the Novels of Toni Morrison,* New York and London: Greenwood, 1987

Mbalia, Doreatha Drummond, *Toni Morrison's Developing Class Consciousness,* Selinsgrove, Pennsylvania: Susquehanna University Press, and London: Associated University Presses, 1991

McKay, Nellie (ed.), *Critical Essays on Toni Morrison,* Boston: G.K. Hall, 1988

Page, Philip, *Dangerous Freedom: Fusion and Fragmentation in Toni Morrison's Novels,* Jackson: University Press of Mississippi, 1995

Peach, Linden, *Toni Morrison,* London: Macmillan, and New York: St. Martin's Press, 1995

Rigney, Barbara Hill, *The Voices of Toni Morrison,* Columbus: Ohio State University Press, 1991

Discussion of Toni Morrison's work generally addresses her status among African-American literary figures and the wider literary critical problem of how to read the relationship between the politics and aesthetics of her work. She appears in most collections of essays on African-American writing, and there are several collections of essays on her work.

McKAY's book is the earliest of these and contains commissioned and republished essays, reviews, interviews, and several pieces on each of Morrison's novels up to *Tar Baby.* McKay's introduction articulates the complex and contestatory location of Morrison's work within and against dominant literary and cultural traditions in the United States, with a special focus on the reception of the novels there. BLOOM collects a number of important essays that concentrate on the novels' thematic concerns such as place (and the move from familiarity to the uncanny) and notions of innocence; questions of otherness; history; canonicity and the specificity of African-American traditions; literary and cultural inheritances; and the problems of self-representation. Bloom's own introduction frames the collection with a concern for the question of aesthetics versus politics in Morrison's work. GATES and APPIAH provide another excellent collection that brings together reviews, essays, and interviews. A short introduction notes Morrison's literary achievements in terms of her formal sophistication, complex thematics, and engagements with both dominant and submerged cultural traditions.

COSER considers Morrison alongside Paule Marshall and Gayl Jones in an examination of the question of "inter-American characteristics" in the work of these writers. The focus on the shared history of colonialism and racism in what she calls "the extended Caribbean" produces readings of Morrison's work that take account of her position in broader traditions of African experiences and cultures in the Americas, thus allowing for different understandings of the possibilities of liberation.

Most of Morrison's critics, on the other hand, stress the significance of local African-American communities in her work. BJORK provides a useful account of the significance of questions of tradition in Morrison's novels, reading them as a broadly conceived American search for self and place, but articulating the specifics of this search for African-American communities and writers. For Bjork, tradition is conceived carefully as the intertextual relationships within a span of African-American writing from nineteenth-century slave narratives through the Harlem Renaissance to the work of Richard Wright, James Baldwin, and Ralph Ellison. African-American feminist critiques of white feminism provide a parallel tradition for Morrison.

PAGE addresses questions of individual and community identities, of representing experiences of fragmentation and displacement, as well as the significance of tradition and the centrality of theorising around cultural and racial differences in each of Morrison's novels. MBALIA provides a careful and engaged reading of

Morrison's novels in terms of a race-conscious aesthetics and a wider consideration of the concepts and literary understanding of oppression and struggle. In particular, class consciousness is read alongside questions of race and community as informing the representations of African-American experiences in the novels.

PEACH structures her discussion around an insistence on the question of rhetoric and literature, that is, on the particular nature and functions of figurative language as manifested in African-American cultural traditions. Peach argues (after H.L. Gates Jr.) that literary texts never simply refer to a reality outside themselves in any simple way. Peach discusses each novel as a rhetorical structure, with a focus not so much on the subject matter in the novels, as on the ways each novel engages with literary and fictional traditions and conventions. This provides a careful context for the biographical and other contextual information provided in this work. HEINZE discusses the novels under the headings of beauty and love, families and family relations, questions of tradition, community and social resistance, and the dimension of the supernatural and the spiritual. The discussion engages with critics of Morrison and African-American writing generally, and the introduction discusses the complexities of Morrison's popularity and the more important criticisms of her.

Feminist readings of Morrison generally place her work within traditions of female writers. RIGNEY defines a black feminine/feminist aesthetic and locates Morrison at the intersection of issues of race and gender, demonstrating her significance for feminist literary criticism in this way. For Rigney, Morrison's work defines a space "outside" of literary convention, producing a possibility for critiquing race and gender hierarchies. While Rigney notes white U.S and African-American criticisms of the dominance of French feminism, she stops short of exploring the political gap between the metaphors and the experiences of "blackness."

HOLLOWAY and DEMETRAKOPOULOS read explicitly against this feminist tradition, instead putting forth a notion of bicultural intersubjectivity as a starting point for reading literature "differently." They engage with dominant feminist literary criticism's long-standing blindness to questions of race, opting instead for what they call "encultured feminist criticism." The chronological organisation of this book reflects not just what the authors see as the increasing complexity of Morrison's work, but also their own background as readers from different academic traditions of African-American writing. The care devoted to such questions of positionings, and the discursive and institutional production of meanings, is useful for students wanting to engage in a complex way with the politics of reading.

—BRIGITTA OLUBAS

Mother-Daughter Relationships

Bell-Scott, Patricia (ed.), *Double Stitch: Black Women Write about Mothers and Daughters,* Boston: Beacon, 1991

Davidson, Cathy, and E.M. Broner (eds.), *The Lost Tradition: Mothers and Daughters in Literature,* New York: Ungar, 1980

Hirsch, Marianne, *The Mother/Daughter Plot: Narrative, Psychoanalysis, Feminism,* Bloomington: Indiana University Press, 1989

Lowinsky, Naomi Ruth, *Stories from the Motherline: Reclaiming the Mother-Daughter Bond, Finding Our Feminine Souls,* Los Angeles: Tarcher, 1992

van Mens-Verhulst, Janneke, Karlein Schreurs, and Liesbeth Woertman (eds.), *Daughtering and Mothering: Female Subjectivity Reanalysed,* New York: Routledge, 1993

Walters, Suzanna Danuta, *Lives Together, Worlds Apart: Mothers and Daughters in Popular Culture,* Berkeley: University of California Press, 1992

The mother-daughter relationship has often been ignored or relegated to the footnotes of male-defined history and scholarship. Over the past 20 years, though, the lamented lack in mother-daughter literature has been obviated by the publication of a wealth of studies in different disciplines, which sanction its centrality in feminist scholarship.

The collection of essays edited by DAVIDSON and BRONER has become a standard among the writings that deal with textual analysis of literary representations of mothers and daughters. Although often criticized for the sketchy quality of some of its essays, its breadth and scope, as well as its extensive historical framework make of this book a necessary introduction to the field. The essays range from an analysis of the story of Ruth and her mother-in-law Naomi in the Bible to Shakespeare's condemnation of his heroines, and from the description of British and American nineteenth-century tradition, with its erasure of the mother from the text and with its motherless daughters, to the dramatization of the conflict between mothers and daughters in the twentieth-century tradition. The last section of the collection, dedicated to minority literatures, stresses a greater empathy between mothers and daughters, in a celebration of their common "Matrilineage."

HIRSH's work is a standard text in the literary criticism of the mother-daughter relationship from a feminist psychoanalytic approach, and it "takes as its point of departure the intersection of familial structures and structures of plotting, attempting to place at the center of inquiry mothers and daughters." The text focuses on the analysis of novels by nineteenth- and twentieth-century female writers from North America and western Europe (including Jane Austen, the Brontës, Kate Chopin, Virginia Woolf, Margaret Atwood, and Toni Morrison), to trace the emergence and transformation of female family romance patterns, while at the same time revealing that the maternal story (and voice) remains the unspeakable plot of western culture, displaced in favor of the daughter's. Hirsh identifies three stages in the development of these familial and plot structures. In nineteenth-century realist novels by women the maternal is repressed or devalued and substituted with compensatory fantasies of brother-sister bonding. In modernist novels the mother becomes a central figure, celebrated from the point of view of an ambivalent artist-daughter in the daughter's text and family romance. In the fictional and theoretical writing that stemmed from the feminist movement of the 1960s and 1970s, there is still a failure to redress the balance between the voices of the mother and of the daughter that are within each woman. Hirsh finds a possible alternative to this feminist erasure of maternity, however, in the contemporary postmodern fiction of Alice Walker and Toni Morrison, which introduces a feminist discourse of identity that begins to speak a maternal discourse together with the daughter's.

The collection of essays edited by VAN MENS-VERHULST offers a perspective on the mother-daughter relationship that had so far been neglected. Its main premise is that both daughters and mothers participate actively in the shaping of the relationship. The three sections of the book provide a wide array of multidisciplinary essays on daughtering and mothering, introduced by insightful analyses of current theoretical debates and the role these new approaches play. The first section focuses on the side of the daughter in the relationship, and object relations theories are the primary frame of reference. The main question addressed in this first part relates to the "sexual dimension of female subjectivity and the role of the mother therein." The contributors emphasize the importance of the contextualization of the mother-daughter relationship, and provide possible alternatives to object relations theory for approaching the relationship. The second section's main focus is the mother, and the essays critique the notion of "universal motherhood." The contributors in this section consider maternal practices (in their biological and social implications) in historic and cultural contexts, and refuse the identification of mothering with a biological or social necessity. They stress the importance of representing the mother as an autonomous and at the same time relational subject, as "subject-in-development." The third part of the collection rethinks mothering and daughtering from a framework that is alternative to object relations theory. It introduces the concepts of relational paradigm and multiple subjectivity paradigm, which reveal "alternative norms for a healthy development of women," and affirm that the idea of "good-enough mothering" is an idealized version of the mother-daughter relationship, supporting relations of dominance between classes, races, and cultures. This book presents an interesting challenge to the established psychoanalytic view, from perspectives as diverse as clinical, social, and cultural psychology, and cultural anthropology.

WALTERS examines the changes in the representation of the mother-daughter relationship in popular media, from a perspective that distances itself from the traditional psychological interpretation of this relationship. It is the author's working thesis that "the mother-daughter relationship is formed, at least in part, by the cultural images that give it meaning," and it has largely been portrayed in terms of conflict and separation. Historically, the analysis covers the period from after World War II to 1990, and the author stresses the importance of a historical, contextual, and intertextual approach to identify the specific "ways of seeing" the relationship that are characteristic of certain periods. This contextualization helps the reader understand how this relationship is socially (re)constructed in accordance with current ideologies and political practices. This book provides an interesting analysis from a cultural studies perspective.

LOWINSKI's analysis of the mother-daughter bond distances itself from the other texts mentioned here, insofar as it weaves in her personal encounters with the experiences of patients and other women she has interviewed in an effort to describe every woman's journey to find her female roots. The central concept of the text, the "motherline," is identified as "a woman's female lineage reaching backward from her mother and her mother's mother, and forward to her daughters and granddaughters." Each of the book's ten chapters delineates an aspect of the feminine self and how it can be reclaimed, from the conceptualization of the motherline as the source of women's stories, to the analysis of the problem of differentiation between mother and daughter, which forces both women to sort between self and other. The purpose of the text is to suggest that, to be fulfilled, a woman needs to acknowledge the profound influence exerted on her by other women, and to recognize both the mother and the daughter in herself.

BELL-SCOTT and the other editors of this important volume have compiled a collection of essays, personal narratives, poetry, and fiction that concerns itself with the experience of African-American mothers and daughters. The diversity of the pieces challenges the notion of a uniform model of black motherhood and daughterhood: deep differences emerge based on class, sexual preference, and age. This collection fulfills an important need in the field, too often dominated by the white, middle-class perspective that is central to so many other texts. Each of the six parts of the collection deals with different moments in the relationship, including the formation of the mother-daughter bond, the acknowledgment of the extended female community in the practice of mothering, and the portrayal of unconventional images of black mothers, women who challenge the stereotype of the devoted, self-sacrificing, all-powerful, perfect matriarch. This book is a valuable resource for all those interested in the analysis of the mother-daughter relationship from an African-American point of view.

—DAVIDA GAVIOLI

See also Motherhood

Motherhood

Bassin, Donna, Margaret Honey, and Meryle Mahrer Kaplan (eds.), *Representations of Motherhood,* New Haven, Connecticut: Yale University Press, 1994

Chang, Grace, Evelyn Nakano Glenn, and Linda Rennie Forcey (eds.), *Mothering: Ideology, Experience, and Agency,* New York: Routledge, 1994

Chodorow, Nancy, *The Reproduction of Mothering: Psychoanalysis and the Sociology of Gender,* Berkeley: University of California Press, 1978; London: University of California Press, 1979

Kaplan, E. Ann, *Motherhood and Representation: The Mother in Popular Culture and Melodrama,* New York and London: Routledge, 1992

Knowles, Jane Price, and Ellen Cole (eds.), *Motherhood: A Feminist Perspective,* New York: Haworth Press, 1990

Rich, Adrienne, *Of Woman Born: Motherhood as Experience and Institution,* New York: Norton, 1976; London: Virago Press, 1977

The question of motherhood and the maternal is a subject of considerable debate in feminist theories. Mothering has often been subject to essentialist interpretations, seen as universal, natural, and unchanging. Metaphors of sisterhood ("sisterhood is powerful") or of friendship became the dominant images in the representation of female and feminist relationships in the 1970s, in a rejection of the maternal as a continued bondage to men and patriarchy. The mother was thus stigmatized as the "root of all evil," either feared as the all-powerful phallic mother or criticized as the powerless mother, helpless in the face of a patriarchal society that she is seen as perpetuating. The texts examined here try to go beyond this stigmatization of the maternal, advocating a need to see the mother as subject in her own right.

RICH's groundbreaking text analyzes motherhood as a social institution created in patriarchy, in the contexts of cultures and traditions that it reflects and reinforces, and as the reproductive capability to which it can not be reduced. Rich's distinction between the female experience on the one hand, and the male cultural expectations and structures that shape it on the other, allows for an examination of the ways in which women have been controlled by the institution of motherhood. She sets up the contrast and struggle between women's potential to be in control of their lives, as well as of their reproductive capability, and the limits imposed by the institutional control that hinder its development. Her critique draws on areas as diverse as literature, psychology, anthropology, myth, history, and theology, as well as on her own experience as a mother, and on experiences of other women who, in their efforts to live up to the expectations imposed by the institution, deny themselves as well as their children. Rich's discourse goes so far as to examine the violence of infanticide, and the depression that comes from trying to conform to the prescribed role of the "good mother." This text highlights the struggle between the realities of institutionalized motherhood on the one hand, and on the other, alternatives to the patriarchal institution that might inspire increased female autonomy.

In a feminist revision of Freudian theory, CHODOROW tries to answer the question: Why do women mother? What psychological operations come into being to ensure the reproduction of mothering by women in our culture? She considers the reproduction of mothering as central to women's oppression, and to the developmental stages she describes as characteristic of men and women in patriarchy. Her psychoanalytic feminism draws on object relations theory, which stresses the centrality of maternal presence and plenitude in the initial state of unity between mother and child, established in the first stages of childhood development, which the child will have to outgrow in the process of subject-formation But while traditional object relations theory identifies her with the stereotypical image of the self-sacrificing mother who has no interests or needs of her own, but lives only for her child, Chodorow is more interested in the mother herself, recognizing in her a certain degree of ambivalence about her role. Although Chodorow's work has been repeatedly criticized for its a-historic, a-specific approach, it remains one of the standard texts on motherhood.

GRACE, GLENN, and FORCEY's collection of essays addresses the question of what constitutes mothering, with special attention to the historical and social variations of the concept. These essays demonstrate how motherhood is a socially constructed, not a biologically determined, relationship. The essays included in this volume document and analyze the different constructions of motherhood that coexisted alongside the dominant white, middle-class, American, idealized model of motherhood in nineteenth- and twentieth-century U.S. cultures. Relying on approaches as diverse as ethnic studies, women's studies, sociology, anthropology, history, and literary studies, these essays highlight the problematic and dialectic relationship that exists between traditional and alternative ideas about motherhood, whether on the grounds of race, class, or sexual orientation. Paradigmatic of several of the studies collected here is Patricia Hill Collins's essay "Shifting the Center: Race, Class, and Feminist Theorizing about Motherhood,"which demonstrates how often feminist theories of motherhood have failed to recognize class- and race-related differences in the idea of mothering, and have identified white, middle-class women's concerns and ideals as universal. Collins suggests that focusing on the experience of women of color brings to the front very different concerns. This collection constitutes a very useful introduction to an examination of motherhood as a concept determined by historical and social specifity, as opposed to a universal, all-inclusive ideal.

The essays collected by BASSIN, HONEY, and KAPLAN explore the maternal experience from the mother's own point of view, positing her as a subject with her own needs, feelings, and interests in an attempt to rescue her from her status as object. Of particular interest is the introduction (complemented by an exhaustive bibliography), which looks extensively at the conflicting positions on motherhood within the feminist movement over the past 30 years. Contributors from diverse fields focus their attention on how motherhood is represented, drawing on psychoanalysis to discuss the psychological experience of mothering and being mothered, confronting the ways in which new achievements in medicine have influenced the meaning of motherhood, addressing specific mothering experiences in non-white, non-middle-class environments, and examining how maternal representations in visual art, literature, film, law, and technological culture have influenced women in their construction of a maternal subject. This work presents interesting and challenging ideas on the notion of the potentially subversive character of the mother as subject, which subvert long held notions, both of women and of motherhood.

KAPLAN focuses on the representation of the mother in literary and film texts in American culture. The book analyzes these representations of the maternal within three different spheres: The first is the historical sphere, in which the author charts the changing representations of motherhood from Rousseau to postmodernism. The second is the psychoanalytic sphere, which pertains to the different kinds of psychoanalytic ideas about motherhood from Freud to the most recent revisionary feminist discourses. And finally, the third sphere deals with fictional representations of the mother in North American texts from 1830 to 1990, such as *East Lynne, Herland, Stella Dallas, Now Voyager, The Handmaid's Tale,* and *Look Who's Talking.* Within the "Master Motherhood Discourse"that she identifies in white, middle-class, North American culture in the time period she has studied, Kaplan problematizes the opposing images of the mother as Angel versus the mother as Witch, and analyzes the often contradictory "mother-representations" in postmodern America, by examining both popular and feminist materials through a cultural studies perspective.

The collection of essays edited by KNOWLES and COLE is the result of the first Women and Therapy conference held in 1988 at Goddard College, titled "Woman-Defined Motherhood: A Conference for Therapists." The main aim of the conference was to define motherhood from a feminist perspective, and to examine the implications of such a definition. The essays and poems included here expose the monodimensional myth of traditional motherhood, and outline the multidimensional nature of being a mother in a woman-defined view of motherhood. Particularly interesting and valuable is the section devoted to an analysis of mother-blaming, and of the personal, social, political, and clinical issues linked to it. Perhaps more clinically oriented than the other texts introduced here, this collection is nevertheless very useful.

—DAVIDA GAVIOLI

See also Child Custody; Family; Mother-Daughter Relationships; Surrogate Motherhood

Mother Jones 1836–1930

American Activist

Fetherling, Dale, *Mother Jones, the Miners' Angel: A Portrait,* Carbondale: Southern Illinois University Press, 1974

Gilbert, Ronnie, *Ronnie Gilbert on Mother Jones; Face to Face with the Most Dangerous Woman in America,* Berkeley, California: Conari Press, 1993

Long, Priscilla, *Mother Jones, Woman Organizer, and Her Relations with Miners' Wives, Working Women, and the Suffrage Movement,* Boston: South End Press, 1976

Steel, Edward M. (ed.), *The Court-Martial of Mother Jones,* Lexington: University Press of Kentucky, 1995

The life and work of Mary Harris "Mother" Jones has suffered from lack of feminist critical attention because of her opposition to woman suffrage and her support of women's traditional roles. Deflected from her own path of motherhood and homemaking in 1867, when she lost her husband and four children to yellow fever, Jones devoted the rest of her long life to the fight for economic protection of her "boys," chiefly miners and mill workers, and their families. Her legacy also includes her speeches, significant, original rhetorical art, her correspondence, and her *Autobiography,* one of the first by a working-class American woman.

In what is still the standard biography of Mother Jones, FETHERLING depicts Mary Harris Jones as an economic warrior whose ubiquitous presence and organizational skills made her a legend among American workers. While presenting a well-researched analysis of historical events in her life, Fetherling develops a multifaceted characterization of his subject: the endorsement of violence contrasted with the "armchair philosophy of nonviolence," the asceticism, the prostitution charges, the courage, and the individualistic stance against all institutions, including at times the Socialists and the United Mine Workers of America (UMWA). If his is not a woman-centered approach, it is rigorously researched, balanced, and intelligent, and it seems to do justice to its subject. The author addresses the issue of Jones's complex attitudes to women, from her opposition to suffrage to her variously-formulated assertion that women could play a valuable part in government, could "shake it up," could prevent World War I. He concludes that for Mother Jones, all other struggles were subjugated to the great one: the economic welfare and security of the working-class family. Fetherling provides a comprehensive source guide, including archival collections, government documents, pamphlets and labor union proceedings, and theses and dissertations up to 1974.

Although LONG's title indicates her focus on women, her largely admiring study, a brief book of 40 pages including notes and references, criticizes Jones directly only once, as Long concludes that her lack of concern about union practices toward women, and about men's attitudes toward women, marred her committed advocacy of the working class. The author levels her strongest critique against a society that has ignored or neglected working-class heroes; she sees Jones as utilizing in her political persona the traditional role of motherhood, fighting for the traditional family against those who would exploit it, and retaining conservative views on women's place in society, views that, in fact, matched those of the men and women she led.

Twenty years after Long's complaint about the difficulty of finding works by or about heroes of the labor movement, many of the egregious gaps are being filled. Of special note in this case are the definitive collections of primary materials by STEEL, who provides for each an extended and substantive introduction. In the book cited, for example, this introduction runs to 95 pages: Steel sets the 1913 court-martial of Mother Jones against the background of the Paint Creek and Cabin Creek strikes of 1912–13, in which she played such a crucial role. The author describes and illustrates his subject's independent spirit and her flair for dramatic action, and he contrasts her actions (empowering, crusading for civil rights, organizing women to support male wage earners) with the paternalism of even the most benevolent of the mine operators. Steel's account is detailed, conscientious, and fully annotated, yet written with narrative skill, and it paints a picture of an extraordinary woman, although its broad focus is on union, state, and national politics.

One of the chief interests of GILBERT's 40-page introduction and substantial notes to her one-woman play lies in its partisan approach. Socialist in orientation, Gilbert gives us an exploration of the moral and political struggles of Mother Jones that is both emotionally committed and honestly probing. Although her tone is not scholarly, and at times veers into the sarcastic and the colloquial, Gilbert also raises important questions about the male labor leaders, critiques the tunnel vision of the suffragists, and emphasizes and explicates the oppositional positions of the suffrage and labor movements. Disturbed by the lack of attention paid to the gifts and example of Mother Jones, Gilbert hopes, ultimately, to see her claimed by feminists, as they continue to challenge a patriarchal society. Incidentally, the play that follows is composed mainly of Mother Jones's own words.

Recent years have seen an extraordinary proliferation of books on Mother Jones for the middle-school and young adult reader. From among several authors, works by Linda Atkinson, Madelyn Horton, Judith Josephson, and Betsy Kraft have received particularly enthusiastic attention.

—MARY O'CONNOR

Multinational Corporations

Dobbing, John (ed.), *Infant Feeding: Anatomy of a Controversy 1973–1984,* London and New York: Springer-Verlag, 1988

Farley, Jennie, and Alice Hanson Cook (eds.), *Women Workers in Fifteen Countries,* Ithaca, New York: ILR Press, Cornell University, 1985

Fuentes, Annette, and Barbara Ehrenreich, *Women in the Global Factory,* Boston: South End Press, 1983

Kumar, Krishna, *Transnational Enterprises: Their Impact on Third World Societies and Cultures,* Boulder, Colorado: Westview Press, 1980

Nash, June C., and Marcía Patricia Fernández-Kelly, *Women, Men and the International Division of Labor,* Albany: State University of New York Press, 1983

Women Workers in Multinational Enterprises in Developing Countries, Geneva: International Labor Office, 1985

The multinational corporation became controversial in the international system in the 1970s because of the dual role that it seemed to play. On the one hand it was portrayed as an engine of growth for developing countries in need of foreign investments to spur economic growth in various industries. The rise of multinational corporations provided employment, managerial skills training, and income for various economies. At the same time these corporations were also viewed as evil mechanisms that drove away local entrepreneurial skills, stunted domestic savings and investment, depressed wages, and widened the gap between the rich and the poor. The evils of multinational operations in the Third World are exemplified in the classic infant formula controversy examined by DOBBING in great detail. Dobbing's work is an excellent coverage of the issues from many angles.

It was not until the 1980s that some attention was paid to the plight of women in multinational enterprises. KUMAR's book of readings contains an article on female workers in multinational corporations, especially in one classic case study of the electronics industry in Malaysia. However, most of the readings focus on the impact of the corporations on society as they affect the relationships among social classes, the working class, and the entrepreneurial class. The readings address the ways social and economic inequities and ethnic stratification have an impact on culture, knowledge and skills, and cultural identity.

The International Labor Organization and the United Nations Industrial Development Organization contracted studies regarding the impact of multinational corporations, especially in Third World development, and some of the data include women. One study cited by NASH shows that in Asia alone, more than 300,000 women labor in electronics plants in export processing zones. The role of gender in the growth of multinational corporations should not be underestimated. The various studies in Nash's book show that young women workers have a tendency to be segregated into the new industrial compounds where they are subject to the patriarchical control of managers. And because of the loss of their traditional sources of employment in agriculture, they often have no alternative but to be dependent upon factory work, which offers no security of position, and no long-lasting employment. Most of the readings show that the global integration of production brought about by multinational operations has sharpened the inequalities between women and men, and between minorities and dominant racial and ethnic groups. And the readings seem to point out that the liberation of female workers as women and as workers can only be achieved when they struggle against capitalist, imperialist, and patriarchal exploitation.

The study on women workers in multinational enterprises in developing countries conducted by the INTERNATIONAL LABOUR OFFICE shows the ways in which women have moved from reproduction to production. It provides a historical view, showing that women are not new in the labor market, since they were employed by the colonial corporations in extractive industries, mining, lumbering, and the trade in raw commodities. They went into plantation agriculture as well, and lately employment of women by multinational corporations in agriculture and agribusiness abound. Women in the manufacturing and service sectors are also investigated, and data is provided for various parts of the world in comparative perspective. Their terms and conditions of employment vary, as well as the degree of unionization. The work takes a positive perspective on the effects of multinational corporations by indicating that they help improve women's status, provide them with more opportunity for upward mobility, and give them a greater degree of independence and a wider range of social activities.

FARLEY's work is a collection of essays about women in such countries as the former Soviet Union, the People's Republic of China, and Yugoslavia. The collection is mostly from developed economies, although there is one essay on low-income countries, which discusses the developing world. Although it is a western-centered work, some of the conclusions drawn are also true about female workers in the Third World. Women's changing perceptions of their roles and the extraordinary increase in their participation in the paid labor force, as well as the substantial gap between women's and men's earnings, are well documented here. But more importantly, there is a focus on the agonizing delays in their acceptance as workers, and the major difficulty they face at home to get men to share in the home care and child care.

FUENTES and EHRENREICH's book examines the current status of women in the global factory and concludes the same things that were said in the 1970s and the 1980s. Factory women are the unseen assemblers of consumer goods. These women on the global assembly line are paid lower subsistence wages, which are justified by the rationale that they are supplementers to household income rather than the major breadwinners. Because they are perceived to be docile and easily manipulated, they are given boring, repetitive assembly work, based on the notion of women's natural patience and manual dexterity. Thus they are relegated to work in the electronics, textiles, and food processing industries. Often they are subjected to health hazards, stress and high anxiety, and even sexual harassment. Their jobs do not have stability, and therefore the women join the ranks of marginal employees, who are in fear of losing their jobs for whatever cause or reason. These abuses show the need for organizing for better wages and working conditions. The book goes beyond the descriptive and becomes prescriptive, suggesting the use of organized pressure, information exchanges among Third World countries, and creation of direct links among women of the world. Some of these actions began to take place as a result of the Fourth International Conference on Women held in Beijing.

—CECILIA G. MANRIQUE

Munro, Alice 1931–

Canadian Writer

Blodgett, E.D., *Alice Munro*, Boston: Twayne, 1988

Carrington, Ildikó de Papp, *Controlling the Uncontrollable: The Fiction of Alice Munro*, Dekalb: Northern Illinois University Press, 1989

Carscallen, James, *The Other Country: Patterns in the Writings of Alice Munro,* Toronto: E.C.W. Press, 1993
MacKendrick, Louis K. (ed.), *Probable Fictions: Alice Munro's Narrative Acts,* Toronto: E.C.W. Press, 1983
Martin, W.R., *Alice Munro: Paradox and Parallel,* Edmonton: University of Alberta Press, 1987
Redekop, Magdalene, *Mothers and Other Clowns: The Stories of Alice Munro,* London and New York: Routledge, 1992
Ross, Catherine Sheldrick, *Alice Munro: A Double Life,* E.C.W. Press, 1992

It has been said that Alice Munro's fiction invites analysis of content rather than form, and yet the criticism associated with the Munro canon would seem to refute the claim. The essays in the collection edited by MacKENDRICK, for instance, specifically address questions of style, structure, and genre to emphasize the risks Munro takes with linear narrative. The "mystery" behind the "real" in Munro's stories is often signalled by linguistic texture, and the essays in this volume reveal the enormous creative range of her work, as does an interview in which Munro discusses her own concerns with the art of creating fiction.

Munro's stories are often set in southern Ontario and told with a familiarity that brings an authentic, personal quality to her work. The life of Alice Munro is delineated in a small illustrated biography written by ROSS. Despite Munro's statement about *Lives of Girls and Women* that "this novel is autobiographical in form but not in fact," an intimate relation between the life and the fiction can be discerned. Biography is therefore of interest. It is usual to divide Munro's life, so far, into three parts: her young life in Wingham; her two years at the University of Western Ontario, and her departure with her first husband to British Columbia, where she lived for 20 years; and finally her return to southwestern Ontario, where she has resided since. This biography provides a useful account of Munro's girlhood in "Lower Town" where, Ross suggests, Munro perfected a mask of ordinariness with which to shield the secret world of the imagination in the community of outcasts in which she lived. It follows her formative years at the University of Western Ontario as an English major, and her struggle to balance writing and parenting. The work traces the development of her writing as a movement away from the personal and toward the wider, and perhaps universal, canvas.

In a comprehensive study of the Munro corpus, MARTIN presents a work designed to be of use to the common reader. Denying any particular critical approach, other than that of close reading, Martin, nevertheless, adheres to a notion that the reader can be "unprejudiced and attentive" while simultaneously remaining paradoxically passive in order to "receive" meaning. Martin's work is often simply descriptive, but it functions as a useful introduction.

REDEKOP's work is also comprehensive, but here Munro's experimentation has led to an iconoclastic approach to criticism. Describing itself as a narrative criticism, this stimulating study is simultaneously an appreciation of Munro's developing aesthetic and the author's own understanding of that aesthetic. The work argues for a relation between the hallucinatory quality of Munro's magical realism and a perceived obsession with mothering. Her devastation of patriarchal institutions remains unassociated with any overt feminist agenda in Redkop's study, but the book celebrates the courageous comedy with which Munro's stories make their way to a "progress of love."

BLODGETT contends that the art of creating fiction is the subject of Munro's work, and in an exciting poststructuralist analysis, the author eschews the obvious appeal of Munro's fiction, with its empathy for ordinary lives, to view her primarily as a super realist. Demonstrating Munro's concern with the role of the narrator as a figure who orders material and establishes relationships, Blodgett defines Munro's fundamental structure, in her early work, as that of an interplay between the continuous and the discontinuous, so that, if analogy and metaphor lead to relationships which may only be illusory, then Munro's concern must lie with the illusory relation between self and being. Exploring the way in which the narrators of Munro's fiction reveal their perceptions of self and how they accommodate change, Blodgett reveals that their recollections of the past ultimately prove its illusory quality. Munro's canon tests the limits of storytelling.

CARSCALLEN considers the form of Munro's work specifically in relation to its mythic patterning. Dividing his book into two parts, Carscallen first delineates an interpretive model for Munro's stories. In Part Two he extends his theory from individual stories to focus on groupings perceived in terms of discernable patterns. Carscallen contends that, consciously or unconsciously, Munro creates, within the body of her work, an analogue to the cycles of sacred text—calling, achievement, failure, chaos. Within an accepted variation, the cycles are seen as consistent throughout the Munro canon.

CARRINGTON, however, in a first American book-length study of Munro's fiction, demonstrates the unity of her canon via a paradoxical theme: controlling the uncontrollable—a theme inextricably linked to Munro's personal and cultural ambivalence toward language. This ambivalence is reflected in her often voyeuristic narrators and protagonists, who divide themselves, and their retrospective points of view, in an attempt to control a suddenly fractured world. Carrington explores Munro's repeated words and metaphors, in particular recurrent metaphors of splitting, such as lightning or earthquakes, to insist that they are intrinsically linked to Munro's conception of the artist who can only resist fragmentation, in a chaotic and uncontrollable world, by an act of self division. Her characters struggle for control amid a series of offensives on experience that is perpetually humiliating. The characters' struggles are part of an ongoing artistic process enacted by way of a wealth of biblical, literary, operatic, and historical allusions.

—JAN PILDITCH

Murdoch, Iris 1919–

British Writer

Byatt, A.S., *Degrees of Freedom: The Early Novels of Iris Murdoch,* London: Chatto and Windus, and New York: Barnes and Noble, 1965

Conradi, Peter J., *Iris Murdoch: The Saint and the Artist,* revised edition, London: Macmillan, 1985; New York: St. Martin's Press, 1986

Johnson, Deborah, *Iris Murdoch,* Brighton: Harvester, and Bloomington: Indiana University Press, 1987

Rabinovitz, Rubin, *Iris Murdoch,* New York: Columbia University Press, 1968

Spear, Hilda D., *Iris Murdoch,* London: Macmillan, and New York: St. Martin's Press, 1995

Todd, Richard, *Iris Murdoch,* London and New York: Methuen, 1984

Iris Murdoch herself has explained that she generally writes from the point of view of a man because she feels that, while a woman is always a woman, a man represents ordinary human beings. What might at first seem to be an anti-feminist stance appears to have created for the critics who have written about her a difficulty of nomenclature. Rabinovitz constantly refers to her as "Miss Murdoch," with the occasional "Iris Murdoch" thrown in; more surprisingly, Byatt does the same; yet neither refers to men novelists as "Mr." Johnson, for different reasons, was exercised as to how to name her author, and states that "with some hesitation" she chose to use "Iris Murdoch" throughout her book. Conradi, Todd, and Spear, perhaps bowing to modern feminist demands, have all accepted that, for a major novelist of our time, the use of "Murdoch" is more acceptable, with the occasional use of "Iris Murdoch" as well.

To some extent RABINOVITZ demonstrates the problems that some male critics have with Murdoch's novels: she is not a feminist writer, and her protagonists are generally men. He is reduced, therefore, to a cursory discussion of philosophic ideas in Murdoch's writing, and his comments on the novels rarely rise above an outline of the plot.

Published three years earlier than Rabinovitz, BYATT's full-length study was written when only seven novels had been published, so it is essentially limited to a discussion of Murdoch's early work. As its title suggests, the book explores the idea of freedom, particularly in personal relationships, but also in social, and to some extent, political contexts. She emphasizes that freedom is only significant when captivity and domination are also present, and she examines the various kinds of oppression and subjugation—physical, mental, and spiritual—that Murdoch imposes upon her characters, particularly the women. A separate chapter is devoted to each of the seven novels, and a final chapter offers a broad critical comment on the novels thus far. Byatt is by no means merely adulatory; she praises Murdoch's narrative originality and vigor, her respect for the individual, the reality of her world, and her marvelous comic vision, but she criticizes what she sees as the poorly integrated use of symbol and action, and the often careless use of cliché and overworked keywords.

By the time TODD's study was published in 1984, there were 21 novels to write about. Todd maintains rightly that Murdoch is not interested in radical feminism. He fails, however, to comment on the more subtle feminism that shows us the plight of the many women characters—generally minor—dominated by their marital partners. Murdoch's oeuvre is here divided into four phases, which Todd himself admits are to some extent arbitrary. The most interesting aspect of this book are the various themes that Todd begins to discuss—the relationship between money and power, the feyness of many of the girls or young women, the erotic overstepping of the barriers of age, gender, and kinship, the complexity of the moral dilemmas within the novels, and what Todd himself describes as "the nature of the symbol-making process." The most irritating aspect is that these themes are not pursued. Instead, Todd, rather like Rabinovitz before him, spends a great deal of time outlining the complicated plots of the novels.

In a much more adventurous and considerably longer book, CONRADI examines a number of themes that bind together certain of Murdoch's novels. Of the critical books under consideration, this is the most academic, although that is not to say that it is difficult or esoteric in its style or content. Conradi admires particularly Murdoch's use of the male first-person narrators, and the sense of veracity of representation that she achieves with them, a feat which he is probably correct in asserting is unusual for a female writer. At the same time, he emphasizes particularly what he suggests is the essential truth of Murdoch's depiction of her characters in general: the eccentricities that make us at first believe that such people cannot exist, and make us later realize that they are only too real. In a very balanced "Conclusion," Conradi dismisses the more outlandish criticisms of Murdoch's work, which have castigated it, for instance, for not being like Tolstoy or George Eliot, and he avoids any submission to "the anarchy of deconstruction." He then proceeds to outline the more positive aspects of the novels—the recognizable characters, the comedy, the direct address to the readers, and the ability to integrate the inner and outer worlds.

JOHNSON is the first, and so far the only, author to write a book-length study of Murdoch from a feminist perspective. She draws attention at the outset to the way in which gender identity is continually questioned and gender boundaries transgressed. Like Conradi, although from a different emotional angle, she discusses how the male narrators inevitably place themselves at center stage but, taking her illustration from *The Italian Girl*, she suggests that their point of view is frequently undermined by the women. Throughout her novels, Murdoch is shown placing her female characters in emotionally difficult and miserable predicaments, while the men's lives are generally conducted with some degree of self-confidence. There is an excellent discussion of *The Bell* from a female-centered perspective, in which Johnson shows Dora overcoming her husband's patriarchal desires and finally escaping from the male domination of her life.

In the most recent book on Murdoch, SPEAR discusses all the novels except the latest, *Jackson's Dilemma*, which was published after her book was put into print. She examines particularly the theoretical dimension of the novels, showing how Murdoch employs her dramatic effects to give the reader a double perspective, in which the action both takes place and is observed taking place. From this she proceeds to illustrate how dual themes and reversals of themes proliferate throughout the novels: the captors are the ones in moral and spiritual captivity; Good and Evil are never the straightforward white and black of romance; religion and philosophy can fail to offer solace. In giving an overview of 25 novels, Spear has attempted to suggest Murdoch's chronological progression, and in her conclusion she sums up what she sees as the good qualities, as well as the problems, of the whole canon of Murdoch's work.

—HILDA D. SPEAR

Music: Classical

Blackmer, Corinne, and Patricia Juliana Smith (eds.), *En Travesti: Women, Gender Subversion, and Opera*, New York: Columbia University Press, 1995

Citron, Marcia, *Gender and the Musical Canon*, Cambridge and New York: Cambridge University Press, 1993

Clément, Catherine, *Opera, or, The Undoing of Women*, translated Betsy Wing, Minneapolis: University of Minnesota Press, 1988; London: Virago, 1989

Cook, Susan C., and Judy S. Tsou (eds.), *Cecilia Reclaimed: Feminist Perspectives on Gender and Music*, Urbana: University of Illinois Press, 1994

McClary, Susan, *Feminine Endings: Music, Gender, and Sexuality*, Minneapolis: University of Minnesota Press, 1991

Solie, Ruth (ed.), *Musicology and Difference: Gender and Sexuality in Music Scholarship*, Berkeley: University of California Press, 1993

Scholars who have approached gender issues in music have tended to adopt one of two complementary avenues of research. While one practice seeks to expose new facts regarding women in music and illuminate their oft-forgotten lives through archival studies, the second adopts a more interpretive and speculative posture in attempts to understand gender roles and their relationship to and presentation through music. The secondary literature reviewed in this essay is representative of the second domain of study.

The modern study of women in classical music begins with CLÉMENT. The Frenchwoman's theories remain problematic for many American scholars, yet few would deny the seminal force of Clément's book. For Clément, opera powerfully transmits masculine, hegemonic paradigms. Music, a mental soporific, bypasses the rational thought of spectators, and, therefore, audiences uncritically accept the masculine world encoded in opera. Through feminist recasting of libretti, Clément demonstrates how opera punishes women for their supposed transgressions. Her critics typically argue that Clément's analyses neglect comic opera, in which women typically fare much better than in serious opera, and that, as a literary critic, she fails to engage the music itself.

BLACKMER and SMITH respond to Clément in another fashion. Rather than focusing on the ways in which women are undone in opera, the essays in their anthology explore the "unparalleled range of opportunities for women to subvert and, often, overturn traditional gender roles." Their arguments are not confined to libretti, but rather expand to include more abstract musical, social, and psychosexual phenomena such as diva-worship, the voice of the castrati, and the portrayal of feminine eroticism. Perhaps because almost half of the contributors style themselves as English or literature professors, Blackmer and Smith's book bring a methodological freshness to opera criticism. For that very reason, however, the authors' command of facts is occasionally shaky, and their engagement with the music is limited.

The anthology has been a preferred choice among gender scholars in music, and SOLIE brings together many of the most respected names in musicology in order to appraise the significance of difference throughout the history of music. In essays whose subject matter encompasses material as disparate as medieval chant, the music of Robert Schumann and Johannes Brahms, and the music criticism of Roland Barthes, the authors examine and question the gendered aspects of musical and musicological discourse. The finest essays (those by Leo Treitler, Carolyn Abbate, Lawrence Kramer, and Susan

McClary, to select but a few) chart unexplored territories and speculate about the ideological constraints in society and musicology that have actively worked to forestall such research in the past. This book is a standard text in graduate courses; likewise its articles have become compulsory reading for specialists.

Although the individual essays are often inspiring, COOK and TSOU's volume lacks a sense of direction. Despite the congratulatory tone of the title and introduction, the book fails to map an agenda for feminist criticism, although the reader may find valuable research in areas as diverse as the English Renaissance, women in seventeenth-century France, American modernism, and even images of women in rap music.

CITRON delineates the methods by which hegemonic male paradigms have suppressed the activity of women in the realm of professional music. Canons have received extensive treatment in many branches of the humanities, and Citron draws widely upon interdisciplinary and feminist research. Although the study of music is often resistant to methodologies cultivated in other fields, analyses of canon formation from other disciplines prove germane to Citron's task. Juxtaposing the personal psychological issues women must confront against the well-documented ideological nature of the public canon, Citron exposes the complementary aspects of a dual mechanism designed to suppress women: a public canon and an individual psychological assault upon women who transgress societal boundaries in order to compose.

McCLARY's book has proven to be the most controversial of the works listed here, but the truest estimate of her success is that many of her conclusions now seem commonplace. She begins by arguing that gender discrimination and even misogyny pervade all branches of musical study—music theory, music history, and representations of gender and sexuality in western music itself. Although gender studies in music are often confined to sociological, cultural, or political treatment of music and society, McClary demonstrates that direct engagement with music may fruitfully coexist in the same book with these other areas of inquiry. Her success in "reading" Absolute Music of the nineteenth century and revealing its hidden ideological content is particularly noteworthy, as is her analysis of Bizet's *Carmen*, in which she displays her virtuosity in relating issues musical and cultural.

—DONALD B. CHAE

Music: Folk/Traditional

Block, Adrienne Fried, and Carol Neuls-Bates (eds.), *Women in American Music: A Bibliography of Music and Literature,* London and Westport, Connecticut: Greenwood, 1979

Ericson, Margaret D., *Women and Music: A Selective Annotated Bibliography on Women and Gender Issues in Music: 1987–1992,* London: Prentice International, and New York: G.K. Hall, 1996

Giglio, Virginia, *Southern Cheyenne Women's Songs,* Norman: University of Oklahoma Press, 1994

Marshall, Kimberly (ed.), *Rediscovering the Muses: Women's Musical Traditions,* Boston: Northeastern University Press, 1993

MARSHALL's book tries to uncover an obscure past, a history with great potential to influence the direction of the future. The purpose of this book is to restore to history some of the forgotten traditions of ritual and dance music that were created and performed by women. Most of the essays in this work concern musical cultures that have left little, if any, notated music, such as those of ancient Israel and Egypt, of Australian Aboriginals, of Central Javanese "wayang," of Classical Greece, and of the Byzantine Empire. The articles on European music in this collection bring together many types of sources to highlight the musical work of women. The inclusion of such diverse topics in one book provides examples of female musical activity at many points within a continuum ranging from purely oral traditions to precisely notated compositions. The title of this work alone evokes a powerful image of female creativity, which has been, for the most part, omitted from the historical record. The essays in this book attempt to balance the scale, to show that the creative abilities accorded the symbols and mythologies of female musicians have been, and continue to be, translated into real musical cultures.

ERICSON provides an annotated guide to publications issued during the period between 1987 and 1992, which investigates issues with regard to women, gender, and traditional music. While this bibliography does not include biographical studies of individual female musicians, it does bring to light publications (including books, essays, and periodicals) that consider not only the collective musical activities of women in history and contemporary cultural contexts, but also the manner in which gender, as a sociocultural construct, has been an influential factor in the formation and production of musical culture. This also influences a woman's role in relation to that culture. This book contains over 1,800 citations to sources on women, gender, and music.

Editors BLOCK and BATES provide a bibliography about American women in traditional music from colonial times to the present. Women have contributed in important ways to musical life in the United States. The study of women in music is a relatively new field. The focus of this book is on the contributions of women to traditional music.

GIGLIO's book focuses on the Native American tribe of the Cheyenne. Women are shown to have made many musical accomplishments. However, this musical culture has little actual notated music. The Cheyenne culture is rich with ritual and dance music that was created and learned through performance, without requiring a written score. Women were often quite active in preparing and leading performances of such music. Unfortunately, most of their endeavors are not acknowledged because they did not produce notated repertoire. The purpose of Giglio's book is to restore some of the rich history of the Cheyenne, and their almost forgotten traditions of music and dance.

—SUSAN M. TAYLOR

Music: Jazz and Blues

Bourgeois, Anna Stong, *Blueswomen: Profiles of 37 Early Performers, with an Anthology of Lyrics, 1920–1945,* Jefferson, North Carolina: McFarland, 1996

Dahl, Linda, *Stormy Weather: The Music and Lives of a Century of Jazzwomen,* London: Quartet, and New York: Pantheon, 1984

Gourse, Leslie, *Madame Jazz: Contemporary Women Instrumentalists,* New York: Oxford University Press, 1995

Harrison, Daphne Duval, *Black Pearls: Blues Queens of the 1920s,* New Brunswick, New Jersey: Rutgers University Press, 1988

Placksin, Sally, *American Women in Jazz: 1900 to the Present; Their Words, Lives, and Music,* New York: Seaview, 1982

Unterbrink, Mary, *Jazz Women at the Keyboard,* Jefferson, North Carolina: McFarland, 1983

Jazz and blues music overlap. Both evolved in the early twentieth century as parts of the culture of black Americans, especially those in and around New Orleans. Jazz was predominantly instrumental music, with strong rhythm and frequent improvisation. "The blues," expressing sadness, anger, and distress, were mostly sung, but often with an instrumental accompaniment. Blues belongs as much to folk music as to jazz, but jazz musicians have found the simple 12-bar blues chord sequence a very fertile inspiration for improvisation. Women have been active, although not prominant (except as blues singers) in both genres.

PLACKSIN's pioneering study is extraordinarily comprehensive, combining history, biography, a cross-section of women active in the 1970s, and 20 pages of discography. There are brief biographical sketches of 66 women (and incidental references to far more), relying extensively on interviews as well as printed sources. There are 43 photographs. The material is organized by decades beginning with the 1920s, and each is introduced by a brief but well-focused sketch of developments both in and out of music. There is a fascinating account of the International Sweethearts of Rhythm, which originated at Piney Woods School in Mississippi in 1937.

DAHL's book parallels Placksin's in its comprehensive scope but gives more attention to people and developments after 1960. An interesting chapter analyzes sex-role stereotyping in the choice of instruments—why are wind instruments perceived as more suitable for males? The power of discrimination is illustrated by the contrasting careers of Blanche Calloway and her brother Cab.

Dahl's study is organized topically rather than chronologically, but much of it, like Placksin's, tells stories about individual women. A section on female vocalists covers both the blues craze of the 1920s and the later band "canaries." An overview chapter on the contemporary scene is followed by profiles of ten active jazzwomen, based on interviews done between 1979 and 1981. Of the 15 photographs, the most striking shows the family orchestra that gave Lester Young his start—the other four members being all women. There is a 48-page discography.

The book by HARRISON complements those by Placksin and Dahl. A superb chapter looks at the "Blues Decade" of the 1920s from the perspective of "Toby": the Theater Owners' Booking Association, which organized live stage performances by black artists. Harrison's discussion dramatizes the opportunities as well as the exploitation. There follows an excellent history of the "race records" boom of the 1920s. The chapter on "Blues from the Black Woman's Perspective" reflects careful listening to numerous records. Four chapters present biographies of Sippie Wallace, Victoria Spivey, Edith Wilson, and Alberta Hunter.

BOURGEOIS concentrates on women in blues in the period ending 1945. An 18-page discussion of themes of women's blues enumerates relationships, drugs and alcohol, illness and disease, superstition, work, and racism. Most of the book provides biographies of the 37 major figures, with much attention to their lyrics. There is an eight-page discography.

GOURSE's book argues that improvement in women's opportunities and participation in instrumental jazz has been striking since the late 1970s. This book is primarily a cross-section of women active in jazz in the 1980s and early 1990s, mostly presented as profiles. Twenty-eight women are named in chapter titles, but a vast number of others find mention. The book is mostly based on interviews. Brief but interesting chapters deal with women in the business end of jazz, and with "love, marriage, and motherhood." There are 30 photographs.

UNTERBRINK's earlier study of female jazz pianists follows a similar format. There are brief overview sections on jazz beginnings, New Orleans, and 52nd Street, but the text is mainly profiles. Fifty-five women are featured. Most were still active and available to be interviewed. There are 30 portrait photographs.

—PAUL B. TRESCOTT

Music: Rock

Gaar, Gillian G., *She's a Rebel: The History of Women in Rock and Roll,* Seattle, Washington: Seal Press, 1992; London: Blandford, 1993

McDonnell, Evelyn, *Rock She Wrote: Women Write about Rock, Rap and Pop,* London: Plexus, and New York: Delta, 1995

O'Brien, Lucy, *She Bop: The Definitive History of Women in Rock, Pop, and Soul,* London and New York: Penguin, 1995

Raphael, Amy, *Never Mind the Bollocks: Women Rewrite Rock,* London: Virago Press, 1995; as *Grrrls: Viva Rock Divas,* New York: St. Martin's/Griffin, 1996

Reynolds, Simon, and Joy Press, *The Sex Revolts: Gender, Rebellion, and Rock'n'Roll,* Cambridge, Massachusetts: Harvard University Press, and London: Serpent's Tail, 1995

If rock and roll were indeed the soul kitchen, it would seem that men have been the only chefs for several decades. Recent scholarship, however, has shown that women have played an integral and essential part of the movement since its slow birth out of blues and rhythm and blues from the 1920s to the 1950s. While today, women rockers grace nearly as many covers of rock periodicals, such as *Spin* or *Rolling Stone,* as do their male counterparts, their treatment via "trends" and "charts" fails to show a comprehensive view of the experience of women in rock and roll.

GAAR's survey considers prototypical women in rock as they lived through and created the distinct phases of rock's evolution, beginning with rhythm and blues (Big Mama Thornton, Lady Bo), and moving to girl groups (Shirelles, Shangri-Las), revolutionary Motown and folk rock vocalists (Martha Reeves, Aretha Franklin, Janis Joplin, Joan Baez), women's emergent, independent identities (Holly Near, Joan Armatrading), punk (Patti Smith, Kate Bush) and post-punk (Chrissie Hynde, Laurie Anderson). Gaar then considers current modern artists as image makers (Madonna) and image breakers (from Suzanne Vega and Michelle Shocked to Queen Latifah and Salt-n-Pepa). Gaar so differentiates the experiences of women rockers in order to fight the tendency to lump all female performers together, and then move them to the margins. She includes biographical information, and the social, cultural, and political issues that were central in each artist's time.

Perhaps even more marginalized than women in rock is the experience of female journalists who have been writing about rock, rap, soul, and blues. McDONNELL has compiled a playful, yet meaningful sampling of the writers, and autobiographical essays from women as creators and performers, "on the scene" essays which have covered musical trends over the years, the narrative experiences of (backstage) fans, the "dissection" of male rock heroes and their iconographies, the exposition of sexism and racism in music, and analyses of the creative processes of female rock journalists. It is a valuable resource for those who would pursue varied and non-mainstream sources, or early influential writers like Ellen Willis. The collected essays range from the humorous "On Stage With Kiss in My Maidenform Bra," to the historical-cultural "Madonna: Soul Sister or Plantation Mistress?"

O'BRIEN's book, like Gaar's, is a historical continuum of women in rock, which analyzes women's presence in the early movements (gospel, blues), as well as their roles in the spin-off trends that have occurred (jazz, swing, disco, pop, rap). O'Brien focuses mostly on the experiences of New York and London, and includes the same artists as Gaar, but she also includes an interesting discussion of an international focus—the influence of rock in Mali and Zimbabwe, among others. She has documented the struggle between the female rocker's public persona, an image often strategically created, and her private struggles to keep her creative psyche intact in a typically inconstant and sexist business. O'Brien also offers a more in-depth inclusion of women who work on the periphery of the stage as managers, executives, publicists, and producers.

In the aftermath of the punk movement, women post-punkers in the 1990s felt a particular sense of deflation and abandonment. Out of these ashes, they created Riot Grrrl, a raucous and rebellious musical movement that continued to fight for political and social causes on distinctly female terms. RAPHAEL's book selects a handful of those who are continuing in the counter-cultural Riot Grrrl tradition, as well as those who are creating contemporaneous expressions, like Queercore and New Wave of New Wave: Courtney Love, Echobelly's Madan and Smith, Bjork, Veruca Salt's Post and Gordon, Raincoat's Birch, Kim Gordon, Sister George's Ellyot Dragon, Huggy Bear, Belly's Donnelly, Doll's Hogg, Kristin Hersh, and Liz Phair. The introduction is written by Debbie Harry. Raphael's compilation of interview essays is a compelling blend of the artists' autobiographical reflections and the defiant attitude that inspires them to storm the rock arena.

Using a psychoanalytic approach, REYNOLDS and PRESS uncover the subliminated images of repression and rebellion in the interplay between gender, sexuality and mainstream rock from the 1960s onward. Their critical analysis is three-fold: first, how male rock artists (Led Zeppelin, Jim Morrison, the Rolling Stones) typify women's connections with the eternal whore in the creation of their own archetypal mythic identities; second, how other male rock artists (Jimmie Hendrix, Pink Floyd, the Birds), with their oedipally styled lyrics and music, regress into the eternal mother and her "oceanic womb;" and third, how women enact their own gender rebellions through either machismo (Patti Smith), catharsis (Janis Joplin), mysticism (Nicks and Bush) or androgyny and masquerade (Madonna, Queen Latifah). Even if the language of psychoanalysis seems a bit heavy-handed at times, the energetic language and interesting studies certainly question whether "good old time rock and roll" was ever just that.

—ANNMARIE PHILLIPS

Musicians

Baldauf-Berdes, Jane, *Women Musicians of Venice: Musical Foundations, 1525–1855*, Oxford: Clarendon Press, 1993

Bowers, Jane, and Judith Tick (eds.), *Women Making Music: The Western Art Tradition*, London: Macmillan, and Urbana: University of Illinois Press, 1986

Hyde, Derek, *Newfound Voices: Women in Nineteenth-Century English Music*, Liskeard: Belvedere Press, 1984

Kendrick, Robert, *Celestial Sirens: Nuns and Their Music in Early Modern Milan*, Oxford: Clarendon Press, and New York: Oxford University Press, 1996

Monson, Craig, *Disembodied Voices: Music and Culture in an Early Modern Italian Convent*, Berkeley: University of California Press, 1995

O'Brien, Lucy, *She Bop: The Definitive History of Women in Rock, Pop, and Soul*, London and New York: Penguin, 1995

Pendle, Karin (ed.), *Women and Music: A History*, Bloomington: Indiana University Press, 1991

The first initiatives into musicological gender issues were primarily compensatory studies, that is, they engaged in a search for forgotten data needed to illuminate the lives of forgotten female musicians. Because the categories of traditional musical historiography undervalue the contributions and accomplishments of female musical activity, the scholars who had undertaken the compensatory archival research were forced either to superimpose the women's history onto traditional historiographic models, or to formulate new methodologies for the study of women. Through a negotiation of the tensions described above, the most successful of the books reviewed here challenge prevailing musicological models and thought.

BOWERS and TICK provide an excellent initiative in understanding the contributions of women throughout western musical history. Although the editors do not intend to produce a comprehensive historical narrative, the contributors to this volume assess the work of women in different geographical areas and historical eras. Some essays introduce the lives of important female composers. Barbara Strozzi (1619–ca.70), Clara Schumann (1819–96), and Ruth Crawford Seeger (1901–53) are treated by leading scholars in individual essays. Other essays discuss women's participation in musical life in specific times and places. The finest of these, by Anthony Newcomb and Julie Anne Sadie, are concerned with female musicians in sixteenth-century Italy and seventeenth- and early eighteenth-century France, respectively.

Like Bowers and Tick, PENDLE's anthology traces the history of women in music, and fully a third of her work is dedicated to modern music, particularly in English-speaking countries. Conceived as a textbook, Pendle's treatment of historical periods is painted in broad strokes. The seventeenth and eighteenth centuries, for example, are discussed in a single essay. Informative essays on women in popular music, blues, and jazz might be useful as introductions to the subjects. A final section groups articles on patronage, feminist aesthetics, and women in non-western cultures; thus, Pendle encompasses a very broad range of gender issues.

In the last few years, authors have favored studying the contributions of female musicians in particular cities. KENDRICK's book, which explores the musical life of Milanese nuns, is the finest in this genre. He sets out to outline the ways by which nuns attempted to establish musical space in which they could find spiritual fulfillment, despite strict religious guidelines and the often oppressive rule of a succession of archbishops. He reconstructs the repertory of Milanese female houses, illustrates the musical life of the sisters, and outlines the sociological, cultural, and economic importance of the "celestial sirens" to Milanese life. Building his conclusions upon such research in neglected archives, Kendrick renders the accepted historiographic basis of sixteenth- and seventh-century Italy inadequate.

Two other books also concentrate on female musicians in Italian cities of the early modern period. Like Kendrick, MONSON studies the nuns of a particular city, Bologna. Whereas Kendrick focuses on the practice of the nuns without structuring his narrative around a single individual, Monson frames his argument around the life of a single nun, Lucrezia Orsina Vizzana (1590–1662), whose life and activities were emblematic of Bolognese musical life. He concludes that the nuns "developed a kind of agency by evolving informal rules and customs that interpreted, challenged, and subverted the external patriarchal authority of the church."

BALDAUF-BERDES studies the uniquely Venetian *ospedali* and their choirs. She devotes a substantial section to the cultural context of Venetian history in which the *ospedali* flourished, and she then moves on to a lengthy consideration of the *cori*, their repertory, and their status in Venetian society and Italy at large. The larger implications of her work reveal that Venetian musical life was not centered in San Marco to the same degree that the traditional view assumed.

HYDE treats the women of nineteenth-century England, by attempting to demonstrate the creative outlets available to musical women. As the century progressed, Hyde claims, women were able to become involved more deeply and in more ways with professional musical life. He argues that female performers were the first to challenge the hegemonic male control in professional music, and that the efforts of ballad composers and female educators contributed to these trends. A chapter on Ethel Smyth (1858–1944) considers her status as the first "professional woman composer in England whose main aim was that her music and its performance be received on equal terms with that of male composers."

Women in popular music of the twentieth century are also beginning to receive attention from scholars. O'BRIEN surveys the roles of women in popular styles of music, from jazz to Courtney Love. Her account is straightforward and reads easily, yet it tends to avoid deeper discussions of problematic issues. In addition to rock and jazz, O'Brien considers women's contributions to disco, rap, reggae, world beat, and the music industry itself. Despite its simplistic tendencies, it remains a useful and thorough account of women in popular music.

—DONALD B. CHAE

Musicology

Citron, Marcia, *Gender and the Musical Canon,* Cambridge and New York: Cambridge University Press, 1993

Clément, Catherine, *Opera, or, The Undoing of Women,* translated by Betsy Wing, Minneapolis: University of Minnesota Press, 1988; London: Virago, 1989

Cook, Susan C., and Judy S. Tsou (eds.), *Cecilia Reclaimed: Feminist Perspectives on Gender and Music,* Urbana: University of Illinois Press, 1994

Kallberg, Jeffrey, *Chopin at the Boundaries: Sex, History, and Musical Genre,* Cambridge, Massachusetts: Harvard University Press, 1996

McClary, Susan, *Feminine Endings: Music, Gender, and Sexuality,* Minneapolis: University of Minnesota Press, 1991

Solie, Ruth (ed.), *Musicology and Difference: Gender and Sexuality in Music Scholarship,* Berkeley: University of California Press, 1993

Although discussions of female musicians and composers began in musicology in the late 1970s, feminist critiques of music and music history did not appear until the 1990s, long after similar work in other fields. In the years that followed, numerous writings employing feminist methodology have appeared. For some authors, feminist theory provides a new approach to traditional topics. For others, it opens avenues of new research admitting subjects into the discipline that had been previously ignored. And for still others, feminist theory functions as a tool with which to critique the field of musicology itself. These listings, while not including all of the work that has been done, provide representative examples of the impact feminist theory has had on the discipline of musicology in the last decade.

In perhaps the first work in the field to use feminist methodology, McCLARY offers a compelling critique of the structure of the field, giving several reasons why musicology may have resisted techniques used in other fields as early as the 1970s. In the five chapters of her book, McClary focuses on different aspects of gender and sexuality in music ranging from Monteverdi to Madonna. This work provoked an extremely strong reaction in the field. Although its methodology has been attacked in the years following its publication, McClary's work is essential for those wishing to understand the development of feminist criticism in the field as a whole.

A work that has proved influential in the realm of opera scholarship is that of CLÉMENT. Published first in France in the late 1970s, Clément's volume is particularly indebted to the work of Claude Lévi-Strauss and psychoanalytic theory. Using Freudian and Lacanian psychoanalytic models, Clément critiques the roles of heroines in operas such as *Carmen, Don Giovanni, La Bohème,* and the Ring Cycle, to name a few. For Clément, women in opera have been victimized, and the calm acceptance of their situations in our culture needs to be reexamined. Although virtually unknown to American musicologists until its translation into English in the late 1980s, this work has become somewhat of a standard, and it has provoked a number of responses in the field.

CITRON chooses as her subject the formation of canon in classical music—specifically music written since 1800—examining possible reasons for the general exclusion of women from the ranks of these well-known composers. In the first chapter of the book, Citron discusses the notion of canonicity, while the last chapter shows how thinking about canon formation might speak to the discipline of musicology as a whole. In the middle chapters, Citron examines factors such as gender, sexuality, reception, professionalism, and creativity, suggesting ways these variables might determine which pieces of music are perpetuated throughout history. Citron's work highlights some of the issues musicologists have wrestled with in the 1990s and offers an interesting perspective about the challenges that changing—or eradicating—an accepted canon entails.

A volume that examines women within the larger context of difference and otherness is the collection of essays by SOLIE, which interrogates ideas of difference in relation to music. In her thought-provoking introduction, Solie offers an extremely useful overview of the debate among scholars over the concept of "otherness" and discusses the relationship of music to this concept. The subjects of the essays themselves are extremely varied, but gender and sexuality emerge as prominent themes throughout much of the collection. Charles Ives, female musicians, and seventeenth-century Italian opera are only a few of the topics under consideration. Additionally, an essay by Carolyn Abbate on the prominence of women in opera provides an interesting counterpoint to Cléments's work.

The collection of essays by COOK and TSOU provides many good examples of how feminist theory has affected historical study in musicology. Like those Solie brings together, the essays are unified not by subject, but by ideology: all espouse feminist perspectives and methodologies. The book illustrates well the impact these approaches have had in musicology. Some essays try to call attention to female musicians, such as Amy Beach or Anna Maria della Pietà, who have been overlooked. Others showcase the role of music in creating representations of gender: the relationship between music and the controversy over women in the English Renaissance, for example, or images of women in American balladry. Also interesting is a discussion of possible feminist approaches to the field of musicology in general. Cook and Tsou's work is helpful, both to specialists focusing on one of the subjects, and also to those searching for models of various feminist approaches to music in general.

While more limited in subject than others on the list, KALLBERG's volume offers extremely intelligent and thoughtful illustrations of how gender might mediate in the meaning music holds. Writing exclusively on the music of Chopin and its reception history, Kallberg offers interesting insights into how notions of gender and sexuality might create ideas about significance in music—and, ultimately, how the reverse might be true as well. The topics Kallberg covers range from specific works of the composer to discussions of genre, musical form, and techniques of marketing and dissemination, to name a few. In addition to scholars of Chopin and nineteenth-century piano music, this volume will also be interesting to those thinking about questions of canon formation and the social construction of meaning.

—JENNIFER MORE

N

National Woman's Party, United States

Becker, Susan D., *The Origins of the Equal Rights Amendment: American Feminism between the Wars*, Westport, Connecticut: Greenwood, 1981

Ford, Linda, *Iron-Jawed Angels: The Suffrage Militancy of the National Woman's Party, 1912–1920*, Lanham, Maryland: University Press of America, 1991

Gillmore, Inez Haynes (Irwin), *The Story of the Woman's Party*, New York: Harcourt Brace, 1921

Rupp, Leila J., and Verta Taylor, *Survival in the Doldrums: The American Women's Right's Movement, 1945 to the 1960s*, New York: Oxford University Press, 1987

Stevens, Doris, *Jailed for Freedom*, New York: Boni and Liveright, 1920

The National Woman's Party was founded by Alice Paul, who had become disillusioned with the tactics of the National American Woman Suffrage Association in its attempt to gain the right to vote for women in the United States. She believed the fight for suffrage had to be waged much more militantly, and formed a group initially called the Congressional Union, which staged parades, and pickets of the White House. In 1917 the group changed its name to the National Woman's Party (NWP).

Stevens and Ford both describe the intensive campaign of the suffrage militants to win the amendment enfranchising women. STEVENS was a participant-observer. She was one of those jailed for civil disobedience, and also served on the NWP executive committee. She tells a story of victimization as political prisoners. The pickets were among the earliest victims of the abrogation of civil liberties in wartime. The anti-suffrage men who attacked the female demonstrators were themselves not arrested. Her account ends with the passage of the Nineteenth Amendment (granting women the right to vote) by Congress in 1919, rather than with the 14-month campaign for state ratification.

FORD focuses on the 168 suffragists who chose jail rather than comply with the law that forbade their disruptive demonstrations. Many were professionals or wives of prominent men, and many were wealthy. Those jailed protested against the illegality of their arrests, the bad conditions, and the brutality of their treatment. They resorted to hunger strikes, leading the authorities to resort to force feeding. Ford suggests that their militancy was based on nonviolent principles of protest.

GILLMORE has told Alice Paul's NWP story several times over the years, concentrating on the period from the party's birth to the ratification of the Nineteenth Amendment, but with some updating to include the later Equal Rights Amendment campaign. Paul reactivated the NWP in 1921, turning its attention from suffrage to other feminist issues. At a commemorative convention in 1923 at Seneca Falls, New York where the first equal rights convention was held in 1848, Paul presented a proposal for an equal rights amendment. Over the years the NWP, a feminist pressure group, rather than a political party, took no stand on issues such as divorce, access to birth control information, or abortion. After the 1960s it concentrated all its efforts on securing passage of the ERA.

BECKER elaborates on the bifurcation between two strands of feminist activism, the more moderate group interested in issues such as temperance, consumer protection, and education, and those who insisted on political equality, represented by the NWP. She follows this schism to World War II. The moderate social feminists became New Dealers. The NWP egalitarian feminists concentrated on the ERA as a litmus test. The former group resisted the constitutional amendment, believing it would be used to strike down all protective legislation for working women. At various points in the early 1920s, it was proposed that the NWP become involved in disarmament, birth control, or the pursuit of voting rights for black women. Paul, however, regarded these goals as diversionary, peripheral issues that would dilute the drive for legal equality between the sexes. The NWP endorsed women for elective and appointive office, promoted the writing and teaching of women's history, and commemorated women's past achievements. By 1941 the NWP had become ingrown in its membership, less democratic in its structure, and increasingly rigid in its ideology. After World War II,

Doris Stevens led an abortive effort to capture leadership away from the hero-worshipped autocratic Paul. Becker faults the NWP for its mistaken strategies and failures of judgment, while praising it for fighting courageously for equal political, legal, and economic rights for all women.

RUPP and TAYLOR credit the NWP for its contributions to the survival of a women's movement into the 1960s, by launching and nursing the ERA. From the 1920s to the 1960s, as the ERA faded from public view, the NWP had kept the faith. The authors, a historian and a sociologist, combine a historical narrative with a sociological framework. They investigated pockets of feminism in a period of extreme domesticity for American women. Rupp and Taylor argue that the unique composition and style of the women's rights movement in this period was "elite-sustained." The movement in its doldrums was comprised of a small, relatively affluent, well-educated, and highly dedicated core of women, who, despite little support and strong opposition from the wider public, carried on the struggle for women's rights.

—MARTIN GRUBERG

See also Suffrage: United States

Native American Women

Albers, Patricia, and Beatrice Medicine (eds.), *The Hidden Half: Studies of Plains Indian Women,* Washington, D.C.: University Press of America, 1983

Allen, Paula Gunn, *The Sacred Hoop: Recovering the Feminine in American Indian Traditions,* Boston: Beacon Press, 1986

Bataille, Gretchen M., and Kathleen Mullen Sands, *American Indian Women, Telling Their Lives,* Lincoln: University of Nebraska Press, 1984

Brown, Jennifer S., *Strangers in Blood: Fur Trade Company Families in Indian Country,* Vancouver: University of British Columbia Press, 1980; Norman: University of Oklahoma Press, 1996

Green, Rayna, *Women in American Indian Society,* New York: Chelsea House, 1992

Klein, Laura F., and Lillian A. Ackerman (eds.), *Native American Women and Power,* Norman: University of Oklahoma Press, 1995

Mankiller, Wilma, and Michael Willis, *Mankiller: A Chief and Her People,* New York: St. Martin's Press, 1993

Niethammer, Carolyn, *Daughters of the Earth: The Lives and Legends of American Indian Women,* New York: Macmillan, 1977

Powers, Marla N., *Oglala Women: Myth, Ritual, and Reality,* Chicago: University of Chicago Press, 1986

Van Kirk, Sylvia, *Many Tender Ties: Women in Fur-Trade Society in Western Canada, 1670–1870,* Winnipeg: Watson and Dwyer, 1980: Norman: University of Oklahoma Press, 1983

Despite the long history of Native American studies in anthropology, research on Native American women is relatively recent, with few books published before the early 1980s. While numerous dissertations and journal articles have appeared, the number of general books is still small. One of the early popular books for the general reader is NIETHAMMER's. It has great breadth, jumping from culture to culture in covering topics from war to motherhood. The book suffers from two weaknesses. First, Native American cultures are quite varied, and any attempt to view American Indians as a whole is doomed to overgeneralization. Second, the research and data available in 1977 were severely limited, and the author was forced to search for women in literature that did not feature them. It remains a good starting place for looking at Native American women, but it should not be the only book read on the subject.

GREEN's book, despite its short length, is a valuable modern introduction to Native American women. It is especially good at examining and destroying widely held stereotypes of squaws and princesses. Green, drawing on personal experience as well as research, focuses on the roles of Native American women today in addition to the past. The importance of the colonial experience in the process of change in sex roles is clearly presented. The book concludes with examples of successful contemporary Native American women from a wide number of fields from chiefs to poets. The book is well illustrated and written.

KLEIN and ACKERMAN bring together a collection of essays that span the different culture areas of the United States and Canada. Each article focuses on the power of women in specific traditional cultures and discusses the changes under colonization. While power is described differently in each culture, it is clear that women were uniformly allotted areas of power that were essential for their society. The image of the meek woman walking paces behind her husband is refuted completely.

Another approach is employed by BATAILLE and SANDS, who are responsible for this important scholarly guide to research on American Indian Women. Their book offers an interdisciplinary orientation to understanding Native American women, with a focus on autobiographies and life histories. Two introductory chapters on literary and ethnographic approaches are followed by the stories of several Native American women from different cultures. The last third is an annotated bibliography, which is very useful for scholars.

ALLEN, a well-known Laguna scholar, also uses both humanities and social science approaches. Her assertion that gynocratic societies were common before colonization, and that the Euro-American fear of gynocracy was a key factor in the genocide and ethnocide that befell so many Native Americans societies, is interesting, if debatable. A second topic is the endurance of Native American people and their literature and spirituality. Allen's final point is the flexibility of gender roles in many Native American societies, which welcomed lesbians as equals. Throughout this book, Native American women are presented as central actors in their societies.

Another approach to the study of Native American women is to limit the investigation to specific cultures. ALBERS and MEDICINE compiled their classic collection of articles on Northern Plains women, which concentrates on the roles of women in this culture area from the time of contact. This volume offers a valuable critique of earlier work on the Plains that "hide" the women, and it challenges popular stereotypes. Albers's article that shows the government's hand in reforming gender roles is especially informative. Likewise, Medicine, a respected elder of Native American studies, offers an article on warrior women that demonstrates the acceptance of alternative gender roles in traditional culture. A strong use of ethnographic and ethnohistorical data runs through this volume. The critiques and coverage of literature on gender go far beyond the one-culture area.

POWERS also focuses on the Plains and takes an ethnographic view of women of the Oglala band of the Lakota. The first half of the book examines traditional Lakota life, focusing on changes in the life cycle and religious roles. The description of the importance of the mythic figure White Buffalo Calf Woman as a role model is compelling. The fundamental belief in the complementarity of men and women, which is often found in Native American cultures, is seen as imbedded in the social structure. The second half of the book uses interviews with a wide variety of contemporary Oglala women. This section allows the reader to hear the authentic voices, although they, understandably, do not coalesce into the same clear picture the traditional section does. Powers asserts that Lakota women had an easier transition than men in the acculturation to western society, and that women encourage the image that men are in charge.

Another approach to the study of Native American women is to focus on a particular historical topic. The reality of intermarriage and colonization is important to the understanding of Native American women, and BROWN and VAN KIRK have each written books that focus on American Indian women in the fur trade. The significance of Native American women as wives and daughters of European traders and their roles in negotiation and trade are well-researched and presented in both books. Each rewrites an important part of history by adding both ethnic and gender factors where they had been previously ignored. Both should be read.

A final and popular approach is biography or life history. A number of life histories of Native American women have been published. One of the most popular is the book by MANKILLER and WILLIS, which is a powerful look at the life of a prominent, contemporary Native American woman. Wilma Mankiller, a former principal chief of the Cherokee Nation, intertwines her personal history with that of her nation. Her own story moves from an impoverished childhood in California, where she faced both class and racial sexual prejudice, through a difficult marriage, to her ethnic and personal awakening at the Native American takeover of Alcatraz. After her return to Oklahoma she remarried and became chief. The history of the Cherokee through the "trail of tears" to contemporary success echoes her own. This is not the story of all Native American women today, but of an extraordinary woman, who follows in the footsteps of earlier important Cherokee female leaders.

—LAURA KLEIN

Nature

Adams, Carol J., *The Sexual Politics of Meat: A Feminist-Vegetarian Critical Theory,* London: Polity Press, and New York: Continuum, 1991

Carson, Rachel, *Silent Spring,* Boston: Houghton Mifflin, 1962; London: Hamish Hamilton, 1963

Dillard, Annie, *Pilgrim at Tinker Creek,* New York: Harper's Magazine Press, 1974; London: Cape, 1975

Griffin, Susan, *Woman and Nature: The Roaring inside Her,* New York: Harper and Row, 1978; London: Women's Press, 1984

Haraway, Donna, *Primate Visions: Gender, Race, and Nature in the World of Modern Science,* New York: Routledge, 1989; London: Verso Press, 1992

Hogan, Linda, *Dwellings: A Spiritual History of the Living World,* New York: Norton, 1995

Macy, Joanna, *World as Lover, World as Self,* Berkeley, California: Parallax Press, 1991

Merchant, Carolyn, *The Death of Nature: Women, Ecology, and the Scientific Revolution,* San Francisco: Harper and Row, 1980; London: Wildwood House, 1982

All nature writing, no matter how it seeks to be ecocentric, is human-centered, and no matter how it addresses the questions that are beyond human boundaries, it is a human occupation and preoccupation. The questions of nature ask the ultimate human riddles of love, beauty, ethics, and knowledge. However, these questions have historically been formulated, over and over, in ways that diminish human beings who fall on the "natural" side of the divide in theories of race, gender, and class. Writers who take up both the categories of women and nature make it their task to undo that violence of language, which has had profound consequences on the lives of women and the life of nature. Women writing about nature tend to take exception with two of the clichés of much popular nature writing: nature as metaphor for woman, and nature as arena of conquest. The works referred to here, from the theoretical to the lyrical, have in common a familiarity of style, even intimacy in the writing, that brings biology and physics into anthropology and psychology, and that brings history into poetry.

CARSON, a marine biologist, taught America about the detrimental effects of pesticides. Her book influenced the United States Congress to investigate and impose stricter regulations. As a scientist and as a writer, she had a profound effect on the development of ecological action and studies; her book has become a classroom classic that still has a voice in environmental politics. ADAMS connects the oppression of women with the symbolic behavior of meat eating and meat taboos; this connection is made by the significance of violence in patriarchal cultures. Her troubling argument is well-defined historically, theologically, and anthropologically; her bold polemic is ecofeminist in perspective.

Nature studies are necessarily multidisciplinary, drawing upon various scientific disciplines, historical and cultural studies, and gender and language inquiries. HARAWAY achieves an original and seamless interdisciplinary expertise. Her study is an astonishingly refreshing and stimulating analysis, ranging from the primate studies of the twentieth century to Theodore Roosevelt and the teddy bear, from commerce to language, and from gender to science fiction. In her work feminist theory informs biological assumptions, and biological science critiques cultural assumptions. Haraway claims that nature, as we participate in it now, is played out in a cyborg world, by means of a discourse made up of gender, race, technology, and war, wherein ideas about animals, human animals, and humans' machines are all a language of contested nature.

Among the numbers of historians and feminist analysts of western patriarchy is MERCHANT, who critiques the hidden biases in scientific assumptions involving gender and nature. Merchant's influential book meticulously traces the historical contexts of the scientific revolution and demonstrates how the influences of those historic cultural paradigms persist in today's assumptions about women and nature. She argues for her readers to take a close and critical look at the mechanistic worldview and reevaluate the organic, or holistic worldview.

DILLARD meditates on the divine through describing every detail of life at Tinker Creek, down to the very cells, and she won the Pulitzer Prize for her poetic essay. All of her work links theological questions with ecological ones, observations of the natural world with the life of a writer. HOGAN's book is a collection of learned, personal essays from a contemporary Chickasaw novelist and poet, unifying moral politics and mystical insight. Hogan is a fine poet and novelist, who addresses the beauty of eagles and bats, knowledgeably discusses Mayan myth and contemporary science, and reflects on animal thought and human relationships. GRIFFIN's work is also polemical and poetical, also from a writer who has two ways of looking: as biological observer and as visionary. She objects to the dualism of patriarchal culture, in which "man" is separate from nature, and she reembodies woman without falling prey to that dualism in which women are relegated to the unconscious stuff of the planet. Hogan, Dillard, and Griffin are exemplars, each in her own voice, of the essay form that characterizes the genre of nature writing in which the writer represents the biologist's observation, combined with the theologian's (or metaphysician's) interpretation. They are poetic books that demand and grant the reader's participation. The work of many of these female nature writers, by means of that poetic participation, necessitates political participation.

MACY captures the fundamental Buddhist philosophical term, *paticcasamuppada* (or dependent co-arising, the idea that every aspect of reality is interdependent upon every other aspect for its own existence), and translates it into the term "deep ecology," thereby transforming a Buddhist concept into a western imperative. Her book is a brilliantly theoretical and practical statement. As with other feminist theorists on nature, Macy rejoins categories of discourse that had become disjointed and incompatible in western thought. Her book delivers systems analysis, history, philosophy, practical guides for grief and empowerment, and poetry. Her poetic interlude, "Bestiary," first published in the journal *Corona*, is a litany of extinct animals, which culminates in a plea from the human destroyers, "Wait. Wait. Don't leave us alone in a world we have wrecked."

Theories of nature and environmental questions have a close connection to theories of gender and feminist social histories. Each of these writers, in her various ways of addressing the question, informs her readers that nature involves a theory of the world as well as the world itself; a crisis of human decision-making as well as the ecosystem in which humans are put in their interdependent places; a basis of cultural myth and something radically outside our narratives. Nature is not merely the "trees out there," but also the books that take up the world's dialogue.

—LYNDA SEXSON

See also Ecofeminism

Nevelson, Louise 1899–1988

American Sculptor

Glimcher, Arnold B., *Louise Nevelson,* London: Secker and Warburg, and New York: Praeger, 1972
Lipman, Jean, *Nevelson's World,* New York: Viking, 1983
Lisle, Laurie, *Louise Nevelson: A Passionate Life,* New York: Summit, 1990
Wilson, Laurie, *Louise Nevelson: Iconography and Sources,* New York and London: Garland, 1981

Just as she created her public persona of the beautiful and flamboyant artist, Louise Nevelson for years attempted to control the way in which her art was seen and thought about. She wrote the text herself for many books about her art, and gave countless published interviews about her own processes and ideas. During her lifetime, it was extremely difficult to find book-length studies about Nevelson to which she had not contributed largely and directly. There are few major studies of the work itself; Nevelson has always been as fascinating for her remarkably unrestrained life as for her art.

LIPMAN's book is a large and heavy volume, echoing the scale of Nevelson's most important work. This book is primarily a study of the development of Nevelson's sculpture over her lifetime; when her drawings and paintings are occasionally mentioned, it is usually to illustrate how the small two-dimensional works led to or echo the large sculptures, and how her representational work led naturally to the abstract. Most of the pages of the book are filled with large photographs of the sculptures, accompanied by quotations from Nevelson; Lipman contributes an interpretive essay to each chapter. In his introduction, Hilton Kramer places Nevelson's work squarely in the constructivist tradition in terms of the syntax of the pieces, but not in terms of her artistic or thematic vision. Lipman sees two opposites—cubism and expressionism—meeting in Nevelson's work.

Part of "Garland's Outstanding Dissertations in the Fine Arts" series, WILSON's book is a bound and reduced reproduction of the author's typewritten pages. In spite of the inelegant presentation, the book provides an important analysis of the artist's mature work, particularly her walls of black boxes and the *Moon Garden + One* exhibit. Noting the air of mystery that surrounds Nevelson's mature work, arising from the suggestiveness of her titles and the abstract nature of the pieces, the author examines the artist's childhood for keys to the symbolism or iconography. She finds three major artistic themes in Nevelson's work—royalty, death, and marriage—and shows how they arise from her childhood fantasies and experiences, and from her identification with her father as an empire builder, and with her mother as a beauty. A chapter on Nevelson's attraction to the theater and dance (she considered a career in theater in her youth), and on the theatricality of her sculpture, is original and illuminating.

Although Nevelson herself wrote the text for many volumes of her work, she gave GLIMCHER many hours of interviews and access to her personal papers, writing only a short prologue for this lavishly illustrated biography, which focuses primarily on her progression as an artist. It does not reveal much about Nevelson's private life, or attempt an assessment of her character. Glimcher is best known as an art dealer, and he brings an expert's knowledge and insight to his analyses of Nevelson's artwork. His descriptions of sculptures, drawings, rooms, and costumes are vivid, but the rest of his writing is flat. Nevelson was a long-time patron and friend of the author, and he clearly respects her restless creativity and indomitable spirit. Admiring her as he does, he is willing to accept everything Nevelson says at face value.

The definitive biography of Nevelson as a person is LISLE's book, which is an important study of her life as it informs her art. Lisle shows clearly the state of American sculpture in the early twentieth century, placing Nevelson's accomplishments in context. The book stresses the importance of assistants, especially Diane MacKown, in Nevelson's work; the artist did her best and most prolific work when she had assistants to handle the more tedious tasks, and when there were no distractions from the men in her life. Her early struggles to be both married and independent, a respected artist and a woman, a public persona and a private person, are well documented here. Nevelson had no great wish to have her private life written about, as Lisle's first encounter with her unwilling subject makes clear. Although the public persona was consciously created to keep the inner self private, Lisle turns to quotations from some of Nevelson's poetry to find glimpses of the inner self.

—CYNTHIA A. BILY

Nightingale, Florence 1820–1910

British Nurse

Baly, Monica E., *Florence Nightingale and the Nursing Legacy,* London and Dover, New Hampshire: Croom Helm, 1986
Bullough, Vern, Bonnie Bullough, and Marietta P. Stanton (eds.), *Florence Nightingale and Her Era: A Collection of New Scholarship,* New York: Garland, 1990
Cope, Zachary, *Florence Nightingale and the Doctors,* Philadelphia: J.B. Lippincott, and London: Museum Press, 1958
Hebert, Raymond G. (ed.), *Florence Nightingale: Saint, Reformer or Rebel?* Malabar, Florida: Robert E. Krieger, 1981

Huxley, Elspeth, *Florence Nightingale,* New York: Putnam, and London: Weidenfeld and Nicholson,1975
Selanders, Louise C., *Florence Nightingale: An Environmental Adaptation Theory,* Newbury Park, California, and London: Sage, 1993
Smith, F.B., *Florence Nightingale: Reputation and Power,* New York: St. Martin's Press, 1982; London: Croom Helm, 1984
Ulrich, Beth T., *Leadership and Management According to Florence Nightingale,* Norwalk, Connecticut: Appleton and Lange, 1992
Woodham-Smith, Cecil, *Florence Nightingale, 1820–1910,* New York and London: McGraw-Hill, 1951

Florence Nightingale is best known for her nursing in British army hospitals during the Crimean War, but she devoted her long life to a range of reform efforts, including schools for nursing and army medicine, hospital design, and sanitary reform in India. The legend of the "Lady with the Lamp" quickly took shape, and early biographers praised her saintly qualities. Recent studies have offered more complex portrayals of Nightingale's work and character, often disagreeing about her motivations, her personality, and the cause of her almost lifelong invalidism.

WOODHAM-SMITH's lengthy biography is filled with quotations and detailed discussions of every aspect of Nightingale's life, from her childhood through her death. Woodham-Smith is generally sympathetic to Nightingale, concluding that she "brought about a revolution" while overcoming constant family pressures and bad health. He nevertheless notes that Nightingale displayed contradictory qualities of exaggerated emotions and uncompromising realism, and that she sometimes exploited her illness.

COPE focuses primarily on Nightingale's relationships with the doctors she encountered in her reform efforts. Indeed, the book seems to be more about the doctors than about Nightingale herself, although it contains many excerpts from her letters. Cope argues that while Nightingale certainly influenced the medical profession, her own work was equally dependent on the help of those doctors. Like Woodham-Smith, Cope sees two sides to Nightingale's personality: a discreet public face and an uninhibited private one. He diagnoses her illness as a stress-related neurosis, one which she subconsciously made habitual after recognizing its advantages.

HUXLEY's biography features lavish illustrations, many in color, appearing on nearly every other page and including Nightingale, her family and friends, and places she lived and visited. Her text is comparatively brief and simplistic, but it does include helpful background information. Huxley argues that while Nightingale is best known today for founding the modern nursing profession, she herself would have ranked her efforts to improve the health of soldiers and Indian peasants higher. Ultimately, although Huxley acknowledges the "mass of contradictions" in Nightingale's character, she portrays her as a woman "of genius" and a "saint."

SMITH devotes her well-documented study to analyzing Nightingale's motivations and strategies in her reform efforts, giving relatively little attention to her private life. Smith's critical descriptions of Nightingale emphasize her "talent for manipulation," her persistent efforts to gain and wield power behind the scenes, and her readiness to cover up failures and exaggerate successes for public relations purposes. In Smith's view, Nightingale was much less interested in actual nursing, and did much less of it, than other biographers have thought. Her work to reform the nursing profession had only limited success, with increasing prestige not matched by practical or technical innovation. In conclusion, Smith argues, "Nightingale served the cause of nursing less than it served her."

BALY evaluates Nightingale's long-term achievements in different nursing fields: hospital nursing, midwifery, poor law nursing, military nursing, and district (or public health) nursing. Baly argues that Nightingale's reforms were less dramatic in reality than in popular legend, and that they often represented substantial compromises between Nightingale and the hospitals and doctors who opposed her. Nightingale herself tended to be intolerant of criticism, and personal conflicts sometimes impeded reform efforts. However, her skill with public relations meant that her schemes enjoyed prestige and publicity even when their enrollments, and records, wavered.

ULRICH, a nurse and hospital administrator, turns to Nightingale for insight into current dilemmas in nursing policy. Her book consists of brief commentaries accompanied by numerous (but undocumented) quotations from Nightingale's own writings. Her brief biographical information is based on earlier works. Ulrich is less interested in evaluating Nightingale's life and work than she is in finding parallels between nineteenth- and twentieth-century health care issues and describing them in up-to-date business jargon. Nightingale, in Ulrich's view, is a "change agent" skilled in dealing with "organizational structure," "participative management" and "stakeholders."

SELANDERS explores the theoretical aspects of Nightingale's views in hopes of inspiring nursing students to learn more about their profession's roots. Her biographical information is brief and mainly derived from other works, though she includes a good bibliography. Selanders sees Nightingale's "establishment of the principles for modern nursing education and practice" as her most important work. Among the values underlying these principles were her religious views, work ethic, belief in the possibility of progress, and emphasis on caring for patients rather than diseases. Using diagrams, Selanders develops these ideas into a theoretical model based around control of the patient's environment.

Selanders admires Nightingale's ideas and sees them as still relevant but faults her for not empowering future nurses to a greater degree.

HEBERT has edited sixteen articles about Nightingale, ranging from primary sources and early twentieth-century biographies to more modern analyses. These are divided into five sections, dealing with nursing in Victorian England, Nightingale's personality, her work in the Crimean War, her subsequent reform work, and her work in the nursing profession. Hebert's introduction portrays Nightingale as a "multi-faceted woman" who, although no saint, was an extremely effective reformer. Although he praises her work to improve the army, public health, legislation, statistics, and the status of women, Hebert considers her work to professionalize nursing the most far-reaching and important. The book also contains a good although somewhat outdated annotated bibliography.

BULLOUGH, BULLOUGH, and STANTON offer nineteen recent articles. Despite the book's title, not all are concerned with Nightingale or even with nursing in Britain. One whole section is devoted to American nursing, while others deal with tangential subjects such as Nightingale's influences on religious organizations and on psychiatric care. The most relevant articles are those in the first section, entitled "New Scholarship." These editors portray Nightingale as a "visionary" but also a "manipulative, often erratic, and dedicated woman." They conclude that Nightingale's continuing acclaim in the nursing profession has depended on the ability of her successors to modify her original views.

—NAN H. DREHER

Nin, Anaïs 1903–1977

American Writer

Deduck, Patricia A., *Realism, Reality and the Fictional Theory of Alain Robbe-Grillet and Anaïs Nin*, Washington, D.C.: University Press of America, 1982

Evans, Oliver, *Anaïs Nin*, Carbondale: Southern Illinois University Press, 1968

Franklin, Benjamin V., and Duane Schneider, *Anaïs Nin: An Introduction*, Athens: Ohio University Press, 1979

Hinz, E., *The Mirror and the Garden: Realism and Reality in the Writings of Anaïs Nin*, Columbus: Ohio State University Press, 1971

Knapp, Bettina L., *Anaïs Nin*, New York: Frederick Ungar, 1978

Nalbantian, Suzanne, *Aesthetic Autobiography: From Life to Art in Marcel Proust, James Joyce, Virginia Woolf and Anaïs Nin*, London: Macmillan, and New York: St. Martin's Press, 1994

Scholar, Nancy, *Anaïs Nin*, Boston: Twayne, 1984

Spencer, Sharon, *Collage of Dreams: The Writings of Anaïs Nin*, Chicago: Swallow Press, 1977

Zaller, Robert (ed.), *A Casebook on Anaïs Nin*, New York: New American Library, 1974

Coverage of Anaïs Nin's work is usually inflected with commentary on her life and literary relationships in such a way that her work is often subsumed into accounts of her life and psychology. Most commentators keep the diaries separate from more literary material in organising their books; however, the intimate connections between these two spheres make it difficult and perhaps ultimately unhelpful to try to keep the two separate. In light of this, there exists a continuing concern for accounts of Nin that explore at a critical and theoretical level that commonplace of traditional literary studies—the relationship between life and art—rather than just assuming it as a given. Other continuing areas of interest are Nin's ambiguous place within feminist literary and cultural traditions, and the long-standing and widespread critical neglect of her work.

FRANKLIN and SCHNEIDER offer an introduction to the writer and her work, which perhaps provides the most comprehensive coverage. However, they do not furnish any detailed analysis of her position within her period or literary coterie nor, indeed, with feminism. Franklin and Schneider instead aim to address the question of Nin's continuing neglect by literary critics and to touch upon some of the lingering editorial confusion that surrounds her work. The discussion hinges very closely upon Nin's own comments on her writing, which are supported by quotations from the diaries. The authors trace Nin's motivations for writing different texts, and their analysis is largely confined to discussion of the meanings of symbols.

EVANS provides the first serious study of Nin and establishes Nin's originality, her femininity, and her emphasis on "feelings" as key elements for study. The book is a useful text, provided its context is kept in mind. ZALLER offers a collection of important essays ranging from a piece by Lawrence Durrell to the often-mentioned Edmund Wilson review that finally brought Nin's fiction to public attention. He also includes a 1971 interview. Collectively, these essays tie Nin's work not so much to her biography as to the very public psychological construction of "Anaïs Nin." Zaller's introductory essay provides a biographical narrative and a useful starting point for reading Nin's work by tracing the substantial revision of each work from one edition to the next. Readers should not expect clear-cut divisions between works, nor a straightforward continuity from one to the next. However, the discussion is informed and engaging.

SPENCER offers a more conventional account and opens with the diary quote, which states that life and art are not separate for Nin. The book structures itself around a notion of literary and creative "ragpicking," citing Nin's sartorial style and her thrift in producing a humanist metaphor about art. KNAPP reads Nin's work as a series of quests exploring the self, with analysis confined to an unpacking of symbolism and a (proto-feminist) tracing of narrative order based on the coming to consciousness of the protagonists. HINZ provides another classic and sympathetic account that considers Nin's work and life together in terms of literary experimentation and achievement.

SCHOLAR considers the public's reception of Nin's diary alongside the critical silence concerning her fiction. She comments on the seductiveness of the diary form in relation to readers' desires for authenticity and Nin's own representations of herself as presenting many masks as forms of "allurement and protection." Like other critics, she reads Nin's work according to the principle that the boundaries between dreams and life are not fixed; her analysis does not simply take this at face value, but rather as a way of charting the literary construction of the meanings of women's experiences, questions of literary narcissism, and the textual strategies of self-revelation and concealment.

Nin's work and life are also usefully located in comparative accounts. DEDUCK reads Nin's fictional theory alongside that of the avant-garde French writer Alain Robbe-Grillet in terms of the crisis concerning the nature of reality as addressed by twentieth-century modernist writers and thinkers. The emphasis on Nin's theories about writing and her thinking through of questions of modernity is useful, but should be most useful when read in light of other writers on Nin. NALBANTIAN takes on the topic of the modernist autobiography as an aesthetic and cultural category, aiming to develop a theory to account for the work of transmutation and transposition in autobiographical writing. Nin provides her with a kind of limit-text of the interconnectedness of life and art; the approach is particularly useful in the ways it provides the beginnings of a theorised response to this fundamental concern in Nin's work.

—BRIGITTA OLUBAS

Nontraditional Jobs

Addis, Elisabetta, Valeria Russo, and Lorenza Sebesta, *Women Soldiers: Images and Realities,* New York: St. Martin's Press, 1994

Deaux, Kay, and Joseph Ullman, *Women of Steel: Female Blue-Collar Workers in the Basic Steel Industry,* New York: Praeger, 1983

Harlan, Sharon, and Ronnie Steinberg (eds.), *Job Training for Women: The Promise and Limits of Public Policies,* Philadephia: Temple University Press, 1989

Martin, Molly, *Hard-Hatted Women: Life on the Job,* Seattle: Seal Press, 1990

Martin, Susan Ehrlich, and Nancy Jurik, *Doing Justice, Doing Gender,* Thousand Oaks, California, and London: Sage, 1996

Milkman, Ruth, *Gender at Work: The Dynamics of Job Segregation by Sex during World War II,* Urbana: University of Illinois Press, 1987

Reskin, Barbara, and Patricia Roos, *Job Queues, Gender Queues: Explaining Women's Inroads into Male Occupations,* Philadelphia: Temple University Press, 1990

Schroedel, Jean, *Alone in a Crowd: Women in the Trades Tell Their Stories,* Philadelphia: Temple University Press, 1985

Stiehm, Judith, *Arms and the Enlisted Woman,* Philadelphia: Temple University Press, 1989

Walshok, Mary, *Blue-Collar Women: Pioneers on the Male Frontier,* Garden City, New York: Anchor Press, 1981

Williams, Christine, *Gender Differences at Work: Women and Men in Nontraditional Occupations,* Berkeley and London: University of California Press, 1989

Zimmer, Lynne, *Women Guarding Men,* Chicago and London: University of Chicago Press, 1986

The study of women in nontraditional jobs is a new field. Social movements of the last 30 years have made possible women's entry into male-dominated work, for which in the past women were recruited only during wartime. The increase of women in the paid labor force during the last 25 years has been accompanied by challenges to occupational segregation by gender and race. It is important to note that conceptualizing work as nontraditional is culturally relative. While it is not unusual for women to work as agricultural or construction laborers in some countries, like Thailand, the same work would fall under the U.S. Department of Labor's definition of nontraditional in the United States: namely, that less than 25 percent of the workers in that occupation are women.

Much of the work written in the 1980s features the voices and experiences of female workers. SCHROEDEL's collection of interviews with women in the Seattle area is an early example of vivid first-person narratives that ground the reader in the diverse range of women who take nontraditional jobs. The stories provide three-dimensionality as women describe, for example, what it was like to go from being a shipyard worker during the war, to later a nursery school teacher and active trade-unionist in a bindery. The interviews are grouped in categories that highlight the issues of feminism, occupational safety and health, race, unions, and family. MARTIN's book includes narratives that go beyond the trades to jobs such as firefighter and subway conductor. Women from across the United States explore the themes of racism, sexual harassment, sexual orientation, family obligations, and coping mechanisms.

A critical question in this field of research is why there are so few women who have penetrated nontraditional work. Conventional explanations that women are not interested or are not willing to undertake the extra training commitment are refuted by many of the studies discussed here. WALSHOK interviewed 117 women in nontraditional jobs to challenge the middle-class and male bias in research on women, and to identify factors that motivated women to break away from female-dominated jobs. She makes the argument that women who had early experiences of autonomy, who were risk takers in terms of preparing themselves for paid employment, and who were not tied up in having an "elaborate" domestic role, were more frequently found among women in nontraditional jobs.

MILKMAN's study of wartime female workers offers a structural argument to explain how industries become sex-segregated. Her in-depth analysis of automobile versus electronic manufacturing concludes that the early stages of an industry are critical for sex-typing of jobs. Concern on the part of unions during World War II that women would become cheap replacements for men led to struggles for equal pay for equal work by the United Autoworkers, and equal pay for jobs of comparable worth by the United Electrical Workers. Women's loss of jobs from both industries is described in the auto industry as male collusion with management over the violation of women's seniority rights, and in the electrical industry as a result of the union's postwar weakness after anti-Communist attacks.

Several studies of the contemporary period focus on how affirmative action has affected the numbers of women in nontraditional jobs, and the opportunities available to women for training and employment. DEAUX and ULLMAN's research on female steel workers shows that the consent decree did make a difference for women, as it did for men of color. But the decline of the steel industry and its subsequent reorganization made it difficult to know longer-term effects. RESKIN and ROOS both have done a great deal of research on sex segregation; the work cited here argues that when women have successfully penetrated an occupation, for example, bus-driving, it becomes stereotyped as a woman's job and loses status and wages. Finally, HARLAN and STEINBERG's collection of essays investigates a range of government policies that affect women's job options, especially in light of the contemporary issues of welfare and workfare. The four essays specifically targeting nontraditional work analyze the relationship of female workers to union apprenticeship, public sector uniformed jobs, and state and federal training programs.

The last group of books concern women in police, military, and correctional services. WILLIAMS's study of female marines and male nurses is a psycho-sociological investigation of the importance of gender identity, in which the author finds that men rely greatly on their occupational status to define their masculinity. Gender identity for women works differently, she finds, since women tend to transcend gender stereotyping because working at a male-dominated job does confer material benefits. One of the themes from this work is echoed in many related studies of uniformed women, that is, how to reconcile different views of what is feminine, and how that affects a woman's ability to do the job and survive in a hierarchical male environment.

ZIMMER's book on female prison guards explores the different strategies women have for keeping their jobs. She identifies an institutional or rule-keeping model, a modified role, in which women allow men to "protect" them, and an innovative model, in which women rely more on interactional skills dealing with inmates and less on their fellow guards. She notes that race and ethnicity are important factors that influence the choice of strategy.

MARTIN and JURIK's book discusses this question as well as pointing out parallels for female guards, lawyers, and police, a revealing comparison. Analysis draws from Martin's extensive past studies of women in the police force, and she also explores the force of homophobia and the enactment of masculinity through work. The theoretical use of social constructionism to explain how gender relations are reproduced makes this a provocative study. STIEHM examines the contradictions of policy about soldiering and creating a cohesive military system by looking at the history of women in the U.S. military. Like Williams, she argues that inconsistencies prevail when jobs are used to demonstrate manhood rather than to get the work done.

Finally, another book on women in the military shows that there are rich areas to explore beyond the United States regarding women in nontraditional jobs. The collection of essays edited by ADDIS, RUSSO, and SEBESTA documents the number of women in militaries around the world (the United States and China are highest in numbers of female soldiers), as well as examining theoretical and cultural issues affecting women primarily in service in the United States, Italy, and Libya. An extensive international bibliography is included in the text. The contributors to the book are European and American economists, political scientists, historians, and philosophers, who consider the broad questions of how the debate over equality and difference in gender relations manifests itself in the institution of the military, from concrete strategies for survival to the consequences on the institution of women's inclusion. They study the question of acceptance being exended to women in the form of status as the assimilated, obedient, professional warrior in lipstick, and the integration of women in the military as a legitimation of the state's use of force rather than as a democratizing, transforming element that could contribute to shifting the power of the state away from war-making. The one essay that focuses on the non-western experience of women in the military in Libya considers the phenomenon as Ghaddafi's attempt at modernizing patriarchal society, with support from the Koran in the form of an allusion to Ayesha, Mohammed's favorite wife, who personally led an army. Since women in military and police service are growing in numbers internationally, the contradictions and issues they raise could become the focus of many future studies.

—VIVIAN PRICE

See also Military

O

Oates, Joyce Carol 1939–

American Writer

Bloom, Harold (ed.), *Joyce Carol Oates,* New York: Chelsea House, 1987

Creighton, JoAnne, *Joyce Carol Oates,* Boston: Twayne, 1979

Grant, Mary Kathryn, *The Tragic Vision of Joyce Carol Oates,* Durham, North Carolina: Duke University Press, 1978

Johnson, Greg (ed.), *Joyce Carol Oates: A Study of the Short Fiction,* New York: Twayne, 1994

Wagner-Martin, Linda (ed.), *Critical Essays on Joyce Carol Oates,* Boston: G.K. Hall, 1979

Wesley, Marilyn C., *Refusal and Transgression in Joyce Carol Oates' Fiction,* Westport, Connecticut: Greenwood, 1993

There are many reasons for considering Joyce Carol Oates a feminist writer. Her works vividly articulate modernity's war against the feminine. She has created many memorable female characters. Her style revises canonical literature, often giving voice to the silenced woman. Her article, "At Least I Have Made a Woman of Her: Images of Women in Yeats, Lawrence, and Faulkner," employs a decidedly feminist strategy in her analysis of the use of images of women. And she has feminist friends in high places. Yet in "(Woman) Writer," Oates rejects classification as a "woman writer," claiming that it is too confining, in that an author writes about human themes without consciousness of her embodied gender. In short, the relationship of Joyce Carol Oates to feminism is at best qualified, and often in spite of her own protests.

JOHNSON's work sets up the terms of the debate about Oates's feminism. His chapter "Early Feminism" details Oates's argument rejecting the label "woman writer," and then applies Oates's own standard of humanism to *Wheel of Love* and *The Goddess and Other Women.* His reading reveals that despite Oates's disavowal of feminist leanings, the women of her stories, even those who are contemporary manifestations of such powerful figures as Kali and Magna Mater, are rendered impotent in the face of our culture's objectification of women.

The arguments for Oates's feminist qualifications are made by Elaine Showalter in BLOOM's collection. Showalter agrees that "woman writer" often condescendingly presumes a narrow subject, a second-rate talent, and a limited treatment, but that in Oates's revision of canonical works, in her allusions to literary mothers, and in her exploration of women's concerns, she deserves "acknowledgment from feminist readers." Also in Bloom's book is Mary Allen's "The Terrified Women of Joyce Carol Oates," which argues that Oates's realism is essentially economic. It is lack of economic opportunities that atrophies women into passive children, vulnerable to our culture's violence.

GRANT's study of Oates, heavily informed by Oates's own reading of herself and other authors, projects the thesis that Oates's works are tragedies, in that they depict the isolated individual's efforts to achieve identity in the wasteland of modernity. Oates's female characters—women who are passive, self-destructive, childlike—are caught in this tragic condition. Grant acknowledges that the lack of liberated female characters does not strengthen Oates's feminist standing, but she argues that the very absence of strong characters suggests a not-yet-realized presence. While Oates's works offer no answers, the act of writing (for Oates) and reading (for her readers) offers hope: coming to terms with what now exists as the first step in a revolution that Oates describes in terms such as "awakening" and "redeem[ing] the time."

In her introduction, WAGNER-MARTIN describes the critical responses to Oates as incredibly varied. Wagner-Martin's collection samples a range of that variety, including JoAnne Creighton's "The Unliberated Women of Joyce Carol Oates' Fiction." Creighton's reading is one common to many feminist readings of Oates: the desire to appropriate Oates as feminist because of her powerful portrayal of modernity's war on the feminine, but the inability to stretch Oates's feminism beyond its cataloguing of female victimization. For Creighton, it is not the cultural objectification of women, nor lack of economic opportunity, but the female characters themselves who are to blame for the trademark Oatsian passivity, according to Creighton because of their dissociation from their own sexuality.

CREIGHTON has also published several volumes on Oates. The book listed here studies Oates's early work and argues that Oates is a naturalist writer with a visionary thesis: contemporary culture is moving from its focus on the individual to a recognition of a larger collective family. Creighton does concede that readers often miss Oates's utopian thesis, being blinded by her violence.

WESLEY's post-modernist Marxist psychoanalytic feminist reading of Oates begins by citing Showalter's claim that feminists have not recognized Oates, and then sets out to right that omission. Her claim is that Oates is a feminist author because her work looks at the creation of gender roles through its portraits of the patriarchal institution of the family. Oates's characters who refuse to play their prescribed gender roles uncover the exploitative power relations behind the family, and in their acts of transgression, gesture toward what does not yet exist, what Wesley calls, in an allusion to Frederick Jameson, "feminist consciousness": the strong and loving mother, the powerful and nurturing father.

In spite of the attention that has been paid to Oates's relationship to feminism, the convincing argument that links her work to feminism has yet to be written. In part this is due to the volume and diversity of Oates's work. Oates's oeuvre does not fit easily into a formula, even one as diverse as women's literature. But it also seems clear that Oates finds value in feminism's strategy of playful pluralism, even if she finds its label confining.

—PAMELA SMILEY

O'Connor, Flannery 1925–1964

American Writer

Asals, Frederick, *Flannery O'Connor: The Imagination of Extremity*, Athens: University of Georgia Press, 1982; London: 1987

Baumgaertner, Jill P., *Flannery O'Connor: A Proper Scaring*, Wheaton, Illinois: Harold Shaw, 1988

Brinkmeyer, Robert H., *The Art and Vision of Flannery O'Connor*, Baton Rouge: Louisiana State University Press, 1989

Di Renzo, Anthony, *American Gargoyles: Flannery O'Connor and the Medieval Grotesque*, Carbondale: Southern Illinois University Press, 1993

Feeley, Kathleen, *Flannery O'Connor: Voice of the Peacock*, New Brunswick, New Jersey: Rutgers University Press, 1972

Friedman, Melvin J., and Beverly Lyon Clark, *Critical Essays on Flannery O'Connor*, Boston: G. K. Hall, 1985

Johansen, Ruthann Knechel, *The Narrative Secret of Flannery O'Connor: The Trickster as Interpreter*, Tuscaloosa: University of Alabama Press, 1994

Rath, Sura Prasad, and Mary Neff Shaw (eds.), *Flannery O'Connor: New Perspectives*, Athens: University of Georgia Press, 1996

Spivey, Ted R., *Flannery O'Connor: The Woman, the Thinker, the Visionary*, Macon, Georgia: Mercer University Press, 1995

Whitt, Margaret Earley, *Understanding Flannery O'Connor*, Columbia: University of South Carolina Press, 1995

Despite the relatively small canon of works (two novels, two collections of short stories, and some occasional writings and letters) from this short-lived Southern woman, there is a large mass of criticism on her writings. Many of the early critics focused on O'Connor's religious beliefs and how they are represented in her works, and newer views often examine O'Connor's social/economic/cultural contexts and their influences. Her works continue to fascinate and to defy easy explanation. The book-length studies here represent a small percentage of the resources available and are drawn from both standard studies and more recent criticism.

FEELEY's study, one of the best religious readings of O'Connor's works, is presented from the point of view of a Catholic Sister. She uses much of O'Connor's own nonfiction, including letters, essays, and annotations from O'Connor's personal library volumes as commentary on the fiction. The volume uses biblical references, writings of early Catholics, and analysis of Christian symbolism in its well-written study of what O'Connor herself called that most important aspect of her fiction, the perspective of faith.

Representing a good selection of reviews, personal accounts of writers who knew O'Connor, critical essays, and an annotated bibliography, FRIEDMAN and CLARK's volume is a helpful resource for the study of the author. The anthology shows the diversity of responses that greeted O'Connor's writings during her lifetime and afterward, ranging from lavish praise to discussion of her weaknesses, and from examination of her Catholic orthodoxy to studies of her Freudian insights. One essay of note is by Alice Walker, who, discovering that she had once unknowing lived near O'Connor in Milledgeville, went back to visit her former house and O'Connor's, writing the account in a letter to her (Walker's) mother. Walker admires O'Connor for writing about racism and "destroying the last vestiges of sentimentality in white Southern writing."

Using a Bakhtinian approach, BRINKMEYER discusses the dialogic qualities of O'Connor's fiction. In other words, according to Brinkmeyer, instead of presenting herself as "the sole possessor of truth," O'Connor is willing to test her faith by bringing in different voices and points of view. Thus, in opposition to some studies that see O'Connor as too moralistic and monolithic in her writings, this work views the author as critical of much of other Catholic fiction and open to challenges of her beliefs. Besides the dialogues between different religious and philosophical beliefs in her works, Brinkmeyer sees O'Connor as engaging in a dialogue with her readers as well. This volume may be too theoretical for the nonliterary student, but it does present an interesting corrective to the sometimes simplistic religious allegorical criticism.

ASALS concentrates on the dualism of O'Connor's fiction, her inclusion of the opposites of good and evil and the sacramental and grotesque in particular. He uses a New Critical approach to examine plot closely as well as to assess the aesthetic qualities of O'Connor's works, combined with a psychological study of her characters. References to O'Connor's Catholic sources, such as Augustine's and Thomas's works, are also provided. The chronological study is very complete and scholarly, although fairly easy to read. Asals concludes that O'Connor saw herself as a modern-day prophet.

BAUMGAERTNER's biography and literary analysis concentrates on O'Connor's religious beliefs and their primacy in her works. Written primarily from a New Critical perspective, the volume portrays the author as conveying "Truth" in her fiction. This very accessible study is punctuated with the delightful cartoons O'Connor drew for her college newspaper, pictorial representations that are then tied into the emblematic qualities of her writings. The analysis also provides scriptural references for many of O'Connor's works, treating them almost as artistic sermons.

Di RENZO's book is written in an engaging, lighthearted fashion, as it examines O'Connor's fascination with the grotesque and sense of the comedic. Far from being a bleak, dour writer, O'Connor is presented here as a brilliant satirist, who, like the medieval sensibility that informs her Catholic imagination, sees the humor in the midst of the darkness. Di Renzo actively engages in quarreling with critics who want to make O'Connor into a serious preacher, and he draws from François Rabelais and Mikhail Bakhtin in his discussion of her individual works. O'Connor's wit is what makes her iconoclasm and social criticism palatable.

O'Connor's narrative secret, according to JOHANSEN, is her use of the "trickster" as the basis of her works to produce timeless stories rooted in enduring myth. What this means is that O'Connor frequently uses a character descended from the "outsider," such as Prometheus in classical literature and the Vice figure in Medieval morality plays. This character, for example, the Misfit in her short story "A Good Man is Hard to Find," subverts the actions of the "normal" principle characters, drawing aside the curtain on their hypocrisy and shallowness. The trickster then is the one who sees more clearly the foibles of humankind and comments on the sins of and necessary correctives for society. Johansen concludes that O'Connor herself acts as trickster in incorporating the Christian idea of the Incarnation, the Divine act that ultimately "turns the world upside down," into her works. The volume presents a provocative archetypal, religious, and literary antecedent study.

SPIVEY's ambitious biography of O'Connor combines his personal knowledge of the author through encounters and correspondence with a Jungian study of her and her works, as well as a sociological study of O'Connor's South. He portrays the writer as a social critic, religious philosopher, and as even a feminist unaware of her feminism. This last hypothesis is the most interesting aspect of Spivey's study, as he sets out to prove that despite her conservatism, O'Connor was concerned with gender as well as racial equity. A weakness of the book is that it sometimes has too much of Spivey and too little of O'Connor.

For a beginning student of O'Connor, WHITT's volume in the "Understanding Contemporary American Literature Series" is a good place to start. Whitt provides a chapter of basic biography and a chapter on each of O'Connor's works, including her essays in *Mystery and Manner: Occasional Prose* and the collection of her letters, *The Habit of Being: Letters*. The chapters on her writings include publication information, plot summary, and Whitt's brief interpretation of O'Connor's works. Also included is a very helpful annotated bibliography.

In a collection of essays that updates Friedman and Clark's volume, RATH and SHAW prove that O'Connor continues to draw the attention of scholars in a postmodern world that may disagree with her religious views. The introduction presents an insightful chronological overview of earlier criticism, as well as a preview of the essays included in this anthology. The approaches of these current essays include gender studies, contemporary rhetorical approaches, and reader-response criticism, as well as views on O'Connor's asceticism and "aesthetics of torture." Two of the essays on gender, by Marshall Bruce Gentry and Richard Giannone, conclude that O'Connor presents a primarily androgynous view in her stories.

CAROL BLESSING

O'Keeffe, Georgia 1887–1986

American Painter

Hoffman, Katherine, *An Enduring Spirit: The Art of Georgia O'Keeffe*, Metuchen, New Jersey: Scarecrow Press, 1984

Hogrefe, Jeffrey, *O'Keeffe: The Life of an American Legend*, New York: Bantam, 1992

Lisle, Laurie, *Portrait of an Artist: A Biography of Georgia O'Keeffe,* New York: Seaview, 1980; revised edition, Albuquerque: University of New Mexico Press, 1986; London: Heinemann, 1987

Lynes, Barbara Buhler, *O'Keeffe, Stieglitz and the Critics, 1916–1929,* Ann Arbor, Michigan: UMI Research Press, 1989

Pollitzer, Anita, *A Woman on Paper: Georgia O'Keeffe,* New York: Simon and Schuster, 1988

Robinson, Roxana, *Georgia O'Keeffe: A Life,* New York: Harper and Row, 1989

Unlike many other women artists of this century, O'Keeffe preferred to live her private life out of the public eye. She did not offer interviews or entertain critics, and kept her personal papers to herself, with the exception of her own book, *Georgia O'Keeffe* (1976). Consequently, there is a greater body of published material focusing on her work than on her life, which is surely how she would have liked it.

HOFFMAN emphasizes the importance of early twentieth-century New York as the formative environment of O'Keeffe's artistic vision. O'Keeffe's contacts with intellectual and artistic circles that rebelled against Victorian values, and called for modernism and individuality, gave her freedom to develop as a woman and as an artist that no previous period would have afforded her. In the middle section of the book, titled "The Critics and Their Background," the author accepts as true O'Keeffe's statements about her own work, particularly her denials of the assumed sexual imagery in her work, and examines the critics to see how they developed a mythology about the art. She finds that criticism of O'Keeffe is of three main types: discussion of her work as emblematic of the feminine experience, attempts to decipher perceived symbolism in the work, and descriptions of the relationship of nature to her work. A third section of Hoffman's book describes individual paintings and sculpture from a technical standpoint. An extensive annotated bibliography, although now outdated, gives excellent guidance through six decades of reviews and criticism.

LYNES shows how O'Keeffe, herself a private, even isolated, figure, gained widespread acclaim through the promotion and advocacy of Alfred Stieglitz. The book examines the contemporary criticism of O'Keeffe's work, describing it as a collection of writings that demonstrates how New York's male-dominated art community dealt with a woman whose talent they could not deny but whose imagery they could not interpret. Lynes argues that Stieglitz himself promoted the idea that O'Keeffe's work should be interpreted in Freudian terms, as an expression of female eroticism—an interpretation O'Keeffe always refuted. The story of the criticism is the story of O'Keeffe's struggle to define the terms under which her art would be examined, and her eventual success. This is an essential study of the relationship between O'Keeffe and Stieglitz, and between O'Keeffe and her work.

The two major biographies are those by Robinson and Hogrefe, both written recently enough to make use of sources not available to scholars during O'Keeffe's lifetime, and to include extensive and current bibliographies. ROBINSON is an art historian and a novelist, and she has written previously about other members of Stieglitz's circle. Her volume is enormous, a detailed and well-documented feminist study, written with the assistance of the O'Keeffe family. With a novelist's expansiveness, the author describes the places O'Keeffe lived and the people who lived there with her, particularly the women who shared her life at every stage. Robinson is always conscious of O'Keeffe as a woman, defying the expectations set for her as artist, wife, and celebrity, and struggling to find a balance between love and work. The book traces the importance of the women's movement of the early part of the century to O'Keeffe's thinking, the embracing of her art and career by the renewed women's movement in the 1970s, and her ultimate rejection of feminists, if not feminism. Robinson has little new to offer about O'Keeffe's relationship with Stieglitz, but presents new and valuable information and insight into the companion of her old age, Juan Hamilton.

HOGREFE is a longtime arts columnist, and he approaches O'Keeffe's life as a journalist looking for secrets and answers. While Robinson had the help of the O'Keeffe family, Hogrefe met O'Keeffe personally, and conducted several interviews with Juan Hamilton. The emphasis in this book is on O'Keeffe's life, how she was able to achieve such admiration and celebrity while flouting all the expectations society had for a woman and an artist, and how she was able to draw around her such devoted friends and lovers despite being so difficult to get along with. While O'Keeffe's lesbianism is only hinted at in other studies, or raised as a possibility and then dismissed, Hogrefe recounts several sexual relationships the artist had with women. He makes an interesting argument that several facets of O'Keeffe's art and life, including the sexual imagery of the flower paintings, were expressions of the sexuality that she felt compelled to repress.

Another useful biography is that by LISLE, the first serious attempt at presenting O'Keeffe's life, but no longer the most complete. According to the author, O'Keeffe's drawings express her conflicts over wanting to be a mother and an artist; she was persuaded by Stieglitz and others that she could not be both. The book emphasizes the ways in which O'Keeffe was held back by her gender and by the politicization of her art, and her struggles to make her own choices.

An important look at the early years of O'Keeffe's career is provided by POLLITZER, the friend who first showed O'Keeffe's drawings to Stieglitz. As the biography explains in some detail, the two women became friends in art school in 1915; O'Keeffe encouraged Pollitzer to write a memoir in the 1950s and then refused permission for the completed manuscript to be published. It remained unpublished but available to scholars until both women had died. The memoir does not, apparently, present O'Keeffe's early years as she would have liked them to be remembered—certainly Pollitzer saw only the rewarding and happy side of O'Keeffe's marriage. The author presents a portrait of an independent, vulnerable artist, who deeply admired and loved her husband and mentor. Unlike some other books, this shows a relationship in which O'Keeffe was as important to Stieglitz's artistic development and personal contentment as he was to hers.

—CYNTHIA A. BILY

Oral History

Gluck, Sherna Berger, and Daphne Patai (eds.), *Women's Words: The Feminist Practice of Oral History,* New York: Routledge, 1991

Kennedy, Elizabeth Lapovsky, and Madeline D. Davis, *Boots of Leather, Slippers of Gold: The History of a Lesbian Community,* New York: Routledge, 1993

Personal Narratives Group (ed.), *Interpreting Women's Lives: Feminist Theory and Personal Narratives,* Bloomington: Indiana University Press, 1989

Ritchie, Donald, *Doing Oral History,* New York: Twayne,1995

Tonkin, Elizabeth, *Narrating Our Pasts: The Social Construction of Oral History,* Cambridge and New York: Cambridge University Press, 1992

Within women's studies, oral history has been extremely important because of its ability to illuminate the experiences of people who are usually overlooked, or about whom written sources rarely exist. For the beginner to oral history, RITCHIE provides step-by-step instructions, and even sample questions for use in an oral-history project. Chapters in his work deal with starting an oral-history project, preparing and conducting interviews, using oral history in research and writing, videotaping, teaching, and collecting oral history. His bibliography consists of sections on methodology as well as other topics, including one section that lists 22 titles concerned with women's studies. In addition, women's studies and other disciplines are indexed so that users can easily find references to relatively obscure compilations of oral-history narratives and other oral-history publications.

Many oral-history works contain introductory chapters on methodology and, for this reason, should also be consulted both by beginners and more advanced scholars concerned with theory and practice in oral history. KENNEDY and DAVIS, for example, provide a thorough discussion of their choices, as well as a good model of an attempt to establish an oral history archive. Kennedy and Davis also discuss the necessity of repeat interviews, anonymity, and the narrators' input in making written transcriptions.

The introduction to GLUCK and PATAI's essay collection notes that women's studies scholars have offered work that has not only added to the body of knowledge about women's lives, but also has contributed important theoretical discussions about knowledge itself, power and privilege, and the linguistic turn within traditional academic disciplines. To illustrate these points, Gluck and Patai compiled the essays of sixteen scholars who had been originally trained in anthropology, history, folklore, literature, psychology, sociology, linguistics, and speech communication. Drawing on their experiences in a variety of national and international contexts, these scholars discuss the process of conducting interviews and analyzing findings while also noting problems related to presuppositions, contradictions, and the goals of feminist scholars. The essays range in subject from interviewing techniques and explorations of narrative structure to the use of oral history in activism. Other discussions underscore some of the typical pitfalls of fieldwork in general.

For a detailed discussion of the problems inherent in interviewing and the use of textual analysis of interviews, TONKIN supplements Gluck and Patai's by urging researchers to proceed despite some problematic procedures. Tonkin encourages researchers to address these problems when necessary and to discuss any changes as part of an ongoing conversation on methodology. Tonkin uses her work with West African communities to show how ideas of self originate in oral narration, a concept important to many researchers in women's studies. She extends this approach by demonstrating that narrators are active participants in the construction of these stories, whether the stories are told to researchers or to others in their own community. Noting theories by Louis Althusser, Laurence Thompson, Jan Vansina, and other anthropologists (most of whom are male), she shows how frequently discussed theories are limited by cultural specificity. This argument, long posited by feminist researchers, has its most complete discussion in Tonkin's book, although women's studies and feminism are not specifically treated.

Tonkin also reconciles two opposing problems for feminist researchers—that narratives are cultural constructs, which serve to stabilize existing social relationships, and that those speaking are, nevertheless, free to construct variations that express their own personal desires for change. Tonkin insists that oral histories are not written texts, and that transcriptions miss so many nonverbal cues and "connotative speech acts" that written oral history can only be seen as an incomplete record. Women's studies scholars of oral history, then, might turn to Tonkin for the use of oral history in performance and for methods that emphasize the actual voices of people rather than the written record of them.

Finally, for various attempts to construct both theory and practice in a way that aids activism as well as academic inquiry, the PERSONAL NARRATIVES GROUP discusses conception and process in biographical research, which includes oral history. They discuss the process of selecting respondents, setting the context of researchers' involvement, and choosing methodology. In the chapter called, "Narrator and Interpreter," the author considers the very names for subject/interviewee and researcher/interviewer. In another chapter, an anthropologist discusses her experience gained from fieldwork and interviewing, and indicates that the development of a friendship between herself and her informant was mutually beneficial. Other essays by other anthropologists ask questions about various research projects involving African women, Mary Leakey, pro-choice and anti-abortion activists, and hospital workers. By focusing on ethical and academic concerns, the contributors provide a varied range of approaches.

—SUSAN TUCKER

P

Pankhurst, Christabel 1880–1958
Emmeline 1858–1928
and
Sylvia 1882–1960

British Suffragists

Bullock, Ian, and Richard Pankhurst (eds.), *Sylvia Pankhurst: From Artist to Anti-Fascist*, London: Macmillan, and New York: St. Martin's Press, 1992

Castle, Barbara, *Sylvia and Christabel Pankhurst*, London: Penguin, and New York: Viking, 1987

Kamm, Josephine, *The Story of Emmeline Pankhurst*, New York: Meredith Press, 1968

Marcus, Jane (ed.), *Suffrage and the Pankhursts*, London: Routledge, and New York: Macmillan, 1967

Mitchell, David, *The Fighting Pankhursts*, London: Cape, and New York: Macmillan, 1987

———, *Queen Christabel: A Biography of Christabel Pankhurst*, London: Macdonald and Jane's, 1977

Romero, Patricia, *E. Sylvia Pankhurst: Portrait of a Radical*, New Haven, Connecticut: Yale University Press, 1987

Winslow, Barbara, *Sylvia Pankhurst: Sexual Politics and Political Activism*, New York: St. Martin's Press, and London: UCL, 1996

Emmeline, Christabel, and Sylvia Pankhurst are best known for their involvement in the struggle for women's suffrage in Britain. Much of the literature on the Pankhurst women concentrates on this part of their lives. Yet, after suffrage, each of them focused on different political activities. For example, Emmeline and Christabel ran for Parliament, Christabel became religious and lectured on the apocalypse, and Sylvia supported the Russian Revolution and Ethiopian independence. While the chosen works do focus on the Pankhursts' political activities beyond suffrage, more has been written about Sylvia, most likely because her interests were not only more diverse but more successful. Books about them reflect conflicting portraits of these three women, as well as speculation about their sexualities. The main consensus on the Pankhursts is that in terms of their political ideals, they were dedicated and determined women, each demonstrating capable leadership.

MITCHELL's study of the Pankhurst women (1967) demonstrates that their fight for suffrage was based on the issue of equal rights for men and women. All three women needed drama, public recognition, loyalty from their followers, and rapid resolutions to all of their campaigns. Mitchell describes the Women's Social and Political Union as "the largest and most efficient of any political organization in Britain." The author believes the Pankhurst women were neither lesbian nor feminist, but were political activists whose gender was incidental.

Conversely, CASTLE suggests that Christabel and Sylvia Pankhurst exemplify two distinct feminisms. Their differing personalities caused a rift in their relationship, and led them to dichotomous activisms. The only similarity she points to is their determination. She describes Christabel as confident, extroverted, calculated, obsessed with the importance of her leadership, and later in life, morbid and apocalyptic. She shows that Christabel endorsed the movement's militant activities, while securing her own safety by moving to Paris. The author also raises the question of the sisters' sexualities. While she sees Christabel's hatred of men as a political strategy rather than an indication of lesbianism, she presents Sylvia as sensuous and heterosexual. Sylvia was also independent, but in addition nervous, depressive, and torn between art and suffragism, that is, between loyalty to her mother's and her father's causes. The author believes that Sylvia's social vision was much broader than Christabel's because it encompassed wider reform than women's suffrage.

KAMM's biography focuses primarily on Emmeline's suffrage activism, and shows that even as a child she was interested in oppression and revolution. Emmeline demonstrated qualities of leadership that would serve her in her reform work as a Poor Law guardian, as well as in the suffrage movement. While Emmeline was an eloquent speaker and a capable leader, the author tells us that she was dictatorial in her running of the Women's Social and Political Union. Yet, she was worshiped as a hero by the Union members. The author also describes

Emmeline's relationship with Ethel Smyth, who taught the suffrage leader how to aim and throw stones.

MITCHELL's biography of Christabel (1977) presents her as a calculating leader, yet a troubled person. He connects the personal and political by suggesting that she was trapped in her extremist rhetoric, while protected from the violent consequences of suffrage militancy, a fact that limited her personal growth. As a suffrage leader, she was encouraged in her personal and political extremism by the suffragists' and her mother's adoration for her. Christabel's possible lesbianism stemmed from the ambivalent feelings for "a neurotic mother." The author's portrait of her is concluded by a comparison between Christabel and Ulrike Meinhof of the Baad-Meinhof terrorist group.

BULLOCK and PANKHURST state that the difficulty of writing a good biography of Sylvia lies in the diversity of her activities. Therefore, each essay in the collection focuses on one aspect if her life, including her art, her suffrage activism, her pacifism, her communism, and her anti-fascism. Particularly useful are the two essays on Sylvia's art, where we are given accounts of her artistic education, analyses of her designs for the Women's Social and Political Union, her mural for the Independent Labor Party hall, and her series on working women.

ROMERO interprets Sylvia's life in terms of her personal and political radicalism. She shows that Sylvia's relentless nature, compounded with the ethic of social activism inherited from her father, made her shift her loyalties to different causes many times during her life. The author provides an alternative to Sylvia's autobiography, by trying to balance Sylvia's achievements in suffragism, socialism, and anti-fascism with a picture of a woman who is a political naif, an emotional campaigner, a poor financial manager, a poor organizer, and a flawed writer. She describes the split among the three Pankhursts as rooted in political differences, Sylvia's jealousy of Emmeline's relationship with Christabel, and Sylvia's illegitimate son.

Instead of interpreting Sylvia's politics as discontinuous, WINSLOW sees Sylvia as the first to connect feminism and socialism. While her political activism began with the woman's suffrage movement, Sylvia became increasingly concerned with the plight of the working class women and men. She saw the issue of women's suffrage in terms of class as well as gender. Sylvia is described as an international feminist whose London organization, the East London Federation of the Suffragettes, later known as the Workers' Suffrage Federation, was both feminist and working class. Sylvia also took stands against racism, imperialism, and colonialism when few people were following suit. While the author believes that it is probable that Emmeline and Christabel were lesbians, she also suggests a lesbian relationship between Sylvia and Zelie Emerson.

Studies of the suffragists can reconfigure notions of women's autobiography, issues of class, and perspectives on the women's movement. MARCUS's introduction to source materials in the Fawcett Library comments on distortions inherent in accounts of the suffragists by both historians of and participants in the suffrage movement. She says that instead of viewing the suffragists as hysterical women, we should read their outspokenness as disruptive of masculine discourse at a time when women were expected to be silent. The hunger strikes, women's refusal to eat and nourish the body, are refusals of motherhood. The author begins and ends with images of forcefeeding as rape.

—HELEN THOMPSON

See also Suffrage: Britain and Ireland

Patriarchy

Boserup, Ester, *Women's Role in Economic Development*, London: Allen and Unwin, 1970

Delphy, Christine, *Close to Home: A Materialist Analysis of Women's Oppression*, translated and edited by Diana Leonard, London: Hutchinson, and Amherst: University of Massachusetts Press, 1984

Dworkin, Andrea, *Pornography: Men Possessing Women*, London: Women's Press, and New York: Perigee, 1981

Firestone, Shulamith, *The Dialectic of Sex: The Case for Feminist Revolution*, New York: Morrow, 1970; and London: Cape, 1971

Millett, Kate, *Sexual Politics*, New York: Doubleday, 1970; London: Hart-Davies, 1972

Rich, Adrienne, *Of Woman Born: Motherhood as Experience and Institution*, New York: Norton, 1976; London: Virago Press, 1977

Walby, Sylvia, *Patriarchy at Work*, Minneapolis: University of Minnesota Press, and Cambridge: Polity Press, 1986

———, *Theorising Patriarchy*, Oxford: Basil Blackwell, 1990

Patriarchy has been a central concept in feminist theory, although there has been considerable debate as to what exactly its nature is. Patriarchy is a trans-historical, cross-cultural political system in which women are subordinated, exploited, and controlled by men. Women's reproductive role has been seen as the central site of women's subordination, where their labour is exploited by the men who control them in the biological family. One of the issues has been the extent to which patriarchy is a universal, unchanging system, one that changes historically and cross-culturally.

BOSERUP provides an empirical account of the sexual division of labour on a world-wide basis. Her account, which focuses on agricultural societies, demonstrates that while the roles women perform differ cross-culturally, women are exploited and dominated in all societies.

FIRESTONE argues that reproduction is the real basis of human society, and therefore the basis of women's subordination by men. The division of the sexes is at the root of all social and cultural divisions. Women's reproductive capacity makes them vulnerable to male control, and as a result they have been subordinated throughout history. Reproductive technologies, she suggests, will make the differences between men and women increasingly irrelevant, but men would not give up their power without a struggle.

Many feminists reject the biologism of Firestone, and argue for a material base for patriarchy. DELPHY analyses patriarchy using a materialist framework. She explores women's economic exploitation within families in the domestic mode of production. MILLETT emphasises patriarchy as a universal ideology of male superiority, reinforced by scientific "knowledge." The social construction of gender, resulting in the differential treatment of the sexes, forms the focus of male power over women.

Sexuality and power are seen by Dworkin and Rich as the basis of male power. DWORKIN points to two major historical forms of patriarchy, both based on sexuality, but differing according to the ways in which sexuality and reproductive capacity are regulated. In the first, "family mode," women are kept and exploited for life, and in the second, "brothel mode," they lose support from men when their sexual and reproductive period is over. RICH suggests that heterosexuality as an expectation for all women is a patriarchal institution. Compulsory heterosexuality makes female friendship difficult, as all female bonding is seen as threatening patriarchal control. Male sexuality is forced on women, and women are controlled by force and physical fear.

WALBY has developed an analysis of patriarchy that takes account of different forms of gender inequality historically, across cultures and among classes and ethnic groups. In her study (1986), she focuses on patriarchal relations in the workplace, arguing that the labour market situation of women confirms women's subordinate position in the household. She argues that the relationship between patriarchy and capitalism is one of tension and conflict.

In WALBY's other book (1990), she outlines six structures where patriarchy operates in articulation with capitalism: the patriarchal mode of production, patriarchal relations in paid work, patriarchal relations in the state, male violence, patriarchal relations in sexuality, and patriarchal relations in cultural institutions. Walby argues that patriarchy is not unchanging. She distinguishes between private patriarchy (men's control of women in the domestic sphere) and public patriarchy (men's control of women in the marketplace). She argues that while it is in men's interests to exploit and control women in the domestic sphere, capitalists want to exploit women in the labour market. The conflict between patriarchy and capitalism since the nineteenth century has resulted in a move away from private patriarchy, and toward public patriarchy.

—PAMELA ABBOTT

Paul, Alice *see* National Women's Party; Suffrage: United States; League of Women Voters

Pavlova, Anna 1881–1931

Russian Dancer

Dandré, Victor, *Anna Pavlova,* New York: B. Blom, 1932

Fonteyn, Margot, *Pavlova: Portrait of a Dancer,* New York: Viking, 1984

Franks, A.H. (ed.), *Pavlova: A Biography,* London: Burke, and New York: Macmillan, 1956

Kerensky, Oleg, *Anna Pavlova,* London: Hamilton, and New York: Dutton, 1973

Lazzarini, John, and Roberta Lazzarini, *Pavlova: Repertoire of a Legend,* London: Collier Macmillan, and New York: Schirmer, 1980

Money, Keith, *Anna Pavlova: Her Life and Art,* London: Collins, and New York: Knopf, 1982

Oliveroff, André, *Flight of the Swan: A Memory of Anna Pavlova,* New York: Dutton, 1932

There is no doubt that Anna Pavlova is one of the best known dancers of all time. Yet surprisingly, little is known about Pavlova the dancer and even less about Pavlova the woman. FONTEYN has tried to show the gradual transformation from eager child, through dedicated student, fledgling ballerina, and excited young celebrity, to supreme artist, mature woman, and eventually to the pure essence of dance. Fonteyn attempts to illuminate Pavlova's magical personality by drawing on her spoken word in interviews, and on the written words attributed to her in articles. Observations from the memoirs of Victor Dandré, Theodore Stier, and André Oliveroff are included for added depth to the portrait of Anna Pavlova.

LAZZARINI and LAZZARINI's book is devoted to Anna Pavlova in performance. The authors document her vast repertoire and picture her in some 90 of her roles. The material generally follows the chronology of the photographs rather than the chronology of first performance. In this way, readers may gain a clearer idea of the evolution of Pavlova's artistry and of the progress of a life virtually spent on the stages of the world. The body of this book is divided into two parts. In part one, Pavlova's development is traced from talented, faltering beginner to prima ballerina in a series of short essays based on descriptions and impressions from contemporary sources. Part two is purely documentary: following brief statements of data pertinent to Pavlova's roles are extracts from press releases from around the world. This work not only celebrates Pavlova's centennial year, but it also attempts to inspire a more profound awareness of the remarkable woman who in the early part of this century became the most famous ballerina in the world, and who remains a perpetual inspiration for dancers everywhere.

The primary function of FRANKS's book is to commemorate the 25th anniversary of the death of Anna Pavlova, and to establish a clear picture both of the ballerina and of the woman. Each of the contributors has written about diverse aspects and qualities of Pavlova's life. Some were her friends over a period of years, some knew her professionally, and others only met her a few times. This book provides a detailed picture of Pavlova by use of press cuttings and hours of conversations with people who knew her. Franks has attempted to develop a three-dimentional picture of Anna Pavlova.

DANDRÉ wrote Anna Pavlova's biography shortly after her death. However, as her husband, he naturally and understandably colored his narrative, so that it is noted more for its adulation than its insight into her character. Dandré presents an image of Pavlova that is full of spiritual beauty. The book proceeds naturally from the early days through Pavlova's last day, stopping periodically to comment on her views and ideas, her favorite charities, some of the people she met, and on a more personal note, her favorite flowers and pets. Dandré wrote this book from the vantage point of being Pavlova's closest associate. Nobody knew her as well as Dandré. After spending a lifetime in the company of Anna Pavlova, Dandré produced a book that is utterly devoted, very detailed, almost like a monument symbolizing an ideal.

Anna Pavlova had a mysterious, enigmatic, indefinable quality. Her impact was felt throughout the world. KERENSKY has tried to present Pavlova in this way, as a woman full of mystery. The author's admiration for her dancing and her personality shine clearly through the pages of this book. Most who write about Pavlova have an amazing devotion and loyalty to her memory; some of them simply are not willing to discuss any faults she may have had and indeed scarcely wish to acknowledge that she was a mere mortal. However, Kerensky makes no attempt to conceal her blemishes, nor does he solve all the mysteries. This book attempts to dissect Pavlova. It examines different aspects of her in isolation from the whole. It also dispels the image of Pavlova as a kind of nun. It shows her as a magnetic and versatile dancer who lived a full life and took an immense and lively interest in the world around her. One of the features of this book is the list of references used, several of which are out of print and not available. Also, there is a list of dancers and others who worked with Pavlova who supplied information for this writing.

MONEY charts the course of Pavlova's life and the effect she had on the history of dancing. There came a point in Pavlova's career at which world events finally played a decisive hand in the direction of her aims, and the book describes these changes. Because Pavlova survived by carrying with her secure, unshakable traditions, Money back-steps a little to talk about her surroundings and the influences that formed her. This book contains so much detail that a determined reader will understand the full implication behind the mere mention of a country or a brutally stark itinerary and know that Pavlova's energy never faltered. She was a missionary for her art and she served it faithfully, above everything and everyone. Money looks at Pavlova's progress as being meteoric, because so much detail subsequently has been pared away. She is often presented as some disembodied head of thistledown, skimming along above rougher pasture as if she never came from any base. However, Money shows that this is not true. He tells the reader that Pavlova grew out of a dense and competititve field, and that she flowered in much the same way as her fellow dancers.

Certainly readers will question the method used in OLIVEROFF's book. This is not a biography of Anna Pavlova, but a first-person-narrated, fictionalized account. This work is somewhat weakened by putting in the foreground a character who is vastly less interesting than the great ballerina actually was. Oliveroff shows Pavlova as a woman with a personality that at an astonishingly early age had succeeded in transmuting itself into terms of the impersonal. Hence, the reader is deprived of an intimate soul-revealing biography. There is no dramatization of the early years. Pavlova, in this account, did not have early conflicts and failures, which tend to make the most interesting pages of the typical biography. This is not a complete biography of Anna Pavlova, but only pages from the lives of the dancer and her company.

—SUSAN M. TAYLOR

Peace Movements

Alonso, Harriet Hyman, *Peace as a Woman's Issue: A History of the U.S. Movement for World Peace and Women's Rights*, Syracuse, New York: Syracuse University Press, 1993

Elshtain, Jean Bethke, *Women and War*, Brighton: Harvester, and New York: Basic Books, 1987

Harris, Adrienne, and Ynestra King (eds.), *Rocking the Ship of State: Toward a Feminist Peace Politics*, Boulder, Colorado: Westview Press, 1989

Jones, Lynne (ed.), *Keeping the Peace*, London: Women's Press, 1983

Liddington, Jill, *The Road to Greenham Common: Feminism and Anti-Militarism in Britain since 1820*, London: Virago, 1989; Syracuse, New York: Syracuse University Press, 1991

McAllister, Pam (ed.), *Reweaving the Web of Life: Feminism and Nonviolence*, Philadelphia: New Society, 1982

Pierson, Ruth Roach (ed.), *Women and Peace: Theoretical, Historical, and Practical Perspectives*, London and New York: Croom Helm, 1987

Ruddick, Sara, *Maternal Thinking: Toward a Politics of Peace*, Boston: Beacon Press, 1989; London: Women's Press, 1990

Warren, Karen J., and Duane L. Cady (eds.), *Bringing Peace Home: Feminism, Violence, and Nature*, Bloomington: Indiana University Press, 1996

Women have been involved in peace work since the beginning of the organized movement at the start of the nineteenth century in Europe and the United States. Three major areas of investigation in this field have been apparent since the 1970s: works on the historical role of women in the peace movement worldwide; works on the theoretical basis of women's relationship to peace and war; and works that include the voices of women who are active in peace work.

Alonso, Liddington, and Pierson incorporate a feminist critique of how and why women participated in the peace movement, and what was unique about women's historical contribution to peace work. ALONSO traces the history of women in the peace movement in the United States from the 1820s to the 1980s. She connects women who worked for peace with feminism and women's rights throughout that period. LIDDINGTON covers the same period for Great Britain. Like Alonso, Liddington was inspired to trace the historical and theoretical underpinnings of women's peace work of the 1980s. PIERSON has edited essays on specific examples of women's peace work from North America, Europe, and Asia. These essays make connections between peace and contemporary movements for women's rights. Essays on the theoretical background of women's work for peace, and on patriarchal society, are also included. All three works conclude that while there are deep philosophical and historical connections between feminism and peace, not all feminists have a commitment to working in the peace movement.

Elshtain and Ruddick tackle the connection between women and their roles in war and peace. ELSHTAIN critiques the various feminist positions on the issue of peace that traditionally identify women as the "lifegivers," and thus, the antithesis of war. She presents the complex relationship women have had with war over time. As women have often supported war efforts, Elshtain concludes that women cannot be simply characterized as naturally peaceful.

RUDDICK contends that women's everyday maternal functions contrasts sharply with militarism as an institution. She acknowledges the role women have had in supporting war efforts. Ruddick goes on to trace how materialism and the role of mothers have been important in the conducting of war and peace. She notes that because peace, rather than war, is more likely to ensure the survival of their children, "maternal practice is a natural resource for peace politics."

WARREN and CADY have edited a volume of essays centered on how feminism may be used to analyze violent and oppressive behavior. They show that an aim of feminism is to end the domination and subordination of women. They also define war as a system of domination promulgated by the extreme use of force. A feminism-based peace politics, they argue, would have to critique a system of domination and oppression. The essays include feminist analysis of environmental violence, theories of war, individual male acts of violence against women such as rape and incest, and women's participation in patriarchal systems of violent domination.

HARRIS and KING, in their collection of essays, have attempted to link history, theory, and stories of activism with their book. Their authors see women's peace efforts as intrinsic to the future existence of the human race. The first section includes essays that bring feminist theory to grassroots peace politics. These authors relate how feminism and a "women's peace movement" bring new perspectives to the intricate questions surrounding peace, war, a just society, and the nature of future civilization. Some of the authors express concern with the need for women to act as nonviolent "warriors" to combat their own oppression. The essays in the second section offer feminist challenges to militarism and military culture. Some authors identify the culture of militarism with a super-masculinity, and as an absence of the feminine and the female. Others recount the difficult relationship that women have had with military culture as dependents of military men or as military personnel themselves. The third section presents examples of women's group actions for peace, such as the efforts of Women Strike for Peace and the women's peace camps at Greenham Common in England and Seneca Falls, New York in the United States. These efforts are presented as successful challenges to patriarchal militaristic culture.

JONES has edited a volume of essays from women all over the world who have worked against nuclear weapons during the 1980s. She includes autonomous women's groups that organized around peace issues in Europe, Asia, and North America. These essays relate the variety of actions and tactics women have used in their antinuclear resistance. Some contributors organized with like-minded mothers as a way to counter the terrible threat of nuclear war and the possible destruction of their children. Others squarely placed a feminist critique of a militaristic, patriarchal society at the center of their actions for peace.

This volume ends with specific plans and suggestions for women on how to organize their own actions.

McALLISTER has edited a book of 56 essays, interviews, and histories of women who have been involved in nonviolent action for social change. As the subtitle suggests, these women connect their work for peace with a feminist analysis. Some pieces are first person accounts, such as Marion Bromley's account of her work for peace and for racial and gender justice from the 1940s onward. Others present analysis and information on how to make connections between nonviolence and feminism, such as Priscilla Prutzman's "Assertiveness, Nonviolence, and Feminism." McAllister has provided a multifaceted book of the voices of women who work for peace.

—WENDY E. CHMIELEWSKI

See also Women's International League for Peace and Freedom; Greenham Common Women's Peace Camp

Pedagogy, Feminist

Culley, Margo, and Catherine Portuges, *Gendered Subjects: The Dynamics of Feminist Teaching,* London: Routledge and Kegan Paul, 1985

Gallop, Jane (ed.), *Pedagogy: The Question of Impersonation,* Bloomington: Indiana University Press, 1995

Gore, Jennifer, *The Struggle for Pedagogies: Critical and Feminist Discourses as Regimes of Truth,* New York: Routledge, 1993

hooks, bell, *Teaching to Transgress: Education as the Practice of Freedom,* New York and London: Routledge, 1994

Lather, Patti, *Getting Smart: Feminist Research and Pedagogy With/in the Postmodern,* New York: Routledge, 1991

Luke, Carmen, and Jennifer Gore, *Feminisms and Critical Pedagogy,* New York: Routledge, 1992

There is not just one feminist pedagogy, but rather a variety of ways of thinking about teaching and learning. Feminist educators have been interested historically in the ways in which formal educational settings are useful in the struggle for gender equity, and the ways in which teaching strategies can aid or inhibit this educational process. For some feminists, this process is seen as important to consciousness-raising and, ultimately, political action. To others, it is seen as a means of gaining qualifications that provide access to some of the powerful institutions that structure people's lives. Feminist pedagogy is a relatively new field, and the books chosen here offer an overview of historical and contemporary approaches.

CULLEY and PORTUGES were forerunners in focusing specifically on the issues surrounding teaching and feminism. Their framework is radical, in the sense that education is seen as having the potential to liberate women—in both a personal and a collective sense. The book focuses on women's studies in the academy, and on the potential for radical pedagogy within this context. An example of the difficulties of this tension is offered by Freidman's essay, in which she argues against the dissolving of the teacher/student power inequity that has been advocated by feminist educators. This approach is committed to increasing the investment of women in the education system, and by so doing, increasing women's ability to merge more successfully with the available power structures, albeit in a feminised form.

LATHER tackles many of the problems and contradictions that are apparent in the collision between feminist theory as a totalising paradigm and ideas about the politics of emancipation. Lather locates her work within the postmodern. The focus of the book is consciousness and its transformation, and Lather certainly concurs with some postmodern notions about the decentred subject, the futility of metanarratives, and the plurality of power and discourse formations. She offers an interrogation of the connections between power, discourse, and consciousness, the purposefulness of such an interrogation and, perhaps most importantly, an implicit insistence on the structures that order the world and their role in the dissemination of power. It is this affirmation of meaning and the crucial importance of engagement with power structures that distinguish her work as being both politically engaged and undermining of postmodernism's relativism and playfulness.

LUKE and GORE's book is a collection of essays by some of the most interesting writers on feminist pedagogy and is firmly placed within feminist poststructuralism. The contributors do not offer any grand plans or methods through which the classroom can be transformed into a truly liberating place, but offer instead some thoughts about the myriad issues that confront anyone thinking seriously about feminist pedagogy. The relationship between pedagogy and wider political struggle is explored, as is the place of women in the academy as a whole. Between these wide issues comes work on the feminist classroom, on the empowerment seen as so crucial, and on the possibilities for change within individuals as well as in practice. The question of empowerment raises many issues, such as how to create an environment in which it might take place within a patriarchal institution; how the power differentials between students and teacher are to be managed when the teacher marks students' work; what happens when the students do not want to be empowered and are only interested in grades; and how the relationships between the students themselves are to be negotiated—especially when they are from disparate social groups.

GORE's book explores the issue of resistance to radical pedagogy in much more depth. Throughout, she considers feminist pedagogy alongside critical pedagogy, which makes for an interesting comparison between two disciplinary branches whose aims seem not dissimilar. In particular, Gore is interested in the ways in which writing about pedagogy, if not pedagogy itself, can be seen as a discourse in the Foucauldian sense. What seems to emerge is the suggestion that such writing can be seen as a discourse—it has an attachment to an institution (usually a university), and through a process of demarcation produces an object of enquiry (education), which exists in opposition to other discourses. This object of enquiry is investigated and analysed, and the knowledge this process produces is sanctioned by the institution that has the capacity for deeming it true. The crux of all this is the carving out of an object and a set of discursive practices relating to it, which at once deem other objects illegitimate. At any rate, Gore confronts some salient issues for educators—particularly those who, like Gore, work in teacher education and thus confront difficult decisions about politics, teaching, and ethics each day.

HOOKS's book is an inspirational text, because it attempts to locate teaching and learning in both a political and a spiritual framework. In terms of politics, hooks is interested in the ways in which racism and sexism are approached and negotiated within classrooms, in connections between power and knowledge, and ultimately in the ways feminist pedagogy assists in the wider struggle for social justice. Unlike the other books treated here, hooks writes of learning as a deeply personal and spiritual experience in which life histories, emotions, and psychologies all play a part in the process of change that feminist education can precipitate. It is not a process that involves only an intellectual shift, but one which involves every part of a human being, and which, because of this, can have a profound effect on people's lives.

GALLOP's book offers a number of papers delivered at a conference called "Pedagogy: The Question of the Personal." She furnishes a very wide selection of essays, and all are characterised by an interest in the influences on the learning/teaching process that cannot be dealt with simply by interrogating structures. Instead, there is an emphasis on the personal—on clothes, the erotic, maternity, sexuality, speaking positions, and the roles played by those intent on teaching and those intent on learning. Cutting across these broad areas are a number of essays that deal with the ways such things affect students of gay studies, the "postmodern Jewish identity," the ethos of multiculturalism, and so on. This book is emblematic of the future direction of feminist writing about pedagogy—a shift from the structural to the personal and the ways this shift relates to wider political concerns.

—KATE PRITCHARD HUGHES

See also Curricular Transformation; Science: Teaching to Women; Mathematics: Teaching to Women

Performance Art

Allsopp, Ric, and Scott deLahunta, *The Connected Body?: An Interdisciplinary Approach to the Body and Performance*, Amsterdam: Amsterdam School of the Arts, 1996

Carr, C., *On Edge: Performance at the End of the Twentieth Century*, Hanover, New Hampshire: Wesleyan University Press, 1993

Champagne, Lenora, *Out from Under: Texts by Women Performance Artists*, New York: Theatre Communications Group, 1990

Hart, Lynda, and Peggy Phelan (eds.), *Acting Out: Feminist Performances*, Ann Arbor: University of Michigan Press, 1993

Juno, Andrea, and V. Vale (eds.), *Angry Women*, San Francisco: Re/Search Publications, 1991

Roth, Moira, *The Amazing Decade: Women and Performance Art in America, 1970–1980*, Los Angeles: Astro Artz, 1983

Ugwu, Catherine (ed.), *Let's Get It On: The Politics of Black Performance*, London: Institute of Contemporary Arts, and Seattle: Bay Press, 1995

Performance art has grown immensely in recent decades, and women have been at the forefront of its growth. One of the best resources for the earlier days of women's performance art in America is by ROTH. The book begins with a general essay that briefly describes the history of the art form, presents the larger issues that led to the creation of this work, and forecasts what most likely will happen in the future. Following the essay, an extended timeline begins in 1770 and lists events in American history, women's history, and women's performance art. The bulk of the book consists of short essays arranged in alphabetical order that describe each woman's background along with an explanation and photograph of one of her primary performance pieces. Finally, Roth and other women complete a bibliography of more general sources related both to women's performance art and the related works of specific women.

CARR, an arts writer for the *Village Voice,* brings together several essays she has written on performance art since she joined the newspaper in 1984, continuing in many ways the work started by Roth. Alhough the book includes essays on both men and women, the largest amount of space is given to work by women such as Ann Magnuson, Lydia Lunch, Annie Sprinkle, and many others. Carr, an artist herself, describes how when she joined the *Village Voice* staff, she knew she wanted to cover performance art. She felt drawn to this open territory and wanted to have a part in defining and describing this innovative new movement in art. The essays are presented in chronological order, a choice that relates the changes in the performance art scene in New York specifically and the art world at large.

HART and PHELAN edit a collection that highlights an academic perspective on performance art that is informed by feminist theory; many of the authors also work in the newer field of "Performance Studies." Next to essays on playwriting and stand-up comedy, many chapters center on performance artists such as Anna Deavere Smith, Karen Finley, and Holly Hughes. In two separate introductions, Hart and Phelan each focus on the political nature of performance and the way that these artists directly address issues of race, gender, disease, and censorship. One key issue that runs throughout many of these essays concerns the issue of identity and how these artists use their work to explore what it means to be a woman.

ALLSOPP and DELAHUNTA also deal with more theoretical and academic issues in their collection of pieces that address the use of the body in art and performance. Essays are written by artists and scholars, and this work draws upon the scholarship of dance, performance, and installation art. Essays center on the work of women such as Linda Montano and Valie Export.

With an emphasis on both American and British work, UGWU brings together pieces that center on multicultural perspectives. Most of these pieces focus on the place of cultural issues in the practice of performance. Ugwu describes the risks these artists take on and the challenges they face in their fights to perform. Essays by scholars such as Coco Fusco, Paul Gilroy, and bell hooks frame descriptions of work by artists such as Susan Lewis.

CHAMPAGNE brings together nine pieces by prominent American female performance artists including Holly Hughes, Karen Finley, and Laurie Anderson. Champagne introduces each of the short scripts with a concise essay that places each woman's work within the larger context of contemporary performance art. In the introduction, she writes of the subversive nature of these performances and the ways these women use the stage to try on various personae in an effort to explore women's complicated social positions. Champagne sees this work not as confessional but as revelatory, and she commends these women for breaking the silences that have been imposed on women for generations.

The overt political nature of women's performance art also comes across in a collection of interviews by JUNO and VALE. The authors interview 16 women, most of whom are performance artists themselves, although all speak about the role that performance plays in both art and women's lives. The women interviewed include Diamanda Galas, Karen Finley, Susie Bright, bell hooks, and Carolee Schneemann. Juno and Vale sought out these women because, as they see it, these artists all use their work to deal directly with the most important issues facing women at the end of the twentieth century.

—NELS P. HIGHBERG

Perkins, Frances 1882–1965

American Politician

Bernstein, Irving, *A Caring Society: The New Deal, the Worker, and the Great Depression,* Boston: Houghton Mifflin, 1985

Grossman, Jonathan, *The Department of Labor,* New York: Praeger, 1973

Martin, George, *Madam Secretary: Frances Perkins,* Boston: Houghton Mifflin, 1976

Mohr, Lillian Holmen, *Frances Perkins: "The Woman in FDR's Cabinet!,"* Croton-on-Hudson, New York: North River Press, 1979

Severn, Bill, *Frances Perkins: A Member of the Cabinet,* New York: Hawthorn, 1976

Ware, Susan, *Beyond Suffrage: Women in the New Deal,* Cambridge, Massachusetts: Harvard University Press, 1981

Frances Perkins has an ambiguous position in historical scholarship. Her appointment as Franklin Roosevelt's Secretary of Labor made her the first female member of the Cabinet, hence one of the great pioneers of modern American politics. However, her status as a pioneer has not earned her a central role in American political history, labor history, or women's history. Perkins's efforts to intervene in the tumultuous labor politics of the 1930s are generally ridiculed or ignored. Only a few historians of the period have raised her above the status of historical footnote.

The most detailed accounts of Perkins's career appear in biographical treatments. Three biographies of Perkins exist; all were published within a three year span in the late 1970s. Martin, Mohr, and Severn provide positive treatments of Perkins and focus their attention on her career as an Industrial Commissioner in New York and as Secretary of Labor. They point to the constructive influence of the settlement house movement on Perkins's attitudes toward the working class and demonstrate her ambivalence toward organized labor. Her appointment to the Cabinet marked Roosevelt's decision to emphasize the Department of Labor's mission to gather health and employment statistics, and its charge to study children's welfare through the Children's Bureau. Under her tenure as Secretary, the Department of Labor shifted its efforts away from prosecution of illegal aliens and embraced efforts to provide a comprehensive statistical examination of the standard of living in the United States. Perkins sought to expand the department's constituency beyond unionized workers and serve the entire working class. The Department of Labor continued to intervene on behalf of organized labor but increasingly submitted to a shared responsibility with detached agencies, notably the National Labor Relations Board.

Among these biographies, MARTIN's analysis displays the most sophisticated understanding of the driving forces in Perkins's life and offers the most compelling examination of her career as a social reformer. He portrays her as a woman inculcated in the nineteenth-century standards of Victorian gentility and later transformed by work with Jane Addams, Florence Kelly, and Al Smith. Martin demonstrates, better than her other biographers, Perkins's pragmatism when dealing with hostile businessmen, politicians, and labor leaders. He aptly discusses her role as a traditional Secretary of Labor, mediating disputes and championing the cause of collective bargaining. In addition, he provides a thorough discussion of her efforts outside the Department of Labor, including her advocacy of Social Security.

The biographies by MOHR and SEVERN are in basic agreement with Martin's analysis. They both benefit from the virtue of brevity, providing succinct accounts of Perkins's career as a social reformer and government official. Although both cover the primary policy conflicts as well as the more personal battles over political turf, neither provides a rich understanding of the dynamics motivating Perkins. Nor do they examine the political implications of policy formulated under Perkins.

GROSSMAN's history of the Department of Labor provides a concise history of Perkins's tenure as the longest-serving Secretary of Labor. More critical than Perkins's biographers, Grossman agrees with their emphasis on the Secretary's efforts to shift the department's mission to one of broad social service for the working class. However, he focuses on the negative institutional ramifications for this policy shift. Under Perkins's tenure the Department of Labor actually shrank in terms of personnel and budget, ceding responsibilities to other departments and accepting shared authority with temporary New Deal agencies.

Perkins regarded the social policy missions of the department as her primary charge. This emphasis is recognized in BERNSTEIN's study of relief policies during the Roosevelt era. Bernstein notes Frances Perkins's role in supporting a policy of federal activism on behalf of the poor. She was an early supporter of Harry Hopkins and his commitment to resolute federal action to provide poor relief. This support of federal relief went beyond the advocacy for key federal appointments to Harry Hopkins and extended to the establishment of principles governing federal social policy. Under Perkins's leadership, the Council on Economic Security proposed a system of shared power between the national and state governments that became the foundation of the Social Security system.

Most historical treatments of Frances Perkins fail to link her to the broader movements in modern American political history. However, WARE places Perkins in the context of women's politics in the Democratic Party. She has identified a network of female political leaders who helped to mold the policies of the Roosevelt administration. Members of this network were dedicated to the dual objectives of placing women in policy-making positions and shifting responsibility for social policy to the federal government. Ware's analysis positions Perkins within a generation of suffragists who had been active in the settlement house movement. Perkins's role as Secretary of Labor exists within the context of a broad women's movement focused on minimum wage issues. Her tenure in the Roosevelt Cabinet is linked to the earlier efforts of private organizations such as the National Consumer's League and the Women's Trade Union League. Her cohort includes Mary Dewson, Katharine Lenroot, and Rose Schneiderman, all women with careers dedicated to establishing standards for minimum income of working families. By providing a broad context for her career as Secretary of Labor, Ware has led the way in pushing Frances Perkins into the mainstream of historical analysis.

—KAREN A.J. MILLER

Peron, Eva 1919–1952

Argentinian Public Figure

Barnes, John, *Evita: First Lady,* New York: Grove Press, 1978

Fraser, Nicholas, and Marysa Navarro, *Evita: The Real Lives of Eva Peron,* London: A. Deutsch, 1996; published as *Eva Peron,* New York: Norton, 1980

Main, Mary, *Evita: The Woman with the Whip,* London: Corgi, 1977; New York: Dodd Mead, 1980; published as *The Woman with the Whip: Eva Peron,* New York: Doubleday, 1952

Martinez, Tomas Eloy, *Santa Evita,* New York: Random House, 1995

Ortiz, Alicia Dujovne, *Eva Peron,* New York: St. Martin's Press, 1996

Since her death at the age of 33, interest in Eva Peron has grown rather than diminished. She has been the subject of a musical play and two films. Her life is now part history and part mythology, and in the years since her death a cult has developed around her life and work. A number of biographies and even a novel try to reconstruct her life, her legacy, and the myth of Evita.

Most of the books rework some of the same material, but each offers a glimpse of the "real" Eva or Evita, as she was affectionately called. Eva Duarte Peron was born poor and illegitimate in rural Argentina and overcame incredible odds to become the first lady of Argentina and a larger than life legend. As many other celebrities create public alter egos, Eva Peron created the personality that became known as Evita. She shaped and carved her image, making it a living legend that became further embellished after her untimely death. All sources seem to agree on the essential character of Eva Peron as an ambitious woman who, against great odds, became the wife of the President of Argentina and possibly the most powerful woman ever in the history of the country. Although frustrated in her attempts to become Vice President of Argentina in her husband's presidency, she soared to even more powerful heights with her official renunciation of power, the martyrdom of her illness and death, and the rise of a cult of Evita that persists long after her demise.

Each of the various major studies makes a contribution to the study of Peron. FRASER and NAVARRO attempt to separate fact from legend in the life of Eva Peron. In particular, they attempt to trace her movement as a teenager from Junin to Buenos Aires. They cast considerable doubt on the legend of her discovery by the Argentinian singer Augustin Magaldi. The work traces her radio career, her work as an actress, and her historic union with Juan Peron. Fraser and Navarro also discredit much of the notorious legend surrounding the young Eva struggling to survive in Buenos Aires in the 1930s. Based on careful research and interviews, the book presents the authors' interpretation of her life and work.

ORTIZ offers a well-researched new addition to the library of works on Peron and spends considerable time discussing and debating various versions of the major occurrences in her life. For example, she explores four different theories of how Peron came to Buenos Aires. She also attempts to chronicle when Eva met Colonel (later General) Juan Peron, offering a hypothesis that it may have been a year before the official meeting in 1944. She even probes the real time of death, which she does not believe to be 8:25 P.M. on July 26, 1952, but sometime earlier on the same day.

Another interesting new contribution to the study of Peron is the work of MARTINEZ, who uses the vehicle of fiction to explore the myths surrounding Peron after her death in 1952, including the saga of the disappearance of her body and its discovery in Milan, Italy in 1971. Martinez's extensive research on both Perons is well-reflected in this work.

BARNES's well-known book focuses on Eva Peron as first lady of Argentina. He highlights her political skills, especially her leadership of the workers (the *descamisados*) and the women of Argentina. He also traces the almost tragic political comeback of Peron and his inability to lead without his Evita in the 1970s.

MAIN presents a far more negative view of Evita. Main was born in Argentina, left Argentina for some years, and returned there in 1951. Her book, written in 1952, under a pseudonym to protect her family, has the flavor of the on-site observer rather than the detached historian. She describes the tyranny and hardships of the Peron years, and the role of Eva in Argentine politics. She removes the romance of the legend and shows the Perons as merciless dictators, who ruined the lives of millions of people. The book was republished in 1980 because of the interest in Eva Peron occasioned by the musical play, *Evita.*

—NORMA NOONAN

Photography

Davis, Keith F., and Kelle A. Botkin, *The Photographs of Dorothea Lange,* Kansas City: Hallmark Cards, 1995
Gernsheim, Helmut, *Julia Margaret Cameron: Her Life and Photographic Work,* London: Fountain Press, and New York: Transatlantic Arts, 1948
Goldberg, Vicki, *Margaret Bourke-White: A Biography,* New York: Harper and Row, and London: Heinemann, 1986
Gover, C. Jane, *The Positive Image: Women Photographers in Turn of the Century America,* Albany: State University of New York Press, 1988
Lorenz, Richard, *Imogen Cunningham: Ideas without End,* San Francisco: Chronicle, 1993
Mitchell, Margaretta K., *Recollections: Ten Women of Photography,* New York: Viking, 1979
Moutoussamy-Ashe, Jeanne, *Viewfinders: Black Women Photographers,* New York: Dodd Mead, 1986
Sullivan, Constance (ed.), *Women Photographers,* New York: Abrams, 1990

The burgeoning presence of female photographers, women's exhibitions, and books of and about female photographers symbolizes that women triumphantly have built a "dark-room of their own," as it were. The history of women in photography, however, remains predictably sparse. Most of the works below detail the separate struggles of the early artists to integrate themselves into the male-run world, at the same time they demanded to be recognized for their own sense of aesthetics. These are the artists who made their emergence from the restrictive "safe-light" that men cast on traditional women's photography, their aesthetic development, and their cultural exposure.

DAVIS neatly captures both Dorothea Lange's philosophy that the camera was an instrument that taught people how to see, and Lange as the visionary who enabled Depression-era America to see itself. He shows Lange's place in the historical/pictorial landscape, with his selection of her photographs of migrant camps and dustbowl victims. But her work is not merely a historical chronicle of the United States; photos taken in Viet Nam and Korea also communicate the universal, primal feelings of pain and isolation. Davis shows the duality inherent in Lange's approach to her work—it belonged to the separate spheres of documentation and interpretation, society and soul, fact and feeling. Lange's own text accompanies the photos, providing subjective yet revealing critical analysis in terms of her inspiration and technique. Davis includes biographical information.

GERNSHEIM chronicles the work and life of the foremost pioneer female photographer, Julia Margaret Cameron. Not only does his book reprint her autobiographical fragment "Annals of My Glass House," but it also reprints a fabulous catalogue of Cameron's unique work. He explores Cameron's associations with the pre-Raphaelites, and her subsequent inspirations to photograph staged tableaus of their poetical and allegorical subjects, most notably those of her friend Alfred, Lord Tennyson's "Idylls of the King." Gernsheim's compilation reveals Cameron's profoundly sensitive vision to things unseen, and her conviction that a photograph should be an embodiment of prayer. Gernshem's work contextualizes the Victorian society that viewed Cameron as an eccentric woman, and the "photographic fathers" who criticized her intentions as "forced art" and her "soft focus" technique as faulty. He allows the modern critic to reevaluate the works of Cameron, a woman who might have been well known in her time, except that she was not considered a "true" artist.

Margaret Bourke-White is sometimes remembered as the "sweetheart" of American photojournalism. GOLDBERG's book shows how this is merely a superficial representation of the driven personality who overcame social, emotional, and financial struggles before achieving success as a *Life* magazine photographer. Even in the 1930s and 1940s, photography continued to be the province of male creative powers. Goldberg tells how Bourke-White defied this rule, taking on typically male "global" assignments like World War II bombing missions, concentration camps, and the British Empire's dissolution in India. While it includes a few of Bourke-White's trademark "sharp focus" architectural and industrial pieces, this account is an intensely personal one, accessing exclusive journals as well as Bourke-White's autobiography, in order to demonstrate personal situations underneath her public persona: her childhood, her family and the Jewish roots she tried to conceal, her failed marriages, and finally the disease that defeated her.

When George Eastman made the camera accessible to the general population in the 1880s, he could not have imagined how quickly it would become a tool of rebellion for Victorian-era women. GOVER's impressive book is less important for its revelation of pictorial representations of the domestic feminine than for its discussion of the feminist network of women that emerged during this time. It shows the united strengths of women who vigorously pursued their new interests, ideologically rather than individually, and who sought to support one another in the spheres of culture, technology, sociology, and art as a means of remaining visible in an all-male system. It includes biographical information of key photographers Gertrude Kasebier, Frances Benjamin Johnston, Alice Austen, Catherine Weed Ward, and other women, both in front of and behind the camera, who were creating their "positive images"—often subversive, androgynous, and homoerotic.

Imogen Cunningham, when asked about her role as a female photographer, quickly responded that "photography has no sex." LORENZ's compilation of her ethereal compositions confirm that she was perennially intrigued by the freedoms of the spirit, rather than the restrictions of the body. His explication of the life and works of this blithe spirit places her as part of a resolute West Coast avant-garde movement that naturally refused to merge with the pragmatic realism of photojournalism in the early twentieth century. Her photographic style and liberated imagination snubbed the bounds of bourgeois mentality, and persisted in creating a charmed, atmospheric body of work that is well represented here. Her inspirations are traced, as well as her evolution from rural naturalism—sensual nudes, evocative botanicals, expressive landscapes—to the mythical and mystical, injecting commonplace scenes with a sense of other-worldliness. Lorenz also shows her later influences of a Picasso-like cubism.

As if in prescient response to the ill sentiment of agism, MITCHELL lauds then octogenarian artisans (Berenice Abbott, Ruth Bernhard, Carlotta M. Corpron, Louise Dahl-Wolfe, Nell Dorr, Toni Frissell, Laura Gilpin, Lotte Jacobi, Consuelo Kanaga, and Barbara Morgan), both through exhibition of their works and the accompanying text, as testament to the "wisdom of the elders." Mitchell has compiled lives and works of 10 pioneer American women photographers, all who were born near the turn of the twentieth century, and who subsequently witnessed and participated, through their cameras, in the major social, cultural, and technological advancements of the century. She highlights those who have remained essentially unrecognized, despite the profundity of their under or unexhibited works. This book is important for photographic history, women's history, the display of varying techniques and, not least of all, artistic inspiration.

MOUTOUSSAMY-ASHE's work documents the triple oppressions of race, sex, and class that afflicted 34 black female photographers from 1839 to 1985. Because of the fact that their work was treated as insignificant for a long time, first belittled by the "white" culture they were struggling to work in, and then all but lost to history as no one thought it important to preserve their work (and only white photographers kept records), Moutoussamy-Ashe has done an incredible amount of necessary research unearthing their rare photos, portraits, and ads; their work prevails and these women have emerged victorious. This monumental book contains striking images of slave daguerreotypes, early portraiture, Harlem social clubs of the 1920s and 1930s, and the network of beauty shops and choirs. It also shows the spiritual proximity between photographer and subject, both in their photographic capturing of key figures of the civil rights movement like King, Ghandi, and Jackson, and in the images of modern African-America's urban life.

SULLIVAN's anthology serves its capacity as a springboard for those wanting to familiarize themselves with the vast scope of women's photography. First, it spans 200 years of women's photographic history, and the variety of cultural influences and artistic intentions therein. Second, the collection of photographs documents several cultures, and its subjects originate anywhere from Mexico to Manila, involving everything from soup kitchens to surrealism. Third, it provides a representative index of photographers whose autobiographies and exhibitions can usually be pursued separately. Accompanying critical analysis by Eugenia Parry Janis considers the symbolism, representation, and language in the photographs' lines, forms, and color, and how this asserts the temperament and imagination of their photographers.

—ANNMARIE PHILLIPS

Physical Fitness

Cooper, Kenneth H., and Mildred Cooper, *The New Aerobics for Women,* New York: Bantam, 1988

Everson, Corinna, and Jeff Everson, *Cory Everson's Workout,* New York: Perigee, 1991

Fahey, Thomas D., and Gayle Hutchinson, *Weight Training for Women,* Mountain View, California: Mayfield, 1992

Mayghan, Jackie Johnson, and Kathryn Collins, *The Outdoor Woman's Guide to Sports, Fitness, and Nutrition,* Harrisburg, Pennsylvania: Stackpole, 1983

Newby-Fraser, Paula, and John M. Mora, *Paula Newby-Fraser's Peak Fitness for Women,* Champaign, Illinois: Human Kinetics, 1995

Rosenzweig, Sandra, *Sportsfitness for Women,* New York: Harper and Row, 1982

Wells, Christine, *Women, Sport and Performance,* Champaign, Illinois: Human Kinetics, 1985

Literature on women and physical fitness falls into five general categories: 1) books on the physiological effects of exercise for women; 2) how-to books written expressly for women; 3) books on the physiological effects on exercise for both sexes; 4) how-to books for both sexes; and, finally 5) theses, dissertations and other reports of new research. This essay is limited to the first two types of literature. If space permitted, there are a number of titles from the three latter categories that are useful and should be included. However, as a starting point for reading in the field of women and fitness, the following can be highly recommended.

WELLS's text was an important landmark in the history of women and physical fitness. Hers was the first to organize and analyze what research had discovered about the effects of exercise on women. As Wells points out in her introduction, "The fact that this book is necessary speaks to the notion that accurate information is either severely limited or not sufficiently indexed to be readily available." Furthermore, throughout the work she points out where new research is needed to fill the gaps in our knowledge of women and exercise. Organized into five sections, Wells's book examines the differences between the sexes, the effects of exercise on menstruation, exercise in pregnancy and menopause, nutrition and weight control, and the use of exercise to enhance sport performance. Although primarily written for fellow exercise scientists and coaches, Wells's prose is clear and lively, making this an accessible text for even the lay person.

ROSENZWEIG approaches women's fitness from several angles in her popular text. She begins with sound advice on general physical conditioning principles and then moves into a lengthy analysis of forty-five different sporting activities. For each sport included, Rosenzweig includes a brief history, training information, warnings about potential injury sites, an evaluation of the sport's physiological requirements, and comments about its effectiveness as a physical conditioner. In addition, Rosenzweig includes an eighty-page sports medicine guide, which is among the most comprehensive in the field of women's fitness.

COOPER and COOPER have done an outstanding job of blending scientific information and personal testimonials into their book on aerobic exercise. Based on their work at the Cooper Aerobics Center in Dallas, Texas, the books explains how to apply the FIT (frequency, intensity, and time) formula to a variety of exercise activities. In addition, the Coopers give detailed advice on nutrition and weight loss, the connections between exercise and cardiovascular disease, and the effect of weight-bearing exercise on osteoporosis. Filled with graphs to allow the reader to chart progress, the Cooper text is a good place to begin the process of getting in shape. Their section assessing one's physical condition is particularly helpful.

MAUGHAN and COLLINS have written an engaging testimony to the value of outdoor sports as a lifetime approach to physical fitness. With the help of nutritionist Mary Echo and exercise physiologist Alex Urfer, Maughan and Collins clearly explain how to get in shape for such outdoor activities as backpacking, hiking, snowshoeing, rock climbing, mountaineering, canoeing, rafting, kayaking, and Nordic and cross-country skiing. Furthermore, they assess the relative merits of these outdoor activities as physical conditioners. Filled with inspirational stories of women who enjoy outdoor sports, this is a book that can be read for enjoyment and then returned to again and again as reference.

South African triathlete Newby-Fraser has won the grueling Hawaii Ironman triathlon more times than any other woman. In this book, NEWBY-FRASER and MORA present not only the former's personal story but a scientifically sound training regimen for women interested in triathlon training. This book is not for beginners, but for those who wish to move to higher levels. As one would expect, the book contains advice and many insider tips on running, cycling and swimming—the three main events of the triathlon. It also contains excellent sections on strength training, stretching, and sport psychology. For those with time and motivation to achieve what Newby-Fraser defines as "peak fitness," this is an inspirational blueprint.

There are several dozen books now available on women's bodybuilding, but they are of varying usefulness. Most books in the field are written by celebrity bodybuilders and are really little more than photo albums. In contrast, the book by EVERSON and EVERSON can be recommended for its useful, frequently lighthearted text. Cory Everson is the most successful female bodybuilder of all time. Following her many wins in the Ms. Olympia competition, she has done film work and has had her own fitness show on ESPN television. Ex-husband Jeff has a Ph.D. from the University of Wisconsin, is a respected writer in the field of resistance exercise, and was for many years a competitive bodybuilder. Targeted at beginners, this book opens with a seven-page glossary of words and nicknames used in the field of weight training. It then takes the reader step-by-step through the process of deciding where to train, what to do, what to eat, and how much to rest. The illustrated exercise section of this book is particularly well done. For each exercise both the starting and finishing positions are shown, making it easy to follow the Eversons' tips and instructions. Also notable are the detailed weight programs for athletes who want to improve their performance in sports such as archery, badminton, softball, basketball, bowling, boxing, canoeing, field hockey, gymnastics, handball, and soccer.

FAHEY and HUTCHISON have also written a useful and accurate text on women and resistance exercise. The authors present a detailed physiological assessment of the effects of weight training on women, a good overall statement of the general principles of resistance exercise, and an excellent guide to nutrition for women involved in exercise. The heart of the book, however—the programs and exercise descriptions—is illustrated only by sketchy line drawings, which, while accurate, do not inspire. However, for those looking for a textbook to be used in a women's physical education class, this is the best choice now available.

—JAN TODD

Physicians *see* Doctors

Piercy, Marge 1936–

American Writer

Keulen, Margarete, *Radical Imagination: Feminist Conceptions of the Future in Ursula Le Guin, Marge Piercy, and Sally Miller Gearhart,* New York: Peter Lang, 1991

Shands, Kerstin W., *The Repair of the World: The Novels of Marge Piercy,* Westport, Connecticut: Greenwood, 1994

Walker, Sue, and Eugenie Hamner, *Ways of Knowing: Essays on Marge Piercy,* Mobile, Alabama: Negative Capability Press, 1991

A prolific feminist author, Marge Piercy's contributions to contemporary literature are numerous. She has published 13 volumes of poetry, including *What Are Big Girls Made Of* (1997), *Available Light* (1995), and *Mars and Her Children* (1992). Her novels, also totaling 13, include *City of Darkness, City of Light* (1996), *The Longings of Women* (1994), and *Woman on the Edge of Time* (1976). In 1990, she received the Golden Rose, the oldest poetry award in the United States. Her work is the subject of numerous articles and has, more recently, been the focus of book-length works of criticism.

SHANDS offers an important examination of Piercy's first 12 novels. In one of the few full-length critical works devoted to Piercy's fiction, Shands focuses on the thematic elements within the novels, specifically the manner in which power is portrayed. Shands articulates Piercy's central theme as a battle between connection, creation, and healing; and separation and destruction. Examining specific characters within each of the novels, Shands discusses the essential human qualities Piercy presents as necessary for human connection and continuity. Shands also attempts to place Piercy's work in cultural and ideological context, as well as to map her literary heritage within the American literary tradition. This book is an important source for readers interested in imagery, theme, and characters within Piercy's novels.

A particularly helpful collection, WALKER and HAMNER's book provides a variety of essays that cover both Piercy's novels and poetry. These essays are quite accessible and are without the difficult academic apparatus that might hinder introductory researchers. Organized around Piercy's publication chronology, this text begins with Eleanor Bender's examination of Piercy's first six volumes of poetry (1968–78) and the primary theme of love. In the following two articles, which focus on Piercy's novel *Small Changes* (1973), Maddone Miner provides insight into the novelist's exploration of the social construction of language, while Nancy Topping Bazin examines Piercy's development of the feminist "woman-hero." Karen C. Adams and Franziska Gygax offer interpretations of *Woman on the Edge of Time,* Piercy's utopian science fiction.

Piercy's poetry collection *Stone, Paper, Knife* is the focus of the essays by Lebow and Nelson. Jeanne Lebow examines Piercy's use of tools to encourage positive change, and the evolution of her worldview from anger to hope. Ronald Nelson also focuses on Piercy's move toward the positive, discussing the healing imagery in her poetry. Eugenie Lambert Hamner approaches *Fly Away Home* and Piercy's interest in women's experience in contemporary society. Additional essays focus on Piercy's feminist tarot reading *Laying Down the Tower,* the political themes in Piercy's novels, and the significance of place in her poetry and novels. Sue Walker also offers a chronological overview of Piercy's life and work, examining the autobiographical influences in her work. The collection concludes with a brief interview with Piercy and a bibliography of works by and about Piercy (to 1989). This collection offers a good overview of Piercy's themes and a good introduction to the critical issues surrounding her work.

KEULEN approaches feminist utopian fiction, discussing Piercy's *Woman on the Edge of Time* in conjunction with works by Ursula Le Guin and Sally Miller Gearhart. Contextualizing the utopian literary genre and female writers' adaptations of the utopian tradition, Keulen discusses these feminist utopias and the connections between them and contemporary feminist theories. Defining Piercy's novel as conventional, relying on traditional elements of utopian fiction, Keulen further classifies the novel as a social utopia, designed to stimulate readers' interest in contemporary political and social problems and illuminate the available solutions to current problems. Keulen also offers an in-depth comparison of the critiques offered by these contemporary feminist utopians. While this study has a very specific focus, it would aid readers interested in Piercy's place in feminist science fiction and utopian fiction.

In addition to the published critical works concerning her oeuvre, Piercy has been the focus of many dissertations and master's theses, including Pia Theilmann's socialist feminist interpretation, *Marge Piercy's Women: Visions Captured and Subdued,* published by R.G. Fisher, Germany. As well as the works included here, Patricia Doherty's forthcoming (1997) *Marge Piercy: An Annotated Bibliography* will soon be available in the Greenwood Press series Bibliographies and Indexes in American Literature. While unavailable at this time, this text should prove invaluable to researchers.

—AMY L. WINK

Pizan, Christine de *see* Christine de Pizan

Plath, Sylvia 1932–1963

American Writer

Bassnett, Susan, *Sylvia Plath,* Totowa, New Jersey: Barnes and Noble, and London: Macmillan, 1987

Malcolm, Janet, *The Silent Woman: Sylvia Plath and Ted Hughes,* New York: Knopf, and London: Picador, 1994

Rose, Jacqueline, *The Haunting of Sylvia Plath,* London: Virago Press, 1991; Cambridge, Massachusetts: Harvard University Press, 1992

Stevenson, Anne, *Bitter Fame: A Life of Sylvia Plath,* Boston: Houghton Mifflin, 1989; London: Penguin, 1990

Wagner-Martin, Linda, *The Bell Jar: A Novel of the Fifties,* New York: Twayne, 1992

———, *Sylvia Plath: A Biography,* New York: Simon and Schuster, 1987; London: Chatto and Windus, 1988

In the preface to her influential *Literary Women* (1976), Ellen Moers wrote of Sylvia Plath, "no writer has meant more to the current feminist movement." Since her death in 1963, Plath's life and work have become critical political and legal battlefields, on which the stakes are more than usually high. Bitter though many of the struggles have been, they continue to raise vital questions about the nature, scope, and appeal of biography, the relationship between the life of the author and the meanings of a literary text, and the politics of gender, genre, and interpretation.

In the late 1980s, two very different biographies of Plath were released within a year of one another. Readers of these biographies might be forgiven for suspecting that there is, in fact, more than one Sylvia Plath. WAGNER-MARTIN's biography offers a broadly feminist representation of its subject. It is sympathetic to the difficulties of combining marriage, motherhood, and a driving literary ambition in 1950s Britain and America—and expresses admiration for the talent and courage with which Plath negotiated these difficulties.

However, while Wagner-Martin's Sylvia Plath is a courageous and sympathetic heroine struggling against the odds, STEVENSON's Sylvia Plath is manipulative, self-destructive, and self-obsessed, with a breezy exterior only partially concealing pathological jealousy and "a seething core of inexplicable fury," making impossible demands on those closest to her. Stevenson calls a succession of witnesses to testify to Plath's "tiresomeness," "rancour," and unreasonable behavior. While Wagner-Martin's Sylvia Plath is "a feminist, in a broad sense of the term," Stevenson insists that to read Plath as a feminist writer "is to misunderstand Plath with a degree of perversity equal to her own." And, in its penultimate paragraph, Stevenson's biography expresses contempt for "those women for whom the legacy of Sylvia Plath was no more than a simplified feminist ideology."

While it is Stevenson's name that appears on the cover of *Bitter Fame,* authorship is never so simple or singular.

In a prefatory note, Stevenson acknowledges (or warns) that this is "almost a work of dual authorship." The story of Stevenson's uneasy collaboration with Ted Hughes's sister Olwyn is complex and controversial—and is discussed by both Malcolm and Rose. The reader will notice, however, that while Wagner-Martin's biography is often distinctly sceptical of the Hughes's version of events, Stevenson's appears to be very much informed or even dictated by it. What is striking and significant is that each of these mutually contradictory versions of Plath's life claims to offer access to the "real Plath." Stevenson's preface promises that hers is "as far as possible . . . an objective account," whereas Wagner-Martin's book is heralded as "a welcome return to the facts." Cashing in on the seductive illusion of the god's-eye view, biography, it seems, rarely acknowledges its inevitably partial and self-justificatory nature, and generally refuses to entertain the suspicion that it may actually constitute the subject which it purports to describe.

MALCOLM's bizarre 1994 book sets out to explore the machinations and excesses of biography in general, and of Plath scholarship in particular. The mass appeal of biography, Malcolm argues, lies in its transgressive and intrusive nature, its appeal to the gossip and the busybody. In a perverse turn of the tables, she proceeds to intrude into the lives of Plath's acquaintances, critics, and biographers, offering the reader descriptions of the clothes, hairstyles, homes, and even the cooking of Anne Stevenson, Jacqueline Rose, and others. In these ways, Malcolm knowingly participates in the voyeuristic and partisan tendencies that she exposes. For example, she confides, unashamedly—and with none of the straight biographer's affectation of impartiality—that she finds Plath physically unappealing, but feels "intense sympathy and affection" for the "electrically attractive" Ted Hughes.

BASSNETT's concise and lucid study does something to disarm this escalation of sensationalist, contradictory and often trivial "revelations." Focusing primarily on the poetry, Bassnett makes the useful point that Plath's controversial life story functions as both an inducement to read, and a stumbling block to interpreting her literary works. So, rather than reading Plath's writing as a transparent expression of her personal suffering, Bassnett concentrates instead on its negotiations with contemporary cultural configurations of gender, and its interrogation of categories such as nature, the family, love, and motherhood. Her emphasis is on the inspirational and enabling aspects of this writing, which is represented as a multifaceted exploration of struggle and survival.

WAGNER-MARTIN's "Reader's Companion" to *The Bell Jar* offers a detailed and accessible exploration of Plath's compelling best-seller. Like Bassnett, Wagner-Martin on the whole eschews narrow readings of Plath's writing as little more than thinly disguised autobiography—situating it instead as both product and critique of its broader literary and socio-political contexts. Notably, she offers an illuminating historical interpretation of America at mid-century, a useful account of the novel's critical reception, and an interesting analysis of the ways in which it draws on and subverts various conventions of genre and gender.

ROSE's book is possibly the most thought-provoking, theoretically sophisticated, and intriguing study of Plath to date. Rose focuses on the ways in which the figure of Sylvia Plath has been constructed and contested by literary criticism and literary biography, and on how her work has been interpreted, edited, censored, and enlisted. She analyzes the violent and polarized reactions that Plath provokes, and what these reactions may reveal about the implicit assumptions and investments of various critical approaches. Rose herself reads on behalf of (post)Freudian psychoanalysis and—while she has some extremely interesting things to say about culturally specific constructions of gender and sexuality—is at times critical of what she sees as feminist attempts to "clean up" certain aspects of Plath's life and writing. However, the primary appeal of Rose's book lies in the strong case that it makes for the radical and transformative potential of Plath's work—work which, in the words of the preface, "regularly unsettles certainties of language, identity, and sexuality, troubling the forms of cohesion on which 'civilized' culture systematically and often oppressively relies."

—ANNA TRIPP

Political Activism see Politics: Local; Politics: National

Politics: Local

Bookman, Ann, and Sandra Morgen (eds.), *Women and the Politics of Empowerment*, Philadelphia: Temple University Press, 1988

Edwards, Julia, *Local Government Women's Committees: A Feminist Political Practice*, Aldershot and Brookfield, Vermont: Avebury, 1995

Flammang, Janet A. (ed.), *Political Women: Current Roles in State and Local Government*, Beverly Hills: Sage, 1984

Garber, Judith A., and Robyne S. Turner (eds.), *Gender in Urban Research*, Thousand Oaks, California: Sage, 1994

Hollis, Patricia, *Ladies Elect: Women in English Local Government 1865–1914*, Oxford: Clarendon Press, and New York: Oxford University Press, 1987

Stewart, Debra W., *The Women's Movement in Community Politics in the U.S.: The Role of Local Commissions on the Status of Women*, New York: Pergamon Press, 1980

——— (ed.), *Women in Local Politics*, Metuchen, New Jersey: Scarecrow Press, 1980

The relationships between women and local politics are among the best established in the literature of women's studies. Because of an association with the home and family, it is within community politics that women have traditionally faced fewer cultural barriers and role conflicts. In a feminist movement dedicated to grass-roots empowerment of women, local politics is an appropriate venue.

HOLLIS has recovered the fascinating story of over three thousand British women between 1870 and 1914 who ran for local office. Those familiar with contemporary scholarship will be struck by the parallels: women on poorhouse and school boards, and, to a lesser extent, town councils advocating for women and children, the poor, the elderly, the sick, and the disabled, and making an impact disproportionate to their numbers; female candidates actively canvassing, speaking, and pamphleteering in their campaigns, building complex networks of group and party support, and often leading the ticket in cumulative election systems; and women spending far more time than men in fulfilling their duties in office and sponsoring innovative policies while their male colleagues ran the business side of these institutions. The early officeholders were a mix of philanthropic women and suffragists such as Emily Davies, Annie Besant, and Lydia Becker, who viewed local office as a steppingstone to the Parliamentary vote. Referring to her extremely detailed study, Hollis wisely urges the reader to "bear with it."

STEWART's collection of nine articles, *Women in Local Politics,* was the first to focus on U.S women's attainment of local office and their performance in that public role. The five authors, primarily political scientists, examine female office-holding in a variety of arenas: legislative, judicial, bureaucratic, and political party. The findings here foreshadow the eventual disappearance of many barriers to female office-holding at all levels of government. Similarly, the now well-established attributes of female elected officials appear here: women and men do differ on policy positions and representative role perceptions, women are more feminist and liberal, and housewives (but not employed women) spend more time on official duties.

United States women also have gained direct representation in local government through local commissions on the status of women (CSWs). STEWART, in *The Women's Movement in Community Politics in the U.S.,* using survey methodology and case studies of five effective commissions, found that many CSWs have been effective advocates for women through public education and lobbying. They brought new persons, resources, and issues into politics. However, their agendas were dominated by issues having the broadest appeal (for example, employment, education, domestic violence, rape, and child care) and screened out issues such as abortion and sexual preference in order to maintain the broad base of support needed for policy effectiveness.

EDWARDS examines a parallel form of feminist political action in Great Britain, the creation of Local Government Women's Committees (LGWCs) to promote women's public employment as well as equality for all women in that locality. Using a methodology similar to that of Stewart, Edwards did field research on six LGWCs and collected information on others. She utilizes feminist theory to link the subordination of women with patriarchal forms of British democracy and local government. In contrast, these LGWCs used the model of equal participation and collective decisionmaking to create a constituency of women to form their agenda. Edwards envisions this feminist model as an archetype for transformative politics in coalition with other disadvantaged groups. Stewart and Edwards do not write for the general reader but do provide essential information.

FLAMMANG provides an excellent overview of women's policy accomplishments, office-holding, and group activism in sub-national politics. Of the 13 chapters, eight deal with the local level. Here female officials and activists have expanded and reshaped the political agenda by defining politics in terms of the connectedness born of family, work, and community. Grass-roots women's groups fulfill roles left vacant by weakened political parties. Issues such as domestic violence, abortion, child care, welfare, and child custody and support are addressed. Feminist leverage in local politics is linked with the visible gender gap and taxpayer demands that local taxes meet human needs.

BOOKMAN and MORGEN also expand the meaning of "the political" by focusing on U.S. working-class women, ethnic women and women of color, and community and workplace organizing. The 15 contributors are both academics and political activists involved in the movements they studied. This collection bridges the gap between an organized middle-class feminism, which focuses on government and elected officials, and working-class women, who primarily have been empowered in venues of workplace, church, neighborhood, and streets. The varied workplaces examined here include home (household work), factory, office, hospital, and street vending. Community groups covered focus on education, health, crime, and social services.

The pioneering GARBER and TURNER volume combines an interest in urban studies with feminist consciousness and analysis. The twenty-two contributors, mostly social scientists in the United States and Canada, assume that the local environment is experienced differently by men and women, and that women can change this setting or design a new one. The essays in the first section argue that urban theory would be improved if issues of gender were incorporated into standard definitions of community, the local political economy, and regime theory. The contrast between the private patriarchy of the suburbs and the public patriarchy of the large central city will resonate with women's studies students.

Ideas advanced in the section on local politics are equally provocative. For example, the formerly peripheral roles of women in local politics as volunteers and organizers in nonprofit organizations, churches, and schools may become more important in a postindustrial economy. Those with a policy orientation will find essays on crime, education, domestic violence, housing, campus date rape, welfare, child care, transit and commuting, and downtown development. It is clear from this innovative book that women must be considered by those concerned with the responsiveness of local politics.

—JANET K. BOLES

Politics: National

Borrelli, MaryAnne, and Janet M. Martin (eds.), *The Other Elites; Women, Politics, and Power in the Executive Branch,* Boulder, Colorado: Lynne Rienner, 1997
Bystydzienski, Jill M., *Women in Electoral Politics: Lessons from Norway,* Westport, Connecticut: Praeger, 1995
Davis, Rebecca Howard, *Women and Power in Parliamentary Democracies: Cabinet Appointments in Western Europe, 1968–1992,* Lincoln: University of Nebraska Press, 1997
Foerstel, Karen, and Herbert N. Foerstel, *Climbing the Hill: Gender Conflict in Congress,* Westport, Connecticut: Praeger, 1996
Genovese, Michael A. (ed.), *Women as National Leaders,* Newbury Park, California: Sage, 1993
Kelber, Mim (ed.), *Women and Government: New Ways to Political Power,* Westport, Connecticut: Praeger, 1994

At the end of the twentieth century, women's presence in national politics remains strikingly low. With the exception of a handful of world leaders, in most countries women hold few national offices, and in some countries they remain completely absent from national political office. Because of this, the literature on women in national politics has emerged primarily in the last two decades of the century as women's participation rates have begun to increase. One can now find numerous studies on women's participation in national politics, including traditional methodological studies of participation rates and voting analysis, as well as more recent studies which combine statistical methodologies with feminist and gender-based theoretical perspectives.

One particular interesting study of women's participation in U.S. national politics can be found in FOERSTEL and FOERSTEL's study. This book looks exclusively at women's participation in the U.S. Congress. The authors begin by tracing the electoral victories and legislative influence of the first female congressional representatives, and continue with a contemporary discussion of women elected to the 104th Congress. Their research combines descriptive statistics, qualitative discussion, and personal comments from female legislators. This study provides considerable insight into the difficulty women face, first in getting elected to Congress and subsequently in the gender bias they face once they take their positions. This book contains little analysis of women's voting patterns in Congress but provides valuable insight into women's involvement and influence on legislative outcomes.

Women's participation in national politics through political appointment also remains low but politically important. Only in the last two administrations of the century have there been more than two women appointed to cabinet positions in any U.S. administration. They have fared only marginally better at the subcabinet level. Because of the low number of female political appointees, few books have focused specifically on women's participation through this channel of national politics. BORRELLI and MARTIN have compiled a series of interesting articles in their book, which helps bridge the gap between the literature on women and politics and the study of executive branch politics. The articles in their book vary significantly in their approach to the topic, with some of the authors using traditional methodological approaches to the study of women and politics, and others building on this approach with the inclusion of feminist political theory. This book adds considerably to our understanding of women's influence and participation in executive branch politics.

All but one of the articles in Borrelli and Martin's book focus on executive politics in the United States. For a more extensive study of women and national politics around the world, one should see the study edited by KELBER. This book looks at the historical, cultural, and political factors that contribute to women's absence in national politics worldwide, while also providing some recommendations for increasing women's leadership in national governments and electoral politics. Although this is a global study, included in the volume are specific case studies of Norway, Sweden, Finland, Denmark, Iceland, and Germany.

The predominance of Scandinavian case studies selected for the above-mentioned volume is not coincidental. The emphasis in Scandinavian culture on equality and justice have contributed to women's high political participation rates in these countries. Presently, there are more women represented in Scandinavian parliaments than in almost any other national parliaments in the world. Even in Scandinavia, however, women work within a political system numerically and culturally dominated by men. In addition to a discussion of why women have been far more effective in securing national office in Norway, BYSTYDZIENSKI's book extends her study of women's participation in formal political institutions to an analysis of women's political participation in informal political channels associated with feminist political activism and other informal institutional structures. Her discussion of the relationship between increased political representation and political outcomes is valuable for anyone interested in women's influence in national politics in any country.

For a broader study of women in parliamentary democracies, one should look at DAVIS's book. Davis studies women's participation in 15 western European parliamentary and parliamentary-type systems in Europe. Davis uses statistical analysis to draw conclusions about the relationship between recruitment patterns and political culture in these parliamentary governments. Although the focus of her study primarily examines women's participation through the appointment process, she also addresses the connection between political appointments and the electoral cycle and appointments and political party affiliation.

One of the weakest areas of scholarship on women in national politics remains comparative studies of female heads of government. This is partly a product of numbers. Because so few women have reached this level of political leadership, and because they have obtained office under such different conditions of national political and economic development, research in this area has often been limited to idiosyncratic or biographical studies with little comparative analysis. Such comparative studies, however, would have the potential to illuminate how gender affects the dynamic of leadership and shapes women's continued political empowerment. GENOVESE's book is an edited volume that utilizes case studies of female heads of government as a starting point for just such a comparative study of women's leadership. Ultimately the book suffers from many of the same difficulties other scholars have had in trying to find similarities in women's leadership experiences. But the case studies in this book, along with the final two articles, make an important contribution to our understanding of similarities in leadership experiences and subsequent political outcomes. More importantly, the book raises a vast number of questions for further research, as scholars seek to better understand the impact and potential of women's leadership at the highest positions of national governments.

—SHARON L. SPRAY

See also League of Women Voters; National Woman's Party, United States; United Nations

Polygamy

Bretschneider, Peter, *Polygyny: A Cross-Cultural Study*, Uppsala: Uppsala University, 1995

Clignet, Remi, *Many Wives, Many Powers: Authority and Power in Polygynous Families*, Evanston, Illinois: Northwestern University Press, 1970

Constantine, Larry L., and John M. Constantine, *Group Marriage: A Study of Contemporary Multilateral Marriage*, New York: Macmillan, 1973

Polygamy is a general term referring to several kinds of plural marriage. It is frequently used interchangeably with the term polygyny, the marriage of one man to several wives. Polyandry is also included as a subset of polygamy. This is the marriage of one woman to several husbands. A rare type of polygamy is group marriage, where a group of people marry each other. Monogamy, the marriage of one man to one woman, is the most widely practiced type of marriage in the world today. While most cultures allow for polygamy, it does not occur frequently because it requires considerable wealth, and it may be prevented by a shortage of either males or females. Usually polygamy is reserved for people of high status. Thus, plural marriage is widely accepted in world cultures but increasingly less practiced. Polygamy is found in some Asian societies, throughout the Middle East, and in many parts of Africa. It is virtually absent from societies dominated by Christianity. An exception is the case of fundamentalist Mormons who continue living in polygynous marriages despite the fact that it has been officially banned by the church.

The literature on polygamy is surprisingly sparse. Very few books have been devoted solely to this topic, although there are many journal articles and chapters in books on polygamy. Most of these focus on polygamous marriages in particular societies. There are a few general books about polygyny and group marriage, with virtually nothing of any significance on polyandry. Especially distressing is the small amount of attention given to the effects of polygamy on women. There has yet to be a thoroughly comprehensive and theoretically sophisticated work on this topic.

CLIGNET has published a study of polygynous societies in Africa. The book has an excellent overall general chapter on polygyny. The author contrasts negative stereotypes about polygyny with ideas about it held by Africans. According to Clignet, Africans argue that the western custom of remarriage subsequent to a divorce is merely another form of polygyny. Another stereotype is that polygyny involves a merciless domination of women by men. The author uses a comparative approach to contrast two African societies that practice plural marriage. Urban versus rural factors are compared. This work is dated, pays little attention to the role of women, and does not probe deeply enough into the nature of polygyny.

CONSTANTINE and CONSTANTINE explore the phenomenon of group marriage, a "radical adventure" that emerged in the United States during the counter culture period of the 1960s and 1970s. The first chapters describe the matrix of American marriage and family life. This is followed by several chapters describing the general features of group marriage. The book concludes with chapters about problems with group marriage and a general discussion on the future of the family. The volume is a product of an experimental period in American society. It is optimistic about the future possibilities for different marriage configurations. Despite its unreserved idealism, the book reports some interesting results of observations and interviews of people who have experienced group marriage. The Constantines see the experimental marital patterns of the 1970s as attempts to expand the boundaries of the family. Thus, group marriage, communal living, and swinging are attempts to transform the family. Today group marriage has vanished from popular view and communes are rare. Swinging, or open marriages, are still active and quite popular in some circles.

The most valuable and up-to-date work on plural marriage is the volume by BRETSCHNEIDER, a cultural anthropologist who compares polygyny in a worldwide sample of 186 societies. Particularly important here are several chapters exploring theories of polygyny. In this volume the author examines attempts to correlate the incidence of polygyny with a number of variables, such as types of agriculture, climatic conditions, postpartem sex taboos, warfare, and female captives. The author concludes by asserting that polygyny is a multidimensional phenomenon. Cultural, economic, environmental, and demographic factors must be combined to understand it. Single factor theories will not suffice. Polygyny is most strongly predictable in societies that have bridewealth payments, high dependency on fishing or plow agriculture, war for plunder, and captives. The occurrence of polygyny is not related to either the sex ratios in a society, the high evaluation of women's reproductive capacity, or long postpartem sex taboos. Even though Bretschneider's book is a valuable source at the macro level for the study of polygyny, it is very abstract and insensitive to the emotional impact of polygyny on human lives. Once again there is little discussion of the impact of polygyny on women. The rather arid and highly theoretical nature of this volume is probably related to the fact that it was originally submitted as a doctoral dissertation in anthropology to Uppsala University in Sweden.

—JAMES J. PRESTON

See also Concubinage

Polygamy, Mormon

Altman, Irwin, and Joseph Ginat, *Polygamous Families in Contemporary Society*, Cambridge and New York: Cambridge University Press, 1996

Anderson, J. Max, *The Polygamy Story: Fiction and Fact*, Salt Lake City: Publishers Press, 1979

Embry, Jessie L., *Mormon Polygamous Families: Life in the Principle*, Salt Lake City, Utah: University of Utah Press, 1987

Iversen, Joan Smyth, *The Antipolygamy Controversy in U.S. Women's Movements, 1880–1925: A Debate on the American Home*, New York: Garland, 1997

Polygamy has thrived in one form or another in many societies throughout the world. However, in Europe and North America it has remained an anathema, except among the early Mormons. Wherever Christianity is found the practice of polygamy has been heavily suppressed. From its very first instance, polygamy among the early Mormons was heavily persecuted. Not until 1890 under duress did the Mormon Church prohibit the practice of polygamy. Yet, it still thrives among various enclaves of dissident Mormons.

ANDERSON's book examines the validity of "Fundamentalist" Mormon claims of legitimacy for the practice of polygamy today. Tracing the history of plural marriage among the Latter Day Saints, the author notes that the practice had to be kept secret in Ohio, Missouri, and Illinois during the early years (1830s) because of antibigamy laws. However, later, after years of persecution, Mormons were driven west outside the confines of the then United States. Polygamy was then declared from the Mormon pulpit a divine law and a necessary commandment. In 1862 the federal government passed the first law outlawing the custom. Church authorities were quick to contest it. Polygamists were actively hunted down and there was a threat by the federal government to confiscate church property. Even the United States Supreme Court supported legislation against the practice of polygamy among Mormons. As a consequence of these measures, the Mormon Church was forced in 1890 to declare an official end to the practice of polygamy. Some members continued their polygamous lifestyles by leaving the country, while others remained active in parts of Utah. Anderson examines the survival of Mormon "fundamentalists" who even today continue to believe that polygamy is a God-given cornerstone of the Mormon faith. "Fundamentalists" claim to be custodians of the gospel revealed to the Prophet Joseph Smith and legitimate heirs to the priesthood of the Church of Jesus Christ of Latter Day Saints. This volume concludes with a strong condemnation of Mormon "fundamentalism" and its claims to legitimacy.

EMBRY has written an impressive and comprehensive volume on Mormon polygamous families. It is a good general source, with chapters on topics such as polygamy on a worldwide scale, Old Testament polygamy, opposition to the practice, underground Mormon polygamy, and a survey of the survival of this practice in Mexico and Canada. There is a good analysis of the demographics of polygamy. Embry tries to answer the difficult question of why these European-Americans decided to practice such a controversial custom. There are several good chapters on women's roles. The scholarly approach taken in this book corrects for a large number of biased works on the topic, mostly condemning it. Embry draws on both historical and sociological sources to sketch a thorough and relatively unbiased treatment of this sensitive topic. Particularly valuable is the breaking of stereotypes accomplished by the book. Mormon polygamous families are not much different than monogamous ones. According to Embry, interviews with Mormon families do not support stereotypes like the oppressed plural wife, the first wife being forsaken for a younger woman, or the "emancipated woman" who becomes independent because she has co-wives to help with household duties.

A well-researched study of Mormon polygamy has been written by ALTMAN and GINAT. In this work a social psychologist and an anthropologist use extensive observations and interviews to present a comprehensive analysis of present-day Mormon polygamous families in American society. This interdisciplinary approach sheds light on how husbands and wives in plural families cope with their complex lifestyles. The most recent estimates suggest there are as many as 20 to 50,000 members of Mormon "Fundamentalism" who condone or practice polygamy today in the western United States, Mexico, and Canada. Topics covered include living arrangements, weddings, honeymoons, husbands' rotations among wives, psychological attachments, relationships between husbands and wives, and emotional ties between wives. This is the best overall source on the contemporary practice of Mormon polygamy. It is well-documented and very accessible to readers. Particularly valuable is the dispassionate and objective approach of the book.

IVERSEN examines the history of the antipolygamy controversy in the United States women's movements. The volume has an excellent review of the literature on Mormonism and women. Iversen finds that the major women's organizations of the nineteenth and twentieth centuries did not respond monolithically during the antipolygamy controversy. Some Mormon women did not challenge the ideal of male supremacy, even though they identified strongly with the women's rights movement and were active suffragists. Iversen argues that polygamy forged strong relationships between women, as well as close mother-child bonds. Anti-polygamy, however, became a national women's issue. This volume is scholarly, well-written and very useful as a historical source on Mormon polygamy and women.

—JAMES J. PRESTON

See also Polygamy; Mormonism

Pornography

Church, Pamela Gibson, and Roman Gibson (eds.), *Dirty Looks: Women, Pornography, Power*, London: BFI, 1993

Dworkin, Andrea, and Catherine A. MacKinnon, *Pornography and Civil Rights: A New Day for Women's Equality*, Minneapolis: Organizing Against Pornography, 1988

Foster, Thomas, Carol Siegel, and Ellen E. Berry (eds.), *Sex Positives? The Cultural Politics of Dissident Sexualities*, New York and London: New York University Press, 1997

Hunt, Lynn (ed.), *The Invention of Pornography: Obscenity and the Origins of Modernity 1500–1800*, New York: Zone Books, 1993

McElroy, Wendy, *XXX: A Woman's Right to Pornography*, New York: St. Martin's Press, 1995

Russell, Diana E.H. (ed.), *Making Violence Sexy: Feminist Views on Pornography*, New York: Teacher's College Press, 1993

Siegel, Lynne, and Mary MacIntosh (eds.), *Sex Exposed: Sexuality and the Pornography Debate*, New Jersey: Rutgers University Press, 1993

Strossen, Nadine, *Defending Pornography: Free Speech, Sex, and the Fight for Women's Rights*, New York and London: 1995

Pornography evokes a range of responses from women, whose views on pornography, whether pro or anti, are often charged and complex because pornography usually contains images and representations of women. Another significant point is that because there is no one accepted definition of pornography, what pornography is shifts depending upon the author's (and viewer's) own definition. However, pornography began as a genre of writing specifically about prostitutes and prostitution.

HUNT shows that authors and readers of pornography once navigated the boundaries between virtue and vice, suggesting that pornography required a viewer to interpret it. Part of the tension surrounding pornography, then as now, was the desire of people to test standards of decency juxtaposed with the desire of others to regulate those standards. Hunt's collection of essays show how attitudes towards bodies and sexuality, gender, sexual practices and their representations changed due to pornography, and addresses the political implications of being a pornographer (especially in France). Areas discussed range from Renaissance Italy to Restoration and Enlightenment England, including 17th and 18th century Dutch pornography.

In contrast to Hunt, RUSSELL sets out to define pornography, recognizing that some women do not delineate between pornography and erotica, while others find it vitally important to do so, asserting that what is primarily objectionable in pornography is the use of degrading, racist, and abusive representations of females and female sexuality, not the sex itself. Russell is interested in separating the consequences of pornography from the issues of censorship. The text is broken into four sections, beginning with first-person accounts of victims and survivors of pornography. Section two is an overview of the issues surrounding pornography, reprinting some of Andrea Dworkin and Catherine A. MacKinnon's anti-pornography work, as well as including essays focusing on the significance of pornography for African-Americans. The third section contains feminist research on pornography, and the final section recounts the experiences of anti-pornography activists.

DWORKIN and MacKINNON are well-known often-cited anti-pornography authors, and their groundbreaking text contains a legal definition of pornography, includes a list of frequently asked questions about pornography and censorship, and reprints four Ordinances. In the mid-1980s, Dworkin and MacKinnon asserted that pornography was a violation of women's civil and human rights, and as such, should be legally banned. Most of Minneapolis agreed; an ordinance to ban pornography was twice passed, then vetoed by the mayor both times. Indianapolis passed the ordinance, it was signed into law, and the city was subsequently sued. The text discusses civil rights, calls for social change through power redistribution, and demands that people recognize the serious harm pornography, through objectification and subordination, causes.

GIBSON and GIBSON focus on representation and theory, asserting that pornography is a representation, and representation requires interpretation. Being offended by pornography is not the same thing as declaring that the pornographic materials in question are harmful. According to Gibson and Gibson's text, the political consequences of the pro-censorship, anti-pornography movement, fall on minority or dissident sexualities. The blame, they state, of harm, thus shifts from the perpetrator of said harm to the pornographer, and deflects attention from the also harmful gender influence of the media and advertising. Their text, composed entirely of essays by women, includes articles debating theory as well as practice, and calls attention to the shifting boundaries between art and pornography through including articles on Annie Sprinkle and photographic essays.

FORSTER, SIEGEL, and BERRY attempt to redefine the terms of feminist debates about pornography, centered around the gulf between pro-censorship groups and sex positives (prosex radicals), which they posit is the primary division between scholars of gender and sexuality. Their text is divided into three sections, the first focusing on pornography, postmodernism, and the complications of feminist opposition to pornography. The second section includes discussions of sexualized racism and colonialism in pornography from Chicana, African, and African American perspectives. Section three repositions the claims of pro-censorship groups and sexual radicals through looking at modern sexual representation and the repression of those expressions. The text calls for a non-oppositional, non-assimilationist politics of pornography, one that does not treat all representations of sexuality as oppressive, or necessarily alike. The text contains many well annotated references for further reading.

SIEGEL and MacINTOSH, like Gibson and Gibson, emphasize that discussions of pornography must remain open because to simplify discussions about pornography would result in the possibility of further censorship and the loss of women's agency in understanding and expressing the complexities of their sexuality. In contrast, Siegel and MacIntosh come from a primarily British perspective. Siegel and MacIntosh ask why discussions of feminism commonly boil down into debates about pornography. They also emphasize that issues surrounding sexuality are not the issues surrounding pornography. Essays included discuss the pornography-erotica debate, as well as the pornography-art debate. Other topics discussed are issues of race and gender, video pornography and the growing women's market, pornography and psychoanalysis, and interviews with women who create and use pornography.

STROSSEN's text contains sections reacting directly against Andrea Dworkin and Catherine MacKinnon's works, but is more anti-censorship than pro-pornography. Strossen discusses anti-censorship movements, including a detailed discussion of the rift between pro and anti-censorship feminists. She calls attention to the lack of any clear definition of pornography, due to what she terms American culture's sex panic. Strossen includes discussion of Canadian censorship law, issues of prostitution and abortion, as well as Margaret Sanger. Strossen also makes mention of McElroy's discussions of filmed pornography.

McELROY, a Canadian, from an individualist feminist perspective, provides a picture of the pornography industry, focusing on hard-core films, and offers suggestions for how the industry could be changed to benefit women further. She also includes a historical overview of pornography in discussing the negative effects of nineteenth-century anti-pornography legislation on the women's rights movement while paralleling this legislation with radical feminism (which, McElroy posits, destroys individualist feminism), presents a condensation of anti-censorship and anti-pornography arguments, reports on a meeting of a national sex workers' advocacy group (COYOTE), and, finally, presents the results of her survey of sex workers.

—ANNE N. THALHEIMER

Porter, Katherine Anne 1890–1980

American Writer

Brinkmeyer, Robert H., *Katherine Anne Porter's Artistic Development: Primitivism, Traditionalism, and Totalitarianism*, Baton Rouge: Louisiana State University Press, 1993

DeMouy, Jane Krause, *Katherine Anne Porter's Women: The Eye of Her Fiction,* Austin: University of Texas Press, 1983

Givner, Joan, *Katherine Anne Porter: A Life,* New York: Simon and Schuster, 1982; London: Cape, 1983; revised edition, Athens: University of Georgia Press, 1991

Nance, William L., *Katherine Anne Porter and the Art of Rejection,* Chapel Hill: University of North Carolina Press, 1964

Stout, Janis P., *Katherine Anne Porter: A Sense of the Times,* Charlottesville: University Press of Virginia, 1995

Tanner, James T.F., *The Texas Legacy of Katherine Anne Porter,* Denton: University of North Texas Press, 1990

Warren, Robert Penn (ed.), *Katherine Anne Porter: A Collection of Critical Essays,* Englewood Cliffs, New Jersey: Prentice Hall, 1979

From the time of her earliest publications in the 1920s, Katherine Anne Porter has presented a puzzle for biographers and literary critics alike. Claiming to be a member of "the guilt-ridden white pillar crowd" of Southern aristocracy, Porter was, in fact, born Callie Russell Porter in rural Indian Creek, Texas. Her creation of a fictional self is as interesting to many of her readers as the creation of her exquisite stories, novellas, and novel, and has become the central focus both for biographers and for scholars of her fiction. Studies of her life and of her fiction tend to look for ways to unify the apparent contradictions found in both—contradictions ranging from political ideology to personal background and identity.

GIVNER, the biographer Porter hand-picked to record her almost century-long life, published the first full-scale biography in 1983, three years after Porter's death. Revised and reprinted in 1991 to include newly accessible material, this thoroughly researched, detailed account of the writer's life acknowledges a fascination with Porter's invented background and fragmented, contradictory sense of self, but moves beyond this fascination to examine the causes and purpose of this fragmentation. Givner concludes that Porter's life story is one of a woman who, against all odds, managed to survive and create, to live a life for which there was no existing pattern, a life "more heroic than anything she invented."

In a more recent biography, STOUT explores the contradictions in Porter's shifting politics, ideas about gender, and conflicted regional and class identity. In this "intellectual biography" Stout identifies the South as the anchor of Porter's fragmented and varied life, but also examines her place near, if not at, the center of international twentieth-century thought. From the executions of Sacco and Vanzetti, to the Mexican revolution, to the rise of Hitler, to Cape Canaveral (where Porter covered a spacecraft launch for *Playboy Magazine*), Porter's involvement in and reactions to the history around her are well-documented.

BRINKMEYER also examines the development of Porter as a thinker and observer, but focuses more narrowly on how this development affected her fiction. Concurring with the aforementioned writers that Porter's perspective is consistent only in the broadest sense of the word, Brinkmeyer locates this consistency in her inquiring and dissenting sensibility, and in her constant struggles with memory. He focuses on three crucial turning points in Porter's life: her interest in revolutionary Mexico of the 1920s, her reacknowledgment of her Southern—specifically Texas—roots after some years of regional denial, and her detestation and fear of totalitarianism sparked by its international rise in the 1930s and 1940s. While he places her work most clearly in the Southern literary tradition, he also acknowledges Mikhail Bakhtin's theories of fiction as providing a framework for his examination of Porter's works.

Arguing that the genteel Southern aspects of Porter's work have been overemphasized, TANNER more narrowly focuses on Porter as "a Texas writer first and last." His book, part of the Texas Writers Series, examines Porter's Texas connection and her apparent denial of her Texas roots. Tanner argues that the decision to distance herself from her native state and become an international figure was necessary to Porter's artistic career. She aspired to become more than a regional writer, and she succeeded. However, she never lost her deep affinities with the region that shaped her earliest memories, her sense of self, and her art. By focusing on Porter's settings and characters, Tanner examines the conflict between the Texas Porter and the cosmopolitan Porter.

Shifting from regionalism to feminism, DeMOUY identifies Porter's territory in terms of psychology and myth, not geography. Noting that practically all of Porter's protagonists are women in search of independence and identity, Demouy argues that Porter's fiction chronicles her own "double" experience as a woman. Her protagonists, like Porter herself, experience a basic psychological conflict between the desire for independence and emotional freedom—as exemplified by the artist figure, and the desire for security and love—as exemplified by the wife/mother figure. Because this conflict is ancient as well as contemporary, many of Porter's stories might be interpreted as statements of "archetypal truths" involving various female archetypes.

In an earlier study of Porter's works, NANCE identifies the central unifying pattern of her fiction as "the principle of rejection." Dividing Porter's stories into two groups, those that contain a semi-autobiographical protagonist such as Miranda (the alpha group) and those that do not (the beta group), Nance acknowledges the close connection between biography and fiction. However, he focuses primarily on analysis of Porter's fiction and the ways in which her characters reject various institutions and beliefs.

The collection of essays edited by WARREN includes reminiscences, criticism, an interview, and one essay by

Porter herself. Contributors include Southern writers Eudora Welty, Cleanth Brooks, George Core, and Warren. However, the essays are not limited to scholars primarily associated with the South: Mark Schorer, Edmund Wilson, and Edward G. Schwartz also contribute to this useful collection of now classic essays.

—ELIZABETH COOLEY

Poverty

Abramovitz, Mimi, *Regulating the Lives of Women: Social Welfare Policy from Colonial Times to the Present*, Boston: South End Press, 1988

Berrick, Jill Duerr, *Faces of Poverty: Portraits of Women and Children on Welfare*, New York and Oxford: Oxford University Press, 1995

Goldberg, Gertrude Schaffner, and Eleanor Kremen (eds.), *The Feminization of Poverty: Only in America?* New York: Praeger, 1990

Kingfisher, Catherine Pélissier, *Women in the American Welfare Trap*, Philadelphia: University of Pennsylvania Press, 1996

Rowbotham, Sheila, and Swasti Mitter (eds.), *Dignity and Daily Bread: New Forms of Economic Organizing among Poor Women in the Third World and the First*, London and New York: Routledge, 1994

Scheper-Hughes, Nancy, *Death without Weeping: The Violence of Everyday Life in Brazil*, Berkeley: University of California Press, 1992

Since Diane Pearce first referred to the "feminization of poverty" in 1978, poverty has been recognized as a global phenomenon that affects women disproportionately. It blurs our facile distinction between the First and Third Worlds, and also cuts across racial divisions (although non-whites are themselves disproportionately represented among the poor). Although it is impossible to represent the sheer volume and scope of the literature on gender and poverty in a short essay, the listings reviewed here have been chosen to touch on the situation in industrialized as well as developing nations, and to represent both macro and micro approaches to understanding gender and poverty.

While "the feminization of poverty" originally referred to the proportional rise in poverty among women and their children in the 1960s and 1970s in the United States, it is probable that poverty as a woman's problem has deep historical roots in many nations. According to ABRAMOVITZ, this is certainly the case in the United States, in which poverty has been feminized since colonial times. Abramovitz does two things that are particularly useful: first, she traces the history of gender and poverty in the United States; and second, she provides an analysis of the structures and ideologies that set the parameters of that history. Specifically, she discusses the interaction of capitalist industrialization and its ethic of work, on the one hand, with patriarchal family structure and its ethic of women as caretakers, an interaction that, on the other, produces a powerful and fundamentally disempowering mix for women.

GOLDBERG and KREMEN expand the geographic focus to encompass a number of socialist and capitalist countries in what is often referred to as the industrialized west, including Canada, Japan, France, Sweden, Russia, and Poland, as well as the United States. The basic goal of their cross-national statistical comparisons is to determine the extent to which the feminization of poverty cuts across the industrialized world. The comparisons are based on analyses of four variables: labor market factors, policies to promote gender equality in the labor market, social welfare, and demographic factors (e.g., rates of single motherhood). This choice of variables reflects the authors' conviction that we must attend not only to women in poverty, but also to the majority of women who are threatened by poverty as a result of gendered inequalities in the domestic and public divisions of labor. Indeed, their results indicate that, while the feminization of poverty is most severe in the United States, women in all the other countries studied are economically vulnerable and more or less "at risk" of becoming poor. What precisely contributes to this risk is a combination of demographic factors with employment and policy issues. An excellent documentation of factors related to the feminization of poverty, this volume provides the larger context within which any micro analysis of gender and poverty must be situated.

SCHEPER-HUGHES's in-depth study of poverty in northeast Brazil provides the kind of textured and nuanced analysis that gives life to the more macro studies discussed above. What do women do when they cannot possibly procure what is necessary to keep their children alive? Scheper-Hughes outlines her controversial thesis that, in a situation characterized by chronic hunger and malnutrition, mothers put more energy into babies who appear to be "thrivers"—who have a determination to live—than those who seem dull, listless, and passive. The latter are thereby condemned to death. It is a story of great complexity—linking culture, economy, and politics, and bringing them to bear in an analysis of dire need and desperation.

Berrick and Kingfisher also provide micro analyses of women's experiences of poverty, this time in the U.S. context. Both books are, fundamentally, about the connections among culture, policy, and lived poverty. BERRICK's case-study approach exemplifies the heterogeneity of women in poverty/on welfare (which she sees as synonymous), most of whom do not fit a single stereotype. The case studies provide the grounds to contest a number of myths about welfare and welfare recipients, including the assumptions that financial assistance programs for the poor are generous and cause family disintegration, that recipients have more children in order to increase their benefits, that all recipients are non-white, and that they are lazy. On the contrary, Berrick recounts stories of hard work, persistence, and hope against all odds.

Drawing on work with women in two welfare rights groups, KINGFISHER provides women's stories in their own words. The stories make it clear that, in many cases, poor women both understand and resist the gendered nature of their poverty; they have unique insight, and often work informally to disrupt the linkages between their relationships with men, paid work, childcare, and poverty. In addition to documenting the experiences of poor women, the book explores the lives of the women in the welfare system whose job it is to provide financial assistance to the poor. Located at the bottom of the welfare hierarchy in terms of both pay and status, the latter exemplify the women "at risk" discussed by Goldberg and Kremen.

Such women also provide the focus of ROWBOTHAM and MITTER's review of organized responses to poverty among First and Third World women involved in "casualized" labor—nonunionized or otherwise unregulated labor, such as that in Free Trade Zones, sweatshops, or the informal market (e.g., street vendors)—in the context of global economic change and the concomitant rise of market ideologies and policies. The book provides seven case studies—two historical, five contemporary—of poor women's organizing around production (work) in Britain, India, Mexico, Tanzania, and the Free Trade Zones of Malaysia, the Philippines, and Sri Lanka. Successes, failures, and lessons learned are documented. The most important lessons concern the critical nature of alliances (often across class and gender), and of creating linkages between the workplace and the community. Indeed, women's work lives cannot be divorced from the rest of their lives, and their needs and demands must perforce address the workplace, the family, the state, and the international economic system. The book thus emphasizes two points made in a number of the works discussed here; namely, that poor women are also poor workers, and that poverty must be situated in the larger socio-economic contexts of its occurrence.

The feminization of poverty is a real and growing phenomenon. It points to one of the major material manifestations of misogyny. Accordingly, gender asymmetry, in terms of both patriarchal culture and political economy, is appropriately the explicit focus of the books described here. Incremental policy changes can reduce the burden of poverty on women and their children and should by all means be pursued. However, only a radical (root) change in our understanding and organization of society—in both social and economic terms—will cure the problem. The ideas outlined in these books—both the authors' and those of the women whose lives they explore—provide a good starting place.

—CATHERINE PÉLISSIER KINGFISHER

See also Welfare; Feminization of Poverty

Pregnancy and Childbirth

Arditti, Rita, Renate Duelli Klein, and Shelley Minden (eds.), *Test-Tube Women: What Future for Motherhood?*, London and Boston: Pandora Press, 1984

Eakins, Oamela S. (ed.), *The American Way of Birth*, Philadelphia: Temple University Press, 1986

Jordan, Brigitte, *Birth in Four Cultures: A Cross-Cultural Investigation of Childbirth in Yucatan, Holland, Sweden, and the United States*, St. Albans, Vermont: Eden Press, 1978

Leavitt, Judith Walzer, *Brought to Bed: Childbearing in America, 1750–1950*, New York: Oxford University Press, 1986

Martin, Emily, *The Woman in the Body: A Cultural Analysis of Reproduction*, Boston: Beacon Press, and Milton Keynes: Open University Press, 1987

Oakley, Anne, *The Captured Womb: A History of the Medical Care of Pregnant Women*, New York: Basil Blackwell, 1984; Oxford: Basil Blackwell, 1986

Rothman, Barbara Katz (ed.), *Encyclopedia of Childbearing: Critical Perspectives*, Phoenix, Arizona: Oryx Press, 1993

The majority of women become involved in the reproductive processes at one point or another in their lifetimes. Although these biological processes are therefore somewhat customary or commonplace, JORDAN illustrates how each group of individuals and every culture shapes these biological processes according to its own values and norms. Jordan's data consist of qualitative research on birth experiences in Sweden, Holland, Yucatan, and the United States. Jordan points out that general knowledge about the management of pregnancy, labor, delivery, and the postpartum period is, by and large, the knowledge of one particular birthing system: western obstetrics. Jordan explains that the United States' definition of birth as a medical event has served to focus research on the physiological aspects of childbearing. Jordan compares the United States experience of birth to that of three other cultures in order to illustrate how very skewed our definition of childbirth is. In Sweden, women's choices in childbirth are weighed heavily even though technology is used quite often. In Holland, birth is seen as a natural event that is best handled with a minimal level of medical interference. In Yucatan, midwives are still traditionally the birth attendants but currently face the pressures of dealing with an influx of modern obstetrics into their villages. Jordan's book is an excellent example of how contextual childbirth practices are, and how much variation there is across cultures in dealing with commonplace biological processes.

Continuing with this idea that reproductive processes are socially-constructed, LEAVITT accurately details the United States' history of childbirth, documenting how childbirth moved from a woman-centered event to one that is medically-controlled and defined. Not only does Leavitt track the development of hospitals and various medical procedures such as the use of forceps, cesarean section deliveries, and anesthesia, she also discusses the decline of traditional midwifery and the rise in the attendance of physicians at childbirths. Leavitt is able to show the reader the changing historical definitions of childbirth, and how these coincided with the rise of modern medicine in the west. This work provides readers with a very good historical base for understanding the issues that have arisen around childbirth today.

For a more current look at American birthing practices, EAKINS's edited book is a good asset to any readers' knowledge of childbirth. Eakins includes chapters that deal with many pressing issues surrounding birth today, such as male doctor-female patient interactions, the rise in the number of cesarean deliveries, the effect that social class has on birth experiences, the revitalization of midwifery in recent decades, and the differences between lay- and nurse-midwifery practice. Eakins's collection of articles provides the reader with a comprehensive picture of the wide range of birthing experiences that women can have even within the United States. This volume is especially useful in acquainting students with basic issues in childbirth and will provoke discussion on numerous topics relating to reproductive experiences.

MARTIN develops a feminist critique of the western scientific community while analyzing women's reproduction. She explores the fragmentation of women's bodies as female processes such as birth, pregnancy, menstruation, and menopause are medicalized and pathologized. Martin utilizes data from a total of 165 interviews with women in their reproductive years to illustrate this fragmentation of body and self, and she allows these women to speak from their own vantage points about the various stages in their reproductive lives. Martin's book is essentially a call for resistance against medical images and health practices that oppress women. Her book is extremely useful in showing the power imbalances between those in the health care professions and women themselves, and how reproductive processes are defined by those who have power.

OAKLEY approaches the study of pregnancy in much the same way as have other feminist scholars. Her book is an attempt to write the history of the medical care pregnant women receive in Britain in preparation for childbirth and motherhood. Oakley is mainly concerned with the fact that pregnancy is separated off from other types of social behaviors or processes, and "reconstituted as a special, technical subject under the external jurisdiction of some expert authority." Once redefined or "captured," to use the author's terminology, pregnancy facilitates the wider social control of women. Oakley states that the most characteristic aspect of modern prenatal care over the last ninety years is the clinical insistence on the potential for pathology in all childbearing. Once childbearing is seen as pathological, those in the medical profession have a license over the bodies and approved lifestyles of women. Oakley documents the process by which pregnancy became defined as a medical phenomenon in Britain and other countries in the early twentieth century. She attempts to link the changes in the treatment of pregnancy to larger changes in medicine and the position of women as mothers through history.

ARDITTI, KLEIN, and MINDEN offer a very different perspective toward pregnancy and childbirth. Their edited collection deals with the question of whether technology has gone too far. Various chapters in this book show how women have actually been removed from many parts of the reproductive process. From egg farming and surrogacy to abortion and the insemination of lesbians, Arditti, Klein, and Minden canvass the intense debates that are currently going on about the future of motherhood. This work is an intensive introduction to reproductive technologies and their impact on the motherhood role, but also to the definition of "woman" in general. Arditti, Klein, and Minden's book puts forth a very different critique of current reproductive practices, showing that processes like pregnancy or childbirth are no longer solely female or biological.

There is fairly little critical feminist study dedicated solely to pregnancy, or the gestational role of motherhood. However, secondary sources analyzing childbirth often include sections on pregnancy, as it is a crucial stage of the reproductive process, before moving on to a discussion of birth. For a general description of all aspects of pregnancy, childbirth, and related medical care, the reader should consult ROTHMAN's encyclopedia. Rothman's edited reference volume provides essays on all issues and a list of sources that can be utilized.

—HEATHER DILLAWAY

See also Midwifery

Professions

see Clergywomen; Doctors; Lawyers; Military; Nursing; Scientists; Teaching: Primary and Secondary; Teaching: University

Property Rights

Coontz, Stephanie, and Peta Henderson (eds.), *Women's Work, Men's Property: The Origins of Gender and Class*, London: Verso Press, 1985

Hirschon, Renée (ed.), *Women and Property—Women as Property*, New York: St. Martin's Press, 1983; London: Croom Helm, 1984

Holcombe, Lee, *Wives and Property: Reform of the Married Women's Property Law in Nineteenth-Century England*, Toronto and Buffalo, New York: University of Toronto Press, and Oxford: Martin Robertson, 1983

Morris, Anne, and Susan Nott, *All My Worldly Goods: A Feminist Perspective on the Legal Regulation of Wealth*, Aldershot and Brookfield, Vermont: Dartmouth Publishing, 1995

Murray, Mary, *The Law of the Father?: Patriarchy in the Transition from Feudalism to Capitalism*, London and New York: Routledge, 1994

Salmon, Marylynn, *Women and the Law of Property in Early America*, Chapel Hill: University of North Carolina Press, 1986

Shanley, Mary Lyndon, *Feminism, Marriage, and the Law in Victorian England, 1850–1895*, London: I.B. Tauris, and Princeton, New Jersey: Princeton University Press, 1989

Property ownership is a crucial indicator of the balance of power between women and men. Property is basic to a materialist interpretation of social phenomena. HIRSCHON's book is based on the assumption that property would illuminate important dimensions of gender relations. By placing women and property as the central focus of this book, she seeks to explore wider dimensions of the topic and open it up for further investigation. The questions addressed here are: In what ways have relationships between women and men been structured by access to, control over, and transmission of property? To what extent and in what respects do women themselves, or their children, constitute property? Other points considered here are ideological constructs, the effect of plural legal systems, and changes in types of property.

According to SALMON's book, women's legal history focuses on three primary concerns that indicate the influence of the new legal history as well as women's history. First, one needs to understand how the laws functioned in practice, as well as in theory, in order to know how legal rules affected women's day-to-day lives. To that end, the reader is given cases as well as commentaries. Second, one needs to understand the meaning of change over time. The third concern encompasses the working of the law in practice. This book focuses on these concerns of women's legal history in a study of property law between 1750 and 1830. Salmon uses several areas of law, including divorce, contract, and inheritance, in order to develop a comprehensive definition of the property rights of American women. Although a woman's legal rights constitute only one of several strands necessary for defining her status, control over property is an important baseline for learning how men and women share power in the family. Salmon tries to unravel the rules on women's ownership and control of property, in order to arrive at a general understanding of women's changing role in the family and society at large.

The English common law, which deprived married women of the right to own and control property, had far-reaching consequences for the status of women in many areas of law, education, employment, and in family life. HOLCOMBE explores the story of the reform campaign in the context of its time. Holcombe gives particular attention to the many important men and women who worked for reform, and to the debates on the subject, which contributed greatly to the formulation of a philosophy of feminism.

SHANLEY studies the Victorian feminists, in order to expose the falsity of the idealization of marriage, and to show how repressive marriage and family life could be for women. In order to modify popular views of marriage and liberal theory's distinction between the private world of family and the public world of politics, feminists had to gain acceptance for their contention that the family was a locus of male power sustained by the judicial authority of the state. No piece of legislation ever fully reflected the principle that the only proper basis for marriage law was full legal equality between husband and wife. This book examines both the theory that motivated these remarkable feminists, and the practical successes and failures of their efforts to translate the ideal of spousal equality into law.

MURRAY's book is about the long-standing debate in feminist and social science literature: the relationship between class and patriarchy. It is also about the transition from feudalism to capitalism. Chapter One considers the theoretical parameters of the structural debate over class and patriarchy. Chapter Two discusses the nature of the relationship between class and patriarchy. Chapter Three outlines the main features of feudal society, and key moments in its development. Chapter Four considers patriarchy and rights in and to property. The author begins the chapter by looking at material relating to the Anglo-Saxon situation. However, more attention is paid to post-conquest times. Chapter Five looks at the patriarchal structuring of politics and political power (or its absence). Chapter Six considers the relationship between property and familial relations, concentrating on the extent to which, and ways in which, women's positions as equal sisters, and as subordinate daughters and wives, can be characterized in a feudal and a capitalistic society. Finally, Chapter Seven offers a critical appraisal of feminist contentions that women themselves were property in precapitalist England.

COONTZ and HENDERSON compile a group of essays that examine why men were able to privatize the services of women and why women, in many societies, did not successfully resist. These questions are analyzed from the standpoint of the authors' respective disciplines (history and anthropology) and scholarly traditions (French and American). The authors agree that while male dominance was not present in the earliest communal societies, it was already present in the earliest class societies as defined in the traditional sense of the term. One final point that is made in this book is that female subordination actually preceded and established the basis for the emergence of true private property and the state. The authors disagree on issues such as how to explain the development of a division of labor by gender, and the degree to which male dominance was a conscious creation of men who wished to exploit female labor.

Equality in the workplace is vital, but it is only part of a much wider problem that must be addressed if women are to be equal participants in the working environment, according to MORRIS. She attempts to draw together an exploration of how the law deals with this fundamental issue. The aim here is not to look at the technicalities of the law, but to examine its objectives and consequences. By doing this, the reader can study the intricacies of the different areas and will be able to view more critically the underlying assumptions and aims of lawmakers. This book actually makes the law more accessible and does a good job at answering many legal questions. By drawing attention to the difficulties women still face, the author does not provide a mere litany of complaints or present women as victims. Rather, she shows that there are many successful women. She writes in a positive tone, indicating that progress for all women is more likely where obstacles are identified and there are constructive remedies offered.

—SUSAN M. TAYLOR

Prostitution

Barry, Kathleen, *Female Sexual Slavery,* Englewood Cliffs, New Jersey: Prentice-Hall, 1979; London: New York University Press, 1984

Bernheimer, Charles, *Figures of Ill Repute: Representing Prostitution in Nineteenth-Century France,* Cambridge, Massachusetts: Harvard University Press, 1989

Bullough, Vern, and Bonnie Bullough, *Women and Prostitution: A Social History,* Buffalo, New York: Prometheus, 1987

Butler, Anne M., *Daughters of Joy, Sisters of Misery: Prostitutes in the American West, 1865–1890,* Urbana: University of Illinois Press, 1985

Corbin, Alain, *Women for Hire: Prostitution and Sexuality in France after 1850,* translated by Alan Sheridan, Cambridge, Massachusetts, and London: Harvard University Press, 1990

Davis, Nanette J., *Prostitution: An International Handbook on Trends, Problems, and Policies,* Westport, Connecticut: Greenwood, 1993

Goldman, Emma, *The Traffic in Women and Other Essays on Feminism,* New York: Times Change Press, 1970

Hicks, George, *The Comfort Women: Sex Slaves of the Japanese Imperial Forces,* New York: Norton, and London: Souvenir Press, 1995

Mahood, Linda, *The Magdalenes: Prostitution in the Nineteenth Century,* London and New York: Routledge, 1990

Sanger, William, *History of Prostitution,* New York: Harper and Brothers, 1858

Spongberg, Mary, *Feminizing Venereal Disease: The Body of the Prostitute in Nineteenth-Century Medical Discourse,* Washington Square: New York University Press, and London: Macmillan, 1997

Walkowitz, Judith R., *Prostitution and Victorian Society: Women, Class, and the State,* Cambridge and New York: Cambridge University Press, 1980

Even if one resists calling prostitution "the world's oldest profession," writings on prostitution have been in existence for centuries. Whether the prostitute was said to fulfill a social need, as in Augustinian writings or St. Thomas Aquinas's imagery of the sewer in a palace, prostitutes have been defined in numerous ways, tolerated, regulated, monitored, examined, and surveyed. Prostitutes have been seen as carriers of disease, seductresses, victims of the moral corruption of patriarchal societies, and individual agents of their own liberation. The literature on prostitution in ancient and premodern societies could generally be categorized as prescriptive, defining certain women's roles either in the context of their function in society or their relationship to the church and to authority. More analytical, historical, and sociological literature dates only from the nineteenth century when researchers began to explore sexuality and deviance from the perspective of contagious diseases (that is, sexually transmitted diseases) and growing bourgeois sensibilities.

Among the more significant nineteenth-century studies of prostitution is SANGER's study of 6,000 prostitutes in New York City. Beginning with a history of prostitution from ancient civilizations to contemporary Europe, Sanger asserted that it was an absurdity to suggest that prostitution could be eradicated. Instead, in this report to the Board of the Almshouse Governors of the City of New York, the author recommended the regulation and legalization of prostitution with a surveillance system modeled either on London or Paris. Slightly earlier in the century, in fact, William Acton (London, 1857) and Alexandre Parent-Duchâtelet (Paris, 1836) had published statistical and prescriptive studies of their own respective cities.

At the turn of the century a new literature of prostitution emerged, encouraged again by concerns about contagious diseases, the agendas of reformers and feminists, and moral crusades. Building on the "scientific" studies of the nineteenth century, new histories of prostitution were written, including Abraham Flexner's 1914 work, which covered no new ground but provided a solid synthesis. The most significant work, however, came from a different source: GOLDMAN's anarchist analysis of patriarchy and marriage. "Red Emma," as she came to be called, published her series of essays condemning the commodification of women as sex objects, their prostitution in and outside of marriage, and the impossibility of their escape from such a system in its present form. With Goldman's deportation to Russia in 1919 after a series of arrests, however, her work was widely discredited.

Beginning in the 1970s, a new, more inclusive literature developed, spawned at least partially by the women's rights movement. Histories, like BULLOUGH and BULLOUGH's synthetic work, established again the historical stage on which prostitution was played out. Treating prostitution as the "institutionalized marketplace for the sale of sex," the authors noted the persistence of that marketplace throughout history, the double standard that has supported it, and the need for the decriminalization of prostitution.

Early in this more recent period of prostitution studies also came the still classic study by WALKOWITZ on prostitution in Victorian Plymouth and Southampton. Framing her study around the class and gender issues inherent in the debates and realities of the late nineteenth-century Contagious Diseases Acts, Walkowitz dispelled the myth of a unitary Victorian culture and a unitary "Josephine Butler crusade" against the Acts. Casting aside interpretations of prostitutes as "fallen women" alongside "male pollutants," Walkowitz argued that the "technologies of power" that were constructed to deal with issues of prostitution were key factors in its analysis.

A companion work is CORBIN's recently translated work on prostitution and sexuality in France after 1850. Anchoring his work in Parent-Duchâtelet's nineteenth-century study of Paris and heavily influenced by Michel Foucault, Corbin delved into the well-organized business of prostitution, treating it not as a crime or vice. Rather, in his both anecdotal and statistical study, he created the analogy that the brothel was to prostitution as the factory was to manufacturing. Furthermore, Corbin hypothesized that the longevity of prostitution was a product of male fantasies and male desire.

A number of significant period and national studies of prostitutes and of various aspects of prostitution have also been published during the last several decades. BUTLER's study of prostitutes in the American west defined four archetypes: brothel dweller, saloon or dance hall worker, crib woman, and street walker. Throwing aside the "dash of spice" aura of many works dealing with prostitution, Butler wrote a narrative of women's roles, debunking the myths that have characterized prostitution as a job of choice or means of social stability.

MAHOOD's work on Scottish prostitutes in the lock hospitals and magdalene houses deals less with actual prostitutes than with the nineteenth-century discourse on prostitution, which labeled, defined, and confined women of the streets. Using a Foucaultian model, Mahood attempts to deconstruct the prostitute, while at the same time, somewhat less satisfactorily, attempting to analyze her agency. In a similar genre, BERNHEIMER turns to the ubiquitousness of prostitution in nineteenth-century French art and literature. To Bernheimer, Manet's "Olympia," Zola's "Nana," and Degas's brothel images were all concerned with making private fantasies public. Although deeply steeped in the language of literary criticism, the author used only two categories for the women in his study: prostitute and courtesan.

A more compelling work is SPONGBERG's analysis of the body of the prostitute in nineteenth-century medical discourse. Beginning with nineteenth-century assertions of women's congenital defects and pathologies, Spongberg analyzed the cultural assumptions that defined women as the "contaminated other." Interestingly her conclusion takes the reader far from the nineteenth century into the discourse of HIV/AIDS. Spongberg concludes that, regardless of the discourse, the heterosexual male remains the standard, and that a strong misogyny and homophobia informs biomedical discourse.

While much of the literature on prostitution outside of western Europe and America is found in collections of essays and periodical literature (for example, journals like *Signs*), BARRY's 1979 work on female sexual slavery broadened that analysis. Using the INTERPOL report of 1974 and historical and sociological studies, Barry's work framed the debate inside and outside traditional boundaries, including sexual terrorism, the slave trade, pimping, pornography, and perversion. Also moving outside the traditional geography of prostitution studies, HICK's 1995 study of the now well-known case of Korean comfort women is based on military records and interviews. Fortunately, the author's somewhat glib view of military prerogative (Mars and Venus "hand in hand" in the encampment) is countered by a recognition of the victimization of the comfort women and decades of Japanese "amnesia" relative to them.

A more comprehensive view of prostitution is found in DAVIS's international handbook. Collecting studies of scholars from Latin America, western Europe, China, Vietnam, and Yugoslavia, Davis challenges the outmoded enforcement terminologies that condemned prostitutes to criminalization, treatment as victims, or objects of various legislative initiatives. Organizing each chapter around definitions, legal issues, and forms of prostitution, the book demands a recognition of the changing nature of prostitution. Instead of the traditional analysis framed around poverty, lack of education, unemployment, minority group membership, and labor market exploitation, new categories of analysis should be developed, she argues, for example, AIDS-related issues, child prostitution, self-help political movements, and international tourism.

—SUSAN P. CONNER

See also Sex Tourism, Sexual Slavery

Protective Legislation

Baer, Judith A., *The Chains of Protection: The Judicial Response to Women's Labor Legislation*, Westport, Connecticut: Greenwood, 1978

Boris, Eileen, *Home to Work: Motherhood and the Politics of Industrial Homework in the United States*, Cambridge and New York: Cambridge University Press, 1994

Hart, Vivien, *Bound by Our Constitution: Women, Workers, and the Minimum Wage*, Princeton, New Jersey: Princeton University Press, 1994

Kessler-Harris, Alice, *Out to Work: A History of Wage-Earning Women in the United States*, Oxford and New York: Oxford University Press, 1982

Lehrer, Susan, *Origins of Protective Labor Legislation for Women, 1905–1925*, Albany: State University of New York Press, 1987

Sklar, Kathryn Kish, *Florence Kelley and the Nation's Work: The Rise of Women's Political Culture, 1830–1900,* New Haven, Connecticut and London: Yale University Press, 1995

Skocpol, Theda, *Protecting Soldiers and Mothers: The Political Origins of Social Policy in the United States*, Cambridge, Massachusetts: Harvard University Press, 1992

Wikander, Ulla, Alice Kessler-Harris, and Jane Lewis (eds.), *Protecting Women: Labor Legislation in Europe, the United States, and Australia, 1880–1920*, Urbana: University of Illinois Press, 1995

At the turn of the nineteenth century, industrial nations adopted laws to protect female workers from workplace hazards and employer exploitation. In the United States, as progressive impulses spread, most states enacted at least some type of protective laws, such as maximum-hour laws, minimum wage laws, night work bans, or occupational exclusions. Since the 1970s, protective legislation has attracted the attention of historians, sociologists, and political scientists. In one of the first studies, a survey of judicial decisions, BAER examines a long string of state and federal cases, starting in the 1890s, that involved women's labor laws. Assessing such cases from the egalitarian stance of the new feminism, Baer assails efforts to embody in law notions of sexual difference. Her commentary includes a critique of the Brandeis brief of 1908 and indictments of pivotal Supreme Court decisions that endorsed classification on the basis of sex. Concluding chapters consider the rejection of such classification by the courts in the late 1960s and early 1970s.

Did protective legislation help or harm female workers? Several studies of the 1980s provide cogent analyses of the problematic nature of protective laws. KESSLER-HARRIS's chapter on protective legislation, part of a larger work on women's labor history, offers a useful overview of the origins of protective laws and the controversies that the laws provoked. It also explores their impact on female wage-earners in the early twentieth century and thereafter. Kessler-Harris stresses the ambivalent or hostile attitudes of labor unions toward working women, and the impact of such attitudes on protective policies. Classification by sex, she concludes, limits economic opportunity; the perils of protection thus outweigh whatever benefits protective laws may have provided.

LEHRER analyzes the conflicting views on protective laws put forth in the Progressive era by a spectrum of interest groups including social reformers, members of the National Woman's Party, labor unions, and employers' associations. In Lehrer's view, protective laws were intended neither to benefit nor to oppress women, but rather to mediate contradictions between women's roles as paid labor and as "maintainers of domestic reproduction in the family." Her commentary, if less judgmental than that of Kessler-Harris, is similarly insightful.

Scholarship of the 1990s focuses on specific aspects of protective legislation. In the first volume of her biography of Florence Kelley, SKLAR reveals the roots of protective legislation in the 1890s. She examines in particular the passage in 1893 of a pioneer Illinois law that provided maximum hours for female workers, a law that female reformers promoted, that employers challenged, and that the Illinois Supreme Court quickly upset. Kelley, however, went on to lead the National Consumers' League and to promote nationwide the policies that had failed in Illinois. Gender-based labor laws, Sklar contends, were a "surrogate" for class-based laws, to which legislatures and courts objected.

BORIS deals with a subset of protective laws, those that regulated or banned industrial homework. Rejected by trade unions and exploited by employers, homeworkers in industrial America included the disabled, the aged, and those who cared for others, old or young, but mainly they were (and are) mothers of young children. Boris discusses their motives, occupations, working conditions, and failure to find a public voice. She also explores reformers' efforts to enact homework laws, the role of industrial homework in New Deal legislation, legal cases involving homework, and debates over homework policies.

HART examines another facet of protective legislation, the minimum wage, once the most controversial type of protective law. Tracing the development of minimum wage policies in Britain and the United States, she presents the common origins of these policies in the early twentieth century and compares their divergent subsequent histories. The American constitutional system, Hart contends, long hampered efforts to achieve a minimum wage but ultimately served workers better than did the British system.

Several more recent works exploit comparisons in order to analyze the United States experience with protective legislation. SKOCPOL argues that uniquely, the United States developed little in the way of "paternalistic" policies, those that provide for the populace in general, such as other industrial nations developed around the turn of the nineteenth century. The government policy of pensions for Civil War veterans ultimately failed, she contends, through wastefulness and corruption, and the failure made further "paternalistic" measures unlikely. In contrast, an extensive array of "maternalistic" legislation, that is, measures promoted by female reformers, such as protective labor laws, mothers' pensions, and support for maternal-child health care, succeeded and had far more impact on the modern state. Skocpol stresses the roles of women's organizations, such as women's clubs, that promoted protective legislation at the state level.

The anthology edited by WIKANDER, KESSLER-HARRIS, and LEWIS brings together essays by historians on protective laws in many nations. Early in this century, Europe, Australia, and the United States all enacted labor laws that affected industrial workers, the editors contend, in order to reconcile patriarchal concepts of family with women's wage work in industry. Similarities abound. All the nations considered envisioned women as "mothers of the race." In all cases, too, female workers took little part in debates over protection. The particulars of the politics of protection, however, vary, as do the policies enacted. The United States alone, for instance, failed to provide maternity leaves, as did Britain, France, Sweden, and other nations. Moreover, as Kessler-Harris's concluding essay contends, despite reformers' rhetoric about motherhood, American night work provisions offered little to aid working mothers. A comparative perspective, the editors show, has much to offer to scholars of protective laws.

—NANCY WOLOCH

Psychological Theories about Women: Pre-Feminist

Chesler, Phyllis, *Women and Madness*, Garden City, New York: Doubleday, 1972; London: Allen Lane, 1974

Lerman, Hannah, *A Mote in Freud's Eye: From Psychoanalysis to the Psychology of Women*, New York: Springer, 1986

Lewin, Miriam (ed.), *In the Shadow of the Past: Psychology Portrays the Sexes: A Social and Intellectual History*, New York: Columbia University Press, 1984

Sayers, Janet, *Mothers of Psychoanalysis: Helene Deutsch, Karen Horney, Anna Freud, and Melanie Klein*, London: Hamish Hamilton, 1991; as *Mothering Psychoanalysis: Helene Deutsch, Karen Horney, Anna Freud, and Melanie Klein*, New York: Norton, 1991

Showalter, Elaine, *The Female Malady: Women, Madness, and English Culture, 1830–1980*, New York: Pantheon, 1985; London: Virago Press, 1987

Schuker, Eleanor, and Nadine A. Levinson, *Female Psychology: An Annotated Psychoanalytic Bibliography*, Hillsdale, New Jersey: Analytic Press, 1991

LERMAN has conducted an extensive investigation of Sigmund Freud, the person, the physician, and the theoretician. In this book, she sheds light on the women in Freud's life, and on his views on sex, women, and marriage. Grounded firmly in the context of Freud's personal and professional milieu, Lerman theorizes about influences on Freud's thinking on women. In her description of Freud, the physician, she describes Freud's patients, his stance toward female patients, and his views on "enlightened" child-rearing. She provides both an understanding and critical analysis of Freud's abrupt change from his original position in which he believed the incest accounts of his female patients to his later position that such stories were fantasies of psychosexual development. Lerman outlines the evolution of Freud's theory of female psychosexual development and cleverly frames the historical period from Freud to feminism in terms of developmental stages (for example, "a latency period"). This book is an excellent resource for understanding Freud's theories concerning women.

After Freud came his "dutiful daughters"—as well as those who were not so closely aligned with his theories and who broke quite clearly from his influence. SAYERS vividly illustrates the prefeminist contributions of Helene Deutsch, Karen Horney, Anna Freud, and Melanie Klein, demonstrating how they redefined psychoanalysis based on their own experiences as daughters, mothers, and simply as women in the cultures in which they lived. She also describes how these women affected the development of "mothering" theories of Margaret Mahler, Heinz Kohut, and Donald W. Winnicott. She portrays Deutsch as a socialist rebel and describes her theories of madness and mothering, female sexuality, lesbianism, and narcissism. Horney, the adored mother, theorized about innate femininity, womb envy, and maternal culturalism, and she was exiled from the psychoanalytic community for her views. Anna Freud, seen as her father's child, focused on child analysis, ego psychology, adolescence, war nurseries, and child custody. Klein, whose motherhood was fraught with depression, later underwent analysis and then analyzed her own children. Her work included the development of early object relations theory as well as foci on sex, art, depression and loss, war, and schizoid mechanisms. The reader will find this book rich with an understanding of the personal influences on psychological theories.

SCHUKER and LEVINSON have written an annotated bibliography in the area of psychoanalytic and developmental theories of the psychology of women. In this comprehensive text, the authors provide over 600 pages of annotations on original writings of psychological, psychoanalytic, and developmental theories about women. In the first section, they address historical views, with a focus on Freud and other early psychoanalytic theories, as well as historical writings from 1900 to 1940. In the second section on developmental perspectives, they address gender differences as well as psychoanalytic constructs, such as preoedipal and oedipal development, latency and adolescence, reproductive and sexual development, early and later adult development, and family relationships. Section three addresses sexuality and various conditions and disorders predominantly ascribed to women, such as masochism, narcissism, eating disorders, and sexual abuse. The last two sections address clinical concepts and reading lists. The book is an excellent research tool and reference work on psychoanalytic ideas about female development and psychology.

LEWIN describes the manner in which the young science of psychology was shaped by social, political, and economic forces, as well as the social and intellectual perspectives of the nineteenth and twentieth centuries. She and her contributing authors illustrate vividly the ways that gendered assumptions of the times influenced psychological thought about women. The authors integrate the history of social relations between women and men over a vast time period and examine Freud in a new light. Lewin then sets the social and intellectual stage for understanding the development of psychology in terms of four major currents or "hidden presuppositions" of Victorian thought. The authors also illustrate the contributions of pioneer female graduate students and psychologists who questioned beliefs of female inferiority. Additional topics include the influence of "father figures" in psychology on male-female relations and parenting, analyses of early psychological theories of masculinity and femininity, the mystification of motherhood and mother blaming, behaviorism, and working mothers. The text is an excellent overview of major themes in early psychology concerning women, gender, and relations between women and men.

The final two books in this review of prefeminist psychological theories about women deal with women and madness. SHOWALTER, in her text on women, madness, and English culture from 1830 to 1980, focuses on three historical periods in the treatment of women and madness. In the first, psychiatric Victorianism, she addresses what she calls the domestication of insanity, when the first lunatic asylum was opened in England. Women occupied a special place in the asylum by numbers alone—women comprised about 60 percent of asylum populations at that time. Victorian psychiatry produced an immense array of female maladies, most often related to women's reproductive cycle. In part two of the book, Showalter addresses psychiatric Darwinism, with particular emphasis on "nervous" women, who evolved as a result of defying their "nature" as appropriate women, wives, and mothers. It was during this time that, throughout Europe, psychiatrists such as Jean Martin Charcot and Freud gained renown for their treatment of hysterics—invariably women. Finally, in her section on women and psychiatric modernism, the author addresses women and madness from 1920 through 1960, focusing on such treatments as electroconvulsive ("shock") therapy as well as the development of the antipsychiatry movement and the implication of the family, notably mothers, in the genesis of mental illness. The book is rich with history and extensive references for further reading.

CHESLER's ground-breaking work on women and madness brought to the attention of the American public both attitudes toward and treatment of women in the mental health system. She begins with the question, "Why madness?" and relates the accounts of four historical women in asylums from the 1800s through 1963. Her account is imbedded in mythology and weaves a captivating account of women's plight throughout the ages. She then turns to a discussion of asylums, women's gender roles, and psychiatric symptoms (depression, frigidity, suicide, and schizophrenia). In her discussion of "the clinicians," she critiques the theories of Freud, Carl Jung, Wilhelm Reich, Erik Erikson, Ronald D. Laing, and others, and identifies attitudes of contemporary clinicians based on those theorists. She traces women's careers as psychiatric patients, addressing issues such as sex between therapist and patient, psychiatric institutionalization, lesbian women, and Third-World women. She ends with a discussion of the past, present, and future of psychology.

—SUSAN L. MORROW

Psychological Theories about Women: Feminist

Belenky, Mary, Blythe Clinchy, Nancy Goldberger, and Jill Tarule, *Women's Ways of Knowing: The Development of Self, Voice, and Mind,* New York: Basic Books, 1986

Bem, Sandra Lipsitz, *The Lenses of Gender, Transforming the Debate on Sexual Inequality,* New Haven, Connecticut: Yale University Press, 1993

Brown, Lyn Mikel, and Carol Gilligan, *Meeting at the Crossroads: Women's Psychology and Girls' Development,* Cambridge, Massachusetts: Harvard University Press, 1992

Gergen, Mary, and Sara N. Davis (eds.), *Toward a New Psychology of Gender,* New York: Routledge, 1997

Gilligan, Carol, *In a Different Voice: Psychological Theory and Women's Development*, Cambridge, Massachusetts: Harvard University Press, 1982

Hare-Mustin, Rachel, and Jeanne Marecek (eds.), *Making a Difference, Psychology and the Construction of Gender*, New Haven, Connecticut: Yale University Press, 1990

Kitzinger, Celia, *The Social Construction of Lesbianism*, London and Newbury Park, California: Sage, 1987

Landrine, Hope, *Bringing Cultural Diversity to Feminist Psychology: Theory, Research, and Practice*, Washington, D.C.: American Psychological Association, 1995

Unger, Rhoda, and Mary Crawford (eds.), *Women and Gender: A Feminist Psychology*, New York: McGraw-Hill, 1992

The variety of texts written from a feminist perspective about women and gender issues in psychology can be divided among three different categories: empirical, feminist standpoint, and postmodern, according to their underlying philosophical assumptions about the nature of science, reality, and language. The empiricists, who are the majority of feminist research psychologists, maintain an allegiance to traditional scientific methods, but are vigilant against sexist biases; feminist standpoint theorists celebrate women's special qualities and vest scientific truth in women's descriptions of their own experiences; and feminist postmodernists, a small but growing group of psychologists in the United States and United Kingdom, generally adopt a social constructionist framework. Social constructionism emphasizes the centrality of language in the development of the subject matter of psychology, including the creation of gender categories. The books selected for review represent these three groupings.

UNGER and CRAWFORD have created a very comprehensive and politically sensitive compilation of the literature within feminist psychology. A popular textbook in psychology of women courses, this book introduces a range of empirical studies of girls and women, covering both biological and cultural influences over the life span. The authors highlight feminist issues such as sexual harassment, violence, and the sexist biases in the diagnoses of mental disorders. Despite the inclusion of much empirical work, including that of feminist standpoint researchers, the authors introduce social constructionist ideas more consistently than any other textbook writers in this genre, and propose the merging of these intellectual pursuits.

LANDRINE's volume is unique within gender psychology, for bringing multicultural influences into mainstream feminist psychology, rather than containing them as tributaries of a predominantly Eurocentric body of literature. An introductory chapter by the editor stresses the strengths of offering a great range of perspectives and styles produced by the diverse set of authors; additionally, she urges feminists committed to cultural diversity to go beyond narrow empirical methods toward a contextualist approach to psychology. The four major sections of the book include: theoretical and methodological perspectives on diversity; therapeutic practice issues concerning diversity; American Indian, Latina, Asian American, and black women's perspectives on their roles within feminist psychology; and three investigations on health, language, and pornography. A concluding chapter by Rhoda Unger deals with the difficulties of integrating social constructionist, contextualist, and empirical approaches to feminist psychology. Besides reporting on the range of primarily empirical research undertaken with and by minority peoples, this book serves as a continual reminder of the importance and difficulty of meeting the challenge of a culturally diverse feminist psychology.

BEM's volume collects and refines the ground-breaking work she began in the 1970s on the concept of androgyny, a personality trait measured by one's scores on the femininity and masculinity scales on the Bem Sex Role Inventory. The book covers her shift in the 1980s, from a study of personality traits to a cognitive model of gender schemas, and to her recent examination of the cultural lenses that influence sex-stereotyped behaviors. While continuing to defend her own empirical research history, she has opened up a space for discussions of the construction of gender in terms of male-dominated discourses.

The work of GILLIGAN and her students and colleagues, which is perhaps the most highly visible feminist scholarship in psychology, represents one strand of the feminist standpoint position. While this work has raised controversy within psychology, the texts of Gilligan and her associates reach a large and responsive audience. The book scarcely needs an introduction; here, Gilligan develops a point of view in contrast to the dominant psychological literature on morality, justice, and personal development. Through interview studies on issues of abortion, moral dilemmas in everyday life, and moral choices over the lifespan, Gilligan describes how women's ways of honoring human connections produce an "ethic of care," in contrast to masculine notions of justice, which depend upon the application of abstract principles of moral reasoning.

BROWN and GILLIGAN's book focuses on the development of identity in girls. Through their specialized interview and analytical process, they discover that girls, who are outspoken and confident in childhood, lose their voices in adolescence as they confront societal demands to become proper young women. Exploring the silences of women, BELENKY, CLINCHY, GOLDBERGER, and TARULE's book made a strong impact on feminist readers, and influenced many educators to alter classroom practices to become more sensitive to women's needs. The authors posit that women, who have been made to feel insecure through subjection to male-dominated forms of learning, are better able to learn in settings that emphasize cooperative relationships, and that are accepting of intuition and personal experience as proper modes of expression, rather than through more traditional models of learning hierarchies, competition, and argumentation.

Writing from a postmodern position, HARE-MUSTIN and MARECEK focus on a cardinal question in feminist psychology: what shall we make of the difference between the sexes? The title is a pun derived from this dilemma: empiricists often tend to minimize and dismiss sex differences; feminist standpointers to emphasize and laud them; postmodernists to deconstruct them. This book emphasizes how the differences are socially constructed, and why. The chapter by Jill Morawski is especially cogent in historicizing these viewpoints and pointing to feminist strategies for reinventing psychology.

KITZINGER's book pioneered the development of a radical lesbian stance in feminist psychology. Her constructionist arguments challenge both nativist and social learning approaches to homosexuality. Although she uses scientific methodologies herself to explore lesbian identities, her book critiques traditional models of science, and emphasizes the importance of political commitment in feminist psychology. Kitzinger suggests that the liberal humanist tolerance of alternative lifestyles ironically contributes to a denial of male oppression rather than a confrontation with it.

GERGEN and DAVIS have edited the first volume that explicitly illustrates forms of social constructionist research, including narratives, discourse analysis, case studies, and interviews in feminist psychology. Encompassing work from related disciplines, the book illustrates how focal areas of interest (for example children's development, sexuality, masculinity, eating disorders, mental health, cultural differences, and power) can be explored from this perspective. The international list of contributors brings a multicultural dimension to this book as well.

—MARY GERGEN

See also Ethic of Care; Psychotherapy, Feminist

Psychotherapy, Feminist

Brown, Laura S., *Subversive Dialogues: Theory in Feminist Therapy,* New York: Basic Books, 1994

Comas-Díaz, Lillian, and Beverly Greene (eds.), *Women of Color: Integrating Ethnic and Gender Identities in Psychotherapy,* New York: Guilford Press, 1994

Greenspan, Miriam, *A New Approach to Women and Therapy,* New York: McGraw-Hill, 1983

Mander, Anica Vesel, and Anne Kent Rush, *Feminism as Therapy,* New York: Random House, 1974

Rawlings, Edna I., and Dianne K. Carter, *Psychotherapy for Women: Treatment toward Equality,* Springfield, Illinois: Charles C. Thomas, 1977

Worell, Judith, and Pam Remer, *Feminist Perspectives in Therapy: An Empowerment Model for Women,* Chichester and New York: Wiley, 1992

In 1974, MANDER and RUSH published their classic work, the first book dealing with feminist therapy. During this early period in the second wave of feminism in the United States, the focus of feminist therapists was upon consciousness-raising and a critical analysis of traditional models of psychotherapy. After an introduction to feminism, the authors define feminist therapy and critique Freudian, Jungian, Reichian, and Gestalt therapies from a feminist perspective, offering an alternative model that stresses power, body-mind healing, and social change. The book is written from a personal perspective by both authors and includes their "herstories." It concludes with a feminist holistic approach to body-mind healing.

Also in the early years of the evolution of feminist therapy, RAWLINGS and CARTER published the first edited book on feminist therapy. During this period, feminist therapy continued to focus on consciousness-raising, as well as on assertiveness training and therapy issues concerning lesbians. The purpose of the book was "to provide the professional community with a guide to psychotherapeutic treatment which encourages women to develop as complete human beings." The authors themselves wrote introductory chapters on values in feminist psychotherapy, addressing such issues as reciprocal influence in psychotherapy and comparing sexist, nonsexist, and feminist psychotherapies. Succeeding chapters cover nonsexist approaches to psychotherapy, assertion training for women, career counseling, psychotherapy for lesbian women, feminism as therapy, radical feminism's challenge to professional psychotherapy, and social activism as therapy. In the concluding chapter, Rawlings and Carter discuss psychotherapy as a means of social change and investigate ways in which psychotherapists can participate in creating a more just and humanistic society.

As feminist therapy evolved in the 1980s, authors continued to conduct critical analyses of Freudian and other traditional therapies as well as psychotherapy in general. GREENSPAN provided a scathing analysis of traditional psychotherapy, pointing to its many ills: overmedication of women, treating women's socially and environmentally induced distress as intrapsychic and pathological, and placing the psychotherapist in the role of expert. She points out the failure of humanistic therapies. Proposing a new approach to women and therapy, she addresses women's bodies and sexuality, femininity and victimization, and work and relatedness. In the final section of the book, she describes how she works as a feminist therapist, stressing the client-therapist relationship, the importance of therapist self-awareness, and helping the client see the ways in which her own power is inextricable from the collective power of women. She integrates her own and other women's stories throughout her book and concludes with case examples from her own work with clients.

WORELL and REMER's work follows the tradition of early feminist therapy theory. They begin with important and basic consciousness-raising regarding the need for a feminist approach to psychotherapy, changing gender roles in society and implications for counseling, and female socialization. They offer the reader several opportunities for self-assessment regarding issues related to women and therapy. Their chapter on principles of empowerment in feminist therapy captures both historical and current thinking on what constitutes feminist counseling. In part two, they address lifespan issues in counseling women, including depression, sexual assault, abuse, careers, and multiple oppressions in the lives of lesbian and ethnic-minority women. Finally, they address ethical and practice issues as well as a model of training. This book is extremely useful as a training text in feminist therapy.

The final two books in this review reveal a focus on what may be the most important perspective to emerge in feminist therapy in the 1990s. Working to respond to criticisms raised by womanist and feminist women of color, both white feminists and women of color have integrated a multicultural perspective into the theory and practice of feminist therapy. COMAS-DÍAZ and GREENE, along with their contributing authors, paint what they term an "ethnocultural mosaic" that informs the reader about the unique concerns of women of color: African-American, American Indian, Asian and Asian-American, Latina, West Indian, and women of the Indian subcontinent. Within these chapters, the authors address the complexities of women's lives, including the effects of racism, mainstream culture's standards of (white) beauty, economic hardship, family, sexuality, and ethnic identity on women of color. They do not avoid such difficult issues as alcoholism, woman and child abuse, and lesbianism. They introduce therapeutic approaches that are congruent with the cultures of women of color. In the second section of the book, traditional therapeutic approaches are transformed into relevant perspectives for women of color, and both feminist and integrative approaches are explained. The final section describes the "labyrinth of diversity," focusing on professional women, lesbian women, women in battering relationships, mixed-race women, and refugee women. This book is an essential addition to the professional libraries of both feminist and mainstream therapists.

Finally, BROWN provides an integrative, multicultural perspective on feminist therapy. Beginning with a "subversive dialogue with the reader," the author notes, "Feminist therapy is the practice of a genuinely revolutionary act in which both lives and society are changed." In her first chapter, Brown defines feminist therapy as that which is informed by both feminist political analysis and multicultural feminist perspectives on women and gender. She grounds feminist therapy in radical feminist political theory and action. Her integration of multicultural perspectives clearly places this book in the forefront of sophisticated thinking about feminist therapy. After describing the benefits of multiculturalism to both therapist and client, she identifies ways in which the feminist therapist may obtain knowledge about human diversity. Brown provides a complex look at the client-counselor relationship, including the place of symbolic relationships (termed "transference" and "countertransference" by traditional psychodynamic theorists), equality, power, and empowerment. In her chapters on diagnosis and assessment, she again addresses power and offers feminist visions and alternatives to traditional models. Brown is the consummate feminist ethicist. Refusing to deal simply or in a rules-based manner with ethics, she proposes ethical dilemmas and delineates the core components of feminist ethical perspectives: boundary issues, failures of respect and mutuality, and therapist self-care. This book is essential reading for every therapist aspiring to practice feminist multicultural therapy.

—SUSAN L. MORROW

See also Psychological Theories about Women: Feminist

Purdah

Abdullah, Tahrunnessa A., and Sondra A. Zeidenstein, *Village Women of Bangladesh: Prospects for Change*, Oxford: Pergamon Press, 1982

Abu-Lughod, Lila, *Veiled Sentiments: Honour and Poetry in a Bedouin Society*, Berkeley and London: University of California Press, 1986

Chowdhry, Prem, *The Veiled Women: Shifting Gender Equations in Rural Haryana 1880–1990*, Delhi and New York: Oxford University Press, 1994

Göçek, Fatma Müge, and Shiva Balaghi (eds.), *Reconstructing Gender in the Middle East: Tradition, Identity, and Power*, New York: Columbia University Press, 1994

Jeffery, Patricia, *Frogs in a Well: Indian Women in Purdah*, London: Zed, 1979

Mernissi, Fatima, *The Veil and the Male Elite: A Feminist Interpretation of Women's Rights in Islam*, Reading, Massachusetts: Addison-Wesley, 1991

———, *Dreams of Trespass: Tales of a Harem Girlhood*, Reading, Massachusetts: Addison-Wesley, 1994

Minturn, Leigh, *Sita's Daughters: Coming Out of Purdah: The Rajput Women of Khalapur Revisited*, New York: Oxford University Press, 1993

Mumtaz, Khawar, and Farida Shaheed (eds.), *Women of Pakistan: Two Steps Forward, One Step Back?*, London and Atlantic Highlands, New Jersey: Zed, 1987

Nanda, Bal Ram (ed.), *Indian Women: From Purdah to Modernity*, New Delhi: Vikas, 1976; London: Sangam, 1990

Wikan, Unni, *Behind the Veil in Arabia: Women in Oman*, Chicago: University of Chicago Press, 1982

A rich variety of works exist on purdah, the traditional harem, and the related practice of veiling women in order to symbolize their bounded seclusion. The diversity of works reflect the broad range of cultural contexts in which these practices prevail. MERNISSI (1991) explores the religious significance of the word *hijab,* the Quranic curtain that descended to place a barrier between two men (rather than a man and a woman), as well as its symbolism in dividing spatial dimensions. Her lyrical autobiographical work (1994) portrays the distressing psychological constraints and vivid pleasures of a girlhood spent in the enclosed purdah of her extended family's courtyard home.

ABU-LUGHOD's rich ethnographic enterprise deals with the different meanings of veiling among Bedouin women for their preservation of modesty in relation to gender, sexuality, and matters of identity. She offers a fascinating examination, in the context of Bedouin women's lived experience, of their critical and empowering use of poetry as it relates to contestations over gender and sexuality.

In a work that describes how rural women in Bangladesh villages are integrating into rural development processes, ABDULLAH and ZEIDENSTEIN concentrate upon the ways in which women perceive their lives. The authors are not concerned with the religious significance of purdah but with the way it affects the behavior and ideas of rural women. Purdah is understood to be a social and religious ideal, maintained through ideologies of women's need for male protection, and the status aspirations of both rich and poor families.

CHOWDHRY situates her study of oral sources in the northern Indian state of Haryana to determine people's perception of reality and social life as it has been personally experienced. Her broad-ranging field work shows that sexual references in language reaffirm the ideology of seclusion of women, and that judgment is passed on non-observers of the custom. Known as *ghunghat* in Haryana, Chowdhry argues that purdah is based on a set of avoidance rules between a woman and her male affines, and is observed by over 72 percent of women. She also notes that male response to non-observance is verbal aggression and indecent behaviour.

A work that covers a broad range of topics concerning Middle Eastern women is that edited by GÖÇEK and BALAGHI. In this book, the editors present a collection of essays that reexamine and reconstruct the ways in which gender is being renegotiated in the power relations of men and women of the Middle East, with the intention to create dialogue both within and across diverse areas of intellectual investigation. In problematising the relationship between tradition and gender, in which women have been portrayed as "mute followers of tradition," various authors explore the use of veiling, female passivity, and contestations of power between family members to propose a reconsideration of static and powerless Orientalised women.

In JEFFERY's definition of purdah as seclusion through use of a "curtain," she not only substantiates Mernissi's definition but also focuses upon the "rather dull everyday reality" experienced by Muslim women who are the hereditary custodians of a shrine in Delhi, India. She documents the subtle complexities and ambivalences that surround women's experience, and the institutions of a society dominated by the rigid separation between men and women. She focuses on objections to the *burqa* which, in her case study, signifies a head-to-toe garment worn over normal dress.

MINTURN's ethnographic account of field work in Uttar Pradesh analyzes the complex factors influencing the roles and customs that shape women's lives. Using quantitative and qualitative evidence, the work covers the customary beliefs supporting purdah, an exploration of its functions as enforced obedience to authority, and changing attitudes to purdah, including urban and rural differences, increasing affluence, easy transportation, and the influence of the media.

MUMTAZ and SHAHEED draw upon personal experience and that of fellow activists in Pakistan's Women's Action Forum to review the theoretical and tactical approaches required to challenge existing patriarchal structures. They clarify the diverse conditions shaping Pakistani women's lives, centring particularly on veiling practices, legally imposed notions of Islamic dress, and the segregation and seclusion of women.

NANDA's collected edition is a re-publication of essays first printed in 1976. Its values lies in its historical rather than contemporary theoretical value. One essay, contributed by Rama Mehta, concentrates on the theme suggested by the title, yet it effectively substantiates Chowdhry's more recent work on the *ghunghat*, by focusing upon the Oswal peoples of Udaipur.

Embedded in WIKAN's classic ethnography of Sohari women in Oman are frequent references to the *burqa* facial mask (as opposed to Jeffery's treatment of the *burqa* as full garment). Building on an understanding gained from the meanings that Sohari women attribute to the *burqa*, she describes the fashioning and use of this individualised garment as the epitome of female modesty and pride. Wikan's representation of Sohari women's perceptions adds complexity to and contests western convictions that purdah practices are inherently suppressive.

—HELEN JOHNSON

Q

Queer Theory

Abelove, Henry, Michele Aina Barale, and David Halperin (eds.), *The Lesbian and Gay Studies Reader*, New York and London: Routledge, 1993

Butler, Judith, *Gender Trouble: Feminism and the Subversion of Identity*, New York and London: Routledge, 1990

Fuss, Diana (ed.), *Inside/Out: Lesbian Theories/Gay Theories*, New York and London: Routledge, 1991

Jagose, Annamarie, *Queer Theory*, Melbourne: Melbourne University Press, and New York: New York University Press, 1996

Queer theory had its genesis in the 1990s within western discourses of sexuality, although queer politics, arguably, can be traced back to the later 1960s and early 1970s. Queer theory's origins are elusive and are likely to be identified according to the particular interests of the person speaking or writing. JAGOSE indicates a movement between gay and lesbian studies and queer theory through the 1980s and into the 1990s. For Jagose, this movement with all its ambiguities is signified by the reissue, in 1992, with a new preface, of Eve Kosofsky Sedgwick's study of the historical discourse of "homosexual desire," *Between Men* (1985). Sedgwick's title epitomises a central difficulty that queer theory poses to a determinedly women's studies perspective: it is a theory founded on a challenge to sex-specific categories.

Jagose is virtually unique in offering a full-length introduction to queer theory. In so doing, she provides brief, accessible references to some of the major contributions to the field, which are largely, but not entirely, to be found in journal articles. Among those she discusses are feminist cultural studies writer Teresa de Lauretis's engagement with queer theory over a brief period of three years. Jagose attempts both to be coherent and to offer firm handholds into theory. Jagose also advocates the potential of queer theory as an agent for change and, while giving careful and detailed attention to a number of critiques, retains a regard for its ability to look forward "without anticipating the future." One of the many useful distinctions offered by Jagose is the idea of "queer" as a process of critiquing identity rather than as an established identity in its own right.

The fundamental questions around identity formation and identity politics raised by queer theory are a central focus for writers in the field and their critics. Jagose examines some lesbian-feminist contestations with queer theory, such as those represented by Sheila Jeffreys. Jeffreys offers one example of an assertively lesbian-feminist position, which contests any politics or theory that emphasizes an alliance of interests between lesbians and gay men. Jeffreys points out the strong historical association of the term "queer" with *male* homosexuality and argues that there must be a strong commonality of lesbians with other women against a male oppression of women, an oppression with which gay men as men must be complicit. Jagose offers an extended critique of Jeffreys's and similar lesbian-feminist positions.

While FUSS does not use the term "queer" in her title, the title does signal the blurring of sexual boundaries and definitions that are characteristic of queer theory. This edited collection addresses and critiques a range of issues, including some of those represented by Jeffreys. Drawing, as do many queer theorists, on Foucaultian analyses and perspectives, the contributors examine issues of identity from many different positions. Catherine Saalfield and Ray Navarro ("Shocking Pink Praxis: Race and Gender on the ACT UP Frontiers") explore issues of unexamined racism within gay and lesbian politics and suggest that campaigns such as "ACT UP" (from which the movement "Queer Nation" was formed) reveal an ethnocentrism that limits their radical openness. In drawing attention to the marginalisation of some sexual identities, they ask, does "queer" necessarily recognise its own capacity for marginalisation?

ABELOVE, BARALE, and HALPERIN's book is a useful and wide-ranging reader, offering a compilation of important discussion that contributes to the ongoing development of queer theory. The contestation of terms within this emerging field is explicitly noted by the editors in their introduction, in which they explain their choice of "lesbian/gay studies" rather than "queer studies" as their framing term, on the basis of contemporary usage; however, the introduction also makes clear that they consider this reader to be part of queer theory. This collection is particularly valuable in the editors' explicit recognition of the reader's limits, which leads them to provide an introductory "User's Guide" and concluding, excellent "Suggestions for Further Reading." From a women's studies perspective, perhaps the most interesting essays are those by recognised feminist contributors: Teresa de Lauretis, Monique Wittig, Gayle S. Rubin, Audre Lorde, and many others. The book is well-organised by themes that collect together a range of different perspectives, indicating the transdisciplinary nature of the field: political, representational, psycho-social, historical, and cross-cultural perspectives are all included. This book includes an extract from Sedgwick's frequently cited text *Epistemology of the Closet* (1990). This essay offers a detailed and complex discussion of the historical development of identities constructed around sexuality and the emergent epistemological arguments from the nineteenth and twentieth centuries. The closing comments of this essay sum up the central difference of queer theory from fixed sexual-identity politics, suggesting that there is less to be gained from a search for essentialist definitions than from a "study of the incoherent dispensation itself."

It is this project that has largely engaged the contemporary writer who is probably the most frequently cited in queer theory, Butler. BUTLER, heavily influenced by Michèl Foucault, describes gender as discursively formed through repeated acts of performance. Butler offers a fundamental challenge to some areas of women's studies that have built their analysis on a clear distinction between gender and sex, often relying on particular psychological and sociological models. The gendered subject, for Butler, is continuously being maintained through performative acts. One of the difficulties created by Butler's central term is that "performance" tends to be associated with a voluntary role-playing, while Butler in fact wants to remove the idea of voluntarism from her discussion. For Butler, the strength of queer theory lies in its potential to release people from the regulatory categories of identity and thus recognise ideas about subjectivity.

Queer theory is an emerging and contested field, to which Jagose offers an accessible, if somewhat partisan, introduction. For new readers venturing further into the field, a browse in the books by Fuss and Abelove, Barale, and Halperin will provide an excellent range of positions and debates, while Butler offers an example of a leading theoretician within the field.

—BARBARA BROOK

See also Lesbian Studies

R

Race/Ethnicity and Gender

Frankenberg, Ruth, *White Women, Race Matters: The Social Construction of Whiteness*, Minneapolis: University of Minnesota Press, and London: Routledge, 1993

Gunew, Sneja, and Anna Yeatman (eds.), *Feminism and the Politics of Difference*, Boulder, Colorado: Westview Press, 1993

hooks, bell, *Yearning: Race, Gender and Cultural Politics*, Boston: South End Press, 1990

———, *Black Looks: Race and Representation*, Boston: South End Press, and London: Turnaround, 1992

Pettman, Jan, *Living in the Margins: Racism, Sexism and Feminism in Australia*, St. Leonards: Allen and Unwin, 1992

Spivak, Gayatri Chakravorty, *In Other Worlds: Essays in Cultural Politics*, London and New York: Methuen, 1987

Trinh, T. Minh-ha, *Woman, Native, Other: Writing Postcoloniality and Feminism*, Bloomington: Indiana University Press, 1989

———, *When the Moon Waxes Red: Representation, Gender and Cultural Politics*, New York and London: Routledge, 1991

One significant challenge faced by second-wave feminists to the integrity of their social justice agenda has come from women outside the dominant cultures of Europe and America: women of colour, women from non-English-speaking backgrounds, women from the developing world, women from racial and cultural minorities, diasporic women, and indigenous women. For these critics, feminism is critically unaware of its own racial and ethnic biases. Its arguments concerning the universality of patriarchal oppression and the centrality of sex and gender based inequality have either ignored or failed fully to recognise the place of cultural and racial difference alongside gender as determinants of the lives of many women. In addition, Euro-American feminism was seen to bypass the difficult question of the role that women in dominant racial/cultural groups play in the oppression of women from non-dominant racial/cultural backgrounds, and to lack a theoretical framework sufficient to analyse and resist the intersecting oppressions of gender, race, and ethnic difference. The last fifteen years has seen feminism transformed by perspectives of feminists outside dominant Euro-American cultural and ethnic groups, as well as the development of theorisations of difference that are inclusive of issues of race and ethnicity.

A theorised and influential challenge to the uncritical Eurocentrism of the dominant theories and methodologies of Marxism, feminism and deconstruction is provided in SPIVAK's collection of essays. Working across the fields of literary and cultural criticism, Spivak questions the cultural hegemony of western intellectuals, including feminists, and counters the persistently neo-imperial urges of western intellectuals in talking about the non-west. An example is Spivak's critique of the French feminist Julia Kristeva's work *About Chinese Women* (1977) and her consideration of the condition of the subaltern woman, doubly dispossessed by patriarchy and colonial domination.

Hooks has made a substantial contribution in opening feminist discourses to African-American women's perspectives and experiences, and in challenging white feminism to consider the multiple oppressions of gender, race, and class. Hooks's work ranges across literary, cinema, and cultural studies and performs the role of cultural comment and critique, frequently engaging with issues as they emerge. HOOKS (1980) presents 23 essays, which engage variously with the practice and politics of black cultural criticism and the "yearnings" (for social change, for a shared space, for black voices to be heard) that this criticism both addresses and produces. Of particular interest are her work on the intersections of discourses of sex, sexuality, and race; the representation of whiteness; black masculinity; and the politics of feminist solidarity as they are played out among white, black, and diasporic women in North American academic circles.

HOOKS (1992) focuses more steadily on representation in a series of essays that take up the representation of race—that is, both blackness and whiteness—in contemporary culture. The book contains provocative essays on the incorporation by dominant white culture of cultural and racial difference in diverse cultural moves that amount to the "eating" of the other; the persistence of representation of hypersexualised black women in popular culture; and a call for the interrogation of the race and ethnicity of whiteness, the construction of which as racially neutral works to naturalise it and ensure the continued dominance of white culture.

FRANKENBERG's book goes some way in answering hooks's call for an interrogation of whiteness as a racial and ethnic category. Frankenberg's thesis—that racial ideology is a determinant of the lives of white women just as surely as it determines the lives of women from racial and ethnic minorities—is elaborated through her qualitative ethnographic study of thirty white American women. In her analysis of her interviewees' views, Frankenberg reveals the degrees to which racial ideology is embedded and naturalised in their lives. Race, including whiteness, in Frankenberg's work is an issue that must be addressed by all women, not simply women from racial/ethnic minorities.

PETTMAN's book tackles the subject of intersecting systems of oppression along racial, cultural, and gendered lines in Australia, a settler society which has seen indigenous people dispossessed—a dispossession that remains unaddressed through waves of subsequent migration. Working from a sociological perspective, Pettman examines the role of culturally exclusive ideologies in the making of the Australian state; the contours of the colonial encounter for indigenous and settler women; the cultural politics of migration and incorporation of racial/cultural difference into the dominant culture; the intersections of racism and sexism and the culturally differentiated effects of sexism; and the role of the state in policing the lives of women, with the lives of women from non-dominant cultural groups being subject to more state intervention than those of women from the dominant culture. Pettman also takes up the question of how academic feminism has met the challenges to its own culturally exclusive constitution, and the lines along which feminism must transform itself in order to address the racial/cultural differentiation of women's experience in Australia.

TRINH's participation in contemporary debates on ethnic and racial difference and feminism is made as both filmmaker and cultural critic. Trinh works across the fields of cinema studies, cultural studies, postcolonial theory, and feminism. Her books critically challenge the limiting effects of racism, the persistence of colonial ideology in western regimes of knowledge, and the prevailing reductionism in discourses of difference, including feminist discourses. The subjects of Trinh's critical interventions and theorizations are wide-ranging, including academic feminism, the discourses of anthropology, women's writing, the work of Roland Barthes, the discursive production of the Third World ("Third Worldism"), nativist discourse and the cult of authenticity, film, and photography. She argues for a heterogeneous feminist theory and activism capable of resisting and dismantling patriarchy and Eurocentrism.

GUNEW and YEATMAN's anthology includes essays from feminists working in a number of fields (history, literary, cinema and cultural studies, politics, philosophy) and deals with the interconnections of gender and race/ethnicity in several national settings (Australia, New Zealand, Canada, the United States, and Japan). Framed by extremely useful essays by Gunew ("Feminism and the Politics of Irreducible Difference") and Yeatman ("Voice and Representation in the Politics of Difference"), which engages the crucial question of who speaks for whom), the book presents a diverse collection of feminist scholarship that critically extends understandings of difference along the often competing axes of gender, race, ethnicity, class and culture.

—DENISE CUTHBERT

See also Apartheid; Arab Women; Asian Women; Black Women; Holocaust; Jewish Women; Latin American Women; Native American Women; Slavery, Black; White Women

Radcliffe, Ann Ward 1764–1823

British Writer

Grant, Aline, *Ann Radcliffe: A Biography,* Denver, Colorado: Alan Swallow, 1951

McIntyre, Clara Frances, *Ann Radcliffe in Relation to Her Time,* New Haven, Connecticut: Yale University Press, and London: Humphrey Milford, Oxford University Press, 1920

Miles, Robert, *Ann Radcliffe: The Great Enchantress,* Manchester: Manchester University Press, and New York: St. Martin's Press, 1995

Murray, E. B., *Ann Radcliffe,* New York: Twayne, 1972

Rogers, Deborah D., *Ann Radcliffe: A Bio-Bibliography,* London and Westport, Connecticut: Greenwood, 1996

———, (ed.), *The Critical Response to Ann Radcliffe,* London and Westport, Connecticut: Greenwood, 1994

The attention accorded to Ann Radcliffe in her own time as the writer of immensely popular Gothic novels was almost immediately followed by a long period of critical dismissal and neglect, and although Radcliffe scholarship has recently been reinvigorated by the upsurge of critical interest in the Gothic, there are still very few books devoted exclusively to her or her work. This neglect has perhaps been assisted by the extreme paucity of information about Radcliffe's life: although speculation about her abounded among her contemporaries, she lived privately and did not make herself available to the hungry public eye; moreover, her journals disappeared soon after her death. This obscurity, together with the presence of doubts and mysteries (why, at the age of 23, did she start writing? Why, eight years and six books later, did she suddenly stop?) left room for GRANT's folk biography, essentially a piece of historical fiction that weaves Radcliffe's whole life from a few shreds of fact and a great deal of unsubstantiated speculation. Unfortunately, the text does not distinguish between the two, and also pays oddly little attention to Radcliffe's work; as a biography, it has been discredited by more rigorous scholars. Yet Grant's vivid descriptions of the events and circumstances amongst which Radcliffe lived and wrote do succeed in bringing to life the England of Radcliffe's day.

ROGERS' biography (1996) is much more reliable, well researched, and carefully documented. This twenty-page account of Radcliffe's life, including newly discovered details of her final illness and death, is followed by an exhaustive annotated bibliography. All known editions of Radcliffe's novels, reviews, articles, general books on the Gothic or the eighteenth-century novel that include discussions of Radcliffe, and doctoral dissertations are included. Annotations are for the most part minimal but do give the reader a sense of each work's approach and range of coverage; thus, the bibliography can be used not just to locate sources, but also to determine their relevance to particular research interests. Apart from the lists of primary sources and full length works devoted exclusively to Radcliffe, the bibliography is organized chronologically. It is an invaluable research tool, particularly helpful for locating discussions of Radcliffe within more general works.

In a useful companion to this volume, ROGERS (1994) presents a collection of excerpts from secondary works, which give readers a sense of Radcliffe's reception in her own day, as well as the directions recent Radcliffe scholarship has taken. The book contains ninety-three excerpts from reviews, articles, and books written between 1789 and 1989. The chronological organization makes it possible to trace the critical response to each of Radcliffe's novels, from early notices through recent psychoanalytic and feminist interpretations. Occasionally a text is excerpted in a way that makes it difficult to grasp the argument, and although the editor's choices are for the most part judicious, the diversity of recent critical interest in the Gothic novel is underrepresented. Still, this volume is a great asset to readers who wish to obtain an overview of Radcliffe scholarship, or to read early responses from sources difficult to access in themselves.

Although her style and approach are dated, McINTYRE's book on Radcliffe is a solid piece of pioneering scholarship, to which many later critics are indebted. Following a biographical chapter, survey of criticism, and interesting source study, McIntyre argues that Radcliffe's major contribution to the novel as a genre was not her use of landscape or the supernatural, as others had claimed; rather, Radcliffe made sustained, plot-driven suspense central to the structure of the novel by developing narrative techniques that maintain the reader's interest sheerly through suspense of incident. These structural techniques, she asserts, influenced the entire development of the genre; later novelists like Charlotte Brontë and Charles Dickens would adopt and perfect them. Although McIntyre's argumentation is out of step with current critical practice, the thesis remains suggestive; in addition, McIntyre articulates many basic insights about the novels, and offers some historical consideration of Radcliffe as an early female writer.

MURRAY's more recent book provides a standard critical introduction to Radcliffe. The first chapter explores Radcliffe's attitudes toward landscape, sensibility, and the sublime; the second surveys eighteenth-century attitudes toward the elements of Radcliffe's Gothic style, focusing on the tension between sensibility and rational empiricism. Murray then examines each of the novels published during Radcliffe's lifetime, providing synopses followed by fairly schematic analyses of characters, setting, and technique. The book traces Radcliffe's development as a novelist, her emerging strengths, and her persistent weaknesses; its overarching argument is that Radcliffe's work successfully bridged the problematic gap between moral and aesthetic sensibility. Although the book is a worthwhile introduction to Radcliffe's works in relation to the intellectual climate of the late eighteenth century, Murray rarely achieves striking insights, and frequently belittles Radcliffe and her work, assessing her as an influential but mediocre writer, oblivious to the larger implications of her writing, whose successes resulted from accident rather than design.

MILES argues against just such an attitude, asserting that, in fact, Radcliffe's complex novels engaged critically with the culture in which she lived, a culture on the brink of what Miles calls "the Gothic cusp." Part of the stated purpose of his book is to make Radcliffe accessible and interesting to modern students, yet his theoretically sophisticated study will also interest advanced Radcliffe scholars. Drawing on Mikhail Bakhtin and Michel Foucault, Miles analyzes the ways Radcliffe's work makes power visible without resolving its inherent ambiguities and contradictions; he examines the "new topography of the self" mapped by her novels, and pays sustained attention to her Gothicism as a response to the French Revolution. In addition, he devotes a chapter to deconstructing the mythicized figure of "Mrs. Radcliffe," with attention, as throughout the book, to questions of class and gender. One hopes that the depth and complexity of Miles's text will interest future scholars in extending his critical engagement with Radcliffe's fascinating work.

—LORRI G. NANDREA

Rape *see* Child Sexual Abuse; Sexual Assault/Rape: Acquaintance; Sexual Assault/Rape: Marital; Sexual Assault/Rape: Other; Sexual Assault/Rape: War

Rankin, Jeannette 1880–1973

American Politician

Davidson, Sue, *A Heart in Politics: Jeannette Rankin and Patsy T. Mink,* Seattle, Washington: Seal Press, 1994

Giles, Kevin S., *Flight of the Dove, The Story of Jeannette Rankin,* Beaverton, Oregon: Touchstone Press, 1980

Josephson, Hannah, *Jeannette Rankin, First Lady in Congress: A Biography,* Indianapolis, Indiana: Bobbs-Merrill, 1974

Jeannette Rankin was the first woman elected to the United States Congress. Rankin was sent to the House of Representatives by the voters of Montana in 1917, and again in 1941. Several themes are consistent among all these works: Rankin's courage in voting against the entry of the United States into World War I and World War II; her resourcefulness and self-confidence, all acquired from an early age; her pioneering role in elected politics; her interest in progressive social causes, especially women's rights and peace; her place in women's history; her rise to office because of the work of other women; the role of her family in her work; the ethical stands she took during her long political career; and her tremendously active and vital old age. Although DAVIDSON's work is directed toward young readers, it is nonetheless sophisticated enough to be useful to an adult audience as well. The book encompasses two fictionalized feminist biographies of pioneering female politicians, Rankin and Patsy T. Mink. Davidson places emphasis on Rankin's years in various suffrage campaigns as the learning ground for her successful Congressional campaign and her knowledge of the workings of the government. Davidson includes a section on Rankin's life as a lobbyist and pacifist after serving in the government.

JOSEPHSON, who knew Rankin personally, incorporates the same themes into the first full-length biography of the Congresswoman. Josephson contends that Rankin was an astute politician, rather than a naïve idealist that some have called her. Josephson details Rankin's work as a lobbyist for the Women's International League for Peace and Freedom, the National Consumer League, the National Council for Prevention of War, and the Women's Peace Union between her two terms in Congress. A third section deals with Rankin's pacifist beliefs and the last decades of her life outside of Washington. There are no footnotes, nor are sources cited in this work.

GILES begins his biography claiming to place Rankin in the context of feminism and other political movements of the twentieth century, and he also provides additional insights into the development of Rankin's pacifist philosophy through the 1920s and 1930s. Rankin was especially attracted to the pacifist philosophy of Mohandas Gandhi, making several trips to India over a 25 year period. At the age of 88, Rankin marched against the war in Vietnam, at the head of the Jeannette Rankin Brigade, which was organized by Women Strike for Peace. Giles presents Rankin as personally more conflicted than do other biographers. He suggests that Rankin was troubled by androgynous aspects of her personality. Giles sees Rankin as in conflict with her family. He portrays Rankin as domineering over her brother and sisters, rather than as a woman who received the support and financial backing of her siblings. Giles includes Rankin's friendship with writer Katherine Anthony, giving more information on Rankin's personal life and personality. Although there are no footnotes in this book, many primary and secondary sources are cited.

—WENDY E. CHMIELEWSKI

Reproductive Freedom

Dixon-Mueller, Ruth, *Population Policy and Women's Rights: Transforming Reproductive Choice,* Westport, Connecticut: Praeger, 1993

Gordon, Linda, *Woman's Body, Woman's Right: A Social History of Birth Control in America,* New York: Grossman, and Harmondsworth: Penguin, 1976

Greer, Germaine, *Sex and Destiny: The Politics of Human Fertility,* New York: Harper and Row, and London: Secker and Warburg, 1984

Hartmann, Betsy, *Reproductive Rights and Wrongs: The Global Politics of Population Control and Contraceptive Choice,* New York: Harper and Row, 1987

Packer, Corinne A.A., *The Right to Reproductive Choice: A Study in International Law,* Turku/Abo, Finland: Abo Akademi University, Institute for Human Rights, 1996

Raymond, Janice G., *Women as Wombs: Reproductive Technologies and the Battle over Women's Freedom,* San Francisco: Harper, 1993

Sen, Gita, Adrienne Germain, and Lincoln Chen (eds.), *Population Policies Reconsidered: Health, Empowerment, and Rights,* Boston: Harvard University Press, 1994

The subject matter ensconced under the label of Reproductive Freedom has been the centre of dynamic evolution since the turn of the twentieth century. From being a concern dominated by problems in the western world in the early years of the twentieth century, it has grown to become a global issue, seen to be central to the lives of women of all races and classes, and covering a plurality of issues significant to the exercise of women's control in matters related to sexuality and childbirth.

The list of books chosen for this essay aims to highlight the diversity of thought that is prevalent in discussions on reproductive freedom. The first, by GORDON, is a treatise on the genesis of the birth control movement in America around the turn of the twentieth century. Tracing the various ideologies regarding reproduction that have prevailed in American society during this time—from orthodoxy, free love movements, race purists, and population control—Gordon follows the persistent and often militant efforts of pioneering men and women to legalise the right to prevent or terminate pregnancies. Underlying her historical documentation is the aim of highlighting reproductive freedom as more than accessibility to contraceptives; Gordon tries to centre women's reproductive self-determination within the larger context of power relations between men and women in society.

In an impressively researched and lucidly argued book, GREER critiques the consumerism that has permeated western ethics on sexuality and reproduction. The developed world has, in her opinion, distanced the act of sex from the larger cycle of life, birth, children, and community, where it ought to belong. Instead, the overwhelming commercialization of the act of sex has posited sexual gratification as the pivot of all human pleasure. The ensuing creed of recent generations has been, therefore, to laud the orgasm, avoid fertility, and denigrate pregnancy and childbirth. A contorted perception of reproductive freedom has emerged. In the closing chapters of the book, Greer draws attention to the efforts of western governments to pass this perspective on to the Third World.

The western world's paranoia since the 1960s of unchecked population growth edging out material advancement has led to frenzied efforts to institutionalise fertility reduction in the Third World, seen to be the site of this malaise. Planners and politicians have, for decades, been working out on paper how many children families in the developing world ought to have. Their rigid and sometimes coercive methods of reaching this end have led to the emergence of two significant strains of writing on reproductive freedom in recent years: one that sees the inclusion of reproductive freedom as an integral human right and has raised discussions on the role of international law in protecting and ensuring these freedoms, and the other a range of works that explores reproductive freedoms in the Third World in the context of institutionalised anti-natalist population programmes.

PACKER's book falls into the former category. She outlines the major international documents and conventions and the references therein that pertain to the right of individuals and in particular, women, to determine their right to make reproductive decisions. Her book draws attention to the exercise of individual rights within a socio-economic context that may have conflicting interests and priorities. Holding that the individual's right is paramount, she deals also with the state's obligations to the individual, and to the measures within international human rights law that secure the right to reproductive choice.

DIXON-MUELLER also follows on the issue of individual human rights in reproductive decision-making. Using an explicitly feminist critique to analyse the concept of "rights," she contends that for women, sexual and reproductive rights are central to the fulfilment of women's rights in other areas, such as education or employment. Basing her arguments on the experiences of women in developing countries, she also looks at the factors that have shaped international population policies, including, among others, U.S. government support for family planning. The most significant contribution in her work is her effort to draw up blueprints of a feminist population policy that would be responsive to women's reproductive needs.

The other genre of writing has been more vocal in demanding restitution of women's right to choice in reproductive decision-making, independent of demographic goals. An early book of this kind is the one by HARTMANN, in which she looks at the inherent potential for abusiveness in family planning programmes in developing countries. Her study of the Indonesian programme, sterilisation in Bangladesh, the one-child policy in China, and the indiscriminate distribution of hormonal and intrauterine contraceptives in the Third World, among others, shows how the usurpation of reproductive decision-making by institutions has been disastrous to women. The main argument she wishes to pursue is that population control can be more effectively accepted by women through positive development measures, such as by improving standards of living and women's status in society.

SEN, GERMAIN and CHEN'S edited book also presents articles addressing women's reproductive rights in developing countries. The articles contained in this volume deal with various aspects of population policies, from paradigmatic concerns to the redesign of specific programmes. The focal contention in the book is that to be effective, population policies must adopt a "human development approach" in which emphasis is on reproductive health, empowerment, and human rights. The need to reconceptualize women's empowerment is essential; from passive concepts of increasing levels of employment, education, and status of women, governments must move to actions that will radically transform social relations and enhance the power of women in decision-making.

RAYMOND provides a discussion on reproductive freedom of women in the context of technological advances of medical sciences. Coming from a radical feminist perspective, her argument is that modern science purports to project an image of enhanced choices for women with reproductive technologies such as in vitro fertilization. The reality of the risks involved, unimpressive success rates, and the intrusiveness of such methods are often obscured in order to promote the medical miracles they claim to produce. Raymond argues that such technologies have consequences that are insidious—they support a new form of traffic in women's bodies, are a form of medical violence against women, and aim, in the long run, to diminish the role of the mother, except as a provider of a womb. She contends that this is already evident in the language of reproductive technology, which refers to women as "maternal environments," "alternative reproductive vehicles," and "human incubators."

—RACHEL SIMON KUMAR

See also Abortion: Pre-Twentieth Century; Abortion: Twentieth Century; Birth Control Movement; Roe v. Wade (United States 1973)

Reproductive Technologies

Birke, Lynda, Susan Himmelweit, and Gail Vines, *Tomorrow's Child: Reproductive Technologies in the Nineties*, London: Virago Press, 1990

Callahan, Joan C. (ed.), *Reproduction, Ethics, and the Law: Feminist Perspectives*, Bloomington: Indiana University Press, 1995

Chadwick, Ruth F. (ed.), *Ethics, Reproduction and Genetic Control*, London and New York: Croom Helm, 1987

Raymond, Janice G., *Women as Wombs: Reproductive Technologies and the Battle over Women's Freedom*, San Francisco: Harper, 1993

Robertson, John A., *Children of Choice: Freedom and the New Reproductive Technologies*, Princeton: Princeton University Press, 1994

Rowland, Robyn, *Living Laboratories: Women and Reproductive Technologies*, Bloomington: Indiana University Press, and London: Lime Tree, 1992

Spallone, Pat, and Deborah Lynn Steinberg, *Made to Order: The Myth of Reproductive and Genetic Progress*, Oxford and New York: Pergamon Press, 1987

Stanworth, Michelle (ed.), *Reproductive Technologies: Gender, Motherhood and Medicine*, Cambridge: Polity Press, 1987

In its widest sense, the term "reproductive technologies" refers to a range of technological interventions into the processes of conception, pregnancy, and childbirth, as well as such low-tech and traditional forms as the use of forceps or the surgical termination of pregnancy. Within contemporary feminism, however, the emphasis has been on those advanced reproductive technologies (ARTs) that have been developed for the most part during the late twentieth century, and that seem to extend or override what is possible for the "natural" female body. One major focus for public and more recent feminist concern has been the development of various forms of assisted insemination, which started originally with the very simple and efficient technique of "artificial" insemination by donor or husband. Currently, more high-tech and often futuristic interventions such as the genetic manipulation of gametes or ex-utero gestation provide new controversy.

The issues have aroused very strong feelings, and moderation is not a notable feature of several books, written and edited mainly by those who would count themselves as radical feminists. SPALLONE and STEINBERG's collection is almost entirely hostile and sees reproductive technologies as part of a patriarchal plot that variously strips women of real choice, undermines the power of motherhood, and uses female bodies as "testing grounds" for experimental interventions. Several articles are written by supporters of the Feminist International Network of Resistance to Reproductive and Genetic Engineering (FINRRAGE) The possibility that the technologies might benefit women is decisively rejected, with varying degrees of rhetorical flourish.

Both Raymond and Rowland focus on the extent to which women are in control of their own bodies. RAYMOND's book is typical of the contention that women are dehumanised and reduced to a mere procreative function, an idea that surfaces interestingly in Margaret Atwood's futuristic novel, *The Handmaid's Tale*. Raymond is concerned, moreover, not simply with technological practices, but with the marketing and commercialisation of ARTs in the name of medical science. The image of science as not simply lacking in accountability, but as positively malevolent, is at the heart of ROWLAND's book, which takes up the theme of the exploitation of women's bodies by the increasingly unethical demands of biomedical experimentation. Rowland paints a pessimistic and even frightening picture, although some of her predictions may strike readers as far-fetched.

A few writers—in addition to those employed in the field—are wholeheartedly positive regarding ARTs. Commentaries now are, at best, cautious in their welcome, seeing many gains for women—particularly for those who experience difficulties conceiving—but also some serious physical, social, political, and ethical problems. This represents a significant retreat from Shulamith Firestone's early enthusiasm in *The Dialectic of Sex* for the (then) predictive potential of the new technologies. One of the most balanced in its approach is the book by BIRKE, HIMMELWEIT, and VINES, which makes a clear distinction between the ARTs themselves and the uses to which they may be put. They address the problems in a highly accessible way, with a thoughtful assessment of the potential consequences of new developments, which does not negatively prejudge the issue. The authors are wary of the future, however, and insist that in order to gain more control over their own reproductive processes, women must seek a greater involvement with understanding and practising science.

STANWORTH offers an edited collection that is equally measured in tone and is particularly valuable in providing a context for ARTs. Her contributors look at the state of health-care provision in general, at the social meanings of infertility, at the law's inadequacy in dealing with the new parental and familial scenarios that these technologies make possible, as well as at the accountability of science. The impression overall is that the use of ARTs could be handled in a way that is much more sensitive and responsive to the real needs of women. The collection is noteworthy, too, in its occasional attempt to employ postconventional modes of analysis to problems that are undoubtedly characteristic of a break with traditional standards. Stanworth's own essay, for example, on the deconstruction of motherhood, and Petchesky's on foetal imagery, provide highly appropriate reflections on the cultural meanings of the new technologies.

The implicit and sometimes explicit ethical thread that runs all through the works cited above emerges as the focus of the books edited by Chadwick and Callahan. CHADWICK brings together scientific explanation and opinion with both secular and theological ethics. Issues such as the eugenic potential of ARTs are opened up to debate. In a similar way, the ethical considerations dealt with by CALLAHAN centre not simply on whether reproductive technologies are good for women—either individually or generally—but on the ability of existing moral and legal paradigms to make sound judgments about highly innovative developments. Questions concerning the attribution of parenthood or concerns over the status of ex-utero embryos are discussed within a broad range of reproductive technologies. The collection is perhaps more philosophical than others discussed but aims to situate the discussion in the context of some very material social problems, which face not just women but society in general.

From the very different perspective of rights-based procreative liberty, ROBERTSON looks at the issue of freedom of choice within ARTs. His analysis is not from a feminist perspective, but it is useful in covering many of the more up-to-date technologies that raise questions about the use of fetal tissue, the problem of surplus embryos, and the implications of genetic screening.

Given the nature of modern scientific endeavor, it is inevitable that any works dealing with ARTs face the problem of being overtaken by events—what was yesterday's overimaginative anxiety or hope is today's reality. The books outlined here examine some of the perennial issues, but what remains is that in a field where change is so dramatic, so few have attempted to move outside conventional models of analysis.

—MARGRIT SHILDRICK

See also Infertility; Pregnancy and Childbirth; Surrogate Motherhood

Rich, Adrienne 1929–

American Writer

Altieri, Charles, *Self and Sensibility in Contemporary American Poetry,* Cambridge and New York: Cambridge University Press, 1984

Cooper, Jane Roberta (ed.), *Reading Adrienne Rich: Reviews and Re-visions, 1951–1981,* Ann Arbor: University of Michigan Press, 1984

Keyes, Claire, *The Aesthetics of Power: The Poetry of Adrienne Rich,* Athens: University of Georgia Press, 1986

Martin, Wendy, *An American Triptych: Anne Bradstreet, Emily Dickinson, Adrienne Rich,* Chapel Hill: University of North Carolina Press, 1984

Templeton, Alice, *The Dream and the Dialogue: Adrienne Rich's Feminist Poetics,* Knoxville: University of Tennessee Press, 1994

Werner, Craig. *Adrienne Rich: The Poet and Her Critics,* Chicago: American Library Association, 1988

Adrienne Rich's work spans over 40 years, and during this time, she has grown into a major American poet, prose writer, and feminist. She sees her life and her work as processes, constantly undergoing change and revision. Further, Rich believes that poetry ought to make a difference in the real lives of people. Consequently, much of the criticism of her work traces her growth as a writer and as a woman, and includes discussions of both her poetics and her politics.

For anyone beginning a study of Adrienne Rich, WERNER's book is a good starting point. The book provides a comprehensive overview of both Rich's work and her criticism through 1986. Werner opens with a chapter entitled "Poetry and Process: The Shape of Adrienne Rich's Career," in which he traces her growth from the "modernist formalism" of her early work to the "lesbian-feminist reconstructions" of her later work. He identifies three phases in Rich's work and cites *Snapshots of a Daughter-in-Law* (1963) and *Diving into the Wreck* (1973) as transitional volumes. According to Werner, Rich employs three recurring themes: first, the analysis and critique of patriarchy; second, the desire for a "woman centered alternative"; and third, the importance of personal and political fusion in poetry. He explores each of these themes in chapter length discussions, beginning with "Patriarchy and Solipsism: Repression, Rebellion, Revision," continuing with "The Lesbian Vision: 'The Meaning of Our Love for Women Is What We Have Constantly to Expand'" and concluding with "The Radical Voice: From Deconstruction to Reconstruction." In his final chapter, Werner places Rich in an American tradition that both includes and transcends Walt Whitman and T.S. Eliot. Werner's bibliography is comprehensive and serves as an excellent source for further study.

While Werner provides a solid introduction to Adrienne Rich, ALTIERI offers an important introduction to contemporary American poetry, one that is frequently cited as an essential resource for the study of Rich's work. Altieri names Rich as a representative poet of the age, and one of the strongest poets of her day. He evaluates poets based on how well they are able to capture the reality of the writer and reader, and how well they exercise self-consciousness. Altieri's book drives through theory to an extended discussion of Rich's work. For Rich, self-consciousness is a means, not an end. Her self-consciousness, he concludes, becomes the means through which she reaches self-definition. Further, it is through self-reflection that Rich is able to identify and address the needs of women in contemporary culture, providing not only a description of those needs, but also alternative sources of strength and energy.

COOPER offers a comprehensive and representative collection of critical essays and reviews of Rich's work. The first section includes contemporary critical essays, written by noted Rich scholars including Claire Keyes, Joanne Feit Diehl, and Wendy Martin, among others. Judith McDaniel's opening essay traces Rich's choices in the reconstitution of herself and her work. It is Rich's "will to change" that most identifies her as a writer. This essay offers an important overview not only for the book, but for any study of Adrienne Rich. The second section of Cooper's book includes reviews of Rich's poetry appearing in print between 1951 and 1981. The reviews provide historical perspective on the reception of Rich's work. Finally, the third section of the book includes both critical essays and reviews of Rich's prose. The final essay in the book situates Rich as a feminist theorist, one who early on called attention to the gaps in feminist thought that overlooked both lesbian and racial issues in the women's movement. Cooper's book concludes with an extensive and comprehensive bibliography, including annotations of secondary sources, listings of Rich's work, listings of all reviews of Rich's work, organized by work, and reference sources.

MARTIN suggests that Rich continues traditions begun by Anne Bradstreet and Emily Dickinson. Martin demonstrates the ways each woman's work is tied not only to her own historical moment, but also to early American thought. The section on Rich is extensive, and based on conversations between Martin and Rich. Martin concentrates on Rich's writings, beginning with *Snapshots of a Daughter-in-Law* (1963), and concluding with *A Wild Patience Has Taken Me This Far* (1981). She begins her discussion of Rich with a biographical overview, stressing Rich's relationship to her father and his influence on her early poetry. Martin suggests that Rich's ideology finds its sources in the Puritan utopian ideal, although clearly not in the patriarchal ideal. Further, Rich's work demonstrates her evolution from a woman dependent on men to a woman who depends on herself. Rich's work concentrates on women's lived experience; her vision is a "society where all women can be at home."

KEYES opens her discussion by asserting that the women's movement has been the central force in the United States for social and political change, and that Adrienne Rich's work has played a significant role in those changes. As the title suggests, Keyes uses the idea of power as the central concern of her book. She argues that notions of power form the central core of Rich's aesthetic. Social, political, and cultural forces shape Rich's work, work that indicts any power structures that limit human potential. Keyes traces Rich's development as a poet, by tracing her growing awareness of the power of women and of the power of poetry. Rich envisions a society informed by feminist ideals and cognizant of womanly power; she imagines the transformative power of poetry changing the material lives of women.

TEMPLETON's goal is to connect Rich's feminist thinking with her poetic practice, in order to examine how one informs the other. She asserts that the reading of poetry is a cultural act, and she questions the ways Rich's feminist poetics affect our reading of her work. Templeton opens her book with "The Lyric Self in a Feminist Moment," a chapter demonstrating the ways in which Rich transforms the romantic emphasis on the individual, private self to a lyric emphasis of the self in relationship to others. Chapter-length examinations of Rich's major collections of poems follow, arranged chronologically. Throughout the book, Templeton returns to the dream and the dialogue of her title, demonstrating the ways Rich imagines change to be the result of the interaction between the dream of an alternative future and the dialogue with the world as it is.

—DIANE ANDREWS HENNINGFELD

Roe v. Wade (United States 1973)

Craig, Barbara H., and David O'Brien, *Abortion and American Politics*, Chatham, New Jersey: Chatham House, 1993

Faux, Marian, *Roe v. Wade: The Untold Story of the Landmark Supreme Court Decision That Made Abortion Legal,* New York: Macmillan, 1988
Garrow, David J., *Liberty and Sexuality: The Right to Privacy and the Making of Roe v. Wade,* New York: Macmillan, 1994
Herda, D.J., *Roe v. Wade: The Abortion Question,* Hillside, New Jersey: Enslow, 1994
Krason, Stephen, *Abortion: Politics, Morality and the Constitution: A Critical Study of Roe v. Wade and Doe v. Bolton and a Basis for Change,* Lanham, Maryland: University Press of America, 1984
Luker, Kristin, *Abortion and the Politics of Motherhood,* Berkeley and London: University of California Press, 1984
McCorvey, Norma, with Andy Meisler, *I Am Roe: My Life, Roe v. Wade, and Freedom of Choice,* New York: HarperCollins, 1994
Milbauer, Barbara, and Bert N. Obretz, *The Law Giveth: Legal Aspects of the Abortion Controversy,* New York: Atheneum, 1983
Rubin, Eva R., *Abortion Politics and the Courts: Roe v. Wade and Its Aftermath,* New York: Greenwood, 1982; revised edition, 1987
Solinger, Rickie, *Wake Up Little Susie: Single Pregnancy and Race before Roe v. Wade,* New York: Routledge, 1992
Tribe, Lawrence, *Abortion: The Clash of Absolutes,* New York: Norton, 1990

In 1973 the U.S. Supreme Court, by a vote of 7–2, in the case of *Roe v. Wade*, held that the constitutional right of privacy included the right of a woman to decide whether or not to terminate her pregnancy. The decision prevented state interference with a woman's determination to have an abortion in the first trimester of pregnancy, but allowed restrictions in the subsequent periods. The Court adopted the view that an unborn fetus did not possess legal personality and therefore was not entitled to constitutional protection. State anti-abortion statutes were struck down.

GARROW starts his account with a presentation of the nineteenth-century enactment of anti-contraceptive and anti-abortion laws. His substantial treatment (more than seven hundred pages of text and two hundred pages of footnotes) is a story of how control over having children moved from an issue of public morals to one of private choice. The author feels that the *Roe* decision was the legal and moral equivalent of *Brown v. Board of Education*, which required public school integration in 1954, and presents the dispute as a new civil rights struggle.

SOLINGER makes vivid the times before *Roe*. The author takes a close look at a few of the slim alternatives open to a single pregnant woman in the two decades after World War II "to show that the treatment of unmarried pregnant girls and women in the era that preceded *Roe* reflected a powerful and enduring willingness of our culture to use women's bodies to promote conservative political goals." Many politicians and academicians, the popular media, social service professionals, and sizable segments of the public at large assigned unmarried mothers political value by race. To this day, he argues, policy makers and social critics regularly ascribe poverty in black communities to the "wanton" breeding of black women.

Several books concentrate on the case of *Roe v. Wade*. FAUX initially tried to write a more general account on abortion, dealing with its ethical, moral, religious, and philosophical aspects. However, she ultimately shifted to a smaller scale, a telling of the story of the *Roe* case. In the course of her presentation, however, she also documents the position in favor of legalization. Faux writes a good portrait of the milieu in which the case arose, and of several of the participants. She shows the alliances with the demographics and eugenics movements. There were 42 friend-of-the-court briefs in favor of legal abortion, and four from anti-abortion groups, which came from medical and legal organizations, academics, and churches. The two attorneys, Sara Weddington and Linda Coffee, had searched to come up with a suitable client to challenge state abortion laws. *Roe* was the first case Weddington had ever argued in court, yet she wound up speaking to the highest tribunal in the country.

The plaintiff, "Jane Roe," was Norma McCorvey, a 21-year-old carnival worker. McCORVEY's autobiography is dedicated "for all the Jane Does who died for Choice." Her life story is depressing. She was repeatedly raped by a distant relative when she was a teen. She gave up two children for adoption and lost custody of a third (tricked into it by her mother). She held dead-end jobs and was in abusive relationships. After her victory she even worked as a telephone counselor in an abortion clinic. When she went public, she traveled around the country speaking at colleges and to women's groups. "I take comfort and pride," she states, "that many women (and men!) have supported and protected me from the pro-lifers." Eventually, however, she allied herself with the pro-lifers.

Whereas "Jane Roe" would not speak with Faux without being paid, she did cooperate with MILBAUER. Milbauer and her collaborator were both 1980 graduates of New York Law School. They discuss cases, arguments, and issues regarding the abortion controversy, with a goal of helping the reader see how the legal process works in the United States. That pedagogic goal is shared by HERDA, whose book on the *Roe* case is part of a series on "Landmark Supreme Court Cases," aimed at a young adult audience. She discusses the persons involved in the *Roe* case, and the opposing arguments made before the courts.

The Supreme Court received more mail on its abortion decision than on any case it had ever handed down. Instead of settling a controversy, it seemed only to escalate the battle. KRASON, an attorney, has prepared his guide for the anti-abortion movement. He attacks the Supreme Court for misreading history, misunderstanding prenatal life, and misconstruing legal precedents.

He has an appendix with a proposed federal statute to criminalize abortion.

LUKER, a professor of women's studies and sociology, argues that abortion is a widespread issue today because of women's increased ability to incorporate children and marriage into a long-term career plan. Her book studies activists in California and describes how moral choices are illuminated by an examination of their social setting, and how the debate over the constitutionality and social validation of abortion may affect activists' senses of identity and esteem.

RUBIN takes the controversy up to 1986. Hers is an impact study of the consequences (political, governmental, medical, social, religious, moral, organizational), intended and unintended, of the Supreme Court decision. She looks at the roles played by the courts and the use of litigation and other means to instigate changes in public policy on divisive social and political issues. The *Roe* decision was a quick and stunning victory. However, it was followed by efforts by right-to-lifers to roll back the gains, and by freedom-of-choice supporters to resist the rollback.

Two books examine the possibilities of reconciliation of the warring camps. CRAIG and O'BRIEN outline how the system might overcome the obstacles to reconciliation, despite the depth of feelings by activists on both sides of the issue. Both sides talk in terms of competing rights, and use the legal and political processes for their own advantage. The authors cover the important constitutional cases and make a dispassionate and unbiased analysis of a controversial and divisive issue.

TRIBE, a Harvard professor of constitutional law, notes that this conflict is a clash of absolutes, life against liberty. His book is a search for a way of resolution that maintains respect for the deepest values on both sides of the equation. Is there common ground? He explores the legal framework in which the constitutional questions of abortion rights must be decided. In addition to summarizing two centuries of abortion positions in America, Tribe reports on how other cultures and nations dealt with the question.

—MARTIN GRUBERG

See also Abortion: Twentieth Century; Reproductive Freedom

Romance

De Rougemont, Denis, *Love in the Western World,* London: Faber and Faber, and New York: Harcourt Brace, 1940

Holland, Dorothy C., and Margaret A. Eisenhart, *Educated in Romance: Women, Achievement, and College Culture,* Chicago: University of Chicago Press, 1990

Illouz, Eva, *Consuming the Romantic Utopia: Love and the Cultural Contradictions of Capitalism,* Berkeley and London: University of California Press, 1997

Lees, Sue, *Losing Out: Sexuality and Adolescent Girls,* London and Dover, New Hampshire: Hutchinson, 1986

Modleski, Tania, *Loving with a Vengeance: Mass-Produced Fantasies for Women,* Hamden, Connecticut: Archon, and London: Methuen, 1982

Seidman, Stephen, *Romantic Longings: Love in America, 1830–1980,* New York and London: Routledge, 1991

Wexman, Virginia Wright, *Creating the Couple: Love, Marriage, and Hollywood Performance,* Princeton, New Jersey: Princeton University Press, 1993

The nature of romance, or romantic love, has captured the interest and imagination of philosophers, poets, and playwrights for centuries. Western writing about romantic love has tended to idealize and celebrate it as a mysterious force or essence ordained by nature and characterized by intense attraction, longing, and passion. But historians have identified the historical origin and evolution of romantic love, calling into question its essential nature. Other scholars have exposed it as a symbolic system of meaning that varies across cultures, and within societies by race and class, undermining claims of its universality. Both historical and cultural analyses have revealed romance as a construct, opening it up to feminist analyses of its political dimensions and consequences.

Written more like a philosophical essay than a historical account, DE ROUGEMONT provides a useful overview of the roots and development of the western conceptualization of romance. He identifies the Tristan and Iseult story as the mythological source of romantic love and locates its historical origin in the twelfth-century troubadours of Provençal. Analyzing its relationship to Christian love, Celtic myths, and religious mysticism, he traces the further evolution of romantic love from its medieval beginnings through to its representation in nineteenth- and twentieth-century literature.

SEIDMAN's study focuses on a more recent past. It offers a cultural analysis of the changing meaning of love in America from the early nineteenth century through the twentieth. Analyzing advice literature and popular medical texts, Seidman focuses specifically on the early twentieth-century sexualization of love that viewed eroticism as a source of romantic bonding. The focus on erotic pleasure that derives from this period has become a source for attacks from many critics on current expansive notions of sexual choice and sexual diversity. Seidman takes issue with these assaults, arguing that they depend on nostalgia for an idealized Victorian intimate culture. This study is particularly useful for its analysis of the meaning and patterns of "gay love," and for its comparison of same-sex notions of intimacy and love to heterosexual ones.

One important trend in feminist studies has been to demystify romantic love, treating it as an ideological construct reinforcing women's secondary position in western societies. LEES's ethnographic study of youth culture in Britain, for example, isolates a gender system couched in terms of romance as a primary force in adolescent women's continued oppression. She shows how a sexual double standard and institutionalized sexism, especially as they operate in the school system, drive young women into exclusive heterosexual relationships for fear of being branded whores, thus constraining their sexual and career options.

HOLLAND and EISENHART's more recent study also identifies the pervasive culture of attraction and romance as a primary factor leading young American women into low-paying occupations and traditional domestic roles, thereby perpetuating women's subordinate position. The study follows two groups of women, one predominantly white, the other black, attending universities in the American South. Collecting data from ethnographic observations, formal interviews, and surveys, it isolates young women's peer culture as the main force motivating these women to interpret gender relations and sexual attraction in terms of romantic love, and their own social worth in terms of their attractiveness to men. Concerned more with relationships than with academic matters, many young women's educational goals and career aspirations erode. This study provides a very useful overview of theoretical approaches for analyzing how social structures, especially gender hierarchies, are reproduced.

Another important line of inquiry in feminist analyses of romance focuses on how culture, the domain in which people search for meaning and construct identity, is subject to commodification, and how commodified cultural production is related to the distribution of power within societies. ILLOUZ's book assesses the implications of the commodification of romance that has occurred under capitalism since the end of the nineteenth century, emphasizing the relationship of romantic love to the American class structure. She reveals a wide range of American romantic symbols and practices (including red roses, candlelight dinners, and the weekend getaway) as deeply embedded in commodity culture, constructed in advertising, movies, songs, novels, magazine advice columns, and self-help books. Drawing on data from these sources and from interviews, she shows how romantic love has become a central component of the democratic ideal in American society, offering a utopian vision of abundance, individualism, and creative self-fulfillment to those who participate in it.

Working within the same tradition, MODLESKI emphasizes women's active role in resisting patriarchal conceptualizations of romance. Her book is a classic in feminist cultural studies. Modleski focuses on mass-produced popular culture designed specifically for female audiences: the Harlequin Romance, female Gothic novels, and soap operas. She rejects the influential Marxist view of consumers as "cultural dupes" who passively imbibe images that produce false consciousness. Rather than see mass-produced romantic fantasies as ones that simply trap women into a celebration of feminine selflessness, Modleski suggests that their immense popularity is best explained by recognizing how they address very real problems and conflicts in women's daily lives. Drawing on filmic and psychoanalytic theory, Modleski concentrates her analysis on the narrative structures of these novels and television serials, claiming that they provide women with a source of pleasure distinct from the typical masculine ones permeating American and British society. Modleski thereby posits an alternate female aesthetic, one that grants women satisfaction through offering them a utopian fantasy of community.

Like Modleski, WEXMAN is concerned with the narrative structure and context of popular culture, but she emphasizes the function of Hollywood movies in defining and portraying socially acceptable ways of falling in love. She focuses specifically on how a romantic notion of "the couple" is constituted in popular films, and on its relationship to a changing conceptualization of marriage from one based on patriarchal assumptions to a more companion-based model. Contending that earlier film studies have treated romance, sexuality, and the couple monolithically, she reveals how changes in these constructs have been produced through an interaction of audiences with specific performers, performance styles, and cinematic techniques. Her introduction provides a brief but informative overview of approaches to film, romance, marriage, and the family.

—FRANCES E. MASCIA-LEES

See also Literature: Romance Fiction

Roosevelt, Eleanor 1884–1962

American Activist

Beasley, Maurine H., *Eleanor Roosevelt and the Media: A Public Quest for Self-Fulfillment,* Urbana: University of Illinois Press, 1987

Black, Allida M., *Casting Her Own Shadow: Eleanor Roosevelt and the Shaping of Postwar Liberalism,* New York: Columbia University Press, 1996

Cook, Blanche Wiesen, *Eleanor Roosevelt,* New York: Viking, 1992; London: Bloomsbury, 1993

Goodwin, Doris Kearns, *No Ordinary Time: Franklin and Eleanor Roosevelt: The Home Front in World War II,* New York and London: Simon and Schuster, 1994

Hershan, Stella K., *A Woman of Quality: Eleanor Roosevelt,* New York: Crown, 1970
Hickok, Lorena, *Eleanor Roosevelt: Reluctant First Lady,* New York: Dodd, Mead, 1980
Kearney, James R., *Anna Eleanor Roosevelt: The Evolution of a Reformer,* Boston: Houghton Mifflin, 1968
Lash, Joseph P., *Eleanor and Franklin: The Story of Their Relationship Based on Eleanor Roosevelt's Private Papers,* New York: Norton, 1971; London: Deutsch, 1972
———, *Eleanor: The Years Alone,* New York: Norton, 1972; London: Deutsch, 1973
Scharf, Lois, *Eleanor Roosevelt: First Lady of American Liberalism,* Boston: Twayne, 1987
Youngs, J. William, *Eleanor Roosevelt: A Personal and Public Life,* Boston: Little Brown, 1985

In her time, Eleanor Roosevelt was one of the most widely admired women in the world. She was more popular with the public than was her husband. COOK acknowledges that Roosevelt seems a mythic character, larger than life but not quite human. The author, who was vice president of the American Historical Association, seeks to combine the personal with the political. She presents a "life and times" of Roosevelt and her generation, showing her subject struggling for social justice and self-realization. Roosevelt learned, rather than inherited, her progressive views. It was only after her husband was paralyzed by polio in 1921 that she developed an interest in politics, replacing her previous focus on social and charitable activities. At this point she was tutored by Louis Howe, her husband's political mentor. She became active in the League of Women Voters, the Woman's Trade Union League, and the women's division of the Democratic party. She went on frequent fact-finding trips for her husband. Cook reconstructs the influence Roosevelt had as a feminist with public and private associations. The first volume ends with her husband's first inauguration.

Just before this time, Roosevelt began a 23-year friendship with HICKOK, the foremost woman reporter in the United States and one of the great American journalists of either sex (according to Cook). Both women had triumphed over grim childhoods. Hickok's memoir of a "reluctant first lady" shows Roosevelt's vain attempt to preserve her privacy, as the two went off on vacation motor trips. Hickok authored other books on Franklin and Eleanor Roosevelt for young readers, and collaborated with Eleanor on a book entitled *Ladies of Courage* (1954).

Roosevelt expanded the role of First Lady. She was her husband's advisor, conscience, and eyes and ears. This made her controversial. LASH was active in student movements in the 1930s when he met Roosevelt. His study of her 45-year marriage and partnership with Franklin is objective yet sympathetic. The book won the Pulitzer Prize in Biography, the National Book Award and the Francis Parkman Prize of the Society of American Historians. Lash was the first to use Roosevelt's private papers. He describes how she had to make a special effort of will to keep her own ideals and personality from being smothered by her husband's strength and magnetism. The two supplemented and drew strength from one another, he having a better sense of what could be accomplished, and she thinking of what should be done.

LASH's second book continues where the other volume left off. Lash keeps the woman and the public figure in delicate balance. Contrary to her initial sense that as a widow she would be out of the public arena, Roosevelt continued to champion the poor and oppressed. She felt an obligation to promote her husband's objectives, seeming to become more progressive as she got older. She took on President Harry Truman, Francis Cardinal Spellman, Tammany boss Carmine De Sapio, and Soviet leader Andrei Vishinsky. She was a member of the U.S. delegation to the United Nations, and was instrumental in the drafting of the UN Declaration of Human Rights. She was Adlai Stevenson's political tutor and ally. She was active in the New York City Democratic reform movement.

GOODWIN tells the story of the World War II home front, told through the lives of the First Family, and the circle of friends and associates who lived with them in the family quarters of the White House. Though Goodwin's research took place more than a half century later, she was able to talk with scores of people who had personal knowledge of the events. There are many colorful anecdotes, including those that show Franklin needing to have people around him constantly with whom he could work and/or relax, and Eleanor's agenda (championing refugees, women, blacks, workers) as wearying on him.

A good one-volume tribute to a remarkable woman, published on the centennial of her birth, is YOUNGS's book. She portrays Eleanor as an idealist, projecting a sympathy from the heart, herself a good writer with a sense of humor, a feeling for a good story, and an ability to analyze honestly her own character.

HERSHAN, a refugee from Austria, met Roosevelt once when she was a college student. She was so transformed that she later decided to compile a collection of anecdotes, stories, and memories by others whose lives were similarly effected. She requested assistance from readers of many publications in the United States, United Kingdom, Canada, and Israel, and had hundreds of responses.

Several books concentrate on Roosevelt's role as reformer. KEARNEY's study shows her earlier development, concluding in 1940. His book discusses Roosevelt as: mother to a generation, friend to a neglected promise, partner in a champion political combination, adviser to a nation, and reformer at large.

SCHARF's short, well-written biography is a moving tribute but not a canonization. She argues that Roosevelt and her associates were social reformers, not genuine feminists (for example, they did not support the Equal Rights Amendment). Roosevelt, she argues, was a patrician in rearing and outlook. She was an admirable, awe-inspiring, yet complex and conflicted person. She was a symbol of the efforts to create a humane social order, and a peaceful international community.

BLACK argues that Roosevelt was the most influential liberal powerbroker in the post-World War II era. She examines Roosevelt's efforts to push American liberalism to promote a more inclusive domestic policy agenda: maximizing employment, respecting diversity and dissent, and promoting party reform. Black traces changes in Roosevelt's position on the issues, and the consistency of her vision of an inclusive democracy, arguing that she was not in it for ego and glory.

BEASLEY, a professor of journalism who was editor of *The White House Press Conferences of Eleanor Roosevelt* (1983) and co-editor of a book on the Depression by Lorena Hickok, discusses how Roosevelt emerged as a media personality (one of the greatest personalities and newsmakers of the twentieth century) as well as Roosevelt's own journalistic career. Through the media, she made herself a role model for others, by combining traditional aspects of a woman's role with the requirements of changing times. She framed her message in traditional terms, yet she legitimized and enlarged the boundaries of proper conduct for women. Beasely tells how Roosevelt initiated weekly press conferences with women reporters, lectured widely, was a pioneer radio commentator, and had a newspaper column.

—MARTIN GRUBERG

Rossetti, Christina 1830–1894

British Writer

Battiscombe, Georgina, *Christina Rossetti: A Divided Life,* London: Constable, and New York: Holt Rinehart, 1981

Jones, Kathleen, *Learning Not to Be First: The Life of Christina Rossetti,* Moreton-in-Marsh: Windrush, 1991; New York: St. Martin's Press, 1992

Kent, David A. (ed.), *The Achievement of Christina Rossetti,* Ithaca, New York: Cornell University Press, 1987

Leder, Sharon, and Andrea Abbott, *The Language of Exclusion: The Poetry of Emily Dickinson and Christina Rossetti,* New York: Greenwood, 1987

Marsh, Jan, *Christina Rossetti: A Writer's Life,* New York: Viking, 1995

Packer, Lona Mosk, *Christina Rossetti,* Cambridge: Cambridge University Press, and Berkeley: University of California Press, 1963

Smulders, Sharon, *Christina Rossetti Revisited,* London: Prentice Hall, and New York: Twayne, 1996

Woolf, Virginia, "I Am Christina Rossetti," in *The Common Reader: Second Series,* London: Hogarth, 1932

On the occasion of Christina Rossetti's centenary, WOOLF wrote "I Am Christina Rossetti," an essay that articulates many of the issues still current in contemporary feminist readings of her work. Woolf begins from the biographical details of Rossetti's life: her lost loves, her brother's power, her dark God, her renunciation of the world, her volatile passion. But midway through her exploration of Rossetti's life, Woolf comes across the anecdote of a very dull tea party at which the small, dark figure of Christina Rossetti took center stage with her announcement, "I am Christina Rossetti." This image of Rossetti pushes Woolf to the realization that "rattling" through Rossetti's desk drawers (emphasizing the sensational details of her private life) ignores the very message that Rossetti left for us: her poetry. The passionate voice of Rossetti's poetry is at such odds with the image of the self-renunciatory Christian and the cultural conservative that modern readings, too, often rifle Rossetti's desk drawers, hoping to find explanations that will reconcile her poetry's passion with her life's stoic self-renunciation.

PACKER's study is the earliest of these attempts. To explain the passion of Rossetti's writings, Packer posits a secret love affair with a married man, W.B. Scott. How else to account for the extremity of feeling in her poetry? While the bulk of Packer's biography is useful, bringing to light letters and biographical data that is otherwise not easily available, her thesis is dated and of limited use for interpreting Rossetti's contradictions.

LEDER and ABBOTT read the surface of Rossetti's life against the passion of her poetry. They credit the contradictions to Rossetti's reformatory zeal. They see Rossetti in her poetry taking her culture to task for its moral lapses and shortness of vision. What Leder and Abbott fail to address is Rossetti's own oft-expressed political conservatism—those points where she not only fails to take her culture to task but, in fact, agrees with its conservative vision.

BATTISCOMBE's biography portrays Rossetti as a woman whose character is divided not only between the passion of her poetry and the self-renunciation of her life, but also between such extremes as "natural generosity and conscientious scruple," and "passionate nature and chaste life." This dualism was established early through Rossetti's Anglo-Italian heritage, Battiscombe explains, and continued to inform the whole of her life.

JONES writes against the commonplace notion (a result of Rossetti's brother William's control of her posthumous reputation, and of Mackenzie Bell's biography) of Christina Rossetti as "the daughter and sister, caring for her parents and brothers, shedding light on their lives." Rather, she argues, Rossetti's role as the "perfect woman" was achieved only at a tremendous cost: repression of her sexuality and self-renunciation. Jones credits Victorian definitions of woman—particularly those formed in Rossetti's Christian childhood—with stunting Rossetti's potential.

The collection of essays edited by KENT contains several interesting articles. Flower's piece, "The Kingly Self: Rossetti as Woman Artist," makes the argument that Rossetti's lessons in obedience may seem on the surface to insist upon female subservience. However, because that obedience is to God rather than to human agents, Rossetti effectively places herself above patriarchal control by appealing to a higher standard. Amico's "Eve, Mary and Mary Magdalene: Christina Rossetti's Triptych" traces the pattern of images of these three female characters, claiming that Rossetti privileges Mary Magdalene, the sinner who repents. Through this strategy, Rossetti shifts the focus from the sins of women to women's eventual reconciliation with God. Bentley's "The Meretricious and the Meritorious in 'Goblin Market': A Conjecture and an Analysis" discredits those who trace the origins of "Goblin Market" to the work Rossetti did with the fallen women of Highgate Hill. Rather, he sees the poem as a model for listening to and learning from the stories of others.

Two of the most recent works on Rossetti are the biography written by Marsh and the critical survey by Smulders. Both works have the strength of carefully placing Rossetti in her historical context: the specific terms of Rossetti's religious conversion, the cultural dialogue on fallen women, and other poets against whom Rossetti would be read, for example. SMULDERS suggests that the many voices and genres Rossetti employs are strategies for critiquing the politics, aesthetics, and morality of her time without jeopardizing her position as a Victorian woman. MARSH's biography contains details of many of the subjects that might be of interest to a feminist reader: Rossetti's emotional breakdown, her disfigurement from Grave's disease, and her being kept at home while her brothers were sent away to school. But the most potentially revolutionary suggestion Marsh makes is that Rossetti's personality change at puberty might have been due to paternal incest. Even without her speculation of incest as the cause of Rossetti's contradictions, Marsh's biography is destined to become one of the standard texts in Rossetti criticism because of the detail and the scope of her study.

—PAMELA SMILEY

S

Sacagawea 1784?–1812

American Guide

Clark, Ella E., and Margot Edmonds, *Sacagawea of the Lewis and Clark Expedition,* Berkeley: University of California Press, 1979

Hebard, Grace Raymond, *Sacajawea: A Guide and Interpreter of the Lewis and Clark Expedition, with an Account of the Travels of Toussaint Charbonneau, and of Jean Baptiste, the Expedition Papoose,* Glendale, California: Arthur H. Clark, 1933

Howard, Harold P., *Sacajawea,* Norman: University of Oklahoma Press, 1971

Kessler, Donna J., *The Making of Sacagawea: A Euro-American Legend,* Tuscaloosa: University of Alabama Press, 1996

Schultz, James Willard, *Bird Woman (Sacajawea): The Guide of Lewis and Clark: Her Own Story First Given to the World,* Boston: Houghton Mifflin, 1918

Sundquist, Asebrit, *Sacajawea and Co.: The Twentieth-Century Fictional American Indian Woman and Fellow Characters: A Study of Gender and Race,* Oslo: Solum Forlag, and Atlantic Highlands, New Jersey: Humanities Press, 1991

Waldo, Anna Lee, *Sacajawea,* New York: Avon, 1978

Sacagawea, according to legend and brief mention in records of the Lewis and Clark expedition of 1803–6, which explored the western lands newly purchased by the United States, was a young Shoshone woman who served as guide to the expedition, her infant son on her back. Sacagawea became a popular American cultural subject in both scholarly and popular writings and was elevated to heroic stature and legend during the Progressive Era. Her image has changed over time to reflect the shifting desires and interests of American culture, but her story has been consistently used to validate the U.S. policy of manifest destiny and to point up the dichotomy between "savagery" and "civilization" (although there have been dissenting portrayals since World War II that question frontier policy and the resultant myths). The most important literary treatments of Sacagawea concern the scope and value of her actual participation in the Lewis and Clark expedition, her autonomy during that period, her position between the white and the Native American worlds, and her life, its length, and its meaning after her death.

KESSLER investigates how the Sacagawea story was elevated to the status of both popular and scholarly legend, why her story has endured, and how it has served American policy and ideology, as well as the opposition to these concerns.

In an early, folksy narrative version, SCHULTZ relates the story of Bird Woman (Sacagawea) as told to Hugh Monroe (Rising Wolf), as then told to Schultz (partially Native American himself). Sacagawea is portrayed as the proverbially "good" woman who would do anything to serve the "kind good [white] chiefs."

Although some historians of the period disputed HEBARD's scholarship and findings, her book became the definitive historical text of Sacagawea's life. Hebard was the first historian to take Sacagawea's story beyond the expedition, arguing that she did not die in her early twenties, as was commonly believed, but lived until she was nearly one hundred years old, during which time she demonstrated her esteem for white civilization by arguing for acceptance of their ways by her Shoshone people.

HOWARD attempts to set straight the historical record about Sacagawea by reviewing what has been learned and conjecturing about her life before, during, and after the expedition in order to accord her a realistic (but not necessarily diminished) place in the westward expansion history of the United States. In an attempt to resolve the controversy over her later life, Howard provides evidence that she died shortly after the expedition had gotten back to South Dakota, at a fairly early age, thus eliminating her need to "choose" between the white world and her own.

SUNDQUIST analyzes Sacagawea (and 164 other female Native American characters) as portrayed in twentieth-century imaginative literature from 1911 to 1980, relating those portrayals to comparative gender variables and race. Sacagawea is most often and most strongly portrayed as an angel, but also as a drudge and a strong woman.

CLARK and EDMONDS examine how the legends, "the fog of idolatry" surrounding Sacagawea, have obscured both the person and her very real contributions to the Lewis and Clark expedition, as well as her character and her life after the expedition, which has been little examined.

WALDO writes the modern romantic version of the Sacagawea story, portraying her both as an Indian princess and as an emblem of modern feminism, a heroine of remarkable power and intelligence who resisted dependence on and violence from men, especially Native American men. While lauding Sacagawea as a kind of everywoman, Waldo repeatedly emphasizes racial stereotypes by depicting Native Americans as savages who subordinate women. In Waldo's account, Sacagawea learned to value civilization because it allowed her female independence and white male companionship, a theme found in many versions of the Sacagawea legend.

—JANET M. LaBRIE

Saints

Ahlgren, Gillian T.W., *Teresa of Avila and the Politics of Sanctity,* Ithaca, New York, and London: Cornell University Press, 1996

Chittister, Joan D., *A Passion for Life: Fragments of the Face of God,* Maryknoll, New York: Orbis, 1996

Duby, Georges, Michelle Perrot, Pauline Schmitt Pantel, and Arthur Goldhammer, *A History of Women in the West: From Ancient Goddesses to Christian Saints,* 5 vols. Cambridge, Massachusetts, and London: Harvard University Press, 1992

Flinders, Carol Lee, *Enduring Grace: Living Portraits of Seven Women Mystics,* San Francisco: Harper San Francisco, 1993

Stuart, Elizabeth, *Spitting at Dragons: Towards a Feminist Theology of Sainthood,* New York and London: Mowbray, 1996

Throughout Christian history, certain women have been singled out as especially holy and have thus been canonized, or named as saints, by the Roman Catholic Church. The feelings and actions of female saints are explored by FLINDERS in her study of the western mystical tradition. She relates the lives of Saint Clare of Assisi, Mechthild of Magdeburg, Saint Catherine of Genoa, Saint Theresa of Lisieux, and several others. The account of Mechthild of Magdeburg is particularly interesting, because Mechthild's mode of discourse is described as a different voice, which is extremely feminine. Her life sparks interest for contemporary women because she affiliated herself with the extraordinary women's movement of her day, the Beguines. There was a genuine spiritual nature of this movement in 1210, which sought no authorization from Rome. Mechthild wrote seven poetic books and speaks with assertion, with a preference for the concrete and contextual thinking, for modes of relationship that are connective rather than hierarchical, and with an insistance on embodiedness—a wholistic spirituality. The humanness of other female saints in this work shows their real flesh and blood, which makes it easy for contemporary women to identify with them.

In a most comprehensive study, the editors DUBY and PERROT seek to show an understanding of women's place in the world, the roles they played, and the powers and influence they possessed. The entire study is five volumes and explores those aspects of mythology, philosophy, law, and art that shed light on practices in women's lives associated with sexuality and reproduction, property, and religious ritual and priesthood. Texts written by the Christian Saint Perpetua are discussed in Volume I as an example of an authentic expression of women's feelings.

AHLGREN describes the sainthood of Teresa of Avila within the Counter-Reformation agenda by exploring the complex and conflicting notions of female sanctity in Spain during the sixteenth century. The humanness of Teresa is brought out by noting that during her day she was criticized as either a fraud or an unbearably arrogant woman. However, she shows herself fully as an indomitable woman who struggled for theological authority and the right to write. It was her rugged determination to overcome patriarchal control that enabled her to survive her era and that keeps her story alive today.

Contemporary authors write about saints as everyday people who point the way to God although their own lives may be viewed as far from perfect. This approach differs from the past canonization process, which sought the heroic and pious and wanted miracles as well as a holy life to qualify a person for sainthood. CHITTISTER asks a central question of what qualities are necessary to live a life of integrity and holiness in the twenty-first century. She looks at Eve, Hildegard of Bingen, Catherine of Siena, Joan of Arc, Dorothy Day, and a number of other figures. The humanness of each figure is portrayed.

Rather than discuss specific female saints, STUART develops a feminist reflection on the theology of sainthood itself. She begins by noting all the reasons why feminists have been suspicious of the doctrine of sainthood: stories of female saints may overly emphasize stereotypical virtues of purity and chastity, which could denigrate female sexuality and embodiment, and in other ways reinforce patriarchal stereotypes; they sometimes feature horrid forms of asceticism; they may stress the role of suffering as the price of redemption and in that way foster the sense of a sado-masochistic relationship with God. After this feministic critique of past interpretations of sainthood, Stuart reclaims and reforms a theology of sainthood using a "Sophia/Wisdom" model, in which revelation of God is not handed down from on high, but comes from below emerging as a mist from the ground, not from angels in the heavens but from the ordinary here on earth. Female saints of the past are shown not to reflect stereotypical ideals of submission and obedience, rather they are presented as examples of strong self-assertion and confidence. Stories of female martyrs are discussed as not a simple affirmation of the value of chastity, but as showing the power of women to affirm their own integrity and self-worth. The lives of female saints are portrayed as a challenge for women of today.

—BILLIE SALISBURY BALADOUNI

Sampson, Deborah *see* American Revolutionary Era

Sand, George 1804–1876

French Writer

Barry, Joseph, *Infamous Woman: The Life of George Sand,* New York: Doubleday, 1964

Crecelius, Kathryn J., *Family Romances: George Sand's Early Novels,* Bloomington: Indiana University Press, 1987

Datlof, Natalie, Jeanne Fuchs, and David A. Powell (eds.), *The World of George Sand,* New York and London: Greenwood, 1991

Dickenson, Donna, *George Sand: A Brave Man, the Most Womanly Woman,* Oxford and New York: Berg, 1988

Glasgow, Janis (ed.), *George Sand: Collected Essays,* Troy, New York: Whitston, 1985

Godwin-Jones, Robert, *Romantic Vision: The Novels of George Sand,* Birmingham, Alabama: Summa, 1995

Lukacher, Maryline, *Maternal Fictions: Stendhal, Sand, Rachilde, and Bataille,* Durham, North Carolina: Duke University Press, 1994

Manifold, Gay, *George Sand's Theatre Career,* Ann Arbor, Michigan: UMI Research Press, 1985

Naginski, Isabelle Hoog, *George Sand: Writing for Her Life,* New Brunswick, New Jersey and London: Rutgers University Press, 1991

Powell, David, *George Sand,* Boston: Twayne, 1990

Schor, Naomi, *George Sand and Idealism,* New York: Columbia University Press, 1993

Thomson, Patricia, *George Sand and the Victorians: Her Influence and Reputation in Nineteenth-Century England,* London: Macmillan, and New York: Columbia University Press, 1977

George Sand is a quasi-canonical yet marginal figure. Neither the well-documented misogyny of her literary peers nor the contestatory elements of her writing kept her from achieving critical acclaim, international popularity, and posthumous recognition, albeit narrowly defined, in French literature manuals. However, few twentieth-century scholars gave her work serious attention until Georges Lubin's edition of her correspondence and an increased interest in women's writing in the 1970s highlighted her contribution to postrevolutionary literature. Many articles, book chapters, and conference proceedings have appeared in recent years, but there are still relatively few book-length studies on George Sand in English.

Even as emphasis has shifted from Sand's life back to the works that ensured her fame, biographers continue to study her and interpret the nineteenth century itself through its reactions to this very public figure. In the absence of a life history that would accentuate this author's intellectual and literary evolution, rather than find its organizing principle in her various romantic liaisons, BARRY's volume remains a readily accessible and well-documented biography. Drawing heavily on her voluminous correspondence, it pays noteworthy attention to Sand's early career and her participation in the 1848 Revolution, but its presentation of the last 20 years of her life is weak.

DICKENSON attempts to fill this analytical void in a compact, relatively conversational work that rehearses Sand's biography, while subsuming the chronology to a chapter-by-chapter discussion of several clichés associated with her, notably those of the French Byron, a feminist, a maternal lover, an inveterate autobiographical writer, and a second-rate novelist. Although many Sandian critics contest the conclusions that Dickenson draws a little quickly, the wide-ranging inquiry and frequent comparisons with British authors are informative and suggestive.

THOMSON's book is now critically dated; however, it remains a gold mine for readers interested in tracing the complicated intersections between Sand and Victorian England. References to published letters, critical reviews, and fictional works by lesser-known and famous British authors including Elizabeth Browning, the Brontë sisters, Matthew Arnold, Clough, George Eliot, and Hardy, chart the paths of exchange between this French author and her British peers.

POWELL directs attention more closely to the rich Sandian literary corpus. He introduces almost all of Sand's writings in a series of chapters devoted to her early novels, travel narratives, and texts using her native province, Berry, as their geographical setting. The central chapters are most helpful in presenting works in relation to the ideologically bound questions of social justice and reform, religion, and feminism, and they include a rare discussion concerning the function of music and art in this melomane's fictional writings. Final chapters aid readers by grouping autobiographical writings, plays, and short stories separately by genre.

MANIFOLD's book provides an excellent starting point for those particularly interested in Sand's theatrical productions. Consideration of Sand's basic source material, the evolving manuscript versions of her plays, epistolary records of her dealings with theater owners and actors, and the press reception afforded her performed and published works demonstrate their originality as well as that of Sand as a director. GODWIN-JONES uses genre, narrative, and reader response theories to analyze Sand's attempt to reshape the world through art. His chapter-length studies of paired complimentary novels constitute an intelligent introduction to almost two dozen novels, including several from the late Second Empire period, and a valuable summary of media reactions at the time of their publication.

CRECELIUS distinguishes the ways in which the novel *Indiana* adapts fundamental structures of the romance as identified by Northrop Frye and Frederick Jameson. Subsequent chapters demonstrate the pertinence of this structure for Sand's other representations of postrevolutionary *embourgeoisement* and its effect on gender and family relations. Crecelius's work is particularly enlightening for its examination of the intertextual relations between *Valentine* and *Tristan et Iseut, Leone Leoni* and *Manon Lescaut, Jacques* and Goethe's *Elective Affinities,* and *André* and the Pygmalion story.

NAGINSKI insists on dialogism as the conceptual underpinning to Sandian plots and on androgynous figures in representing an authorial voice both within and beyond gender distinctions. Naginski untangles Sand's complex representations of metaphysical, social, and aesthetic principles popular in the romantic period, exploring, for example, the use of Swedenbourg's theory of spheres in *Valentine* to represent postrevolutionary social dislocation. Particularly interesting from a feminist perspective is Naginski's reading of *Lélia,* in which she compares this reputedly scandalous text to those penned by her male romantic counterparts; of *Spiridion,* whose reputation for being conceived by and partially written by Pierre Leroux inspires a passage on the role of gender stereotypes in literary criticism; of *Consuelo,* for its relationship with Gothic tales of initiation; and of *La Mare au diable* as an aesthetic manifesto.

SCHOR concentrates less on Sand's novels themselves than on their increasingly marginal position within the late nineteenth- and early twentieth-century literary canon. Psychoanalytic concepts and Marxist criticism frame discussions of works spanning Sand's literary career, from *Lélia* to her *Correspondance* with Flaubert. Scholars debate Schor's insistence on the paternal as the organizing principle of George Sand's identity, her valorization of those critics definding idealism, and her characterization of Sand's work as defined within its boundaries; nevertheless, Schor masterfully emphasizes her idealism in opposition to realist representations of gender and class identity, and she argues convincingly that Sand's identification with idealism was crucial in discrediting her work for close to one hundred years. Readers will appreciate the final bibliography.

LUKACHER uses the theories of Freud, Deutsch, Jean-Luc Nancy, Kristeva, and Cixous to understand Sand's conflicted relationship with the maternal and her desire to found a new community through fiction. This essay devotes particular attention to the ways in which *Mauprat, Le Péché de Monsieur Antoine, Consuelo,* and *Histoire de ma vie* oppose postrevolutionary patriarchal hegemony, and it includes a final comparison with Marguerite Duras's *India Song.* Among the proceedings that have appeared in English, the collection edited by GLASGOW, along with that presented by DATLOF, FUCHS, and POWELL, provide insightful analyses of Sand's sources and influences throughout Europe, of her autobiographical writings, and of the political, religious, and philosophical positions articulated in articles and fiction. Final indexes in both works increase their usefulness.

—ANNE E. McCALL

Sanger, Margaret 1879–1966

American Activist

Bachrach, Deborah, *Margaret Sanger,* San Diego, California: Lucent, 1993

Chesler, Ellen, *Woman of Valor: Margaret Sanger and the Birth Control Movement in America,* New York: Simon and Schuster, 1993

Douglas, Emily Taft, *Margaret Sanger: Pioneer of the Future,* New York: Holt, Rinehart and Winston, 1960

Gray, Madeline, *Margaret Sanger: A Biography of the Champion of Birth Control,* New York: Richard Marek, 1978

Whitelaw, Nancy, *Margaret Sanger: Every Child a Wanted Child,* New York: Dillon Press, 1994

Of the many truths about Margaret Sanger one stands above all else—she had a complex personality. She was a pioneer, champion, activist, and heroine who gained the adoration of some, the contempt of others, and respect from all. Sanger's biographers have been faced with the daunting task of bringing to light her darker side while still acknowledging her momentous accomplishments. Her multifaceted nature consisted of conflicting images—she was egotistical, selfish, radical, and ruthless, yet charming, intelligent, caring, diligent, and witty. All five of the biographers chosen here have provided a consistent picture of the major episodes in Sanger's public life and the progress of the birth control movement. However, they differ with respect to the detail, accuracy, and openness of her private life—the part of her that lends significant insight into the motives and directions of her public persona. What is known of Sanger's private life is revealed through her extensive correspondence with close friends—most of whom were her lovers—and family members. These letters were left by Sanger to the Smith College Library and the Library of Congress for use by her numerous biographers to paint a more complete picture of this champion of birth control. The biographies of Margaret Sanger that are viewed as the most detailed and historically accurate are discussed first.

CHESLER's book represents the most comprehensive biography of Sanger and the movement to which she gave birth. The author takes great care to provide a detailed and objective account of Sanger's life by weaving together a multitude of historical sources to verify or dispel the accuracy of earlier accounts. She uses a triangulation of historical data to offer the most accurate portrait of Sanger and the birth control movement. Finally, Chesler is more open about Sanger's darker side than previous biographers. While most biographers acknowledge Sanger's multifaceted personality, their efforts stop there. Chesler is specific about Sanger's private life—her experiences with many lovers including sexual encounters with her close female friends from Wantley Circle, her clashes with fellow activists, and her failures as a mother and wife. This book, one of the most recent biographies available, is of tremendous value to researchers, historians, students, and other general interest readers.

GRAY's biography of Sanger is the second most informative piece of work on the birth control pioneer. While much less concerned with historical accuracies, Gray concentrates on Sanger's own thoughts by incorporating a substantial number of her personal letters. Quoted at length, the correspondence reveals Sanger's feelings and desires concerning friends, lovers, and family, as well as her commentaries on the progress of the birth control movement. Gray points out the inaccuracies that Sanger herself communicates in her personal letters about the manner in which events occurred and her role in those events. The author also gives more attention than other biographers to the philosophies by which Sanger lived her life and approached her work. As Gray describes, Sanger believed firmly that the use of one's sexual power led to individual development on a spiritual level. This put her in direct opposition to Mohandas Gandhi's philosophy of complete abstinence, and it is therefore not surprising that they did not find much common ground during her visit to India. Gray's work is an excellent source for those interested primarily in Sanger herself and less in the historical accuracy of her movement.

The biography of Sanger offered by DOUGLAS is much less detailed than those of Chesler and Gray. Douglas relies on a storybook format and describes in more detail the people with which Margaret surrounded herself. The lives of Sanger's parents are described at length, as well as the characteristics of her closest friends. Douglas, however, spends less time than Chesler or Gray in detailing the time line in which events occurred. There is a discrepancy between Douglas and later biographers on Sanger's age at the time of her death. Douglas overlooked Sanger's habit of claiming her younger sister's age as her own—something Chesler and Gray confirmed from birth records and family members. Despite such discrepancies, Douglas provides thoughtful insight into Sanger's personality and motives through her relationships with the people she loved, admired, or despised.

The biographies of Sanger by Bachrach and Whitelaw serve more as brief summaries of her life story. WHITELAW's book covers only the most basic facts of Sanger's life and is more appropriate for younger readers with a general interest in birth control and its leading activist. BACHRACH's book, part of the "Importance Of . . ." series, includes a helpful timetable; however, inaccuracies render her work marginally useful for more well-informed readers. A major inaccuracy concerns the devastating impact of an interview with a young, ambitious reporter named Mike Wallace. According to Chesler, the interview was nationally broadcast in September, 1957 and astonished her relatives who watched from home. Michael Sanger, long divorced from the woman he so adored, wept quietly at the public defeat of a woman weakened by age and her addiction to pain killers and alcohol. Bachrach, however, reports that the interview was never aired. A more obvious mistake is the referral to Margaret's granddaughter Margaret II, her namesake, as Peggy—Sanger's daughter who died as a child. The books reviewed here all provide consistent snapshots of the pioneer's life and career. Capturing the complexity of Margaret Sanger is a formidable task for any interested biographer and in the books reviewed here, those by Chesler and Gray are the most successful.

—SANDI L. DINGER

See also Birth Control Movement

Sappho ca. 610–580 B.C.

Ancient Greek Writer

Burnett, Anne Pippin, *Three Archaic Poets: Archilochus, Alcaeus, Sappho,* Cambridge, Massachusetts: Harvard University Press, and London: Duckworth, 1983

DeJean, Joan, *Fictions of Sappho, 1546–1937,* Chicago: University of Chicago Press, 1989

DuBois, Page, *Sappho Is Burning,* Chicago: University of Chicago Press, 1995

Jenkyns, Richard, *Three Classical Poets: Sappho, Catullus, and Juvenal,* London: Duckworth, and Cambridge, Massachusetts: Harvard University Press, 1982

Snyder, Jane McIntosh, *The Woman and the Lyre: Women Writers in Classical Greece and Rome*, Carbondale: Southern Illinois University Press, and Bristol: Bristol Classical, 1989

As the list suggests, it is not unusual in Sappho scholarship to find books that combine their study of Sappho with the study of other ancient poets. JENKYNS's book on Sappho, Catullus, and Juvenal is not primarily comparative, though he does draw some useful parallels among the three poets. His study of Sappho is valuable for its close, detailed readings of the fragments. Jenkyns begins his discussion of Sappho's poetry by focusing on her controversial reputation throughout history, and on readers' fascination with her biography. Since we know so few facts about Sappho's life, however, we should not let biographical speculation inform our readings of her work. Nor, Jenkyns argues, should we approach her work with assumptions about archaic poetry and expect hers to conform. In his careful attention to Sappho's individual works, Jenkyns argues that we must consider her poetry on its own terms, in order to appreciate her importance as a poet of "exceptional subtlety and power."

The book by SNYDER also focuses on some minor poets in addition to Sappho, but the author begins her study with a long discussion of Sappho as the major female poetic voice of the ancient world. She describes the many legends and misconceptions about Sappho's life, and examines attitudes towards Sappho and her work as reflected in paintings, sculpture, and literature throughout the centuries. Snyder discusses some selections of the poetry to illustrate Sappho's range of subject matter, and she concludes with a very helpful discussion of Sappho's influence on nineteenth- and twentieth-century poets, such as H.D., Amy Lowell, Olga Broumas, and Edna St. Vincent Millay.

BURNETT's study considers Archilochus and Alcaeus as well as Sappho; all three poets, she claims, have been inappropriately measured against the standards of the epic "Greek spirit." Sappho's poetry, Burnett says, uses "a lyric way of thinking to extract truths from experience." Burnett's main premise is that Sappho's poems are neither direct autobiographical self-revelations nor poems merely written for specific social occasions, except for the epithalamia (wedding poems). Burnett focuses on the six best-preserved songs of Sappho, arguing that they employ conventional song patterns and metrical forms in a conscious, meditative fashion. Burnett's study, like Jenkyns's, eschews biographical readings of Sappho's work in favor of close, detailed textual interpretations.

DuBOIS argues that we must read Sappho's work from a historicist perspective instead of a formalist approach. She discusses Sappho's critical role in the history of subjectivity: Sappho was among the first to use the first person singular in poetic diction, the first to create a "cultural space for individual subjectivity." While that sense of interiority may be a given in contemporary society, it was a subversive phenomenon in a society that conceived of identity as collective. Sappho's poetry, DuBois argues, is important not only for its new emphasis on the individual but for its revision of "preexisting poetic materials." For example, Sappho's representation of Helen of Troy is very different from Homer's, as is her concern with the subjects of love and desire instead of military conflict. One of the most important aspects of DuBois's book is her reading of Sappho against Michel Foucault's theories of sexuality. DuBois criticizes Foucault for ignoring Sappho and the idea of female desire in the classical age, but she acknowledges that his work on the history of sexuality can be very useful in understanding Sappho's strategies and rhetoric.

DeJEAN'S focus is how Sappho's work has been treated by readers, critics, and editors from the sixteenth to the twentieth centuries. DeJean demonstrates that in the early modern period, French translators and editors exercised enormous influence in their careful translations and editions of Sappho's work. They presented Sappho as an amorous woman and a well-respected poet among her Greek contemporaries; they did not suppress evidence of same-sex love in Sappho's poetry. It was in later centuries, according to DeJean, that editors and translators were unwilling to acknowledge the homoerotic context of Sappho's work, and often tried to alter her works in a way that would disguise lesbian subject matter. DeJean's study is indispensable to an understanding of Sappho's work in a modern context.

—JO ELDRIDGE CARNEY

Sarton, May 1912–1995

American Writer

Evans, Elizabeth, *May Sarton, Revisited*, Boston: Twayne, 1989

Hunting, Constance (ed.), *May Sarton: Woman and Poet*, Orono: National Poetry Foundation, University of Maine at Orono, 1982

——— (ed.), *A Celebration for May Sarton: Essays and Speeches from the National Conference "May Sarton at 80: A Celebration of Her Life and Work,"* Orono, Maine: Puckerbush Press, 1994

Kallett, Marilyn (ed.), *A House of Gathering: Poets on May Sarton's Poetry*, Knoxville: University of Tennessee Press, 1993

Schwartzlander, Susan, and Marilyn R. Mumford (eds.), *That Great Sanity: Critical Essays on May Sarton*, Ann Arbor: University of Michigan Press, 1992

The criticism of May Sarton's work revolves around four issues: the contributions she has made to feminist thought as a woman, an artist, and a lesbian, and the influence such ideas have had on her; the unity of the author and her landscape; the reasons she has found little acclaim in the academy; and the need to understand Sarton's biography and autobiography in assessing her work.

HUNTING's 1982 book was the first volume of critical essays on Sarton. Containing contributions by 20 authors in the form of 20 essays, four interviews, and a bibliography, it focuses on the need to consider the author's life, views, and interaction with her audience and her landscape in evaluating her work. The intent of the book is to begin to establish a body of critical work on Sarton and thereby present her to academia as a writer worthy of serious consideration. Beginning with a biography stressing Sarton's eccentric upbringing, it moves to a consideration of her autobiographical work. Sections discussing her novels and poetry follow. The essays range from explication of her journals to discussions of the messages she conveys, some reviews of her artistic concerns, and an examination of the risks she undertook in working with traditional poetic forms.

EVANS's book is a solid critical biography of Sarton, which updates the first critical biography of her, written by Agnes Sibley in 1973. It is arranged by genre, beginning with a biography, and then moving to her journals, novels, and poetry, although it does not cover all of her work to 1989 in depth. The final section explores the lack of critical acclaim for Sarton. The book's concern is to demonstrate that Sarton was aware of the journal as an artistic form that expresses the struggle between the public and private, and to emphasize the importance of Sarton's upbringing and her relationships with other authors and artists, as well as her friendships, in forming and sustaining her feminism.

SCHWARTZLANDER's collection of essays is more scholarly in approach and content than the other collections. This book contains 12 essays divided into four sections, based on critical approaches. The focus of the text is to place Sarton squarely within the academic and artistic communities. It maintains the need for biographical context, and identifies her authorial, social, and personal communities, as well as providing an artistic context. Several essays discuss a variety of feminist critical concerns, including aesthetics, her focus on feelings, her lesbianism in relation to her art, and her sense of communion and community. One essay take a reader-response approach, suggesting that Sarton's work has remained outside the academy and resists "canonization" because her readership is predominantly women, and women read in different ways and for different purposes than do men.

KALLETT's book is the only critical anthology to focus primarily on the poetry. Stressing that Sarton regarded poetry as her most serious written work, the essays range from a testimonial from a former student of Sarton's, underlining her discipline and craft as well as her genius, to an analysis of her work and processes, to explications of specific works. The book also delineates the compelling qualities of her poetry, citing the musicality of her language, her meticulousness, her sense of humanity, and her eloquent use of silence. Kallett attempts to place Sarton within a poetic artistic community, and thus demonstrate that her work is worthy of serious artistic consideration.

HUNTING's 1994 book is the most recent study of the author. A collection of all the papers presented at the conference at Westbrook College in Portland, Maine, celebrating Sarton's 80th birthday, it is the least traditional of the volumes on Sarton's work, and in large part because of that, it is perhaps the most valuable. As the title notes, it is a celebration, so the essays honor rather than criticize Sarton. The text is eclectic—not all the contributors are English professors or authors. A social worker commends Sarton for all she has contributed to the process of aging with dignity, thus recognizing her voice as one that affects large numbers of people in their daily lives. As the text is not divided into sections, it presents a more holistic view of Sarton's work than do those that differentiate among the genres in which she worked. The aging process and Sarton's views on it are central to a number of the works here, but others cover her place and role in the artistic community, investigating her muses, the influence various authors had on her, and feminist concerns such as the need for a holistic view of life, a celebration of solitude, and female autonomy. Carolyn Heilbrun's article is valuable, as she postulates that Sarton has been overlooked by the academy because her life, her work, and her attitudes do not reflect those of either men or of "conventional" women.

Whatever the focus of each text, several issues appear consistently. Sarton made great contributions to feminist thought, particularly by vindicating solitude for women and celebrating lesbianism. She defined a number of issues surrounding aging with dignity, embraced a solitary life in the face of a society that condemns women for choosing solitude, and dealt with topics surrounding domesticity. She was deeply connected to her landscape, whether in Nelson or on the coast of Maine, rooted in gardening and natural beauty, and sensitive to the changing of seasons. She dared to work with form in poetry when form was not in vogue, and to value the personal reflective journal as art. All of these issues, and many other social and artistic ones, are essential in assessing Sarton's work, and it may be primarily these choices of topics, genre, and form that have barred her from acceptance by the academy. The writers of all these works insist that her work is worthy of scholarly consideration.

—KAREN LYONS

Sati

Anand, Mulk Raj, *Sati: A Writeup of Raja Ram Mohan Roy about Burning of Widows Alive,* Delhi: B.R. Publishing, 1989

Gaur, Meena, *Sati and Social Reforms in India,* Jaipur, India: Publication Scheme, 1989

Hawley, John Stratton, *Sati, the Blessing and the Curse: The Burning of Wives in India,* New York: Oxford University Press, 1994

Narasimhan, Sakuntala, *Sati: A Study of Widow Burning in India,* New Delhi and New York: Viking, 1990

Singh, Santosh, *A Passion for Flames,* Jaipur, India: RBSA, 1989

Sunder Rajan, Rajeswari, *Real and Imagined Women: Gender, Culture, and Postcolonialism,* London and New York: Routledge, 1993

Thompson, Edward, *Suttee: A Historical and Philosophical Inquiry into the Hindu Rite of Widow-Burning,* London: Allen and Unwin, and Boston: Houghton-Mifflin, 1928

The word "suttee" or "sati" (as is most often spelled by contemporary Indian writers on the subject) has now come to mean the Hindu religious ritual of a widow climbing onto the funeral pyre of her dead husband and being burned alive. It is seen as a manifestation of extreme loyalty, virtue, and godliness. It is also the name given to the woman who has performed a sati. The word was derived from *sat,* meaning the essence of truth and virtue, and a sati or *satimata* was a woman who was so imbued with truth, purity, and virtue that she had the divine ability voluntarily to give up her life on the funeral pyre of her dead husband. Even in modern India, some religious and political leaders (often men) truly believe that sati is an act of self-sacrifice that can be performed only if a woman has been bestowed with the super-human gift of *sat.* Therefore they support the practice in the belief that this is a religious right, should such a divinely blessed widow voluntarily wish to become a *satimata.* Outspoken feminist critics, including those of Indian origin (often women) call it murder or suicide under coercion, and even if it is not, they argue that societal and religious acceptance of such an act subjugates and demeans womanhood. Sati has indeed been illegal in India since the late nineteenth century, although practiced quietly in remote villages, once in a while. However, when Roop Kanwar, a young widow, committed sati in a small village in Rajasthan in 1987, Indian feminists as well as other groups immediately took a stance on the subject. They were quite outspoken in their criticism against the practice, and the episode brought much national and international attention to the subject of sati immediately.

One of the earliest English writers on the topic, THOMPSON provides a historical overview of the origins of suttee based on Hindu scriptures. The appendix gives an interesting chronological account of suttee, performed from 317 B.C. through A.D. 1520 and right up to the nineteenth century, as gleaned from references and quotes from well-researched documents. ANAND's reissue of the writings of Raja Ram Mohan Roy's classical writings on the theme of sati clearly demonstrate that even as early as 1818, the great Indian social reformer was attempting to bring a new social conscience to the British government of the time. He ends the book with an addendum, including the published records of the journalistic reporting in the Indian media following the 1987 Roop Kanwar sati, which may have triggered the resurgence of the interest in this subject. The addendum offers an excellent set of original articles representing the immediate reaction of the Indian media, published in such well-known magazines and newspapers as *Seminar, India Today, Indian Express, The Illustrated Weekly,* and *Times of India.*

Gaur, Sunder Rajan, Narsimhan, and Singh are four contemporary Indian female writers, each of whom brings in her own unique perspective on the subject. GAUR does a rather scholarly treatment of the origin of sati in non-Indic civilizations, reviewing the history of social reforms in nineteenth-century India. The historical survey of the status of women in early civilizations leads to an explanation of the ritual of burning widows. Although widow self-immolation was practiced in many parts of India, she focuses on its impact in Rajasthan, where it was upheld and honored as a sacred ritual.

SUNDER RAJAN's book is a collection of feminist critical essays, and the focus is on the post-colonial Indian woman in contemporary India, with a chapter on sati, which documents the feminist approach to this ritual. In Chapter One, she reviews the writings of Indian feminist scholars like Lata Mani and Gaytri Spivak. She notes that they "shift the emphasis from Sati-as-death (murder or suicide, authentic or inauthentic) to Sati-as-burning, and investigate both the subjective pain and the objective spectacle that the shift reveals." NARSIMAHAN goes into greater detail about the cultural influences surrounding widow burning. The work provides an introduction to the subject of sati, but much of the author's focus is on the cultural issues surrounding the subject, such as the subjectivity of the rural Indian women who tend to perform sati.

For a reader who wishes a more comprehensive study of sati, SINGH discusses the issues from several points of view, seriously attempting to present an impartial review of the various perspectives in this highly controversial topic. As the preface succinctly summarizes, she describes the genesis of sati in the Hindu religion, its evolution from prehistoric times to the present day, the various factors that were responsible for promoting the custom, and the problems that confront Hindu women in general and Hindu widows in particular. This work incudes chapters on the concept of sati in Hindu religion and its history and evolution, the various forms of related rituals, the psychological, social, and legal aspects of sati, and issues concerning the reform movements. There is a listing of 202 titles referring to works on women in Indian society, but most of them appear to have been published by India publishers and are not likely to be available outside India.

As editor and contributor of perhaps the most comprehensive collaborative recent work on sati, HAWLEY has successfully brought together from around the globe some of the most knowledgeable contemporary scholars in the field, who treat the subject as objectively as a group of scholars can. Each chapter provides some unusual perspectives (for example, description of the iconography of sati; a survey of European sources on the topic; a detailed chronological listing of the events surrounding the Roop Kanwar case; an explanation of the values of sati, and an appreciation of the wifely self-sacrifice that celebrates the power of women), and why it could conceivably be applauded (the original essay on which this chapter was based provoked a storm of criticism from Indian feminists). A couple of the collaborators respond to each other's comments, providing further insights from different perspectives, thereby enlightening the reader interested in seeing all sides of this issue. The book contains excellent bibliographies and notes after each chapter.

—INDRA M. DAVID

Sayers, Dorothy Leigh 1893–1957

British Writer

Brabazon, James, *Dorothy L. Sayers: A Biography*, New York and London: V. Gollancz, 1981

Coomes, David, *Dorothy L. Sayers: A Careless Rage for Life*, Oxford: Lion, 1992

Dale, Alzina Stone, *Maker and Craftsman: The Story of Dorothy L. Sayers*, Grand Rapids, Michigan: William B. Eerdmans, 1978

Durkin, Mary Brian, *Dorothy L. Sayers*, Boston: Twayne, 1980

Gaillard, Dawson, *Dorothy L. Sayers*, New York: Frederick Ungar, 1981

Hitchman, Janet, *Such a Strange Lady: A Biography of Dorothy L. Sayers*, New York: Harper and Row, and London: New English Library, 1975

Hone, Ralph E., *Dorothy L. Sayers: A Literary Biography*, Kent, Ohio: Kent State University Press, 1979

Kenney, Catherine, *The Remarkable Case of Dorothy L. Sayers*, Kent, Ohio, and London: Kent State University Press, 1990

Reynolds, Barbara, *Dorothy L. Sayers: Her Life and Soul*, New York: St. Martin's Press, and London: Hodder and Stoughton, 1993

Tischler, Nancy M., *Dorothy L. Sayers: A Pilgrim Soul*, Atlanta, Georgia: John Knox Press, 1973

Dorothy Sayers's writing career began with detective stories, moved on to religious drama and theology, and ended with translation and criticism of Dante. Some scholars have focused upon explaining these transitions in her professional interests or debating which form of her work is best or most important. Others have targeted mysteries in Sayers's private life, including an illegitimate son she never acknowledged and an unlikely marriage.

HITCHMAN wrote the first biography of Sayers. Although she did not have access to Sayers's personal papers, she discovered and disclosed the existence of Sayers's son for the first time. Hitchman is critical of Sayers's private life, suggesting that she and her son would have been happier if she had put him up for adoption. Nevertheless, Hitchman praises Sayers's work, most importantly for bringing "amusement and fun into the lives of millions" with her detective stories.

DALE's biography offers good historical context on Sayers's times and is written in a lively, easy-to-read style suitable for the least informed reader. This is not an academic biography, and it contains few details on Sayers's life, but the author has consulted some archival collections. Dale calls Sayers "an energetic and enthusiastic person at home in many worlds," and unlike Hitchman, considers her religious work to be her most important and her real calling.

HONE calls his work a "literary biography" and gives most of his attention to events in Sayers's professional life, spending less time discussing her private life. He attributes both her professional changes of emphasis and her private travails to a conflict between her love of religion and her desire for physical sensuality. Hone defends Sayers against charges of apathy in her treatment of her son, suggesting that the opposition of her husband or efforts to spare her parents humiliation explain her failure to bring him into her home. Like Dale, Hone sees Sayers's religious work as her best and most important.

TISCHLER focuses more specifically on Sayers's religious character. Her book describes Sayers as a "pilgrim soul" whose importance lies not so much in her writings as in the example her spiritual journey set and her commitment to work and Christian ethics. Tischler argues that Sayers's "experience in sin and its consequences"(her illegitimate son) helped deepen her knowledge of emotional truth and evil, although her intellectual approach to Christianity was, in Tischler's view, a failing.

DURKIN, a nun, echoes this religious emphasis. Durkin devotes more effort to summarizing Sayers's writings than to analyzing them, but she does identify an overall theme of integrity in Sayers's writing: "integrity of work, of the mind, of right relationships with others, one's self, and with God." She dismisses controversies over Sayers's private life as unimportant "trivia" in comparison with Sayers's work, especially her religious writings. Durkin often repeats that Sayers's works contain important lessons for our times, although she never discusses the specifics of those lessons.

BRABAZON, an acquaintance of Sayers, was the first biographer authorized by Sayers's son and the first given access to her personal papers. Brabazon appears fairly objective in his work, and his biography is well footnoted, but he admits that certain things were suppressed at her son's request, including the identity of his father. Brabazon attributes Sayers's lack of interest in her son to the isolation of her childhood, contradicting earlier portrayals of her husband as an incompetent rogue. Brabazon considers Sayers a "first-rate scholar, first-rate theologian and highly competent dramatist," but concludes that her detective novels will be her longest-lasting legacy.

GAILLARD's book concentrates on Sayers's detective novels. She traces the development of Sayers's recurrent characters and of Sayers's attitude toward detective fiction over time. Gaillard is a great admirer of Sayers and begins her study with the stated goal of expressing that admiration in print. Like other commentators, Gaillard argues that Sayers's writings stress her commitment to work, but she also notes an enduring interest in male and female relationships. Gaillard attributes Sayers's move away from detective fiction not to a religious call, but to the realization, after two World Wars, that "the detective pattern of problem-solving" was no longer adequate.

KENNEY is also attracted by Sayers's detective novels and feels earlier scholars have not properly appreciated Sayers's work as "literary art." Kenney concentrates on assessing Sayers's contributions to modern literature. These, she concludes, are her "transformation of the modern detective story into a serious novel," her "critique of the situation of modern women," and her work as "a lay theologian and interpreter of Christianity." Rather than explain Sayers's moves from detective fiction to religious topics and then to Dante, Kenney argues that Sayers's work shares the common themes of a Christian worldview and commitment to Christian values.

COOMES devotes his biography to demonstrating that Sayers had more emotional depth than previous biographers thought. He takes issue with Brabazon's portrayal of Sayers's religious devotion as primarily intellectual, arguing that Sayers's religious faith came from her heart. Coomes admires Sayers and praises her repeatedly. He suggests that her moves from fiction to religion to Dante are due to a propensity for intense, short-lived obsessions. Because of her personal tragedies, he argues, she devoted her life to pursuing truth rather than happiness.

REYNOLDS has written the most recent and most detailed biography. Reynolds was a close friend of Sayers, and although she has clearly done a great deal of research, her book does not include detailed footnotes on this. Reynolds does what all earlier biographers have failed to do; she discloses the name of the father of Sayers's son. Reynolds takes issue with scholars who feel that Sayers's lifelong guilt over her son's birth influenced her work, arguing that Sayers would have expiated that guilt through confession and been left with merely a sense of responsibility. Reynolds concludes that Sayers is most admirable for her "intellectual ardour."

—NAN H. DREHER

Scholarship/Research, Feminist

Bowles, Gloria, and Duelli-Klein, Renate (eds.), *Theories of Women's Studies*, London and Boston: Routledge, 1983

Fonow, Mary, and Judith Cook (eds.), *Beyond Methodology: Feminist Scholarship as Lived Research*, Bloomington: Indiana University Press, 1991

Harding, Sandra (ed.), *Feminism and Methodology: Social Science Issues*, Milton Keynes: Open University Press, 1986; Bloomington: Indiana University Press, 1987

Maynard, Mary, and June Purvis (eds.), *Researching Women's Lives from a Feminist Perspective*, London and Bristol, Pennsylvania: Taylor and Francis, 1994

Reinharz, Shulamit, *Feminist Methods in Social Research*, New York: Oxford University Press, 1992

Roberts, Helen (ed.), *Doing Feminist Research*, London and Boston: Routledge, 1981

Stanley, Liz (ed.), *Feminist Praxis: Research, Theory, and Epistemology in Feminist Sociology*, London and New York: Routledge, 1990

Discussions and descriptions of western feminist research and scholarship can be broadly divided between textbooks outlining methods, methodological studies that shade into epistemology/ontology debates, and more "grounded" versions of such debates, often based around specific research projects. There are, of course, numerous studies within specific disciplinary fields, but they are beyond the scope of this brief introduction. The discussion here is of writers interested in the construct of new forms of a specifically feminist research, rather than those more concerned with the critique of existing research paradigms.

BOWLES and DUELLI-KLEIN were arguably the first to address questions of what characterizes a methodology as feminist. Their title signals the book's pioneering place in publishing, mapping out a place for women's studies just prior to the massive expansion of publications in the field that took place in the 1980s. Among its germinal essays is Maria Mies's "Towards a Methodology for Feminist Research." Mies centrally addresses the need for feminist research to engage with positivist claims for a "value-free," "neutral" observer/researcher.

She argues for a less theoretical view in research, and puts her theory into practice by applying her theoretical position to a specific action-research project. Mies introduces themes and concerns that continually return through subsequent discussions of feminist research. Bowles and Duelli-Klein's book is also of historical interest in that it predates the debates around the (im)possibilities of a "common language" that have become so central within women's studies over the last 10 years.

As an introduction to the establishment of the field, Bowles and Duelli-Klein can be usefully read along with REINHARZ. It is interesting to see the origins of Reinharz's later text in her contribution to the above book. Reinharz's work is explicitly a textbook for feminist social researchers: it is a survey of issues and approaches offered in a lucid and well-indexed format. Its pedagogical intentions are clearly marked in the introductory comments. Reinharz hopes that feminist researchers will begin to develop new approaches rather than fall back into a reactive position of "fighting patriarchy." She also stresses her attachment to pluralism, and to a positive definition of what makes research feminist based on its inclusions. The approaches reflect Reinharz's own background in North American sociology, but she draws on examples from across a wide range of disciplines and makes some reference to British feminist researchers. This book is, to date, the most comprehensive textbook in the field, but the inevitable limitations of any textbook need to be kept in mind, and her extensive bibliography should be consulted for supplementary reading.

Edited collections necessarily offer more complex and diverse perspectives. FONOW and COOK present a range of articles that provide some definitive moments in the marking out of feminist research methodology over the last decade or so. Their clear and sophisticated introduction posits some of the central questions for feminist research, and signals recent moves to attempt some deconstruction of the boundaries between epistemology (theory about knowledge) and ontology (theory about being). Many, if not all, of the contributors engage with issues of their own reflective research practice, and with the ethics of (re)constructing others' lives within research paradigms. Patricia Hill Collins's "Learning from the Outside Within" argues for the significance of black research experience in reformulating some central problems in mainstream sociological models of participant observation. Many of the contributors share with the editors a belief in the importance of biography. This is also increasingly a focus of the British feminist theorist/researcher Liz Stanley.

STANLEY, like Fonow and Cook, offers a collection of articles prefaced with a complex but lucid exploration of some of the contemporary problems and issues for feminist researchers. Stanley's editorial introduction is an exemplary piece of reflective feminist research, which also clearly defines "feminist praxis" as the production of a kind of knowledge which is "knowledge for." This would be one point of agreement for all the editors and writers cited: one difference of feminist research is its commitment to changing the world for women. Stanley's introductory essay, co-authored with Sue Wise, "Method, Methodology and Epistemology in Feminist Research Processes," offers an excellent survey of the field and an impressive bibliography. It could be usefully followed by a reading of their book-length study, *Breaking Out Again: Feminist Ontology and Epistemology* (1993). Stanley's other contributors provide a diverse series of case studies of research projects with reflective commentaries: these are notable for including detailed discussion of failures and problems, as well as successes.

Stanley and Wise's essay in this book critiques Sandra Harding and other theorists for their silences, in particular those regarding black feminist and lesbian feminist perspectives. However, Stanley's contributors also seem to speak from predominantly white British positions. The exceptions are Chung Yuen Kay's "At the Palace: Researching Gender and Ethnicity in a Chinese Restaurant," and Australian Jane Haggis's "The Feminist Research Process—Defining a Topic." Haggis succinctly signals the necessity for white first-world feminists to interrogate their own implication in colonization, and to acknowledge debts to the knowledge production of black and non-western women, in the quest for a "qualitatively different research methodology and product."

A central concern for feminist researchers is the rejection of a neutral, value-free position toward the object(s) of inquiry. In challenging this central tenet of traditional western science, feminist research has to face questions about validation and reliability. One major theorising direction has been designated "standpoint theory," although the theorists identified with this have different interpretations of what it means. HARDING, here and elsewhere, argues for a more complete view of the feminist, since she is an outsider (to patriarchy) and therefore more truly objective. "Feminist standpoint" is, therefore, for Harding, a "successor science," working within the science paradigms but doing them better. Nancy Hartsock's description of standpoint, in Harding's book, is positioned squarely within a Marxist-feminist frame of reference, arguing for the crucial inclusion of the material context of research, including its history.

ROBERTS's book is a British collection reflecting British perspectives. It includes sociologist Anne Oakley's influential pioneering work on feminist interviewing, "Interviewing Women: A Contradiction in Terms." It also offers David Morgan's "Men, Masculinity and the Process of Sociological Enquiry," which raises, both explicitly and in its inclusion in this feminist collection, questions about men's relationship to feminist research. Can a man be a feminist researcher? It is an issue which resurfaces from time to time, and highlights a central and important question: that of the authority of experience. The appeal to women's experience as a validation for feminist research is often repeated.

Such questions, and their most recent formations, are usefully collected by MAYNARD and PURVIS. The book includes contributors who write "in the silences": race, class, lesbian, and disability experience. This collection is notable for its sophisticated combination of personal reflection, and its analysis of grounded research within theorised frameworks. Among the essays are: Holland and Ramazanoglu's discussion of the power of the researcher; Skeggs's attempt to define a feminist ethnography; and Marshall's analysis of the problems and urgency of developing black feminist paradigms, methodology and epistemology within social research. The editors bear in mind that the establishment of a literature of feminist research and epistemology risks making abstract the material conditions of women's lives and can turn away from "the dynamics of actually *doing* research."

—BARBARA BROOK

Schumann, Clara 1819–1896

German Composer

Chissell, Joan, *Clara Schumann, a Dedicated Spirit: A Study of Her Life and Work,* New York: Taplinger, 1983

Litzmann, Berthold, *Clara Schumann: An Artist's Life*, 2 vols., translated by Grace E. Hadow, London: Macmillan, 1913; New York: Vienna House, 1972

Reich, Nancy B., *Clara Schumann: The Artist and Woman,* Ithaca, New York: Cornell University Press, 1985

For a variety of reasons, musicologists have tended to present and evaluate the lives and contributions of women and music in essays and journal articles rather than full-length books. Lack of sufficient documentation and a smaller readership have been significant causes of this, but, more importantly perhaps, the categories of traditional musical historiography valorize types of achievement and participation in which women, for many cultural and ideological reasons, have failed to excel. The two major biographies of Clara Schumann that appeared in the mid-1980s, however, testify to Schumann's stature as a musician and artist who transcended any limitations of gender.

LITZMANN's book, the authorized biography written at the behest of Schumann's eldest daughter, remains an invaluable source for Schumann studies. Litzmann dispels many of the persistent nineteenth-century myths that had clung to Clara herself, Friedrich Wieck (Clara's father), and Clara's relationships with male musicians of the times—Robert Schumann and Johannes Brahms. Although the two-volume biography tends to be anecdotal, Litzmann did have access to a number of documents that have since been lost or destroyed. His treatment of Schumann's childhood and adolescence is brief, but he presents the events of her later life thoroughly. Readers should not expect much interpretation or psychological nuance, nor does Litzmann, a self-styled historian of literature, engage Schumann's creative oeuvre. Given to lengthy quotations of Schumann's correspondence, Litzmann, at times, reproduces page after page of Schumann's letters without any interpretation whatsoever.

CHISSELL provides a lively and easily-readable source for those interested in Schumann, but it will not satisfy the serious researcher. Without a bibliography and comprehensive footnotes, readers must take Chissell at her word. Her presentation is anecdotal at times, and like Litzmann, she tends to reproduce correspondence without introducing her own interpretation. Her knowledge of the musical and cultural context of Schumann's life does not measure up to Reich's, nor does she match Reich in psychological insight.

REICH's biography is unparalleled in almost every aspect: command of the events of Clara's life, psychological intuition and nuance, and analysis of Schumann's compositions. Moreover, Reich's knowledge of nineteenth-century music and culture enables her to provide a more thorough assessment of the context in which Schumann lived and worked. Part I recounts the events of Clara's life. In this section, Reich incorporates more psychological interpretation than any of her predecessors. In Part II, Reich considers themes that have defined Schumann's place in music history: her relationships with Brahms and other contemporaries, her activity as a composer and editor, her vital importance and influence as one of the premier pianists of the nineteenth century, and her work as a teacher. Mitigating the significance of her "passionate" friendship with Brahms, Reich settles on the less provocative epithet, "many-layered" friendship. Her decision to separate biography from analyses of Schumann's music is not so helpful. (Chissell provides a more helpful context for the compositions by interweaving discussion of the two.) In what might be the most important of Reich's conclusions, she reassesses Schumann's role as a pianist. She concludes that Schumann was, along with Franz Liszt, the most influential pianist of the century. Her high standards of execution and dedication to great music, Reich claims, are her most lasting contributions to both the musical life of her time and to posterity.

—DONALD B. CHAE

Science Fiction *see* Literature: Utopian and Science Fiction

Science: Gender Bias in Research

Bleier, Ruth, *Science and Gender: A Critique of Biology and Its Theories on Women,* New York: Pergamon Press, 1984
Fausto-Sterling, Anne, *Myths of Gender: Biological Theories about Women and Men,* New York: Basic Books, 1985
Haraway, Donna, *Primate Visions: Gender, Race, and Nature in the World of Modern Science,* New York: Routledge, 1989; London: Verso Press, 1992
Harding, Sandra, *The "Racial" Economy of Science: Toward a Democratic Future,* Bloomington: Indiana University Press, 1993
Rosser, Sue V., *Biology and Feminism: A Dynamic Interaction,* New York: Twayne, 1992
Tuana, Nancy (ed.), *Feminism and Science,* Bloomington: Indiana University Press, 1989

A central focus of feminist science studies has been an examination of gender bias in scientific research. The vast majority of research has focused on the biological sciences, perhaps because of the interconnectedness of biological theories of humans with theories of other animal and plant species. Critiques of biological determinism (the idea that human social behavior and sociology can be explained by biology) are particularly significant because of their impact on women's lives and women's health. The work of feminist scholars shifts the focus from biological sex and "human nature" to gender. These scholars have repeatedly documented how science constructs gender, and how gender constructs science, and how these dual processes reinscribe and naturalize gender norms.

TUANA has put together a collection of essays that are rich and lucid, and that sketch the central arguments of feminist science studies. The volume is divided into one set of essays that explore feminist analyses of epistemological frameworks of modern science and a second set that explores feminist theories of science. It is the latter set of essays that elaborates critiques of the ways in which the practice of science and scientific knowledge are affected by and reinscribe sexist, racist, homophobic, and class biases. The essays explore the use of language (such as the "active sperm/passive egg"), the "dis-easing" of the female body through masculinist biases affecting scientific research of the pre-menstrual syndrome, sex difference research on the brain, gender bias in theories of human reproduction, and the use of corpuscular philosophy in physics and chemistry.

HARDING's volume includes both classic and recent essays that provide a critical analysis on the development of western science. This is a large volume with a rich variety of essays from scholars in both the west and east. The first section explores early non-western science traditions—from China, Egypt, and early Andean cultures. The second section is a collection of essays on how science constructs "race." A third set of essays explores who gets to do science in the United States, exploring the role of race and gender among scientific practitioners. The fourth section focuses on scientific technologies and applications, including essays on the Tuskegee syphilis experiments, the use of Depo-Provera, the practice of masculinist forestry in India, and finally the development of environmental racism. The section on critique of scientific objectivity and value neutrality includes well-developed essays on Nazi medicine, and cultural differences among high energy physicists. This is an important collection of essays that point to the inextricable interconnectedness of gender, race, class, sexuality, and nationality, and that illustrate that a thorough understanding of any one of them must include a complex exploration of them all.

ROSSER's volume focuses on the biological sciences and is a very good introduction to the impact of women's studies on the subdisciplines in the biological sciences. The first section of her book focuses on the history and current status of women in science. In the rest of the book she examines the effects of feminism on theories and methods in biology by systematically exploring the literature in women's studies on each of the following subdisciplines: organismal biology (including evolutionary biology, animal behavior, and ecology) and cellular and molecular biology (including neurosciences, endocrinology, developmental biology, and cell biology).

BLEIER's work weaves together a compelling argument for how science has created an elaborate mythology of women's inferiority as a way of justifying their subordinate position in society. Her chapter on biological determinism and who such arguments serve is well developed. She treats much of sociobiology (which attempts to explain human social behavior and organization by biological theories) as flawed and as bad science. She systematically documents her position by critiquing numerous scientific examples. These include sex difference research on the brain, hormonal effects on brain development, man-the-hunter theories of human cultural evolution, and sexuality research. What Bleier advocates is a new vision of science, one that is not dominated by dualisms and one that does not highlight control, dominance, or linear causality. Instead she advocates a revisioning of science into one that is understanding of complexity, constant change, contextuality, and the interaction of natural and social phenomena.

FAUSTO-STERLING explores how physicians, biologists, and anthropologists have shaped women's place in the world, and she documents how science has created these myths of gender. She examines biological, genetic, evolutionary, and psychological evidence and shows how they fail to support the notion of biologically-based sex differences. One of the important points the author makes is to go beyond the model of good science/bad science. She argues that simply to write off past research as bad science is too simple. She suggests that within a particular cultural context, scientists might well be doing excellent science, which in the wisdom of hindsight seems like bad science. She calls for an understanding of science as a socially-constructed process. This has been a very influential book in feminist science studies.

HARAWAY employs a completely different approach to an exploration of the field of primatology. Using scientific texts as narrative, she uses tools from literary criticism to create a framework to understand how race, sexuality, gender, nation, family, and class have been written into the body of nature in the western life sciences since the eighteenth century. While difficult reading for those not familiar with her writing, the book brilliantly pulls together evidence from as diverse sources as scientific articles, science fiction novels, movies, newspapers, fiction, politics, anthropology, sociology, philosophy, critical race theory, law, advertisements, and so forth. Using the work of several primatologists as case studies, she argues for primatology as a genre of feminist theory.

—BANU SUBRAMANIAM

See also Medical History

Science: History

Abir-Am, Pnina G., and Dorinda Outram (eds.), *Uneasy Careers and Intimate Lives: Women in Science, 1789–1979,* New Brunswick, New Jersey: Rutgers University Press, 1987

Alic, Margaret, *Hypatia's Heritage: A History of Women in Science from Antiquity to the late Nineteenth Century,* London: Women's Press, and Boston: Beacon Press, 1986

Benjamin, Marina (ed.), *Science and Sensibility: Gender and Scientific Enquiry, 1780–1945,* Oxford and Cambridge, Massachusetts: Basil Blackwell, 1991

Jacobus, Mary, Evelyn Fox Keller, and Sally Shuttleworth, *Body/Politics: Women and the Discourses of Science,* New York and London: Routledge, 1990

Keller, Evelyn Fox, *Reflections on Gender and Science,* New Haven, Connecticut, and London: Yale University Press, 1985

———, *Secrets of Life, Secrets of Death,* New York and London: Routledge, 1992

Noble, David, *A World without Women: The Christian Clerical Culture of Western Science,* New York: Knopf, 1992; Oxford: Oxford University Press, 1993

Ogilvie, Marilyn Bailey, *Women in Science: Antiquity through the Nineteenth Century,* Cambridge, Massachusetts: MIT Press, 1986

Rossiter, Margaret W., *Women Scientists in America,* 2 vols., Baltimore: Johns Hopkins University Press, 1982, 1995

Schiebinger, Londa, *The Mind Has No Sex?: Women in the Origins of Modern Science,* Cambridge, Massachusetts and London: Harvard University Press, 1989

———, *Nature's Body: Gender in the Making of Modern Science,* Boston: Beacon Press, 1993

Wertheim, Margaret, *Pythagoras' Trousers: God, Physics, and the Gender Wars,* New York: Times Books, 1995; London: Fourth Estate, 1997

Yost, Edna, *Women of Modern Science,* New York: Dodd Mead, 1959

Seeking to discover previously invisible women in science, historians have combed the archives searching for evidence of a female presence in the world of science, as well as explanations for the paucity of such evidence. Most of their efforts are still in print, testimony to the lively effect of feminist scholarship. The literature is polarized between representations of women as active practitioners, subjects of science, or passive objects.

ALIC covers the endeavors of women in science from the goddesses and heroines of prehistory through the life of Mary Somerville, the last Victorian amateur scientist. Among others, Alic includes short biographies of Hypatia of Alexandria, Trotula of Salerno, Hildegard von Bingen, the Duchess of Newcastle, and Lady Mary Montagu. She explains why botany was dubbed the female science, and what women contributed to the scientific revolution. However, critics have complained that her work typifies outdated attempts to shape women's ventures to meet male standards of scientific accomplishment, thereby obscuring genuine understanding of their careers.

YOST similarly lionizes, in almost quaint biographical form, a handful of scientific women in the first half of the twentieth century, including Lise Meitner and Chien Shiung Wu. Additional information on the lives of over two hundred women in science from antiquity to 1900, from Abella to Anne Sewell Young, can be gleaned from OGILVIE's biographical dictionary and its useful annotated bibliography.

Rather than concentrate on great female scientists throughout history, SCHIEBINGER (1989) explores the rise of modern science in seventeenth- and eighteenth-century Europe and the exclusion of females from that enterprise. Using various historical methods, she examines the institutions, individuals, disciplines, and complementarian culture that produced the gender system in science. SCHIEBINGER (1995) continues to limn the eighteenth century and the problem of gender in the making of modern science, but here she shifts her focus to the historical infusion of nature with sexuality and the ethos of natural history. Plant taxonomies defined female flower parts as inferior to the male; Linnaeus's naming of "mammals" also emerged from the deep cultural roots of gender politics. As the natural sciences gained prestige, European men questioned whether women were even capable of abstract thought and barred them from the public realm of science and scholarship. Both of these books are provocative and replete with ideas for additional reading and research.

NOBLE also investigates the origins and implications of the masculine culture of western science. He reconstructs the first millennium of the Christian era, correcting the common misperception that women were always banned from the community of learning. Denying that this community merely extended ancient patriarchy, Noble blames the ascetic clerical hierarchy in the High Middle Ages for closing the door on female participation in science and indicts the modern secular scientific brotherhood with keeping it shut. This excellent tome has useful citations, but inexplicably it lacks a bibliography.

WERTHEIM's focus is the history of mathematically based science since Pythagoras and the absence of women from it. She attributes part of that exclusion to the religious origins and continuing religious currents in contemporary physics and argues for a new culture of physics more concerned with human needs. Although conditions for women in physics have improved since the 1970s, Wertheim echoes Noble's description of today's secular "mathematical man" as priestly and his world still without women.

A series of scholarly essays edited by BENJAMIN probes three topics: female practitioners of science in the nineteenth century, gender representation in science, and the relationship of feminism to science. Benjamin's review of scholarly literature in an introduction is pithy but cogent. ROSSITER has exhaustively surveyed women's participation in American science from the 1820s to the recent past. Volume one begins with the establishment of women's colleges, created to respond to the needs of the republic by giving females a moral education. Women subsequently infiltrated graduate schools, found scientific work in the federal government, and joined scientific societies, all the while camouflaging their achievements and coping with double standards and discrimination. Heroines in the struggle against professional segregation are featured.

Volume two assays the remarkable generation of female American scientists who wrestled with the injustices of ambivalent encouragement, faculty antinepotism rules, and research marginality during a golden age of science in the United States. Their indignation coalesced in the late 1960s into the movement that spotlighted their isolation and brought needed change.

Seeking to explore the particular difficulties faced by women in science as they balance their personal lives and careers, ABIR-AM and OUTRAM have gathered together twelve international case studies by various scholars on the family situations and strategies of pioneering female scientists. The studies point to the complexity of patterns in gender-science interaction and the need for more historical study to mine the persistence of gender bias in science and society at large.

The most frequently encountered contributor to advanced debate on women and the history of science is Keller, author or co-author of several intellectually charged works to be considered in any serious examination of the topic. KELLER (1985) first posited her charge that the social study of science tacitly supports the divisions between masculine and feminine, which secure the autonomy of science, while a feminist perspective confronts the science-gender system. KELLER (1992) continued to challenge the icons of science in essays that provide re-readings of Francis Bacon, Robert Boyle, Isaac Newton, and others for language bias and that discovers their cultural norms transformed into natural law.

Finally, KELLER labored with JACOBUS and SHUTTLEWORTH to produce an edition of papers by various scholars on the feminine body as defined in literary, social, and scientific discourses from 1800 to the present. Feminist analysis of these discussions has substantiated the metaphor guiding the development of modern science: domination of the female body of nature by the pursuit of scientific knowledge. The more distant the historical period, the easier to identify the determining pressures of social ideology and the ways they have framed scientific dialogue. These articles are intellectually sophisticated and resonate with anger.

—ELIZABETH LANE FURDELL

Science: Teaching to Women

Bleier, Ruth (ed.), *Feminist Approaches to Science*, New York: Pergamon Press, 1986

Kass-Simon, G., and Patricia Farnes (eds.), *Women of Science: Righting the Record*, Bloomington: Indiana University Press, 1990

Kelly, Allison (ed.), *Science for Girls?*, Milton Keynes and Philadelphia: Open University Press, 1987

Reiss, Michael J., *Science Education for a Pluralist Society*, Milton Keynes and Philadelphia: Open University Press, 1993

Rosser, Sue (ed.), *Teaching the Majority: Breaking the Gender Barrier in Science, Mathematics, and Engineering*, New York: Teachers' College Press, 1995

Skolnick, Joan, Carol Langbort, and Lucille Day, *How to Encourage Girls in Math and Science: Strategies for Parents and Educators*, Englewood Cliffs, New Jersey: Prentice Hall, 1982

Tobias, Sheila, *They're Not Dumb, They're Different: Stalking the Second Tier*, Tucson, Arizona: Research Corporation, 1990

Warren, Rebecca Lowe, and Mary H. Thompson (eds.), *The Scientist within You*, Eugene, Oregon: ACI, 1995

Both educators and scientists have recognized the need to address the issue of science education, particularly for women and girls. Sex role socialization affects the skills and confidence of girls in math and science, and much of school science is still seen as appropriate for boys but inappropriate for girls. Improving access to science for women and girls requires both a change in the image of science and more inclusive methods of teaching and practicing science. Changing the way that physical and natural science is taught is a critical component of attracting and retaining girls and women in these fields.

BLEIER begins by questioning what it is about science, or about women, that accounts for the absence of a feminist perspective as an integral part of the sciences. She wonders how science might be different, and how we might have a different perspective of the physical and natural world, if women were, historically and currently, recognized as worthy participants in the sciences. This collection of 12 papers considers the nature and perceptions of modern science and is written primarily by scientists. It presents women with an opportunity to begin to understand how and why science and science research neglects and negates the role of women.

TOBIAS presents a case for why we need to teach more students to do more science, and why we need to recruit and retain those individuals interested in science but unwilling to pursue it. Much of this book is a recounting of the stories recorded during a research project designed to understand why students chose not to do science. For women, school science was found to be too easy (not challenging enough) and tedious. Women also expressed discouragement due to large class sizes where dialogue was not encouraged and often physically not possible. Students who chose not to do science rejected the "culture of competition" in favor of a "culture of competence," felt that science does not provide a well-rounded liberal arts education, had interests and motivations unrelated to science, and were not convinced by "right-answer science." Simply seeing and hearing about these cases will help women in science classes understand why they are uncomfortable with the atmosphere and may help them to persist in spite of the odds.

REISS approaches science teaching by considering what science is (and is not), which helps girls and women to see that science is taught, presented, and perceived within too narrow a focus. He points out the western, male view in which modern science has developed, providing numerous examples intended to help teachers create a more inclusive, multicultural science curriculum.

Changes in teaching science can be as simple as including the accomplishments of female scientists, a topic that is usually not considered in typical science classes. Although people have numerous images of famous male scientists, who often become heroes and role models for aspiring young men, female scientists, who might provide more appropriate role models for girls and young women, have been left out. KASS-SIMON and FARNES present the histories and stories of large numbers of female astronomers, biologists, chemists, physicists, and others that help dispel the myth that women scientists are somehow rare or exceptional. They discuss the numerous and important works by women in many disciplines, the importance of women's colleges in training women scientists, and some of the reasons why women's achievements in the sciences have gone uncelebrated. Presenting these issues to women and girls in science classes would give students an opportunity to see that women can, and do, participate in science and that they should not believe otherwise.

Often, instructors may recognize that female scientists are not visible in science education but have few tools to address this issue. WARREN and THOMPSON have produced a wonderful collection of curricular materials that highlight women's achievements in science and mathematics. There are a total of 23 instructional units, each featuring a hands-on experiment or activity designed to duplicate or demonstrate the relevance of a female scientist's work. Many units contain photographs of the women, presenting a different visual model of who scientists are. This book not only inspires girls to pursue science and mathematics, leading to higher expectations and achievements in these fields, but also teaches boys and men that women have always been participants in science and mathematics.

SKOLNICK, LANGBORT, and DAY look for solutions to inspire girls in math and science, and they provide educators and parents with tools to achieve this. The book provides a variety of educational strategies and almost 70 activities designed to encourage girls. The book identifies particular problems in the socialization of girls that result in learning problems in math and science. The activities present a multitude of ways to apply strategies in building critical math and science skills.

The 12 essays in the book edited by ROSSER are written by female educators and underscore the numerous ways that secondary and post-secondary science courses prevent women's participation in the sciences. The gender-biased language and atmosphere found in science classes is illustrated, and each author provides specific classroom experiences and suggestions for pedagogical change to achieve more equitable instructional methods and a more inclusive learning environment.

KELLY proposes explanations for problematic relationships with school science and stresses the need for changes in school science to meet girls' development. She also discusses teacher expectations of girls in science, the nature of classroom interactions, and the need to change science to make it more attractive to people, in general, and particularly to girls. There are distinctions between girl-friendly science, science packaged to be more friendly to girls, feminine science that demands a change in the classroom to place more emphasis on caring and cooperation, and feminist science that values science for personal development, adopting a more subjective and holistic approach to the natural world, and not privileging science over other forms of knowledge. This book offers a range of materials from philosophical debates to methods of intervention.

—INGRID BARTSCH

See also Mathematics: Teaching to Women; Pedagogy, Feminist

Science: Women as Subject of

Caplan, Paula J., and Jeremy B. Caplan, *Thinking Critically about Research on Sex and Gender,* New York: HarperCollins, 1994

Gilligan, Carol, *In a Different Voice: Psychological Theory and Women's Development,* Cambridge, Massachusetts: Harvard University Press, 1982

Harding, Sandra, *Whose Science? Whose Knowledge?: Thinking from Women's Lives,* Ithaca, New York: Cornell University Press, 1991

Keller, Evelyn Fox, and Helen E. Longino (eds.), *Feminism and Science,* Oxford and New York: Oxford University Press, 1996

Longino, Helen E., *Science as Social Knowledge: Values and Objectivity in Scientific Inquiry,* Princeton, New Jersey: Princeton University Press, 1990

Tavris, Carol, *The Mismeasure of Woman: Why Women Are Not the Better Sex, the Inferior Sex, or the Opposite Sex,* New York: Simon and Schuster, 1992

TAVRIS provides a wealth of fascinating information about the mismeasure of women by scientists. She includes a detailed account of much of the recent history of empirical research on women. Tavris's book is painstakingly accurate, comprehensive, and highly readable. Although less scholarly in tone than the other books discussed here, her research and discussion are solid. Some of the topics she covers include fables of female sexuality, premenstrual syndrome, and the problems with traditional classifications for mental illness. Her analysis of the strengths and weaknesses of Carol Gilligan's research on the moral development of girls and women is superb. One of the book's many highlights is the background she provides about the role that scientific politics has played in promoting the flawed research on sex differences in the brain. Tavris is a thorough researcher, a smooth writer, and a great wit.

Like Tavris, CAPLAN and CAPLAN provide a critical look at how sex differences are magnified, distorted, and in some cases manufactured by scientists. This pithy 125-page volume evaluates classic and contemporary research on the sexes. Caplan and Caplan discuss important flaws in research on women. They elaborate on how psychological myths (like the myth of women's masochism) have become reified over the years. The authors include 10 chapters critically examining such issues as mother-blame in therapy, the thin basis of the claim that males are superior in math and females are superior in verbal skills, and the flaws in hormone research. They raise awareness of how scientists' personal values may wittingly or unwittingly obfuscate logic and evidence in gender research. The most vital contribution of this volume is its instruction in how to become a more critical consumer of all gender research.

Like Caplan and Caplan's book, LONGINO's thoughtfully-titled volume identifies how social values influence scientific endeavors. Science, she writes, is influenced by the particular social and historical atmosphere in which it occurs. Her elegant discussion of how scientific endeavors have "degrees of objectivity" is illuminating. She critiques methodology and scientific models in a manner that engages the reader. Her incisive text includes analysis of vivid case examples. Her most unique and notable contribution is her philosophical analyses of the relation between social values and scientific inquiry. She discusses how the work of a number of philosophers (from Carl Gustav Hempel to Helmut Kuhn) informs this dialogue. For the majority of the book, Longino details many of the issues touched on by Caplan and Caplan. However, Longino's work highlights the role of social values in science and is more in-depth and inclusive of sciences besides psychology. A central theme of the book is her caution to all scientists: be aware of your social and political ideas and how these may influence your work. She pointedly states that replacing an androcentric bias with a feminist bias is anathema. She argues that scientists need to identify their political allegiances and consider how these commitments influence research topics, research methods, and interpretation of results. This sensible approach (which has been the norm for most feminist researchers) should be the first lesson in scientific training.

GILLIGAN's book has become a classic. Gilligan began with the noble premise of challenging Lawrence Kohlberg's measurement of moral development, which used the male as standard. She succeeded in drawing an enormous amount of attention to the androcentric bias of psychological measurement. This was no small feat, especially considering the popularity of Kohlberg's assessment, and how uninformed the populace had been about psychology's sexism. Gilligan first took issue with Kohlberg's finding that the highest rung on the moral ladder was abstract morality (characterized by pursuing ethical principles regardless of what other people think). Gilligan believed that this theory favored a "male-centered morality" and devalued the moral reasoning she believed was typical of females: favoring relationships with others over abstractions. Gilligan's work was an attempt to right the male-as-norm, female-as-deficient view of the sexes in psychology. Gilligan's voice had a powerful effect on sensitizing a broad audience to the fact that pioneers (like Jean Piaget and Sigmund Freud) and modern-day psychologists studied men, excluded women, and concluded that women were inferior morally, intellectually, and behaviorally. Her book has fascinating excerpts from many interviews with girls and women about morality. While Gilligan's thought-provoking work is roundly celebrated in popular feminist circles, it does have some drawbacks. She too often slips into language that generalizes and describes women one way (relationship-oriented) and men the other way (abstraction-oriented). A substantial number of feminist scientists have criticized Gilligan for asserting gender differences in morality based upon small samples of subjects (most of her studies have focused on fewer than 40 individuals). Another criticism is that Gilligan does not problematize the issue of gender. Perhaps the apparent gender differences in morality are not gender differences at all. It may be more parsimonious and correct to state that what she observes in her female subjects is solely due to status/power differences between men and women. Nonetheless, Gilligan's book is a thoughtful examination of the entrenched patriarchal attitudes in psychology.

The KELLER and LONGINO book is an edited collection of 17 carefully abridged essays on issues related to feminist critiques of science. The authors of the essays reveal the permeating effect of gender ideologies on scientific endeavors. While the essays are diverse, they have in common the goal of demonstrating how social hierarchy and social roles make all science a subjective endeavor. For this important lesson alone, these essays should be required reading of any student in the sciences. The essays address such varied and important issues as feminism and science, pretheoretical assumptions in evolutionary explanations of female sexuality, the role of values in science, and the scientific construction of a biological romance based on stereotypical male-female roles. Probably the most noteworthy aspect of this collection is that both science as a whole and individual sciences are astutely critiqued.

HARDING's book provides important missing components to the previously discussed works. Specifically, hers is the only book that incorporates a global feminist view into the critique of science dialogue. She includes perspectives of women of color, women of the Third World, and lesbian/bisexual women. Her book is the only one that discusses the role that the "labor and lives" of Third World people have had in advancing scientific knowledge and technology. She reminds the reader of how the scientific endeavor is warped without the perspectives of a wide variety of individuals. Harding's book is valuable because she provides a critique of both the androcentric and Eurocentric points of view of science. As she beautifully demonstrates, these biases have a synergistic effect. Understanding these biases individually and collectively makes the reader even more aware of how subjective science is, and how science's findings elevate those in power and subordinate those without power. She provides one of the best discussions of standpoint epistemologies (how historical and social conditions influence scientific questions, scientific methods, and the answers scientists "find") to date.

—KAROL MAYBURY

Sciences: Biological

Abir-Am, Pnina G., and Dorinda Outram (eds.), *Uneasy Careers and Intimate Lives: Women in Science 1789–1979,* New Brunswick, New Jersey: Rutgers University Press, 1987

Alic, Margaret, *Hypatia's Heritage: A History of Women in Science from Antiquity to the Nineteenth Century,* London: Women's Press, and Boston: Beacon Press, 1986

Grinstein, Louise S., Carol A. Biermann, and Rose K. Rose (eds.), *Women in the Biological Sciences: A Bibliographic Sourcebook,* Westport, Connecticut: Greenwood, 1997

Harding, Sandra G., *The Science Question in Feminism,* Milton Keynes: Open University Press, and Ithaca, New York: Cornell University Press, 1986

Hubbard, Ruth, *The Politics of Women's Biology,* New Brunswick, New Jersey: Rutgers University Press, 1990

Merchant, Carolyn, *The Death of Nature: Women, Ecology, and the Scientific Revolution,* San Francisco, Harper and Row, 1980; London: Wildwood House, 1982

———, *Earthcare: Women and the Environment,* New York: Routledge, 1996

Rossiter, Margaret W., *Women Scientists in America: Before Affirmative Action, 1940–1972,* Baltimore, Maryland: Johns Hopkins University Press, 1995

———, *Women Scientists in America: Struggles and Strategies to 1940,* Baltimore, Maryland: Johns Hopkins University Press, 1982

Schiebinger, Londa, *Nature's Body: Gender in the Making of Modern Science,* Boston: Beacon Press, 1993

Shepherd, Linda Jean, *Lifting the Veil: The Feminine Face of Science,* Boston: Shambhala, 1993

Challenging the value neutrality that many scientists claim for their disciplines is an important element in modern feminist theory. Several of the above books have been influential in drawing the attention of scholars to the hidden historical, social, and psychological roots of scientific knowledge. Some of these books deal specifically with how the ideologies of gender and science have shaped society's views of biological knowledge. Other authors wrote their books to remove the veil they see as masking the masculine face of science. With regard to the biological sciences, several writers want to show how the interaction of nature (historically treated as female) and science (historically dominated by males) has constituted the central metaphor of scientific discovery. Since ideas have consequences, there are several important results of the historical relationship between gender and science. Women interested in studying biology have, when compared to men, faced obstacles in getting an education. Once educated, these women have had to accept slower advancement in the few jobs open to them, restricted recognition for their accomplishments, and fewer supervisory and administrative opportunities. Most striking is the salary differential between men and women in the biological sciences, which increases with increasing educational level, academic and industrial rank, and seniority. Despite these and other obstacles, women continue to enter the biological sciences in increasing numbers, and there exists some evidence for small improvements in their status.

No book specifically detailing the history of the biological sciences has yet been written, but ALIC's history of women in science from prehistoric times to the end of the nineteenth century treats the natural sciences as an important part of her general account of female scientists during this period. For example, since botany was deemed a subject appropriate for women to study, women made contributions to this field, particularly as illustrators of scientific herbals and bestiaries. Because of these and other achievements of female naturalists, Alic calls botany "the female science."

The ABIR-AM and OUTRAM collection contains an essay specifically devoted to American female botanists, but the authors of other essays are also concerned with women's work in biology, for example, female ornithologists in the first half of the twentieth century, and women who played important roles in the development of molecular biology. The general goal of the Abir-Am and Outram book is to discover how certain women devised ways to combine intensive work in science with time for "family duties and pleasures." Indeed, one of their conclusions is that, for two centuries, science and family have, for women, been closely intertwined. They found science being done not only in laboratories, but also in kitchens and parlors. The lifestyles of female biologists described in the book are quite diverse, and the children of these families range from the fulfilled and happy to the neglected and resentful.

The GRINSTEIN, BIERMANN, and ROSE book contains specific biographical and bibliographical information on a larger number of female biologists from several different countries and time periods. The authors selected their subjects on the basis of their scientific achievements and leadership in their fields. In this massive reference work, entries consist of three sections: a biography, an assessment of the subject's scientific work, and a bibliography of works by and about the subject. Useful appendices also list the women by country of birth and field of interest.

ROSSITER's two volumes tell the story of the struggles of American women to become scientists from about 1820 to 1972. Women in the biological sciences are very much a part of this story, and she explores in great detail the career experiences of female botanists, plant pathologists, zoologists, biochemists, and entomologists in acquiring their education, obtaining employment in academia, industry, government, and participating in various professional organizations. Even though women in the biological sciences tended to outnumber women in the physical sciences, female biologists were also forced to accept the same partial acceptance into scientific work. This situation was not due to a lack of merit on the part of these women, but to discrimination both hierarchical (preventing the career advancement of women) and territorial (segregating women in low-prestige subfields).

SCHIEBINGER's book is more sharply focused than those of Alic and Rossiter. She restricted herself to eighteenth-century European natural historians, in order to discover how "the politics of participation" molds scientific knowledge. She feels strongly that who does science influences the kind of science that gets done. Natural history was popular in the eighteenth century, and it was also big business, since it was an essential part of Europe's commercial and colonial expansion. Schiebinger shows how gender actively shaped biological science. Although female naturalists existed, they were scarce, and natural history was dominated by men. Schiebinger believes that the biology created by these European males would have been vastly different had female naturalists done the collecting and classifying. Who was included (males) and who was excluded (females) determined what biological projects were pursued and whose observations were validated. Schiebinger thinks that the shortsightedness of these male naturalists harmed biology and, in the long run, resulted in a crippling loss of scientific knowledge.

MERCHANT, a historian of science, makes the biological sciences a central theme of her book (1980). Because males were the principal proponents of the Scientific Revolution of the sixteenth and seventeenth centuries, they devised a mechanical universe to suit their predilections. Since the earth was no longer seen as a nurturing mother, it became something to be exploited. The organicist conception of nature popular in the Middle Ages (God's creation, ensouled and alive) was, in the sixteenth century, inappropriate for new experimental methods and practical applications. When male scientists replaced the earth-centered universe with the sun-centered one, they also replaced a woman-centered world with a man-centered one. Merchant is thus able to interconnect ecology and women's issues, a theme that is also extensively developed in her book (1995) on "earthcare," which explores the historical connections of woman and nature and relates this to the role of women in the environmental movement. Her study reveals the positive and negative ways in which both women and nature have been constructed over time by science and society, and she concludes that gendering nature as female (for example, as in the Gaia hypothesis) is at present too problematical to be useful in emancipatory movements.

HARDING believes that earlier feminist critiques of science have not gone far enough in envisioning a gender-free science. The biological sciences are very much a part of her argument, since she thinks that masculine bias pervades the life sciences in a specific way. For example, she discusses the arguments of male biologists that their studies of biological sex differences, the evolution of various animals, and human neuroendocrinology make a powerful case for biologically determined sex roles. She tries to show that androcentric assumptions permeate these studies. To replace this old androcentric science, she wants a new science that will accept people with different backgrounds who will then conceive of the natural world in different ways. She does not want a "woman's science." She seeks an end to androcentrism, not to systematic inquiry. Some critics do not think Harding's arguments for a new science are convincing, but they believe that she may have provided the conceptual tools necessary for designing such a science in the future.

Such feminists as HUBBARD suggest that the category of "sex differences" is a "fabrication supported by sexism," and in her book she tries to reconceptualize biology in order to expose male scientists' hidden prejudices and ideologies. Hubbard, a biologist, believes that nature is part of history and culture, and not the other way around. Biological facts have been expounded mostly by white, economically privileged males, and their background explains why, for example, DNA's operation in cells have been interpreted as hierarchic, mechanistic, and reductionist. Unless things are changed, these ideas will continue to characterize these scientists' mechanistic approach to women's role in the reproduction of life. In the past, biologists presented their science as separate from society in order to obscure its close relationship to political power, but she believes that biology, a social construct, is profoundly political in its power to tell all of us, men and women, what is natural and what is human.

SHEPHERD, whose background is biochemistry, also spent time studying Jungian psychology, and this training informs her discussion of the ways in which qualities associated with "the feminine principle" can help to change both male and female scientists and even science itself. Like many of her feminist colleagues, Shepherd thinks that the language and metaphors of traditional science reflect the masculine idea of objective, rational, logical, and linear understanding, whereas the subjective, emotional, intuitive, and holistic understanding associated with the feminine ideal has been subordinated, undervalued, and denigrated. As examples she uses the modern molecular biological picture of DNA's functioning, which, many scientists claim, is responsible for all we are as human beings. However, Shepherd points out that when a human being is reduced to molecules, the person's essence is lost. Similarly, she shows that Darwin's brutal view of nature as inherently competitive and warlike led scientists to neglect examples of the harmonious cooperation that characterizes the relations of many living things. Her goal is to make science into a force for truth, freedom, and creativity for all human beings. She believes that feminism can bring about a transformation of science. All human beings, both male and female, can build cooperative networks based on curiosity, trust, and love.

—ROBERT J. PARADOWSKI

See also Biological Determinism; Ecofeminism; Franklin, Rosalind, and the DNA Controversy; Medical History; Nature; Reproductive Technologies; Scientists

Sciences: Physical

Alic, Margaret, *Hypatia's Heritage: A History of Women in Science from Antiquity to the Late Nineteenth Century,* London: Women's Press, and Boston: Beacon Press, 1986

Gornick, Vivian, *Women in Science: Portraits from a World in Transition,* New York: Simon and Schuster, 1983

Grinstein, Louise S., Rose K. Rose, and Miriam H. Rafailovich (eds.), *Women in Chemistry and Physics: A Biobibliographic Sourcebook,* Westport, Connecticut: Greenwood, 1993

Kass-Simon, G., and Patricia Farnes (eds.), *Women of Science: Righting the Record,* Bloomington: Indiana University Press, 1990

Keller, Evelyn Fox, *Reflections on Gender and Science,* New Haven, Connecticut, and London: Yale University Press, 1985

Hanson, Sandra L., *Lost Talent: Women in the Sciences,* Philadelphia: Temple University Press, 1996

Mattfeld, Jacquelyn A., and Carel G. Van Aken (eds.), *Women and the Scientific Professions: The M.I.T. Symposium on American Women in Science and Engineering,* Cambridge, Massachusetts: MIT Press, 1965

Rossiter, Margaret W., *Women Scientists in America: Before Affirmative Action, 1940–1972,* Baltimore, Maryland: Johns Hopkins University Press, 1995

———, *Women Scientists in America: Struggles and Strategies to 1940,* Baltimore, Maryland: Johns Hopkins University Press, 1982

Wertheim, Margaret, *Pythagoras' Trousers: God, Physics, and the Gender Wars,* New York: Times Books, 1995; London: Fourth Estate, 1997

Zuckerman, Harriet, Jonathan R. Cole, and John T. Bruer (eds.), *The Outer Circle: Women in the Scientific Community,* New York: Norton, 1991

Because of the male dominance of the physical sciences throughout most of their history, the role of women in the development of these sciences has been largely neglected. With the growth of the feminist movement, particularly since the 1960s, scholars have begun to investigate the topic of women in science, and the items on the above list reflect this new interest. Several of these studies treat the subject of women in the physical sciences as part of the general issue of women in science, but some are principally dedicated to the analysis of the achievements and difficulties of women in such physical sciences as physics and chemistry. Some scholars investigate this subject historically, others use a sociological approach, and still others use the personal essay. A common theme throughout these analyses is the gradual increase in the numbers and influence of women in the physical sciences, but with a cautionary warning that serious problems remain, for example, the under-representation of women in the upper echelons of industry and academia.

Although such women as Hypatia and Marie Curie had been discussed, albeit briefly, in traditional histories of science, male scientists were the prime focus, and ALIC felt that these histories neglected many female scientists, and that their few discussions of the accomplishments of female scientists were done "in a masculinist way." To rectify this distorted view, Alic's history of western science deals mainly with women, especially those who worked in astronomy, physics, chemistry, geology, and other physical sciences, for example, the astronomer Caroline Herschel and Mary Somerville, "The Queen of Nineteenth-Century Science," whose book on "the connexion of the physical sicences" went through several editions.

ROSSITER's two volumes tracing the experiences of female scientists in America from the beginning to 1972 contain extensive analyses of female astronomers, physicists, geologists, and chemists, although she also discusses women in other fields. Her well-documented study deals with the various types of discrimination that women encountered, resulting in their segregation into certain fields that were unpopular with men, and their restriction to less prestigious positions in their professional advancement. During World War II, female scientists' participation in higher education, professional organizations, and industry dramatically increased, but in the postwar period male dominance reasserted itself. A theme in Rossiter's discussions in both volumes is that patriarchal structures in such American institutions as universities and government agencies erected barriers that subordinated and frustrated women. Despite these obstacles, female physicists and chemists continued to grow in numbers and professional stature.

In contrast to the historical approach of Alic and Rossiter, the symposium edited by MATTFELD and VAN AKEN is dedicated to investigating problems confronting female scientists and engineers in the 1960s, with the goal of helping these women to separate the mythical from the actual difficulties they might encounter. The symposium attracted such distinguished speakers as Bruno Bettelheim, Erik Erikson, Lillian Gilbreth, and James R. Killian, Jr., and the analyses provided by these and other scholars give an interesting description of the problems women faced in entering the physical sciences at a time when the modern feminist movement was just beginning.

GORNICK's book, which explores the emotional, intellectual, and professional experiences of women struggling for opportunity and recognition in various fields of science, uses a number of secondary sources and interviews with scientists to delineate the complex environment of modern science, which often promotes so much self-doubt and anxiety in women that it hinders them from fulfilling their true potential. Her interview with the Nobel Prize-winning physicist I.I. Rabi is revelatory (he feels that because of "their nervous systems," women "will never do great science.") Gornick, on the other hand, sees science in transition to a new era in which women will be able "to succeed in their scientific work while retaining their full humanity and individuality as women."

In contrast to Gornick, KELLER believes that female scientists are made, not born. Keller, who was initially trained as a physicist, uses the experiences of several physical scientists to examine a scientific culture that she sees as saturated with the "norms of masculinity." She explores the question of what science would be like if subjectivity, feeling, and the understanding of nature as organism (views traditionally characterized as "female") replaced objectivity, reason, and the understanding of nature as mechanism (views that have characterized male-dominated science). This male conception of science, Keller believes, has made it impossible for female scientists to succeed in their struggle for equal treatment, but she does not want to replace a "masculine science" by a "female science." Rather, she wants a science characterized not by gender, but by an approach that encourages "diverse conceptions of mind and nature."

In the volume edited by ZUCKERMAN, COLE, and BRUER, the editors and other authors explore the question of why female scientists, despite significant increases in their numbers, have not acquired anything close to parity with men in research opportunities. Their sociological study also investigates such questions as why women publish only about half as much as their comparable male peers. Their conclusion is that an alien male environment creates barriers to success throughout a female scientist's career.

GRINSTEIN, ROSE, and RAFAILOVICH take advantage not only of recent increases in the number of women in the physical sciences, but also of three centuries of achievement by women in these fields, to provide a biobibliographic sourcebook that will be useful for both established scholars and women seeking information about careers and career models in the physical sciences. The editors selected female physicists and chemists on the basis of such criteria as innovative research, quantity and quality of scientific publications, and leadership in professional societies. Entries, which are alphabetically arranged, have three sections: a biography, an account and assessment of the scientist's important discoveries, and a bibliography of primary and secondary sources.

The KASS-SIMON and FARNES book originated from the observation that the standard histories and biographical reference works contained a paucity of information about female scientists. Was this because female scientists had produced little of importance? To answer this question, the editors called upon prominent female scientists to investigate the achievements of women in their disciplines. A substantial portion of the book is devoted to describing the accomplishments of women in geology, astronomy, physics, chemistry, and crystallography, leading to the conclusion that women in the physical sciences have actually produced much of genuine importance.

WERTHEIM's sociocultural study of science attempts to explain the exclusion of women from the sciences throughout history as a direct consequence of science's long association with religion. She sees male scientists as "high priests" who have repeatedly compaigned against women's advancement in physics, her discipline of focus. Her attempt to tie the church to women's exclusion from science met with considerable criticism from reviewers of her book.

HANSON, a sociologist, asks a different question from previous writers about women in the physical sciences. She asks not why they were excluded from science, but why so many talented young women leave science once they have embarked on their careers. The recovery of this "lost talent" is the central concern of her book. The dominant image is the pipeline leading from elementary and high school through undergraduate, graduate, and postgraduate education into the scientific positions in academia, government, and industry. This pipeline "leaks women" at all stages, and the reasons for this are quite complex. Women's experiences in science are not "snapshot events" that can be frozen in time; therefore it is necessary that scholars follow aspiring female scientists over time to capture the dynamics of their experiences. Hanson believes that the "gender effect" remains powerful in the sciences. Families, schools, government agencies, and industries continue to view science as a male preserve. Not until members of these institutions become convinced of the real value of both genders to the advancement of science will a qualified and creative workforce be achieved.

—ROBERT J. PARADOWSKI

See also Technology; Scientists; Geography

Science Studies, Feminist

Haraway, Donna, *Simians, Cyborgs, and Women: The Reinvention of Nature,* New York: Routledge, and London: Free Association, 1991

Harding, Sandra, *Whose Science? Whose Knowledge?: Thinking from Women's Lives,* Ithaca, New York: Cornell University Press, 1991

Keller, Evelyn Fox, *Reflections on Gender and Science,* New Haven, Connecticut and London: Yale University Press, 1985

Keller, Evelyn Fox, and Helen Longino (eds.), *Feminism and Science,* Oxford and New York: Oxford University Press, 1996

Schiebinger, Londa, *The Mind Has No Sex?: Women in the Origins of Modern Science,* Cambridge, Massachusetts, and London: Harvard University Press, 1989

Traweek, Sharon, *Beamtimes and Lifetimes: The Word of High Energy Physicists,* Cambridge, Massachusetts: Harvard University Press, 1988; London: 1992

Over the last two decades, feminist scholars have created a rich framework in which to understand the institution of science, the scientific method, knowledge construction, and the role of male and female scientists within a larger cultural and political context. This growing interdisciplinary field, named feminist science studies (including works from the social studies of science and the cultural studies of science) shifts from an understanding of science as an objective and value-free enterprise to one that is socially constructed. The field includes the work of scientists (who critique the inadequacy of some scientific work as bad science and bad scientific practice), historians (who document the history of women in science, recovering forgotten female scientists and highlighting the systematic exclusion of women from scientific pursuits), sociologists (who describe the social organization and development of the institution of science and scientific knowledge construction), anthropologists (who explore social relations in scientific culture), literary critics (who explore language in science and science as narrative), and philosophers (who examine the epistemologies of science). While the individual scholars might employ disciplinary or interdisciplinary approaches, this body of work carefully documents how science has not been and is not "value-neutral," and how it has continued to serve the interests of the socially and politically powerful. It also explores how science has historically been dominated and shaped by men and "masculine" ideals, and as a result the contemporary institution and culture of science reflects that history.

KELLER is a very important figure in feminist science studies, and in this ground-breaking work she sketches out the project of gender and science in three sections: historical, psychological, and scientific/philosophical. By exploring the historical role of Plato and Francis Bacon in the development of modern science, and by careful analysis of language, Keller documents how science developed during the sixteenth century into a "masculine" enterprise committed to a project of studying nature by dominating "her." Using object relations theory (which explores the relationship between cognitive and affective processes) she stresses the importance of understanding issues of objectivity, power, and knowledge in science. In her essay on theories of aggregation in cellular slime mold, she cautions how we might read into nature frameworks that seem familiar to us in our times. Her essay on Barbara McClintock suggests an alternate vision of science as one driven by "a feeling for the organism."

LONGINO and KELLER have put together an important collection of essays. The writers include some of the most influential figures in feminist science studies, and the essays represent a diverse range of approaches and disciplines. The introduction by the editors is a good introduction to feminist science studies and locates the essays and essayists within the larger field, naming and elaborating how and what various approaches contribute to the project of feminism and science.

SCHIEBINGER, a historian, sketches out the contribution of women to the development of early modern science. She does the important task of recovering the forgotten contribution of women in science during this period, and of exploring how women maneuvered within the gender boundaries prescribed by society. In addition, she documents how cultural meanings of femininity and masculinity (that is, gender) became embedded in scientific readings of "women's nature" and were used to argue against the participation of women in science, thus showing us how historical forces systematically excluded women from science. Although the book focuses on the origin of modern science, this work helps our understanding of how science is shaped by social forces and how that history shapes contemporary science.

HARDING, a philosopher, sketches the project of feminism and science by asking the basic question of who creates science and who that knowledge serves. This is an accessible book, especially the section on feminist philosophy of science (here she elaborates her notion of "strong objectivity" as a more rigorous version of scientific objectivity). In this book she stresses that in order to understand the development of western science, we need simultaneously to understand the erasure and marginalization of other forms of knowledge (for example, indigenous forms in "other" cultures and peoples) and that feminist movements must influence and be influenced by other liberatory movements.

HARAWAY approaches the study of science by treating scientific texts as stories, using literary analysis to explore the creation of meanings of nature, living organisms, and cyborgs (cybernetic organisms: systems that embrace organic and technological components). Her "A Cyborg Manifesto" has become a cult classic. Rather than dismissing technology as a masculine project antithetical to feminism, she uses the cyborg (where nature and culture are reworked) as a way out of the maze of dualisms (machine/organism, male/female, self/other, mind/body) and as a site for a progressive politics. A second essay on "situated knowledges" in this volume makes an important contribution to feminist epistemologies of science.

TRAWEEK, an anthropologist, studies the elite and elusive world of high energy physicists. While physicists claim to have no culture, no mutually agreed upon rules of social relations, Traweek describes this "culture of no culture" as a community of mythmakers. This book weaves together a fascinating story of physicists by exploring their lab spaces, how physicists train new physicists, social relations within the community (hierarchies of countries, universities, labs, and experimentalists/theorists). This anthropological exploration paints a coherent picture of the culture of science and how it reproduces itself generation after generation.

—BANU SUBRAMANIAM

Scientists

Gabor, Andrea, *Einstein's Wife: Work and Marriage in the Lives of Five Great Twentieth-Century Women*, New York: Viking, 1995

Keller, Evelyn Fox, *A Feeling for the Organism*, San Francisco: W.H. Freeman, 1983

McGrayne, Sharon Bertsch, *Nobel Prize Women in Science: Their Lives, Struggles, and Momentous Discoveries*, New York: Carol, 1993

Sime, Ruth Lewin, *Lise Meitner: A Life in Physics*, Berkeley: University of California Press, 1996

Sonnert, Gerhard, and Gerald Holton, *Who Succeeds in Science: The Gender Dimension*, New Brunswick, New Jersey: Rutgers University Press, 1995

Stille, Darlene, *Extraordinary Women Scientists*, Chicago: Children's Press, 1995

Wadsworth, Ginger, *Rachel Carson, Voice for the Earth*, Minneapolis, Minnesota: Lerner, 1992

Only recently have historians began to compile the accomplishments of female scientists. These efforts are largely the result of the women's movement of the late 1960s when women began to realize their own inferior status in many fields of business, industry, and academia. In science, people began to ask: Were so few scientific achievements attributed to women because so few women had participated in science? Or, had women failed to receive acknowledgement for their achievements in science? Fortunately, much of the research revealed the latter condition, and we now have a relatively large resource base about the lives of female scientists.

Often, the female scientists we read about are those who have achieved exceptional status within their scientific disciplines. The book by McGRAYNE fits this model by providing biographical sketches of 14 women, eight of whom were awarded Nobel Prizes. The book begins by asking why so few women have been awarded Nobel Prizes (only nine of over 300, although this number has risen to 10 since the book was published) and goes on to examine the lives and achievements of the women. The stories portray the struggles against gender discrimination faced by female scientists, both as students of science and as researchers, as well as the personal sides of the women as they raised families and became political and religious leaders. Although they come from different disciplines and lived during different periods, these women share a love for science itself and a passionate determination to succeed.

Keller and Sime continue to explore the lives of famous female scientists but do so for only one individual each. KELLER discusses Barbara McClintock, a geneticist whose insight into and understanding of genetic organization was far ahead of those of her contemporaries. She often worked alone and developed ideas about (corn) chromosomes that made little sense to her colleagues in the 1940s and 1950s but that later became cornerstones in molecular biology. Her ideas were eventually recognized in 1983 when she received the Nobel Prize.

Lise Meitner, discussed by SIME, was not awarded a Nobel Prize, although her male partner did receive this recognition for the project she initiated. Like McClintock, Meitner's work was critically important, and equally revolutionary, in physics: she determined that atomic nuclei can be split. Unlike McClintock, Meitner worked in collaboration with a number of physicists, both in Europe and then in the United States. Meitner, along with other Jewish scientists, was forced to leave Europe during the Second World War.

Rachel Carson was a zoologist, perhaps better known for her writing and work as an environmentalist. Several biographies have been written about her, and her books, *The Sea Around Us* and *Silent Spring*, continue to be classics. WADSWORTH presents a complete story of Carson's life, from her early work as an author for the school newspaper, to her research to document the effects of DDT, to her personal bouts with cancer. Rachel Carson was one of the most influential people of this century, educating people about the environment through her books.

GABOR profiles the lives of five twentieth-century women, including scientists Mileva Maric Einstein and Maria Goeppert Mayer, both physicists. It is both interesting and important that these women be placed alongside women such as Sandra Day O'Connor, because it provides them with a legitimacy that they might not otherwise receive. Einstein fell under the shadow of her more famous husband, who had little sympathy for the difficulties she faced as a scientist who was also a mother. Mayer explored the idea that the atomic nucleus was organized into the shells and valencies, a concept now taught and supported in chemistry. She also raised two children and, although her research was extraordinary, she was unable to get a job that paid her until shortly before winning the Nobel Prize in 1963.

Not all female scientists are recognized for their work, and STILLE presents the biographies of both famous and less-known women in her book. She addresses the book to young women, stating that "these scientists are role models for today's young women." Indeed, role models are important motivators, providing an image of science that girls and women in science can pursue. All of the women in this book can be role models for girls and women who wish to pursue a career in the physical or natural sciences. Each biographical sketch is concise, one to three pages, and often a photograph is provided.

SONNERT and HOLTON present a very different approach to scientists, one that recounts the detailed career paths of male and female scientists, with a particular emphasis on women. The twenty participants in the study were questioned about gender influence in their careers. The women noted lack of mentorship and direction and lack of access to both professional and social networks. This type of information is important for those wishing to pursue a career in science, because it alerts them to the gender biases that persist in the physical and natural sciences and allows them to make decisions about their own lives. Their success will depend, in large part, on how well they meet the criteria of "success" and how much they are willing to tolerate to become successful.

—INGRID BARTSCH

See also Franklin, Rosalind, and the DNA Controversy; Inventors

Sculpture

Fine, Elsa Honig, *Women and Art: A History of Women Painters and Sculptors from the Renaissance to the 20th Century*, Montclair, New Jersey: Allanheld and Schram, and London: Prior, 1978

Kasson, Joy S., *Marble Queens and Captives: Women in Nineteenth-Century American Sculpture*, New Haven, Connecticut: Yale University Press, 1990

Kleiner, Diana E.E., and Susan B. Matheson (eds.), *I, Claudia: Women in Ancient Rome*, New Haven, Connecticut: Yale University Art Gallery, 1996

Rubinstein, Charlotte Streifer, *American Women Sculptors: A History of Women Working in Three Dimensions*, Boston: G.K. Hall, 1990

Schmoll, Josef Adolf, *Auguste Rodin and Camille Claudel*, Munich: Prestel-Verlag, 1994

Slatkin, Wendy, *Women Artists in History: From Antiquity to the 20th Century*, Englewood Cliffs, New Jersey: Prentice-Hall, 1985

Women have been the object of sculptors' carvings for thousands of years. Although they have been and always will be objects of art, women were, for the most part, not taken seriously as artists or sculptors themselves until the nineteenth century. Before that time social, cultural, and economic restrictions prevented most women from any professional endeavor. Therefore, most chronicling of the history of female sculptors, for all intents and purposes, does not start until the mid- to late 1800s. Two elements make up the study of sculpture as it is related to women: women in sculpture as the primary inspiration for most works of art, and women as sculptors and artists themselves.

KLEINER and MATHESON look at women as viewed through Roman art, from empress to slave. Roman women had power through their husbands, and with this association, they commissioned works of art that both utilized and depicted women in everyday life. The virtues of Roman society were embodied in the ideal of womanhood as depicted in Roman art. Roman women were not only instrumental in the development of art, but in the practice as well. Although most ancient artists remained anonymous, the most famous within Rome was thought by scholars to have been a woman. Ancient sculpture cannot be fully appreciated unless one understands the context in which it was created. This includes not only the locale, but the purpose of the creation as well. These works of art were inseparable from their purpose or function and from the lives, towns, and residences in which they were placed.

KASSON examines nineteenth-century images of women as objects of sculpture. The nineteenth-century concept of sculpture idealized women as fragile, protected, and helpless. This ideal was occurring ironically at the same time women started working toward expanding legal and political rights. These conflicting concepts created tensions between the elements of domesticity and desire, best depicted in Hiram Power's *The Greek Slave*—a work of the best-known American sculptor of the mid-nineteenth century.

Demographic, cultural, and economic factors have historically influenced the availability and ability of female artists. SLATKIN notes that the nineteenth century marked an increase in women moving toward the forefront of artistic achievement, because these factors started to become more favorable. It was not until the nineteenth century that women were allowed to become apprentices. Slatkin moves the reader through each epoch, from the oldest known sculpture *(Venus of Willendorf)* to the post-World War II era. A threshold was crossed when a group of female sculptors settled in Rome in the last quarter of the 1800s and became known as the "White Marmorean Flock." They established the foundation for women becoming recognized and respected as professional sculptors. Of this group, Harriet Hosmer became the most famous, particularly for her *Zenolia in Chains*, which created a standard within the neoclassocial style. Slatkin continues by highlighting the most important female sculptors of the twentieth century. Of these, perhaps Germaine Rithier and England's Barbara Hayworth are the most influential. Both employed abstract style and surrealism in their works. Louise Nevelsen, perhaps the most innovative twentieth-century female sculptor, developed the methodology to create large scale or monumental sculpture.

RUBINSTEIN confines her studies to American female sculptors, tracing their history from its neoclassical roots to modernism and the renaissance of black artists. She delights over the quality and quantity of female artists' products on display throughout the country. From Maya Lin's *National Vietnam Veterans Memorial Wall* to public sculptures in small town America, the author chronicles the depth, complexity, and broad spectrum of artwork created by women. However, Rubinstein feels the public acceptance of female sculptors peaked during the suffrage movement of the 1920s and 1930s and has since declined in comparison to male artists of the same period. Her goal appears to be to include as many female artists as she can within the confines of the periods she defines, and particularly within the scope of the overall text.

FINE tracks the history of female artists from the Renaissance to the twentieth century. Like Slatkin and Rubinstein, she divides her text into the chronological periods of artistic development. However, Fine sets the tone for her review by lamenting over the lack of great contemporary female artists compared to earlier periods of art. Outstanding historical figures include Anne Seymour Damer, the most important female sculptor in England until the twentieth century. Elisabet Ney came from Bavaria to Texas and pioneered art development in that state. She worked in isolation from the outside world and so preserved the outdated neoclassical tradition. Edmonia Lewis was one of the "White Marmorean Flock" although she was part black and American Indian. Her best known works involved studies representing her cultural heritage.

No review of female sculptors would be complete without an analysis of the life of Camille Claudel. As a recognized sculptor in her own right, she was overshadowed by her mentor and lover Auguste Rodin. She left a small body of work scattered about, fragmented in total just as were her own later years. SCHMOLL's book sees her life as a tragedy representing the struggle of all female artists over the decades. She relied on Rodin for everything, and in the end he cast her aside. After their breakup, both professionally and personally, she drew inside herself, foregoing her art, and spent her remaining years in an insane asylum. She was completely dependent on her benefactor, a man who was responsible for her greatest triumphs and her deepest misery. Just now are her accomplishments being seen in a light outside of the shadows cast by the dominance of Rodin.

—GARY D. CRANE

Secretaries *see* Clerical Work

Self-Defense

Atkinson, Linda, *Women in the Martial Arts: A New Spirit Rising,* New York: Dodd Mead, 1983

Brewer, James D., *The Danger from Strangers: Confronting the Threat of Assault,* New York and London: Insight, 1994

Caignon, Denise, and Gail Groves (eds.), *Her Wits about Her: Self-Defense Success Stories by Women,* New York: Perennial Library, 1987; London: Women's Press, 1989

Sugano, Jun, *Basic Karate for Women: Health and Self Defense,* Tokyo and New York: Trans Pacific, 1976

Violence against women is one factor in the growing wave of alarm about violence in society. BREWER has taken a positive approach to writing about methods to help women reduce their exposure to violence. This book is full of facts and figures supported by Brewer's analysis. There are exercises to help the reader prepare to confront potentially dangerous circumstances. Brewer guides readers through discussions about who the criminals are and what they look for in a victim. The author provides guidance for community-based support groups in order to put a stop to victimization, hoping to deliver a clear message to the reader that violence is not inevitable, and one can do something about it. This book can serve as a supplemental reference in schools, colleges, and service organizations. It was published just after the passage of the "Brady Bill" by the U.S. Congress.

CAIGNON and GROVES have compiled a book written by women who have faced violence. It is the story of how women have fought back. This book begins with women who were attacked during childhood. Part II deals with women fighting back with words. Parts III through V talk about women who maneuver and fight for self-protection. Women talk about how they have worked with others in self-defense. Finally, the book contains a cornucopia of self-defense tactics. This book is designed to teach and inspire. The authors give readers insight into the minds and actions of attackers. The work also shows how women can successfully defend themselves if they think clearly. One of the basic premises here is that women can fight back and feel proud of themselves for what they did instead of guilty about the things they did not do. This is a book about ordinary women from many cultures around the world, who used a variety of self-defense tactics and survived.

For most of history, women did not (and could not) take advantage of what the martial arts had to offer. ATKINSON's book profiles eight contemporary women who are among the most accomplished martial artists. She talks about their pioneering efforts, classes, and competitions in the martial arts. The book discusses why these women became involved in the martial arts. Some were drawn to study their particular fighting skills by temperament or need, while others came somewhat by accident, feeling timid and ill-suited. The book also discusses more than simply the "art" of martial arts, but martial arts as a means of self-defense for women.

SUGANO's book contains all the basic karate techniques that a woman needs to know. Also included are applications of the techniques to specific situations where self-defense is called for, and exercises related to karate practice, which are excellent for developing the body and maintaining health. This book is completely illustrated in simple step-by-step sequence; the techniques are the ones most commonly used in this art of self-defense. The author stresses stability, balance, and the application of power. Considering a variety of situations in which a woman may be attacked, the author indicates the response to each situation. From these, the reader can imagine other situations and the applications of the basics to them. This is a simple, easy-to-follow guide that will be valuable to women who want to know more about self-defense.

—SUSAN M. TAYLOR

Self-Esteem

Bordo, Susan, *Unbearable Weight: Feminism, Western Culture, and the Body,* Berkeley: University of California Press, 1993; London: University of California Press, 1995

Boyd, Julia A., *In the Company of My Sisters: Black Women and Self-Esteem,* New York: Dutton, 1993

hooks, bell, *Sisters of the Yam: Black Women and Self-Recovery,* London: Turnaround, and Boston: South End Press, 1993

Hyman, Jane Wegscheider, and Esther R. Rome, *Sacrificing Our Selves for Love: Why Women Compromise Health and Self-Esteem— and How to Stop,* Freedom, California: Crossing Press, 1996

Orenstein, Peggy, *Schoolgirls: Young Women, Self-Esteem, and the Confidence Gap,* New York: Doubleday, 1994

Rapping, Elayne, *The Culture of Recovery: Making Sense of the Self-Help Movement in Women's Lives,* Boston: Beacon Press, 1996

Sadker, Myra, and David Sadker, *Failing at Fairness: How America's Schools Cheat Girls*, New York: Scribner, 1994
Sanford, Linda Tschirhart, and Mary Ellen Donovan, *Women and Self-Esteem: Understanding and Improving the Way We Feel and Think about Ourselves*, Garden City, New York: Anchor Press/Doubleday, 1984
Saussy, Carroll, *God Images and Self-Esteem: Empowering Women in a Patriarchal Society*, Louisville, Kentucky: Westminster/John Knox Press, 1991

In the past few decades of the recent feminist movement, one of the central discussion topics to appear continuously is self-esteem. One of the most fundamental books on the subject has been written by SANFORD and DONOVAN. Their text aims directly at women, providing much practical advice. They begin their work with the premise that how individual women view and live their personal lives affects women as a community. In detail, they discuss every facet of a woman's life: family, childhood, education, friendship, religion, career, and more. Each section concludes with "Blueprints for Change," which offers questions and exercises to guide women in reflecting upon their own lives, finding the areas they want to change, and actually enacting these changes. In their view, such acts empower individual women, in addition to helping women as a community both personally and politically.

Studies of female self-esteem often focus on girls as they participate in the educational process. SADKER and SADKER have been studying women in education since their own graduate school days in the late 1960s. Originally, they planned for this book to focus on textbooks and their representation of gender issues. However, they extended their study to include an analysis both of how teachers treat children and children regard each other, after noticing the attention and preferential treatment that boys and men continually received. After years of study, they had collected field notes and data from hours of observations at elementary, middle, and high schools, and colleges. The resulting book relates stories of girls and women who continually feel a lack of support in their schools.

ORENSTEIN deals with similar issues. She responds directly to the influential study by the American Association of University Women that determined the importance of adolescence in the development of a woman's self-esteem. To analyze the results of this report herself, Orenstein conducted a long-term study in 1992 of girls in the eighth grade at two schools. Through interviews and observations of classrooms, athletic fields, and other sites at the schools, she discovered articulate and insightful girls of diverse races and classes who downplayed their own academic achievement, suffered from eating disorders, and expressed desires to join a gang.

With a strong background in the deeply complex academic theories of feminism and post-structuralism, BORDO offers an intense study on representations of women's bodies. She looks, for example, at magazine advertisements for exercise clubs, dolls, spring water, food, eye shadow, and other products to connect visual symbols and characters to societal attitudes. Chapters on eating disorders and the singer Madonna explore a range of issues that intersect in their vital emphasis on how women relate to the bodies they inhabit.

HYMAN and ROME also write about body image, but in a way that offers more practical advice that women can use in their daily lives. They focus on the actual health hazards that can result from a woman's search for love and acceptance. Women can risk their health in the need to be liked, to find love, and to grasp approval. For example, the authors discuss what women go through to change their looks with dieting and cosmetic surgery. Staying in abusive relationships and putting oneself at risk for diseases like AIDS are also topics that are covered in some detail.

Taking an approach between the academic theories of Bordo and the practical advice of Hyman and Rome, RAPPING centers on the "industry" of the contemporary recovery movement. She watched numerous television talk shows such as Oprah, observed hours of 12-step program meetings including Overeaters Anonymous and Sex Addicts Anonymous, and read many self-help books. She connects the self-esteem issues in these and other media forms with the goals of the feminist movement in enhancing women's lives and fighting for their survival.

SAUSSY utilizes a somewhat different approach by specifically focusing on issues of faith and spirituality. She begins with a personal narrative, chronicling her early life in a family in which both parents suffered from self-esteem problems and a church-school system that inspired her to immerse herself in religious ideas and issues. Understanding that religion can both help and hurt women, she conducted interviews with 21 women connected to an east coast seminary. The women come from a variety of religions, ethnic backgrounds, and sexual identities. Still, Saussy does not intend to make general conclusions about women from these few interviews, but to offer a starting place for continued explorations. She discusses parent/child relationships, the various ways women conceptualize a deity, and the inter-connections between aspects of a woman's life and beliefs and how that affects self-esteem.

In recent years, several books narrow the focus to scrutinize the self-esteem issues prevalent in the lives of specific groups of women. BOYD focuses on African-American women. Like Saussy, she begins with her personal experience and explains how she learned early on that her life was different from those of the white girls she saw on television. However, unlike other studies, Boyd maintains her personal voice throughout the text. The purpose of this book is to present her search for identity, strength, and understanding, hoping that it helps other African-American women. Many of the ideas in the book arose out of monthly discussions with a close network of friends, her "sister circle" as she calls it. Their voices also appear in the story, and this personal perspective highlights the real, lived experience of women as they face these real issues.

HOOKS, one of the strongest voices in the contemporary feminist movement, also concentrates on African-American womanhood. Out of a respect for self-help literature and a belief that "academic" or analytical writing can reach beyond the scholarly audiences who generally read it, hooks conceptualizes this book as one of healing, as a map that can lead to the places of love that African-American women hold inside of them. She writes of literature, the act of writing, and discussions she has with family and friends. Her book will be one that others writing or talking about self-esteem will continuously refer to because of the power of hooks's voice and the ideas she encourages others to consider.

—NELS P. HIGHBERG

Separate Spheres

Cott, Nancy F., *The Bonds of Womanhood: "Women's Sphere" in New England, 1780–1835,* New Haven, Connecticut: Yale University Press, 1977

Fox-Genovese, Elizabeth, *Within the Plantation Household: Black and White Women in the Old South,* Chapel Hill and London: University of North Carolina Press, 1988

Guildford, Janet, and Suzanne Morton (eds.), *Separate Spheres: Women's World in the Nineteenth-Century Maritimes,* Fredericton, New Brunswick: Acadiensis Press, 1994

Harris, Barbara J., *Beyond Her Sphere: Women and the Professions in American History,* Westport, Connecticut: Greenwood, 1978

Rosenberg, Rosalind, *Beyond Separate Spheres: Intellectual Roots of Modern Feminism,* New Haven, Connecticut: Yale University Press, 1982

Smith-Rosenberg, Carroll, *Disorderly Conduct: Visions of Gender in Victorian America,* New York: Knopf, 1985

Historically, cultural conceptions of women have focused on theories of sexual difference. From the late eighteenth through the nineteenth centuries, the prevalent ideology of separate spheres influenced women's social, political, and cultural status. According to this theory, women belonged to the private sphere, which was concerned with domesticity and other personal issues. Men belonged to the public sphere and concentrated on social, political, and cultural concerns. Many feminist studies have focused on understanding separate spheres and women's experiences with this ideology. One of the most influential texts in women's history, COTT's book investigates women's sphere in New England during the late eighteenth and early nineteenth centuries. Rather than examine how women were oppressed by the concept of separate spheres, Cott discusses how they used the domestic sphere to form an empowering women's culture within an oppressive environment. Her purpose is to understand the formation of women's experience, and to provide a framework for the recovery and future interpretations of women's history. Using diaries and letters, Cott details how women viewed work, domesticity, education, religion, and sisterhood, and explores how the concept of womanhood derived from the experience of Northern women became a cultural ideal. This book is a standard text for research in women's history.

Another critical text essential to the study of women's sphere is that by SMITH-ROSENBERG. Smith-Rosenberg's collection of essays investigates the creation of the middle-class ideology in the nineteenth-century United States, and its influence on the lives of bourgeois women. Smith-Rosenberg examines the economic changes during the nineteenth century that led to the formation of the "Cult of True Womanhood" ideology, which limited women to a world of domestic concerns. The book delineates the political and cultural movements that alienated women from social power and how women responded to their shifting social position. Reprinted in this text, Smith-Rosenberg's influential article "The Female World of Love and Ritual" transforms many critical conceptions of nineteenth-century women's lives by examining women's friendships and how the domestic sphere created a women's culture. Smith-Rosenberg also explores women's disempowerment during the nineteenth century, arguing that separate spheres ideology made bourgeois woman an icon of cultural degradation. She offers powerful interpretations of nineteenth-century views of religion, sexuality, education, and medicine, which influenced, and were influenced by, the social construction of "woman."

To counter the narrow view of "women's culture" based exclusively on white, middle-class women in the North, FOX-GENOVESE offers an examination of black and white women in the ante-bellum American South, challenging the idea that a "women's culture" crossed racial and class distinctions. Using a Marxist-feminist approach, Fox-Genovese argues that the experience of black and white women in patriarchal society in the South differed greatly from that of other women, and therefore from what she defines as the accepted "women's experience" in women's history. Fox-Genovese argues that the social system based in slavery and patriarchal ideology "reinforced gender constraints," and that the distinct class divisions precipitated by the slave system led to a very different "women's culture." Complicating the conception of home and domesticity, Fox-Genovese articulates the extreme difference among the women of the "household" systems of the South, focusing on plantation households which included twenty or more slaves. Fox-Genovese challenges the ideal of a harmonious women's culture by examining the intimate relationships between female slaves and their female owners. She also discusses the distinct divisions among the planter/slaveholding class, yeoman farm women, and the poor white women of middle classes of southern towns. Fox-Genovese's book is an excellent source, which expands the historical conception of women's experience beyond the limits of previous studies.

Another departure from studies of women's sphere in the U.S. middle class is GUILDFORD and MORTON's book. This fascinating collection of essays examines women's sphere in the nineteenth-century Canadian Maritimes (Nova Scotia, Prince Edward Island, New Brunswick), and looks at how the ideology of separate spheres influenced women's personal experiences in these provinces. The essays analyze the political, legal, and social restrictions on women resulting from the ideology of separate spheres, and collectively argue, in opposition to Cott's analysis of empowerment, that this ideology had a negative impact on women. Investigating issues such as women's involvement in local and national politics, married women's property law, women's religious organizations, and African-Nova Scotia women, this text offers a broad spectrum of topics relating to the ideology of separate spheres. While not a complete historical study of women in the nineteenth-century Maritime Provinces, Guildford and Morton offer a compelling introduction to women's lives in Canada.

A more general study of separate spheres is offered by HARRIS. Detailing women's entrance into the world of professional work, Harris describes the lengthy European history of domestic ideology that formed the concept of separate spheres in the United States. Harris offers a general discussion of the cult of domesticity, and uses the ideology of separate spheres as a framework for her discussions of the women's suffrage movement, post-suffrage struggles, the influence of World War II, and the "New Feminism" of the 1960s and 1970s. This text is a good introduction to the history of the feminist movement in the United States.

Focusing on the challenges to the influential ideology of separate spheres, ROSENBERG offers a compelling history of the study of sex differences during the late nineteenth and early twentieth centuries. This book focuses on the scientific investigations concerning sexual difference and the efforts of women scientists to debunk the nineteenth-century sexist theories of women's sexual difference and "women's nature," which had influenced the political, social, and legal position of women. Rosenberg examines the early feminist social scientists who resisted standard interpretations of women's difference, and launched studies of cultural influences on women's identity, providing new theories and challenging claims about women's nature as prescribed in the ideology of separate spheres. This text specifically discusses Marion Talbot, Helen Bradford Thompson, Leta Stetter Hollingworth, Jessie Taft, Virginia Robinson, Elsie Clews Parsons, Clelia Duel Mosher, Mary Roberts Smith Coolidge, and Margaret Mead.

—AMY L. WINK

See also Cult of True Womanhood; Dual Labor Markets; Division of Labor by Sex; Victorian Era

Seton, Elizabeth Ann Bayley 1774–1821

American Nun and Saint

Barberey, Helen Bailly de, and Helene Roederer, *Elizabeth Seton,* translated and adapted by Rev. Joseph B. Code, New York: Macmillan, 1927; originally published as *Elizabeth Seton et les Commencements de l'Église Catholique aux États Unis,* Paris: Poussielgue, 1868

Dirvin, Joseph I., *Mrs. Seton, Foundress of the American Sisters of Charity,* New York: Farrar Straus, 1962

———, *The Soul of Elizabeth Seton: A Spiritual Portrait,* San Francisco: Ignatius Press, 1990

Laverty, Sister Rose Marie, *Loom of Many Threads: The English and French Influences on the Character of Elizabeth Ann Bayley Seton,* New York: Paulist Press, 1958

Melville, Annabelle M., *Elizabeth Bayley Seton, 1774–1821,* New York: Scribner, 1951

White, Charles I., *Life of Mrs. Eliza A. Seton,* New York: Edward Dunegan, 1853; as *Mother Seton: Mother of Many Daughters,* revised and edited by the Sisters of Charity, New York: Doubleday, 1949

The granddaughter of an Episcopalian rector, Elizabeth Seton was raised in that faith, but in 1805, after the death of her husband, and impressed by the Catholic faith she had witnessed in Italy, she and her five children became Catholics, in spite of family opposition. As a widow with no financial means, she at first relied on the generosity of relatives and friends to support her family. Later she ran a boarding house for boys attending a local school to provide for herself and her three daughters. When the boarding venture failed in 1808, she moved her family to Baltimore and established St. Joseph's Academy, a school for Catholic girls, in Emmitsburg, Maryland. Together with a few dedicated women, she founded the American Sisters of Charity. Not only was Elizabeth Seton a prolific correspondent during her adult life, but after moving to Emmitsburg, she spent many hours translating French religious works for the Sisters, since Catholic religious books were not available in the United States.

The first biographer of Elizabeth Seton, WHITE not only had access to her papers but also interviewed her two surviving children and other individuals who had known her in New York, Baltimore, and Emmitsburg. White's biography was popular enough during the nineteenth century to warrant many editions from different publishers, the last in 1904. In his first preface, White states: "In the construction of this narrative, I have quoted, whenever it was possible, Mrs. Seton's own words, in order to render it as much as possible an autobiography, and thus present a more lifelike portraiture of her character." The most complete version of her Italian journal (1803–4) is found only in White's first edition; subsequent editions omit the entries about her return trip to New York. Although he provided no documentation for his sources, a check of the original documents verifies his accurate transcriptions, an accuracy not always found in later biographies and collections. He does provide some background notes as well as a brief, updated account of the Sisters of Charity and their establishments, either as a final chapter in the first edition or as an updated appendix in all editions. To appeal to readers in the present century, the revision by Sisters of Charity of New York sought to achieve greater accuracy, conciseness, and simplicity, while providing a valid representation of his original work.

Code's translation adheres closely to BARBEREY's own text; however, in introducing his translation, he notes that he did not translate Barberey's direct quotations from Elizabeth Seton's writings. Instead he made use of the original manuscripts; however, a comparison of his text with those originals reveals his extensive liberties with those documents. This biography does include a condensed account of the return from Italy and an updated history of the American Sisters of Charity, as well as a list of the deceased Sisters from Emmitsburg with date and place of death. Although Code included some photographs, neither he nor White provided separate bibliographies.

Both Dirvin and Melville follow the birth-to-death chronology established by White, but their accounts end with the death of Mother Seton. DIRVIN (1962) includes many creative embellishments, especially in the early chapters where factual data is scarce. His citations, limited to direct quotations, are difficult to follow. He includes not only photographs but also some of Father Bruté's sketches; one of St. Joseph's grounds forms the end papers in the hard-cover edition.

Although the Vatican acclaimed White's biography the "Bible of the Cause of the Canonization of Mother Seton," actually MELVILLE's work provides the definitive text. Her study, directed by John Tracy Ellis, has thirteen chapters crammed with data as she traces Seton's life. Melville meticulously documents every fact and quotation and provides significant photographs. Like White and Code, Dirvin and Melville had access to the original documents from various archive collections and also furnish extensive bibliographies.

Aware that Elizabeth Seton's grandson had investigated and published the family history of the Setons, but convinced that Elizabeth's own family background was central to her character, LAVERTY brings together these threads, describing the histories of Seton's maternal and paternal ancestors, the LeContes, Bayleys, Charltons, and Bayeux. The Huguenot family of Susanne LeConte, her paternal grandmother, had escaped Catholic persecution in Normandy and settled in New Rochelle, New York. The parents of Mary Bayeux, her maternal grandmother, fled similar persecution against the Huguenots in St. Kitt, West Indies, and established themselves in New York. Her maternal grandfather, Rev. Richard Charlton, born in Ireland, was ordained to the Episcopal ministry in England before coming to New York. William Bayley, her paternal grandfather, left his family home in Hoddesdon, Hertfordshire, England, to settle in Fairfield, Connecticut. Laverty traces this French and English heritage in the first two sections of her study. The third section on Elizabeth Seton's life, similar to the biographies, includes many of the same quotations.

DIRVIN's analysis of Elizabeth Seton's soul (1990) offers additional information. Beginning in 1975 when she was canonized as the first American-born saint, the author provides interesting factual information on the canonization process. He uses her life and writings to reflect various spiritual aspects: her faith and adherence to God's will, and her attitudes toward death, eternity, prayer, and discipleship. His documentation in this study is easier to follow than that in his biography of Seton.

—ELLIN M. KELLY

Settlement House Movement

Beauman, Katherine Bently, *Women and the Settlement Movement*, New York and London: Radcliffe Hall, 1996

Carson, Mina, *Settlement Folk: Social Thought and the American Settlement Movement, 1885–1930*, Chicago: University of Chicago Press, 1990

Crocker, Ruth Hutchinson, *Social Work and Social Order: The Settlement Movement in Two Industrial Cities, 1889–1930*, Urbana: University of Illinois Press, 1992

Davis, Allen Freeman, *American Heroine: The Life and Legend of Jane Addams*, New York: Oxford Press, 1973

Deegan, Mary Jo, *Jane Addams and the Men of the Chicago School*, New Brunswick: Transaction, 1988

Lasch-Quinn, Elisabeth, *Black Neighbors: Race and the Limits of Reform in the American Settlement House Movement, 1890–1945*, Chapel Hill: University of North Carolina Press, 1993

Lissak, Rivka Shpak, *Pluralism and Progressives: Hull House and the New Immigrants, 1890–1919*, Chicago: University of Chicago Press, 1989

Trolander, Judith Ann, *Professionalism and Social Change: From the Settlement House Movement to Neighborhood Centers, 1886 to the Present*, New York: Columbia University Press, 1987

The settlement movement was begun in 1884 in England by university men. Toynbee Hall was the first settlement house, where university-trained volunteers lived among the poor to meet the cultural and social needs of the poor. Although the movement was begun by men, women soon joined by helping in the settlements founded by men as well as by starting settlement houses of their own. BEAUMAN's work is a historical analysis of the role played by women in Britain where the settlement movement began. Beauman focuses on the major personalities and the most renowned houses of the British settlement movement such as Octavia Hill and Toynbee Hall. She explores the long-term national influence female settlement workers had on the development of training for social workers and the contributions women's settlements made in both World Wars. Beauman demonstrates the impact female settlement workers of the past have on social welfare in Britain today.

Just a few years after the British settlement movement began, both men and women in the United States were founding settlement houses. Although Hull House, founded by Jane Addams and Ellen Gates Starr, was not the first settlement house in the United States, it is the most famous. Jane Addams's charismatic personality and her talents as a writer made her the best-known settlement leader in the early twentieth century. DAVIS writes a unique biography of Jane Addams, which not only tells the story of her life and work, but also examines the legends created around her and the immense impact she had on American society. The first four chapters of his book are a detailed account of the circumstances that influenced her decision to found Hull House in 1889. Davis then looks at the symbolic role Jane Addams has played for many Americans. He discusses her reputation and demonstrates her unique position as a representative American woman and a cultural sounding board. He aspires to examine the American attitudes towards social reform, women, and poverty in the early twentieth century, by examining the changing reputation of Addams.

DEEGAN sets out to redefine Jane Addams as a major academic thinker, in particular a sociologist. She argues that Addams and her contemporaries—many of whom were based at Hull House—have had their contributions omitted from the early development of sociology or relegated to social work. Deegan claims that within the early development of sociology, specifically the Chicago School, there was a distinct female tradition growing out of the settlement movement. She argues to define Jane Addams as a sociologist for many reasons: Addams taught college courses, she was offered academic positions in sociology, she was a member of the American Sociological Society, she was published, and she had her books reviewed in sociological journals. Deegan calls attention to the role Addams held as a leader of female academics and as a feminist thinker. This book is a comprehensive look at the social thought and political activities of Jane Addams, as well as an analysis of the role of gender in the history of sociology.

Using Addams as a reference point, CARSON focuses on the role played by the American settlement movement in adapting, testing, re-articulating, and refining specific Victorian values in the early construction of twentieth-century social welfare paradigms. Her study is fundamentally an intellectual history of the ideology forged by the most prominent settlement leaders. She begins by discussing the roots of American settlement philosophy in the moral values of Victorian England. The two elements of Victorianism that Carson stresses are Christianity and the cult of character. She demonstrates how early settlement leaders were influenced by the "service ideal." Furthermore, she argues that the old Victorian ideals of personal service and the importance of personality continued to be central to twentieth-century social welfare ideology, even while they were tested and adapted through experience. Carson also identifies the conflicts within settlement ideology, particularly between assimilation and cultural pluralism.

While many feminist works have focused on the achievements of the female settlement workers, more recently some feminists have begun to examine more critically the contradictions within the work of those first-wave feminists. LISSAK, in her book, does not focus on the role Jane Addams and Hull House played in improving the social conditions for poor immigrants, but rather she looks at their impact in the national debate surrounding the position of immigrants in American society. Unlike other authors who have focused on the social beliefs of the settlement workers, Lissak also sets out to consider the viewpoints of the immigrants. She focuses on the debate between sociocultural assimilation and cultural pluralism. She reevaluates the claims that Jane Addams embraced cultural pluralism. She argues that Hull House was predominantly committed to complete assimilation of immigrants into American culture. Lissak also discusses the response of immigrant communities and their leaders to the ideas and policies of Hull House.

Recently, feminists have begun to study the valuable contributions of the less-known settlement houses and workers. LASCH-QUINN sets out to demonstrate that a variety of African-American organizations, which have not been considered a part of the settlement movement, did practice settlement work in black communities. She begins her study by examining the mainstream settlement movement's neglect of its black neighbors. She explains that mainstream settlements were limited by their secular values, northeastern and urban focus, and racist beliefs. In the second part of her study Lasch-Quinn works to revise settlement history and demonstrate the role of race in American reform. She contrasts the often racist attitudes of white settlement workers with black activists who focused on battling discrimination, segregation, and the withholding of education, employment, and social services from black communities. Her work strives to expand the definition of settlement work to include the reform work of black women.

CROCKER offers a reassessment of the settlement movement, which, like Lasch-Quinn's work, focuses its attention away from the work of famous settlement leaders. Crocker attempts to interpret settlements from the perspective of the poor as well as the settlement workers. She examines seven settlements in Indianapolis and Gary, Indiana. All of the settlements she studies worked for reform, but each had a unique agenda. Crocker stresses the variety that characterized the settlements on which she focuses. For example, two of the settlements were black settlements, and one of these was founded by both black and white reformers. Others were founded by religious organizations, women's universities, and employers. Her study also address the connection between social work and social order.

TROLANDER not only broadens the criteria for the settlement movement but also extends her study of it beyond the Progressive era. Her first chapter summarizes the formation and accomplishments of the settlement movement until World War II, and the main focus of her book is on the decline of the settlement movement after the war. She examines how the professionalization of social work and the transition from a white female leadership to black male leaders affected settlement houses. She demonstrates the important impact settlements have had on social reform, while documenting their transformation into neighborhood centers. Overall, her story is one of major change involving both workers and their clients in their ability to produce social change within a diminishing social movement.

—JULIE K. JOHNSTON

Sévigné, Marie, Marquise de 1626–1696

French Letter-Writer

Aldis, Janet, *The Queen of Letter Writers: Marquise de Sévigné, Dame de Bourbilly, 1626–1696*, London: Methuen, and New York: Putnam, 1907

Allentuch, Harriet Ray, *Madame de Sévigné: A Portrait in Letters*, Baltimore, Maryland: Johns Hopkins University Press, 1963

Boissier, Gaston, *Madame de Sévigné*, translated by Henry Llewellyn Williams, London: Routledge, 1887; Chicago: A.T. McClurg, 1888

Farrell, Michele Longino, *Performing Motherhood: The Sévigné Correspondence*, Hanover, New Hampshire: University Press of New England, 1991

FitzGerald, Edward, *Dictionary of Madame de Sévigné*, 2 vols., London: Macmillan, 1914; New York: B. Franklin, 1971

Megaw, Arthur Stanley, *Madame de Sévigné, Her Letters and Her World*, London: Eyre and Spottiswoode, 1946; Folcroft, Pennsylvania: Folcroft Library Editions, 1976

Mossiker, Frances, *Madame de Sévigné: A Life and Letters*, New York: Knopf, 1983

Ojala, Jeanne, and William T. Ojala, *Madame de Sévigné: A Seventeenth-Century Life*, Oxford: Berg, and New York: St. Martin's Press, 1990

Recker, Jo Ann Marie, *"Appelle-moi Pierrot": Wit and Irony in the Letters of Madame de Sévigné*, Philadelphia: J. Benjamins, 1986

Ritchie, Anne I., *Madame de Sévigné*, London: Blackwood, and Philadelphia: J.B. Lippincott, 1881

Williams, Charles G.S., *Madame de Sévigné*, Boston: Twayne, 1981

Madame de Sévigné, born Marie de Rabutin-Chantal in 1626, led an unusual life in the France of Louis XIV. Famed for her winning intelligence and her stubborn personal independence, she participated in several salons including those of the *précieuses*, and became the most famous letter-writer of her time. Understandably, biographers have been fascinated by her life and letters, creating a small library of works in French and English about Madame de Sévigné and her society. All of the following books are still in print, as are several editions of the marquise's renowned messages. OJALA and OJALA have produced the most recent, conventional, and pithy Sévigné biography, chronicling her years from her youth as the ward of a beloved uncle through her marriage to a Breton nobleman, motherhood, and early widowhood to her status as habitué of the most stimulating Parisian intellectual circles. Madame de Sévigné would approve of the woman the Ojalas describe, particularly their emphasis on her full engagement with life, ebulliently enthused even into her dotage with books, journeys, and friends. Although Madame de Sévigné acted in an overbearing fashion toward her only daughter, Madame de Grignan, the Ojalas argue that it is precisely because of their troubled relationship that the mother's marvelous letters are so regular and lengthy. Their otherwise admirable book is marred by two lamentable production decisions: the use of in-text citations and the absence in the bibliography of page numbers for journal articles.

MEGAW's breezy book will appeal to the general reader because of its present-tense style, which mellifluously permits profuse application of letters to text. It also has attractive illustrations of Madame de Sévigné's friends and houses. However, it altogether lacks documentation and a bibliography.

More than twice as long as the Ojalas's tome, MOSSIKER's effort reconciles the writer and her oeuvre by combining biography with autobiography. Despite the attention of generations of scholars, Mossiker laments the lackluster quality of translated Sévigné correspondence, which she calls works of genius, and relies on her own translation. The happy result is a book as much by the subject as about her, replete with erudite, ardent, and earthy comments by Sévigné herself, set off in italics from the historian's narrative. Excerpts from the Sévigné missives reveal the marquise's anger over the inferior education and depressed legal status of females, her insistence that women ought to resist frequent motherhood, and her pride in her books, recipes, remedies, and business affairs.

Several Sévignistes have attempted to situate the illustrious letters in the literary culture of seventeenth-century France. RECKER mines the wit and irony in the "*spirituelle marquise,*" the epithet given Sévigné by Voltaire, and finds more intellectual rigor than previously appreciated, as well as a remarkable connection to Molière and French theater. This book is aimed at language specialists and uses modern literary criticism to unmask the hidden core of the letter-writer.

So does WILLIAMS's scholarly work, the theme of which is paradox and controversy in Madame de Sévigné's letters. He finds that because of imperfect records and partial readings, her writing was assessed by critics as "literature of gossip." He rejects those who would categorize the marquise as a Balzacian "monster of maternity" because of her devotion to her daughter. Instead, Williams locates her literary influence in the poetry of Lamartine and in the novels of Proust.

ALDIS revels in the pleasure and gaiety of the French elite, making no apologies for the brilliance and charm of Madame de Sévigné nor for her faithful correspondence to an absent daughter. Her focus is less literary and more social, giving the reader the most complete setting for the marquise's life. FITZGERALD's dictionary alphabetizes and describes key persons, places, and things (from Abbé to Vitré) found in the Sévigné epistles.

A reading knowledge of French is essential for appreciating ALLENTUCH's sophisticated sketch of Madame de Sévigné, because although the text is in English, the epistles are untranslated. Employing the methods associated with the Dutch-French characterological school of Peter Heymans, William Wiersma, and René Le Senne, Allentuch probes the nature of the letter-writer, attempting to investigate the discordant dimensions exhibited in the Sévigné correspondence. She concludes that after an imprudent youth and disappointing family fortunes the insouciant marquise sought equilibrium in her later life by reading austere philosophy and embracing Jansenism.

Written more than a century ago, the biographies by Ritchie and Boissier show their age. RITCHIE's slight work is all breathless admiration, punctuated by short English passages from the letters, while BOISSIER's undocumented essay flaunts an anti-female bias, particularly in the Victorian assumptions of the author about gender, education, and Madame de Sévigné's behavior. Boissier relies heavily on the malicious memoirs of Roger de Bussy-Rabutin, while tacitly acknowledging the rejected suitor-cousin as a slanderer; indeed, parts of the tract are more about Bussy than the marquise and castigate "the Marchioness" for not always behaving like a lady.

At the opposite end of the spectrum is the study by FARRELL of more than 500 of Madame de Sévigné's dispatches through a feminist perspective. Farrell contends that the marquise's correspondence gained acceptance in the seventeenth-century French canon not only because of its brilliance, but because Sévigné represented the appropriate generic code of her time. According to Farrell, Sévigné restricted her writing to the epistolary margin and posited her authority within the acceptable maternal sphere. The notes and their creator were celebrated in their own time, shared within salon circles at points of inception and reception, lending Sévigné a discreet, controlled identity in the public performance of her maternal role. She cultivated the notion of a culture and language specific to women, thereby representing and reinforcing conservative tradition. What is missing from the Sévigné profile, proffers Farrell, is any response from the marquise's daughter, whose faithful replies were destroyed by Madame de Simiane, granddaughter and editor of Madame de Sévigné and daughter of Madame de Grignan; the troubling mother-daughter tensions discernible in the Sévigné letters evidently continued in the next generation. However, Farrell ingeniously tries to restore the textless voice of the addressee by "inventing" the daughter's reactions through a closer reading of the mother's content. Madame de Sévigné's letters are quoted both in their original French and in English; the book boasts scholarly endnotes and a substantial bibliography.

—ELIZABETH LANE FURDELL

Sex Customs in China, Japan, and India

Gichner, Lawrence E., *Erotic Aspects of Hindu Sculpture,* New York: privately published, 1949

———, *Erotic Aspects of Japanese Culture,* New York: privately published, 1953

Levy, Howard S., *The Lotus Lovers: The Complete History of the Curious Erotic Custom of Footbinding in China,* Buffalo, New York: Prometheus, 1966

Van Gulik, R. H., *Sexual Life in Ancient China: A Preliminary Survey of Chinese Sex and Society from ca. 1500 B.C. till 1644 A.D.*, Leiden and Kinderhook, New York: E. J. Brill, 1961

The paucity of material written in English on the subject of sex customs in China, Japan, and India is largely due to the difficulty of reading classic sources in the original languages. Thus, the four works in English cited here are especially welcome, for they can provide readers with much useful information that can serve as a gateway to deeper understanding and appreciation of the sexual mores of Asian peoples.

GICHNER's book on India (1949) studies the Hindu people's erotic customs and the philosophy that explained their acts, through an examination of the exuberant carvings on the outer walls of rock-cut temples in the land. While discussing these carved figures—records in stone of the lives and loves of the myriad gods—and the meanings they convey, the author has placed this phase of art in the larger context of an architectural whole, it being an eloquent expression of the religious beliefs long entrenched in the legends and lives of the people. The book has two parts. The first part furnishes the reader with background information on foreign invasions, Hindu thought and habits, a general description of two classic manuals on sexual love (*Kama Sutra* and *Ananga Ranga*), and basic tenets of Hindu belief that have governed artists. It also provides historical background for sculpture, artistic standards of criticism, and temple construction methods. The second part concentrates on the meaning behind the sculptures. The author classifies various interpretations into four categories: judgments based upon foreign standards; the "good life," similar in principle to epicureanism; "practical" usage; and sculpture as a way to obtain spiritual knowledge. Gichner explores the sexual relations of Hindus as reflected in divine subjects, with special emphasis on the importance of sex and its physical manifestations. He also discusses issues specifically important to women, such as early marriage, child bearing, fecundity, the ideal of female beauty, and the place of female forms in Indian sex-mysticism. The book contains many photos and illustrations that demonstrate the various positions of the marital embrace. Readers seeking a general orientation on Hindu erotic art and sex customs will find the book very useful. It is of great help particularly to western readers, as the author constantly compares eastern and western modes of thought and alerts western scholars, including modern feminists, to the wide divergence between the two cultures. The usefulness of the book is further augmented by a bibliography that identifies some of the locations of the temples mentioned.

As in his book on India, GICHNER (1953) adopts a survey approach to the subject. When discussing pertinent issues, he is mindful of the thinking and behavior patterns peculiar to Japanese culture. The scope and content of this book is extended to embrace a variety of art forms, notably picture scrolls, wood-block prints, ivory carvings, and literary writings. He presents relevant information in terms of subject matter, theme, history of development, and elements of stylization. The book contains a generous number of illustrations, which are usually accompanied by lengthy descriptions, critical appraisal, and keys to fuller appreciation and comprehension of the artistic works. The choice of illustrations, according to the author, is meant to indicate the huge variety in the vast field of erotica, and, thus, he includes both items of superior quality and secondary merit to give an idea of the range. The book's central theme—that sex is not a destructive, disruptive agency for evil, but rather a function to be enjoyed for procreation and pleasure—underlines and unifies the material being treated. But the author stops well short of unambiguous approval when discussing issues such as women's position in Japanese society, prostitution, and the role of the geisha. The book's bibliography lists master works in English, French, German, and Japanese for further study.

VAN GULIK's book surveys the interrelationship between sex and society in China from antiquity through the end of the Ming dynasty (1368–1644). The book adopts a broad cultural perspective and develops arguments along a general sociological line, with relevant sexual, cultural, economic, artistic, and literary data arranged in a historical sequence. The book is composed of four major parts, which are further subdivided into ten chapters, each of which treats one period in Chinese history. The first part gives an account of the fundamental Chinese ideas on sex and society as a general introduction. The second part focuses on sex and the influence of Confucianism, Taoism, Buddhism, and family life. The third part deals with the handbooks on sex (manuals teaching the head of the household how to conduct relations with women), their popularity and decline, high-class and low-class prostitution, sexual relations in the palace, medical and erotic literature, the custom of footbinding, and the influence of Neo-Confucianism on sexual relations. Finally, the fourth part centers around sex relations under the Mongol occupation, with special reference to Lamaism and sex in art and letters. The book is richly illustrated. It also contains an essay on Indian and Chinese sexual mysticism, which aims to formulate a theory on the historical connection between these two ancient cultures in the matter of sex mysticism. One of the professed goals of the book is to rectify the western misconception of the "depraved" and "abnormal" sexual habits of the ancient Chinese. The author also argues that after 1644 Confucianist puritanism succeeded in fostering an attitude of prudery and secretiveness about sex matters among the Chinese. However, until that date China's history of Taoism had, on the contrary, favorably influenced the development of sexual relations and consequently had enhanced the position of Chinese women in general. Readers can usually find references to particular subjects in the general index. The author has refrained from discussing purely medical and sexological subjects on the grounds that he perceives himself as an orientalist with a general interest in anthropology. However, readers interested in medical and sexological topics can still find in the translated texts sufficient primary material to form their own conclusions.

Until the publication of van Gulik's book, very little was known by the western audience of sexual relations in China. But van Gulik's research does not cover the past three hundred years of Chinese history. LEVY's book, when coupled with the work of van Gulik, will help to round out that picture. The institution of footbinding thrived in China for a millennium. It originated in the tenth century as a fashion developed by court dancers and was subsequently adopted by court circles and upper-class ladies. The practice reached the masses in the course of the following centuries and evolved into an ingrained custom. Footbinding waned at the start of the twentieth century and was abolished in the 1930s. In dealing with this subject, Levy brings together pertinent information from the erotic works of traditional China and sentimental novels of the time. He also delves into modern magazines and newspapers. The book records the history and development of the custom, campaigns to abolish the practice, critical comments by abolitionists and counterarguments by proponents, sexual implications, relevant social customs and superstitions, descriptions of varieties and principal styles, and interviews with and biographies of women who had their feet bound. The author contends that footbinding was a part of a set of mores in a society of male dominance that saw women as intellectual inferiors and insisted on coercing them into self-mutilation and self-mortification in order to please men. Levy's book, therefore, provides interested readers with valuable material in the fields of general anthropology and sexual psychology. It is also rich in illustrations and concludes with a selected bibliography of works in Chinese, Japanese, English, and French.

—SHARON SHIH-JIUAN HOU

Sex Discrimination in the Workplace

Arputhamurthy, Savitri, *Women, Work, and Discrimination*, New Delhi: Ashish, 1990

Brown, Claire, and Joseph Pechman (eds.), *Gender in the Workplace*, Washington, D.C.: Brookings Institute, 1987

Cockburn, Cynthia, *In the Way of Women: Men's Resistance to Sex Equality in Organizations*, London: Macmillan, and Ithaca, New York: ILR Press, 1991

Figes, Kate, *Because of Her Sex: The Myth of Equality for Women in Britain*, London: Macmillan, 1994

Madden, Tara Roth, *Women vs. Women: The Uncivil Business War*, New York: American Management Association, 1987

Rantalaiho, Liisa, and Tuula Heiskanen (eds.), *Gendered Practices in Working Life*, London: Macmillan, and New York: St. Martin's Press, 1997

Schroedel, Jean, *Alone in the Crowd: Women in the Trades Tell Their Stories*, Philadelphia: Temple University Press, 1985

Scott, Hilda, *Working Your Way to the Bottom: The Feminization of Poverty*, London and Boston: Pandora Press, 1984

The realities of life in the working world for women differ from country to country and job to job; however, the writers whose books are included in this essay describe problems of equality and advancement that are remarkably similar. Whether the subject is women in corporate America or farmers in rural India, the conclusion the writers come to is that women are still subordinate to men and are still a long way from equality in the workplace.

BROWN and PECHMAN's book, sponsored by the Brookings Institute and the Committee on the Status of Women in the Economics Profession, contains essays on a variety of gender issues. Individual chapters examine consumption patterns of families as women enter the workforce, occupational segregation, internal labor markets, unions and the female workforce, part-time versus full-time work, the problems of single parents, and comparisons of the work experiences of women in the United States with those of women in Mexico and Sweden. Each chapter also contains comments by other experts in the field, which point out both strengths and weaknesses with data and/or conclusions. For this reason, the book does more than provide data on women and the workforce; it also illustrates the problems with assessing the status of women and provides alternative information and arguments.

SCHROEDEL's purpose in writing a book about women in the trades was, she says, to help bridge the isolation experienced by such women, to create a picture for women considering nontraditional work, and to give voice to working-class women whose stories had not been viewed as worth recording. The result is a fascinating oral history of women in the United States working as pipefitters, steel haulers, plumbers, and firefighters—to name just a few of the occupations.

COCKBURN's book is an examination of the attempts by men to stop feminism from appealing to women. Although she conducted her study in England, Cockburn's findings are not unique to that country. She describes reactions toward feminism and actions against it that are not uncommon elsewhere. After a thorough discussion of feminism, Cockburn examines in depth four organizations for their equal employment policies and practices and their views on domestic and sexual issues. She concludes that women's bid for visibility, recognition, and equality is being actively and passively obstructed by men.

FIGES contends, after examining women's lives in Britain today, that discrimination against women has not improved but worsened in recent years, and that despite rhetoric of equal opportunity, women are still second-class citizens. She cites as causes overt exclusion of women from jobs, the labeling of women as either careerists or noncareerists, and myths still running rampant that women will quit to have children, that women are less dedicated than men, that women have men to take care of them, and that men are the "technologists." Figes explores the concept of the glass ceiling, differences in male and female management styles, and the lack of accommodation for working mothers. Her discussions concluding the book about the ineffectuality of discrimination lawsuits and the backlash against feminism support her thesis that for women, the working world has not improved of late.

SCOTT's book focuses primarily on salary inequity between men and women in England. Scott examines job segregation, pay, and effects of technology to illustrate the ways in which women work their way into poverty. She says that many people—primarily men—still believe that it is not normal for women to work outside the home and blame women for taking away jobs that rightfully belong to men. Women's poverty, according to Scott, comes from their having to bear primary responsibility for childrearing, and from occupational segregation, sex discrimination, and sexual harassment.

MADDEN's book illustrates that women's problems in the workplace are not created entirely by men. Madden believes that working women are engaged in a "form of unacknowledged urban guerrilla warfare" in the corporate world, that women who have risen above middle management do not want the company of other women, and that they purposely undermine their female colleagues and engage in backstabbing, character assassination, and sabotage. She backs up her beliefs with historical precedent, her own observations during seventeen years in the American corporate world, and the research of others.

A study of gendered practices in the work world in Finland, RANTALAIHO and HEISKANEN's book is a compilation of essays by Finnish academics, researchers, and government officials. It includes discussions of patriarchy, male domination of the present gender systems, and the "iron law of gender," not uncommon in other countries. This "law" states that when women enter a male-dominated profession, wages and status fall, but the reverse happens when men enter female-dominated professions. Other essays look at women and technology, case studies of organizations, and everyday working life for women, including the interaction of work and family life. Finally, the authors examine the concept of comparable worth and make recommendations for improving the status of women in Finland.

ARPUTHAMURTHY takes us to rural India and describes the discriminatory socioeconomic practices in this Third World country. She points out that job segregation is more prevalent in agrarian under-developed societies than in more developed societies. Because of the strict division of labor, agricultural women constitute the most exploited segment of laborers, and their levels of employment and wages remain significantly below those of men. While the primary focus of the book is women in India, individual chapters include comparisons with other countries and discussions of economics in general.

—KATE PEIRCE

See also Glass Ceiling; Sexual Harassment in the Workplace; Earnings Gap; Nontraditional Jobs; Protective Legislation; Workplace Equity Legislation

Sexism

Davies, Miranda, *Women and Violence: Realities and Responses Worldwide,* London and Atlantic Highlands, New Jersey: Zed, 1994

Davis, Angela Y., *Women, Race and Class,* New York: Random House, 1981; London: Women's Press, 1982

French, Marilyn, *The War against Women,* New York: Summit, and London: Hamish Hamilton, 1992

hooks, bell, *Ain't I a Woman: Black Women and Feminism,* Boston: South End Press, 1981; London: Pluto Press, 1982

Pharr, Suzanne, *Homophobia: A Weapon of Sexism,* Inverness, California: Chardon Press, 1988

Wittig, Monique, *The Straight Mind and Other Essays,* Boston: Beacon Press, and New York and London: Harvester Wheatsheaf, 1992

The most basic definition of sexism includes three parts: social relationships in which male authority presides over female authority; discrimination in favor of the male sex; and a set of beliefs that promote men while stifling women. However, feminists have theorized beyond this definition and examined the ideologies of sexism from many different angles. Instead of merely looking at individual acts of sexist behavior, feminists have viewed sexism as existing in governing institutions in society. FRENCH uses this perspective of institutionalized sexism in her work to analyze the beginnings of global sexism. She begins with a discussion of the history of sexism and cites patriarchal societies, dating back to the fourth millennium B.C., as the breeding ground for male authority. Approaching each topic as globally as possible, the author also investigates how various world religions foster sexist thinking and behavior. In addition, French argues that sexism is not only ingrained in societies because of visible discrimination, but many languages, especially the English language, are structured and used to instill sexist values. French argues her points in four parts including: systemic discrimination against women; institutional wars against women; cultural wars against women; and men's personal wars against women. The author provides an easy to understand linear discussion of sexism.

Many feminist discussions of sexism, such as French's work, eventually lead to the linkage of sexist behavior and ideologies with actual violence against women. DAVIES furthers French's work by providing explicit details showing how sexism, that is structural relationships of domination by men, leads to violence against women. She also takes a global approach and argues that wife-beating is the most universal violent act by men to occur across the globe. The author interviews feminists worldwide and reports on how sexism, which manifests into violence against women, is being dealt with in their communities. Not only does Davies present the vast array of problems occurring as a result of sexist ideologies, but she also presents many solutions. For example she discusses women-run police stations in Brazil—their strong points as well as their weak points. From her text, it becomes obvious sexism is a worldwide issue with dangerous and immediate repercussions. Some of the communities Davies includes in her work, each making a separate chapter, are Papau New Guinea, Northern Ireland, Brazil, and India.

Analyzing issues with a global perspective in feminist and women's studies is an approach that has been practiced most often in recent years. Along with subverting the traditional ethnocentric lens, feminists have also been challenged to analyze issues from various class and race perspectives. Sexism is a major issue, which feminists have argued cannot be understood only by examining issues of sex and gender. With this challenge in mind, DAVIS examines sexism through the lens of race and class. The author is one of the first pioneers to examine the connections between racism, sexism, and classism, and to determine that one category cannot be analyzed autonomously of other oppressions. Davis addresses the rise of the women's suffragist movement and the antislavery movement together. Here the relationship between sexism and racism becomes extremely apparent. Her first chapter begins with the legacy of slavery. Although she does not focus exclusively on sexism, Davis argues that one cannot separate sexism from classism or racism and fully understand what happened in history, or what might happen in the future.

HOOKS is another feminist who has done extensive writings on issues pertinent to black women. In her work she dispels many myths regarding sexism and how it relates to black women. Her work, along with Davis's, is important for understanding the many facets of sexism today. Hooks investigates the impact of sexism on the social status of black women, asking such questions as: Where do black women fit when theorizing about sexism? The author uses her own experience as a black woman to begin theorizing about what types of analyses are missing from literature regarding sexism, racism, and experiences of black women. She discusses historical black women, such as Anna Cooper and Sojourner Truth, who were instrumental in fighting against the sexist oppression of black women. In addition, she argues that sexism was an integral part of the social and political order that white colonizers brought with them from Europe and used to oppress black and white women. Finally, hooks discusses how sexist behavior throughout history affects the status of black women today.

Along with the proliferation of feminist writings about women, race, and class came a body of literature that added sexual orientation to the list. PHARR not only adds sexual orientation to the identities in her work, but she directly links homophobia to sexism. Her argument is the first of its kind to plainly state that homophobia is a tool used by patriarchal societies to keep sexist values and behaviors in place. The chapters focus on the problems, effects, strategies for change, commonalities of oppressions, and lesbian experience of sexism and homophobia. Even though Pharr discusses theoretical issues, her focus is much more of a practical one. The author takes her personal experience as a lesbian and a director of domestic violence shelters to articulate her theories and back her arguments. Although her work focuses on the United States, her theories can be applied to various communities worldwide.

WITTIG, a French feminist, also focuses on the interrelation between sexism and homophobia. However, her work is much more theoretical. She takes a materialist feminist approach in examining sexism and the oppression of women in general. The author includes in her book nine essays written between 1976 and 1990. She discusses how the category "lesbian" disrupts the typical way sexism plays out, because it does not fit the patriarchy's values, which insist on women's dependence on men. She also provides an extensive analysis of the difference between sex and gender. She argues that the "sexes have been artificially constructed into political categories—categories of oppression [sexism]." In addition, she investigates how sexism seeps into language, briefly discussing the difference between the French and English languages.

—MELANIE G. GREEN

Sex-Segregated Education

Conway, Jill Ker, and Susan C. Bourque (eds.), *The Politics of Women's Education: Perspectives from Asia, Africa, and Latin America*, Ann Arbor: University of Michigan Press, 1993

Eschbach, Elizabeth Seymour, *The Higher Education of Women in England and America, 1865–1920*, New York: Garland, 1993

Horowitz, Helen Lefkowitz, *Alma Mater: Design and Experience in the Women's Colleges from Their Nineteenth-Century Beginnings to the 1930s*, New York: Knopf, 1984

———, *Campus Life: Undergraduate Cultures from the End of the Eighteenth Century to the Present*, New York: Knopf, 1987

Howe, Florence, *Myths of Coeducation: Selected Essays, 1964–1983*, Bloomington: Indiana University Press, 1984

Kelly, Gail P. (ed.), *International Handbook of Women's Education*, New York and London: Greenwood, 1989

Sadker, Myra, and David Sadker, *Failing at Fairness: How America's Schools Cheat Girls*, New York: Scribner, 1994

Solomon, Barbara Miller, *In the Company of Educated Women: A History of Women and Higher Education in America*, New Haven, Connecticut, and London: Yale University Press, 1985

Tyack, David, and Elisabeth Hansot, *Learning Together: A History of Coeducation in American Schools*, New Haven, Connecticut: Yale University Press, 1990

Until the nineteenth century, most education was a privilege extended only to boys and men. This privilege remains, today, influenced more or less by sex segregation in education and/or differing philosophies about the education of males and females. The fairly quiet appearance of the U.S. coeducational public school system in the nineteenth century marked, therefore, one of the most important events in gender history, as TYACK and HANSOT point out. Tyack and Hansot provide a good starting place for the history of sex-segregated education. They discuss the history of single-sex schools, gender policies and practices in schools, and differences within education as determined by class, race, and region within the United States.

For an analysis of contemporary theoretical and practical issues surrounding some of these same concerns, SADKER and SADKER's book includes an analysis of every level of American schooling. Two chapters trace arguments concerned with the psychological differences between boys and girls and how these differences are affected by schools. Some studies on boys involved in sex-segregated education, for example, find such schooling to purvey even stronger notions of boys' superiority to girls than they receive in coeducational schools. Other studies find such boys to be more inclined to value nontraditional subjects such as literature and art than boys in coeducational schools. For schools segregated to girls, the authors report on a wide range of qualities but conclude that, overall, academically rigorous girls' schools promote healthier self-esteem than do coeducational institutions.

The Sadkers' work builds upon two decades of inquiry that began with HOWE, who addresses problems inherent within a system designed exclusively for males. Her essays discuss the myth that access is the key to content and quality of education. She notes that often both coeducational and sex-segregated institutions teach girls and women to accept their subordinate position in a male-centered world.

SOLOMON considers the American schooling of girls and women from colonial times to the late 1970s. Solomon explores women's struggles for access to institutions, the dimensions of the collegiate experience, the effects of education upon women's life choices, and the complex interaction between feminism and women's education. Solomon also emphasizes the social conditions around which women's colleges were created, a review of the historical differences in male and female education, and an examination of twentieth-century changes in the character of female education. In so doing, she draws attention to a number of earlier sources on the history of women's education within single-sex institutions and to more recent studies comparing the achievements of female graduates of single-sex institutions to those of coeducational institutions. Although the book emphasizes northeastern women's colleges in some chapters, Solomon also explores other geographic regions, and discusses higher education for working class and ethnic minority women as well.

HOROWITZ (1984) provides a concentrated, and clearly chronological approach to sex-segregated education through an in-depth history of the Seven Sisters colleges. In examining architecture, curriculum, and campus administration, Horowitz provides a thorough and sometimes lyrical examination of the motives of the founders of women's colleges, as well as successive administrators. Much more so than other historians, she incorporates lengthy and telling data from biographical sources and primary documents about the passionate appeal of the early administrators and faculty members who sought to educate women in single-sex institutions that were as rigorous as those for men. As her title suggests, Horowitz shows each campus as it was created to mirror philosophies concerned with the education of women apart from men.

HOROWITZ (1987) continues this approach by providing a chapter comparing single-sex and coeducational institutions. The influence of the past, individual reasons for attendance at particular institutions, and curriculum and social changes are all considered important in assessing how student behavior and experiences are shaped. She also discusses such topics as the development of sororities and political activity among women students.

ESCHBACH furnishes a brief overview that supplements many of the points made by both Solomon and Horowitz. She incorporates European themes within the educational theories of the United States and England. Looking at the preparation of women for motherhood and paid work responsibilities, Eschbach discusses the search for equity in education and the reaction to a single-sex education for women that imitated men's education. While other authors also provide comments from male critics of women's colleges, Eschbach quotes such people as Mary Putnam Jacobi, who sought to reassure parents about active, well-educated daughters.

The reader may turn farther afield to KELLY's book for an international approach to understanding women's schooling, both within coeducational and single-sex institutions, in Africa, Asia, Australia, Europe, Latin America, the Middle East, and North America. For example, the chapter on Japan details the founding of the sex-segregated Joshi Eigaku Juku. A number of articles in Kelly's book discuss in depth the importance of religion in influencing the continuing philosophies of single-sex schools. Kelly also supplies an extensive bibliography.

Another international perspective is found in the book by CONWAY and BOURQUE, which discusses, among other topics, colonialism within the organization of education. In addition, this book also looks more closely at specific instances of racial inequities, elitist education, and vocational programs. In perusing these topics, one can glean a number of approaches to understanding sex-segregated education in Asia, Africa, and Latin America. A chapter on methodology also considers further implications of the elusive goal of gender equity in education. The book is hampered by the lack of an index.

—SUSAN TUCKER

See also Coeducation

Sexton, Anne 1928–1974

American Writer

Colburn, Steven E. (ed.), *Anne Sexton: Telling the Tale,* Ann Arbor: University of Michigan Press, 1988

George, Diana Hume, *Oedipus Anne: The Poetry of Anne Sexton,* Urbana: University of Illinois Press, 1987

———(ed.), *Sexton: Selected Criticism,* Urbana: University of Illinois Press, 1988

Hall, Caroline King Barnard, *Anne Sexton,* Boston: Twayne, 1989

McClatchy, J.D. (ed.), *Anne Sexton: The Artist and Her Critics,* Bloomington: Indiana University Press, 1978

Middlebrook, Diane Wood, *Anne Sexton: A Biography,* Boston: Houghton Mifflin, and London: Virago Press, 1991

Morton, Richard E., *Anne Sexton's Poetry of Redemption: The Chronology of a Pilgrimage,* Lewiston, New York: Edwin Mellen Press, 1988

Although all writers' works are influenced by their experiences, Anne Harvey Sexton's life and art merge and mesh more significantly than most. As a confessional poet, Sexton was painfully honest about herself in her writings; as someone struggling with mental illness, writing was a prescribed therapy that necessitated introspection. Anne Sexton is the subject of her own poems. Secondary sources on her, therefore, usually tie together criticism with biography, for a holistic view of this intriguing woman.

The first of the full-length studies of Sexton, McCLATCHY's compendium provides glimpses of Sexton through her own words (in interviews), through the eyes of her contemporaries, and through critical reviews of her work. Sexton's annotated manuscripts for the poem "Elizabeth Gone" are also included. The resulting volume provides more a multi-faceted portrait than a standard biography, and it accomplishes McClatchy's goal of showing the many contradictions that constituted Sexton. The section of Sexton's poet-peers is the most interesting and reads like a Who's Who list of later twentieth-century poets, including Robert Lowell, Denise Levertov, and Maxine Kumin, her closest friend and advisor. No interview of W.D. Snodgrass is included, but many of the selections mention the influence of his *Heart's Needle* on her work. The reviews show a mixed reception to her work, from adulation to condemnation as overly self-indulgent. Two especially helpful chapters are Jane McCabe's feminist critical study of Sexton's poetry (McCabe says Sexton was not a feminist), and McClatchy's summation of the volume and the artist.

GEORGE (1987) provides a study of Sexton's work that combines psychoanalytical and feminist theory, using Sexton's life as a way of reading her poetry, rather than the reverse approach that most of the other works on Sexton take. Less emphasis is placed on the externals of Sexton's life, and more on Freudian insight into the universals of her psyche. Sexton's preoccupation with death is especially emphasized and is seen as an inability on the poet's part to be dishonest about her own mortality; her unflinching honesty and quest for self-knowledge is what ties her to Oedipus, and she ends tragically as well. George sees many of Sexton's psychic disturbances as linked to being female, including her hidden incestuous desires for her father and her victimization by the male-privileged society in which she lived and wrote.

COLBURN's volume is a follow-up to McClatchy's work, reproducing some of the same material—the personal glimpses of Sexton by her peers and reviews—but the editor has amassed a plethora of additional reviews and later critical essays as well. Alicia Ostriker's piece "That Story: The Changes of Anne Sexton," is a good commentary in miniature on Sexton's canon, particularly her movement toward religious themes. An extensive bibliography is included as well.

GEORGE (1988) presents a sampling of critical approaches to Sexton, including Freudian, Jungian, religious, and biographical. The editor's introduction provides an overview of Sexton's works, as well as a helpful chronology of her life. One interesting essay is by Stephanie Demetrakopoulos on the goddesses in Sexton's works, seen as a way of overcoming an image of God as male and looking to herself as a legitimate source of meaning. Several of the essays are original to this collection, while the majority are reprinted from journals.

The thesis of MORTON's slim volume is that Sexton moved from "alienation to order" in the progression of her poetic canon. The author takes a religious/philosophical approach to Sexton's works, ultimately seeing the poet as searching for and coming to a knowledge of or relationship with the Divine. Morton asserts that Sexton's work could be considered together as a "conversion narrative," tied to the religious traditions of Protestant New England from which the poet originated.

HALL's accessible book provides a good introduction to Sexton's life and works. The author focuses on three main ideas in Sexton's works: "the nature of the mid-twentieth-century female experience, the lineaments of madness, and the character of confession." Hall assesses Sexton positively, feeling that her poetry showed a movement toward feminism, and that it went beyond self-indulgence into helping readers gain their own self-awareness. The work interweaves explications of the poems, in chapters organized volume by volume, with biography. Also included is a helpful annotated bibliography.

The latest full-length work on Sexton, MIDDLEBROOK's ground-breaking biography uses audio tapes, notes, and unpublished poetry from Sexton's therapy sessions with one of her psychiatrists, Dr. Martin T. Orne, whom Sexton saw from 1956 through 1964. The work was written by the invitation and cooperation of Sexton's family and provides the most detailed look into all aspects of Sexton's life, from sexuality to religion, from mental breakdowns to teaching techniques. Photos, recollections from friends and family members, letters, previously published interviews with Sexton, and unpublished notebooks and other materials about Sexton are used to give a well-rounded look at the poet. Middlebrook provides scrupulous documentation and an actual transcription of one of Sexton's therapy tapes. To read this volume is to remove much of the mystery from Sexton's life and poetry.

—CAROL BLESSING

Sex Tourism

Enloe, Cynthia, *Does Khaki Become You?: The Militarisation of Women's Lives,* London: Pluto Press, and Boston: South End Press, 1983

———, *Bananas, Beaches and Bases: Making Feminist Sense of International Politics,* London: Pandora Press, 1989; Berkeley: University of California Press, 1990

Matsui, Yayori, *Women's Asia,* London and Atlantic Highlands, New Jersey: Zed, 1989

Murray, Alison J., *No Money No Honey: A Study of Street Traders and Prostitutes in Jakarta,* Singapore and New York: Oxford University Press, 1991

Phongpaichit, Pasuk, *From Peasant Girls to Bangkok Masseuses,* Geneva: International Labour Office, 1982

Richter, Linda, *The Politics of Tourism in Asia,* Honolulu: University of Hawaii Press, 1989

Truong, Tranh-Dam, *Sex, Money and Morality: Prostitution and Tourism in Southeast Asia,* London and Atlantic Highlands, New Jersey: Zed, 1990

Tourism is a complex term that defies easy categorisation. Many tourists are drawn to visit other countries through representations of "unspoilt colourful tribal life" and the possibility of having "authentic" cultural experiences. Some wish to conduct business, and some wish to be "entertained" by available young women and children. Notwithstanding these individual desires, the particular practice of sex tourism is supported and institutionalised by the ideological, social, economic, and political systems of particular nation-states, and the expansion of global capitalism.

ENLOE (1989) documents the commodification of women's and children's bodies through the processes of militarisation and global tourism, for their consumption by men. The work examines how representations of Third World women as passive and erotic are circulated globally, associating male adventure with female sexual availability in order to sell Third World tourism. ENLOE (1983) elucidates the ways in which the military manipulates "femininity" as a negative contrast to presumptions of "virile masculinity," and how women have supported men in the armed forces through recent western history. The book traces the development of militarised psychosocial and structural practices, which move from racism to rape to prostitution.

Through the eyes of a Japanese woman, MATSUI's work describes the poverty that results from ill-conceived development policies and dehumanising economic structures, and their traumatic effects upon indigent Asian women. With a journalist's informal style, she describes the effects of expanding tourism and militarisation, patriarchal traditions and religious values that foster contempt for women, and the international trafficking of women and children that occurs due to advances in transport and communications.

Conceptual changes introduced by feminist anthropology have challenged and modified anthropology as an arena for knowledge-making. Although MURRAY's ethnography does not deal specifically with sex tourism, she gives substance to theoretical understandings of working-class women's lives in southeast Asian cities through her methods of informal participant-observation and spontaneous dialogue. Focusing on the everyday life of Jakarta's street traders and prostitutes, Murray provides an incisive analysis of the intersections of class, the ordering of power relations, the creation of "universal" gender roles through mediated images of women, and the development of capitalist relations of production and ideology, as they shape the lives of impoverished urban women.

PHONGPAICHIT's study concentrates on the masseuses who work in Bangkok, finding that their migration to urban environments is an entrepreneurial move designed to better their own situations and those of their families. A comparison of earnings for "unskilled" work is made. There are also reports on field trips to the women's villages to examine rural attitudes. The study lists the physical and psychological hazards experienced by the women.

A particularly useful focus on Thailand is included in RICHTER's broader analysis of the power relations implicated in tourism and global capitalism. She is insightful in showing the embeddedness of sexuality in state activities and development. She argues that sex tourism is now greater in scale than the (ab)use of women's bodies throughout Thailand's history of concubinage, multiple wives, and *mui tsai* domestic service. She writes that the Thai government's marketing and evaluation of the tourist industry solely in economic terms gives little attention to unequal distribution of income among Thai citizens and ignores the social and cultural impact of rapid tourism growth. Richter critically analyses the ways in which minimal financial backing and legislative authority for concerns about women's health issues have resulted in the commodification of women's and children's bodies. She assesses the sociocultural and economic effects of privileging the sex consumer as the primary factor in economic planning for Thailand's tourist industry.

TRUONG's work shows how fantasy and meaning centre around east-west differences in the advertising campaigns of tour operators. Differences are constructed to emphasise the sexual availabilty of Thai women, which, in turn, is determined by the market and local sexual norms, the supremacy of male sexual satisfaction through the domination of females, and the justification of prostitution by poverty, charity, and curiosity. Truong critically analyses the influence of Buddhist beliefs, which categorise sex workers as being of "low birth" or as having imperfect karma, demonstrating the ways in which the Buddhist discourse of female sexuality is interwoven with Thai state structures, laws, and relations of production.

—HELEN JOHNSON

See also Sexual Slavery

Sexual Assault/Rape: Acquaintance

Estrich, Susan, *Real Rape*, Cambridge, Massachusetts: Harvard University Press, 1987

Ferguson, Robert, and Jeanine Ferguson, *A Guide to Rape Awareness and Prevention: Educating Yourself, Your Family, and Those in Need*, Hartford, Connecticut: Turtle Press, 1994

Francis, Leslie (ed.), *Date Rape: Feminism, Philosophy and the Law*, University Park: Pennsylvania State University Press, 1996

Parrot, Andrea, and Laurie L. Bechhofer (eds.), *Acquaintance Rape: The Hidden Crime*, New York: John Wiley and Sons, 1991

Russell, Diana E.H., *The Politics of Rape: The Victim's Perspective*, New York: Stein and Day, 1974

Sanday, Peggy Reeves, *A Woman Scorned: Acquaintance Rape on Trial*, New York and London: Doubleday, 1996

Schwartz, Martin D., and Walter S. Dekeseredy, *Sexual Assault on the College Campus: The Role of Male Peer Support*, Thousand Oaks, California: Sage, 1997

Warshaw, Robin, *I Never Called It Rape: The Ms. Report on Recognizing, Fighting and Surviving Date and Acquaintance Rape*, New York: Harper and Row, 1988

Wiehe, Vernon R., and Ann L. Richards, *Intimate Betrayal: Understanding and Responding to the Trauma of Acquaintance Rape*, Thousand Oaks, California: Sage, 1995

Although greater media attention is given to instances of stranger rape, women are much more likely (five to ten times more likely) to be raped by someone they know than by a stranger. Surveys indicate that 25 percent of college women have had an experience that meets the legal definition of acquaintance rape, although the women themselves may not have labeled the experience as rape. The impact of acquaintance rape on women is frequently profound and long-lasting. Women are likely to blame themselves, to question their judgment, and to have pervasive problems in feelings of trust and safety. Because of societal attitudes and misconception, women are also less likely to get the support that they need to overcome the impact of the experience.

SANDAY describes how rape, primarily acquaintance rape, has been addressed in the courtroom for the past 400 years. Although some changes are outlined, there is still resistance on the part of the many courts and police investigators to believe that a woman can be raped by someone whom she knows and with whom she voluntarily agreed to spend time. The book by WARSHAW is one of the earliest books to present information about acquaintance rape in a clear form that is readily accessible to women, men, parents, educators, counselors, and those in the legal system. It includes a thorough description of Dr. Mary Koss's well-known survey of date rape on the college campus, which indicates both its high prevalence and the failure of both men and women to accurately identify rape experiences. It also includes narratives by rape survivors, educational information for both rape survivors and rapists, and a description of preventive techniques.

The book by PARROT and BECHHOFER is a more current one, which attempts to bridge the gap between empirical findings published in scholarly journals or presented at professional conferences and the needs of interested persons outside of academic circles. The title "Hidden Crime" comes from the observation that "forced sex between people who know each other is often not viewed as a legitimate crime by its assailants and victims, or by the society at large." A wealth of information about the occurrence and prevalence of acquaintance rape, contributing factors, the characteristics of assailants, and the effects on victims is included.

An essay by philosopher Lois Pineau, which seeks to redefine acquaintance rape, with companion essays supporting or criticizing Pineau's thesis, comprise the book by FRANCIS. Pineau describes how the current American legal system focuses on what a man believes about a woman's desire to engage in sexual activity (or what a "reasonable man" in such a situation would be likely to believe) in determining whether or not a rape has occurred. She finds this approach seriously flawed. She proposes that women can be considered to consent to sexual activity only when clear communication exists about the sexual desire of the two persons. This is a thoughtful, provocative book. It is also quite theoretical and abstract.

An extremely clear and interesting book describing the legal foundation of both acquaintance rape and stranger rape is that by ESTRICH. Some of the shocking implications of recent legal rulings and writings are described, as well as a thoughtful proposal for meaningful legal reform. The role of social attitudes and prejudices in the definition, perception, and prosecution of rape is described by RUSSELL. This book also includes a well-written section describing the roles of both racism and reverse racism in the perception and occurrence of rape. This material in particular does not appear to be readily available elsewhere.

Factors that lead college men to commit acquaintance rape are described in the book by SCHWARTZ and DEKESEREDY. Sexual dominance and aggression are considered positive characteristics in North American society, and sexually aggressive men in college will frequently seek out other men who uphold the same values and attitudes, such as members of a fraternity or sports team. These men then form a male peer support group that encourages them, as individuals or as part of a group, to do whatever it takes to "score." The use of alcohol either to persuade a nonconsenting girl to agree to sex, or to facilitate sex with a nonconsenting, unconscious female, is also described. The importance of education for both men and women in preventing acquaintance rape is emphasized.

How to prevent rape is the subject of the book by FERGUSON and FERGUSON. They believe that most of the material written about preventing acquaintance rape includes too few descriptions of techniques and approaches that may be taken by women. Because each situation is unique, Ferguson and Ferguson describe over 130 practical and effective safety tips that women of all ages can easily implement in their daily lives. These approaches include creating and projecting a strong self-image, and simple yet powerful tactics for fighting back. It is emphasized that a woman need not be strong to escape her attacker. This book is important for any women who wishes to explore, define, and protect the boundaries of her sexuality and herself.

For victims of acquaintance rape, and those close to them, the book by WIEHE and RICHARDS will be helpful. A number of narratives by persons who have been raped are included, as well as discussion of what kinds of behaviors are most likely to be helpful and not helpful. Cases of marital rape are also described, and the special problems that women in this situation encounter.

—JANE CONNOR, ANNA NG, AND SUE GILBERT

Sexual Assault/Rape: Marital

Bergen, R.K., *Wife Rape: Understanding the Response of Survivors and Service Providers,* Thousand Oaks, California: Sage, 1996

Finkelhor, Davis, and Kersti Yllo, *License to Rape: Sexual Abuse of Wives,* New York: Holt, Rinehart, and Winston, 1985

Hall, Ruth, Selma James, and Judit Kertesz, *The Rapist Who Pays the Rent,* Bristol: Falling Wall Press, 1981

Russell Diana E.H., *Rape in Marriage,* New York: Macmillan, 1982

At the time of this writing, only four book-length studies of marital rape have been published, all of them appearing after 1980. Like many other forms of sexual violence, marital rape has only recently gained legitimacy in scholarly and activist circles, due largely to feminist efforts in the late 1970s to end legal and cultural sanctioning of sexual violence in marriage. Despite such efforts, the general population continues to regard marital rape as a contradiction in terms, and, as late as 1996, 33 states in the United States still had laws excusing rape in marriage under certain circumstances.

The text by HALL, JAMES and KERTESZ is a self-described "handbook on rape in marriage" designed specifically for changing . . . .(British) law on rape." Despite its compactness (68 pages), it incorporates important issues overlooked in longer works, including reference to race, class, and sexual orientation as factors affecting the quality of treatment accorded survivors by social institutions. It also exposes the double standards, stereotypical thinking, and circuitous reasoning undergirding biased legal and cultural responses to survivors of all forms of rape. Hall, James, and Kertesz make a major contribution to the literature of wife rape by demonstrating how marital rape exemptions serve as a linchpin for holding together a variety of discriminatory practices toward survivors of all kinds of rape, both within and outside of marriage.

RUSSELL's study summarizes findings in existing literature and presents data from interviews conducted with 87 wife rape survivors. The study is noteworthy for its rigorously tested research methods and narrowly applied definition of rape, as well as for the extent of Russell's efforts to ensure that interviewers were trained and sensitized to the subject matter. Russell argues that wife rape occurs because some men abuse power, authority, and sexual access they derive from the patriarchal family structure. Her analysis of the unequal power relationship between husbands and wives leads her to critique social science perspectives that ignore differences between male-initiated assaults and female acts of self defense by collapsing them under the rubric "family violence." Russell also presents compelling evidence that marital rape survivors are a distinct group of abused wives whose experiences and needs differ significantly from those of women encountering other forms of marital violence. She also argues that despite the tendency of battered women's shelters to overlook the needs and concerns of survivors of wife rape, they are the service providers best equipped to administer to the needs of this population.

Findings from FINKELHOR and YLLO's interviews with 323 Boston area women are similar to those cited in Russell's study. Like Russell, Finkelhor and Yllo found that sexual assault by husbands occurred at all socioeconomic levels and that, within the sample surveyed, marital rape was the most common form of sexual violence experienced. Like Russell again, these scholars use accounts from interviewees to highlight the isolation and self-blame marital rape survivors endure because of their own and others' misconceptions about what constitutes "real" rape. This latter issue forms the cornerstone of their book and represents their major contribution to the literature on marital rape. Finkelhor and Yllo make important connections between nineteenth- and twentieth-century feminist challenges to laws giving husbands a literal license to rape their wives. More importantly, they provide a systematic and comprehensive analysis of rationalizations used to deny wives legal protection against husbands who rape them. They discuss the faulty assumptions underlying arguments to retain marital rape exemptions, examine the recodification of rape laws in various states where marital rape exemptions have been removed totally or in part, and offer data in support of eliminating both cultural and legal biases that allow for sexual assault of any kind in marriage.

BERGEN develops a somewhat different perspective by exploring women's understandings of their experience of marital rape, as well as the often inadequate response of helping agencies when marital rape survivors contact them for assistance. Bergen bases her study on interviews with 40 survivors and 37 service providers, experience as a participant observer at a battered women's shelter and a rape crisis agency, and a national survey of 621 service providers. She looks at the varied nature and causes of wife rape and the ways women define, manage, and end the violence perpetrated against them by their husbands. While she furthers marital rape research by giving systematic attention to survivors' strategies for coping with or managing their husbands' sexual violence, Bergen's major contribution is her discussion of ways in which survivors of marital rape are frequently revictimized by social institutions they turn to for help. In particular, Bergen finds that while battered women's shelters, rape crisis agencies, and combination programs provide an invaluable service by helping survivors understand their experiences of sexual victimization within marriage as rape, staff at these agencies are generally ill-equipped to administer assistance to this population, because each agency tends to view wife rape as the province of some other agency. As a consequence, marital rape survivors are often denied the advocacy, counseling, housing, or educational support they need to get out of their abusive situations. Bergen argues that activists and service providers must move beyond an either/or construction of wife rape, as well as make the structural and procedural changes necessary to include marital rape survivors as integral, yet distinct, members of their client population.

—PAT WASHINGTON

Sexual Assault/Rape: Other

Bart, Pauline B., and Patricia H. O'Brien, *Stopping Rape: Successful Survival Strategies*, New York and Oxford: Pergamon Press, 1985

Benedict, Helen, *Virgin or Vamp: How the Press Covers Sex Crimes*, New York and Oxford: Oxford University Press, 1992

Brownmiller, Susan, *Against Our Will: Men, Women and Rape*, New York: Simon and Schuster, and London: Secker and Warburg, 1975
Cameron, Deborah, and Elizabeth Frazer, *The Lust to Kill: A Feminist Investigation of Sexual Murder*, New York: New York University Press, and Cambridge: Polity Press, 1987
Gordon, Margaret T., and Stephanie Riger, *The Female Fear: The Social Cost of Rape*, New York: Free Press, and London: Collier Macmillan, 1989
Harvey, Penelope, and Peter Gow (eds.), *Sex and Violence: Issues in Representation and Experience*, London and New York: Routledge, 1994
Kelly, Liz, *Surviving Sexual Violence*, Minneapolis: University of Minnesota Press, and Cambridge: Polity Press, 1988
Scully, Diana, *Understanding Sexual Violence: A Study of Convicted Rapists*, London: HarperCollins, and Boston: Unwin Hyman, 1990
Searles, Patricia, and Ronald J. Berger (eds.), *Rape and Society: Readings on the Problem of Sexual Assault*, Boulder, Colorado and Oxford: Westview Press, 1995
Soothill, Keith, and Sylvia Walby, *Sex Crime in the News*, London and New York: Routledge, 1991

Feminist scholarship on sexual assault and rape now has a tradition of over 20 years, and publications have multiplied and taken diverse directions, as initial work has been built on and, in some cases, challenged. The best-seller by journalist BROWNMILLER was the first to widely publicise rape as a serious social issue, but the book is controversial among contemporary feminists. Nevertheless, the book's landmark status alone marks it as an interesting and valuable cultural document of its time, and the text is replete with relevant popular culture references. The broad scope includes rape and the law, rape in war, riots, pogroms, and revolutions, rape as a function of specific forms of authority, and the myth of the heroic rapist, along with a long chapter about rape victims and, finally, suggestions of ways for women to fight back. Brownmiller's book therefore continues to be worthy of study and debate, supplemented by more recent scholarship.

One such collection is that by SEARLES and BERGER, a usefully broad interdisciplinary anthology, which has contributions from many well-known researchers and writers on various kinds of sexual assault, including rape in war, date rape, sexual murder, and child sexual abuse. The book contextualises itself by beginning with a brief overview of the history of feminist activism on sexual violence, and it is then divided into five separately introduced sections: feminist foundations, why men rape, varieties of rape and assault, rape and the (U.S.) legal system, and surviving and preventing rape. The legal section importantly includes an article on rape, racism, and the law, providing important redress for the omissions and implicit racism of earlier white-dominated feminist work on rape. In a similar illustration of the book's contemporary milieu, a male rape survivor relates his experience in the context of his support for the feminist anti-rape movement. Overall the book is an especially good introduction to the scholar wishing to become familiar with what is by now a complex and diverse field of study; it is also a potentially useful and accessible teaching resource, with a style ranging from clearly expressed theoretical pieces to poetry and personal accounts.

KELLY's British feminist sociological research project aimed to give voices to the women studied. Sixty women were interviewed in depth about a range of forms of sexual violence over their lifetimes. Kelly argues that it is important to focus on how women themselves understand and deal with their experiences, and hence that the idea of a continuum is a crucial feminist concept in interpreting both the range of sexual violence and how individual women experience, survive, and resist it in their lives. The continuum concept also allows Kelly to connect sexual violence to ordinary male behaviour and to suggest that therefore all women are affected by sexual violence in some way. The book includes a helpful overview of the recent "knowledge explosion" in research on sexual violence.

BART and O'BRIEN offer one of the few feminist works of research to focus on the immediate avoidance of rape, via documentation of a range of women's situations and strategies. The study interviewed 94 Chicago women who had been attacked and compared the situation for those who managed to avoid rape with those who did not. There is useful discussion of some of the complexities in self-definition of an experience as rape or non-rape, in line with the book's overall radical feminist emphasis on women's own quite diverse interpretations. The authors consider the effect of multiple situational variables like time of day, whether the attempt took place inside or outside, whether the attacker was a stranger, the presence of weapons and multiple assailants, and women's childhood socialisation. The book is a very accessible research back-up for many of the ideas and skills taught in feminist self-defence classes. The book's at times irreverent tone toward would-be rapists and rape-supportive attitudes are refreshing counterparts to the upsetting stories of survivors and victims.

The only feminist study that focuses on the rapists rather than their victims, the book by SCULLY is essential reading. While obviously limited by its focus on prison inmates, the book nevertheless provides compelling evidence for feminist arguments that rapists' behaviour and attitudes are more typical of dominant accepted masculinity than otherwise. Interview data are set in a sociological framework to demonstrate that rape myths are not simply believed by all rapists but are also used by them to manipulate their and others' views of themselves, even after conviction. Men categorised as "deniers" used various justifications to try to present the crime as "not rape," while "admitters" used excuses such as being under the influence of alcohol and drugs. Scully therefore makes a strong case for the impact of sociocultural attitudes on rapists themselves, both before and after their violence.

Other research more generally addresses the relationship between rape and its broader sociocultural milieu. GORDON and RIGER interviewed 299 women and 68 men in three U.S. cities about their fear of rape, in order to try to understand what makes some women more fearful than others and how women cope with their fears. This largely liberal feminist study tends to base its assumptions about the validity of women's fears on official crime data rather than feminist research. However, it does suggest that the myth of stranger danger is still widely held by women, and that this is exacerbated by the media. Gordon and Riger back up their argument with a sub-study of eight major newspapers shown to employ highly selective and often lurid coverage of rape cases.

Media research is more central to BENEDICT, whose work focuses mainly on four major cases to argue that in the 1980s and 1990s the standard of coverage of rape in the mainstream U.S. press declined to match the pre-1970 emphasis on the bizarre and sensational, with the consequent trivialisation and denigration of victims. The book sets its analysis against a backdrop of relations of power in American society and the specific practices and ideologies of the press, including drawing on interviews with journalists and editors. The choice of four cases attempts to represent key themes and time periods: the 1978–79 Greta and John Rideout rape case (marriage), the 1983–84 New Bedford "Big Dan's" gang rape (ethnicity), the 1986 killing of Jennifer Levin (class), and the 1989–90 Central Park jogger case (race). The book's particular political analysis of rape and of what counts as fair journalism will not be shared by all readers, and its interpretation of the place of racism in understanding rape in the United States is contentious and requires supplementation from black feminism. Nevertheless Benedict provides a rare account of some important tendencies in media coverage of rape and is therefore an important beginning for the feminist researcher.

SOOTHILL and WALBY provide an even more rare attempt to analyse systematically the ways in which crimes such as rape are constructed in the media. This book's findings represent part of a larger long-term study of the reporting of sex crime in 40 years of British newspapers, set against a backdrop of changes in the reporting of sexually violent crimes to the police, and legislative and policy initiatives that have attempted to improve media constructions. Soothill and Walby argue that while rape is now being talked about in the press, newspapers of the 1970s and 1980s tended to construct a very narrow version of sex crime in which only a few cases received most of the coverage. Rape was generally not set in its broader social context but instead sensationalised as due to "sex beasts;" and consequently, rather than drawing on feminist analysis, press accounts endorsed conservative "law and order" strategies. This book is a must for the media researchers, not least for its reminder of the complexity of such an undertaking.

CAMERON and FRAZER provide an interdisciplinary cultural analysis that aims to extend more common feminist interpretations of sexual violence to exploring the issue of sexual murder. The book argues that the sex killer is a comparatively recent, western, and exclusively masculine phenomenon, and that as with other forms of sexual violence, both the act and the perpetrator are actually more reflective of modern masculinist culture than they are aberrant. However, representations of the sex killer in popular culture, literature, philosophy, criminology, and clinical pathology tend either to deviantise or glorify the perpetrator. The authors suggest that not only is this typical of post-Enlightenment thought, but that this same framework actually helps to produce the sex killer via its associations of the possibility of mastery and transcendence for the masculine subject with transgression, eroticism, and murder. This book therefore forays into the cultural specificity of western capitalist societies, in which sexual violence must be understood in relation to its location within the particular system of symbolic representation.

This is a theme also addressed in the book by HARVEY and GOW, a collection of papers from anthropological and cultural studies perspectives. All writers are influenced by the idea that violence and sexuality are culturally embedded concepts that may not be able to be translated meaningfully across cultures, and that rather may have very different contextualised interpretations. This is a work that is relevant not only to anthropologists, but to any feminists trying to understand forms of what might be called sexual violence as always products of culturally specific modes of representation. Hence, for example, one of the chapters points out that gang rape in an Amazonian social system cannot simply be understood using western ideas about male domination and the meaning of sexualised violence in a (western) culture that endlessly symbolises women as desirable objects, and that in fact to impose such a framework does its own representational violence, linked to a broader domination by and in the west of its "others."

—CHRIS ATMORE

See also Child Sexual Abuse

Sexual Assault/Rape: War

Allen, Beverly, *Rape Warfare: The Hidden Genocide in Bosnia-Herzegovina and Croatia,* Minneapolis: University of Minnesota Press, 1996

Brownmiller, Susan, *Against Our Will: Men, Women, and Rape,* New York: Simon and Schuster, 1975

Stiglmayer, Alexandra (ed.), *Mass Rape: The War against Women in Bosnia-Herzegovina,* Lincoln: University of Nebraska Press, 1994

From time immemorial, one of the primary weapons of war has been to rape the women of the enemy people, thereby attempting to demoralize the population (including the men who are the women's fathers and husbands), dehumanize the women, and forcibly create offspring for the conquerors. This has been documented since ancient times, and it has been a regular part of warfare throughout human history, but it was not until Brownmiller's groundbreaking book on rape and the feminist movement's raising of the issue of rape and sexual assault as important social issues that the use of rape as a weapon of war has been brought to public attention.

BROWNMILLER discusses sexual assault in many forms, but she was the first to address as a feminist issue the violation of women as a systematic method of warfare. She documents the rape of enemy women as a part of ancient Greek and Roman warfare, the Crusades, the American Revolution, both World Wars, and the war in Viet Nam, among others. She analyzes rape in war as part of the psychology of warfare but also as a tactic that "provides men with the perfect psychologic backdrop to give vent to their contempt for women." Further, the opportunity to rape conquered women has long been, she says, one of the "rewards" of fighting a winning battle, and a further effect of such rapes is to intimidate and demoralize the enemy. This issue had still not, however, really captured public attention until news of mass rapes of women as part of the war in Bosnia-Herzegovina in the 1990s was made public through the international media. Books on the topic of rape and war are therefore limited to discussions arising from this conflict.

ALLEN describes in detail three types of rape practiced by the Serb forces in Bosnia-Herzegovina and Croatia, but her focus is on the genocidal aspect of rape. Allen discusses how the Serbs have used rape as a weapon of war and describes the perverse logic on which its genocidal implications are based: the perpetrators of this form of warfare impregnate their victims in order to erase the mother's cultural identity and have them give birth to "Serbian" offspring. According to this policy, the victimized women become nothing more than vehicles for the production of a future generation of Serbs, a philosophy that demonstrates the extreme nationalism of the Serb cause. Allen discusses this policy of genocidal rape in terms of its implications for international warfare and considers the ways in which it should be defined and prosecuted by the UN's International Criminal Tribunal. Her study is based on the analysis of accounts by concentration camp survivors who are kept anonymous in order to assure their safety.

STIGLMAYER's book consists of 10 essays by various writers, including two by herself. The emphasis throughout is on theory: rape as a weapon of warfare is analyzed in terms of its broader implications for women and for what it says about cultural attitudes toward women. Stiglmayer's own essays are based on her direct experiences in Bosnia-Herzegovina and Croatia and provide a more direct context for the overall topic of rape in war.

—ELEANOR AMICO

Sexual Double Standard

Daly, Mary, *Pure Lust: Elemental Feminist Philosophy,* London: Women's Press, and Boston: Beacon Press, 1984

Dworkin, Andrea, *Intercourse,* London: Secker and Warburg, and New York: Free Press, 1987

Irigaray, Luce, *This Sex Which Is Not One,* Ithaca, New York: Cornell University Press, 1985

Stoltenberg, John, *The End of Manhood: A Book for Men of Conscience,* New York: Dutton, 1993

Tong, Rosemarie, *Women, Sex, and the Law,* Totowa, New Jersey: Rowman and Allanheld, 1984

Wolf, Naomi, *Promiscuities: The Secret Struggle for Womanhood,* New York: Random House, 1997; as *Promiscuities: A Secret History of Female Desire,* London: Chatto and Windus, 1997

The past and present reality of the sexual double standard—the fact that society upholds a different set of normative expectations for the sexual attitudes and behavior of women and men—and the consequences thereof for the disparate treatment of women and men in society, is a basic theme of all feminist theorizing. But the problem of the sexual double standard is understood differently by liberal and radical feminism. To liberals, the sexual equality negated by the double standard means the right of women to enjoy the same sexual freedom that men are allowed. To radicals, this sexual equality means the right of women to define for themselves what "freedom" really means, and in this way to move beyond the false alternative of subservience to men (the double standard) on the one hand, or the freedom to be like men on the other.

A prominent spokesperson for the liberal view is WOLF. Wolf depicts the coming of age of a cross-section of adolescent girls. Their capacity for adventure, experimentation, and pleasure is portrayed against the backdrop of an uncomprehending and unsupportive culture. Thus, they are not permitted to integrate the sexual aspects of themselves—that is, those aspects that are expressed in and through sexual activity—into the totality of their lives and personalities. The state of youthful exuberance ends up being regarded as an episode or a stage to be left behind rather than a true beginning, to be developed or built upon. In this sense the women—and by extension all women—are unfree, that is, they are not free to seize upon and make use of their own experience as part of the process of creating a life for themselves.

A prominent representative of the radical approach is DWORKIN. The underlying theme of her work is that the sexual oppression of women is due not to their exclusion from the world of male sexuality, but to their forced participation in it. The sexual double standard, then, refers to the fact that for men, normal sexuality means eroticized domination. Women "participate" in this as objects of domination; in this sense there is only one (male) standard of normal sexuality. Dworkin argues that male sexuality, and hence socially sanctioned sexuality, establishes and reinforces the subordination of women, primarily by means of the sanctification of heterosexual genital intercourse. Intercourse is a ritual act whose function is the glorification of male power or "manhood" or "man" as symbolized by the phallus. Male supremacy is encoded in the institution of intercourse (the organization of normal adult sexuality around hetersexual genital intercourse as its zenith and goal), whether this takes the form of explicit violence (criminal rape) or implicit violence (the patriarchal marriage, in which intercourse upon demand has traditionally been understood as a husband's right).

The question arises how these patterns can persist in an era in which men as well as women proclaim their belief in gender equality. One way to answer that question is to confront men's deep need to exercise domination over women, and to examine how sexuality functions in men's lives as a way for them to secure their dominant status. It is a task that at least in part must be taken up by men, since it is men who have access to the primary data that must be analyzed—namely, the experience of sexual desire as an eroticized form of the desire to overpower, control, and subdue. STOLTENBERG argues that, while normal masculinity takes a wide variety of forms (which he describes in vivid experiential detail), these forms possess one fundamental unifying element: a self-imposed terror at the thought of being in a position of weakness, that is, a fear of being feminized. This fear, Stoltenberg observes—along with many contemporary feminist theorists—explains the essential role homophobia plays in the male psyche as a defense against the threat of identification with the feminine.

What Stoltenberg does not examine is the role of the unconscious in the formation of homophobia and misogyny. Indeed, he addresses his work to "men of conscience," as if stating the problem were sufficient to solve it. Feminist psychoanalysts, of course, would disagree. The most important among them is IRIGARAY. In a number of works—this listed book is a highly influential collection of her writings on the subject—Irigaray argues that the fusion of sexuality and aggression that is the hallmark of normal male sexuality originates in men's unconscious anxiety over potential loss of the phallus, and that in the male psyche such loss is represented by the figure of the feminine. In subduing and conquering women, men subdue and conquer their own fear of castration. They reassert their own phallic power by means of a negation of one who is without the phallus.

Of course all such Freudian analyses presuppose the significance of the phallus without explaining it; psychoanalysis invariably requires supplementation by sociology. In addition, if there is a connection between "valorization" of the phallus and the normativity of male sexual aggression (as the "practice" of that valorization), it is hard to imagine how a critique of normal male sexuality could be developed from within the limits of a heterosexual worldview (the limits within which Irigaray theorizes). Thus, lesbian-feminist critiques of male sexuality often reach diagnostic depths that are closed off to others. A good example is DALY's book, in which the author analyzes phallic desire as a vehicle of sheer destruction, an embodiment of a commitment to the negation of the authentically affirmative attitude toward life—pure lust—of which only women freed from the phallic mystique are capable. Daly offers a lyrical account of the purified lust for life that is available to those who reject the pseudo-passion of phallocentric lust. In this sense her work refutes the charge that feminist thinking is merely critical. On the other hand, her insistence that free gynocentric existence (freed from the bonds of patriarchal false pleasures) can and does occur in the patriarchal here and now, refutes the charge of utopianism. (Her writing style—full of word play as well as conceptual play—exemplifies that of which it speaks).

For those women who cannot reach such heights, and even for those who can, the concrete question of how to protect themselves against male sexual aggression remains a pressing one. That means, for one thing, that the question of law is relevant to a discussion of the sexual double standard. The role of law is paradoxical: as a patriarchal social institution, it expresses and promotes the interests of men. Yet, as an institution based on universalistic principles, it has the capacity to break through its own boundaries and represent the interests of all citizens, even women. TONG's classic text on gender and the law has become outdated based on later legislation and court cases, for example on sexual harassment. Yet the book is still relevant because it is principally a philosophical analysis of law. She discusses in turn pornography, prostitution, sexual harassment, rape, and battering, focusing in each case on traditional conceptions of these phenomena in law and society, and how these conceptions have influenced the justice system's response (or nonresponse) to them. She shows that the current state of law on any issue invariably reflects the dynamic interplay among philosophical and common-sense conceptions of it, and that these conceptions are subject to change as society continues to debate, both at a philosophical and common-sense level, the meaning of the issue at hand. Pornography, for example, is the subject of especially intense debate; Tong presents a formidable case for the view that pornography should be regarded as "gyno-thanatic," that is, women-degrading.

—JAY MULLIN

See also Sexual Politics

Sexual Harassment in Education

Dziech, Billie Wright, and Linda Weiner, *The Lecherous Professor: Sexual Harassment on Campus,* Boston: Beacon Press, 1984

Gallop, Jane, *Feminist Accused of Sexual Harassment,* Durham, North Carolina: Duke University Press, 1997

Gittins, Naomi E., and Jim Walsh, *Sexual Harassment in the Schools: Preventing and Defending against Claims,* Alexandria, Virginia: National School Boards Association, 1990

Guinier, Lani, Michelle Fine, and Jane Balin, *Becoming Gentlemen: Women, Law School, and Institutional Change,* Boston: Beacon Press, 1997

Lott, Bernice, and Mary Ellen Reilly (eds.), *Combatting Sexual Harassment in Higher Education,* Washington, D.C.: National Education Association, 1996

Paludi, Michele A. (ed.), *Sexual Harassment on College Campuses: Abusing the Ivory Power,* Albany: State University of New York Press, 1990; revised edition, 1996

Riggs, Robert O., Patricia H. Murrell, and JoAnn C. Cutting, *Sexual Harassment in Higher Education: From Conflict to Community,* Washington, D.C.: George Washington University, School of Education and Human Development, 1993

Sandler, Bernice R. (ed.), *The Educator's Guide to Controlling Sexual Harassment,* Washington, D.C.: Thompson, 1993

Although the term "sexual harassment" was coined in the 1970s, the impact and scope of sexual harassment on college campuses were first recognized in the early 1980s. Colleges and universities are expected to provide learning and working environments free of bias or intimidation; however, reports and books like DZIECH and WEINER's publication indicate otherwise. This book was written at a time when the sexual harassment issue was fairly new. Dziech and Weiner reported that sexual harassment of college students by their professors was a fact of campus life that many educators learn to ignore and, in their silence, to accept. This publication no doubt inspired many others to look more closely and cast more light on the issue. The work treats only the subject of sexual harassment of female students by male professors, because the authors saw this form of sexual harassment as the most common and most damaging. The goal was to convince students, parents, and academicians that the problem was serious, and that they could do something about it. The authors suggest that the environment of higher education, myths about college women, the developmental patterns of male professors, and the professional dilemmas of female faculty contribute to the problem. The intense reaction to this book no doubt led to many of the following selections.

According to PALUDI, she wrote her book to value students and to empower them. Contributors to the first edition were asked in the second to update their chapters, focusing on new research, case law, and theory. Also, new contributors offer perspectives on sexual harassment. This edition also illustrates how important a spiritual focus is for many women who are dealing with sexual harassment at school and at work. The goal of this book is to focus on changing the way campuses deal with sexual harassment, rather than on changing victims' perceptions of their experiences with their professors and classmates. Major sections of the book include legal and conceptual issues, faculty issues, and consensual relationships (also addressed in relation to mentoring), and effective campus interventions. Appendices are included on counselor training, policy and procedure resources, and education/training resources.

LOTT and REILLY interpret how the decisions and interpretations about workplace sexual harassment affect schools, colleges, and universities. They report what sexual harassment means for the full spectrum of college personnel including students, professors, staff members, administrators, and unions. Authors represent a wide variety of academic disciplines, differing institution sizes and locations across the United States, and a wide assortment of jobs within institutions. The book includes sections on the historical context of opening higher education for women, exploring varying definitions of sexual harassment, problems presented by these definitions, and legal developments and impact on policies and procedures. It was designed to help educators and scholars in research and teaching, and administrators and staff in developing workshops and formulating policy.

Considerable space is devoted to the discussion of consensual relationships and the question of when a power differential negates consensus and actually carries the presumption of coercion, and what a university can legally do to prohibit such relationships. Another section provides a perspective on the contradictions for feminist unionists in the academy where sexual harassment is concerned. There is discussion of the pros and cons of including provisions concerning sexual harassment within a bargaining contract.

RIGGS, MURRELL, and CUTTING report that times have changed. If an organization does not make the issue of sexual harassment a major concern, the results could be very costly. Yet, sexual harassment is more than just a moral, legal, or financial concern. In a condition of fear or emotional discomfort, academic goals cannot be achieved. This report was written for higher education institutions as they address this issue. The authors provide a definition section and explain why sexual harassment is illegal. They also address what kinds of behavior constitute sexual harassment on campuses and who the victims are, including sexual harassment of students, peers, non-faculty employees, and in consensual relationships. There are also specific descriptions of what steps institutions should take to eliminate sexual harassment, from preparing policy to handling grievances. A model policy and complaint resolution plan is included.

GITTINS and WALSH's book was written to assist school attorneys and administrators. The goal was to instill an understanding of the law regarding sexual harassment of employees and students, to serve as a guide in developing policy and preventive measures for reducing incidents of sexual harassment, and to respond appropriately to sexual harassment claims. An overview of the Supreme Court 1986 decision in *Meritor Savings Bank v. Vinson* is included, as well as a discussion of post-Meritor sexual harassment cases and an outline of protocol advice on handling sexual harassment in schools. Although the book does not address education specifically, the contents are quite applicable to education. Also, the appendices include detailed resources.

The book by GUINIER, FINE, and BALIN is an appeal for institutional change. It is the story of women's experience with legal education and how institutions need to transform themselves to benefit women. It contains a description of a study done at the University of Pennsylvania Law School—a story of the insidious effects of gendered stratification. The focus is on the experiences of a law professor and female law students and the impact of self- and structurally imposed silences, denigration of "outsiders'" points of view, and the value of dual or multiple consciousness. The message is that no one should have to become a gentleman in order to be heard—that a genuine commitment to inclusion can become the basis for rethinking how we distribute opportunities in all educational areas.

Higher education administrators were concerned about how educational institutions would be impacted by the Meritor decision. But when the 1992 Supreme Court decision that educational institutions could be financially liable in sexual harassment cases was announced, that concern became a demand to find ways to lessen that liability. One of the results of this widespread demand is SANDLER's training manual. This is an extensive manual that contains sections of information on foundations of sexual harassment legislation, various definitions and explanations of sexual harassment, important factors to consider when developing policy, tips for handling sexual harassment claims, and many resources for further reading. One of the most unique aspects of this work is the inclusion of two complete workshop outlines (a one-hour session and a two-hour session) designed for educational institutions, students, and staff. Each outline contains suggestions for what to include in each section, with transparency masters and handout materials included. The information sections provide for various parts of the workshop to be customized. Handouts include case studies from various occupational perspectives on campus. The manual contains major sections of material for elementary and secondary education settings as well.

GALLOP's publication is the personal story of a feminist professor who was accused by two students of sexual harassment. The accusation is all the more sensational because a female, and a feminist at that, is the accused. The author chose to use her "spectacle," as she calls it, to explore assumptions about sexual harassment and feminism. It was the feminist movement that named the behavior "sexual harassment" and proceeded to make it illegal. Gallop seeks to clarify that feminism is not, in principle, a movement against sexuality. It is, rather, a movement against the disadvantaging of women. Thus, sexual harassment is a feminist issue not because it is sexual, but because it disadvantages women. Included in the work is a consideration of consensual relations and intellectual inquiry. Gallop finds her experiences and the experiences of women she knows to contradict the picture of the lecherous professor described by Dziech and Weiner. She most often finds students initiating the sexual activity, and she is not entirely convinced that banning sexual relations between students and teachers is a good thing. She finds the ban on consensual relations dehumanizing, in the same way that sexual harassment is dehumanizing.

—BEVERLY STITT

Sexual Harassment in the Workplace

Bingham, Shereen G. (ed.), *Conceptualizing Sexual Harassment as Discursive Practice*, Westport, Connecticut: Praeger, 1994

Brant, Clare, and Yun Lee Too (eds.), *Rethinking Sexual Harassment*, London and Boulder, Colorado: Pluto Press, 1994

Farley, Lin, *Sexual Shakedown: The Sexual Harassment of Women on the Job*, New York: McGraw-Hill, 1978; London: Melbourne House, 1980

MacKinnon, Catherine, *Sexual Harassment of Working Women: A Case of Sex Discrimination,* New Haven, Connecticut: Yale University Press, 1978

Pattinson, Terry, *Sexual Harassment: The Hidden Facts,* London: Futura, 1991

Petrocelli, William, and Kate Barbara Repa, *Sexual Harassment on the Job,* Berkeley, California: Nolo, 1992

Segrave, Kerry, *The Sexual Harassment of Women in the Workplace; 1600 to 1993,* Jefferson, North Carolina: McFarland, 1994

Webb, Susan L., *Shockwaves: The Global Impact of Sexual Harassment,* New York: MasterMedia, 1994

Since the late 1970s there has been a steady flow of literature dealing with the sexual harassment of women in the workplace. FARLEY's book, one of the earliest available surveys, documents the widespread occurrence of sexual harassment in traditionally women's jobs, as well as in non-traditional occupations, in the United States. Because it describes working women's experiences of sexual harassment at a time when the problem was not socially recognised, the book is useful for understanding the situation of sexually harassed women prior to the introduction of workplace sexual harassment policies.

Another pathbreaking book on sexual harassment in the workplace is that by MacKINNON. It defines sexual harassment as an expression of power and develops the argument that sexual harassment constitutes a form of sex discrimination, making it illegal in the United States under Title VII of the 1964 Civil Rights Act. Most current discussions of workplace sexual harassment law refer to and engage critically with this very influential book. Therefore, it is particularly useful for anyone wishing to gain an in-depth historical understanding of legal protections against sexual harassment in the United States.

The book by PETROCELLI and REPA is one of many handbooks that now provide practical advice on how to identify and deal with sexual harassment. It focuses on the legal protections against workplace sexual harassment in the United States. The book begins by explaining the legal definition of workplace sexual harassment. It illustrates this by reference to the range of behaviours that the courts have found to constitute unwelcome sexual conduct that creates an intimidating, hostile, or offensive working environment. The authors explain relevant legal terms used when considering the main issues pertaining to a determination of sexual harassment. These include the question of whether the conduct is sexual in nature, unreasonable, pervasive, and unwelcome. A discussion of the causes and effects of sexual harassment makes use of statistical information about the gendered nature of employment practices. A brief political history of the introduction of sexual harassment laws in the United States is particularly useful for understanding the difference between the application of state and federal laws. There is an extensive discussion of the advantages and disadvantages of alternative responses to workplace sexual harassment that are available to the sexually harassed. These range from taking formal action, such as confronting the sexual harasser directly or complaining in writing, to the use of formal complaint procedures. Separate chapters are devoted to employer-implemented complaint procedures, state and federal legal remedies for the recovery of wages, compensation for personal injuries, and workplace reform. The authors also assess the effectiveness of the agency that is responsible for the enforcement of the federal law, the Equal Employment Opportunities Commission.

SEGRAVE traces the long history of sexual harassment of working women, detailing cases from 1600 to 1993 across a range of occupations. These include indentured and domestic servants, industrial workers, clerical and service sector employees, wartime workers, and military and professional women. Drawing on a variety of sources, the author documents the historical association of working women with a failure in their morals and links this to the repeated tendency to blame women's sexual nature for the occurrence of sexual harassment. Although the book does not contain too much by way of theoretical analysis, it is useful for its informative material about the prevalence of sexual harassment.

BRANT and TOO's collection of essays gives an idea of the depth and breadth of current ways of questioning the meanings that feminists have associated with the term "sexual harassment." It does this, however, without abandoning the belief in the prevalence of the social phenomenon. The 11 essays offer an interdisciplinary assessment of current sexual harassment discourses—including legal, sociological, psychological, and literary—as well as considering the role of the media in reinforcing sexual harassment. One of the main concerns of the book is to draw attention to the ways in which feminists' association of sexual harassment with employment, in the late 1970s and early 1980s, has restricted current understanding of it. There is an attempt to expand the traditional emphasis on workplace sexual harassment through the examination of the effects of conceptions of space on the experience of sexual harassment. As well as addressing broad philosophical issues concerning the effects of the dominant ideas about sexual harassment, it deals with the issues of power, consent, and subjectivity that are central to the issue. The book also enables some comparison of the dominant American models of sexual harassment with those operative in other historical and cultural contexts.

PATTISON's book is among those demonstrating that sexual harassment is a very widespread if underestimated social problem. It mentions many published case histories of sexual harassment but focuses on the details of three famous cases. Two draw attention to the hazards for women of working in predominantly male work environments, and the third deals with a male in a position of authority over women. The book also provides much anecdotal evidence of sexual harassment. Although the sources are most often female office workers, they are also women who are in positions of relative power and authority, such as trade union officials. One important theme that is subtly traced through many sexually harassed women's stories is how much their personal response and their decision about whether or not to complain to superiors are shaped by fear of retaliation by male sexual harassers. Other issues that are raised are popular views about the causes of sexual harassment in the workplace, such as sexually harassed women's so-called tendency to dress provocatively, the inadequacy of male-run workplace complaint procedures, and the role of unions, the media, and the courts in addressing the problem of sexual harassment.

BINGHAM's book gives an excellent critical overview of developments in the field of the social sciences. It begins from the observation that the last two decades have produced considerable research into the various aspects of sexual harassment, such as the perceptions and evaluations of harassers and harassees, the role of power, and the significance of gender. Yet attempts to deal with sexual harassment at the institutional and legal level have not been so successful. Bingham suggests that this is due to the fact that public policy has focused on behaviours, their negative material and psychological effects, and the organisational structures that enable them. One issue that is discussed is the view that investigations into the occurrence of sexual harassment represent and serve workplace managerial interests more than the interests of those subjected to sexual harassment. This book is a very useful guide to current efforts to rethink the terms in which social science research into sexual harassment should be undertaken.

WEBB examines sexual harassment as a global phenomenon. Her research suggests that, even though sexually harassing behaviour is not always very severe, it is a serious problem because it occurs too often all around the world. The book contains a wealth of information about the incidence of workplace sexual harassment in over 20 countries across the continents. Webb draws together international media reports and surveys conducted by the International Labor Organisation and other bodies. The information provided covers issues like the numbers of victims, the type of harassment experienced, the impact of sexual harassment on victims' lives, victims' responses, the availability of legal protections, and the effectiveness of legal remedies. The book includes an extensive list of contracts, which provides a global view of the organisations, agencies, and services currently dealing with the problem of workplace harassment.

—TOULA NICOLACOPOULOS

See also Sexual Harassment in Education

Sexually Transmitted Disease *see* AIDS and HIV

Sexual Politics

Beauvoir, Simone de, *The Second Sex,* translated and edited by H. M. Parshley, New York: Knopf, 1952; London: Cape, 1953; originally published as *Le Deuxième Sexe,* Paris: Gallimard, 1949

Butler, Judith, *Bodies That Matter: On the Discursive Limits of "Sex,"* New York and London: Routledge, 1993

D'Emilio, John, and Estelle B. Freedman, *Intimate Matters: A History of Sexuality in America,* New York and London: Harper and Row, 1988

Firestone, Shulamith, *The Dialectic of Sex: The Case for Feminist Revolution,* New York: Morrow, 1970; and London: Cape, 1971

Foucault, Michel, *The History of Sexuality: An Introduction,* translated by Robert Hurley, New York: Pantheon, 1978; London: Lane, 1979

Friedan, Betty, *The Feminine Mystique,* New York: Norton, and London: V. Gollancz, 1963

Grosz, Elizabeth, *Volatile Bodies: Toward a Corporeal Feminism,* Bloomington: Indiana University Press, 1994

Millett, Kate, *Sexual Politics,* New York: Doubleday, 1970; London: Hart-Davies, 1972

Wiegman, Robyn, *American Anatomies: Theorizing Race and Gender,* Durham, North Carolina, and London: Duke University Press, 1995

Sexual politics is a broad field of inquiry, one that makes problematic the easy distinctions between masculine and feminine, men and women, male and female. Because of this, many readings in sexual politics discuss both men and women and their sexual and social relations. The first five books reviewed take this broad approach to sexed bodies, sexual practices, and sexuality. The last four books reviewed focus more specifically on women.

D'EMILIO and FREEDMAN provide a historical overview of sexuality in America (primarily in the United States). The book charts how the meaning and place of sexuality in American life has changed from a family-centered, reproductive sexual system in colonial times, to a conflicted romantic period, to a commercialized sexuality in the modern era. It focuses on both ideology (what was expected) and behavior (what was practiced) by explaining the sexual meanings, sexual regulations, and sexual politics of each of the three "eras" of sexuality. The text presents sexuality as continually reshaped by the changing nature of the economy, the family, and politics. Its citations, index, and bibliography offer the researcher and the curious reader an array of informative places to go.

FOUCAULT has written many works that are concerned with power. His works are useful sources of post-structuralist theory and critique. Foucault suggests that the modern explosion of talk about sex (which is supposedly liberating) is, in actuality, a way of controlling sex practices through discourse. He interrogates scientific discourses on sexuality, and delimits approaches to analysis and critique of discourses of sexuality.

In addition to, and extending upon, her earlier work, *Gender Trouble,* BUTLER argues that bodies "matter" in and through performance. Repeated performances (of sex and gender) participate in a process of materialization that stabilizes over time, giving the appearance of solidity. Using this argument, she reconceptualizes notions of agency, identity, intentionality, and "the subject" central to psychoanalysis, post-structuralism and feminism (footnotes provide a wealth of information and further readings in these three areas). She also reveals how discursive practices mark and form both gender and sex differences. Some "sexes" are so "incredible" to conventional understandings, she argues, that they are unrecognizable, immaterial—they are bodies that do not (have) matter. This text is a challenging philosophical, psychoanalytic, deconstructive inquiry, and well worth the effort.

GROSZ, like Butler, is concerned with bodies. Her goal is to reunite body and mind, which, she argues, have been set in an unproductive opposition. By means of this opposition (dualism), women are associated with the body and subsequently devalued. Using as her ruling metaphor the mobius strip (an inverted three-dimensional figure eight with no determinate interior or exterior), Grosz uses psychoanalytic, phenomenological, and neurophysiological accounts of the lived body to re-connect the body to the mind, and she uses theorists of corporeal inscription to re-connect the mind to the body (and assert the body's productivity). Her final chapter critiques the sexually specific male body posited by the accounts and theorists above, and their condemnation of women's uncontrollable (menstrual and other types of) "flow." In response, Grosz suggests men project fears of their own (seminal) flow and lack of control onto women.

WIEGMAN takes the discussion of bodies a step further by interrogating the visual bias of modernity, and how this concern with vision, the visual, and the visible has helped rationalize social hierarchies by means of race and gender. A major strength of this work is its recognition that sexual politics do not operate in a contextual vacuum but work with and against other politics. Wiegman shows how different "differences" (in this case, race and gender) combine and play off each other at particular historical moments and complicate assessments of politics. Her appreciation for, and extended discussion of, the complexities of identity politics remind readers that sexism is only one part of a larger political ecosystem—one where "isms" and anti-"ism" agendas (including Wiegman's own) are inevitably but not unproductively paradoxical.

DE BEAUVOIR's text is a classic in twentieth-century feminist thought. Its main thesis is that patriarchy, not "natural feminine" characteristics, has placed women in a secondary position in the world in relation to men. As a result, women have not been able to achieve equal status as humans. Her analysis is rooted in existential philosophy and includes critical assessment of the destiny of women, history of women, and myths about women offered by patriarchy. Her detailed and down-to-earth depiction of (French) women's stages of life, which includes discussion of childhood, young girlhood, sexual initiation, lesbianism, marriage, motherhood, prostitution, and old age, sensitively conveys how women are made, and not just born.

FRIEDAN's text, a classic for many American women, addresses the dissatisfaction of women relegated to housewifery, strict femininity, and an underdeveloped self-identity. Her depiction of "the problem that has no name" spoke during the 1960s to a number of (particularly middle-class) women torn between social expectations and personal needs and desires. In the text, Friedan critiques Sigmund Freud, Margaret Mead, social science, psychology, self-help, and advertising, with an accessible writing style, candor, and even humor. She includes the testimony of experts and lay-persons alike, provides examples to fuel her critique, and relates personal anecdotes. This text, perhaps more than any other, fueled the modern women's movement.

MILLETT'S text critiques the relationship between the sexes in the United States in a political light. Millett develops a theory of sexual politics at work in ideology, biology, sociology, class, the economy, education, force, anthropology, and psychology. She charts the evolution of the women's movement from 1830 to 1930 and the counterrevolution from 1930 to 1960. She also critiques the literature of four key male writers of her time: D.H. Lawrence, Henry Miller, Norman Mailer, and Jean Genet, and reveals the sexism, patriarchal bias, and exploitation of women (and the woman-like) in their work.

FIRESTONE emerges from a Marxist tradition. She develops a materialist view of history based on sex itself, locating biology and reproduction prior to and at the origin of dualisms upon which economic class inequalities are built. She recommends a revolt of the underclass (women), seizure of the means of (re)production, and development of technologies that would undermine the impact of genital differences so they would no longer matter culturally. Her discussions of American feminism, Freudianism, childhood and the incest taboo, racism, love, romance, (male) culture, and ecology are gritty and provocative.

—VALERIE V. PETERSON

See also Sexual Double Standard

Sexual Slavery

Altink, Sietske, *Stolen Lives: Trading Women into Sex and Slavery,* London: Scarlet Press, and New York: Harrington Park Press, 1995

Barry, Kathleen, *Female Sexual Slavery,* Englewood Cliffs, New Jersey: Prentice Hall, 1979; London: New York University Press, 1984

Calaguas, Belinda, *Let Our Silenced Voices Be Heard: The Traffic in Asian Women,* Manila: Isis International, 1993

Commission of the European Communities, *Trafficking in Women for the Purpose of Sexual Exploitation,* Brussels, Luxembourg: Office for Official Publications of the European Communities, 1996

Davis, Nanette, *Prostitution: An International Handbook on Trends, Problems, and Policies,* Westport, Connecticut: Greenwood, 1993

Hicks, George, *The Comfort Women: Sex Slaves of the Japanese Imperial Forces,* London: Souvenir Press, and New York: Norton, 1995

O'Callaghan, Sean, *Damaged Baggage: The White Slave Trade and Narcotics Trafficking in the Americas,* London: Hale, and New York: Roy, 1969

Trafficking in women has been practiced for thousands of years. It has been sanctioned by religious custom or has been the result of war or industrial changes. The feminist writer BARRY dispels the notion that "white slavery had become a historical artifact." She puts the international traffic in women and forced street prostitution under the same heading of female sexual slavery. Massive proliferation of pornography has brought prostitution into our daily lives and into our homes, which has changed society's definition of woman. This definition includes her sexual utility. Barry's activities helped place the traffic in women on the United Nations agenda and on women's conference agendas in Mexico and Denmark. To gather information for her book, Barry relied on interviews of women who had escaped from sexual slavery or left prostitution since 1966. She found that markets for womens' bodies exist wherever men congregate in large groups separated from home and family. Such groups include military men, traveling businessmen, sailors, and immigrant laborers. She examines the efforts of Asian and European feminists who were successful in reducing sex tourism in Japan and the Philippines. At the time she finished her book, she noted that sex tourism was appearing in the United States.

O'CALLAGHAN's account certainly proves that female sexual slavery has been a thriving business in the twentieth century. He emphasizes the economic necessity of prostitution, illustrates the deceitfulness of the procurers, and cites cases of whippings and injections of drugs in girls who resisted their fate. His activities were concentrated in South America, where prostitution was still legal, and the demand for girls was fulfilled by a French sexual slave ring until 1958, and since 1961 by a Middle East sexual slave ring. The French traffic was different in that the man in charge would have pretty girls snatched off Parisian streets and delivered to his brothels. Because of the apathy or corruptness of the local authorities, it took undercover work to get information on the traffic activity and to find the missing girls. It took an American businessman in Paris to go undercover to find his missing secretary, which led to the smashing of the French traffic. Because it is often useless and sometimes dangerous to approach the police, O'Callaghan had to go undercover to gather information on the Middle East ring in South America. The girls involved were either already prostitutes in Lebanon and were sent out ostensibly on visits to relatives, or they were cabaret artists, belly-dancers, singers, or chorus girls, lured to South America by promises of stardom and more money.

ALTINK presents a more comprehensive study of female sexual slavery, including the nineteenth and twentieth centuries and the international practice. Working for the Dutch Foundation Against Traffic in Women, Stichting Tegen Vrouwenhandel, Altink talked to more than 100 women. For her book, she interviewed 20 women from Thailand, Indonesia, Colombia, Dominican Republic, Morocco, Poland, Yugoslavia, and the Philippines. She found that the methods used by traffickers in recruiting girls are the same in the different countries. As captives in the brothels and red light districts, the girls could not speak out or talk to one another because it might endanger their parents. Consequently, their stories could not be corroborated. Therefore, Altink did not go undercover but interviewed girls who had run away from their captives or were in contact with the police. To compound the problem, the sexual slaves were seen by the authorities as illegal immigrants rather than as refugees, which made it difficult for them to give evidence against their traffickers. Altink views traffic in women as a human rights issue, because it violates the Universal Declaration of Human Rights.

Despite over two decades of an international women's movement, DAVIS points out that prostitution in many societies represents an extreme case of sexual stratification, where female sexuality serves as the core element of the gender system. Her book brings together the studies of a number of scholars from different societies. She demonstrates that the traditional rationales of poverty, unemployment, and minority group membership do not explain the persistence and new forms of prostitution. New issues, such as the Acquired Immune Deficiency Syndrome (AIDS), child prostitution, and international tourism have made prostitution a sociopolitical reality and dispel the notion that it is a "victimless crime." To achieve a comparative analysis among the 15 countries, interdisciplinary themes included such items as social and legal definitions of prostitution, social organization of prostitution, law enforcement, and intervention.

Davis tries to demonstrate the selective, gender-biased, hierarchical nature of control that exploits and damages women. She discusses the different responses in addressing the problem of prostitution. They include decriminalization, improvement in law enforcement, reeducation, health care, psychological counseling, financial assistance for the victims, and shifting focus from prostitution to the procurers, business operators, and traffickers. Moreover, there is a discussion over the disagreement that exists between feminists and prostitutes on how they perceive the sale of sexual services.

CALAGUAS has complied lists of conferences, periodicals on the problem, and international organizations working on the issue, in addition to stories and statistics on the subject. This work emphasizes economics for the selling of sex. Impoverished women are traded or sold to rich men, and the direction of trade flows from Latin America to southern Europe and the Middle East; from Southeast Asia to the Middle East and central and northern Europe; and from east Europe to west Europe. In the non-western world trafficking in women takes on different forms, such as bridewealth and mail-order brides. Today, in Japan the sex industry is controlled privately, but during World War II, it was state-sponsored. Over 200,000 women, mostly Korean, were dragooned to serve as "comfort girls" by catering to the sexual needs of the Japanese Army throughout Southeast Asia. Calaguas shows that women in Asia are networking, making strategy, and planning tactics to address the issue. Their plans are addressed to other women's groups, governments, and international bodies such as the United Nations.

HICKS first heard about the comfort women when some Korean women took the Japanese government to court in 1991. Through personal contacts among Japanese female activists, he was able to collect practically everything that had been written about the comfort women. Through other contacts Hicks found individuals in Southeast Asia who were the victims. Comfort women were Japanese prostitutes and abducted Southeast Asian women who were gathered to serve the sexual needs of the Japanese Imperial Army between 1930 and 1945. Eighty percent of the abducted women were Koreans. In the late 1980s women's groups in Korea and Japan began to organize, and in 1992 hotlines were set up to collect information about comfort stations and comfort women. Consequently, issues such as sex tourism and the plight of comfort women have become political issues throughout Southeast Asia.

The COMMISSION OF THE EUROPEAN COMMUNITIES points out that sexual exploitation for high profits has become increasingly practiced by organized crime, and the flow of the trafficking of women runs from developing countries to central, eastern, and western Europe. The book points out that it has been the activities of non-governmental organizations, such as the United Nations and the Council of Europe, that have brought the issue to public awareness, and they have emphasized the issue of the violation of basic human rights. The book reports on the activities of European conferences and committees that met in the 1990s to discuss existing activities to combat sexual exploitation, and to discuss how the different agencies can cooperate and coordinate their activities. Lack of cooperation was cited as a weakness in dealing with the problem. It was recommended that improvements need to be made in migration training, law enforcement training, and training in the social field. This training would be undertaken by such agencies as Europol, Interpol, UNESCO, the Council of Europe, and the Task Force for Justice and Home Affairs.

The Commission reported that the Vienna Conference of June, 1996 held a comprehensive session on the causes, countries involved, and the number of women involved in sexual slavery. The purpose of the conference was to establish an integrated multidisciplinary approach to the problem. Such an approach would involve improvement in data and research, national legislation against sexual exploitation, cooperation and coordination among the countries, better training in counseling, safe havens for victims, rehabilitation centers, and other recommendations.

—BILL MANIKAS

See also Sex Tourism; Prostitution

Shakespeare, William 1564–1616

English Playwright and Poet

Bamber, Linda, *Comic Women, Tragic Men: A Study of Gender and Genre in Shakespeare,* Stanford, California: Stanford University Press, 1982

Dreher, Diane Elizabeth, *Domination and Defiance: Fathers and Daughters in Shakespeare,* Lexington: University Press of Kentucky, 1986

Dusinberre, Juliet, *Shakespeare and the Nature of Women,* London: Macmillan, and New York: Barnes and Noble, 1975

Jardine, Lisa, *Still Harping on Daughters: Women and Drama in the Age of Shakespeare,* New York and Hemel Hempstead: Harvester, 1983

Neely, Carol Thomas, *Broken Nuptials in Shakespeare's Plays,* New Haven, Connecticut, and London: Yale University Press, 1985

Williamson, Marilyn L., *The Patriarchy of Shakespeare's Comedies,* Detroit, Michigan: Wayne State University Press, 1986

The women's movement and the development of feminist criticism put new life in Shakespeare studies. Instead of the traditional focus on political structure or history in Shakespeare's plays, a new area of inquiry developed—an examination of the Bard's concepts of women. One of the first to address this new focus was DUSINBERRE. In this work, the author claims that feminism did exist in the sixteenth and seventeenth centuries, and that Shakespeare and other playwrights explored the ramifications of equality in their plays. Dusinberre explores possible causes for Shakespeare's feminism. One of the main influences, she explains, was Calvinism—that is, Puritanism. She includes a long discussion of the Calvinist concept of companionate marriage both in her introduction and in the first chapter. Other topics investigated include ideas of chastity, authority, women as property, and education. In all of these areas, Dusinberre examines the relationship of Shakespeare's society, Protestant theology, and the plays. She believes that, although Shakespeare was not allied with the most zealous arm of the Protestant Church, he, along with other playwrights, was influenced by Calvinist questioning of orthodox beliefs about the nature of women. This book has become a standard text in feminist Shakespeare criticism. It has also sparked an ongoing debate about Shakespeare's ideas about women.

Feminist Shakespeare criticism has generally followed one of two lines: either Shakespeare's genius was able to transcend patriarchy to express the various nuances of the nature of women, or he was a product of patriarchy, and, therefore, his plays reflect chauvinistic attitudes. JARDINE sets out to follow a different path. She explores various cultural issues of the Renaissance, and examines the plays within the contexts of those issues. She begins with a discussion of the problem of the actors who played women's roles, concerned with the possible influence of sexual ambiguity on the development of female characters. She also considers education, the role of inherited wealth, the threat of the shrew, and female heroism. In each chapter, Jardine discusses prevalent cultural concepts and the way they are employed in the creation of female characters. She does not conclude that any of the playwrights she considers is either feminist or chauvinist; rather, she shows how female characters reflect or distort the concepts in question. This is a valuable resource for those interested in Renaissance culture, drama, and feminist interpretation.

BAMBER also deliberately diverges from the two most common approaches to feminist criticism of Shakespeare's works. She notes the difference between Shakespeare's treatment of women in the comedies and in the tragedies. In the comedies, the female characters are often smarter than the men, while in the tragedies, they are often evil. Bamber makes no claims for Shakespeare as a Renaissance feminist; rather, she focuses on the fact that gender relationships are always central to his works, but that in them, the Self is always masculine and the Other is always feminine. In order to make her point, she studies several of the tragedies in depth: *Antony and Cleopatra, Hamlet, Macbeth, Coriolanus, Henry VI, Henry V,* and *The Tempest*, although the comic heroines get only one chapter. Bamber's work is interesting and important because it does not ignore the presence of patriarchy—even misogyny—in Shakespeare's plays; instead, she confronts each issue as it arises.

NEELY is one of the best known and respected feminist critics of Shakespeare's work. This book has become a standard text in the field, focusing on the importance of marriage to Shakespeare's plays. She sees the female characters' position in the marriage process— "maiden/wife/widow"—as their defining trait. Neely does not place Shakespeare's females within the social context of Renaissance England; rather, she sees the variety of female characters and their strengths and weaknesses as his response to the demands of different genres. The book is developed around the theme of marriage and the stages of the marriage process. Neely considers five plays in depth, all of which have marriage as a central issue: *Much Ado About Nothing, All's Well That Ends Well, Othello, Antony and Cleopatra,* and *The Winter's Tale.*

DREHER focuses on another kind of male-female relationship, that between fathers and daughters in Shakespeare's works. Dreher is interested in both the bond of affection, and the conflict that develops as the daughter comes of age. As daughters demand more freedom, fathers begin to face the inevitability of this change, which they experience as rejection. Some of the daughters in Shakespeare's plays continue to submit to their fathers, like Ophelia, and others rebel, like Desdemona and Jessica. Dreher sees the fathers as caught in mid-life crises, often becoming either tyrants or busybodies. Dreher combines Jungian theory with history to explore one of the most important kinds of relationships in Shakespeare's plays.

WILLIAMSON uses New Historical methodology and the theories of Michel Foucault in her book, which she intends as a study of power in the comedies. In this work, the author investigates written cultural artifacts such as manuals, diaries, sermons, and official records to place Shakespeare in a cultural context. Among her concerns is the connection between power and language. She sees history not as background but as a context for the plays. Thus, she examines history along with the plays, which she considers as groups. She believes other feminist critics have neglected historical study of patriarchy, and her intent is to remedy this lack. She traces the development of Shakespeare's plays through a variety of historical events and places them against a historical backdrop. Williamson's book is a valuable study for those interested in the theories of Foucault as applied to literary criticism.

—KATHERINE ROBERTS

Shelley, Mary 1797–1851

British Writer

Bennett, Betty T., *Mary Diana Dods, A Gentleman and a Scholar,* New York: William Morrow, 1991
Blumberg, Jane, *Mary Shelley's Early Novels: "This Child of Imagination and Misery,"* Iowa City: University of Iowa Press, and London: Macmillan, 1993
Dunn, Jane, *Moon in Eclipse: A Life of Mary Shelley,* London: Weidenfeld and Nicolson, and New York: St. Martin's Press, 1978
Fisch, Audrey A., Anne K. Mellor, and Esther H. Schor (eds.), *The Other Mary Shelley: Beyond "Frankenstein,"* New York: Oxford University Press, 1993
Levine, George Lewis, and U.C. Knoepflmacher (eds.), *The Endurance of "Frankenstein": Essays on Mary Shelley's Novel,* Berkeley: University of California Press, 1974
Mellor, Anne K., *Mary Shelley: Her Life, Her Fiction, Her Monsters,* New York and London: Routledge, 1988
Smith, Johanna M., *Mary Shelley,* New York: Twayne, and London: Prentice Hall, 1996
Spark, Muriel, *Child of Light: A Reassessment of Mary Shelley,* London: Tower Bridge Publications, 1951; Folcroft, Pennsylvania: Folcroft Library Editions, 1972; revised as *Mary Shelley,* New York: Dutton, 1987; London: Constable, 1988
Sunstein, Emily W., *Mary Shelley: Romance and Reality,* Boston: Little Brown, 1989; London: Johns Hopkins, 1991
Walling, William A., *Mary Shelley,* New York: Twayne, 1972

Until recently, biographers and critics saw Mary Shelley primarily as the lover, wife, and widow of an important writer, Percy Bysshe Shelley, and as the creator of one important novel, *Frankenstein,* in which the writing was heavily influenced by her husband. Her other writings and her life and concerns apart from her husband's had to wait until the women's movement to receive their deserved critical attention.

WALLING's book is the earliest full-length critical study to feature Shelley as important in her own right, and to treat some of the lesser-known novels as worthy of critical attention. He finds in *Valperga* Shelley's highest achievement in characterization, and a political treatment of the theme of ambition, found also in *Frankenstein. The Last Man* is an idealized biography of Shelley's dead husband, its pessimism attributable to grief and loneliness. Although he does not examine the roles of sex and gender, Walling provides a reliable but somewhat dated introduction to Shelley study.

Making insightful use of letters and other archival material not available to Walling, and looking through the lenses of feminism and Marxism, SMITH also examines Shelley's life and works; although both books present their findings in the standard and helpful Twayne format, they could not be more different. Smith analyzes more of the works, including the verse drama, travel writing, and poetry. In showing how Shelley's work reflects and informs literary history, she demonstrates the weaknesses inherent in the exercise of categorizing literature into genres and periods. Contextualizing and analyzing Shelley's feminist and political concerns, she illuminates the history of the romantic and Victorian periods. As intended, the book is valuable both as a critical work on Shelley and as a work of cultural studies. It includes a briefly annotated bibliography.

Also drawing on archival materials is MELLOR's work, focusing on Shelley's family relationships to illuminate *Frankenstein* and other fiction. Mellor believes Shelley tried throughout her life to create the close and supportive family she never had, and that she wrote *Frankenstein* as an exploration of the consequences of the lack of the nuclear family. She proposes that Shelley's struggles to reconcile a longing for a bourgeois family and her strong sense of the oppression of patriarchy create the central tension of her writing. Mellor presents an important historical and feminist analysis of Shelley's understanding of science and clarifies the nature and extent of Percy Bysshe Shelley's contributions to the novel.

In the introduction to LEVINE and KNOEPFLMACHER's book, the first serious critical study of *Frankenstein,* the editors defend their choice of the novel as a subject for serious attention. The twelve essays place the novel within literary history, trace biographical elements, explore political and social dimensions, consider the text itself, and examine popular adaptations. Most essays were written especially for this volume, and there are many cross-references and internal debates.

Although BLUMBERG approaches *Frankenstein, Valperga,* and *The Last man* from a biographical standpoint, the book is pointedly not a psychological study of Shelley. In a discussion of Shelley's editing of her husband's work, the book demonstrates how Shelley made an intellectual break with the poet's ideas but never wavered in her devotion to the man. Blumberg explores Shelley's relationship with her friend Lord Byron, with whom she was "connected in a thousand ways."

FISCH seeks to correct what the editors perceive as Shelley's having moved, with the increase in feminist criticism of *Frankenstein,* from the shadow of her husband to the shadow of her creation. Fisch's 14 essays and introduction survey the complete works, locate *Frankenstein*'s place within Shelley's body of work, and identify in Shelley a writer resisting romanticism. Part One, "Romanticism and Resistance," includes essays on Shelley's editions of her husband's works, by Mary Favret and Susan J. Wolfson. Part Two, "Culture and Criticism," includes Fisch's "Plaguing Politics: AIDS, Deconstruction, and *The Last Man.*"

The essential biography is that by SUNSTEIN, which claims for Shelley a place among the "stellar" English romantic writers. Her tragedy was that she lived in the wrong time and place: romantic period England, where intellectual, artistic, and sexual opportunities were increasingly within reach, but where society condemned women who took advantage of them. Sunstein treats the full body of Shelley's writing (some works for the first time) and traces the full extent to which Shelley was responsible for establishing Percy Bysshe Shelley's reputation.

BENNETT explores in full detail a strange part of Shelley's life only touched on by Sunstein: Shelley's close relationships with women, and in particular her involvement with Maria Diana Dods, who posed as a man and married Isabella Robinson. This book casts intriguing light on strong woman-centered networks in the nineteenth century, within which Shelley lived the last half of her life.

Published 100 years after Shelley's death, SPARK's first edition was the first important Shelley biography. The revised edition takes into account new insights offered by the journals and letters and yields a readable and sympathetic view of the life and times. DUNN, also seeking to rescue Shelley from her husband's shadow, quotes excerpts from the fiction to "mirror" the facts of Shelley's life. Dunn's Shelley values family and friends over ambition, as shown by her life and extolled in the fiction.

—CYNTHIA A. BILY

Single-Parent Families

Burns, Ailsa, and Cath Scott, *Mother-Headed Families and Why They Have Increased,* Hillsdale, New Jersey, and Hove, United Kingdom: Lawrence Erlbaum Associates, 1994

Dickerson, Bette J., *African American Single Mothers: Understanding Their Lives and Families,* Thousand Oaks, California, and London: Sage, 1995

Dowd, Nancy E., *In Defense of Single-Parent Families,* New York and London: New York University Press, 1997

Edin, Kathryn, and Laura Lein, *Making Ends Meet: How Single Mothers Survive Welfare and Low-Wage Work,* New York: Russell Sage Foundation, 1997

Gordon, Linda, *Pitied But Not Entitled: Single Mothers and the History of Welfare, 1890–1935,* New York: Free Press, 1994

McLanahan, Sara, and Gary Sandefur, *Growing Up with a Single Parent: What Hurts, What Helps,* Cambridge, Massachusetts: Harvard University Press, 1994

Mink, Gwendolyn, *The Wages of Motherhood: Inequality in the Welfare State, 1917–1942,* Ithaca, New York, and London: Cornell University Press, 1995

Polakow, Valerie, *Lives on the Edge: Single Mothers and Their Children in the Other America,* Chicago: University of Chicago Press, 1993

Taylor, Debbie, *My Children, My Gold: A Journey to the World of Seven Single Mothers,* Berkeley: University of California Press, 1994

The term "single-parent families" is often used as a euphemism for "single-mother families" and deployed in contemporary discourse as a symbol of all that is wrong, pathological, or dangerous about modern societies. The trend to female headship, as some of the volumes considered here show, is indeed a worldwide phenomenon. In the social sciences, a great deal of research has been done on single-mother families, much of it assuming, and intending to document, the pathology of single motherhood. The volumes considered here are a refreshing counterpoint to this predominant literature; despite a wide variety of methodological approaches, most of the authors intentionally place the words and experiences of single mothers themselves at the center of consideration.

Both Gordon and Mink provide useful historical analyses of the role of single motherhood in the development of social welfare provision in the United States. GORDON focuses on the role of the development of the field of social work, and the female social reformers at the center of this movement, in the creation of the mother's pension programs that became the (now defunct) Aid to Families with Dependent Children (AFDC) program, the primary vehicle for assistance to poor single mothers from 1935 until 1996. She also discusses the different approach to providing for single mothers among the African-American women involved in social reform and poor relief.

MINK also describes the maternalist policies of the social reform movement in developing mothers' pensions, especially showing the way in which race and the desire for cultural homogeneity played a role in the goals of aid to single mothers. Mink documents the concern for making certain that children of new immigrants embrace "American values," leading to a highly intrusive level of supervision for single mothers who received mothers' pensions, supervision unheard of in programs intended primarily for male breadwinners. Both books are well-researched and written.

As their title indicates, BURNS and SCOTT are concerned primarily with considering the evidence as to why mother-headed families have increased in numbers in the late twentieth century. The book usefully separates discussion of the three major sources of single motherhood: divorce, non-marital births, and widowhood. The authors' primary focus is on western industrialized nations, although the book also includes a chapter on out-of-wedlock births in non-western countries. The book also considers various theories that attempt to explain single motherhood. The authors conclude that what they term "decomplementary theory" provides the best explanatory model. The basic idea is that, due to economic, social, and legal changes, men and women no longer have "complementary" interests. One of the book's greatest weaknesses is its discussion of feminist theories regarding families, which is cursory and certainly does not encompass much recent feminist theorizing in the area. However, its usefulness is in its effort to look at single motherhood as a worldwide phenomenon and provide comparisons among disparate societies.

One of the greatest concerns regarding single parents is the effect of such families on the children raised in them. The issue is so politicized, however, that it is often difficult to decipher fact from fabrication. Some of the most widely cited studies on the subject are deeply problematic due to methodological flaws, including lack of control groups and the use of unrepresentative sample groups. McLANAHAN and SANDEFUR's book is a useful antidote to this problem. Utilizing four data sets representative of the U.S. population—the Panel Study of Income Dynamics, the National Longitudinal Survey of Young Men and Women, the High School and Beyond Study, and the National Survey of Families and Households—the authors set out to compare children of single-parent families, whether formed by divorce or nonmarital birth, with children of two-parent families. For their purposes, the authors defined two-parent families as those in which the child, at age 16, was living with both biological parents. What McLanahan and Sandefur found was that on a variety of indicators, including educational attainment and risk of sustained adulthood unemployment, children of single parents do less well than children in two-parent families. (It should be noted here that most children do well on the indicators studied regardless of family structure.) About half of the disadvantages are explained by income; most of the rest are due to residential mobility and amount of parental supervision. The authors propose policy solutions that include universal programs to support families regardless of family structure, both economically and otherwise.

Two of the texts considered here provide insight regarding the lives of women who are single parents and poor. After a brief survey of the history of childhood and the ideology of motherhood, POLAKOW uses an ethnographic approach to discuss the lives of poor single mothers and their children. She evocatively tells the stories of six teenage mothers and of five other single mothers, giving a clear sense of what life is like for these women. She then turns to a discussion of the lives of poor children, as observed in their classroom settings. Her discussion makes it clear that many poor children are set up for failure by their teachers and school situations, but also that an understanding and skilled classroom teacher can make a world of difference in the life of a child growing up in poverty. This book is highly useful for its ability to humanize single mothers and their children.

EDIN and LEIN provide a more detailed picture of the lives of single mothers in the United States, both those receiving public assistance and those in low-wage jobs. Their study involved intensive interviews with 379 women in four cities: Boston, Chicago, Charleston, and San Antonio. National survey data show that low-income people report more expenditures than they do income; one goal of this study was to find out the sources of the additional income. Edin and Lein found that single mothers and their children regularly experience material hardship, and that low-wage workers actually experience more hardship than women on public assistance, largely because their expenses (for child care, transportation, and so on) are greater. Most of these women receive additional support from off-the-books work, boyfriends, their children's father(s), or other family members. Edin and Lein emphasize that for most of these women, the well-being of their families took priority, which is why they used a wide variety of strategies to provide enough income for basic material needs. The authors see the principal problem of single mothers as the lack of jobs that pay a living wage.

Among the most vilified of single mothers are African-American single parents. DICKERSON provides a very useful source of information on the lives of these women and their families, intentionally placing the experiences of African-American women at the center of consideration. The book includes chapters that place single-parent families in the African-American community in historical perspective, examine attitudes regarding morality in the African diaspora, discuss teenage mothers, provide a "visual analysis" that discusses media presentations of single motherhood, and discuss the relationship between the legal system and single motherhood. A very useful chapter by Suzanne M. Randolph discusses the impact of single motherhood on children; Randolph clearly points out some of the strengths of single-mother families. The book generally succeeds in placing single motherhood in the African-American community in its social, historical, legal, political, and economic context.

DOWD provides a timely and useful defense of single-parent families, including some attention to those headed by men. The book is in three parts. The first part addresses some of the stigmas attached to single-parent families, and presents commonly-held myths about single parents, along with refutation of those myths. The second section addresses law and single parents, looking at divorced and nonmarital families in separate chapters. Dowd also argues that single-parent families offer positive role models, especially because such families have been found to be less hierarchical and to provide greater autonomy to children. The third section of the book suggests policies that would provide greater support to single parents and their children.

TAYLOR tells the stories of seven single mothers in seven different countries. Five of the women are from what the author terms the "Fourth World"— represented are Brazil, China, Egypt, India, and Uganda; the other two are from Scotland and Australia. The author's goal is to put a human face on single motherhood, while also showing that two conditions, patriarchy and poverty, although taking unique forms in each society, shape the lives of single mothers and their children. The stories told here are powerful, illustrating the struggles that single mothers face, as well as their remarkable resiliency and strength.

—JYL JOSEPHSON

See also Child Custody; Child Support; Divorce: Present-Day

Sisterhood

Dunn, Judy, *Young Children's Close Relationships: Beyond Attachment,* Newbury Park, California: Sage, 1993

Mathias, Barbara, *Between Sisters: Secret Rivals, Intimate Friends,* New York: Delacorte Press, 1992

Merrell, Susan Scarf, *The Accidental Bond: The Power of Sibling Relationships,* New York: Times, 1995

Ripps, Susan, *Sisters: Devoted or Divided,* New York: Kensington Press, 1994

Saline, Carol, *Sisters,* Philadelphia and London: Running Press, 1994

Of the many relationships in a woman's life, the bond between sisters is unique. It stretches and bends through periods of closeness and distance, but it almost never breaks. SALINE presents a moving portrayal of a relationship like no other in a series of essays. In the interviews included in this book, the author focuses on sisters who genuinely like each other. However, she also includes a few who do not get along. Both groups express common feelings. They talk about what the world thinks a sister should be and how they wish their relationship reflected that model. These women speak of the wisdom and experience they share with their sisters. They are writers, athletes, students, and teachers. They tell how they share challenges in the same careers, compete in different professions, and battle together against illness. Women of all ages tell how they fought and made up, how they laughed and loved, and how they gave, risked, and resented one another—but never stopped caring. Their stories are poignant and stirring; they are filled with humor, tenderness, and pride.

RIPPS's book includes more than 50 interviews in which women talk about their relationships with their sisters. She includes commentary of psychologists who are experts in the field of family relationships. The reader will meet sisters who share every moment together, and sisters who share little more than the same parents; sisters who have successfully borne a child for a sister unable to conceive on her own; sisters who have stolen a sister's husband or lover; sisters who have been in conflict since childhood; and sisters who have resolved their relationships. This book is divided into two parts. Part one discusses the power of sisterhood, including both competitive and supportive sisters. Part two discusses the prevailing bond of sisterhood, including sections on twins, jealous sisters, and devoted sisters.

Sisters can be the best of friends and the worst of friends. MATHIAS brings both professional and personal insight into the sister connection. She uses colorful stories from real lives as well as interviews with experts in the fields of psychology, family relations, and women's studies. The author illustrates the dynamics of sisterhood. The reader is guided through the maze and mystery of this relationship. Mathias explores the wide range of intricate emotions, from jealousy to guilt, from closeness to compatibility, from diversity to similarity. This is a book about how women relate to their biological sisters. It is both a study of and a reflection on the joy and complexity of being sisters.

DUNN's book examines the differences in family relationships, including the relationship between mother and child, the relationship of siblings, and the special relationship between sisters. Each relationship is first described in terms of the dimensions that appear, on theoretical grounds, to be good candidates for developmental influence. Next is the key issue of the links between children's relationships with mothers, with siblings, and with friends. The author draws on a range of current studies. In these projects, children were studied over several years from preschool, as they grew up with their mothers and siblings, and also with their friends. There is a special section devoted to sisters.

MERRELL writes a book on sibling relationships, paying particular attention to sisters. The author consulted experts when interpreting a particular sibling's behavior. The goal of this book, however, is not to analyze the siblings the author interviewed for this work, but to try to place their stories in the context of the most fundamental aspects of brother-sister, brother-brother, and sister-sister relationships. This book contains 10 chapters. The first chapter deals with the topic of the bond between siblings, which the author calls an accidental bond. The second chapter talks specifically about sisterhood, whereas the third chapter talks about brotherhood. By reading these two chapters, one gets a clear idea of the differences between the relationships of sisters and those of brothers. The fourth chapter discusses the special relationship twins share. The last six chapters deal with stories about siblings, focusing on the power of the sibling relationship.

—SUSAN M. TAYLOR

Slavery, Black

Bush, Barbara, *Slave Women in Caribbean Society, 1650–1838*, Bloomington: Indiana University Press, and London: James Currey, 1990

Brown, Kathleen M., *Good Wives, Nasty Wenches and Anxious Patriarchs: Gender, Race, and Power in Colonial Virginia*, Chapel Hill and London: University of North Carolina Press, 1996

Davis, Angela Y., *Women, Race and Class*, New York: Random House, 1981; London: Women's Press, 1982

Fox-Genovese, Elizabeth, *Within the Plantation Household: Black and White Women of the Old South*, Chapel Hill and London, University of North Carolina Press, 1988

Jones, Jacqueline, *Labor of Love, Labor of Sorrow: Black Women, Work, and the Family from Slavery to the Present*, New York: Basic Books, 1985

Morton, Patricia (ed.), *Discovering the Women in Slavery: Emancipating Perspectives on the American Past*, Athens and London: University of Georgia Press, 1996

Robertson, Claire C., and Martin A. Klein, *Women and Slavery in Africa*, Madison: University of Wisconsin Press, 1983

Stevenson, Brenda E., *Life in Black and White: Family and Community in the Slave South*, New York and Oxford: Oxford University Press, 1996

White, Deborah Gray, *Ar'n't I a Woman? Female Slaves in the Plantation South*, New York and London: Norton, 1985

Black slavery has been the topic of innumerable books since the 1960s, but few have included gender as a category of analysis. Only in the 1980s and 1990s has this paucity of sources been rectified by the publication of a number of books that consider gender first and foremost. The 1980s brought the publication of several works that analyzed the experience of black women in slavery and freedom. Several new books have appeared in the 1990s that use gender and race as their major points of reference and give treatment to both black and white women of the southern United States. Even more rare than books about women in slavery in the United States are works that delve into black female slavery in other areas of the world.

One of the first authors to call for the inclusion of women in slavery studies in the United States was Davis. Although her treatment of women in slavery is brief, Davis set up the parameters of the debate about African-American women. Her book contains one chapter on the legacy of slavery. This legacy consisted of a culture in which women worked like men in the fields, held equal—but not superior—roles within the family and were subject to sexual abuse by their owners. Moreover, she avers, resistance to slavery was not confined to men. Hers was a beginning call for more extensive study, which has been answered by a number of more recent works. Davis's book is a good starting point for reading about black women in slavery in the United States.

BUSH, although writing about women in slavery in the Caribbean, particularly credits Davis for inspiring her to study slave women. She explicates Davis's themes in great detail, showing through her studies of large sugar plantations that women were treated similarly to men in their work lives; that they were sexually exploited (although she adds complexity to this picture by elucidating circumstances under which women benefited from sexual liaisons with white men); and that women also engaged in resistance to slavery. In addition, she believes that the key role of slave women was the creation and preservation of the family.

One of the few book-length studies of women in slavery in the United States is that by WHITE, who has written one of the few secondary works on women which is limited to the period of slavery and to black women. She concludes that all women were oppressed by work, by sexual oppression, by powerlessness, and by lives limited by law and custom, but the suffering of African-American slave women surpassed all other women's travails.

JONES's work spans both slavery and freedom, but it focuses on the family as the center of the black woman's life. All was subordinate to the preservation of the family. Although work in the big house seems to have been the better role for ease of living, Jones shows that living in the slave quarters and working in the fields was preferred because of the autonomy and proximity to children that it offered. Jones treats the post-Reconstruction period fully, showing how sharecropping provided more autonomy for the black family and protected black women from some of the ills of slavery, such as sexual exploitation. Jones's work is a most useful and comprehensive book on black women from slavery to the present.

A number of works have appeared recently that compare white and black women in the slave South. FOX-GENOVESE was one of the first to employ this method. Looking at the plantation household, which she defines as all aspects of plantation production and reproduction, Fox-Genovese shows that although black and white women's lives were connected—sometimes intimately—they were not allies. White women, although thoroughly subordinate to white males, were still the beneficiaries of the slave system. Her work uses the stories of individual women such as Sarah Gayle and Harriet Jacobs to prove her point. The rich detail of their lives makes this a compelling book.

BROWN's book is a comprehensive study of colonial Virginia, which focuses not only on black and white women, but also on Indians and male patriarchs. Hers is a valuable book for seeing the connections between race, gender, slavery, and patriarchal power. STEVENSON'S book is a community study of Loudoun County, Virginia between the Revolution and the Civil War. Part One of the book deals with marriage and family in the white community, and Part Two considers the same variables in the black community. Unlike Jones and White, she finds that black families were unable to stand up to the forces of disintegration that were endemic to Loudoun county during the antebellum period, because of the marginality of free black families and the devastating effects of the domestic slave trade for slaves of the upper South.

MORTON'S book is a collection of essays that shows the diversity of slavery in the United States and the various methodologies that can lead us to a knowledge of slavery. The first section uses the case study method to focus on both black and white women, while the second section, the group study section, explores such groups as black women in New Orleans, in both the colonial and the antebellum period, and black Methodist women. In addition, selected essays in this section investigate the adornment of plantation slave women, breastfeeding and weaning of white children by slave women, interracial sexual relations, the dilemmas of elite white women, and the experiences of German-American women.

Finally, ROBERTSON and KLEIN have collected a number of essays that examine African women's role in slavery in the nineteenth and twentieth centuries. The book deals with women in the Atlantic slave trade, women in the African slave trade, and women as exploiters of the slavery of other women. Males outnumbered females in the Atlantic slave trade by approximately three to one, but female slaves dominated the slave trade in Africa. Case histories of slave women in Africa demonstrate that these women were often used as pawns, had little power, and often led abject lives. More controversial is the evidence that women held other women as slaves and engaged in the slave trade themselves. This collection brings an important dimension to the study of black women in slavery.

—BONNIE L. FORD

Smith, Margaret Chase 1897–1995

American Politician

Fleming, Alice M., *The Senator from Maine: Margaret Chase Smith*, New York: Thomas Y. Crowell, 1969

Graham, Frank, *Margaret Chase Smith: Woman of Courage*, New York: John Day, 1964

Lamson, Peggy, *Few Are Chosen: American Women in Political Life Today*, Boston: Houghton Mifflin, 1968

Wallace, Patricia W., *Politics of Conscience: A Biography of Margaret Chase Smith*, Westport, Connecticut: Praeger, 1995

Often books about women in a "man's world" present them as two-dimensional inspirational role models, exceptional and without failings. This is good neither for readers looking for guidance, nor for the person being portrayed. GRAHAM's work is of that genre. Margaret Chase Smith was the first woman to serve both in the House and Senate of the United States. Eventually she served longer in the Senate than any other woman. She was known for her conscientious attendance on the Senate floor during debates and votes. (Even when running for president in 1964, she did not miss a vote.) Graham's account is a story of devotion to duty, unstinting hard work, refusal to compromise personal principles, and an example of what can be done by a woman in a "man's world." The author sets out to describe the professional life of a U.S. Senator. He admits that he could have chosen as his subject any of the other 99 Senators. However, he decided on Margaret Chase Smith because of the special problems she encountered in the chamber as a woman, and because of her exceptional qualities of independence and dedication. In addition, the author documents her 1964 run for the presidency. She was the first Republican woman in the Senate, and the first woman to seek a major party's presidential nomination.

A similar life of a senator-as-saint was FLEMING's book. It was part of a Women of America series, and also takes the story up to Smith's 1964 candidacy for president. Smith was a former teacher, newspaperwoman, and businesswoman. At 29, she became president of the Maine Federation of Business and Professional Women's Clubs. She married a local newspaper publisher and politician. When her husband went to Congress in 1937, she served as his secretary. When he was dying in 1940, he asked his constituents to elect his wife to fill out his term. She won and was re-elected four times. Smith was elected to the U.S. Senate in 1948 by the highest majority, and the greatest total vote majority, in the history of Maine. She was easily re-elected in 1954, 1960, and 1966. She was one of the first senators to speak out against the excesses of Senator Joseph McCarthy. (He attacked her and her allies as "Snow White and the Six Dwarfs.") She cast a decisive vote that helped Democrats block the president's appointment of Lewis Strauss to be Secretary of Commerce. Although polls showed that most Americans were for them, she voted against the test ban treaty and the wheat sale to the Soviet Union.

Several books included Smith in the company of other women who were exceptions in the political world of men. LAMSON, for example, discusses ten such women: four Congresswomen, one judge, a presidential appointee, an ambassador, a mayor, a state legislator, and Senator Smith. In this book also, the coverage of Smith's career terminates with her 1964 presidential candidacy.

WALLACE's study provides balance to these glowing accounts. The author, a professor of women's history and foreign relations who conducted many interviews with Smith at the twilight of her long life, presents both Smith's strengths and her failings. The author says Smith, a skilled politician, was the most influential woman in the history of American politics (as a policy-maker—whereas Eleanor Roosevelt, the author feels, was influential as a symbol). Wallace's work covers Smith's thirty-two years of congressional service. Wallace finds Smith to be an example for other women, but not a feminist. Smith was supersensitive to press criticism and deliberately separated herself from the women's movement (although she was a sponsor of the Equal Rights Amendment). She was rigid and intolerant, with a need for enemies and a sense of victimization. Some saw her as independent, others as inconsistent. She was a cold warrior, a proponent of the military-industrial complex, and of nuclear power. Wallace discusses the influence on her career and life of her close friend and aide, William C. Lewis, Jr., who honed her image as a feisty, hardworking Maine independent. Theirs was both a political and a personal partnership. One flaw in Wallace's fine book, however, is a recourse to fictionalized conversations.

—MARTIN GRUBERG

Soap Opera

Ang, Ien, *Watching "Dallas": Soap Opera and the Melodramatic Imagination,* London and New York: Methuen, 1985

Brown, Mary Ellen, *Soap Opera and Women's Talk: The Pleasure of Resistance,* Thousand Oaks, California, and London: Sage, 1994

Geraghty, Christine, *Women and Soap Opera: A Study of Prime Time Soaps,* Cambridge: Polity Press, 1991

Hobson, Dorothy, *"Crossroads": The Drama of a Soap Opera,* London: Methuen, 1982

Modleski, Tania, *Loving with a Vengeance: Mass Produced Fantasies for Women,* Hamden, Connecticut: Archon, and London: Methuen, 1982

Mumford, Laura Stempel, *Love and Ideology in the Afternoon: Soap Opera, Women, and Television Genre,* Bloomington: Indiana University Press, 1995

Nochimson, Martha, *No End to Her: Soap Opera and the Female Subject,* Berkeley and Oxford: University of California Press, 1992

Historically, soap operas and their predominantly female fans have been commonly regarded with anything from dismissive amusement to mocking contempt. Recently, however, feminist cultural theorists have called for greater understanding of the pleasures offered by popular media texts such as television soap operas. Responses to this call have varied in their approach—some scholars have examined soap operas themselves for insight into the nature of women's viewing pleasure, while others have studied the significance of this genre to its many female fans.

HOBSON adopts the latter approach, combining insights into the production process of the British soap *Crossroads* with findings from an ethnographic exploration into fans' receptions of this popular "tea-time" serial. Chapter six will be of most interest for its detailed account of the ways in which women's viewing is organized around their domestic responsibilities and household routines. Here, Hobson identifies some of the factors contributing to women's enjoyment of *Crossroads,* and suggests that viewers' interactions with this text largely involve relating it to their own life experiences. She also discusses women's often critical responses to this soap, along with their assessment of its handling of contemporary social issues. This early work has been very important in terms of setting the agenda for subsequent research on women and soap opera, and is a ground-breaking intervention in this field.

Also significant is MODLESKI's text-based analysis, which draws on psychoanalytic theories of spectatorship to analyze the historical relationship between "feminine" narratives and their female readers and viewers. Of most relevance is Chapter four, which attends to the specificity of soap opera as a genre. Here, Modleski develops her thesis that the formal properties of soap opera resonate pleasurably with the rhythms of women's domestic labor—both being characterized by repetition, interruption, and distraction. She argues that additional rewards derive from viewers' anticipation of an ending, which is continually deferred until "tomorrow." Modleski also suggests that soap narratives overturn a more traditional reliance on progression, climax, resolution, and closure—all of which have been theorized as central to the historically dominant "masculine" mode of viewing pleasure. This analysis has been very influential in the development of a theoretical understanding of the spectator-text relationship in soap opera.

Another early audience-based study is ANG's analysis of the various pleasures and displeasures experienced by Dutch viewers of the prime-time American soap, *Dallas.* Ang suggests that one of the key attractions of *Dallas* lies in its construction of a "tragic structure of feeling" which leads fans to experience the drama as emotionally realistic and hence pleasurable. She also considers the implications of women's viewing pleasure for an emancipatory feminist politics, and suggests this pleasure is neither subversive nor regressive, since it stems from women's engagement with the purely fictional world of soap opera at the level of fantasy. This study is an interesting but somewhat limited exploration of the source of *Dallas*'s cross-cultural popularity among a segment of its predominantly female Dutch audience.

A rather more detailed and expansive text-based analysis is offered in GERAGHTY's comparative study of British and American soaps such as *Coronation Street, EastEnders, Dallas,* and *Dynasty.* Geraghty begins by outlining the formal and aesthetic conventions of soap opera, and then discusses the role of female characters in relation to soap's thematic preoccupation with the personal sphere—most specifically the family—and also in relation to the communities featured in particular series.

The utopian possibilities of soap are also addressed in this book. Geraghty suggests that this genre can be used either to maintain the status quo, or to promote change by way of influencing public attitudes and diffusing tensions around differences of race, class, and sexual orientation. One of her central arguments is that the pleasures of watching soaps are grounded in its validation of women's traditional skills within the private sphere of the family and intimate personal relationships. Geraghty maintains, however, that soap's validation of these conventional skills is highly contradictory, and potentially offers feminine "space" or, alternatively, feminine "ghetto," depending upon the nature of women's engagement with this form. In its wide-ranging descriptive nature, this text may bear greater instructional value to teachers of feminist cultural studies than earlier ground-breaking works.

NOCHIMSON adopts an intensively theoretical approach to her text-based analysis of American soap opera narratives and female subjectivity. Drawing from psychoanalytic and feminist film theory, Nochimson first rejects the traditional centrality of the Oedipal saga to both of these theoretical traditions, and focuses instead on the myth of Persephone, which she suggests "clears the way for a female subject." She then reviews and theorizes the narrative structure and content of soap, and outlines the aesthetics of what she terms soap's involuntary feminine discourse. Nochimson's central thesis is that soap opera accentuates a decentered and multiple mode of feminine subjectivity, and creates innovative narratives of female desire, mutuality, and inclusiveness. The feminine politics of soap opera narratives are consequently theorized to destabilize the more traditional "masculine" emphasis on linearity, closure, mastery, and control, a position also taken by Modleski.

In contrast to Nochimson's textual analysis, BROWN's ethnographic study of soap opera fanship networks explores women's resistive pleasures in engaging with the American day-time soap *Days of Our Lives*. She suggests this soap provides a source of empowerment for its female viewers, by helping create and sustain an oral fanship network in which hegemonic constructions of gender, femininity, and womanhood can be critiqued. Brown draws from Foucault's theory of discourse and power, Gramsci's theory of hegemony, and Bourdieu's theory of cultural capital and strategic knowledge to theorize topics such as the politics of women's pleasure, and the power of women's talk, laughter, and friendship networks. Those new to this field will find Chapter Four useful for its concise overview of existing research on soap opera, and will appreciate Brown's inclusion of an extensive bibliography. This text may also be of considerable benefit to those intending to conduct ethnographic research in this area.

The most recent textual analysis is MUMFORD's discussion of soap opera narrative and patriarchal ideology. While much of this work covers similar ground to earlier authors, Chapter Five is noteworthy for its discussion of the centrality of the paternity mystery in soap opera narratives, which Mumford describes as "a fictional reiteration of the power of the father." In her view, such reassertions of male dominance are typical of American daytime soap, the underlying and at times overt agenda of which is to naturalize and hence reproduce patriarchal relations along with racism, classism, and heterosexism.

—CAROLYN MICHELLE

Social Work *see* Settlement House Movement

Spirituality, Feminist

Braude, Ann, *Radical Spirits: Spiritualism and Women's Rights in Nineteenth-Century America*, Boston: Beacon Press, 1989

Carmody, Denise Lardner, *Seizing the Apple: A Feminist Spirituality of Personal Growth*, New York: Crossroad, 1984

Christ, Carol P., *Diving Deep and Surfacing: Women Writers on Spiritual Quest*, Boston: Beacon Press, 1980

Conn, Joanne Wolski (ed.), *Women's Spirituality: Resources for Christian Development*, New York: Paulist Press, 1986

Isasi-Díaz, Ada Maria, and Yolando Tarango, *Hispanic Women: Prophetic Voice in the Church*, San Francisco: Harper and Row, 1988

Sewell, Marilyn (ed.), *Cries of the Spirit: A Celebration of Women's Spirituality*, Boston: Beacon Press, 1991

Solle, Dorothee, *The Strength of the Weak: Toward a Christian Feminist Identity*, Philadelphia: Westminster Press, 1984

Starhawk, *Dreaming the Dark: Magic, Sex, and Politics*, Boston: Beacon Press, 1982

Weidman, Judith L. (ed.), *Christian Feminism: Visions of a New Humanity*, San Francisco: Harper and Row, 1984

Spirituality has been linked to feminism at least since the nineteenth-century interest in the occult practice of Spiritualism. BRAUDE's volume traces "how seances and trance speaking empowered a generation of American women to claim their own voices." Spiritualism held that contact with the spirits of the dead provided empirical proof of the immortality of the soul. Spiritualists advocated women's rights, and women were in fact equal to men in Spiritualist practice, polity, and ideology. Spiritualists appeared throughout the most radical reform movements of the nineteenth century, including movements for the abolition of slavery, the reform of marriage, children's rights, and religious freedom; they supported socialism, labor reform, vegetarianism, dress reform, health reform, and temperance.

In contrast to Braude's nineteenth-century study, SEWELL's book deals with women and spirituality in the twentieth century. Sewell traces the origin of her volume to a course on the "Sources of Faith," which completely omitted any reference to women. Because she believed that "women tend towards a relational sacrality that is based on the natural world of earth and flesh" and that "women's perspective is healing and life-giving," she compiled her anthology of poetry completely from women's words; it is "a book in which female wisdom and power are honored."

CONN's book identifies three issues in women's spirituality: the inseparability of human development and religious development, the unique and problematic situation of women's spirituality today, and the relationship between women's spirituality and feminist spirituality. Conn maintains that "when women become explicitly conscious of the way a male-centered society and church affects their spirituality, they may accept the challenge and rewards of moving toward a feminist spirituality."

CARMODY's volume maintains her two-fold allegiance: to feminism, the commitment to women's full equalization with men, as a moral imperative, and to Christianity, which, despite its patriarchal detritus, is a treasure-house of spiritual resources, a path that can lead to the loving God. Carmody's spirituality contains a vision enlightened by "Lady Wisdom," a call to self-transcendence, freedom, and love, feminist shadings on male transcendentalist thinking, and developmental psychology. She devotes chapters to prayer, work, family life, and politics—what she considers to be the "concrete areas" where women struggle to live out whatever notion of spirituality they have generated.

WEIDMAN, like Carmody and Conn, has produced a collection that affirms its fidelity to Christianity. While acknowledging that "the more one becomes a feminist, the more difficult it becomes to go to Church," she has deliberately drawn together essays by women who believe that the church bears the seeds of its own renewal, and she asserts that "the unifying theme of the volume is community." Ruether has authored the first article, "Feminist Theology and Feminist Spirituality." Her title illustrates how women have blurred the boundaries. Where precisely does spirituality begin and theology end? What precisely is their relationship? Chapters follow by Fiorenza on feminist biblical interpretation, by Brock on the feminist redemption of Christ, and by Russell on women and ministry. Part two addresses wider cultural issues: lifestyle changes among American women, work, sexuality, and global consciousness.

SOLLE's work consists of her reflections on feminist identity, particularly as these illumine its relationship to Christian faith and to human liberation. Divided into two parts, the book provides seven chapters on "Faith and Society" and nine chapters on the "Foundations of a Feminist Theology." She is convinced that "rebellion against banality," against a production-line society, and against isolation and disconnectedness contains in itself the potential for liberation; she holds out the goal of "life without suffering" as a way of overcoming narcissism and replacing apathy with sympathy. She is convinced that love that extends beyond the family and that pursues justice has future possibilities. Solle sees the search for nonauthoritarian relationships and conditions as that which unites feminists, mystics, and advocates of liberation.

With the exception of Solle, the authors cited above are American women—white, middle class American women. But feminist spirituality is far more extensive. The primary focus of ISASI-DÍAZ and TARANGO's work is Hispanic women. This book contains five chapters; after each is a summary in Spanish. The chapter most significant for feminist spirituality is entitled, "In Their Own Words, Hispanic Women's Understandings of the Divine." Here seven women articulate their understanding of the significance of God in their lives.

CHRIST's monograph is concerned with female writers and spirituality. Affirming the value of women's stories and their integral relation to women's spiritual quest, Christ traces that quest through experiences of nothingness, of awakening—often through mystical identification—and of a new naming of one's self and reality that often reflects wholeness, that is, an overcoming of the dualism of self and world, body and soul, nature and spirit, and reason and emotion. She devotes chapters to Kate Chopin, Margaret Atwood, Doris Lessing, Adrienne Rich, and Ntozake Shange. She entitles her final chapter, "Toward Wholeness: A Vision of Women's Culture."

Not all feminist spirituality is Christian. STARHAWK's book articulates a spirituality based on reverence for nature and on a non-patriarchal worldview. She is part of the Neo-Pagan movement that invokes the divine as both feminine and masculine, and that recollects goddesses and gods of many cultures as metaphors for its earth-based and egalitarian spirituality.

—ALICE L. LAFFEY

See also Goddesses; Witchcraft/Wicca: Modern and Neo-Paganism

Sport and Gender

Birrell, Susan, and Cheryl L. Cole (eds.), *Women, Sport, and Culture,* Champaign, Illinois: Human Kinetics, 1994

Cahn, Susan, *Coming on Strong: Gender and Sexuality in Twentieth-Century Women's Sport,* New York: Free Press, 1994

Costa, D. Margaret, and Sharon R. Guthrie (eds.), *Women and Sport: Interdisciplinary Perspectives*, Champaign, Illinois: Human Kinetics, 1994

Hall, M. Ann, *Feminism and Sporting Bodies: Essays on Theory and Practice*, Champaign, Illinois: Human Kinetics, 1996

Hargreaves, Jennifer, *Sporting Females: Critical Issues in the History and Sociology of Women's Sports*, London and New York: Routledge and Kegan Paul, 1994

Lenskyj, Helen, *Out of Bounds: Women, Sport, and Sexuality*, Toronto: Women's Press, 1986

Messner, Michael A., and Donald F. Sabo (eds.), *Sport, Men, and the Gender Order: Critical Feminist Perspectives*, Champaign, Illinois: Human Kinetics, 1990

Vertinsky, Patricia A., *The Eternally Wounded Woman: Women, Doctors, and Exercise in the Late Nineteenth Century*, Manchester: Manchester University Press, and New York: St. Martin's Press, 1990

These selections represent some of the books that focus on women and sport, or more broadly gender and sport written from a feminist perspective. Scholarship on the history and sociology of sport emerged in the late 1960s and early 1970s in an international context. The scholarship on gender and sport, particularly feminist analyses of sport, emerged later in the 1980s. The texts selected here will appeal to scholars and students who have a specific interest in gender and sport, and/or to scholars and students who have a broad interest in feminist perspectives on gender, culture, and society.

LENSKYJ's book, the earliest among the books selected, was one of the first radical feminist analyses that examined the links between women's sport participation and the control of women's reproductive capacity and sexuality. In an engaging historical narrative, Lenskyj explores how the dominant medical discourse from the 1880s to the 1980s operated to limit women's participation in physical exercise and sport. Her well-documented discussions of the female-fragility thesis, sexual innuendoes about female athletes, the female sex-test used in international athletic competition, women's participation in combat sports and self-defense, and the 1980s fitness craze offer readers a rich understanding of the persistent tension between femininity and sport, the mechanisms of control of women's physicality and sexuality, and some of the strategies women have used to empower themselves through sport. This book represents an early theoretical statement on the relationship between compulsory heterosexuality and the rigid masculine/feminine dichotomy within the context of sport. Lenskyj's book, which has become a feminist classic in the area of gender and sport, will appeal to both gender scholars and students alike.

VERTINSKY's text explores the intersections of the social-historical construction of middle-class womanhood, medical practice, and physical culture during the late nineteenth century. Vertinsky interrogates diverse perspectives to build an understanding of the multiple and contradictory relationships between women, doctors, and exercise. Part I documents the male medical discourse on women's physical capacity that is intrinsically connected to women's reproductive function. Part II examines how female doctors provide a different understanding of the value or potential harm of physical exercise for women. Finally, Part III focuses on how the radical views of G. Stanely Hall and Charlotte Perkins Gilman contour the contested terrain of womanhood during the late nineteenth century. Vertinsky's text will be of interest to anyone seeking to understand the historical persistence of biological determinism, the fear of female sexuality, and the control of middle-class women in the realm of physical culture.

CAHN's book is one of the best single texts on the history of twentieth-century women's sport in the United States. Starting with a discussion of the new type of athletic girl at the turn of the century, Cahn offers a well-developed account of the ever-present tension between femininity and sports. Cahn explicates, in an entertaining fashion, the subtleties and nuances of the intersections of race, class, gender, and sexuality through her chapters on the growth of women's sports in the 1920s, the battle of women's competitive sports, the suppression of women's basketball, African-American women in track and field, the All-American Girl's Baseball League, notions about the mannish athlete and the lesbian threat, lesbian identity and community in sports, the negotiation of gender through sports, and the "revolution" in women's sports in the 1970s. The book is recommended to anyone interested in the history of women's sports in the United States and the continual renegotiation of sexuality and femininity by female athletes.

HARGREAVES examines, in great detail, the development of women's sports from their formative years in the nineteenth century to the present day. More than a historical narrative, this text is a critical feminist analysis of the problems and complexities of research on gender relations in sport. This book, which is over three hundred pages long, is an ambitious text that takes up issues ranging from Victorian and Edwardian sports for women to debates in physical education programs and the relationship between sports, structures of capitalism, and ideology. Hargreaves focuses primarily on the United Kingdom, although she uses many examples from other countries. Hargreaves weaves the theme of continuity and change throughout the text and skillfully shows how the relationships between individual and society, women and sport, and agency and structure are constantly shifting relationships that are complex and contradictory. This work will be useful for its thorough critical examination of the theoretical debates and empirical issues of the uneven power relations between women and men in sport, and it will also be useful for its extensive bibliography.

MESSNER and SABO's edited volume represents the emerging scholarship of feminist men's studies. This anthology is founded on the belief that, to fully understand the historical and contemporary meanings of sport, gender must be used as a fundamental category of analysis. The study of men and sport is hardly new; however, this volume forges new ground by examining the relationships between masculinities and sport from a critical feminist perspective. Messner and Sabo bring together scholars from Canada, Australia, the United States, and England who write from a diverse set of disciplines. The text is organized into three parts: theoretical and historical conceptualizations of sport and the gender order; current research on masculinities and sport; and strategies for challenging oppressive structures and practices in sport and developing theories to assist in this process. Messner and Sabo's book offers a series of essays on diverse subjects and thus will appeal to many different readers.

COSTA and GUTHRIE's edited volume is an interdisciplinary book on women and sport. There are 22 chapters that make up the book's three sections. The first section covers the historical and cultural foundations of women's sport history, the second section considers the biomedical factors of sport, and the final section focuses on the psychological and social dimensions of women and sport. The volume contributors, who come from France, the United States, and Canada, work in the following disciplines: sport and exercise sciences, kinesiology, biomechanics, physical education, history, political science, health, medicine, sociology, and women's studies. As a result of this diversity, the theoretical perspectives and methodologies presented in this volume vary. Among all the selections reviewed here, this is the only book that spends considerable time examining the biomedical aspects of women and sport.

BIRRELL and COLE's book, another edited volume, is similar to the above text in that it puts women at the center of the analysis of sport. However, this book differs in that it is more fully grounded in a feminist cultural studies perspective that draws on poststructuralism and postmodernism. Birrell and Cole bring together scholars whose work disrupts the traditional boundaries of the fields of kinesiology, sport studies, and physical education and attempts to reconceptualize sport research to respond to the conditions of postmodernity. The volume contains 24 articles organized into five sections: Women, Sport, and Ideology; Gender and the Organization of Sport; Women in the Male Preserve of Sport; Media, Sport, and Gender; and Sport and the Politics of Sexuality. The volume will appeal to teachers, scholars, and students who want to explore cutting-edge scholarship on gender, sexuality, and the body.

The final selection is HALL's book, the most recent book on the list. Hall reviews the debates and development of feminist scholarship and feminist theory in the area of gender and sport. She uses her own 30-year intellectual history as a researcher of sport and physical education to trace the history, current trends, and future of the area of gender relations and sport. Included in Hall's discussion are liberal, radical, Marxist, socialist, cultural studies, and postmodern feminist perspectives. Hall also devotes two chapters to the discussions of the significance of the body and feminist research as praxis. This book will be most useful to readers familiar with feminist theory and the history and sociology of women and sport.

—CYNTHIA FABRIZIO PELAK

Sport, History of

Cahn, Susan K. *Coming on Strong: Gender and Sexuality in Twentieth-Century Women's Sport*, New York: Free Press, 1984

Costa, D. Margaret, and Sharon R. Guthrie (eds.), *Women and Sport: Interdisciplinary Perspectives*, Champaign, Illinois: Human Kinetics, 1994

Guttman, Allen, *Women's Sports: A History*, New York: Columbia University Press, 1991

LeCompte, Mary Lou, *Cowgirls of the Rodeo: Pioneer Professional Athletes*, Urbana: University of Illinois Press, 1993

Mangan, J.A., and Roberta J. Park, *From "Fair Sex" to Feminism: Sport and the Socialization of Women in the Industrial and Post-Industrial Eras*, London: Frank Cass, 1986; Totowa, New Jersey: Frank Cass, 1987

McCrone, Kathleen E., *Playing the Game: Sport and the Physical Emancipation of English Women, 1870–1914*, Lexington: University of Kentucky Press, 1988

Todd, Jan, *Physical Culture and the Body Beautiful: Purposive Exercise and American Women 1800–1870*, Macon, Georgia: Mercer University Press, 1997

Vertinsky, Patricia A., *The Eternally Wounded Woman: Women, Doctors, and Exercise in the Late Nineteenth Century*, Manchester: Manchester University Press, and New York: St. Martin's Press, 1990

Although the discipline of women's sport history only began in the 1970s, a rich and varied body of literature already awaits the reader. Now well past the "great lady" biographies of the 1970s and early 1980s, women's sport history today draws upon the methodologies of social history, feminist theory, body ideology, and even postmodernism. And, as the books discussed below demonstrate, our understanding of the centrality of sport and exercise to the lives of women has significantly deepened as historical approaches to these activities have become more sophisticated.

To date, GUTTMAN has produced the best, and only truly comprehensive, overview of the international history of women and sport. Winner of the North American

Society for Sport History's 1991 prize for the best book in the general field of sport history, this book—although controversial—has been rightly called a "landmark" by more than one reviewer. Meticulously researched, engagingly written, and theoretically provocative, Guttman's book traces the evolution of women's sport participation from the ancient Egyptians to the 1990s using evidence from art, archaeology, literature, popular magazines, and professional journals to further his analysis. Divided into two parts, the book's first 12 chapters deal with the international evolution of women's sport, an evolution Guttman contends was not as dominated by patriarchal controls as most feminist historians have argued. In the second part of the book, Guttman examines three contemporary controversies: masculinization, eroticism, and the decreasing differences between the performances of male and female athletes.

One of the feminist historians with whom Guttman takes issue is VERTINSKY, whose analysis of the influence of the medical establishment on the sport and exercise interests of nineteenth-century women should not be considered as simply a book on sport history, but rather as an outstanding contribution to the general field of women's history. Using British, Canadian, and American sources, Vertinsky examines the ways in which traditional medical practitioners fostered notions of weakness and debility among upper-class white women in North America and England. As Vertinsky puts it, "the labeling of normal female functions such a menstruation and menopause as signs of illness requiring rest and medical observation did not, in itself, make women sick or incapable of vigorous activity. It did, however, provide a powerful rationale to persuade them from acting in any other way."

McCRONE's book on the evolution of sporting practices in Victorian and Edwardian England makes a good companion volume to Vertinsky's. Although McCrone also touches on the medical debate surrounding appropriate sport for women's sport history, her first three chapters examine sporting practices within the public schools and women's colleges—practices, she rightly argues, that were widely copied throughout the English speaking world. McCrone's other contribution is her analysis of the connections between the British women's movement and sport. According to McCrone, interest in female emancipation tended to coincide with the growth of sport rather than be caused by it.

TODD also examines the nineteenth century, but from a different theoretical perspective. Todd argues that there were at least two opposing visions of appropriate womanhood and appropriate sporting practices for women in the early nineteenth century. Based on popular magazines, guidebooks, diaries, and letters, Todd's research suggests that many lower- and middle-class women did not adopt the upper-class notion that women should be weak and physically incompetent. Instead, these women understood the connections between physical fitness and personal freedom, and some used their new physicality as a springboard to professional lives and greater personal autonomy. Two aspects of Todd's work bear special note: her attempts to assess physiologically the difficulty of some of the early exercise systems, and her reassessment of the career of exercise and women's-rights proponent Dio Lewis.

Many professors pull COSTA and GUTHRIE's book from their shelves to help undergraduates more than any other. Written as a text for courses on women and sport, it contains a 138-page historical section that is accurate, readable, and nicely illustrated. The eight chapters in this section are written by some of the most prominent names in the field of women's sport history. Included are an essay by Catriona Parrat on the state of women's sport history research, June Kennard and John Marshall Carter's analysis of ancient and medieval sport, Roberta Park's study of women's sport in seventeenth- and eighteenth-century Europe, Nancy Struna's essay on eighteenth-century American women, Vertinsky on the nineteenth century, Joan Hult on the evolution of physical education as a profession for women, Lynne Emery on industrial sport, and Paula Welch and Margaret Cista on women in the Olympics.

MANGAN and PARK have complied what most scholars consider to be the most important anthology on women and sport. The 12 essays included in their volume are geographically organized and cover the evolution of sport in Britain, Canada, Australia, and the United States. The book's one drawback is that all but two essays concern the Victorian period. However, without exception, all are well-written, thought-provoking, and thoroughly researched. Scholars of women and sport will find the selected bibliography compiled by the book's 12 contributors to be especially useful.

Those interested in post-Victorian sport history can begin their search with no better tome than CAHN's. Broad in scope and impeccably researched, Cahn's book is the definitive work on the twentieth century. Using feminist theory as her framework, Cahn examines the connections between race, class, and gender in women's sport at the collegiate, amateur, and professional levels. Sport historians have paid only scant attention to the recent past, and so Cahn's analysis, particularly her chapter on the impact of the post-Title IX athletic revolution in the 1970s, is an especially important contribution. Cahn concludes that even though modern women have far more chances to participate, corporate sponsors, sports leaders, and the commercial media continue to use sports as a site "where traditional patriarchal values are upheld and transformed in response to changes in the broader society."

One of the most exceptional contributions to the history of women and sport is the work of LeCOMPTE. Her book, part of the prestigious University of Illinois series on the history of sport, breaks new ground in several significant ways. It is the first major monograph to focus on the world of professional women's sport. It is also the first to concentrate on the sporting lives of women of the American west—women, who, LeCompte points out, were not as captivated by the myths of frailty and invalidism as were their eastern sisters. LeCompte's book is a wonderful mix of personal and institutional histories. Her analysis of the evolution of the professional rodeo associations governing female participants is especially noteworthy as a counterpoint to the evolution of women's sport in the Olympic movement and universities. Drawing from dozens of interviews, diaries, and other primary sources, LeCompte presents a compelling, important, and unique view of the history of women in sport.

—JAN TODD

Staël, Madame de, Anne-Louise-Germaine 1766–1817

French Writer

Besser, Gretchen Rous, *Germaine de Staël Revisited*, New York: Twayne, 1994

Gutwirth, Madelyn, *Madame de Staël, Novelist: The Emergence of the Artist as Woman*, Urbana and London: University of Illinois Press, 1978

Gutwirth, Madelyn, Avriel Goldberger, and Karyna Szmurlo (eds.), *Germaine de Staël: Crossing the Borders*, New Brunswick, New Jersey: Rutgers University Press, 1991

Hogsett, Charlotte, *The Literary Existence of Germaine de Staël*, Carbondale: Southern Illinois University Press, 1987

Isbell, John Clairborne, *The Birth of European Romanticism: Truth and Propaganda in Staël's "De l'Allemagne," 1810–1813*, Cambridge and New York: Cambridge University Press, 1994

There are only a handful of book-length studies of Germaine de Staël in English, and most of them of recent origin, due mostly to the impact of feminist criticism, which has played a crucial role in the reevaluation of this important figure of European romanticism. The first significant scholarly monograph in English devoted to de Staël's fiction is GUTWIRTH's (1978) study, which frames itself as a feminist exploration of the writer's life and work. Skillfully combining historical, biographical, and literary analysis, it begins by placing de Staël in the context of eighteenth century attitudes to women in general and female writers in particular, and then gives a detailed account of the psychodynamics of her childhood and adult family relationships. The mixed messages she received from both parents in terms of her education and the use to which it was put, namely the practice of writing, led to the notes of self-castigation and self-justification that permeate her work. In addition, in her intense love for her father and its impossibility of fulfillment, Gutwirth finds the prototype of de Staël's numerous failed loves. Later chapters chart the progress of her writing career, how in her early works she attempted, not wholly successfully, to stay in the mold of the "lady novelist," and how her romantic tales became ways of mediating her own femininity. Two chapters on *Delphine* and four on *Corinne* continue the psychological analysis of de Staël's mode of female self-consciousness as revealed in the writing. The nameless sorrow and the compulsive search for love and self-worth through others, which distinguish this self-consciousness, is regarded by Gutwirth as a response to society's "depreciation of the female." As well as such biographical and socio-historical analysis, Gutwirth considers the literary contexts of *Delphine* and *Corinne*, and the genres they challenge and in which they participate. In the final chapter of this wide-ranging study Gutwirth argues for the significance of *Corinne* as a myth of female narcissism.

HOGSETT's study explicitly builds on Gutwirth's feminist approach to de Staël. In an introductory chapter, Hogsett signals the ways in which her argument is informed by 1980s feminist theory debates over the concept of "women's writing," and a constructed versus an essential feminine identity. Hogsett sees de Staël's "literary existence," or her writerly identity, as split between her feminine identity and the masculine models on which she seeks to model herself. The body of Hogsett's study offers detailed textual analyses of de Staël's works, considering fictional alongside non-fictional texts. She pairs *De la Littérature* with *Delphine*, and *De l'Allemagne* with *Corinne*, to examine the interplay of masculine and feminine modes and genres. While several of her male contemporaries also worked in multiple genres, de Staël tends to transgress generic boundaries within her works more frequently and radically. Although this leads to a challenging of gender norms in terms of the proper domain of the "lady novelist," Hogsett concludes that however much she sought to do so, de Staël cannot erase her feminine writing identity. Instead, the authentic and authoritative "voice" Hogsett finds in the best of de Staël's work is a necessarily gendered one.

Hogsett is also one of 18 contributors to GUTWIRTH, GOLDBERGER, and SZMURLO's collection of essays. As Szmurlo outlines in her Introduction, the subtitle, "Crossing the Borders," captures the collection's focus on "spacialization," "geo-graphics," and the multiple ways in which boundaries are transgressed in de Staël's works. In contrast to the figures of enclosure and constriction noted by Sandra Gilbert and Susan Gubar as prevalent in nineteenth century women's writing, we find in de Staël "a topos of distance and divergence." This collection is also notable, not only for its representation of a range of methodological and theoretical approaches to de Staël, but also because it makes accessible to English readers the work of several prominent francophone scholars of her work, such as Simone Balayé and Marie-Claire Vallois, who have essays here in translation. The book is divided into four sections. The first, "History and the Imaginary," considers de Staël in the context of the 1789 Revolution; the second, "Articulations of Inwardness" includes an essay by Margaret Higonnet on the figure and rhetoric of suicide as liberation and self-construction in de Staël's work; the third section, "Transgressing Gender and Genre," includes Joan DeJean on *Corinne*'s reworking of traditions surrounding the figure of Sappho; and the final section, "Topographical Surveys," contains essays which, broadly speaking, consider the reception of de Staël's works and their influence on later writers, including an important piece by Kurt Mueller-Vollmer on the huge debt American transcendentalism owed to de Staël's *De l'Allemagne*. This final section also contains several shorter pieces that respond to some of the other essays in the collection.

While not explicitly feminist in focus, ISBELL's book constitutes a major contribution to de Staël studies, establishing beyond doubt her significance to her contemporaries and the huge influence of her writings on male literary figures who have become the major representatives of European romanticism, including George Gordon Byron, Giacomo Leopardi, and Alexander Pushkin. Believing that the impact of de Staël on her contemporaries has been underestimated, he argues specifically for the centrality of *De l'Allemagne* in providing a model of romantic nationalism to the emergent revolutionary nations of Europe. This is achieved by de Staël through the propagandist agenda of *De l'Allemagne*, the immediate effectiveness of which is seen in Napoleon's order to his troops to pulp all copies of the book. In her text, according to Isbell, de Staël misrepresents the truth in order to invent romanticism. By comparing manuscript to published versions, Isbell shows how de Staël edits out facts in order to present a unified German nation-state, an ideal model that would inspire romantic nationalists far and wide. Yet as Isbell is determined to stress, the very extent of this influence—de Staël's fame—is ironically due to a European cosmopolitanism that such romantic propaganda helped to destroy.

BESSER's text may be briefly mentioned as a good basic introduction to the main features of de Staël's life and work. Coming after the feminist and historicist reclamation of de Staël, this book assumes rather than argues for the significance of her writing. It proceeds more or less chronologically and provides useful summaries of de Staël's works.

—SUSAN CONLEY

Stanton, Elizabeth Cady 1815–1902

American Suffragist

Banner, Lois W., *Elizabeth Cady Stanton: A Radical for Woman's Rights*, Boston: Little Brown, 1980

Griffith, Elisabeth, *In Her Own Right: The Life of Elizabeth Cady Stanton*, New York and Oxford: Oxford University Press, 1984

Lutz, Alma, *Created Equal: A Biography of Elizabeth Cady Stanton 1815–1902*, New York: John Day, 1940

Pellauer, Mary D, *Toward a Tradition of Feminist Theology: The Religious Social Thought of Elizabeth Cady Stanton, Susan B. Anthony, and Anna Howard Shaw*, Brooklyn, New York: Carlson, 1991

Oakley, Mary Ann B., *Elizabeth Cady Stanton*, Old Westbury, New York: Feminist Press, 1972

Elizabeth Cady Stanton's place in the history of American feminism, and in particular the suffrage movement, has been charted by several biographers in the last 60 years. In themselves, these texts can be seen as indicators of the development of feminist biography in this century, from early work establishing and mythologising Stanton's place and reputation, to later attempts that see themselves as part of the "renaissance of women's history" in the 1980s, and that reconstruct her established image using a defined critical frame of reference.

LUTZ's substantial 1940 work was the first full-length biography of Stanton to appear, and it is largely laudatory. It covers all the major aspects of Stanton's life and is in some ways the most comprehensive and detailed of her biographies. Lutz gives thorough coverage of the diversity of material pertinent to Stanton's life, including significant attention to the relationships she fostered and maintained (despite periodic differences of opinion) with other prominent figures in the woman's rights movement, particularly Susan B. Anthony. Lutz draws on and quotes extensively from a wealth of primary source material: letters, diaries, and speeches, as well as the popular press, a technique that highlights Stanton's radicalism in the face of conservative popular opinion. Despite its antiquity and lack of critical framework, Lutz's work has stood the test of time and remains a significant resource for information on Stanton.

OAKLEY's biography of Stanton appeared as part of Feminist Press's project of recuperating women's history in the early 1970s. Published thirty years after Lutz's work, Oakley offers a tightly condensed biographical sketch of her subject, written in an almost novelistic style, which, while it gives a general and abbreviated picture of the key events of Stanton's life, lacks Lutz's and later biographers' detail and depth of analysis. However, Oakley's text makes minor steps toward a critical appraisal of Stanton's life and work, and it is of interest for its self-conscious reclamation of feminist history during the "second wave."

BANNER's biography draws on newly available manuscript material and profits from the upsurge of feminist theory since the 1970s, in the construction of a much more critical and rigorous look at Stanton's life. Banner frames the biography in terms of the social and historical influences of Stanton's early life, and she examines the later intellectual sources of her feminist philosophies and utopianism. Loosely chronological, but also mapping the life around consistent themes, Banner in a sense deconstructs the mythologised version of Stanton's life passed on by previous biographers (and Stanton herself). She gives voice to many (and not always positive) aspects of her life ignored by earlier works, such as her relationship with her mother, her recurrent bouts of severe depression, her interest in homoeopathy and phrenology, her love of practical jokes, and her marital problems with Henry Stanton. While acknowledging Stanton to be "the foremost woman intellectual of her generation," Banner provides a critical analysis of her speeches and writings, revealing some interesting contradictions, and explicating her conservatism on certain issues toward the end of her life (by which time, Banner notes, she had become less of a strategist and more of a figurehead of the women's movement). Banner's biography is full of fascinating material; it is also the first to reveal the "family legend" of Stanton's alleged euthanasia.

GRIFFITH's text is the only fully scholarly biography of Stanton available to date. Somewhat unjustifiably downplaying the achievements of previous biographers, Griffith works on the premise that Stanton has been "lost to history" or has been seen primarily as Susan B. Anthony's "sidekick," and she aims to complete the factual record begun by previous "abbreviated" works. In this she is only partially successful: some new anecdotal material makes its appearance alongside additional background details, but for the most part Stanton's life narrative is not materially altered. Calling her work "psychobiography," Griffith draws on psychological theories of social learning as a critical framework underpinning her study, and in this way she examines Stanton's life as a "progression of behaviour patterns based on successive role models." This technique provides some curious insights into Stanton's achievements and motivations. Griffith also continues Banner's work of questioning the myths handed on by earlier biographers, providing several useful appendices, including a "Phrenological Character" of Stanton done in 1853.

PELLAUER's study represents a departure from the biographical format, and concentrates on Stanton's contribution toward a tradition of feminist theology in the nineteenth century. Roughly half of Pellauer's book is devoted to Stanton's critiques of organised religion; it examines the intersection between her social analysis, her religious perspective, and her corresponding notions of justice. Pellauer reveals that Stanton's religious thought was fundamental to her involvement in the suffrage movement, and she views Stanton as an early precursor to the rise of feminist theology in the 1970s. Pellauer cleverly maps the changing currents of Stanton's religious thought over her long life, her ideas on the fourfold bondage of women by family, church, state, and society, and her arrival at an argument for "a more rational religion" based on natural law, individualism, and the central tenet of "a woman's right to think." This is a fascinating analysis of an important aspect of Stanton's intellectual life.

—TIFFANY URWIN

See also Women's Rights Convention, Seneca Falls, New York; Suffrage: United States

Stead, Christina 1903–1983

Australian Writer

Brydon, Diana, *Christina Stead,* London: Macmillan, and Totowa, New Jersey: Barnes and Noble, 1987

Gribble, Jennifer, *Christina Stead,* Melbourne and New York: Oxford University Press, 1994

Lidoff, Joan, *Christina Stead,* New York: Ungar, 1982

Rowley, Hazel, *Christina Stead: A Biography,* Port Melbourne: Heinemann, 1993; New York: Holt, 1994; London: Secker and Warburg, 1995

Sheridan, Susan, *Christina Stead,* New York and Brighton: Harvester, 1988

Christina Stead's international reputation has grown steadily since her death, ensuring her place as one of the major novelists of the twentieth century. Her brilliant novel of family life, *The Man Who Loved Children,* is now recognized as a modern classic, but on the whole the reception of Christina Stead's novels has been uneven. Until recently her work has been misunderstood and ignored by many critics and readers, so much so that Lidoff could open her study of Stead with the rhetorical question "Who is Christina Stead?" The present upsurge of interest in Stead can be attributed to a number of causes, but certainly, the women's movement and the development of feminist literary studies has been a major impetus.

BRYDON's study rightly claims to be the first book-length study to focus specifically on the ways in which Stead's status as a woman affected her fiction, and the first to focus on those elements of her fiction that are most relevant to women. Stead's own concerns in writing were never explicitly feminist. Rather, she preferred to align herself intellectually with the left, and therefore with a class-based analysis of oppression. Brydon's study is sensitive to the complexities of this political alignment, without allowing Stead's own professed antipathy to the women's movement to negate the radical nature of her representation of gender and ideology in the fiction. Brydon recognises that the fiction is political insofar as it questions socially indoctrinated gender differences, but that it is never programmatic or orthodox. Likewise, Stead's novels stylistically defy the conventional critical categories of modernism, socialist realism, bourgeois realism, and feminism. Accordingly, Brydon allows Stead's own creative approach to dictate her critical one, and she offers wide-ranging analyses of eleven novels and the short story collection, *The Salzburg Tales.*

SHERIDAN's study, like that of Brydon, is based on the assumption that Stead's fiction is feminist and as such challenges the assumptions of pre-feminist criticism. It centres on the relation of Stead's writing with feminist theory and criticism; in particular it aims to establish a dialogue between some of the novels and contemporary theories of literary production and of gendered subjectivity. By contrast to other studies reviewed here, Sheridan's approach is highly selective; it focuses on the female protagonists in six novels, with one half of the study devoted to *The Man Who Loved Children* and *For Love Alone.* Sheridan discusses the limitations of an "author criticism" approach to Stead's work and draws attention to the ways in which the autobiographical truth of Stead's fiction has had the effect of authorising certain readings and rendering others illegitimate. Sheridan's book is the most theoretically engaged study to have appeared to date, and it is essential reading for the students of Stead's work.

Unlike Brydon and Sheridan, GRIBBLE's agenda is not explicitly feminist in content or methodology. Rather, her study is primarily focused upon the complex and innovative narrative structure of Stead's fiction. Stead has stressed the importance of stories and storytelling to human happiness; for her, stories were a primary mode of comprehending experience, individually and collectively. Gribble's study is notable for its detailed textual analysis of a wide range of novels and stories, but it is her exploration of narrative as a series of antithetical yet interrelated fictions, each with its interlocking, enclosed, and suppressed stories, that gives the study coherence. One useful aspect of this work is its final chapter on Stead's last American novel, *I'm Dying Laughing: The Humorist.* This work was published posthumously by Virago Press in 1986 and was therefore unavailable to Stead's early critics, with the notable exception of Sheridan, who discusses *I'm Dying Laughing* at some length. In this regard Sheridan and Gribble's commentaries on this interesting and important last work stake out new ground in Stead criticism.

LIDOFF's study is useful as a general introduction to Stead's work as a whole. It covers eleven major works, but the space allowed for discussion of some of these is necessarily restricted: *The Man Who Loved Children* and *For Love Alone* are allocated a chapter each, whereas the other nine works are dealt with in a single chapter, with the result that some works receive little more than summary treatment. Many of Lidoff's local analyses are of enduring interest, for example, her identification of a specifically feminine form of the domestic Gothic in *The Man Who Loved Children.* Lidoff's study is flawed, however, by her attempt to force Stead into an individualistic, and at times, Christian frame of belief. This leads to misreadings of Stead's methods and purposes, as when it is implied that Stead believed that the imagination transcends ideology and politics. Stead would not have conceived of the relationship between ideology and fiction in this way, as artistry and the dramatisation of the ideological consistencies that characterise twentieth-century capitalist societies are interrelated dimensions of her overall project. In this respect, the ideological criticism of such critics as Brydon and Sheridan is better adapted to understanding Stead's work. Both recognize that Stead is neither a propagandist for any particular cause nor a liberal humanist. On the other hand, they also recognise that the idea that the personal is political was more than mere rhetoric for Stead.

ROWLEY's biographical study contains a great deal of useful source material bearing on Stead's life and work. Rowley's analysis of the fiction is limited, but as the first biographer to have been granted access to Stead's private correspondence and most intimate friends, she has been able to make available for the first time a vast archive of unpublished material, as well as to provide new information based on oral sources. This material is meticulously documented in the numerous and detailed notes to each chapter, thus making the work an indispensable book for researchers and interested readers alike.

—JENNIFER McDONELL

Stein, Gertrude 1874–1946

American Writer

Berry, Ellen, *Curved Thought and Textual Wandering: Gertrude Stein's Postmodernism*, Ann Arbor: University of Michigan Press, 1992

Bowers, Jane Palatini, *Gertrude Stein*, London: Macmillan, and New York: St. Martin's Press, 1993

Chessman, Harriet Scott, *The Public Is Invited to Dance: Representation, the Body, and Dialogue in Gertrude Stein*, Stanford, California: Stanford University Press, 1989

DeKoven, Marianne, *A Different Language: Gertrude Stein's Experimental Writing*, Madison: University of Wisconsin Press, 1983

Hoffman, Michael, *Critical Essays on Gertrude Stein,* Boston: G.K. Hall, 1986

Neuman, Shirley, and Ira B. Nadel (eds.), *Gertrude Stein and the Making of Literature,* London: Macmillan, 1987; Boston: Northeastern University Press, 1988

Ruddick, Lisa, *Reading Gertrude Stein: Body, Text, Gnosis,* Ithaca, New York: Cornell University Press, 1990

Souhami, Diana, *Gertrude and Alice,* London: Pandora, 1991; San Francisco: HarperCollins, 1992

Her name almost synonymous with modernism and experimental writing, Gertrude Stein's life reads like a "who's who" amongst intellectuals in the period. Stein is known for discovering several French artists, like Pablo Picasso, Paul Cézanne, and Henri Matisse, and for her friendships with artists and writers of the period, as well as for her experimental writing. Any discussion of Stein must always include a discussion of her relationship to Alice B. Toklas, her lifetime companion and lover. In addition to their personal relationship, Toklas was Stein's amanuensis, typing up manuscripts, making appointments, and even deciding to use the now famous quote, "a rose is a rose is a rose is a rose" as Stein's personal motto. Both Stein and Toklas have written about their lives and time together in Stein's *The Autobiography of Alice B. Toklas* and Toklas's memoirs *What is Remembered.*

A full historical biography of Stein and Toklas's relationship is available in SOUHAMI's book. This work is distinctive, as Souhami presents full biographies of Toklas's early life as well as Stein's, and charts the entire relationship, including Toklas's old age spent finishing the late Stein's projects. Most works cover Toklas's life only as it intersects with Stein's and ignore the work Toklas did for Stein after Stein's death from cancer in 1946.

BOWERS provides a more focused account of Stein's life, with particular attention to, and emphasis upon, Stein's writing. Bowers's book provides an excellent and detailed look at Stein's pre-writing life, especially her young adult years spent with her brother, Leo Stein. Bowers also includes detailed linguistic critical analyses of several of Stein's better known works and relates the works and analyses to events going on in Stein's life at the time of her writing. The combination of biographical, historical, and linguistic analysis clearly delineates Stein's growth as a writer.

HOFFMAN's anthology of criticism provides an excellent overview of the history of Stein criticism, beginning with reviews and articles from her contemporaries, and ending with a fairly comprehensive representation of the major movements in literary criticism applied to Stein's work—modernism, language, postmodernism, autobiography, and feminism. While other works provide a more comprehensive and closer look at these movements as applied to Stein's work, Hoffman's book offers an excellent overview of general trends in Stein criticism.

The critical articles provided in NEUMAN and NADEL's anthology present examples of the various schools of Stein scholarship since 1975. Many of the critical approaches are excellent examples of the various ways that scholars are currently reading and analyzing Stein's texts. Of particular interest in this anthology are articles comparing Stein's experimental writing to the experimental artwork of the period, and an article by Nadel comparing Stein's and James's writing and discussing their influences upon each other.

RUDDICK provides a clearly feminist poststructuralist analysis of a few Stein texts. She mixes criticism of the body and the text. The introduction to Ruddick's book discusses the difficulty readers often have with Stein's experimental use of language. She offers suggestions for reading and understanding some of Stein's more difficult and experimental works, focusing her discussions on *Three Buttons, Three Lives,* and Stein's poetry—insisting that these works should not be reduced by reading and interpreting them in a conventional manner.

BERRY also discusses ways in which to read the more experimental works of Stein. Berry suggests viewing Stein as postmodernist, rather than modernist, as she usually is seen because of the period in which she was writing. Some authors argue that Stein was the inventor of modernism, but Berry classifies her as postmodern, because she feels that Stein was ahead of her time with many of her more experimental uses of language. Berry's book is a good complement to Ruddick's, as she examines different works—*A Long Gay Book, A Novel of Thank You, Mrs. Reynolds,* and *Lucy Church Amiably.* Berry provides a clear and almost step-by-step framework for reading Stein's novels, which would be extremely helpful for those having problems with Stein's unique and often confusing style. The rest of the text focuses on close readings applying specific postmodern theories—performance, metafiction, nonsense—to specific Stein novels. This analysis is interesting, but extremely narrow.

DeKOVEN also examines Stein's experimental writing, which she defines as those works between *Three Lives* and *The Autobiography of Alice B. Toklas.* While others may argue with her definition of Stein's "experimental period," DeKoven examines these works as a package, rather than trying to use a specific theory differently applied to each work. DeKoven devotes an entire chapter to explaining her choice of classification and definitions of experimental. The bulk of her work focuses on tracing chronologically Stein's experimenting and changing styles. DeKoven's analysis is based upon feminist theory and readings—she assumes that Stein's experiments were a way of refusing traditional patriarchal modes of writing, and she therefore examines Stein's experimental work under a feminist assumption. DeKoven's work is unique in Stein criticism and is also helpful for understanding Stein's possible rationales behind her experiments.

It is a common practice in Stein criticism to conflate her work and her personal life. This conflation is decried by CHESSMAN as devaluing both Stein's life and work. Chessman argues that Stein's writing consists of a dialogue between writer and reader, and that Stein's writing persona needs to be examined separately from her life but also needs to be examined as a dialogue. Chessman pays particular attention to the maternal elements in Stein's work and explores at length Stein's use of the body as part of the dialogue in which Chessman is interested. Chessman's application of her theory to Stein's portrait writing is especially interesting and compelling, and it is probably one of the best examinations of the portrait writing available.

—STACEY C. SHORT

Stereotyping *see* Gender Stereotyping

Sterilization

Blank, Robert H., *Fertility Control: New Techniques, New Policy Issues,* New York and London: Greenwood, 1991

Broberg, Gunnar, and Nils Roll-Hansen (eds.), *Eugenics and the Welfare State: Sterilization Policy in Denmark, Sweden, Norway, and Finland,* East Lansing: Michigan State University Press, 1996

Presser, Harriet B., *Sterilization and Fertility Decline in Puerto Rico,* Berkeley: University of California Press, 1973

Reilly, Philip R., *The Surgical Solution: A History of Involuntary Sterilization in the United States,* Baltimore and London: Johns Hopkins University Press, 1991

Robitscher, Jonas B. (ed.), *Eugenic Sterilization,* Springfield, Illinois: Charles C. Thomas, 1973

Shapiro, Thomas M., *Population Control Politics: Women, Sterilization, and Reproductive Rights,* Philadelphia: Temple University Press, 1985

Most recent discussions of sterilization concentrate either on the cultural and political factors that form the basis of sterilization laws and practices in a specific country, or on the moral and societal implications of sterilization. Critical discussions distinguish, first, between voluntary and involuntary sterilization (that is, those procedures enacted for a woman's health or as a chosen means of birth control versus those performed on individuals considered deficient or unfit to reproduce) and second, between sterilization as a state policy and sterilization as a method of individual fertility control. Most studies focus primarily, although not exclusively, on female sterilization since women are sterilized, either voluntarily or not, much more often than men.

ROBITSCHER's collection provides a good overview of the various issues, particularly the social implications, involved in eugenic sterilization, the involuntary sterilization of those individuals considered unfit biologically, mentally, behaviorally, or socially. The text includes papers from a conference held in 1970, whose purpose was to bring together a wide range of perspectives on eugenic sterilization: medical, genetic, legal, psychiatric, historical, political, and moral. Throughout, the focus is on public and scientific attitudes toward sterilization rather than on the prevalence of specific techniques or the implications for individual women. The text presents eugenic sterilization in the context of other "biomedical interventions"—abortion, euthanasia—into social and biological "problems." Individual essays discuss sterilization in terms of other social issues: one discusses the sterilization of "mentally defective" women in terms of concerns about child-rearing, women's sexuality, and the use of IQ tests to determine eligibility for parenthood, while others discuss concerns about race, class, and religion enmeshed in sterilization policies. This book is a good place to start for a broad social view of involuntary sterilization.

REILLY examines the moral and societal implications of involuntary sterilization for institutionalized mentally retarded individuals, primarily women, from the perspective of the history of medicine and social policy in the United States. He is particularly concerned with the origins of legislation and national programs, as well as with the definitions and perceptions of "degeneracy," including the supposed link to criminality, which legitimized U.S. sterilization legislation. Reilly details early debates about sterilization legislation by prominent physicians, scientists, academics, and philanthropists; he also presents the origins and the history of legislation in individual states throughout this century. He notes that during the Depression, a change occurred in the perception and the recipients of sterilization: a majority of those sterilized began to be young women, and sterilization began to be considered less for decreasing the number of degenerate children and more for preventing reproduction by those labeled socially inadequate or unfit to be parents.

SHAPIRO presents the history and social origins of U.S. sterilization policy and considers the implications of that history for current population-control politics and discussions of reproductive choice. His study offers the most extended analysis of sterilization among American women; he investigates sterilization in the context of the American birth control movement, the women's movement, and population control politics (including the ways arguments for sterilization coincided with discussions of the need to limit fertility for certain segments of the population). Shapiro uses an analysis of sterilization and population policies to explore the intersections of gender, race, and class issues in American political history. Yet Shapiro also bridges the gap between social/political history and individual decision-making by analyzing the ways in which women's decisions about voluntary sterilization are grounded in the social constraints created by larger political, cultural, and economic patterns and beliefs.

BLANK examines the cultural and political factors shaping U.S. sterilization policy; he provides a detailed analysis of the ways ideas about sterilization fit into core American political and cultural values. He looks at sterilization in the context of debates about individual choice, self-reliance, and constitutional rights, particularly in the arena of parental control and reproductive choices. He then considers American faith in technology, especially medical technology, as a "fix" for most social problems and as a rationale for state intervention in problems such as poverty, overpopulation, and the "problems" resulting from the perceived inability of individuals to control themselves or care for their offspring. This book is useful for its extended discussion of the complicated nexus of American policy and ideology that supports involuntary sterilization despite the country's stated commitment to individual civil rights. Blank also outlines various factors, including concerns about limited resources and population growth, which make the control of reproduction a social issue that continues to spark debate.

The essays edited by BROBERG and ROLL-HANSEN similarly discuss sterilization within the context of larger social issues, ideology, and cultural forces but focus on early twentieth-century Scandinavian social history. The essays cover the history of legislation and social programs involving sterilization and biomedical politics in Denmark, Sweden, Norway, and Finland, especially in the context of the countries' differing socialist/social welfare policies. Several of the essays discuss the push for comprehensive sterilization policies in terms of other radical political movements from the 1900s through the 1920s, such as feminist and birth control movements. Many of the arguments for eugenic sterilization centered on concerns about declining populations in Scandinavia, particularly concerns about the "quality" of that population if wealthier, more educated women chose to limit their reproduction more than other classes of women did. The book is especially useful because each essay provides some discussion of the ways in which notions about gender extended into concerns about population "quality" and social welfare.

Whereas the other texts concentrate only on involuntary sterilization or on both involuntary and voluntary procedures, PRESSER's sociological study focuses exclusively on voluntary sterilization. This book provides specific demographic data about individual women who chose sterilization, as well as data on perceptions about sterilization within specific communities. Presser analyzes the history of sterilization in Puerto Rico from 1930 to 1965 in order to account for the prevalence of sterilization among Puerto Rican women. She compares Puerto Rican views on sterilization to those of other "developing" countries in Latin America, the Caribbean, Asia, and Africa. Through these comparisons, Presser establishes the specific social conditions in Puerto Rico that allowed sterilization to flourish as a primary means of birth control; a marked desire to limit family size and a positive view of sterilization on the part of medical practitioners are the most important factors. In individual chapters, she analyzes the impact of women's education, awareness of fertility control options, family income, employment status, and location on sterilization patterns.

—KIMBERLY VanHOOSIER-CAREY

See also Reproductive Freedom; Reproductive Technologies

Stone, Lucy 1818–1893

American Suffragist

Blackwell, Alice Stone, *Lucy Stone: Pioneer of Women's Rights*, 1930; reprint, New York: Krause, 1971

Hays, Elinor Rice, *Morning Star*, New York: Harcourt Brace, 1961

Kerr, Andrea Moore, *Lucy Stone: Speaking Out for Equality*, New Brunswick, New Jersey: Rutgers University Press, 1992

Despite Lucy Stone's significant contributions to the women's suffrage movement, there exist a limited number of critical sources on her life. These three biographies offer much overlapping material, but each is an important contribution to the picture of Lucy Stone. The first biography was written by her daughter. Less a critical biography than a collection of primary source material, BLACKWELL offers a compelling, if rather propagandistic view, of Stone based on her letters and speeches. Blackwell devotes much attention to Stone's early life and her education at Oberlin. She includes important primary material concerning Stone's friendship with Antoinette Brown Blackwell, her husband Henry Blackwell, and those influential in both the abolition and suffrage movements.

The first critical biography of Stone, HAYS offers a compelling portrait, including important information about the cultural contexts of Stone's life. In addition to relating Stone's own biography, Hays discusses the historical situation surrounding Stone and the women's suffrage movement, thus providing a compelling portrait of the movement as well as of Stone herself. Hays devotes additional attention to Antoinette Brown Blackwell and her friendship with Stone, offering a brief biography of the first ordained female minister in the United States. Hays also offers biographical information on other significant members of Stone's personal circle, including the Blackwell family and other suffragist leaders. She examines Stone's contributions to the abolition movement, documenting her court appearance for Margaret Garner—whose story would later become the catalyst for Toni Morrison's Pulitzer Prize winning novel, *Beloved*. This biography charts Stone's move from the struggle for abolition to that for women's suffrage. It also documents Stone's later split from Susan B. Anthony and Elizabeth Cady Stanton and their National Woman Suffrage Association, and Stone's corresponding formation of the American Woman Suffrage Association. This text provides an excellent history, not only of Lucy Stone, but of the early years of the women's suffrage movement in the United States.

The most recent biography of Stone, that by KERR provides an intimate portrait of Stone's life and work, and is concerned specifically with her private life and its influences on her public life. Kerr devotes attention to the harsh conditions of Stone's childhood, documenting the physical abuse she suffered and also suggesting the possibility of childhood sexual abuse. Focusing on her private life and public appearance, Kerr examines Stone's difficulties with her family, and her husband's continued financial debacles as she struggled to fight for women's suffrage. Kerr also examines the split between the National Woman Suffrage Association and the American Woman Suffrage Association, detailing the conflict over the Fifteenth Amendment and the racism displayed by Stanton and Anthony that drove Stone to form her own organization. Influenced by contemporary feminist biographical theory, Kerr suggests that Stone's disappearance from the history of women's suffrage was directly related to her philosophical split from Stanton and Anthony, who, in reconstructing their history of the suffrage movement, lessened Stone's significance. Kerr's biography is a powerful discussion of Stone's life, and provides significant information that may have been glossed over in previous biographies.

—AMY L. WINK

See also Women's Rights Convention, Seneca Falls, New York

Stopes, Marie 1880–1958

British Activist

Briant, Keith, *Marie Stopes: A Biography*, London: Hogarth Press, 1962

Hall, Ruth, *Passionate Crusader: The Life of Marie Stopes*, New York and London: Harcourt Brace, 1977; published in London as *Marie Stopes*

Maude, Aylmer, *Marie Stopes: Her Work and Play*, London: P. Davies, and New York: Putnam, 1933

Rose, June, *Marie Stopes and the Sexual Revolution*, London and Boston: Faber, 1992

Marie Stopes began her career as a botanist but became notorious worldwide after publishing her pioneering book *Married Love* (1918), which endorsed sexual fulfillment for women. She opened Britain's first birth control clinic three years later. Throughout her life, the outspoken Stopes placed priority on controlling her public image. Her first two biographers were both intimate friends, and subsequent scholars have devoted much effort to revising these early portrayals. Stopes's biographers have suggested differing motives for her work, but most point to her ironically unhappy personal life: an unhappy childhood, two unhappy marriages, the alienation of her only son, and the impossibly idealistic nature of her goals.

MAUDE published his study in 1933 at Stopes's request, as a counterbalance to negative publicity after she lost a libel case. According to Hall (reviewed below), Stopes financed and even wrote much of the book, forbidding Maude to reveal her age. Maude presents Stopes as an innocent, intelligent woman cruelly victimized first by her impotent first husband and later by the "pertinacious and unfair opposition" of the Catholic Church, the medical profession, and the press. He endorses her claim that her work on sexual relations was only stimulated by her discovery, five years after her first marriage, that the marriage had never been consummated. While he admits that public charges of egomania and neurosis have been made in relation to Stopes's strong-mindedness, he points out that she considered herself a prophet and a revolutionary trying to achieve happiness for others. He himself feels that "her crusade is a necessary one," meriting "respect" and "gratitude." Throughout the book, Maude offers lengthy excerpts from Stopes's own writings and speeches, as well as other people's comments about her, and an appendix offers a list of her published work. While this book offers interesting details, the reader must use it with caution. Although Maude acknowledges that Stopes is a friend, he does not mention that he lived with her and maintained a romantic, if platonic, relationship for some years. This and other omissions discredited the book even at the time of its publication.

BRIANT's biography of Stopes, published some thirty years after Maude's, also suffers from partiality. Like Maude, Briant had a romantic relationship with Stopes, and while his book was published after her death, it was first approved by her family. Nevertheless, Briant claims to have sought "the truth" and not to have omitted anything that "considerably affects" the biography, and his work is somewhat more impartial than Maude's. Like Maude, Briant is a great admirer of Stopes, calling her a "distinguished scientist" and a "Renaissance character" and arguing that her work "revolutionized and enriched the lives of millions." But Briant compares Stopes's life to that in a Victorian melodrama, arguing that the personal tragedies and personality flaws that drove her to achieve paradoxically prevented her from obtaining happiness herself. He concedes that she exhibited "megalomania and sexual vanity" later in life, and was "morbidly self-conscious" of criticism. Briant also suffers from the desire to name-drop; he runs on for several chapters about Stopes's encounters with well-known writers, regardless of their relevance to understanding her life. The book includes a number of photos and lengthy excerpts from Stopes's writings and speeches.

HALL's is the first biography of Stopes by an outsider, and the first based on extensive research using Stopes's many personal papers. She points out numerous deliberate inaccuracies made by Maude and Briant. In addition to greater objectivity, Hall provides much clearer explanations of Stopes's personal and legal crises. In contrast to Maude and Briant, Hall shows little personal sympathy with Stopes, noting that the "aura of saintly altruism" Stopes cultivated was "suffused with an large and equally genuine self-esteem," and that she refused to tolerate criticism. Hall does, however, argue that Stopes was a revolutionary figure, that her struggles were greater than those of the women's movement of the 1970s, and that she created a major change in public opinion about sex. Hall does much more than previous biographers to show how the birth control campaign was, for Stopes, part of a larger commitment to the class- and race-based eugenics movement. Like Briant, Hall uses the idea of paradox to explain Stopes's personal and professional life, "the ideals of love she believed in and advocated for others perpetually eluding her own grasp." While Hall stresses the great impact made by *Married Love,* helping readers appreciate the context in which it was published, she also notes that it had little original content. Stopes was not so much an innovative thinker as a courageous and skillful popularizer. And while Stopes's goal of government-sponsored birth control services became reality in her own country, her larger goal of racial improvement through eugenics has become almost unmentionable.

ROSE offers the most recent study of Stopes, one influenced by psychoanalytic theory, in which actions are repeatedly traced back to childhood events (a distant mother, a schoolgirl crush on a teacher, and a lifelong lack of self-esteem). Rose's book is written in a very clear, almost simplistic style and is less detailed than the others, although it includes more photos. Rose stresses the role of gender relationships in Stopes's life, and has found some new archival evidence about this. Most dramatically, she suggests that Stopes's claim to have begun her campaign after discovering that she was still a virgin five years after marriage—the claim that appeared in *Married Love* to give her respectability, and that was accepted by her first three biographers—may have been false. She also notes that Stopes's public commitment to equality in relationships failed on a personal level, since Stopes insisted on dominating every relationship she ever had, often with disastrous results. Rose attributes Stopes's personal unhappiness to an unrealistic ideal of marriage and her professional obstacles to an inability to work with others. Like the other biographers, Rose concludes that Stopes's success in helping other women came at the price of personal unhappiness.

—NAN H. DREHER

Stowe, Harriet Beecher 1811–1896

American Writer

Caskey, Marie, *Chariot of Fire: Religion and the Beecher Family,* New Haven, Connecticut: Yale University Press, 1978

Crozier, Alice C., *The Novels of Harriet Beecher Stowe,* New York: Oxford University Press, 1969

Gossett, Thomas F., *"Uncle Tom's Cabin" and American Culture,* Dallas, Texas: Southern Methodist University Press, 1985

Hedrick, Joan D., *Harriet Beecher Stowe: A Life,* New York: Oxford University Press, 1994

Kirkham, E. Bruce, *The Building of "Uncle Tom's Cabin,"* Knoxville: University of Tennessee Press, 1977

Lowance, Mason I., Jr., Ellen E. Westbrook, and R.C. DeProspo (eds.), *The Stowe Debate: Rhetorical Strategies in "Uncle Tom's Cabin,"* Amherst: University of Massachusetts Press, 1994

Sundquist, Eric J. (ed.), *New Essays on "Uncle Tom's Cabin,"* New York and Cambridge: Cambridge University Press, 1986

Tompkins, Jane, *Sensational Designs: The Cultural Work of American Fiction, 1790–1860,* New York: Oxford University Press, 1985

Although Harriet Beecher Stowe's 1852 bestseller *Uncle Tom's Cabin* made her world-famous, her work has only in the last two decades received sustained critical attention. As a result of that renewal of scholarly interest, sparked by the development of the disciplines of American studies, women's studies, and African-American studies, *Uncle Tom's Cabin* is now often taught in U.S. history or literature classrooms at the high school or college levels. The novel is routinely included in recent scholarly books on the American Renaissance, and in discussions of race, religion, and domesticity in American history. Yet Stowe's professional career extended 20 years before *Uncle Tom's Cabin* and 25 years after. While most critics still concentrate on Stowe's most famous novel, her other work—novels, essays, stories, and letters—is receiving renewed attention as well.

The single best source on Stowe, and the ideal beginning for anyone interested in learning about Stowe's life, work, and culture, is HEDRICK's magisterial new biography (awarded the Pulitzer Prize). The first scholarly biography of Stowe since 1941, it corrects the chauvinism and speculative psychology of earlier biographers, drawing on insights from recent scholarship in nineteenth-century popular culture and literature to place Stowe's work in the context of her times. While its literary discussions of individual works are somewhat limited, this eminently readable book is unsurpassed in giving a sense of Stowe as a real person in a vibrant cultural moment.

TOMPKINS's book, while not entirely on Stowe, contains the most influential single essay written on her work in the last few decades. Opening and closing chapters, in addition, provide a sustained argument for the value of nineteenth-century sentimental literature such as Stowe's for the twentieth century and beyond. Tompkins's insistence on the need to immerse ourselves in the ways nineteenth-century readers would have understood the sentimentality and didactic evangelical message of works like Stowe's continues to shape literary criticism, and has helped to spur the ongoing recovery of popular nineteenth-century works.

CROZIER's book is still a good brief introduction to the full range of Stowe's work, arguing for Stowe's literary significance far beyond the impact of *Uncle Tom's Cabin*. She shows, for instance, how Stowe's 1870s novels of manners anticipate the social realism for which William Dean Howells and Henry James would later become famous. Ending with a chapter on Stowe's 1869 exposé of Lord Byron's incest with his half-sister—an exposé which caused such an outcry it nearly ended Stowe's career—Crozier argues for the importance of the Byronic figure for Stowe and for her culture.

CASKEY, while undeservedly neglected today, remains the best source on the significance and range of Stowe's theological heritage, in the context of her Beecher family roots and influences. Caskey shows how Stowe's religious experience, as the daughter and sister of some of the most famous theologians and preachers of the nineteenth century, shaped her thinking and her art. Caskey reveals, too, how Stowe's life and work reflect broader trends in the gradual liberalization of nineteenth-century Christianity.

Not surprisingly, *Uncle Tom's Cabin* has received and continues to receive the greatest critical attention. KIRKHAM's pioneering book is a study of how *Uncle Tom's Cabin* was written; it incorporates a detailed study of the surviving manuscript pages, the book's initial serial publication in the *National Era*, and its final version in book form. Arguing for Stowe's seriousness about her craft, he shows how her two decades of previous writing prepared her for what would become a world-famous work.

GOSSETT shows how *Uncle Tom's Cabin* reflects nineteenth-century popular assumptions about (for instance) innate racial characteristics, and how the long history of its many adaptations for stage and screen shows how important this novel has been in reinforcing or commenting on American cultural stereotypes. SUNDQUIST's collection of essays contains several influential treatments, including discussions of Stowe's characterizations of African-Americans, her gothic imagination, and her Christlike maternal heroines.

LOWANCE, WESTBROOK, and DePROSO's collection, a product of a National Endowment for the Humanities Summer Seminar for College Teachers on "Uncle Tom's Cabin and Antebellum American Culture," considers how *Uncle Tom's Cabin* relates to various kinds of nineteenth-century American "rhetorics": evangelical, political, domestic, sentimental, biblical, and racial. DeProspo's afterword is a provocative look at what the future status of *Uncle Tom's Cabin* might be, given readers' continuing unease about whether or not it is a racist work.

—GAIL K. SMITH

Suffrage: Britain and Ireland

Garner, Les, *Stepping Stones to Women's Liberty: Feminist Ideas in the Women's Suffrage Movement 1900–1918*, London: Heinemann Educational, and Rutherford, New Jersey: Fairleigh Dickenson University Press, 1984

Holledge, Julie, *Innocent Flowers: Women in the Edwardian Theatre*, London: Virago Press, 1981

Holton, Sandra Stanley, *Suffrage Days: Stories from the Women's Suffrage Movement*, London and New York: Routledge, 1996

Kent, Susan Kingsley, *Sex and Suffrage in Britain 1860–1914*, Princeton, New Jersey: Princeton University Press, 1987; London: Routledge, 1990

Leneman, Leah, *A Guid Cause: The Women's Suffrage Movement in Scotland*, Aberdeen: Aberdeen University Press, 1991

Liddington Jill, and Jill Norris, *One Hand Tied Behind Us: The Rise of the Women's Suffrage Movement*, London: Virago Press, 1978

Owens, Rosemary Cullen, *Smashing Times: A History of the Irish Women's Suffrage Movement 1889–1922*, Dublin: Attic Press, 1984

Pankhurst, E. Sylvia, *The Suffragette Movement*, London and New York: Longmans Green, 1931

Stowell, Sheila, *A Stage of Their Own: Feminist Playwrights of the Suffrage Era*, Manchester: Manchester University Press, and Ann Arbor: University of Michigan Press, 1992

Strachey, Ray, *The Cause: A Short History of the Women's Movement in Great Britain*, London, G. Bell, 1928

Tickner, Lisa, *The Spectacle of Women: Imagery of the Suffrage Campaign 1907–14*, London: Chatto and Windus, 1987; Chicago: Chicago University Press, 1988

Histories of the women's suffrage movement in Britain have traditionally tended to focus on the events of the early twentieth century, on the metropolitan-based national-political organizations, and on the personalities of their leaders. Critics, however, have recently begun to explore the contradictions and complexities of the movement and its values: the problematics of heroine worship; the exclusions propagated by the national-metropolitan nexus; the deployment of the militant or constitutional categories; and the uneasy elision of the women's suffrage movement with the broader women's movement in Britain.

This elision is demonstrated by the subtitle of STRACHEY's book, first published in the year of women's enfranchisement on the same basis as that of men in Britain. Nevertheless, Strachey ranges widely, from the publication of Mary Wollstonecraft's *The Vindication of the Rights of Women* in 1792 through the nineteenth century's campaigns, arriving at the twentieth century only after some two hundred pages. Strachey's narrative is that of a participant in the movement. More partisan, however, is PANKHURST's book, which recounts the movement through the lens of the Women's Social and Political Union, embedded in the Pankhurst family story.

Although the issue of class had prompted many women to refuse involvement in women's, in favor of adult, suffrage, this issue was marginalized in many early studies of the movement. LIDDINGTON and NORRIS challenge the dominant view of the suffrage movement as a middle-class (and metropolitan) movement, identifying radical suffragists in the industrial north, in Lancashire and Manchester. The analysis of the daily lives and the history of the political activism of working women usefully precedes the account of the campaigns, the suffragists' relationships with the Labour Party and the impact of World War I.

The cultural practices and cultural infrastructure of the suffrage movement were long regarded by historians as independent of, or at least secondary to, the (explicitly) political meetings and activities. GARNER's comparative analysis of the various feminist ideas of the women's suffrage movement excels in its treatment of the diversity of feminist ideas promoted through publications by the suffrage political organizations. Individual activists and organizations are decentered by TICKNER's exploration of the cultural production of the movement. This study comprehensively examines the visual imagery, notably in the banners and posters, of the women's suffrage movement, which provided daily cultural ammunition. A dynamic relationship is identified between the pro- and anti-suffrage campaigners and their art work, its production and its consumption.

The participation of women of the theatre in the women's suffrage movement is introduced by HOLLEDGE in the metaphor of Lady Macbeth's subversive innocent flower concealing the serpent beneath. This history of women in the theatre examines the changing role of the actress in the nineteenth century as a prelude to the involvement of actresses in organizations such as the Actresses' Franchise League (AFL), the Woman's Theatre, and the Pioneer Players (founded by Edith Craig). Three short plays that had been performed by the AFL are reproduced in the appendix. STOWELL analyses "suffrage drama" and the plays written for women's suffrage by a selection of feminist playwrights (Elizabeth Robins, Cicely Hamilton, Elizabeth Baker, and Githa Sowerby) as reworking existing dramatic forms—the romantic comedy and naturalism. The representations of women, the thematic concerns, and the plot dynamics in these plays are effectively linked to broader theatrical and political contexts through explorations of gendered responses in newspaper reviews.

The terms "sex" and "suffrage" dominated the movement and were deployed in diverse ways, as KENT's history demonstrates. Women were defined in terms of "sex," even categorized as "the (fair) sex," and therefore perceived to be controlled by sex. Femininity became a battlefield that positioned suffragists as unwomanly and therefore not women. The ambivalence felt by middle-class suffragists about prostitution and sexually transmitted diseases is usefully explored, identifying and contextualizing the radical identification of some suffragists with the prostitute, and the divisiveness of other suffragists' speaking for, claiming to know better than, women exploited through poverty. The sexual double standard was a prime target of the feminist campaign for the vote.

The need to redress the over-emphasis on London has provided new and urgent perspectives. The Irish women's suffrage movement from 1889 to 1922 is the subject of OWENS's study, which attends to the activism in Ireland in the context of Irish political and religious circumstances. The issue of Home Rule and the promise of equal rights in the 1916 proclamation affected suffragists in Ireland, who found that although they were enfranchised in 1922—six years before women in England—feminism became subsumed into party politics and the issue of nationalism. Nevertheless, the first female Member of the British Parliament was Irish, Constance de Markievicz.

A different national perspective is taken up by LENEMAN, whose study of the suffrage movement in Scotland similarly constructs a new history of activities hitherto marginalized in anglocentric histories. As a Liberal stronghold, Scotland acted very much as a gauge for suffragists of their impact on the Liberal government. The biographical list of suffragists active in Scotland, and a list of recorded attacks against property in Scotland attributed to suffragists, form invaluable appendices.

HOLTON tells the stories of the British women's suffrage movement through seven activists: Elizabeth Wolstenholme Elmy, Jessie Craigen, Elizabeth Cady Stanton, Hannah Mitchell, Mary Gawthorpe, Laurence Housman, and Alice Clark. The different positions of these individuals is shown in their involvement in the movement and their responses to it, demonstrated by their writings, notably in Clark's case from newly discovered papers. The concluding chapter discusses specifically how the histories of each of the seven came to be written, and more generally explores ways in which women's history is constructed. The descriptive list of further reading provides a useful bibliography of work to date, published and forthcoming, on British women's suffrage history.

—KATHERINE COCKIN

Suffrage: United States

Beeton, Beverly, *Women Vote in the West: The Woman Suffrage Movement, 1869–1896*, New York and London: Garland, 1986

Buechler, Steven M., *The Transformation of the Woman Suffrage Movement: The Case of Illinois, 1850–1920*, New Brunswick, New Jersey: Rutgers University Press, 1986

DuBois, Ellen Carol, *Feminism and Suffrage: The Emergence of an Independent Women's Movement in America, 1848–1869*, Ithaca, New York, and London: Cornell University Press, 1978

Flexner, Eleanor, *Century of Struggle: The Woman's Rights Movement in the United States*, Cambridge, Massachusetts: Belknap Press of Harvard University Press, 1959

Kraditor, Aileen S., *The Ideas of the Woman Suffrage Movement: 1890–1920*, New York: Columbia University Press, 1965

Kugler, Israel, *From Ladies to Women: The Organized Struggle for Women's Rights in the Reconstruction Era*, New York and London: Greenwood, 1987

Morgan, David, *Suffragists and Democrats: The Politics of Woman Suffrage in America*, East Lansing: Michigan State University Press, 1972

Nichols, Carole, *Votes and More for Women: Suffrage and after in Connecticut*, New York: Haworth, 1983

Wagner, Sally, *A Time of Protest: Suffragists Challenge the Republic, 1870–1887*, Sacramento, California: Spectrum, 1987

DuBOIS examines the first stage of the campaign for women's suffrage in America, from the Seneca Falls Convention of 1848 to the formation of two rival woman suffrage groups in 1869. The Seneca Falls, New York, meeting was convened by Lucretia Mott and Elizabeth Cady Stanton. The ballot was the single most radical demand of the early movement. The resolution to support it passed with only a narrow majority, because many perceived the demand as too extreme. DuBois, editor of a volume of the correspondence, writings, and speeches of Stanton and Susan B. Anthony, discusses the role of women in the Civil War years, and how Reconstruction caused shifts in political and reform activities. Anthony and Stanton refused to endorse the Fifteenth Amendment, because it did not give women the ballot. Their National Woman Suffrage Association (NWSA) sought a federal amendment for women's suffrage. Lucy Stone and Julia Ward Howe argued that after the black males were enfranchised, women would achieve their goal. The Stone group formed an American Woman Suffrage Association (AWSA), which sought to gain the vote via state legislation.

KUGLER puts the women's suffrage organizations in the context of other rights campaigns in the post-Civil War period in the areas of education, labor conditions, and reform of women's legal status. His aim was to provide a clarifying perspective on the movement in subsequent periods up to the present day. WAGNER's "time of protest" was the 1870s. She presents an account of radical feminist activities in that decade: efforts to form a feminist-labor coalition, tax resistance, and protests during the Philadelphia Centennial and at the dedication of the Statue of Liberty.

FLEXNER integrates the fight for the franchise into the centuries-old struggle for equal rights including equal work and educational opportunities. The author, daughter of a suffragist, packs her work with the contributions of the famous and obscure. A quarter of the book is devoted to the final dozen years of the suffrage campaign. She has an interesting chapter on those who opposed woman suffrage.

There was no official ideology of the woman suffrage movement. KRADITOR's exhaustively documented study includes the arsenal of arguments used in the battle for suffrage, as well as the points of view exchanged in intra- and inter-organizational disputes about principles, strategy, and tactics. The NWSA and AWSA united in 1890 into one organization, a National American Woman Suffrage Association. Most of the leaders of the second stage of the movement, beginning in the 1890s, were more conservative, although more systematic than their predecessors. Kraditor shows that the movement was largely bourgeois, with antiforeign and antilabor feelings among women of the north who were older "native stock" Americans, and white supremacy views on the part of southern suffragists. The ideas they employed combined persuasion and propaganda. There were arguments based on the idea of equity: that suffrage was a matter of simple justice in the light of the nation's democratic tradition. There were also arguments from expediency: that society would benefit if women had the vote. Kraditor concludes that for suffrage to come about required both the movement and the transformation of society.

MORGAN notes that the nineteenth-century feminist elite was never able to secure a sufficient following to bring about women's suffrage. However, economic, social, and legal forces emerged that transformed the situation. Political opportunity and political preparedness combined to achieve the victory. Morgan focuses on the campaign for suffrage at the congressional level after 1912. He deals with the interactions between the suffrage movement, President Wilson, state campaigns, the evolving situation in Congress, and, finally, in the states during ratification. He looks at the considerations that motivated politicians' attitudes toward the suffragists (for example, short-term partisan advantage and disadvantage).

NICHOLS examines how women's suffrage was achieved between 1869 and 1896 in four Rocky Mountain states: Wyoming, Utah, Colorado, and Idaho. She concludes that women were enfranchised in the west as a matter of expediency, not ideology (as a means to attract investors and settlers, to embarrass an opposition or gain supporters, to gain eastern support for statehood, and as a safe social experiment).

BUECHLER shows that, whereas originally the suffrage demand was a symbolic challenge to patriarchal power, in the intervening decades the ballot became detached from a larger agenda of social change. Such a transformation made possible the forging of an alliance with the traditional and conservative woman's club movement, with working-class immigrant women who were recruited by the settlement house movement, and with upper-class club women. His case study concentrates on developments in Illinois, but he makes comparisons with the situation nationally. Buechler argues that to the extent that suffrage and temperance became intertwined, the suffrage movement lost any prospect of a cross-class alliance with an increasingly heterogeneous working class.

—MARTIN GRUBERG

See also Women's Rights Convention, Seneca Falls, New York

Suffrage: Worldwide

Cleverdon, Catherine Lyle, *The Woman Suffrage Movement in Canada*, Toronto: University of Toronto Press, 1950; Buffalo, New York: University of Toronto Press, 1974

Grimshaw, Patricia, *Women's Suffrage in New Zealand*, Auckland: Auckland University Press, 1972

Hahner, June E., *Emancipating the Female Sex: The Struggle for Women's Rights in Brazil, 1850–1940*, Durham, North Carolina: Duke University Press, 1990

Lees, Kirsten, *Votes for Women: The Australian Story*, St. Leonards: Allen and Unwin, 1995

Morton, Ward M., *Woman Suffrage in Mexico*, Gainesville: University of Florida Press, 1962

Oldfield, Audrey, *Woman Suffrage in Australia: A Gift or a Struggle?*, Cambridge and New York: Cambridge University Press, 1992

Tikoo, Prithvi Nath, *Indian Women: A Brief Socio-Cultural Survey*, Delhi: B.R. Publishing, and New York: Apt Books, 1985

Walker, Cherryl, *The Women's Suffrage Movement in South Africa*, Cape Town: University of Cape Town, 1979

Political history is a perennially popular topic, and there is no shortage of works about women in the public arena. Even the countries in which women's studies has yet to catch fire generally have a book on women's suffrage listed among the national literature. Typically, suffrage books cover similar ground regardless of their nation of focus. The first feminist battles waged in a nation have often occurred over the issue of suffrage, because women have believed that they could effect other reforms by using the power of the ballot. Activists involved in crusades for temperance and against vice generally campaigned for the vote as a means to the desired end. Women's suffrage arrived at different times in different countries, and no constant factor in victory has become evident to historians.

WALKER's book is a rarity. One of the very few to deal with South African women, it examines the suffrage movement in this highly conservative country. Although its scope is sufficiently broad to be of use to researchers, this book is essentially a long essay. It was presented in partial fulfillment of the requirements for a baccalaureate degree and, as a result, it is too scholarly in tone and style to appeal to a broad audience.

MORTON's book is a study of woman suffrage in Mexico. This was one of the first histories of Mexican women to emerge, and it suffers badly from an unenlightened tone. By discussing the value of the vote only to wives and mothers, Morton seems to be unaware that women's lives are important in ways that do not relate to men. His emphasis on the men who supported women's suffrage does not contribute significantly to the history of women.

HAHNER provides one of the best studies of Latin American women's political history. This book examines the growth of women's rights activities in Brazil from their early manifestations in the mid-nineteenth century to the successful conclusion of the suffrage campaign in the 1930s. Hahner recognizes that the definition of feminism changes from region to region, and her problematizing of this concept adds to the debate on the historical and ethnic dimensions of feminism. A sophisticated work based on exhaustive research, Hahner's book is essential reading for all students of Latin America.

TIKOO offers an informal study of the world of Indian women. The book gives a somewhat detailed account of the suffrage movement, and it is the only Indian book to do so. However, the survey style and entire absence of historical analysis seriously handicaps this work.

New Zealand women were given the right to vote in 1893, thus making the nation the first country to allow suffrage for women. In a pathbreaking book that has become a classic, GRIMSHAW adds an important voice to the growing women's history field by providing a study of the New Zealand suffrage movement. She examines a group of colonial women who held high hopes for the effectiveness of a civil liberties campaign to transform women's unequal status under the law. Subsequent studies have raised problematic issues about these women's motives and goals, yet Grimshaw's book is worthy of being read for offering a highly readable account of women who were long hidden from history. The bibliography in this brief book is especially strong.

OLDFIELD pieces together the stories of the campaigns for the ballot by women in Australia. As befits a solid historical work, this book contains a chronicle of the development of the wider women's movement. Oldfield argues that the women's groups that coalesced to achieve the vote always retained their individual identity below the surface of unity. She explores the record of unity and disunity while discussing the problems of terminology, particularly the words "feminism" and "feminist." Australian women's history has become a flourishing field, and this book is but one example of the strength of the work being conducted there.

Histories of suffrage have been faulted for focusing on the activities of white women while excluding the stories of women of color. Another Australian historian, LEES, addresses this tendency towards racial blindness by juxtaposing the suffrage struggles of white women against those of Aboriginal and Torres Strait Islander women in Australia. While white women achieved suffrage in 1902, Lees points out that for women of color the vote not only came much later, but when it came it did not afford the same opportunity for advancement or pave the way for justice. A chronology of major events in Australian women's political history and an extensive bibliography further add to the value of this volume.

Although a bit awkward to read, CLEVERDON's book remains the best study of women's suffrage in Canada nearly half a century after its publication. This history follows a chronological pattern and explains the great amount of interest manifested by Canadians in woman suffrage during World War I, after some three decades of general indifference. However, the book suffers from a lack of feminist historical analysis.

—CARYN E. NEUMANN

Surrogate Motherhood

Andrews, Lori, *Between Strangers: Surrogate Mothers, Expectant Fathers and Brave New Babies,* New York: Harper and Row, 1989

Field, Martha, *Surrogate Motherhood: The Legal and Social Issues,* Cambridge, Massachusetts.: Harvard University Press, 1988

Gostin, Larry (ed.), *Surrogate Motherhood: Politics and Privacy,* Bloomington: Indiana University Press, 1990

Rae, Scott, B., *The Ethics of Commercial Surrogate Motherhood: Brave New Families?* Westport, Connecticut: Praeger, 1994

Ragoné, Helena, *Surrogate Motherhood: Conception in the Heart,* Boulder, Colorado: Westview Press, 1994

Although there has been a great deal written about many aspects of surrogate motherhood in the light of the new reproductive technologies, there are still not very many book-length comprehensive treatments of the topic. RAGONÉ's book is one of the few to present an extensive ethnographic study of surrogate motherhood in the United States. She provides a detailed exposition of the processes involved in commercial surrogacy arrangements, and the responses of participants in these processes. The book documents the experiences and perceptions of surrogate mothers, fathers, and adoptive mothers, who gave interviews during the period from 1988 to 1994. Although they were interviewed at different stages in the surrogacy process, all were participants in well-established programs operating in the United States. The book also presents the perspective of program directors, and details the inner workings of what the author refers to as "open" and "closed" programs. The former involve the participants in ongoing close interaction throughout the surrogacy process, whereas the latter conduct meetings between the participants only, for the purposes of finalizing legal matters. Of particular interest in this study is the attempt to reveal the complexity of the motivations of surrogates. Their ambiguous and often inconsistently stated motivations are examined and understood in terms of the suggestion that surrogacy provides working-class women with the chance to move beyond their traditional motherhood roles without having to deny the worth of those roles. The effect of reproductive technologies on notions of motherhood, fatherhood, kinship, and family are also explored.

GOSTIN's edited collection gives an idea of the breadth of legal and ethical issues relating to surrogate motherhood. It includes 13 essays and a number of reviews of the case of the child known as Baby M. One focus of the discussion is the question of whether there is a constitutional right to privacy in making a surrogacy agreement. This, in turn, raises the question of whether and why surrogacy might be understood along the lines of intimate relationships that give rise to privacy issues.

Another focus of some of the essays is the social and economic context in which commercial surrogacy arrangements are often made. Some argue that the legal enforcement of surrogacy contracts is yet another expression of white male privilege. Both the exploitation of poor working-class women who take up the role of surrogate, and the commodification of children as a result of "baby buying" are discussed. Another ethical issue that is explored in the essays is the question of how a policy of either banning or allowing commercial surrogacy contracts affects women's autonomy and control over their own bodies. There is also a section on the impact of surrogate motherhood on the health care professions.

FIELD offers a more detailed feminist analysis of surrogate motherhood, which is concerned with the vulnerable position of surrogate mothers. This work is interesting for the ways in which it advocates what amounts to a strengthening of the legal position of women who enter into surrogacy agreements. In this regard, the book argues for the use of a presumption favoring the surrogate mother in child custody disputes following the breach of a surrogacy agreement.

Views on the appropriateness of enforcing commercial surrogacy agreements differ greatly. RAE critically assesses literature on the ethics of commercial surrogacy arrangements, asking how much the process of conceiving children ought to be linked to profit-making activity. The book argues at length against various defenses of commercial surrogacy and defends the view that the law should prohibit the payment of a fee to surrogates. Further, he says, it should not enforce contracts that deny the surrogate mother parental rights to her child. It offers a redefinition of motherhood in the light of the separation of the genetic and gestational aspects of motherhood, made possible by new reproductive technologies. Taking the position that gestation should define motherhood, an argument is advanced in favor of the view that parental rights to children should be accorded to surrogate mothers in the event of a custody dispute. The author's ethical analysis is also applied to important court decisions, as well as to current state surrogacy laws of the United States. and relevant international laws. The book ends with a draft proposal for legislation that would embody the author's ethical approach.

Rather than construct rigorous ethical arguments, ANDREWS contributes to the development of an understanding of the role that the law should play in the regulation of parenting and reproduction, with a narration of the personal and familial stories of a number of people involved in surrogacy arrangements. The book addresses the ethical, legal, and social issues surrounding surrogate motherhood amidst the presentation of dialogues that reveal the personal convictions, aspirations, and disappointments of surrogate and adoptive mothers and their respective families. It offers a powerful critique of the criminalization of surrogacy, developed in part by way of an interesting comparison of commercial surrogate motherhood with the cultural practice of permitting the adoption of children with the consent of their teenage mothers.

—TOULA NICOLACOPOULOS

Suttee *see* Sati

T

Teaching: Primary and Secondary

Acker, Sandra (ed.), *Teachers, Gender and Careers*, New York and London: Falmer Press, 1989
———, *Gendered Education*, Buckingham and Philadelphia: Open University Press, 1994
Altenbaugh, Richard J., *The Teacher's Voice: A Social History of Teaching in Twentieth Century America*, London and New York: Falmer Press, 1992
De Lyon, Hilary, and Frances Widdowson Migniuolo, *Women Teachers: Issues and Experiences*, Milton Keynes and Philadelphia: Open University Press, 1989
Grumet, Madeleine R., *Bitter Milk: Women and Teaching*, Amherst: University of Massachusetts Press, 1988
Miller, Jane, *School for Women*, London: Virago Press, 1996
Prentice, Alison, and Marjorie R. Theobald, *Women Who Taught: Perspectives on the History of Women and Teaching*, Toronto: University of Toronto Press, 1991
Weber, Sandra, and Claudia Mitchell, *That's Funny, You Don't Look Like a Teacher!: Interrogating Images and Identity in Popular Culture*, London and Washington, D.C.: Falmer Press, 1995

Female teachers have certainly been present throughout the centuries, yet literature concerning them has been conspicuously absent. Written feminist pedagogy tends to concern university rather than primary and secondary education. Women have a long history of teaching at primary and secondary level, and mainstream education theory has largely ignored this until recently. Women as teachers, and teaching for gender equity at primary and secondary level are the issues here. Texts on women and teaching included here are historical, sociological, psychological, psychoanalytic, and philosophical, often with practical suggestions for ongoing research and practice. Major issues include the feminisation of teaching as a career, teaching for gender equity, and the sexual division of labor in the teaching hierarchy.

ACKER (1994) addresses the careers of female teachers and academics in a collection of her own essays spanning 20 years of feminist scholarship. This book is important for its thorough sociological analysis of gender issues and teaching. Acker is interested in making gender central to the sociology of education and frequently reviews the literature on teaching from this perspective. For instance, Acker notes that women as teachers tend to be discussed in terms of their marital status. Acker is critical of the attitude, from her own educational experience, that it is better to write about higher education than lower education. Conventional approaches to the sociology of teaching since 1960 are criticised, and the sexual division of labour in teaching is examined. An important issue for Acker is why teachers resist anti-sexist initiatives. One chapter examines the influence of teachers' working conditions and cultures on their perceptions of their careers.

PRENTICE and THEOBALD edit a collection of essays concerning the history of women as teachers, an area often overlooked until recently in the history of education. Their extensive historiography of female teachers looks at the history of research on teaching. The essays in this book examine women teaching in the private and public sphere in the nineteenth and early twentieth centuries. The hidden, private worlds of female teachers in Australia, Britain, Canada, and the United States are uncovered. Important avenues for future research are suggested. A selected bibliography is provided for further research in this area.

ALTENBAUGH's collection of essays is important for its focus on twentieth-century teachers. These essays are written in relation to the current economic and philosophical education situation in the United States and elsewhere. The use of oral history in these essays means schooling from the perspective of the teacher can be investigated. The first section, on women's work, explores the relation between domesticity and teaching, and equal rights campaigns. In the second section, essays on teachers and their communities discuss events involving race and religion. A third section concerns the debatable issue of whether teachers are professionals or workers, examining this in a historical context. One writer addresses the influence of postmodernism and poststructuralism on historiography. Altenbaugh criticizes policy dealing with the recent "crisis" in education, which overlooks the teacher who occupies a strategic position in schooling and in implementing reform.

Gender is central to the discussion of teachers' careers in the text edited by ACKER (1989). Race, class, and sexual orientation are also discussed. Gender is an important issue when looking at teachers' careers, because there is a significant sexual division of labour in this occupational role. The studies documented in the essays forming this collection take place mainly in England, but also in New Zealand and the United States. This book is valuable for the range of sociological issues discussed in the fields of teaching, gender, and careers. These issues include social reproduction of gender divisions, and the theory that teachers as workers have become deskilled. Some essays have a historical focus.

The "bitter milk" of GRUMET's title is a ritual tonic given to young women in Sri Lanka, who sometimes experience psychotic responses to adolescence. Mothers, too, use bitter milk to wean their babies. Used here, it is a symbol of contradiction and ambivalence, and of Grumet's feelings toward her work as a teacher. Grumet's essays seek to understand what teaching means to women, frequently drawing on a broad range of theory such as psychoanalysis, Marxism, phenomenology, and the work of Jacques Merleau-Ponty. Topics include the feminisation of teaching, "the Look" in parenting and pedagogy, curriculum, transference, the relation of the private domestic sphere and the public teaching sphere, and furnishing education with feminist theory. This collection of essays is interesting and valuable for its exploration of teaching based on informed personal experience.

The essays edited by DE LYON are by female teachers writing about their experiences of primary and secondary teaching. This book is valuable for the information it provides about teacher training, career development, equality issues in teaching, and teacher unions. Controversial issues and experiences are discussed, such as socialisation into primary teaching, sexual harassment, access to teaching for black women, and the experience of lesbian teachers. This book questions the image of teaching as a rewarding career for women.

WEBER and MITCHELL write about the images of school teachers that shape our personal notions of who teachers are and what they do. This provides critical insight into the relationships between schooling, gender, teacher identity, and children's popular culture. Teachers and the image we have of them are central to this interdisciplinary text, which will be of interest to teachers and those considering teaching as an occupation. Influential contemporary theoretical issues are employed, such as the importance of image and metaphor in education and identity. The gendered nature of teacher identity and work is analysed.

MILLER writes that 60 percent of all teachers in Britain are women, yet this significant fact is barely acknowledged in educational discourse. Miller provides an overview of the history of female teachers from the mid-nineteenth century to the present day. This text fluidly brings together historical and sociological themes. Major topics include the feminisation of schooling, teaching as work, and literacy. Contentious issues of the day are discussed. Miller draws on the often unpublished autobiographical writings of female teachers, advocating the importance of autobiography in this field.

—BRIDGET HOLLAND

Teaching: University

Committee on Women's Studies in Asia (eds.), *Women's Studies, Women's Lives: Theory and Practice in South and Southeast Asia*, New Delhi: Kali for Women, and Melbourne: Spinifex Press, 1994; published in the United States as *Changing Lives: Life Stories of Asian Pioneers in Women's Studies*, New York: Feminist Press, 1995

Davies, Sue, Cathy Lubelska, and Jocey Quinn (eds.), *Changing the Subject: Women in Higher Education*, London and Bristol, Pennsylvania: Taylor and Francis, 1994

Gallop, Jane (ed.), *Pedagogy: The Question of Impersonation*, Bloomington: Indiana University Press, 1995

hooks, bell, *Teaching to Transgress: Education as the Practice of Freedom*, New York and London: Routledge, 1994

Middleton, Sue, *Educating Feminists: Life Histories and Pedagogy*, New York: Teachers College Press, 1993

Statham, Anne, Laurel Richardson, and Judith A. Cook, *Gender and University Teaching: A Negotiated Difference*, New York: State University of New York Press, 1991

With increasing numbers of women teaching in universities has come speculation and reflection on teaching as a gendered practice. This interest has been prompted in part by the knowledge that women still predominate in those ranks of the academic profession where teaching loads are heaviest, marginalising them within a higher education culture that consistently values research activities over those of teaching. Feminist commentators have therefore begun to examine the particular experience of women teaching in university and college classrooms, in an effort to validate that experience and to question whether and in what ways women's career paths, motivations, professional practice, and impact might differ from that of their male counterparts. The following references offer broad-based analyses of gender and university teaching, as well as some more personal and autobiographical accounts by individual educators.

The book by STATHAM, RICHARDSON, and COOK addresses itself directly to the question of gender difference and its impact in the classroom by comparing the attitudes and experiences of male and female college faculty. Sociological in its orientation, the study seeks to examine the impact of gender difference on university teaching. Using observation of classroom situations, and interviews and surveys with both staff and students, the authors gather data on gender differences in teaching styles and classroom activities, on differences in managing authority, and on students' methods of evaluating the performance of male and female teaching staff. Their findings indicate that a complex matrix of expectations, rather than fixed gender stereotypes, generally dictates the degree of acceptance and success women professors experience in the classroom relative to their male counterparts.

DAVIES, LUBELSKA, and QUINN provide a wide-ranging collection of essays based on papers from a 1993 Women in Higher Education Network conference. Contributors explore how women survive in the academy and how they can empower themselves, drawing out the various conflicts and contradictions women face within academia, as well as the well-known tensions between personal and professional commitments. The collection is divided into three parts: the experiences of women in higher education, the empowerment of women in higher education, and women challenging the mainstream curriculum in higher education. Both the commonality and difference of women's experiences are stressed, with attention paid to the roles race, sexuality, and maternity play in shaping women's academic lives. Insights offered into the sexual division of labour in universities and the relationship between gender and power in higher education institutions are especially compelling. While space is given to documenting the struggles many women face, successful practical strategies for changing conventional understandings of the "subject" of higher education are also suggested.

GALLOP's collection came out of the conference "Pedagogy: The Question of the Personal," hosted by the Center for Twentieth Century Studies at the University of Wisconsin-Milwaukee. As the title suggests, the essays in this volume examine the act of teaching as a performance, teasing out the links between the personal and impersonation. Influenced by cultural studies and psychoanalysis, contributors analyse the various masks teachers wear, how teachers often play to—and with—their student audiences, and the erotics of the classroom. This is a risky and challenging collection that addresses those elements of pleasure, power, intimacy, and identification in teacher-student relationships that often go unacknowledged in more conventional studies.

By employing life-history methods, MIDDLETON takes a more intimate approach to tracing the personal and political dimensions of an individual teaching career. Writing from New Zealand, she weaves together her own autobiography with contemporary feminist theory and educational philosophy, teasing out the ways in which personal history and lived experience inform pedagogy, and analysing what it means to be at once a woman, a university academic, a graduate student, a mother, and a citizen. These reflexive examinations form an important counterpoint to discussions of the process of feminist teacher education, in which the author is involved professionally, and the broader experience of being a feminist academic seeking social change. This work is of interest to feminist academics generally, but it also has specific applications for those involved in teacher education.

In a similar vein, HOOKS presents a series of highly personal essays and dialogues around the topic of radical feminist pedagogy. Largely autobiographical and reflective in nature, she argues out of her own experiences for the need to rethink teaching practices to meet the needs of increasingly diverse classrooms. Drawing on the liberatory pedagogy of Paulo Freire and her own history as a student and teacher, hooks strongly advocates teaching students to find freedom through transgressing racial, sexual, and class boundaries. Also discussed are hooks's experiences of marginalisation as a black female teacher and scholar, the passion and eroticism she locates in teaching, and the connections between intellectual work and the process of liberation. Hooks's writing is at once engaging and accessible.

The collection by the COMMITTEE ON WOMEN'S STUDIES IN ASIA provides a welcome balance to the Euro-American orientation of many works on women's university teaching experiences. In this collection, distinguished women's studies scholars and practitioners from India, Pakistan, Singapore, Japan, Korea, China, Hong Kong, Taiwan, Vietnam, Indonesia, and the Philippines provide lively autobiographical accounts of their relationships to feminist politics, to activism, and to teaching, particularly in the area of women's studies. Each contributor details her personal path to becoming a feminist educator, examining her intellectual and political development in the context of both family life with its attendant demands and expectations, and the wider cultural and political concerns for feminists in their respective countries. This volume is especially useful for its insights into the lives of individual academic women in South and Southeast Asia, and into the place of women generally within the higher education systems in those areas.

—MARYANNE DEVER

Technology

Faulkner, Wendy, and Erik Arnold (eds.), *Smothered by Invention: Technology in Women's Lives*, London: Pluto Press, 1985

Kramarae, Cheris (ed.), *Technology and Women's Voices: Keeping in Touch*, New York and London: Routledge and Kegan Paul, 1988

Rothschild, Joan (ed.), *Machina Ex Dea: Feminist Perspectives on Technology,* New York: Pergamon Press, 1983
Trescott, Martha Moore (ed.), *Dynamos and Virgins Revisited: Women and Technological Change in History,* Metuchen, New Jersey, and London: Scarecrow Press, 1979
Wright, Barbara Drygulski (ed.), *Women, Work, and Technology: Transformations,* Ann Arbor: University of Michigan Press, 1987
Zimmerman, Jan (ed.), *The Technological Woman: Interfacing with Tomorrow,* New York: Praeger, 1983

Interest in how technology relates to women and feminism peaked in the 1980s when a number of relevant conferences were held. The books from this period deal mostly with white, middle-class women of the nineteenth and twentieth centuries in both Europe and the United States. As a result, the focus of the books is most often on Western science and recent high technology.

FAULKNER and ARNOLD claim that the exclusion of women from technology is a recent event. Throughout history, women have been inventors, builders, and scientists; women were most likely responsible for the harnessing of fire, the development of agriculture, and the advancement of medicine. Only with the advent of capitalism and industrialization have women been driven out of technological occupations. Major topics covered in the book are medicine, birth control, housework, the Green Revolution, word processing, computers, and employment.

KRAMARAE focuses on communication and transportation, positing that women are restricted in activity, socializing, speech, and movement. Kramarae's topics include the exclusion of women from computer programming, and the lack of communication and interaction among women assigned to word-processing pools. Another chapter, which anticipates the communication possibilities of the Internet, claims that interaction among women can increase with the introduction of a worldwide computer communication system. Other articles deplore women's lack of adequate access to transportation.

ROTHSCHILD focuses on abstract feminist theories and plans for future growth. The book includes a chapter on Lillian Moller Gilbreath, a twentieth-century engineer who was notable for her consideration of all aspects—including those that were ergonomic or psychological—of a worker's life in her management theories. Other topics include the exclusion of women from the field of engineering and the still-prevalent notion that women are merely consumers confined to the home without the proper technology to complete domestic tasks. Additional topics include mining as a male-dominated and ecologically unsound activity, ecology as a feminist issue, and science as an essentially feminine, synthetic activity as exemplified by Barbara McClintock's work. Further chapters discuss the future of technology and what women might do to make technology more acceptable.

TRESCOTT has published the results of work done by Women in Technological History, a subgroup of the Society of the History of Technology. It is dedicated to the years after the Industrial Revolution and concentrates upon the last years of the nineteenth century and the early years of the twentieth. The first part of the book presents the effect of mechanization on women's work in the textile, carpet, and paper industries. The next section provides a look at nineteenth-century U.S. women inventors and scientists, including an article about Julia B. Hall's role in assisting her brother Charles Martin Hall, the inventor of the electrolytic method of producing aluminum. Trescott also compares how housework has changed with the introduction of labor-saving machines. The book concludes with a study of birth control technology and an account of childhood toys, particularly those designed to mimic adult sex roles.

WRIGHT devotes most of her text to careful explanation of statistical analysis as she seeks to determine whether there is really a sex difference in various occupations. The book discusses technology as it affects women's work, both paid and unpaid. Mechanization brought women into the factory as production was deskilled with the introduction of the assembly line. The increase in international commerce brought female workers into offices to do low-paid clerical work. Farm women's lives changed when they became less needed in the fields as agribusiness' big machines and monoculture took over. Highlights include a commentary on the sexism inherent in forbidding women of child-bearing age to work with lead and a revealing article that deals with the omission of women inventors' names in the history books.

ZIMMERMAN focuses on the future of women in technology. She believes that women will become empowered by designing effective technology that addresses their concerns. An interesting chapter details the achievement of black women inventors. One section explores the dilemma of the housewife and contains a fascinating look at Frances Gabe's self-cleaning house, a totally workable and effectively designed system that keeps all parts of a typical house clean. Possibilities in women's paid employment are also explored. As new technologies create different jobs, women need to know how to prepare themselves to be employable in the future. The book ends with a discussion of feminism in the future and with articles about the computer revolution.

—ROSE SECREST

See also Inventors

Tekakwitha, Kateri 1636–1680

American Indian Christian

Bechard, Henri, *Kateri Tekakwitha,* Kahnawake, Quebec: Kateri Center, 1994

Bunson, Margaret R., *Kateri Tekakwitha: Mystic of the Wilderness,* Huntington, Indiana: Our Sunday Visitor, 1992

Sacred Congregation of Rites, *The Positio of the Historical Section of the Sacred Congregation of Rites on the Introduction of the Cause for the Beatification and Canonization and the Virtues of the Servant of God: Katherine Tekakwitha, the Lily of the Mohawks,* New York: Fordham University Press, 1940

Weiser, Francis X., *Kateri Tekakwitha,* Kahnawake, Quebec: Kateri Center, 1972

In 1980 Pope John Paul II presided over the beatification ceremony for a Mohawk Christian woman known as the "Lily of the Mohawks." Her name was Kateri Tekakwitha, daughter of a Mohawk chief who lived in upstate New York during the seventeenth century. Kateri Tekakwitha was converted to Christianity and suffered persecution for her beliefs. She moved to Kahnawake, a Mohawk Christian community established by the Jesuits near Montreal on the St. Lawrence River. Noted for her great piety and deep faith, she declined marriage and lived a penitent life. She died at an early age after a long illness. After her death there were many miracles reported, and over the years she has remained a focus of pious devotion. During the twentieth century there has been great interest on the part of the Roman Catholic Church in canonizing individuals from ethnic groups other than European. Kateri Tekakwitha is the first Native American to be elevated to the rank of Blessed by the Roman Catholic Church.

The lives of the saints are often highly distorted by faithful admirers. The literature on Tekakwitha is no different. It consists of a variety of hagiographies. Many of these are fanciful and over-romanticized; some, however, are well-documented, using many historical sources. It is interesting to trace the transformation of these hagiographies into biographies, a phenomenon that reflects a gradual shift in the Roman Catholic concept of sainthood. Today saints are not placed as high on pedestals are they once were. They are less distant and are portrayed in a more realistic manner than in earlier times.

WEISER's book on Kateri Tekakwitha has been the standard reference since 1972. The author is a Jesuit scholar. Unlike other earlier biographies, this one pictures her against the background of her own time and people. Weiser's hagiography is much less fanciful than earlier ones. It attempts to tell the story of Tekakwitha's spiritual journey with great attention to detail. For the first time we have a work that attempts to be authentic, relying heavily on good documentation.

BUNSON tries to sketch a general picture of Native American populations. She places Kateri Tekakwitha in a historical context. While this is a relatively lightweight treatment of a complex topic, at least it attempts to transcend the stereotyping found in most earlier biographies.

BECHARD's hagiography is particularly useful because it is documented better than any other source. The most well-researched and highly competent treatment of the life of Tekakwitha was written by this Jesuit historian, who was the Canadian Vice Postulator for the cause of this potential saint. It is the best biography for those interested in examining the saintly life of Blessed Kateri Tekakwitha.

The elaborate volume by the SACRED CONGREGATION OF RITES, the Vatican group in charge of the making of saints, documents with great detail the life of this future saint. It consists of letters from the two Jesuit fathers who baptized and guided Tekakwitha's spiritual life. Unlike other biographies, this book attempts to be accurate in recording details about the canonization process itself. It is clearly the most authentic source on this Mohawk woman.

The canonization of Tekakwitha represents an important event for Catholic Indians. Despite the fact that it has been over 300 years since her death, she remains a vibrant spiritual force. Three major shrines are devoted to her in Canada and the United States, and she has devotees all over the world. Today Blessed Kateri Tekakwitha is a symbol of the blending of Native American traditions with the Catholic faith.

—JAMES J. PRESTON

Television, Images of Women in

Brown, Mary Ellen (ed.), *Television and Women's Culture: The Politics of the Popular,* Sydney: Currency, and London: Sage, 1989; Thousand Oaks, California: Sage, 1990

Geraghty, Christine, *Women and Soap Opera: A Study of Prime Time Soaps,* Cambridge: Polity Press, 1991

Gunter, Barrie, *Television and Sex Role Stereotyping,* London: John Libbey, 1986

Heide, Margaret J., *Television Culture and Women's Lives: "thirtysomething" and the Contradictions of Gender,* Philadelphia: University of Pennsylvania Press, 1995

Rowe, Kathleen, *The Unruly Woman: Gender and the Genres of Laughter,* Austin: University of Texas Press, 1995

Tuchman, Gaye, Arlene Kaplan Daniels, and Benét James (eds.), *Hearth and Home: Images of Women in the Mass Media,* New York: Oxford University Press, 1978

The social significance of television portrayals of women has been an ongoing issue for feminist research since the 1970s. Initially, investigations focused on television's sex-role stereotyping of women, arguing that representations communicated messages to viewers about appropriate forms of behaviour, appearance, and occupation for women. TUCHMAN, DANIELS, and JAMES's edited collection is representative of this approach. Tuchman's introduction argues that media images of women are reflective of dominant social values, and that the very limited range of roles occupied by women in television encourages viewers to consider women as of little importance in American society. Tuchman claims that where women are portrayed in positions of public power and authority, the representation will very likely be a negative one. Thus, television is theorised as participating in the "symbolic annihilation" of women. This "symbolic annihilation" thesis is supported by other essays in the collection, through textual content analyses of where and how women are represented across a range of television formats. The book also includes an annotated bibliography of research on television images of women up to 1975.

GUNTER's overview of research on television sex-role stereotyping discusses investigations conducted up to the period of the mid-1980s. The studies combine to indicate a gross underrepresentation of women in action-drama programmes and show that women's roles were largely restricted to home, rather than work-based, contexts. Content analyses of television texts as well as laboratory based psychological studies and survey research on the effects of television gender stereotyping on children and adult viewers are discussed. Gunter argues against the notion that audiences passively absorb television messages about appropriate sex roles, concluding that television's stereotyped images of women do not have a direct impact on perceptions of women in real life.

BROWN's edited collection demonstrates how feminist research into television representations of women moved in new directions in the 1980s. For example, Ang explores how fans of *Dallas* related to one of the soap opera's central female characters, Sue Ellen, concluding that the programme offered forms of progressive pleasure for women who identified with such an essentially powerless figure. Clark's article provides an in-depth feminist textual analysis of the detective series *Cagney and Lacey*, which is theorised as transgressing traditional narrative representations of women and as being politically empowering for female viewers. A range of other television images of women are also discussed in the book, which incorporates both textual and reception-based research, and places an emphasis on understanding how female audiences negotiate and relate to television images of women.

More recently, feminist television criticism has increasingly come to identify different television genres as providing for different representations of women. Consequently, some theorists have emphasised the study of those programme types that attract proportionally large numbers of female viewers. GERAGHTY illustrates this approach in an examination of women's roles in prime time soap operas. She argues that, unlike other television genres, soap opera portrays women in rational terms, and in concentrating on the emotional lives of characters, it legitimates this sphere of existence. Geraghty also explains that not all women are treated equally in soaps. She claims that British programmes, for example, have exhibited an awkward handling of career women, nonwhite women, and lesbians, who are treated as marginal to the central community of the narrative. Geraghty's feminist textual analysis also argues that soaps have become a less "safe" genre for female characters and viewers. She claims that the drive for ratings and attempts to attract male viewers to the genre have resulted in the development of stronger male characters and crime-based storylines which portray women as vulnerable and suffering rather than assertive and in control of their lives.

Romantic comedy is a genre that ROWE argues shows instances of being appropriated by feminism. Using semiotic and narrative theory in analyses of *The Muppet Show*'s Miss Piggy and *Roseanne*'s Roseanne Conner, Rowe argues that these characters are examples of "the unruly woman," a carnivalesque figure representing resistance to patriarchal control over the female body through an exhibition of the grotesque, which celebrates fatness, eating, and wild sex. Her book presents an exploration of Roseanne's television career and an in-depth analysis of media responses to her as a female star and television character. This includes consideration of how Roseanne's disclosures of sexual abuse as a child and her reshaping of her body affect the theorising of her persona as oppositional. This is a detailed and very thorough textual discussion of romantic comedy and the possibilities it offers for disruptive feminist expression.

Thirtysomething, a U.S. drama series that ran from 1987 to 1991, has been heavily criticised as representing women from within a framework of the backlash against feminism. HEIDE, however, argues that its representations need to be considered in relation to the programme's target audience—aging baby boomers—which, she claims, comprise many women who have been unable to resolve tensions between their family and work lives. Heide investigates how *thirtysomething* portrays different "life choices" available to women through its four principle female characters. She then presents an audience reception study of these characters and concludes that, while offering points of identification for female viewers, *thirtysomething* encourages women to consider traditional female roles as providing the resolution to their tensions and frustrations. Heide's research is a useful example of textual and reception analyses being combined in a consideration of how certain television images of women come into being, and how these might affect female viewers' perceptions of their own personal and social situations.

—C. KAY WEAVER

See also Advertising, Images of Women in

Teresa of Avila 1515–1582

Spanish Saint

Bilinkoff, Jodi, *The Avila of Saint Teresa: Religious Reform in a Sixteenth-Century City*, Ithaca, New York, and London: Cornell University Press, 1989

Chorpenning, Joseph F., *The Divine Romance: Teresa of Avila's Narrative Theology*, Chicago: Loyola University Press, 1992

Clissold, Stephen, *St. Teresa of Avila*, London: Sheldon Press, 1979; New York: Seabury Press, 1982

Green, Deirdre, *Gold in the Crucible: Teresa of Avila and the Western Mythical Tradition*, Dorset: Element, 1989

Gross, Francis L., Jr., and Toni Perior Gross, *The Making of a Mystic: Seasons in the Life of Teresa of Avila*, Albany: State University of New York Press, 1993

Lincoln, Victoria, *Teresa, a Woman: A Biography of Teresa of Avila*, Albany: State University of New York Press, 1984

Peers, E. Allison, *Handbook to the Life and Times of St. Teresa and St. John of the Cross*, Maryland: Newman Press, and London: Burns Oates, 1954

Walsh, William Thomas, *Saint Teresa of Avila: A Biography*, Milwaukee, Wisconsin: Bruce, 1943

Scholarship about Saint Teresa of Avila initially tended to take one of two positions: works were either strictly biographical, directly relating the facts of Teresa's life in a respectful manner, or they revolved around interpretations of her writings and mysticism. WALSH's book falls into the first category, as it is a lengthy and detailed volume about Saint Teresa and her life. It is very straightforward and direct in recounting the life of this Spanish mystic, using specific anecdotes and tales in order to present a full picture of the saint. The text is dated, but its age does not affect the facts of Teresa's biography. Sections of the text read like a story, which is beneficial as the work is rather long, and it does leave out certain then-controversial details about her life, even though there are numerous references to the biographies of those who actually knew Teresa of Avila. There are an index and detailed footnotes, but no supplementary information, such as maps or chronologies.

CLISSOLD's text is also a biography in the vein of Walsh, but it includes portraits, maps, a list of primary characters in Teresa's life, and a chronology (useful, but not as detailed as some of the other works in this entry). Clissold is often cited by other scholars of Teresa. Whereas Walsh leans toward recounting episodes of Teresa's life, writing some as dialogue as well as quoting extensively from her writings in an effort to retain what he regards as her natural vitality on paper, Clissold tends to take more of a distanced and objective voice in his work. The book is much more condensed than Walsh's, but not dense; it is easy to read and follow.

PEERS's purpose is to provide a history of the Discalced Carmelite Reform, discussing the roles of Teresa as well as Saint John of the Cross, rather than providing a direct point-by-point biography of Teresa's life. However, the real strength of this text is Peers's extensive biographies of the people to whom Teresa referred in her writings, as well as the people with whom those people were closely connected. Peers also roots the text in historical facts, including lists of convents and priories founded between 1562 and 1594 that Teresa was involved with or helped found, in addition to a list of places of importance to both Teresa and the Discalced Carmelite Reform. This text emphasizes Teresa's role in Carmelite reform, rather than centering only on her personal spiritual development.

BILINKOFF's text is a combination of the historical tack that Peers uses, with the inclusion of Clissold's use of diagrams and maps. Bilinkoff also includes a detailed selected bibliography to conclude her work, which centers around not Teresa, per se, but Avila itself, where Teresa spent most of her life. Bilinkoff's point is that biographies of Teresa may astound modern readers, and rightly so, as it is commonly agreed that she was a remarkable and influential woman, but those same modern readers should also consider Teresa and her work in the context of both where and when she lived. Doing so grants the reader a fuller, more profound picture of Teresa's life and influence, a perspective that one might miss if not encouraged to consider the town of Avila and Teresa's connection to it.

After the early 1980s, works about Teresa of Avila began to expand from the two emphases mentioned earlier, and they began to be concerned with other aspects of Teresa's life. As feminist scholarship increased, and after the Second Vatican Council, saints began to become regarded as humans who did extraordinary acts, rather than as distant and exceedingly holy beings. Many early texts about Teresa, such as Walsh's, while very respectful, glossed over certain details that could help Teresa become more vivid to readers, especially those of her own gender.

LINCOLN's text was one of the first to delve into Teresa's own work and begin to answer questions deliberately avoided in early scholarship. Lincoln uses a novel-like format to address issues of sexuality, race, and psychology, all of which factored into and were important facets of Teresa, the woman who later became the saint. For example, she notes that Teresa was not a virgin when she entered the convent, and she also had Jewish ancestors. Lincoln emphasizes Teresa's humanity in this biography, as well as the issues that address being a woman, through using Teresa's own writing (especially her extensive correspondence). A detailed biography and list of people and places important to Teresa is also included.

Lincoln's text also paved the way for works such as GREEN's, which places Teresa, as a woman, mystic, and human being, in western mythical tradition and women's spirituality. Green attempts to model her bio-graphy after Teresa's own writings; that is, clear, honest, and direct. Attention is paid to Teresa's Jewish roots and their influence on her life and work. Green positions Teresa in the context of sixteenth-century Spain (discussing also the treatment of female mystics), and emphasizes Teresa's insights regarding visions and visionary experiences. Green does not discuss Teresa's connections to Discalced Carmelite Reform in detail, or theological doctrines, but she provides enough background so the reader is not lost (Peers's text works well with Green's).

GROSS and GROSS present a biography of a different sort than most scholarship of Teresa of Avila: this biography is developmental, in the sense of the theories of Jean Piaget and Sigmund Freud. Gross and Gross compare Teresa to an array of characters ranging from J.D. Salinger's Holden Caulfield to Dorothy Day, focusing on Teresa's psychological development. Gross and Gross aimed to write a text, like Lincoln's, that reads like a novel. They directly refer to Bilinkoff's work, encouraging the reader to consider their own text, which breaks Teresa's life into four distinct seasons (childhood, adolescence, adulthood, and old age), in conjunction with other biographies of Saint Teresa of Avila, in order to gain a more detailed understanding of her life and her work.

—ANNE N. THALHEIMER

See also Saints

Thatcher, Margaret 1925–

British Prime Minister

Harris, Kenneth, *Thatcher,* London: Weidenfeld and Nicolson, and New York: Little Brown, 1988

Jenkins, Peter, *Mrs. Thatcher's Revolution: The Ending of the Socialist Era,* London: Cape, 1987; Cambridge, Massachusetts: Harvard University Press, 1988

Kavanagh, Dennis, *Thatcherism and British Politics: The End of Consensus?* Oxford and New York: Oxford University Press, 1987

Mayer, Allan J., *Madame Prime Minister: Margaret Thatcher and Her Rise to Power,* New York: Newsweek Books, 1979

Ogden, Chris, *Maggie: An Intimate Portrait of a Woman in Power,* New York: Simon and Schuster, 1990

Riddell, Peter, *The Thatcher Decade: How Britain Has Changed during the 1980s,* Oxford and Cambridge, Massachusetts: Blackwell, 1989; 2nd edition, as *The Thatcher Era and Its Legacy,* Oxford and Cambridge, Massachusetts: Blackwell, 1991

Smith, Geoffrey, *Reagan and Thatcher,* London: Bodley Head, 1990; New York: Norton, 1991

Watkins, Alan, *A Conservative Coup: The Fall of Margaret Thatcher,* London: Duckworth, 1991

Young, Hugo, *One of Us: A Biography of Margaret Thatcher,* London: Macmillan, 1989; as *The Iron Lady: A Biography of Margaret Thatcher,* New York: Farrar, Straus, 1989

Margaret Thatcher was the first British Prime Minister in more than 150 years to win three successive elections. She was also Britain's first woman Prime Minister and the longest-serving Prime Minister in the twentieth century. She reshaped the image of her Conservative party and altered the political and economic landscape. The daughter of a grocer who became a mayor, she had been a Conservative activist since her school days. She became a research chemist and later a lawyer, was elected to Parliament in 1959, and served as Secretary of State for Education and Science from 1970 to 1974. After her party's loss of two general elections in 1974, she successfully challenged Edward Heath for the party leadership in 1975, becoming the first woman to lead a major British party. She led it to victory in 1979, 1983, and 1987, profiting from a divided opposition. Thatcher was hostile to welfare state policies, favored reduced taxes, promoted privatization (of gas, electricity, water, and telecommunications), sought restrictions on trade unions and immigration, and championed a strict monetarist policy.

Americans compared her to her friend and collaborator, Ronald Reagan. However, as SMITH notes, they had both similarities and differences. Both made much of their humble origins (both were born in apartments above stores). They each had a populist emphasis on patriotism, the family, and the pernicious legacy of the 1960s. Both Reagan and Thatcher came at a time of malaise, a sense of their nations in decline. Both were relative outsiders to the political establishment, and spoke with moral fervor about restoring national pride, and reducing the role of the state at home, while enhancing its capacity to counter threats from abroad. They used a language of nineteenth-century individualism. Both were seen at first as aberrations, brought to power through the default of opponents. They stayed atop the political heap because their divided, dispirited foes lacked better ideas to offer.

Smith, long a reporter for the *Times* of London (his book is stronger on anecdotes than on analysis), noted that their durable special relationship was asymmetric. Thatcher needed Reagan's support more than he needed hers. He valued her approval and advice. She was the more aggressive partner, he the more powerful. Reagan gave active support to the United Kingdom in the Falklands war; Thatcher allowed U.S. planes bound for Libya to use British bases for staging.

Yet while Reagan was loved, Thatcher was respected. She was adored by some, detested by others. She had a capacity to work but was not a great communicator. Her politics were identified with her personality. While she supported capital punishment, she also was for the right to abortion. She was never a supply-sider. (American supply-siders criticized her austerity measures to counter inflation.)

MAYER, who covered British politics for *Newsweek*, tells the story of her assent to political power. She came to leadership when Britain was deeply demoralized, unsure of its role in the world, and drained by 30 years of economic inflation, labor unrest, and industrial decay. She was highly visible and often controversial. When she was Minister of Education, there was a controversy about terminating "free" milk in primary schools. She is portrayed as a passionate believer with a prickly sense of personal pride and self-worth, at war with the "Socialist State," more a nanny than a mommy, a woman of single-minded drive and determination, the strongest "man" in her cabinet.

KAVANAGH places the Thatcher government in the perspective of postwar British politics. There had been a consensus covering full employment, welfare, conciliation of the trade unions, and a mixed economy with state intervention and social engineering. Harold Macmillan later described her privatization program as "selling off the family jewels." The post-Attlee Conservatives became a socialized party after 1951. There was talk of "Butskell," an amalgam of the names of the Conservative Chancellor of the Exchequer and his Labour predecessor. The consensus broke down because of economic problems, changes in policies and personnel in the parties, and the challenge to the intellectual bases of the consensus mounted by groups on the New Right.

HARRIS, a leading British journalist with the *Observer*, gives a laudatory account of the Thatcher record, an adoring portrait. He considers her to be a phenomenon, and explores how this came about and whether she gave Britain a new lease on life. He chronicles how she turned away from a bipartisan public policy consensus, regarding leaders like Heath as surrendering to the other side. Thatcher was indifferent to the modern feminist agenda, yet was a role model for women and an example to males of female success on "their" turf. She flattened local government, sold more than a million municipal homes to their tenants, and spoke of the millennium as though she expected to be in charge until the year 2000.

OGDEN, an American journalist based in Britain (*Time* bureau chief in London after an earlier stint with United Press International), is a sympathetic biographer. He interviewed her extensively for the book and accompanied her campaign in 1987 and on overseas trips. His economic analysis, though, is superficial.

A model biography is that of YOUNG. His work is well organized, comprehensive, intellectually astute, and dramatic. He regards her as the most important Prime Minister since Winston Churchill. He notes a number of paradoxes. She was enormously effective without being personally popular, a woman who seemed to have no use for others of her sex, and successful at the polls with a people who did not share her political values. She was concerned with solutions, not the convolutions of problems. She believed in the values passed on to her by her aldermanic father. She was inflexible. The Russians labeled her "the Iron Lady" for her fierce anti-communism. Young's book was a bestseller in the United Kingdom. He was political editor of the *Sunday Times* and later the *Guardian*, and produced a documentary to mark Thatcher's tenth anniversary as Prime Minister, which was shown on Public Television.

JENKINS, a social democrat, a reporter for *The Independent*, authors a 10-year political history describing the decline of the British left. He is no admirer of Thatcher, noting that almost a fifth of all Britons were living on welfare in 1987, the casualties of the Thatcher revolution. Yet she was successful at the polls, in 1983 because of the victory over Argentina and of voter distaste for the Benn camp of left Labourites. In 1986 the nuclear issue blew apart the alliance between the Liberals and the Social Democratic party, and severely damaged any chance Labour might have had of winning the 1987 general election.

To widespread surprise, though, Thatcher's ascendancy came to an end. She was brought down because of her hostility to the European Community. Thatcher was a reluctant member of the European Community, and resisted infringements on British sovereignty. She opposed fixing the exchange rate of the pound. WATKINS, a political columnist for the *Observer*, is hostile to Thatcher's program, but straight-forward in reporting on her fall as a human tragedy. She discovered that she was expendable. Thatcher felt she was ousted because of a collective failure of nerve by her cabinet ministers. Another view, though, is that scores of Conservative Members of Parliament decided that her continued leadership would lose them the election.

RIDDELL, a political columnist and commentator for the *Times* of London, published in 1989 a book entitled *The Thatcher Decade*. After her fall from office in November, 1990, he extended his account of the Thatcher years to include an assessment of her legacy and its consequences for Britain. He examines how Britain changed during the Thatcher period, discussing the gains and the costs. He approves of the needed shake-up she gave to British industry. However, he is critical of many of the social consequences of Thatcherism. There were Achilles' heels: high unemployment, inflation, a poll tax in place of property taxes, and attempts to reform the National Health Service. Riddell has a good grasp of economic matters.

—MARTIN GRUBERG

Theater: Images of Women in

Case, Sue-Ellen, *Feminism and Theater,* London: Macmillan, and New York: Routledge,1988

Cima, Gay Gibson, *Performing Women: Female Characters, Male Playwrights, and the Modern Stage,* Ithaca, New York, and London: Cornell University Press, 1993

Ferris, Lesley, *Acting Women: Images of Women in Theatre,* New York: New York University Press, 1989; London: Macmillan, 1990

Finney, Gail, *Women in Modern Drama: Freud, Feminism, and European Theatre at the Turn of the Century,* Ithaca, New York and London: Cornell University Press, 1991

Goodman, Lizbeth, *Contemporary Feminist Theatre: To Each Her Own,* London and New York: Routledge, 1993

Hart, Lynda (ed.), *Making a Spectacle: Feminist Essays on Contemporary Women's Theater,* Ann Arbor: University of Michigan Press, 1989

Hart, Lynda, and Peggy Phelan (eds.), *Acting Out: Feminist Performances,* Ann Arbor: University of Michigan Press, 1993

Tait, Peta, *Converging Realities: Feminism in Australian Theatre,* Sydney: Currency Press, 1994

During the 1980s feminist scholars began to rewrite western theater history from the perspectives offered by women's studies. At the same time, female theater practitioners were finding new ways of making women-centered theater. The work of feminist scholars and women in theater is now well-documented in a number of published texts.

CASE's book is one of the first in this area. It offers a revision of traditional male-centered theater history, and begins with a reading of images of women in Greek drama. Case finds that in the absence of real women from the stage and theater production as a whole, images of women were created by and for a misogynist culture. Although the issue of women's absence from the classical theater remains under dispute, the book is an important starting point for feminist readings of female characters in drama. The book is also concerned with the recuperation of the silenced voices of early women dramatists, such as the tenth century Hrotsvit von Gandersheim. Turning to the present, Case sets up a critical framework for women's theater practice, and anticipates an emerging feminist poetics for the theater.

FERRIS argues that while images of women have been generated through all periods of theater history, for the most part, women have been denied access to participation in that image making. The book offers extensive research into the history of performance, and analyses dramatic and other relevant texts in terms of their attitudes to women. The book not only discusses women's official exclusion from performance, but also attempts to understand the impact of this practice on the creation of female characters. The discussion of female archetypes as the creation of a male-dominated culture is detailed and fascinating. An epilogue provides a brief account of contemporary women's theater, and welcomes attempts to challenge and subvert inherited archetypal images such as the virgin warrior and the willful woman.

FINNEY's book is also a text-based study of images of women. This study focuses on the powerful and complex female characters who emerge in dramatic literature at the turn of the twentieth century. The book examines these characters in relation to the intellectual and social developments of the period, in particular, Sigmund Freud and the study of human sexuality on the one hand, and feminism and the early women's movement on the other. Dramatists studied include Oscar Wilde, George Bernard Shaw, John Millington Synge, Henrik Ibsen, Hugo Hofmannsthal, Gerhard Hauptmann, August Strindberg, and Benjamin Franklin Wedekind.

CIMA is also concerned with female characters in modern dramatic literature, but her study concentrates on the performance of these characters by female actors. Although its focus is on canonical male playwrights—Ibsen, Strindberg, Bertolt Brecht, Harold Pinter, Sam Shepard, and Samuel Beckett and the female characters they created—the emphasis is on the innovative and artistic potential of the female actors who realize these characters in performance. There is particular interest in the way in which the female actor can challenge male constructions of the feminine. This is particularly so in the case of a dramatist such as Brecht, who is found to be sexist in both his artistic and his personal life. In other instances, such as for Beckett, there is a recognition of the close and productive tension between the male dramatist and the female actor. This is a detailed and sophisticated study, densely written and theoretically well informed, and it is a good example of the complexity of feminist performance studies.

The Hart and Hart and Phelan books are both collections of essays by feminist scholars and critics on women's theater practice from the 1970s to the present. The introduction to the HART (1989) collection provides a very useful survey of the state of feminist theater criticism, and identifies some of its major concerns as the politics of representation and the problem of inherited dramatic structures. The essays in the collection discuss the work of a range of contemporary and mostly American women playwrights at the same time as they resist the establishment of a women's canon. The playwrights are discussed in relation to their creation of powerful, subversive and multi-dimensional images of women, and for the way in which they challenge conventional theater practice.

The HART and PHELAN (1993) collection differs in quite significant ways from the other titles in the list. This book represents a move away from the text and the playwright as the object of study to a performance-centered study. The interest is in the self-devised work of performers in non-traditional theater spaces, in the work of theater collectives, and in performance art and artists. Performances that challenge mainstream social, sexual and aesthetic paradigms are privileged as sites for the contestation of dominant images of female sexuality, identity, gender and the body. The book contains interesting and informative introductions by both editors.

GOODMAN's book is a study of British feminist theater from 1968 to the early 1990s. Like Hart and Phelan's, this book focuses on performance by collectives and individuals of new and largely unpublished works. The research is extensive, and makes an original contribution to the field of women's theater studies; the study of collaborative performance making is particularly informative. The book focuses on the social and cultural context for the production of diverse contemporary images of women, and notes the role of race, sexuality, ethnicity, and class in the production of those images. The book argues that women's image-making in theater is a critique of mythical and stereotypical images of the feminine, and a reclaiming, a revisioning, and a renegotiation of performance-making in the interests of self-representation and difference.

TAIT similarly offers a survey of women's performance making. Her study is based in Australia, and begins with the New Theater movement of the 1930s, which was inspired by leftist politics, and moves to the present day in which women's theater is produced by a multi-faceted feminist movement. The book notes the development from storytelling and biographical approaches to women's lives, to satirical takes on traditional images of women, to postmodern representations of the fragmented, elusive, and fluid subject. Tait is particularly interested in non-mainstream theater, and provides interesting sections on the formation of alternative cultural identities in lesbian and multi-cultural theater groups.

—DENISE VARNEY

Theater: Women's Activity in

Aston, Elaine, *An Introduction to Feminism and Theatre*, London and New York: Routledge, 1995

Case, Sue-Ellen, *Feminism and Theatre*, London: Macmillan, and New York: Methuen, 1988

——— (ed.), *Performing Feminisms: Feminist Critical Theory and Theatre*, Baltimore: Johns Hopkins University Press, 1990

Holledge, Julie, *Innocent Flowers: Women in the Edwardian Theatre*, London: Virago Press, 1981

Loomba, Ania, *Gender, Race, Renaissance Drama*, Manchester: Manchester University Press, and New York: St. Martin's Press, 1989

Parker, Andrew, and Eve Kosofsky Sedgwick (eds.), *Performativity and Performance*, London and New York: Routledge, 1995

Wandor, Michelene, *Carry On, Understudies: Theatre and Sexual Politics*, London and New York; Routledge and Kegan Paul, 1986

———, *Look Back in Gender: Sexuality and the Family in Post-War British Drama*, London and New York: Methuen, 1987

Feminist work on women's theater, indeed the emergence of women's theater, is a phenomenon that gained momentum from the 1970s onward, with critical publications having their first heyday during the 1980s. WANDOR (1986) was one of the first playwrights and poets, as well as one of the first critical writers, to chart the history of women's theater in the United Kingdom. In the Anglo-American feminist tradition of uncovering the hidden histories of women's cultural production, she surveyed the movement of women's theater from being politically motivated street theater in the 1970s, to the formation of grant-aided, building-based women's theater groups in the 1970s and 1980s, to the emergence of feminist playwrights such as Caryl Churchill in the 1980s, whose work is performed in mainstream, prestigious theater venues. Referring to both women's and men's work, Wandor tries to show how gender politics informs theater, and in her second book (1987) offers readings of a wide range of contemporary playwrights' work to highlight the inter-relationship between political and cultural realities in post-war Britain. There are feminist essays on the work of the "angry young men" of the 1950s, such as John Osborne, Arnold Wesker, and Harold Pinter, as well as readings of works by women playwrights like Shelagh Delaney and Ann Jellicoe and many others, which index the changing sexual politics of the post-World War II period, with women increasingly becoming the subjects rather than the objects of theater. Wandor's discussions of individual plays are brief, but the focus on gender relations within the sexual politics of the family has remained pertinent in a political climate where the family as a social unit remains under sustained scrutiny.

CASE's volume (1988) offers an analysis of the history of women's theater that reaches back to the early twentieth century and, briefly, earlier to figures such as Hrotsvit of Gandersheim. Case's writings embrace a critique of heterosexuality and engage with the critical discourses about performance that have become much more prominent in the 1990s, when critical writings on women's theater have moved beyond the unveiling of a chronology of cultural activity. Case intersperses interpretive readings of women's plays with general arguments about the specificities of women's theater. This includes discussions of theater by women of color. Like Wandor, she uses categories such as "radical" and "materialist" to describe particular types of feminist theater. This method of organizing discussions of women's work is very much a phenomenon of the 1980s.

HOLLEDGE discusses women's theater of the early twentieth century. Like Wandor, and typically of British feminist writing, she takes a materialist approach and reads theater in its socio-political context. Her focus is, however, less on plays by women than on the women and theater companies, such as the Pioneer Players, who produced divergent theater work that might be described as feminist, usually by virtue of being interested in women's issues. Holledge thus offers a particular view of the theater world of the early twentieth century, detailing the ways in which women as actors and directors attempted to change the conventions that had governed naturalistic theater until that time.

In the 1980s, feminist criticism of Shakespearean theater and the Renaissance became increasingly established in academe, in part in response to the fact that drama from the Renaissance is commonly taught in literature courses, as well as in the context of theater studies. LOOMBA belongs to the group of feminist writers who were promoting a critical review of the representation of gender and sexuality in the Renaissance, explicitly augmented in her case by a focus on the intersection between sexuality and race, and by a discussion about how conventional study of the Renaissance reinforced and reproduced notions of racial difference. Ranging widely across plays from the period, Loomba discusses the "disorderly woman" and the simultaneous elevation and degradation of women within Renaissance drama, and sets these in a racially informed context.

ASTON provides an introduction to feminism and theater that focuses on British material, utilizing this to discuss theater history, "m/othering the self," and the impact of French feminist theory on theater, black women's work in theater, and material practices within it. Her book is a useful introduction to the issue of women and theater. It offers both general sections on the impact of feminist criticism and work on theater, and case studies on individual plays and playwrights, to discuss how this impact concretely manifests itself.

Recent feminist or gender-conscious anthologies of theater criticism, such as CASE's collection (1990), contain a wide range of essays that utilize psychoanalytic theory, semiotics, and other contemporary theoretical frames, to read both dramatic texts and performances. This volume has sections on marginality, on class and ethnicity, on the figure of the father, and on performing gender, and within those sections, essays range from Jacobean drama to Caryl Churchill's plays. All are informed by a feminist stance.

PARKER and KOSOFSKY SEDGWICK focus on performance and the meaning of that term in their collection, which is informed by the emergence of "queer" and its notions of performativity and iterative acts. All action is regarded as (potentially) performative, with the consequence that boundaries between theater and other spaces are broken down. Thus AIDS activism constitutes one kind of performance, rituals and rites another. One important focus of this volume's essays is the way in which particular uses of language create, and indeed are effects, in the material world. These essays exemplify one major trend in work on the notion of performance within the 1990s, which is to move away from the idea that theater is a rarefied space in which performance happens. The experience of performance from trauma to catharsis thus becomes the object of enquiry in a context where doing is regarded as performing.

—GABRIELE GRIFFIN

See also Acting

Theology, Feminist

Daly, Mary, *The Church and the Second Sex*, Boston: Harper and Row, and London: G. Chapman, 1968

Heschel, Susannah (ed.), *On Being a Jewish Feminist: A Reader*, New York: Schocken, 1983

Hinsdale, Mary Ann, and Phyllis H. Kaminski (eds.), *Women and Theology*, Maryknoll, New York: Orbis, 1995

Johnson, Elizabeth A., *She Who Is: The Mystery of God in Feminist Theological Discourse*, New York: Crossroad, 1992

McFague, Sallie, *Models of God: Theology for an Ecological, Nuclear Age*, London: SCM, and Philadelphia: Fortress, 1987

Plaskow, Judith, *Standing Again at Sinai: Judaism from a Feminist Perspective*, San Francisco: Harper and Row, 1990

Ruether, Rosemary Radford, *New Woman, New Earth: Sexist Ideologies and Human Liberation*, New York: Seabury Press, 1975

———, *Sexism and God-Talk: Toward a Feminist Theology*, Boston: Beacon Press, and London: SCM, 1983

———, *Womanguides: Readings toward a Feminist Theology*, Boston: Beacon Press, 1985

———(ed.), *Religion and Sexism: Images of Woman in the Jewish and Christian Traditions*, New York: Simon and Schuster, 1974

Ruether, Rosemary Radford, and Rosemary Skinner Keller (eds.), *In Our Own Voices: Four Centuries of American Women's Religious Writing*, San Francisco: Harper, 1995

DALY's name is almost synonymous with feminism's critique of religion. In this first of her monographs, she considers feminism a moral issue the church needs to address for its own sake as well as for the sake of women. While Daly believes that the church is a significant instrument of women's oppression, she also believed, at the time of this book, that the oppression could be overcome. Basing her argument on the development of doctrine, she posits that the church can modify those aspects of Christianity that have been harmful to women. Although Daly herself later rejected this position, the argumentation she uses in this volume has been incorporated by many Jewish and Christian feminists who wish to understand themselves as both feminists and faithful members of their respective religions.

RUETHER (1975) recognizes the interrelation of ideology and social structure in the history of sexism. She shows how reigning ideologies, such as patriarchal religion and psychology, are the cultural superstructure for a system of male domination that is socioeconomic and systemic in character. RUETHER (1983) exposes the patriarchal social context of both the Old and New Testaments; because she places feminist claims within the prophetic teachings of the Bible she is thus able to reject any assumption or assertion of patriarchy as authoritative.

RUETHER (1985) provides a collection of texts that she intends to serve as a resource for doing feminist theology. Although she believes that feminist theology cannot be done from the existing base of the Christian Bible because of how it successfully sacralizes patriarchy, she nevertheless includes certain biblical texts that can be read between the lines to find fragments of women's experience that were not completely erased. She also includes noncanonical texts from alternative communities, texts that reflect either the greater awe and fear of female power that was denied in later patriarchy, or questionings of male domination in groups where women did enter into critical dialogue. Ruether's object is to provide a new norm out of which to construct a new community, a new theology, and perhaps even a new canon.

RUETHER's first edited volume (1974) contains eleven articles, each of which sheds light on how women have been presented, represented, and understood in the Jewish and Christian traditions. These essays discuss cultural images that have degraded and suppressed women. Topics include depictions of women in the Old Testament, the New Testament, the Fathers of the Church, the Talmud, Medieval Theology, Canon Law, the Continental Reformation, and the theologies of Barth and Tillich. RUETHER (1995) allows four centuries of American women to give voice to their own religious beliefs. Included are collections of documents by Catholic women, Protestant laywomen who were active members of institutional churches, Jewish women, black women, evangelical women, American Indian women, and women who were members of utopian and communal societies. Each of the collections is preceded by an informative introduction. A final chapter authored by Ruether deals with the contemporary context of growing pluralism, which calls for a new dialogue.

HINSDALE and KAMINSKI have together edited a collection of essays. After Kaminski's introduction, "Theology As Conversation," the volume proceeds in three parts: "Entering the Conversation," "Adding Voices," and "Changing the Terms." M. Shawn Copeland's essay, which calls for a critical feminist theology of solidarity, precedes articles on the theologies of Cornelia Connelly and Maisie Ward and an essay on the women at Vatican II. Mary Rose D'Angelo's essay challenges its readers to listen to the silenced voices in history. The final section calls for conversations between the fields of religious studies and women's studies, and between feminist theory and feminist theology; it re-envisions, with a fully integrated feminist perspective, ecclesial discernment, theological anthropology, and Christian symbols.

JOHNSON re-examines the symbol of God using analogies drawn from female experience and from the wisdom tradition. She explores the Trinity under the rubric of "Sophia." Johnson depicts each of the persons of the Trinity, and the Trinity as a whole, through the metaphor of a lively and enlivening relational divine nature. God is among us, she says, intimately and empoweringly, providing for and sustaining human life from moment to moment. MCFAGUE's volume, set out in two parts, situates herself and her readers in an ecological, nuclear age, one which demands a new sensibility. She offers, in part two, models of God for our time, non-dominating relational models. God, metaphorically speaking, is mother, lover, and friend.

Feminist theology is hardly the exclusive domain of Christian women. PLASKOW develops a feminist Judaism. This involves the reshaping of Jewish memory (Torah); the development of a new concept of community (Israel); the re-imaging of God; and the development of a new theology of sexuality. Feminist Judaism involves political and social responsibility, what Plaskow calls "repair of the world." HESCHEL has collected essays from more than twenty Jewish feminists. The book reflects on some of "the old myths and images" (and their consequences for women), the new identities being forged by contemporary Jewish women, and the task and challenge of creating a feminist theology of Judaism.

—ALICE L. LAFFEY

See also Spirituality, Feminist

Trade Unions *see* Labor Unions

Transgenderism

Allen, Mariette Pathy, *Transformations: Crossdressers and Those Who Love Them*, New York: Dutton, 1989

Bornstein, Kate, *Gender Outlaw: On Men, Women, and the Rest of Us*, New York and London: Routledge, 1994

Bullough, Vern, and Bonnie Bullough, *Cross Dressing, Sex and Gender*, Philadelphia: University of Pennsylvania Press, 1993

Burke, Phyllis, *Gender Shock: Exploding the Myths of Male and Female*, New York: Anchor/Doubleday, 1996

Feinberg, Leslie, *Transgender Warriors: Making History from Joan of Arc to Dennis Rodman*, Boston: Beacon Press, 1996

Herdt, Gilbert, *Third Sex, Third Gender: Beyond Sexual Dimorphism in Culture and History*, New York: Zone, 1994

Transgenderism is a newly-emerging and diverse subject. There is some difference of opinion on its meaning, but the most compelling and widely accepted definition—and the first to gain popular acceptance—is that proposed by BORNSTEIN. She suggests that transgenderism be thought of as "gender transgression," transgression of prevailing norms of gender behavior and appearance. This definition has proven both popular and politically powerful. Bornstein, in talking about her own male-to-female transsexuality, also makes the case that she is neither exactly male nor female, but rather inhabits a space of "other." In so doing, she challenges most presumptions about what is normal and natural with regard to a person's sex and gender. This work is outstanding in its explanation of a transgender perspective, using warmth and humor to enhance its accessibility.

A follow-up work to her earlier work of fiction, *Stone Butch Blues* (1993), FEINBERG's book provides a broad overview of the case for a legitimate transgender presence in society. The text argues for a socialist perspective, blaming capitalism and property ownership for moving society from a communal to a competitive basis, and consequently suppressing gender transgression. Its historical review of transgenderism is sketchy, and in at least one case—citing the Welsh "Rebeccas," rebel men who wore women's clothes, as "cross-gendered warriors"—strains credibility. This weakness notwithstanding, the work serves as a sound vehicle for a somewhat radical transgender political perspective. The author is a leading activist in the movement to change the social view of gender from a strict binary system to one that recognizes and encourages diversity in gender expression and identification.

HERDT's monumental book provides a gallery of investigations into, and revelations of, the existence of persons who cannot be categorized in a simple binary scheme of male/female. The essays in this volume (which is extensively footnoted) explore the different cultural definitions of a third sex or gender—a diverse and shifting category of people who have been at various times abhorred, celebrated, repressed, fully integrated into society, or confined to its margins. The volume brings together historical and anthropological studies, challenging the usual emphasis on sexual dimorphism and reproduction, and providing a unique perspective on the various forms of socialization of people who are neither "male" nor "female." It features an impressive range of cross-cultural materials in a seriously adventurous collection.

Detailed history of transgender behavior is provided by BULLOUGH and BULLOUGH, probably the most complete and lucid work on the subject. Although the final few chapters on recent history are somewhat narrow in their perspective, the bulk of the book contains a detailed investigation of countless instances of transgenderism in history. Starting with mythology and ancient history, and working up through the centuries to the modern day, Bullough and Bullough present compelling evidence of a transgender presence in virtually every time and culture. No other work presents as comprehensive a case for the normalcy of transgenderism in society.

ALLEN's work remains the most sympathetic and enlightening portrait of men who crossdress. It was published prior to the transgender movement and lacks the political awareness that has since come into being, but nonetheless it provides a glimpse into the real lives and feelings of men who feel compelled to transgress gender norms and spend at least some of their time as women. A classic work, it provides a profoundly intimate and very real portrait of the world of crossdressers, including their lives in their home settings, with their families.

BURKE makes a case for the elimination of formal "gender identity disorder" (GID) pathology. She relates several case histories of children subjected to abusive practices aimed at curbing their gender-transgressive appearance and behavior. The cases are compelling, if disappointingly few. Nonetheless, this work has stimulated a substantial movement to eliminate GID from the American Psychiatric Association's standard for diagnosis. The book presents the perspective that variation in gender identity is a natural phenomenon, and that attempts to constrain individuals' gender identities according to their genital configurations are not just ineffective, but also terribly abusive. Although weak in some aspects, this is to date the only work to make a clear case for eliminating the medical pathologizing of gender variation.

—NANCY R. NANGERONI

Transsexualism

Benjamin, Harry, *The Transsexual Phenomenon*, New York: Julia Press, 1966

Brown, Mildred L., and Chloe Ann Rounsley, *True Selves, Understanding Transsexualism*, San Francisco: Jossey-Bass, 1996

Cameron, Loren, *Body Alchemy: Transsexual Portraits*, Pittsburgh: Cleis Press, 1996
Denny, Dallas, *Gender Dysphoria: A Guide to Research*, New York: Garland, 1994
Hausman, Bernice L., *Changing Sex: Transsexualism, Technology, and the Idea of Gender*, Durham, North Carolina: Duke University Press, 1995
Stuart, Elizabeth, *The Uninvited Dilemma: A Question of Gender*, Lake Oswego, Oregon: Metamorphous Press, 1983

The issue of transsexualism has gone through a significant revolution in the mid-1990s, created by the greatly increased visibility of transsexual persons. Prior to this time, transsexuals were commonly advised by medical authorities to create a false past when they changed genders, and such persons disappeared into the fabric of society. In the 1990s, communication among transsexuals made it clear that this was an unhealthy tactic, and that being "out" about one's past was the more successful alternative. As a result, more transsexuals are now available for study and dialogue, and knowledge of them has increased dramatically. New books are being released at a brisk pace, so the reader is encouraged to seek out new works of quality.

The most authoritative work on the subject is the book by BROWN. It presents the characteristics and issues faced by transsexual persons, from childhood to adulthood to transition and beyond. It clearly presents an extensive catalogue of the typical emotions and desires felt by transsexuals. While noting that "there is no such thing as a typical transsexual," it presents extensive insight into typical childhood experience, family relations, feelings about self, and much more. It presents a friendly and balanced perspective on the unique and diverse characteristics of transsexual people, in an easily digested style, with the most knowledgeable content available. It falls short only in understating the presence and impact of post-transition homosexuality and bisexuality among transsexuals, and completely ignoring the challenge to the binary norm—and all categorization—that is presented by the existence of the transsexual. Like much medical-based knowledge, it fails to question the norm against which it measures pathology, in particular, the presumption that a person must be either man or woman. This lack notwithstanding, it remains the most comprehensive text available. For any student of the topic, this is the essential text, unsurpassed in clarity, accuracy, insight, and organization.

A less comprehensive but still insightful book is that by STUART. Based on a study of about one hundred transsexuals, it presents important information unavailable elsewhere, like the fact that, in this survey, about fifty percent of parents were accepting and loving in the face of their child's transsexualism. This book remains an excellent choice for those seeking to better understand a transsexual friend or family member, or to educate others about one's own situation. Within the community of transsexuals, this has long been a text of choice for educating loved ones.

A book of photography provides strikingly personal glimpses of transsexual men (female-to-male). The text by CAMERON is a beautifully produced, striking work of unusually high integrity. In dramatically sparse text, with diverse subjects, Cameron provides the viewer with an authentic feel for what it looks and feels like to be a transsexual man. He presents portraits of himself and other transsexual men in their native environment, whether the gym, or a police cruiser, or a construction site. If there were any preconceptions or presumptions about what transsexual men must be like, this book should dispel most of those. These men come from all walks of life and inhabit all sizes and shapes and all races and ethnicities. Cameron's book comes at a time when transgenderism is out of the closet and growing in popularity. It is daring and beautifully presented.

For a comprehensive guide to research, DENNY'S volume stands alone. Denny is a transsexual woman and long-standing educator to the transsexual community. Her reference work is painstakingly thorough and a reliable guide for anyone who seeks greater depth on any area of transsexualism. Focusing on gender identity disorders, this authoritative bibliography incorporates articles and books from medical, legal, and psychological sources. The book also offers such special interest categories as transsexual surgery, follow-up studies on transsexualism, intersexuality, and crossdressing.

HAUSMAN traces the history of changes in concepts, treatments, and terminology around cross-sex and cross-gender phenomena. She argues that endocrinological and surgical advances enabled the emergence of transsexualism, and also that "gender" produces "sex," not the reverse. BENJAMIN's book was for many years the definitive work on the subject, originally published in the 1960s. Alhough now somewhat dated (written when homosexuality and bisexuality were still considered disorders), it has been returned to print and provides a perspective on the development of the field over the past 30 years.

—NANCY R. NANGERONI

Tristan, Flora 1803–1844

French Activist

Cross, Máire, and Tim Gray, *The Feminism of Flora Tristan*, Oxford and Providence, Rhode Island: Berg, 1992
Desanti, Dominique, *A Woman in Revolt: A Biography of Flora Tristan*, New York: Crown, 1976
Dijkstra, Sandra, *Flora Tristan: Feminism in the Age of George Sand*, London and Concord, Massachusetts: Pluto Press, 1992

Gattey, Charles Neilson, *Gauguin's Astonishing Grandmother: A Biography of Flora Tristan*, London: Femina, 1970

Strumingher, Laura S., *The Odyssey of Flora Tristan*, New York: Peter Lang, 1988

Flora Tristan, the messianic feminist and advocate for the working class, was all but lost from studies of activism and socialism in the nineteenth century until she was rediscovered by Jules Puech, whose *La Vie et l'Oeuvre de Flora Tristan, 1803–1844* (1925) has become a standard in the field, although it has never been translated from the French. Among standard works on Tristan is GATTEY's treatment of the woman as painter Paul Gauguin's extraordinary grandmother. Beginning with Gauguin's analysis of Tristan as a bluestocking anarchist-socialist who was "not good at cooking," Gattey builds his biography of Tristan around her "turbulent personality," her poor relations with men, including the sensational murder trial when her husband attempted to kill her, and her innovative ideas that position her as a "political precursor of Marx." Gattey's work, which is most frequently catalogued under "art," however occasionally verges on hagiography and reverts to Gauguin in the conclusion.

DESANTI's biography of Tristan, which was originally published in French in 1972, treats Tristan as a forgotten nineteenth-century socialist whose work was buried under the greater reknown of Marxism. Desanti's study begins with the rediscovery of Tristan by mid-twentieth-century women's rights activists and focuses on Tristan's opposition to capital punishment, her refusal to see women as "sex objects" even when sexuality was lauded by utopians, her insistence on an international women's movement, her demands for economic independence, and her pressures for companionate marriage.

STRUMINGHER's interpretation of Tristan builds on the Peruvian/French woman's evolution as an activist worker. Framing her biography as a cross-cultural analysis of Tristan, Strumingher views the key issues of the 1830s through the lens of Tristan's feminism and her proletarian identification as a pariah. Tristan's contributions to modern feminism, therefore, were her pressures for women's equality in both the workplace and the home, and her debt to French revolutionary Olympe de Gouges, English writer Mary Wollstonecraft, and others.

To DIJKSTRA, Tristan was not a socialist at all. Moving away from socialist interpretations of Tristan's role in the nineteenth century, Dijkstra asserts that Tristan sold out to the emerging capitalism of the time. Obsessed by her divine mission, devastated by the continual attacks on her self-esteem and on her person, and frustrated by her inability to find human love, Tristan was unable to deal with other nineteenth-century feminists. Instead she turned to ideological fantasies, replacing her own lack of domestic security with the strength of workers' palaces. Ultimately her separation from more mainstream socialism and feminism brought her failure, a martyrdom she had created from the beginning.

Also among the recent, revisionist works on Tristan is CROSS and GRAY's historiographic, critical, and polemical analysis of Tristan's feminism. While "no one doubts that Flora Tristan was a feminist," according to authors Cross and Gray, there has never been a study that defined the kind of feminism Tristan espoused. Her civic feminism was exemplified by her petitions on divorce and the death penalty; her romantic feminism, by her novels. Her economic feminism was defined by the *London Journal*, her socialist feminism, by the *Workers' Union*. Cross and Gray further posit that Tristan's feminism was always prior to her socialism; and, in the most controversial portion of the study, they assert that Tristan's ideology was as deeply rooted in liberalism as it was in socialism. A secondary message is that feminists should look, therefore, to liberalism instead of the customary alliance with socialism.

—SUSAN P. CONNER

Truth, Sojourner c. 1797–1883

American Activist

Bernard, Jacqueline, *The Journey toward Freedom: The Story of Sojourner Truth*, New York: Norton, 1967

Fauset, Arthur Huff, *Sojourner Truth: God's Faithful Pilgrim*, Chapel Hill: University of North Carolina Press, 1938

Mabee, Carleton, and Susan Mabee Newhouse, *Sojourner Truth: Slave, Prophet, Legend*, New York: New York University Press, 1993

Painter, Nell Irvin, *Sojourner Truth: A Life, a Symbol*, New York: Norton, 1996

Stetson, Erlene, and Linda David, *Glorying in Tribulation: The Lifework of Sojourner Truth*, East Lansing: Michigan State University Press, 1994

Sojourner Truth was born Isabella Baumfree in about 1797, changing her name in 1843 in response to a voice she attributed to God. Although illiterate, Truth was well known as an itinerant preacher, an abolitionist, and an outspoken advocate for women's rights. Although she was unable to write her own autobiography, Truth's narrative of her life was recorded by Olive Gilbert in 1850. This narrative, along with contemporary newspaper accounts of her speeches, letters dictated by her, and letters written to her, form the core material from which later writers have drawn their information.

FAUSET, the first writer to attempt a book-length biography of Truth, divides his book into three sections. "Isabella" contains the account of her early life as a slave in the Dutch-speaking Hardenbergh household with her parents, Mau-Mau Bet and Baumfree, and her subsequent sale to the Nealy household where she was beaten for her failure to understand English. In this section, Fauset also describes the conditions of Truth's escape from slavery. The second section, "Matthias," details her involvement with the religious fanatic Robert Matthews, also known as Matthias. A scandal concerning illicit sexual affairs and murder swirled around the Matthias group. During this period, Truth sued a white man for slander and won her case. The final section, "Sojourner," traces the last 40 years of her life, including her name change, her itinerant preaching, her work for women's suffrage, and her final days. Fauset's work is highly imaginative and dramatic, filled with dialogue and description. Although lively to read, the book offers little other than a place to start for the serious student of Truth's life.

Truth's life has been the subject of many novels, poems, and films, as well as young adult and juvenile biographies. Most notable among these is BERNARD's work. This book is the result of extensive primary resource research and, although written for the adolescent reader, provides an accessible, well-researched basis for further study. The 1990 edition includes an introduction by Nell Irvin Painter, a professor of history and a Sojourner Truth scholar herself, who calls attention to the importance of words and rhetoric in any study of Sojourner Truth's life. In addition, Painter provides an overview not only of Truth's life, but also of the publication of *Journey Toward Freedom*, noting that in 1967, the *New York Times Book Review* listed it as one of the best books of the year.

MABEE and NEWHOUSE offer the first scholarly biography of Sojourner Truth. The authors note that much of the previous writing on Truth was done without proper documentation or citation. As a result, earlier biographical writing contributed to the Sojourner Truth mythology, rather than attempting to discern the historical reality behind the legends. Mabee and Newhouse also demonstrate the ways in which Truth's life has been appropriated to serve a variety of political and psychological purposes. The authors have exhaustively searched the records and primary sources for their construction of Truth's life and the work is extremely well documented. In addition to covering the familiar ground of Truth's life as Isabella the slave, they also explore the question of why Truth never learned to read. In a particularly notable chapter, Mabee and Newhouse examine Truth's famous 1851 Akron speech, commonly known as the "Aren't I a Woman?" speech. They note that Frances Gage's report of the speech has long been regarded as the definitive source for the text. However, by careful examination of other newspaper accounts of the speech, the writers are able to unravel the threads of what Truth probably said. Mabee and Newhouse also discuss Truth's role in the relocation of freed slaves to the North, and her involvement in the women's rights movement. In the closing chapter, Mabee and Newhouse examine Truth's involvement in the Spiritualist movement.

STETSON and DAVID situate Sojourner Truth within an analysis of her public discourse. Although they follow chronological organization in their biography, Stetson and David focus on Truth as a speaker and performer, and on the ways she defined herself by her speech. Stetson and David acknowledge that Truth's illiteracy means that there are no written texts in her own hand on which to base a biography; however, this absence provides their very means of entry into Truth's life. They place Truth within the tradition of women speakers whose voices take their authority from lived experience. Further, by close and careful reading of what others report as Truth's speech and actions, the writers are able to construct a life for Truth that is illustrative not only of the way Truth was able to influence people, but also of the way she was able to construct herself for others. They suggest that Truth remained illiterate deliberately, as a way of focusing attention on her spoken words. While the book is theoretical in its treatment of rhetoric, intertextuality, and gender, it is written in a clear and readable style. This is an important book for anyone interested in Truth; further, it is an important book for anyone interested in the construction of feminine biography.

PAINTER acknowledges both the mystery and the myth surrounding the life of Sojourner Truth, as well as noting the difficulty of preparing an academic biography for a woman who left no personal papers of her own. She begins her biography with the familiar ground of Truth's girlhood as Isabella. In the second section, she focuses on Isabella's mid-life reconstruction as Sojourner Truth, a woman single-mindedly dedicated to her causes. Truth's Akron speech is discussed as well, connecting her to the women's rights movement. She notes that as a woman, Truth did not fit neatly into abolitionist notions of slavery; as a black woman, she did not fit neatly into the overwhelmingly white women's suffrage movement. In the final section, Painter examines the ways in which Sojourner Truth's life has become a symbol for generations of Americans. Painter draws extensively on the photographs of Truth to help her reconstruct a life out of mystery.

—DIANE ANDREWS HENNINGFELD

Tsvetaeva, Marina 1892–1941

Russian Writer

Feiler, Lily, *Marina Tsvetaeva: The Double Beat of Heaven and Hell*, Durham, North Carolina: Duke University Press, 1994

Hasty, Olga Peters. *Tsvetaeva's Orphic Journeys in the Worlds of the Word*, Evanston, Illinois: Northwestern University Press, 1996

Karlinsky, Simon, *Marina Tsvetaeva: The Woman, Her World and Her Poetry*, Cambridge: Cambridge University Press, 1985

Makin, Michael, *Marina Tsvetaeva: Poetics of Appropriation*, Oxford: Clarendon Press, and New York: Oxford University Press, 1993

Shveitser, Viktoriia, *Tsvetaeva*, London: Harvill, 1992; New York: Farrar, Straus and Giroux, 1993

———, *Marina Tsvetaeva: One Hundred Years*, Oakland, California: Berkeley Slavic Specialties, 1994

Taubman, Jane A., *A Life through Poetry: Marina Tsvetaeva's Lyric Diary*, Columbus, Ohio: Slavica, 1988

The Soviet image of Marina Tsvetaeva was tailored to fit the socialist need for a viable female artist who could appeal to the sentimental romanticism and puritanism of the general public and at the same time express anti-fascist, pro-Russian sentiments despite years abroad. The breakdown of the Soviet Union, which allowed greater openness about previously censored writers and the publication of heretofore inaccessible or unpublished works and correspondence, has, together with the women's movement, led to revisionist criticism that totally rejects this view and to greater interest in the west in the psychology and achievement of Marina Tsvetaeva. She is now recognized as one of Russia's major and most original poets of the first half of this century—passionate, contentious, and enigmatic.

KARLINSKY's pathbreaking and comprehensive biography of Tsvetaeva, the most authoritative of its time, provides a solid base of documented research (much previously unpublished) that traces Tsvetaeva's life and literary development (her entire canon) in the light of their historical, political, and literary background. In particular, he stresses her personal relationships with literary contemporaries, her affairs, her collision course with the post-Revolutionary Soviet literary establishment and with both liberal and conservative Russian émigres in Paris, and her response to Soviet political and literary pressures. His Tsvetaeva is an egocentric, quixotic personality, insensitive and devious, but a "splendid" poet.

Asserting that Tsvetaeva lived in, by, and for poetry, TAUBMAN focuses on the writer as an artist who transformed her life into art, and whose inner life and voice speak through her nonnarrative poems—a continuously-unfolding, self-referential lyric diary whose self-contradictory opposites reflect the inner conflicts and turmoil of an enigmatic poet. Taubman explicates difficult poems in terms of the artist's search for self-definition, her image of her poetry as an ocean ever renewing itself, her mythmaking, her paradoxes, her intriguing mix of the highly traditional ("despising modernity") and the highly innovative ("at the cutting edge of modernism"), and, most significantly, the illuminating sequence of her poems. Taubman also addresses her importance to feminist scholarship as a creative genius who purposefully ignored sex roles and gender limitations.

Based on 20 years of research, including work in the Mayakovsky Museum, and participation in compiling the poet's *Complete Works*, SHVEITSER's (1992) full-length biography of Marina Tsvetaeva is the first by a specialist from Russia, one with access to archival sources, relatives, friends, and literary associates unavailable to western scholars. Shveitser's approach is personal and speculative, with reminiscences and reflections as she makes a personal pilgrimage to Tsvetaeva's grave in Elabuga and then traces the tragic patterns of Tsvetaeva's life, graced by quotations from her poetry and prose. She captures the passion, pride, complexity, and enigmas of a multifaceted personality, whom Shveitser as enthusiast/critic clearly views with fascination. Although criticized by western scholars for its unscholarly tone and inadequate footnoting, this book provides useful raw material for future studies and a truly Russian view of Tsvetaeva as a woman who disdained conventional values and who asserted her unique personal ideas in her art.

Arguing that much of Tsvetaeva's work resists exclusively biographical interpretation, MAKIN seeks meaning instead in the writer's brilliant and purposeful use of eclectic literary sources, including myth, history, folklore, and legend, particularly during her most productive period (1917–26). To illuminate her "fascinating but sometimes impenetrable or totally inaccessible" poetry, he demonstrates her "appropriation" and "revision" of her European and Russian readers' familiar literary heritage, to actively involve them in her own symbolic and mythical poetics. Makin shows her purposefully creating tensions between the traditional and the innovative and dislocating the familiar to explore personal themes of transformation and magic. He concludes that her rewriting of inherited material makes visible the process of poetry and the creative functions of literary systems.

FEILER, encouraged by Karlinsky, breaks new ground in her Freudian psychoanalytical explorations of the forces that shaped Tsvetaeva, her psyche, and her art. Feiler relies on a close reading of Tsvetaeva's texts, interpreted intuitively and psychoanalytically, to understand the writer's persona: she treats Tsvetaeva's life as a literary study. The chapters follow the chronology of Tsvetaeva's life from her loveless childhood and conflicted adolescence to her fanciful escapes in art and sexuality, her lesbian affair with Sofia Parnok, her flirtation with Mandelstam in the shadow of revolution, her life under Communism, her Parisian experiences, her growing isolation, alienation, and indigence, the fatal year before her return to the Soviet Union, and her final despair and suicide. Feiler theorizes that Tsvetaeva's emotional deprivation as a child (the indifference of her father and the rejection and criticism of her mother) produced her early fixation on mother-child symbiosis and the contradictory drives (duty versus rebellion; poet versus woman; control versus freedom) that tore her apart. Feiler describes her as alternating between depression and contempt, love and rage, intensity and self-annihilation, and she concludes that the passion that fed her poems destroyed her life. Tsvetaeva was not a feminist, asserts Feiler, but she avoided gender-specific pronouns and reversed or combined gender distinctions. She was the embodiment of nineteenth-century romantic values, yet radical and experimental in her poetry. Feiler captures her contradictions and complexity in two examples: her reading of her work glorifying the White Army to an audience of Red Army soldiers, and her writing of a long poem lamenting the execution of the last Czar when her husband was a Soviet agent and assassin.

SHVEITSER (1994) compiled and edited papers from the 1992 Tsvetaeva Centenary Symposium at Amherst College. Although only five of the essays are in English (the others are in Russian by noted Russian scholars), these five provide close textual studies of specific poems, compare and contrast two significant poems by Tsvetaeva and Alexander Blok, and explore Tsvetaeva's place in the feminine tradition in Russian poetry. Jane Taubman, in particular, traces the influence of three sister poets—Anna Akhmatova, Adelaida Gertsyk, and Sofia Parnok—and Tsvetaeva's change of voice from hesitancy at using the female voice to self-confident development of a grammatically feminine lyric voice.

To HASTY, Tsvetaeva was a carefully observant, systematic, intellectually responsible thinker engaged in an avant-garde Hegelian dialectic of generative contraries (particularly her bisexual erotic analogies, the dichotomy of body and soul, and the living poet's confrontations with death); these contraries subvert conventional significance, expand the domain of sensibility, and engage the fundamental questions of poetic discourse. Hasty concentrates on Tsvetaeva's use of the Orpheus myth to erode the issue of gender, and to create her own mythos of self-realization that offers Ophelia and Eurydice, transformed from the traditionally passive to active, authoritative voices, as correctives to the male stance represented by Orpheus and Hamlet (and tied to Aleksandr Blok and Rainer Maria Rilke). As creative artist Tsvetaeva places reality into a mythic framework that transforms death into the inciter of creative activity.

—GINA MACDONALD and PAULINA BAZIN

Tubman, Harriet c. 1820–1913

American Abolitionist

Bradford, Sarah Elizabeth, *Harriet Tubman: The Moses of Her People*, New York: Lockwood, 1886

Conrad, Earl, *Harriet Tubman*, Washington, D.C.: Associated Publishers, 1943

Nies, Judith, *Seven Women: Portraits from the American Radical Tradition*, New York: Viking, 1977

Petry, Ann, *Harriet Tubman: Conductor of the Underground Railroad*, New York: Crowell, 1955

Although Harriet Tubman is arguably one of the best-known figures of the nineteenth-century United States, very few book-length scholarly studies of her life have been written. There are a number of reasons for this; most commonly cited is Tubman's illiteracy–obviously she would not have left written documents of her life. Further, her work in helping slaves escape from the South was illegal, and any written accounts of this would have put her and her helpers in danger. However, while there is a dearth of scholarly studies on Tubman, there is an increasing number of excellent young adult, juvenile, and children's biographies available, assuring that Tubman will continue to grow in stature among young people looking for heroes. Tubman is also the subject of many novels, poems, films, and pieces of art, which also contribute to her important place in women's history.

Any serious study of the life of Harriet Tubman inevitably begins with BRADFORD's biography. This volume is a revised edition of Bradford's quickly written 1869 biography and provides a fuller account of Tubman's life than did the earlier edition. Basing the book on conversations she had with Tubman herself, Bradford's purpose for writing the biography was to raise money in order to pay off the mortgage on Tubman's home. As such, the book is unabashedly hagiographic in tone. Bradford seems to be conscious of some of the shortcomings of her work; although she states that she attempted to corroborate the incidents related to her by Tubman, she also notes the difficulty Tubman's illiteracy presented. Bradford's work, then, is largely based on Tubman's recollection of events long past, and therefore, the book must be used with this in mind. There is the additional problem of Bradford's role in the shaping of the text. For example, Bradford chooses to transcribe Tubman's words in dialect, in the style of many nineteenth-century writers who recorded the speech of African-Americans. A further problem is that the book itself is a series of chronologically unordered reminiscences, making the book difficult to use. Nevertheless, Bradford provides the reader with ample anecdotal evidence of Tubman's life, and it remains the source upon which most later work is based. Although it should not be the only source consulted for any serious student of Tubman's life, it is nonetheless an indispensable place to begin.

While drawing heavily on Bradford's work, CONRAD arranges his material in a more useable chronological order. In addition, Conrad uses letters, newspaper articles, and other primary sources to support his construction of Tubman's life. Conrad's volume is footnoted and carefully documented; he clearly followed every path to glean more information about Tubman's life. Nevertheless, it is not what one would consider an "academic" biography. For example, although he drops Bradford's use of dialect when he recounts anecdotes illustrating Tubman's adventures, Conrad still includes dialogue for the characters of his book. Further, he attempts to provide for his readers the emotional and psychological state of Tubman, historical figures, escaping slaves, and a variety of characters who played roles in Tubman's life. Nevertheless, his exhaustive research and his careful sifting through the myths surrounding Tubman's life make this an important book. His bibliography is also useful in identifying additional primary sources for the study of Tubman's life.

PETRY provides a valuable resource for teachers who wish to introduce young people to Harriet Tubman's life. Although written for adolescent readers, Petry's work is generally cited as an important resource. As the title suggests, the book emphasizes Tubman's contribution to the Underground Railroad. She is pictured heroically as someone who risked her life to help bring others to freedom. Petry also discusses Tubman's time with the Union Army during the Civil War, when she acted as a spy and a nurse. The book provides an easily accessible overview of Tubman's life and work.

Focusing on the idea of the "radical woman," NIES has gathered portraits of seven American women who dared to act in the public sector to change society. She characterizes Tubman as the leader of "guerrilla operations" in the southern states in the years preceding the Civil War. Like Scruggs, Nies constructs Tubman as an actor, a woman who believed that she must seize freedom, not wait for it to be granted her. Nies also emphasizes Tubman's role as a model of black resistance, as well as her connections to Susan B. Anthony and the suffragist movement. As should be obvious from the above discussion, Tubman's life remains an important but largely unexplored area for the student of women's history.

—DIANE ANDREWS HENNINGFELD

U

United Nations

Hevener, Natalie Kaufman, *International Law and the Status of Women*, Epping: Bowker, and Boulder, Colorado: Westview Press, 1983
Iglitzin, Lynne B., and Ruth Ross (eds.), *Women in the World 1975–1985: The Women's Decade*, Santa Barbara, California: ABC-CLIO, 1986
Kardam, Nuket, *Bringing Women in: Women's Issues in International Development Programs*, Boulder, Colorado, and London: L. Rienner, 1990
Lynn, Naomi B. (ed.), *United Nations Decade for Women World Conference*, New York: Haworth Press, 1984
Winslow, Anne, *Women, Politics, and the United Nations*, Westport, Connecticut: Greenwood, 1995

The United Nations (UN) is an international organization formed after World War II, in order to promote peace and prevent another world war. Despite the fact that its main concern was the maintenance of world peace, the 51 chartering members of the United Nations believed that world stability could also be achieved by promoting economic and social progress and human rights, which included not discriminating because of race, sex, nationality, or religion. Thus, almost immediately, "women's issues" began to appear on the UN's agenda.

For a compilation of the different international legal instruments dealing specifically with women, HEVENER's book is valuable. The documents included in the book reflect the consensus on the part of the world's nations on the role of women in society. These legal documents were formulated, negotiated, and ratified, and serve as protective, corrective, nondiscriminating attempts at reaching a consensus regarding particular problems in the treatment of women that require legal solutions.

Various attempts have been made to assess the effectiveness of the UN when it comes to women's issues. WINSLOW's book is an update on the strength and cohesion of the international women's movement, especially as women have worked with the UN to achieve some of their goals. The various chapters focus on the major instruments for action used by women within the UN system. It reviews the developments in five of the major UN-associated specialized organizations with which women have been most concerned: the International Labor Organization, the Food and Agriculture Organization, the UN Educational, Scientific and Cultural Organization, the World Health Organization, and the World Bank.

KARDAM's book looks at how three international organizations—the United Nations Development Program, the World Bank, and the Ford Foundation—have responded to the incorporation of women into development activities. Their responses to different women in development issues depends on how much advocacy is undertaken by the staff members in each of the organizations. Should the staff not make a conscious choice to address these issues, then the issue does not get to the forefront of the international agenda, and responses to them may never be formulated.

IGLITZIN and ROSS's book looks at how the UN Decade for Women, and the various attempts in the international system to focus upon the social, economic, political, and legal status of women have had an impact on women's lives in individual countries. This book of readings brings together the works of contributors who investigate the emergence of "women's issues" in the forefront of the political agenda everywhere, showing how they are being implemented, and how they are changing the status of women in different countries.

LYNN's book provides a different perspective, in its attempts to assess the progress of the decade for women. Except for the compilation of data about the status of women in different countries, many countries have only paid lip service to the objectives of the decade. The country studies in this book confirm the critical importance of culture in determining female political status and behavior, which for some countries may be difficult to change.

—CECILIA G. MANRIQUE

V

Victoria 1819–1901

British Queen

Hardie, Frank, *The Political Influence of Queen Victoria,* London: Cass, 1935; New York: Oxford University Press, 1938

Longford, Elizabeth, *Victoria R.I.,* London: Weidenfeld and Nicolson, 1964; as *Queen Victoria: Born to Succeed,* New York: Harper, 1965

Marshall, Dorothy, *The Life and Times of Victoria,* London: Weidenfeld and Nicolson, 1972; New York: Praeger, 1974

Mullen, Richard, and James Munson, *Victoria: Portrait of a Queen,* London: BBC Books, 1987

Munich, Adrienne, *Queen Victoria's Secrets,* New York and Chichester: Columbia University Press, 1996

Plowden, Alison, *The Young Victoria,* London: Weidenfeld and Nicolson, 1981

Thompson, Dorothy, *Queen Victoria: Gender and Power,* London: Virago Press, 1990

Weintraub, Stanley, *Victoria: An Intimate Biography,* New York: Dutton, and London: Allen and Unwin, 1987

Queen Victoria was England's longest-ruling monarch and, as such, has sparked a wealth of volumes that cover items from her personal life to her governing style. There are many works from the time of Victoria herself, but they may not be available widely to readers; further, they show a Victorian interpretation of the subject. This list, therefore, contains recent works on the queen, in an attempt to cull the best from more available and possibly more objective perspectives.

HARDIE's study, although originally written in 1935, has not been replaced by a more contemporary work. He examines the period from 1861 to 1901, the time of Victoria's rule, focusing on affairs of state rather than analyzing the queen's personality. The author is a constitutional historian, writing a political historical overview of the effect Victoria's reign had on moving powers of state from sovereign to Parliament. He concludes that Queen Victoria, in an era dominated by the middle classes, was the penultimate middle-class monarch.

LONGFORD presents a somewhat daunting portrait of Victoria, at 600 plus pages, yet her writing is accessible. Her desire is to write a biography that is neither sentimental nor overly critical of the queen. The main impression the work gives of Victoria is as a down-to-earth woman, who worked hard and strove to improve herself and her ruled lands. Heavily detailed chapters include coverage of her childhood as well as her period of reign. The author relies primarily on sources from the royal archives, although the finished work is for both general and academic audiences.

A good popular history and biography is MARSHALL's work. The volume consists of almost as many illustrations as it does text, from photos of Victorian architecture to engravings from the Great Exhibition of 1851; from royal portraits to cartoons of the queen. Marshall's main undertaking is to contextualize Victoria's life against the major events of the age for a general audience. The work does mainly reinforce generalities and stereotypes of Victoria, rather than probing them.

PLOWDEN's work covers the period from the death of Victoria's father's first wife, Princess Charlotte, to Victoria's wedding day. The work is entertaining reading, as the author tries to humanize the queen by providing background on her early years, rather than presenting her as merely a head of state. Plowden uses accounts of those surrounding Victoria when she was a child; although most of her research is from secondary sources, she does use published versions of Victoria's letters and journals. The work is very detailed, including aspects of Victoria's appearance, dress, play, relations with her friends and relatives, and romance with Albert.

MULLEN and MUNSON's biography had as its genesis a BBC radio series. Their well-researched work draws heavily from primary sources, including the letters and journals of Victoria, as well as correspondence from other Victorians about the queen. The volume is good at providing detailed accounts of Victoria and her activities without minutiae, for its lack of sentimentality, its apt choice of quotations from Victoria, and its fluid yet intelligent prose style. The emphasis is more on Victoria's personality than on political affairs.

A well-researched and constructed recent biography, readily available in paperback, is WEINTRAUB's work. The author has made use of materials only recently made available on Victoria, such as her *album consolatium*, and more letters and journals of her relatives and others who came in contact with her. The author's goal is to bring out the many sides of Victoria's personality, and he does so by concentrating more on her private life and ways of dealing with problems than on her politics and rule. The narrative style of the work makes it easily accessible to a general audience. The author offers his assessment of her flaws and strengths, concluding that she was partially responsible for the transformation of the British monarchy to more of a ceremonial than ruling position.

In an excellent book that explores Victoria's reign from a guardedly feminist perspective, THOMPSON attributes much of Victoria's success to the fact that she was a woman. As a female figurehead, the queen was seen as less threatening and more nurturing than a male, and was more able to unify the British empire at that time. Thompson is quick to note that Victoria did not work for the rights of women, but through her powerful presence, she did provide a positive role model and antecedent for the female reform movements of her day. The author also tries to separate the myth of Victorian narrowness from the "complex" person of the queen. Marvelous cartoons from *Punch* punctuate the text.

MUNICH's volume is the best of the very recent scholarly work on Victoria. It is scrupulously researched and documented, with illustrations and a very complete chronology. The author uses contemporary cultural theory and revisionist historical methods to explore visual, media, and literary images associated with Victoria in her era, images which helped to maintain an aura of mystery around the queen, while at the same time reinforcing her sovereignty. Munich contrast the paradoxes surrounding Victoria: domestic mother, yet ruler of distant lands; staunch moralist, yet obviously a sexually active and fertile female. The work seeks not to uncover the real Victoria, but to explore ideas held about her.

—CAROL BLESSING

Victorian Era

Banta, Martha, *Imaging American Women: Ideas and Ideals in Cultural History,* New York: Columbia University Press, 1987

Basch, Françoise, *Relative Creatures: Victorian Women in Society and the Novel, 1837–67,* New York: Schocken, and London: Allen Lane, 1974

Burstyn, Joan, *Victorian Education and the Ideal of Womanhood,* Totowa, New Jersey: Barnes and Noble, and London: Croom Helm, 1980

Campbell Orr, Clarissa (ed.), *Women in the Victorian Art World,* Manchester and New York: Manchester University Press, 1995

Dijkstra, Bram, *Idols of Perversity: Fantasies of Feminine Evil in Fin-de-Siècle Culture,* New York and Oxford: Oxford University Press, 1986

Douglas, Ann, *The Feminization of American Culture,* New York: Knopf, 1977; London: Papermac, 1996

Jalland, Pat, *Women, Marriage and Politics 1860–1914,* Oxford and New York: Oxford University Press, 1988

Poovey, Mary, *Uneven Developments: The Ideological Work of Gender in Mid-Victorian England,* Chicago: University of Chicago Press, 1988; London: Virago Press, 1989

Showalter, Elaine, *The Female Malady: Women, Madness, and English Culture, 1830–1980,* New York: Pantheon, 1985; London: Virago Press, 1987

Vicinus, Martha, *Independent Women: Work and Community for Single Women 1850–1920,* Chicago: University of Chicago Press, and London: Virago Press, 1985

Scholarly sources reclaiming and documenting previously unarticulated aspects of Victorian womanhood have burgeoned in the last three decades, progressing from charting the limitations and restrictions circumscribing women's lives during the period to more recent studies that have begun the process of questioning and deconstructing the rigidity of the governing bourgeois ideology of the separate spheres (private/feminine and public/masculine). The works listed here attempt to span several disciplines and represent a very small sample of the large body of excellent material available on the subject.

SHOWALTER's groundbreaking feminist history of psychiatry examines the status of madness as "female malady" through nineteenth-century legal, medical, literary, and visual discourses. Showalter demonstrates that the aligning of women with madness was a pervasive cultural association and an appealing, even sexually charged cultural icon. Sections dealing with the nineteenth century cover psychiatric Victorianism and psychiatric Darwinism and reveal how the detection, definition, treatment, and confinement of "mad" women were influenced by constructions of gender in particular cultural contexts. Building on Sandra Gilbert and Susan Gubar's study of female madness in literature, Showalter's text is an essential cultural history of madness.

As its title indicates, POOVEY's book is concerned with deconstructing the idea of a unifying Victorian social ideology, an ideology that she sees as "fissured, self-contradictory, [and] contested." The study focuses on the constructions of gender and the separate sphere ideology in the Victorian period, and the contradictions of class and race such constructions implied. To this end, the separate spheres ideology is examined at work in five major Victorian institutions: medicine, the law, literature, education and work, and nursing. Poovey's incisive interdisciplinary analysis of Victorian culture provides extremely valuable insight into the social construction of femininity during the period.

JALLAND's text examines women's place and influence in British politics from the Victorian period to 1914. Jalland draws on a large body of primary source material—correspondence, diaries, and other family papers—to examine both the public and private experiences of women belonging to key political families. Jalland maps both particular cases of individual women and general patterns in political families through various phases in the life cycle: courtship and marriage, childbirth, motherhood, and spinsterhood, as well as devoting a discreet section to the "special roles" and attitudes of political wives of the period. The study cleverly reveals the ways in which women's lives in the governing classes conformed to and diverged from the prescribed social roles of the period.

Despite being published more than two decades ago, BASCH's book remains an informative and useful source of introductory material on women in Victorian society and literature. Basch traces the construction of the "pure" (wife/mother) literary heroine of the first thirty years of Victoria's reign alongside the antipathetic fallen woman and the single or working-class woman, reading such constructions or representations against the social, religious, legal, and ideological climate of the day. Focusing primarily on "major" Victorian novelists (George Eliot, the Brontës, Gaskell, Dickens, Thackeray, Trollope), Basch's text is a penetrating early study of literary and social stereotypes of Victorian women, which has played a significant role in opening up subsequent scholarly debate on the woman question.

BURSTYN's text is a valuable introductory social history of women's education in the Victorian period. Focusing largely on the middle classes but giving some attention to lower-class women, Burstyn delineates the prescriptive nature of women's education and its self-conscious perpetuation of an ideal social and domestic role for women. The study outlines the major social, ideological, scientific, economic, sexual, and religious arguments posed against the move toward women's higher education and relates such debates to the aggressive formation and maintenance of middle-class values during the Victorian period. Burstyn's analysis reveals a schism between the ideal and the reality of womanhood that has fed into other critical studies of the period.

CAMPBELL ORR's collection of essays situates discussions of women's roles in the production and consumption of Victorian art within contemporary debates about the separate spheres ideology. The essays examine the ways in which women of the period combated a male-centered art world and skirted the boundaries of bourgeois ideology by forging networks and opening artistic spaces, despite the lack of formal training and artistic recognition. Drawing on women's lives of the period (particularly Barbara Leigh Smith Bodichon), the book discusses the status and education of female amateur and professional artists, and women's roles as critics, scholars, collectors, connoisseurs, and benefactors of art. It is an excellent example of recent feminist art thinking about the period.

Of the two books listed that center on women in the United States during the Victorian period, DOUGLAS's study examines nineteenth-century American culture through extra-canonical literature of the period between 1820 and 1875. Douglas asserts that such literature, the textual productions of northeastern clergymen and middle-class literary women, sought to exert a religious influence and to propagate feminine/matriarchal values within society through the mass medium of the press. Douglas's study reveals that the roots of contemporary American popular culture can be traced in the sentimentalizing of theological and secular culture in this mass-produced nineteenth-century literature.

As its title suggests, BANTA's copiously illustrated work is as much a visual as a written record and analysis of representations of American women, particularly types or allegories of womanhood from 1876 to 1918. Banta draws on images from both popular and high art and literature of the period to examine the cultural values and contradictions inherent in such images. Issues surrounding representations of women, such as gender play, patriotism, the organization of private and public space, and the merchandising of femininity, are explored.

VICINUS's contribution to feminist history is a significant one. In this text, she examines the lives of two generations of single bourgeois working women, the communities they formed, and the institutions they founded. Beginning at the mid-century, Vicinus maps the uneven struggle away from a constraining ideological view of Victorian womanhood and toward the opening of spaces in which single women could undertake meaningful and fulfilling paid work. Her study centers on the ways in which marginalized and "redundant" women began to support themselves outside the nuclear family, to define new roles and occupations for themselves, and to establish an active movement that worked toward intellectual, social, and political freedom for women.

Like other authors in this listing, DIJKSTRA draws on both visual and written material to look at the cultural war waged on woman at the turn of the century. Written in a lively intellectual style, Dijkstra's analysis of the "iconography of misogyny" produced by artistic productions of the period from 1875 to 1900 ranges over national boundaries and reveals that in a period in which artistic images of feminine evil were mass-produced through photography, art played a significant role in the dissemination of the dominant ideological thinking about women. Dijkstra explores ideological attitudes toward women through the pervasive images of such figures as the wasting woman, the mythological woman, the whore, the virgin, and the lesbian, which dominated artistic representations of women at the *fin-de-siècle.*

—TIFFANY URWIN

See also Cult of True Womanhood; Separate Spheres

Virgin Mary

Brown, Raymond E., and Paul J. Achtemeier (eds.), *Mary in the New Testament: A Collaborative Assessment by Protestant and Roman Catholic Scholars,* Philadelphia: Fortress Press, and London: Geoffrey Chapman, 1978

Cunneen, Sally, *In Search of Mary: The Woman and the Symbol,* New York: Ballantine, 1996

Hamington, Maurice, *Hail Mary? The Struggle for Ultimate Womanhood in Catholicism,* New York: Routledge, 1995

Pelikan, Jaroslav, *Mary through the Centuries: Her Place in the History of Culture,* New Haven, Connecticut: Yale University Press, 1996

Ruether, Rosemary Radford, *Mary: The Feminine Face of the Church,* Philadelphia: Westminster, 1977; London: SCM Press, 1979

Warner, Maria, *Alone of All Her Sex: The Myth and Cult of the Virgin Mary,* New York: Knopf, and London: Weidenfeld and Nicolson, 1976

The Virgin Mary, or Mary of Nazareth, or Mary, mother of Jesus has been the object of speculation and reverence in Christian history, doctrine, legend, and art since the first century. Countless volumes deal with apparitions of Mary (Guadalupe, Lourdes, Fatima, Medjugorje) and devotional accounts of spiritual experiences attributed to Mary. The literature surveyed below is limited to more scholarly Marian studies whose perspective ranges from gender-sensitive to feminist.

Using the historical critical method of biblical analysis, the collection by BROWN and ACHTEMEIER surveys the New Testament texts that refer to Mary, mother of Jesus. These texts include a fragmentary reference in Galatians, brief familial references in Mark, Matthew, and Luke, a comparative study of Mary in the birth narratives of Jesus in Matthew and Luke, Mary at Cana and at the foot of the cross in John, and a cryptic reference perhaps to Mary in Revelation 12. This book explores roots for the theology of virginal conception in the birth narratives. It also builds a bridge to later traditions of Mary by describing the portrayal of Mary in early Christian non-canonical texts, especially the Protevangelium of James. The cataloguing of biblical references and non-canonical and Patristic references are especially helpful.

CUNNEEN'S search for a Mary appropriate for today recognizes the role of the lived experience of ordinary people in developing images of Mary, rather than the role of the hierarchical church in formulating Marian doctrine. Cunneen traces the development of Marian traditions since the New Testament through art, drama, poetry, and devotional piety. Since the author's purpose is to make thematic connections between tradition and today, she credits sources less rigorously than more scholarly writers. In her treatment of modern Marian thought, Cunneen describes the work of modern iconographers, some of whom are outside of Christianity. Cunneen paints a broad landscape with the goal of rediscovering an image of Mary that speaks to various cultures today.

HAMINGTON explores the ethical implications of the images of Mary, which historically have primarily been formulated by a patriarchal Church. Hamington deconstructs these patriarchal images by placing them within their historical framework and discussing the symbolic worldviews that gave rise to them. For example, the image of Mary as the new Eve created a dualism that claimed that women were either evil like Eve or good like Mary. The implications of this dualism have perpetuated a justification for violence against women identified as evil and an unattainable image for women identified as good. Hamington reconstructs an interim model of Mary, which he names "Mary, Everywoman." This image sees Mary as "woman" emphasizing power, Mary as" sister" emphasizing relationship, and Mary as "mother" emphasizing creative harmony. This image undermines the traditional sexual stereotypes of Mary that have valorized the celibate lifestyle over others. This is a well-annotated book reflective of the recent feminist scholarship on Mary.

PELIKAN's approach to the traditions of Mary is to describe the developed traditions and then to trace them backward to biblical and doctrinal sources. This strategy illuminates the interpretive methodology of the development of Christian thinking, which freely used typology and allegory to support tradition. Likewise, Pelikan places the development of Marian traditions within the broader framework of the development of Christian doctrine. His purpose is to help the reader gain an appreciation for what he terms the "eternal feminine" that leads one to what is holy. While the patriarchal nature of religious institutions is recognized, this book attempts to move beyond feminist critique to a more mystical appreciation of Mary. Of special interest to inter-faith dialogue, Pelikan compares Surah 14 of the Qur'an with the biblical statements about Mary and suggests that Mary functions as a bridge between Islam and Judaism and Islam and Christianity. While Pelikan's interpretation may not satisfy many feminist readers, he presents a comprehensive treatment of Mary as the "eternal feminine."

RUETHER presents a concise and accessible volume outlining the roots for Marian theology in ancient goddess traditions, the Hebrew Bible, and the New Testament. She traces the development of the doctrines of Mary such as Mary as the New Eve, Perpetual Virgin, Mother of God, Mediator of Grace, and the Mary of the Assumption and of the Immaculate Conception. Since this volume is intended primarily for Protestant readers, it describes the status of Marian devotion among the reformers and the basis of theological differences between Protestants and Roman Catholics with regard to Mary. Ruether seeks a theology of Mary that can empower women in the church. Discussion guides make this book useful for adult study groups.

WARNER undertakes a historical interpretation of the development of the traditions of Mary, namely Mary as Virgin, Queen of Heaven, Bride, Mother, and Intercessor. For example, in her discussion of Mary as Virgin, Warner surveys pre-Christian mythologies of miraculous births, early Christian apologetics in defense of Mary's virginity, medieval reinterpretation of Aristotelian anthropology relevant to woman's role in reproduction, medieval devotional poetry, selected anthropological studies involving belief in divine conceptions, and artists' depictions of virgin birth. Warner discusses the implications of Mary's virginity as it became the moral sanction for the celibate lifestyle over marital sexuality. While each chapter is rather concise, Warner's extensive footnotes provide ample reference to primary sources. The book contains over fifty color and black-and-white depictions of Marian art and a detailed chronology of Marian references.

—BARBARA B. MILLER

Volunteerism

Ellis, Susan J., and Katherine H. Noyes, *By the People: A History of Americans as Volunteers,* Philadelphia: Energize, 1978

Jedlicka, Allen, *Volunteerism and World Development: Pathway to a New World,* New York: Praeger, 1990

Kaminer, Wendy, *Women Volunteering: The Pleasure, Pain and Politics of Unpaid Work from 1830 to the Present,* Garden City, New York: Anchor Press, 1984

Karnes, Frances A., and Susan M. Bean, *Girls and Young Women Leading the Way: 20 True Stories about Leadership,* Minneapolis, Minnesota: Free Spirit, 1993

McCarthy, Kathleen D., *Lady Bountiful Revisited: Women, Philanthropy, and Power,* New Brunswick, New Jersey: Rutgers University Press, 1990

O'Donnell, Lydia, *The Unheralded Majority: Contemporary Women as Mothers,* Aldershot: Gower, and Lexington, Massachusetts: Lexington Books, 1984

Scott, Anne Firor, *Making the Invisible Woman Visible,* Urbana: University of Illinois Press, 1984

Throughout the history of civilization, women have answered the call to improve the quality of life for the community-at-large. With change being the only constant as society has progressed, women have joined forces to tackle the problems that neither government nor industry has been willing to solve. Women realized early on that through a shared vision and the strength of organization, they could create better communities at a local level, which would affect society as a whole.

ELLIS and NOYES provide a detailed history of volunteerism as a concept in America. Beginning in the 1600s with the Pilgrims and following through to the 1970s, this book emphasizes the thousands of individual citizens and their role in shaping the future of America. It pays homage to those individuals who have been historically unrecognized for their contributions to community, despite their lack of financial recompense, and recognizes the human concept of taking responsibility for a community need on a local level and through actions affecting the community-at-large. Through divisions in historical time periods, Ellis and Noyes examine how volunteerism has affected our social history and has produced the volunteer community we see today.

JEDLICKA provides an analysis of the role of volunteerism in world development. While this source does not necessarily come from a women's studies' perspective, it does address the historically important role of volunteers versus bureaucratic entities in creating true world development and education for our progressively global community. Jedlicka also proposes solutions, through a restructuring of the role that bureaucratic intstitutions can play in supporting volunteerism.

KAMINER provides one of the few histories of women as volunteers in America. While volunteering is often thought of as reinforcing the traditional roles of women in society, Kaminer illustrates how the volunteer efforts of middle-class American women gave rise to the nineteenth-century feminist movement. Combining a historical perspective, which began around the industrialization of America and the subsequent rise of the middle class, with personal interviews from full-time and part-time female volunteers from diverse backgrounds, Kaminer shows that throughout history, volunteerism has been a source of work outside the home for married, middle-class women. While some of the information is dated, this is a quality source for a socio-political history of female volunteerism.

Through the examples of 20 girls, ranging from elementary to high school age, KARNES illustrates the power of a woman at any age. The leadership and organizational skills presented in these examples will serve not only as inspiration, but also as an action agenda for what can be accomplished, even at a young age, in our communities through the efforts of girls. By telling the stories of these 20 girls who have addressed community needs such as homelessness and hunger, Karnes provides an insight into the leadership capabilities and resources available to women in any community.

McCARTHY examines how women's volunteer efforts have affected society at large, offering a multi-cultural and socio-economic cross section of examples. With national and international examples, this book provides an insightful history into the power and influence that organized women have had over the last 200 years. By discussing the history of women's volunteer organizations from the inception of the Society for the Relief of Poor Widows with Small Children in 1797 forward, McCarthy provides one of the most comprehensive and broad histories of women in volunteerism published to date.

O'DONNELL takes volunteerism and places it in the context of career women as mothers and community housekeepers. By examining the changing sex roles and the resulting images of woman and mother, as well as the importance of women feeling fulfilled, O'Donnell explains in Part IV how the change in social convention and new employment opportunities have placed a new responsibility on women to be social agents and community-builders, in combination with the more traditional roles of women. O'Donnell emphasizes the importance of neighborhood supports, and women's role in establishing them, as an enhancing element of parenting and social interaction. The book also evaluates women as volunteers in child-related (for example, schools) and non-child-related organizations (for example, League of Women Voters), and their fulfillment, obligations, and impact on the nuclear family.

Through a collection of essays, the social historian and pioneer in women's history SCOTT emphasizes the important role that voluntary societies have played in the history of American women. Scott argues for the importance of a comprehensive social women's history. Arranged by subject and chronologically, the reader is able to gain access to the three main themes of the text, particularly the examples of individual women as integral to reconstructing the past, the role of the education of women, and the opportunities provided by and impact of the women's voluntary associations throughout history.

—MELISSA HELLSTERN

W

Wald, Lillian D. 1867–1940

American Reformer

Daniels, Doris Groshen, *Always a Sister: The Feminism of Lillian D. Wald,* New York: Feminist Press, 1989
Duffus, R. L., *Lillian Wald: Neighbor and Crusader,* New York: Macmillan, 1938
Eiseman, Alberta, *Rebels and Reformers: Biographies of Four Jewish Americans: Uriah Phillips Levy, Ernestine L. Rose, Louis D. Brandeis, and Lillian D. Wald,* Garden City, New York: Zenith, 1976
Epstein, Beryl Williams, *Lillian Wald: Angel of Henry Street,* New York: Julian Messner, 1948
Siegel, Beatrice, *Lillian Wald of Henry Street,* New York and London: Macmillan, 1983

One of the best-known women of her day, Lillian D. Wald has largely been forgotten by scholars. A contemporary of Jane Addams, Wald moved in the same social work and pacifist circles as the Hull House leader. Among the first generation of professional nurses, Wald founded the Visiting Nurse Service and the Henry Street Settlement in New York City in 1893. Besides battling for greater training and enhanced status for nurses, Wald also found time to lobby for women's suffrage, organize female workers into unions, oppose the corruption of Tammany Hall, and work for peace in the years leading up to World War I. Much of the material on Wald consists of newspaper and magazine accounts penned by contemporaries. Studies of the settlement house and Progressive movements often note Wald's endeavors, but only a few historians have attempted longer evaluations of the life of this reformer.

DUFFUS has written a highly sympathetic biography of Wald. A close friend of the famed nurse, Duffus wrote his book with Wald's cooperation and consent. He makes no attempt at evaluating Wald's career, but his book has interest because it represents Wald's view of her life and work. Much of Duffus's material comes from oral history interviews with Wald and from access to her private papers. Duffus does not write a history of the Henry Street Settlement, of the Visiting Nurse Service, or of any period or movement. This is an older-style biography, focusing exclusively upon Wald as an individual and as a symbol of American generosity.

EPSTEIN has aimed her book at a young adult audience. She creates dialogue to bring Wald to life and does so effectively. A good introduction to Wald and to the lives of the poor in New York City, this book is too simplistic to appeal to those scholars who are seeking a more critical examination of Wald and her impact upon the world. Epstein wrote several decades before the flowering of women's history, and her work thus suffers from being uninformed by the insights of feminist scholarship.

By examining the problems of immigrants and the poor in New York City at the turn of the nineteenth century, EISEMAN sets Wald's work in context in a brief, accessible book. Eiseman's descriptions of the terrible conditions of tenement life in the city explain very well why Wald was so determined to better the lives of the poor. Eiseman is less successful, however, in examining the motivations of this famous nurse. Particularly surprising, since ethnicity is mentioned in the subtitle of this book, is Eiseman's total failure to explore whether a belief in Judaism influenced the way in which Wald conducted her life and career.

SIEGEL's biography is one of the best available books on Wald. In preparing to assist with Duffus's book, Wald may have destroyed many of her personal papers. Much of her early life is shrouded in mystery, making the biographer's task all the more difficult. Despite these challenges, Siegel has produced a historically sophisticated work. This book is based on a wide variety of sources, including personal remembrances and archival papers. Siegel traces the life of Wald, showing how she became an urban pioneer who developed new concepts of public health, and how she pressed the United States government to assume responsibility for the economic well-being of all its citizens. In addition to being a fine work of scholarship, this biography is exceptionally well-illustrated.

Another superb book is DANIELS's study of Wald's feminism. It is perhaps the best study of Wald's career.

Daniels provides a short introduction to Wald's life before focusing almost entirely upon her Henry Street work. She argues that Wald's pragmatism blocked her from developing a consistent, comprehensive philosophy of life. Wald's chief aim was to support the Henry Street movement, and she refused to antagonize potential sources of financial aid, many of whom espoused conservative views. While friends like Florence Kelley and Lavinia Dock took unpopular public stands, Wald kept her controversial opinions as quiet as possible. Daniels finds that although an overt feminist in private, Wald's writings are sometimes contradictory as to the role and place of women in society. Additionally, Daniels finds that while Wald supported legalized birth control and, possibly, abortion as well, she did not take a leading part in this particular battle for "married women's freedom." Wald took particular care to emphasize that her endorsement of birth control was "a personal not a Henry Street matter." The most recent of the Wald books, this biography tackles several difficult topics. Wald never married and, since many of her contemporaries were romantically involved with women, the question of Wald's possible lesbianism has been raised. Daniels addresses this difficult question with sensitivity, arguing that although Wald chose to spend her life among women, she was probably not a lesbian. Daniels also explains why neither religious urges nor a sense of mission were important factors in Wald's decision to enter the nursing field.

—CARYN E. NEUMANN

Walker, Alice 1944–

American Writer

Bell, Roseann P., Bettye J. Parker, and Beverly Guy-Sheftall (eds.), *Sturdy Black Bridges: Visions of Black Women in Literature*, Garden City, New York: Anchor/Doubleday, 1979

Bloom, Harold (ed.), *Alice Walker*, New York: Chelsea House, 1989

Butler-Evans, Elliott, *Race, Gender, and Desire: Narrative Strategies in the Fiction of Toni Cade Bambara, Toni Morrison and Alice Walker*, Philadelphia: Temple University Press, 1989

Walker's work, while widely and enthusiastically read, has not been as well served by critical readings as that of other African-American female writers. Discussion of her work so far has been largely confined to journal essays, many of which, however, have been republished in edited volumes devoted to the work of several writers. One major collection is the volume edited by BLOOM, which brings together many important essays on Walker, organised chronologically according to year of first publication and culminating in an essay by bell hooks, published for the first time in this volume. The framing of this collection with Bloom's own careful but ultimately evasive introductory essay, and hooks' equally careful assertion of the extensive cultural implications of a work like *The Color Purple*, suggests at once the complexity of this field of criticism and its multiple effects. While Bloom does not engage with either the nature of Walker's popularity or the particulars of her indebtedness to Zora Neale Hurston, hooks' essay is always cognisant of the implications of the larger cultural traditions of reading and writing, both for Walker as a writer and for her readers. Hooks is also careful to locate Walker's success within the traditions of misdirected readings of African-American writings that have marked the white academy, arguing, for instance, that reading *The Color Purple* simply as "a modern day slave narrative" constitutes a form of continuing discursive and institutional control. The other essays in Bloom's collection, written by many of the major figures in African-American women's literary analysis and criticism, cover a range of possible reading contexts and traditions, addressing the question of influence and inheritance between generations of African-American women, the complexities of race and gender as figured in Walker's writing, and the celebratory and polemic interest of Walker's work.

Walker's work is more often considered alongside that of other African-American female writers. BUTLER-EVANS brings a range of critical theoretical perspectives to bear on a reading of the discourses of race and gender on the writing of Toni Cade Bambara, Walker, and Toni Morrison. In particular, psychoanalytic theory's account of desire and subjectivity provides a useful perspective on the significance of narrative in these works. Furthermore, Butler-Evans is able to interpret Walker's key term "womanist" not as a fixed or closed statement, but rather more carefully in terms of the openness of an "ideological position in progress." Walker's work is well served by being addressed in terms of a carefully articulated black aesthetic discourse, drawing on the linguistic work of M.M. Bakhtin, narrative theory, and the work of New Historicists such as Stephen Greenblatt and theorists of history such as Hayden White, as well as the more obvious traditions of feminist and African-American literary analysis.

BELL, PARKER, and GUY-SHEFTALL's book is partly of archival interest, having been published in the 1970s. It includes the important early essay by Mary Helen Washington that discusses the full range of Walker's work published up until the mid-1970s, and it can be seen from this discussion how crucial it is to read Walker's novels alongside her poetry and essays, particularly for the combined focus they provide of her concern with and for black women. This essay also takes up the question of Walker's indebtedness to other writers and provides in this sense a useful counterpoint to the discussion in Bloom's book. Also included is another key essay from the 1970s by Chester J. Fontenot, which considers one of Walker's stories, "The Diary of an African Nun," in the context of a consideration of the continuing significance of theorising around "double consciousness" in black local and international communities.

—BRIGITTA OLUBAS

Warren, Mercy Otis *see* American Revolutionary Era

see American Revolutionary Era

Weil, Simone 1909–1943

French Writer

Allen, Diogenes, and Eric O. Springsted, *Spirit, Nature, and Community: Issues in the Thought of Simone Weil,* Albany: State University of New York Press, 1994

Brueck, Katharine, *The Redemption of Tragedy: The Literary Vision of Simone Weil,* Albany: State University of New York Press, 1995

McLane-Iles, Betty, *Uprooting and Integration in the Writings of Simone Weil,* New York: Peter Lang, 1987

Nye, Andrea, *Philosophia: The Thought of Rosa Luxemburg, Simone Weil, and Hannah Arendt,* London and New York: Routledge, 1994

Veto, Miklos, *The Religious Metaphysics of Simone Weil,* translated by Joan Dargan, Albany: State University of New York Press, 1994

White, George Abbott (ed.), *Simone Weil: Interpretations of a Life,* Amherst: University of Massachusetts Press, 1981

Winch, Peter, *Simone Weil: "The Just Balance,"* Cambridge and New York: Cambridge University Press, 1989

Simone Weil wrote and lectured extensively during her short lifetime. Yet her writings and lectures were not published, for the most part, until well after her death. Hence, the critical writings about her life and work did not begin to appear until well after her primary writings were published and examined. The book most scholars consider the standard work on Weil is that by VETO, whose recent translation into English allows for a wider readership. Veto reconstructs Weil's entire philosophy, focusing, as much of Weil scholarship still does, on her philosophy as theology, although he sees the unity of her thought in her development of the ideas of the role of beauty, time, and the self. Identifying René Descartes, Plato, and Immanuel Kant as influential to her development, Veto concentrates his study on Weil's use of the Platonic sense of "conversion" as the individual's return to God through a study of the problems of necessity, time, attention, and purposiveness without purpose. Although these themes were discussed in her earlier writings, Veto argues that her later, mature writings offer the greatest depth and beauty. He also offers an extremely useful chapter on Weil's notion of "decreation."

One decade later, the first full collection of papers treating various impressions and reflections on Weil and her life from diverse perspectives was published. WHITE is recognized for his insightful exploration of significant parallels between writings and experiences relating to the concept of work, that of Simone Weil in northern industrialized France, and that of Dorothy Day of the Catholic Worker's Movement in New York. The essays here treat Weil's political thought, especially two essays that relate her labor experiences and her critique of Marxism to some of the concerns of the American New Left. They also investigate her psychology, her biography, her "anti-politics," her bibliography, and her death. Notable is Michael Ferber's interpretation of *L'Iliade ou le Poème de la Force.* His reading, which explores the theme of necessity, sees in this work an anticipation of later religious concepts.

McLANE-ILES extends the discussion of all aspects of Weil's philosophy, organizing her writing around the metaphors of uprooting and integration, problems Weil refers to as *déracinement/enracinement.* The author hopes to express the essential value of Weil's philosophy, imitating in the structure of her own book a pattern of deconstruction she feels is at the heart of Weil's work. Not entirely chronological, the book discusses in its first two chapters works representative of two consecutive periods of development in Weil's philosophy, which McLane-Iles believes laid the groundwork for Weil's later writings. She also separates her analyses of Weil's writings on science and religion, two topics that are often combined to show Weil as a predominantly religious writer. Especially useful are McLane-Ile's references to sources and influences and her interpretation of Weil's relationships to thinkers such as Alain, Paul Valéry, Jean Paul Sartre, and others.

WINCH provides a fresh perspective on the complete span of Weil's work and discusses the fundamental difficulties of tracing the dividing line between philosophy and religion, while examining Weil's religious, social, and political thought. While many critics find Winch overzealous in his lengthy comparison between Weil and Ludwig Wittgenstein, most would agree that Winch provides an interesting and complete philosophical treatment of Weil's epistemology and metaphysics. He closely details Weil's problem in conceiving the relation between human beings and nature while attempting to explain mutual understanding and justice. Wrestling with this difficulty coincided with a considerable sharpening of her religious sensibility and led to a new conception of the natural and social orders, involving a supernatural dimension. Indeed, instead of passing over Weil's early work in philosophy, Winch shows how it is related to her later political and religious writing.

ALLEN and SPRINGSTED move between biographical and textual criticism, considering the many ways in which Weil is seen as an outsider. They argue against the portrayal of Weil as marginalized in her own time as sickly, female, and Jewish; they also question those who believe she was not baptized before her death. They further the philosopher Charles Taylor's ideas on moral philosophy by positing a connection between Taylor's concept of a person and Weil's focus on the good. They attempt to uncover Weil's understanding of the human person and Weil's own distinctive political philosophy through discussions of George Herbert's poetry and Platonic conceptions, concluding that Weil can be considered a marginal figure no longer.

NYE provides the only consciously feminist approach to Weil's work, through which she attempts to recover an alternative tradition of women's thought. The three female writers whose work she examines have received only marginal attention from feminists and philosophers. Like the others, Weil was pressed by violence and catastrophe to rethink the nature of reality, knowledge, and the self, projecting a metaphysics that reconciled a world ruled by force and reestablished the condition for justice. The questions all of these women ask—about the future of goodness, the progression of social theory, and the relationship between science and human freedom—connect them to one another and highlight their distinction from the mainstream philosophical tradition.

BRUECK offers the first full-length study of Weil's approach to literature, arguing that Weil uses literature to think philosophically and religiously. In her discussions of *Antigone, King Lear, Oedipus Rex,* and *Phèdre,* Brueck convincingly employs a distinctive Weilian approach she calls "supernatural," in which tragedy not only retains its tense moral elements, but in which that tension is also seen as redemptive. Little noticed elsewhere in tragic criticism, it offers an interesting alternative to present theories of tragedy. This book is a valuable study for those interested in the relations between the religious writings of Weil and tragic literature.

— HOLLI G. LEVITSKY

Welfare

Berrick, Jill Duerr, *Faces of Poverty: Portraits of Women and Children on Welfare,* New York: Oxford University Press, 1995

Dujon, Diane, and Ann Withorn (eds.), *For Crying Out Loud: Women's Poverty in the United States,* Boston: South End Press, 1996

Edin, Kathryn, and Laura Lein, *Making Ends Meet: How Single Mothers Survive Welfare and Low-Wage Work,* New York: Russell Sage Foundation, 1997

Kingfisher, Catherine Pélissier, *Women in the American Welfare Trap,* Philadelphia: University of Pennsylvania Press, 1996

Miller, Dorothy C., *Women and Social Welfare: A Feminist Analysis,* New York: Praeger, 1990

Quadagno, Jill, *The Color of Welfare: How Racism Undermined the War on Poverty,* New York: Oxford University Press, 1994

Rose, Nancy E., *Workfare or Fair Work: Women, Welfare, and Government Work Programs,* New Brunswick, New Jersey: Rutgers University Press, 1995

Sidel, Ruth, *Keeping Women and Children Last: America's War on the Poor,* New York: Penguin, 1996

Aid to Families with Dependent Children (AFDC), commonly known as welfare, has been one of the most controversial social programs in the United States, to the point that AFDC was dismantled and welfare programs radically overhauled beginning in 1996. Over the years, there have been numerous accounts of welfare's history, design, and significance, along with continuing calls for reform. Criticisms of the program have spanned the political spectrum; what is new today is the emergence of works, such as the above listings, analyzing public assistance from feminist viewpoints.

These books share a number of similarities. Each one denounces current reforms as an assault on single mothers who are wrongly blamed for overall social problems, and for their own poverty. There is general agreement that the welfare system must be vastly improved rather than curtailed or eliminated. And the authors conclude that high quality training and education, affordable and reliable day care, health care, and assorted other support services must be part and parcel of any serious effort to aid the poor. Nearly all of them recognize a commonality of interest among women, regardless of class, income, or current marital status, although a few pay special attention to the question of race.

Most of the books, in contrast to previous studies, focus on the stories of women as told through their own voices: how they perceive their world, themselves, and their lives. The portraits tend to be strikingly at odds with the prevailing views and stereotypes of society toward welfare and its recipients.

KINGFISHER explores the attitudes of the predominantly female welfare workers (whom she calls street level bureaucrats), and their clients, especially those who are politically active. Through in-depth interviews, she attempts to listen to how these women experience the welfare system and their place in it. She notes that recipients and employees do not share a sense of solidarity with each other. In fact, front-line workers tend to reproduce commonly held attitudes, such as the distinction between the deserving and undeserving poor. However, both groups view themselves as well-intentioned, plodding victims of the system.

The words of unskilled, single mothers and their children are highlighted by EDIN and LEIN, who compare welfare recipients and low-wage workers, focusing on how these two groupings of women survive economically. After carefully piecing together details on their actual consumption of goods and services, the authors conclude that neither welfare nor low-wage work provides enough income to cover basic needs. These women are forced to rely on additional sources of income to survive: boyfriends, absent fathers, relatives, off-the-books work, and the like. However, hardship is widespread, with the workers facing even more material deprivation than those who rely primarily on AFDC: wage-reliant mothers have greater expenses (day care, health care, transportation, and so forth) that outweigh any gains from wages. Moreover, because of the unstable nature of the low-wage job market, combined with the demands of raising a family, a large percentage of single mothers are forced to cycle between low-wage employment and public assistance. Despite the problems, almost all of the respondents indicated that they would choose to work if they could.

DUJON and WITHORN also present a picture of welfare recipients through stories. They warn that it is vital for all women to understand their common needs and vulnerabilities, and to communicate and work together on a broad-based movement to defend mothers on welfare. On the other hand, the structural causes of poverty affect different categories of women in distinct ways, thereby requiring varied solutions. Dujon and Withorn stress that caring for children is legitimate work: welfare recipients must be allowed the choice between meaningful employment and full-time child care.

SIDEL also provides an analysis of welfare recipients, through interviews, detailing the many faces of poverty. She cogently argues that the widespread campaign against welfare mothers is a form of scapegoating—to deflect attention from the real causes of the social and economic ills that afflict American society today: profound changes in technology and international trade; the inadequacy of our social policies; diminishing jobs with decent wages and benefits; and deteriorating infrastructure. Debate should center on ways to improve conditions for the poor rather than blame them and the welfare program for their situation.

BERRICK provides narratives of five representative types of single mothers living on welfare, including tales by their children. The author shows how they are affected by public assistance, their attitudes toward the program, and the ways in which they cope. The women range from Ana, who slips into dire economic need because of a work injury, and requires only temporary aid, to Darlene, whose emotional instability interferes with her ability to function productively. Berrick maintains that none of the women want to be on the dole, and that relatively few recipients fit the welfare stereotype.

MILLER takes a more theoretical approach, assessing the function of gender in the social welfare system historically and today. She charges that policies have been shaped primarily by women's relationships to men (anything that disrupts women's economic dependency is threatening), although class and racism play a role as well. Meaningful change is blocked because of inherent cultural and institutional biases, including patriarchal domination and control, the needs of capitalism, and white supremacy. Miller emphasizes that we must recognize the interdependence of home and workplace, allowing women to lead their lives holistically.

In contrast, QUADAGNO forcefully argues that race is the defining feature of the American welfare state. She analyzes policies from the New Deal and Great Society programs through the 1990s, concluding that ongoing racial issues and racial conflict not only have impeded the development of decent and comprehensive national welfare programs, but that such factors continue to shape (and limit) welfare reform today.

ROSE also assesses relief and government work programs through the decades. She explores two distinct approaches to publicly supported employment: current workfare and the earlier 1930s fair work programs. The author observes that workfare programs, which are primarily directed at women, are mandatory, punitive, and stigmatized. They pay very low or no wages. In contrast, fair work programs are voluntary, assume that participants are deserving and want jobs, and are based on prevailing local wages. The author lambastes the paternalism of the welfare system, moralistic criticisms of recipients, and current approaches to reform as mean-spirited, punitive, and harsh.

—LAURA KATZ OLSON

See also Poverty; Feminization of Poverty

Welty, Eudora, 1909–

American Writer

Bloom, Harold (ed.), *Eudora Welty*, New York: Chelsea House, 1986

Devlin, Albert J., *Eudora Welty's Chronicle: A Story of Mississippi Life*, Jackson: University Press of Mississippi, 1983

Kreyling, Michael, *Eudora Welty's Achievement of Order*, Baton Rouge: Louisiana State University Press, 1980

Mark, Rebecca, *The Dragon's Blood: Feminist Intertextuality in Eudora Welty's "The Golden Apples,"* Jackson: University Press of Mississippi, 1994

Pingatore, Diana, *A Reader's Guide to the Short Stories of Eudora Welty,* New York: G.K. Hall, and London: Prentice Hall, 1996

Trouard, Dawn (ed.), *Eudora Welty: Eye of the Story Teller,* Kent, Ohio, and London: Kent State University Press, 1989

Vande Kieft, Ruth M., *Eudora Welty,* New York: Twayne, 1962; revised edition, Boston: Twayne, 1987

Westling, Louise, *Eudora Welty,* London: Macmillan, and Totowa, New Jersey: Barnes and Noble, 1989

It is evidence of Eudora Welty's stature as a major American writer that there are many full-length critical texts to aid the understanding of her work. Early criticism tended toward formalist and archetypal critique, followed by biographical and psychological approaches in the 1970s and 1980s. More recently, critics are using a wide variety of postmodern readings to illuminate and interpret Welty's work.

VANDE KIEFT's revised edition of her 1962 text (which was the first book-length study of Welty) includes a biography, a condensation of the discussion of Welty's early work from Vande Kieft's earlier versions, and a thorough discussion of Welty's work since 1955. Vande Kieft identifies Welty's central themes as the "mysteries of the inner life," as she demonstrates how Welty opposes order, stability, and control with disorder, chaos, and unpredictability. Included are extended discussions of *Delta Wedding, The Golden Apples, The Bride of the Innisfallen and Other Stories, Losing Battles,* and *The Optimist's Daughter.* The book closes with an analysis of *One Writer's Beginnings* (autobiography). By all accounts, Vande Kieft's text is the standard introduction to Eudora Welty, the place where all who wish to learn more about Welty's work should begin.

WESTLING presents Welty as uncomfortable with labels such as "woman writer," because she sees herself as a writer, without reference to gender. Westling also emphasizes that Welty is an intensely private person. Welty's favorite subject is the family; thus Westling aligns her with Anton Chekov, Jane Austen, Virginia Woolf, Katherine Anne Porter, and Elizabeth Bowen. Also included in this book is a discussion of Welty as a photographer during her days as a Works Progress Administration publicity agent, and extended examinations of *Delta Wedding* and *The Golden Apples.* Westling argues that the latter ought to be considered in its entirety, as the stories function so closely as to "constitute a sort of loose novel." Finally, although Welty rejects the label of feminist, Westling pictures her as providing a "major new feminine vision."

PINGATORE offers a comprehensive overview of the criticism written about the stories that appear in *The Collected Stories of Eudora Welty.* For each story, Pingatore provides a publication history, background information concerning the composition of the story, any relationships between the story and the rest of Welty's work, a summary and evaluation of the criticism each story has received, and a bibliography of criticism. Because of the scope of the book, the treatment of each story is necessarily brief. In addition, the discussion of the critical approaches taken to each story is highly condensed and summarized. Nevertheless, Pingatore's book is a valuable contribution to Welty research, offering a useful, comprehensive reference tool for anyone undertaking a study of Welty's short stories. Further, the bibliographies at the end of each chapter lead the reader to the most important critical studies of Welty's work written before 1995.

Another valuable resource is BLOOM's collection of representative criticism. Included in this volume is Katherine Anne Porter's introduction to *A Curtain of Green,* often cited as an essay that contributed significantly to Welty's stature as a writer. In another essay, Robert Penn Warren examines Welty's narrative voice while essays by such notable scholars as Ruth M. Vande Kieft and Cleanth Brooks, and novelists Reynolds Price and Joyce Carol Oates examine Welty's subject matter, themes, and Southern tradition. Feminist scholar Patricia Meyer Spacks closes the volume with a discussion of "Gossip and Community in Eudora Welty." Bloom's book provides the reader with some of the most important examples of Welty scholarship, arranged chronologically.

DEVLIN emphasizes Welty as a writer of place. The book examines the importance of Jackson, Mississippi, to Welty's work, identifying the Southern quality of her writing. Devlin discusses Southern historiography, and analyzes Welty's aesthetic, placing her with William Butler Yeats, James Joyce, and Virginia Woolf. Devlin also attempts to establish the grounds for unity in her work, in spite of the fact that Welty herself finds little to suggest that her work is a "unified whole," other than the presence of a "lyric quality." It is this very quality, Devlin argues, that serves to unify Welty's writing. He thus chooses to demonstrate the ways Welty mines the cultural-historical material of her region to produce a body of aesthetically pleasing, lyrically unified work.

Like Devlin, KREYLING tries to find unifying elements in Welty's work; he focuses on Welty's aesthetic technique in her choices of setting, image, character, and plot. For Kreyling as well as Devlin, it is Welty's style that provides the integrative structures of the stories. In the early stories, he finds Welty's use of the grotesque to be another integrative factor. Throughout his text, Kreyling demonstrates the oppositions Welty constructs in her stories: connectedness and disillusionment, imagination and reality, Appollonian reason and Dionysian passion, and order and chaos. Kreyling provides an important chapter on *The Robber Bridegroom,* connecting it to the American pastoral image. Kreyling argues that the achievement of the work is its "integrating vision" of the "continuity of time."

MARK offers an explicitly feminist reading of *The Golden Apples*. Although she acknowledges the use of mythological allusions in the work, she also calls attention to the use of cultural artifacts. She attempts to demonstrate that Welty both confronts and transforms the myths of patriarchy that underpin the culture, and argues that in so doing, Welty is both a feminist and a postmodernist. It is as such, Mark asserts, that Welty will leave her mark, not as a regional writer. Like other critics, Mark notes the oppositions in Welty's work: individual and community, tradition and innovation, tragedy and comedy, and the technological and natural worlds. However, for Mark, it is the dynamic interchange between the oppositions that gives Welty's work its power. Mark's work is theoretical, yet accessible for readers familiar with postmodern critique.

TROUARD's collection provides a number of essays that attempt to look at Welty in new ways. The essays deal with the less studied of Welty's works, and many essays are based on Bakhtinian, feminist, or culture theory approaches. The categories into which the essays are divided demonstrate the range of approaches: part one concentrates on Welty's use of language and culture; part two examines Welty's female characters (including discussions of mother-daughter relationships); part three focuses on connections between perception and reality; and part four considers the importance of place in Welty's fiction. The book closes with a highly readable and useful discussion of Welty pedagogy by Ruth M. Vande Kieft.

—DIANE ANDREWS HENNINGFELD

Wharton, Edith 1862–1937

American Writer

Bauer, Dale, *Edith Wharton's Brave New Politics*, Madison: University of Wisconsin Press, 1994

Bell, Millicent (ed.), *The Cambridge Companion to Edith Wharton*, Cambridge and New York: Cambridge University Press, 1994

Bendixen, Alfred, and Annette Zilversmit (eds.), *Edith Wharton: New Critical Essays*, New York: Garland, 1992

Benstock, Shari, *No Gifts from Chance: A Biography of Edith Wharton*, London: Hamish Hamilton, and New York: Scribner, 1994

Goodman, Susan, *Edith Wharton's Women: Friends and Rivals*, Hanover, New Hampshire: University Press of New England, 1990

Joslin, Katherine, *Edith Wharton*, New York: St. Martin's Press, and London: Macmillan 1991

Singley, Carol, *Edith Wharton: Matters of Mind and Spirit*, Cambridge and New York: Cambridge University Press, 1995

Waid, Candace, *Edith Wharton's Letters from the Underworld: Fictions of Women and Writing*, Chapel Hill: University of North Carolina Press, 1991

Wolff, Cynthia Griffin, *A Feast of Words: The Triumph of Edith Wharton*, Oxford and New York: Oxford University Press, 1976; revised edition, 1994

Long overshadowed by those of her friend Henry James, the works of Edith Wharton have in the past 20 years become the focus of intense critical scrutiny. The listings here primarily reflect reassessments of Wharton's work, many in light of current feminist thought. They encompass but a few of the many recent works on Wharton, however; those looking for additional sources should consult Kristin Lauer and Margaret Murray's *Edith Wharton: An Annotated Secondary Bibliography* (1990), the review essays in *American Literary Scholarship*, and the annual bibliographic essays in *The Edith Wharton Review*.

The field of Wharton biography was one of the first areas to benefit from the opening of Edith Wharton's papers in 1975. Following R.W.B. Lewis's groundbreaking and still essential *Edith Wharton: A Biography* (1975) and the edition (with Nancy Lewis) of Wharton's letters (1988), WOLFF's influential critical biography uses Erik Erikson's theories to analyze the language of oral deprivation and isolation in Wharton's works. The revised edition collects two previously published essays, and includes a new introduction. One of the first of the standard critical works focusing solely on Wharton, Wolff's book is a central text in Wharton studies.

In addition to Eleanor Dwight's pictorial biography *Edith Wharton: An Extraordinary Life* (1994) and Alan Price's *The End of the Age of Innocence: Edith Wharton and the First World War* (1996), BENSTOCK's feminist approach focuses on the process by which Wharton came into her own as a writer. Meticulously researched, and the first full biography to be completely annotated, this book addresses such problematic issues as the nature of Wharton's ill health during the 1890s, her supposed breakdown in 1898, and her anti-Semitic attitudes, while providing a revealing picture of Wharton as a financially astute businesswoman and professional author.

Intended for general as well as scholarly readers, JOSLIN's book includes a biographical sketch, as well as a useful brief overview of major criticism; this section is especially strong in outlining the controversies engendered by feminist criticism of Wharton. For Joslin, Wharton's characters emerge from Emersonian autonomous selfhood, only to be caught up into a "social web" of relationships; they must learn instead "relational selfhood," or the ability to achieve individualism within, rather than against, a social fabric. Using scientific discourse as a stylistic tool, Wharton corrected the errors of two genres in her fiction: the female domestic novel, which seeks to enforce social bonds, and the male pastoral romance, which celebrates the protagonist's escape from them.

Another valuable starting place for both general and scholarly readers is BELL's collection of essays. Beginning with an excellent critical overview of Wharton's career and the reception of her works by Bell, a noted Wharton critic and biographer, the essays comprise a collection of new views on Wharton, ranging from cultural studies perspectives on *The Age of Innocence*, a psychoanalytic view of *Summer*, and genre criticism of *The House of Mirth*, *The Valley of Decision*, and *The Fruit of the Tree*. Especially provocative is an essay by Elizabeth Ammons, who extends the sociological examination of her important study *Edith Wharton's Argument with America* (1980) to an exploration of Wharton's implication in her culture's racial attitudes. Like Joslin, Bell includes a bibliography of important works about Wharton.

An equally indispensable collection is BENDIXEN and ZILVERSMIT's. Ranging beyond the major novels, the eighteen essays in this volume examine narrative strategies (Nettels, Blackall), Miltonic allusions (Carlin), the literary influence of naturalism (Pizer), female selfhood (Funston, Faery), and questions of genre, especially of Wharton's ghost stories (McDowell, Zilversmit). This collection provides a good introduction to a host of well-known Wharton critics and critical approaches; careful readers can gain a good sense of the state of Wharton criticism through its careful perusal.

Of single-author studies, SINGLEY provides a comprehensive overview of Wharton's moral philosophy and intellectual life. Refuting the common belief that Wharton concerned herself only with aesthetic principles, Singley argues that Wharton is a "novelist of spirit" as well as of manners. Contextualizing works against their corresponding philosophical bases, she examines Wharton's use of deterministic philosophy in her early works, an austere Calvinism to create a modern aesthetic in *Ethan Frome*, the interfusion of Platonic idealism into *The Age of Innocence*, Whitmanian and Emersonian transcendentalism in *Summer*, and a fascination with Roman Catholicism in her late work (*Hudson River Bracketed* and *The Gods Arrive*).

Addressing Wharton's cultural, rather than intellectual and spiritual milieu, BAUER uses Bakhtin's concept of "cultural dialogics" to explore the social and intellectual dimensions of Wharton's often-dismissed later novels. Bauer examines *Twilight Sleep*, *The Children*, and other late works as Wharton's responses to such 1920s social movements as eugenics and birth control, which masked concerns about immigration and racial purity under the banner of scientific rationalism. In misunderstanding Wharton's "mapping," as well as critiquing of such movements, Bauer argues, critics have oversimplified Wharton's complex politics and missed her attempt to "[foreground] the consequences of mass culture and the anxieties it generates." Calling as it does for the reassessment of the second half of Wharton's career, Bauer's book points toward a new direction in Wharton studies; however, it should supplement, not supplant, works on Wharton's more critically accepted novels.

WAID considers another set of Wharton's dialogues with her culture, placing her in a nineteenth-century American context, as Bauer does in a twentieth-century one. Waid traces Wharton's use of the Persephone myth as a figure for the female writer, who must leave the mother's world of feminine aesthetics to reside in the underworld of experience. In a series of excellent readings, Waid analyzes extensively both Wharton's poetry and her major novels, including a thorough investigation of allusions noted in passing by previous critics. For example, her discussion of Andrew Marvell's poetry animates the chapter on *The Custom of the Country*, and her exemplary reading of Mary E. Wilkins Freeman's "Old Woman Magoun" at once illuminates *Summer* and reveals Wharton's complex relationship with the author she unwillingly considered her "predecessor."

GOODMAN breaks with earlier critics who saw Wharton's women primarily as isolated and competitive. She analyzes the "crucial moments," when female characters in Wharton's fiction must decide between cooperation and competition. Seeking to dispel the vision of Wharton as a female author who surrounded herself only with male intellectuals, a subject she explores further in *Edith Wharton's Inner Circle*, Goodman examines Wharton's female relationships, including the problematic one with her mother and the warm friendship she shared with Sara Norton. Addressing a broader range of subjects, this book complements, rather than replaces the more intensive discussion of similar themes in Wolff and Waid.

—DONNA M. CAMPBELL

Wheatley, Phillis 1753–1784

American Writer

Richmond, Merle A. (ed.), *Bid the Vassal Soar: Interpretive Essays on the Life and Poetry of Phillis Wheatley and George Moses Horton,* Washington, D.C.: Howard University Press, 1974

Robinson, William Henry, *Phillis Wheatley in the Black American Beginnings,* Detroit: Broadside Press, 1975

———, *Phillis Wheatley and Her Writings,* New York: Garland, 1984

——— (ed.), *Critical Essays on Phillis Wheatley,* Boston: G.K. Hall, 1982

Phillis Wheatley, the first black female poet in America, had her book of poetry published in 1786, but it is only recently that she has begun to receive serious critical attention. The collection of essays edited by RICHMOND is a biographical and critical study of Phillis Wheatley and

George Moses Horton. Poems by Wheatley and Horton, both black slaves, were published together in a single volume during the nineteenth century to advance the abolitionist cause. Richmond discusses the significant social, historical, and philosophical differences between the two poets, as well as the contrast in their poetics. Nonetheless, he argues, the fact that both poets wrote for a white audience raises some interesting questions about black-white relationships and black identity in this country. Richmond claims that their poetry is not aesthetically impressive, but it is important for what it reveals about the status of slaves and the institution of slavery. Puritan ideology was imposed upon Wheatley, but because she was enslaved, she received none of its compensations. According to Richmond, Wheatley's poems are therefore thematically vicarious and stylistically imitative, because she was not allowed to develop her own voice as a black poet.

Author of three of the books under consideration, ROBINSON has made an impressive contribution to Wheatley scholarship. Robinson's first book (1975) begins with a brief outline of Wheatley's life and then continues with a discussion of her poetry. In the past two centuries, readers and critics have responded to Wheatley's work in a variety of ways. Robinson's discussion of the reasons for these differences in critical opinion is especially useful; he is interested in why Wheatley has provoked such a controversial reputation among both blacks and whites. In contrast to Richmond, Robinson argues that Wheatley did indeed assert her worth as a black poet, and that she was responsible for creating the black American literary tradition.

ROBINSON's collection of critical essays (1982) is essentially a history of Wheatley criticism. The book is a chronological compilation of a wide variety of responses to Wheatley, from newspaper reviews, anecdotes, and memoirs to more formal critical essays. Of particular interest are the responses to Wheatley by a number of historical figures, including Benjamin Franklin, Voltaire, and George Washington. The section of critical essays includes close readings of individual poems, her theories of prosody, discussions of Wheatley's knowledge of major aesthetic ideas of the eighteenth century, and her use of the elegiac mode. This is an extremely useful collection for anyone interested in Wheatley's life or work.

ROBINSON's most recent book (1984) includes a biographical sketch of Wheatley, as well as an account of her Boston milieu and a consideration of her poetry through close readings of several individual poems. This volume also contains a selection of her variant poems and letters in facsimile; her complete volume of poetry in facsimile; and a memoir of Wheatley written by a descendent of Wheatley's mistress. The annotations for these original documents are particularly helpful.

—JO ELDRIDGE CARNEY

White Women

Castiglia, Christopher, *Bound and Determined: Captivity, Culture-Crossing and White Womanhood from Mary Rowlanson to Patty Hearst,* Chicago: University of Chicago Press, 1996

Fowlkes, Diane L., *White Political Women: Paths from Privilege to Empowerment,* Knoxville: University of Tennessee Press, 1992

Frankenberg, Ruth, *White Women, Race Matters: The Social Construction of Whiteness,* Minneapolis: University of Minnesota Press, and London: Routledge, 1993

Jayawardena, Kumari, *The White Women's Other Burden: Western Women and South Asia during British Colonial Rule,* New York: Routledge, 1995

Segrest, Mab, *Memoir of a Race Traitor,* Boston: South End Press, 1994

Strobel, Margaret, *European Women and the Second British Empire,* Bloomington: Indiana University Press, 1991

Ware, Vron, *Beyond the Pale: White Women, Racism and History,* London and New York: Verso Press, 1992

Historically, writing about women in the west has largely centered on the lives and experiences of white women. In this sense there are tens of thousands of works by and about white women. Critical reflection on white women and white womanhood, however, can best be understood both as the product of post-colonial studies, and as a response to claims of women of color that white women are reluctant to examine their own condition as it contributes to the interlocking nature of sexism, racism, classism, and homophobia. In response to the growing literature by and about women of color, many white academics have turned their attention to issues of white privilege, the role of white women in colonial projects, and intersections of whiteness and gender.

Among the many texts exploring the philosophical, sociological, and historical dimensions of whiteness, FRANKENBERG's work stands out as the most complete discussion of how race shapes white women's lives in the United States. Arguing that white people and people of color live racially structured lives, she sets out to explain the socially constructed invisible nature of whiteness in the lives of 30 women. Paying special attention to the ways in which these women talk about race, Frankenberg explores how race shapes white women's racial discourse, childhood, and views on interracial sexuality and intimacy. Her chapter, "Thinking Through Race," makes a useful distinction between essentialist, color/power-evasive, and race cognizant discourses.

FOWLKES's project answers the questions "How do white female political activists understand themselves in terms of their race and gender?" and "How do they understand feminism and politics?" Her theoretically informed exploration of the lives of 27 political activists is used to explain how white political women of various groups (Democratic, Republican, radical lesbian, Marxist, etc.) have come to understand how their lives are shaped by both privilege and oppression. Her research yields an extensive classification of the relationships between being a woman and having a feminist/anti-feminist consciousness, which she uses to illustrate possible models for white women's political activism. The book has a useful bibliography.

Unlike the sociological approaches above, SEGREST's book is autobiographical. Her haunting memoir details her life and work as a racially aware white lesbian with North Carolinians Against Racist and Religious Violence (NCARRV). Her story is a rare account of grassroots interracial coalition building and organizing in a climate of emerging white supremacist activities. The book includes first person accounts of the 1979 Greensboro massacre, encounters with the White Patriot Party, and the Shelby Bookstore murders. Her penultimate chapter, "A History of Racism in the United States," is an excellent socio-historical account of the political construction of whiteness in the United States.

An extremely unique approach to the topic is CASTIGLIA's examination of white womanhood through the genres of American captivity narratives and later captivity romances. Captivity themes, which the author argues flourish in moments of racial "crisis," provide a useful way of examining themes of containment and community, border-crossings, and the shifting boundaries of culture and identity. Traditionally these genres tell the story of brutal, murderous savages who capture frail, vulnerable white women and threaten to rape and enslave them. To restore white patriarchal order, white men must kill the "savages" and rescue the white woman.

Beginning with Mary White Rowlandson's 1682 capture by Narragansett Indians, Castiglia analyzes popularization and wide circulation of captivity narratives as a means of maintaining the interlocking hierarchies of race and gender. Just as tales of white women's capture by Native Americans justified westward expansion, he argues, Patricia Hearst's narrative detailing her abduction by "dark" men was used to create the social climate necessary to mobilize American sentiments against radical feminist and black nationalist demands, and to justify aggression against Arab nations during the oil crisis. Castiglia also examines romantic versions of captivity themes authored by white women. The final chapters examine how Ann Eliza Bleecker, Susanna Rowson, Catharine Maria Sedgwick, and popular romance novels have been used by female novelists to invent a "literary wilderness" in which women are released from rigid gender conventions.

Other works examine the emergence and importance of white womanhood in the context of colonial empire building. WARE uses British women's participation in abolitionist movements, British campaigns against lynching in the United States, and British imperialism in India to explore issues of race, nation, and gender in historical memory. Instead of exploring white understandings of race, this book concentrates on the development of the racial components of white femininity. Key themes include: the identification of images of white womanhood embedded in familiar racist discourse, the politics of anti-slavery as a useful way to examine the problematic category of "woman," and the relationship between feminism and imperialism.

Focusing on the British Empire in sub-Saharan Africa and India, STROBEL's monograph examines both the lives of European women as missionaries, reformers, anthropologists, travelers, teachers, and wives of colonial administrators in the process of British colonial expansion, and their relationships with indigenous women. Topics of focus include female sexuality, home and work, women's roles as administrators and policy makers, and the status of indigenous women. Strobel focuses almost exclusively on the lives of Christian missionaries, *memsahibs* (wives of diplomats), educators, and well-meaning spinsters who were bringing western education and values, social reform, women's rights, and modernization to the colonies.

JAYAWARDENA's book highlights the contributions of European women critical of colonial rule. The book casts an Asian "feminist gaze" on European women's activities in India and Sri Lanka during British colonialism. Jayawardena problematizes white western feminist identity by retrieving the histories of western women theosophists, Orientalists, Holy Mothers, Socialists, Communists, supporters of local nationalist struggles, and Buddhist and Hindu devotees who find India's cultures more liberating than their own. The subjects of this work rejected Christianity and western values and often perceived Asia as the model for an alternative society. Leading independent lives and breaking away from traditional roles, these women were seen by colonizers as undermining white supremacy by consorting with the colonized. Their book includes extensive bibliography and photographs.

—ALISON BAILEY

Wicca *see* Witchcraft/Wicca: Modern and Neo-Paganism

Widowhood

Bremmer, Jan, and Lourens van den Bosch (eds.), *Between Poverty and Pyre: Moments in the History of Widowhood*, New York and London: Routledge, 1995

Lieberman, Morton, *Doors Close, Doors Open: Widows, Grieving and Growing*, New York: Putnam, 1996

Lopata, Helena Znaniecka, *Current Widowhood: Myths and Realities*, Thousand Oaks, California, and London: Sage, 1996
Lund, Dale A., *Older Bereaved Spouses: Research with Practical Applications*, New York: Hemisphere, 1989
Morgan, Leslie A., *After Marriage Ends; Economic Consequences for Midlife Women*, Newbury Park, California, and London: Sage, 1991
Owen, Margaret, *A World of Widows*, London and Atlantic Highlands, New Jersey: Zed, 1996
Rose, Xenia, *Widow's Journey: A Return to the Loving Self*, New York: Henry Holt, 1990; London: Souvenir, 1992
Wilson, Lisa, *Life after Death: Widows in Pennsylvania, 1750–1850*, Philadelphia: Temple University Press, 1992

Widows are probably one of the most misunderstood groups. However close her friends and family may be, a woman experiences the death of her husband by herself, in a unique way. LIEBERMAN's book is based on solid research and interviews of over seven hundred widows over the course of seven years. He shares the wisdom he has gained, retelling the women's stories about the pain, the anger, and the challenges they face in the first few months of being widowed. But, most important, he has made discoveries that expose many of the pernicious myths about widows. He discloses the surprising sources of help for widows and the fact that there is light at the end of the tunnel.

LOPATA explores a wide range of subjects and issues surrounding widowhood, including myths, emotions, identity, roles, external relationships, and support systems. Her book is organized with an initial comparative and historical perspective on the situation of widows in various parts of the world and in special communities in the United States. She shows the effects on a woman of the role of wife and the circumstances by which a woman experiences the illness and death of her husband. Following this discussion are analyses of the effects of widowhood on the roles of mother, kin member, friend, and participant in the larger community. The book ends with an overall picture of the major themes of the effects of social development and of the myths surrounding widowhood. To pull this together, Lopata used interviews, questionnaires, participant observations, personal experiences, census, and other statistical resources.

LUND's 16 chapters are organized into four parts. The first part addresses questions dealing with the degree of impact that bereavement in later life has on the mental and physical health of the surviving spouse, the periods of time when difficulty and distress are the greatest, and the proportions of people who experience major coping difficulties. The second part focuses on the role of social support in alleviating the stress and threats to mental health functioning that can accompany the bereavement process. Part three compares bereavement, or widowhood, with divorce. And part four focuses on extremely important aspects of bereavement and comes to some conclusions that cover issues about the impact, course, and predictors of bereavement adjustments among older spouses.

Since time immemorial widows have been associated with notions of ambiguity. They often represented a marginal group whose lives were controlled by rules. This might explain the small amount of attention they received in scholarly research in the past. This lack of interest is the motivation for BREMMER and VAN DEN BOSCH's collection of essays, which focus on the position of widows throughout the centuries in the Mediterranean and western Europe, and in the religious traditions of Islam and Hinduism. This collection is viewed from the perspectives of historians, jurists, philologists, anthropologists, and theologians. While not broad enough to be considered standard, the collection is useful for those studying widowhood in different countries.

The purpose of OWEN's book is to open up the neglected subject of Third World widows and to create an awareness of the topic's importance. This book provides a global overview of the status of widowhood. Owen explores the process of becoming a widow: poverty and Social Security in the context of widowhood; differing laws and customs regarding widows' inheritance; the situations of widows who remarry; and issues of sexuality and health. She examines the needs for specific groups of women, including refugees, older widows, and child widows. She also looks at widowhood in the context of AIDS. Throughout the book, Owen shows the prevalence of discrimination against widows in inheritance rights, land ownership, child custody, security of home, and nutrition and health. The book closes with a summary of widowhood as a human rights issue and an overview of widows organizing for change.

MORGAN's book demonstrates that the diversity and complexity of women's lives defy general statements. She explores the economic protection of marriage among mid-life women by comparing several marital transitions—separation, divorce, widowhood, and remarriage. Rather than simply comparing the financial straits of women in different marital statuses, she followed them over the course of several years. She examines the consequences for women in midlife when their marriages end, focusing on economic change. The core of this book outlines the sometimes dramatic and socially significant changes occurring to women as their marriages end.

WILSON's book takes a somewhat different approach. She carves out a one hundred year period, between 1750 and 1850, and she uses Pennsylvania, namely Chester and Philadelphia Counties, as a backdrop against which many widows can be observed in different and changing contexts during a pivotal time in women's history. The first part of the book addresses womanhood through the prism of widowhood, and in particular, the abilities and priorities of widows and the contradictions and difficulties widowed women presented for the concept of separate spheres. The last portion of the book tries to account for these apparent contradictions through an examination of the family's reaction to the loss of the husband and father. The conclusion makes a case for the importance of the family perspective in assembling the puzzle of gender-based descriptions of women's lives.

ROSE's work is extremely useful in explaining what women must go through after the death of their husbands. She takes the reader on a journey, beginning with the immediate challenges widows must face in the first few months after the husband's death. She discusses some very frightening questions, such as "Who is really going to take care of you?" and "Who are my friends, and where have they gone?" Rose does not paint a picture of despair, but rather her journey is one of hope. She explains the living with loneliness and dispels some of the myths associated with the length of the grieving time. Finally, Rose openly looks at feelings of intimacy, fear, and loving again. Her book presents an easy-to-read discussion of the journey through widowhood.

—SUSAN M. TAYLOR

See also Sati

Willard, Emma 1787–1870

American Educator

Campbell, Karlyn Kohrs (ed.), *Man Cannot Speak for Her, Volume One: A Critical Study of Early Feminist Rhetoric,* New York and London: Greenwood, 1989

Eschbach, Elizabeth Seymour, *The Higher Education of Women in England and America, 1865–1920,* New York: Garland, 1993

Faragher, John, and Florence Howe (eds.), *Women and Higher Education in American History,* New York: Norton, 1988

Goodsell, Willystine (ed.), *Pioneers of Women's Education in the United States: Emma Willard, Catherine Beecher, and Mary Lyon,* New York: McGraw-Hill, 1931

Lutz, Alma, *Emma Willard: Daughter of Democracy,* New York: Houghton Mifflin, 1929

———, *Emma Willard: Pioneer Educator of American Women,* Boston: Beacon Press, 1964

As one of the first advocates of higher education for females, Emma Hart Willard deserves much more study than has been the case. Although she is often mentioned in passing by authors more generally about the history of education and women's rights, little time is solely devoted to this educator. Only Goodsell and Lutz have produced detailed biographies of Willard. The remaining three works cited above have been included as more general references on female education in the United States and abroad. Although these authors examine Willard's influence in the United States, they spend more time recording the broader origins and history of female education. However, it is important to note here that from these works a sense of the more general setting for Willard's life can be found. Campbell, Eschbach, and Faragher and Howe do an excellent job of analyzing the careers of Willard and others who were deeply entrenched in the initial movement for female education, and they simultaneously provide adequate background for understanding why these individuals were so important.

Why does Emma Willard figure so prominently in the history of women? Willard, along with a few select others, was directly responsible for educating the generation of women who would organize and seek rights for women for the first time. In particular, CAMPBELL states that such an influential woman and well-known feminist as Elizabeth Cady Stanton received her secondary education at Emma Willard's Troy Female Seminary in the early 1830s, just prior to her active pursuance of women's rights. While Campbell dedicates most of her analysis and discussion of early feminist texts to those of the next generation, she emphasizes the crucial role that Emma Willard and other female educators played in facilitating women's rights. Some feminist historians argue that individuals like Emma Willard planted the seed, so to speak, from which early feminism would grow. Campbell believes that Willard and others facilitated the professionalization of women's sphere by creating institutions in which young women could receive a respectable education and then advocating the placement of these women in schoolrooms across the United States and abroad. Female education, from this point of view, provided women with a gradual means of power—first allowing them to be moral arbiters for the family or private sphere and eventually giving them access to independence and the public sphere as well. At base, women's rights agitation began in the classroom, and the mere existence of young women in classrooms was the result of the efforts of Willard and only a few others.

In order to be fair to Willard's accomplishments, it is also critical that the reader peruse ESCHBACH's work. Eschbach describes how, when Willard began her work to further female education, the nation was in the midst of vast economic and social changes. Industrialization, urbanization, and improvements in transportation were transforming the way many Americans led their lives, as movement—from country to city, from home as a work place to factory, and from east to west—became a national trend. Eschbach explains how these changes necessitated or at least encouraged the development of new gender roles. Since men no longer worked within the home, many people began to credit the nation's women with the ability to shape the future character of the U.S.

population. Mothers became the sole arbiters of family life and were given responsibility for raising children. Since maintaining the morality of children had fallen to female hands, women like Willard realized the importance of academic training for women.

FARAGHER and HOWE also set the stage for Willard's actions. These authors explain how Willard furthered higher education as a means for improving women's status. Willard's mission, according to Faragher and Howe, was to elevate the female character and bring it within reach of the privilege males held at that time and which "unreasonably distinguished the leading sex from theirs."

Besides providing a fully-detailed account of Willard's life in her 1929 and 1964 books, LUTZ describes the delicate line that Willard had to walk in order to further female education but also remain a decent, acceptable woman in the eyes of others. This was a dilemma of all early feminists to be sure, but it was magnified for the women of Willard's generation, who had not asked for any rights as of yet. Opposition came from all corners, and many declared that education would not help women in accomplishing their domestic tasks. Others claimed that education would encourage women to compete with men and therefore upset the established social order. Lutz explains how Willard took "A Plan for Female Education" to the New York State Legislature in order to secure funds for a school for female students. The Legislature only responded with praise and a charter, but no money. Private donors eventually funded Willard's Troy Female Seminary, which opened in 1821 and offered secondary education to women for the first time. Lutz does well in illustrating the fact that Willard met with many pitfalls along the way to securing secondary education for females yet did not falter. She stood quiet yet firm against opposition and thus should be remembered as a pioneer of women's equal opportunities in education.

GOODSELL's work offers the reader the unique opportunity of comparing three initial advocates of female education: Emma Willard, Catharine Beecher, and Mary Lyon. Each woman influenced female education in a slightly different way; Willard's impact was that she furthered the professionalization of women outside the home. Goodsell states that one of the greatest services Emma Willard rendered was in training and sending out to the nation's newly established schools a crop of efficient and knowledgeable teachers. Goodsell informs the reader that in a very real sense, Troy Female Seminary was a pioneer normal school, performing a public service of teacher training. The young women who graduated from Willard's school, with a certificate signed by Willard herself, were equipped with the highest recommendation for a teaching position that the country offered before the founding of normal schools in 1837. In fact, Goodsell notes that Emma Willard sent forth from Troy 200 trained teachers before even one was graduated from a public school in the United States. Goodsell concludes that although Willard cannot be credited fully with the foundation upon which every women's college and coeducational college may be said to rest (as Lutz proposes), she was a vitalizing influence and one of the builders of the solid base upon which female education rests today. Considering the influence that she had on female education and also the professionalization of women in the field of teaching, the lack of secondary sources written on Emma Willard is inexcusable.

—HEATHER DILLAWAY

Willard, Frances 1839–98

American Reformer

Bordin, Ruth, *Frances Willard: A Biography,* Chapel Hill and London: University of North Carolina Press, 1986

———, *Woman and Temperance: The Quest for Power and Liberty, 1873–1900,* Philadelphia: Temple University Press, 1981

Earhart, Mary, *Frances Willard from Prayers to Politics,* Chicago: University of Chicago Press, and London: Cambridge University Press, 1944

Gordon, Anna A., *The Beautiful Life of Frances E. Willard: A Memorial Volume,* Chicago: Woman's Temperance Publishing Association, 1898

Trowbridge, Lydia Jones, *Frances Willard of Evanston,* Chicago: Willett, Clark, 1939

Tyrrell, Ian, *Woman's World/ Woman's Empire: The Woman's Christian Temperance Union in International Perspective 1880–1930,* Chapel Hill and London: University of North Carolina Press, 1991

Frances Willard has until recently been relegated to relative obscurity because of the cause most associated with her name, prohibition. Her work, however, was not limited to heading the Woman's Christian Temperance Union (WCTU) for many years; she was also a women's college president, author, and a proponent of reforms in labor and health. There are several older biographies of Willard, written early in the century. More currently, renewed interest in female led social and political reforms has led to rediscovery of Willard as a strong, active, articulate woman.

The first biography of Willard was commissioned by the Woman's Christian Temperance Union and written by GORDON. It is a highly subjective Victorian work focusing on the spiritual piety of Willard, but it is helpful in presenting the words of those who were her friends and co-workers. The volume is divided into sections of biography, speeches from Willard's memorial service, and writings of others about Willard.

TROWBRIDGE's biography is essentially a volume of praise for Willard, listing her accomplishments as not only her work in the WCTU, but also her work for women's right to vote and equal pay, for labor reforms, such as the minimum wage and an eight-hour day, for required education for citizenship, for physical education programs in the schools, and for vocational training for girls. The book also includes a helpful chronology of Willard's life.

EARHART's book is a very cogently written older biography that probes what she terms the "myth" of Frances Willard, particularly as perpetuated by Gordon's book and other works written for the Woman's Christian Temperance Union. While this myth constructs a portrait of Willard as a "saint," Earhart wishes to portray Willard as a woman of remarkable leadership ability who was responsible for a "whole women's movement." Thus, Earhart emphasizes the arenas Willard was involved in besides the WCTU, including politics, labor, and education.

Although TYRRELL's work is not exclusively on Willard, but on the WCTU, Willard's life is so interwoven with the organization that she is referenced on the majority of the pages. Tyrrell presents Willard as a woman who was concerned not only with the cause of temperance, but also with being a strong, positive female role model. She was against marriages based on economic reasons, against traditional male dominated marriages, and in support of males and females working together. However, Tyrrell acknowledges that Willard did have conflicting views of women's complete equality in the public sphere.

If one reads only one work on Willard, BORDIN's biography (1986) should be the one. The author is a manuscript librarian, archivist, and historian, and as such, makes use of original sources only recently rediscovered. This is the only contemporary full-length reappraisal of Willard, and it avoids the sentimentality of older biographies. Bordin sees Willard's work in the WCTU as significant because it opened the way for American women to move from the domestic to the public sphere. The volume includes a helpful bibliography, photos, and extensive coverage of Willard's life and work.

BORDIN (1981) offers a discussion of Willard in the context of the Woman's Christian Temperance Movement, hypothesizing that Willard used the platform of the WCTU to showcase her talents and promote women's rights. The work is helpful in showing Willard in the setting of the community of women with whom she worked. Bordin conducts meticulous historical research, drawing from primary sources.

—CAROL BLESSING

See also Woman's Christian Temperance Union

Witchcraft: Ancient

Baroja, Julio Caro, *The World of the Witches,* London: Weidenfeld and Nicolson, and Chicago: University of Chicago Press, 1964

Dukes, Eugene D., *Magic and Witchcraft in the Dark Ages,* Lanham, Maryland: University Press of America, 1995; London: University Press of America, 1996

Frazer, James George, *The Golden Bough: A Study in Magic and Religion,* New York and London: Macmillan, 1900

Harrison, Michael, *The Roots of Witchcraft,* London: Muller, 1973; Secaucus, New Jersey: Citadel Press, 1974

Kittredge, George Lyman, *Witchcraft in Old and New England,* Camridge, Massachusetts: Harvard University Press, 1929

Marwick, Max G. (ed.), *Witchcraft and Sorcery: Selected Readings,* New York and Harmondsworth: Penguin, 1970

Rose, Elliot, *A Razor for a Goat: A Discussion of Certain Problems in the History of Witchcraft and Diabolism,* Toronto: University of Toronto Press, 1962; London: University of Toronto Press, 1989

Russell, Jeffrey B., *A History of Witchcraft: Sorcerers, Heretics, and Pagans,* London and New York: Thames and Hudson, 1980

———, *Witchcraft in the Middle Ages,* Ithaca, New York, and London: Cornell University Press, 1972

Summers, Montague, *The History of Witchcraft and Demonology,* London: K. Paul, Trench, Trubner, and New York: Knopf, 1926

There are many texts on ancient magic, witchcraft, medicine, paganism, and religion, and while several such articles and books freely mix and separate these words in highly inconsistent ways, there are far more texts on modern (post-Middle Ages) practices and beliefs than upon ancient. One person's paganism is another person's religion; one person's religion is another person's witchcraft, and so on. Even the adjective "ancient" is relative to a person's discipline: it could be referring to the Middle Ages, to the Greco-Roman Era, or even to the Neolithic Period. This issue is further complicated by the fact that much contemporary witchcraft is inspired by, or is a revision of, ancient institutions. Finally, the historical transition toward contemporary dominant religions (Christianity perhaps at the forefront) and the evolution from oral traditions into literacy means a void in understanding ancient witchcraft; indeed, much of our knowledge is based upon interpretations of Christian-biased texts and the archaeological and anthropological studies of both artifacts and "modern-primitive" societies. Portrayal is further inconsistent and unduly biased because some scholars are so rooted in their western or Puritanical traditions.

FRAZER, whose book has had a great impact upon witchcraft studies in this century, is one such scholar. Furthermore, while it can certainly be argued that Frazer's work is comparable to that of Freud or Darwin, like Freud, he is now more aligned with, and used in, literary criticism than for the purposes of scientific or historical factual study. Indeed this book is considered a major influence upon twentieth-century poetry and fiction. As an anthropologist, Frazer's studies have been considerably less impressive, frequently proving to be little more than a reworking of the research of other scholars.

KITTREDGE, a noted scholar in the field, is less biased in his taxonomy, rooting his scholarship in a more folkloric and historical approach, but he still oversimplifies—referring to societies as either "civilized" or "uncivilized," with the latter being essentially anything that is not remotely analogous to twentieth-century England. In addition, his primary scholarship is rooted in medieval and folkloric literary studies, which is reflected in his excellent and enjoyable, although equally intuitive and subjective, work.

Furthermore, today most scholars agree that the concept of witchcraft being equivalent to devil worship is a derivative of sixteenth-century paranoia, and SUMMERS's book is a beautiful example of such inaccuracy. However, that it has been republished testifies to its impact as a well-known work, although by a questionable authority (for example, while he claimed to be a priest—and wore vestments—there is no record of his ordination). RUSSELL, an established scholar on several subjects, which he closely relates, including the two listed texts on witchcraft, also provides an inaccurate portrayal. For example, he regards sorcerers and pagans as tightly associated with witchcraft. In that sense, he is caught up in the "old school" of scholarship. That he is trapped within the boundaries of such biases is further evidenced by his scholastic trend away from witchcraft toward Satanism in his later research. However, both books also take pains to also differentiate the practice of ancient witchcraft from other beliefs, including earth-worshiping pagan as well as more modern practices.

ROSE discusses the problems of this dualistic (good beliefs vs. bad beliefs) thinking that seems to have, until recently, permeated scholarship on witchcraft. Roughly half of this historically emphasized text is devoted to ancient witchcraft in particular, and it covers witchcraft right up into modern times. Rose's criticisms of past scholarship are sound and rooted in excellent documentation—this is a frequently cited text.

BAROJA provides another one of the more frequently cited works in this field, a scholarly, detailed history on the rise, crisis, decline, and rise again of witchcraft. Careful to cut away from the good (Christianity) versus evil (witchcraft) he is also just as careful in backing the theory that witchcraft is an ancient cult. This text is among the more objective approaches available, especially in that it fully recognizes the limitations of what we can and cannot possibly know looking back from the twentieth century.

Three texts that clearly break away from the dualistic thinking of earlier research are those by Harrison, Marwick, and Dukes. HARRISON focuses on the fertility cult aspect of witchcraft, with a Celtic emphasis, from pre-Christian Europe to modern times. MARWICK takes a world-wide approach with a selection of various articles on witchcraft in mostly primitive/ancient societies. While DUKES provides a highly scholarly text with an extremely narrow focus (Europe between A.D. 392 and 814), this work has a historical emphasis that discusses the politics of witchcraft and the church in a seemingly unbiased (un-dualistic) manner.

—CAROL L. ROBINSON

See also Witch Hunts

Witchcraft/Wicca: Modern and Neo-Paganism

Adler, Margot, *Drawing Down the Moon: Witches, Druids, Goddess Worshippers, and Other Pagans in America Today,* New York: Viking, 1979

Harvey, Graham, and Charlotte Hardman (eds.), *Paganism Today,* London: Thorsons, 1995

Jones, Prudence, and Nigel Pennick, *A History of Pagan Europe,* London and New York: Routledge, 1995

Lewis, James R. (ed.), *Magical Religion and Modern Witchcraft,* Albany: State University of New York Press, 1996

Luhrmann, Tanya M., *Persuasions of the Witch's Craft: Ritual Magic in Contemporary England,* Cambridge, Massachusetts: Harvard University Press, and Oxford: Basil Blackwell, 1989

York, Michael, *The Emerging Network: A Sociology of the New Age and Neo-Pagan Movements,* Lanham, Maryland: Rowman and Littlefield, 1995

It is only since the 1980s that academic texts on neo-pagan movements have begun to appear. Even now the term "neo-pagan" remains problematic; it is welcomed by some within such movements, but rejected by others. For our purposes it is best viewed as an umbrella term, including within it a variety of "pathways," among which is modern witchcraft, also known as the Craft or Wicca. One of the elements that holds these pathways together is a recognition, in some way or other, of the female divine principle as an intimate part of the theophany of nature.

Only the first and last chapters of JONES and PENNICK's work relate directly to neo-paganism. However, the remainder of the text is valuable in tracing the history of the goddess in Europe in belief, rites, and iconography. This focus on the female deity serves to show the extent of neo-paganism's roots, stretching back through most European cultures to ancient history, and the processes by which the Judeo-Christian-Islamic hegemony has sought to replace the female with a male deity. This text establishes the contemporary relevance of neo-paganism's concern with the goddess in social, cultural, and ecological terms.

The best and most comprehensive introduction to American neo-paganism is provided by ADLER. She relates the evolutionary history of the various groups and indicates the commonalities and differences between them. As well as presenting an account of the origins of neo-paganism from a 1960s counterculture, she also illustrates the ways in which neo-paganist lifestyles and beliefs intersect with feminist, libertarian, and ecological movements. Her treatment leads her to the conclusion that neo-paganism's concern with the Earth Mother, and the centrality of the goddess, have empowered women and women's experience in ways not possible in New Age or traditional religions. The appendices give accounts of pagan rituals and details of where resources on neo-paganism might be obtained.

LUHRMANN's book is probably the most readable text on the Craft. She works as a "psychological anthropologist," having joined a number of covens and magical groups in the London area in the 1980s and recorded her experiences. She sensitively portrays the women and men she encounters, and the activities in which she participates. The strength of this work is in its ethnographic rigour and in its humanising of the members of Wiccan groups. These two elements are bonded together by the difficult task, given a materialist academic methodology, of attempting to explain why intelligent people practise and believe in magical rites. Luhrmann gives accounts of her membership in feminist covens, her participation in feminist rituals, and the techniques used in the Craft for communion with the goddess. This is a superb book and an invaluable resource, presenting primary liturgical texts and high-order qualitative accounts.

HARVEY and HARDMAN's volume brings together academics and practitioners of neo-paganism. The articles serve as a general introduction to neo-paganism, its defining characteristics and core theological constructs, a study of aspects of a variety of neo-pagan movements, and accounts of neo-pagan practices. There is a sustained exposition of beliefs and practices relating to the goddess in neo-paganism, and several chapters that are focused on women and the goddess. Consideration is given to the psychological and social effects on female believers of a female deity, the ways in which a feminist witchcraft empowers women, and the membership and organisational structures of neo-pagan groups. The multi-faceted nature of this work makes it an excellent resource for the study of neo-paganism.

Many of the contributors to LEWIS's book are academics who are also practitioners of neo-paganism. The articles are diverse, some discussing generic features of religion as they relate to neo-paganism (ethics, ritual, myth), and others narrating first-hand qualitative and experiential accounts. This multi-layered approach complements the acceptance of plurality that is at the heart of Wicca and also makes this a readable text that can be accessed at different points. For example, one might read about the process and components involved in the construction of a Wiccan ritual, or one could read about how neo-pagan festivals involve gender, sexuality, and dress-codes, and allow for the forging of "magical selves." There are entries on ethics and on neo-paganism's interface with Christianity, areas not covered in other texts. These build on the section detailing the witches' worldview and the centrality accorded to the goddess and the Earth Mother in the Craft and its theology. The book concludes with a survey of significant researchers on neo-paganism and an analysis of the characteristics of neo-pagans and Wiccans drawn from a variety of sources.

YORK presents a more thorough-going sociological analysis of neo-paganism than any of the preceding works. He is concerned with how the movements emerge, who joins them, their leading exponents, and their relationship with the New Age movement. He presents a substantial literature review and detailed accounts of the work of neo-pagan representatives, all of whom are women. In looking at differences between neo-paganism and the New Age movement, York sees a tendency for neo-paganism to use female metaphors for divinity, to be generally more feminist, more supportive of lesbians, and less inclined to use patriarchal, hierarchical, or binary symbol structures. A useful inclusion in this volume is statistical data relating to the size of groups, the gender, marital status, sexual orientation, education, occupation, and attitudes to abortion, of members from a selection of neo-pagan groups.

—ANDREW CLUTTERBUCK

See also Goddesses; Spirituality, Feminist

Witch Hunts

Barry, Jonathan, Marianne Hester, and Gareth Roberts (eds.), *Witchcraft in Early Modern Europe: Studies in Culture and Belief,* Cambridge and New York: Cambridge University Press, 1996

Hoffer, Peter Charles, *The Devil's Disciples: Masters of the Salem Witchcraft Trials,* Baltimore: Johns Hopkins University Press, 1996

Karlsen, Carol, *The Devil in the Shape of a Woman: Witchcraft in Colonial New England,* New York: Norton, 1987

Klaits, Joseph, *Servants of Satan: The Age of the Witch Hunts*, Bloomington: Indiana University Press, 1985
Levack, Brian P., *The Witch-Hunt in Early Modern Europe*, London and New York: Longman, 1987
Roper, Lyndal, *Oedipus and the Devil: Witchcraft, Sexuality, and Religion in Early Modern Europe*, London and New York: Routledge, 1994
Williams, Gerhild Scholz, *Defining Dominion: The Discourses of Magic and Witchcraft in Early Modern France and Germany*, Ann Arbor: University of Michigan Press, 1995
Willis, Deborah, *Malevolent Nurture: Witch-Hunting and Maternal Power in Early Modern England*, Ithaca, New York: Cornell University Press, 1995

Anthropologists and historians have demonstrated that nearly all pre-modern societies believed in witchcraft and made some attempts to control witches. It was only in early modern Europe and the English colony in Massachusetts, however, that these beliefs led to large-scale hunts and mass executions. This upsurge in witch trials, which occurred in waves from the late fifteenth through the seventeenth centuries, is often termed the "Great Witch Hunt" or the "Witch Craze." We have no way of knowing exactly how many people were executed—the best scholarly estimates are between 50,000 and 100,000 in Europe—but we do know that in most areas of Europe and in Massachusetts, the vast majority of those who were investigated, tried, and often executed for witchcraft were women.

Despite the predominance of women among the accused, much of the scholarship on the witch hunts has until very recently focused on other issues, primarily concentrating on the question of why the upsurge of accusations and trials occurred when it did. New concepts of demonology, new legal structures, and social, economic and political changes have all been investigated; some of these studies do not consider gender at all, or view it as of only minor importance. Both KLAITS's and LEVACK's books, on the other hand, include good discussions of the relationships between ideas about women and ideas about witchcraft, and of the actual role of women as both accused and very often accuser. Both of these are designed to be used in the classroom, and serve as reliable introductions in a field that has often produced some fanciful linkages. (Students need to beware of works that view the witch hunts as a move to wipe out knowledge of birth control, or describe witches as worshippers of a pre-Christian cult of Diana, or list the number of witches executed in the millions; none of these has been borne out by reliable historians.)

Older explanations of the witch hunts tended to privilege either intellectual or social explanations, but newer studies often combine these two in a more comprehensive cultural analysis, reflecting changes in historical scholarship more generally. The book by BARRY, HESTER, and ROBERTS includes 13 essays with this cultural emphasis, by some of the best-known contemporary scholars in the field, ranging widely across Europe (and the Spanish New World), some of which focus specifically on issues of gender, and some of which do not.

ROPER's book is also a collection of essays, all of them by the same author, which situates witch accusations within a more general religious, cultural, and symbolic context. Roper argues that many of the accused women actually regarded themselves as witches, but attributes this to fantasies that emerged in the long judicial interrogations. She uses psychoanalytical terminology and categories, for which she has been criticized, but she presents individual cases in ways that are both compelling and complex; more advanced students might be fascinated by some of the connections she draws.

Both Roper and, in more detail, WILLIS, use the actual language of witchcraft trials and other discussions of witchcraft to argue that malevolent motherhood was a much more common image than female sexuality in descriptions of the crime of witchcraft. Willis uses both nonliterary and literary texts, including William Shakespeare, and finds that while gentry-level and aristocratic texts often make reference to witches as enemies of God, in village-level discourse, witches were more often accused of introducing childlike demonic imps that brought sickness and death into another household. The accusers were often younger women, and Willis skillfully explores their actions within the context of neighborhood quarrels and household activities, rather than seeing such women simply as mouthpieces for patriarchal authority. Like Roper, Willis uses some psychoanalytical theory in her analysis, though this is primarily drawn from Melanie Klein rather than Sigmund Freud.

WILLIAMS also uses both literary and non-literary texts, this time from France and Germany rather than England, to uncover other female imagery linked to witchcraft. Accused of being bad mothers and satanic seductresses, many of those tried as witches were women who refused to become wives, preferring to be alone, or who were wives only part of the year, such as the women in the coastal areas of western Europe whose husbands were away fishing much of the time. Williams unearths one of the most novel explanations provided by a contemporary for why the witch hunts happened when they did; in the opinion of Pierre de Lancre, a French magistrate and witchhunter of the early seventeenth century, it was because demons and the devil had returned to Europe from the New World once Christian missionaries were there!

Apparently some demons remained in America, however, or so many of the residents of Salem, Massachusetts, believed, for in 1692 and 1693, hundreds of people in and around Salem were accused of witchcraft, and 20 were executed. This was the largest witch hunt in the

American colonies, and has been the focus of many books as well as several plays and movies. Because there are so many more records available for Salem than there are for most European witch hunts, studies can include very detailed analyses of personal and family relationships, and their social and economic setting. KARLSEN provides just that, exploring the demographic and economic bases of the Salem witch hunts using quantitative methods, but also analyzing Puritan ideas about witchcraft and about women. She sees witchcraft not only as shaped by ideology and social structures, but also as shaping these in turn. HOFFER focuses on social relationships and the dynamic of the trial itself. Like Roper and Willis, he uses some contemporary psychological theory, but he also takes a number of other factors into account, explicitly rejecting any monocausal explanations, whether socio-economic or psychological. Both Karlsen's and Hoffer's books would be useful texts for advanced undergraduates.

—MERRY WIESNER-HANKS

See also Witchcraft: Ancient

Wollstonecraft, Mary 1759–1797

British Writer

Conger, Syndy McMillen, *Mary Wollstonecraft and the Language of Sensibility*, Rutherford, New Jersey, and London: Fairleigh Dickinson University Press, 1994

Falco, Maria J. (ed.), *Feminist Interpretations of Mary Wollenstonecraft*, University Park: Pennsylvania State University Press, 1996

Ferguson, Moira, and Janet Todd, *Mary Wollstonecraft*, Boston: Twayne, 1984

Flexner, Eleanor, *Mary Wollstonecraft: A Biography*, New York: Coward, McGann and Geoghegan, 1972

Poovey, Mary, *The Proper Lady and the Woman Writer: Ideology as a Style in the Works of Mary Wollstonecraft, Mary Shelley, and Jane Austen*, Chicago: University of Chicago Press, 1984

Sapiro, Virginia, *A Vindication of Political Virtue: The Political Theory of Mary Wollstonecraft*, Chicago: University of Chicago Press, 1992

Sunstein, Emily W., *A Different Face: The Life of Mary Wollstonecraft*, New York: Harper and Row, 1975

Taylor, G.R. Stirling, *Mary Wollstonecraft: A Study in Economics and Romance*, London: M. Secker, and New York: Haskell House, 1911

Tomalin, Claire, *The Life and Death of Mary Wollstonecraft*, London: Weidenfeld and Nicholson, and New York: Harcourt Brace Jovanovich, 1974

Mary Wollstonecraft has been long thought of as a forerunner in the women's rights movement. Born into a time period where women were deemed subservient, Wollstonecraft broke down many of the boundaries established by her societal contemporaries and was decidedly egalitarian in her view of women and men. Her writings, particularly *A Vindication of the Rights of Woman*, reflected her objective to redistribute political and economic power equally between men and women. A woman whose life ended tragically short with suicide, Wollstonecraft wanted everything out of life and made every possible effort to achieve as much, particularly in her personal life. She has been credited as the mother of feminism, long before the women's movement came into being. Regardless of the labels given to her, there is much to be learned from the life and works of Mary Wollstonecraft.

CONGER resists the three primary classifications of Wollstonecraft—a daughter of Enlightenment, a forerunner of Romanticism, and a feminist—and takes a cumulative approach to understanding the woman and her works through a new definition of her relationship with the "language of sensibility." Conger attempts to explain these three distinctions and eliminate the paradoxes they create when juxtaposed through this more broad definition. Conger defines Wollstonecraft's personal life and her individual works through the language of sensibility and its fictions (metaphors, metonyms, and myths). While this book is written for a well-read, academic audience, it raises intriguing insights about who Wollstonecraft was and how her life and writing was affected by her time period and the societal norms of her surroundings. Citing several specific excerpts from her letters and examples from her works, Conger evaluates the use of language in its time period and the role it played in Wollstonecraft's life work.

FERGUSON and TODD explore each of Wollstonecraft's works chronologically, in an effort to explain the influences of her life and how they are imbedded in her writings. Perhaps most unique to this biography is the combined involvement of authors who have written other significant texts on Wollstonecraft, including two primary biographers Ralph Wardle, who is often credited with writing the first good modern biography of Wollstonecraft in 1951, and Emily Sunstein. Ferguson and Todd provide a superior overview, concise and well-researched, of the writings and life of Wollstonecraft.

Writing during the beginning of the women's movement in the 1970s, FLEXNER, a distinguished woman's rights historian, offers another historical context and interpretation of the life and work of Wollstonecraft, predominately from a feminist perspective. Flexner draws on sources that were not included in previous biographies, particularly letters, to explore the influences of Wollstonecraft, her challenges and adversities, and the cumulative works' relevance to the feminist movement.

While not solely focused on Wollstonecraft, POOVEY delves into an examination of three female writers, particularly how these three created ideology through the use of their styles. Viewing Wollstonecraft in relation to the well-chosen writers Shelley and Austen offers new information regarding how the preconceived notion of a lady produced female writers who struggled with the ambiguities of their work and their lives. Perhaps this book's greatest value is in placing the female writers within the context of women's issues without declaring them either feminist or antifeminist. Through the examination of these writer's works accompanied by a variety of substantial sources (books, diaries and letters, magazine articles, and novels), the observations presented here are acute and well-deserving of further examination and study.

A political scientist and scholar of women's studies, SAPIRO attempts to define the significance of *A Vindication of the Rights of Women* and other works two centuries later. Sapiro looks at Wollstonecraft through the context of feminist thought, but most uniquely, in relation to the history of political theory. Written in clear, accessible language, Sapiro believes that it is impossible to separate the individual life from the resulting work, and she therefore evaluates Wollstonecraft's writings and her life through the dimensions of both then and now. Without labeling her as one kind or another of political or feminist theorist, Sapiro explores the substance and relative political implications of her writings through extensive examples and comparative elements, which, in the end, grant a more current, fresh insight into the woman and her works.

An active participant in political reform herself, SUNSTEIN asks the question, "What kind of life should a woman ask for herself?" Through a detailed, well-researched biography, Sunstein explains how Wollstonecraft wanted it all—"career and family, independence and attachment, intellectual achievement and love"—and how these dichotomies are resonant in her life and work. Exploring the motivations and ambitions of the personal woman, Sunstein declares that "Wollstonecraft's existence was an attempt to make life conform to her needs, and her expectations and demands were so unrealistic as to be self-defeating" explaining that "she spent her life looking for a peace of mind that her own ambivalence made difficult." While Sunstein critiques and credits her biographical predecessors, she claims not to let these previous texts influence her current one, divining her own interpretations strictly from the events of Wollstonecraft's life and her works, both public and private.

TAYLOR's older book is a rare excursion into the interpretations of Wollstonecraft throughout history, an intriguing accompaniment to understanding the various interpretations of her life and works throughout the social history that followed. Taylor begins, "But it so happens that she is of doubled interest at the moment; for the turmoil which is expressing itself is on all sides today, under the general phrase of 'The Women's Movement,' could scarcely be more tersely summarized than in the words which Mary Wollstonecraft wrote during the eighteenth century." Perhaps one of the first biographical investigations into how the life of Wollstonecraft is reflected in her work, Taylor's book provides an enlightening glimpse into the historical context of her life and how it was interpreted in the early stages of the feminist movement.

TOMALIN utilizes several excerpts and passages from the writings of Wollstonecraft, as well as a wealth of basic historical information, to tell the story of Wollstonecraft and her life. While less objective than many of the other accounts—the text seems slanted more toward opinion—Tomalin utilizes not only the personal and public writings of Wollstonecraft, but also of individuals influential in Wollstonecraft's life. One of this biography's strengths is its ability to give context to the many individuals present in Wollstonecraft's life. This method works to give a broader scope to her position in society and the resulting influences of these people in her works.

FALCO's book encompasses many of the viewpoints previously expressed regarding Wollstonecraft, in essays from prominent scholars related to her work. Ferguson and Sapiro are two of the contributing essayists on this project, in which the titles range from "Wollstonecraft and Rousseau: The Gendered Fate of Political Theory" to "Women's Rights and Human Rights: Intersection and Conflict." Perhaps most intriguing is the final essay by Wendy Gunther-Canada, who reflects on the previous study and interpretation of Wollstonecraft in "'The Same Subject Continued': Two Hundred years of Wollstonecraft Scholarship." This is certainly a worthy addition to any study of Wollstonecraft.

—MELISSA HELLSTERN

See also Feminist Theory, Formative Works

Womanism

Cannon, Katie G., *Katie's Canon: Womanism and the Soul of the Black Community,* New York: Continuum, 1995

Sanders, Cheryl J. (ed.), *Living the Intersection: Womanism and Afrocentrism in Theology,* Minneapolis: Fortress Press, 1995

Townes, Emilie M. (ed.), *A Troubling in My Soul: Womanist Perspectives on Evil and Suffering,* Maryknoll, New York: Orbis, 1993

Walker, Alice, *In Search of Our Mothers' Gardens: Womanist Prose,* New York: Harcourt Brace Jovanovich, 1983; London: Woman's Press, 1984

Weems, Renita J., *Just a Sister Away: A Womanist Vision of Women's Relationships in the Bible*, San Diego, California: LuraMedia, 1988

Williams, Delores S., *Sisters in the Wilderness: The Challenge of Womanist God-Talk*, Maryknoll, New York: Orbis, 1993

In 1983, WALKER introduced the term "womanist" to feminist theory. Drawing from the black folk expression—"you acting womanish"—used by mothers to their inquisitive and willful daughters, she imbued the expression with collective and political identity. For Walker, a womanist is a black feminist or feminist of color who is pro-women, but who also cares about men and is committed to the liberation of all people. By introducing the term, she created a space for women of color to align themselves with an inclusive feminism that was neither white supremacist nor separatist. At the same time, she pressed white feminists to confront the ways in which racism and separatism kept many women of color from the women's movement. Walker's championing of a feminism that draws from and centers on the experiences of black women is embraced and pursued by many scholars. Yet, no group of scholars has more actively employed the concept of womanism than the growing network of black feminist theologians and womanist preachers.

One of the first to adopt the concept, WEEMS joins feminist biblical criticism—particularly the project of reconstructing the lives of ancient women—with the African-American oral tradition's emphasis on participatory story-telling to explore women's relationships in the Bible. Focusing on women's relationships with each other—as friends, sisters, in-laws, mothers, daughters, mistresses, and maids—Weems creatively reconstructs biblical passages to illuminate the possible motivations behind their struggles and triumphs with each other. Designed as a study guide for religious women, the nine chapters close with questions written to illuminate parallels between biblical and contemporary women, as well as to shed light on the intersections of race, class, gender, and religion.

Using the Old Testament story of Hagar as a point of departure, WILLIAMS pursues connections between the ancient woman and black women throughout U.S. history. Like Hagar, black women have faced and continue to deal with the legacy of slavery, forced motherhood, and homelessness. In addition, Williams argues, many black women have faced Hagar's "wilderness experience," in which a near-destruction situation leads to a life-saving encounter with God. The first part of the book explores these issues through an examination of social and religious history, literature, and music. Shifting emphasis and tone, the second part of the book engages black men involved in black liberation theology in "womanist god-talk," a discussion of theological methodology, doctrine, and ethics, and their relation to black women's lives. After addressing this group, Williams turns to white feminists and other feminists of color and opens a dialogue about differences and commonalities among feminist and womanist theological approaches. She discusses concepts such as virginity, patriarchy, and oppression.

TOWNES's collection reveals the breadth of interests and approach among womanist thinkers in the Christian Church. Her volume brings together fourteen womanist scholars and practitioners whose essays address the complexities of evil and suffering as they relate to the lives of African-American women. Sources as diverse as spirituals, folk sermons, slave narratives, spiritual autobiographies, and writings from the black woman's club movement are analyzed to uncover the ways black women have used the language of morals and ethics in their attempts to shape a humane social order. Other essays focus on the politics of contemporary black churches to show how they contain both liberatory and repressive elements. Contributor Frances Wood explores how African-American churches can perpetuate the suffering of black women by supporting misogyny and reinforcing internalized racism, and she closes her essay with a framework for change.

Christian social ethicist CANNON employs womanism as a methodological framework for challenging the religious canon. Using a "systemic analysis of race, sex, and class from the perspective of African American women in the academy of religion," she both critiques dominant religious scholarship for its collusion with racism and sexism, and presses the field to expand its concerns. In particular, she calls for analysis of the moral wisdom and agency of black women. Comprised of essays written over a decade, which meld personal narrative, history, folklore, literature, and biblical interpretation, Cannon is concerned with theorizing black women's religious consciousness and their work as moral agents from slavery to the present. Frequently drawing from black women's literature, particularly the work of Zora Neale Hurston, she uses this wellspring to map a tradition of womanist ethics and to encourage both its growth and analysis.

The essays in the collection edited by SANDERS explore relationships between womanism and Afrocentrism—particularly as delineated by Molefi Asante in his *Afrocentricity* (1988)—in the field of religion. Most of the writings are responses to an early 1990s call by Howard University's School of Divinity for work examining the intersections of Afrocentric and womanist perspectives. Divided into three sections, the essays grapple with the complexities of being black and female in the United States, examine implications of womanist and Afrocentric perspectives for biblical and literary analysis, and discuss teaching strategies that are consistent with womanist and/or Afrocentric thought. Divided about the intersection between the two perspectives, some of the authors point to sexism within Afrocentric thought, and are wary of womanist participation with it. Others believe that womanism is inherently Afrocentric, but that tensions exist because Afrocentrism relies on patriarchal ideas. Contributor Lorine Cummings captures this tension by stating, "Afrocentrists are not womanist, but womanists are Afrocentric." Still others focus on the ways African-American women have utilized what might now be called Afrocentric ways of knowing and acting throughout U.S. history.

—LISA GAIL COLLINS

Woman's Christian Temperance Union

Blocker, Jack S., Jr., *"Give to the Winds Thy Fears": The Women's Temperance Crusade, 1873–1874*, Westport, Connecticut and London: Greenwood, 1985

Bordin, Ruth, *Frances Willard: A Biography*, Chapel Hill and London: University of North Carolina Press, 1986

———, *Woman and Temperance: The Quest for Power and Liberty, 1873–1900*, Philadelphia: Temple University Press, 1990

Cook, Sharon Anne, *"Through Sunshine and Shadow": The Woman's Christian Temperance Union, Evangelicalism, and Reform in Ontario, 1874–1930*, Montreal and Buffalo, New York: McGill-Queen's University Press, 1995

Rose, Kenneth D., *American Women and the Repeal of Prohibition*, New York and London: New York University Press, 1996

Tyrrell, Ian, *Woman's World/Woman's Empire: The Woman's Christian Temperance Union in International Perspective, 1880–1930*, Chapel Hill and London: University of North Carolina Press, 1991

The public image of the Woman's Christian Temperance Union (WCTU) as a collection of narrow-minded cranks obsessed with alcohol consumption has undoubtedly contributed to the paucity of studies of the organization. Unlike female suffragists, women temperance advocates attracted comparatively little attention until the publication of Bordin's two works in the early 1980s. Yet the WCTU pioneered in politics, becoming the first sizable organization controlled exclusively by women. As the nucleus for the development of a distinct women's middle-class culture, the WCTU deserves much credit for bringing women into public life. The Union, particularly the American and World's branches under the dynamic administration of Frances Willard, attacked social, economic, and political evil from all directions and at all levels. The works cited will be useful to scholars in the fields of religion, history, and alcohol and temperance studies.

Formed in 1874, the WCTU emerged from a grassroots movement of 1873–74, known as the Woman's Temperance Crusade. BLOCKER argues in his exhaustive study that the success of the Crusade, the largest women's movement up to its day, shows the willingness of nineteenth-century women to protest the conditions facing them in a patriarchal society. Threatened individually or collectively by male drinking, women by the tens of thousands in the United States enlisted in this effort to peacefully shut down saloons. The Crusade sparked the birth of the WCTU by showing women the results that were possible with effective organization and powerful leadership. Bordin believes that women were attracted to the Crusade for the same reasons that they would later join the WCTU—their special vulnerability at the hands of (male) abusers of alcohol, the congeniality of temperance to the doctrine of separate spheres, and the acceptability of temperance work to many Protestant churches.

While the Crusade relied upon prayer and moral suasion to effect temperance reform, Blocker and Bordin agree that the American WCTU appealed to women more optimistic about political action. In the WCTU, women were encouraged to do everything except march upon liquor dealers. BORDIN (1990) points out that the Union effectively used political influence and employed a range of sophisticated political weapons to achieve primarily legislative aims. Both of her books, examining the American branch during the nineteenth century, are essential reading for students of the Union. Bordin redefined WCTU members as early feminists pushing a broad social agenda. In this book, the only full-length study of the nineteenth-century American WCTU, she identifies its members as following a model of gender-conflict. Deeply distrustful of men's ability and willingness to protect women, the Union leadership sought power in order to guarantee an improvement in the situation of women. Yet they did not dispute women's separate sphere, arguing for suffrage and temperance on the grounds of "home protection." In her biography of the public life of Frances Willard, BORDIN (1986) theorizes that this political maverick led American women so successfully because she did not appear to challenge society's accepted ideals. Willard sought to remake the world to benefit women, yet phrased her demands in such a manner as to unite those with both liberal and conservative views of women's proper place.

COOK, in her work on the Canadian WCTU, also concludes that the Crusade helped crystallize the methodology and organizational structure to be adopted by the Union. Particularly useful for bringing the Canadian Union out of the shadow of its American sister, Cook's work looks at the effect of Protestant evangelical ideals on women. She traces Canadian women's involvement with a religion-based feminism, and suggests that evangelicalism's emancipating theology originally empowered women and caused them to approach temperance as a moral and religious issue, not simply a social one. The history of the Ontario WCTU, in her view, demonstrates that the tradition of feminine piety created discontent in women. By promoting female moral superiority and righteousness, the WCTU did not encourage an unquestioning acceptance of clerical and male authority, but spread dissatisfaction with a society that apparently rejected the primacy of the home and family. In the case of the Canadian Union, evangelical piety provided self-identity, collective consciousness, and organizational strategies for women. Cook's analysis of Letitia Youmans, described as a Canadian Frances Willard, is particularly helpful in explaining the different paths followed by the two North American WCTUs. More decentralized in structure, more evangelical in ethic, and less inclined to fight legislative battles, the Canadian branch had a distinct identity from its American mother.

As TYRRELL makes clear, no organization has ever done more than the World's WCTU to promote the emancipation of women around the globe. The Union embraced an international and occasionally ecumenical vision that included a critique of western materialism and imperialism. But, at the same time, its mission inevitably promoted the Anglo-American cultural practices and Protestant evangelical beliefs that were deemed morally superior by the WCTU leaders. Tyrrell also considers, from a comparative perspective, the links between feminism, social reform, and evangelical religion in Anglo-American culture that made it so difficult for the WCTU to export its vision of a woman-centered mission to other cultures.

ROSE's work, although seriously flawed in its treatment of the introductory stages of women's temperance activism, is the best book-length study of the twentieth century WCTU in the United States to date. The class composition of the American WCTU leadership slipped steadily downward during the 1920s, and Rose submits that many of the middle- and upper-class women who, in a different generation, might have joined the Union, instead enrolled in the women's groups devoted to the repeal of Prohibition. Both the WCTU and the groups who opposed it, he concludes, supported a maternalist philosophy, and asserted women's higher moral authority, but in a society increasingly enamored of personal liberty, the restrictions on the freedom to drink promoted by the WCTU no longer appealed to great masses of women.

—CARYN E. NEUMANN

Woman's Club Movement

Blair, Karen J., *The Clubwoman as Feminist: True Womanhood Redefined, 1868–1914*, New York: Holmes and Meier, 1980

Croly, Jane Cunningham, *The History of the Woman's Club Movement in America*, New York: Henry G. Allen, 1898

Martin, Theodora Penny, *The Sound of Our Own Voices: Women's Study Clubs, 1860–1910*, Boston: Beacon Press, 1987

Scott, Anne Firor, *Natural Allies: Women's Associations in American History*, Urbana: University of Illinois Press, 1992

Watts, Margit Misangyi, *High Tea at Halekulani: Feminist Theory and American Clubwomen*, Brooklyn, New York: Carlson, 1993

Wedell, Marsha, *Elite Women and the Reform Impulse in Memphis, 1875–1915*, Knoxville: University of Tennessee Press, 1991

Wells, Mildred White, *Unity in Diversity: The History of the General Federation of Women's Clubs*, Washington, D.C.: General Federation of Women's Club, 1953

Wood, Mary I., *The History of the General Federation of Women's Clubs for the First Twenty-Two Years of Its Organization*, New York: General Federation of Women's Clubs, 1912

The roots of the Woman's Club movement can be found as early as colonial times in the informal philanthropic associations of women working together toward a common end. During the Civil War, women in both the North and South worked in focused groups on various war efforts. After the war many of these groups continued and, combined with the somewhat increased amount of leisure time for middle-class women and a desire for self-improvement, the club movement burgeoned and grew. The groups took a number of forms, from charitable groups whose activities involved working to provide kindergartens, libraries, and educational programs, to social, literary, and study groups that promoted self-education, to more politically focused groups where women discussed current events. These groups became very powerful, leading eventually to political action organizations that fought for suffrage for women and to other powerful organizations such as the Woman's Christian Temperance Union, which eventually brought about the Prohibition laws.

Eventually it became apparent that the clubs needed a national federation so that they could combine efforts under a single umbrella. Thus, in 1890, the General Federation of Woman's Clubs was formally organized. The General Federation was, however, primarily a white women's association. A parallel organization for African-American women grew alongside it, and in 1896 the National Association of Colored Woman's Club was formed. Both organizations exist today.

No study of the Woman's Club Movement can be undertaken without looking at CROLY's book. Jennie Croly was the president of Sorosis, the largest woman's club in New York City. Her book is a thorough (over 1,000 pages) chronicle of the formation, bylaws, membership, and activities of the federation and of local groups. Interesting in itself is the desire on Croly's part to document the history of an organization that had only been in existence for eight years. Even then she was well aware of the historical importance of the movement, for she dedicates the book to "Twentieth Century Women" in order for them to understand the struggles of those in the nineteenth century.

Fourteen years later the history was updated in WOOD's book. The introduction to this book attempts to place the federation in a historical context. Indeed the analysis begins with the dawn of time. By the middle of the eighteenth century, middle-class women had more leisure and did not need to be at home so much. Wood emphasizes particularly the study club, which was somewhat sarcastically known as the "middle-aged woman's university."

WELLS's book updates the history of the federation. The book is particularly interesting for its perspective on club activities during World War II. Wells also details some of the legislation that the federation worked for on a national level, particularly after women got the vote and the federation became more of a political force. Some of these included statehood for Alaska and an equal rights amendment. Wells talks about the growth of foreign branches of the federation, which proliferated after World War I.

BLAIR's analysis focuses on the movement in the late nineteenth century. She sees the literary clubs as a way for women to gain autonomy, which then led to an increasing awareness of the potential to gain power through collective action. She sees the woman's club movement as an important historical force that shaped the course of women's lives from that time forth.

SCOTT's book takes a more comprehensive look at women's organizations in general. The book is divided into two sections, pre- and post-1866. Scott discusses the several strands of organizations that eventually came together to form the "Woman's Club Movement." The book is heavily illustrated.

MARTIN emphasizes the educational aspects of the club movement. Her study examines how the movement touched women's educational aspirations, and how the desire to learn was passed down to the daughters of club women, and this, in turn, led to the increase of college-educated woman around the turn of the century.

Besides these works, there are numerous studies that focus on the histories of local groups, such as those by WATTS and WEDELL. These and others have excellent introductions that put the local club histories into the context of the broader movement.

—ROBIN S. LENT

See also Black Woman's Club Movement

Women at Work during World War II, United States

Campbell, D'Ann, *Women at War with America: Private Lives in a Patriotic Era,* Cambridge, Massachusetts: Harvard University Press, 1984

Gluck, Sherna Berger, *Rosie the Riveter Revisited: Women, the War and Social Change,* Boston: Twayne, 1987

Hartmann, Susan M., *The Home Front and Beyond: American Women in the 1940s,* Boston: Twayne, 1982

Honey, Maureen, *Creating Rosie the Riveter: Class, Gender and Propaganda during World War II,* Amherst: University of Massachusetts Press, 1984

Milkman, Ruth, *Gender at Work: The Dynamics of Job Segregation by Sex during World War II,* Urbana: University of Illinois Press, 1987

Rupp, Leila J., *Mobilizing Women for War: German and American Propaganda, 1939–1945,* Princeton, New Jersey: Princeton University Press, 1978

Wise, Nancy Baker, and Christy Wise, *A Mouthful of Rivets: Women at Work in World War II,* San Francisco: Jossey-Bass, 1994

In the 1970s, social historians began to examine the impact of World War II on the status of women and gender roles in the United States. The earliest work argued that the roles women played in the war years created a favorable environment for re-assessing and re-defining women's traditional roles. More recent work has challenged this view, arguing that the war did not radically change the role of women. According to some scholars it actually increased the focus on domesticity for women, ushering in the era of the "feminine mystique."

Many books re-examining women at work in the war years began to appear in the 1980s. HARTMANN's book was one of the first. This text deals not only with women's paid employment during wartime, but also examines the experience of women in the military, in education, in politics, in the family, and under the law. She argues that the war did not produce dramatic change but did sow seeds that would bear fruit in the 1960s. Among the reasons she identifies for the undermining of the radical potential of the war experience is the desire for a return to "normalcy" after a decade of Depression and then a decade of wartime disruption. The economic revival of the 1940s made it possible for working-class white men to support a family on one wage.

CAMPBELL's book also stresses continuity when examining the war years. Drawing on a rich data base that includes surveys and polls taken during the 1940s, she stresses women's own desire for domesticity and a return to the private sphere. Particularly interesting is her discussion of the failure of government-supported day-care facilities. She argues that while the war altered specific activities of women and changed individual women, it did not alter women's interpretation of their primary role. In this view, the legacy of the war years is the 25 years of intense domesticity, not the rebirth of feminism.

MILKMAN's study is based on two industry-specific historical case studies. Although she focuses on the automobile industry and the electrical manufacturing industry during the war years, she places the changes in job assignments in historical context, examining how "men's" jobs came to be so labelled. She too finds continuity between the decades before the war and the experience of women after the war. The pattern of women's employment in these industries changed only for the duration of the war and then returned to pre-war patterns. Indeed, she notes, the striking thing about women's employment is how little patterns of employment have changed—even into the 1980s. Milkman argues that occupational sex-typing is "deeply rooted in industrial structures and can only be understood historically." The sexual division of labor that develops, and the gender ideology that justifies and supports that division, are resistant to change even when it would be profitable to do so.

Studies relying on oral histories also began to appear in the 1980s. GLUCK's book presents 10 oral histories of former California aircraft workers, framed by a thoughtful introduction and conclusion. Her conclusion, based on 45 oral histories, also finds continuity in pre-war and post-war experience for most workers, but she emphasizes the change that women themselves reported in their attitudes toward work and their pride in "holding their own with men." Although all the authors reported here are sensitive to class, race, and ethnic differences in the experiences of female workers and do their analysis accordingly, it is in the oral histories that these differences find their fullest expression. Gluck emphasizes the important impact that even temporary lowering of racial barriers had on women of all races. She concludes that women's wartime experiences did not create a social transformation, but that they played a vital role in the future process of redefinition. She argues that the mothers' wartime experiences may have "helped foster the development of a working-class feminist consciousness among working women."

WISE and WISE's book is a thematically organized history of women's experiences during the war. Drawing on nearly 150 interviews with women (including one of the authors) who worked in all types of jobs during the war, the book presents an interesting array of experiences. It is a particularly useful source of classroom materials, but the authors do not provide much analysis of their information, preferring perhaps to let the women speak for themselves.

Also of interest is the use of propaganda to encourage women to do their patriotic duty and go to work for the war effort. "Rosie the Riveter" was a creation of the wartime media. HONEY's fine book is a study of the use of propaganda to create a myth of Rosie that has lasted well into the post-war era. She describes both the efforts of the Office of War Information to create a favorable picture of the housewife turned war worker, and the effort to send Rosie home after the war. An earlier work by RUPP is a similarly excellent comparative study in the use of propaganda. Both the United States and Germany manipulated images of womanhood to encourage women's paid work, while upholding traditional gender role definitions.

—PAMELA J. NICKLESS

See also British Women during World War II

Women's History Movement

Davis, Angela Y., *Women, Race, and Class,* New York: Random House, 1981; London: Women's Press, 1982

Degler, Carl N., *At Odds: Women and the Family in America from the Revolution to the Present,* New York: Oxford University Press, 1980; Oxford: Oxford University Press, 1981

DuBois, Ellen Carol, and Vicki L. Ruiz (eds.), *Unequal Sisters: A Multicultural Reader in U.S. Women's History,* New York: Routledge, 1990

Flexner, Eleanor, *Century of Struggle: The Woman's Rights Movement in the United States,* Cambridge, Massachusetts: Belknap Press of Harvard University Press, 1959

Kelly, Joan, *Women, History, and Theory: The Essays of Joan Kelly,* Chicago: University of Chicago Press, 1984

Kessler-Harris, Alice, *Out to Work: A History of Wage-Earning Women in the United States,* Oxford and New York: Oxford University Press, 1982

Lerner, Gerda, *The Majority Finds Its Past: Placing Women in History,* Oxford and New York: Oxford University Press, 1979; Oxford: Oxford University Press, 1981

Scott, Joan W., *Gender and the Politics of History,* New York: Columbia University Press, 1988

Groups of feminist scholars began in the late 1960s to consciously define themselves by a particular choice of subject—women—and created the field of women's history. The readings listed above are an attempt to identify the major trends of historical inquiry in the field since the late 1950s. The readings document feminist historians' attempts to change both the theory and practice of history. With the publication of FLEXNER's book, which focused on the suffrage movement, and the birth of the second women's movement in 1963, scholarship in women's history has experienced an unprecedented explosion of research and publication.

LERNER, the recognized mother of women's history, writes of the prevailing interest of feminist historians in groups that lack power. She also notes the problems associated with constructing a conceptual framework of women's history. She calls for a paradigm shift that would challenge traditional scholarship. Her 1969 pathbreaking essay, "New Approaches to the Study of Women in American History," is the first essay reprinted in the book.

KELLY's book is a collection of essays begun in the 1970s. The essays trace her efforts to create a Marxist feminist consciousness and an analysis that would make social relationships of the sexes as fundamental a category of historical thought as class. Kelly's exuberance led her to believe that the findings of feminist scholars would restore women to history and create a wholly new vision of history, especially in terms of the meaning of major events and periodization.

Concern with women's private sphere led many feminist historians to look to family history, which also dealt primarily with the private rather than the public sphere. DEGLER attempts to locate women's history within the field of family history. His work became a standard text, but feminist historians quickly moved away from family history, because it continued to make men and men's affairs the main component of their analyses.

Historical scholarship during the 1970s was also concerned with the movement of women into the public sphere, and KESSLER-HARRIS's book is an example of this concern. She attempts to pinpoint the structural determinants of change in women's status. While many historians studied a variety of means by which women "entered" the public sphere—education, profession, and reform movements—the largest number, however, including Kessler-Harris, focused on labor. She, like other liberal and Marxist feminist scholars, believed women would achieve emancipation only if they achieved financial independence and fought against capitalism. Kessler-Harris therefore provides a history of female wage labor and explores its interrelationship with economics and family lives.

By the early 1980s, many feminist historians began to advance a new case for the importance of difference. Many African-American, Hispanic, Native American, and Asian-American women, including DAVIS, did not believe that they were a part of the mainly white middle-class women's history that had been written. Davis's book attempts to address this issue from an African-American point of view. DuBOIS and RUIZ claim that women's history has replaced the "universal man" of U.S. history with the "universal woman," and they advocate a biracial or multicultural approach that will allow historians to explore conflict among women as well as between men and women. They advocate "multiple narratives."

The latest challenge women's historians face is from feminist scholars who are shaping a new subfield called "gender history." SCOTT, a poststructuralist, believes that all that remains is the representation of gender in discourse. Her work is entirely theoretical, and she discounts the earlier work of feminist historians, not for its lack of cultural diversity, but for its philosophical shortcomings.

Feminist historians have not transformed the standard narrative, but they have contributed to the restoration of women to history.

—PATRICIA McNEAL

See also Oral History

Women's International League for Peace and Freedom

Adams, Judith Porter, *Peacework: Oral Histories of Women Peace Activists*, Boston: Twayne, 1990

Alonso, Harriet Hyman, *Peace as a Women's Issue: A History of the U.S. Movement for World Peace and Women's Rights*, Syracuse, New York: Syracuse University Press, 1993

Bacon, Margaret Hope, *One Woman's Passion for Peace and Freedom: The Life of Mildred Scott Olmsted*, Syracuse, New York: Syracuse University Press, 1993

Bussey, Gertrude, and Margaret Tims, *Pioneers for Peace: Women's International League for Peace and Freedom, 1915–1965*, London: Allen and Unwin, 1965

Foster, Carrie A., *The Women and the Warriors, the U.S. Section of the Women's International League for Peace and Freedom, 1915–1946*, Syracuse, New York: Syracuse University Press, 1995

Foster, Catherine, *Women for All Seasons: The Story of the Women's International League for Peace and Freedom*, Athens: University of Georgia Press, 1989

Randall, Mercedes M., *Improper Bostonian: Emily Greene Balch, Nobel Laureate, 1946*, New York: Twayne, 1964

For some women, the mid-nineteenth and early twentieth centuries marked a significant move into the national and international political sphere. Women created associations, campaigns, and conferences and traveled globally for leisure, missionary, political, and educational purposes. This movement of, for the most part, educated middle-class women into the public political arena presents important questions for historians of women and gender. Literature on the Women's International League for Peace and Freedom (WILPF) illuminates themes applicable to this general development. The WILPF, created out of the 1915 response of women to World War I, provides a rich opportunity to study, among other developments, female support networks, the politicalization of women, women's social movements, and relationships of women to violence.

BUSSEY and TIMS provide a highly detailed organizational and political history of the founding, international proceedings and peace missions, and policies of the international WILPF through the period of World War II. WILPF's various responses to major global conflicts, like the Ethiopian War, Manchurian crisis, events in Palestine, advent of fascism, outbreak of World War II, and the Korean War are detailed. Bussey and Tims's work, although not analytical, underscores the broad scope of the organization's work, and is the only book-length treatment of it as an international entity. It provides important information on international WILPF leaders and the creation and demise of numerous national sections. Bussey and Tims illuminate struggles among national sections over various external and internal issues, including pacifism, nationalism, leadership, and membership.

CARRIE FOSTER covers the same time period as Bussey and Tims, but her sole focus is the U.S. section of the WILPF. Her treatment, more analytical, critiques the WILPF women's progressive, reformist, pacifist approach to domestic and international military and economic conflicts and repression. In Foster's treatment of the U.S. section during the inter-war years, she details organizational, educational, lobbying, and reform efforts in relation to U.S. economic imperialism in Haiti, Nicaragua, and Mexico; naval expansion and big business involvement in the burgeoning munitions industry; and the rise of repression at home (against organized labor, African-Americans, and pacifists) and the spread of fascism abroad. WILPF's role in 1930s coalition campaigns to keep the United States from entering World War II is discussed in detail. Throughout this study, Foster situates WILPF at the intersection of the history of the peace movement, the first-wave women's movement, and Progressive reformers. Foster's work contributes to our understanding of the development and transformation of Progressive-era female social reformers as they moved into the post-suffrage political era.

ALONSO contextualizes and problemitizes the history of the U.S. section of WILPF more than any other works currently published. The first few chapters treat the development of a "feminist peace consciousness" out of the abolitionist and suffragist traditions starting in the mid-nineteenth century. Alonso sees a continuity of feminist thought and action during the inter-war years, which are also the years connecting the first and second waves of the women's movement. In this time period, which until recently historians considered lacking in feminist activity, Alonso argues that feminist peace activists maintained feminism, because they educated women to be political agents, they maintained female support and political networks, and they used theories and strategies developed during the first wave of feminism. In chapter three, Alonso analyzes Jane Addams's (first international president of WILPF) influence on the burgeoning women's peace movement in comparison to the influence of the more conservative Carrie Chapman Catt. Alonso, in chapter five, presents a thorough treatment of the affects of McCarthyism on WILPF, the only women's peace organization to survive World War II. Organizational struggles with issues of race, class, religion, and ethnicity receive important attention, as do debate over the new radical feminism that emerged in the late 1960s. While WILPF is not the only organization of "suffragist peace activists" Alonso studies, WILPF figures into all of the chapters. The appendix contains a comprehensive list of women's peace associations since 1820 and a chronology of the Metropolitan New York Branch of the WILPF. The bibliography is very useful.

CATHERINE FOSTER's book, thematically and analytically, is an offspring of the 1980s flourishing of grassroots cultural feminist women's peace action. The first half updates Bussey and Tims's chronicle of organizational policies and responses to global issues. The second half profiles eighteen international WILPF leaders based on oral histories conducted by Foster. Collectively, they tell rich stories of women's political coming of age. A central focus of the profiles are WILPF leaders' views on feminism—whether they identify as feminists; the role of feminism in the current and past work of WILPF; and the debate over women's "inherent" peace-mindedness. As critical text, the interviews emphasize a divergence of opinions on the nature versus nurture debate. Other themes include nonviolence, internationalism, movement building, and women and aging. National sections represented include Israel, Lebanon, Costa Rica, Japan, the United States, Sri Lanka, and Austria, among others. Read against one another, the profiles propose multiple points of entry and philosophies on the relationships of women to politics, leadership, nurturance, and community building. This book is useful for gaining a sense of the current status of international WILPF sections. ADAMS's collection of oral histories of U.S. female peace activists over 60 years of age features many WILPF members. The women interviewed represent diverse racial and economic backgrounds and WILPF branches across the country.

Randall and Bacon provide insight into the lives of two generations of "new women" who helped shape and direct the organization for its first 50 years. Emily Greene Balch, the first international secretary general of WILPF, a U.S. section president during the 1930s, and a Nobel peace prize recipient in 1946 at the age of 78—personified the first generation new woman. RANDALL, through use of diaries, organizational records, and Balch's published writings, illuminates her development as a teacher, scholar, and international stateswoman in the areas of peace arbitration, immigration, and nationalism. Balch is best known and rewarded as a tireless thinker on and advocate of transnationalism. Randall chronicles more than analyzes Balch's life work. Balch's role and association with and in the WILPF and other organizations, her dealings with proponents of more radical 1920s responses to war, and her socialism are pursued. Her leisure and political world travel, literary interests, and familial responsibilities are a subtext of this biography.

BACON's biography of Mildred Scott Olmstead, WILPF member for 70 years, is a significant addition to the literature because it weaves together Olmstead's public and private lives. Born in 1890, Olmstead struggled with the social conservatism of her Smith College classmates and lingering Victorian expectations of women's roles as wife and mother. Although she married, Olmstead maintained a lifelong relationship with a college crush, Ruth Mellor, who lived, for a time, with the Olmsteads and accompanied them on all their vacations. Olmstead served as a WILPF staff member for 60 years. Remembered for her sometimes overpowering effort to change WILPF from a small elite organization to a large one with popular appeal, Olmstead's general organizational leadership and some of her more spectacular achievements are highlighted. The latter includes a 1934 trip to fascist Germany to check on the welfare of members, missions in 1930 and 1960 to the Soviet Union, and civil rights work in the 1950s and 1960s. Bacon's treatment of Olmstead's reflections on the strategies and styles of the young upstarts of the New Left and the women's liberation movement contextualizes Alonso's treatment of WILPF during this period.

—MELINDA PLASTAS

See also Peace Movements

Women's Liberation Movement

Bambara, Toni Cade, *The Black Woman: An Anthology*, New York: New American Library, 1970

Evans, Sara, *Personal Politics: The Roots of Women's Liberation in the Civil Rights Movement and the New Left*, New York: Knopf, 1979

Firestone, Shulamith, *The Dialectic of Sex: The Case for Feminist Revolution*, New York: Morrow, 1970; London: Cape, 1971

Friedan, Betty, *The Feminine Mystique*, New York: Norton, and London: V. Gollancz, 1963

Hole, Judith, and Ellen Levine (eds.), *Rebirth of Feminism*, New York: Quadrangle, 1971

Morgan, Robin, *Sisterhood Is Powerful: An Anthology of Writings from the Women's Liberation Movement*, New York: Random House, 1970

In the late 1960s and early 1970s, interest in feminism, which had deteriorated after the battles for women's suffrage were won, began to revive. Women who had been active in the great social movements of the 1960s, such as the civil rights movement, the anti-Vietnam War movement, and the New Left, began to see that, even within these social causes, their own rights as women were being denied. Out of this atmosphere of activism was born a new wave of feminism, which, during its early years, was called the women's liberation movement.

MORGAN's collection is described as itself an activist project, as it broke traditional norms, having been "conceived, written, edited, copy-edited, proofread and designed by women," as she claims in the introduction. Important primary documents are contained—a statement on birth control by a black women's liberation group in New York, early theories of female sexuality, a statement on the politics of orgasm, Mary Daly's early discussion of women and the Catholic Church, an analysis of experiments regarding women in China, looked to as a model for liberation, and an essay on Mexican-American women. Excerpts from the SCUM manifesto, a statement by Chicago Women's Liberation, the Redstockings Manifesto, WITCH documents, and a photo section of WITCH demonstrations, women's liberation marches, and a nude sit-in protesting a *Playboy* representative on campus round this out as one of the best examples of the spirit of the outbreak of the women's liberation movement in the United States.

BAMBARA's early collection points the way for researchers into the roots of this movement in the United States. Alice Walker's "The Diary of an African Nun," and poetry by Audre Lorde and Nikki Giovanni, among other of these collected writings, indicate a strong African-American women's presence at these early stages of the movement. She discusses the involvement of all the authors in the struggle for liberation from the "exploitative and dehumanizing system of racism, from the manipulative control of a corporate society, and liberation from the constrictive norms of mainstream culture." Hence the collection belies later critiques of the early movement as purely white and middle class. Bambara's own criticism of Leroi Jones's *The Great White Hope*, and texts such as "Poor Black Women's Study Papers" and "A Historical and Critical Essay for Black Women in the Cities," by Pat Robinson, indicate that many active women were thinking about racism at this time in the early dialogue that created second-wave feminism. Views on the black revolution in America, black romanticism, the black university, the pill, contradictions of black pride, and the application in Harlem of revolutionary techniques from the Battle of Algiers, are all useful for showing the extent of black women's struggle with what Frances Beale calls the "double jeopardy" of being black as well as female. Also cogently exposed and discussed are "Mississippi politics," and the politics of motherhood and survival on welfare.

Although later criticized for rejection of pregnancy and motherhood as innately oppressive, and for lauding test tube babies as the ultimate in women's liberation by technology, FIRESTONE's book was a significant early text of the women's liberation movement. Based on historical research, and grappling with European progressive thinkers, she first posited the notion of "sex class," thus overcoming the dichotomy that located oppression either in one's sex or in one's class position. She broke boundaries in thinking and was a forerunner in breaking taboos about what was possible to question. For example, Firestone first posited the theoretical perspective that the connection between sex and racism was deeper than societal consensus was able to contemplate. The work is useful for showing the active, engaging critiques of the times in which the women's liberation movement was coming to voice.

Challenging what would later become revisionist history of the early women's liberation movement, EVANS looks to early cracks in the mold by going south and tracing the Southern white woman's position in a Southern black movement. She sees Black Power as a catalyst for feminism, and traces the reassertion of the personal in the struggle to define women's role in the black liberation movement. Looking at forms of women's activism in the pre-women's movement climate, in class and race-based politics, she shows how the dam broke, and how in that context, women's liberation with "personal politics" developed. Valuable primary documents include the Student Non-Violent Coordinating Committee (SNCC) position paper on women in the movement, "Sex and Caste."

HOLE and LEVINE introduce and discuss the historical precedents of the women's liberation movement. Furthermore, they offer feminist analysis of the period's ideas on issues such as biological differences, technology, sex-role stereotyping, the image of women in media, professional status of women working in the media, media coverage of the women's movement, child care, resistance to the women's movement, education, women in the professions, abortion, and the church. Valuable historical documents are included, such as the 1848 Seneca Falls declaration and a 1969 New York Radical Feminist manifesto on the politics of the ego. Hole and Levine have also brought together a photography section of shots of early consciousness-raising groups, sit-ins and demonstrations. The volume as a whole is excellent for grounding later revisions of this history in the experiential testimony of this stage of the movement.

FRIEDAN wrote what was widely hailed as the book that started the women's movement. This book named "the problem that has no name," and exposed the fallacy of the "happy housewife," by documenting the very real crisis in women's identity. The book contains one of the earliest and most vocal critiques of Sigmund Freud. Friedan interviewed housewives, and used their responses to critique and condemn the consumer-based ideology of the times. Later biographers have traced Marxist roots in Friedan's thinking, and pointed to her activism in the civil rights movement as well. Certainly her criticism of the time that housework takes set the basis for later discussions of housework as consumption work, leading some to posit the notion of wages for housework as an activist programmatic demand. Hence, this book has become a standard for tracing emergent feminist thinking, and for laying the groundwork for the incipient movement for women's liberation.

—BATYA WEINBAUM

See also Feminism: Liberal; Feminism: Radical; Feminist Movements: Twentieth Century

Women's Organizations

Barrett, Jacqueline K. (ed.), *Encyclopedia of Women's Associations Worldwide,* London and Detroit: Gale Research, 1993

Brennan, Shawn, and Julie Winklepleck, *Resourceful Woman: Contacts and Connections on Politics, Arts, Kinship, Sexuality, Health and Spirituality,* Detroit, Michigan: Visible Ink Press, 1994

Ferree, Myra Marx, and Patricia Yancey Martin (eds.), *Feminist Organizations: Harvest of the New Women's Movement,* Philadelphia: Temple University Press, 1995

National Council for Research on Women, *NWO: A Directory of National Women's Organizations,* New York: National Council for Research on Women, 1992

Remington, Judy, *The Need to Thrive: Women's Organizations in the Twin Cities,* St. Paul: Minnesota Women's Press, 1991

Scott, Anne Firor, *Making the Invisible Woman Visible,* Urbana: University of Illinois Press, 1984

While there was a surge in growth of women's organizations as women asserted their individuality in the 1970s, the history of women uniting to create societal change is a long and extensive one, filled with examples of how these unions have affected our local and global society in a wide variety of areas, including, but not limited to, health, civil rights, justice, education, culture, housing, and care for the elderly and children. Through shared vision and the collaborative process, women have provided for the needs of people, raised questions as to right versus wrong, and led crusades for the betterment of humanity as a whole.

BARRETT provides a comprehensive reference that gives names, addresses, and summaries of thousands of women's organizations, both in the United States and elswhere. This directory is a comprehensive tool for the study of current women's issues, and a great resource for further secondary research. The entries are listed first by continent and secondly by country but are also indexed by subject area to make any area of interest accessible.

BRENNAN and WINKLEPLECK have put together a directory that shows organized women in a wide range of areas, including aging, arts, community, education, global issues, health, history, kinship, politics, sexuality, spirituality, sports and recreation, violence against women, work, and youth. Here, readers and researchers can find easy access to more information about any number of women's collaboratives in their state or on a national scale.

FERREE and MARTIN provide a detailed overview of the social changes attributed to the power of women's organizations and then discuss the impact of the feminist ideal through these organizations' movements in the realm of politics. The references cross all cultural and geographical boundaries and illuminate their affects not only on society, but also on the women involved. Discussions range from explaining the most effective tactics and policies of women's organizations to evaluating the impact of popular media and its resulting effects. In Part IV, Ferree and Martin attempt to define what constitutes social movement success and cite specific examples relating to this broad question. Perhaps one of the book's greatest strengths is that, through the examples and subject headings, a history of wars waged and the resulting societal impact forms in the reader's mind. The extensive bibliography also provides more than adequate secondary source materials on a wide variety of topics.

The NATIONAL COUNCIL FOR RESEARCH ON WOMEN has created a comprehensive listing of women's groups, networks, and organizations in the United States. Each entry includes a brief abstract of the organization, including a description of the organization, areas of focus, services offered, publications, target population, and scheduled organization meetings. In order to qualify for entry, each organization must be non-profit, national in scope, and hold a primary focus on women and women's issues. While providing a well-researched assimilation of the most recent and up-to-date information on women's organizations, this listing also provides an extensive, source-filled bibliography for further study.

REMINGTON examines women's organizations, primarily those with roots in Minneapolis and St. Paul, with an overriding focus on the infrastructure of women's organizations as a whole. By examining the power and societal effects of some of the oldest organizations in the United States, Remington describes the collaborative process, the impact that women have when they stand together for an issue, the difficulties inherent in a changing infrastructure combined with a changing society, and the resulting need to remain cohesive or to disband.

Through a collection of essays, the social historian and pioneer in women's history, SCOTT, emphasizes the important role that voluntary societies have played in the history of American women. Scott argues for the importance of a comprehensive social women's history. Arranged by subject and chronologically, the reader is able to gain access to the three main themes of the text, particularly the examples of individual women as integral to reconstructing the past, the role of the education of women, and the opportunities provided by, and impact of, women's voluntary associations throughout history.

—MELISSA HELLSTERN

Women's Rights Convention, Seneca Falls, New York

Banner, Lois W., *Elizabeth Cady Stanton: A Radical for Woman's Rights*, Boston: Little Brown, 1980

Bernhard, Virginia, and Elizabeth Fox-Genovese (eds.), *The Birth of American Feminism: The Seneca Falls Woman's Convention of 1848*, St. James, New York: Brandywine Press, 1995

Davis, Angela Y., *Women, Race and Class*, New York: Random House, 1981; London: Women's Press, 1982

Dubois, Ellen, *Feminism and Suffrage: The Emergence of an Independent Women's Movement in America, 1848–1869*, Ithaca, New York and London: Cornell University Press, 1978

Flexner, Eleanor, *Century of Struggle: The Woman's Rights Movement in the United States*, Cambridge, Massachusetts: Belknap Press of Harvard University Press, 1959

Griffith, Elisabeth, *In Her Own Right: The Life of Elizabeth Cady Stanton*, New York and Oxford: Oxford University Press, 1984

Gurko, Miriam, *The Ladies of Seneca Falls, The Birth of the Woman's Rights Movement*, New York: Macmillan, 1974

Marilley, Suzanne M., *Woman Suffrage and the Origins of Liberal Feminism in the United States, 1820–1920*, Cambridge, Massachusetts: Harvard University Press, 1996

The first woman's rights convention took place in Seneca Falls, New York in 1848. Although contemplated by Elizabeth Cady Stanton and Lucretia Mott at the World Anti-Slavery Conference in London in 1840, preparation for the convention itself took only one week. An advertisment was placed in the Seneca Falls newspaper on July 14, 1848 for a meeting to be held in the Wesleyan Methodist Chapel on July 19 and 20 to discuss women's rights. Yet on such short notice, 300 attendees were motivated to appear. This convention is used as a convenient shorthand to date the beginning of organized feminism in the United States, although there had been individual feminists in the United States and Europe before this time. The uniqueness of the Seneca Falls convention owes to the manifesto written by Elizabeth Cady Stanton, which crystallized feminist demands, and to the reaction it drew from women all over the country who held similar conventions in the following years. Invoking Seneca Falls means more than just that one occasion.

GURKO shows the antecedents of the convention from Mary Wollstonecraft to the abolition movement, and how they led to women's rights. She writes an entire chapter on the immediate precursors to the convention and a chapter on the convention itself. She continues with the Civil War, the schism in the women's movement, and the eventual reconciliation of the women who had been divided by the struggle over the Fifteenth Amendment to the United States Constitution. The book ends with the deaths of Stanton and Susan B. Anthony. This is a readable work that serves as an indispensable starting place for an understanding of nineteenth-century feminism.

FLEXNER'S book covers much of the same territory in the beginning but goes much farther and carries the thread to its final conclusion with the achievement of suffrage. Hers too is required reading for anyone interested in the first women's rights movement and the ramifications of that movement in the early twentieth century. Her emphasis is on both the development of the movement and its crowning achievement. It is a more complex and detailed work than Gurko's, including the early involvement of women in labor organizations as well.

Another fruitful area for information on the Seneca Falls Convention can be found in biographies of Elizabeth Cady Stanton. BANNER shows how Stanton was the major philosophical and rhetorical force behind the convention. It was Stanton's idea to use the Declaration of Independence for the manifesto of the convention."The Declaration of Rights and Sentiments," as it was called, was read time and time again at other conventions. It was Stanton who favored advocacy of woman suffrage, much to the chagrin of her husband and to the trepidation of Lucretia Mott. Banner illustrates in many ways what a radical Stanton was.

Another biographer of Stanton, GRIFFITH, goes into more detail about the convention itself and discusses the convention both in the life of Elizabeth Cady Stanton and in the history of feminism. She sees the convention as a major turning point in Stanton's life, insofar as it coalesced her thinking about women's rights in the "Declaration of Rights and Sentiments," and because it set Stanton's career on the path of feminist leadership. This is a most useful work because of its clear explication of the Seneca Falls Convention.

A recent work edited by BERNHARD and FOX-GENOVESE is unique in its approach. It has an introduction that gives the basic facts of the convention, followed by primary documents that give texture to the surrounding times. The first section of readings is devoted to discourse prior to the convention; the second part contains readings about the Seneca Falls convention itself; and the third part consists of selections from 1849–56 all taken from *The Lily,* a periodical published by Amelia Bloomer in Seneca Falls, as well as a selection that includes readings from succeeding conventions between 1848 and 1855. Most of the readings have a brief introductory note from the editors.

DUBOIS focuses on the brief span from Seneca Falls in 1848 to the split in the women's movement that occurred in 1869 over the adoption of the Fifteenth Amendment, which prohibited states from using race as a barrier to the elective franchise. Dubois sees this fissure as a bitter experience that ultimately led to a more highly developed, organized, and radical movement than would have been the case if women had easily won the vote. This book is essential reading for the political intricacies of this painful moment in women's history.

DAVIS calls the Seneca Falls Declaration "the articulated consciousness of women's rights at midcentury," a white middle-class women's consciousness that did not include working-class women and slave women. Davis devotes two chapters to the racism of the early women's movement. The first criticizes the Seneca Falls convention for not including the needs of working-class or slave women in its manifesto, and the second excoriates the stance of Stanton and Anthony when they demanded that the Fifteenth Amendment include women as well as men. This is an important critique of the early feminist movement, and Davis discusses fully the positions of the leaders of the abolition movement after the Civil War.

MARILLEY takes it for granted that the leaders of the first women's rights movement would be elite, educated, and white. Only those women would have the confidence to begin such a movement. Marilley's book is about suffrage. In considering the meaning of suffrage for women, she begins with its origins in the liberal feminism of Stanton and the other women of the antislavery movement. She analyses the "Declaration of Rights and Sentiments" from a political point of view and traces the movement's philosophical bends and turns from Seneca Falls to the Nineteenth Amendment in a new and sophisticated way.

In all these accounts of the Seneca Falls convention, there is no disputation of the facts. The accounts are similar, but the interpretations vary greatly. Each author puts her perspective on this most important marker in feminist history. By reading all the accounts and seeing the event from many different vantage points, one can begin to appreciate the impact of this hastily convened meeting, which provoked strong opposition as well as imitation.

—BONNIE L. FORD

See also Feminist Movement, Abolitionist Origins of; Feminist Movements: Nineteenth Century

Women's Studies: General Works

Aaron, Jane, and Sylvia Walby (eds.), *Out of the Margins: Women's Studies in the Nineties,* London and New York: Falmer Press, 1991

Arnot, Madeleine, and Kathleen Weiler (eds.), *Feminism and Social Justice in Education: International Perspectives,* London and New York: Falmer Press, 1993

Bowles, Gloria, and Renate Duelli Klein (eds.), *Theories of Women's Studies,* Berkeley: University of California Press, 1980; London: Routledge amd Kegan Paul, 1983

Cosslett, Tess, Alison Easton, and Penny Summerfield (eds.), *Women, Power and Resistance: An Introduction to Women's Studies,* Buckingham and Philadelphia: Open University Press, 1996

Hinds, Hillary, Ann Phoenix, and Jackie Stacey (eds.), *Working Out: New Directions for Women's Studies,* London and Washington, D.C.: Falmer Press, 1992

Stone, Lynda (ed.), *The Education Feminism Reader,* London and New York: Routledge, 1994

Books in the field of women's studies tend either to examine the discipline by looking at its parameters, methodologies, politics, and practices or by offering an overview of the material one would expect to find in a women's studies course—particularly an introductory one. The books discussed here mostly fall into the first category. Since the early 1970s, when the first women's studies courses appeared in the United States, there has been a huge proliferation in the number of courses available. Recently, discussion has concentrated on the meaning and function of these courses and the part they play in the academy and in women's lives. Are they about getting women credentials? Are they important for raising consciousnesses? Do they have a different approach to knowledge, to power? What is their role within the wider movement for women's liberation? These are some of the questions dealt with in the following texts.

BOWLES and KLEIN's book is pivotal in the area of feminist education. It is comprehensive, covering the autonomy/integration debate, the relationship between academic feminism and the women's movement, and feminist research and pedagogy. It addresses the political implications for women of traditional epistemologies, which necessitate the separation of the objective and the subjective, and ask where such notions leave a discipline like women's studies, which has as its very raison d'être the understanding that the enquirer cannot be separated from her enquiry, that knowledges are partial, and that knowledge has a liberating potential. At issue in many of the essays in the book is the construction of a body of knowledge about women, which is for women. Thus, research methodologies are discussed, as is the standing of such a body of knowledge within a patriarchal institution like a university. Bowles and Klein also examine the classroom environment in which women are empowered to "see through" patriarchal discourse and to construct their own version of the truth.

AARON and WALBY offer a broad introduction to some of the issues confronting feminist educators in the 1990s. The book is divided into four sections, each dealing with a key issue for women's studies practitioners. The first section, "Women's Studies Today," looks at the breadth and depth of women's studies teaching in Europe—not just in universities but also in adult education. Following this is "Women's Studies and the Feminist Movement," in which the contributors tackle some of the important questions for a discipline that arose from a social movement and, as some would argue, answers to it. The third section, "Working with Diversity," investigates the issues of racism in women's studies, lesbianism, and the international flavour of feminism in terms of their meaning for those who seek unity of purpose and methodology. The final section summarizes the influence that women's studies, and feminist theory more generally, has had on other academic disciplines.

HINDS, PHOENIX and STACEY's book is part of the same series as Aaron and Walby's, and covers a similar range of issues. These are "The Politics and Practice of Women's Studies," "Commonalities and Differences," "International Feminisms," and "Theories and Methods." There are some very intriguing pieces of writing here—all have the backdrop of the politically conservative 1990s and show an awareness that, although feminist theory and practice is constantly developing, it does so under threat of erasure. There is a chapter on men in women's studies, which poses questions such as whether men should teach feminist courses, and whether they should be allowed in as students. Some chapters look at issues that cut across gender, such as disability, race, and sexuality. The focus then moves outside the west to examine feminist perspectives in development theory, women's rights in Muslim countries, and women's studies in eastern Europe. Finally, the contributions focus on the ways in which the discipline produces itself—the epistemologies and methodologies that render it different from mainstream academic disciplines.

ARNOT and WEILER's collection of essays looks at education in Australia, Britain, New Zealand, and the United States from a feminist perspective. Although obvious similarities exist among these nations—economically they might all be described as "First World"—sexual and racial relationships are diverse. The book's perspective is that education—whether in a primary school, a university, or an adult education setting—provides an environment where groups struggle for power. It covers, then, the role of teachers, pupils, academics, and teacher trainers—seeing education as both a contested arena and one where feminists must make their mark if they are not to be consumed by "malestream" philosophies and philosophers whose purpose it is to control and discipline.

STONE gathers together an impressive collection of articles originally published in journals that have been key to the development of feminist education. They deal with issues of self and identity, education and schooling, knowledge, curriculum and instructional arrangement, teaching and pedagogy, and diversity and multiculturalism. Through the selected articles it is possible to trace changes in thought over a number of years and to see the development of particular ways of conceptualizing problems in education.

COSSLETT, EASTON, and SUMMERFIELD give readers an excellent example of a text perfectly suited to any introductory course in women's studies. Their book is written in an engaging style (by a number of people) and covers the social organization of gender relations, the cultural representation of women, gender and social identity, and women and political change. It is a comprehensive book that covers issues such as religion, the visual arts, and ecofeminism. For those working in modern environments, it is also extremely useful to see a text that places ethnicity and race issues at centre stage. These topics are not only dealt with on their own, but are integral to each chapter.

—KATE PRITCHARD HUGHES

Women's Studies: Introductory Works

Buikema, Rosemarie, and Anneke Smelik (eds.), *Women's Studies and Culture: A Feminist Introduction*, London and Atlantic Highland, New Jersey: Zed, 1995

Cosslett, Tess, Alison Easton, and Penny Summerfield (eds.), *Women, Power and Resistance: An Introduction to Women's Studies*, Buckingham and Philadelphia: Open University Press, 1996

Freeman, Jo (ed.), *Women: A Feminist Perspective*, Mountain View, California, and London: Mayfield, 1975; 5th revised edition, 1995

Gunew, Sneja Marina (ed.), *Feminist Knowledge: Critique and Construct*, New York and London: Routledge, 1990

Hughes, Kate Pritchard (ed.), *Contemporary Australian Feminism*, Melbourne: Longman Chesire, 1994; 2nd revised edition, Melbourne: Longman, 1997

Jackson, Stevi (ed.), *Women's Studies: A Reader*, New York and Hemel Hempstead: Harvester Wheatsheaf, 1993

Madoc-Jones, Beryl, and Jennifer Coates (eds.), *An Introduction to Women's Studies*, Oxford and Cambridge, Massachusetts: Basil Blackwell, 1996

Richardson, Diane, and Victoria Robinson (eds.), *Thinking Feminist: Key Concepts in Women's Studies*, New York: Guilford Press, 1993; published in Britain as *Introducing Women's Studies: Feminist Theory and Practice*, London: Macmillan, 1993

The rapid development of women's studies programs internationally over the last two decades has sponsored a dynamic period of writing and publishing on related topics. There are now numerous general introductions to the field of women's studies available, and they encompass a broad range of perspectives and disciplinary standpoints. Many are sufficiently comprehensive to provide the basis in themselves for an introductory course on women's studies and some of the more popular works have reappeared in revised and updated editions. The following list represents only a small cross-section of the works currently available.

COSSLETT, EASTON, and SUMMERFIELD provide one of a number of available collections designed for use in first-year undergraduate women's studies courses. The book serves to introduce students both to the idea of women's studies as a field of interdisciplinary endeavour, and to a series of key analytical concepts. The book is divided into four parts, each containing essays by various contributors: the social organisation of gender relations; the cultural representation of women; gender and social identity; and women and political change. These parts are linked through a common focus on questions of women, power, and resistance. Tailored appropriately to the early undergraduate level, individual essays succeed in introducing often quite complex ideas through clear and accessible terminology. Each essay also contains sections listing questions and further exercises, as well as recommended reading. This collection distinguishes itself by its ability to expose students to an exciting range of issues within a coherent framework of inquiry.

In a similar vein is the book by MADOC-JONES and COATES, accurately described by the editors as an introductory "taster," rather than a comprehensive overview of feminist concerns. The book centres around women's lives, offering students a range of analytical and theoretical tools with which to examine them. Each of its themed chapters maps a different aspect of women's lives (for example, growing up, girls and schooling, understanding sexuality) and uses extracts from novels, poems, and historical and sociological works, combined with thoughtful commentary and carefully designed exercises to encourage students to reflect on and document their own histories and experiences using the conceptual frameworks offered. More directed than many works of its kind, this textbook offers a sound basis both for independent study and for more interactive classroom learning.

JACKSON provides one of a number of readers designed for use in undergraduate women's studies programs, although more advanced students wishing to familiarise themselves with particular issues would also no doubt find this work a useful starting point. Arranged around 14 key themes including feminist social theory, cross-cultural perspectives on women's lives, sexuality, women and the law, and feminist literary criticism, the book offers extracts of varying lengths from important works by key scholars and theorists in those areas. Each section is accompanied by a brief introductory essay outlining the central issues and debates and a list of suggested further reading. This reader is especially useful for introducing students to the diversity and complexity of modern feminist thought.

Now in its fifth edition, the collection by FREEMAN has been an especially popular work, possibly because it is one of the most lively and comprehensive introductory works available. This edition is arranged in seven parts covering body politics; relationships, family and the life cycle; work and occupation; words and images; institutions of social control; feminism in perspective; and feminism and diversity. Each part contains up to six separate essays representing different disciplinary standpoints and reflecting on different aspects of the chosen theme. Among the topical issues addressed are body image, sexuality and sexual harassment, labour and workplace issues, the effects of advertising and the media, and diversity among women. Considerable effort is made both to historicise issues and to link them to contemporary legal and policy debates in the U.S. context. New emphases in the fifth edition are the history of feminism as a social movement, and critiques of dominant, white, middle-class feminist perspectives.

The second, recently revised edition of the book by HUGHES directs itself to the impact of feminism in the Australian context but has wider applications too. Specifically designed for introductory women's studies programs, this collection of essays begins by outlining some of the contemporary debates surrounding the politics of feminism in Australia and overseas. The following 12 chapters deal in detail with a broad range of issues such as the ideology of the family, changing perceptions of gender roles, sex and sexualities, working women, gender and justice, women's health care, and ecofeminism. As the book introduces students to the discourses and institutions that structure women's lives, considerable emphasis is placed upon recognising diversity among women and among feminist theories. Overall, the collection succeeds in presenting complex ideas and concepts in an accessible and meaningful way for students encountering them for the first time.

RICHARDSON and ROBINSON's book is organised in a similar fashion to that by Hughes. It opens with two essays examining the nature of contemporary women's studies, taking particular note of how questions surrounding racial and cultural difference and feminist pedagogy have reshaped the area in recent years. The 12 essays that follow are characterised by the editors as attempting to provide an overview of past, present, and future developments in feminist knowledge and theory and include contributions by leading British women's studies practitioners such as Mary Maynard, Stevi Jackson, and Jackie Stacey. Broad, introductory accounts of topics such as violence toward women, sexuality and male dominance, feminist literary criticism, popular culture, motherhood, reproduction, and women's health conclude with short, usefully annotated lists of further reading. While key concepts are presented clearly and concisely, this volume is arguably best suited to slightly more advanced undergraduate students.

BUIKEMA and SMELIK take a different approach than the other titles listed, by examining the impact of feminist thought on a wide range of academic disciplines. Produced by staff of the women's studies program at the University of Utrecht, a leading European program, the collection provides an overview of the full range of contemporary feminist theories, including detailed coverage of the equality/difference debate, and the impact of postmodernism on feminist thought. Individual chapters then examine feminist interventions in the fields of linguistics, literary theory, popular culture, history, film theory, art history, theatre studies and musicology, psychoanalysis, semiotics, and black criticism. The volume concludes with a section on suggested student exercises, a glossary, and a bibliography. This work would be of particular interest to those teaching in women's studies and feminist cultural studies programs with an emphasis on contemporary theory.

Another volume with a strong theoretical orientation is that by GUNEW, which developed out of the women's studies program at Deakin University in Australia and is broadly international in its scope and application. Originally intended to be used in conjunction with its companion volume *A Reader in Feminist Knowledge* (1991), also edited by Gunew, this text has developed considerable popularity as an independent work. It is arranged in four parts: feminist knowledge, contemporary theories of power and subjectivity, discourses of definition, and feminist interventions. Each part contains a number of introductory essays by well-known theorists and women's studies practitioners, including Elizabeth Grosz and Renate Klein, and covers topics such as sexual difference, psychoanalysis and feminism, debates surrounding essentialism, feminist philosophy, radical feminism, feminism and religion, and theories of subjectivity. Individual essays conclude with detailed notes and recommendations for further reading on each topic. This work is particularly valuable for demystifying contemporary feminist theories and is recommended for both undergraduate and advanced students wishing to gain a general familiarity with key theoretical concepts.

—MARYANNE DEVER

Woodhull, Victoria 1838–1927

American Activist

Brough, James, *The Vixens: A Biography of Victoria and Tennessee Claflin*, New York: Simon and Schuster, 1980

Johnston, Johanna, *Mrs. Satan: The Incredible Saga of Victoria C. Woodhull*, New York: Putnam, and London: Macmillan, 1967

Marberry, M.M., *Vicky: A Biography of Victoria C. Woodhull,* New York: Funk and Wagnalls, 1967
Sachs, Emanie, *"The Terrible Siren": Victoria Woodhull (1838–1927),* New York: Harper and Brothers, 1928
Underhill, Lois Beachy, *The Woman Who Ran for President: The Many Lives of Victoria Woodhull,* Bridgehampton, New York: Bridge Works, 1995

Victoria Woodhull can best be described as one of the most controversial American women of the nineteenth century. The first woman to run for President of the United States, in 1872 on the Equal Rights Party ticket, Woodhull was both fearless and reckless in her pursuits and her publicly-voiced opinions. By advocating free love, romance without the restrictions imposed by marriage, Woodhull created a tremendous uproar. By printing an expose of the extra-marital affair of the Reverend Henry Ward Beecher, the most popular clergyman of the day, with one of his parishioners, she created an even bigger uproar. Arrested by the anti-vice crusader Anthony Comstock for publishing the Beecher story in her *Woodhull and Claflin's Weekly,* Woodhull eventually served time in jail while awaiting trial on obscenity and libel charges. Woodhull's image provoked such strong emotions that Thomas Nast, America's most popular editorial cartoonist, drew her for *Harper's Weekly* as a harpie with black wings. Nast called her "Mrs. Satan" and the label stuck despite Woodhull's legal victory against Comstock, her contributions to the woman suffrage movement, her immense success as a stockbroker on Wall Street, and her later marriage to a British nobleman. Such a colorful individual has proved to be an irresistible target for biographers.

SACHS researched her book when many of Woodhull's associates were still living. Based on oral history interviews, newspaper accounts, and court records, her biography is an invaluable sourcebook for any study of the life of Woodhull. Sachs was able to talk with the men and women who knew Woodhull, and she was the first to track down the facts of Woodhull's life. Unfortunately, she missed a few points: Sachs neglects to report Woodhull's role in the suffrage movement, despite her domination of four national suffrage conventions, held in 1871 and 1872. This biography is a biased account by an author who does not maintain a scholarly distance from her subject and who concludes that Woodhull's life was worthless. The weaknesses of the work are largely related to its age. First published in 1928, this book does not benefit from the feminist scholarship of later eras. Sachs accepts unflattering descriptions of Woodhull's contemporaries, such as Catherine Beecher, at face value and is unable to incorporate gender analysis. In a sexist turn, Sachs presents Woodhull's ambition as a fatal character flaw. Additionally, her prose often takes on the purplish hue that was popular in that day.

Heavily based on Sachs's work, JOHNSTON's biography is a highly readable account of the lives of Woodhull and her equally notorious younger sister Tennessee Claflin, and it contains the same flaws as the earlier book. Designed for a popular audience, the writing style of this book is reminiscent of that of a novel. Johnston incorporates quite a bit of dialogue into her story, all of it drawn from memoirs and newspaper reports, and maintains a tone of historical impartiality. This would be, however, an excellent reading choice to introduce young adults to the life of Woodhull.

MARBERRY spins a narrative of Woodhull's life from her days in New York City to her sojourn in England, from 1870 to 1927. Written more in the style of a novel than as a serious study of a woman's life, Marberry's book is entertaining but not particularly analytical. Woodhull's life is not set in historical context and the movements with which she was involved, free love and Comstockery, are not explored in any depth.

BROUGH's book is a semi-fictionalized history of the lives of Woodhull and Claflin. The author creates dialogue and puts thoughts into the minds of his subjects to create a book that often reads like a cheap novel. As its less-than-enlightened title indicates, this is not a particularly good work of history and it is best left alone on the bookshelf. An added damning factor is that the book is not even particularly well-written.

UNDERHILL has written the best available biography of Woodhull. The quality of the book is such that it may be many years before it is surpassed. Based on a wealth of archival material, Underhill's book entertainingly explores Woodhull's life from beginning to end and includes feminist historical analysis along the way. In a particularly interesting inclusion, Underhill explores why Woodhull has been dismissed from most histories of the suffrage movement and concludes that she has been poorly served by the elitist memoirists who were intent upon disassociating themselves from Woodhull's numerous scandals. A extensive bibliography finishes this excellent work.

—CARYN E. NEUMANN

Woolf, Virginia 1881–1941

British Writer

Bell, Quentin, *Virginia Woolf: A Biography,* 2 vols., London: Hogarth Press, and New York: Harcourt Brace, 1972
Caramagno, Thomas C., *The Flight of the Mind: Virginia Woolf's Art and Manic-Depressive Illness,* Berkeley: University of California Press, 1992
Caws, Mary Ann, *Women of Bloomsbury: Virginia, Vanessa, and Carrington,* New York: Routledge, 1990

DeSalvo, Louise, *Virginia Woolf: The Impact of Childhood Sexual Abuse on Her Life and Work,* London: Women's Press, and Boston: Beacon Press, 1989

Hanson, Clare, *Virginia Woolf,* London: Macmillan, and New York: St.Martin's Press,1994

Hussey, Mark (ed.), *Virginia Woolf and War: Fiction, Reality, and Myth,* Syracuse, New York: Syracuse University Press, 1991

Laurence, Patricia Ondek, *The Reading of Silence: Virginia Woolf in the English Tradition,* Stanford, California: Stanford University Press, 1991

Marcus, Jane, *Virginia Woolf and the Languages of Patriarchy,* Bloomington: Indiana University Press, 1987

Moore, Madeline, *The Short Season between Two Silences: The Mystical and the Political in the Novels of Virginia Woolf,* Boston: Allen and Unwin, 1984

Since the 1970s, criticism of Virginia Woolf has widened from the previous vision of a writer concerned only with high art, to one that acknowledges and studies Woolf as a writer with deeply felt and widely resonant views about the world.

Even before her death from suicide in 1941, Virginia Woolf's life engaged readers. BELL, Woolf's nephew, details that life in his biography. The first volume looks at Virginia's upbringing, the death of her beloved mother, sister Stella, and brother Thoby, and her efforts to educate herself. The second volume explores her adult life, complete with her breakdowns, her marriage to the Jewish Leonard Woolf in an increasingly anti-Semitic time, and the onslaught of World War II, during which Woolf and her husband planned to commit suicide if England were invaded.

DeSALVO's book, controversial when it first came out, focuses in more depth on the details Bell describes, and on the treatment afforded girls, the license given men, and the failure of heterosexual bonds. DeSalvo looks at Leslie Stephen's turning to his stepdaughter Stella for affection after the death of his wife; the similar recourse to Virginia's sister, Vanessa, by Stella's husband after she too dies; and the sexual abuse of Virginia and her sister by their half brother, George Duckworth. DeSalvo traces the influence of these events on Woolf's efforts to find a language that could express what was deemed inexpressible, and on her imagery.

CARAMAGNO takes exception to DeSalvo's study, arguing that it presents a simplistic neurotic model of Woolf's life and art as constrained by childhood trauma. These objections clear the ground for his own reading of the interconnection between Woolf's mental states and her work. His interdisciplinary "neurobiography" tries to determine from Woolf's and her husband's descriptions of her mental states what the clinical cause could have been. Manic-depression, or bipolar affective disorder, Caramagno argues, both accounts for the states of mind and symptoms which Woolf describes, and more accurately fits her great sensitivity to the world around her and the acuity of her thought. Trauma or neuroses, Caramagno argues, would taint all of Woolf's work, whereas the episodic nature of manic-depression allows us to read her as a self-aware, perfectly sane, but sensitive writer.

Because of Woolf's position as a pioneer in feminist thinking, critics have tended to respond to her quite personally. This response CAWS turns to good account in her presentation of, and innovative, personally-based, impressionistic reaction to the three women of her title. She traces their relationships, and the texture of their daily lives as found in their journals and letters to each other, and uses this background to illuminate their writing and painting. Caws sees all three women as struggling against convention to develop domestic relationships that would feed their emotional desires without swallowing them up into angels of their hearths.

MARCUS uses her study of Woolf in a different way. Collecting essays spanning the decade before the book' s publication, she invites readers to chart her growth as a feminist critic against her culturally-based readings of Woolf's essays, novels, and life. Particularly striking is her resurrection, in "The Niece of a Nun," of Caroline Stephens, Virginia's aunt. Marcus sees Stephens's influence not only in the vision of a woman writing at a table in *The Waves*, but in the happiness of characters such as Mrs. Dalloway in her nunlike attic bedroom. Stephens's negotiation of patriarchal bonds and the desire to accomplish meaningful work in the service of humanity, Marcus convincingly argues, gave Woolf a pattern and even a vocabulary to articulate her own similar vision.

Unabashedly feminist is HANSON's volume, which adopts a theoretical reading for the published writing and the personal experience central, as Hanson claims, to women's work. Woolf's early novels, Hanson argues, support the sense that women are excluded from patriarchy's symbolic order, and must therefore subscribe to the notion of the feminine-as-difference, in order to undercut patriarchal definitions. But her later work reflects discomfort with an unproblematic definition of the female as opposition, perhaps recognizing, in a proto-post structuralist way, that such a creation simply reaffirms the other term of the opposition. Instead, Hanson points out, Woolf's later work constructs a world in which meaning is flexible, fluid, and unfixed—in contrast to the fixed stability patriarchy tries to impose on the world. This little book is a readable and useful introduction to the increasingly theoretical treatments of Woolf's writing.

MOORE takes as her subject the opposition of Woolf's spiritual beliefs and the reality she depicts in her novels. The former is grounded in an appreciation of nature, and establishes a transcendent utopic ideal: pantheistic, egalitarian, and humane. Against this Moore posits the life experienced by Woolf's characters, and from which they must retreat: oppressive and hierarchical. Moore sets her analysis in the context of Woolf's own political activism: her public lectures and support for social reform.

In contrast, LAURENCE's work is the most literary of those here surveyed: Laurence positions Woolf's effort to write about silence in the milieu of "interiority" in the English literary tradition, equating it with the ongoing project of articulating and redefining psychological or mental states. Laurence also compares Woolf's work to contemporaneous studies by Freud and others, as well as to surrealist painters. She explores what silence means for Woolf—presence, rather than absence. That presence, Laurence convincingly argues, then subverts any "realist" effort of the novels, underscoring in its unknowability the always-already contextual and constructed quality, not just of the language which conveys these silences, but of reality itself.

HUSSEY's collection of 14 essays on Woolf and war go further than Laurence. They argue that Woolf not only implicitly, but explicitly, and throughout her work, from *The Voyage Out* to the more obvious *Three Guineas* and *Between the Acts*, challenged the notions of reality, and the constructions of oppositional codes that inexorably lead to battle.

—VICTORIA CARCHIDI

Work

Bradley, Harriet, *Men's Work, Women's Work: A Sociological History of the Sexual Division of Labour in Employment*, Minneapolis: University of Minnesota Press, and Cambridge: Polity Press, 1989

Davidson, Marilyn J., and Cary L. Cooper (eds.), *Working Women: An International Survey*, Chichester and New York: John Wiley, 1984

Dubeck, Paul J., and Kathryn Borman (eds.), *Women and Work: A Handbook*, New York and London: Garland, 1996

Dunn, Dana (ed.), *Workplace/Women's Place: An Anthology*, Los Angeles, California: Roxbury, 1997

Farley, Jennie, and Alice Hanson Cook (ed.), *Women Workers in Fifteen Countries*, Ithaca, New York: ILR Press, Cornell University, 1985

Kahn-Hut, Rachel, Arlene Kaplan Daniels, and Richard Colvard, *Women and Work: Problems and Perspectives*, New York and Oxford: Oxford University Press, 1982

Kemp, Alice Abel, *Women's Work: Degraded and Devalued*, Englewood Cliffs, New Jersey: Prentice-Hall, 1994

Kessler-Harris, Alice, *Out to Work: A History of Wage-Earning Women in the United States*, Oxford and New York: Oxford University Press, 1982

Lloyd, Cynthia B., and Beth T. Niemi, *The Economics of Sex Differentials*, New York: Columbia University Press, 1979

Reskin, Barbara, and Irene Padavic, *Women and Men at Work*, Thousand Oaks, California: Pine Forge, 1994

Stromberg, Ann H., and Shirley Harkess (eds.), *Women Working: Theories and Facts in Perspective*, Palo Alto, California: Mayfield, 1978

Ward, Kathryn (ed.), *Women Workers and Global Restructuring*, Ithaca, New York: Cornell University Industrial and Labor Relations Press, 1990

In addition to their household work, most women around the world work long hours in fields, factories, and offices growing food, making goods, and rendering services. Nonetheless, work done by women has routinely been viewed as less important (and less worthy of study) than work done by men. However, led by sociologists and economists, and complemented by work by anthropologists, historians, and political scientists, research on women's employment has increased dramatically during the last two decades.

While almost 20 years old, LLOYD and NIEMI's book still represents one of the essential treatises in the economic perspective toward women's work. This book provides not only an overview of socioeconomic issues (work and economic status, home versus market work, socialization for labor force participation, labor market dynamics, discriminations and inequalities, effects of law and policy), but also some of the core theoretical foundations (labor supply and human capital) that continue to influence study and research in this area.

Western women, especially American and British women, are the focus of some of the most widely available books. KESSLER-HARRIS's history of wage-earning women in the United States and BRADLEY's history of employment among British women remain among the best surveys from a historical perspective. Even though some of the books focusing on western women include a section on cross-cultural issues and international comparisons, readers should note that works with an international focus are quickly dated. For example, the books edited by DAVIDSON and COOPER on the position of women at work in developed western countries (six European Common Market countries and the United States, compared with the Soviet Union) and by Farley on 15 countries (China, Yugoslavia, low-income countries, and the Federal Republic of Germany) predate the revolutionary political changes in those countries over the last decade. Periodicals are better resources for more current cross-cultural research.

Also, as with too many other edited books, Davidson and Cooper fail to provide sufficient integration or synthesis in the form of introductions or summaries for the individual chapters (which are simply placed in one of three parts: "Six EEC Countries," "Three Other European Countries," "The Two Superpowers"), or even a concluding chapter. The reader is not assisted in understanding the variation between (or within) gross categories, as for example what difference a country's membership status respective to the European Economic Community (EEC) makes with regard to women's work.

On the other hand, FARLEY's edited book does provide a helpful introductory chapter, but that is exclusively from the perspective of the International Labour Organization. Alice Hanson Cook (in whose honor the essays are offered) authors an afterword, albeit brief, in which she comments on issues of work that are shared by all women, east and west (for example, comparable worth, segregation, and training).

The place of women's work in development has benefited significantly from comparative study. In another edited book, sociologist WARD not only brings together nine fine essays on the role of women in global economies but also provides an introduction that offers definitions, specifies major issues (including the "third shift," which is the informal labor that occupies women in addition to formal employment and the "second shift" of housework), frames critical questions such as the paradox of women's employment as liberation or subjugation, and sensitizes the reader to the difficulty of understanding women's resistance (for example, to unionization). Ward's consideration of the situation of female off-shore assembly workers powerfully demonstrates the essential nature of women's work in an interconnected global context.

This genre includes a variety of books that are useful both as secondary sources and as textbooks or readers (primarily for undergraduates). KEMP applies a strong feminist perspective, as reflected in the discussion of methodology and the inclusion of feminist theories along with functional, neoclassical economic, and Marxist and socialist theories. Kemp's feminist perspective and intended scope are clearly reflected in her subtitle ("Degraded and Devalued") and her closing chapter ("The Plight of Third World Women and a Feminist Agenda for the Future").

RESKIN and PADAVIC offer a survey of the influence of gender in the workplace and stratification by sex. This book includes a chapter on the social construction of what has come to be called the "gendered" workplace and devotes special attention to discrimination. Reskin and Padavic also close with a chapter on the future, but unlike Kemp, Reskin and Padavic's final chapter examines trends in women's work and implications for both women and men. Reskin and Padavic also integrate a glossary into their index, which undergraduates and other non-specialists will appreciate.

KAHN-HUT, DANIELS, and COLVARD's edited reader examines women's work from a variety of standpoints—macro and micro, and liberal and radical perspectives—including feminist perspectives. STROMBERG and HARKESS's edited volume contains review essays (authored primarily by economists and sociologists) on women in the labor market, occupations, women's role in the family, and pay equity.

Two of the newer edited readers on women and work are of particular note. First, the contributors to the "handbook" edited by DUBECK and BORMAN represent an unusually wide variety of disciplines (accounting, communication, criminal justice, education, French, geography, journalism, management, marketing, psychology, religion, and social work) beyond "the usual suspects" (anthropology, economics, history, political science, and sociology). While the book considers women's labor force participation only in the United States, the chapters do represent the wide diversity of U.S. women's social lives: immigrant, working class, young, retired, Appalachian, Greek, and black and other women of color. Dubeck and Borman also include a fairly comprehensive discussion of issues related to women's work, including occupational diversity, socialization, legal factors, the organizational context of work, and work/family linkages.

Second, DUNN's anthology is organized around major themes in the sociology of work: socialization to employment, stratification and inequality, workplace dynamics, occupation and segregation, and work-family linkages. The volume is introduced by an excellent overview to the study of women and work, and each of the five units is prefaced by a concise overview of the subspecialty and the readings that follow. Asian, black, and Chicana women are included in multiple readings. However, like other books in the field, the work lives of Native American women are ignored.

—MEG WILKES KARRAKER

Workplace Equality Legislation

Blank, Robert H., *Fetal Protection in the Workplace: Women's Rights, Business Interests, and the Unborn*, New York: Columbia University Press, 1993

Bouchier, David, *The Feminist Challenge: The Movement for Women's Liberation in Britain and the U.S.A.*, London: Macmillan, 1983; New York: Schocken Books, 1984

Conway, M. Margaret, David W. Ahern, and Gertrude A. Steuernagel, *Women and Public Policy: A Revolution in Progress*, Washington, D.C.: CQ Press, 1995

Fogel, Walter, *The Equal Pay Act: Implications for Comparable Worth*, New York: Praeger, 1984

Greene, Kathanne W., *Affirmative Action and Principles of Justice*, New York and London: Greenwood, 1989

Lehrer, Susan, *Origins of Protective Labor Legislation for Women: 1905–1925*, Albany: State University of New York Press, 1987

Lewis, Jane, *Women in Britain since 1945: Women, Family, Work and the State in the Post-War Years*, Oxford and Cambridge, Massachusetts: Blackwell, 1992

McGlen, Nancy E., and Karen O'Connor, *Women, Politics, and American Society, Englewood Cliffs*, New Jersey: Prentice-Hall, 1995

In order to understand workplace equality legislation for women, one must first understand that at the turn of the twentieth century, the emphasis was on protecting the female worker in such matters as maximum hours, minimum wages, and better working conditions. That is what LEHRER writes about in her book. She attempts to show that this movement was the result of changes in the nature of work, such as mechanization and specialization of labor, which had detrimental effects on workers. However, women were not united in their efforts because the suffragists opposed this type of legislation. In the United States, the National Woman's Party in particular led the opposition as it felt that its cause of equal voting rights for women would suffer if women were to be the beneficiaries of special legislation in the workplace. There were other women's groups who supported the legislation, such as the Women's Trade Union League. Labor generally opposed protective legislation, especially the powerful American Federation of Labor, although the International Ladies Garment Workers' Union supported it, even though its primary objective was socialism. The book also points out that employers' associations such as the National Association of Manufacturers opposed it, whereas the National Civic Federation did not take a stand. This is a useful book to start to study workplace equality legislation for women.

FOGEL's book is important because the U.S. 1963 Equal Pay Act was the start of equality legislation by Congress for women. Fogel shows the need for the law and the congressional support for it, and he writes about the meaning of equal work and what the plaintiff must do to win a case. He then gives three cases that went to the courts, including one that went to the Supreme Court. One of the highlights of the book is his discussion of the market as a defense for unequal wages. He also addresses the question of whether, if women do, in fact, have equal job access and job equality, the Equal Pay Act has any meaning. His answer is that if there is equal access, the courts usually do not find the jobs equal, but if there is not equal access, the jobs are likely to be found equal, thereby necessitating equal pay. The book ends with a look at the Act and at wage discrimination once Title VII of the 1964 Civil Rights Act was implemented.

GREENE's book devotes the entire second chapter to a legislative history of Title VII and the role played by President Kennedy in the need for the law, as well as the action taken in its passage by the House of Representatives and the Senate. She discusses the law's initial implementation with the realization that the law needed corrective legislation. She therefore spends the next part of the book writing about the 1972 Equal Employment Opportunity Act. Under the 1964 Act, even though workplace discrimination against women was prohibited, the agency created to enforce the law, the Equal Employment Opportunity Commission, could only try to obtain voluntary compliance. With the 1972 law, it could initiate lawsuits. In addition, employees of educational institutions came under the law. She discusses the implementation of the law during the Reagan years and the role of the Supreme Court, and concludes the book with a look at case law in the affirmative action area, including the Court endorsement of affirmative action for women.

BLANK's book is important because it describes the need for the U.S. 1978 Pregnancy Discrimination Act and the trend in court cases toward recognition of maternal responsibility for the well-being of the unborn child. Because of a history of sex discrimination as well as reproductive hazards in the workplace, women were excluded from certain jobs. However, with the passage of the law as well as Supreme Court decisions such as in the Johnson Controls case, such exclusion is now illegal. Nevertheless there is still uncertainty about claims for compensation for harm to a fetus from workplace hazards, which causes the author to discuss alternatives such as cleaning up the workplace, education and full disclosure, job transfers, guaranteed access to prenatal care, and maternity and parental leave. He concludes by discussing the building of a rational policy to prevent fetal injury and to create an accident compensation fund.

In McGLEN and O'CONNOR's book, chapters three and four are especially relevant. Chapter three discusses the drive for protective legislation at the turn of the century, and how equality in the workplace was not an aftermath of winning the vote. Therefore, women in the United States lobbied for and saw the passage of such laws as the Equal Pay Act, the Civil Rights Act, the Equal Employment Opportunity Act, and the Pregnancy Discrimination Act. Chapter four discusses the economic status of women and includes the 1993 Family and Medical Leave Act, which does provide most workers with up to 12 weeks unpaid leave each year. Although applying to both sexes, women probably benefit more from this law due to their role as mother and often as caregiver of a parent.

In CONWAY, AHERN, and STEUERNAGEL's book, chapters four, five, and eight are the ones that most bear upon workplace equality legislation. Besides going into a history and an implementation of equal opportunity policy, chapter four examines the problem of sexual harassment and how it comes under Title VII, the criteria for proof of discrimination, and the concept of comparable worth and its relationship to Title VII. Chapter five takes an in-depth look at the Equal Credit Opportunity Act and its results, and chapter eight studies the Pregnancy

Discrimination Act and the Family and Medical Leave Act along with some important Supreme Court cases in those areas.

BOUCHIER's book is most interesting in that it looks at the resurgence of feminism in the 1960s and especially looks at the years from 1966 to 1983. Although Bouchier compares the United States and Great Britain, the core of the book is about Britain. He traces the origins of the current movement there with the formation of the Women's Social and Political Union in 1903 and the passage of the Sex Disqualification Removal Act in 1919, which gave women access to professions and professional associations. However, welfare was the dominant theme then, not equal rights. In 1931 women suffered a setback when the British Anomalies Regulation cut married women off from unemployment benefits; later, in 1946 a report from the Royal Commission on Equal Pay implied that only professional women really deserved the same pay as men. Then in 1961 Britain adopted the equal pay principle for teaching and civil service, and in 1970 came the Equal Pay Act, which was to be implemented by 1975. In the early 1970s British feminists staged the Night Cleaners Campaign, because the women who cleaned office buildings at night were mostly poor immigrants who were exploited by contractors.

In 1974 British women adopted a 10 point charter for working women, focusing on such issues as wages, promotions, training, and working conditions, and the following year they waged a campaign for financial and legal independence.The result was the passage of the Social Security Pensions Act, the Social Security Benefits Act, and the Employment Protection Act, which protected pregnant workers. In 1978 women were given greater autonomy in tax affairs, equal treatment in Social Security, and the Supplemental Benefits Review modified the strict definition of the man being the family breadwinner. The author examines the 1975 Sex Discrimination Act, under which there is to be no discrimination in such work-related areas as job advertising, recruitment, fringe benefits, and promotion. In addition, trade union sexual equality and equality in mortgages are mandated. The book concludes by looking at opposition in Britain to women's equality by men, women, organized groups, mass media and commercial culture, and some intellectuals, and it studies the women's movement today and points out what the future might hold.

LEWIS's book opens with a discussion of gender and family politics, and the so-called permissive movement of the 1960s, and then it focuses upon women and work. Lewis takes a good look at Britain's Equal Pay Act and shows that there is still a persistence of low pay due to the high level of sex segregation in the workplace. In addition, unpaid work in the family has remained women's work. She next looks at women's welfare and the state, including the passage in 1975 of the Invalid Care Allowance, which is payable if one must give up paid employment in order to care for a sick or elderly person at home. She points out that the allowance excludes married and cohabiting women because that is part of their normal household duties. This was not changed until a court case in 1986. She offers the interesting insight that women's self-help efforts are important in getting legislation passed for them, but they do not get much support from trade unions due to women's weak position there. Thus much depends upon the willingness of the state to support these efforts, but she contends there has been little political commitment.

Lewis studies the Equal Pay Act, which when written mandated equal pay for equal work. It was amended in 1983 to call for equal pay for work of equal value, but she contends that is not much help when female skills are undervalued in female jobs. She also studies the Sex Discrimination Act, which covers both direct and indirect discrimination, but it is only applicable in the public sphere, has a "genuine occupational qualification" clause (permitting male-only jobs for good reasons), and does not cover social security, tax, and pension rights. She also examines the Employment Protection Act, under which a woman cannot be fired for being pregnant, can return to the job after birth, and must get maternity pay. However, under all three laws, the individual must bring the case, which makes it difficult for women to realize the laws' benefits.

—ROBERT W. LANGRAN

See also Sex Discrimination in the Workplace

World Wars *see* Women at Work during World War II; British Women during World War II; Holocaust

Wright, Frances 1795–1852

American Social Reformer

Bartlett, Elizabeth Ann, *Liberty, Equality, Sorority: The Origins and Interpretation of American Feminist Thought—Frances Wright, Sarah Grimke, and Margaret Fuller,* Brooklyn, New York: Carlson, 1994

Egerton, John, *Visions of Utopia: Nashoba, Rugby, Ruskin, and the "New Communities" in Tennessee's Past,* Knoxville: University of Tennessee Press, 1977

Heineman, Helen, *Restless Angels: The Friendship of Six Victorian Women,* Athens: Ohio University Press, 1983

Kissel, Susan, *In Common Cause: The "Conservative" Frances Trollope and the "Radical" Frances Wright,* Bowling Green, Ohio: Bowling Green State University Popular Press, 1993

Lane, Margaret, *Frances Wright and the "Great Experiment,"* Totowa, New Jersey: Rowman and Littlefield, and Manchester: Manchester University Press, 1972
Morris, Celia, *Fanny Wright: Rebel in America,* Cambridge, Massachusetts: Harvard University Press, 1984
Pease, William, and Jane Pease, *Black Utopia: Negro Communal Experiments in America,* Madison: State Historical Society of Wisconsin, 1963
Perkins, Alice, and Theresa Wolfson, *Frances Wright Free Enquirer: The Study of a Temperament,* New York and London: Harper, 1939
Waterman, William Randall, *Frances Wright,* New York: Columbia University Press, 1924

Despite her compelling story, Frances Wright's role in American history has often been ignored, dismissed, or misunderstood. Contemporary feminist scholars suggest that this disregard for her social and political contributions is a result of her radically unpopular ideas about marriage, religion, education, and race relations. Most of the works about Wright seek to reestablish her position as a pioneering feminist through an examination of her complex private and public lives.

WATERMAN's book is one of the earliest attempts to redeem Wright by "securing for her a definite niche in the social history of the people of the United States." Although she was never an active participant in the suffrage movement, Waterman characterizes Wright as a women's rights pioneer and a role model for contemporary feminists. This work is well researched, relying heavily on Wright's papers and conversations with her grandson.

ECKHARDT's biography is the most authoritative and comprehensive examination of Wright's life, and as such, is used as a source for all the works that post-date it. This book offers a balanced analysis of an extremely complex woman, by moving past an attempt to make Wright a hero and, instead, examining her personal pain and public failures. Eckhardt's suggestion that Wright's fanatic devotion to her vision of social reform, in part, was a result of manic-depression offers a unique explanation for a life presented as a series of paradoxes.

PERKINS and WOLFSON tell the story of Wright's life with particular attention to the private influences of friends and family on her radical philosophy and activities. This work offers a romanticized account of Wright's life, focusing on her adventurous feats and romantic liaisons. While it is well researched, drawing extensively on Wright's publications, lectures, diaries, and letters, as well as newspaper accounts of her activities, its focus on drama necessitates a critical reading.

LANE's book is a concise and complete biography of Wright, which frames Wright's fascination and dedication to America's "great experiment" with democracy as the force that drove her public and private activities. Characterizing Wright's public life as "intoxicated by the atmosphere of danger," and her private live as disillusioned by interpersonal and financial losses, Lane, like Eckhardt, presents Wright as a complex and troubled hero.

HEINEMAN portrays six "relatively obscure" nineteenth-century women as "striving to define themselves in areas women are still exploring." Frances Wright is the most well known of this circle of friends, which also includes Frances's sister Camilla, Harriet and Frances Garnett, Julia Garnett Pertz, and Frances Trollope. It quickly becomes evident that Wright serves as the pivotal figure in this collective biography. More specifically, Heineman characterizes Wright's founding of the utopian community of Nashoba as a determining factor in the lives of each of the women, separating them both geographically and ideologically depending on their level of support and commitment. The focus on sisterhood and female forms of expression (the primary archival source is letters the friends wrote to each other) makes this book a valuable resource for scholars of women's status in Victorian England and America.

KISSEL examines the political theories of two powerful nineteenth-century women—Frances Wright and Frances Trollope. Kissel charges historians with simplifying and dismissing Wright's and Trollope's complex ideologies by incorrectly labeling them as "radical" and "conservative" respectively. In contrast to what Kissel calls the "myth of opposition," she concentrates on how Wright's and Trollope's ideals "overlap and parallel" to form a complex mix of conservative, liberal, and radical political theory. After identifying Wright's and Trollope's personal and ideological differences and commonalities, Kissel considers the influences they each had on the literature of their time, as well as contemporary political philosophy. Another of Kissel's conclusions is that Wright's feminism was essentialist, and that she would be dismayed to find twentieth-century women "rushing to emulate men rather than modulating capitalist selfishness through female leadership in cooperation and nurturance."

BARTLETT's book examines the intellectual roots of three nineteenth-century feminists by identifying the patriarchal philosophical traditions that influenced them, as well as the ideas and approaches that represent original feminist thought. Bartlett analyzes how the political thought of each woman weaves three concepts, which she identifies as "the core of feminism"—liberty, equality, and sorority. Bartlett concludes that Wright's feminism is a "balanced tension between equality and liberty," while it fails to address sorority. While she explains that this exclusion is due to Wright's emphasis on the equality of humanity without regard to gender, Bartlett is critical of Wright's failure to recognize that a "rejection of women's ways of knowing was perpetuation of a male-defined reality that denied the quality of women's experiences and perceptions."

Two works of interest to Wright scholars focus on one particular chapter of her life—Nashoba. EGERTON's book contextualizes Nashoba historically and geographically as part of a utopian movement in Tennessee, extending from 1736 to the present day. This focus on Nashoba, rather than on Wright herself, provides the reader with details about the practical aspects of communal life encountered by Wright, including the search for land, dealings with the local population, and the daily management of failing agricultural and educational enterprises. Excerpts from the diaries and letters of Nashoba's residents introduce the issue of the abuse of Nashoba's slaves at the hands of their white caretakers, but leaves unanswered the extent of Wright's involvement in and knowledge of these events.

The work by PEASE and PEASE offers readers a unique perspective by focusing on nineteenth-century America from the perspective of African-Americans. The authors examine Nashoba as an example of "Negro communities" formed as alternatives to an unsuccessful abolition movement. In addition, they present one of the most critical analyses of Wright and her plan for gradual abolition of America's slave population. The authors concentrate on the failure of Nashoba, and attribute it to the incompatibility of Wright's two primary goals—the elevation of the social status of ex-slaves, and the liberation of the human mind. Through a critical analysis of Wright's complex belief system, which advocated the equality of all humans, while simultaneously supporting the colonization of ex-slaves outside of America, Pease and Pease conclude that Wright's plan for gradual abolition ultimately fostered an inferior position for African-Americans. While the authors stop short of accusing Wright of supporting the abuse of Nashoba's slaves, they place the blame for the community's failure, not on poor crops, financial mismanagement, or malaria infested land as do other authors, but on Wright's failure to overcome European and American belief in the essential inequality of Africans.

—LINDA C. BRIGANCE

Y

Yourcenar, Marguerite 1903–1987

French-American Writer

Farrell, C. Frederick, Jr., and Edith R. Farrell, *Marguerite Yourcenar in Counterpoint*, Lanham, Maryland: University Press of America, 1983

Galey, Matthieu, *With Open Eyes: Conversations with Matthieu Galey*, translated by Arthur Goldhammer, Boston: Beacon Press, 1984

Horn, Pierre L., *Marguerite Yourcenar*, Boston: Twayne, 1985

Howard, Joan E., *From Violence to Vision: Sacrifice in the Works of Marguerite Yourcenar*, Carbondale: Southern Illinois University Press, 1992

Savigneau, Josyane, *Marguerite Yourcenar: Inventing a Life*, translated by Joan E. Howard, Chicago: University of Chicago Press, 1993

Shurr, Georgia H., *Marguerite Yourcenar: A Reader's Guide*, Lanham, Maryland: University Press of America, 1987

Since Cardinal Richelieu founded the French Academy in 1635, no woman had ever been elected to join the "40 immortals" until 1980, when Marguerite Yourcenar was invited to become a member, even after she had refused to lobby the 40 academicians and warned the academy that she would neither wear their gold-embroidered uniforms (she wore a skirt and cape by St. Laurent instead) nor carry a sword at her inaugural. This pivotal event in her life illustrates the problems Yourcenar posed, not only for conservative men but also for radical feminists, since she did not chide the academy for its neglect of female writers throughout the previous three-and-a-half centuries. Indeed, she was a woman of many paradoxes. Honored as a French writer, she had been born in Belgium and later spent over half her life in the United States (where she became a citizen in 1947). She eschewed the Parisian literary scene to live a hermit-like existence on Mount Desert Island in Maine, yet she needed and enjoyed the company of a wide variety of people. Even though most of her time was spent in the United States and France, her books are located in other countries, including Greece, Spain, Italy, China, and India. Although she was in many ways a woman of the twentieth century, she set her works in other times, especially antiquity and the Renaissance. She believed that the present was deeply rooted in the past, and much of her work seeks to link the past to the present. These paradoxes, some of which were culled from the books in the above list, are connected with Yourcenar's belief in the "nobility of refusal," a trait that also characterizes several of her protagonists.

FARRELL and FARRELL wrote their book to call the attention of American readers to the works of a French woman whom they viewed as a major twentieth-century writer. They also wished to encourage admirers of the *Memoirs of Hadrian* and *The Abyss* (her best-known books) to read and enjoy her other writings. Finally, they wanted to correct some common misconceptions about her, especially her supposed neglect of women. It is certainly true that she created important male protagonists, including the emperor Hadrian, but she also created a wide variety of aggressive as well as passive women characters, and these women occupy various social classes from peasant to empress. In her novels and short stories the reader will find women from history, myth, and legend, as well as from life itself.

By using his series of interviews with Yourcenar over many years, GALEY seeks to introduce new readers to the personality of the author and the complexity of her works. He first brings out her extraordinary intelligence. She was a very well-read woman, conversant in the literatures of France, Germany, Spain, Greece, Italy, and the United States, as well as several Asian countries. Although she loved literature, she disdained being a member of any literary coterie. Galey also tries to clarify her relationship to feminism. Yourcenar has stated that the feminist movement never interested her. Indeed, she had "a horror of such movements," because she was opposed to every kind of particularim, whether based on nationality, religion, species, or sex. She saw things simply: "a good woman is worth as much as a good man." She favored the equality of women in education, politics, and all other areas of human endeavor, but she also pointed out that "equality does not mean identity." Furthermore, she voiced her strong objection to "modern feminism," since, she said, it is usually aggressive, and "aggression rarely succeeds in bringing about lasting change."

SHURR's work on Yourcenar grew out of an intensive study of her writings. She found that even advanced students in French literature needed a guide to appreciate how Yourcenar created her novels. Like some other feminists, Shurr is disconcerted that Yourcenar's central characters are almost always men, and that the male worldview is the most distinctive element in her writings. On the other hand, her female characters are often colorless, shadowy creatures who exist only to serve as agents of conflict. Critics of Shurr's book have disputed some of her main points, arguing that, in searching for autobiographical clues in Yourcenar's novels, she has confused the author with her characters. Yourcenar herself has stated that she has not "hidden behind the men in her writings." She also points out that in some of her novels, *A Coin in Nine Hands,* for example, male and female characters balance each other, and she has also written poems about such strong women as Antigone and Mary Magdalene.

HORN, who believes that Yourcenar is "one of the most original writers of the second half of the twentieth century," emphasizes the subversive themes in her novels. Yourcenar believed that any seeker of truth and goodness inevitably comes into conflict with established values. Her protagonists often rebel against traditional cultural limits and engage in radical thought. Sometimes they are destroyed by this conflict; other times they are unable to resolve the conflicts between society's demands and their passions. Horn finds the critique of some feminists that Yourcenar exhibits contempt for women in her works false and unfair. He gives examples of female characters who play important roles in Yourcenar's fiction. He also argues that her objection to "a new ghettoization" of women (she did refuse to be published by Virago Press in England because "they publish *only* women") has not precluded her from committing her energy and talent to numerous good causes, including equality of women in politics and various other professions.

HOWARD views Yourcenar as a radical and a feminist, and she wants to correct the picture of her as a conservative (Yourcenar herself has stated that she is neither a rightist nor a leftist). By analyzing several of Yourcenar's principal novels, Howard focuses on the theme of sacrifice that she feels is central to Yourcenar's vision of the world. In the *Memoirs of Hadrian,* for example, this Roman emperor, as he nears death, reflects on weakness, failure, and sacrifice in a world that admires strength, success, and self-interest. Hadrian thus illustrates one of Yourcenar's dominant themes—the artist's struggle to maintain and express his sensibilities in a hostile environment. Howard sees Yourcenar's vision of the world s "a horrible gift," since it exposes a western culture that victimizes creative individuals. In this way Yourcenar, who spent much of her time studying the past, has something to say to the present. Her novels are mirrors held up to our own times, helping us to recognize the oppressive powers that we must fight. Therefore, according to Howard, Yourcenar's art spurs us to move from violence toward a life-enhancing vision.

Yourcenar, who once expressed her concern about becoming "the prey of biographers," destroyed many of her papers during her last years, and many of those that she left have been sealed for a period of 50 years after her death. This has made the task of SAVIGNEAU and other biographers more difficult. As Savigneau realizes, her biography cannot be definitive, since the lost and restricted documents cannot be used to confirm or invalidate some of her ideas about her subject. Despite these obstacles, Savigneau has used the many letters, diaries, and other manuscript material to which she did have access, along with interviews with Yourcenar's friends, to reconstruct a life that her subject did a lot to obscure (even in her autobiographical writings Yourcenar was less than candid about several aspects of her life and work). Savigneau interprets Yourcenar as a woman who played by her own rules. She does not attempt to give a detailed analysis of Yourcenar's work, choosing instead to emphasize the events of her life (which are certainly related to what she created, but which are insufficient to explain the provenance and meaning of these writings). Savigneau disagrees with those critics who think they can find the autobiographical roots to Yourcenar's writings, since she thinks that Yourcenar blurred the boundary between fiction and reality. What comes across in this biography is that Yourcenar possessed a luminous and magnetic intelligence that attracted many friends in her life and many readers to her fiction. In both her life and writings, she sought to discover those deep human truths that encourage compassionate feelings for human beings in all their frailty. For Yourcenar, her life and her books were ways of learning to feel more deeply, acutely, and precisely, and in doing this she has provided all of us with a deeper understanding of our common human condition.

—ROBERT J. PARADOWSKI

Z

Zaharias, Mildred "Babe" Didrikson

1911–1956

American Athlete

Cayleff, Susan E., *Babe: The Life and Legend of Babe Didrikson Zaharias,* Urbana: University of Illinois Press, 1995

Johnson, William O., *Whatta-Gal: The Babe Didrikson Story,* Boston: Little Brown, 1977

Schoor, Gene, *Babe Didrikson: The World's Greatest Woman Athlete,* Garden City, New York: Doubleday, 1978

Perhaps the most versatile athlete of the twentieth century, Babe Didrikson Zaharias has been celebrated for both her unparalleled athletic accomplishments and her courageous struggle against the cancer that ultimately claimed her life. Zaharias's renown largely rests on her gold medal track and field performances in the 1932 Olympic Games and her unprecedented string of amateur and professional gold victories, including three U.S. Open titles. Yet she also gained visibility and widespread notoriety endorsing products and performing athletic stunts around the country. Accounts of Zaharias's life range from young adult biographies (not cited here) that simplistically laud her as sports hero to more complex portraits of her complicated relationship to the society that both vilified her and made her into a cultural phenomenon.

SCHOOR presents a conventional narrative of Zaharias's life, relying on telling anecdotes to illustrate what he considers her most remarkable attributes, including her perseverance, dedication, courage, and strength. His biography opens, for example, with the "defining moment" in Zaharias's career and life: her single-handed victory in the team Amateur Athletic Union track and field championships, which qualified her to compete in three events in the 1932 Olympics. This account is chronological and dramatic, focusing almost exclusively on her athletic accomplishments and her struggle with cancer. A brief nod is given to the criticism faced by female athletes during this period, but Schoor primarily glorifies Zaharias as a cultural hero. This biography is useful for gaining a general understanding of Zaharias's athletic career, and as an example of traditional accounts of her life.

JOHNSON and WILLIAMSON's biography, which intersperses a narrative of Zaharias's life with contextual observations, is somewhat more detailed and carries a more critical perspective. Drawing on a very general understanding of women's history and the history of organized sports and spectatorship, Johnson and Williamson develop a picture of the cultural milieu amidst which Zaharias attained her fame, and amidst which this fame quickly became inseparable from legend. In discussing the factors that contributed to the Zaharias legend, they also seek to qualify it; they demonstrate, for example, that Zaharias could be abrasive and arrogant as well as charming. And they show that Zaharias was not unquestioningly considered a hero; as frequently she was invoked as a negative example by parents who feared their daughters might become "muscle molls." In showing Zaharias—and the Zaharias legend—to be a product of her times, this account points out how many of the struggles she faced parallel those faced by contemporary athletes.

In reading Zaharias through a feminist lens, CAYLEFF's recent work presents the most thorough and scholarly treatment of Zaharias's life. Cayleff extensively analyzes the perilous climate of women in sports during Zaharias's lifetime and discusses the significance of both Zaharias's career and her image. She reads Zaharias as a kind of trickster figure, highly aware of her public image ands constantly—and consciously—negotiating between her conventionally feminine self and her androgynous, rebellious self. This account draws on contemporary feminist and cultural theory to consider Zaharias within a "historical context of women's sports, gender, homophobia, and culturally constructed sex-role expectations." This sympathetic but not uncritical portrayal is valuable for showing Zaharias as a pioneer in challenging gender roles, as well as for elucidating the ways in which she suffered as a result of these challenges.

—CAROL E. DICKSON

See also Athletes

BOOKLIST INDEX

BOOKLIST INDEX

Books and articles discussed in the entries are listed here by author/editor name. The page numbers refer to the lists themselves, where full publication information is given.

GENERAL INDEX

GENERAL INDEX

Page numbers in **bold** indicate subjects with their own entries.

A

B

D

E

H

I

J

N

O

P

Q

R

S

NOTES ON CONTRIBUTORS

NOTES ON CONTRIBUTORS

Abbott, Pamela. Professor and Director of Social Sciences, University of Teesside, Middlesbrough. Author of *Women and Social Class* (1987) and, with Claire Wallace, *The New Right and the Family* (1993) and *An Introduction to Sociology: Feminist Perspectives* (1990). Series editor, Social Sciences for Nurses and the Caring Professions. **Essays:** Class and Gender; Family; Feminism: Marxist/Socialist; Patriarchy.

Ahern, Susan Kiernan. Associate Professor and Chair, Department of English, University of Houston, Downtown, Texas. Contributor to *ANQ, Journal of English and Germanic Philology, Eighteenth-Century Current Bibliography,* and *Theatre Review.* Consultant in literature, *Women's Studies Encyclopedia* (1990–92). **Essay:** Literature: Modern Children's.

Airheart-Martin, Tria. M.A. candidate in English, Texas A and M University, College Station. Contributor of short fiction and poetry to *Snowy Egret, Soundings East,* and *Concho River Review.* Poetry editor, *Twice Removed.* **Essays:** Literature: Folklore and Fairy Tales; Literature: Mythology.

Amberg, Julie S. Assistant Professor of English, York College of Pennsylvania, York. **Essays:** Adams, Abigail; American Revolutionary Era.

Armstrong, Elisabeth. Visiting Instructor, Wesleyan University, Middletown, Connecticut. **Essay:** Labor Unions.

Atmore, Chris. Lecturer in Anthropology and Sociology, Monash University, Clayton, Victoria. Contributor to *Journal of Homosexuality, Media Information Australia, Feminism and Psychology,* and *Child Abuse Review.* **Essays:** Child Sexual Abuse; Incest; Sexual Assault/Rape: Other.

Bailey, Alison. Assistant Professor of Philosophy, Illinois State University, Normal. Author of *Posterity and Strategic Policy: A Moral Assessment of Nuclear Policy Options* (1989). Contributor to *Journal of Social Philosophy, Hypatia,* and *APA Newsletter on Feminism* and *Philosophy.* **Essays:** Greenham Common Women's Peace Camp; White Women.

Baladouni, Billie Salisbury. Assistant Director, Institute for Ministry, Loyola University, New Orleans, Louisiana. **Essays:** Christianity: Post-Reformation; Saints.

Balakier, Ann Stewart. Associate Professor of Art History, University of South Dakota, Vermillion. Author, with James J. Balakier, of *The Spatial Infinite at Greenwich in Works by Christopher Wren, James Thornhill, and James Thomson* (1995). **Essay:** Art, Images of Women in.

Barton-Kriese, Paul. Associate Professor of Political Science, Indiana University, East, Richmond. Author of *Nonviolent Revolution* (1995), *The Politics of Diversity in the United States: Positive Dreams and Phyrric Victories* (1987), and *Truth-Speaking and Power: Ethical Alternatives and Political Consequences* (1987). Contributor to *International Third World Studies Journal and Review, Dialogue and Universalism, Extrapolation, Indiana Journal of Political Science, Foundations for Peace, Political Methodology,* and numerous edited collections. **Essays:** Arendt, Hannah; Dyer, Mary; Jordan, Barbara; Mandela, Winnie.

Bartsch, Ingrid. Assistant Professor of Women's Studies, University of South Florida, Tampa. **Essays:** Science: Teaching to Women; Scientists.

Baskin, Judith R. Professor and Chair, Department of Judaic Studies, State University of New York, Albany. Author of *Women of the Word: Jewish Women and Jewish Writing* (1994) and *Pharaoh's Counsellors: Job, Jethro, and Balaam in Rabbinic and Patristic Tradition* (1983). Contributor to *Shofar, Studia Judaica, Associa-*

tion for Jewish Studies Review, Jewish History, and numerous other journals and edited collections. **Essays:** Jewish Women; Judaism.

Bazin, Paulina. Instructor in Russian, Modern Foreign Languages Department, Loyola University, New Orleans, Louisiana. Coauthor, with Gina Macdonald, of numerous contributions to edited collections. President of the Eastern European and Slavic Interest Section of SCMLA (1996–97). **Essays:** (with Gina Macdonald) Akhmatova, Anna Andreeva; (with Gina Macdonald) Tsvetaeva, Marina.

Belmonte, Frances R. Associate Professor, Institute of Pastoral Studies, Loyola University, Chicago, Illinois. Author of *Women and Health* (1997). **Essays:** Codependency; Medical History.

Benson, Linda. Professor of History, Oakland University, Rochester, Michigan. Author of *The Ili Rebellion: Moslem Challenge to Chinese Authority in Xinjiang 1944–1949* (1990). Contributor to *Toronto Studies in Central and Inner Asia, The Muslim World, Bulletin of the Association for the Advancement of Central Asian Research, Central Asian Survey, Central and Inner Asian Studies,* and numerous edited collections. **Essay:** Jiang Qing.

Bily, Cynthia A. Instructor, Adrian College, Adrian, Michigan. Contributor to numerous reference books. **Essays:** Barton, Clara; Cassatt, Mary; Catherine the Great; Duncan, Isadora; Joan of Arc; Kollwitz, Käthe Schmidt; Millay, Edna St. Vincent; Nevelson, Louise; O'Keeffe, Georgia; Shelley, Mary.

Blessing, Carol A. Assistant Professor of Literature, Point Loma Nazarene College, San Diego, California. Contributor to *Daughters of Sarah* and the edited collection *Celebrating Women's History.* **Essays:** Burney, Frances; Julian of Norwich; Language, Gender Inclusive/Exclusive; Mary Stuart; O'Connor, Flannery; Sexton, Anne; Victoria; Willard, Frances.

Boles, Janet K. Professor of Political Science, Marquette University, Milwaukee, Wisconsin. Author of *Historical Dictionary of Feminism* (1996), *American Feminism: New Issues for a Mature Movement* (1991), *The Egalitarian City* (1986), and *The Politics of the Equal Rights Amendment* (1979). President, Section on Women and Politics Research of the American Political Science Association (1994–95) **Essays:** Antifeminism; Politics: Local.

Bona, Mary Jo. Associate Professor of English, Gonzaga University, Spokane, Washington. Editor of *The Voices We Carry: Recent Italian/American Women Writers* (1994), and, with Anthony Tamburri, of *Through the Looking Glass: Italian and Italian/American Images in the Media* (1996). Contributor to *MELUS, VIA, Feminist Teacher,* and *Differentia: Review of Italian Thought.* **Essays:** Bradstreet, Anne; Gilman, Charlotte Perkins.

Bond, Beverly Greene. Assistant Professor of History, University of Memphis, Memphis, Tennessee. Author of "African American Women in Memphis, Tennessee 1840–1915" (Ph.D. dissertation). **Essays:** Bethune, Mary McLeod; Black Woman's Club Movement; Davis, Angela Y.

Bordwell, Marilyn. Ph.D. candidate in communication studies. University of Iowa, Iowa City. Contributor to *Journal for the Anthropological Study of Human Movement.* **Essay:** Graham, Martha.

Bresnahan, Eileen. Assistant Professor of Political Science and Women's Studies, University of Utah, Salt Lake City. Contributor to *Women's Studies Quarterly* and *NWSA Journal.* **Essays:** Lesbian Community; Lesbian Identity.

Brigance, Linda Czuba. Ph.D. candidate in communication studies, University of Iowa, Iowa City. Past director, Women's studies, University of Memphis, Memphis, Tennessee. **Essays:** Anthony, Susan B.; Wright, Frances.

Brod, Harry. Assistant Professor of Philosophy, University of Delaware, Newark. Author of *Hegel's Philosophy of Politics: Idealism, Identity, and Modernity* (1992). Editor of *The Making of Masculinities: The New Men's Studies* (1987), *A Mensch among Men: Explorations in Jewish Masculinity* (1988), and *Theorizing Masculinities* (1994). **Essays:** Masculinity; Men and Feminism.

Brook, Barbara. Senior Lecturer in Women's Studies, Victoria University, Melbourne. Contributor to *Southern Review* and *Contemporary Australian Feminism.* Editor, *Australian Women's Book Review.* **Essays:** Queer Theory; Scholarship/Research, Feminist.

Brusco, Elizabeth E. Associate Professor of Anthropology, Pacific Lutheran University, Tacoma, Washington. Author of *The Reformation of Machismo: Evangelical Conversion and Gender in Colombia* (1995). Contributor to *American Journal of Sociology, Feminist Issues,* and numerous edited collections. **Essays:** (with Laura Klein) Anthropology: Traditional; (with Laura Klein) Benedict, Ruth; Female Genital Mutilation.

Burgess, Susan R. Director, Center for Women's Studies and Associate Professor of Political Science, University of Wisconsin, Milwaukee. Author of *Contest for Constitutional Authority: The Abortion and War Powers Debates* (1992). Contributor to *Polity, Review of Politics,* and *Legal Studies Forum.* Editor, *Women's Caucus for Political Science Quarterly.* **Essay:** Jurisprudence, Feminist.

Byrne, Deirdre C. Lecturer in English, University of South Africa, Pretoria. Contributor to *UNISA English Studies* and *Journal of Literary Studies.* Coeditor, *Probe.* **Essay:** Le Guin, Ursula K.

Cameron, Jenny. Lecturer in Geography and Environmental Science, Monash University, Clayton, Victoria. Contributor to *Rethinking Marxism.* **Essay:** Homemaking and Housework.

Campbell, Donna M. Assistant Professor of English, Gonzaga University, Spokane, Washington. Author of *Gender and Genre: Local Color and the Naturalists in American Fiction, 1885–1915* (1997). Contributor to *Legacy, Studies in American Fiction, American Literary Realism,* and *Speaking the Otherself: American Women Writers,* edited by Jeanne Campbell Reesman (1997). **Essay:** Wharton, Edith.

Carchidi, Victoria. Lecturer in English, Massey University, Palmerson North, New Zealand. Contributor to *MELUS* and numerous edited collections. **Essays:** Head, Bessie; Woolf, Virginia.

Carleton, Francis. Assistant Professor of Social Change and Development, Political Science, and Women's Studies. University of Wisconsin, Green Bay. Contributor to *Women and Politics, Wisconsin Women's Law Journal, Race, Gender, and Class,* and *Review of Education/Pedagogy/Cultural Studies.* **Essays:** Affirmative Action; Ethic of Care.

Carney, Jo Eldridge. Assistant Professor of English, Trenton State College, Trenton, New Jersey. Contributor to numerous edited collections. **Essays:** Bishop, Elizabeth; Christine de Pizan; Hildegard of Bingen; Kempe, Margery; Sappho; Wheatley, Phillis.

Carter, Allison. Instructor of Sociology, Rowan University, Glassboro, New Jersey. Contributor to *Women's Issues, Clinical Sociology Review,* and *Journal of Ideology.* **Essay:** Beauty Pageants.

Chae, Donald Baird. Graduate student in Music, University of Chicago, Illinois. **Essays:** Music: Classical; Musicians; Schumann, Clara.

Charbonneau, Joanne A. Humanities Coordinator, General Education, James Madison University, Harrisonburg, Virginia. Author of *Middle English Romance: An Annotated Bibliography, 1955–1985* (1986). Contributor to *American National Biography* (1977) and *Magill's Ready References: Women's Issues* (1997). **Essays:** Hypatia and Early Philosophers; Laurence, Margaret; Marie de France.

Chmielewski, Wendy E. Curator, Swarthmore College Peace Collection. Author of *Women in Spiritual and Communitarian Societies in the United States* (1993). Editor of *Guide to Sources on Women in the Swarthmore College Peace Collection* (1988). Contributor to *Peace and Change.* **Essays:** Intentional Communities; Peace Movements; Rankin, Jeannette.

Christian-Smith, Linda K. Professor of Education, University of Wisconsin, Oshkosh. Author of *Becoming a Woman through Romance* (1990), and, with Leslie Roman, *Becoming Feminine: The Politics of Popular Culture* (1988). Contributor to *English Journal, Curriculum Inquiry, New Advocate,* and *Contemporary Education.* **Essay:** Literature: Romance Fiction.

Cicero, Dawn M. Graduate student in Women's Studies, San Diego State University, San Diego, California. Contributor to *Stepjazz.* **Essay:** Ancient Egalitarian Cultures.

Classen, Albrecht. Professor of Germanic Studies, University of Arizona, Tucson. Author of *The German Volksbuch* (1995), *Eroticism and Love in the Middle Ages* (1994). Editor, *Tristania* (1993–); coeditor, *Mediaevistik* (1992–); book review editor, *Journal of the Rocky Mountain Medieval Review* (1995–). **Essay:** History: Medieval.

Clutterbuck, Andrew. Senior Lecturer in the Study of Religion, University of Hertfordshire, Aldenham. Author of *Growing Up in Sikhism* (1990). Contributor to *International Journal for Human-Computer Studies, Sikh Bulletin.* **Essays:** Islamic Fundamentalism; Witchcraft/Wicca: Modern and Neo-Paganism.

Cochrane, Helena Antolin. Adjunct Lecturer in Spanish, University of Pennsylvania, Philadelphia. Contributor to *Mosaic.* **Essay:** Isabella I.

Cockin, Katherine. Lecturer in English, University of Hull. Author of *Edith Craig: Dramatic Lives* (1997). **Essays:** Hall, Radclyffe; Literature: Biography and Autobiography; Suffrage: Britain and Ireland.

Collins, Lisa Gail. Lecturer in Women's Studies, Bowdoin College, Brunswick, Maine. Contributor to *Colors: Opinion and the Arts in Communities of Color,* and *International Review of African American Art.* **Essay:** Womanism.

Conley, Susan. Assistant Professor of English, Australian National University, Canberra. Contributor to *Victorian Women Poets: A Critical Reader* (1996). **Essays:** Moore, Marianne; Staël, Madame de, Anne-Louise-Germaine.

Conner, Susan P. Professor of History, and Chair, History

Department, Central Michigan University, Mount Pleasant. Contributor to *Eighteenth-Century Studies, Journal of Women's History, Journal of Social History, Eighteenth Century Life,* and numerous edited collections. **Essays:** Marie Antoinette; Prostitution; Tristan, Flora.

Connor, Jane. Professor of Psychology, State University of New York, Binghamton. **Essays:** (with Alison Thomas-Cottingham) AIDS and HIV; Breastfeeding; Homophobia and Heterosexism; (with Anna Ng and Sue Gilbert) Sexual Assault/Rape: Acquaintance.

Cooley, Elizabeth. Assistant Professor of English, Gonzaga University, Spokane, Washington. Contributor to *South Atlantic Review, Studies in Short Fiction, Spectator Magazine, Contemporary Literary Criticism, Limestone: A Literary Journal, Carolina Quarterly,* and numerous edited collections. **Essays:** Angelou, Maya; Porter, Katherine Anne.

Coppola, Carlo. Professor of Modern Languages and Linguistics, Oakland University, Rochester, Michigan. Editor of *Marxist Influences and South Asian Literature* (1974) and *Anthology of Mohan Rakesh* (1975). Contributor to *Literature East and West, Journal of South Asian Literature, South Asian Review, Annual of Urdu Studies,* and *South Asia.* **Essays:** Aung San Suu Kyi; Bhutto, Benazir; Catherine de Medici; Freud, Anna; Freud, Sigmund; Horney, Karen; Keller, Helen; Klein, Melanie; Luxemburg, Rosa; Meir, Golda.

Crane, Gary D. Chair, Department of Business Administration, Ivy Technical State College, South Bend, Indiana. **Essays:** Aviation; Feminism: Radical; Sculpture.

Crane, Ralph J. Senior Lecturer in English, University of Waikato, Hamilton. Author of *Inventing India: A History of India in English-Language Fiction* (1992), and *Ruth Prawer Jhubvala* (1992). Editor of *Passages to Ruth Prawer Jhubvala* (1991). Coeditor, *SPAN.* **Essay:** Jhabvala, Ruth Prawer.

Cuthbert, Denise. Director, Centre for Women's Studies, Monash University, Clayton, Victoria. Author of *Andrew Marvell* (1993). Contributor to *Cultural Studies, Thamyris, Australasian Drama Studies,* and *Australian Women's Book Review.* **Essay:** Race/Ethnicity and Gender.

Cyganowski, Carol Klimick. Associate Professor of English, Director of American Studies Program, DePaul University, Chicago, Illinois. Author of *Magazine Editors and Professional Authors in Nineteenth Century America: The Genteel Tradition and the American Dream* (1988). Contributor to *NWSA Journal, Arizona Quarterly,* and numerous reference books and edited collections. Consulting editor in literature, *Women's Studies Encyclopedia* project. **Essays:** Hellman, Lillian; Inventors.

Darling-Wolf, Fabienne. Ph.D. candidate and instructor in Communication Studies, University of Iowa, Iowa City. Contributor to *Journal of Communication Inquiry, Herizons,* and *Woman Rebel.* **Essay:** Beauty Standards.

David, Indra M. Associate Dean, Library, Oakland University, Rochester, Michigan. Contributor to *Proceedings of the Sixth National Conference of the Association of College and Research Libraries* and *Discovering Librarians: Profiles of a Profession,* edited by M.J. Scherdin (1994). **Essay:** Sati.

D'Cruz, Doreen. Senior Lecturer, Department of English, Massey University, Palmerson North. Contributor to *Studies in the Novel, Renascence,* and *SPAN.* **Essay:** Fashion.

Dever, Maryanne. Lecturer, Centre for Women's Studies, Monash University, Clayton, Victoria. Editor of *Wallflowers and Witches: Women and Culture in Australia 1910–1945* (1994) and *Australia and Asia: Cultural Transactions* (1997). Founding member of the Women's Studies Research Centre, University of Hong Kong. **Essays:** Teaching: University; Women's Studies: Introductory Works.

DeZwart, Mary Leah. Career Programs Coordinator, Norkam Secondary School, Kamloops, British Columbia. Author, with L. Peterat, of *An Education for Women: Home Economics Education in Canada 1900–1990* (1995). Contributor to *Education Research Forum* and *Canadian Home Economics Journal.* **Essay:** (with Linda Peterat) Home Economics.

Dickson, Carol E. Lecturer in English, University of Wisconsin, Madison. **Essays:** Eddy, Mary Baker; Howe, Julia Ward; Zaharias, Mildred "Babe" Didrikson.

Dillaway, Heather Elise. Ph.D. candidate in sociology, Michigan State University, East Lansing. **Essays:** Doctors; Hutchinson, Anne; Midwifery; Pregnancy and Childbirth; Willard, Emma.

Dinger, Sandi L. Ph.D. candidate in management, State University of New York, Binghamton. **Essay:** Sanger, Margaret.

Dingley, Robert. Senior Lecturer, Department of English, University of New England, Armidale, New South Wales. Author of *The Land of the Golden Fleece,* edited by George Augustus Sala (1995). Contributor to *Victorian Literature and Culture, AUMLA, Durham University Journal, Notes and Queries, Victorian Review, Art*

Bulletin, and *Cahiers Victoriens et Edouardiens.* **Essays:** Brontë, Charlotte and Emily; Eliot, George; Gaskell, Elizabeth.

DiPalma, Carolyn. Assistant Professor, Department of Women's Studies, University of South Florida, Tampa. **Essays:** Biological Determinism; Health: Gender Politics of.

Dixon, John C. Ph.D. in English, Boston University, Boston, Massachusetts. Contributor to *On the Market: Ph.D.s Tell Their Stories of the Academic Job Search,* edited by Christina Boufis and Victoria C. Olsen (1997). **Essay:** Capitalism.

Donaldson, Colleen T. Grants Development Director, State University of New York, Brockport. Contributor to *Society of Research Administrators Journal.* Assistant Editor, *Society of Research Administrators Journal.* **Essay:** Abortion: Twentieth Century.

Dreher, Nan H. Assistant Professor of History, Marquette University, Milwaukee, Wisconsin. Contributor to *Victorian Periodicals Review* and *Albion.* **Essays:** Byron, Ada, Countess of Lovelace; Curie, Marie; Nightingale, Florence; Sayers, Dorothy Leigh; Stopes, Marie.

Evans, Ruth. Lecturer in English Literature, University of Wales, Cardiff. Editor of *Simone de Beauvoir, The Second Sex: New Interdisciplinary Essays* (1997) and coeditor of *Feminist Readings in Middle English* (1994). Contributor to *Reader's Guide to English Literature,* edited by Mark Hawkins-Dady (1996), *Encyclopedia of Translation Studies* (1996), *Feminist Criticism: Theory and Practice,* edited by Susan Sellers (1991), *Leeds Studies in English,* and *Textual Practice.* **Essays:** Chaucer, Geoffrey; Feminist Theory, Formative Works; Misogyny.

Ewell, Barbara C. Professor of English, City College, Loyola University, New Orleans, Louisiana. Author of *Kate Chopin* (1986). Editor, with Dorothy Brown, *Louisiana Women Writers: New Critical Essays and a Comprehensive Bibliography* (1992). Contributor to *Louisiana Literature, Southern Literary Journal, Modern Language Quarterly, Centennial Review,* and *New Orleans Review.* **Essay:** Chopin, Kate.

Farrell, Amy S. Ph.D. candidate in law, policy, and society, Northeastern University, Boston, Massachusetts. Author, "Women, Crime, and Drugs: Testing the Effect of Therapeutic Community Participation and Social Support" (master's thesis). Contributor, with Ruth Horowitz, to *Gender and Society.* Student Editor, *Law and Human Behavior.* **Essay:** Gender-Role Socialization; Lawyers.

Feldman, Susan B. Ph.D. candidate in literature and psychoanalysis, State University of New York, Buffalo. **Essay:** Bisexuality.

Fensham, Rachel. Lecturer, Centre for Drama and Theatre Studies, Monash University, Clayton, Victoria. Contributor to *Cultural Studies, Writings on Dance.* Editor, *Antithesis* and *Real Time: National Performing Arts Magazine.* **Essay:** Dance.

Ford, Bonnie L. Professor of History and Women's Studies, Sacramento City College, Sacramento, California. **Essays:** Divorce: History; Slavery, Black; Women's Rights Convention, Seneca Falls, New York.

Foss, Vivian. Lecturer in English, University of Wisconsin, Oshkosh. **Essays:** Higher Education; Literature: Renaissance.

French, Brigittine M. Ph.D. candidate in anthropology and graduate instructor of rhetoric, University of Iowa, Iowa City. **Essay:** Communication Styles and Gender.

Furdell, Elizabeth Lane. Associate Professor of History, University of North Florida, Jacksonville. Contributor to *Sixteenth Century Journal, Historian, Historical Dictionary of Stuart England* (1996), and *Historical Dictionary of the British Empire* (1995). **Essays:** Healers and Herbalism; Science: History; Sévigné, Marie, Marquise de.

Gaul, Theresa Strouth. Ph.D. candidate in American Literature, University of Wisconsin, Madison. Contributor to *Literature/Interpretation/Theory.* **Essay:** Fuller, Margaret.

Gavioli, Davida. Visiting Assistant Professor of Italian and Comparative Literature, Oberlin College, Oberlin, Ohio. Contributor to *Gendered Contexts: New Perspectives in Italian Cultural Studies,* edited by Laura Benedetti, Julia Hairston, and Silvia Ross (1996), and *Reader's Guide to Literature in English,* edited by Mark Hawkins-Dady (1996), and *Rivista annuale dell'Associazione Italiana di Studi Nord-Americani.* **Essays:** Mother-Daughter Relationships; Motherhood.

Gergen, Mary M. Associate Professor of Psychology and Women's Studies, Pennsylvania State University, Media. Author, with K.J. Gergen, of *Social Psychology* (1981) and, with J. Suls, R. Rosnow, and R. Lana, *Psychology: A Beginning* (1989). Editor of numerous collections of essays. Contributor to *Psychology of Women Quarterly* and numerous edited collections. **Essay:** Psychological Theories about Women: Feminist

Gibson, Amelia. Radio Journalist. **Essay:** (with Katharina von Ledersteger and Barbara Penner) Architecture.

Gordon, Sharón. M.A. candidate in geography, San

Diego State University, San Diego, California. **Essay:** Geography.

Gough, Val. Lecturer in English, University of Liverpool. Coeditor of *Optimist Reformer: Studies on the Fiction of Charlotte Perkins Gilman* (1997). Contributor to *Woolf Studies Annual.* Editor, *Liverpool Studies in Language and Discourse;* International Associate Editor, *Woolf Studies Annual.* **Essay:** Cixous, Hélène.

Green, Melanie G. Graduate student in women's studies, San Diego State University, San Diego, California. Contributor to *Aesthetic Voice* and numerous edited collections. **Essay:** Sexism.

Griffin, Gabriele. Author of *Feminist Activism in the 1990s* (1995), *Gender Issues in Elder Abuse* (1996), *Pulp and Other Plays by Tasha Fairbanks* (1996), *Stirring It: Challenges for Feminism* (1994), and *Heavenly Love?: Lesbian Images in 20th Century Women's Writing* (1993). **Essays:** Elder Abuse; Literature: Lesbian; Theater: Women's Activity in.

Gross, Rita M. Professor of Comparative Studies in Religion, University of Wisconsin, Eau Claire. Author of *Buddhism after Patriarchy: A Feminist History, Analysis, and Reconstruction of Religion* (1993), *Feminism and Religion: An Introduction* (1996), and, with Nancy Aver Falk, *Unspoken Worlds: Women's Religious Lives* (1989). Coeditor, *Journal of Buddhist-Christian Studies.* **Essays:** Buddhism; Goddesses; Hinduism.

Grossman, Michèle. Senior Lecturer in Communications and Language Studies, Victoria University of Technology, Melbourne, Victoria. Contributor to *Cultural Studies, Thamyris, Arena Journal, Age Monthly Review,* and numerous edited collections. **Essay:** Aboriginal Women.

Gruberg, Martin. Professor of Political Science, University of Wisconsin, Oshkosh. Author of *Women in American Politics.* Contributor to numerous reference books. Senior editor, 2nd and 3rd editions of *Encyclopedia of American Government.* **Essays:** Catt, Carrie Chapman; League of Women Voters; Luce, Clare Boothe; National Woman's Party, United States; Roe v. Wade (United States 1973); Roosevelt, Eleanor; Smith, Margaret Chase; Suffrage: United States; Thatcher, Margaret.

Haffey, Deborah Bush. Associate Professor of Communication Arts, Cedarville College, Cedarville, Ohio. **Essays:** Business and Entrepreneurship; Dual Career Families.

Hall, Joan Wylie. Instructor of English, University of Mississippi, University. Author of *Shirley Jackson: A Study of the Short Fiction* (1993). Contributor to *Legacy: A Journal of American Women Writers, Studies in Short Fiction, Faulkner Journal,* and *Mississippi Quarterly,* and *Renascence.* **Essay:** Cather, Willa.

Hames, Gina L. Assistant Professor of History, Pacific Lutheran University, Tacoma, Washington. Contributor to *Feminist Literary Theory: A Dictionary* (1996), *Encyclopedia of World History* (1995), *Encyclopedia of Social History* (1994), and *Hispanic American Historical Review.* **Essay:** Latin American Women.

Hart, Alexandra M. Graduate student in Latin American studies, San Diego State University, San Diego, California. Contributor to *Latinos Magazine.* **Essay:** Bernhardt, Sarah.

Heaphy, Leslie. Assistant Professor of History, Kent State University, Stark Campus, Canton, Ohio. Contributor to *NINE, Journal of Sport History, International Journal of Sport History, Journal of Interdisciplinary Studies,* and *Northwest Ohio Quarterly.* **Essay:** Athletes.

Hellstern, Melissa. Freelance Writer. Editor of *When Women Lead the Way* (1996) and *Teacher's Manual to Accompany Citizenship through Sports and Law* (1996). Contributor to *St. Louis Magazine* and *St. Louis Business Journal.* **Essays:** Mentoring; Volunteerism; Wollstonecraft, Mary; Women's Organizations.

Henningfeld, Diane Andrews. Assistant Professor of English, Adrian College, Adrian, Michigan. Contributor to numerous reference books. **Essays:** Christianity: Pre-Reformation; Eating Disorders; Rich, Adrienne; Truth, Sojourner; Tubman, Harriet; Welty, Eudora.

Herzog, Melanie A. Assistant Professor of Art History, Edgewood College, Madison, Wisconsin. Contributor to *International Review of African American Art* and *School Arts.* Editor, Women's *Caucus for Art National Honor Awards Exhibition Catalogue.* **Essays:** Art and Gender Issues; Artists: Twentieth Century.

Highberg, Nels P. M.A. in women's studies, Ohio State University, Columbus. **Essays:** Comedians; Literature: Drama; Performance Art; Self-Esteem.

Holland, Bridget D. Ph.D. candidate in education, University of Auckland. Contributor to *The Economics of Education* (1995) and *Revisiting the "Reforms" in Education* (1994), both authored and edited by Bridget Holland and James Marshall. **Essays:** Ecofeminism; Teaching: Primary and Secondary.

Horowitz, Sara R. Associate Professor and Director, Jewish Studies Program, University of Delaware, Newark. Author of *Voicing the Void: Muteness and Memory in*

Holocaust Fiction (1992). Coeditor of *Jewish Women Writers* (1994) and *KEREM.* **Essay:** Holocaust.

Hou, Sharon Shih-jiuan. Associate Professor of Modern Languages and Literatures, Pomona College, Claremont, California. Author of *Intellectual Ferment in China: The Hu Shi Reader* (1990). Contributor to *Indiana Companion to Traditional Chinese Literature,* edited by William H. Nienhauser, Jr. (1986). **Essay:** Sex Customs in China, Japan, and India.

Hughes, Kate Pritchard. Senior Lecturer, Social and Cultural Studies, Victoria University, Melbourne, Victoria. Author of *Contemporary Australian Feminism 2* (1996) and *How Do You Know? An Overview of Writings on Feminist Pedagogy and Epistemology* (1994). Assistant Editor, *Australian Women's Book Review.* **Essays:** Pedagogy, Feminist; Women's Studies: General Works.

Jamsen, Kirsten. Ph.D. candidate in English, University of Wisconsin, Madison. **Essays:** Child, Lydia Maria; Grimké, Angelina and Sarah.

Johnson, Helen. Lecturer in Anthropology and Women's Studies, Monash University, Clayton, Victoria. Contributor to *Australian Journal of Anthropology.* **Essays:** Concubinage; Dowry Murder/Bride Burning; Female Infanticide; Femininity; Gender Stereotyping; Hunting/Gathering Cultures; Purdah; Sex Tourism.

Johnston, Julie K. Ph.D. candidate in women's studies, San Diego State University, San Diego, California. **Essays:** Hurston, Zora Neale; Settlement House Movement.

Josephson, Jyl J. Assistant Professor, Department of Political Science, Texas Tech University, Lubbock. Author of *Gender, Families, and State: Child Support Policy in the United States* (1996). Contributor to *Women and Politics.* Editor of *PEGS* (1991–94). **Essays:** Child Support; Divorce: Present-Day; Single-Parent Families.

Kalny, Cheryl Toronto. Lecturer in Women's Studies, University of Wisconsin, Green Bay. **Essays:** Criminal Punishment; Female Offenders; Gender as a Social Construct.

Karraker, Meg Wilkes. Associate Professor of Sociology, University of St. Thomas, St. Paul, Minnesota. Contributor to *College Teaching, International Journal of Social Studies Education, Urban Education,* and *Race, Gender, and Class.* Review Editor for *Gender and Society* and *Teaching Sociology.* **Essay:** Work.

Keith, Carolyn. Housing Social Services Specialist, Milwaukee, Wisconsin. Contributor to *Women and Environments, Journal of Marriage and Family,* and *NASW Practice Journal.* **Essay:** Aging

Kelly, Ellin M. Professor Emeritus of English, DePaul University, Chicago, Illinois. Author of *Elizabeth Seton's Two Bibles* (1977), *Numerous Choirs: A Chronicle of Elizabeth Bayley Seton and Her Spiritual Daughters,* 2 volumes (1981, 1996), and, with Stanley Damberger, *A Look at Brittany: Its Calvaries, Its Faience.* Coeditor, with Annabelle Melville, of *Elizabeth Seton: Selected Writings* (1987). Contributor to *English Language Notes, Notes and Queries, American Benedictine Review, Listening: Journal of Religion and Culture, Comparative Drama,* and numerous edited collections. **Essay:** Seton, Elizabeth.

Kelly, Erna. Professor of English, University of Wisconsin, Eau Claire. Contributor to *Seventeenth Century Wit,* edited by Claude Summers and Ted-Larry Pebworth (1995), *Selected Proceedings: Conference on Cultural Emblematics,* edited by Ayres Bagley et al. (1996), and numerous other edited collections and journals. **Essay:** Literature: Diaries and Journals.

Kenschaft, Lori J. Graduate student, Boston University, Boston, Massachusetts. Contributor to *A Companion to American Thought,* edited Richard Wightman Fox and James Kloppenberg (1995). **Essays:** Abortion, Pre-Twentieth Century; Coeducation; Feminist Movements: Nineteenth Century; History: American.

Kenschaft, Patricia Clark. Professor of Mathematics, Montclair State University, Upper Montclair, New Jersey. Author of *Math Power: How to Help Your Child Love Math Even If You Don't* (1997) and numerous other books. Editor of *Winning Women into Mathematics* (1991). Contributor to *Signs, American Mathematical Monthly,* and *1997 Yearbook, National Council of Teachers of Mathematics.* First National Chair, Committee on Participation of Women, Mathematical Association of America. **Essays:** Mathematics: General; Mathematics: Teaching to Women.

Keown, Michelle Maria. Tutor and Assistant Lecturer, Department of English, University of Waikato, Hamilton. Contributor to *SPAN.* **Essay:** Frame, Janet.

Kingfisher, Catherine Pélissier. Lecturer, Women's and Gender Studies, University of Waikato, Hamilton. Author of *Women in the American Welfare Trap* (1996). Contributor to *Discourse and Society* and *Annual Review of Anthropology.* **Essays:** Citizenship; Poverty.

Klein, Laura F. Professor of Anthropology, Pacific Lutheran University, Tacoma, Washington. Coeditor, with Elizabeth Brusco, of *The Message in the Missionary: Local*

Interpretations of Religious Ideology and Missionary Personality (1994), and, with Lillian Ackerman, *Women and Power in Native North America* (1995). Contributor to *Arctic Anthropology* and numerous edited collections. **Essays:** (with Elizabeth Brusco) Anthropology: Traditional; (with Elizabeth Brusco) Benedict, Ruth; Matriliny; Mead, Margaret; Native American Women.

Kulbicki, Melvin A. Professor of History and Social Science, York College of Pennsylvania, York. **Essay:** Military.

Kumar, Rachel Simon. Graduate student in women's studies, University of Waikato, Hamilton. Contributor to *Twentieth Century Romance* (1993), *Economic and Political Weekly*, and *Indian Journal of Labour Economics*. **Essay:** Reproductive Freedom.

Kurian, Priya A. Lecturer, Department of Political Science and Public Policy, University of Waikato, Hamilton. Coeditor of numerous edited collections. Contributor to *Asia Pacific Journal on Environment and Development, Environmental Professional, North Dakota History*, and numerous edited collections. **Essays:** Feminization of Poverty; Migrant Labor.

LaBrie, Janet M. Lecturer, University of Wisconsin Center, Rock County, Janesville. Contributor to *Agricultural History* and numerous volumes and editions of *Masterplots*. **Essays:** Glasgow, Ellen; Literature: Mysteries and Crime Fiction; Migration; Sacagawea.

Laffey, Alice L. Associate Professor of Religious Studies, College of the Holy Cross, Worcester, Massachusetts. Author of *An Introduction to the Old Testament: A Feminist Perspective* (1988). Contributor to *Horizons, Bible Today, The Way*, and numerous articles in religious reference works. **Essays:** Bible: General; Bible: Old Testament/Hebrew Bible; Convents and Nuns; Spirituality, Feminist; Theology, Feminist.

Langenheim, Ralph L., Jr. Professor Emeritus of Geology, University of Illinois, Urbana. Contributor to *Bulletin of the Geological Society of America* and *American Journal of Science*. Book Review Editor, *Journal of Geoscience Education*. **Essay:** Franklin, Rosalind, and the DNA Controversy.

Langran, Robert W. Professor of Political Science, Villanova University, Villanova, Pennsylvania. Author of *The United States Supreme Court: An Historical and Political Analysis* (1989). Contributor to *Teaching Political Science* and numerous reference works. **Essay:** Workplace Equality Legislation.

Ledersteger, Katharina von. M.A. in architectural history and theory; student of architecture, University College, London. **Essay:** (with Amelia Gibson and Barbara Penner) Architecture.

Lent, Robin S. Head of Collection Development, University of New Hampshire, Durham. Contributor to *Short Fiction by Women* and *College Composition and Communication*. Managing Editor, *Journal of the Experimental Analysis of Behavior*. **Essays:** Blackwell, Elizabeth; Woman's Club Movement

Levin, Carole. Professor of History, State University of New York, New Platz. Author of *The Heart and Stomach of a King: Elizabeth I and the Politics of Sex and Power* (1994) and *Propaganda in the English Reformation: Heroic and Villainous Images of King John* (1988). Coeditor of numerous books. **Essays:** Elizabeth I; Mary I.

Levitsky, Holli G. Associate Professor of English, Loyola Marymount University, Los Angeles, California. Author of *Contemporary Jewish American Novelists* (1997) and *Masterpieces of Women's Literature* (1997). Contributor to *Women's Studies*. **Essay:** Weil, Simone.

Li, Jian. Research Associate, Southern Methodist University, Dallas, Texas. Contributor to *South Carolina Historical Magazine* and *Anthropological Quarterly*. **Essays:** Adultery; Friendship; Matrifocal Cultures.

Locy, Sharon A. Professor of English, Loyola Marymount University, Los Angeles, California. Contributor to *Metanoia, Women's Studies Encyclopedia* (1990), *Victorian Britain*, edited by Sally Mitchell (1988). **Essays:** Cameron, Julia Margaret; Lowell, Amy.

Lutes, Jean Marie. Ph.D. candidate in American literature, University of Wisconsin, Madison. **Essay:** Bly, Nellie.

Lyons, Karen V. Lecturer in English, University of Nebraska, Lincoln. **Essay:** Sarton, May.

MacCormack, Patricia. Ph.D. candidate in women's studies, Monash University, Clayton, Victoria. Contributor to *Bloodsongs*. **Essay:** Ancient Classical World.

Macdonald, Gina. Visiting Assistant Professor, Loyola University, New Orleans, Louisiana. Author of *James Clavell* (1996), *Robert Ludlum* (1997), and *Mastering Writing Essentials* (1995). Coauthor, with Paulina Bazin, of numerous contributions to edited collections. Coeditor of *IEP Newsletter* (1995). **Essays:** (with Paulina Bazin) Akhmatova, Anna Andreeva; (with Paulina Bazin) Tsvetaeva, Marina.

MacRae, Suzanne H. Faculty of English Department, University of Arkansas, Fayetteville. Contributor to numerous journals. **Essay:** Gordimer, Nadine.

Malone, Edward A. Assistant Professor of English, Missouri Western State College, St. Joseph. Contributor to *Milton Quarterly, Faulkner Journal,* and *English Language Notes.* **Essay:** Milton, John.

Manikas, Bill. Professor of History, Gaston College, Dallas, North Carolina. **Essays:** Dix, Dorothea; Sexual Slavery.

Manrique, Cecilia G. Associate Professor of Political Science, University of Wisconsin, La Crosse. Contributor to *Kaleidoscope, Proteus, Wisconsin Political Scientist, PS: Political Science and Politics, Social Science Computer Review,* and numerous edited collections. **Essays:** Asian Women; Economic Development: Asia; Multinational Corporations; United Nations.

Marston, Catherine L. Ph.D. candidate in journalism and mass communication, University of Iowa, Iowa City. **Essay:** Disability Issues.

Mascia-Lees, Frances E. Professor of Anthropology, Simon's Rock of Bard College, Great Barrington, Massachusetts. Author of *Toward a Model of Women's Status* (1984). Coeditor, with Patricia Sharpe, of *Tattoo, Torture, Mutilation, and Adornment: The Denaturalization of the Body in Culture and Text* (1992). Contributor to numerous journals and edited collections. **Essay:** Romance.

Maybury, Karol. Assistant Professor of Psychology, Whitworth College, Spokane, Washington. Contributor to *Omega: Journal of Death Dying.* **Essays:** Science: Women as Subject of.

McCall, Anne E. Associate Professor of French, Tulane University, New Orleans, Louisiana. Author of *De l'être en lettres: l'autobiographie épistolaire de George Sand* (1996). Editor of George Sand, *Histoire de ma vie,* vol. 4 (1996). Contributor to *L'esprit créateur.* Editorial board, *George Sand Studies.* **Essay:** Sand, George.

McCay, Mary A. Professor of English, Chair of English Department, Loyola University, New Orleans, Louisiana. Author of *Rachel Carson* (1993). Contributing editor of *The Feminist Companion to Literature in English* (1990). Contributor to numerous edited collections. Book Review Editor, *New Orleans Review* and *New Orleans Times Picayune.* **Essay:** Carson, Rachel.

McDonell, Jennifer. Lecturer in English and Communication Studies, University of New England, Armidale, New South Wales. Contributor to Southerly and *South Asia: Journal of South Asian Studies.* **Essays:** Beauvoir, Simone de; Martineau, Harriet; Stead, Christina.

McNeal, Patricia. Director, Women's Studies Program, Indiana University, South Bend. Author of *Harder than War: Catholic Peacemaking in Twentieth Century America* (1992) and *The American Catholic Peace Movement 1928–1972* (1978). Contributor to numerous journals and edited collections. **Essays:** Day, Dorothy; Women's History Movement.

Michelle, Carolyn. Postgraduate student in the Department of Women's and Gender Studies, University of Waikato, Hamilton. **Essays:** Advertising, Images of Women in; Soap Opera.

Miles, Angela R. Professor of Adult Education, Ontario Institute for Studies in Education, Toronto, Ontario. Author of *Integrative Feminisms: Building Global Visions, 1960–1990s* (1996). Coeditor of *Feminism: From Pressure to Politics* (1989). **Essay:** Feminist Movements: Global.

Miller, Barbara B. Assistant Professor of Religious Studies, Edgewood College, Madison, Wisconsin. Contributor to *Deadly Deference: Women's Issues* (1997). **Essays:** Bible: New Testament; Virgin Mary.

Miller, Karen A.J. Assistant Professor of History, Oakland University, Rochester, Michigan. **Essay:** Perkins, Frances.

Mohanram, Radhika. Lecturer, Department of Women's and Gender Studies, University of Waikato, Hamilton. Coeditor of *Postcolonial Discourses and Changing Cultural Contexts* (1995) and *English Postcoloniality: Literatures from around the World* (1996). Contributor to *NWSA Journal, New Zealand Women's Studies Journal,* and *Indian Journal of Gender Studies.* Coeditor of *SPAN* (1994–). **Essay:** Literary Criticism, Feminist.

Moore, Jennifer R. Postgraduate student, researcher in English, University of Sydney, New South Wales. **Essay:** Doolittle, Hilda (H.D.)

More, Jennifer. Ph.D. candidate in the history and theory of music, University of Chicago, Chicago, Illinois. **Essays:** Composers; Musicology.

Morrow, Susan L. Assistant Professor of Counseling Psychology, University of Utah, Salt Lake City. Author of *Living Our Visions: Building Feminist Community* (1996). Contributor to *Journal of Vocational Behavior, Journal of Counseling Psychology, Journal of Counseling and Development,* and *Journal for Specialists in Group Work.* **Essays:** Psychological Theories about Women: Pre-Feminist; Psychotherapy, Feminist.

Mullin, Jay. Associate Professor of Sociology, Queensborough Community College, City University of New

York, Bayside. Contributor to *Encyclopedia of Women's Issues* (1997). **Essay:** Sexual Double Standard.

Nandrea, Lorri G. Graduate student in English, Northwestern University, Evanston, Illinois. **Essay:** Radcliffe, Ann Ward.

Nangeroni, Nancy R. Secretary, International Foundation for Gender Education. Contributor to *Gender Bending*, edited by Bullough et al. (1997), *Transgender Tapestry*, and *Sojourner.* **Essays:** Transgenderism; Transsexualism.

Narayan, Shyamala A. Reader in English, Jamia Millia Islamia, New Delhi. Author of *Raja Rao: The Man and His Work* (1989). Contributor to *Ariel, World Literature Today, Indian Literature*, and *Journal of Indian Writing in English.* Adviser, *Reference Guide to Short Fiction* (1994). **Essay:** Gandhi, Indira.

Neumann, Caryn E. Managing Editor, *Journal of Women's History;* Ph.D. candidate in women's history, Ohio State University, Columbus. Contributor to *Journal of Women's History.* **Essays:** Feminist Movement, Abolitionist Origins of; Feminist Movements: Twentieth Century; Goldman, Emma; Great Depression; Kelley, Florence; Lesbian History; Suffrage: Worldwide; Wald, Lillian; Woman's Christian Temperance Union; Woodhull, Victoria.

Nickless, Pamela J. Associate Professor of Economics, University of North Carolina, Asheville. Contributor to *Journal of Economic History* and *Women in Spiritual and Communitarian Societies in the United States*, edited by W. Chemielewski, L.J. Kern, and M. Klee-Hartzell (1993). **Essays:** Dual Labor Markets; Earnings Gap; Lee, Ann, Mother; Women at Work during World War II, United States.

Nicolacopoulos, Toula. Assistant Professor, School of Philosophy, LaTrobe University, Bundoora Campus, Bundoora, Victoria. Contributor to *Alternative Law Journal.* **Essays:** Feminism: Liberal; Sexual Harassment in the Workplace; Surrogate Motherhood.

Noonan, Norma C. Professor of Political Science, Augsburg College, Minneapolis, Minnesota. Coeditor and contributor to *Russian Women in Politics and Society* (1996). Contributor to numerous reference books. Senior editor, *Russian Women's Movements.* **Essays:** Leadership; Peron, Eva.

Nováková, Soňa. Assistant Professor of English Literature and British Cultural Studies, Charles University, Prague. Contributor to *Litteraria Pragensia, Prague Studies in English*, and numerous reference books. **Essays:** Astell, Mary; Behn, Aphra; Magazines and Periodicals.

O'Connor, Mary. Associate Professor of English, South Dakota State University, Brookings. Contributor to *Eire/Ireland, Krino*, and numerous edited collections. **Essay:** Mother Jones.

O'Grady, Christine. Social Worker, Group Home for Teenage Girls, Puslinch, Ontario. **Essays:** Addictions; Caregiving.

O'Grady, Kathleen. Ph.D. candidate, Trinity College, University of Cambridge. Author, with Paula Wansbrough, of *A Sweet Secret: Telling the Story of Menstruation* (1997). Contributor to *Literature and Theology.* **Essays:** Irigaray, Luce; (with Paula Wansbrough) Menstruation.

Olson, Laura Katz. Professor of Political Science, Lehigh University, Bethlehem, Pennsylvania. Author of *Public Policy and Aging: The Politics of Growing Old in America* (1983) and *The Political Economy of Aging: The State, Private Power, and Social Welfare* (1982). Contributor to numerous journals. **Essay:** Welfare.

Olubas, Brigitta. Lecturer, School of English, University of New South Wales, Sydney. Contributor to *Australian Literary Studies* and *New Literatures Review.* **Essays:** Mansfield, Katherine; Morrison, Toni; Nin, Anaïs; Walker, Alice.

O'Reilly, Andrea. Adjunct Professor, York University, North York, Ontario. Contributor to *African American Review, AFRAM Newsletter, Everyday Acts against Racism: Raising Children in a Multiracial World*, edited by Maureen Reddy (1996), and *Feminism and Education*, edited by Paula T. Bourne. **Essay:** Black Women.

Orr, Catherine M. Ph.D. candidate in speech communications and women's studies, University of Minnesota, Minneapolis. Contributor to *Women Public Speakers in the United States, 1925–1993: A Bio-Critical Sourcebook*, edited by Karlyn Kohrs Campbell (1994). **Essays:** Consciousness-Raising; Feminist Activism.

Ortel, Jo. Lecturer, Department of Art, University of Wisconsin, Madison. Contributor to *SPOT.* Editorial board, *SPOT.* **Essays:** Carr, Emily; Kauffmann, Angelica; Morsiot, Berthe.

Oxendale, Stephanie. Ph.D. student and teaching assistant in European women's history, State University of New York, Binghamton. **Essays:** Industrial Revolution; Mormonism.

Paradowski, Robert J. Professor, College of Liberal Arts, Rochester Institute of Technology, Rochester, New York. Contributor to *The Nobel Prize Winners: Chemistry*

(1990) and *Journal of Chemical Education.* **Essays:** Hodgkin, Dorothy Mary Crowfoot; Sciences: Biological; Sciences: Physical; Yourcenar, Marguerite.

Pease, Bob. Senior Lecturer, Department of Social Work, Royal Melbourne Institute of Technology, Bundoora Campus, Victoria. Author of *Men and Sexual Politics* (1996). Contributor to *Issues in Social Work Education* and numerous edited collections. International editor for Australia, *Masculinities: Interdisciplinary Studies on Gender.* **Essay:** Men's Movements.

Peirce, Kate L. Professor of Mass Communications, Southwest Texas State University, San Marcos. Contributor to *Journalism Quarterly, Journalism Educator,* and *Sociological Spectrum.* **Essays:** Adolescence; Girlhood; Sex Discrimination in the Workplace.

Pelak, Cynthia Fabrizio. Ph.D. candidate in sociology, Ohio State University, Columbus. **Essay:** Sport and Gender.

Penner, Barbara. **Essays:** (with Amelia Gibson and Katharina von Ledersteger) Architecture.

Peterat, Linda. Professor of Home Economics Education, University of British Columbia, Vancouver. Contributor to *Canadian Home Economics Journal, Journal of Consumer Studies and Home Economics, Journal of Curriculum Theorizing, Journal of Vocational Home Economics Education,* and numerous other journals and edited collections. **Essay:** (with Mary Leah DeZwart) Home Economics.

Peterson, Barbara Bennett. Professor Emeritus, University of Hawaii, Honolulu. Author of *John Bull's Eye on America* (1995), *America: 19th and 20th Centuries* (1994), *American History, 17th, 18th, and 19th Centuries* (1993), *The Pacific Region 1990* (1991), *America in British Eyes* (1988), and *Notable Women of Hawaii* (1984). Numerous articles and essays in journals, edited collections, and reference books. Associate Editor, *American National Biography.* **Essay:** Flaubert, Gustave.

Peterson, Valerie Victoria. Ph.D. candidate in communication studies and rhetoric, University of Iowa, Iowa City. Contributor to *Iowa Journal of Communication.* Chair, editorial board, *The Sextant.* **Essay:** Sexual Politics.

Phillips, AnnMarie. Adjunct Professor of Composition, State University of New York, New Paltz. Contributor to *SUNY Graduate Review, Ulster Magazine.* **Essays:** Arts and Crafts, Traditional; Boadecia; Health: Women's Health Movement; Music: Rock; Photography.

Pilditch, Jan. Senior Lecturer in English, University of Waikato, Hamilton. Author of *The Critical Response to Katherine Mansfield* (1996). Contributor to *Literature and Philosophy, Landfall, SPAN, Scotlands,* and numerous edited collections. **Essays:** Browning, Elizabeth Barrett; Dickinson, Emily; Lessing, Doris; Munro, Alice.

Plastas, Melinda. Visiting Instructor in Women's Studies, Bowdoin College, Brunswick, Maine. Contributor to *Circles: The Buffalo Women's Journal of Law and Social Policy.* **Essay:** Women's International League for Peace and Freedom.

Plichta, Stacey B. Assistant Professor of Health Sciences, Old Dominion University, Norfolk, Virginia. Author of *Women's Health: Results from the Commonwealth Survey* (1996). Contributor to numerous journals. **Essay:** Mental Health.

Poxon, Judith L. Ph.D. candidate in religion, Syracuse University, Syracuse, New York. Contributor to numerous reference books. **Essays:** Church Fathers; Feminism: Cultural.

Preston, James J. Professor of Anthropology, Chair, Religious Studies Program, State University of New York College at Oneonta. Author of *Mother Worship: Theme and Variations* (1982), *Cult of the Goddess: Religious Change in a Hindu Temple* (1985), and, with B. Misra, *Community, Self, and Identity* (1978). Contributions to numerous journals and edited collections. **Essays:** Blavatsky, Helena Petrovna; Cabrini, Mother Frances; Dowry; Feminine Archetypal Theory; Matriarchal Theory; Polygamy; Polygamy, Mormon; Tekakwitha, Kateri.

Price, Victoria. Professor of English and Director of English as a Second Language, Lamar University, Beaumont, Texas. Author of *Christian Allusions in the Novels of Thomas Pynchon* (1989). Contributor to numerous reference books. **Essay:** Alcott, Louisa May.

Price, Vivian. Ph.D. candidate in politics and society, University of California, Irvine. Contributor to *Zheziang Academic Journal.* **Essay:** Nontraditional Jobs.

Raaberg, Gwen. Associate Professor of English, Western Michigan University, Kalamazoo. Coeditor of *Surrealism and Women* (1991). **Essay:** Feminism: Postmodern.

Reagan, Bette Adams. Professor of English, Kutztown University, Kutztown, Pennsylvania. Contributor to *Rhetoric Society Quarterly, Journal of the American Studies Association,* and numerous reference books. **Essays:** Literature: Letters; Literature: Travel Writing.

Reaves, Michaela Crawford. Assistant Professor of History, California Luthern University, Thousand Oaks,

California. Contributor to numerous reference works. **Essays:** Ancient Near East; Hatshepsut.

Renfro, H. Elizabeth. Teacher, Center for Multicultural and Gender Studies, and Director, Literacy and Learning Program, California State University, Chico. Author of *The Shasta Indians* (1992) and *Basic Writing: Process and Product* (1985). Contributor to *Western American Literature, Puerto del sol,* and numerous edited collections and reference books. **Essay:** Heterosexuality.

Roberts, Katherine. Associate Professor of English, University of Wisconsin, Oshkosh. Author of *Fair Ladies: Sir Philip Sidney's Female Characters* (1993). Contributor to *Classical and Modern Literature, Sidney Newsletter and Journal,* and *Wisconsin English Journal.* **Essays:** History: Renaissance; Shakespeare, William.

Robinson, Carol L. Assistant Professor of English. Middle Georgia College, Cochran. Contributor to *Studies in Medievalism V, Post Script: Essays in Film and the Humanities,* and *Cinema Arthuriana,* revised edition, edited by Kevin J. Harty. **Essays:** Filmmaking; Witchcraft: Ancient

Russell, Rinaldina. Professor of European Languages and Literatures, Queens College, City University of New York, Flushing. Author of *Generi poetici medioevali* (1982) and *Tre versanti della poesia stilnovistica: Guinizzelli, Cavalcanti, Dante* (1973). Coeditor and translator of Tullia d'Aragona, *Dialogue on the Infinity of Love* (1997). Editor of *The Feminist Encyclopedia of Italian Literature* (1997) and *Italian Women Writers* (1994). **Essay:** Grandma Moses.

Sanders, Vicki A. Director of Drama and Assistant Professor of English, Paine College, Augusta, Georgia. Contributor to numerous reference books. **Essays:** Acting; Bourke-White, Margaret.

Saunders, Rebecca. Assistant Professor of English, Illinois State University, Normal. Contributor to *PMLA, Romantic Review, Novel: A Forum on Fiction, Journal of the Hellenic Diaspora,* and numerous edited collections. **Essays:** Apartheid; Duras, Marguerite.

Schraefel, Monica C. Senior Instructor, Computer Science, University of Victoria, Victoria, British Columbia. **Essay:** Computers and Cyberspace.

Secrest, Rose. Independent scholar, Signal Mountain, Tennessee. **Essays:** Literature: Utopian and Science Fiction; Technology.

Sergi, Mark. Psychology Intern, Veterans Affairs Outpatient Clinic, Los Angeles. **Essay:** Depression.

Sexson, Lynda. Professor of Humanities, Montana State University, Bozeman. Author of *Ordinarily Sacred* (1982), *Margaret of the Imperfections: Stories* (1988), and *Hamlet's Planets: Parables* (1997). Contributor to *Kenyon Review, Carolina Quarterly, Story Quarterly, Manoa,* and numerous edited collections. Coeditor, *Corona.* **Essays:** Literature: Fiction; Nature.

Shildrick, Margrit. Honorary Research Fellow, Department of Primary Care, University of Liverpool. Author of *Leaky Bodies and Boundaries: Feminism, Postmodernism, and (Bio)Ethics* (1997). Contributor to *Journal of Medicine and Philosophy* and *Body and Society.* **Essays:** Health: General Works; Reproductive Technologies.

Short, Stacey C. Ph.D. candidate, Texas A and M University, College Station. **Essays:** Brooks, Gwendolyn; Colette; Stein, Gertrude.

Simmons, Donald C., Jr. Assistant Director, Mississippi Humanities Council, Jackson. Contributor to *Historical Dictionary of the Modern Olympic Movement,* edited by John E. Findling and Kimberly D. Pelle (1996). Coeditor of *Latin America and the Caribbean in Transition* (1995). President, Association of Third World Studies. **Essays:** Cleopatra; History: British.

Smiley, Pamela M. Associate Professor of English, Carthage College, Kenosha, Wisconsin. Contributor to *College English, Hemingway Review,* and *Asian Journal of Women's Studies.* **Essays:** Kahlo, Frida; Oates, Joyce Carol; Rossetti, Christina.

Smith, Angela K. Lecturer in English, University of Plymouth, Devon. **Essay:** Battlefield Nursing.

Smith, Gail K. Assistant Professor of English, Marquette University, Milwaukee, Wisconsin. Contributor to *American Women Short Story Writers: A Collection of Critical Essays,* edited by Julie Brown (1995). **Essay:** Stowe, Harriet Beecher.

Spear, Hilda D. Honorary Research Fellow and Senior Lecturer Emeritus in English, Dundee University, Dundee. Author of *Iris Murdoch* (1995), *Remembering, We Forget* (1979). Contributions to *Essays in Criticism, Durham University Journal, Literature of Region and Nation, Lines Review, Scottish Review, English Literature in Transition,* and others. **Essays:** Austen, Jane; Murdoch, Iris.

Spray, Sharon L. Assistant Professor of Political Science, Associate Dean of Students, University of the South, Sewanee, Tennessee. Contributor to *The Other Elites: Women, Politics and Power in the Executive Branch,* edited by Mary Anne Borelli and Janet M. Martin. **Essay:** Politics: National.

Staudt, Kathleen. Professor of Political Science, University of Texas, El Paso. Author of *Women, International Development, and Politics: The Bureaucratic Mire* (1990) and *Managing Development* (1991). Contributor to numerous journals and edited collections. **Essays:** Economic Development: Africa; Economic Development: Latin America; Home-Based Work; Management.

Stitt, Beverly A. Coordinator, Women's Studies Program, Southern Illinois University, Carbondale. Author of *Gender Equity in Education: An Annotated Bibliography* (1994). Contributor to *CUPA Journal, NEA Higher Education Advocate, American Technical Education Journal, Continuing Higher Education Review,* and *Journal of Aviation Education.* **Essays:** Gender Bias in Education; Sexual Harassment in Education.

Stoner, Carla A. Teacher of English, adult education and correctional education, Rosemont School District, San Diego, California. Contributor to numerous reference books. **Essay:** Infertility.

Stott, Annette. Associate Professor of Art History and Women's Studies, University of Denver, Denver, Colorado. Contributor to *American Art, Prospects, Art Journal,* and numerous edited collections. **Essays:** Artists: General Surveys; Artists: Nineteenth Century.

Striff, Erin. Ph.D. candidate in feminist theater, University of Wales, Cardiff. Contributor to *Women's Studies International Forum, Journal of Law and Society,* and *Reader's Guide to Literature in English,* edited by Mark Hawkins-Dady (1996). **Essay:** Atwood, Margaret.

Subramaniam, Banu. Research Assistant Professor in Women's Studies/Ecology and Evolutionary Biology, University of Arizona, Tucson. **Essays:** Science: Gender Bias in Research; Science Studies, Feminist.

Sullivan, Timothy E. Associate Professor of Economics, Towson State University, Baltimore, Maryland. **Essays:** Division of Labor by Sex; Glass Ceiling.

Taylor, Susan M. Professor of Law, Indiana University, South Bend. Contributor to numerous reference books and journals. **Essays:** Amazons; British Women during World War II; Child Custody; Clerical Work; Fonteyn, Margot; Girls' Organizations; Hill, Anita; Music: Folk/Traditional; Pavlova, Anna; Property Rights; Self-Defense; Sisterhood; Widowhood.

Thalheimer, Anne N. Ph.D. candidate in English. University of Delaware, Newark. **Essays:** Lesbian Separatism; Lesbian Studies; Pornography; Teresa of Avila.

Thomas-Cottingham, Alison. Ph.D. candidate, State University of New York, Binghamton. Contributor to numerous edited volumes. **Essays:** (with Jane Connor) AIDS and HIV; (with Jane Connor) Homophobia and Heterosexism.

Thompson, Helen. Instructor of English, Auburn University, Auburn, Alabama. Author of *Necessary Heresies: Women, Disavowal, and Desire in the Works of Edna O'Brien* (forthcoming). **Essay:** Pankhurst, Christabel, Emmeline, and Sylvia.

Todd, Jan. Assistant Professor of Kinesiology, University of Texas, Austin. Author of *Physical Culture and Body Beautiful* (1997), and *Lift Your Way to Youthful Fitness* (1985). Coeditor of *Iron Game History: Journal of Physical Culture.* **Essays:** Physical Fitness; Sport, History of.

Todd, Mary. Assistant Professor of History, Concordia University, River Forest, Illinois. Contributor to *Daughters of Sarah, The Cresset,* and the collection *Lutheran Women in Ordained Ministry, 1970–1995: Reflections and Perspectives* (1995). **Essays:** Clergywomen; Fundamentalism: Christian.

Toussaint, Sandy. Lecturer in Anthropology, University of Western Australia, Nedlands, Western Australia. Contributor to *Social Analysis, Arena, Environment, Aboriginal History, Australian Journal of Social Issues, Alternative Law Journal,* and numerous others. **Essay:** Menopause

Trescott, Paul B. Professor of Economics, Southern Illinois University, Carbondale. Author of *Money, Banking and Economic Welfare* (1960), *Financing American Enterprise* (1963), *Thailand's Monetary Experience* (1971), and *The Logic of the Price System* (1970). **Essay:** Music: Jazz and Blues.

Tripp, Anna. Lecturer in Literature, University of Hertfordshire, Aldenham. Contributor to *Women: A Cultural Review, English Review,* and *Reader's Guide to Literature in English,* edited by Mark Hawkins-Dady (1996). **Essays:** Literature: Poetry; Plath, Sylvia.

Tucker, Susan. Curator of Books and Records, Center for Research on Women, Newcomb College, Tulane University, New Orleans, Louisiana. Author of *Telling Memories among Southern Women: Domestic Workers in the Segregated South* (1988). Contributor to *Frontiers, Monthly Extract, A Room of One's Own,* and numerous edited collections. Book review editor, *Cultural Vistas: The Magazine of the Louisiana Endowment for the Humanities.* **Essays:** Domestic Service; Oral History; Sex-Segregated Education.

Urwin, Tiffany. Ph.D. candidate in English, University of Queensland, Brisbane. Editor of *Australasian Victorian*

Studies Annual. **Essays:** Stanton, Elizabeth Cady; Victorian Era.

VanHoosier-Carey, Kimberly A. Brittain Fellow in Teaching, Georgia Institute of Technology, Atlanta, and Ph.D. candidate, University of Texas, Austin. Contributor to *D.H. Lawrence Review.* **Essays:** Birth Control Movement; Cult of True Womanhood; Gynecology, History and Development of; Sterilization.

Varney, Denise. Lecturer in Theatre Studies, Victorian College of the Arts, University of Melbourne, Parkville, Victoria. Contributor to *Antithesis, Shakespeare's Books,* edited by Philip Mead and Marion Campbell (1993), and *Studies in Performance Processes* (1997). **Essay:** Theater: Images of Women in.

Walter, Lynn. Professor of Social Change and Development, University of Wisconsin, Green Bay. Author of *Ethnicity, Economy, and the State in Ecuador* (1981). Contributor to *Gender and Society, Feminist Review, American Ethnologist, Journal of Comparative Family Studies, Feminist Collections,* and *America Indigena.* **Essays:** Anthropology: Feminist.

Walters, Cecil. Graduate student in psychology, State University of New York, Binghamton. **Essay:** (with Tanya Williamson) Body Image.

Wansbrough, Paula. Young women's youth worker and public health educator, Toronto, Ontario. Coeditor of *A Sweet Secret: Telling the Story of Menstruation* (1997). **Essay:** (with Kathleen O'Grady) Menstruation.

Washington, Pat. Assistant Professor of Women's Studies, San Diego State University, San Diego, California. Contributor to *The Womanist: A Newsletter for Afrocentric Feminist Researchers,* and *SAGE.* **Essay:** Sexual Assault/Rape: Marital.

Weaver, C. Kay. Lecturer in Film and Television Studies, University of Waikato, Hamilton, New Zealand. Coauthor of *Cameras in the Commons* (1990) and *Women Viewing Violence* (1992). Contributor to *Continuum: The Australian Journal of Media and Culture.* **Essays:** Film, Images of Women in; Television, Images of Women in.

Weinbaum, Batya. Editor and Publisher, Angel Fish Press, Montpelier, Vermont. Author of *Curious Courtship of Women's Liberation and Socialism* (1978), *Pictures of Patriarchy* (1983), *The Island of Floating Women* (1993), *Jerusalem Romance* (1993), *Fragments of Motherhood* (1996). Contributor to *Science Fiction Studies, NWSA Journal, Women's Studies International Forum,* and *Feminist Review.* **Essays:** Curricular Transformation; Israeli-Palestinian Conflict; Women's Liberation Movement.

Wiesner-Hanks, Merry E. Professor of History, University of Wisconsin, Milwaukee. Author of *Women and Gender in Early Modern Europe* (1993) and *Working Women in Renaissance Germany* (1986). Editor, *Oxford Encyclopedia of the Reformation* (1995). Contributor to *Colloquia Germanica, Journal of Medieval and Renaissance Studies, Feminist Collections, Archiv für Reformationsgeschichte, Journal of Social History, Exemplaria, Memoria, Sixteenth Century Journal,* and numerous edited collections. **Essays:** History: Prehistory; Witch Hunts.

Williamson, Tanya E. Graduate student in Psychology, State University of New York, Binghamton. **Essay:** (with Cecil Walters) Body Image.

Wilsch, Kerstin. Arabic Instructor, St. Anthony's College, University of Oxford. **Essay:** Arab Women.

Wink, Amy L. Postdoctoral Lecturer in English, Texas A and M University, College Station. Contributor to *Borderlands: The Texas Poetry Review.* **Essays:** Pierce, Marge; Separate Spheres; Stone, Lucy.

Woloch, Nancy. Adjunct Associate Professor of History, Barnard College, Columbia University, New York, New York. Author of *Women and the American Experience* (1994), *Early American Women: A Documentary History* (1997), and *Muller v. Oregon: A Brief History with Documents* (1996). Coauthor of *The Enduring Vision* (1996) and *The American Century* (1992). **Essay:** Protective Legislation.

Yiannopoulou, Effie. Lecturer in English, University of Wales, Cardiff. Contributor to *Gramma* and *European Journal of English Studies.* **Essay:** Dinesen, Isak.